MATTHEW AND THE MARGINS

The Bible & Liberation

An Orbis Series in Biblical Studies

Norman K. Gottwald and Richard A. Horsley,
General Editors

The Bible & Liberation Series focuses on the emerging range of political, social, and contextual hermeneutics that are changing the face of biblical interpretation today. It brings to light the social struggles behind the biblical texts. At the same time it explores the ways that a "liberated Bible" may offer resources in the contemporary struggle for a more human world.

Already published:

The Bible and Liberation: Political and Social Hermeneutics (revised edition), Norman K. Gottwald and Richard A. Horsley, Editors

Josiah's Passover: Sociology and the Liberating Bible, Shigeyuki Nakanose

The Psalms: Songs of Tragedy, Hope, and Justice, J. David Pleins

Women and Jesus in Mark: A Japanese Feminist Perspective, Hisako Kinukawa

Liberating Paul: The Justice of God and the Politics of the Apostle, Neil Elliott

Becoming Children of God: John's Gospel and Radical Discipleship, Wes Howard-Brook

Discovering the Bible in the Non-Biblical World, Kwok Pui-lan

Biblical Hermeneutics of Liberation: Modes of Reading the Bible in the South African Context, Gerald West

Apocalypse: A People's Commentary on The Book of Revelation, Pablo Richard

Go Preach! Mark's Kingdom Message and the Black Church Today, Brian K. Blount

Shall We Look for Another? A Feminist Rereading of the Matthean Jesus, Elaine M. Wainwright

Contesting the Interpretations: Asian Biblical Hermeneutics and Postcolonialism, R. S. Sugirtharajah

Unveiling Empire: Reading Revelation Then and Now, Wes Howard-Brook and Anthony Gwyther

The Bible & Liberation Series

MATTHEW AND THE MARGINS

A Sociopolitical and Religious Reading

Warren Carter

ORBIS BOOKS

Maryknoll, New York 10545

The Catholic Foreign Mission Society of America (Maryknoll) recruits and trains people for overseas missionary service. Through Orbis Books, Maryknoll aims to foster the international dialogue that is essential to mission. The books published, however, reflect the opinions of their authors and are not meant to represent the official position of the society. To obtain more information about Maryknoll and Orbis Books, please visit our website at www.maryknoll.org.

Published by Orbis Books, Maryknoll, NY 10545-0308
Manufactured in the United States of America

Library of Congress Cataloging-in-Publication Data

Carter, Warren, 1955-
    Matthew and the margins : a sociopolitical and religious reading / Warren Carter.
        p.   cm. — (Bible & liberation series)
    Includes bibliographical references and index.
    ISBN 1-57075-324-5 (pbk.)
    1. Bible. N.T. Matthew—Commentaries.   2. Bible. N.T. Matthew—Social scientific criticism.   I. Title.   II. Series.

BS2575.3 .C38 2000
226.2'067—dc21
                                                                00-044128

Contents

Part I
THE FIRST NARRATIVE BLOCK
GOD COMMISSIONS JESUS (1:1-4:16)

Part III
THE THIRD NARRATIVE BLOCK
RESPONSES TO JESUS' MINISTRY (11:2-16:20)

Part V
THE FIFTH NARRATIVE BLOCK
JESUS IN JERUSALEM: CONFLICT AND DEATH (21:1-27:66)

Part VI
THE SIXTH NARRATIVE BLOCK
GOD RAISES JESUS (28:1-20)

Abbreviations

ABD	*Anchor Bible Dictionary.* Edited by D. N. Freedman. 6 volumes. New York: Doubleday, 1992.
ANRW	*Aufstieg und Niedergang der römischen Welt.* Berlin and New York: Walter de Gruyter.
ANTJ	Arbeiten zum Neuen Testament und Judentum
ARW	*Archiv für Religionswissenschaft*
ASTI	*Annual of the Swedish Theological Institute*
BA	*Biblical Archaeologist*
BAGD	Bauer, Arndt, Gingrich, Danker. *Greek-English Lexicon*
BAR	*Biblical Archaeologist Reader*
BARIS	British Archaeological Reports, International Series
BDF	Blass, Debrunner, Funk. *Greek Grammar*
BETL	Bibliotheca ephemeridum theologicarum lovaniensium
BEvT	Beiträge zur evangelischen Theologie
Bib	*Biblica*
BTB	*Biblical Theology Bulletin*
BZ	*Biblische Zeitschrift*
BZAW	Beihefte zur Zeitschrift für die alttestamentliche Wissenschaft
BZNW	Beihefte zur Zeitschrift für neutestamentliche Wissenschaft
CBQMS	Catholic Biblical Quarterly Monograph Series
CBQ	*Catholic Biblical Quarterly*
CurTM	*Currents in Theology and Mission*
EDNT	*Exegetical Dictionary of the New Testament.* Edited by H. Balz and G. Schneider. 3 volumes. Grand Rapids: Eerdmans, 1990-93.
EThL	*Ephemerides Theologicae Louvanienses*
ExpT	*Expository Times*
FRLANT	Forschungen zur Religion und Literatur des Alten und Neuen Testaments
HBT	*Horizons in Biblical Theology*
HDR	Harvard Dissertations in Religion
HeyJ	*Heythrop Journal*
HTKNT	Herders theologischer Kommentar zum Neuen Testament
HTR	*Harvard Theological Review*
HUCA	*Hebrew Union College Annual*
IBS	*Irish Biblical Studies*
ICC	International Critical Commentary
JAAR	*Journal of the American Academy of Religion*

JAC	*Jahrbuch für Antike und Christentum*
JBL	*Journal of Biblical Literature*
JECS	*Journal for Early Christian Studies*
JETS	*Journal of Evangelical Theological Studies*
JHS	*Journal of Hellenic Studies*
JPTSS	Journal for Pentecostal Theology Supplement Series
JRAS	*Journal of the Royal Asiatic Society*
JRS	*Journal of Roman Studies*
JSJ	*Journal for the Study of Judaism*
JSNT	*Journal for the Study of the New Testament*
JSNTSup	*Journal for the Study of the New Testament* Supplement Series
JSOT	*Journal for the Study of the Old Testament*
JSOTSup	Journal for the Study of the Old Testament Supplement Series
JSP	*Journal for the Study of the Pseudepigrapha*
JTS	*Journal of Theological Studies*
LXX	Septuagint
MT	Masoretic Text
NICNT	New International Commentary on the New Testament
NCB	New Century Bible
NovT	*Novum Testamentum*
NTOA	Novum Testamentum et Orbis Antiquus
NTS	*New Testament Studies*
OBO	Orbis biblicus et orientalis
OBT	Overtures to Biblical Theology
RAC	*Reallexikon für Antike und Christentum.* Edited by T. Klauser. 1950-78.
RevQ	*Revue de Qumran*
RNT	Regensburger Neues Testament
SBEC	Studies in the Bible and Early Christianity
SBL	Society of Biblical Literature
SBLDS	Society of Biblical Literature Dissertation Series
SBLSP	Society of Biblical Literature Seminar Papers
SBT	Studies in Biblical Theology
SJT	*Scottish Journal of Theology*
SNTSMS	Society for New Testament Studies Monograph Series
TDNT	*Theological Dictionary of the New Testament.* Edited by G. Kittel. 10 volumes. Grand Rapids: Eerdmans, 1964-76.
THKNT	Theologischer Handkommentar zum Neuen Testament
TS	*Theological Studies*
TynBul	*Tyndale Bulletin*
WBC	Word Bible Commentary
WUNT	Wissenschaftliche Untersuchungen zum Neuen Testament
ZNW	*Zeitschrift für neutestamentliche Wissenschaft*

Biblical and Classical Sources

Citations of biblical, including so-called apocryphal texts, generally refer to the New Revised Standard Version (NRSV) (though in a few instances I have supplied my own translation). Citations of so-called pseudepigraphical literature refer to J. H. Charlesworth (ed.), *The Old Testament Pseudepigrapha* (2 vols.; Garden City, N.Y.: Doubleday, 1983, 1985). Abbreviations generally follow those listed in *JBL* 117 (1998) 559-67, and *ABD,* "List of Abbreviations," lii-lxxviii. Most citations of Greek, Roman, and other Jewish authors refer to the Loeb Classical Library editions (Cambridge, Mass.: Harvard University Press; London: William Heinemann). Abbreviations are listed below. The following texts should also be noted:

Aristides, *Roman Oration.* Text and Commentary in J. H. Oliver, "The Ruling Power: A Study of the Roman Empire in the Second Century after Christ through the Roman Oration of Aelius Aristides." *Transactions of the American Philosophical Society* ns 43 Part 4 (1953) 871-1003.

Cynics. A. J. Malherbe. *The Cynic Epistles.* Missoula, Mont.: Scholars Press, 1977.

Menander. D. A. Russell and N. G. Wilson. *Menander Rhetor.* Oxford: Oxford University Press, 1981.

Musonius Rufus. C. Lutz, *Musonius Rufus: The Roman Socrates.* Yale Classical Studies 10. New Haven, Conn.: Yale University Press, 1947.

Abbreviations of Ancient Texts

Abr	Philo, *De Abrahamo*
Anab	Xenophon, *Anabasis*
Ann	Tacitus, *The Annals*
Ant	Josephus, *Jewish Antiquities*
Apoc	Seneca, *Apocolocyntosis*
Apollonius	Philostratus, *Life of Apollonius*
Att	Cicero, *Letters to Atticus*
AUC	Livy, *Ab Urbe Condita*
Chron	Malalas, *Chronicles*
Coac	Hippocrates, *Coacai* (Κωακαί)
Con Ap	Josephus, *Contra Apion*
De Ben	Seneca, *De Beneficiis*
De Cherub	Philo, *De Cherubim*
De Clem	Seneca, *De Clementia*
De Const	Seneca, *De Constantia*
De Dec	Philo, *De Decalogo*
De Div	Cicero, *De Divinatione*
De Leg	Cicero, *De Legibus*
De Off	Cicero, *De Officiis*

De Prov	Cicero, *De Providentia*
De Prov	Seneca, *De Providentia*
Disc	Dio Chrysostom, *Discourses*
Diss	Epictetus, *The Discourses*
Ep	Horace, *Epistles*
Ep	Pliny, *Epistles*
Ep	Seneca, *Epistulae Morales*
Epig	Martial, *The Epigrams*
Fam	Cicero, *Ad Familiares*
Gaium	Philo, *De Legatione ad Gaium*
Hist	Diodorus Siculus, *Library of History*
Hist	Herodotus, *History*
Hist	Polybius, *Histories*
Hist	Tacitus, *The Histories*
In Cat	Cicero, *In Catalinem*
In Verr	Cicero, *Verrine Orations*
Instit	Quintilian, *Institutia Oratoria*
Jos	Philo, *De Josepho*
JW	Josephus, *Jewish War*
Mig	Philo, *De Migratione Abrahami*
NH	Pliny, *Natural History*
P Oxy	The Oxyrhynchus Papyri
Pan	Pliny, *The Panegyricus*
Pol	Aristotle, *Politics*
Rom Ant	Dionysius of Halicarnassus, *Roman Antiquities*
Sat	Horace, *Satires*
Sat	Juvenal, *Satires*
Silv	Statius, *The Silvae*
Somn	Philo, *De Somniis*
Spec Leg	Philo, *De Specialibus Legibus*
Vita Cont	Philo, *De Vita Contemplativa*

Preface

This reading of Matthew is a selective reading. I do not attempt, as some recent commentaries do, to be "encyclopedic."[1] I recognize that all readings, including this one, are perspectival, partial, and shaped by the questions, experiences, and location of various communities of readers. I am concerned with some questions but not with others. I recognize that Matthew can be read in various ways and that any one reading can be enriched by other readings.

This reading, then, like Matthew's gospel, has an agenda. That doesn't make it unusual. All readings of Matthew have agenda. Some commentators make their agenda explicit, while others do not. Daniel Harrington, for instance, wants to understand Matthew as a gospel written from a post-70 Jewish-Christian community wrestling, as other Jewish groups were, with the pressing issues raised by the overthrow of Jerusalem and the temple by the Romans in 70 C.E.[2] Elaine Wainwright reads Matthew with the explicit goal of examining its presentation of women and of seeking to understand what circumstances or experiences in the Matthean community and society shaped these presentations.[3]

My particular agenda concerns reading Matthew from the cultural margins. Throughout I will pursue a reading that takes this reality of marginality seriously. My reading perspective is *that Matthew's gospel is a counternarrative. It is a work of resistance written from and for a minority community of disciples committed to Jesus, the agent of God's saving presence and empire. The gospel shapes their identity and lifestyle as an alternative community. It strengthens this community to resist the dominant Roman imperial and synagogal control. It anticipates Jesus' return when Jesus will complete God's salvific purposes in establishing God's reign or empire over all, including Rome.*

I will explain what I mean by "margins" (and the rest of this statement) in the Introduction. It is sufficient here to employ some synonyms: exclusion, periphery, powerlessness, "over-against," critique, alternative visions, living in several worlds, tension, a "both-and" existence. To speak of preferences for the margins implies "dis-ease" with some centers. I will identify two significant centers, a synagogue and the Roman empire.

A focus on Matthew and the margins has not been prominent among interpreters of Matthew. Even when it has been noted or at least noticed, as in the use of the term "sectarian" for Matthew's community,[4] it has not been given much force or attention in detailed discussions of the gospel's content and function.

This neglect is not surprising. To read from and live on the margins is to see life in ways that it is not seen at the center. It is hard for those who do much of the scholarly writing and publishing on Matthew, members of university and seminary faculties in the Western world, with access to immense educational resources, numerous scholarly and publishing opportunities, prestige in scholarly guilds or ecclesial groups, stable political and social environments, and often comfortable salaries and lifestyles, to think about Matthew on and from the margins. But, while difficult, it is not impossible. We can learn to see as others see, at least to some extent. We can listen to others' experiences of the cultural margins because of gender, sexual orientation, ethnicity, national origin, religious affiliation, political views, economic realities, age, relational and professional experiences. We can learn from our own experiences of exclusion and powerlessness.

Several factors suggest to me that pursuing this reading of Matthew from the margins might be worthwhile. *Historical factors* indicate that it is a sustainable approach to this gospel. Matthew's gospel originates in and is addressed to a small, minority group probably living in the large city of Antioch. The community from which the gospel originates was not a numerical majority, was not constituted by the ruling elite, and did not share its central focus on Jesus with most of its society. In fact, the religious and imperial elite, whose power is constituted by birth (priests), wealth (Sadducees, elders), training (scribes, Pharisees) and military-political power (Rome, elders), expel Jesus from their society with a form of execution reserved for those suspected of treason and of disrupting civic and political order. The community of Jesus' disciples follows one commissioned by God but without any institutional legitimation or social status, who was in fundamental respects "out-of-step" with his society, though a participant in that society. Being attentive to this complex sociohistorical reality of marginality produces insight into numerous aspects of the gospel.

Literary factors also suggest that attention to aspects of marginality in the gospel's story world might be important. The gospel's plot concerns a main character who is involved in constant conflict with the religious elite, and who is finally put to death by an alliance of religious and political elites. Along with this conflict, Jesus calls into being a group of disciples who are to live his teaching. This teaching, more often than not, resists conventional wisdom with an alternative vision of human existence. Being attuned to the conflict, to what is resisted and advocated, to the continual settings of elites and marginals, opens up further dimensions of marginality.

No reading of a biblical text is removed from an interpreter's circumstances. *Contemporary ecclesial factors* also suggest that pursuing this reading of Matthew from the margins might be worthwhile. In the United States, actual church attendance and participation have consistently dropped since the high point in the 1950s. Then the church was a significant social institution, a status quo player. But increasingly church participation and influence have declined. Most clergy in so-called mainline denominations know firsthand the situation in which about one-third of the membership forms, in reality, the actual worshiping, participating congregation. Church members know firsthand the declining influence of the church. Some are aware of increasing hostility, violence, and persecution.[5] Numerous denomination agencies have lamented, studied, and programmed to arrest this situation of decline. But there is a widespread sense of the continued loss of the center or socially dominant position.

These churches are in transition in a polyreligious and increasingly diverse society to a social role of much less influence and status. They are in transition toward the edges, the cultural margins.

It is worth reflecting on the role of the Bible in this transition. It is widely acknowledged that in the heyday of church membership in the 1950s and 1960s the use of the Bible declined in churches, with doubts over its relevance. That is not surprising. The biblical documents by and large do not derive from communities of faith that occupy powerful or central social, political, or historical locations. The biblical material, such as Matthew, mostly originates in social locations of weakness and cultural marginality, among a minority, from the poor. Generally it does not offer the powerful who occupy the status quo much comfort or encouragement, affirmation or support.

If, then, it is true that the church in the United States is increasingly becoming culturally marginalized, perhaps we will find some affinity again with biblical material such as Matthew, which originated on the cultural margins. Perhaps we will rediscover some different locations and strategies for reading the Bible. Perhaps our location on the cultural margins might offer not so much cause to lament as new opportunities for understanding and living biblical faith.

Churches in other parts of the world know this location well. In Britain and Europe, for instance, churches have long known such locations in what has been called a post-Christian world. Churches in numerous other parts of the world, in Central and South America, Africa, Asia, and the Pacific, have read the Bible as the witness of the poor and the oppressed against those who have tried to co-opt the biblical tradition against them. They have also frequently read it as members of larger cultures which do not share their commitments. Increasingly, published scholarly and liturgical resources from these locations, and personal encounters with church leaders, members, and scholars, make available the hard-earned wisdom of those who live faithfully in such locations.

A fourth factor suggests to me that pursuing this reading of Matthew from the margins might be worthwhile. *My own experience* has been of reading from the margins. I have lived most of my life in New Zealand, where the church has long occupied the cultural margins. It was "normal" for me to be one of few kids, if not the only kid, in my class to attend Sunday school or church. Church membership and participation have been around 10 to 15 percent. I learned to read the Bible, to think about and live faith, as a member of a marginal community. Moreover, in that context I have witnessed the continuing destructive legacy of British imperial practices on New Zealanders, especially among Maori people. Subsequently, as an immigrant in the United States, I, along with numerous immigrants, know what it is to be socially and culturally marginalized on the basis of national origin, appearance, accent, customs, traditions, and legal status. These experiences shape my living and writing.

The reading of Matthew from the margins is, then, the guiding agenda for this book. This focus, along with limits of length which result from publishing realities, has shaped various decisions about the book's content.

1. I have not included comprehensive bibliography with each pericope. In the notes I cite some key works and those with which I particularly interact.

2. With a few exceptions, I do not engage in text-critical discussion. I have generally followed the NRSV as a base text, though I have freely departed from it and used my own translation in a number of places.

3. I have not cited the Matthean text at the beginning of each section. The old adage remains true, though, that commentaries always make much more sense when read simultaneously with the biblical text.

4. Though I have constantly engaged the marvelous resources of Matthean commentators such as P. Bonnard, W. D. Davies and D. C. Allison, H. Frankemölle, D. Garland, J. Gnilka, W. Grundmann, R. Gundry, D. Hagner, D. R. A. Hare, D. J. Harrington, D. Hill, U. Luck, U. Luz, D. Patte, A. Sand, E. Schweizer, and D. Senior, and have consulted numerous wonderful studies of aspects of the gospel, I have omitted catalogues and evaluations of their various positions on each item. More often than not, I have (regrettably) included only the outcome and not the process of much of that debate.

5. I do not undertake a source and redaction study of each pericope. As the introduction explains, I utilize an audience-oriented approach that attends to the interaction of the final text form and a sociohistorically located audience.

6. In referring to biblical and Jewish and Greco-Roman writers, I have supplied the reference but usually not the full citation. I include these references not because I think the gospel's author or audience were necessarily aware of these exact references, but because they indicate diverse cultural perspectives and contexts among which the gospel's presentation finds its place.

7. For a long time I have disliked the practice in commentaries of referring readers to discussions in other parts of the commentary (the ubiquitous "see 2:5," for example). This practice often contributes to a choppy, detached, "random thoughts/no coherence" feel, and it overlooks the dominant "dip and pick" reading habit of many users of commentaries. Nevertheless, space concerns have regrettably forced me to it.

8. I have included Greek terms only when necessary for the discussion.

I want to thank A. K. M. Adam, Dennis Duling, Keith Hohly, Amy-Jill Levine, Kathy Neary, Mark Allan Powell, and Stan Saunders for astute responses to earlier drafts. To have people who are willing to take the time to offer detailed and insightful critique is indeed a gift. I have learned much from their comments. Nicole Schoenhals and LeeAnn Ahern rendered valuable assistance. Much of the writing was made possible by a 1998-1999 Lilly-sponsored Faculty Fellowship Award from the Association of Theological Schools. I am most grateful for this financial support. I also wish to thank the president, Dr. Lovett Weems, Jr., and the trustees of Saint Paul School of Theology, Kansas City, Missouri, for sabbatical leave. Susan Perry and Catherine Costello have been skilled and helpful editors. I am very grateful for the opportunity to write this book.

WARREN CARTER
September 21, 1999
Feast of St. Matthew, Apostle and Evangelist

Introduction

I read Matthew's gospel* as a counternarrative. It is a work of resistance, written for a largely Jewish religious group. It "stands and/or speaks over against"[1] the status quo dominated by Roman imperial power and synagogal control.[2] It resists these cultural structures.[3]

But it is also a work of advocacy and of hope. The gospel constructs an alternative worldview and community. It affirms a way of life marginal to the dominant structures. It challenges its audience to live this resistant way of life faithfully in its present circumstances. And it promises that Jesus will return to establish God's empire and salvation in full.

I will argue that the gospel addresses disciples who live in the time after Rome's defeat of Jerusalem in 70 C.E. It interprets this defeat as God's punishment of the religious leaders for misleading the people into rejecting Jesus, God's commissioned agent or Christ. Rome, ironically an ally of the religious elite, is the agent of God's punishment (see 22:7). But this punishment is not God's final word. The gospel promises that Jesus will "save his people from their sins" (1:21). God's salvation or empire is partly experienced in the present in proclamation, healing, exorcism, and so on (10:7-8), and through the community of disciples and its alternative way of life. It will be completed at Jesus' imminent return. Then Rome's imperial arrogance will end and God's just and merciful new creation, God's empire, will be established. God's salvation from Roman imperialism will be accomplished. In depicting the coming triumph[4] of God's salvific purposes and the defeat of Rome, the gospel ironically co-opts the very imperial paradigm it resists.

Nine factors that I will elaborate in this introduction contribute to this reading of the gospel. The first three factors concern the gospel's function of shaping identity and lifestyle:

1. Reading is an active process. Reading this gospel exposes the world of the center and unveils the alternative world of God's empire or reign. It imagines a different present with distinct practices and relationships, and anticipates the future, overpowering triumph of God's salvific purposes at Jesus' return.
2. The gospel uses the form of a biography to legitimate and shape the resistant and alternative identity and lifestyle of a community of disciples of Jesus.
3. The gospel employs a range of strategies to accomplish this identity-forming work: various names, a focus on Jesus as the center, rituals,

---

*For a plot outline of Matthew's gospel, see the Appendix.

1

attacks on opponents, an apocalyptic worldview, and a presentation of the origin, governance and practices of the community.

Factors 4 through 9 concern the circumstances of the gospel audience:

4. Matthew's gospel was probably written in the 80s C.E., in the city of Antioch in Syria, by an author unknown to us.
5. The gospel's audience lives its discipleship in the tough, rural-urban, hierarchical environment of Antioch.
6. The gospel's audience is a socioeconomic cross-section of this society.
7. The gospel's audience is a small group.
8. The gospel's audience is in tension with other members of the city's Jewish community.
9. The gospel's audience resists the values, commitments, and agendas of the Roman empire.

In a final section I will argue that a sociologically informed notion of marginality accurately names the alternative counterexistence which the gospel proposes for its audience.

1. READING AND HEARING A COUNTERNARRATIVE

Reading is a complex process. We work hard to formulate meaning. We notice features of the text. We construe words and fill gaps. We supply content and understandings that the text assumes of us. We attend to the actions, conflicts, characters, settings, and point/s of view of the individual subunits that comprise the gospel's episodic structure. We discern and evaluate different points of view, different behaviors and values. We link scenes, attend to settings, construct sequences, identify causality, determine temporal relations, and create unity. We assess the relative importance of actions, combine character traits, and discern intra- and intertextual connections. And in connecting these elements, we construct an expanding narrative world as we interact with the text.[5]

The audience quickly discovers that resistance plays a prominent role in this narrative. Throughout, Jesus engages in continual conflict with an alliance of religious leaders. The central issues involve contrasting visions of society and Jesus' legitimacy or authority. The religious elite, typically allied with the political elite in an imperial society, comprises the status quo in Jerusalem and upholds the current social hierarchy (Matt 2:1-6; 15:1).[6] Because of their birth, wealth, training, gender, and social position, they have the power. As an outsider without noble or priestly birth, wealth, specialized religious training, or social standing, Jesus resists their authority and social vision. They do not find his actions or teaching persuasive; and with the help of the Roman governor and political elite, they put him to death in Jerusalem (chs. 26-27). Jesus warns his disciples that such is the way of the world until his return. Moreover, this conflict reflects a cosmic struggle between God and Satan. The audience discovers from the gospel's opening chapters that God has authorized Jesus to live as he does. To welcome or follow Jesus is to agree with God. To oppose Jesus is to oppose God and to side with Satan (4:1-11).[7]

Through this struggle, the audience understands the gospel to advocate certain perspectives, structures, and practices associated with Jesus and God, while rejecting those associated with the religious leaders and the devil. Reading the gospel is a world-advocating and world-rejecting, world-unveiling and world-decentering, world-affirming and world-exposing process.

This reading process unveils and resists a center that comprises the powerful political and religious elite. The gospel's divine point of view exposes and evaluates this center negatively as a world that dominates, oppresses, marginalizes, destroys. It elevates male above female, king above people, ruler above ruled, rich above poor, religious leaders above people, violence above compassion, the center above the margins. As the Roman vassal king Herod demonstrates in chapter 2, the center uses greed, deception, inequality, violence, conquest, power, rank, division, control, derision, and propaganda to further its goals. The gospel shows the powerful center at work, reveals its goals and methods as illegitimate in God's view, and portrays its ultimate decentering. This center is not, contrary to its propaganda, the only or inevitable or desirable or permanent or normative world. The gospel resists and subverts the center.

To speak of a center suggests life that is marginal to it. Reading the gospel text unveils an alternative world of the margins. The gospel reveals God's empire to be breaking in to challenge the center, to liberate, and to offer life (4:17, 23; 5:5, 10). It creates alternative systems and ways of being: nonhierarchical structures; "one-flesh" male-female existence; communal sufficiency in shared economic resources; the reversal of inequities; the inclusion of ethnically different groups; and practices of worship, compassion, mutual service, and nonviolent resolution of conflict. One of the effects of reading this story of Jesus is to see God's reign or empire at work, to notice it in unlikely places, to understand its goals and methods, to hear its call to live in and for a just and compassionate world, and to participate in its final triumph over all.

In so doing, the conflict of the two worlds and their quite different values, structures, and practices becomes very apparent. The genealogy of chapter 1, for example, utilizes but undermines the dominant system of patriarchy. First by the inclusion of women and then in the astonishing account of Mary's conception of Jesus without any male agent, it becomes clear that God works in and through and around male dominance. In the story of Herod's murderous resistance in chapter 2, it is evident that the imperial center is not pleased with God's disruptive presence and empire. The "empire strikes back" when God threatens its (in)vested interests. The temptation narrative in 4:1-11 reveals Satan's control over Rome and other worldly powers. For those with eyes to see, the gospel stories expose inadequacies of the status quo, offer visions of God's life-giving alternative, realistically warn of the conflict, and sustain its consenting readers to live this counternarrative on the margins.

The verbs of "unveiling," "exposing," and "seeing" are important. Paulo Freire argues that perception, the recognition of one's current situation, is the beginning of transformation.[8] But he recognizes that the experience of the oppressive present is often precisely that which hinders perception. Only as the true nature of the present is discovered, reflected on, and actively challenged is there any hope of and motivation for resistance and liberation. Accurate perception means seeing "the reality of oppression not as a closed world from which there is no exit, but as a limiting situation which they can transform."[9] Such perception emerges through reflection and praxis, dialogue and explanation.

G. Soares-Prabhu emphasizes the role of Jesus' "liberative pedagogy" in this process. He argues that Jesus' "non-elitist, transforming, prophetic, dialogical and critical pedagogy" is liberative in two ways. It makes the gospel's audience

> conscious of their worth as children of one Father in heaven whose value derives not from personal ability or social status but from the inalienable reality of the Father's love (Mt 6:26; 18:10-14). And as prophetic and critical teaching it freed them from the manipulative myths which legitimize their oppressive and alienating society, and points them towards a new and non-exploitative world in which men and women could live together. . . .[10]

J. D. Kingsbury has also highlighted the gospel's emphasis on perception in discussing the gospel's "rhetoric of comprehension." He argues that it is a literary strategy through which readers assess characters in terms of whether they understand Jesus. To understand Jesus is to agree with God's verdict of him as God's agent commissioned to manifest God's saving presence, the empire of the heavens (1:1, 21, 23; 4:17).[11] But to understand Jesus in God's perspective involves understanding the nature of the present world as a world of sins (1:21) in which the devil actively opposes God's purposes (4:1-11; 6:13b) often through human agents (13:38-39) and oppressive religious and political structures (2:1-23; 4:8). People need saving and delivering from this world. To "see" or "understand" God's empire manifested in Jesus and in the alternative community Jesus forms is the decisive issue in this counternarrative.

Not surprisingly, God's blessing resides not in knowing the emperor or the central elite, not in acknowledging their power as the ultimate sovereignty, but in experiencing God's empire and in "seeing" God (5:3, 8). The gospel reveals that Rome's empire is doomed. Disciples who follow Jesus "know the secrets of the reign/empire of the heavens" present among them but not yet complete. They "see" and "hear," while those who do not follow, who do not "see" or "hear," do not understand (13:10-17). The women, the only characters to understand Jesus' teaching on resurrection, "see" the empty tomb for what it is, a demonstration of God's life-giving power, presence, and empire which are not contained by death (28:1).[12] To discern God's transforming work under way but not yet completed is a fundamental challenge.

But Be Careful

To consent to God's point of view on Jesus, the world, and the empire of the heavens is precisely what the author wants from us as readers. Authors write with an assenting "model" audience in mind, an "authorial audience" who, they imagine, agrees with every word, who supplies every missing "gap," who has the cultural knowledge necessary to provide the relevant information or experience, who finds every rhetorical strategy appealing and convincing.[13]

We as an actual audience will at times find ourselves in agreement with the authorial audience. At other times we may be open to what is being commended to us, and/or challenged to reconsider what we think important or "normal," and to contemplate other ways of being, thinking, feeling, and looking. At still other times we will resist the counternarrative.

This gospel asks us to agree with some very questionable assertions. Consider these three examples:

1. In places it encourages its audience to regard all synagogues as places of hypocrisy and violence, and Jewish religious leaders as hypocrites and murderers. It encourages us to view Jews who do not follow Jesus as faithless and deserving of destruction. It expects us to accept its demonization of the Jewish leaders accomplished by describing them in the same terms as the devil and by presenting them as the devil's agents (4:1-11; 12:34; 16:1-14; 19:3; 22:15, 34). It expects us to share its co-option of Jewish history and traditions with its claim that their significance resides only in their relation to Jesus.

2. More often than not, the gospel is androcentric in focusing on men more than it does on women. Only men, it seems, are "disciples." Women are often invisible. The gospel does reject patriarchy (see 19:3-12; 23:8-12), yet by frequently calling God "Father" it seems to suggest that the world should be a divine patriarchy ruled benignly by Father God.[14]

3. The gospel resists and exposes the violent and oppressive ways of empires (ch. 2; 14:1-12) which "lord it over" people (20:20-28). It recognizes that "the things of Caesar" are not coextensive with "the things of God" (22:15-22). The alternative to Rome's empire is God's empire, present in Jesus and soon to be victorious over all. But in using the identical language of "empire" and the concept of supreme power, the gospel seems to imitate precisely what it rejects! In its supreme confidence of the enforcement of God's will, its use of "bully tactics" of "do it—or else" to solicit compliance (see 18:35), and in its violent destruction of those who resist, God's empire resembles, rather than offers an alternative to, Rome's power. The gospel and God's empire seem co-opted by that which they resist, rather than, for example, offering an alternative model of inclusion and reconciliation.[15]

These issues of ethnicity, gender, and power need extensive discussion. The point here is that the authorial audience is assumed to "go along with the story" and accept its violence, hatred, and oppression, warts and all.[16] But those of us who are readers from the Christian tradition must be careful not to be uncritically co-opted by our respect for this text. Our "consent" can only be temporary, just as for the sake of "going along with the story," we temporarily accept that in musicals and opera people break into song simultaneously and in apparently spontaneous harmony and identical words! As an actual audience we know that this dramatic, highly rehearsed, and very skillful act is not to be mistaken for the everyday world!

Likewise, we must utilize, not suspend, the insights of our own experiences as we engage the gospel. As real readers, we know historical circumstances, literary realities, values, and consequences which collide with these aspects of the gospel world, which put them in a different perspective, and which undermine some of the gospel's claims and the roles it assumes of its audience. There are specific sociohistorical reasons for such presentations of synagogues and religious leaders (see sections 7 and 8 below). We dare not generalize the gospel's verdict. All synagogues are not places of violence and hypocrisy, whatever this gospel may claim. We have witnessed in the twentieth century's holocaust some of the terrible consequences of such sinful thinking and hatred. As an actual audience, we can understand, but reject, what is expected of us as the authorial audience.

In response to the gospel's androcentricity, we must make visible the women's experiences and roles that have been rendered invisible by male preoccupations. It is obvious that with the "Father" language for God and the use of the image of God's "empire," the language and patriarchal and imperial categories of its own time influence the gospel. Such influence is true for all human endeavor, but it is also true that human creativity can look beyond the conventional to different worlds. And in places the gospel does so. The commands to love enemies (5:44) and practice mercy (9:13; 12:7), the partial redefining of "father" in terms of God's indiscriminate favor to all (so 5:45), and the reformulation of "empire" as compassionate and transforming (so 4:17-25)[17] suggest resistance to dominant cultural norms (section 9 below) and a struggle for a different world. Even if we finally decide that the gospel does not go far enough, at least it has joined the struggle for different forms of human community not based on dominating one's neighbor by birth, power, wealth, gender, status, and training. At least, albeit inconsistently, it has pointed to inclusion, mercy, and service as basic forms of human interaction in a world that knows God's goodness to all (5:45).

There is another, quite different, danger in joining the authorial audience. To assent is one thing, but it is not the same as experiencing the reality of which we read. Matthew's authorial audience is expected not just to agree to love its enemy (5:43-44), to refuse to serve wealth (6:24), not to dominate others (20:20-28), and to worship God (22:37-39). The members of this audience are to live these realities in their everyday lives. To assent without considering *how* to do so in the context of our particular circumstances and experiences of abusive power and demanding gods is futile. Assent without reflection, without probing the implications for our present, is cheap assent. And like its theological cousin "cheap grace," cheap assent short-circuits encounter with God and the transformed life created by God's saving presence and empire.

Hence, I understand joining the authorial audience as the beginning half of the reading process. An author warrants a "fair" hearing, a careful reading from readers who are willing to be open to the experience and reality which the story world will depict.

But joining the authorial audience, as much as we can reconstruct those roles and knowledge for a two-thousand-year-old text, is only half the story. It is a strategy that enables the rest of the work to be done, the evaluation of the interaction of the gospel and our lives as "real readers." Real readers can agree with, reject, explore, scorn, tentatively endorse, be intrigued by, ignore, meditate on, and live out any or some of the authorial audience's roles. We might find the fundamental vision of marginal existence generally convincing, or we may prefer to read without committing to either its truth or its falseness. If we find it generally convincing, we then have to determine, using both the gospel and our experiences of the contemporary world, what it looks like to live this way in the twenty-first century, some two thousand years after this document was written.

Clearly my reading of Matthew's gospel cannot do that work for all real readers since it is work that belongs to each reader's circumstances and communities of faith. My hope is that I can at least facilitate some of that interaction with this text by attending particularly to my sense of the authorial audience's interaction with the text. That interaction is always a construct, always one reader's work, even though it is informed by the knowledge and experiences of other readers and scholars. But without claiming that is the only or a comprehensive reading, I do hope, helped by the work of numerous other readers, at least to demonstrate its plausibility.

2. WHAT DO GOSPELS DO?
LEGITIMATING AN IDENTITY AND A WAY OF LIFE

What, then, does Matthew's gospel "do" for consenting readers?[18] One unconvincing approach claims that the gospel provides a historical account of the life of Jesus. But discrepancies with the other gospels and the gospel's own distinctive and consistent emphases (observed in detailed comparisons with the other gospels) rule this out. The gospel itself attests that conveying information is not its primary function (7:24-27; 12:46-50). Equally implausible is a view that claims an evangelistic function. While some of the material might be used to gain new followers of Jesus, the gospel material is generally concerned with forming disciples out of those already committed.

The gospel is best understood, then, as oriented to those who are already disciples of Jesus. Can we be more specific about its function or functions? G. D. Kilpatrick thought it was written as a "revised Gospel lectionary" to be read and expounded in worship.[19] But his efforts to identify sufficient, distinctive liturgical elements falter, and our ignorance of both synagogal and early Christian worship patterns renders his claims unpersuasive. Kilpatrick did, though, draw attention convincingly to the gospel's educative role and communal orientation. The gospel seeks to shape a community of disciples. An obvious feature of the gospel is its five teaching blocks (chs. 5-7, 10, 13, 18, 24-25) in which Jesus provides disciples with instruction on the distinctive practices of discipleship and exhorts them to faithful perseverance. It seeks to nurture and grow the "little faith" of followers into an active and faithful way of life.

This formational rather than informational function and communal orientation have been a constant focus in studies of the gospel over the last half century. Most scholars understand the gospel to have some sort of teaching and pastoral function, though they debate whether it is concerned with repudiating other Christian groups, defining relationships with the rest of Judaism, or distancing disciples from Judaism.[20] Redaction critics in particular have attempted to identify the gospel's distinctive teaching and exhortation.[21]

In addition to this attention to the gospel's content, studies of the gospel's genre point to the same formational function and communal orientation. Richard Burridge persuasively argues that the gospels belong to the genre of *bioi* (βίοι, "lives").[22] These "ancient biographies" are not the same as modern "kiss-and-tell" biographies with their strong psychoanalytic approach. Burridge identifies four types of features that are typical of Greco-Roman biographies[23] and are very evident in this gospel.[24] In terms of the gospel's function, Burridge observes that "biography is a type of writing which occurs naturally among groups of people who have formed around a certain charismatic teacher or leader, seeking to follow after him."[25] True to their genre, the gospels focus on "the person of their subject, Jesus of Nazareth."[26] Like *bioi,* they function not only to instruct about or elicit praise or admiration for Jesus but also to offer "a model for the audience to follow."[27] They provide examples, instruction, and apologetic and polemical material for communities of disciples. Burridge cites Graham Stanton in saying that Matthew is "primarily concerned to set out the story and significance of Jesus in order to encourage and exhort Christians in his own day."[28] As *bioi,* the gospels have a "community building" function.[29] Talbert observes that the gospels "find it necessary to correct misunderstanding about Jesus at the same time that they set him forth as the expression and the norm of a community's values."[30]

These functions could be stated succinctly in claiming that the gospel is an identity-forming, lifestyle-shaping narrative. By "identity" I refer to that which defines the central commitment or investment of members of Matthew's audience, namely, their allegiance to Jesus as God's agent. This commitment, or following, constitutes their center or focus, their way of experiencing the world and interpreting it, their boundaries or relationships with other groups and people not members of the community of disciples (see 4:18-22; 13:10-17). It also defines their ways of being in the world. It shapes an appropriate way of life or set of practices or behaviors. These actions constitute a lifestyle that embodies their identity as disciples of Jesus.

In performing this identity-forming, lifestyle-shaping work, the gospel continues something that is already under way for the gospel's audience. The gospel assumes that the members of its audience are well familiar with Jewish scriptures, traditions and piety which, interpreted by Jesus, shape their identity and lifestyle. As followers of Jesus, they already know his teachings. The written gospel continues, affirms, and expands this communal work in circumstances that we will describe in sections 4-9 below.

3. HOW DOES THE GOSPEL FORM
COMMUNAL IDENTITY AND SHAPE LIFESTYLE?

How does the gospel do this identity-forming, lifestyle-shaping work? Studies have identified a variety of complex and interrelated methods that groups—and opponents—employed to define themselves and other groups in the Greco-Roman world.[31] The gospel evidences many of these as it outlines its vision of a marginal community.

    i. *Naming.* The gospel employs various names for its audience: disciples, blessed, children, *ekklēsia,* brothers and sisters, prophets, scribes, the wise, infants, little ones, etc. These names secure separation from other communities, reinforce group identity, and warn this community not to be like other groups.[32]

   ii. *Central Focus.* The gospel reinforces commitment to Jesus as the central feature of the community's identity.[33] Jesus calls disciples to "follow me/him" (4:19-22; 9:9; 10:1-4; 19:21) and to take *his* yoke, not that of oppressive powers (11:29). Disciples are to act on his behalf and in his name (5:11; 10:18, 22, 39; 16:25; 18:5; 19:29; 24:9). They obey his teaching (7:24-27; 12:46-50) which separates them from those who do not (13:10-17).

  iii. *Claims of Exclusive Revelation.* The gospel presents Jesus as the definitive revealer of God's presence (1:23; 18:20; 28:20), will (5-7, 10, 13, 18, 24-25), reign (4:17) and forgiveness (1:21; 9:1-8; 26:28).[34] He provides definitive interpretation of the scriptures, of the future, and teaching for "the meantime." This revelation derives from Jesus' relationship with God (11:25-27). As recipients of revelation about God's mysteries or purpose, the community of disciples is separated from all others (13:10-17).

  iv. *Rituals and Association.* Associating with this group, complying with its entrance ritual of baptism (28:19), accepting its teaching (7:24-27), worshiping (2:1-12; 5:23-24),[35] interacting with other members in appropriate ways (e.g., with forgiveness [6:14-15; 18:21-35], love [22:38-39]), participating in its governance (18:15-20) and ritual meals (26:26-29), praying its prayer (6:9-13), and living its praxis of inclusive mercy (10:7-8; 19:16-30; 25:31-46) forge identity for participants in this community.[36] Rituals create order, sustain a community in an alternative way of living, and effect transformation.[37]

   v. *Social Organization.* The gospel shapes the community's governance. There is no recognized leadership, teaching office (23:8-12), or hierarchical control (20:20-28). The community (at least ideally) is to be an egalitarian community in which all imitate Jesus in serving one another (20:25-28). The community makes decisions about appropriate behaviors and practices (18:18). It has its own disciplinary structure (18:15-17). Yet the audience is to continue to interact with and participate in its larger society and religious traditions (e.g., 5:43-48).[38]

vi. *Invective against Opponents.* Matthew vilifies Jesus' opponents, the religious leaders. He names them as enemy, hypocrite, blind guides, evil,[39] serpents, brood of vipers, and so on.[40] They fail to understand the scriptures and the power of God (22:29). They oppress, rather than lead, the people (9:36). They are disqualified from leadership (21:43; 23:38). They have no place socially in the Matthean community or eschatologically in God's future (15:13; 23:13).[41] The gospel also defines its desired way of life "over against" dominant groups. The audience is not to emulate the perceived hypocrisy of the synagogue (6:2-6, 16-18). Nor can disciples heap up empty phrases in prayer "as the Gentiles do" (6:7) or secure the material necessities for life as the Gentiles do. They are to seek first God's empire (6:33). Disciples are not to structure their community relations and exercise power as the leaders of the Gentiles do (20:25). It is a resistant way of life.

vii. *Apocalyptic Eschatology.* Apocalyptic eschatology is a way of understanding the world. It views human experience in a fundamental temporal, cosmic, and social dualism. There are two ages: the present evil age, which disregards God's purposes, and the future glorious age, when God's purposes will be triumphantly established (13:36-43). There are two cosmic forces: Satan, who opposes God's purposes, and God, who will assuredly establish God's reign (4:1-11). There are two social groups who are aligned with this cosmic struggle and who experience the present in two fundamentally different ways. The righteous or just are faithful to God but are powerless in a crisis of oppression and tyranny inflicted by the wicked. The righteous and wicked have two quite different destinies. In the new age, which could dawn at any moment, God will punish the wicked and vindicate the oppressed righteous (25:31-46). Matthew reinterprets this common Jewish worldview in relation to Jesus. In Jesus' ministry, the new age marked by God's reign or empire is beginning to dawn. At Jesus' return, it will be established in full through judgment and vindication (see chs. 13; 24-25).

Such a worldview functions to legitimate Jesus' disciples as the group that is faithful to God's purposes. Though oppressed in the present, they will be vindicated in the future at God's coming triumph. This apocalyptic worldview provides them with a cosmic perspective on their experiences of the present and offers encouragement and hope in God's future. Then the righteous will get their reward and the wicked will be punished. The constant emphasis on future accountability in the judgment functions to strengthen group solidarity and to control group behavior and practices.

This apocalyptic mind-set reinforces their identity as recipients of God's favor, fashions a lifestyle according to God's will, warns of dire consequences for failing to live accordingly, but promises reward and salvation for continued faithfulness.[42]

viii. *Community Definition by Origin, Governance, and Practices.* A common pattern for defining a group or people in the ancient world consisted of describing its origin, accomplishments (especially governance), and deeds or way of life.[43] This pattern is evident, for instance, in the first-century B.C.E. historian Dionysius of Halicarnassus (*Rom Ant* 1.9-2.29), in the first-century Jewish historian Josephus (*Con Ap* 2.145-295), in the second-century encomia on Rome and on Athens by Aristides, and in the third-century C.E. instructional treatise on encomia by Menander of Laodicea.[44] This definitional pattern of focusing on origin, accomplishments, and deeds affirms and strengthens shared perceptions of a community's identity by renewing visions of what a people holds to be important.

Matthew's gospel incorporates these topics of origin, governance and practices to shape and legitimate the marginal identity and lifestyle of a community of disciples.

a) Origin

The gospel begins by setting out Jesus' genealogy (1:1-17), miraculous conception (1:18-25), birth (2:1a), early childhood (2:1b-21), and settlement in Nazareth (2:22-23)—conventional topics for encomia and *bioi*.[45] Jesus originates in Israel's history with God (1:1-17) and in God's purposes (1:18-25), which protect him in a hostile and dangerous imperial world (2:1-23). God commissions him for a special task (1:1, 21-23; 2:15; 3:17).

Echoes of Joseph and of Moses link Jesus with Israel's origins in liberation from slavery.[46] Like Joseph, Jesus travels to Egypt. Like Moses, Jesus is born into a world of empire and a murderous ruler (ch. 2). Both Pharaoh and Herod learn of the baby from scribes. Moses and Jesus dwell in Egypt. God thwarts the destructive actions taken against them and keeps them safe to carry out the tasks to which they are commissioned. Jesus, like Moses and his people, passes through water (3:13-17) and encounters temptation "in the wilderness" (4:1-11). Jesus seems to reprise the exodus story (see 2:15). To invoke Joseph and Moses is to associate Jesus with the founding of an ancient people.

Jesus too brings a community into existence. He is a son or child of Abraham (1:1), and God brings into existence more children of Abraham (3:9). As a child or son of God (2:15; 3:17), he brings into existence a community of children of God (5:9, 43-45). He who is descended from David and is a king (1:1; 2:2) and who announces a kingdom or empire has subjects (4:17-22), a people being saved from sin (1:21). He establishes this community by calling disciples (4:18-22; 9:9; 10:1-4),[47] disrupting their "normal" existence, teaching them

(5-7; 10; 13; 18; 24-25), creating a new community and family (12:46-50), commissioning them for mission (4:19b; 10:5-14; 28:19-20). The genealogy and connections with Abraham, Joseph, and Moses locate Jesus and his community within Israel, a people of great antiquity (1:1-17).

b) Accomplishments/Governance

The gospel provides teaching on communal governance.[48] This governance is a theocracy, focused not on offices and officials but on the community of disciples who do God's will revealed by Jesus (1:21; 11:25-27; 12:46-50).

Jesus does not reveal God's will for the community *ex nihilo*. He interprets traditions (5:21-48) and appeals to antiquity, God's will "from the beginning" (19:3-6), and to the teaching of Moses (8:1-4), David (12:3; 22:42-45), and the prophets (9:10-13). These appeals cohere with Jesus' interpretive principles expressed in 5:17-20.[49] He has not come to "abolish" the scriptures. Rather, using the language of "Greek political discussions of a state's or a people's constitution,"[50] he has come to "fulfill," to interpret appropriately and justly,[51] the existing law and the prophets (5:17). Jesus is the definitive and reliable interpreter for disciples (5:21-48; 7:23-27; 12:46-50), while his opponents, the religious leaders are sadly deficient since they know "neither the scriptures nor the power of God" (22:29).

Jesus' instruction is not for his own time only, since his words will never pass away (24:35). They are to be faithfully taught to successive members and generations of the community (28:19-20). But they must also be reinterpreted. Dionysius and Josephus uphold a utopian idea from earlier writers that the founder's constitution remains for the people's history and only the impious and unjust would abolish or alter it.[52] Yet both historians recognize that new circumstances bring revisions, even the abolition of laws. While Matthew's Jesus declares that he will not abolish the law, he seems, while fulfilling it, to do almost that (5:43-48). And in 16:19, utilizing further vocabulary from Greek political discussions about a state's constitution,[53] Jesus authorizes Peter, the community's representative "to bind and loose," to have the power to determine which laws and teachings are or are not to be observed.[54] The gospel demonstrates this provision to revise communal practice. In new circumstances, Jesus legitimates the Gentile mission (28:18-20), having earlier limited preaching to Israel (10:5). The teachings are "adaptable for life."[55]

The same vocabulary from Greek political discussions about a state's constitution appears in chapter 18. Now, speaking to the whole community, Matthew's Jesus authorizes the community "to bind and loose" (18:18), to decide which laws and teachings are or are not to be observed, and if so how. The community is given a procedure for disciplining members who do not live appropriately (18:15-20). Ultimately disciples are accountable to God, who will reward and punish disobedient and obedient disciples at the judgment (chs. 24-25). Each teaching section ends with scenes depicting reward for faithful discipleship and punishment for unfaithfulness (7:15-27; 10:32-42; 13:47-50; 18:21-35; 25:31-46).

As part of this communal governance, the gospel also attests concern with household order. Philosophical traditions claim the household as a basic unit of a state or kingdom. Those who encounter the empire of the heavens (βασιλεία, *basileia*) are to live in appropriately structured households.[56] Matthew 19-20 subverts the four standard elements of philosophical discussions of household order to offer an alternative household structure.[57] Instead of unrestricted patriarchal power, more "egalitarian" structures are proposed. There are severe warnings against lust, adultery, and male power in divorce (5:27-32; 19:3-12). Children are important (19:13-15; cf. 2:1-23; 18:1-14).[58] Excessive wealth is to be redistributed and used for the poor (19:16-30; 6:19-34). The audience is to live as slaves (20:17-28).

c) Actions

Jesus' five major teaching sections (chs. 5-7; 10; 13; 18; 24-25) outline actions envisioned for disciples.[59] The experience of God's saving presence and empire is fundamental to this way of life (1:21-23; 4:17). Numerous stories depict the transforming experiences of those who encounter God's merciful and saving reign in Jesus. People are healed, sight is restored, demons are cast out, marginalized people are accepted, the dead are raised, the speechless have speech restored (4:18-25 following 4:17; chs. 8-9).

One of the primary actions or virtues evident in the community is not domination but justice or righteousness.[60] Some interpreters have claimed that this term refers to God's saving action; others have argued that it refers to human ethical action, while still others have suggested that its meaning is not consistent. More accurate I think is the view that it denotes God's will or saving reign enacted in human actions. The term "justice" is used seven times (3:15; 5:6, 10, 20; 6:1, 33; 21:32), though in contexts such as 5:20 and 6:1 it serves as an inclusive term for other virtues which the subsequent material describes (5:21-48; 6:2-18). Righteousness or justice (3:15; 5:6) means reconciling and faithful relationships (5:21-26, 27-32), integrity of one's word (5:33-37), nonviolent resistance to evil (5:33-37), love and prayer even for one's enemy (5:43-48), mercy in giving alms (6:2-4), prayer (6:5-15; 7:6-11), fasting (6:16-18), an anxiety-free existence trusting God (6:19-34), refraining from judging others (7:1-5). It creates a distinctive way of life not shared by the wider society and for which disciples are persecuted (5:10).

Closely related are love and mercy. Disciples are to love God (22:37). They are also to love one other and their enemy, in imitation of and in response to God's indiscriminate love (22:38-39; 5:43-48; 7:12). On the same basis, disciples who know God's forgiveness of sin forgive one another and maintain community relationships (6:14-15; 18:21-35). Likewise the experience of God's mercy (5:7) means a life marked by mercy and peacemaking (9:13; 12:7; 6:2-4; 5:7, 9). The expression of love and mercy is practical (5:42; 6:1-4; 19:20-22; 25:31-46). Jesus sends disciples to continue his mission of preaching, healing, and casting out demons among the marginalized and Gentiles (5:13-16; 10:7-8;

24:14; 25:31-45; 28:18-20). Jesus warns, though, of hostility and rejection; courage and perseverance are needed (10:14-25).[61]

These distinctive practices of the community frequently collide with and resist dominant societal practices and commitments. Nonviolent resistance, not passivity or violence, comprises a basic social strategy (5:43-48). Justice—not birth, wealth, and social prestige—is the priority (6:34). Service replaces domination (20:20-28). Practical mercy is normal praxis (9:12; 12:7). God's empire, not Rome's, is supreme (chs. 24-25).

The gospel seeks, then, to define the identity and way of life of the community of disciples by presenting its distinctive origin, governance, deeds, and practices which are to mark its everyday life. What, then, are the circumstances of the audience called to such a way of life?

4. MATTHEW'S GOSPEL: WHO? WHERE? WHEN?

Through the millennia the church has attributed the gospel's vision-giving power to the Holy Spirit. That affirmation invites questions. Through what circumstances did the Spirit first work to bring such a document, such a vision and challenge into existence?

I am not investigating the gospel's place of origin, date, and author because I think that this original context is the only context in which to understand the gospel. Nor do I think that we in the twenty-first century can somehow recover "the original" meaning. Nor do I think that the original meaning, even if we could capture it, determines all subsequent readings.

Rather, I do it because as I have noted above in relation to its hostility toward the synagogue and its images of "Father" for God and "empire" for God's purposes that the gospel bears the marks of the world in which it was created and to which it addressed. It cannot help being culturally shaped in its language, settings, characters, events, perspectives, constructs of power, gender, social relations and ethnicity, and the knowledge and experience it assumes of its audience.[62] Being attentive to these and other aspects of the gospel will help us understand this text which comes from a distinctive and different time and place. It will also prevent us from absolutizing our own time and place, from committing the sin of literary xenophobia, which dismisses a foreign world as unworthy of our attention. It will give us distance and perspective, which help us to reflect on our own sociohistorical location as we interact with this gospel.

Who?

We simply do not know who wrote Matthew's gospel.[63] In all likelihood it was probably not the disciple Matthew named in 9:9. This disciple has no other prominence in the gospel, no privileged meetings with Jesus. He is not, for example, a special witness of private events such as Jesus' baptism or the transfiguration (see 17:1). He appears eighth on the list of disciples in 10:2-4, hardly a rank of preeminence. Moreover, this gospel probably relies significantly on

Mark's gospel, written around 70 C.E. Matthew's gospel was probably not written until the 80s or 90s of the first century (as I will demonstrate shortly). In an age in which forty was considered old age for many, an eyewitness disciple of Jesus would have been long dead by then.

In addition, the first evidence of a link between this gospel and the name "Matthew" comes from Irenaeus near the end of the second century, a hundred years after the gospel was written. He refers to this gospel as "according to Matthew" (*Against Heresies* 3.1.1).[64] The intriguing question is why this link is made. Why does Matthew's name come to be associated with this gospel?

Several good guesses can be made. The name "Matthew" means "gift of God," an appropriate designation for the good news that this story offers. The name Matthew also sounds somewhat similar to the word "disciple" in Greek (μαθητής, *mathētēs*), a word that literally means "a learner." That too is appropriate for a gospel which seeks to train disciples to live an alternative existence.

Another guess takes us in a somewhat different direction. Perhaps the name Matthew is associated with this gospel because the disciple Matthew was, after the crucifixion of Jesus and before the writing of the gospel, a significant figure for the community to whom the gospel was addressed. Perhaps Matthew founded this community with his preaching or nurtured it with his teaching. Perhaps that instruction forms the basis of the traditions which are brought together in the gospel. The name Matthew, then, would recall this past and invoke the authority and memory of this distinguished leader. But as the frequent use of the words "guess" and "perhaps" in this paragraph indicate, in the final analysis, we do not know who wrote it.

I will continue to refer to Matthew's gospel and "Matthew" while recognizing that we do not know who this Matthew may have been as a historical figure.

Where?

Nor can we be entirely sure about where it was written.[65] Suggestions include Jerusalem or Palestine,[66] Caesarea Maritima,[67] Sepphoris or Tiberias in Galilee,[68] the Transjordan at Pella,[69] or Syria.[70] There are some good reasons for thinking that Matthew's gospel was written in the city of Antioch-on-the-Orontes river in the Roman province of Syria in the last decade or two of the first century.[71] The earliest citations of this gospel are found in writings that have connections with Syria, and Antioch in particular. Ignatius, the "bishop" of Antioch in the first decade of the second century, utilizes material found only in Matthew in his letters to several churches.[72] And the *Didache*, written about the same time, cites the Lord's Prayer in its Matthean, not Lukan, version (compare *Did* 8:1-3 with Matt 6:9-13 and Luke 11:1-4). These apparent uses of Matthew's gospel in material originating from Antioch and widely used in Syria suggest a similar place of origin for the gospel. Matthew 4:24 refers to Jesus' fame spreading "throughout all Syria." This reference is absent from the likely source passage in Mark 1:28, 39 and is unusual given the emphasis on

Galilee in Matt 4:12-15, 23, 25. It suggests local color, an act of writing one's own place and audience into the story.

It has also been noted that Peter plays a more prominent role in this gospel than in Mark. He is the first disciple to be called (4:18-20), the first named on the list of disciples (10:2), the one who imitates Jesus in walking on the water (14:28-32), the disciple who confesses Jesus as "Christ the son of God," the one on whom Jesus will build his church (16:16-18), one of the three disciples who witnesses Jesus' transfiguration (17:1-8). He accompanies Jesus in Gethsemane (26:36-46) and plays a prominent if not glorious role in the crucifixion (26:33-35, 58, 69-75). This emphasis may reflect the significant role that Peter played in the church at Antioch (so Gal 2:11-14).

While other places have been suggested, none makes a stronger case than Antioch. We cannot be certain about this location, and in arguing for Antioch I do not rule out that the gospel may have been written for various communities of disciples in the vicinity of Antioch or Syria.[73] Nor do my claims in this reading depend on an Antiochene provenance. But in the absence of a better suggestion, I will focus on Antioch. I will shortly discuss the implications of locating the gospel's audience in and around Antioch.

When?

Just as no manuscript exists that indicates the gospel's place of origin and author, so no manuscript notes its date of composition. Several criteria point to a likely date in the 80s or 90s of the first century C.E., some fifty or sixty years after the crucifixion of Jesus around the year 30. First, the citation of this gospel by Ignatius and by the *Didache* indicates that at the latest it was written by the beginning of the second century. Two factors point to 70 C.E. as the earliest possible date for Matthew's gospel. Scholars have generally, though by no means universally, accepted that Matthew's gospel uses Mark as one of its sources. Matthew rewrites Mark, eliminating, editing, abbreviating, and adding material. Mark was probably written around 70, or perhaps in the last years of the decade of the 60s.[74] Matthew's gospel was written some years after Mark, perhaps a decade or two, when Mark's gospel, probably written in Rome, had become known to Matthew's community in Syria.

A further factor indicates a time of writing after 70 C.E. Matthew's gospel refers to the destruction of Jerusalem, carried out in 70 C.E. by the Romans and interprets it as God's punishment. In 22:1-14, Jesus tells the parable of the king who hosts a wedding feast for his son. Those invited do not come. Verse 7 records the king's violent response. He sends troops to destroy them and burn their city; then he invites others to the feast. The king's response is extreme. The scenario of the king celebrating his son's wedding among the city's smoking ruins is quite unrealistic. Verse 7, moreover, disrupts the sequence between v. 6 and v. 8, and it is missing from Luke's version of the parable (Luke 14:15-24). It looks as though Matthew added v. 7 to the rest of the parable to provide a theological interpretation of Rome's destruction of Jerusalem. The gospel's writer, along with other Jewish interpreters of the time,[75] views Jerusalem's destruction by the Romans as God's punishment. For Matthew, the punishment is for the elite's sin in rejecting God's agent or son Jesus (see also 21:12-13, 18-19, 41-43; 22:7; 23:37-39; 24:15; 27:25).

These dates, then, provide a "window of opportunity" for the writing of the gospel. Sometime after 70 C.E. but before 100 C.E., perhaps in the 80s, an author now unknown to us, probably living in the city of Antioch in Syria, wrote a gospel which sometime in the second century came to bear the name Matthew.[76]

5. DISCIPLESHIP IN ANTIOCH

What experiences of living in this large city in the late first century are assumed of the gospel's audience? Understanding some of the dynamics of pre-industrial or ancient cities provides crucial information in engaging the gospel's vision of discipleship as marginal existence.[77]

Antioch in Syria was perhaps the third largest city of the Roman empire behind Rome and Alexandria.[78] The city had been founded about 300 B.C.E. by Seleucus I on the Orontes River on the southwest corner of the Amuk plain, some fourteen or so miles inland from the Mediterranean Sea. Subsequent expansion onto the island in the river to the north, toward Mt. Silpius to the east, and the suburb of Daphne to the south, had increased its size. It was laid out in a typical grid pattern with the main axis, the famous colonnaded main street, running northeast to southwest.

Antioch was the capital of the Roman province of Syria. Consistent with Roman practice elsewhere, the city was the key unit for maintaining control over a much larger area. As was typical of the empire's practices, Rome cooperated with and utilized the local elite in exercising control.[79] This alliance had a(n in)vested interest in ensuring political and socioeconomic privileges. As a commercial center, Antioch was the point of convergence for several major north–south and east–west trade routes.[80] Its location on the then navigable Orontes River some fourteen miles from the Mediterranean Sea also ensured its economic significance. The legate or governor was responsible for the administration of Roman law. Appeal to him meant, at least in theory, legal process and rights. But as numerous ancient authors recognized, judges and verdicts could be bought. Those with wealth and greater status received more favorable treatment than those of lower ranks.[81] Reputation and money functioned for one and against the other.

Though large by ancient standards, Antioch was small both in population and in area when compared to modern cities. Estimates put Antioch's population at about 150,000 to 200,000 at the end of the first century.[82] The city's area comprised about 3.2 km. (2.0 mi.) in length and 1.2-1.5 km. (0.75-1.0 mi.) in width.[83]

Population density was intense. R. Stark estimates a density of 117 people per square acre, compared with 21 people per square acre in contemporary Chicago or 37 in New York. But given that about 40 percent of the city area was taken up with public buildings such as an agora/forum, market buildings, streets (mostly narrow), basilica, gymnasia, baths, temples and monuments, the density of living space increases to 205 per acre (compare 183 in Bombay and 122 in Calcutta).[84] With such density of population, privacy was minimal, scrutiny intense, and conflict imminent.

Moreover in social structure, the city resembled any city of the empire in that its population consisted essentially of two groups, the small elite, perhaps up to 5 to 10 percent of the population, who controlled city life for their own advantage, and the nonelite, comprising a spectrum of the very poor to the somewhat wealthy, who served the needs of the elite.[85] In this structure, the elite's societal dominance rested essentially on power (economic, political), considerable wealth (particularly from land), and public repute (Plutarch, "How to Tell a Flatterer," *Moralia* 58C-D "power or wealth or repute").

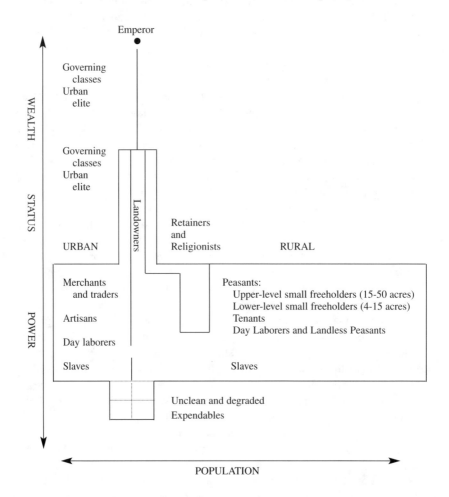

Figure 1[86]

At the very top, the governor or legate, appointed from Rome (see Josephus, *JW* 7.58-59), represented the emperor. He commanded the legions, collected taxes, and maintained public order. Below the legate was the governing elite, allies of Rome. The elite in Antioch comprised several groups which reflected the city's political, military, administrative, and commercial roles. Prominent were the great landowners, whose wealth derived from their control of land and raw materials. The elite's political power was exercised through the *boulē,* or council, which comprised perhaps up to five hundred members,[87] and was responsible for legislative and executive matters (in consultation with the legate), including appointments to various civic positions.

Economic support for this elite group of consumers came from taxes, interest on loans, and rents (often paid in kind). Defaults on loans made to small farmers provided one means of increasing landholdings.[88] The elite may also have derived some income from trade and commerce.[89] While some of the wealthy regarded trade as inferior and saw landed wealth as preferable, trade nevertheless seems to have provided a subsidiary source of revenue.[90] Some merchants without land could make considerable wealth but often lacked social or political power.

The elite were assisted in their exercise of power by two groups. One of these comprised priests and priestesses, who were appointed or elected to city temples, often as reward for acts of beneficence to the city. They might be supported by produce from temple land or by a salary.[91] The second group, retainers, carried out the elite's wishes as bailiffs, tax collectors, government bureaucrats or administrators/clerks, educators, judges, and soldiers. Their power was derived from their association with the elite, and so they were subject to their favor. Antioch was home to three or four legions, approximately fifteen to twenty thousand soldiers, and was a "staging ground" for troops in the 66-70 C.E. war.[92] Since Roman control or peace (*Pax Romana*) resulted from intimidation and war ("peace with bloodshed," to misquote Tacitus, *Ann* 1.10.4),[93] the legions had a vital and visible role to play in securing it from outside threat and internal turmoil. The considerable economic support needed for this imperial presence came from taxes and levies (often in kind), as was typical of the Rome's tributary political-economic system.[94] Josephus records that Syria supplied corn and other necessities to Titus's army attacking Jerusalem in the 66-70 C.E. war (*JW* 5.520).

Around and beneath the elite lived the nonelite, most of the city's population. The nonelite included the free, the freed, and slaves. They comprised small merchants, artisans (who could not produce enough to gain significant wealth), and laborers. They supplied the skills, labor and goods which sustained the elite's way of life.[95] R. MacMullen lists a cross-section of possible occupations in an ancient city:

> sailors, pilots, bargees, divers, longshoremen, caulkers, shipwrights, cordwainers; joiners, inlayers, ebonists, cabinetmakers, sawyers, millhands, coopers, carpenters; mosaicists, fresco-painters, floor-layers, plasterers; cleaners, weavers, dyers, clothiers, ragpickers, bag-makers,

tailors, felterers; tanners, cobblers, bootmakers, hosiers; farriers, bronze-, silver-, gold-, iron-, and nail-smiths; dancers, tragedians, comedians, singers, flutists, harpists, choristers, and many, many other specialists untranslatably named according to what they did for a living.[96]

Such a list, as the last lines indicate, is not complete. Food vendors, providers of transport, and unskilled day laborers need to be added. The work of the non-elite was family-based. A male usually learned the trade or skill of his family. Kinship and dependence on wealthy but benign patrons were crucial though unpredictable strategies for survival.

A large group of involuntary marginals comprises the bottom level of society. Often coerced by socioeconomic and political forces beyond their control, this lower social strata included the unclean and the expendables, who did despised and sporadic work: day laborers, the destitute, some slaves, those dependent on alms, women without familial support, the diseased and physically maimed, criminals, bandits, and prostitutes. Outside the city were the peasants, heavily taxed and always scraping for even a subsistence existence. Some were freeholders with varying sizes of landholdings; others were tenant farmers, day laborers (see Matt 20:1-16) and slaves.

Socially, then, the city reflects a vertical, hierarchical, and interconnected social structure ranging from a few extremely wealthy families to the much larger numbers of free and freed poor and slaves.[97] While there was some social mobility (Petronius's Trimalchio represented the *nouveau riche,* who gained wealth through manumission, an inheritance, marriage, or perhaps trade), for many there was no thought of "improvement." The struggle was to maintain one's existence and social position, often in a new urban environment without the status and protection accorded by their previous rural and family connections.[98]

In addition to being hierarchical, vertical, and interconnected, the social structure was marked by hostility. The writings of the elite indicate that they generally despised the nonelite. One social historian observes, "We may note in passing the categories that are held up for derision: in cities, petty artisans and people of no fixed place of business, the unpropertied; in the countryside, peasants; also, everywhere, slaves, children, and women."[99] While some members of the elite, not the city or empire, provided handouts for selected groups of "deserving poor" and often with an eye to the provider's honor or advantage, the general view seems to be that it was impossible to do enough and that most poor generally deserved nothing more or less than their poverty.[100]

Less well attested are the feelings of the nonelite, the witnesses of the elite's conspicuous consumption. Plutarch imagines that the nonelite are resentful, jealous, violent, and contemptuous toward the rich ("Precepts of Statecraft," *Moralia* 822A). Lucian's cock claims that the rich find the nonelite to be ungrateful and physically threatening (*The Cock,* 20-23). And Diogenes sends a message from the realm of the dead which mocks the rich and encourages the poor that in death they will "see rich men, satraps, and tyrants so humble and insignificant with nothing to distinguish them but their groans" (Lucian,

Dialogues of the Dead, 1.330, 333, 334; also 4.336-37; 22.437-47). Josephus records the desperation of a fire around 70 in Antioch which "burnt down the market-square, the magistrates' quarters, the record-office, and the law courts-exchange." It was started by some men "who, under the pressure of debts, imagined that if they burnt the market-place and the public records they would be rid of all demands" (*JW* 7.55, 61). One can imagine a range of attitudes: desperation, hostility, resentment, envy, resignation, disregard, determined efforts to survive, obsequiousness, and gratefulness for occasional handouts.

Social relations are further complicated by the honor-shame code typical of ancient urban societies.[101] One's status, one's prestige in the eyes of others or lack thereof, rested partly on ancestry (including place of origin), on one's social rank or *ordo* reflecting wealth, and on political office or power. Also important were language and accent, freedom (not slavery), education, occupation, gender (male dominated female), ethnicity and age.[102] But status or honor is not a permanent commodity. It must constantly be demonstrated and renewed. One's achievements, housing, clothing, and social connections and interaction, especially one's place in networks of patrons and clients, played a huge role in demonstrating one's status. The city provided the elite with opportunities to perform their duty in spending money to display and maintain status: through public service and office, through public displays of beneficence in funding a statue, a festival, a public building or entertainment, religious observance, or handout to some poor residents, through sponsorship of a voluntary association or organization, and through carefully prescribed social interactions of obligation and subservience (so Cicero, *De Off* 2.54-63). By these means members of the elite maintained their rule over others. Males tended to represent the household in the public domain while women's roles tended to be restricted to the private sphere, though this division was by no means strictly enforced, especially for elite women.[103]

Organization of Physical Space

The physical organization of the city reinforced this social verticality. According to Pausanias, people expected to find certain buildings in a city (*Description of Greece* 10.4.1). He doubts that "one can give the name of city to those who possess no public buildings, no gymnasium, no theatre, no market-place, no water descending to a fountain, but live in bare shelters just like mountain huts on the edge of ravines." Antioch clearly included all of these buildings and more. W. L. MacDonald identifies the public buildings typical of an ancient city: administrative (basilica), commercial (market, shops, storehouses), cultural (library, theater, amphitheater), hygienic (baths, latrine, cistern), recreational (bath, theater, circus, stadium), and religious (temples, cult buildings).[104]

Antioch seems to have had several "centers of power": near the river (including the island), which was the site of the original agora and royal residence, along the famous colonnaded main street running northeast to southwest, and within the "new" quarter Epiphania started by Antiochus Epiphanes and developed in the first century by the emperor Tiberius. In addition to the agora near the river, Epiphania included an agora and *bouleutērion,* or meeting and council hall burned in 23/24 C.E.[105] G. Downey suggests the agora near the river was devoted to trade, while the "tetragonal" agora in Epiphania served political and educational purposes.[106]

Attention to the spatial organization of cities such as Antioch illuminates its social organization. As Dominic Perring argues, "space is structured to meet the needs of society, and gives shape to social life."[107] He argues that the elite of cities such as Antioch used space for several purposes: to include and exclude, to provide for legitimate activities and to discourage unacceptable actions, to ensure social cohesion and differentiation.

The imposing residences of the elite tended to cluster near the center, and the nonelite more toward the periphery. MacMullen notes, "The closer to the heart of the city, the more respectable; the farther away, the more scorned, until the suburbs melted into the countryside."[108] Social distinctions reinforced by location, however, were not rigid because the elite needed the nonelite for practical (supplying goods and services) and for social reasons (maintaining their status).[109] Patron–client relations were, as noted above, a basic form of social intercourse, permitting, controlling, and restricting contact.[110] A client's commitment to a wealthier patron benefited both, the former materially and socially, the latter socially and politically through displays of the patron's influence and wealth that brought honor. The nonelite tended to cluster in areas according to ethnic and occupational groups. Street, trade, burial, and religious associations provided some social cohesion (section 10).[111]

The elite's control of the physical space is evident in considering the theater and amphitheater. They were started by emperors in the first century B.C.E. and were located on the slopes of Mt. Silpius. The theater was expanded by Agrippa, Tiberius, and, early in the second century, by Trajan. Its expanded capacity included more citizens but controlled their activities through entertainment. In the case of the amphitheater, the greater capacity removed more inhabitants from the center of the city.[112] By the first century Antioch also included several walls, both internal and external.[113] Defense was an obvious function, but walls also defined the boundary between city and country. Gates provided places of control at which to levy tolls on market goods, and, through inscriptions and visual images, a means of displaying sovereignty (see 7:13-14).

City and Country

Evident in the description so far is the agricultural basis of Antioch's economy, and the close relationship between the city and the surrounding countryside of the plain of Amuk and the lower Orontes valley.[114] The nature of this connection is, though, debated. Some scholars, such as McMullen, view the relationship between city and country as symbiotic, in which both were mutually dependent, the empire supplying order, security, and entertainment in return for food.[115] Others, though, see the relationship much more convincingly in terms of conflict and the oppression of the country by the city and rural elites. The relationship existed for the benefit of the consuming elite and at the expense of the rural producers. The city-based elite controlled the surrounding rural villages, land, and yield and gained wealth through predatory or tributary economic practices: rents (for land use), interest on loans, requisitions, and taxes (on markets, livestock, produce).[116] In addition to these urban demands, peasants also had to supply family needs, provide for stock, and acquire seed for the next year's crop. Any surplus of grain, wine, oil, hides, and so on, though taxed and irregular especially in times of drought and famine as in the mid-40s in Antioch, benefited the nearby city, though if K. Hopkins is right, some inter-regional trade also occurred.[117] The city was the "central space," drawing to itself the surrounding countryside's resources. Corbier comments that "cities could only live by siphoning off the resources of the country, and this did not only take the form of rents. They derived profit from the collection of taxes . . . [and] levies such as the requisition of grain."[118]

City and country seem to have had ambivalent attitudes toward each other. Peasants are often suspicious of cities and regarded Antioch as a place of vice, lazy pleasure, and control, which removed food and imposed taxes, while being necessary for ordered existence. Rural areas were often viewed with derision as inferior places, uncultured and marked by scorned manual work. Yet there was some nostalgia for rustic virtues and the realization of the social and economic importance of owning land.[119] Interaction between the two favored the urban elite. Their wealth meant that the rural village poor, who formed the bulk of the population, moved in the narrow sphere between famine and subsistence. In seeking abolition of debt or the redistribution of land, peasants could and did revolt at times with acts of violence against landowners, tax collectors and buildings holding debt records (as in Antioch in 69-70).[120] But revolts occurred only sporadically. Perhaps the fear of force, failure, or retaliation and trained deference, which socialized people into "knowing one's place" and not dreaming of alternatives account for the lack.[121] The elite could stave off revolts through patronal relationships and calculated acts of social goodwill. By remitting some debt or sponsoring a festival or entertainment, oppression could be alleviated enough to secure compliance through gratitude and dependence.

Physical Conditions

While the city could be a comfortable place for the wealthy, conditions were not pleasant for most inhabitants, the nonelite population. Rodney Stark provides a graphic description of life in first-century Antioch.[122] While the elite lived in large mansions, some of which have been partially excavated,[123] or in spacious upper-level apartments, most people lived in smaller houses or in small-roomed apartments in multistoried tenement buildings, often very smokey from cooking. Streets were narrow and served as public living space and shop fronts. Intense population density placed heavy demands on sewage disposal and water supply. Water, brought to the city by aqueducts from springs, was piped to wealthy houses and to public baths, latrines, fountains, and storage tanks.[124] Most people carried it to their living quarters from fountains or storage tanks in which the stagnant water grew algae and other organisms that endangered health. While public baths and toilets were available, most relied on chamber pots, if that. Sewage was disposed of in open ditches or emptied out windows onto the street. Given numerous animals and warm temperatures, the city was filthy and smelly. It was a breeding ground for disease, for high mortality rates, and short life span. Stark notes that diseased and physically disabled people were very visible, and that men outnumbered women.

In such space lived people of various ethnic groups—Romans, Syrians, Greeks, Jews, Gauls, Germans. Stark estimates eighteen identifiable ethnic quarters. In addition to the social tensions outlined above, ethnic tensions ran high.[125] Jews experienced considerable hostility, for example, around 69-71 C.E. (see section 8). Moreover the population was transient with a constant flow of newcomers, including people from rural areas either dispossessed of land through debt or forced from small family farms unable to supply enough produce. Diversity and an influx of newcomers are, sociologically, prime conditions for crime and disorder. Riots resulting in death and destruction were not uncommon. Residents were vulnerable to fires, which swept through the closely built, predominantly wooden structures. Antioch also experienced famines, earthquakes, and floods from the river and from water pouring down Mt. Silpius. Stark summarizes his picture of life in Antioch:

> Any accurate picture of Antioch in New Testament times must depict a city filled with misery, danger, fear, despair and hatred. Antioch was a city where the average family lived a squalid life in filthy and cramped quarters, where at least half of the children died at birth or during infancy, and where most of the children who lived lost at least one parent before reaching maturity. The city was filled with hatred and fear rooted in intense ethnic antagonisms and exacerbated by a constant stream of strangers. This city was so lacking in stable networks of attachments that petty incidents could prompt mob violence. Crime flourished and the streets were dangerous at night. And, perhaps above all, Antioch was repeatedly smashed by cataclysmic catastrophes. A resident could expect literally to be homeless from time to time, providing that he or she was among the survivors.[126]

Among these socioeconomic, political, and physical realities exists the audience addressed by Matthew's gospel. Who comprised this audience? From what social strata, ethnic groups, and gender were they drawn? How were they to live?

6. WHERE IN ANTIOCH ARE MATTHEW'S CHRISTIANS?

The gospel's narrative world reflects numerous aspects of this societal structure. The tributary economy, based on the retainers' collection of rents, taxes, and tributes for the ruler, is the basis for the parable in 18:23-35. The parable of the householder in 20:1-16 brings together a very wealthy landowner and day laborers. Tax collectors from the retainer level appear in 9:9-13. D. Duling has collected numerous references in the gospel to the large group of involuntary marginals which comprise the bottom level of society.[127]

But where in this urban society are we to locate the Matthean audience addressed by the gospel? While the gospel makes frequent reference to Jesus' involvement with "involuntary marginals" and to the sending of disciples among this group (10:7-8; 25:31-45), we cannot conclude that Matthew's audience thereby consists only or even predominantly of "involuntary marginals." The text's concern with "involuntary marginals" may not reflect the audience's present reality but may sensitize a more privileged audience to mission responsibilities among this group. The relationship between "story world" and audience is not a one-on-one correlation.

Matthew's Audience: A Cross-section of Society

Recent scholarship argues that Matthew's audience probably did not consist predominantly of "involuntary marginals" from the lowest social level, but of a cross-section of urban society. By focusing on numerous, apparently incidental details, some scholars have noted in the gospel, for instance, some features of urban wealth and prosperity.[128]

1. Kingsbury suggests that the gospel's use of Greek, not Aramaic, probably points to an urban, more educated environment.
2. He draws a similar conclusion from the gospel's use of the word "city" twenty-six times (compare Mark's eight), while it uses "village" only four times (compare Mark's seven times).[129]
3. Matthew's audience is assumed to have some familiarity with wealth. Whereas Mark's disciples are not to take "copper coin" on the mission journey (Mark 6:8), Matthew's disciples are not to take the upmarket currency of "gold, silver, or copper coin" (10:9). Whereas Luke's Jesus speaks in a parable about low-valued "minas" (Luke 19:11-27), Matthew's Jesus speaks about "talents" (25:14-30), worth fifty times as much. Whereas in Mark and Luke Joseph of Arimathea is a member of the council (Mark 15:43; Luke 23:50-51), in Matthew he is a "rich man" (27:57).
4. Matthew's language for money is much more varied and elevated in value than that of Luke or Mark. Matthew refers to "silver," "gold," and "talent" twenty-eight times compared with Mark's single and Luke's fourfold reference to "silver" alone.

It is difficult to evaluate these observations. How much do these terms reflect the actual world of members of the Matthean community, or do they reflect aspects in their wider environment of which they are aware but with which they are not personally familiar? One can know that gold is valuable and that wealthy people have it, without having it oneself. Perhaps these details indicate numerous wealthy members. Perhaps they do not.

In the absence of certain and specific information about Matthew's audience, we need to draw from other data about the early Christian movement. An older view saw early Christian groups as comprising predominantly slaves and the very poor.[130] E. A. Judge was one of the early challengers of this view. He examined the names, ranks, and occupations in the Christian documents and concluded that the movement embraced a much broader constituency, a cross-section of society from which the most socially and politically powerful as well as the most underprivileged were largely absent.[131]

Various pieces of evidence can be invoked to support this view.[132] The famous text in 1 Cor 1:26-28 ("not many of you were wise . . . powerful . . . of noble birth") indicates the presence of the more privileged, though in fewer numbers than those without power, wealth, or noble birth. We would expect such a situation, given the societal structure (see section 5).[133] The dispute over the Lord's Supper in 1 Cor 11:17-34, in which some have plenty to eat and drink while others do not, suggests a similar range. The dispute seems to reflect the common social practice whereby order of seating, type and quantity of food, and quality of eating utensils reinforced social distinctions and status.[134] Erastus (Rom 16:23; 2 Tim 4:20), as "the city treasurer" in Corinth, is part of the city's governing elite yet is clearly a member of the church.[135] Christians from the elite, including possibly two senatorial families, are probably part of the church in Rome.[136] The movement utilizes wealthy benefactors (Phoebe, Rom 16:1-2) who provide meeting places in homes big enough to host a number of people, and who support leaders and itinerant teachers and preachers.[137]

The language and style of the writings suggest an audience of some education and literary experience.[138] Stark observes that women are prominent, especially higher-status women.[139] He also argues sociologically (and from contemporary, not ancient, data) that new religious movements often recruit more successfully among the more privileged.[140] This is not to suggest that the Christian movement consisted only of more upper-status members, but it is to observe their presence as part of communities that seemed to include a cross-section of society.

Meeks's analysis of the available data relating to the sixty-five people named in Paul's letters supports this conclusion.[141] While noting the paucity of the evidence, he observes merchants, a physician (perhaps a former slave), people of some wealth, traders, artisans, slaves and freed, skilled and unskilled manual workers. These names indicate diverse social and civic status, ethnic identities, levels of wealth, and gender. Absent generally are the extreme top (e.g., wealthy powerful senators) and the very poor (day laborers, peasants). These Christian communities appear to be a cross-section of society. In the absence of any other data, it seems safe to conclude that the audience for whom Matthew writes was probably similar.

Matthew's audience, then, was probably not constituted predominantly by "involuntary marginals." We cannot of course assume their absence either, especially since the gospel narrates Jesus' extensive mission among them. And, given the common experience of indebtedness, loss of land, and loss of status and kinship networks as rural people moved to the city seeking some means of staying alive, it is likely that some such people comprised Matthew's audience. But the older view that early Christian communities comprised almost exclusively the economically and socially wretched does not seem sustainable. Rather, the audience seems to represent a cross-section of their society.

7. MATTHEW'S AUDIENCE: SMALL IN NUMBER

In addition to being a cross-section of their society, Matthew's audience was probably small in number, a minority community within the larger dominant society. This social experience impacts their hearing of the gospel.

Several images in the gospel affirm smallness as a constituent part of the experience of living as disciples of Jesus. Jesus declares that only a *few* find the narrow and difficult road of discipleship. Assuming Mark's gospel as a source for Matthew's gospel, Matthew retains from Mark the term "little ones" (18:6 = Mark 9:42) as a term for disciples. But Matthew intensifies its use. He adds it to both the beginning (18:10) and the end (18:14) of the Q parable about the ninety-nine sheep (Luke 15:3-7). Whereas in Luke's gospel this parable expresses Jesus' searching out of sinners (Luke 15:2, 7), Matthew redirects its message by placing it in the community discourse of chapter 18. In the previous verses Jesus has warned against causing "one of these little ones who believe in me" to stumble (18:6-7). In this context, and with the addition of the term "little ones" to its introduction (18:10), the parable now concerns disciples caring for every valuable member of the community of disciples. The addition and repetition of "little ones" underline the identity of disciples as vulnerable and at risk, yet very valuable.

Matthew 10:42 adds the term "little ones" to another Markan passage (9:41). In the context of instruction to disciples about their mission to the larger society, the term refers to disciples as missionaries. The verse focuses on their reception.

Two more terms indicate smallness and vulnerability in 11:25. Matthew retains Q's designation of disciples, the recipients of Jesus' revelation, as "infants" (cf. Luke 10:21), and he retains and expands Mark's image of disciples as "children" in 18:1-5 (Mark 9:36-37; 10:15) and 19:13-15 (Mark 10:13-16).

In the subsequent discussion of each section of the gospel, I will unpack these images. It is sufficient to note here that they denote small size, vulnerability, powerlessness but specialness in God's purposes. The combination of "small but special" builds on a Hebrew Bible tradition that is reinterpreted for the Matthean community of disciples of Jesus. The Hebrew scriptures attest the tradition of God's election of Israel precisely because they were "the fewest of all peoples." Moses tells the people:

It was not because you were more numerous than any other people that the Lord preferred you and chose you—you were the fewest of all peoples; it

was because the Lord loved you and kept the oath that the Lord had sworn
to your ancestors that the Lord redeemed you from slavery in Egypt. (Deut
7:7-8)

The gospel continues to affirm the value of smallness and minority experience
in God's liberating purposes (cf. Amos 7:1-6).

How Many?

It is impossible to say how many members or disciples comprised the community or communities addressed by the gospel. While precision is impossible,
it is possible to make some guesses. I will offer two estimates, both of which
indicate a very small number and percentage of Christians in Antioch.

We know from other New Testament writings such as 1 Cor 16:19 and Rom
16:5 that the early Christian groups met in the larger houses of wealthy patrons
or in rented halls. Since most city dwellers lived in small, cramped apartments
in tenement buildings, only the more wealthy with larger houses had space to
host a gathering. J. Murphy-O'Connor has argued that in excavated houses in
Corinth the average size of the triclinium (dining room) was thirty-six square
meters and of an atrium fifty-five square meters. He calculates that it could
accommodate about forty to fifty people for a gathering.[142]

No first-century houses have been excavated at Antioch, but some work has
been done on houses from the second century to the fifth century. R. Stillwell
notes dining rooms ranging from twenty-five to ninety square meters, an average size of about fifty square meters, which would accommodate forty to forty-
five people.[143] If the Christians in Antioch gathered in only one house,[144] there
may have been no more than forty at the time Matthew was written. Perhaps
several groups from within and outside the city gathered in several houses,
which might include up to two hundred Christians at most.

Great care, though, must be taken with this approach. The calculations
depend on average figures, but the sizes of triclinia vary significantly and so
affect the estimate of how many people may have gathered. Moreover, several
of the excavated houses in Antioch have several triclinia, which would increase
the numbers. D. Balch and C. Osiek are critical of J. Murphy-O'Connor's calculation for a third reason.[145] They argue that his focus on the size of the triclinium is too restrictive and overlooks other features of houses that allowed
much larger numbers to gather. They note, for example, that the preference for
as much outdoor living as possible is reflected in the common use of courtyards
or peristyles and gardens with numerous adjoining rooms.[146] They cite the
example of one very large house in Pompeii which incorporated three peristyles, with fifteen rooms opening onto them (six + three + six). They calculate
that the total area of gardens and adjacent rooms could handle 1,135 people.
Another large house with two gardens and a large dining hall could cater for
360 people. Stillwell's discussion of the Antioch houses notes the frequent existence of (though not the measurements of) peristyles and courtyards, as well as
a house with two triclinia.[147] The significance of Balch and Osiek's analysis

lies in expanding the possible number of Christians who might have gathered in a wealthy person's house. While groups of thirty to forty could fit into a triclinium, public spaces in larger houses could clearly handle hundreds of people. These factors create a range from thirty to hundreds, even to a thousand! But without knowing the plan of the exact house or houses in which Christians met, or the number of houses, we have to be content with such a spectrum.

A second method, based not on house size but on percentage of population and growth ratios, encourages us to think of numbers in the bottom of this range. Rodney Stark has calculated that in the year 100 C.E. there were 7,530 Christians in the Roman empire. He reaches this figure by noting that shortly after the year 300 C.E. there were enough Christians in the empire that the emperor Constantine identified with the church. Stark casts about to try to identify how many were "enough" to cause an emperor to act in this way. From the estimates of a number of scholars, he establishes a "range of 5-7.5 million" Christians, and finally settles on 6.3 million, about 10.5 percent of the empire's estimated population of about sixty million. He then asks what growth rate would have been needed for Christianity to reach this figure. His calculations indicate that a growth rate of about 40 percent per decade was needed. Using this figure he calculates that in the year 100 there were about 7,530 Christians in the empire, or 0.0126 percent of the empire's population.[148]

How many Christians in Antioch? Using the figures of T. Chandler and G. Fox, Stark estimates that around the year 100, Antioch had a population of about 150,000.[149] How many Christians were there? On the basis of Stark's figure that in the year 100, 0.0126 percent of the empire were Christian, we can estimate that 0.0126 percent of 150,000 means that there were nineteen Christians.

This figure is perhaps too low. The calculation for Antioch assumes an even percentage of Christians throughout the empire. But this assumption seems unrealistic. Both Acts (chs. 11-13) and Galatians (2:11-14) indicate that Antioch was an important and early center for the Christian movement.[150] A group or groups of followers of Jesus had probably existed there since the 30s. Acts notes the conversion of "a great number" of people in Antioch (11:21, 26) and reports that Antioch was the place where disciples were first called "Christians" (11:26). It also names at least five "prophets and teachers" (Acts 13:1). We have to be somewhat cautious, though, with Acts' numerical claims. While it is tempting to think of large numbers, Acts' general triumphant tone and the frequent use of numbers in antiquity for rhetorical effect rather than for literal information speak against doing so.[151]

These two methods have produced a wide range of possible figures depending on how many groups of Christians we imagine gathering in Antioch and in what size houses. Determining the accuracy of any of these figures is difficult simply because we have so little data. But whether we settle for nineteen or 150 or even a thousand Christians, the Christian community remains a tiny one in a city of 150,000 to 200,000. This experience of being few in number is assumed of the gospel's audience.

8. TENSION WITH A SYNAGOGUE

So far I have sketched the larger urban and societal context of the community addressed by this gospel. In this section and the next, I will outline two significant aspects of the audience's experience in Antioch which deeply impact the way in which the audience hears Matthew's story of Jesus.

Scholars have often noted that Matthew's gospel is a very "Jewish" gospel.[152] They have pointed, for example, to the frequent Hebrew Bible citations, to Jesus' interpretations of the traditions, to the Jewish practices it advocates (such as almsgiving, prayer, and fasting in 6:1-18), to the opening genealogy, which assumes detailed knowledge of the biblical traditions, to references to key Jewish figures like Solomon (6:29; 12:42), Jonah (12:39-41), and David (12:23; 22:42-46). The gospel does not need to argue for the authority and importance of such material. It assumes that its audience values this tradition. Most probably, this audience was Jewish, or at least predominantly so. The gospel indicates some openness to Gentiles (2:1-12; 8:5-13; 15:21-28; 28:19-20), so some Gentile presence is also likely.[153]

There was a significant Jewish population in Antioch.[154] According to Josephus (*Con Ap* 2.39; *Ant* 12.119-24; *JW* 7.44), Jews were among the city's first settlers, mercenaries in the army of Alexander the Great (*Con Ap* 1.192, 200). Those willing to worship the city gods could be enrolled as citizens, but most Jews in the late first century probably lived as a *politeuma,* a largely autonomous neighborhood that was administered by a presiding elder or ruler (*JW* 7.45) and council, with rights of assembly, sabbath observance (cf. *JW* 7.51-53), their own judges, freedom to follow and administer their own laws and customs (cf. *Ant* 14.235), and exemption from military service.[155]

The regard in which Antioch's Jewish residents were held varied over the centuries. Josephus indicates a long tradition of Syrian conflicts with Jews (*JW* 1.88; 2.266, 461-65, 477-78; 5.550-51), yet he notes that Herod had paved Antioch's main street (*JW* 1.425) and claims numerous Gentile adherents at a synagogue (*JW* 7.45). J. M. G. Barclay suggests that the differences may reflect the experiences of different social levels, with upper levels being more accommodationist and lower levels more antagonistic.[156]

The circumstances of Jews declined significantly in 40 C.E. and 66-70 C.E. In 40 C.E. Antiochene Jews protested against Gaius Caligula's attempts to establish a statue of himself in the Jerusalem temple. They were attacked, some were killed, and synagogues were burned. Similar disturbances in Palestine and Alexandria saw Claudius guarantee Jewish observance of their customs (Josephus, *Ant* 19.286-91).

The situation deteriorated in 66-70. Cestius Gallus, the governor of Syria, failed in 66 to take Jerusalem and had retreated in a disastrous flight (Josephus, *JW* 2.499-555). Jewish protests against Roman actions in Galilee and Judea, and divisions within the Jewish community in Antioch, saw a prominent Jew, Antiochus, accuse other Jews of responsibility for a disastrous fire which destroyed a number of public buildings. Though not found to be responsible, some were massacred in the theater (Josephus, *JW* 7.47, 60-61). For a short time sabbath observance was suspended and some were forced to sacrifice (to the city gods? [Josephus, *JW* 7.50-53]). Calls to revoke Jewish privileges and demands to have Jews expelled were denied by Titus in 70-71 (Josephus, *Ant* 12.119-24; *JW* 7.43-62, 100-111).[157] To have agreed to these demands would have threatened every ethnic group and destabilized the whole city. Yet Titus did not hesitate to display in Antioch signs of the Jewish defeat, and Vespasian minted *Judea capta* coins, which celebrated his victory (see section 9).

At least two synagogue buildings seem to have existed, one in the city and one in nearby Daphne.[158] Jewish groups may also have met in houses, as other religious associations (*collegia*) did. As noted, Josephus claims numerous Gentile adherents (*JW* 7.45). Synagogue buildings functioned as a type of community center for the ethnic group, being a place not primarily of worship but of political organization, communal self-regulation, and social and educational interaction.[159] These multiple meeting places and the instances of conflict among Jews testify that the Jewish community in Antioch was, like the rest of first-century Judaism, diverse and multifaceted in its beliefs, practices, interactions with the Hellenistic world, and responses to the events of 70 c.e.[160] To be in tension with a synagogue is not simply a religious matter, not simply a matter of not being welcome in a building. It means estrangement from one's people and community. It involves political, social, economic, and familial dimensions.

Matthew's audience is part of the diversity of the Antiochene Jewish community. But the gospel attests considerable tension between the Jesus group and some others within the synagogue community. These tensions are evident, for example, in the changes that Matthew makes to his sources, Mark and Q. Many, but not all, scholars think that in writing the gospel, Matthew redacts Mark and Q to address the particular circumstances of its audience and to reflect the author's perspective on that situation.[161]

Six types of changes seem to reflect recent disagreements between Matthew's group and the synagogue.[162]

1. Some changes increase negative and hostile references to the synagogue. Compared with Mark's single use, Matthew uses the phrase "their synagogue" five times (4:23;[163] 9:35; 10:17; 12:9; 13:54) and "your synagogue" once (23:34) to underline distance between Jesus and the synagogue community. Several of these passages emphasize hostility between the synagogue and Jesus' disciples. In 10:17 Jesus warns disciples that they will be flogged in *their* synagogues. In 13:54-58 *their* synagogue rejects Jesus, and in 6:2 and 5 and 23:6, the behavior of "the hypocrites in the [not 'your'] synagogues" is condemned and contrasted with that of "you" in Christian groups.

2. Some changes omit favorable references to the synagogue from the sources. (a) Whereas Jairus is a "ruler of the synagogue" in Mark 5:22, 35, 36, 38, in Matthew the synagogue disappears and he is simply a "ruler" or "official" (Matt 9:18, 23).[164] (b) Luke's version of the Q tradition about the healing of the centurion's servant presents the centurion as a lover of the Jewish people

and a builder of a synagogue (Luke 7:5). Matthew omits these references but retains praise for the man's faith (Matt 8:5-13).

3. Changes especially target the religious leaders and heighten their negative presentation.

- Matthew intensifies Mark's references to the religious leaders' role in opposing and killing Jesus.[165]
- He adds "scribes" to Mark's one reference to the Pharisees as hypocrites to ensure more encompassing condemnation (Mark 7:6; Matt 15:1, 7).
- He adds seven references to "hypocritical" Pharisees.[166]
- Four times he replaces Mark's references to "scribes" with references to Pharisees, suggesting a particular target.[167]
- Unique to Matthew are his descriptions of the scribes and Pharisees as "blind guides" and "blind fools" (23:16, 17, 19, 24, 26; cf. 15:14). Since "seeing" is associated with comprehending disciples (13:10-17) and wisdom with Jesus (11:25-30), these epithets condemn them for not allying themselves with Jesus.

4. The term "rabbi" becomes a negative term used only by false disciples and religious leaders. Matthew removes Peter's two uses of it in Mark by changing one to "Lord" (Mark 11:21 and Matt 21:20) and omitting the other (Mark 9:5 and Matt 17:4). Matthew retains its use by the traitor Judas (Mark 14:45; Matt 26:49). Two added references reinforce its negative associations with betrayal and false discipleship. In 26:21-25 Judas calls Jesus "rabbi" while the remainder of the disciples call him "Lord" (compare no title in Mark 14:19). And in 23:7 "rabbi" is a title that the self-seeking and hypocritical scribes and Pharisees prefer (23:2-7). Matthew's Jesus forbids its use in the Christian community (23:8).

5. Similar dynamics are involved in Matthew's heightened negative portrayal of "scribes" (γραμματεύς, *grammateus*). (a) While Mark contrasts Jesus' teaching authority with that of "*the* scribes" (Mark 1:22), Matthew intensifies the distance between them by changing "*the* scribes" to "*their* scribes" (7:29). (b) Matthew changes the Q tradition of the *person* who volunteers to follow Jesus (Luke 9:57) into a *scribe* who is rejected by Jesus (Matt 8:19). The rejected scribe addresses Jesus as "teacher," while the disciple addresses him as "Lord" (8:21).[168]

(c) In chapter 2 (material unique to Matthew), the scribes do not link the scriptures to Jesus, nor do they act on their knowledge (2:4-6) to pay him homage (cf. 22:29; 7:24-27; 12:46-50).

(d) Matthew significantly recasts Mark's sympathetic account of the scribe whom Jesus declares to be "not far from the kingdom of God" (Mark 12:28-34). Matthew's account (22:34-40) turns the scribe into a Pharisee (22:34), removes Mark's double reference to the scribe's appreciation for Jesus' answers (Mark 12:28, 32), and removes Jesus' commendation of the scribe (Mark 12:32-34). (e) Overall Matthew adds eleven references to "scribes," ten of which are negative.[169] Chapter 23 is very harsh in its condemnation.

6. Some changes intensify polemic against the religious leaders.[170] (a) Matthew contrasts the superior lifestyle of his readers with the justice of the "scribes and the Pharisees" (5:20). (b) In two contexts (21:43; 22:7) Matthew adds verses to parables from Mark (12:1-12, esp. v. 11) and Q (Luke 14:15-24, esp. v. 21) to underline judgment on the religious leaders. (c) The final woe announced against the hypocritical scribes and Pharisees in chapter 23 (23:29-36) identifies them more explicitly than in Q as murderers of followers of Jesus (cf. 23:34 with Luke 11:49).

How do we explain Matthew's consistently heightened negative presentation of the synagogue and the religious leaders? Most redaction critics argue that it reflects the community's experiences of a bitter conflict within at least part of the Jewish community in Antioch. Their present situation reflects some distance and hostility. The intensity of the hostility in the gospel suggests recent and bitter conflict.[171]

The intense polemic is not addressed directly to the "scribes and Pharisees." Rather, as Stanton argues, it is "in-house" for the benefit of Matthew's audience.[172] In its context of conflict in which it feels persecuted (5:10-12; 10:17-18), Matthew's community struggles to make sense of the pain and hostility. It seeks to articulate its own place as a beleaguered minority, but nevertheless a special group in God's scheme of things. The gospel story provides a symbolic universe, a context for making sense of its past, and direction to shape its present and future as a community marginal to the rest of the Jewish community.[173]

Scholars have connected this conflict with the devastating circumstances resulting from Rome's destruction of Jerusalem, the temple, and the priesthood in 70 C.E. (Matt 22:7; 23:38; 24:2; 26:61). The following decades were a time of much anguish and debate as various Jewish groups wrestled with what had happened, why it had happened, and with what the future would look like.[174] Significant for the gradual reformulation of Judaism was the emergence of Pharisaic leadership to provide new focus, new theological understanding, and patterns of worship centered on synagogues.[175] Their emergence as leaders suggests the failure of Matthew's group to carry the day, and may explain Matthew's increased negative references to them.

Issues Involved in the Conflict

There are some clues in the gospel about issues involved in this conflict. Rome's destruction of the Jerusalem temple in 70 required significant reformulation of important theological ideas and religious practices. The temple's destruction shattered a way of worship and understandings of life lived in relation to God. As contemporary works such as *4 Ezra* and *2 Baruch* attest, questions arose about God's faithfulness and power, about encountering God's presence, about experiencing atonement and God's forgiving mercy, about knowing God's revealed will and avoiding God's punishment. Within this debate, Matthew's community/ies made claims about Jesus who had been crucified some forty to fifty years previously but whose presence they encountered. They claimed that Jesus was the one who answered these questions and provided God's salvation (1:21).

Heightened emphasis on three claims in the gospel may attest their role in the conflict.[176]

(i) Jesus Forgives Sin

Various writers interpreted Rome's defeat of Jerusalem and destruction of its temple in 70 C.E. as God's punishment (Josephus, *JW* 4.386-88; *4 Ezra* 3:24-36; 4:22-25; 5:21-30; *2 Bar* 1:1-5; 4:1; 6:9; 32:2-3). Matthew agrees, but particularizes the sin as the elite's rejection of Jesus and misleading of the people (21:12-13, 18-19, 41-43; 22:7; 27:25). But God's wrath does not last forever. God's saving work, displayed previously in release from Egypt, Assyria, and Babylon (see 22:7), continues in Jesus, who "will save his people from their sins" by making forgiveness available now, and by establishing God's empire in the future, which will mean the demise of Rome (1:21; chs. 24-25).[177]

Matthew takes over the Marcan controversy stories about Jesus forgiving sin,[178] and heightens the claim that Jesus forgives sin. (a) The unparalleled opening passage about Jesus' conception names Mary's baby Jesus, "for he will save his people from their sins" (1:21). Jesus' name expresses his divine mission. Usage of the name "Jesus" throughout the gospel recalls for the audience this meaning and role and provides a perspective from which to understand Jesus' actions and words.

(b) Matthew removes Mark's reference to John preaching a baptism of repentance *for the forgiveness of sins* (cf. Mark 1:4 and Matt 3:1). Matthew has John call for repentance (3:2) and people "confess their sin" (3:6; so Mark 1:5), but he restricts forgiveness of sin to Jesus. (c) In Matthew's version of the Last Supper, Jesus describes the cup as "my blood of the covenant which is poured out for many *for the forgiveness of sins*" (26:28). Matthew adds the italicized words to Mark 14:24. The cross and Jesus' death, as well as Jesus' life (9:1-8), are a means of forgiveness. (d) Matthew adds several sections which remind the community that God's forgiving mercy in Jesus leads to forgiveness within the community (5:23-24; 18:23-35; cf. 6:12, 14-15).

(ii) Jesus Manifests God's Presence

In addition to saving from sins (1:21), Jesus is to manifest God's presence among human beings (1:23). Though Jerusalem has been destroyed because of sin, God has not withdrawn God's presence but has manifested it in Jesus. This theme is woven through the narrative in sections that are unique to Matthew. Its initial assertion in the form of a scriptural citation in 1:23 not only provides an authoritative statement, but its initial placement provides perspective on all that follows. Jesus' subsequent actions of calling disciples, healing the sick, teaching, casting out demons, and so on, manifest God's presence. God's presence is also encountered among the community which gathers in Jesus' name for worship (18:20), in its mission of mercy among the dispossessed (25:31-46), and in its teaching and preaching mission (28:18-20).

(iii) Jesus Interprets God's Will

Matthew presents Jesus as the one who brings the definitive interpretation of God's will. If Jerusalem's destruction was God's punishment for sin, how can people know God's will with certainty and avert future disaster? The gospel's answer lies with Jesus.

In a section unique to Matthew (5:21-48), Jesus quotes Jewish traditions six times and presents their definitive interpretation. The interpretations amplify the claim made in 5:17 that Jesus has come not "to abolish the law and the prophets . . . but to fulfill [them]." Jesus interprets the scriptural traditions to indicate their "true" meaning (9:11-13; 11:10; 12:1-8; 12:9-14; 13:14-17; 15:1-20; 19:3-12; 22:34-40; 22:41-46). Jesus' life also demonstrates a complete consistency with the scriptures: his birth (1:23; 2:6, 15, 18), where he lives (2:23; 4:15-16); his healing (8:17); his teaching methods (parables, 13:35); his actions of going to Jerusalem (21:5), his arrest (26:56) and betrayal (27:9-10). Jesus interprets these scriptural traditions.

Jesus' followers are to live his teaching (7:24-27; 12:46-50) and not that of the religious leaders whose traditions and practices are not God's will (12:1-14; 15:1-20, esp. v. 13; 16:1-12; 23:2-4). "Hearing and doing my words" is the criterion by which people are vindicated or condemned in the judgment (7:24-27). Jesus' words continue as authoritative teaching for the community (24:35; 28:20). In the post-70 era the Matthean community understands that in Jesus' interpretation of the traditions, not in Moses' or some other revealer figure's interpretation, and not in the religious leaders' teaching and praxis, is the definitive and authoritative manifestation of God's will.[179]

Post-70 Debates

In a situation of crisis and reformulation in post-70, post-temple Judaism, numerous documents in the names of such authoritative figures as Abraham, Enoch, Moses, Baruch, Ezra, and Solomon claim definitive revelations and teaching. The Mosaic tradition was central among Pharisaic circles. Within this matrix Matthew's community makes claims about encountering God's saving, forgiving presence and empire in Jesus and in the community committed to him. Hence Matthew explicitly presents Jesus using Jewish symbols and traditions. He is descended from David and Abraham (1:1). He is wisdom (11:19, 25-27). He is greater than the temple (12:6), than Jonah (12:41), than Solomon (12:42). Commitment to him, and not claims of ethnic descent and privilege based on descent from Abraham (3:7), provides the basis for God's people (cf. 12:50; 21:43; 22:7). Moreover, Jesus' manifestation of God's forgiveness, presence, and will is important for Gentiles also. Jesus is a descendant of Abraham through whom God promised to bless all the nations of the earth (Gen 12:1-3).

But the leaders of the synagogue seem to have found such claims to be unacceptable. In the gospel's story world, these leaders declare Jesus' forgiveness of sin to be "blasphemy" (9:3). They attribute his claimed manifestations of God's empire to the devil (9:34; 10:25; 12:24). They identify his association with "tax collectors and sinners" as indicating that he is a "glutton and a drunkard" (11:19). They view his breaking of sabbath traditions as deserving of death (12:14). They question his authority and its source (21:23-27) and certainly do not appreciate his denouncing their origins (15:13-14), their performance as leaders (21:28-46), and their ignorance of God's power and word (22:29). They think he is a deceiver (27:63), not an agent of God's salvation.

Whether these views reflect in detail actual responses from the synagogue is not clear. A situation of rising tension and antagonism, of accusation and allegation, means the growing refusal of both groups to recognize the legitimacy of the other. The tension is bitter and socially disruptive. Theological or ideological conflicts are never exclusively a matter of the mind. Broken relationships, divided households (10:34-36), and loss of socioeconomic networks, honor, and political influence are part of the price. The margins are where those rejected by the dominant and more powerful center cluster.[180]

It is important to emphasize that this scenario of conflict within a synagogue community does not mean separation from Judaism. First-century Judaism was not monolithic with one official synagogue, one clearly recognized leadership group, one set of practices, and one set of beliefs.

Crucial to understanding the situation of Matthew's (largely) Jewish community committed to Jesus, is the recognition that it is involved in a local fight within a synagogue over its place in a common tradition. They share the same scriptural traditions. They share the same focus on divine presence, with knowing the divine will, with encountering divine favor and forgiveness, with worship, with living faithfully. Yet along with this common history, traditions, relationships, and practices is ground which divides—namely, the claims that Jesus occupies a central role in those traditions, that he interprets them definitively, and that he manifests God's saving presence and empire. The synagogue of origin increasingly rejects these claims and practices and does not see any preeminent place for Jesus. Matthew's audience is thus a Jewish group in tension with a synagogue community yet shaped by and committed to shared Jewish traditions.

9. ROMAN IMPERIAL PRESENCE

In addition to this struggle within the Jewish community, Matthew's audience encounters another difficult context in Antioch, that of Roman imperial presence, or what Walter Wink has called the "Domination System."[181] Remarkably, Matthean scholars have paid little attention to this dimension of the gospel's world, in part because Rome is not mentioned and the emperor receives only a brief reference in 22:15-22.[182] Yet unmistakably, the experience of Roman power is very real for the gospel's audience.[183] It lives in a world in which Roman power was very evident (see below). It reads a story in which the main character, Jesus, offers an alternative, inclusive social vision and conflicts with the religious leaders, members of the ruling elite, allies of Rome, and defenders of a hierarchical structure sanctioned by Rome.[184] It reads a story in which the main character is crucified by Rome. The question is, How does it live in this context? Does the gospel present Rome as benign and urge compliance? Or does it advocate violent revolt? Or does it reveal Rome to be Satan's agent, recognize its days to be numbered, and urge the gospel audience in the meantime to live an alternative and subversive, though patient, existence shaped by God's empire and in anticipation of its full establishment and God's final salvation? I will argue this last position.

As the capital of the Roman province of Syria, Antioch was a significant military and administrative center. It played a crucial role in the defense of the Roman empire's eastern borders, especially against Parthia, and in maintaining internal peace and security (for example, against Jews in Galilee and Judea in 66-70). As an administrative center, it was responsible for the four functions of provincial government: taxation, jurisdiction, supervision of local government, internal order and defense.[185] Roman presence and imperial ideology were pervasive in the city, a constant reminder of Rome's sovereignty and enactment of Cicero's sentiment that Jews and Syrians were born for servitude (*De Prov* 10). The legate and his staff, as well as the legions, were visual displays of Roman control. Several actual and future emperors visited Antioch in the first century —Augustus and Tiberius in 20 B.C.E., Vespasian in 66 C.E., Titus in ca. 71. Trajan made Antioch his headquarters in preparation for the war against Parthia in 114 C.E. and was present during the major earthquake of 115. No doubt the emperor's birthday and other significant Roman occasions such as the founding of the city were celebrated.

Extensive building activity represented Roman control, displayed the benefits of Roman presence, and attempted to assuage resentment or ensure cooperation through gratitude. Some building was new, while various natural disasters required the rebuilding of damaged parts of the city. Tiberius was involved in extensive rebuilding after the 23/24 C.E. fire, Gaius Caligula after the earthquake in 37, and Claudius after another earthquake in the 40s. Early signs of Roman presence included the building of a circus and palace on the island.[186] Subsequent emperors through the first century, especially Tiberius, Domitian, and Trajan, added, extended, or improved residential quarters, administrative buildings, baths, water supply, drainage, aqueducts, the theater, temples, the hippodrome, gates, statues, fountains, and streets.[187]

Several specific buildings emphasized Roman control. Tiberius added a gate at the northeastern end of the main colonnaded street, on top of which was located a statue of Romulus and Remus being nursed by the she-wolf. The statue attested Roman sovereignty over the city. Later in the second decade of the second century, Trajan would add an arch to the middle of this street, which also bore the same symbol.[188] A statue of Tiberius erected along the same street and of Vespasian in Daphne further demonstrated Roman presence.[189] Such building testified to Rome's "ubiquitous power and the benefits it could bring."[190]

Signs of military victories made the same point. After his victory over Jerusalem in 70 C.E., Titus set up bronze figures outside the city gate leading to Daphne, which were understood to be cherubim from the Jerusalem temple. On the gate facing toward Jerusalem, he displayed a bronze figure of the moon and four bulls, a symbol of *Aeternitas,* of Rome and the Flavians forever.[191] These figures located near Jewish quarters in the southern part of the city and in Daphne were humiliating for Jews and a clear warning to all of the cost of not submitting to Roman control.

Coins also demonstrated Roman sovereignty. The mint at Antioch played a significant role in Augustus's attempts to reorganize coinage in the eastern part of the empire. From Augustus and Tiberius on, coins bore the image of the emperor as a reminder of Rome's authority. In the mid-first century Claudius and Nero seemed to find it necessary to strengthen this display of sovereignty. They issued coins that bore not only the emperor's name and titulature in Latin but also the name of the city and of the legate in Greek. Coins symbolized Roman accomplishments and the blessings of the gods which the emperor mediated to the people. There was no escaping Roman presence even in daily transactions.

Particularly humiliating for the Jewish community were the *Judea capta* coins issued by the emperor Vespasian, and then again around 80 C.E. by Titus. Using various figures, especially a bound female personifying Judea, they celebrated the victory of Vespasian and his son Titus over Jerusalem.[192] Also a humiliating reminder of its status as a people defeated by Rome was the tax which Vespasian levied on all Jews (Josephus, *JW* 7.218; Dio 65.7.2; cf. Matt 17:24-27). Whereas previously this had been paid to the Jerusalem temple, Vespasian co-opted it to rebuild the temple of Jupiter Capitolinus, victorious over Judea's God.[193]

Downey observes that the coming of Roman rule, "the dawn of the golden age," meant many years of material prosperity for Antioch.[194] Numerous scholars have identified undeniable benefits of *Pax Romana.* Keith Brannigan refers to Reg's speech in *The Life of Brian* in which Reg, the leader of the fictional People's Front of Judea, consistently opposes the Romans, yet reluctantly concedes that they have provided "better sanitation, medicine, education, irrigation, public health, roads, freshwater system, baths and public order."[195]

This view of Roman beneficence is akin to that of the second-century orator Aristides.[196] In his oration in praise of Rome, he extravagantly lauds Rome's blessings of justice and harmony (*Roman Oration* 31-39), the absence of envy and hatred (65), order based on military power and Roman presence (81, 87), cities (92-93), material gifts (98), security (100):

> one can say that the civilized world, which had been sick from the beginning, as it were, has been brought by the right knowledge to a state of health. (98) . . . You have measured and recorded the land of the entire civilized world; you have spanned the rivers with all kinds of bridges and hewn highways through the mountains and filled the barren stretches with posting stations; you have accustomed all areas to a settled and orderly way of life. (101)

Such a positive assessment of *Pax Romana,* though, begs consideration of who benefits from empire. It is a very selective view "from above." But as K.

Wengst demonstrates, the view "from below" was by no means so optimistic.[197] As I have noted, Roman control meant for provinces like Syria and cities like Antioch taxes, tolls, and levies on goods and labor. Taxes were calculated on the basis of a census and were collected on land value, on the exchange and circulation of goods, per head, and on the use of public facilities.[198] Tacitus supplies a Briton chief Calgacus with a very passionate speech in which Calgacus protests against the common burdens of provincials: slavery, conscription, tax, tribute, forced labor, and Roman arrogance. "To plunder, butcher, steal, these things they misname empire: they make a desolation and they call it peace" (*Agricola* 29-31).

This oppressive burden on the provinces and their peasants and artisans paid for Rome's military presence, the elite's wealth, Rome's splendor and food supply, Antioch's building projects and infrastructure, and of course entertainment and games. Aristides boasts about Rome: "For whatever is grown and made among each people [throughout the empire] cannot fail to be here at all times and in abundance" (*Roman Oration* 10-13, esp. 11). But he does not stop to consider at whose expense and deprivation Rome's abundance was provided. The center and upper levels of the empire benefited at the expense of the periphery and lower levels. Wengst summarizes the military, political, and economic situation of Antioch: "Internal conditions ordered by Rome, security from external enemies guaranteed by Rome, paid for by tribute, maintained by obedience. . . ."[199]

Pax Romana was expressed through these political, military, cultural, legal, and social means. But it was also legitimated as the will of the gods. Rome was destined by the gods to rule.[200] Vergil recognizes that the gods have given Rome an empire without limits (*Aeneid* 1.277-79). Looking "from above," Aristides recognizes that "the gods, beholding, seem to lend a friendly hand to your empire in its achievement and to confirm to you its possession." He goes on to invoke their blessing that "this empire and this city flourish forever and never cease" (*Roman Oration* 104-5, 109). Pliny calls the gods "the guardians and defenders of our empire" and prays for "the safety of our prince"[201] since the human race's "security and happiness depends [*sic*] on your safety."[202] Seneca has Nero recite a soliloquy which extols the emperor's divine election and divinely given immense power over the destinies of individuals and nations:

> Have I of all mortals found favor with heaven and been chosen to serve on earth as vicar of the gods? I am the arbiter of life and death for the nations; it rests in my power what each man's [*sic*] lot and state shall be: by my lips fortune proclaims what gift she should bestow on each human being: from my utterance peoples and cities gather reasons for rejoicing; without my favor and grace no part of the whole world can prosper; all those many thousands of swords which my peace restrains will be drawn at my nod, what nation shall be utterly destroyed, which banished, which shall receive the gift of liberty, which have it taken from them, what kings shall become

slave and whose head shall be crowned with royal honor, what cities shall fall and which shall rise—this is mine to decree. (*De Clem* 1.1.2)[203]

The Jewish writer Josephus adds further divine sanction. He recognizes "that Fortune has transferred her favors" to the cause of Rome over all other peoples (*JW* 2.360; 4.622), or, in a different formulation, that "God has been behind the growth of her empire" (*JW* 2.360) and "without God's aid, so vast an empire could never have been built up" (*JW* 2.390-91; so also 3.400-404; 5.60, 363-419 esp. 367-68, 378, 396, 412; 6.310-15).[204] This divine sanction means that Jews should not resist Rome. "To war against Rome is to war against God" (Josephus, *JW* 5.378). God used Rome in the 70 C.E. defeat of Jerusalem to punish and cleanse God's people (*JW* 5.559; 6.99-110; 7.323-36, 358-60; see Matt 22:7).

After Vespasian became emperor in 69, succeeded by one son Titus in 79, and his other son Domitian in 81, writers such as Tacitus, Suetonius, and Dio, and poets such as Martial, Silius Italicus, and Statius utilize traditional themes to claim divine legitimation for the emperors (as Pliny will do in his *Panegyricus* when Trajan becomes emperor in 98).[205] They celebrate the special relationship between the emperor and the gods, and the emperor's mediatorial role. The gods, especially Jupiter, are sovereign in human affairs and have predestined Rome to rule. They have elected the Flavian emperors to represent their rule on earth, and they protect their chosen one. The emperors manifest the gods' presence and make their blessings and favor available among humans. The earth is blessed, and societal well-being results from the gods' favors mediated by the emperor.[206] Statius writes about Domitian:

a god is he, at Jupiter's command he rules for him the happy/blessed world . . . Hail ruler of men [*sic*] and parent of gods, foreseen by me and foreordained was thy godhead. (*Silv* 4.3.128-29, 139-40)

These claims of divine sovereignty, presence, agency, and societal well-being comprise an imperial theology or ideology that legitimates Rome's exercise of power. This is the propaganda articulated not only by historians and poets but by numerous coins, buildings, taxation, military and governmental presence, statues, and so on, to gain compliance and obedience. It was these values and claims that were displayed in Antioch after the defeat of Jerusalem in 70: by Roman legions, *Judea capta* coins, Vespasian's tax for the temple of Jupiter Capitolinus, the spoils of war displayed at the south gate, and by Titus's visit in 71 C.E.

How to Respond?

How was Matthew's largely Jewish community to respond to such Roman claims and actions? Jewish groups and writers evidence a variety of responses to Roman imperialism.[207] Some welcomed Roman presence, especially the elite, and opposed any military act (Agrippa's speech in Josephus, *JW* 2.345-

401).[208] Others like Josephus, though recognizing that Jews lost their liberty to Rome, cooperated (*Ant* 14.77). Priests offered sacrifices for the emperor; Bar 1:11-12, in effect, urged prayers for Vespasian and Titus. But there were also various forms of resistance: diplomacy (Philo's delegation to Gaius Caligula, with positive attitudes [*Gaium* 13]), nonviolent mass protest (against Gaius Caligula's proposed desecration of the temple; Josephus, *JW* 2.184-203), banditry,[209] the refusal by lower-ranked priests to offer sacrifices "for Caesar and the Roman people" (Josephus, *JW* 2.197), and the war of 66-70 C.E.[210]

Debates about the 66-70 war highlight the range of strategies. "The wealthier, more hellenized, more powerful men and those close to Agrippa (cf. his speech in Josephus, *JW* 2.345-404) were against the war."[211] So too was Rabbi Yohanan ben Zakkai, a significant leader after the war (*Aboth de Rabbi Nathan* A 4, B 6).[212] Its advocates, mainly from the lower levels, comprised those with various motives who saw an opportunity to change the status quo.

Matthew writes after the war. He, like many others, saw the fall of Jerusalem and its temple in theological terms. It was God's punishment for various sins.[213] As I noted in section 4, Matthew refers to Jerusalem's fall in 22:7 in the context of condemning the religious leaders for their rejection of God's messengers, especially Jesus, God's son, and for misleading the people (also 21:12-13, 18-19; 27:25). In this view, Matthew continues a Deuteronomic understanding that God's blessings or curses take effect through historical events (Deut 28). God brings judgment on the people for unfaithfulness to the covenant. The Deuteronomist accounts for the sixth-century Babylonian exile in these terms (Deut 28-30; 1 Kgs 9:1-9; cf. Jer 25). Just as imperial powers such as Assyria (Isa 10:1-7), Babylon (Jer 25:1-11), and Antiochus Epiphanes (2 Macc 6:12-17) functioned as God's punitive agent, so does Rome. In this view of Rome as God's punitive agent, Matthew agrees with the writers of *Psalms of Solomon* (2:1-15; 8:9-22), of *4 Ezra,* of *2 Baruch,* of Bar 1:15-17, and Josephus (see above).

But punishment at Rome's hands is not the end. There is divine salvation from Rome. The tradition of recognizing imperial powers as God's punitive agents also sees their eventual demise for failing to honor God, for overstepping the mark. God (equally an imperial tyrant in this tradition) judges and destroys Assyria (Isa 10:12-34), Babylon (Jer 25:12-14; 27:7; Isa 44:28; 45:1) and Antiochus Epiphanes (2 Macc 7:32-36). So too God will judge Rome (*Pss. Sol.* 2:16-25, 30-33; 17:21-34; *Sib. Or.* 3:46-53). For Matthew, this salvation is already under way. Jesus provides forgiveness of sins (1:21), which includes the sin of rejecting Jesus (12:32). But the goal of God's salvific purposes is yet future. The gospel's repeated visions of the final establishment of God's empire (e.g., the judgment scene of 13:37-43 and the eschatological discourse of chs. 24-25) indicate this destiny. Rome's might will be crushed at the coming of Jesus (see 24:27-31), and God's sovereignty over heaven and earth in which Jesus already shares (28:18) will be established in full.

In the light of this future, how then do followers of Jesus live in the meantime? Active support of Rome, which is under Satan's power (see 4:8), is not possible. Nor is violence an option as the terrible events of 66-70 attest (see 5:38-42; 26:52-53).[214] Rather, the gospel's approach is to celebrate that God's empire, manifested by Jesus, is already at work in the world. It sketches for its audience what that empire or reign looks like now. It offers them appropriate daily practices which embody this reign. It depicts the predominantly resistant and rejecting nature of the present world under Roman control (which crucifies Jesus). There will be conflict with this world, mission to it, and no retreat from it. Acts of apparent compliance such as paying Vespasian's tax on Jews are necessary, but are redefined as subversive acts which attest God's alternative empire (see 17:24-27). The gospel warns of terrible consequences if they are unfaithful and encourages (bullies!) them into faithfulness. Throughout, the gospel builds an alternative worldview which shows the imperial claims of Rome to be limited. Rome is not ultimate. Rome, agent of Satan (4:8), will succumb to God's purposes. The community of disciples lives its distinctive existence in the midst of, yet in tension with this Roman world, knowing that one day God's empire will be established.

A crucial element of this strategy is to reframe the audience's thinking, their way of viewing the present and the future.[215] The gospel contests every one of Rome's imperial claims about divine sovereignty, presence, agency, and societal well-being. The gospel's apocalyptic framework answers the question, "to whom does the sovereignty of the world belong?"[216] with an unequivocal assertion of God's sovereignty and reign. God, not Jupiter, not the emperor, is "Lord of heaven and earth" (11:25), and the risen Jesus shares his total authority over "heaven and earth" (28:19). God's empire or reign, not Rome's, is manifested (partially now) in Jesus, claiming human allegiance (4:17-22) and overcoming sin (1:21; 9:1-8), disease (4:23-25), and Satan's reign (12:28). This empire, not Rome's, will last forever (chs. 24-25).

Divine presence is manifested by Jesus (1:23; 28:20) and in the community committed to him (18:20). The revelation of God's presence in Jesus' conception and birth (1:18-25) brings a violent response from one of the empire's vassal kings (ch. 2). The scene's theme and vocabulary are reminiscent both of Pharaoh's opposition to Moses' freeing God's people from slavery in Egypt and of Jesus' crucifixion by the religious and political elite.

Agency is clearly decided in Jesus' favor. From the opening verse, Jesus, not the emperor, is God's commissioned agent, the Christ or Son. He manifests God's reign/empire, blessing, saving presence, justice in his teaching, miracles, death, resurrection, and imminent return.

Societal well-being results not from imperial actions but from God's indiscriminate blessing, which supplies and sustains human life (5:45). Jesus' prayer seeks the hallowing of God's name, the coming of God's empire, the doing of God's will, the gifts of bread and forgiveness, deliverance from temptation and evil (6:9-13). Prominent among the recipients of God's blessing are the sick, the marginalized, the insignificant, not the powerful and privileged (4:17-25). In God's blessing is the possibility of a new and different way of life. God's blessing disrupts, not legitimates, the hierarchical and unjust status quo (5:3-12).

The gospel contests these claims about divine sovereignty, presence, agency, and societal well-being. Its strategies are theological and communal. The gospel narrative subverts the imperial propaganda by showing that Rome's empire is not ultimate. The gospel tells a story of a prophetic figure who suffers the worst that the empire can do to him, execution by crucifixion. But his resurrection and subsequent coming in power expose the limits of Roman power. The gospel constructs an alternative world. It resists imperial claims. It refuses to recognize that the world has to be ordered on those lines.[217] It offers an alternative understanding of the world and human existence centered on God manifested in Jesus. It creates an alternative community and shapes an anti-imperial praxis. This identity and lifestyle embody God's empire and anticipate its full establishment when Jesus returns to complete his mission to save his people from their sins.

10. ADVOCATING A MARGINAL EXISTENCE

We have noted the gospel's function of shaping the identity and lifestyle of a community of disciples. We have located the gospel's audience in Antioch, a small distinctive community in an urban, hierarchical, imperial society. We have identified a struggle within a synagogue community and with Roman imperial propaganda. Given these factors, what sort of identity and lifestyle does the gospel shape?

I suggest that the gospel legitimates a *marginal* identity and way of life for the community of disciples. What does it mean to speak of "marginal" and "margins" in this context? What are the center/s and what is it about them that is so inadequate that it necessitates affirming a life of marginality as worthwhile human existence? With minimal sociological jargon, I will describe several social-scientific views of marginality and assess their relevance for reading Matthew.[218]

Robert E. Park (1928) and E. V. Stonequist (1937) presented marginality as the experience of living simultaneously in two different, antagonistic cultural worlds but not fully belonging to either.[219] These cultural worlds might consist of "historic traditions, languages, political loyalties, moral codes or religions."[220] Basic to their analysis of marginality is the sense of ambivalence, of "discords and harmonies, repulsions and attractions" which result from participating in both worlds but not belonging fully to either.[221]

Jung Young Lee, writing from an Asian-American perspective, has revised this model. Lee argues that while this definition of marginality as "in-between" is helpful to a point, it presents only half the story. He notes that it is formulated from the perspective of the dominant group, which constitutes the normative center. This group decides who does and does not belong to the center, and it chooses to stylize the experiences and traits of the marginalized in a consistently negative way (inferior, cultural schizophrenia, self-alienation).[222]

Lee argues that there is another perspective on marginality, that of those who live on the margins. He proposes a self-affirming definition of marginality, which he labels "in-both." This notion recognizes the existence of both the center and the margins, allows for an experience of the margins that is at times negative and at times positive, but affirms the reality and the strengths and richness of simultaneously participating in diverse worlds.[223] To not belong to the center does not mean not belonging elsewhere. To not belong to the center may mean gladly choosing the margins as well as participating in the center at times. Rather than "not belonging" to several worlds or living in-between them, Lee affirms marginal existence as living "in-both" worlds.

G. Germani's 1980 work highlights another element of marginality beyond that of the positive and negative experience of living simultaneously in several worlds. He focuses on individuals and subgroups with norms, values, and practices that differ from the majority.[224] These groups, while related to and members of the larger society, are excluded from the center of power and exist on the periphery. They do not participate "in those spheres in which according to determined criteria, they might be expected to participate." They do not participate in "the normative scheme" because of a lack of resources (education, purchasing power, jobs) and/or because of a lack of suitable "personal conditions" (attitudes, motivations, knowledge, behavior patterns, and so on).[225] Duling calls this "involuntary marginality," which arises not so much from one's own choices as from larger forces which impose it on a person or group.[226] Basic to this view of marginality is an antithetical relationship or oppositional stance to the "normative scheme" of the center.

Victor Turner's notion of liminality also emphasizes this quality of "over-againstness" as the relation between the margins and the center.[227] He speaks of "structure" and "anti-structure." "Structure" consists of "differentiated, and often hierarchical systems of politico-legal-economic positions with many types of evaluation" and positions with fixed "relationships between statuses, roles and offices."[228] "Anti-structure" consists of the absence of these structures. It comprises an existence that is "spontaneous, immediate, concrete," without highly structured hierarchical roles and status, a *communitas* marked by more egalitarian comradeship.[229] This *communitas* can be spontaneous, or it can be normative, that is, "organized into a perduring social system," or ideological, in which this way of life is conceived and presented as a social vision.[230]

A major difference, though, exists between Turner's understanding and that of Germani. While Germani identifies enforced or "involuntary marginality," Turner highlights marginality that can be chosen, either as a temporary experience or organized as a way of life, or envisioned as a form of human existence. Because it is an alternative to societal structures and norms freely chosen by those who embrace it and not socially imposed on them, Duling calls it "voluntary marginality."[231]

These definitions of marginality have been developed in the twentieth century from experiences such as immigration and tribal initiation rites which differ significantly from the realities of the first century. Hence it is not possible to apply them in detail or uncritically to a reading of an ancient text such as Matthew's gospel. Yet these scholars, especially Germani and Turner, indicate that their analyses extend far beyond the immediate context in which they were developed. The same might be said for Lee's discussion of Asian-American experiences, which highlights the "in-both" dimensions of marginal experiences. They offer us three useful perspectives on marginality.

1. "In-both": Marginal groups live an ambivalent existence, "in-both" worlds, simultaneously existing in their larger cultural context and in that of their own group ethos.
2. "Over-Against": These worlds exist in tension with different values and commitments. The dominant center excludes the marginal group from the "normative scheme" ("involuntary marginality"), or the group chooses to exclude itself by its own ideology, commitments, and visions of reality ("voluntary marginality"). To be marginal is to exist out of the center, on the edge, at the periphery in an antithetical relationship in which groups live in some opposition to the dominant or central reality (structure/anti-structure).
3. Alternative Existence: Not all worlds are created equal. As Lee points out, for the marginal group this "in-both" yet "over-against" existence can be quite positive. But it is positive precisely because it allows a group to favor one world over another. The group fosters and maintains its own commitments, practices, and worldview, as alternatives to those of the dominant or central world.

Marginality and Matthew

I suggest that these factors ("in-both" existence; "over-against" existence; an alternative existence) provide helpful perspectives from which to understand the vision of discipleship and human existence offered by Matthew's gospel. To embrace and live this vision means being part of a marginal community because it exists "in-both" its larger cultural context of urban-rural, hierarchical Antioch as well as within the ethos of its own community. It belongs to both worlds yet is on the edge of, is peripheral, is marginal to the dominant cultural context, or normative scheme. Its communal life, centered on following Jesus, is its primary world. Its chosen marginality in relation to the larger society is ideological and social. It lives as participants in the wider society, but in tension with, over against, as an alternative to its dominant values and structures.[232]

More specifically, the two particular centers of the "normative scheme" "over-against" which disciples live are a synagogue community with which it is in tension, and the Roman imperial system with its sociopolitical practices and ideological claims, which are antithetical to the community's theological, christological, eschatological, and ecclesial understandings and practices.

From these dimensions emerge the alternative identity and lifestyle or practices of these followers of Jesus:

1. Instead of looking to Abraham, Enoch, Moses, Baruch, Ezra, and Solomon, or to the synagogue's leadership, or to imperial ideology for revelations about acceptable teaching and praxis, this community looks to Jesus to manifest God's will.

2. Instead of commitment to the emperor as head of the empire, this community is to follow Jesus crucified by the empire (chs. 26-27).
3. Instead of embracing *Pax Romana,* this community encounters, proclaims and prays for God's empire (4:17; 6:10; 12:28; 24-25).
4. Instead of understanding the emperor as manifesting the will of the gods, this community finds God's saving presence and will manifested in Jesus, Emmanuel (1:23; passim; 18:20; 28:20).
5. Instead of gladly embracing imperial power, this community is to critique kingship and leadership (ch. 2; 14:1-12; 20:20-28; 27).
6. Instead of supporting imperial power as the sustainer of order, this community sides with the prophetic tradition (John the Baptist, ch. 3) in calling it to account.
7. Instead of emulating the exercise of power over others exhibited by the Gentiles and "their great men," this community is to live as a community of slaves (20:20-28).
8. Instead of maintaining hierarchical, patriarchal households, this community is to embrace an alternative, more egalitarian household structure (chs. 19-20).
9. Instead of paying taxes as an act of submission to the empire, this community is to pay them as an act which recognizes God's sovereignty over the earth (17:24-27; 22:15-22).
10. Instead of using violence to retaliate, this community is to be committed to active, nonviolent resistance (5:43-48).
11. Instead of pretending the empire has brought health to the world (Aristides; Matt 4:24), this community is to be an inclusive community, adopting in the fragmented urban chaos and hardship of Antioch a praxis of indiscriminate mercy, actively responding to need regardless of social, gender, or ethnic boundaries (chs. 8-9; 9:13; 12:7; 25:31-46).
12. Instead of seeking wealth to establish status, this community is to seek God's reign and use wealth in alternative, lifegiving practices of loans and almsgiving to those in need (5:42; 6:19-34; 10:9-15; 19:16-30).

My thesis is that the gospel calls its audience to such an existence. It offers the audience a vision of life as voluntary marginals, confirms and strengthens those who already embrace such an existence, and challenges them and others to greater faithfulness.

The Appropriateness of a Vision of Voluntary Marginality

Perhaps four factors provide some appropriate context for such a call to a marginal existence.

1. Numbers

As we have already noted in section 7, the experience of being few in number is probably assumed of the gospel's audience. It is one factor which provides an appropriate context for a vision of discipleship as the marginal existence of a minority community "over-against" the normative scheme.

2. Urban Unconventionality

The sociologist Claude Fischer argues that one result of urban size and density is the existence and maintenance of "viable unconventional subcultures . . . which exist within a larger social system and culture."[233] Urban dwellers are more prone to "diverge from the predominant norms of society" and to violate "the normative rules, understandings, or expectations of social systems"[234] and to form alternative communities and networks. Fischer argues that population size encourages "competition, comparative advantage, and associative selection," thereby creating and maintaining subsystems.[235] As a "central space," cities attract more population. Subcultures become more intense as they are sustained by numbers, legitimated by their own institutions, and contrasted (especially in conflict) with other groups. Deviant or unconventional religious groups are one such expression.[236]

If Fischer's work on contemporary urban environments is applicable to ancient cities, a large, densely populated city such as Antioch provides the environment in which an unconventional religious group such as Matthew's audience might exist (see section 5 above). Members of this group participate daily in city life. They speak its language. They work. They walk its streets. They participate in various social and economic networks in order to survive. They pay taxes. They experience urban poverty and ethnic tensions. Yet in profoundly significant ways, while participants in their society, they comprise another group, a religious community committed to Jesus and addressed by this gospel which offers a different vision of reality, an ideological perspective which, focused on God's empire, shapes an alternative identity and set of practices and social structures for a voluntary marginal existence.

3. Religious Groups

A third factor points to the appropriateness of this vision of voluntary marginality. In first-century, polyreligious Antioch, religious groups were commonly environments for such alternative visions and unconventional practices.

Antioch was a multireligious city. Temples dedicated to Dionysius, Artemis, Aphrodite, Ares, Herakles, and Asclepius existed in the city. Zeus had a prominent place with a temple, patronage of the games, his image on coins, and depiction in a mosaic.[237] We have noted the presence of synagogues. No doubt there were also religious celebrations for the empire and the emperor, though their extent in Syria is not clear.[238] Various itinerant religious teachers and wonder-workers, such as Apollonius of Tyana (Philostratus, *Apollonius* 6.38), also operated in the city.

Much religious observance, of course, reinforces pervasive cultural values, maintains the status quo and ensures a society's survival. Antioch was dedicated to *Tychē* (fortune or chance), the city's protector and guarantor of prosperity. A bronze statue and coins bearing her likeness reminded residents of her role and helped to elicit sacrifices at her shrine.[239] A temple in Antioch for the worship of Demeter sought a regular supply of grain, absolutely basic for the city's survival. A temple of Jupiter ensured the worship of the patron god of the Flavians and of the Roman empire.

But some religious groups point to other realities and social patterns. Though we do not know the precise situation for Antioch, some synagogues in the diaspora affirmed women's leadership.[240] The worship of Isis was well established in Antioch.[241] Women especially participated in the worship of Isis, the "goddess of women." Her protection of female domestic relationships and roles meant that "You have made the power of women equal to men."[242] By the first century some women also held office as priestesses in the Isis cult.[243] R. Witt notes that within Isis groups, different patterns of social interaction emerged as people from various social, gender, and ethnic groups mixed on somewhat equal terms. Within the confines of a group's liturgy and symbolic world, "fellow slaves could band themselves together and feel free, colored Africans could join with Romans, and women could claim the same power as men. But Isis could allure men of far more exalted rank than slaves . . . [including] . . . Domitian [who] . . . built her a temple in Rome."[244] Not surprisingly, opposition to the Isis cult and to other foreign, including Egyptian and Jewish, religious groups arose (Dio Cassius 6.52.36; Suetonius, *Augustus* 93; *Tiberius* 36). They were perceived to be seedbeds of "conspiracies, factions and cabals" (Dio Cassius) and to undermine political and social structures such as male power over women (patriarchy), the division of free and slave, and the hierarchy of Roman and provincial.[245]

The existence, then, of other religious groups as structures of unconventionality, as places of alternative understandings and structures, offers a third context in which a call to and vision of an alternative and voluntarily marginal existence might be offered through this story of Jesus.

4. Voluntary Associations

Discussion of these religious groups involves a very common social structure called "voluntary associations."[246] These groups were known by the Latin term *collegia* or by various Greek terms such as *thiasos, ekklēsia* (cf. 16:18!), *synagōgē, synodoi,* or *koinon.* They came into existence for political, social, and religious or cultic reasons. One scholar has identified three basic (but overlapping) types of groups:[247] funerary associations, which provided social gatherings and guaranteed an honorable funeral for members; religious associations such as synagogues[248] and Isis groups noted above; and professional or guild associations comprising artisans or trades people.

A history of suspicion accompanied voluntary associations. Since 64 B.C.E., associations were regularly banned (64, 56, 55; 19 C.E.) or placed under various restrictions or controls, though measures were not consistently or uniformly implemented.[249] But clearly, the xenophobic suspicion of political subversion and of violating the social order by having women in prominent leadership roles, and in which slaves and free, poor and wealthy mixed equally, was not appreciated by members of ruling elites.

Numerous similarities exist between these groups and early Christian groups:

- voluntary membership, not based on birth
- groups are founded by private initiative
- meet in the houses of members
- small in size;[250] intimate, face-to-face fellowship
- regular meetings, shared meals, celebrated special days
- membership is open to male and female, slave and free/freed, and people of all social levels
- locally based with some translocal connections[251]
- prominent role of a deity in founding the group, in offering salvation and security, in cultic practices, and in reinforcing moral standards with threats of punishment
- a mixture of hierarchy and equality: wealthy patrons often play a prominent role; internal governance is often democratic and egalitarian; broad social mix
- discipline and exclusion for inappropriate behavior[252]

It would seem reasonable to conclude that in terms of these features, Matthew's community(ies) look(s) like a voluntary association to outsiders, and feels like one to insiders. In tension with some parts of the Jewish community in Antioch, it could form its own meeting group in a well-established social structure. Opposed to fundamental claims and structures of the empire, it could form a group that nurtures alternative worldviews, structures, and practices. This structure is most appropriate to a vision of voluntary marginality.

These factors of small size, urban unconventionality, the nature of religious groups, and structure and societal posture of *collegia* indicate that a vision of a voluntary marginal existence is appropriate to the circumstances of the gospel's audience. Already in its social experience the commuity knows marginality. The gospel confirms and legitimates its social experience, interprets it theologically, and challenges it to a more consistent and faithful marginal identity and alternative way of life in anticipation of the completion of God's salvific purposes and establishment of God's empire in full at Jesus' return.

PART I

The First Narrative Block

God Commissions Jesus (1:1-4:16)

CHAPTER 1

The Origins of Jesus Messiah
and His Followers

1:1-17—THE GENEALOGY

The opening narrative block (1:1-4:16) presents Jesus' conception, his commissioning by God, and his compliance with this role. What is the contribution of the genealogy in 1:1-17?[1]

Genealogies in ancient biographies do much more than pass on historical-biological information.[2] By associating the hero with prestigious ancestors, a genealogy enhances his prestige or shows that the subject has lived up to his heritage or made it more noble.[3] A genealogy defines the relationship of the main character to the past and shows something important about the present. Tacitus defines Agrippa's prestige in terms of wealthy political connections (*Agrippa* 4). Josephus defines his own prestige in terms of priestly ancestors (*Vita* 1-6).

But this genealogy takes an alternative path. It establishes Jesus' significance not by wealth, power, or social status but by locating him in Matthew's version of the biblical story. The genealogy retells and interprets the biblical story. It is not a complete rendition of that story. It makes no mention of Moses or of the prophets, for example, both of whom will be important in the gospel. But its selectivity and partiality indicate the agenda or perspective that controls the retelling.[4]

The genealogy sets Jesus' origin, and that of his followers, at the center of God's purposes.[5] Every name evokes larger stories of encounters with Israel's God.[6] Polemic is integral to this approach. The genealogy does not testify to Rome's control of human destiny or to the emperor's oversight of human affairs at the gods' behest, as Nero's opening soliloquy in Seneca's work *De Clementia* claims (1.1.2; see Introduction, section 9). It depicts God's sovereign will and guiding promises.

God's purposes involve the formation of a people for whom God intends blessing and life. Named at the head of the genealogy is Abraham, to whom God promised blessing for all the peoples of the earth (Gen 12:1-3). God's intent of blessing, of providing people with a just and abundant life (as the tradition elaborates it, e.g., Deut 28), stands over the genealogy and the gospel.

God's purposes are, accordingly, wide-ranging and inclusive. They extend over Jewish (Israel, Judah) and Gentile territory (Ur of the Chaldees, Babylon). They involve males and females (five women; see 1:3, 5, 16), Gentiles and Jews, those who are giants in the tradition (Abraham, David) and nobodies that even the tradition seems to have forgotten (see 1:3b-4, 13-15), the powerful (kings) and those with relatively little power and status (the women).

God's purposes are constant and faithful. The initial reference to Abraham and David evokes two guiding promises of descendants, blessing to all nations (Gen 12:1-3), and an eternal reign (2 Sam 7). God intends to bless all people with plentiful fertility, food, health, prosperity, and freedom from imperial powers (as Deut 28-29 elaborates the blessing). *God* blesses the earth, not Jupiter, and God blesses "all people" not just a powerful and privileged elite. David's reign is to be marked by righteousness and justice with no place for oppressive and exploitative practices (Ps 72). This vision of kingship differs radically from Rome's rule. The genealogy shows that God's commitment to these promises is undeterred by resistance and rejection. There is a line of kings after David (1:6b-11) and life after exile in Babylon (1:12-16). Imperial power cannot derail God's purposes.

But while God's purposes are constant, human allegiance is not. The characters are not selected as models of perpetual faithfulness. Most know faithfulness *and* unfaithfulness, like Abraham and David and some of the kings. Other kings are remembered only as unfaithful. Yet though God's purposes are threatened by human fickleness and evil, they are not thwarted.

God's purposes are not predictable. At times God works through cultural conventions of patriarchy and primogeniture. But at other times God breaks these established patterns and works around them. Male-centered structures are not always normative.

Nor are God's purposes complete. The genealogy bears witness that God's purposes have not been accomplished. The post-Babylon sequence indicates that the promise to David of a reign that will last forever is not yet realized (1:12-16). And the promise to Abraham of blessing for all people has not taken place while most live under Rome's control in a world that favors the elite at the expense of the rest.

Hence the genealogy locates Jesus' birth in the context of what God has committed to do among humans, what is resisted, and what God has not yet accomplished. Jesus, "child of Abraham, child of David" (1:1), is God's Christ or agent, commissioned to continue what God has promised, started, but not yet completed. And as both 1:11-12 and chapter 2 will show, it locates Jesus in a world in which the elite and powerful, namely, the religious and political leaders, continue to resist God's purposes.

Those who are committed to follow Jesus live in a world blessed because God is at work in it, but troubled because God's purposes are not completed nor always welcomed. The genealogy offers the gospel's audience, Jesus' community marginalized by political, cultural, social, and religious structures represented by a synagogue and the Roman empire,[7] a central place in God's purposes. It shapes and strengthens their identity as people who live according to God's purposes in circumstances of hostility, and vastly different cultural values.

The genealogy has, then, a theological agenda, a sociological and pastoral function, and a narrative contribution. Its theological agenda identifies God's purposes as paramount and locates Jesus in relation to God's previous and ongoing salvific relationship with Israel. The "genealogy is not a record of (human) biological productivity but a demonstration of God's providence. . . . (It) reflects the working out of God's plan of creation in a history of salvation."[8] Its sociological and pastoral function locates the gospel's audience in these same purposes and affirms its identity as followers of Jesus in a cultural, social, political, and religious context of alienation.

For the narrative, the genealogy provides an interpretative framework which shapes the understanding of the rest of the story.[9] God's purposes determine the actions of the main character, Jesus, and provide the evaluative point of view by which all characters and actions will be assessed.

While the genealogy's identity-forming function is good news for Jesus' followers, it has unfortunate implications which must be lamented. The genealogy co-opts and reframes Jewish traditions and history to serve its christological perspective. But in claiming Jesus and his followers as central to God's purposes, it disenfranchises all those who do not follow Jesus. Ironically, the very same co-opted traditions indicate that God's faithfulness to covenant commitments is much more steadfast and inclusive than the genealogy's exclusionary claims.

• 1:1

The gospel opens by naming the main character, **The book of the origin of Jesus Christ**.* The term **origin** is a better translation than "genealogy" or "birth" since the same word is repeated in 1:18 to introduce Jesus' conception, not birth (1:18-25). Jesus' **origin** is the initial, predictable focus of this ancient biography. Verses 1-17 delineate his **origin** in terms of ancestry, while vv. 18-25 identify God's initiative through the Holy Spirit.

In addition to this focus on origin, Jesus' importance is asserted in five ways.

1. The phrase **book of the origin** evokes the book of origins and creation, Genesis (Gen 2:4, "the generations of the heavens and the earth"; Gen 5:1, Adam's descendants, not ancestors as here). The phrase suggests a new creation. Some Jewish apocalyptic texts unveiled God's intent to end this sinful and oppressed world by starting over with a new world in which God's presence and will reign (*4 Ezra* 5-10; *2 Bar* 26-30). In some (but not all) apocalyptic scenarios, a messiah was understood to have some role in the events leading up to this new age (*1 En* 46-48; *Pss. Sol.* 17; *T. Reu.* 6:8; *2 Bar* 29:3; 30:1; 72:2; *4 Ezra* 12:32).[10]

At several points, the gospel invokes this hope of new creation. The descending Spirit at Jesus' baptism (see 3:16) suggests the hovering Spirit of creation

---

* All boldface words within the text are taken directly from the Gospel of Matthew.

(Gen 1:2). Jesus' calming of the storm and walking on the water (8:23-27; 14:22-33) recall God's separation of the waters from dry land (Gen 1:6-10) and keeping them in their place (Pss 69:1-2; 77:16-20; 77:23-32). In 19:3-9 Jesus invokes the Creator's will from the beginning and cites Gen 2:24. And in 19:28 he refers to this "new world." By invoking Genesis, the phrase **book of the origin** establishes Jesus as one who will have a key role in God's new creation. See 14:32.

Apocalyptic thinking is not escapist or "pie in the sky." It addresses fundamental questions of human allegiance and power: "To whom does the sovereignty of the world belong?"[11] It seems as though the world belongs to the powerful Romans (see Introduction, sections 2, 9). But invoking Genesis reveals a counterperspective, not of *Pax Romana* but of God's creation vision for the world, in which all things are justly related to each other and to God. Jesus' **origin** is linked to this claim of God's sovereignty.

2. The main character is identified as **Jesus**. This Greek form of the Hebrew name Joshua means "God saves." Jesus' work of accomplishing God's salvation from all that resists God's purposes, including Rome, will be elaborated throughout the gospel (1:21).

3. Jesus is **Christ**, a Greek form of the Hebrew-derived term "messiah," which means "anointed." An anointed or "christed" or "messiahed" person is one whom God has commissioned or set apart to serve God. That service can take all sorts of forms. (i) In the Hebrew scriptures, God anoints or commissions kings to represent God's reign, justice, and righteousness (see Ps 2, esp. v. 2; also 89:20, 38, 51; Ps 72). (ii) Priests are anointed to lead worship (Lev 4:3, 5, 16). (iii) Prophets are anointed to speak God's will and challenge sinful practices (3:1; 1 Kgs 19:16). (iv) The Gentile Persian ruler Cyrus is designated "anointed" or "messiah" because God was understood to have given him the task of setting the sixth-century exiles in Babylon free to return home (Isa 44:28-45:1, esp 45:1a). He was God's agent. (v) Some writings, but by no means all, look to a future figure to carry out a special role in God's purposes for a new world. The expectations are diverse and by no means universal. In Dan 9:25 an "anointed prince" will rebuild Jerusalem. In *Psalms of Solomon* (17:32; 18:5, 7), an anointed one, a king, will drive the Romans out "by the word of his mouth" (17:24). In *1 Enoch* 37-71, the anointed messiah is a heavenly figure who will carry out judgment (*1 En* 48:10; 52:4) by vindicating the righteous and punishing the wicked, who include oppressive kings and rich landowners. In *4 Ezra* 7:26-44, a messiah reigns for four hundred years, and, after a week of silence, God creates a new world and executes judgment.

There was no standard expectation of a messiah, nor did every Jew look for a special anointed figure. Thus, to call Jesus "messiah" or **Christ** does not evoke a fixed checklist of what "the messiah" is to do. Rather, the term raises a question. For what special task or role has God anointed or designated Jesus? The answer will be revealed in 1:21-23 and in the gospel story.

4. Jesus is a **descendant of David**. David was a major political and religious figure in Israel's history and traditions (1 Sam 16:1-1 Kgs 2:11). David was a shepherd who by God's choice became Israel's king. As king, he composes music to praise God, commits adultery and murder, yet seeks God's mercy (Ps 51), receives God's promise of a kingdom that will last forever (2 Sam 7) and from whose line a messiah was expected (*Pss. Sol.* 17:21). He was the father of Solomon (6:29), reputed to be wise, and associated with acts of power and magic (*T. Sol.*). The gospel will elaborate in what ways Jesus is **descendant of David** (see 9:27; 15:22; 20:30-31). Kingship or rule will be an important dimension (2:2; 4:17).

5. Jesus is **descendant of Abraham**. Again Jesus is linked with a major figure in Israel's history. The phrase evokes a rich narrative of God's grace and demand, and Abraham's faith and faithlessness. God called Abraham (a Gentile) to journey from Ur of the Chaldees (Gen 12:1). Through him, God promises to bless all the nations of the earth (Gen 12:3; 18:18). Abraham struggles with God's promise that he will have many descendants (Gen 16), but he puts the promise to the test in offering up his son Isaac as an act of obedience (Gen 22). Abraham is circumcised as a sign of belonging to the covenant and so is the forebear of Israel, God's covenant people (Gen 17). As **descendant of Abraham**, Jesus, not the emperor (see Introduction, section 9), enacts the blessing of God (not of Jupiter) on all the nations of the earth.

The gospel's opening verse, then, locates Jesus in relation to God's eschatological purposes for a new creation (**book of origin**), asserts his role as one who saves (**Jesus**), identifies him as one anointed or commissioned by God (**Christ**), and allies him with two towering figures in Israel's past, **David** and **Abraham**. These connections assure a community in tension with a synagogue and living in a world over which Rome reigns supreme (Introduction, sections 8 and 9) that, though marginal to both these realities, it is caught up in God's purposes as followers of Jesus.

• 1:2

The line of Jesus' ancestors begins with **Abraham**, repeated for emphasis from v. 1 (cf. 1:17). **Abraham was the father of Isaac.** The genealogy is selective. Each name means the exclusion of others. It does not begin with Adam (Luke 3:38) nor does it mention Sarah. Its focus predominantly on men reflects a patriarchal culture that values descent through the male line (but see v. 3).

The phrase "A **was the father of** B" will recur some thirty-nine times. It expresses this patriarchal focus and employs a pattern evident in genealogies in Ruth 4:18-22, which (along with 1 Chr 2:10-15) may have been the partial source for this genealogy.

The line of blessing flows from **Abraham**, not the unnamed females Sarah or Hagar (Gen 16-17). It does not follow primogeniture (Ishmael, Hagar's son) but elevates the younger **Isaac**, Sarah's son (Gen 12:1-3; 15:1-6; 18-21). **Isaac was the father of Jacob.** The line continues with the younger **Jacob**, not the older Esau. Perfection is not necessary for inclusion. Jacob joined with his mother Rebekah to deceive his father in stealing Esau's birthright (Gen 25:19-34; 27). **Jacob was the father of Judah and his brothers. Judah**, Jacob's fourth son, is elevated above his brothers and is promised a reign (Gen 49:1-12; 1 Chr 2:1). Omitted are the three older sons Reuben, Simeon, and Levi.

The addition of **and his brothers** creates a break in the "A **was the father of** B" pattern. The break draws attention to something unusual which exists along with the conventional. For similar breaks, see **and Zerah** in 1:3 (**Perez**'s brother), and in v. 11, **Jechoniah and his brothers**. The addition of **and his brothers** underlines God's sovereignty in choosing a particular person Judah to continue the line (Gen 49:8). But the choice of one for a task is not the rejection of the others. Jacob's twelve sons (Judah's **brothers**) originate the twelve tribes that comprise Israel, God's chosen people (Gen 49). Their inclusion, along with **Zerah** and **Jechoniah's brothers** in 1:3, 11, widens the focus beyond the named person to significant moments in Israel's history: twelve tribes called by God (Gen 49), but disenfranchised in going into Egypt (Perez, Gen 46:12) and exiled in Babylon (Jechoniah). The term **brothers** will subsequently describe Jesus' disciples. Those who do the will of God are Jesus' "brother and sister and mother" (12:50).

• 1:3a

Judah was the father of Perez and Zerah by Tamar. Judah's three sons (Er, Onan, and Shelah) are omitted (Gen 38; 1 Chr 2:3). The line continues through Judah's two sons from his daughter-in-law **Tamar**, especially the older **Perez** (who) **was the father of Hezron**, not the younger **Zerah** (Gen 38:15-30; Ruth 4:18; 1 Chr 2:4).

So far, the genealogy exhibits ambivalent attitudes to the cultural patterns and structures of patriarchy and primogeniture. God is both conventionally patriarchal in elevating the male and the firstborn, but quite subversive in choosing several younger brothers. No explanations are offered. The genealogy asserts God's initiative and intervention in ways at times consistent with normative cultural patterns and at times quite contrary to them.

This ambivalence continues with a further break in the "A was the father of B" pattern with the addition of **by Tamar**. While the inclusion of women in biblical genealogies has precedent (Gen 11:29; 22:20-24; 1 Chr 2:18-21, 24, 46-49), it is unusual in an androcentric world, and only two of these women, Tamar and Bathsheba, are named in Matthew's possible source 1 Chr 1-3. In all, five women break up the pattern: **Tamar**, **Rahab,** and **Ruth** (1:5), **the wife of Uriah** (Bathsheba, 1:6), and **Mary of whom Jesus was born who was called Christ** (1:16). Who are these women?

In Gen 38, Judah mistakes his daughter-in-law **Tamar,** the widow of Judah's eldest son Er, for a prostitute. She conceives the twins **Perez and Zerah**, after Er's brother fails to perform his duty of producing children with her (according to levirate marriage, Deut 25:5-6). **Rahab,** in Josh 2, was a Canaanite prostitute who provided protection for Joshua's spies on the edge of the city of Jericho. She hid them, confessed faith in their God as the liberator of the exodus and giver of the land, and enabled their escape from the king of Jericho, in return for assurances that her household would be safe in the invasion. **Ruth** was a Moabite (they originated from Lot's incest with his daughter, Gen 19:30-38) who, despite Moses' decree (Deut 23:3), became part of God's people through marriage to **Boaz** (1:5). The genealogy does not name Bathsheba, but in referring to her as **the wife of Uriah**, it underlines both David's terrible abuses of power in his acts of adultery and murder, and Uriah's Gentile identity as a Hittite (2 Sam 11-12). **Mary** gives birth to Jesus, conceived of the Holy Spirit while she was betrothed to Joseph (1:18-25).

What is the significance of the women's inclusion? Numerous explanations have been offered.[12]

1. The naming of these women, like the brothers of 1:2, reminds the audience of other unnamed women like Sarah, Rebekah, Leah, and numerous others who played important roles in Israel's history but are not named specifically in the genealogy.

2. An old explanation, at least since Jerome (d. 420 C.E.), was that the women were sinners. Their inclusion is variously claimed to contrast with Jesus the righteous savior, to indicate that God can work through the sinful Davidic line, and/or to answer charges about Mary's alleged adultery by showing other sexually sinful people in God's purposes. There are several difficulties with this approach. It evokes an obvious negative stereotype of women. Women have no monopoly on sin, as the inclusion of numerous sinful men in the genealogy indicates (e.g., David, Ahaz, Manasseh). More significantly, Rahab was subsequently understood to be a model of faith (Heb 11:31)[13] and Tamar of righteousness (Gen 38:26). Tamar is also positively associated with Ruth (Ruth 4:12). Moreover, Mary is not regarded as sinful.

3. A view from the sixteenth-century Reformation sees the women's significance as being Gentiles who participate in God's purposes and salvation. Rahab was a Canaanite (Josh 2) as probably was Tamar (Gen 38:1-6). Ruth was a Moabite (Ruth 1:4). But Bathsheba was an Israelite. Her father was Eliam (2 Sam 11:3) from Giloh in the Judean hills south of Hebron (2 Sam 23:34).[14] But her marriage to Uriah the Hittite at least links her with a Gentile (2 Sam 11:3). The inclusion of Gentiles as well as Jews in God's purposes and covenant people is emphasized by Abraham (1:1-2), and by the magi, visitors from the east, in chapter 2. There is, though, no hint of Mary being a Gentile.

4. A widely supported view sees something unusual, even scandalous, in their actions. Their relationships with men are not culturally approved: a seducer (Tamar), a prostitute (Rahab), a possible seducer (Ruth; see Ruth 3:1-18), an adulterer (Bathsheba), and a pregnant betrothed virgin (Mary). In these circumstances, the women must "use sex as a tool either for economic existence (Rahab; Ruth), for political safety (Bathsheba), or for a reason to exist (Tamar). . . ."[15] The focus in part falls on the women's initiative and faith in employing unusual means to protect their

own interests and overcome obstacles created by men. Despite these irregularities God surprisingly intervenes to accomplish God's purposes. Yet Mary does not fit well, since she does not initiate her circumstances.

5. Another view, developed by Elaine Wainwright, rightly recognizes that the genealogy is androcentric (focused on males) and patriarchal in that it upholds descent through the male line, and largely ignores women and daughters.[16] She argues that the four women are included because they occupy situations that endanger this patriarchal structure. The women named here exist outside of legitimated relationships with specified men (wife, mother, daughter). When Judah fails to give his son Shelah to the widowed **Tamar**, Tamar remains an unprotected widow without a son, outside the structure of levirate marriage. **Rahab** the prostitute is neither a virgin daughter nor a wife. **Ruth** commits herself to the protection not of a man but of another woman, her mother-in-law Naomi. **Bathsheba**, the wife of Uriah, is involved in an adulterous relationship with David, outside a normative patriarchal marriage. Mary conceives without the supposedly determinative male agency. All five situations are subversive, "over-against" prevailing norms, marginal to the patriarchal line and structures. God's actions are not contained by or bound to these structures. God breaks them open to work on the margins. The margins are not God-forsaken or cursed, but crucial to God's purposes.

6. Amy-Jill Levine argues that social categories of marginals and elites, rather than gender or ethnic divisions, provide a key clue. The women are "socioeconomically and culturally powerless, yet they exhibit the faith by which the divine program is accomplished." They contrast with the powerful males who do not fulfill their roles. The women become examples of the "greater justice/righteousness" which Jesus requires in 5:20. They also indicate that "marriage is not . . . the prerequisite for righteous or just action or salvation."[17] **Tamar** seduces Judah because by withholding his son Shelah, Judah unjustly does not fulfill his levirate obligations. **Rahab**, on the social and physical margins of the city, welcomes the spies and commits herself to their God, unlike the king of Jericho, who seeks to capture them and resist God's purposes (Josh 2). He is defeated but she is vindicated. **Ruth**, a poor widow and foreigner, is forced as a disenfranchised person to glean from the fields. She persuades the wealthy and powerful Boaz to act on her behalf. The argument is less convincing for Bathsheba (Levine actually discusses Uriah's faithfulness), though it is clear that **Bathsheba** occupies a far less powerful position than King David, who misuses his power to break the commandments concerning adultery and killing. **Mary** conceives through the Spirit, while Joseph, at least initially, plans to divorce her, before acting obediently to the angel's revelation. The excluded women who demonstrate active faith contrast with the powerful and privileged elite males who fail to live out their responsibilities. Again it is the margins where God's action is encountered, a theme that will continue throughout the gospel. The women represent the inclusion of the marginal and the excluded, the community's

welcome to "all denied status or privilege by members of elite groups, to all whose higher righteousness is undervalued by structures of hierarchy."[18]

While all the suggestions are not of equal value (often because they fail to apply to all five women), interpreters often make the mistake of seeking only one explanation. Of the six views, all but no. 2 contain some valid insight, with options 4 to 6 being especially helpful.

• 1:3b-4

Perez (was) **the father of Hezron, Hezron the father of Aram, and Aram the father of Aminadab, Aminadab the father of Nahshon, and Nahshon the father of Salmon.** Apart from genealogical references, little is known about the characters between **Perez** and **Salmon** (cf. Ruth 4:20-21 and 1 Chr 2:9-11).[19] Several have some link with God's liberating action in the exodus. **Hezron** is associated with Joseph and his going into Egypt (Gen 46:8, 12). **Aminadab,** the only son of **Aram** in Ruth 4:19 and 1 Chr 2:10, is also linked with Moses and the desert wanderings (Num 1:7), as is **Nahshon** (Num 1:7; 2:3). Their names evoke the larger story of disenfranchisement as slaves in Egypt, of God's victory over the Egyptian pharaoh and liberation of the powerless from the oppressive political powers, and of God's faithfulness to the promise of a new land.

• 1:5-6a

Salmon was the father of Boaz by Rahab. Boaz was the father of Obed by Ruth, and Obed the father of Jesse and Jesse the father of King David. It is most unlikely that **Salmon** and **Rahab** produced **Boaz.** Over a century separates them. **Salmon** is the great-grandfather of Jesse, David's father (1 Chr 2:11-13; Ruth 4:21-22), but **Rahab** lives at the earlier time of the invasion and occupation (Josh 2). The focus continues to be on theological and social legitimation rather than historical information. Rahab's absence from the Ruth and Chronicles lists underlines Matthew's addition. Likewise, while **Boaz, Obed,** and **Jesse** appear in the same lists at Ruth 4:21-22 and 1 Chr 2:11-12, Ruth is absent. On the inclusion and importance of the women **Rahab** and **Ruth,** see 1:3.

According to 1 Chr 2:11-12, **Jesse** has seven sons and two daughters. The line continues by God's election through **David,** the seventh. The reference to **David** completes the first section of fourteen generations (1:17). The addition of **the king** to **David**'s name emphasizes his political, social, economic, and religious prominence. It recalls his divine commission to be king (1 Sam 16; 2 Sam 5), God's promise of a line and a kingdom that will last forever (2 Sam 7), David's violation of the Decalogue (Exod 20:13, 14) and abuses of his position through adultery and a murderous coverup (2 Sam 11-12). It also recalls the vision of kingship in royal psalms such as Psalms 2 and 72. The king represents God's reign, justice, and mercy. The righteous king, faithful to God's commission, protects the poor and needy from oppression and violence (72:12-14). This vision of kingship hangs over the next section (1:6-11) as the benchmark for Israel's kings, who mostly fail to live up to it. Jesus' association with David as a descendant or son (1:1) prepares for an emphasis on Jesus' kingship and rule (see 4:17).

• 1:6b-11

And David was the father of Solomon by the wife of Uriah. The repeated **David** begins the second group of **fourteen generations**, from David to the tragic Babylonian exile in 587 B.C.E. (1:17). This section focuses on the socially elite kings but tells the story of failed kingship. The genealogy assumes the audience's knowledge of each king from the narratives of 1-2 Kings and 1-2 Chronicles. These narratives assess the political performance of the kings from the theological perspective of their faithful representation of God's will and justice (Ps 72).

Solomon, son of David (see 9:27), is the first of the failed kings. Both Moses in Deut 17:14-20 and Samuel in 1 Sam 8:1-17 warn that kings must attend to God's just and merciful will and not imitate "the ways of the kings" of the nations, which consist of military conscription, forced labor, requisitioned property, and slavery. But Solomon disobeys. Precisely by these exploitative and oppressive means he gathers excessive wealth (see 1 Kgs 1-11; 2 Chr 1-9; also Matt 6:29).[20] On **the wife of Uriah,** see 1:3.

• 1:7

Solomon was the father of Rehoboam, the first king of the southern kingdom Judah after the division from the northern kingdom Israel in 922 B.C.E. (1 Kgs 12-14; 2 Chr 10-12). The narratives evaluate him negatively for continuing the oppression of his father, Solomon, and allowing pagan worship (2 Chr 12:1, 14). **Rehoboam was the father of Abijah** (1 Kgs 15:1-8; 2 Chr 13; also called Abijam). He "committed all the sins that his father did before him" (1 Kgs 15:3, though 2 Chr 13 is more positive). **Abijah was the father of Asa.** After two wicked kings, **Asa**[21] generally receives positive comments because he encourages the worship of God (1 Kgs 15:9-24; 2 Chr 14-16, though note 16:7-14).

• 1:8

Asa was the father of Jehoshaphat, who is praised for walking in God's ways (1 Kgs 22:1-50, esp. v. 43a; 2 Chr 17-20). But he does not remove pagan worship (1 Kgs 22:43b) and is condemned for an alliance with the wicked king Ahaziah of Israel (2 Chr 20:35-37). **Jehoshaphat was the father of Joram**. Joram does not do God's will (2 Kgs 8:16-24; 2 Chr 21). In naming **Joram the father of Uzziah**, the genealogy omits three kings and a queen (Ahaziah, 2 Kgs 8:25-9:28; Queen Athaliah; Jehoash/Joash; Amaziah). It jumps over some sixty years (see 2 Kgs 8:16-25; 9:27-28; 11:1, 12, 16, 21; 12:1, 21; 14:1-20; 2 Chr 22-26:1). **Uzziah**, like **Asa** and **Jehoshaphat**, receives a mixed evaluation for doing what was right, but he is ineffective against pagan worship and usurps the role of priests (2 Chr 26; also called Azariah in 2 Kgs 14:21; 15:1-7[22]).

• 1:9

Uzziah was the father of Jotham. Jotham too receives a mixed evaluation (2 Kgs 15:32-38; 2 Chr 27). **Jotham was the father of Ahaz,** who is ranked among the evil kings (2 Kgs 16; 2 Chr 28). **Ahaz was the father of Hezekiah** (2 Kgs 18-20; 2 Chr 29-32), who rules faithfully and encourages the worship of God.

• 1:10

Hezekiah was the father of Manasseh, who is strongly condemned for encouraging pagan worship and injustice (2 Kgs 21:1-18; 2 Chr 33:1-20 including his repentance, 33:12-13; see also *The Prayer of Manasseh*). **Manasseh was the father of Amos,** who continues the evil (2 Kgs 21:19-26; 2 Chr 33:21-25). Amos's son **Josiah** seeks to restore faithful worship (2 Kgs 22-23:30; 2 Chr 34).

• 1:11

Josiah was the father of Jechoniah and his brothers at the time of the Babylonian exile. This second section, which has featured kings, ends with military defeat and Babylonian exile (597/587-539 B.C.E.). **Jechoniah** (whose regnal name was Jehoiachin) is actually **Josiah**'s grandson. **Josiah** had four sons (1 Chr 3:15-16), the second of whom, Jehoiakim, had two sons **Jechoniah** and Zedekiah. The omission of the generation of Josiah's four sons ensures fourteen generations (see 1:17). **Jechoniah** (or Jehoiachin; 2 Kgs 24-25), who is identified as doing evil, surrendered to the Babylonian Nebuchadnezzar in 597 and was exiled with leading officials to **Babylon** after Nebuchadnezzar laid siege to Jerusalem. Jechoniah's uncle, Zedekiah (so 2 Kgs 24:17, not his brother as in 2 Chr 36:10), was appointed king but was taken in exile in 587. For **and his brothers**, see 1:2b.

The reference to the **Babylonian exile** names a key perspective on imperial power. The noun **exile** appears in the LXX text of 2 Kgs 24:16, 1 Chr 5:22, and Ezek 12:11, in contexts that interpret this event as divine punishment. God uses Babylon to punish the kings for their failure to represent God's justice and will by not worshiping God and by exploiting the people (contrary to the vision of Ps 72). **Babylon** was God's agent in enacting punishment (1 Kgs 9:6-9). But in turn, God judges and punishes Babylon (Isa 44:28-45:1) and saves the people from Babylonian rule (44:21-24; 45:15b). The Babylonian situation, like the exodus from Egypt, is analogous to the crisis under Rome in 66-70 C.E. God has used Rome to punish the people (Matt 21:12-13, 18-19, 41; 22:7; 27:25; Introduction, section 9). But God will again save them in Jesus' life, death, and future return (1:21; 11:29-30; 20:28; 24:27-31; 26:28). Imperial power is evil, but it is always subject to God's power, even though it may temporarily serve God's purposes.

From **David** to **Jechoniah** fifteen kings are named. Only two, Hezekiah and Josiah, are understood in 1-2 Kings and 1-2 Chronicles to be good kings. Six (David, Solomon, Asa, Jehoshaphat, Jotham, Uzziah) receive mixed evaluations. The remaining seven do evil things. They fail to represent God's reign. Jesus, son of David, will subsequently manifest God's reign or empire in his ministry (4:17) and establish it in full at his return (24:27-31).

• 1:12

Verse 12 begins the third section of fourteen generations (1:17), though in fact there are only thirteen.[23] That there is any post-deportation story to tell at all indicates God's faithful salvific action. The phrase **And after the deportation to Babylon** recalls the prophets who declared God's liberating power at work through the Persian ruler Cyrus (Isa 44:28; 45:1; Ezek 33-39). God is trustworthy and powerful. As in the exodus, God acts on behalf of an oppressed group under the control of the Babylonian empire to save them and return them to the land. Babylon performed its role as God's agent but is subject to God's judgment. The power of empire, whether Babylonian or Roman, is not final. The gospel's audience is reminded that, despite their claims and all appearances to the contrary, empires such as Rome do not control human history and destiny but are subject to God's sovereignty.

The phrase **Jechoniah was the father of Salathiel** marks continuity from the exile (1:11). **Salathiel was the father of Zerubbabel.**[24] **Zerubbabel** was appointed governor of Jerusalem by the Persians after the return from exile. He restored the temple. For some he was God's servant chosen to overthrow and destroy "the strength of the kingdoms of the nations" (Hag 2:20-23). His inclusion continues the emphasis on God's control of human affairs despite the seeming power of empires. Jesus' subsequent proclamation of God's empire enacts that sovereignty in the context of Rome's control and anticipates Rome's demise (cf. 24:27-31).

• 1:13-15

Eleven names (**Zerubbabel, Abiud, Eliakim, Azor, Zadok, Achim, Eliud, Eleazar, Matthan, Jacob, Joseph**) cover the nearly six hundred years between **Zerubbabel** and **Joseph**. Most of these names do not appear in the genealogies of 1 Chronicles. For example, **Abiud** is not one of the five sons of **Zerubbabel** mentioned in 1 Chr 3:19-20. Several characters in biblical traditions bear the names of **Eliakim, Azor, Zadok** (including David's priest, 2 Sam 15:24-29), and **Eleazar**.

• 1:16

Jacob is the father of Joseph. This genealogy names **Jacob** as **the father of Joseph,** whereas Luke names Eli (3:23). This **Jacob–Joseph** link recalls the Genesis story in which another Jacob fathers a son called Joseph (Gen 37:1-4). This Joseph, like the Joseph of Matt 1-2, travels to Egypt, faces danger under imperial rule, interprets dreams, is faithful to God, and serves a key role in God's purposes. The Genesis link again evokes a context of oppression from which God liberates the people.

Joseph is **the husband of Mary from whom Jesus was born.** By *not* saying that Joseph is "the father of Jesus," and by defining him only in terms of

Mary, the "A was the father of B" pattern is broken to signal something unusual. The next clause **from whom Jesus was born** elaborates the unusual. While Mary's gender ensures continuity with the four previous women in the genealogy (see 1:3), she is distinguished from them. The construction **from whom** uses a *feminine* singular pronoun to restrict attention to Mary as Jesus' mother, without any reference to Jesus' father. Moreover, the passive verb **was born** breaks the active-voice construction of the "A was the father of B" pattern which has been used thirty-nine times to focus on the male actor. The patriarchal framework, already qualified by the four previously named women (see 1:3), is compromised by this sudden silence on male agency. The passive voice often implies God's action. The next section (1:18-25) will clarify that the Holy Spirit, not Joseph, is the actor in Jesus' origin,[25] and that Joseph has a legal, but not physical, role. The name **Jesus** is repeated from 1:1, as is **Christ** (see 1:1).

• 1:17

The three artificial sets of **fourteen generations** (**Abraham to David**, 1:2-6a; **David to the deportation to Babylon**, 1:6b-11; **Babylon to the Messiah**, 1:12-16) summarize the unit (see n. 2).

Why **fourteen**? (1) Various writers thought of history as a series of eras, with the present as a stage close to the final or new era that God would introduce. Daniel 2 and 7 know four eras plus one. *1 Enoch* has ten periods (93:1-10; 91:12-17). *2 Baruch* has twelve eras plus two (chs. 27, 53-74). The use of three groups of fourteen generations emphasizes God's sovereign control over human history. With Jesus, God's new creation begins to dawn (see 1:1, **book of origins**). See 14:32.

(2) In Hebrew, letters also double as numbers. Each consonant has a numerical value. The numerical values of the consonants in the name **David** add up to fourteen.

$$d + v + d = 4 + 6 + 4 = 14$$

This observation, along with the repeated name **David** in 1:1, 6, and 17, the use of the title **king** in v. 6, and the appearance of the name **David** in fourteenth position (1:6), suggests that the structure underlines links between Jesus and David. Both are chosen to perform significant roles in God's purposes. Jesus will be identified as a king in 2:2 as **David** is in 1:6. Jesus will proclaim an empire or reign (4:17; cf. 2 Sam 7). The royal tradition saw the king as representing God's merciful reign, which protected the poor and needy from oppression (Ps 72). The link with David suggests that Jesus will enact God's reign or empire.

The summary emphasizes (1) Jesus' descent from **Abraham** and **David**, (2) Jesus' place in God's history with God's people, (3) God's faithfulness, initiative, and saving presence throughout this history in freeing the people from tyranny in Egypt (exodus) and **exile to Babylon**, (4) God's new and unusual action in the conception of Jesus, which follows in the line of other unusual actions (Tamar and Judah, Rahab and Salmon, Ruth and Boaz, Bathsheba and David), yet which is the high point of that history. (5) Not only is this the story of God's actions and of Jesus' origin; it is, by implication, also the story of the origin of Jesus' followers. The one whom God calls into being will call them into being and to a distinct way of life yet to be outlined (4:17-25; chs. 5-7). The genealogy locates them in this account of the interaction of God and the people. This inclusion, though, comes at a price. By making Jesus central to God's purposes, the genealogy co-opts Israel's history, recasts it as the exclusive property of this small group of Jesus' followers, and does not recognize a legitimate place for those who do not follow him.

1:18-25—JESUS' CONCEPTION AND COMMISSION

The genealogy locates Jesus' origins in the story of God's dealings with God's people. Specifically, Jesus originates from Mary, whose husband is Joseph from the line of David. But the unusual passive construction **was born** in 1:16 has not identified Jesus' father. How is Jesus son of David? Verses 18-25 answer this question. The elaboration of 1:16 in 1:18-25 somewhat resembles the double creation story in Genesis: the brief reference to the creation of humans in Gen 1:26-31 is elaborated in 2:4b-25. God's creative initiative, which impacts the whole of creation, is operative.

This section (1:18-25) is the first key incident in the plot. God's act through the Holy Spirit (by whom Mary conceives) provides the "foundation for what follows,"[26] the event that cannot be deleted without damaging the narrative logic. *God* (not Joseph and Mary [1:18c, 20d, 25a]) begins the story.

This scene continues to legitimate the gospel audience's place in God's purposes. It assures followers of Jesus that they follow one who is brought into being at God's behest to carry out God's commission and will (1:21-23). In the roles that Mary and Joseph play, and especially in the setting aside of male agency, vv. 18-25 also offer a powerful example that God's ways are distinctive and out of step with conventional human behaviors. The example challenges the community to a difficult but faithful way of life.

• 1:18

Now the origin of Jesus the Messiah took place in this way. The word **origin** is often translated "birth," but the section's focus is on Jesus' conception by the Spirit,[27] and only incidental attention is paid to his birth in 1:25b (naming is more important) and 2:1 (Herod's response matters more). The repetition of **origin** from 1:1 again evokes Genesis 1, Abraham, and David. See 1:1. On **Jesus Christ**, see 1:1, 16, 17. Repetition, a common feature of this gospel, underlines important information.[28]

The explanation of Jesus' origin focuses on a certain time period, **When his mother Mary had been betrothed to Joseph.** In 1:16 **Joseph** is identified as **the husband of Mary** but not Jesus' father. On **Mary**, see 1:3, 16. The audience is assumed to know the cultural practice of **betrothal**, which begins the marriage agreement into which families entered. During the year or so before the marriage, the couple were referred to as "husband" and "wife" (Joseph is **husband** in 1:16, 19; Mary is **wife** in 1:20), the woman stayed with her family, and the couple did not live together or engage in sexual intercourse. If the woman has sex with another man, she commits adultery. To break the betrothal meant a bill of divorce.

The placement of the terms **his mother** and **betrothal** in the same clause is unusual. But there is a further complication. **Before they came together, she was found to be pregnant.** The first clause **Before they came together** has a double meaning: (i) before living together (between the agreement and the public ceremony), and (ii) before they had intercourse. Joseph and Mary have not had intercourse, yet **she was found to be pregnant**. She is not identified as a virgin until 1:23. Without this information, Joseph would conclude that she has had intercourse (willingly? seduced? raped?) with another man.[29] This was a serious breach of community values (cf. Deut 22:23-27). Pregnant and betrothed, **Mary** is by conventional cultural standards on the social, economic, and religious margins. Jane Schaberg notes curses on such women and their children in Sir 23:22-26 and Wis 3:16-19; 4:3-6.[30]

The addition of **from/through the holy spirit** establishes (for the audience but not for Joseph) that the conception did not result from Mary's unfaithfulness and/or from a man. It results from the **spirit**, God's creative power at work, the agent of God's will, as in Gen 1:2.[31] This conception without male agency and outside marriage circumvents the patriarchal household structure emphasized in 1:1-17. God is not bound by a structure that privileges male power. God seems to counter it, a theme that will continue as Jesus creates a new community in which the household is "not ruled by or even defined by a male head of the house"[32] (see 4:18-22; 12:46-50; chs. 19-20). And, second, the removal of human fatherhood anticipates the theme that membership in Jesus' new community is not constituted by descent through the father's biological or ethnic line.[33] Jesus is descendant of Abraham and David not by physical descent but by God's action. God's action prepares the way for two central dimensions of the "over-against" identity of the community of disciples. This community will be nonpatriarchal and ethnically inclusive.[34]

The notion of what scholars call "Mary's virginal conception"—conception by some action of a god—has a number of parallels in the ancient world.[35] These stories often account for the special abilities and deeds of a great hero:[36] Plato, Alexander the Great, Romulus, Augustus.[37] While Jesus' conception is unique in breaking the "A was the father of B" pattern in 1:2-17, it is not unique in the ancient world. The mode of his conception begins to show that he is one of the greats, in the company of outstanding human beings. But the narrative moves on. What matters is the divine purpose for this yet unborn child. For election in the womb, see Jer 1:5; Isa 49:1.

• 1:19

The focus moves to **Her husband Joseph** and his response to Mary's pregnancy.[38] The designation **husband**, appropriate terminology for a betrothal agreement, indicates Joseph's perspective. He, unlike the audience, knows nothing of God's intervention. He also knows that he is not the father (knowledge which the audience shares from **before they came together** [1:18]).

He is described further as **being just/righteous and not wishing to expose her to public disgrace**. The Greek participial construction does not clarify the relationship between these two attributes. (i) Are the two clauses in conflict? Being **righteous/just** he could instigate a public procedure to determine whether she has been seduced or raped (Deut 22:23-27), but **not wishing to disgrace her,** he could simply issue her a bill of divorce (cf. Deut 24:1). (ii) Or are the two clauses in agreement, with **righteous** essentially meaning "merciful"? Because he is **righteous/just** he will show kindness to her by **divorcing her quietly.**[39] The first seems more consistent with the meaning of **just/righteous,** which signifies to do the just/right thing. It is to act toward others according to a norm, to be faithful to one's responsibilities and commitments, especially in relation to God's will (Deut 16:18-20; Tob 14:9; see Matt 3:15).[40] In Joseph's view, Mary has dishonored him by violating the betrothal agreement. Divorce is the only option (cf. Deut 22:20-27). But righteousness or justice is not separated from mercy, so, **not wishing to expose her to public disgrace**, Joseph prefers a quiet divorce. Joseph exemplifies the mercy required of Jesus' followers (5:7; 9:13; 12:7).

• 1:20

But just when he had resolved to do this, behold an angel of the Lord appeared to him in a dream. The word **behold**, which appears some sixty-two times, frequently signals something unusual. Joseph receives a revelation and new perspective from **an angel of the Lord**, a messenger sent from God, who speaks God's will and so makes God audible to humans. This is a world in which divine presence and direction are very accessible and intrusive. The messenger's origin (**of the Lord**) guarantees its truth. In chapter 2, **angels** and/or **dreams** will figure four times to communicate the divine will to humans (2:12, 13, 19, 22). Both are common means of revelation in Jewish traditions. An angel helps Hagar (Gen 16:7-14) and another Joseph learns God's will through a dream (Gen 37:5-11). Among Greco-Roman writers, Plutarch calls dreams "our most ancient and respected form of divination" ("Dinner of the Seven Wise Men," *Moralia* 159A; see also Cicero, *De Div* 1.20-32).[41]

Angels often announce births (Ishmael, Gen 16:7-12; Isaac, Gen 17:1-19; Samson, Judg 13:3-22). Such annunciations usually include five common elements:[42] (1) the angel appears; (2) the human expresses fear; (3) the angel delivers a message (names and/or defines the recipient, reassures, announces forthcoming birth, names the child and interprets name, articulates the child's future great acts); (4) the recipient objects; (5) the angel gives a sign.

This section employs features 1 and 3.

The **angel** from God greets **Joseph** by name and by lineage, **son of David**, recalling 1:16. The angel assures him, **Do not be afraid**, and commands him, **take Mary as your wife**. To obey this order will directly counter what Joseph has decided. To be **righteous/just** means to do God's will as understood in the new circumstances created by Jesus' origin. For Joseph and Mary it means an action (marrying) which is contrary to societal expectations and which might be widely misunderstood and evaluated as shameful. By completing their marriage and not divorcing, Joseph and Mary are called to live a difficult existence against the cultural grain.

The angel identifies the basis for Joseph's action by revealing to him what the audience learned in 1:18, **for that which is conceived in her is of the holy spirit**. For the third time, the narrative states that Mary's pregnancy does not result from human actions. This is God's act.

• 1:21

The angel declares Jesus' future actions. Such prophecies of great accomplishments were, like miraculous conceptions, common features in accounts of the origins and youth of heroes in the Greco-Roman and Hellenistic Jewish worlds.[43]

The angel announces that **she will bear a son and you will call his name Jesus.** In naming the baby, Joseph, son of David, will acknowledge paternity and make Jesus "son of David." The name **Jesus** is explained: **for he will save his people from their sins**. The term "savior" is commonly associated with gods such as Asklepios[44] and Zeus (e.g., Plutarch, "That We Ought Not To Borrow," *Moralia* 830B), as well as with emperors. Josephus reports that the new emperor Vespasian is hailed as "savior" and "benefactor" as he approaches Rome in 70 C.E. (*JW* 7.71). It is also commonly used for Israel's God (Deut 32:15; Pss 24:5; 25:5; Isa 12:2). The choice of this name for Jesus reflects his God-given mission (based on Ps 130:8 [LXX 129]). It is the Greek form of the Hebrew name Joshua, the person who was God's agent in completing the people's redemption from Egypt by overcoming Canaanite power and occupying the land. The name signals Jesus' task of overcoming Rome. The naming commissions the yet-unborn baby. Jesus is the Christ (1:1, 16, 17), whom God has commissioned or anointed to save from sins. How he will carry out this mission will be narrated through the gospel. The explanation of his name suggests, though, that as the name is used in the gospel, the audience recalls this commission and evaluates his actions and words in relation to it.

Who are the **people** he will **save**? The invoking of Ps 130:8 suggests Israel, since 130:7-8 assures Israel of God's redemption.[45] Moreover, in Matt 2:6 the term **people** refers to the covenant people Israel ("his people Israel"). From what do they need **saving**? The gospel is written after the fall of Jerusalem in 70 C.E., an event that Matthew regards as God's punishment for the religious elite's rejection of Jesus (21:12-13, 18-19, 41; 22:7; 27:25; Introduction, sections 4, 8-10). Their rejection of Jesus, God's commissioned agent, is the elite's typical response to God's messengers (21:34-39, 45; 22:2-7; 23:29-39). While the gospel is concerned with all and any sins (cf. 5:21-48; 19:18-19),[46] the sin of the rejection of God's messengers and its consequences of neglecting God's will in its social, economic, political, and personal dimensions seems to be paramount. The leaders who will not be led by God cannot lead the people (9:36), except to lead them astray in persuading the Jerusalem crowds to call for Jesus' crucifixion (27:20).

But a world under Rome's rule does not embody God's purposes. Rome also rejects God's anointed.[47] Chapter 2 will show that Herod, Rome's ally and puppet king, murderously fails to welcome God's purposes. His tyranny prefigures that of rulers like the "governors and kings," who persecute disciples (10:18); Herod Antipas, who beheads John (14:1-12); and Pilate, who crucifies Jesus (27:11-37). The world needs saving from this oppressive rule.

However, while the elite and the people misled by the religious elite have sinned, God has not ended the covenant relationship with Israel. Just as punishment follows sin, so salvation or restoration follows punishment. This is the Deuteronomic understanding of salvation history: after the wilderness comes the promised land (Num 14:20-35), after exile in Babylon the return home (1 Kgs 9:6-9; 2 Kgs 25:27-30; Isa 40:1-11; 48:14-22), after punishment by Antiochus Epiphanes there is victory (2 Macc 6:12-17), after the punishment of Rome's occupation of Judea under Pompey, salvation must follow (*Pss. Sol.* 2; 17). Punishment is not final. The gospel proclaims that the rejection of Jesus, punished in the fall of Jerusalem, was not God's final offer. Through the proclamation of the community of disciples, Israel has a chance to repent, to be forgiven, and to find salvation in following Jesus, who will return to overcome Rome and to complete God's salvific purposes (cf. 24:27-31). The gospel seems to suggests that Israel will welcome Jesus as Messiah (see 23:39).

Further, God's purposes have never only involved Israel, as the references to Abraham (1:1-2) and the women (1:3-5) indicate. Israel is a light to the nations (Isa 49:6) that will cause the Gentiles to worship God (Isa 2; Mic 4:1-4; Matt 2:6). Israel's salvation will mean the nations' salvation also. The **people** that will be saved from their sins includes Jews and Gentiles.

But while this universal focus is apparent, the force of **his** (Jesus') cannot be overlooked. The gospel writer knows that in the present only some Jews and Gentiles follow Jesus. While **his people** potentially embraces all people, in the present it actually comprises the community of followers of Jesus. This community has a mission to the rest (5:13-16; 28:18-20) in anticipation of Jesus' completion of God's purposes.

• 1:22

The angel's announcement of the divine will is initially guaranteed by its origin from God (1:20). Now Jesus' conception and commission are shown to be consistent with God's will previously declared in the scriptures. This is the first of a series of "fulfillment citations" in which events in Jesus' life are shown to be consistent with God's will declared in the scriptures (2:5-6 [?], 15, 17-18, 23; 4:14-16; 8:17; 12:17-21; 13:35; 21:4-5; 26:54, 56 [?]; 27:9-10). The scriptural verses address, in the first instance, the circumstances in which they were written. But in each case the scripture is also seen to be significant for the time of Jesus and his followers. It is understood to declare beforehand God's will for Jesus, to which God is now being faithful. This perspective on the scriptures is shared only by those committed to Jesus. Other groups (e.g., Qumran) read the scriptures with a similar method and found in it references to their own history. This strategy assured the audience of Jesus' key place, and its key place, in God's purposes.

The initial **All this has happened** refers, as v. 23 indicates, not only to

Jesus' origin but also to the significance of his name. All of this is God's work. Thus, **to fulfill what was spoken by the Lord** means more than doing God's will, or being guided by the scriptures or bringing out their true or original meaning. It means bringing into being what God has previously promised in an action that expresses God's faithfulness.

The prophet (**through the prophet**) is Isaiah of Jerusalem, who lived in the eighth century. Invoking a **prophet** can be dangerous in an imperial context, since prophets keep alive hopes and different visions of the present and future which challenge the claims made by the powerful Roman and religious elite. Just as the eighth-century prophet Isaiah countered imperialist claims, so does the prophet's word for the Matthean audience.[48]

• 1:23

Look, the virgin shall conceive and bear a son and they shall name him Immanuel. The quotation is from Isa 7:14 (essentially following the LXX). It was originally addressed to King Ahaz of Judah (see 1:9), who was threatened by the greater northern powers of Syria and Israel (Isa 7:1-2; cf. 2 Kgs 16). Isaiah assures Ahaz that their imperial plans to conquer Judah will fail because of God's faithfulness. God offers Ahaz and the people a sign, the birth of a child named Immanuel, which signifies that the king's Davidic line will continue, that the Syro-Ephraimite imperialism is doomed, and that God is present with the people. God promises a stunning reversal—that during the baby's life, the lands of Israel and Syria will be laid waste (Isa 7:1-17). God's sign invites the king to trust God but he does not do so. Judgment follows. Isaiah announces that Assyria will punish the people.[49]

Many have debated the identity of the pregnant young woman. In the Isaian context it is not Mary. The Hebrew text refers to "a young woman," uses a noun that indicates her age (*almah*) not her sexual status (*betulah* would mean "virgin"), and indicates that she is pregnant without any hint of anything unusual. Most likely, the mother was Ahaz's wife and the baby was Hezekiah.

But in the context of Matt 1:18-25, the text refers to Jesus. **Behold** as in 1:20 underlines the unusual. Both the LXX and Matthew use the word *parthenos* (**virgin**) to underline one who has not had intercourse; this refers to Mary's conception by the spirit (**The virgin will conceive and bear a son**). Several traditions link Romulus, Rome's founder, with a virginal conception (Plutarch, *Romulus* 2.3-6; 3.1-5; see n. 37 above). Jesus' mission outdoes that of Rome.

To **call/name** the baby is not merely to give a name but to confer God's commission that this baby will save from sins (see 1:21). The Septuagint's "you will call" is changed here to the third person plural **they**. The **they** may refer to disciples who in using Jesus' name participate in his mission. Jesus gets a second name, **Immanuel which is interpreted "God with us."** No conflict exists with "Jesus" in 1:21, since to save from sins is to encounter God's saving presence.

The claim that Jesus manifests God's presence is partially polemical. It challenges Roman imperial theology, which understood the Flavian emperors to mediate the presence of the gods, and it is clearly not the synagogue's perspective (see Introduction, sections 8-9). To assert God's presence among humans is not new (so Isa 7-8; Isa 43:5; Ezek 34:24-31, esp. v. 30). The issue, post-70, is how God is known now after the devastation by Rome of Jerusalem and its temple. Josephus declares that God left the temple when it was destroyed (*JW* 5.412; so also, with modifications, Tacitus, *Hist* 5.13). Verse 23 proclaims that God's presence is known in Jesus, Emmanuel. Isaiah 7:14, forged in one situation threatened by imperial power, provides an analogy with the gospel audience's situation, also under imperial power, that of Rome. It offers the same assurance that, despite all appearances to the contrary, the empire does not hold sway, it is not sovereign, and God is not powerless. God's saving presence is now known through God's agent, Jesus. He is not God but makes God's presence known (see 18:20; 28:20) until God's reign is established in full (24:27-31).

• 1:24-25

These verses again focus on Joseph's response, as v. 19 did. But now **he did as the angel of the Lord commanded**. For Joseph's obedience as a counter-cultural action, see 1:20. Joseph's righteousness is seen in doing the will of God as it pertains to Jesus, revealed by the angel and the scriptures read in relation to Jesus. **He took her as his wife** completes the marriage process, as the angel requires (1:20). The biblical idiom of sexual intercourse as intimate experiential knowing (Gen 4:1; **but he did not know her**) shows his obedience to the scripture about a virgin bearing a son (1:23). Mary's virginal status, and thereby God's intervention, is emphasized by the repetition. God's will announced by the angel and the scriptures is accomplished, **until she bore a son**. God is faithful to the word. Joseph names the child (**he called his name Jesus**). The use of the same words (with a change in verb tense) as in the angel's instruction in 1:20-21 highlights Joseph's careful obedience. The verb **call** is used three times (1:21, 23, 25) to depict the accomplishment of God's will. In naming the child, Joseph assumes paternity, confers the status of descendant of Abraham and David on Jesus, and formally adopts him. "Jesus is incorporated into a lineage not his by birth."[50] Jesus' identity and function are derived from God's action, just as they are for his followers.

This is Jesus' origin in the promises, purposes, and effective word of God, made known through the angel and the scriptures and performed by the Holy Spirit. In the context of imperial threat (see Introduction, section 9) God acts. There is continuity with the past, but something decisive for the present and future is enacted as Jesus is commissioned by God to manifest God's saving presence (1:21, 23). In obeying the will of God as it is made known to them, Joseph and Mary live in tension with cultural norms, a fundamental aspect of this vision of marginal existence (see Introduction, section 10).

CHAPTER 2

The Empire Strikes Back

In the context of a long and uneven relationship with Israel (1:1-17), God has taken a new action in the conception of Jesus and in commissioning him to manifest God's saving presence (1:18-25). This action, in an imperial world dominated by sin (1:21), continues God's purposes to restore creation to its just order and relationship with its creator.

Chapter 2 contrasts two responses to God's initiative. (1) The empire strikes back as Herod, Rome's vassal king, and Jerusalem's settled elite of chief priests and scribes respond negatively. Herod employs military, religious, and social resources and strategies to thwart God's work. His murderous actions, allied with the inaction of the religious elite, demonstrate the oppressive structures from which Jesus is to save the world (1:21).[1]

(2) The new creation expands through unlikely people who embrace God's purposes: the very mobile magi, Gentiles who have neither power nor valued knowledge, witness to the dawning of God's new age. And the nonelite and mobile Joseph and Mary receive angelic revelations, guard the life of "the child," and protect the divine purposes against Herod. God's purposes prevail with Herod's death, though the ominous phrase "Archelaus reigned . . . in the place of his father" (2:22) warns the audience that the pernicious threat of empire is omnipresent for a marginal community of disciples.

These responses are sometimes falsely presented as a contrast between "rejecting Jews" and "believing Gentiles." The role of Joseph and Mary, and Herod's origin as an Idumean, clearly indicate that this division is not convincing. Rather the division consists of a sociopolitical dynamic between the powerful settled center (Herod, the religious elite) and the apparently powerless, insignificant, and mobile margins (magi, Joseph and Mary).[2]

2:1-12—ELITE OPPOSITION AND MAGI WORSHIP

• 2:1

The repeated reference to Jesus' birth (**When Jesus was born in Bethlehem of Judea in the days of Herod the king**), like 1:25, confirms the efficacy of God's words spoken through the angel (1:20-21) and declared previously in the scriptures (1:22-23).

73

The birth notice identifies the geographical and temporal locations of Jesus' birth. It took place in **Bethlehem of Judea**, a small village, not a center of power like Jerusalem (see 3:5; 4:5, 25; 5:35). The place, though, has a regal history. David was anointed king in **Bethlehem** by Samuel to replace the rejected king Saul (1 Sam 16:1-13). Jesus, David's son (1:1, 17, 20, 25), is born there **in the days of Herod the king**, Rome's representative and puppet. No information about Herod is given;[3] his character will be revealed in the subsequent events. He was appointed by the senate in 40, gained control in 37, and died in 4 B.C.E. Josephus has him acknowledge Rome as "masters of the world" (*Ant* 15.387). His brutality, political skill in maintaining his throne, and grandiose building projects, which included temples for God in Jerusalem and for Roma and Augustus in Caesarea Maritima (also in Sebaste), were well known. While Herod financed some of this building activity (see Josephus, *Ant* 15.380), and while it provided employment for many, much of it was funded by taxation and requisitions of material and labor.

The negative presentation of Herod in chapter 2 is consistent with the mostly negative view of kings in 1:6b-11. Moreover, various connections between this story and that of Moses leading the people out of slavery in Egypt (see 2:13) show Herod to resemble Pharaoh, another ruler who resists God's purposes in vain. Herod, then, represents the "kings of the earth" who resist God and God's anointed but are thwarted by God (Ps 2:1-6; also Matt 17:24-27). His resistance contrasts with Jesus' obedient kingship and the **magi**'s worship.[4]

Something unusual happens (so **behold**; see 1:20, 23), namely, the appearance of new characters: **magi from the east came to Jerusalem.** If Juvenal's stereotypical presentation is any guide, the **east** and easterners were often perceived negatively as slaves or freedmen and were associated with the "low" life of drinking and brothels, and with superstition, astrology, and other fantastic or unpredictable happenings.[5]

Magi were not kings or "wise men."[6] The narrative presents them as ambivalent or liminal figures (Introduction, section 10). **Magi** were originally members of the Persian priestly class serving the ruler (Herodotus, *Hist* 1.101, 132; Philostratus, *Epistle of Apollonius* 17). They had access to the centers of power as these magi do to Herod (cf. Dan 2:2-10). Yet **magi** could be threats to royal power[7] with a destabilizing influence in predicting events that threatened the empire, such as a short reign or an emperor's imminent death, or the birth of a new king.[8]

With astrological insight, they claimed supernatural knowledge and powers. Some dismissed their claims. Tacitus calls them "absurdities" (*Ann* 2.27-33; though more ambivalent in *Ann* 6.20-22, a prophecy that Galba would be emperor!). Seneca laughs at the astrologers who have been predicting Claudius's death "every year, every month" (*Apoc* 3.2). Pliny mocks the "Magian deceits" of a physician Asclepiades as "surpassing even Magian nonsense" (*NH* 26.7-9). He intends to "refute the fraudulent lies of the magi." Philostratus finds it necessary to defend Apollonius against the insulting charge that he is a "magus" (*Apollonius* 1.2). And in the only use of **magi** in the LXX

(Dan 2:2-10), King Nebuchadnezzar's magi, despite being threatened with loss of property, limb, and life, can not recall the king's dream (2:5).

Knowledge from the stars was also viewed negatively in many Jewish traditions. See Exod 7-9; Isa 47:12-15; *Jub.* 12:16-24, where Abram learns that God, not the stars, is to be trusted. And Philo has Balak describe the magus Balaam as "the most foolish of all men" (*Moses* 293). **Magi**, then, are supposedly skilled and learned in matters that are variously regarded by some as nonsense and by others as unreliable![9]

Yet various emperors took the magi's astrological knowledge very seriously. Nero is alarmed at a comet's appearance "because it is commonly believed to portend the death of great rulers" (Suetonius, *Nero* 36). Juvenal attacks a woman who gossips about a comet threatening the kings of Armenia and Parthia (*Sat* 6.407-12). The emperor Tiberius expels astrologers from Rome in 19 C.E., as do Vespasian in 70-71 and Domitian ca. 89-90.[10] Seneca claims that "on even the slightest motion of heavenly bodies hang the fortunes of nations, and the greatest and smallest happenings are to accord with the progress of a kindly or unkindly star" (*To Marcian on Consolation* 18.3). Herod is threatened by their knowledge from a star and takes it very seriously.

The **magi from the east** are Gentiles.[11] They respond positively to God's actions with Jesus while some other Gentiles do not (6:7; 8:34; 18:17; 27:27-31). They are itinerant, in contrast to **Jerusalem,** the fixed seat of political (Herod) and Jewish religious and social (chief priests, scribes) power.[12] **Jerusalem** and its temple were regarded in the Zion traditions as God's chosen dwelling place (Isa 2:2-4; Ps 48). For some it was therefore inviolable and indestructible (Isa 31:4-5; Jer 7:4; Ps 48:8), though Isaiah recognized trust in God as a condition for its survival (Isa 1:19-28). Neither Micah (3:12) nor Jeremiah (7:1-15; ch. 26) hesitated to predict Jerusalem's fall because of its sin and corruption in using its political, religious, and economic power for the benefit of the priests and elite, not the people. The **magi** travel, then, to a city that is called to be a "holy city" (Matt 4:5; 27:53), God's special city (5:35), but whose political and religious leadership betray this calling. The negative response in **Jerusalem** evidenced here in chapter 2 anticipates the crucifixion narrative (e.g., 27:25; the title **King of the Jews** will also be prominent: 27:11, 29, 37, 42).

• **2:2**

This verse discloses the magi's purpose, threat, political naïveté, and ignorance. Their knowledge that a special king has been born comes from a star:[13] **Where is the one born king of the Jews for we observed his star at its rising?** They do not know, though, who the **king** is or where he is (not until v. 9, guided primarily by the scriptures).

On one hand, their use of a star does not attest unique or special knowledge. Pliny reports (though does not seem to believe) that widespread popular belief understood a **star** to brighten at a person's birth and dim at death, the richer the person the brighter the star (*NH* 2.28). Many stories associate stars and heavenly phenomena with the birth of significant figures: teachers and wonder workers such as Apollonius of Tyana (Philostratus, *Apollonius* 1.5 [a thunder-bolt]), and emperors such as Augustus, Tiberius, and Nero (Suetonius, *Augustus* 94.2 ["the ruler of the world"]; *Tiberius* 14.2; Nero, Dio Cassius 61.2.1-4 [stars]). Virgil had written that a star guided Aeneas to the site on which Rome was to be built (*Aeneid* 2.692-704). Josephus indicates a comet and a star over Jerusalem at its destruction in 70 C.E. (*JW* 6.289; for other portents, see Pliny, *NH* 2.91-94). The **magi** have observed what anyone could have observed.

Yet the magi *are* observant enough to notice it (no one else does), motivated enough to travel some distance to identify the special person to whom the star bears witness, astute enough to know that the star attests a new king, and discerning enough to know that worship is the appropriate response (2:2). Ironically, God reveals something very significant to these **magi** by this means (see 2:4 for a contrast with the Jewish religious leaders who know the scriptures). Throughout the gospel the natural world, properly interpreted, attests God's presence and purposes (5:45; 6:26, 28, 30; 10:29; 24:32-33) including Jesus' crucifixion (27:45), death (27:51-53), and return (24:29-30).

The magi state their motive: **And we have come to worship him** (see 2:8, 11; 4:9; 28:9). Worship expresses allegiance to God, as the first commandment, using the same verb, makes clear (Exod 20:5; Deut 5:9). But the term **worship** or *proskynesis* is also a political one which designates the prostration required, especially in the east since Alexander, when greeting a ruler (see 4:9-10).[14] The magi have not extended any such submission to King Herod. They have made their choice.

• 2:3

When King Herod heard this, he was frightened, and all Jerusalem with him. Herod's position as **king** is emphasized by repetition. He is **frightened** by the magi's report of a star and question about a king. The verb **frightened** may recall King Belshazzar's response (same verb) in Dan 5:9 to his advisers' inability to interpret "the writing on the wall," a message of doom for his kingdom (see also Matt 14:26). As an Idumean without a royal genealogy (in contrast to King Jesus, 1:1-17), Herod is especially touchy despite Roman support. The **magi** and **star** are dangerous in that they challenge political stability by witnessing to an alternative **king**.

The magi may lack political astuteness in reporting the star to Herod and in asking him about a king! But in the tradition of magi in conflict with kings (such as Balaam's opposition to King Balak and Gaumata's opposition to King Cambyses[15]), their question signals inevitable conflict, since King Herod (2:1) was also known as **King of the Jews** (Josephus, *Ant* 16.311). In addition, Josephus notes a Jewish tradition that someone from their "country" would become "ruler of the world" (*JW* 6.310-13; also Tacitus, *Hist* 5.13). They interpret it as an oracle fulfilled when Vespasian becomes emperor (cf. Suetonius, *Vespasian* 4.5). The gospel points to Jesus' different kingship as son of David (1:1, 17, 20, 25).

Herod is joined in his fear by **all Jerusalem**. Given the contrast between the marginal **Bethlehem** and center **Jerusalem** in v. 1 and the prominence of

Joseph in 1:18-25 (and the subsequent Jewish disciples), **all** cannot mean that all Jews fear because of this threat to Herod's position and reject Jesus, in contrast to the worshiping Gentiles. Rather the contrast, as in v. 1, is between the powerful but now troubled center/elite and the inconsequential and supposedly powerless and insignificant margins. In God's scheme, **Bethlehem** is the place of new creation, **Jerusalem** the place of fear because God's actions challenge (in)vested interests and power.

• 2:4

Herod takes the initiative, as he will do often throughout the scene.[16] **He assembled all the chief priests and scribes of the people,** his advisory council, the Sanhedrin (see 26:3, 57).[17] As was typical in imperial societies, **the chief priests and scribes** as religious leaders (along with the Pharisees and Sadducees who appear in 3:7) are part of the elite. Together they are members of the governing classes, who in alliance with Rome and its representatives (Herod, Pilate) uphold the present hierarchical societal structure (see Introduction, sections 1, 5). Josephus consistently locates the chief priests, the "most notable Pharisees," and the Sadducees among the ruling group ("the notables" or "powerful ones," οἱ δυνατοί, *hoi dynatoi*) as defenders of the status quo and as allies of Rome (*Ant* 13.297; 18.17 [Sadducees]; *JW* 2.197, 320, 411, 414 [chief priests and Pharisees]). J. Kautsky argues that in interpreting sacred texts and representing sacred traditions, **scribes** typically maintain and support, rather than change, the status quo.[18] This first appearance of the religious leaders, significant characters through the gospel,[19] is ominous. They are linked with Jerusalem's **fear** (2:3), allied with Herod, and introduced by the verb **assembled**. The verb **assembled** is the verbal form of "synagogue," an institution from which Jesus will be distanced ("their synagogue," 4:23; 9:35; 12:9; 13:54; 23:34) and which will consistently receive bad press (e.g., 6:2, 5; 10:17; 23:6; see Introduction, section 8). The verb appears six times in the passion narrative, four times of the religious leaders carrying out Jesus' execution (26:3, 57; 27:62; 28:12), once of the crowd under their control (27:17, 20), and once of the Roman soldiers (27:27). The verb here, then, refers to an alliance of religious leaders that, with Rome's support, will oppose Jesus and put him to death. Moreover, the verb **assemble** designates in Ps 2:2 the earth's rulers who assemble against "the Lord and his anointed." Its use here presents the alliance's opposition to God and Jesus as the typical but doomed behavior of centers of power.

The plural **all the chief priests** is unusual, since there was one high priest. It probably indicates the religious leaders in Jerusalem, including not only the chief priest but also former priests, members of priestly families and those involved with the weekly and daily rotations in the temple. That is, it evokes the central power structure of the priestly elite whose power and status derive from their birth into the priestly line. The **scribes of the people** were the professional class of legal experts, the teachers, interpreters, and administrators of the Mosaic law.[20] Their authority derived from their knowledge and training. Herod summons the religious, social, and intellectual leadership.

It should be noted that the scene is historically improbable. Josephus reports that Herod massacred many of these religious leaders and allowed them little influence (*Ant* 17.41-45). Some have suggested that the antipathy to the religious elite in the narrative reflects the socioreligious experience of the audience post-70 in Antioch in a struggle against a synagogue (see Introduction, section 8).

Herod inquires from this elite **where the Christ was to be born**. The narrative equates "king of the Jews" in 2:2 with **Christ** here (see on 1:1, 17, 18). His question does not mean that there was a common expectation of one place for the Messiah's birth (see 1:1). Rather the question sets up the subsequent explanation of Jesus' birth in Bethlehem as one born of the line of David.

• 2:5

The religious leadership immediately names **Bethlehem of Judea**. From Jerusalem's perspective, any other place and personnel are marginal. The reference to the small town **Bethlehem** as the place of Jesus' birth indicates that God's action is encountered in a supposedly inconsequential place among marginal people, not in the center of power among the elites.

The elite's information comes not from the star (the magi don't know, 2:2) but from the scriptures (**for so it has been written by the prophet**). The **prophet** is not named (as in 1:22), but the verse comes from Mic 5:2, combined with a line from 2 Sam 5:2. The reference to **prophet** repeats the understanding of the scriptures articulated in 1:22, namely, that God's previously revealed will is now enacted in Jesus. The irony is that while Matthew's audience is to consent to this way of reading the scriptures, the religious leaders do not. The prophets are a source of dangerous and destabilizing material about God's purposes, which challenges the claims and interests of the political and religious elite and their theological legitimations.[21]

• 2:6

The citation is from Mic 5:2. As part of Mic 4:1-5:15, the verse was probably a postexilic addition to the Micah tradition. It anticipates a time after the exile when Gentiles will come to Jerusalem to worship Israel's God, and all people, Jew and Gentile, will walk in God's ways (Mic 4:1-4). God will also provide a shepherd-ruler who will rule faithfully (Mic 5:2). This hopeful claim contrasts with the despair of the setting: the overthrow of Jerusalem and the exiling of its citizens to Babylon (Mic 4:10). There seems no hope against the imperial ambitions of the nations (Mic 4:11). But God's purposes are otherwise (4:12). Ironically, Micah uses imperial rhetoric to detail God's plans to rescue and redeem the people (4:10b; 5:9) by means of a shepherd-ruler from Bethlehem (5:2). God's (imperial) purposes are that all will submit to and worship God, will learn of God's ways and live under God's reign in peace (4:1-4; see Introduction, section 1).

Micah's word, proclaimed centuries earlier for the postexilic situation, is used to interpret what is happening in the events of Jesus' birth. The Gentile magi have come to worship, and a king from David's line has been born in Bethlehem. God keeps the promise, and the new creation is under way. The verse highlights again the importance for God's purposes of the seemingly insignificant, and God's resistance to imperial power. In a location that seems from the center (Jerusalem) to be marginal and inconsequential, God's saving presence is revealed.

The citation does not strictly agree with either the Hebrew (MT) or the Greek (LXX) version. The gospel's author shapes details to fit this context. The first line, **But you Bethlehem (in the) land of Judah** substitutes **Judah** for Ephrathah. The change underlines that Bethlehem is the focus, not Jerusalem. Matthew's second line, **are by no means least among the rulers of Judah**, rewrites the second line of Mic 5:2, which affirmed "Ephrathah" as "one of the little clans of Judah." The verse in Micah as a whole emphasized the importance of insignificant Bethlehem because of the promised birth. The change in Matt 2:6b highlights the reversal from Bethlehem's apparent insignificance to its present great importance because of God's action. This reversal too emphasizes the contrast between the supposedly great center (Jerusalem) and insignificant Bethlehem alluded to in vv. 1-3. The change from "clans" to **rulers** focuses the chapter's concern with the effect of political power. **For from you will come a leader/ruler.** Matthew omits several words from the original, including the phrase "a ruler in Israel," because the genealogy and the magi have indicated the universal significance of Jesus. The **ruler** is Jesus, not Herod and his allies, not the emperor who secures Herod's throne.

As agent of God's rule, Jesus **will shepherd/govern my people Israel**. This line comes from 2 Sam 5:2. It quotes God's election of David as king and promise of a reign that will last forever. This reign represents God's covenant faithfulness to the people. It enacts God's justice by defending the poor and needy, and by having mercy on the weak (so Ps 72). Jesus as David's descendant is elected by God to **shepherd/govern my people Israel** (cf. 1:21).

How he will do these tasks is a pressing question. In a world that knows oppressive rule, will God's rule manifested in this new king be any different? Micah's imperial rhetoric, which insists on the submission of all to God's triumphant will, raises doubts. The gospel will also often resort to this rhetoric but will at times glimpse a different reign or empire in contrast to the ruthless Herod and Roman empire. While the verb **govern/shepherd** will not appear again, the cognate noun **ruler/shepherd** will be used of Jesus in 9:36 to designate a rule not of oppression and exploitation but of compassion for "the harassed and helpless." In such ruling/shepherding, Jesus Immanuel reflects God's compassionate and life-giving shepherding/ruling (Ps 23:1).

The style of his rule is also clarified by Ezek 34, a chapter evoked by the **shepherd** image.[22] God condemns the leaders as false shepherds because they look after themselves but harm the sheep/people (Ezek 34:2-10; see Matt 9:36). God promises to search and care for the people (34:11-22) and will send a Davidic shepherd to shepherd (same verb, *poimanei*, as Matt 2:6) "my sheep," God's people (Ezek 34:23-34, 30-31). The religious leaders, in quoting this verse and invoking Ezekiel's critique of false and oppressive leaders, inadvertently condemn themselves and agree with God's verdict. They will oppose and crucify God's shepherd, Jesus (cf. 26:31).

• 2:7

Then Herod secretly called for the magi. The religious leaders suddenly disappear! They quote the scripture but they do nothing. In contrast to the Gentile and marginal **magi** (v. 2), the elite religious leaders know where the Christ is to be born. Just as Joseph can interpret Pharaoh's dreams when the Egyptian magicians cannot (Gen 41), just as Daniel can interpret Nebuchadnezzar's dreams when his Babylonian wise men cannot (Dan 2), the Jewish religious leaders know what these ignorant Gentiles do not. The magi's tradition of special knowledge seems not so stellar.

But in quoting scripture, the religious leaders fail to do two things. (1) The religious leaders do not connect the scripture to Jesus. Matthew 1:19-20; 1:21, 22-23 have made it clear that the scriptures reveal things about Jesus and have to be understood in relation to him. The audience knows from v. 1 that Jesus is born in Bethlehem and from chapter 1 that he is descendant of David. But the religious leaders do not make the link with Jesus. (2) The religious leaders do nothing with their knowledge. They know the Christ is to be born in Bethlehem, but they do not go there. The powerful center resists God's purposes, while the lowly (Bethlehem) and marginal (the Gentile magi) embrace them.

The narrative follows **Herod**. He acts on what he has learned, but inappropriately. Taking the initiative as in 2:4, he **summoned the magi secretly**; the adverb **secretly** indicates some subterfuge and deception. The **magi** are treated not as valued guests but as servants as Herod instructs them to do his bidding. He seeks **to learn from them the exact time of the star's appearance**. This strange inquiry is not explained. It will be clarified by the death commands in 2:16.

• 2:8

Then he sent them to Bethlehem saying, "Go and search diligently for the child; and when you have found him, bring me word so that I may also go and worship him." With his fear in v. 3, the secret gathering of v. 7, and the mimicking of the **magi's** genuine purpose (2:2), the king's sincerity seems dubious. Jesus is referred to here not by name or by a title but as **the child**, the first of eight such references to him in the chapter (2:8, 9, 11, 13 [twice], 14, 20, 21; note also **children** in 2:16, 18).

The term **the child** is significant. It evokes the audience's knowledge of widespread (though evolving) attitudes to children in the Greco-Roman world. These cultural values contrast sharply with post-Enlightenment understandings of children as sweet, innocent, good, and harmless. Without denying parental love in patriarchal households, children were often viewed with suspicion as a threat to adult (male) civic order.[23] They were weak, irrational, ignorant, unpredictable, of little present value, but significant for the future. Children were to be obedient and respectful, learning their important future roles as an adult. Until then their place was on the margins of the adult male world. The frequent and repeated references to Jesus as a **child**, weak and vulnerable to the murderous power of King Herod, evoke such experiences of marginality and vulnerability. The world of empire and of political and religious power is a dangerous one. But the context shows that it is with the marginal, not the powerful and elite of the center, that God's power, protection, and presence are encountered.

• 2:9-10

When they had heard the king, they set out, and behold the star that they had seen at its rising went ahead of them, until it stopped over the place where the child was. The **star,** which had signaled a significant birth (2:2, 7), now leads them to **the child** whose birthplace the scriptures have revealed. God's guidance ensures that they are able to worship in the midst of Herod's counterplans. Their response, extravagantly described in the clause **they rejoiced with exceeding great joy** is typical of the experiences of those who recognize God's presence, guidance, or protection (Pss 5:11; 30:11-12; 47; 63:5-9; 66; etc.; Matt 5:12). It is also a feature of God's anticipated new creation (Isa 65:17-19) and of the existence of those vindicated in judgment (Matt 25:21, 23). The magi display desirable discipleship features.

• 2:11

On entering the house, they saw the child with Mary his mother. Jesus' birthplace is a **house.** Since the household was a basic unit of society, socially, religiously, economically, this is an important location. Numerous important things will happen in houses (see 8:14; 9:10, 23, 28; 17:25; 26:6). In various ways (see chs. 19-20), the gospel will challenge the normative patriarchal and hierarchical household patterns and offer disciples a vision of restructured relationships and more equitable use of resources.[24]

The magi **saw the child with Mary his mother**. This phrase reappears in 2:13, 14, 20, 21. Joseph is not named. The phrase recalls Exod 4:19 LXX (also 2:20-21), in which Moses goes to Egypt with his wife and sons. Increasingly, echoes of the Moses story appear in this scene as Jesus relives events in Moses' and Israel's past. A new exodus, a new liberation from slavery and oppression is under way. Pharaohs/emperors do not have the final say, no matter how much they resist God's purposes.

The magi **fall down and worship, and opening their treasure chests, they offered him gifts of gold, frankincense, and myrrh.** Their act recalls scenarios of Gentiles journeying to Jerusalem to worship either the king as a representative of God's justice (Ps 72:10-11) or God (Mic 4:1-2, so 2:5-6 above; Isa 2:1-4; 60; *Pss. Sol.* 17:31; *1 En* 53:1). The coming of the Gentiles (nations and kings) is part of a vision of the restoration of God's wholeness and justice on earth which is recognized by Gentiles including those who formerly "oppressed . . . and despised you" (Isa 60:14). In this pilgrimage the Gentile kings bring **gifts**: "gold" (Ps 72:10, 15), "the abundance of the sea" (Isa 60:5), "gold and frankincense" (Isa 60:6), "flocks" (Isa 60:7), "silver and gold" (Isa 60:9), "wealth" (Isa 60:11).

But while the magi's act may recall this tradition and anticipate the worship of the Gentiles, the scene subverts the tradition. (i) Kings such as Herod do not come to worship Jesus or welcome God's intervention, because they have much to lose (cf. Ps 2:2). Instead of kings, their servants and dangerous adversaries, the marginal magi, come to **worship** (see 2:2, 8; 4:9-10). (ii) Further, they do not come to Jerusalem and the temple to worship. They travel instead to insignificant Bethlehem to worship Jesus. Jesus appears in the post-70 context after Rome had destroyed the Jerusalem temple as a new temple where God's presence is encountered and acknowledged (1:23; 12:6).

Do their gifts of **gold and frankincense and myrrh** have special signifi-cance? U. Luz helpfully notes that the gifts have been seen by readers over two millennia to say something about either Jesus or about the magi as disciples.[25] The christological readings have seen gold indicating Jesus' kingship, frankin-cense variously his divinity or his high priestly office, and myrrh his humanness or his death. But Matthew does not declare Jesus to be divine or a high priest, or attribute these meanings to the gifts. The discipleship or parenetic readings have seen the gifts representing desirable qualities such as faith, reason, good works, prayer, mortification of the flesh, love, hope, mercy, purity, and a believing heart. Again the gospel does not make these or any identifications.

It is preferable to see the **gifts** as signifying other realities: (i) some Gentiles come to worship as part of God's universal purposes; (ii) the magi give their treasure to Jesus (6:21). Gold, linked with common folks in 10:9, does not indi-cate excessive wealth. They give what they have.[26]

• 2:12

And having been warned in a dream not to return to Herod, they with-drew into their own country by another road. The focus returns to vv. 8-9a and Herod's schemes. His attempts to thwart God's purposes are thwarted through **a dream** (God's activity in 1:20-21).

Magi are renowned for interpreting dreams (Herodotus, *Hist* 1.107, 120; Cicero, *De Div* 1.23.46-47). The magi obey the dream's warning. True to the traditions of Balaam and Gaumata (see 2:3), the magi work against their kingly master.

The section 2:1-12 has maintained key emphases from chapter 1. Theologi-cally it has continued to assert God's initiative and intervention. God's new cre-ation is under way (1:1). It is God's world (not the empire's or Jupiter's) and God's reign is being asserted. Christologically, Jesus' significance is underlined by the scriptures, the worshiping Gentiles, the hostile Herod, and the unmoved religious leaders. God's purposes involve Gentiles as well as Jews, as the magi demonstrate. Ecclesially, or in discipleship terms, the section continues to shape identity and lifestyle. There is a basic contrast between the urban elite, the powerful center which resists God's purposes, and those marginal to this center (the magi, the town of Bethlehem) who encounter God's purposes. The magi model important dimensions of discipleship: their marginality, their dis-covery of God's purposes, worship, faithfulness, and obedience to God's pur-poses in the face of Herod's actions. The world of empire is a dangerous place for those who seek God's purposes and respond positively to God's initiative. God's vision of human society and justice differs so greatly with its preference for the margins. It is to such an existence that the gospel calls its audience as voluntary marginals, warning that it is dangerous but assuring that it is divinely guided and protected (see Introduction, section 10).

2:13-23—MURDEROUS HEROD AND FAITHFUL JOSEPH AND MARY

• 2:13

The repeated reference to the magi's **withdrawal** emphasizes God's guidance of them, God's protection of Jesus (and of God's purposes) in circumstances of threat, God's partial blocking of Herod's opposition, and the magi's obedience and subversion. **Behold** (cf. 1:20; 2:1; something marvelous or unusual) **an angel of the Lord appeared to Joseph in a dream**. The wording essentially repeats 1:20 (cf. 2:19) and is a typical angelophany. The angel sent by God supplies divine guidance and protection for Jesus. **Joseph** plays the key role. As befits Matthew's interest in redefining traditional patriarchal household roles (see 2:11; 12:46-50; chs. 19-20), Joseph does not rule over his family but serves it faithfully or righteously in protecting it from danger (cf. 1:19).[27] For the association of Joseph, dreams, and Egypt, see Gen 37-41.

Get up, take the child and his mother (see 2:8, 11) **and flee to Egypt, and remain there until I tell you.** Though under Roman control since 30 B.C.E., Egypt traditionally provided refuge for those who were fleeing the deathly power of rulers: Jeroboam from Solomon (1 Kgs 11:40), the prophet Uriah from King Jehoiakim (Jer 26:21), the high priest Onias from Antiochus (Josephus, *Ant* 12.387). Itinerancy and distance from the center mean safety.

The reference to **Egypt** evokes other stories of people whom God delivers from Egypt. (1) Several similarities exist between this scene and the experiences of Joseph, son of Jacob, in Egypt ("The Lord was with him," Gen 39:2): danger, dreams, divine protection in the midst of political power, family bonds, deliverance. (2) Many readers have noted echoes in chapter 2 of the story of Moses.[28] These include the following:

- similar events: attacks on male children (Exod 1; Matt 2:16-18); conflict with rulers (Exod 2; Matt 2:1-12), exile and God's protection (Exod 2:15; Matt 2:13-14), return from exile after a revelation of the tyrant's death (Exod 2:23; 4:19; Matt 2:19-20)
- the citation of Hos 11:1 in Matt 2:15
- verbal similarities: compare the accounts of Moses' and Jesus' return in Exod 4:19-20 (LXX) and Matt 2:19-21

(3) The specific links with Moses evoke both the exodus or liberation from slavery and oppressive rule and the wilderness and Sinai events, in which Moses reveals God's will (the Ten Commandments). Ironically, Egypt, the place of bondage in Moses' story, becomes for Jesus a place of refuge, so great is the Jerusalem elite's resistance to God's purposes. But, like Moses, Jesus is given the task of saving a people (1:21) and of revealing God's will (cf. chs. 5-7). Jesus seems to relive the exodus story in a further expression of God's

saving work. But God's salvation is as yet only partial and selective, as the murdered babies and reign of Archelaus, Herod's successor, indicate.

This is not the only or first time the biblical tradition conceives of God's saving activity as a new exodus. In talking about the return from exile in Babylon in the sixth century, Deutero-Isaiah uses a "new exodus" theme, and, as here in Matt 1-2, associates it with a new creation (Isa 51:9-11).

The angel tells Joseph the reason for their flight: **for Herod is about to search for the child, to destroy him**. The angel discloses, for the first time, Herod's motivation for collecting information from the religious leaders (2:4-6) and from the magi (2:7-11). This motivation accounts for the warning to the magi not to return to Herod (2:12-13a). Herod's hypocrisy in claiming that he wants to worship (2:8) and his outright rejection of God's purposes are clear. So too are the danger to **the child** and God's greater power to thwart Herod's destructive power. The empire lashes out against perceived threats, but it cannot prevail despite all appearances of power. The verb **destroy** will be used in both 12:14 and 27:20 to describe the goal of the religious leaders' opposition to Jesus. The center elite remain united against God's purposes, but the angel and Joseph protect Jesus for his divinely commissioned mission (1:21-23).

• **2:14-15a**

The repetition of much of the angel's instruction from v. 13 (**Then Joseph got up, took the child and his mother by night, and withdrew into Egypt, and remained there until the death of Herod**) underlines Joseph's obedience (cf. 1:24). The phrase **by night** emphasizes the immediacy of his obedience to the angel's appearing in a dream as well as its danger.

The verb **withdrew** appears for the third time (2:12, 13) to denote a response to hostility. But as in 2:22-25, 4:12-16, 12:15-21, a fulfillment citation follows the hostility and withdrawal. The action of **withdrawing** enacts the divine will and ensures Jesus' safety so that he can carry out the mission for which God has commissioned him.[29] The verb similarly denotes Moses' and Judas Maccabeus's withdrawal before imperial hostility in Exod 2:15 and 2 Macc 5:27.

Joseph, Mary, and Jesus **remain** in Egypt **until the death of Herod**. This is the first of three references to Herod's death (2:19, 20). Ironically, the death of the one who seeks Jesus' death (2:13b) is the means by which God finally thwarts Herod's opposition and threat.

• **2:15b**

Another fulfillment citation follows (see on 1:22-23): **so that what was spoken by the Lord through the prophet might be fulfilled, saying** . . . . The prophet is Hosea (Hos 11:1), and the citation follows the Hebrew (MT) not the Greek (LXX) version: **from Egypt I have called my child/son.** The citation's reference to Egypt connects it to vv. 13-15a. But the event to which it refers, Jesus' return from Egypt to Israel, will not occur until 2:19-21 (in 2:15 Jesus is going *into* not *from* Egypt).

In Hos 11, the verse does not refer to Jesus. It refers both to the exodus from Pharaoh's oppressive power, and to the covenant people of Israel as God's

child/son whom God loves with a maternal love (Hos 11:3-4). But despite God's liberating the people from slavery, Hosea laments that the people do not heed God's call and have practiced injustice and unfaithful worship (Hos 10:13; 11:2) so they will be punished.

Here in 2:15b, the verse underlines God's protection of Jesus from the dangerous threat of Herod (anticipating 2:16-17) and portrays Jesus in coming out from Egypt as reliving the (exodus) story of Israel. Like Israel, he is in filial covenant relationship with God and is freed from oppression.

The term **son/child** does not indicate that Jesus is divine. The same term identifies Israel in Hos 11:1, the wise person in Wis 2, the king in Ps 2:7, none of whom is divine. Rather it indicates that Jesus enjoys a faithful relationship with God and has a significant function or role in God's salvific purposes. (So in 2 Sam 7:14 the king as God's son is to rule faithfully in God's love). The term is used here essentially as a synonym for "Christ" (1:1, 16, 17, 18) in highlighting Jesus' role as God's agent (see 16:16; 4 Ezra 7:28-29; 13:32, 37). The fifth appearance of the verb **call** also emphasizes Jesus' role and relationship with God. In three previous uses, it denotes, as here, God's summons of and purposes for Jesus (1:21, 23, 25; also 2:23).

• 2:16

From God's guidance exercised through two "dream" revelations (2:12, 13), Joseph's obedient action (2:14), and God's will revealed in the scripture (2:15), the focus returns to **Herod** (2:1, 3, 7, 12, 13, 15) as he pursues his futile resistance. He represents the scenario of Ps 2:1-2 played out frequently in the history of God's people:

> Why do the nations/Gentiles conspire
> and the peoples plot in vain?
> The kings of the earth set themselves
> and the rulers take counsel together
> against the Lord and his anointed . . .

He reenacts the role of Pharaoh in resorting to murderous violence against male babies to destroy an opponent (Exod 1:15-16). The invoking of these texts from Exodus and Psalms serves two purposes. It portrays again the pervasive oppressive and destructive way of rulers in misusing their power. But it also evokes God's opposition to such misuse. In Ps 2 God mocks the rulers and their fate is destruction. In Exod 1, the midwives subvert the royal decree and disobey it (Exod 1:15-22). Here the obedient magi, Joseph, and God's actions thwart Herod's attack on Jesus.

Herod **sees that he has been deceived/mocked by the magi**. In obeying their dream's warning not to return to Herod (2:12) rather than Herod's instruction to do so (2:8), the magi acknowledge God's authority, rather than Herod's. Herod does not know that God's intervention has thwarted his plans. In describing Herod's recognition that he has been **deceived/mocked** (having the sense of "made a fool of," "ridiculed"), the narrative uses a verb that appears in the exodus story. In talking with Moses, God uses it to describe God's thwarting of Pharaoh (Exod 10:2). The verb will appear again in association with Jesus' death in Matt 20:19; 27:29, 31, 41. When Herod is **mocked**, death follows. When Jesus is **mocked**, death and life follow.

Herod **became very angry** not only because the magi do not return but also because, as in 2:2-3, he cannot tolerate a rival. The empire never can. His intolerance is manifested in his action. Not knowing exactly *where* this "king of the Jews" was born, he **sent and killed all the children**[30] **in Bethlehem and in all that region**. And not knowing exactly *when* this "king of the Jews" was born, he has killed all those **two years old or under according to the time that he had learned from the magi.** Bethlehem might be on the margins of the powerful center Jerusalem, but it is a threat, and the empire viciously strikes. Herod's desperation creates what he imagines is a geographical and temporal safety zone.

• 2:17-18

A third fulfillment citation appears, **Then was fulfilled what was spoken through the prophet Jeremiah.** Its introduction is significantly different from 1:22 and 2:15. Those citations begin with a word (ἵνα, *hina*) which denotes purpose and indicates the carrying out of God's previously declared will: "this happened *so that* the word . . . might be fulfilled" (or "in order to fulfill" or "to fulfill"). But this citation in vv. 17-18 begins not with ἵνα/*hina* denoting purpose ("in order to") but with a word expressing a time sequence **then** (τότε, *tote*).

Why the different introduction? Most interpreters suggest that the change from purpose to time indicates an unwillingness to see Herod's terrible event as something God actively willed or brought about. Herod's act contrasts with God's life-giving purposes. But while God did not will Herod's murders or bring them about, God does not stop them from happening.[31] It is the way rulers and empires typically behave until God's sovereignty is established in full. God predicted it in the scripture and permitted it in the present. Conversely, while it was not Herod's purpose to fulfill the scriptural word, his murderous rage enacted it. The same change (from purpose to temporal sequence) will appear for the same reason in 27:9 in reference to Judas's death.

The citation derives from **the prophet Jeremiah,** the first of three references to him (16:14; 27:9), two of which introduce citations in relation to destructive responses to God's purposes enacted in Jesus (2:18; 27:9). This citation, like that in 2:15, seems closer to the Hebrew (MT) than to the Greek (LXX) text of Jer 31:15, but does not follow either exactly. As with the previous citations, this text also has nothing to do with Jesus in its originating context. For Jeremiah, it refers to two significant defeats of Israel by imperial powers: the exile of people from the northern kingdom defeated in 722 by Assyria, and the exile of those from Jerusalem and the southern kingdom defeated in 587 by Babylon (see 1:11-12, and 2:5-6). These events of exile, along with the exodus evoked in 2:15, meant great suffering caused by imperial power, but they were also followed by displays of God's saving power. After declaring for much of his prophetic ministry that God will punish the people for their sin by sending them into exile in Babylon, Jeremiah sounds a note of hope in chapters 30-33 by declaring that God will overcome Babylon and bring them back from exile. God's action will reverse the situation for which Jerusalem weeps (31:16) by liberating the people.

Place provides the immediate link between Jer 31:15 and Matt 2: **A voice was heard in Ramah, wailing and loud lamentation, Rachel weeping for her children.** Gen 35:16-19 and 48:7 locate Rachel's tomb "on the way to Ephrath[ah] (that is, Bethlehem)", the site of Herod's violence. In Jer 40:1, Ramah is a marshaling place for exile to Babylon, associating the place with loss. Her weeping for the exiles continues in Bethlehem's weeping.

The reversal of which Jeremiah speaks is not immediately apparent in Matt 2:18. The verse emphasizes only her **weeping** and the deep agony Herod has inflicted on his people in order to maintain his power. **She refused to be consoled, because they were not**. Why, then, has a verse that in its original context promised reversal and offered hope been used here to highlight grief?

Weeping expresses pain, sorrow, and outrage. It recognizes that what has happened is not acceptable, not normal. Humans weep to protest against something unacceptable or to try to cope with or make sense of something abnormal. The use of Jer 31:15 highlights the pain, but it also evokes the rest of Jeremiah 31 with its message of hope that God will liberate and return those sent into exile. Herod's actions, though brutal and painful, are not the final word. While they may be the typical actions of imperialist rulers, they are not how it will always be in God's world. The verse underlines the incompleteness of God's purposes. God's reversal, though, is under way in another king, one who represents God's justice and presence (1:21-23; 4:17). In establishing God's empire in full, he will overcome the oppressive rule of tyrants like Herod. The gospel again in part mirrors what it rejects.

• 2:19-20

A sign of God's reversal follows, **Then Herod died**. No details indicate how much time has elapsed (**then**) or how he died. The one who sought to put to death the "king of the Jews" (2:2)—in whom God's new creation is under way, the one commissioned (Christ, 1:1, 16, 17, 18) to save from sins (Jesus, 1:21) and manifest God's presence (Emmanuel, 1:23)—meets the fate that he planned for Jesus! The phrase closely echoes Exod 2:23 (LXX), the death of Pharaoh, as God thwarts another who misuses their power (cf. Ps 2).

Herod's death provides the opportunity for Jesus to return to Israel (so 2:13-15): **the angel of the Lord suddenly appeared in a dream to Joseph in Egypt and said, "Get up, take the child and his mother and go to the land of Israel, for those seeking the child's life are dead."** For the third time (1:20; 2:13) an angel reveals the divine will. The reference to **Egypt** ensures continuity with 2:13-15. On **Joseph**'s crucial role, see 2:13. The plural **those seeking** suggests the alliance of the central elite, Herod and those with military and religious power (2:3-6, 16).

• 2:21

Joseph's obedience is emphasized in that the narrative of the return to Israel closely resembles the angel's instructions of 2:20 (as they did in 2:13 and 14). The words also resemble the instructions given to Moses to return to Egypt to liberate the people (Exod 4:19-20). God is again saving people from tyranny. See on 1:20; 2:13. The phrase **and he went into the land of Israel** echoes God's leading of the people into the promised land after the exodus (Exod 12:25; Num 32:9; Deut 4:21, spoken by Moses), as well as the return from Babylonian exile (Ezek 20:36-38). Jesus relives the people's history of liberation from oppression in anticipation of the full accomplishment of God's purposes.

• 2:22

Just when there seems to be some security, there is ominous news. Joseph **heard that Archelaus reigned over Judea in place of his father Herod**. The narrative doesn't supply any details about the division of Herod's kingdom into three regions after his death (Archelaus ruling Judea and Samaria, Herod Antipas ruling Galilee and Perea, and Philip ruling the area north and east of the Sea of Galilee). Nor does it include any of the information that Josephus notes about Archelaus's vicious rule. Protests to Rome against his "cruelty and tyranny" saw Archelaus removed and exiled to Gaul (*Ant* 17.342-44). The clause **reigned . . . in place of his father Herod** recalls Herod's paranoia, opposition to God's reign, and massacre of the children. The ways of empire do not end with the death of one ruler. The verb **reign** uses the same root as **king**. It recalls this designation for Jesus in 2:2 and so continues the contrast between Jesus and Herod, the center and the margins, God's empire and Rome's empire.

Joseph **was afraid to go there**, to Judea, especially to Bethlehem (2:1), where he and Mary have a house (2:11). As in 1:19, when Joseph hears bad news and **is afraid** (1:20), he receives a further divine revelation: **And after being warned in a dream, he withdrew to the region of Galilee.** The revelation guides his actions (cf. 1:20) and protects God's purposes. Like the magi (the same language is used in 2:12), he is **warned in a dream**. On **withdrew**, see 2:14. No information is added about **Galilee;** see 4:12-16. For the moment it is safer than Judea, but not completely, as 4:12-16 will indicate. For now it is out of Archelaus's sight, away from the center of power, on the margins. Its apparent insignificance is its importance for God's purposes.

• 2:23

More specificity follows. **He went and dwelt in a city called Nazareth. He**, though singular, continues to include Mary and Jesus with Joseph. The same grammatical construction "into + a place" (εἰς, *eis* with an accusative) binds Israel (2:20), Galilee (2:22), and Nazareth (2:23) together in increasing specificity. **Nazareth** will subsequently act like Jerusalem and reject Jesus (13:53-58).

While this city affords escape from Archelaus, there is no escape from Herodian-Roman control based in Sepphoris (and later Tiberias), the economic and military centers which consume peasant production through taxes, rents, levies, and so on. Royal pretender figures—Judah son of Hezekiah, Simon, and

Athronges—had at the time of Herod's death in 4 B.C.E. led attacks against royal palaces (including Sepphoris) and Herodian and Roman troops, but retaliation was brutal (Josephus, *Ant* 17.271-85; *JW* 2.56-58).[32]

Predictably (so 2:4-6) this small and inconsequential place (despised in John 1:45-46) is in accord with the divine will revealed previously in scripture, **so that what was spoken through the prophets might be fulfilled**. See on 1:22-23; 2:15, 17. This citation, unlike 2:17, is introduced by a word indicating purpose (ὅπως, *hopōs,* not ἵνα, *hina,* as in 1:22 and 2:15). Jesus' move to Nazareth enacts or **fulfills** the divine will that **he shall be called a Nazarene**.

The citation is difficult because it does not exist as a specific citation anywhere in known writings. Moreover, whereas all the other introductions to citations use either the singular **prophet** or name the prophet, only this one employs the plural **prophets**. And missing is the participle **saying** (replaced by ὅτι, *hoti,* the only time in a citation introduction). These factors suggest that 2:23 makes a general claim that Jesus' dwelling in Nazareth is in accord with the divine will, but without invoking a specific scriptural reference. To call Jesus a **Nazarene**, one from Nazareth, is an ambivalent designation. It identifies him, in the eyes of the Jerusalem urban elite, as coming from an insignificant, irrelevant, powerless little place, on the margins away from the real action, "nowhereland"[33] near somewhereland. But in the world of this gospel, such places, like Bethlehem, are vital to God's purposes.

Some interpreters, though, think particular scriptures are in view. (1) Some have suggested that **Nazarene** indicates that Jesus is a Nazirite. This term refers to a tradition of people consecrated to serve God, who take a vow not to cut their hair or to drink wine (Num 6; Samson, Judg 13:5-7). Samson the Nazirite did God's will and saved the people, a task given to Jesus (1:21). Since Nazirite means "set apart" for God's service, the same meaning as the word "holy," some scholars point to Isa 4:3, which reads, "you will be called holy" as being a likely source of 2:23. With this context, the term **Nazarene** also indicates that Jesus is holy in that he is consecrated or set apart to serve God by saving from sin and manifesting God's presence (1:21, 23). If this connection establishes Jesus as a "Nazirite," the accusation which Jesus reports in 11:19 that he is a "glutton and a drunkard" indicates how seriously "they" misunderstood him, and perhaps how much Jesus redefines the term.

(2) Others have noted a connection to the word *nēṣer,* meaning "branch" in Isa 11:1. The verse describes a king from David's line. A "shoot [will come] from the stump of Jesse" and a "branch (*nēṣer*) . . . from his roots." In this context, **Nazarene** recalls that Jesus is David's son (1:1) and a king (2:2) whose reign will be very different from that of Archelaus.

God's initiative in the conception and birth of Jesus (1:18-25) is met by two responses: resistance, violence, and rejection from the center elite of political and religious power in Jerusalem, and worship, trust, and obedience from those who, in the perspective of the center, occupy the insignificant margins where God's purposes of liberation are being accomplished. The danger and evil of empire constantly threaten and oppose those purposes, places, and people. But the empire does not have the final word. God's purposes are protected.

CHAPTER 3

John's Ministry

3:1-12—JOHN THE BAPTIST

In two ways chapter 3 elaborates the key incident of the first narrative block, God's initiative in commissioning Jesus (1:18-25). First, John's testimony about Jesus (3:11-12; cf. 1:21, 23; 2:15) expands on God's commission (3:11-12; cf. 1:21, 23; 2:15). Second, the conflict between the center (the political, economic, social, and religious elite) and the margins (the locus of God's action) continues as the prophet John confronts some resistant religious leaders in the wilderness.[1]

The prophet John occupies a liminal place (Introduction, section 10). The narrative locates him in the wilderness, a place marginal to the centers of power. His call for repentance (3:2) and scathing denunciation of the religious elite (3:7-10) indicate a role antithetical to the center's interests. Yet he interacts with both the religious (3:7-10) and political (14:1-12) centers.

This liminal location and role are akin to those experienced by Israel's prophets, who spoke against the society in which they lived. They interacted with kings, prophets, and priests, yet in speaking of an alternative world, they did not say what the elite wanted to hear. Elijah's confrontation with Ahab and the prophets of Baal over false worship is a classic scenario (1 Kgs 17-19). Amos, perhaps a wealthy landowner,[2] condemned greed and injustice, militarism and shallow piety (Amos 2:4-16; 4:1-13; 6:1-7; 7:10-17; 8:4). Isaiah of Jerusalem spoke *with* and *against* kings (Isa 7-8). Jeremiah, the son of a priest, confronted nations, the people of Judah, and the unjust kings (Jer 22:10-30; ch. 23), and countered prophets and priests (5:31; 6:10, 13-15). Ezekiel the priest attacked the abuses of the temple (Ezek 8-11; 40-48), countered other prophets (13:1), spoke to the "elders of Israel" (14:1), condemned the kings and envisioned Israel's future without a king (ch. 34). John the prophet exists in this tradition.

John's stance against and challenge to the elite link him with numerous other figures who employed various strategies against Roman power and injustice. An assortment of figures looked for God to intervene to retake Judea from Rome.[3] Others found hope, even incentive for war, in predictions of a figure from the east who would rule the world (Josephus, *JW* 6.312; Suetonius,

90

Vespasian 4.5; Tacitus, *Hist* 5.13). A slave from Pontus, "remarkable for [his] eyes, hair, and grim face," enacted Nero's return and envisaged a return to Nero's rule (Tacitus, *Hist* 2.8-9). The German prophetess Veleda offered a vision of Roman vincibility by predicting German success over the Roman legions (Tacitus, *Hist* 4.61).[4] In his preaching and confrontation with the local Jerusalem elite, allies of Rome, John proclaims judgment on the world dominated by Rome.

In addition to his liminal location and role, conflict with the elite, and rejection (3:7-10; 14:1-12), several other prophetic features mark the presentation of John the Baptist.

1. John is, like many prophets, primarily a proclaimer. Verse 1 introduces him by naming this activity; v. 2 identifies its content; v. 3 supplies scriptural support for his preaching activity; vv. 5-6 narrate its effect; and vv. 7-10 offer an example of his preaching against the religious elite.

2. Like the prophets, John sees a bleak contemporary situation which requires change. His preaching has a prophetic theme, **repent** (3:2) or "turn around," "return" to faithful relationship with God. Compare Moses (Deut 30:2, 10), Hosea (Hos 2:7; 3:5; 6:1; 11:15), Amos (Amos 4:6, 8-9), Isaiah (Isa 6:10; 9:13; 31:6), Jeremiah (Jer 2:27; 3:10, 12, 14, 22), and Ezekiel (Ezek 14:6; 18:30, 32).[5] Dire consequences of judgment result from the refusal to embrace the prophet's message (3:10-12).

John's proclamation also prepares for and bears witness to Jesus' ministry. In 3:2 repentance is necessary because of "the empire/reign of the heavens". The section 4:17-11:1 will indicate that proclaiming and enacting God's empire is central to Jesus' commission to manifest God's saving presence (1:21, 23). In 3:11-12 John expands on aspects of Jesus' mission. Jesus will baptize with the Holy Spirit and with fire (3:11) and will judge (3:12).

3. Like the prophets, John performs sign-actions in his baptism, location, diet, and clothing. Hosea enacts his message in marrying a prostitute and in the naming of their children (Hos 1). Isaiah is naked for three years (Isa 20:1-4). Jeremiah does not marry or have children (Jer 16:1-4). Ezekiel eats a scroll (3:1), makes a model of the siege and fall of Jerusalem (4:1-3), lies on one side for 390 days and the other for 45 days to symbolize punishment (4:4-8), shaves his head (5:1-4), and does not mourn his wife's death (24:15-27).

4. The description of John's clothing (Matt 3:4) echoes that of the prophet Elijah in 2 Kgs 1:8 almost word for word. Evoking Elijah suggests that John may share aspects of Elijah's prophetic role, especially Elijah's call for repentance in his life-and-death confrontation with the political and religious powers of Ahaz, Jezebel, and Baal. Subsequently, 11:14 and 17:11-13 will identify John with Elijah.

5. Echoes of the prophetic traditions sound in phrases (in those days, preaching), images (in the desert, fruit, fire, water, winnowing wheat), themes (repentance, prophetic critique of false piety, the Spirit), and rhetorical techniques (stating a position in order to reject it, 3:9; perceiving what is already

taking place, 3:10a; stating the destructive consequences of not heeding the prophetic warning, 3:10b). See further below.

• 3:1

In those days John the Baptist appeared in the wilderness of Judea, proclaiming. The opening phrase **in those days** connects this scene with chapter 2. While Jesus dwells in Nazareth (2:23), John's ministry begins. The phrase often denotes a special time of God's action, whether present (Dan 2:10) or future (Jer 3:16, 18; 31:33; 50:4, 20; Zech 8:23).[6] Here God acts through John. The verb **appeared** (παραγίνεται, *paraginetai*), which was used in 2:1 for the appearing of the magi to worship Jesus, allies the magi and John in their concern with God's purposes.

John is introduced as the **Baptist,** but, with nothing said about his baptism until v. 5, initial attention focuses on his **preaching.** Numerous prophets are commanded to **preach** (κηρύσσειν): Hosea (5:8), Jonah (1:2; 3:2, 4, 5), Joel (1:14; 2:1, 15; 3:9), Trito-Isaiah (61:1). John preaches **in the wilderness of Judea.** Given the reference to the Jordan in 3:5, this geographical area is probably east of Jerusalem to the Dead Sea, and north through the Jordan Valley.[7] It is removed from the central location of the powerful elite, Jerusalem (2:1-4), which cannot control or contain his mission (3:5). John frequents the geographical margins. Compare other apparently insignificant places (Bethlehem, 2:6; Nazareth, 2:23) which are central to God's purposes.

The **wilderness** has further theological significance. It played a key role in God's liberation of the people from the imperial tyrant Pharaoh (Exod 5:1, 3; 7:16; 13:18, 20; 14:3, 11, 12; etc.). It frequently appears in the prophetic traditions (over thirty times in Isaiah and Ezekiel, nearly thirty in Jeremiah) with rich and diverse associations. The wilderness is a place of

    i. Redemption in the exodus from Egypt, God's faithful guidance to the promised land, and the people's faithlessness (Hos 2:14; 9:10; 13:5; Amos 2:10; 5:25; Ezek 20:10, 13, 15)
    ii. Revelation (Exod 19:1-6; 1QS 8:12-14; Josephus, *JW* 2.250; 7.438)
    iii. Punishment (Hos 2:3; 13:15; Isa 1:7; 5:9; 6:1; 14:23; Jer 9:10, 12; Isa 50:2; Ezek 5:14; 6:14; 20:35; 29:9)
    iv. Testing (Exod 16:4; 20:20; Deut 8:2)
    v. God's redemption in a new exodus and new creation (Isa 40:3; 41:18; 43:19-20; 48:21; 51:3; Ezek 36:33, 35, 38)
    vi. Attempted escape for Elijah (1 Kgs 19:4, 15)
    vii. Danger where demons reside (Lev 16:10; Tob 8:3; *1 En* 10:4; 4 Macc 18:8a)

John's **preaching in the wilderness of Judea** offers a different sort of danger. The use of **Judea** recalls Jesus' birth in Bethlehem of **Judea** (2:1, 5) and its threat to Jerusalem (2:3) and to Herod. That threat continues because, while "Archelaus reigns over (βασιλεύει, *basileuei,* 2:22) **Judea** in the place of his father Herod," John proclaims the imminent reign or empire of God (βασιλεία, *basileia,* 3:2) in Judea. The cognate terms sharply juxtapose two reigns present in **Judea**. Conflict seems inevitable.

• **3:2**

John proclaims, **Repent**, a prophetic call (see above, no. 2) to abandon lives of unfaithfulness, injustice, and false allegiance, and to turn back to faithful living in the covenant. The call assumes that life as it is currently constructed by the ruling elites, life structured to benefit the elite at the expense of the rest (Introduction, sections 5-10), is not how God wants it to be. The call expresses the divine will for change and is a means of averting judgment and disaster. Josephus warns that repentance will avert Jerusalem's destruction by Rome in 70 (*JW* 5.415).

The reason **for** this call is that **the empire**[8] **of the heavens has come near.** At first glance this is a troubling image since it employs the imperialist language of oppressive rule and suggests that God's action is more of the same. Norman Perrin and others have indicated from their study of Jewish sources that this phrase does not refer to a stable concept with fixed content. It is, rather, a symbol that is tensive, open-ended, expanding.[9] It evokes the general memory of God acting in diverse ways and circumstances on behalf of God's people.[10] Given that **empire** will recur frequently through the gospel (over fifty times), any adequate understanding of God's actions must take account of the whole gospel.

At this point, one thing is clear. In the context of chapters 1-2, the imminent **empire of the heavens** relates to the revelation of God's saving presence, which God commissions Jesus to carry out (1:21, 23). **Heaven** is the abode of God (cf. 5:34; Isa 66:1). The genitive **of the heavens** points to God as the origin of this **empire**, just as God initiates the saving work Jesus is to perform. God's saving presence, then, constitutes an empire that asserts God's claim on and reign over human existence. God's reign, as presented in Ps 72 for example, liberates and protects people from oppressive allegiances, structures, relationships, and powers which usurp God's role and claim. It establishes God's life-giving and just order in their place. Chapter 2 has demonstrated the threat and challenge of God's action to the imperial powers. Now, from a prophetic figure in the wilderness, comes a declaration of God's purposes which challenge the unjust commitments and self-interest of the political and religious centers (Matt 3:7-10). The rest of the gospel will elaborate the mysterious, disturbing, and transformative power of God's life-giving and just empire.

The reign is **at hand**. Numerous scholarly contributions have debated whether the verb ἤγγικεν (*ēngiken*) indicates "nearness" or "arrival." Does it denote that the reign is approaching, or that it is already present? R. Berkey's helpful survey of the data concludes that it is impossible to limit the verb to one of these meanings, or even to distinguish precisely between them. The verb holds these ambiguous time elements together, denoting both arrival and nearness, present and future dimensions.[11]

• 3:3

This is the one of whom the prophet Isaiah spoke when he said. . . . The origin of John's prophetic role and message from God is confirmed with a citation from the **prophet Isaiah**. As with earlier references (1:22; 2:5, 15, 17, 23), **the prophet** speaks a dangerous and challenging word. The citation claims that John's appearing is not a surprise or an accident but enacts the divine will stated in Isa 40:3. The five other citations of **Isaiah** evoke contexts of imperial domination (see 1:22-23; 4:14-16; 15:7-9). They underline God's saving work (which includes Gentiles, 4:14-15; 8:17; 12:17-21) and its rejection by some (13:13-15; 15:7-9).

The citation of Isa 40:3 is taken not from the Masoretic (Hebrew) Text but from the Greek Septuagint.[12] Its use here maintains significant continuities with its Isaian context, but new elements are present. In Isaiah 40, the reference is not to John. The text addresses the community exiled in Babylon after Babylonian imperial expansion had conquered Jerusalem in 587. The text promises God's salvific reversal of this situation. There, the identity of **the voice who cries** is not clear, perhaps the Lord, or a member of the heavenly council, or another proclaimer. But the voice asserts that God will end Babylonian power. God will "anoint" (the cognate verb of the noun "Christ" in Matt 1:1, 16, 17, 18; 2:4) the Persian ruler Cyrus to overthrow the Babylonians and liberate the exiles (Isa 44:28-45:1). The voice urges its hearers to prepare for God's action.

The new context in Matthew ensures some obvious differences: the voice is now John; the focus is on Jesus, not Cyrus; the place is Judea, not Babylon; Rome, not Babylon, is in power; the time is six centuries later. Biblical texts are polyvalent, capable of new and different meanings in different circumstances (see on 1:23; 2:6, 15, 18, 23). But there is a fundamental continuity. God continues to assert God's empire in liberating people from oppressive imperial power. Babylon no longer holds power. Rome, like Babylon, cannot resist God's purposes and will experience the same fate. God's liberating work is encountered now in John's ministry in the wilderness, on the margins not the center, just as it was in the liberation from Egypt's Pharaoh and from Babylon.

The verse underlines John's preaching (**voice crying**) and its location (**in the wilderness**). It also elaborates John's call to **repent**. By repenting, people **prepare the way of the Lord and make his paths straight**. Both **way** and **path** are metaphors for God's will and purposes (Deut 5:33; Jer 7:23; Matt 7:13-14; contrast with Roman ways and roads).[13] God's purposes, manifested in Jesus, will be experienced either as salvation or as condemnation depending on one's response to John's call to repent. To repent signifies, then, not only specific changes in structures and ways of living, but a basic receptivity to God's purposes.

Here **Lord** probably points to the coming of Jesus, but since his task is to manifest God's presence (1:23), the distinction cannot be pushed. Jesus' **way** and **straight paths** are his mission of manifesting God's saving presence and empire.

• 3:4

Now John wore clothing of camel's hair with a leather belt around his waist. John is an Elijah look-alike (see comment no. 4 above). **His food was locusts and wild honey**, food that derives from a desert or wilderness location. His food denotes poverty, as well as his commitment to and trust in God by not being distracted from the reign because of concern with daily food (cf. 6:25-34, 11). He is indebted to no one.

John has good company in not letting food distract him from serving God: the levitical purity laws, the Nazirite refusal of strong drink (Num 6:3; Judg 13:4-5, 14), heroes and heroines who maintained faithfulness to God in not eating meat (Dan 1:12, 16; Jdt 10:5; 12:2-4, 17-20), and the Rechabites, who renounced wine, houses, and agriculture (Jer 35). Among Gentiles, Apollonius renounces a flesh diet and wine in favor of dried fruits and vegetables since flesh was unclean, gross, and endangered mental balance (Philostratus, *Apollonius* 1.8). Dio Chrysostom provides parallels with Stoic-Cynic philosophers (*Disc* 1.61-62; 4.70; 6.12, 14; 13.10-11; 60.7-8). Even John's unusual food, then, attests a different way of life centered on faithfulness to God. It presents a critique of the economic extravagance of the powerful elite, who maintain their own abundance at the expense of the poor (see Matt 11:8; 12:1-8; 14:13-21; for his critique of fine clothing and the palaces of the wealthy and powerful, see 11:9).

• 3:5-6

From John's preaching and lifestyle, the narrative now elaborates the term by which he was first introduced in 3:1, **the Baptist. Then the people of Jerusalem and all Judea were going out to him, and all the region along the Jordan, and they were baptized by him in the river Jordan, confessing their sins.**

Three regions are personified as **going out** (the imperfect tense indicates an action recurring over a period of time) to John to be **baptized by him**. The first group comes from **Jerusalem**—somewhat surprisingly, given the alliance between Jerusalem and Herod in responding negatively to Jesus' birth (2:3). But 3:5 drops the "all" of 2:3 in reference to Jerusalem; despite the opposition of the political and religious elite, some in Jerusalem respond positively to John. Two other groups—**all Judea,** the area around Jerusalem, and **all the region along the Jordan**—also respond positively.

Scholars have suggested various possible sources for the practice and meaning of John's baptism.[14] But the lack of precise parallels (compare the repeated washings with John's once-only baptism) attests little more than the widespread use of water in various religious rituals.

More useful is to interpret the baptism in the context of Matthew's presentation of John. John baptizes in **the Jordan**, the river through which the Israelites passed as they entered the land after their journey in the wilderness (Josh 3:14-17). These echoes of the exodus from Egypt indicate that John's baptism is, at least in part, an act of liberation from the oppressive political and religious leadership exemplified in chapter 2. There is also some unspecified relationship between John's baptism and **sins,** since in baptism they **confess their sins** (3:6). No mention is made of forgiveness (cf. Mark 1:4) so it does not seem to effect that. As a response to John's proclamation of repentance, the baptism seems to demonstrate the baptized ones' acceptance of John's verdict on the present as sinful, their recognition of participating in the people's sins, and a commitment to turn from sinful living and to live differently. Water symbolizes a clean start. Baptism in water may also express, as in Ps 69:1-3, being saved by God from a terrible situation. John's preaching and sign action make no mention of the temple cult. He bypasses the religious elite's central institution.

Further, what is the relationship of the act of baptism to the empire of the heavens? Given that John proclaims the imminence of the reign, which will be evident in Jesus' mission of saving from sin (1:21) and manifesting God's presence (1:23), John's baptism also seems to express the baptized ones' openness to that empire to be manifested in Jesus. It anticipates the baptized ones' participation in that reign, in which they will encounter present and final (or eschatological) salvation from sin through Jesus.

• 3:7

A particular group is now identified as **coming for baptism, many Pharisees and Sadducees**. These groups have not appeared previously in the narrative. Historical information about each group (e.g., Josephus, *JW* 2.162-66) indicates some theological, social and political differences,[15] though Josephus attests the membership of both Pharisees and Sadducees among the wealthy (*Ant* 13.297; 18.17) and politically powerful (*JW* 2.410-14), including the chief priests. But here any differences are set aside. The groups are united by one thing. As religious leaders, they are united opponents of John and his preaching. That opposition renders them opponents of God's purposes and, in turn, allies them with the chief priests and scribes in 2:4-6 who, in support of Herod, do not welcome Jesus' birth. Chapters 2 and 3 thereby create a coalition of religious and political leaders that is allied against John and Jesus. On these religious leaders as members of the imperial society's ruling elite, defenders of the current hierarchical social order, allies of Herod and Rome, and opponents of Jesus, see Introduction, sections 1 and 5, and comments on 2:4; 5:20.

Why do they come to John? The NRSV translation, "**coming for baptism,**" suggests that they intend to be baptized. John's harsh response in 3:7b would foresee that they would undergo an external washing that would leave their commitments and practices unchanged (cf. 23:25-26); John would reject their role-playing. While this approach is possible, there is no indication yet that the audience is to suspect them of hypocrisy. And the **many Pharisees and Sadducees** are named as a group separate from the positive respondents identified in 3:5-6. John's immediate hostility to them in 3:7b also suggests that it is unlikely that the phrase **coming for baptism** means "coming to be baptized."

The phrase **coming for baptism** can also be translated, **coming against the baptism**. The Greek preposition translated **for** (ἐπί, *epi*) can mean **against**.[16]

John's prophetic identity suggests likely conflict with the religious elite, and in 2:4-6 the religious leaders are introduced as resistant to God's purposes. More likely, then, is that they come to oppose John's baptism and persuade others not to be baptized.

John immediately rebukes them personally (**You**) and graphically (**brood/offspring of vipers/poisonous snakes**) with a metaphor that emphasizes evil and destructiveness (see 12:34; 23:33). Since social standing and honor have to do with birth, this harsh insult places "them at the lowest levels of illegitimacy."[17]

His rhetorical question, **Who warned you to flee from the wrath to come?** is ironic since they oppose John's baptism and have not repented (3:8-10). The notion of **wrath** refers to God acting righteously and in holiness against Israel and the nations to judge injustice, idolatry, and rebellion. These acts counter God's will and covenant relationship of love. Humans are accountable to God. This action of **wrath** can be expressed in the present (disease, pestilence, weather disturbance [drought, flood], devastation of land, famine, death, defeat in battle, exile) or in God's future judgment which ushers in a new age. The notion is evident in historical (Exod 4:14; Deut 4:25; 6:15; 1 Kgs 14:15; 16:33; 1 Chr 13:10), cultic (Ps 2:5, 11; 78:31), prophetic (Hos 13:9-11; Jer 4:4, 8, 26; Ezek 5:15; 6:12), and apocalyptic traditions ("the day of the Lord," Isa 13:9; Zeph 1:14-16; 2:2; Dan 8:19; 11:36; *1 En* 90:15-27; *Apoc. Ab.* 29:14-21).[18]

From the margins and contrary to the perceptions of the religious center, John sees the corrupt nature of the present and the inevitability of God's **wrath to come,** which holds people accountable, and for which repentance is the only preparation. Interpreters usually assume that John sees a cataclysmic apocalyptic, future scenario (supported by "in those days" in 3:1). While this is probably correct, several factors do not rule out his warning against expressions of God's wrath also in the present. (1) The Hebrew Bible traditions outlined above do not reserve God's **wrath** only for an end-time event. (2) The participle **to come** or **coming** (μελλούσης, *mellousēs*) indicates a future event that will certainly, or is (divinely) destined to, take place, but it does not automatically assume an eschatological occurrence.[19] (3) John's proclamation of God's imminent empire holds together present and future dimensions. John sees God's approaching wrath or judgment, which may be expressed within imminent history and as a cataclysmic apocalyptic event. The fall of Jerusalem expresses God's wrath (Introduction; 22:7). The religious elite do not see **wrath** at all.

• 3:8-10

Their presumption that all is well provides the basis for John's condemnation of them. John exhorts the leaders to **bear fruit worthy of/that befits repentance**. The image of **bearing fruit** denotes behavior that embodies God's will (Ps 1:1-3; Hos 9:16 [its absence]; Isa 27:6; Jer 17:7-10; Ezek 17:8-9, 23). John does not think they have repented and calls them to a way of life marked by covenant values of trust, worship, and justice. John's preaching and baptism divide the repentant and unrepentant.

The religious leaders belong to the latter. John warns them: **Do not presume to say to yourselves, "We have Abraham as our ancestor."** John employs a common prophetic technique of quoting a position only to refute it (Jer 8:8-9, 11, 18-21). Wherein lies the presumption of claiming God's chosen one Abraham as ancestor, Israel's forebear (cf. 1:1)? John's comment seems to suggest that they think being a descendant of Abraham, being born a Jew, ensures their participation in God's covenant and salvific purposes (cf. Sir 44:19-21).[20] John's objection seems to be that they have separated this blessed identity as a descendant of Abraham from the obligations and demands of covenant (**fruit**). John attributes to the Pharisees and Sadducees a valuing of ethnicity or physical descent from Abraham that overlooks **fruit**, a life of faithful and just living that shows repentance. Ethnicity (race) or social prestige as educated religious leaders (class) will not save the religious center from God's wrath.

Whether they do presume this is not clear; the religious leaders do not speak for themselves in this scene. John's charge and the gospel's presentation are polemic—the charges of one religious group against another. Polemic is always about a group's perceptions of others and of themselves, not about historical accuracy or just charges. We cannot rely on John (or Matthew) to give us an accurate picture of all religious life in the first century.

God's power and action, not human descent, are central to the explanation (**for**) John offers, **for I tell you, God is able from these stones to raise up children to Abraham**. The link between stones and Abraham derives from Isa 51:1-2: those who pursue righteousness and seek God are instructed, "Look to the rock from which you were hewn . . . Look to Abraham your father and to Sarah who bore you, for he was but one when I called him, but I blessed him and made him many." The passage emphasizes God's action in calling, blessing, and multiplying Abraham. The rock is lifeless and cannot of itself produce offspring, just as it seemed the aged Abraham and Sarah were too old to bear a child, but God ensured it would happen (Gen 16:2; 17:17; 21:6). God's action in human lives (Jew and Gentile) determines Abraham's children, not physical descent (so Jesus, 1:1, 18-25). Descent from Abraham by itself is not what ultimately matters, but God's action in the lives of those who live faithfully to God's gift and demand.

The exhortation to fruit is reinforced in v. 10 with a warning of immediate and inevitable punishment. God's wrath is imminent: **even now, the axe is lying at the root of the trees**. The marginal prophetic figure John sees something that the religious center cannot see. John borrows this image of judgment from the prophets, where it describes the fall of the powerful nations (Isa 10:33-34 ["the lofty" Assyrians]; Ezek 31 [Assyria]; Dan 4:9-27 [the Babylonian ruler Nebuchadnezzar]). He turns back on the religious leaders an image previously used against Israel's enemies and opponents of God's rule and purposes (so Amos 1-2).

Further, the **axe** was a symbol of Roman authority and a means of Roman execution. It was part of the *fasces,* a bundle of wooden rods enclosing an **axe**, which functioned for Roman officials as "a portable kit for flogging and decapitation," a "symbol and instrument of executive [and executing] power." The *fasces* denoted the Roman official's authority to maintain public order and exact punishment. They were paraded in Rome and in the provinces as "a vivid . . . symbol of subjection to Rome," as "tokens of absolute, imperial power" (cf. Josephus, *JW* 2.365-66).[21] But in John's image, it is God who defines acceptable order, whose reign is to be encountered, and who wields the **axe** of punishment against all, including the elite. Again the gospel borrows imperial images, that which it resists, to present God's empire.

John continues to bully them into repentance. **Every tree that does not bear good fruit is cut down and thrown into the fire.** The exhortation to **bear good fruit**, to repent and to live according to the divine will, is now presented in a description of judgment for failing to repent. The singular **every tree** (after the plural **trees** in v. 10a) individualizes the warning. The warning is expressed in negative terms (**does not bear**) and the element of punishment is intensified by adding a new dimension to **cut down**, the image of being **thrown into the fire**. Fire is also a prophetic (Isa 10:15-19 [Israel]; Amos 7:4 [Israel]; Ezek 38:22 [Gog]) and apocalyptic reference to judgment (Zeph 1:18; *1 En* 90:24-27; 48:9; 54:1-2 [destruction of "kings and potentates"]). The intensely negative statement in 3:10b, which recognizes the lack of fruit and the inevitability of judgment, suggests little hope that the religious leaders will change their ways. Their fate—judgment by God (the passive verbs **is cut down and thrown** imply God as the agent)—seems sure. Not all who think they are children of Abraham by birth are part of the people who escape God's wrath.

• 3:11-12

John continues to proclaim, but the audience changes. Having harshly rebuked the religious leaders, he now addresses the other group of those whom he baptizes: **I baptize you with water for repentance** (see 3:5-6). He talks to them about another who comes with a different baptism. In explaining the relationship of the two baptisms, John testifies about this coming figure.

This other is introduced—**one who is more powerful than I is coming after me**. Who is this one? In the context, it must be Jesus, born in chapter 2 and living in Nazareth at the time of John's ministry ("in those days," 3:1), who appears in 3:13-17 for baptism.[22] Jesus is **more powerful** in that he saves from sins (1:21) through healings and forgiveness (9:1-8; 8:17), death and resurrection (26:28), and his return in power to establish God's empire over all including Rome (24:27-31). He is **coming after me** in the temporal sense that his ministry begins after John's. Perhaps there is an echo of Ps 118:26 ("Blessed is the one who **comes** in the name of the Lord"), which the crowds will shout as Jesus approaches Jerusalem (see 21:9). If so, the phrase also underlines Jesus' identity as God's agent. John witnesses to Jesus' greatness (**I am not worthy to carry/remove his sandals**) by declaring himself not worthy to do this slave's task.

John presents Jesus' ministry to the repentant baptized (**you**) in terms of another baptism: **he** (emphasized with a pronoun αὐτός, *autos*) **will baptize you with the holy spirit and with fire**. Jesus' ministry/baptism is elaborated by two elements **with** (ἐν) **the holy spirit** and **fire**. How do these two elements relate to each other? Do they form one entity denoting judgment (a fiery spirit)? Is one positive (**spirit**) and the other negative (**fire**)? Or is each term positive and negative in representing judgment and salvation?[23]

This last option seems more likely. **Spirit/breath** signifies God's punishment (Isa 4:4; Jer 4:11-16). But it is also a gift of God's covenant with a holy and faithful people, who with God's Spirit or abiding presence and a new heart know and do God's will (Ezek 36:25-28; 39:29; Isa 32:15; 44:3; Joel 2:28-29). **Spirit** is God's life-giving power, which empowers people to proclaim and live God's justice (Isa 61:1-3) and accomplish God's will (Matt 1:18-25).

Fire refines and cleanses (Zech 13:9; Mal 3:1-3 [cf. 3:18-4:1 for judgment]; 1QS 4:21). Often it expresses punishment (see Matt 3:10; 13:40-43; 25:41 in reference to the final judgment). This double meaning of blessing and destruction represented by each term would suggest that John presents Jesus' entire mission (including his role in the final judgment, 25:31) as one that has a double effect: some are blessed and purified (so 1:21 "save his people from their sins"); some are punished and destroyed.

Why does John offer those who are being baptized this mixed news? What, then, does John's baptism guarantee? John's point is that his baptism guarantees nothing. To guarantee those who are being baptized only blessing is quite inconsistent with John's tough rejection of presumption and insistence on a repentant way of life. While their baptism by him is a step in the right direction, it is not the final baptism. Their response to Jesus and subsequent faithful way of life, of hearing and doing God's will and of being purified, are much more significant.

Jesus will carry out judgment, now imaged as separating **wheat** and **chaff**. **His winnowing fork is in his hand, and he will clear his threshing floor and will gather his wheat into the granary/ storeroom; but the chaff he will burn with unquenchable fire.** How and when this judgment is to be exercised is not indicated. The subsequent narrative will clarify that judgment is exercised in Jesus' present and future ministry. **Winnowing**, threshing, and harvest are frequent images of judgment (Prov 20:26; Isa 18:4-5; 27:12-13; Jer 51:33; Mic 4:12-13; *4 Ezra* 4:26-27; *2 Bar* 70:1-2; see Matt 13:24-30, 36-43). Since Jesus has **his winnowing fork . . . in his hand** (cf. the axe in 3:10), the judgment is imminent. It involves two related tasks. **He will gather his wheat into the granary/storeroom** (the word is used to denote storerooms in the temple in 1 Chr 28:11, 12, 13, 20). The harvest of **wheat** is a metaphor for faithful discipleship in 13:23, 38. But the **chaff**, often identified as the wicked (Ps 1:4; Isa 17:13), will be **burned with unquenchable fire** (cf. Isa 34:8-10; as an image of judgment, see Matt 3:10). If the **chaff** are the wicked in general, and in this context the Pharisees and Sadducees who oppose John's baptism, the **wheat** must be those who respond to John's message by repenting and who follow Jesus, hearing and obeying his teaching.

Matthew's John envisions himself, then, preparing for the ministry of Jesus, who effects judgment. One of the effects of John's ministry is to redescribe the center and the margins. Political, social, economic, and religious power does not define the center. John's marginal location and role (from the perspective of Jerusalem and the religious leaders) are a temporary center for God's purposes. By not being allied with the religious leaders, he is marginalized, but on the margins he is allied with Jesus, who is central to God's purposes.

3:13-17—JOHN BAPTIZES JESUS:
THE SPIRIT DESCENDS

Jesus appears. Nothing is said of the years since his infancy (2:23). The one for whom John prepares, and the one about whom he testifies, comes to John for baptism. In the context of 3:1-12, we might expect the scene to show Jesus' baptism following his repentance from sin. But three factors indicate that the emphasis is elsewhere. (1) The scene is silent about Jesus' sin or repentance. (2) Jesus' authority and John's subservient role are maintained as Jesus instructs John to baptize him (3:15b). John's protests at baptizing the more powerful one with the superior baptism are overcome by Jesus' statement that for "now" this reversal is appropriate to enact God's saving will previously manifested ("fulfills all righteousness," 3:14-15). (3) After the baptism (3:16-17), a revelatory event occurs. A vision of the opened heavens and a heavenly voice disclose Jesus as God's agent, anointed and empowered by God to carry out God's purposes. With its focus on Jesus and its presentation of his identity, the scene continues the elaboration of 1:18-25.

• 3:13

Jesus performs his first action in the gospel (recall the passivity and help-lessness of "the child" in ch. 2). **Then Jesus came from Galilee** (2:22-23) **to the Jordan to John to be baptized by him** (see 3:5-6). As with the magi in 2:1 and John in 3:1, the verb **came** (παραγίνεται, *paraginetai*) denotes Jesus' action. The three characters, in contrast to the static center Jerusalem with its political and religious elite, are concerned with God's will. This alliance between John and Jesus suggests their agreement on the imminence of God's judgment, the sinfulness of the present, and the need for a repentance to escape God's wrath.

• 3:14

John would have prevented him. John recognizes Jesus as the one about whom he had spoken in 3:11-12. John's prediction of "one . . . coming after me" is correct. John's proclamation is reliable. Moreover, John's resistance to baptizing Jesus is consistent with the humility or unworthiness he expressed in 3:11. In acting consistently with his own words, John exhibits an integrity of word and action which this gospel values (5:37; Jesus does his own teaching [see 6:10b and 26:42b]; the condemnations of hypocrisy [ch. 23]). Further, his recognition that he needs Jesus' baptism (**I need to be baptized by you and do you come to me?**) exhibits the receptive response to which John exhorts his baptizands in vv. 11-12. The Greek emphasizes the pronouns **I . . . by you . . . you . . . me** which contrast the two figures.

• 3:15

But Jesus answered him, "Let it be so now." Jesus' response exhibits his authority. His opening word is an imperative (**Let it be**), which requires immediate obedience (**now**). His explanation (**for**) declares that his baptism **is proper for us in this way to fulfill all righteousness/justice.**[24] The verb **fulfill** does not mean, as some have suggested, merely to do God's will. The gospel more commonly employs three other verbs to express "doing," or "keeping," or "observing" God's will.[25] The verb **fulfill** has already appeared in 1:22; 2:15, 17, 23 to introduce a citation from the Hebrew Bible (so also 4:14; 5:17; 8:17; 12:17; 13:35; 21:4; 26:54, 56; 27:9). It indicates that what is happening in Jesus' ministry (or accompanying circumstances) is consistent with, and so enacts or accomplishes, God's will previously declared in the scriptures. What is the righteousness that Jesus' baptism enacts?

The gospel uses the term **justice/righteousness** seven times (3:15; 5:6, 10, 20; 6:1, 33; 21:32); four meanings have been suggested. (1) Some argue that the term always refers to God's saving activity. (2) Some suggest that it always refers to humans doing God's demand. (3) Others suggest that both elements are present: God's gift and human action. (4) Still others argue the uses are inconsistent and need to be determined case by case. Which one is correct?

At root, **righteousness/justice** is not, as in Greek thought, an ideal by which actions can be measured, but refers in Hebrew tradition to actions that are faithful to commitments and relationships.[26] God is righteous or just in that God acts faithfully to the covenant commitments to save and deliver the people. So, for example, "salvation/savior" and "deliverance/righteousness" (δικαιοσύνη, *dikaiosynē*) are parallel terms for God's saving actions in Pss 51:14; 65:5; Isa 46:13; 51:5-8. God's people or Israel's kings are righteous or unrighteous, just or unjust in that they are or are not faithful to the covenant demands. So in Ps 72, the Psalmist prays that the king will act with "righteousness" (vv. 1, 2, 7), will act faithfully to the covenant in defending the poor, delivering the needy, crushing the oppressor, and exercising life-giving dominion over the earth (vv. 2, 3, 4, 8-14, 16). Unrighteous or unjust actions are actions not faithful to the covenant requirements.

God's righteousness and human righteousness are not isolated from or independent of each other. God gives righteousness or justice to the king (Ps 72:1); the actions which the king is to perform are actions that are repeatedly attributed to God; and the psalm finishes by acknowledging God as the one who "alone does wondrous things" (v. 18).

This material suggests that option 3 (God's gifts and human actions) is the best choice for 3:15.[27] God is very active in the scene (3:16-17), as are Jesus and John in deciding for and undertaking the baptism (**for *us* to fulfill**). Jesus' instruction to John indicates that God's saving action, previously stated by the scriptures, is being enacted in Jesus' and John's actions. On this basis, John **consented** to baptize Jesus.

• **3:16-17**

How does Jesus' baptism enact God's saving will (**fulfill all righteousness**)? Verses 16-17 answer the question by presenting Jesus as the one whom the scriptures had previously revealed to be the agent of God's saving purposes. The explanation comes after **Jesus had been baptized just as he came up from the water**. It comes as a revelation to Jesus: **suddenly the heavens were opened to him**. The opening of the heavens to reveal heavenly or divine knowledge was a common motif in both Jewish (Ezek 1:11; 3 Macc 6:18; *2 Bar* 22:1; *T. Abr.* 7:3) and Roman literature (Virgil, *Aeneid* 9:20; Cicero, *Div* 1.43.97). The passive **were opened** indicates God's action. The almost exact citing of Ezek 1:1 in this phrase, along with the similar location beside a river for the vision, links Jesus and Ezekiel. The link evokes the exile of 587 B.C.E. at the hands of Babylonian imperial power and God's liberation from it. The liberation from exile recalls the exodus, God's liberation of the people through water from Pharaoh (Isa 43:14-21).

In Jesus, God continues these purposes of saving and liberating from tyranny. His ministry initiates the time and events that will lead to salvation from Rome's punishment of Jerusalem and the people. Jesus forgives sin (9:1-8; 26:28), creates an alternative community which acknowledges God's empire (4:17-22), and anticipates his return to establish God's reign in full (24:27-31). The gospel replaces one form of empire with another, albeit one marked by justice and mercy.

The revelation is presented as a visual (**and he saw**) and an auditory (**a voice**) experience. Jesus **saw the Spirit of God descending like a dove and alighting on him**. The **Spirit of God**, already active in Jesus' conception (1:18, 20), is now linked to his ministry. It recalls John's promise in 3:11 of one who would baptize in the Spirit. True to John's word, Jesus receives the Spirit, which he will make available to others. He belongs to a long line of other figures on whom the Spirit has descended: Gideon (Judg 6:34), Samson (Judg 15:14), Saul (1 Sam 10:6), the Davidic king (Isa 11:1-6). God thus anoints Jesus to proclaim and to set free the oppressed (Isa 61:1; also 42:1). He is the Christ/Messiah ("anointed one," 1:1, 16, 17, 18) through whom the Spirit is at work, as several traditions expected (*Pss. Sol.* 17:37; 18:7; *1 En* 49:3 [the Elect one is the Messiah, 48:10]; 62:2).[28]

The **Spirit of God** also echoes Gen 1:2 ("the Spirit of God hovered over the water"). The Genesis links of water and spirit (and **like a dove,** so Gen 1:2[29]) continue the new creation theme from chapter 1. If **the dove** evokes Noah's sending out of a dove (Gen 8:8), the theme of a new creation/new start is strengthened.

Since Homer (*Odyssey* 12.62) the **dove** has been identified as Zeus's servant who represents divine presence and love and conveys Zeus's messages. Here, in contrast to such claims, the dove is linked with the Spirit which empowers Jesus, God's beloved child, as God's commissioned agent.[30] God is beginning a whole new world, an alternative way of life, because the present structures of Rome's empire allied with Israel's social and religious elite are not what God intends. God will complete God's salvation in the yet-future return of Jesus to establish God's empire in full.

• 3:17

The auditory revelation follows: **And behold a voice from the heavens said**. While John is a voice in the wilderness (3:3), this **voice** is **from the heavens**, the abode of God (cf. 5:34; Isa 66:1). God speaks directly. Numerous traditions celebrate the power and efficacy of God's word in creation (Gen 1) and in human affairs (Ps 29; Isa 55:11). God's word here concerns Jesus' identity: **This is my son, the beloved, with whom I am well pleased**. Jesus is identified as God's **son/child** in 2:15, but the term's repetition in a direct word from God underlines its importance.

What does it mean to name Jesus as **my son/child** (see 2:15)? God's words seem to echo four biblical passages: (1) the suffering servant: Isa 42:1 **my son/servant, the beloved** (παῖς [*pais*] in Isaiah becomes υἱός [*huios*] in Matthew; and Isaiah's ἐκλεκτός [*eklektos*, chosen] becomes ἀγαπητός [*agapētos*, **beloved**]); (2) the king: Ps 2:7 υἱός μου (*huios mou*, **my son**); (3) perhaps **beloved** derives from the story of Abraham offering Isaac in Gen 22:2, τὸν υἱόν σου τὸν ἀγαπητόν (*ton huion sou ton agapēton*, "your beloved son"; also Gen 22:12, 16); (4) Israel (Exod 4:22-23, υἱός μου [*huios mou*, "my son"]). These four significant texts associate Jesus with four very important figures and moments in Israel's history.

1. Isaiah 42:1-4 identifies a child/son or servant who seems at times to be Israel (Isa 49:3) and at times a person or group in mission to Israel (Isa 49:5-6). This figure is not divine. He is anointed by the spirit to save Israel and the Gentiles not through destructive military and imperial power but through proclaiming justice and through suffering its consequences. This passage is applied to Jesus in Matt 12:18-21, as is Isa 53:4 in 8:17. Jesus is the chosen servant who liberates from oppressive forces and establishes God's justice for Jews and Gentiles.

2. Psalm 2, a royal psalm, celebrates the coronation of the Davidic king, whose task as God's chosen son (2:7) or agent is to represent God's just rule on earth. The Spirit settles on Jesus as descendant of David (1:1, 6, 17; cf. 1:20) who as God's son was promised an eternal kingdom and God's love (2 Sam 7:14-15). Jesus' task in saving from sin and manifesting God's presence (1:21, 23) is to represent God's rule (4:17). The combination with Isa 42 is interesting because while Ps 2 envisions God's dominating reign over all others, Isa 42 offers some critique of this view of power and points to another way of working, through gentle care and endurance of suffering.

3. Genesis 22 is the famous (and troubling) story of Abraham's near sacrifice of his son Isaac. The story evokes God's promises to Abraham of blessing all the nations, a promise that would be placed in jeopardy by Isaac's death. Abraham trusts God in being willing to sacrifice his son, and God proves faithful in providing deliverance. Jesus has a mission of blessing all nations, which will also involve his sacrifice.

4. Exodus 4 is part of the struggle to set God's son/child, the nation Israel, free from Pharaoh's oppressive rule. In passing through water, Jesus continues God's liberating work.

The servant and the king represent Israel. Jesus, baptized in the river Jordan, represents Israel and reenacts Israel's exodus story. The references to Abraham and the servant indicate his significance for both Jews and Gentiles.

God is **well pleased**. God's revelation of Jesus' identity (cf. 1:18-25; 2:15) occurs not in the center, not in the presence of the political, social, economic, and religious elite, and not with their approval or permission. God is at work on the margins with those who dare to see a different present and an alternative way of life and future. People are given the chance through his ministry and the narrative of it to participate in God's just and liberating reign in anticipation of its full establishment.

Jesus' baptism by a marginal figure in a marginal place, then, **fulfills all righteousness/justice** in disclosing that God has chosen Jesus (**my son the beloved**) to carry out these roles concerning God's liberating justice and reign, God's new creation. These various scriptural traditions expand on his task of saving people from their sins and manifesting God's presence (1:21, 23). In being baptized Jesus consents to this mission. Those who follow him are to continue this task of proclaiming and embodying God's just and liberating reign in the face of the opposition that inevitably results from those with (in)vested interests in defending the status quo.

CHAPTER 4A

Diabolical Opposition and Imperial Darkness

4:1-11—THE DEVIL'S TEMPTATION OF JESUS

This scene continues to elaborate God's initiative in conceiving and commissioning Jesus to save from sins and manifest God's presence (1:18-25). God's purposes conflict with the empire's interests in chapter 2, but God protects Jesus. In chapter 3, from the margins and resisted by the religious elite, John calls for a changed society and testifies to God's coming wrath and to Jesus' decisive role, a blessing to some and destruction to others (3:11-12). God confirms and empowers Jesus as God's child or agent in the baptism with the Spirit's descent (3:13-17).

In 4:1-11, the devil challenges the relationship of Jesus and God, which was declared in 3:16-17. The central issue concerns allegiance: Who will determine Jesus' actions? Will Jesus be faithful in carrying out God's commission, or will the devil, God's opponent, define his actions and claim his allegiance? By causing Jesus to act in a way contrary to God's will, the devil would dishonor Jesus and God. By resisting the devil's temptations, Jesus shows himself worthy of, and faithful to, God's commission, and so honors God.

This scene discloses a further dimension of the Roman-dominated world. In the third temptation, Satan claims control of "all the kingdom's/empires of the world" (4:8-9). This startling revelation means that Satan controls the Roman empire. Moreover, linguistic links connect Satan, the Roman vassal king Herod, and the religious elite as opponents of God's purposes enacted in Jesus. In 4:8-9 Satan refers to the world's empires as *basileias* (βασιλείας). In 2:1, 3 Herod is introduced as king (βασιλεύς, *basileus*). The two related terms identify Herod as Satan's ally and agent. His kingship, derived from the devil and allied with Rome, contrasts with Jesus who is king (βασιλεύς, *basileus*, 2:2) by God's calling. The verb "tempt" provides a second link. It denotes the devil's actions in 4:1, 3, and describes what the religious leaders do to Jesus in 16:1; 19:3; 22:18, 35.

The temptation story discloses this diabolical alliance and the devilish nature of these opponents. The devil portrays the inner spirit of the empire and the reli-

106

gious elite. The political and religious leadership is the visible institutional form of an inner reality which resists God's purposes and pursues its own agenda through injustice and oppressive power.[1]

The narrative does not explain who the devil is. It is assumed that the audience knows various traditions that identify nonhuman powers and forces (angels and demons by various names) which impact institutions, structures, nations, and individuals and resist God's purposes. Daniel 10:10-21 identifies conflict among the angels or "princes" of Persia, Israel, and Greece. In *Jub.* 15:31-32, God appoints spirits over all the nations, which lead them astray. But no spirit rules Israel because God rules it directly. In *Jub.* 12:20 evil and misleading spirits "rule over the thought of (human) hearts." In the *Testament of Solomon,* numerous demons led by Beelzeboul (*T. Sol.* 3:6) cause people to commit evil actions and to suffer various physical deformities and sicknesses. Each demon has a thwarting angel. This temptation scene assumes this invisible world of supernatural opposition.

The scene thus exposes a cultural norm. It enables the audience to consider afresh the issues of control and allegiance implicit in their world. (1) It depicts the diabolical nature of the imperial status quo which opposes God's purposes, is oppressive, and is committed to the elite's self-interest. (2) The scene depicts Jesus' resistance to this structure. If Jesus yields to Satan's temptations, he becomes Satan's agent and, as such, would be an ally with Rome! His resistance to Satan signals his resistance to, not his cooperation with, Rome. Jesus' actions, guided by the scriptures and vindicated by ministering angels, focus on God's will, resist the devil, and advocate an alternative existence constituted by God's purposes.[2]

• 4:1

Then Jesus was led into the wilderness by the Spirit. The temptation immediately follows the baptism (**then**). John disappears until chapters 11 and 14 (cf. 4:12). The name **Jesus** recalls his God-given mission from 1:21-23. This mission is now at stake.

While Jesus is the focus, God moves the action forward (as in 1:18-25). The **Spirit** is God's agent (1:18, 20), which descended on Jesus (3:16) in accord with John's promise (3:11). The Spirit now **leads** Jesus. The verb is used as God **leads/brings** plagues on Pharaoh (Exod 8:5, 6, 7; 10:14) and **leads** Israel from Egypt into the wilderness and to the land (Exod 33:12, 15; Num 14:13; 16:13; Josh 24:17). **Wilderness** further echoes the exodus story. After passing through water in their liberation from slavery (compare Jesus' baptism in 3:13-17), the people were tested in the wilderness (cf 3:1). Jesus relives the wilderness experience of God's child Israel (cf. Hos 11:1; Matt 2:15), though Jesus remains faithful. The **wilderness** setting further links Jesus and John (see 3:1, 3). Again God's preferred location is the margins, outside and threatening to the centers of power.

The **Spirit** leads Jesus **to be tempted/tested by the devil**. The wilderness is associated with evil spirits and demons (Lev 16:10; Tob 8:3; 1 *En* 10:4; 4 Macc

18:8a). The verb **tempted** denotes God testing Israel to reveal faithfulness (Exod 16:4; 20:20; Deut 8:2), and Israel's illegitimate attempts to test God (Exod 17:2, 7; Num 14:22). Here the agent of the testing is **the devil**. Note the two parallel phrases **by the spirit** and **by the devil**. The devil, once a member of the heavenly court, accuser of humans (Zech 3:1-10; Job 1-2) and inciter of sin (1 Chr 21:1), becomes known under various names in Hellenistic-Jewish traditions as an evil opponent of God's purposes, who tempts people to sin and thwarts God's plans.[3] His tempting of Jesus, ironically, serves the divine purposes in showing Jesus' commitment to do God's will.

• 4:2

Like Moses (Exod 34:28), Jesus **fasted forty days and forty nights**, a valued act of devotion. See Lev 16:29, 31 (Day of Atonement); Ps 35:13 (with prayer); Tob 12:8; Jdt 4:9; *T. Jos.* 3:4; Dan 10:3; 5:7-3:4 (fasting precedes visions); Suetonius's use of the phrase "fasting as a Jew" (*Augustus* 76) attests a widespread practice; Matt 6:16-18. The time period **forty days and forty nights** echoes Exod 34:28, but the number **forty** evokes numerous significant events and underlines themes of judgment and testing:

- The length of Noah's flood (Gen 7:4, 12, 17), an event of judgment and of new creation
- Israel's forty years in the wilderness (Exod 16:35) after slavery, a time of divine presence (Deut 2:7), faithfulness (Deut 29:4-5), and testing (Deut 8:2-3)
- Ezekiel lies on his right side for forty days, portraying the punishment of Judah (Ezek 4:6)
- Jonah predicts Nineveh's destruction in forty days (Jonah 3:4)

And afterwards he was famished. Jesus relives Israel's experience of hunger in the wilderness (Deut 8:3). But whereas Israel murmurs against God in its hunger (Exod 16:3-8), Jesus does not.

• 4:3

Jesus' devotion in fasting provides an opportunity for the devil. **The tempter** (same verb as v. 1) **came[4] and said to him, "If you are the son of God, command these stones to become loaves of bread."** The devil's words echo God's designation of Jesus as **son** (3:17; 2:15). The reference to stones recalls John's reference to God's power in 3:9. The devil tempts Jesus to display God's power to satisfy his hunger. The goal is commendable: food shortages were a major issue in the first century, often arising from the elite's control of food sources, supplies, and prices.[5] But while food would be God's blessing (cf Prov 9:1-5; Wis 16:26), it would be procured at the devil's command.

The temptation consists not in doubting that Jesus is God's son or agent, or that he can perform a miracle, or in provoking a display of miracle-working power (no crowd is present). Rather it resides in causing Jesus to act at the devil's behest. To do so would mean that Jesus does not act according to God's will as God's Christ and son (1:1, 17, 21-23; 2:15; 3:17). The devil seeks to control Jesus through obedience (4:3-4, 9) and worship (4:9). If Jesus supplies his own bread at the devil's command, he acts for his own benefit as the elite do. He ceases to trust and obey God, contrary to his own subsequent teaching (6:25-35). In not trusting God, he yields to the devil's directives.

• 4:4

Jesus resists by evoking the exodus (Deut 8:3b LXX; cf. Exod 16),[6] **One does not live by bread alone but by every word that comes from the mouth of God**. The verse does not disparage human hunger; its context, Deut 8:1-3a, indicates an intertwining of, not a dualism of, physical and spiritual needs. It recalls God supplying food to hungry people in a situation that challenged their trust. God's life-giving word ensured their survival (see 14:13-21; 15:32-39; cf. 25:31-46). Jesus cites the verse to express his trust in, dependence on, and obedience to God. God, not the devil nor Jesus' desire, will define his mission and use of power.

• 4:5

Then the devil took him to the holy city. The devil instigates a second temptation at a new location. He **took him** (how?) from the margins of the wilderness to the center, **the holy city** (Isa 48:1; 52:1; Neh 11:1; Tob 13:9; 2 Macc 3:1; Sir 49:6). In addition to being the political-social-religious center (see 2:1-3), several traditions identified Jerusalem as the center of the world (Isa 2:2-4; Mic 4:1-4 [to which the nations come]; Ezek 5:5; 38:12; *Jub.* 8:19; *1 En* 26:1). To be **holy** does not mean to be perfect or sinless but to be set apart to serve God.[7] The description **the holy city** is ironic in recalling Jerusalem's calling to serve God yet Jerusalem's resistance to God's action in 2:3, 4-6.

The location emphasizes this calling and failure (the priests in 2:4-6). The devil **placed him** (Jesus) **on the pinnacle of the temple**. In addition to sanctioning or being co-opted by political power (2:4-6), the **temple** was a place of encounter with divine presence (Isa 31:4-5; Jer 7:4; Pss 95; 125), forgiveness (Ps 51), and protection (Pss 61:4-5; 91). It legitimated both worship and living in accord with God's will. The devil places Jesus above this cosmic, political, and religious center and tempts him again.

• 4:6

The devil repeats God's declaration of Jesus' role: **"If/since you are son of God** (see 4:3; 3:17; 2:15), **throw yourself down."** The command does not seek Jesus' destruction, but tempts him to act at the devil's request and trust God (4:4). The devil mimics Jesus by quoting scripture to show that the command is God's will (Ps 91:11a, 12): **"for it is written, 'He will command his angels concerning you,' and 'On their hands they will bear you up so that you will not dash your foot against a stone.'"** The devil omits v. 11b ("to guard you in all your ways") because Jesus must be unguarded if he is to comply with the devil's ways. The psalm celebrates God's protection of the faithful. Presumably the **angels** (see 1:20, 24; 2:13, 19) will catch the falling Jesus. But the devil perverts the psalm in suggesting that it guarantees God's protection, regardless of human faithfulness. Jeremiah counters such deception in warning those who think God will not punish Jerusalem because "the temple of the Lord" is there (Jer 7:4). The events of the Babylonian exile of 587 and of Rome's destruction of city and temple in 70 C.E. indicate no place for such presumption.

• 4:7

As with 4:4, Jesus cites scripture, the address of Moses to Israel in the wilderness: **"Again it is written, 'Do not put the Lord your God to the test.'"** The text from Deut 6:16b refers to the people testing God at Massah (Exod 17:1-7). Lacking water, they doubt God's faithfulness, life-giving purposes, and presence. God provides water to reassure them. In citing the verse Jesus declares that he will not demand any display from God, that he will trust God, and that he will act at God's direction, not the devil's. The devil has misused the scripture by confusing trust in God with a presumption that makes God a servant of human bidding. Jesus will later refuse angelic aid to escape the crucifixion in 26:53, and will refuse the calls to descend from the cross (27:40, "if you are the son of God") because he knows he must die (16:21) in accord with God's will.

• 4:8-9

A repeated clause (**the devil took him**; see 4:5) and a new location (**to a very high mountain**) introduce the third temptation. This first mountain scene (see 5:1; 8:1; 14:23; 15:29; 17:1; 21:1; 28:16) evokes important mountain scenes in Israel's traditions: Abraham is tested (see 1:1-2; 3:17) and promised descendants and blessing for all the nations (Gen 22:2, 14-18); Moses receives the Decalogue on Mt. Sinai (Exod 19:20); Elijah retreats to Horeb/Sinai (1 Kgs 19:8). In addition, the gods were thought to reside on Mt. Olympus.

The devil **showed** Jesus **all the empires/kingdoms of the world and the glory of them. All these I will give you**. The offer is staggering. The devil claims to control the world's **empires/ kingdoms** including Rome, the chief empire. Roman imperial theology declares that Rome rules by Jupiter's will (see Introduction, section 9).[8] Here Rome is shown to be allied with the devil's reign. The devil's claim discloses the hidden power manifested in the external actions of the empire and vassals such as Herod (ch. 2).

The **world** is the realm of everyday political, social, economic, and religious life. Though created by God and the object of God's purposes (Ps 24:1), it is claimed by the devil and in need of saving (5:14; 13:38; 24:21). While **glory** often denotes the splendor of God's power and presence in the world especially in liberating people from Pharaoh (Num 14:10-12, 22, linked with testing God), here it is usurped by the devil.

This is not how it should be, not a faithful embodiment of God's purposes. In Ps 2 (see Matt 3:17), God invites the king, God's child or son, to ask *God* for "the nations" and "the ends of the earth" (Ps 2:8; cf. 72:8). Such rule is God's to give, not the devil's. The risen Jesus will receive this authority in 28:18, but not yet, and not from the devil. In making his offer, then, the devil usurps God's authority and violates the first commandment (Exod 20:3). At issue is sovereignty—"To whom does the world belong?"[9] To God (cf. Gen 1; Lev 25:23; Ps 24:1) or to the devil? If Jesus receives the devil's offer, he acknowledges the devil's authority and rule. But it is God's empire that Jesus is commissioned to manifest (1:21, 23). John has already announced that God's **reign/empire** is at hand (3:2), and Jesus will soon declare its presence (4:17). The play on the noun βασιλεία (*basileia,* reign) in 3:2 and 4:17 and the plural form used by the devil in 4:8 (βασιλείας, *basileias,* **empires/kingdoms**) must not be missed. God, not the devil, has commissioned Jesus to this role.

The price of Jesus' receiving this empire from the devil is **if you will fall down and worship me**. Worship makes explicit the issue of allegiance. But worship belongs to God, as the first commandment, using the same verb, states (Exod 20:5; Deut 5:9). Echoing but not imitating the exodus (Exod 32), Jesus refuses this idolatry. Herod uses the same verb (**worship**) to declare (falsely) that he wants to worship Jesus (2:8; cf. the magi in 2:2, 11). Herod and the devil are allies in false worship and in using worship as means to their own ends. Subsequently, people seeking Jesus' help will worship *before* making a request (8:2; 9:18; 15:25).

Further links between the devil's challenge to Jesus and the empire are evident. The noun **worship** (*proskynēsis*) designates the prostration required, especially in the east since Alexander, when greeting a ruler such as the emperors Gaius Caligula, Nero, and Domitian.[10] Gaius Caligula had forced Jews to make a decision comparable to that of Jesus when he tried to replace worship of God in the Jerusalem temple with worship of himself (Josephus, *JW* 2.184-203; Philo, *Gaium* 116). Attacks on faithful worship are evident in Titus's destruction of the Jerusalem temple, Vespasian's use of the former temple tax to rebuild the temple of Jupiter Capitolinus (see on 17:24-27), and his destruction of a synagogue in Daphne, a suburb of Antioch, to build a theater which included a statue of himself (Malalas, *Chron* 260-61). The Flavian imperial theology (see Introduction, section 9) collides with worship of God as sovereign of heaven and earth. Followers of Jesus know the same test (10:17-18, 32-33).

• 4:10

Jesus dismisses the devil, **Away with you, Satan!** (cf. 16:23). The new name (**Satan**) underlines the adversarial nature of the scene by evoking Satan's accusatory role in the heavenly council (1 Chr 21:1; Job 1; Zech 3:1-2). Jesus demonstrates his faithfulness to God and authority over the devil. This victory, though, is not absolute; Jesus will later confront the devil's reign in exorcising demons, the devil's agents (4:23; 12:28).

Jesus again (cf. 4:4, 7) is directed by the scriptures: **for it is written, "Worship the Lord your God and serve only him**." He quotes Moses (Deut 6:13) with two changes: replacing "fear" with **worship** to be consistent with the devil's temptation in 4:9b, and adding **only** to underline exclusive allegiance.

Moses' address to Israel reminds the Israelites not to forget God's liberating action in the exodus and to reject idolatry. Jesus reminds the audience not to forget its foremost loyalty.

• 4:11

Jesus' authority is efficacious, **Then the devil left him**. The scene has exposed the devil's claim to control the world's empires, the devil's dangerous resistance to God's purposes which is hidden within and operative through the political and religious powers, and the devil's limited power. While not yet the end of Satan, God's purposes prevail. **And suddenly angels came** (the same verb has the devil as subject in 4:3) **and were waiting on him**. The translation **waiting on** represents a view that the verb διακονέω (*diakoneō*) denotes "serving food." While this is likely, the verb indicates primarily the actions of a go-between, of an agent who represents or acts on behalf of another.[11] The scene presents them as agents of God who convey God's care and provision to Jesus.[12]

Jesus remains faithful to his identity as God's son/child or agent in the face of the devil's temptations and attempts to claim Jesus' allegiance. Jesus demonstrates God's sovereignty over the devil and anticipates its establishment over all resisting powers.

The uniting of the devil with the political and religious leaders is one troubling aspect of this scene. The history of anti-Judaism attests the tragedy of the demonization of the Jewish religious leaders, especially its extension by Christian readers to demonize all Israel. The gospel does not make this leap. An extensive discussion is not possible here,[13] but Matthew's readers must in their thinking, talking about, and living of this gospel be extremely careful not to continue this destructive history.

Equally troubling is the already noted question of how Jesus will manifest God's empire. Will this reign imitate Rome's in being oppressively enforced? Where is the good news in an image such as empire or reign, which readily evokes oppression and tyranny?

4:12-16—JESUS THE LIGHT SHINES
IN IMPERIAL DARKNESS

The first major section or narrative block concludes with a scene that draws together several main themes of 1:1-4:16. (1) The scene uses the image of light to recapitulate Jesus' commission to manifest God's saving presence (1:21, 23). (2) God's initiative in Jesus challenges an imperial world and asserts God's sovereignty. Jesus' presence in Capernaum means "light" in the midst of darkness and death, an image of divine presence and salvation in the midst of the political and socioeconomic hardship of imperial rule.[14] Evoking Isa 9 recalls the expansionist threats of Syria, Israel, Assyria, and now Rome. But God provides a way of salvation. (3) Jesus' presence in Capernaum enacts the divine will previously made known by the scriptures in Isaiah (4:14-16). (4) The scene emphasizes the universal extent of God's purposes by identifying Galilee as "Galilee under the Gentiles" (4:15). This reference continues the theme of Gentile inclusion: "son of Abraham" (1:1), the Gentile women in the genealogy (1:3, 5, 6), the magi (2:1-12), Egypt (2:13-23), John's attack (3:9), and the devil's offer to Jesus of "all the kingdoms of the world" (4:8).

• 4:12

Now when Jesus heard that John had been arrested. Not explained are how Jesus **heard**, what time has elapsed since the events narrated in 3:13-17 or between 4:11 and 4:12, why John should be arrested, or by whom (see 14:1-12). The cryptic reference to his arrest, though, indicates the elite's negative response to John's baptism (see 3:7) and call for repentance. In speaking of God's empire, John is perceived to be a threat. The aorist passive form (**had been/was**) commonly attests divine action and suggests that John's arrest results from God's commission. Further, his arrest anticipates Jesus' ministry. Jesus' ministry, to which John bears witness (3:11-12), will so threaten the status quo that the empire will subsequently **arrest** Jesus (17:22; 20:18-19; 26:2, 15-16, 21, 23-25, 45-46, 48; 27:2-4, 18, 26).

John's arrest causes Jesus **to withdraw into Galilee** (see 14:13). The magi (2:12-13) and Joseph (2:14, 22) withdraw from the dangerous rulers Herod and Archelaus. But Jesus' withdrawal from the wilderness (around the Jordan) to Galilee is not for safety reasons (as in 2:12, 13, 14, 22). The citation in 4:15-16 identifies **Galilee** as occupied territory, with its own centers of power, and 14:1-12 indicates that John is killed by its ruler, the Roman client Herod Antipas. Jesus **withdraws** into a dangerous situation created by John's arrest, in which he will now carry out God's purposes. Jesus' withdrawal means opportunities and danger (so also 9:24; 12:15[?]; 14:13; 15:21). After 70, Vespasian and Titus claimed control of **Galilee** (Josephus, *JW* 7.216-17), redistributed land among loyal supporters, and ensured economic control of land and resources through taxation of the largely peasant economy.[15] Loyal local elites who secured their own social and economic power through cooperation with Rome assisted in maintaining control. The powerful few benefit at the expense of many. This injustice, sustained by the threat of military violence and reinforced by the presence of Vespasian's and Titus's images on coins,[16] was a far cry from the vision of the promised land, which acknowledged God's sovereignty and justice.

Galilee is also geographically distant from and marginal to hostile Jerusalem (ch. 2). It symbolizes "the periphery [which becomes] the new, non-localized center of divine presence."[17] As in 2:14, 22, and 12:15, a scripture citation confirms the move.

• 4:13

Jesus left **Nazareth** (see 2:23) and made his home in **Capernaum by the sea**, a small agricultural and fishing village (population around one thousand) on the northwestern shore of the Sea of Galilee. He does not move to the larger cities, Tiberias (built to honor and named after the emperor Tiberias) or Sepphoris, the centers of imperial political, economic, social, and cultural power in Galilee, which maintain the elite's interests and control over the surrounding villages through taxation.[18] As a Jew in Roman-controlled territory, Jesus locates himself among the marginal, with the poor not the wealthy, with the rural peasants not the urban elite, with the ruled not the rulers, with the powerless and exploited not the powerful, with those who resist imperial demands not enforce them. He continues the gospel's preference for the apparently small and insignificant places and people who, nevertheless, are central for God's purposes (2:5-6, 22-23; 3:1).

Capernaum is **in the territory of Zebulun and Naphtali**. These are the names of two of the twelve tribes and designate tribal allocations of the land which God had sworn to Abraham, Isaac, and Jacob, shown to Moses (Deut 34:1-4), and apportioned under Joshua (Josh 18:3; 19:10-16 [Zebulun in the Galilean highlands] and 19:32-39 [Naphtali, to the west and north of the Sea of Galilee]). This was land for a people who recognized God's reign. **Capernaum** was in **Naphtali**. The tribal names prepare for the citation from Isaiah in 4:15-16; they also continue from 3:13-4:11 the echoes of the exodus and occupation narrative. The nomenclature locates Jesus in the promised land, which God gave to the people and over which God has sovereignty. It is a daring reminder of God's sovereignty in the face of Roman claims on Galilee and the presence of Roman client rulers like Herod. The terms expose and challenge Roman claims by evoking but not explicitly articulating God's perspective.

• 4:14

Jesus' move to Capernaum happens **so that what was spoken by the prophet Isaiah might be fulfilled**.[19] Jesus again enacts the previously declared will of God (see 4:1-11; 1:22-23; 2:15). The term **prophet** introduces a destabilizing voice that challenges the self-interest of the status quo (see 1:22-23; 2:5-6, 15, 18, 23; 3:1-3). The citation of Isa 9:1-2 has a geographical focus (as do the four scripture citations in ch. 2), but, as in Matt 1:22-23, Isa 7-9 evokes God's salvation from imperial aggression. **Isaiah** was quoted in 3:3 concerning liberation from exile.

• 4:15-16

The citation of Isa 9:1-2 does not exactly follow either the Masoretic Text (Hebrew) or the Septuagint (Greek).[20] In Isaiah the passage concerns the Syro-Ephraimite crisis of 735-733 B.C.E. (Isa 7-8), in which the northern kingdom (Ephraim/Israel) and Syria threaten Judah. Isaiah's word of hope to Judah is that God will use another imperial power, Assyria, to destroy the two northern powers (Isa 7:1-9; 8:1-4), and that God will be present with the people, symbolized in the birth of a child called Immanuel (Isa 7:14; see on 1:22-23). But unbelief means that Assyria will punish the people (7:17-25; 8:5-15). Isaiah's word partly comes to pass when the capital, Samaria, falls in 722 to Assyria, who exiles the leadership and occupies **Zebulun and Naphtali** (2 Kgs 15:29).

Isaiah 8:16-22 narrates the terrible results for a people subjected to imperial power. "Greatly distressed and hungry" because of appropriated resources, they know "distress and darkness, the gloom of anguish; and they will be thrust into thick darkness" (Isa 8:22). Isaiah 9:1 repeats the impact of Assyria's punishment, but offers hope for a reversal of the "anguish" and "contempt" as the "rod of their oppressor" is broken through one who will embody God's reign of justice, righteousness, and peace (Isa 11:4-7).

Matthew transfers the Isaiah text from one situation of imperial aggression to another.[21] **Zebulun and Naphtali**, land given by God to the people (Deut 34:1-4; Josh 19:10-16, 32-39), remain under imperial control. It is no longer Assyria's control, but Rome's, tightened since the successes of Roman troops in Galilee in 67 C.E. **Galilee of the Gentiles**, a synonym for **Zebulun and Naphtali**, designates occupied status, a land *under* the power of, possessed by, belonging to, ruled by Gentile imperialists (cf. 2 Kgs 17:24-27).[22] The term does not emphasize, as some have claimed, that **Galilee** was inhabited by non-Jews or was susceptible to hellenization (though both are true), or that Jewish ethnicity and piety had almost disappeared, or that Jesus was looking only for Gentiles (both of which are not true; cf. 4:18-22, 23-25!).[23] It signifies Roman control (Josephus, *JW* 7.216-17).

Imperial control is imaged in describing **Galilee under the Gentiles** as a place of **darkness** and **death** into which **light** shines (4:16). **Darkness** symbolizes various realities,[24] especially that which is contrary to God's life-giving purposes: the chaos before God's creative light and life (Gen 1:2), the oppressive reality of slavery in Egypt (Exod 10:21, 22; 14:20), Assyria's rule (Isa 8:22), exile in Babylon (Isa 42:7; 47:5; 49:9). Those who walk in darkness are the wicked who do injustice to the weak and needy (Ps 81:5); by contrast the righteous, those who fear the Lord, who deal in justice, who are secure in the Lord, and who give to the poor, are lights in the darkness (Ps 111:4). **Darkness** denotes political, social, economic, and religious acts and structures such as imperialism that are contrary to God's purposes. Darkness is the rejection of God's call to a changed society, the call to repentance which John brings, and for which he is arrested (4:12).

Darkness is **death**, as the parallelism of Matt 4:16a and b indicates. To **sit in darkness** or **death** is to live in the midst of actions and structures contrary to God's will (cf. Isa 9:9 "inhabitants of Samaria"). Yet **darkness** is not the final word, even though it seems to be. **Light**, an image of God's life and saving power (Ps 27:1), **dawns** and rescues people from darkness, whether political oppression (Exod 10:21, 22; 14:20; Isa 9:2; 42:7; 45:7; 47:5; 49:9; *1 En* 1:8-9) or personal misery (Ps 90:6; 106:10-16 LXX) such as hunger or affliction (Isa 58:10). Jesus manifests God's salvation by transforming personal misery, by announcing God's empire, by forming an alternative community, and by anticipating the future establishment of God's empire in full (chs. 24-25).

The imperial poet Statius praises the emperor Domitian, "that present deity" (*Silv* 5.2.170), by noting his "immortal brightness" (1.1.77), which shone even when he tried to dim it (4.2.41-44). He outshines constellations and the sun.

People reflect his light (4.1.3-4, 23-27). Martial greets Domitian's return to Rome as restoring light to the darkness (*Epig* 8.21).[25] But the **light** in 4:16 is not the presence of the Roman emperor who "rules" Galilee. Roman rule is part of the **darkness** and **shadow of death** under which **Galilee of the Gentiles** now suffers. The gospel offers a counternarrative. The **light** is Jesus' presence, which manifests God's empire. His public ministry is to commence. As the light of the world (5:14), the community of disciples will continue his salvific mission.

PART II

The Second Narrative Block

Jesus Manifests God's Empire
and Commission in Words
and Actions (4:17-11:1)

CHAPTER 4B

The Beginning of Jesus' Public Ministry

4:17-25—HOW JESUS CARRIES OUT HIS MISSION

With this scene the plot takes a new turn. The opening section (1:1-4:16) has established *what* God has commissioned Jesus to do (1:21, 23). It has not, though, indicated *how* Jesus carries out his mission to manifest God's saving presence.[1]

The second major section of the gospel's plot (4:17-11:1) answers this question in its account of Jesus' public ministry. The narrative block's key scene (4:17-25) presents the answer in three subsections. Jesus manifests God's saving presence in a world of darkness and death (4:12-16) by (i) declaring that God's empire is at hand (4:17), (ii) by calling people to follow him in an alternative community (4:18-22), and (iii) by showing God's transforming reign at work through teaching, preaching, and healing (4:23-25). The rest of the narrative block (5-11:1) will elaborate his teaching in chapters 5-7, miracles in chapters 8-9, and mission call to "fish for people" (4:18) in chapter 10.

• **4:17**

Jesus begins his public ministry by proclaiming, **Repent, for the empire/reign of the heavens has come near.** The imperative **repent** indicates that God can be encountered either as judge or as savior (2 Chr 7:13-22; Jer 4:1-10; 7:5-34; 17:24-27) and points to what is necessary for the latter option. Jesus' use of the same words that John used (see 3:2) allies the two figures and confirms the reliability of John's preparatory testimony (see 3:1-12).

What is the relationship between Jesus' commission and God's **empire/reign**?[2] The narrative has shown God commission Jesus to save from sins (1:21) and manifest God's presence (1:23); it has shown Jesus loyal to God's will (4:1-11) and has designated him "light" (4:16), a metaphor for God's saving presence. Jesus' announcement of the **empire** refers, then, to this commission. The **empire of the heavens** is God's saving presence. God's reign has **come near** (ἤγγικεν, *ēngiken;* see 3:2), a verb that holds together both arrival and nearness, present and future dimensions.[3] The perfect tense suggests that

119

God's empire is displayed in the ministry of Jesus with continuing but not yet completed impact. The name **Jesus** in 4:17 explicitly evokes his naming and commissioning from 1:21-23.

What does God's empire look like? As noted in 3:2, at first glance the term is troubling because it employs the imperialistic language of oppressive rule. Yet (following N. Perrin; see 3:2) it is not a steno-symbol, a stable concept with fixed content. It is, rather, a tensive, open-ended, expanding symbol. It evokes the general memory of God acting on behalf of God's people, the display of God's sovereignty among people (*T. Mos.* 10:1; *Pss. Sol.* 17:3; 1QM 6:6; 12:7). At times this display is overwhelming and destructive; at other times it is gentle and merciful (see Ps 72).[4] In a world dominated by Roman rule, Jesus will manifest God's empire in proclamation (4:17), in creating an alternative community (4:18-22), in acts that transform misery and brokenness (4:23-25) in anticipation of the full establishment of God's reign over all imperfection, sickness, and want (13:39-43, 49-50; 19:28; chs. 24-25). The proclamation that soon the world will acknowledge God's sovereignty, not Rome's, threatens the status quo but encourages the gospel's audience.

• 4:18-22

The immediate, but partial, demonstration of the impact of the reign comes in a call narrative.[5] This scene is reminiscent of Elijah calling Elisha in 1 Kgs 19:19-21. Elisha and the fishermen hear the call in the midst of everyday life. The call is a demand from God, and both abandon their way of life.[6]

In his study of prophetic call narratives, N. Habel shows that call stories proclaim "the prophet's claim to be Yahweh's agent at work."[7] This call story demonstrates Jesus doing God's work and legitimates the disciples as God's agents. A. J. Droge examines call narratives in Greek biographies, especially in Cynic writings.[8] They include similar features: a call to follow (ἀκολουθέω, *akoloutheō*) initiated by a founder figure, in the midst of everyday life, which elicits an immediate response and effects a transition to a new identity. These stories show the significance of the main figure, and they present features of the lifestyle of followers, often in contrast to nonfollowers. The double call narrative in 4:18-22, then, utilizes a common form to present Jesus as God's agent enacting his commission to manifest God's saving presence, the empire of the heavens, and to legitimate the beginning of an alternative community of disciples called to live on the basis of this reign.[9] The calls occur in the midst of the empire's close control of fishing whereby licensing, quotas, and taxation secure Rome's sovereignty over the water and its contents (see below). Jesus' call contests this dominant reality by asserting God's sovereignty and offering an alternative way of life.

• 4:18

As he walked by the sea of Galilee, he saw two brothers. The unspecified pronoun **he** requires the audience to review 1:1-4:16 and 4:17 to identify Jesus as its referent. The one commissioned to manifest God's saving presence (1:21-

23), the one who has announced the reign of the heavens (4:17), carries out this action. He performs it by God's authority, in response to God's commission. Calling disciples embodies his God-given commission. The location **by the sea of Galilee** continues the emphasis on places away from the powerful center and clarifies the act's significance. Both 4:13 and 15 connect the region **by the sea** with **Galilee under the Gentiles** (see 4:12-16), the place of oppressive darkness and death in which the light of God's saving presence now shines.

That oppressive darkness is evident in the political and economic structures implicit in the scene. Jesus **saw two brothers, Simon, who is called Peter, and Andrew his brother, casting a net into the sea—for they were fishermen**. **Simon Peter** appears first. His prominence continues in the rest of the story (see 10:2; 16:15-20, 22-23).[10] Their identity as **fishermen** means involvement in the imperial economic and political monopoly. Fish were claimed as revenue for the empire. ". . . [E]very rare and beautiful thing in the wide ocean . . . belongs to the imperial treasury" (Juvenal, *Sat* 4.51-55).[11] As **brothers,** and possibly members of a cooperative with James and John (4:21), they have purchased a lease or contract with Rome's agents that allows them to fish and obligates them to supply a certain quantity of fish. They pay taxes on the catch and transportation. The elite—retainers like tax administrators and collectors (see Introduction, section 5), Herod Antipas (until 39 C.E.), the emperor— benefit.[12] While the fishermen have some economic resources, their social ranking is very low. In Cicero's ranking of occupations (*De Off* 1.150-51), owners of cultivated land appear first and fishermen last. Athenaeus indicates that fishermen and fishmongers are on a par with moneylenders and are socially despised as greedy thieves (*Deipnosophistai,* 6.224b-28c).[13] The two characters have a socially inferior and economically precarious existence under Roman control. It is among such vulnerable people that God's empire is first manifested.

• 4:19

Demonstrating his authority as the one commissioned by God (Christ, 1:17; agent or Son, 2:15; 3:17), Jesus takes the initiative, **And he said to them, "Follow me, and I will make you fish for people."** One cannot volunteer to be a follower. Nor does one belong by birth, wealth, gender, or training. Jesus' call invades and challenges their everyday world controlled by imperial economics. His words make available God's empire/reign and create for those who **follow** an alternative community and way of life with a different center, values, and structure.

The location **beside the sea** is a threshold, a transition from death and darkness into God's reign and presence (cf. 4:14-16). Peter and Andrew are commissioned to a new lifestyle, **I will make you fish for people**. Prophets use the fishing image to denounce the elite's false worship (Jer 16:16) and unjust lifestyle of "oppressing the poor and crushing the needy" (Amos 4:2). Ezekiel decries Egypt's imperial power and uses a fishing image to promise God's judgment (Ezek 29:3, 4-16; see Matt 13:47). Peter and Andrew's lifestyle, as part of a new community, will resist imperial abuses and oppressive privilege. The term **people** signifies those who are not disciples. The mission will be clarified in chapters 5-7 and 10.

• 4:20

Immediately they left their nets and followed him. They turn from one way of life to another. Their instant (**immediately**) and sacrificial (**their nets**) response makes sense because the audience knows from 1:1-4:16 that Jesus' words express his God-given commission. The verb **follow**[14] denotes his authoritative call and their commitment of entrusting themselves to him at considerable social and economic cost. It is the basis for the new community of **brothers and sisters** (4:18). The term denotes both the blood relationship of Peter and Andrew and membership in the community of followers of Jesus. Jesus starts to build an alternative community in the midst of the imperial world.

• 4:21-22

The scene of 4:18-20 is repeated. **As he went from there he saw two other brothers, James son of Zebedee and his brother John, in the boat with their father Zebedee, mending their nets, and he called them. Immediately they left the boat and their father, and followed him.** The gospel often repeats important material.[15] There are two new elements. The verb **called** (4:21) replaces Jesus' direct address to the fishermen (4:19, "Follow me"). In its five previous uses this verb expresses God's electing salvific activity in the origin and destiny of Jesus, and designates Jesus' purpose and mission as agent of God's saving presence. See 1:21 (naming), 23 (naming), 25; 2:15 (God calls), 23. Its use in 4:21 to describe Jesus' activity indicates that Jesus is doing his God-given commission.

Further, this second call scene (4:21-22) identifies the **father of James and John** three times (**son of Zebedee**; **with their father Zebedee**; **and their father**). By retaining the term **brothers** and adding these references to leaving their **father**, the scene heightens the issue of the new disciples' relation to their family. Family and household obligations were basic aspects of both the Decalogue (Exod 20:12) and civic responsibility.[16] Producing children was, among other things, an insurance policy for care in one's old age.[17] Yet these new disciples abandon their father, an act that challenges cherished household values.

Their actions, while unusual, are not unique. Musonius Rufus urges disobeying a father who resists the study of philosophy and Zeus's command to philosophize (Lutz, *Musonius Rufus,* 16). Epictetus celebrates his freedom from household and possessions (*Diss* 3.3.5-9). Various religious and philosophical traditions in the Greco-Roman world (Philo, Essenes, Cynics, Stoics) recognized that familial obligations can be transcended by and subordinated to a greater obligation to God.[18]

But the subsequent narrative will show that they do not completely abandon economic and household ties (see 10:2; 20:20; 15:1-9), that followers do not leave everything (cf. 8:14-15). This scene (4:21-22) sets up what will emerge as a basic feature of following Jesus. Commitment to Jesus takes precedence over all other allegiances, but it does not mean that all ties are broken. Wholehearted allegiance to Jesus also involves continuing participation in socioeconomic structures.[19]

• 4:23-25

This third subsection offers a further demonstration of the transforming impact of God's empire. After the very narrow focus of 4:18-22 (beside the sea, four disciples, a call), the view broadens with regard to geography (**Jesus went throughout all Galilee**; see 4:14-16), new actions (**teaching in their synagogues, proclaiming . . . healing**), and people affected (**crowds**). Jesus teaches the non-elite. He does not have a fixed geographical center like the Jerusalem elite. He is an itinerant preacher and healer, like Cynic philosophers and miracle workers (Philostratus, *Apollonius* 3.38-39).

The first activity is **teaching in their synagogues** (cf. 9:35; 13:54). **Synagogues** were Jewish places of communal and religious activity (Introduction, section 8). Yet the word **their** (also 9:35; 10:17; 12:9; 13:54; "your" in 23:34) distances Jesus from them, hinting at the subsequent opposition (10:17; 12:9-14) and attacks on hypocrisy (6:2, 5; 23:6). Jesus' **teaching** is not reserved for academics, nor does it consist of esoteric secrets; rather it centers on ethical matters, involves his interpretation of the commandments of the law (5:17-19), and requires obedience to his teaching (28:20).[20] It can be directed to and involve disciples (5:2, 19; 28:20), but is often a public activity (11:1; 21:23; 26:55).

Jesus also **proclaims the good news of the empire/reign**. Both John (3:2) and Jesus (4:17) **proclaim**. As God's commissioned agent (1:1, 21-23), Jesus makes known God's **empire** (3:2; 4:17) or saving presence. God's action is **good news** in offering transformation, new sovereignty, commitments and community (cf. 4:18-22, 24). The Psalms, using the cognate verb "to announce good news" celebrate the **good news** of God's salvation from personal troubles and enemies (Pss 40:9; 68:11; 96:2). Deutero-Isaiah proclaims the **good news** of God's salvation from Babylon's empire (Isa 40:9; 52:7; 61:1; Josephus, *Ant* 11.65). The exiles can return home because "Your God reigns" (Isa 52:7). The term also has imperial uses. Various texts (Josephus, *JW* 4.618, 656, concerning Vespasian) and inscriptions (the Priene inscription concerning Augustus's birth) celebrate the emperor's birth, coming of age, and rule over the empire as **good news**.[21] Jesus' **good news**, as 4:23-25 will show, is not the emperor's oppressive and exploitative rule but God's life-giving empire, which brings salvation from all that resists God's purposes and claim. It is bad news for those who do not welcome God's claim.

Jesus **heals every disease and sickness among the people**. L. Wells's argument that his "healing is primarily for the anguish of the soul" goes beyond the evidence. Jesus is very concerned with physical well-being.[22] But Wells rightly indicates that his healing is multidimensional. What is its significance? In the context of the proclamations of 4:17 and 23b, Jesus' healings manifest God's life-giving empire or reign (cf. Isa 35:5-6; Matt 11:2-6).

Numerous health care systems were operative in the ancient world. Some saw sickness as resulting from physical or lifestyle factors. Plutarch's elitist view contends that sickness is caused by immoderate living and excessive pleasure ("Advice About Keeping Well," *Moralia* 129D-130A; 134C-D). The elite usually employed physicians (so Plutarch, "Advice About Keeping Well," *Moralia* 128B; 136F; 137A-B; for Herod's physicians, see Josephus, *JW* 1.657), though physicians were also available to poorer people. A medical tradition from Hippocrates to Galen trained physicians in knowledge about causes, prevention, and medicinal and surgical treatments (see Tob 2:10; 11:8; Sir 38:1-15 for Jewish variants; see *JW* 2.136 for Josephus's reference to Essene practice; see also Pliny, *NH* 20-32; Matt 9:12). A lack of success ensured physicians' ambivalent status, and numerous "quacks" added to their disrepute.[23]

Many understood **disease and sickness** to have nonphysical causes. (1) Sin was regarded as one cause (9:1-7; cf. Jn 5:14; 9:2; Philo, *Vita Cont* 1-2 [the Therapeutae]). Josephus interprets Apion's sickness and death as God's punishment for Apion's attack on Jews (*Con Ap* 2.143-44). He views the sickness and death of the "wicked" Catullus, Roman governor of Libya, in similar terms (*JW* 7.451-53). God is deemed to punish the tyrant Antiochus with sickness (4 Macc 9:5-18). Other similar causes include a person's evil eye,[24] displeasing God or a god (Deut 28:21-22, 27-28, 35), demons and other hostile cosmic forces (Tob 3:8, 17; *T. Sol.; Jub.* 10; the magic formula in the Greek Magical Papyri[25]).

(2) Social and economic structures also cause disease. Limited resources, poor technology, vulnerability to the weather, harsh taxation, overcrowding, poor hygiene, and the unequal distribution of wealth meant poor nutrition, poverty, hunger, worry, and overwork for many—prime conditions for poor health and death.[26]

(3) Social scientists have argued that in the harsh contexts of social tensions, economic exploitation, and political control, sickness can be psychosomatic. In 4:24 demon possession and paralysis are two such examples (see discussion). *Testament of Zebulon* 9:7 indicates that Gentile conquest brings sickness, tribulation, and oppression. Sickness and health are frequent metaphors for imperial control. Aristides, in praising Rome's accomplishments, credits Rome with bringing health to the nations: "one can say that the civilized world, which had been sick from the beginning as it were, has been brought by the right knowledge to a state of health" (*Roman Oration* 97). Josephus compares new armed revolts against Roman control to "the inflammation, [which] as in a sick man's body, broke out again in another quarter" (*JW* 2.264). The social and political turmoil of the war in ca. 70 is a "contagion" (*JW* 7.260; Tacitus calls Christianity a disease [*Ann* 15.44]). Rome supposedly brings health and wholeness, but this and subsequent healing scenes show how sick is the imperial world.

Some sought healing from physicians. But differences of social status, high fees, prevailing worldviews, and distrust persuaded others to seek healing from various gods and goddesses. Isis and Asklepios, with shrines or temples in many larger cities, were popular.[27] Domitian built a temple for Asklepios in

Antioch; Isis's presence is well established.[28] Numerous Hellenistic and Jewish miracle workers, exorcists, and healers were popular.[29] Apollonius of Tyana visited Antioch in the late first century (Philostratus, *Apollonius* 1.16-17; for miracles, see 3.39; 4.20, 45).[30] The Greek Magical Papyri (see above) attest a long tradition of popular "magical" potions, chants, and rituals, whereby people sought change, solace, or protection.

Jesus' healing miracles belong, then, in a diverse spectrum of means of healing. They are not unusual. They accomplish four things. (1) They restore physical wholeness and so offer the healed person the possibility of an improved way of life. (2) For some, they create new social interaction. The gospel does not usually state this effect but it can be reasonably imagined. Isolating a sick person was one way to manage disease. Distance offered protection against their curse and punishment (cf. 9:28 the demoniacs in the graveyard). Begging was a common though shameful means of support (Sir 40:28-30) if households could not support a nonworking person (20:30, beside the road outside the town). People shunned beggars (Epictetus, *Diss* 3.22.22). Healing removes the fear of becoming sick through association. A healed person can work and contribute to a household.

(3) In healing sickness and casting out demons, Jesus overcomes sin and the devil (9:2-8; 12:24) and manifests God's saving presence and empire (1:21-23; 4:17, 23; 8:17, and Isa 53:3-4; 12:24-28; cf. Ps 103:3: God "forgives all your iniquity and heals all your diseases"). The absence of disease (νόσος, *nosos*) indicates God's blessing (Exod 15:26; Deut 7:15) and the curtailing of Satan's power (*Jub.* 10:12-13). God's reign is stronger than that of the devil, demons, and sin (cf. 4:1-11; 12:28).

(4) Jesus' healings protest the current "sick" imperial world and anticipate the yet-future, complete establishment of God's reign. The absence of sickness forms part of the hope for God's new age in which God's reign removes all that which is contrary to God's purposes (*Jub.* 23:29; *1 En* 96:3; *T. Zeb.* 9:7-8; *4 Ezra* 8:52-55; *2 Bar* 73:1-3). Some expected the Messiah to establish God's reign in ending illness and bringing health (see *2 Bar* 29:6-7; 73:1-2; *4 Ezra* 7:123; 4Q521, line 12.[31] That reign, God's new creation (1:1; 14:32) is already being manifested in part in Jesus' ministry. The present world, "healed" by Rome according to Josephus and Aristides, is very sick. Jesus' actions provide healing and look to God's future action in establishing God's reign over all. The gospel views the causes of disease—namely, political oppression and unjust economic practices and social structures—in this eschatological context. Alternative social relationships (households in chs. 19-20) and practices (nonviolent resistance, 5:38-42; almsgiving, 6:2-4) provide some present relief.

• 4:24

Jesus' ministry has broad impact. **His fame spread throughout all Syria**. The reference to **Syria** continues the Gentile inclusion theme last noted in 4:15 (though a significant Jewish population existed in Syria and its capital Antioch). The reference to **Syria** may reflect the gospel's origin. **Syria** was an imperial province, administered by a legate appointed by the emperor, and the home to three or four legions (see Introduction, sections 4-10). Reports of Jesus' proclamation and demonstrations of God's empire, with their challenge to Rome's sovereignty, reach there.

A further reference to **healing** (see 4:23) follows.[32] Jesus' effectiveness in manifesting the gracious and transforming reign and salvific presence of God is underlined by **all** (also 4:23), and by piling up terms. Three general words (**the sick, those afflicted with various diseases** [repeated from 4:23], and **pains**) are followed by three more specific designations, **demoniacs, epileptics,** and **paralytics**. Disease and deformity appeared in every village and city of the empire. Each word designates personal, social, and economic misery for each victim.

The word translated **pains** (βασάνοις, *basanois*) suggests not only disease but also distress and torment from imperial power and torture by imperial tyrants (cf. Egypt and the exodus [Wis 19:4]; King Ptolemy Philopator [3 Macc 3:27]). In 4 Maccabees, where it is used thirty six times, it refers to the torture that the Seleucid Antiochus Epiphanes imposes on the old man, the seven brothers, and their mother who refuse to obey Antiochus's order to be unfaithful to God.[33] Fourth Maccabees probably originated in Jewish circles in Antioch.[34] For the gospel's audience in Antioch or elsewhere, the term might include, apart from those generally suffering under harsh conditions of daily life, people wounded in or displaced by the war in Galilee in 67 who had moved north, and/or those injured in anti-Jewish outbursts ca. 70 (Josephus, *JW* 7.41-62, 100-111). The naming of **Syria** strengthens such possibilities.

The reference to **demoniacs** (also 8:16, 28-36; 9:32; 12:22; cf. 15:22-28) recalls the devil's resistance to Jesus and God's purposes (4:1-11) and Satan's claim to be the power that controls "all the kingdoms/empires of the world" (4:8). To cast out demons is to defeat the devil's agents and to represent the defeat and rejection of Rome, the devil's ally and agent (4:8-9). Compare Eleazar's exorcism before Vespasian (Josephus, *Ant* 8.46-49).

A number of scholars relate demon possession to circumstances of oppression and colonialism, "social tensions . . . , class antagonisms rooted in economic exploitation, conflicts between traditions . . . , colonial domination and revolution."[35] The behaviors of demon possession are "personal aberrations integrally connected with the breakdown of right social relations in the community." It can be a way of coping with and/or a form of protest against harsh (crazy) circumstances, a refusal to accept and adjust to economic, social, religious, and personal demands. Labeling someone a demoniac may also be a form of social control, an attempt to subvert a threat to the status quo. Hence the elite in 9:34 and 12:24 accuse Jesus of being possessed. Jesus' exorcisms challenge attempts at control and put the exorciser in conflict with the elite.

The term **epileptics** literally means "moonstruck"[36] and reflects an understanding of the harmful effects of the moon (Ps 121:6; Deut 4:19; 17:3; cf. the English term "lunacy").[37] See the Greek Magical Papyri for invoking the moon or goddess Selene to harm people, including making them sick (PGM 4.2241-58, 2622-2707, 2785-90).[38] For the moon and demons, see Matt 17:15-20.

Malalas (*Chron* 260-61) claims that Vespasian set up Cherubim and Seraphim from the destroyed Jerusalem temple outside Antioch and a statue of four bulls in honor of Selene. He honored Selene because moonlight aided the capture of Jerusalem. Jesus' healing of **epileptics,** or "moonstruck" people, demonstrates God's control over the moon (Gen 1:14-19) in defiance of Rome's claims. Jesus overpowers the moon's power, a possible symbol of the reversal of Rome's moon-blessed success with Rome subordinated to God's sovereignty. Hippocrates (2.127-83) rejects popular understanding of this disease as "sacred or divine."

The third term names Jesus' healing of **paralytics** (8:5-13; 9:2-8). J. P. Brown suggests that this condition, like demonic possession, can be understood as a psychosomatic illness. It may reflect the overwhelming impact of imperial control, or it may be a form of resistance to the ruling elite, literally and physically refusing to do their will.[39] Contemporary medical research, and reports on Serbian imperialism in Kosovo in 1999, indicate that paralysis and muteness reflect the trauma and violence of war and occupation.[40] Jesus **healed** them (a verb that will appear sixteen times); he frees such people from the crippling, silencing impact of imperial control to a new existence in God's reign.

• 4:25

And great crowds followed him. The **crowds** (fifty times in the gospel),[41] in contrast to the elite, are frequent recipients of Jesus' compassionate ministry (9:36; 14:13-14, 15, 19, 22-23; 17:14-15; 19:2). They express amazement and some perception that God is at work in Jesus (7:29; 9:8; 15:31). Yet they lack the understanding (12:23; 13:2, 10-11; 21:8, 9, 11) and faith of disciples (8:18, 23, 26; 12:46). They also lack the hostility of the religious leaders (cf. 9:3, 8)—though the crowds will ally with the religious leaders in calling for Jesus' death (26:47; 27:15-26). They reflect the difficulty of mission in a largely rejecting world.

They **follow** Jesus, but in contrast to the commitment to Jesus of disciples (see 4:20, 22), here the verb denotes physical movement. Missing are Jesus' call and a costly response (cf. 4:18-22). The crowds follow **from Galilee, the Decapolis, Jerusalem, Judea and from beyond the Jordan** (cf. 3:5). The response is a mixed blessing. Jesus' impact is claimed to be widespread as he enacts God's commission in the occupied territory of **Galilee . . . and from beyond the Jordan** (cf. 4:15). But there are danger signals. Jesus has already encountered negative responses centered in **Jerusalem** (Herod and the religious leaders, ch. 2) and **Judea** (death, 2:1, 16, 22). Religious leaders resisted John in **Judea** at the **Jordan** (3:1-12), and he has been arrested (4:12).

CHAPTER 5

Jesus Teaches

The Sermon on the Mount Begins

Having been commissioned by God to manifest God's empire and saving presence (1:18-25), Jesus begins (4:17-11:1) his mission by announcing the presence of God's empire or saving presence (4:17), forming a new community of disciples (4:18-22), and teaching, preaching, and healing (4:23-25). Chapters 5-7 elaborate his teaching activity, while chapters 8-9 will expand on his healing.[1]

The focus of Jesus' teaching concerns the "good news of God's empire/reign" (4:17, 23; 5:3, 10, 19, 20; 6:10, 33; 7:21). The sermon is not, though, a comprehensive manual or rule book, not a step-by-step "how to" book. Rather it offers a series of illustrations, or "for examples," or "case studies" of life in God's empire, visions of the identity and way of life that result from encountering God's present and future reign. The sermon is direction-pointing, more than giving commands, suggestive and illustrative rather than comprehensive. Jesus' subsequent discourses (chs. 10, 13, 18, 24-25) and actions will elaborate this vision of life in God's empire.

The scenes in 4:17-25 have indicated that God's empire, present in a world dominated by *Pax Romana,* is disruptive and transformative. The sermon sketches an alternative world marked not by oppression but by restructured societal relationships, and by redistributed and accessible resources.[2] It resocializes disciples into a world of justice (5:6, 10, 20; 6:1, 33) which differs from their previous life (4:18-22) and which conflicts and contrasts with the values, commitments, and practices of the majority who have not encountered it.

In grasping the audience's imagination with these scenarios, the sermon shapes the perspective, practices, and character of the community of disciples, training them to discern and live in ways faithful to and imitative of the reign's just presence and future. Given that these commitments and practices often differ from current cultural practices, the sermon portrays and invites its audience to a voluntarily marginal way of life as a minority community.

This approach also accounts for the sermon's so-called double audience. In 5:1-2 both the crowds and disciples are present, yet Jesus seems to distinguish them and favor the disciples. Yet the crowds do not go away but overhear the sermon and react favorably to it (7:28-29). Given that the disciples and crowds experienced Jesus and the reign in different ways in 4:18-25 (see on 4:25), how do we understand the presence of both groups? In offering a vision of life based on God's empire, the sermon informs and forms disciples further about this existence to which they have committed themselves. For the crowd, the sermon provides the "rest of the story." Having experienced God's gracious presence in healing, they now hear God's vision of life based on God's reign. God's grace precedes God's demand.

For those who belong to the minority and marginal community of disciples of Jesus, the sermon continues the gospel's formational and envisioning work. It shapes and strengthens the community's identity and lifestyle as a small community in a dominant culture that does not share that culture's fundamental convictions. The community is reminded that interactions with God, with one another, and with the surrounding society are important aspects of their existence which embraces all of life, present and future. Mission to, love for, and tension with the surrounding society mark their participation in this society. Integrity or wholeness defines their relationships with one another. Prayer, accountability, and the active doing of God's will are features of their relationship with God and experience of God's empire.

5:1-2—INTRODUCTION

• **5:1-2**

These verses establish the sermon's speaker, audiences, and physical setting. **When he saw the crowds, he went up the mountain.** Jesus, not named, is the subject of the two verbs. The absence of a subject requires the audience to review the previous material to locate the subject in 4:17. This review links the sections and underlines Jesus' identity. Jesus, son of David and Abraham (1:1), the Christ (1:17), commissioned by God to manifest God's saving presence (1:21, 23), King of the Jews and a ruler (2:2, 6), God's child (2:15; 3:17), opposed and endangered by the ruling elites (ch. 2), witnessed to by John as the coming judge (3:11-12), tempted by the devil (4:1-11), the light (4:16), the one who announces and manifests God's reign (4:17-25)—this one speaks the sermon. It expresses his mission and God-given commission (1:21-23).

Jesus **went up the mountain**, a location invested with multiple meanings (see 14:23; 15:29-31; 17:1; 21:1; 24:3; 28:16-20). The devil offered Jesus "all the kingdoms/empires of the world" on a **mountain** (see 4:8). By contrast, on this **mountain**, Jesus will manifest God's reign/empire. Mountains are holy places. Jupiter/ Zeus and the gods dwell on Mt. Olympus. On mountains God is revealed (Abraham [Gen 22:2, 14]; Elijah and Mt. Carmel and Mt. Horeb [1 Kgs 18:18-46; 19:8-18]; see also *2 Bar* 13:1 [Zion]; *Apoc. Ab.* 9:12; 12:2). The phrase **went up the mountain** refers nine times to Moses going up Sinai to receive the Decalogue (Exod 19:3; 24:12, 13, 18; 34:2, 4; Deut 9:9; 10:1, 3).[3]

Jesus relives Moses' and Israel's experience, escaping from Egypt (2:15), passing through water (3:13-17), encountering temptation (4:1-11). Now he brings God's revelation.

The phrase **went up the mountain** also refers six times to Mt. Zion, including God's new age in which the nations will come to Zion and learn of God's ways (Isa 2:3; Mic 4:2; also Ps 24:3; Hag 1:8; 1 Macc 5:54; 7:33). Thus the theme of Gentile inclusion continues (1:1, Abraham; 1:2-17, women; 2:1-12, the magi; 4:24a, 15). Jesus **sat down**, a teaching position for Ezekiel (Ezek 8:1), but more commonly kings **sit** to exercise power and rule, frequently in the service of death (1 Kgs 1:13, 46; 2:12, 19, etc.; Matt 27:19 [Pilate]; Suetonius, *Nero* 13). By contrast, in *1 En* 25:3 God sits on a mountain and reigns at the end. So does Jesus in 19:28; 25:31. King Jesus (cf. 2:2) manifests God's life-giving empire as he **taught them** (the same verb as 4:23).

The phrase **his disciples came to him** provides the first use of **disciples** to identify Jesus' followers. In the Greco-Roman and Jewish worlds the term refers to learners and adherents of a recognized master.[4] Who are **his disciples**? The four brothers called in 4:18-22 and distinguished from the **crowds** in 4:23-25 (and in 5:1) are the obvious candidates, though the list of twelve disciples in chapter 10 indicates that the term is a more open one. While the focus is on the twelve, other characters behave as disciples. So Joseph in 1:18-2:23 and the faithful women in 27:55, 61; 28:1. The term denotes any followers of Jesus. On **came**, see 4:3, 11.

5:3-12—THE BEATITUDES

Jesus' vision of life in God's empire begins with nine beatitudes. This form was widely used in the Greco-Roman world and Jewish wisdom and apocalyptic writings with various functions and contexts.[5] Beatitudes concern not just emotions (the misleading "happy are"), not just personal qualities, but primarily God's favor for certain human actions and situations (Ps 1:1-2). In apocalyptic works they declare God's future transformation or reversal of present dismal circumstances (*1 En* 58:2-3; *Pss. Sol.* 17:44). Beatitudes are directed to the present and future ages.

K. C. Hanson relates beatitudes to the important values of honor and shame. They affirm "conditions and behaviors" which God regards as honorable or esteemed and which are to be practiced by the audience.[6] While they are declarations of favor, they also function as exhortations by identifying favored behavior, and as promises proclaiming God's future actions.[7] Being merciful or peacemaking (5:7, 9) is affirmed and exhorted, while mourning (5:4) is not an ethical behavior to be emulated, but awaits reversal. The beatitudes reassure those who already experience the circumstances or manifest the particular behavior that God's favor is or will be on them. They thereby mark out features of a faithful and favored or blessed and honorable group. They constitute, affirm, and challenge a community's distinctive identity and practices.[8]

The beatitudes are organized into two groups. The first group consists of

four beatitudes (5:3-6). They have thirty-six words, as do vv. 7-10 (without
5:11-12); they close with a reference to righteousness, as does the second group
(5:6, 10); they are influenced by Isa 61 and are bound together by an allitera-
tion of the letter p (or π in Greek; "Blessed are the poor in spirit, the plaintive,
the powerless, and those who pine for righteousness"[9]).

Influenced by Isa 61, these four beatitudes describe not personal qualities
but oppressive situations of distress or bad fortune, which are honored or
esteemed because God's reign reverses them. This reversal is under way in
Jesus' ministry but is not yet complete. The first four beatitudes critique the
political, economic, social, religious and personal distress that results from the
powerful elite who enrich their own position at the expense of the rest. They
delineate the terrible consequences of Roman power.[10]

The remaining four, and the elaboration in vv. 11-12, concern human actions
which, inspired by the experience of God's reign in vv. 3-6, are honored or
esteemed because they express God's transforming reign until God's completion of it. Fundamental to all the beatitudes is the establishment of God's justice
or righteousness by removing oppressive societal relationships and inadequate
distribution of resources.

• 5:3

Blessed are poor in spirit. **Blessed** expresses God's favor and blessing not
on poverty but on "the people who" are poor. The **poor** are not to be spiritualized either by softening the referent ("the voluntary poor") or making it figura-
tive ("the fainthearted," "the humble"). They are the literal, physical poor, the
destitute, those who live in social and economic hardship, lacking adequate
resources, exploited and oppressed by the powerful (Lev 19:10, 15; Prov 14:31;
28:15) and despised by the elite.[11] They include the stranger, the orphan, the
widow, the needy, the physically maimed (blind, lame), and the powerless (cf.
Deut 24:19; Job 29:12-16), who are powerless before the unrighteous, the
wicked, the greedy, the sinners, and the oppressor, who inflict harm on them (Ps
10). They inhabit the Roman (and every) world, including cities like Antioch.

To be **poor in spirit** does not mean "patience" or "humility" in piously
accepting poverty. This common claim (*anawim* piety) runs counter to the conviction that God will save the poor (cf. Isa 61:1-2).[12] More helpful are comparable phrases like "pure in heart" (Ps 24:4) or "the crushed in spirit" (Ps 34:18).
The "heart" is the sphere of the purity or of being crushed. When there is
poverty in the human **spirit**, the spirit is like economic poverty: without
resources and hope, subject to larger forces.

The **poor in spirit**, then, are those who are economically poor and whose
spirits or being are crushed by economic injustice. They can see no hope, but
they know the corrosive effect of hopeless poverty. They are described in several psalms as oppressed by the wicked. Even God seems to have forgotten
them (Ps 10:1-13 [hope comes in v. 14]; 34:17, 22-23; 68:1-2; 82; Job 24). They
do not benefit from God's promised salvation but "fret" because of the wicked
(37:1). They are exhorted to hope because in "yet a little while" God's salvation will come (37:10).

Who are such people? They are the people named in 4:18-22, locked into an exploitative economic (taxation and debt) system with no control over their own destiny. They are the sick, the demon possessed, and moonstruck of 4:24 whose illness means they bear in their very bodies the harmful effects of the imperial system. Denied justice, adequate resources, wholeness, and subject to the power of the ruling elite, there is no hope of change.

Unless God intervenes.[13] Jesus' proclamation of **God's empire** (see on 3:2; 4:17) and demonstration of it in healings (see 4:23, and ch. 8) begin a reversal even now as the present tense indicates (**theirs is**). Jesus' power over demons, sin, and misfortune reveals that the status quo is not ultimate and anticipates the completion of God's purposes. Jesus instigates a new community with the hope of a future heaven and earth in which God's will is done (6:10; 19:28). When **God's rule**, now under way in Jesus, is completed, there will be no **poor in spirit**. The beatitude blesses the ending of current imperial structures through God's action.

• 5:4

The declaration that the hopeless poor are **blessed** (see 5:3) because God is in the process of liberating them is so startling that it is repeated. **Blessed are those who mourn.** They do not lament their own sins, but, on the basis of Isa 61:1-3 (in which the **poor** are also named), they **mourn** or lament the destructive impact of imperial powers such as Babylon (and Rome) which oppress God's people. So they **mourn** evildoers (Ps 34:11), the powerful elite (Isa 3:26; Jer 4:28; 14:2), other nations (Isa 16:9; 19:8), the imperial tyrant Antiochus Epiphanes (1 Macc 1:27; 2:14, 39). Note the impact of Assyria, Babylon, and Herod in 2:18, where Rachel **mourns** their devastating actions. They **mourn** the misrule of God's world by the devil's agents (see 4:8).

Greco-Roman consolation literature generally disapproves of **mourning** as the practice of the uneducated masses. Plutarch employs traditional themes in consoling his wife ("Consolation to His Wife," *Moralia* 608A-612B). He urges restraint in grieving for their two-year-old daughter (608C, F-609A, 609F-610A, 612A-B), and acceptance of Fortune's lot (610D-611AF).[14] But in Matt 5:4 the view of oppressive rule is "from below," the view of those who suffer the pain of unjust societal relationships, and not "from above," the elite who benefit from it.[15] Oppression is not normative. It should be mourned.

Jesus promises that oppression and mourning are not the final words. **They shall be comforted**. The future passive verb suggests a divine action that will end oppression, establish the justice of restored resources and relationships, render mourning unnecessary, and turn sadness into joy (Isa 60:20; 61:1-3; 66:10). The future tense (**shall be**), rather than the present (**is**) in v. 3, points to the future completion of God's empire.

• 5:5

A third situation of desperation is evoked. **Blessed are the meek.** Jesus partially cites Ps 37:11, 22, 29. The unfortunate English word **meek** does not mean

"wimp," "gentle," "doormat," "mild," or "passive." In Ps 37, it names the powerless and humiliated who are entreated to trust in God to save them from "the
wicked" (vv. 1, 9, 10, 12, 13, 14, 16, 17, 20, 21, 28, 32, 34, 35, 38, 40). The
wicked are violent against the poor and needy (vv. 14, 32), borrow but do not
pay back (v. 21), and oppress them (v. 35). But the poor are not to "fret" or imitate the violent wicked. They are not to take justice into their own hands and
effect their own revenge (37:6). Though they are beaten down by unjust economic practices, their strategy is to live an alternative, righteous lifestyle and to
look for God's response, even while God seems slow to act. To be meek is to
renounce retribution and to live faithfully and expectantly. Jesus is among the
meek (11:29; 21:5).[16]

God's promise is that **they will inherit the earth**. This is not to be spiritualized. God, not the meek, **will** overthrow the elite so that all may use **the earth**
(Ps 37:10-11). The present inequitable access to land, based on exploitative
societal relationships, will end. The earth and its resources belong to God (Gen
1; Ps 24:1). As stewards, humans are to nurture it (Gen 1:28-31) as a basis for
a community in which all have access to necessary resources. Resisting economic exploitation, the sabbatical year principle authorized the land to lie fal-
low every seventh year.[17] Resisting massive accumulation of land through taxes
and defaults on high-interest loans, which deprived people of access to necessary resources for living, the jubilee year, every fifty years, returned ownership
of land to kinship groups (Lev 25). The land belongs to God; all people are tenants (Lev 25:23). The issue is sovereignty and the just nature of human community.

When God rules, God will redistribute access to this fundamental resource
(Isa 60:1-2; *1 En* 5:7). The present inequitable use of land will finally end as
the present heaven and earth pass away (5:18; 24:35) and God creates a new
world (19:28). **Earth**, then, refers not only to the land of Israel but to all of
God's creation (so also Matt 5:13, 18; 6:10 etc.). The beatitude envisions God's
empire as it begins to transform the status quo. It challenges a system secured
by Roman power which furthered the interests of local landowning elite at the
expense of peasants forced into a subsistence existence. Rome's way is not the
divine will.

• 5:6

Blessed are those who hunger and thirst for righteousness/ justice. People literally **hunger and thirst** because of unjust practices concerning land,
access to resources, taxes, debt. Dissatisfied with the status quo of exploitative
social relations, those who **hunger and thirst** know that the divine will is not
done on earth (6:10). They cry out for God's help (Ps 107:5-6), for God's presence and empire to liberate them (Ps 42:1-2, 9).

They long for **righteousness/justice**, for God's action to put all things in just
relationship (see 3:15). God's justice punishes a structure that deprives people
of bread and life (*1 En* 62-63, the landowners and rulers). **Righteousness or
justice** signifies right societal relationships and access to adequate resources

for living (5:5, land; 6:11, bread). Isaiah 61:3 sees it as God's salvific action, which establishes God's will (cf. Isa 61:8, 11). This action involves eschatological judgment on the oppressors and wicked who resist God's will and reign, a task entrusted to Jesus (3:11-12; 25:31-45). God's action shapes human activity in accord with God's reign (just or righteous action). For **righteousness/ justice**, see 1:19; 3:15; also 5:10, 20; 6:1, 33. The future passive **they will be satisfied** promises God's reign over all (as in 5:4).

"Those who hunger and thirst for a justice that has been denied them include people who have no reason to hope, no cause for joy, and no access to the resources of this world. Such needs will be satisfied by the eschatological reversals that God's rule brings."[18] These beatitudes provide a vision of the people and circumstances among which God's empire is already at work, and with what sort of outcome. The vision shapes a community that lives in the now and not yet of God's empire, on the basis of and oriented to the completion of God's disruptive and transforming reign.

• **5:7-12**

The focus in the second group of beatitudes moves from the circumstances which God is reversing to human actions that manifest God's empire. These and similar actions (this is not a complete list) enact God's purposes for just societal relationships and access to resources. Such a way of life is blessed now and rewarded by God in the future, at the completion of God's purposes. That is, while the "empire of the heavens" is *God*'s rule, this emphasis on human actions indicates a partnership between God and those living in accord with God's purposes.

• **5:7**

Blessed (see 5:3) **are the merciful**. Being **merciful** is a traditional emphasis (Prov 14:21; Hos 6:6; Tob 4:5-7). God's empire is not oppressive but transformative and life-giving (cf. Exod 34:6). Those who encounter it are to be **merciful**. They provide the destitute with necessary economic resources (Matt 5:42; 6:2-4; 25:31-46). Mercy forgives (6:12, 14-15) and extends love to enemies (5:38-48) and other marginals, foreigners, and women (15:22). It marks God's empire. Jesus' healings (9:27; 17:15; 20:30-31) and exorcisms (15:22) demonstrate mercy (cf. 4:23-25 and 9:36), as do his meals with social outcasts (9:13) and his allowing the hungry to eat (12:7) when religious leaders disapprove.

To be **merciful** is not desirable according to the gospel's religious leaders and some Greco-Roman philosophical traditions.[19] But it is God's will (9:13; 12:7), a "weightier matter" of God's law not to be neglected (23:23). By imitating Jesus, disciples live in a way that the dominant culture does not value.

The merciful are promised that **they will receive mercy**. Most interpreters rightly suggest that the future passive (**will be mercied**) and prominent eschatological scenarios in 5:3-6 indicate a promise of God's mercy in the future judgment. But God's empire is also active already. The beatitude shapes a way of life in the meantime, a community of practical and active mercy.

• 5:8

Blessed are the pure in heart. In Ps 24:4, the **pure in heart** are worshipers with clean hands who are not committed to what is false and do not swear deceitfully.[20] The linking of the external (worship and "clean hands") and the internal (the pure heart and commitment to what is not false) indicates that integrity, or the consistency of inner disposition and outer action, is the issue. The **heart** is the core or center of a person's willing, thinking, knowing, deciding, and doing, given either to God or to some other (Deut 6:4-19), such as money (Matt 6:21). The **heart** may be a place of lust (5:27-28) or love (22:37). Disciples are **pure in heart**. Having encountered God's empire in Jesus, they live a life that manifests it in actions such as mercy, justice, and peacemaking. They know nothing of hypocrisy (7:5; 15:7; ch. 23). External actions must not mask false commitment (6:1-18) but must be consistent with internal commitments and motivations (7:16-20). They are promised that **they will see God.** To **see God** is not possible for humans in the present era, as Moses attests (Exod 3:6; 19:21; 33:20, 23), but it is promised to the righteous (Pss 11:7; 17:15) presumably in the completion of God's purposes (13:43). It is an image of intimate, face-to-face encounter with God.

• 5:9

Blessed are the peacemakers. This peace is not Epictetus's calm detachment from surrounding circumstances (*Diss* 3.13.9-13), and certainly not the empire's "peace with bloodshed" (to misquote Tacitus, *Ann* 1.10.4). It is God's cosmic peace in which all things are in just relation with each other and their creator.

Rome's peace (*Pax Romana*) consisted of Rome's "gift" of order, security, and prosperity, guaranteed by the emperor as commander of Rome's military (cf. Seneca, *De Clem* 1.4.1-3). G. Zampaglione notes that "almost all the Roman writers agreed that spreading peace . . . meant subjecting other peoples to Roman dominion," an expression of the "proud conviction" that Rome had been "vested with the mission of imposing [its] laws and way of life on the rest of the world" (see Introduction, section 9; Matt 27:11).[21] Inscriptions from Priene and Halicarnassus celebrate this peace. Pliny calls it "a gift of the gods" (*NH* 2.117; 27.3; also Pliny the Younger, *Pan,* passim; Plutarch, "Precepts of Statecraft," *Moralia* 824C-D).[22] Vespasian (69-79) built a temple of peace near the forum in Rome (Suetonius, *Vespasian* 9; Josephus, *JW* 7.158-62; cf. the "Ara Pacis Augustae" dedicated in 9 B.C.E.). Vespasian, Titus, and Domitian used coins to celebrate the epiphany of the divinity "peace" in their reigns.[23] Several poets celebrate the emperor Domitian (81-96) as the restorer of peace (Statius, *Silv* 4.1.11-16; 4.3.134; Silius Italicus, *Punica* 14.684-85; Martial, *Epig* 9.70.7-8; 9.101.21).[24] Philo refers to Augustus and Tiberius as peace bringer and guardian (*Gaium* 141, 144-47).

K. Wengst argues that claims about the benefits of Rome's peace reflect the elite's perspectives, not those "from below." He notes the great military, political, social, economic, cultural, and religious cost of a peace based on military might and sanctioned by the will of the god/s, which ensures the elite's social and cultural domination and the economic exploitation of land and resources. Peace "for whom?" is the question.[25] Zampaglione complains that, despite the revulsion for war that Seneca could express (*Ep* 95.30-31) and the appreciation for peace expressed by the Plinys, Dio Chrysostom, Plutarch, and Aristides, "war, as a brutal means of expansion and subjugation of other nations, was not subjected to adequate criticism by the new governing classes."[26] They had no interest in dismantling the ideology and practices that sustained their elitist existence.

In this world, God's reign makes a different **peace**. For Philo God is "peace-maker and peace-keeper . . . who creates plenty and fertility and an abundance of other good things (*Spec Leg* 2.192). Psalm 72 pictures a king establishing God's righteousness and justice by crushing the oppressor and defending the poor and the needy (72:4), by having pity for, not violently exploiting, the weak and needy (72:12-14). Righteousness (God's salvific will) and peace (whole-ness) result (72:7). **Peace** is the well-being that arises from God's will for and rule over the earth. This is not a natural state. It is God's gift and work which will have an eschatological completion. Some Jewish traditions acknowledge a place for war and violence in overthrowing Rome and establishing the "eternal peace" of God's empire (*2 Bar* 39:5; 40:1-2; 72:2-6; 73:1-5), while others cel-ebrate the end of war (*4 Ezra* 13:30-35; cf. the eschatological priest in *T. Levi* 18:4). Peace consists not of exploitation but of all things cosmically in right relation to God. **Peacemakers** enact not the empire's will but God's merciful reign, living toward this wholeness and well-being and against any power that hinders or resists it.

They will be called (by God, a future passive) **children of God**. On the verb **call** as a designation of God's electing and salvific work, see 4:21. To **make peace** is to live as God does (5:48) and as Jesus, child or son of God, does in announcing and enacting God's empire. To act like God is to be one of God's **children** now (5:45; 6:9), which will mean intimacy with God in the future completion of God's purposes. God's children are shaped not by ethnicity (cf. Deut 14:1) but by imitating God (cf. Matt 3:9).

• 5:10-12

Blessed are those who are persecuted for justice's sake. The just way of life envisioned in 5:3-9 challenges the status quo, its commitments, power structures, and beneficiaries. God's reign or **justice/righteousness** seeks dif-ferent societal relationships and an equitable distribution of and access to resources. The empire will certainly strike back, as in chapter 2 (also 5:44; 10:16-23) and as in a tradition of the persecuted righteous, who are "inconve-nient to us" (Pss 35; 37; Wis 2:12-24). The crucified Jesus belongs to this tra-dition. The perfect passive participle indicates past and continuing persecution.

The persecution is **on account of righteousness/justice**, both God's salvific **empire** exhibited by Jesus (5:3-6; **on my account**, 5:11) and human actions which embody that **reign** (5:7-9). See 3:15; 5:6 (on justice/**righteousness**); 3:2; 4:17, 23; 5:3 (on **reign/empire of the heavens**).

The persecution is not an empire-wide policy. Rather its expression, as 5:11-

12 elaborates by directly addressing the audience in the second, not the third, person, is local, but not to be taken lightly. **Blessed are you when people revile you and persecute you and utter all kinds of evil against you falsely on my account.** The verb **revile** can mean physical violence, even death, as its association with "kill," "crucify," and "scourge" in 23:34 indicates. Verbal violence (**utter**) seeks to destroy one's honor and integrity (cf. 5:8) by slander and defaming.

Disciples respond to persecution not by giving up, not by accommodation, not by retaliation: **Rejoice and be glad**. The next clause explains (**for**) the imperative, **your reward is great in heaven**. God's **reward** is not earned but is God's just response to the faithfulness that the disciples exhibit. They will participate in the completion of God's purposes, enjoying the fullness of God's presence and empire. Reward is not different in kind; it continues and intensifies the communion with God experienced already in the faithful service of God.[27] That eschatological goal puts the present in perspective and renders it bearable.

Nor is this persecution new or surprising. It is the way of the world in response to those who live God's claim and gift, **for in the same way they persecuted the prophets who were before you**. The persecution of the prophets is well attested (Neh 9:26; 1 Kgs 18:4, 13; 19:10, 14; 2 Chr 36:15-21; *Lives of the Prophets* 1:1; 2:1; 3:2; 6:2; 7:2; etc.; *Ascen. Is.* 1:9; 5:1-16), and the gospel will return to the theme repeatedly (13:57-58; 21:35-36; 22:6; 23:29-32, 34-37). On John, see 3:1-12; 4:12; and 14:1-12.

While the link does not make disciples **prophets**, it does ally them in the difficult role of speaking and enacting God's claim on their society which does not care for the divine voice. Disciples, like prophets, know a liminal role (Introduction, section 10). They live in but at odds with their dominant culture. Yet they cannot retreat from it because they have a God-given mission to it and in it.

5:13-16—SALT AND LIGHT

Two more images of the communal identity and way of life which follow from encountering God's empire express the community of disciples' difficult and distinct task of mission to a hostile world: salt (5:13) and light (5:14-16).

• 5:13
The second person direct address to disciples of 5:10-11 continues with the emphatic plural and present tense **You are the salt of the earth**. The image of **salt** is polyvalent: Sir 39:26 identifies "salt" as one of "the basic necessities of human life." It seasons food in Job 6:6. In Lev 2:13 and Ezek 43:24 salt and sacrifice are linked. Elisha uses salt to purify drinking water (2 Kgs 2:19-23). In Ezra 4:14 sharing salt seems to suggest loyalty (so also "salt of the covenant" in Lev 2:13 and Num 18:19).

As **salt of the earth**, the community of disciples, not the ruling elite or the synagogue, is to live this flavoring, purifying, sacrificial way of life committed to the world's well-being and loyal to God's purposes. The **earth** is its sphere of action and the object of its mission. **Earth** (5:5, 18, 35; 6:10, 19) belongs to God (Ps 24:1; Lev 25:23) but its inhabitants do not do the divine will (6:10) since the devil has usurped authority (4:8). This is where disciples live, in the midst of the poor in spirit, the mourning, the powerless, and the hungry and thirsty, dominated and exploited by the ruling elite (5:3-6). It is where the community embodies God's empire in mercy, purity, peacemaking and persecution as it lives its alternative existence (5:7-12).

Such engagement brings its challenges. Salt can cease to be salt. **If salt has lost its taste** (the translation is difficult; a more literal and better translation is, **if salt becomes foolish), how can its saltiness be restored?** Saltiness cannot be restored. But it can be lost by being overwhelmed by or mixed with larger quantities of other materials.[28] The translation **becomes foolish** suggests how this might happen. This verb and its cognate noun (fool) refer to behavior that is contrary to God's will (Isa 32:5-6; 44:24-25, esp. 25; Jer 5:21; 11-16, esp. 14; Sir 16:23; 22:12).[29] The community of disciples loses its identity as **salt** when it ceases to live in the world on the basis of God's reign as described in 5:3-12. The result is that **it is no longer good for anything, but is thrown out and trampled under foot** (literally, "treated with disdain by the people"). **People**, as in 4:19, denotes nondisciples who render the salt ineffective. The verse warns disciples in mission (5:14a) against being so overwhelmed, so compromised, so unfaithful that no transforming work is done. The world which disciples seek to save destroys them.

• 5:14-16

A second image identifying the disciples essentially emphasizes the point, continuing the second person plural, present, emphatic direct address: **You are the light of the world**. See 4:16 for light as the image of Jesus' mission in the darkness and death of Galilee ruled by imperial power. Disciples continue his mission of manifesting God's empire and saving presence. Disciples do not exist for themselves.

They continue the task given to Israel. In Isa 42:6; 49:6, Israel is "a light to the nations." Cicero describes Rome as a "light to the whole world" (*In Cat* 4.11). Statius and Domitian describe Domitian as light (see 4:16). But here Jesus' disciples are God's agents in mission to the **world**, created by God (Gen 2:1) but in 4:8 under the devil's control (cf. 13:38).

Two scenarios emphasize this mission identity and activity. **A city on a hill cannot be hid**. Some have seen a reference to the present or new Jerusalem on Mt. Zion, to which all people will be drawn (Isa 2:2).[30] If the Matthean audience lives in Antioch, it could refer to that city on the slopes of Mt. Silpius. But equally it could refer to any city.

In 5:15, the opposite point is made in the household sphere. It is possible, but unnatural, to hide a light. **No one after lighting a lamp puts it under the bushel basket but on the lampstand and it gives light to all in the house**.

Verse 16 supplies the application and exhortation. **So let your light shine before others/people so that they may see your good works**. The **others/ people** (5:13) are the **world**, Jew and Gentile, male and female, the powerless and the powerful, the arena and focus of the community's mission (4:19). Presumably **light shines** as disciples live in the way outlined in 5:3-12. Further **good deeds** are outlined in 5:21-48.

The impact is that **others/people see** God's empire manifested in their actions. To **see** does not indicate spectators but those who discern (2:2; 4:16; 13:10-17; 28:1) and encounter (5:8) God's saving presence. They will **give glory to your Father in heaven**. To **give glory** is to respond with worship (contrast the devil's plea for worship in 4:9-10). To enable others to **give glory** to God is the very purpose of the community's existence (ch. 10; 28:18-20).

God, whose sphere is **heaven** and whose reign is manifested by Jesus (4:17), is known as **your Father**. This is the first use in the gospel of this very important image for God, an image common in the Sermon as Jesus addresses disciples (see 5:45, 48; 6:1, 4, 6, 8, 9, 14, 15, 18, 26, 32; 7:11, 21; 23:9).[31] Jewish traditions associated the image with the formation and obedience of God's people (Deut 32:6; Isa 63:16; Jer 3:19-20; Mal 1:16; Tob 13:4; Philo, *Gaium* 115 ["Father and Maker of the world"]). Conjoining imperial and patriarchal power, it was commonly used of Jupiter/Zeus (Musonius Rufus 16 ["the common Father of all people and gods"]; Epictetus, *Diss* 1.37-41 ["Father, King, Protector of Cities, Guardian of the Race"[32]]), and emperors such as Augustus and Vespasian (Seneca, *De Clem* 1.14.2-3 ["Father of his country"]; Suetonius, *Vespasian* 12) and Domitian (Statius, *Silv* 3.4.48; 4.1.17 ["renowned father of the world"]; see Introduction, section 9). It denoted origin, kinship, loyalty, and protection.

Like **empire**, **Father** at first glance does not seem to be a positive image for God, if the patriarchal and authoritarian father of the political realm and ancient androcentric household is in view (see chs. 19-20). The image occurs, however, after four chapters that have presented God as resisting oppressive power structures and as manifesting mercy and life (cf. 7:13-14). The image is then defined by this context and by subsequent material (cf. 5:45-48).

What do these two images of **salt** and **light** contribute? They emphasize the missional identity and lifestyle of disciples. While participation in God's empire is blessed, it mandates an alternative way of life that challenges the status quo. This is a costly demand for a minority and marginal community, vulnerable to being overpowered by, or accommodating itself to, the dominant culture. The two images strengthen that identity and direct its way of life in a hostile context.

5:17-20—JESUS INTERPRETS SCRIPTURE

More examples of the identity and way of life created by God's empire will follow in 5:21-48. But first comes this difficult section concerning Jesus' interpretation of "the law and the prophets." This section seems to interrupt the vision of God's empire articulated in 5:3-16, 21-48, but it is an integral part of this chapter. Several factors make it necessary.

1. Jesus has not articulated the relationship between his vision of God's empire and the scriptural tradition with which the gospel's audience is familiar. Or, to put it in other terms, since life in the reign is a righteous or just life (so 5:10, 20), what is the basis for the justice that Jesus teaches? Verses 17-20 attest the importance of the scriptures.

2. The scriptural tradition has not been absent from 5:3-16. Frequently Jesus cites, alludes to, or evokes verses or images from the scriptures. How Jesus uses and interprets the scriptural tradition needs to be made explicit.

3. Nor has the scriptural tradition been absent from chs. 1-4. Various events in Jesus' conception, birth, and life "fulfill the scriptures" (cf. 1:22-23; 2:15 etc.). He has debated them with the devil (4:1-11). How does Jesus' teaching relate to the scriptures?

4. The six examples of life shaped by God's empire set out in 5:21-48 derive *explicitly* from the scriptures—or, more accurately, from Jesus' interpretation of the scriptures. On what basis does Jesus interpret scripture? What authority does it (and he) have? This section (5:17-20) prepares for 5:21-48 by establishing that Jesus interprets, and does not abolish, scripture. One outcome of this formulation is the impossibility of calling 5:21-48 "antitheses."

5. The formulation of 5:17 ("Do not think . . .") suggests a possible response to criticisms made by opponents of the community of disciples. Perhaps an issue in its alienation from the synagogue involved Jesus' interpretation of scripture (see Introduction, section 8). Perhaps some thought Jesus' teaching undermined the authority of the scriptures. In the post-70 era, various Jewish groups debated questions about the meaning and practice of scripture and about the authority to interpret. This section asserts answers not for the benefit of outsiders but to reassure the community of disciples that Jesus taught God's will, and that he is the definitive interpreter of the tradition. His vision of life in God's empire is reliable and binding.

• 5:17

The negative imperative **Do not think** counters a mistaken perspective, namely, that Jesus' mission (**I have come**[33]) is **to abolish the law and the prophets**. **Abolish** means "destroy" (as in the destruction of the temple in 24:2; 26:61; 27:40, Matthew's only other uses of the verb) or in a legal context the annulling or making invalid of, or the refusal to "recognize and implement,"[34] scripture as a binding authority (2 Macc 2:22; 4:11). D. Balch observes that the verb appears as "a key term in Greek political discussion of a state's or a people's constitution and laws," affirming that the founder's constitution is binding on the people's entire history even when it must be revised.[35]

The law and the prophets are the scriptures, the Mosaic Pentateuch and the prophets (so Sirach, prologue [three times]; 2 Macc 15:9; 4 Macc 18:10; Rom 3:21; Luke 16:16; Matt 7:12; 11:13; 22:40). Jesus' disclaimer that he does not

abolish scripture coheres with the gospel's use of scripture to define his mission: 1:21 alludes to Ps 130:8, while 1:23 cites Isa 7:14.

Jesus' denial is repeated for emphasis (**I have come not to abolish them**) and contrasted with an affirmative declaration **but to fulfill them**. How does he fulfill them?[36] (1) The verb (πληρόω, *plēroō*) means more than simply "do" or obey the scriptures, for which Matthew prefers verbs like ποιέω (*poieō,* "do") and τηρέω (*tēreō,* "keep"). (2) Nor can it mean that Jesus brings into being something that was only promised or foreshadowed in the past. The use of Isa 7:14 (Matt 1:23) to refer to Hezekiah's birth or Hos 11:1 (Matt 2:15) to refer to the exodus renders this impossible. (3) Some have suggested that Jesus fulfills the law and prophets in teaching and doing love (22:34-40). But while Paul makes this claim (Rom 13:8-10; Gal 5:14), the verb πληρόω (*plēroō*) is absent from Jesus' teaching about love in Matt 22:34-40.

(4) Apart from 5:17, the verb appears fifteen times (see 3:15), twelve of which introduce a scriptural citation (1:22; 2:15, 17, 23; 4:14; 8:17; 12:17; 13:35; 21:4; 26:54, 56; 27:9). And in 11:13 **the law and the prophets** form the subject of the verb "prophesied." These two observations suggest that the gospel understands the scriptures in a double prophetic sense. They address their own age and circumstances (see, e.g., 1:22-23; 4:14), and they point to God's future salvific action, which is now dawning in Jesus' ministry. Jesus **fulfills** the scriptures by implementing or accomplishing God's previously revealed, salvific will in his proclamation of God's empire and in his actions.

Jesus recognizes and implements scripture as a binding authority. Interpreted in relation to Jesus, the scriptures are the authoritative source of the justice or righteousness (5:20) which he teaches (cf. 5:21-48).

• 5:18
Jesus states a consequence (**for**) of the recognition that the scriptures are understood in relation to his life and actions. The introductory **truly I tell you** is a legitimation formula which asserts the authority of one of greater status.[37] He asserts the scripture's authority: **not one letter, not one stroke of a letter, will pass from the law**. The exact meaning of **letter** and **stroke** is not clear— Is **letter** (literally, **iota**) the Greek letter or the Hebrew *yodh?* Either way, he values even the smallest letters or markings.

This assertion of the scripture's lasting authority is qualified by two temporal clauses. The first evokes the end of the age: **until heaven and earth pass away**. This is not a synonym for "never," since they do pass away at the end of the current created order dominated by evil (so also Isa 51:6; 65:17; *1 En* 45:4-5; 2 Pet 3:10-12; Rev 20:11; 21:1; cf. Matt 5:5; 19:28; 24:35). A time limit for the scriptures is set. They are authoritative until God's empire is established in full. Nothing will **pass from** them until this new creation, the completion of God's purposes.

The second limit is expressed as **until all is accomplished**. The verb **accomplished** regularly means **happen**. It especially refers to the "happening" of what is written in the prophets *now* in Jesus' existence (so 1:22; 21:4; 26:54,

56). This clause, then, is not a parallel reference to the future completion of God's purposes, but provides another limit. Nothing from the scriptures passes away until everything prophesied **happens** in the existence of Jesus. That time is under way, so the time of passing away is beginning.

How to reconcile the two limits? As with God's empire, which is under way now but not yet completed, so with **passing from the law**. Now that the scriptures are being fulfilled in Jesus' ministry, the passing away begins, but not yet fully because heaven and earth have not yet passed away. This process means that Jesus, through his fulfilling and interpreting of the scriptures, determines that some parts pass away, but others do not.

• 5:19

An implication from 5:18 (**Therefore**) is now drawn for teachers of Jesus' teaching. **Whoever breaks/looses one of the least of these commandments and teaches others to do the same.** Jesus' position in regard to the scriptures has been established. They are to be read in relation to him. He is the key to interpreting them (so 5:21-48), to determining what is already passing from the law and what is not. This verse warns followers (**whoever**) against ignoring his teaching by **breaking/loosing** scripture and so **teaching** it. The task of teachers is to ensure the doing of the scriptures as fulfilled by Jesus. To **break** seems to be the same as **abolish** in 5:17, but the focus is now on individual **commandments,** which Jesus teaches have continuing value (so 15:3-4 [honor for parents]; 19:17-19 [do not kill, commit adultery, steal, bear false witness; honor parents, love neighbor]; 22:36, 38, 40 [love God and neighbor]). **To teach others to** ignore Jesus' teaching is not permitted.

The punishment is to be **called least in the reign/empire of heaven**. The future passive indicates God's response at the judgment.[38] To be **called** is to encounter God's action (see on 4:21; 5:9) as punishment. This does not mean total exclusion, for which the gospel has graphic and unambiguous language (13:41-42, 49-50; 25:31-46), but there are degrees of reward (5:12; 10:41-42) and rank in heaven (20:23).

The second half restates the scenario positively. **Whoever does them and teaches them** (the commandments as interpreted and taught by Jesus) **will be called great in the reign/empire of heaven**. Jesus emphasizes the congruity of action and teaching (7:24-27; 12:46-50). Faithfulness meets with great reward.

• 5:20

For I tell you (see 5:18) **that unless your righteousness/ justice exceeds that of the scribes and Pharisees, you will never enter the empire of the heavens.** The goal of Jesus' accomplishing and interpreting God's previously revealed, salvific will is **justice/righteousness**, the doing of God's salvific will by his followers (see 3:15; 5:6, 10). This doing is defined over against **that of the scribes and Pharisees**. On **scribes**, see 2:4; on **Pharisees**, see 3:7. Their views on **justice/righteousness** are not given. The verse assumes that they think justice important and ascribes some doing of it to them, but somehow it is not adequate. Disciples are to **exceed** their **justice/righteousness**.[39]

The inadequacy is perhaps clarified first of all by recalling that in the imperial society **Pharisees and scribes** belong to the societal elite, the governing group in alliance with Rome, with a vested interest in maintaining, not reforming, the current, hierarchical, unjust societal structure (see Introduction, sections 1 and 5; also Matt 2:4; 3:7; 5:3-12; 7:28). Further clarification comes from 5:21-48. Their practice is presented as being based on a narrow reading of the scriptures which ignores its implications for wider aspects of human living (cf. 23:23, "justice, mercy, and faith"). Jesus' teaching upholds the written text but develops these justice implications. That is, the problem with the justice that the **Pharisees and scribes** practice may be that it leaves the status quo of Roman domination intact. They do not practice a transformative "justice, mercy, and faith" as an alternative way of life that challenges the status quo and reflects the presence and triumph of God's empire over all, including imperial ways.

How do disciples **exceed** their **justice/righteousness**? First in quantity, as 5:21-48 will demonstrate. Not murdering is a good start, but more is required, namely, the absence of relationship-destroying anger (5:21-26). This also involves a qualitative difference shaped by Jesus' interpretation of the scriptures. The beatitudes have set out God's transformative will which confronts and changes the status quo. This **exceeding** will be identified in 5:48 as perfection or wholeness. If the community does not live this way, **you will never enter the kingdom/empire of heaven**. It will not participate in the completion of God's purposes already encountered in part in Jesus' proclamation and healing (4:17-25). This eschatological goal provides motivation for the present. Present living is to be shaped by God's just will upheld in the judgment. The gospel frequently employs a "bully" approach in using eschatological threats to procure compliance. See 7:13.[40]

5:21-48—SIX "FOR EXAMPLES"

These six scenes provide examples of the exceeding righteousness or life of justice which God's empire requires.

5:21-26	On Anger and Relationships
5:27-30	On Adultery and Male Lust
5:31-32	On Divorce and Male Mistreatment of Women
5:33-37	On Integrity of Word and Action
5:38-42	On Non-Violent Resistance to Evil
5:43-48	On Love for Enemies

Each section begins with a citation of scripture (**you have heard it said**) followed by a statement from Jesus (**but I say to you**). What is the relationship between these two statements? (i) Since Marcion in the second century, some have argued that the two statements are antithetical. The second statement replaces the first. But this is not adequate. Jesus does not replace the command against murder in v. 21, for example. (ii) Another approach sees no replacement. Jesus adds to the first statement with his second.[41] This makes sense of most, but may stumble on the fourth (vv. 33-37) and fifth (vv. 38-42). (iii) Some suggest, more convincingly, that replacement occurs in some, while in others Jesus intensifies the demand. They argue about which examples and how many.[42]

Jesus uses the scriptures as a point of departure to demand more from disciples. In most cases he extends the scripture by interpreting its ethical and societal implications for human living. But in the fourth (vv. 33-37) and fifth (vv. 38-42) "case studies," he allows part of the scriptures to "pass away" (vv. 18-19). Oaths and revenge are not part of life in God's empire.[43]

5:21-26—ON ANGER AND RELATIONSHIPS

• 5:21

You have heard that it was said to those of ancient times, 'You shall not murder'; and 'whoever kills shall be liable to judgment.'" Jesus' first example of exceeding righteousness derives from the Decalogue and Moses (Exod 20:13). The commandment is known to the audience (**You have heard**) as God's word (the passive **it was said**) entrusted to previous generations (**to those of ancient times**). Added to this command is its consequence of punishment (**liable to judgment**; see Exod 21:12; Lev 24:17).

• 5:22

Jesus' contribution begins with the authoritative **But I say to you** (see 5:18). As God's anointed agent (1:1, 17; 2:15; 3:17), Jesus' teaching is spoken on behalf of God, as the will of God. **But I say to you that if you are angry with a brother or sister, you will be liable to punishment.** The but (δέ, *de*) is not contrastive in replacing or superseding Moses. Jesus does not say murder is good. Rather, he elaborates the commandment by showing that anger expressed in violent speech is like murder in that it destroys relationships and people. At heart is a fundamental commitment to relationships and human beings which refuses their "murder" in any shape or form. The sanction is again a threat (5:19-20). Jesus declares the same punishment for anger as for murder (**liable to judgment**, 5:21). Some think **judgment** may refer to a local court or council; an ascending pattern of punishment leads to the final judgment (**hell of fire**). But since the same offense is in view, this seems unlikely. Given that Jesus indicates the sort of life God's empire creates, a hyperbolic reference to eschatological judgment seems preferable. Breaking relationships with anger is this serious! The extreme reference stimulates reflection and insight.[44] The **brother or sister** is both a family member and a follower of Jesus (4:18-22). Jesus does not merely identify or elevate an internal dimension of murder— namely, anger—but he asserts anger's comparably destructive impact.

What sort of **anger** is in view? After all, John refers to God's wrath or anger in the coming judgment, and in 18:34-35 the king's angry action portrays God's response. Two examples illustrate unacceptable, destructive expressions of **anger**—public actions that provoke violence, and anger that writes a person off, consigning him or her to hell. The first example concerns anger expressed in insults, **if you insult** (literally, **say "rhaka"**[45]). This is a very public way of dishonoring someone and a serious offense in a society that values public honor. It also provokes retaliation. The cycle of anger and violence must be broken. If it is not, **you will be liable to the council**.

A further serious insult follows: **If you say, "You Fool," you will be liable to the hell of fire.** A **fool** (see 5:14) is one who says, "There is no God" (Pss 14; 53:1). To so label someone is to judge them, a task that belongs to God (7:1-5). It is to regard someone as beyond all hope. Anger means the loss of perspective on the other and on oneself. **Hell or Gehenna of fire** is the place of fiery punishment for the condemned wicked (*1 En* 27:1-2; 54:1-6; 90:26; *2 Bar* 85:13; *4 Ezra* 7:26-36).[46] This destructive consequence underlines the importance of controlling anger.

Jesus' teaching is not unique. Proverbs, very concerned with social interaction, warns against anger expressed in harmful actions (Prov 6:34; 14:17, 29; etc.). Note also Sir 34:25, where depriving the poor of bread is murder; *2 En* 44:2-3; the Cain and Abel story is a classic example of anger leading to murder (Gen 4:1-16). Philosophical traditions (Seneca, *De Ira;* Plutarch, "On the Control of Anger," *Moralia* 452F-464D) identify causes of the "disease" and offer means of control.[47] Compare Plutarch's dismay at brotherly hatred especially over inheritances ("On Brotherly Love," *Moralia* 478C) and his plea for reconciliation (481B-E, 489C).

• **5:23-24**

A second scenario concerning worship and broken relationships is offered. Like v. 22 there are hyperbolic features. The improbabilities,[48] the stopping of worship and journey of reconciliation, grasp the audience's imagination to emphasize the gravity and importance of unresolved anger. Worship is in progress: **when you are offering your gift at the altar and you remember that your brother or sister has something against you, leave your gift at the altar there and go; first be reconciled with your brother or sister and then come and offer your gift.** Worship without reconciled relationships is not possible. The offended **you** is charged with the responsibility of effecting reconciliation. See 6:12, 14-16, and Sir 28:3, which links anger and the unreasonable expectation of God's healing.

• **5:25-26**

A third scene follows, this time involving an **accuser** and **court. Come to terms quickly with your accuser while you are on your way to court with him.** The dispute is neither described nor condemned. But the appropriate action involves not anger but reconciliation. The verb translated **come to terms** has the sense of "being well disposed to" or "showing good will" to someone, the opposite of anger. As an incentive to pursuing reconciliation, terrible consequences of continuing in anger are narrated: **Or your accuser may hand you over to the judge and the judge to the guard and you will be thrown into prison. Truly I tell you, you will never get out until you have paid the last**

penny. The **last penny** may refer to some debt (cf. 18:23-35) or to punitive fines. Anger that leads to murderous actions, literally or metaphorically with words and in relationships, is not behavior envisaged for God's reign (contrast 1 Macc 2:44). The alternative is not compliance at any cost. It is reconciliation or peacemaking (5:9).

5:27-30—ON ADULTERY AND MALE LUST

• **5:27-28**

The second "for example" follows the command against murder in the Decalogue, **"You have heard that it was said, 'You shall not commit adultery'"** (Exod 20:14; Deut 5:18). The short introduction (compare 5:27 and 21) appeals to the audience's knowledge (**You have heard**) and its recognition of the authority of God's word (the passive **it was said**). As in the first "for example" (see 5:22), Jesus interprets the citation. His interpretation is introduced by the authoritative **But I say to you**, which places Jesus on par with Moses and claims the function of speaking the divine will. Again **but** (δέ, *de*) is not contrastive in replacing or superseding Moses. Jesus does not say adultery is good; in fact it is destructive of the "one flesh" relationship, which is an act of God (19:4-6) and which is not to be violated at will by males, either by adultery or divorce (for an exception, see 5:31-32).

Jesus' addition redefines adultery by focusing not just on the physical act but on the eye (**everyone who looks at a woman**) and heart (**has already committed adultery with her in the heart**) where the sin begins. The **everyone** are males. The androcentric language reflects a society in which male concerns dominate and in which marriage is commonly patriarchal. Attitudes to adultery were ambivalent. There are strong condemnations: see Horace, *Sat* 1.2.37-46; Suetonius, *Augustus* 67 [Augustus' death sentence for adulterers]). But there are also accommodations. See Plutarch's "Advice to Bride and Groom," in which the wife is to accommodate herself to her husband's wishes (e.g., *Moralia* 140B, 144E, passim), since his "leadership and preferences" dominate (139D). He is to "rule" her (ἄρχειν, *archein;* 142E).[49]

Adultery begins with a type of looking: **at a woman in order to desire her** (translated in the NRSV as **lustfully**).[50] Note Exod 20:17, "You will not **desire** your neighbor's wife." Love for neighbor, whether male or female, not lust, is Jesus' command (22:39; 7:12). Lust against the woman is sin because it is predatory in seeking to exploit her. Jesus' focus on "looking to desire" is not unique (*T. Issachar* 7:2; *T. Isaac* 4:53; Sir 41:21). This looking derives from the **heart**, the very center of a person's being (see on 5:8). The heart is where the adultery has **already** happened, before the physical act.

Jesus counters such culturally sanctioned dominance. God's empire creates different male-female relationships. In these verses, the woman is not blamed (cf. Sir 26:9, 11; 23:22-27; 42:9-14); male responsibility and self-control are required; male infidelity is not excused;[51] and male power is restricted by asserting a woman's integrity. The woman's dignity, not just her husband's marriage, is protected. She is sinned against with adulterous looks. The "for example" nature of the scene challenges women to the same standards.

• 5:29-30

Such evil requires drastic actions. Prayer for God to purify evil desires is one option (Ps 51:10; Sir 23:5). So too is male responsibility. **If your right eye causes you to sin, tear it out and throw it away. Right** was regarded as the favored or good side, the left the bad. The valued has been contaminated. It is to be **torn out and thrown away**. Literally? Probably not, since Jesus' emphasis is on the origin of adultery in the heart. Tearing out the **eye** will not change this. The hyperbole underlines the seriousness of the eye's role and the need to attend to it. So too do the eschatological consequences. **It is better for you to lose one of your members than for your whole body to be thrown into hell** (cf. 5:22, hell of fire). The little eye jeopardizes the well-being of the whole person (**body**). Verse 30 repeats the scenario for emphasis, with **cutting off the right hand**.

Adultery violates God's will and social relationships. It is one example of the evil which the heart conceives and enacts (cf. 15:18-19). God must rule the heart (6:21-24), but it is able to be forgiven (6:12, 14-15).

5:31-32—ON DIVORCE AND
MALE MISTREATMENT OF WOMEN

The third "for example" continues the focus on household relationships and male power. This is a difficult and much-debated section; the implications of its interpretation are far-reaching in human lives. The bibliography is enormous. Its assumption about the indelible and continuing effect of the marriage union, which cannot be canceled even when marriage ends with divorce, is strange to modern ears. Yet in a culture that knew almost unlimited male power and generally assumed the inferiority of women, the passage's restriction of male power points to much more mutuality in male–female relationships. See 19:3-12.

• 5:31-32

The introduction is shorter than 5:21 and 5:27, retaining only the divine authorization for the statement, **It was also said**. Unlike 5:21 and 27, in which Jesus quoted the Decalogue, here he summarizes Deut 24:1-4, **Whoever divorces his wife, let him give her a certificate of divorce**. Whereas Deut 24:1-4 is concerned to prevent the divorced woman from remarrying her first husband after she has married a second, Jesus' summary highlights divorce (and assumes a certain view of marriage). As with 5:27-30, the perspective is androcentric. Households and marriages were generally structured on patriarchal lines with the power and interests of the husband/father/master to the fore.[52] Though Gentile and some Jewish women could initiate divorce (cf. Mark

10:12; Plutarch, "Advice to Bride and Groom," *Moralia* 144A, who advises the "jealous" woman not to file for divorce because her rival wants her to "abandon my very home and chamber"),[53] the focus here is on the dominant practice of male-initiated divorce. Deuteronomy 24 recognized that a man could divorce his wife if he found "something objectional" about her. This phrase was interpreted as referring to various behaviors including premarriage impropriety (Deut 22:13-21), adultery (Jer 3:8), or simply disliking (Deut 22:13). By the first century, the school of Shammai had restricted the cause to adultery (*m. Git.* 9:10), but the more dominant position held by the school of Hillel interpreted it much more widely to refer to anything displeasing to the husband.[54] The latter view meant that a husband exercised virtually unlimited power over "his" wife.

Jesus' response (**But I say to you**; see 5:18, 22, 28) restricts this male power because of the consequences it brings on the woman: **anyone who divorces his wife . . . causes her to commit adultery**. The assumption is that the divorced woman remarries to survive, though some women could return to their father's house or to a relative. She commits adultery in remarrying because the bill of divorce cannot cancel the permanent union which her marriage creates (see 19:4-6). For the same reason, a man **who marries a divorced woman commits adultery** against her first marriage. Against a prevailing cultural climate of easy divorce, Jesus (in line with Mal 2:14-16) takes a restrictive and seemingly harsh approach.

Jesus, does permit divorce, however, in the exceptive clause **except on the ground of unchastity/adultery**. The noun πορνείας (*porneias*) is difficult. Some think it refers to incest on the basis of Lev 18:6-18, which forbids marriage with certain relatives. Gentiles who would join the community of disciples, so the argument goes, would not be familiar with these requirements, and would be required to divorce. But this noun (*porneias*) is absent from Lev 18-19. The noun can also refer to various forbidden sexual acts, such as premarital intercourse, but the focus on divorce in 5:31 and Deut 24:1-4 makes **adultery** the most obvious meaning. In these circumstances, Jesus says that divorce is permissible because the marriage union has been broken by the adultery.

This "for example" envisions a type of marriage in God's empire which reins in destructive male power over a woman. A man cannot selfishly and without thought to the consequences "dismiss" his wife. As Jesus will elaborate in 19:3-12 marriage is a "one flesh" reality, and the commitments of both partners are serious. Yet the scene recognizes that divorce is permissible when the union has been fractured through unfaithfulness. Yet the divorce cannot unjoin what "God has joined," so remarriage is not permitted.

Yet while it restricts male power and points to a much more egalitarian understanding of marriage, one consequence of its greater emphasis on the permanence of marriage may be to bind women more tightly into patriarchal and androcentric patterns and expose them to economic hardship and personal restriction in not being permitted to remarry. Both a woman's marital status and her post-marriage situation are problematic if guided only by this scene.

Also strange is that the gospel's emphasis on forgiveness (6:12, 14-15;

18:23-35) and love (22:34-40) is not factored into the discussion. How does the community of disciples hold together this restrictive divorce with the reality of God's love, which enables forgiveness and new possibilities?[55]

5:33-37—OATH-TAKING:
INTEGRITY OF WORD AND ACTION

Oaths were pervasive in swearing loyalty to a city or public appointments; to the judicial system and business contracts; to memberships in clubs, associations, or guilds; for religious activities, and so on. Jesus counters this extensive practice and tradition which encouraged oaths.[56] These scriptures are passing away even now in the time which Jesus has inaugurated but not completed (so 5:18).

• 5:33

Again, you have heard that it was said to those of ancient times (see 5:21). The adverb **again** begins the second three scenarios. As with 5:31, the scripture tradition is summarized (contrast 5:21, 27), **"You shall not swear falsely/break your oaths but carry out the vows you have made to the Lord."** An extensive tradition warned against false oaths and exhorted honoring those made: Exod 20:7, 16; Lev 19:12; Deut 5:20; 23:21, the longer discussion in Num 30:3-15; also Wis 14:28; *Ps.-Phoc.* 16. Oath taking was widely practiced to express commitment to God or to a person; oath breaking risked divine punishment (cf. Deut 23:21; Philo, *Spec Leg* 2.11; *De Dec* 95). The practice, intended to guarantee reliable human communication and trustworthy relationships, ironically undermined them through evasive or deceptive uses of oaths and by creating a category of potentially unreliable communication not guaranteed by oaths.

• 5:34-36

Jesus' view is emphatic (**But I say to you** [see on 5:18, 21]), clear (**Do not swear**), and comprehensive (**at all**). The **at all**, along with the examples in 5:34-36 and repetition in 5:37, bans not only swearing falsely but any oath taking (so Jesus in 26:63-64 and 23:16-22). His total prohibition has some affinity with the aversion (though often qualified) of some philosophers (Plutarch, Quintilian, Epictetus[57]). See Sir 23:9-11; Philo, *De Dec* 84; and Qumran (CD 15:1-5; cf. Josephus, *JW* 2.139-42 ["tremendous oaths"]).

Four examples of forbidden oaths, which span the cosmos, follow in 5:34b-36. A disciple is not to swear **by heaven, for it is the throne of God**. A human cannot presume to co-opt God. Such an oath is akin to the devil's temptation of Jesus which would compel God to act in a particular way (cf. 4:5-7). Oaths are diabolical in their presumption.

• 5:35

The same argument applies in this verse. A disciple is not to swear **by the**

earth, for it is God's footstool (cf. Isa 66:1). The **earth** is the Lord's (Ps 24:1), even though the devil and various empires usurp its control (see 4:8; 5:3-10). God's will is to be done there (5:13; 6:10), and a disciple, committed to doing that will, will not presume to bind God to a course of action.

The argument is repeated a third time concerning **Jerusalem for it is the city of the great King**. The description evokes Ps 48:3 specifically and the Zion tradition in general in which Jerusalem is God's dwelling place (Ps 135:21). The affirmation is made in the face of the city's defeat and destruction by Rome in 70. Rome has violated the city, as have the religious leaders in not welcoming Jesus (see 2:1-3; 4:5-6). God has not finished with Jerusalem; Rome's control is temporary.

• 5:36

This verse adds a further reason. Not only are oaths inappropriate in presuming to compel God to act, but a human cannot enforce them. **You cannot make one hair white or black**. Human limitations (recognized also in 6:27) render an oath useless.

• 5:37

The alternative praxis for the community of disciples is straightforward, sincere, and trustworthy speech, which builds honest and trusting relationships and which derives from a person's integrity: **Let your word be "Yes, Yes" or "No, No"; anything more than this** (the addition of an oath) **comes from the evil one**. The implicit connection with the devil noted in 5:34-35 is explicit. Oaths **come from the evil one**. They presume to invade God's realm, attempt to bind God to a course of action, and overstep human limits. They create mistrust and broken relationships through unreliable communication. Honest communication with God and other disciples is part of the exceeding righteousness (5:20) of God's empire. Relationships of trust and integrity are necessary to sustain the marginal and minority community of disciples in its alternative lifestyle. If the practice applies to societal participation and relations with those outside the community, it will cause difficulty, given the pervasive use of oaths.

5:38-42—ON NONVIOLENT RESISTANCE TO EVIL

• 5:38

The fifth "for example" of life in God's empire envisions "active nonviolent resistance" to the oppressive, imperial context of domination and violence.[58] Jesus summarizes (cf. 5:31, 33) the *lex talionis,* the law of equal retribution, which limited revenge in proportion to the offender's offense (e.g., Philo, *Spec Leg* 3.181-82):[59] **You have heard that it was said** (5:21, 27), **An eye for an eye and a tooth for a tooth** (see Exod 21:23-25; Lev 24:20; Deut 19:21). The chosen items (**an eye for an eye**, not "life for a life"; Exod 21:23; Deut 19:21) suggest bodily harm, not murder.[60] The brief illustrations in 5:39-42 confirm this view.

• 5:39

Jesus' authoritative interpretation (**But I say to you** [see 5:18, 22]) is **Do not violently resist an evildoer**[61] (my trans.). The strange NRSV translation **Do not resist an evildoer** (or **evil**) forbids self-protection and invites the same submissive approach to tyrants which the vassal king Herod Agrippa urges the crowds to adopt, rather than rebel against Rome (Josephus, *JW* 2.345-401).[62] It suggests that God legitimates evil and requires disciples to capitulate to and collude with, not oppose, evil action. This is strange indeed; since 5:21, four scenes have exhorted the audience to resist doing evil! Jesus resisted the devil (4:1-11), enacted God's empire against evil disease (4:17-25), taught that God's reign transforms evil (5:3-6) and creates a community that continues Jesus' mission (5:7-16). Moreover, vv. 39-42 offer scenes of resisting oppressive power.

The translation **Do not violently resist an evildoer** is preferable. The verb ἀντιστῆναι (*antistēnai*) occurs only here in Matthew. W. Wink shows that the term indicates "armed resistance in military encounters" or "violent struggle."[63] Liddell and Scott (p. 140) define it as "to set against, esp. in battle." Hence the translation **Do not violently resist**. The issue is not whether to resist or not ("flight or fight," passive submission or violent retaliation) but *how* evil is resisted. Jesus' teaching offers a third option, nonviolent resistance. Jesus' teaching does not contradict the scriptures in that it continues the mandate of the law and the prophets to not let evil go unchecked. Evil must be countered if justice is to be established (5:20). But in terms of *how* disciples respond to evil, Jesus' approach differs from the *lex talionis* summarized in 5:38. Retribution, in which violence and damage meet and match violence and damage, is set aside. The cycle of violence is broken.

Parts of the scriptural tradition reject strict retribution; see Lev 19:18 (love for neighbor); Prov 24:29; Deut 32:35 (which leaves it to God). Stoics and Cynics (Seneca, Musonius Rufus, Epictetus) urge preserving one's inner calm, bearing the blow or insult without retaliation, though Seneca thinks that physical violence may be necessary to correct (not avenge) evil (*De Const* 12.3)![64] The gospel indicates that the armed revolt against Rome in 70 was a disaster, but the alternative was not submission (22:6-7, 15-22; see on 17:23-27). Resistance, yes; violence, no. Jesus' third way is active nonviolent resistance.

Four somewhat witty yet serious examples of this active nonviolent resistance follow. The illustrations offer specificity to the principle, capture the imagination to envision God's empire at work, and continue to help the audience perceive both the reality of its oppression and the means of liberation.[65]

The first example in 5:39b posits a scene which utilizes physical violence to assert control and maintain societal inequalities: **but if anyone strikes you on the right cheek**. This refers not to a direct blow with a fist but to a blow with an open hand (BAGD, 734), a "slap in the face" (Liddell and Scott, 1565). This was an insulting gesture (Job 16:10; Ps 3:7; Lam 3:30; Isa 50:6; 1 Esdr 4:30; *m. B. Qam.* 8:6). It expresses the power differential of a superior who disdains an inferior: a master with a slave, a wealthy landowner with a poor farmer or artisan, a Roman with a provincial,[66] a wise man with a fool or a child (who like a slave is not considered capable of rational discourse),[67] a government official with a difficult prophet (2 Kgs 22:24), the religious elite with a dangerous preacher (Matt 26:67). This action dishonors and humiliates the inferior. No response except submission is expected. The direct object (**strike you**) suggests a gesture with which Matthew's audience is familiar.

Rather than be subdued into nonresponsiveness, and rather than lashing out in violence and continuing the cycle, Jesus teaches a third response: **turn the other also**. This action shows that one has not been intimidated or provoked into uncontrolled actions. It is a chosen, active, nonviolent response to a system designed to humiliate. The chosen action refuses submission, asserts dignity and humanness, and challenges what is supposed to demean. It refuses the superior the power to humiliate.

• 5:40

A second example concerns loan collection proceedings in a court: **if anyone wants to sue you and take your coat**. Why would anyone want to? In Deut 24:10-13 (also Exod 22:25-27) a loan is to be guaranteed by a pledge. A poor person may have to pledge his cloak, in which case the lending party is to return it by nightfall so that the poor person can keep warm. The scenario assumes the common experience of indebtedness.[68] It posits a poor person, perhaps a peasant farmer, who cannot repay a loan and whose land is about to be seized (if it hasn't been already), being sued by creditors for almost the last thing he has. How is such a poor-in-spirit person to respond? Where is God's empire? (cf. 5:3)

Jesus' response is to **give your cloak as well**. This striking act means giving up one's outer and under garment (for a slave wearing two garments, cf. Josephus, *Ant* 17.136). Why strip oneself naked in court? This gesture represents the stripping away of land and property which the creditor is enacting. By standing naked before one's creditor who has both garments in his hand, one shames and dishonors the creditor. Nakedness exposes, among other things, the greed and cruel effect of the creditor's action and the unjust system the creditor represents. Removing clothing, along with all that it represents (status, social relations, power, gender, etc.), reveals the basic humanity which should unite the indebted and creditor. The act enables the poor to take some initiative against power that seems ultimate. The act protests by unmasking the powerful one's heartless demands as inhuman, and the act offers the possibility of a different relationship, even reconciliation. A changed system is not guaranteed, but God's reign has exposed the nature of the present system and pointed to an alternative.

• 5:41

After social (5:39b) and economic inequalities (5:40), this third scene explicitly addresses a practice of Roman power, **if anyone forces you to go one mile, go also the second mile**. The verb **forces** (ἀγγαρεύσει, *angareusei*) refers to requisitioning labor, transport (animals, ships), and lodging from subject people (called *angaria*). In 27:32 Roman soldiers compel (same verb) Simon of Cyrene to carry the cross of a convicted criminal about to be executed. The emperor Domitian (81-96 C.E.) attempted to use permits to curtail abuses in Syria.[69] Those who lived near a city such as Antioch in which legions were stationed were especially vulnerable. A Roman soldier who abused a subject person could be punished by flogging, reduced rations, pay, or rank, or discharge, but discipline was inconsistent. Here **going one mile** probably means carrying a soldier's pack (Josephus, *JW* 3.95) for one mile.

The response to this imposition of imperial power is not violence but **go also the second mile**. At first glance this might seem to be complicity with the oppressor, the path of least resistance and maximum cooperation as Epictetus urges (*Diss* 4.1.79). But, as with the previous examples, it is a strategy for responding to what is intended to humiliate by refusing to be humiliated. It attempts to regain initiative and human dignity. By **going a second mile**, the person refuses to play the game on Rome's terms. Instead of feeling superior, the soldier is surprised and off guard. Why is the person doing this? Will they file a complaint against him for making them do two miles? The soldier does not know. The subservient has seized the initiative, chosen the action, made the oppressor worry, possibly opened the way to a different relationship, and manifested God's empire.

• 5:42

A fourth example, one of alternative economic practice, follows: **Give to him who begs from you**. The command assumes poverty and exploitative practices of tax and debt. It counters a cultural understanding of giving as benefiting the giver or benefactor's reputation and social position, and obligating the recipient to reciprocate by enhancing the patron's status (see 6:2-4).

Jesus advocates an alternative system without exploitation, reciprocity, and self-aggrandizement. There are two steps. The first involves alleviating the distress caused by the present system. To give to **him who begs** is not a new action (Deut 15:7-11, though not universal, see Sir 12:1-7), but a vital one of mercy for and solidarity with the oppressed. P. Freire notes that oppressed people often turn their humiliation on each other in violent and destructive acts.[70] Jesus' command (cf. 6:2-4) requires people to do what they can to alleviate one another's suffering from debt and taxes, resisting the "divide and conquer" strategy of the elite.[71]

The second step involves creating an alternative system, **do not refuse anyone who wants to borrow from you**. This is not new either (Exod 22:25; Lev 25:36-37; Deut 15:1-3; 4 Macc 2:8), but it is a radical alternative to dominant practices. **Not refusing anyone** means setting aside reciprocity and benefits from repayment, high interest rates, or default. It creates a system intent not on securing wealth but on ensuring justice and economic equality by providing the opportunity for adequate support for all. One's resources are available not only for oneself but also for others.

Jesus offers four examples of nonviolent resistance to oppressive power. They are examples of creative, imaginative strategies which break the circle of violence. The servile refuse to be humiliated; the subjugated take initiative by acting with dignity and humanity in the midst of and against injustice and oppression which seem permanent.

W. Wink describes Jesus' third way in phrases such as: Seize the moral initiative, find a creative alternative to violence, assert your own humanity and dignity as a person, meet force with ridicule or humor, break the cycle of humiliation, refuse the inferior position, shame the oppressor, be willing to suffer. Such actions exhibit different relationships and manifest the destabilizing, transforming reign of God.

5:43-48—ON LOVE FOR ENEMIES

• 5:43

After the familiar **You have heard that it was said** (5:27, 38), the verse cites Lev 19:18b, **You shall love your neighbor**. It omits "as yourself," perhaps because the focus is on imitating God's love for others (5:45). It adds **and hate your enemy,** which is not found in the Hebrew Bible (though somewhat comparable statements appear [cf. Deut 20:1-18; Ps 139:21-22; Qumran 1QS 1:10-11]).

Both statements assume definitions of **neighbor** and **enemy**.[72] In Lev 19 the focus is on Israel (19:2): parents (19:3), the poor and alien (19:10, 33-35), one another (19:11), a laborer (19:13), deaf and blind (19:14), poor and great (19:15), kin (19:17), people (19:18), slaves (19:20), priest (19:22), daughter (19:29), the aged (19:32) are specified. "Neighbor" embraces diversities of gender, wealth, kin, physical condition, age, and ethnicity (cf. alien).

Yet one cannot be sure of one's own. **Enemy** is not limited to national opponents and foreigners (cf. Deut 20) but includes personal foes. The Psalmist lives among the godless and compassionless, the verbally and physically violent who threaten life (see Pss 18, 31, 41, etc.). Sirach recognizes that distinguishing friends and foes is difficult (Sir 6:8-18; 12:9, 17-18). Plutarch assumes that having enemies in everyday life is normal, but instead of seeking revenge against them, one should use them to improve one's own life ("How to Draw Benefits from One's Enemies," *Moralia* 86B-92F). Other groups manifest hate for those who are different, including Jews[73] (outbreaks of violence against Jews occurred in Antioch ca. 70 C.E.[74]). Note the difficulty with strangeness and difference reflected in treatment of "Barbarians" including ambivalent but often hostile attitudes to the "Black African" (*Aethiops*).[75] In Matthew **enemies** include one's household (10:36) and those who cause economic havoc with sabotage (13:25, 28).

• 5:44

Jesus' greater righteousness (**But I say to you** [see 5:18, 22]) offers love not only to neighbors but to all. **Love your enemies and pray for those who persecute you**. Ethnicity, gender, social status, appearance, and wealth are no bases for restricting love (cf. 3:9). **Enemies** are to be treated as neighbors. This is not easy. **Enemies** include **those who persecute** followers of Jesus, opponents of God's purposes enacted in Jesus and his people. See on 5:10-12. **Love**, like hate, is an action. It seeks the enemy's good in **praying**, or with indiscriminate loving actions (5:46) and greetings (5:47). Does praying for **those who persecute you** (so also *T. Jos.* 18:2) embrace prayers for the demise of Rome and its supporters (cf. *Pss. Sol.* 2:25-27; 17:22-25)?

Love for enemies, which rejects the conventional wisdom of helping friends and harming enemies, is not unique (see Exod 23:4-5; 1 Kgdms [1 Sam] 24:16-20; Prov 24:17-18; 25:21-22; Jonah 4:10-11; *T. Iss.* 7:6; *T. Zeb.* 7:1-3; *T. Gad* 6:1-7; *T. Benj.* 4:2-3; *Ep. Arist.* 227, 232; *Jos. Asen.* 29:3-4; Seneca, *De Ben* 7.30.2, 5).[76]

Love does not, though, mean accommodated "niceness" without conflict. It involves challenge (5:3-12; ch. 23 [Jesus' harsh words to correct (?) the religious leaders]), with no guarantee that it will be returned, the love-er benefited, the "other" changed, or that the action will be understood as love (= beneficial). To challenge injustices and oppression and to manifest God's empire (5:3-9, 38-42) may incite conflict and suffering. How the community challenges (loving, creative, and active nonviolence) and to what end (the fullness of God's empire) matter enormously. R. Stark has argued that the early Christian willingness to love actively and indiscriminately, especially in relieving the miseries and hardships of urban life suffered by the majority poor in cities like Antioch, was a major factor in its growth.[77]

• 5:45

The purpose of such indiscriminate and active love is **so that you may be children of your Father in heaven**. This has present and future (eschatological) dimensions. Acting now as peacemakers (cf. 5:9), praying for one's enemies, doing good, and so on, marks the community as God's **children**, in covenant relationship with God as Father (see 5:16; 23:9), constituted not by ethnicity (cf. Deut 14:1) but by following Jesus in imitating God (cf. Matt 3:9) and sharing in the completion of God's purposes. For **heaven** as God's abode, see 5:34; as the origin of God's reign, see 3:2, 4:17.

The basis for indiscriminate loving is God's gracious and indiscriminate action as creator. God makes **his sun rise/dawn on the evil and the good, and sends rain on the righteous and the unrighteous.** For God's control of **sun** and **rain**, see Gen 1:14-19; 2:4-5; Job 38, esp. vv. 24-30; Pss 19:5-6; 104:19-23; Sir 43:2-5; *1 En* 41:4-8; Philo rejects the notion that sun, moon, and stars are gods; God controls them (*Spec Leg* 1.13-20). Jesus' claim, then, counters other claimants. Horace claims that Jupiter provides wind and rain to make the earth fertile (*Secular Hymn,* lines 22-24, 29-32). Seneca ascribes the same task to the gods (*De Ben* 3.31.4-5). The sun-god Helios, widely understood to direct the universe and to whom Apollonius prays (Philostratus, *Apollonius* 2.38), appeared on Nero's coins and in popular religious petitions.[78]

God's life-giving and loving actions in creation attest God's treatment of humans. Just as God makes the **sun rise/dawn**, Jesus the light **dawns** (same verb) in the darkness of oppression, sin, and death (4:15-16). Disciples continue his mission as light (5:14). God gifts life indiscriminately and mercifully through sun and rain to all people (Ps 145:9; Wis 15:1), regardless of moral status (**evil**, **good**; **righteous**, **unrighteous**). Though the **evil** and **unrighteous** are enemies of God's purposes, God's comprehensive and undeserved kindness extends to all. Disciples are to imitate God's loving actions. Seneca among others also urges imitating God's actions of benefiting all (though he was not moved to end slavery! *De Ben* 4.26). Contrast Josephus's comment (*JW* 5.407), "It is surely madness to expect God to show the same treatment to the just and the unjust (δικαίοις . . . ἀδίκοις, *dikaiois . . . adikois*)," and Apollonius is quite sure that the gods bless the holy but express wrath to the wicked (Philostratus, *Apollonius,* 1.11).

• 5:46-47
The emphasis on indiscriminate rather than reciprocal love continues. **For if you love those who love you, what reward do you have?** Reciprocity was a common behavior, binding parties in obligations and securing the patron–client status of each (see 6:2). Indiscriminate loving, part of the greater righteousness required of disciples (5:20), is a countercultural practice, undermining, not securing, social hierarchies and obligations (see 5:37). The ensuing series of four questions engages the audience, forcing it to formulate answers in terms of the principle outlined in 5:44-45, and to imagine behaviors of indiscriminate love.

To **love those who love you** brings no benefit (see 5:12). **Do not even the tax collectors do the same?** This question introduced by οὐχί (*ouchi*) expects a yes answer. This is the first reference to **tax collectors** (see 9:10-11; 11:19; 21:31-32).[79] As members of the retainer class (see Introduction, section 5), they contracted to collect not personal, poll, or land taxes but indirect taxes on transported goods at commercial centers (see 9:9-10). They profited by collecting more, and so increased the oppressive tax burden. They were very unpopular, and social outcasts (Cicero links them with beggars, thieves, and robbers [*De Off* 150-51]; see also Luke 18:11). But this marginalized group found support from each other. Disciples are to do more.

The third question establishes further comparisons: **if you greet** (perhaps involving a prayer, Tob 5:9; 9:6) **only your brothers and sisters**, whether kin or disciples, they do nothing more than tax collectors (cf. 5:20; Sir 41:20 [not returning a greeting is less]). Love is bound by kinship or religious boundaries. Instead of imitating God's indiscriminate love, they copy cultural norms: **do not even the Gentiles do the same?** Further negative contrasts with **Gentiles** follow in 6:7, 32; 18:17, yet **Gentiles** are within God's purposes and the objects of mission (28:19; 5:13-16). The gospel, written in Greek and emanating from a largely Jewish group, seems ambivalent about Gentile culture and practices. The community in which the gospel originated provably lived, as did many Jewish groups, a tension of assimilation and resistance.[80]

• 5:48

This verse sums up all six examples. The greater righteousness (5:20) which embodies God's empire imitates God in *wholeness*. **Be whole/perfect, therefore, as your heavenly Father is perfect.** To be **whole** denotes the undivided heart which truly knows and loyally does God's will (Gen 6:9; Deut 18:13; 3 Kgdms [1 Kgs] 8:61; 11:4; 15:3, 14; 1 Chr 28:9). Relationship with God involves active trust and obedience (cf. 19:21). Such wholeness of heart and living in accord with God's loving purposes or goal (the adjective derives from the verb "to complete") are not natural; they are something that God gives and humans do as they discern and perform God's will of love (Wis 9:6). Wholeness summarizes the way of life envisioned in 5:21-48, which involves the whole person in every sphere doing love toward all, including enemies (5:44), imitating God's love for all, including those who resist God's purposes (5:45). Such love expresses God's justice and empire. On **Father**, see 5:16, 45; 23:9.

This section (5:21-48) thus offers examples of, a vision of, what life in God's empire looks like. These verses illustrate a way of life marked by a comprehensive and constant love even in the face of opposition. In offering examples or a vision, this section trains the audience to imagine the embodiment of God's empire in numerous other situations. It informs and forms a community that is constantly called to discern what life in God's empire might look like in all sorts of situations.

CHAPTER 6

Jesus Teaches

The Sermon on the Mount Continues

6:1-18—LIVING JUSTLY

Two markers indicate continuity with chapter 5. First, the speaker (Jesus), audience (disciples), and location (mountain) continue (4:23; 5:2). Second, the term **justice/righteousness**—unhelpfully translated by NRSV in 6:1 as **piety**—continues as the focus. In 5:21-48 Jesus offered six examples of the "exceeding justice" (5:20) which disciples are to exemplify in an identity and lifestyle that differ from and challenge life under imperial control. Matt 6:1-18 continues this focus by discussing the role of three acts of piety: giving alms or material relief to those in need (6:2-4), prayer (6:5-15), and fasting (6:16-18).[1]

6:1—THE WARNING

• 6:1

This verse sets out the section's basic warning, which will be illustrated with three examples in 6:2-18: **Beware of practicing/doing your justice/right-eousness before others in order to be seen by them**. In an honor-shame society, one's good reputation, sustained by the approval and esteem of others who have benefited from one's public actions, is important. Jesus' command strikes at a fundamental societal pattern.[2] The use of **beware** signals the danger. In four of the five subsequent uses of this verb, danger comes from the synagogue (anticipating 6:2) or religious leaders (echoing 5:20; see 10:17; 16:6, 11, 12; in 7:15 false prophets). Differentiating disciples from the synagogue continues.

The concern is not the public doing of **justice/righteousness**, the doing of what God requires, which includes restructured societal relationships and access to resources; see 5:6, 10, 20. Being merciful, peacemaking, being persecuted (5:7, 9, 10-12), or giving alms (6:2-4) happen in the public sphere. The concern, rather, is with motivation, **in order to be seen by them**. The warning is not against a literal seeing but against making people into spectators by impressing them, or seeking their approval, and sustaining one's own status, as 6:2b will make clear. Such motives turn worship into theater or spectacle.[3] In theater, playing a role and audience approval are appropriate, but not in worship. Acting a part has been ruled out by exhortations to integrity and wholeness (5:21-48). Disciples are to "fish for" people, not impress them (4:19). Disciples witness not to themselves but to God's light in embodying God's saving presence and empire. People are to honor not disciples but God (5:16). For disciples, interaction with society is about mission, not about seeking approval.

God is the only audience for worship. If one seeks to be **seen by** people, the **reward** of **your Father who is in heaven** is lost. On **reward** as that which follows faithfulness, the intensification of communion with God known even now in faithful service, see 5:12, 46; on **Father in heaven,** see 5:16, 45, 48; on **heaven** as God's abode and the origin of God's empire, see 3:2, 16-17; 4:17; 5:3, 34.

6:2-4—A FIRST ACT OF JUSTICE: ALMSGIVING

• 6:2

So whenever you give alms. So links 6:2-4 to 6:1 as the first of three examples. Almsgiving, sharing material resources with the needy, is assumed of disciples (cf. 5:7, 43-48), regardless of economic level. The word **almsgiving** is a cognate of "merciful" and "mercy" in 5:7. This act denotes the presence of God's empire. It is a necessary survival strategy because imperial society distributes resources unequally (so 5:3-12). Seneca attests great poverty in cities: "how great a majority are the poor" (*To Helvia on Consolation* 12.1). Sharing resources provides an alternative socioeconomic practice to dominant societal practices which deny access to resources through greed and oppression.

A. R. Hands has shown that when the wealthy provided relief for some of the poor, giving was often "self-regarding" in that the giver anticipated some benefit and honor. Concepts of reciprocity and of the enhancement of one's reputation and status by conspicuous and calculated kindness (*philotimia,* "acts-of-love-of-honor") dominate, though they do not preclude some concern to provide relief for the destitute.[4] Almsgiving was a linchpin of patron–client relations which maintained the hierarchical social structure by elevating the powerful and prosperous. It enabled them to secure honor and dominate the lower ranks by binding them into dependent relationships (Introduction, section 5).

Hence Seneca's wise man will provide relief, but not feel pity or sorrow (*De Clem* 2.6.6), though Seneca thinks there is no point in helping the undeserving poor (*De Vita Beata* 24.1). Plutarch opposes greed and accumulation of wealth because it will not bring happiness ("On the Love of Wealth," *Moralia* 523C-528B). But he does not propose giving wealth to the destitute, nor does he take their poverty seriously.[5] Musonius Rufus, though, urges moderate housing and furnishing with the rest being used for "public and private charity" (Lutz, *Musonius Rufus,* 19-20). But generally, the Greco-Roman world sought to maintain social stratification, with the more wealthy dominating and depriving the majority poor, whom they generally viewed with disgust, not concern or aid. "Poverty . . . makes people the target of ridicule," not of assistance (Juvenal, *Sat* 3.147-54).[6]

Jewish texts attest **giving alms** as part of what God requires; see Prov 25:21-22; Sir 3:30; 7:10; Tob 1:3, 16-17; 4:6-11; 12:8-10; *Ps.-Phoc.* 22-30, often with prayer, fasting, and righteousness. R. Stark has noted that in the Greco-Roman world the notion that God required worshipers to care for each other was unusual.[7]

Jesus' concern is not with whether to give alms or not, but with *how* to carry out this practice of indiscriminate love (cf. 5:43-47). The *how* contrasts with the incorrect practice of the synagogue: **Do not sound a trumpet before you, as the hypocrites do in the synagogues and in the streets, so that they may be praised by others**. Since there is no evidence for people using **trumpets** to signal almsgiving, the expression must be metaphorical, not literal, and a hyperbolic and polemical claim. It caricatures conventional cultural behaviors which draw attention to the almsgiver: boasting about almsgiving in conversation, identifying oneself as a sponsor of a food distribution, or memorializing oneself in inscriptions and monuments. The sweeping generalization has polemical purposes and discloses considerable antagonism. It does not allow that some in the synagogues might not be **hypocrites**.

The term **hypocrites** derives from the theater, the actor who plays a part. Theaters were common in cities (e.g., Sepphoris in Galilee near Nazareth; Titus built one just outside Antioch in Daphne in the early 70s, possibly on a site of a synagogue; there was one already in Antioch). The term also designates the godless person (Job 34:14; 36:13; Sir 1:29; cf. *Pss. Sol.* 4:1-8) and playing a role (the verb, 4 Macc 6:15, 17). Here the term suggests playing a public role of aiding another in accord with God's will, whereas the real inner interest is in one's own honor and reputation. In pursuing one's own honor, the synagogue practice imitates the dominant cultural patterns of reciprocal and conspicuous giving. The **hypocrites** presumably include the Pharisees and scribes (cf. the contrast in 5:20); subsequently, see 15:7; 22:18; 23:13, 14, 15, 23, 25, 27, 29.[8] This harsh and repeated verdict reflects not a researched and objective view but a polemical verdict. It may reflect a bitter conflict with a synagogue (see Introduction, section 8). Disciples must learn an alternative practice.

Though Jesus ministers in **synagogues** (4:23), there is distance ("their"; also 9:35; 13:54). This is the first of several negative references to hypocrisy (6:5; cf. 23:6) and resistance (10:17; 12:9; 13:54; 23:34) in synagogues. Their motivation and "performance" of almsgiving are pejoratively described **so that they might be praised by others**. The verb **praised** replaces "seen" in 6:1 to sharpen the attack. This verb literally means "glorify." It is used in 5:16 to denote what should be directed to God, not to almsgivers. Hypocrites steal the gratitude and praise due to God, the giver and sustainer of life (5:45; 6:25-34). Public applause is their only **reward** (see 5:12; 6:1).[9] The recipient of their alms benefits them! There is no solidarity or just relationship. The **synagogue** mirrors the larger imperial society, rather than establishes an alternative practice (5:20). Jesus' authoritative **truly I tell you** declares their eschatological destiny as the will of God (so also his teaching, 5:18, 22, 28, 32, 34, 39, 44).

• 6:3-4

In contrast to the synagogue and the larger imperial society that it mirrors, the community of disciples (addressed with a singular pronoun, **you**) has a different practice. The hyperbole underlines it. **But when you give alms, do not let your left hand know what your right hand is doing so that your alms may be done in secret**. Instead of public performance, they imitate God, **your Father who sees in secret**[10] and they act in secret (see Pss 33:13-15; 139:6-16; Prov 25:2; Sir 16:17-23; 23:17-21; 42:15-25; *T. Job* 9:7-8; *T. Gad* 5:3; *2 Bar* 83:3). Note in 2 Macc 3:39; 7:35; 9:5 the notion of the "all-seeing" or "observant" God who sees and punishes the tyrant Antiochus Epiphanes (the same term [ἐπόπτης, *epoptēs*] is used for the emperor [BAGD, 305]). On **your Father**, see 5:16, 45, 48 (the Father and God of Jesus; see 2:15; 3:17; 4:3, 6). For a minority and marginal community that lives an alternative lifestyle, societal acclaim indicates unfaithfulness to its identity and practices. God, not public acclaim or approval, provides their only audience in sharing material support. This is "exceeding righteousness." God **will reward you** in the judgment and completion of God's purposes. On **reward**, see 5:12, 46; 6:1, 2.

6:5-15—A SECOND ACT OF JUSTICE: PRAYER

The ancient world approached its gods in two ways: with prayer and with actions and gifts (sacrifice, votive offerings). This unit on prayer assumes the former as it outlines two errors in praying.[11] In 6:5-6, the error concerns the practice of prayer: Does the community of disciples imitate the synagogue in seeking public approval? In 6:7-15, the error concerns the theology of prayer: Does the community pray as the Gentiles do or in a different manner because of its different understanding of God? Employing polemical language, this section contrasts the disciples' lifestyle with the piety of both the synagogue (Jews) and the Greco-Roman world.[12]

• 6:5

This second practice is introduced in a manner comparable to almsgiving in 6:2 (though **you** is now plural); **when you pray, do not be like the hypocrites.** The assumption is that disciples pray. But their practice is to differ from that of the hypocrites, who **love to stand and pray in the synagogues and at the street corners so that they may be seen by others**. Again the polemic attacks the synagogue in unflattering and generalized terms. Public applause is their goal. The verdict from Jesus (**truly I tell you**) is that they too **have received their reward**. Most of this vocabulary repeats the terms and tone used in 6:2-4.

The polemic is intensified, though, by adding a claim about their delight in seeking public approval. They *love* **to stand and pray**. Love for public approval means that prayer ceases to express love for God (the first command-ment; cf. 22:37), but, like alsmgiving, serves the one praying. For **standing** as common Jewish practice, see Jer 18:20; Pss 134:1; 135:2; Neh 9:4. Persius in *Satire* 2 (lines 8-13) attacks Gentiles who pray "prayers such as all people may hear" for a sound mind, a fair name, good credit. But "under his breath" the pray-er mutters, "O if only my uncle would pop off!" or "if only I could wipe out that ward of mine. . . ."

• 6:6

By contrast to the synagogue, **whenever you pray** (the singular returns, per-haps for personalizing emphasis), **go into your inner room/storeroom and shut your door and pray to your Father who is in secret.** Instead of public places (6:5), prayer happens in the **inner room/storeroom**, a private place of differing functions (Gen 43:30; Exod 8:3; Deut 32:25; Tob 7:16; 8:1; Sir 29:12). Naming the place says little about the types of houses in which the members of the audience live, but much more about being out of the public gaze and space, and in the presence of God. Prayer is not public performance but communication with God. The assurance is that **your Father who sees in secret will reward you**. For **reward,** see on 5:12; 6:1, 2, 4.

• 6:7-8

The second "how to pray" issue defines disciples over against Gentiles. At one level it concerns the choice and number of words in prayer, but at a deeper level is an issue of theology, the nature of the God being addressed. The verse continues to assume the practice of prayer, **when you are praying**. Again a contrast follows: **do not heap up empty phrases as the Gentiles do**. These **empty phrases**, surely a polemical, exaggerated mocking and not to be taken as a fair statement about all **Gentile** practice (as with Jewish almsgiving and praying in 6:2-6), may refer (1) to praying to numerous gods to ensure success and not offend any by omission.[13] A variation on this approach asks a god such as Zeus for guidance on which particular gods to address.[14] (2) The Greek Mag-ical Papyri evidences the use of nonsense sounds believed to be the language of the gods.[15] (3) Both Greek[16] and Jewish texts (Eccl 5:2-3; Isa 1:15; Sir 7:14) urge short prayers and warn against long prayers. Long prayers tried to force gods to listen[17] and wearied them (Statius, *Thebaid*, 2.244). This negative ref-erence to Gentiles follows that of 5:47 (see also 6:32).

But the central issue is not long prayers per se. Jesus prays all night in Matt 14:23-25 and repeatedly in 26:36-46. The explanatory (**for**) identifies the issue: **for they think that they will be heard because of their many words**. This unflattering statement claims that repetition and quantity are needed to get a hearing from gods who seem reluctant to listen or to act. At the heart of this polemic is an issue of theology. The deity(ies) to whom the Gentiles pray are presented as unknowing, reluctant, deaf and uncaring. Many words are needed to get their attention.[18] These are the gods whose will the empire enacts.

By contrast, the God of Jesus and his disciples is **your Father** (so 5:16, 45,

48; 6:4, 6) who **knows what you need before you ask him** (cf. Isa 65:24). The seeing God of 6:4, 6 is also the **knowing** God, or at least the God who **knows** what God's children **need**.

Of course, many Gentiles would not agree with this characterization of their gods. Plutarch refers to the Pythian priestess who delivers oracles before the question is put because her god "understands the dumb and hears when no man speaks" ("On Talkativeness," *Moralia* 512E). But polemic is never interested in fair or accurate presentation. Presumably, as the Father who indiscriminately sustains all life (Matt 5:45), this God will meet the **needs**, not wants, of the praying children. The **needs**, or at least some of them, will be elaborated in 6:11-13, 25-34. The community is exhorted not to imitate the Gentiles (**Do not be like them**) but to enter into trusting prayer with this **Father**. Its identity and lifestyle are constituted by this God over against Gentile and synagogue understandings (theology) and practices.

• 6:9

Since **heaping up empty phrases** (wrong practice) to be **heard because of their many words** (wrong theology) is not the way (6:7), Jesus provides a different practice based on the alternative theology of 6:8 (**God knows what you need**): **pray then in this way**. The plural **pray** indicates a group prayer. The **then** connects it closely to the theological statement about the all-knowing Father in 6:8, while **in this way** suggests that the following prayer is more an example to be imitated than exact words to be recited.

Compare Jesus' prayer with Seneca's instruction to pray for a sound mind and health of soul and body (*Ep* 10.4), or Plutarch's instructions to pray for the productivity of the soil, tempering of the seasons, childbearing by wives, and the safety (σωτηρίαν, *sōtērian*) of the offspring ("Precepts of Statecraft," *Moralia* 824C-D). Epictetus urges submissive prayer, "Use me henceforward for whatever Thou wilt; I am of one mind with Thee; I am Thine" (*Diss* 2.16.42-43). The Magical Papyri and a shrine of Zeus at Dodona attest numerous petitions for health, wealth, love, favor and fame, friendship, knowledge about the future, choice of occupation, business success, daily plans, travel, revenge, and protection against anger, revenge, disease, and so on.[19]

Several questions have featured in interpretations of the prayer:[20] (i) *How* is the prayer answered? Does God answer it on behalf of passive disciples? Or does God respond through the lives and actions of disciples? Or does it vary with each petition?

(ii) *When* is the prayer answered? Is the whole prayer oriented to the future in asking God to complete God's purposes? Or does God respond now through the lives of disciples? Or does God respond both in the present *and* at the eschaton? I will argue that praying the prayer looks to God to respond both now and in the future, and through the lives and practices of disciples. Praying is part of, not removed from nor a substitute for, the lived faithfulness of disciples.

(iii) The meaning of the prayer is significantly impacted by the social location and circumstances of those praying. The petition for daily bread, for instance, is, for those with plenty, a petition against greed and luxury. Prayed by those in the midst of poverty, it is a petition for basic survival. The latter perspective will govern this interpretation.

The prayer begins by addressing **our Father in the heavens**. See 5:16, 45, 48; 23:9. It is the prayer not of followers of Jupiter/Zeus (commonly called father; see 5:16), nor of the emperor as *Pater Patriae* ("father of the fatherland," 23:9), but of the creator and sovereign God who is the Father of and manifested by Jesus (cf. 1:21, 23; 2:15; 3:16-17). As God's child he draws others into the same relationship (5:9, 45). On **heaven**, see 6:1. The **our** indicates a communal prayer. This pronoun (subsequently also v. 11 [twice], v. 12 [four times], 13 [twice]) places all who pray on the same footing before God regardless of social or gender roles and everyday status in a hierarchical world. It draws them into an undifferentiated community in which relationship with God, not cultural markers, provides their identity as children.

Children in the ancient world symbolized not innocence and purity but marginality, vulnerability, threat to and exclusion from the adult (male) world.[21] This community of children, defined by the practices of 5:3-6:8, prays a prayer whose petitions subvert dominant cultural commitments and practices, envisage the transformation of the current order, and anticipate the completion of God's purposes and the establishment of God's empire. This prayer sustains the identity and lifestyle of this community.

The first three petitions seem to concern God (**your**, 6:9-10), while the following four concern those who pray (**us**, 6:11-13). This focus is appropriate for a community that recognizes in the prayer's address that God is its source of life, and that it lives all of life in relation to God. But the first three petitions also have profound implications for how the community lives.

Hallowed be your name, or **May your name be sanctified**. God's **name** refers with reverence to God, especially the revelation of God's presence and liberating will in the midst of distress and oppression (Exod 3:13-15). Likewise in 1:21 Jesus' **name** signifies his mission to save from sin.

To **hallow or sanctify** involves the notion of holiness, in which someone or something is set apart for faithful divine service. Special people (Exod 19:22), animals (Exod 13:12), and things (Exod 30:28-29) are set apart, consecrated, or hallowed (made holy) for divine service (see 4:5). To hallow God's name (God) is to honor God in doing God's will (Lev 22:31-32) and in recognizing God's faithful, saving actions (Isa 29:22-23). Such actions reveal God as God, the one who gives life to humans and who demands that humans live so that all may enjoy life.

According to Ezekiel, God's name (God) is dishonored, shamed, or profaned by sinful disobedience, and the result is exile of the people for not doing God's will. This punishment—defeat and exile by the Babylonians in 587—shames God's name before the nations, but God will sanctify or hallow God's name (God) by liberating the people from their captors and returning them home (Ezek 36:22-37). The Babylonian situation was widely recognized as a parallel to Rome's triumph in 70 (*2 Baruch; 4 Ezra*). The parallel serves to explain the current situation as one of punishment and to offer hope for the future. God's name is set apart or honored in God's saving purposes to be enacted in Jesus (1:21), which will transform oppression into liberation.

This petition is made, then, in circumstances in which God is not honored. It recognizes human sinfulness and unfaithfulness in dishonoring God through injustice, or in giving allegiance to another name such as "Caesar." It recognizes that humans are so trapped by this way of life that we cannot turn ourselves around. Using a divine passive form of the verb **hallowed** or **sanctify**, it asks God to liberate people from such captivity and distress. It asks God to act faithfully. The petition seeks the honoring of God in establishing God's liberating purposes in God's world.

Ultimately this petition has an eschatological response when God's just purposes are established in full and Rome is defeated. But those purposes are now being manifested in Jesus (1:21; 4:17-25) and in the lifestyle of the community of disciples which lives toward this goal (5:3-48). To pray for God to act is to call for a display of God's justice or faithful righteousness and to commit to honor God's name or presence in living God's will or justice even now. God's name is hallowed in acts of liberation, but ultimately in a world that honors God as God.

• 6:10

The second petition, **Your kingdom/empire come**, essentially repeats the first and so underlines its importance and longing for God to recreate the world. The image now moves from God as loving Father (5:43-45) to God who rules. Matthew 4:17-25 and 5:43-48 have established God's **empire** as life-giving, not oppressive, as challenging the devil's claim to exercise authority over the "kingdoms" of the world (4:1-11), including the Roman empire. This situation of widespread refusal to recognize God's sovereignty motivates this petition. It is grounded in the recognition that humans cannot "build" God's reign. God alone asserts God's rule.

God's empire or saving presence (1:21, 23) is now being demonstrated in the merciful and transformative ministry of Jesus especially among the poor and desperate (see on 4:17-25), and is continued through disciples (see 5:3-16). On **kingdom** or **empire**, see 4:17, 23; 5:3, 10.[22] The petition prays that God will actively continue that disruptive manifestation, begun at God's initiative. But it also looks to the completion of God's purposes, when God will establish God's reign over all, including Rome, involving destruction for many (7:13) and life for a few (7:14).

The third petition is similar. **Your will be done on earth as it is in heaven**. This petition also recognizes that God's will is not done on earth despite it being God's footstool (5:35). The suffering in 4:23-25 and the oppressive and exploitative actions in an imperial system which deprives many of the earth's resources in 5:3-6—not to mention the murderous actions of the imperial puppet Herod in 2:13-23, the resistant religious leaders in 3:7-12, or the devil's claim in 4:1-11—have established widespread rebellion against the divine will. This petition, like the previous two, resists this status quo of elitism, imperialism, militarism, and materialism and refuses to recognize it as normative. The petition asserts that **earth**, the realm of humans, does not have autonomy independent of God's reign and will (5:13).

Against this idolatry, the petition asks God to reestablish God's **will** on **earth** in imitation of **heaven**. Already in **heaven** that rule is established (cf. 5:34), demonstrated in the actions of angels announcing the divine will (1:18-25; 2:1-23), in the life-giving and indiscriminate sun and rain which express God's love to all (5:45), or in the actions of the "birds of the heaven" (literal trans.), who live according to the divine will by trusting God's provision of food (6:26). The petition seeks that heavenly reality, God's just rule, be extended everywhere. It is a petition of hope, confident that God's mercy will be overcome human evil.

Stoic (Epictetus, *Diss* 1.12.1-16; 1.14.1-10; Seneca, *Ep* 74) and Pythagorean writers, among others, also sought harmony with the divine will (Iamblichus, *Life of Pythagoras* 137).[23] Here the content of God's will is known in Jesus. His actions of healing (4:17-25) and words of teaching (5:3-16), and especially his interpretation of the scriptures (5:17-48; 6:1-18) display the divine will and justice.

This petition is answered in part by the obedient and faithful lives of disciples of Jesus who live according to Jesus' interpretation of the divine will (cf. 12:46-50) and not according to the conventions of an **earth** that resists God's will. The community is in mission to the **earth** (5:13). But the ultimate doing of God's **will on earth** will be the establishing of God's reign over all, an act that God will perform which will involve a new heaven and a new earth (5:18). The petition expresses the longing of God's people for God to bring about that age and their commitment to live on that basis and to that end in the meantime.

• 6:11-13

After three petitions concerning God, though not without implication for how disciples live, four petitions focus on human needs (food, forgiveness, temptation, overcoming evil).

• 6:11

Give us this day our daily bread. There is much debate over the word translated **daily** (ἐπιούσιαν, *epiousian*).[24] The word is unattested in ancient literature. According to BAGD (pp. 296-97), four meanings are possible: (1) "necessary for existence"; based on a combination of two Greek words (ἐπί and οὐσία, *epi* and *ousia*); (2) "being" or "current," an abbreviation of a phrase involving the feminine singular accusative participle form of the verb "to be" (οὖσαν, *ousan*); (3) "future," if it derives from the Greek word ἐπιέναι (*epienai*); (4) "belongs to," on the same basis. The third option appeals to scholars who see a reference to the end-time banquet (see Matt 8:11, perhaps anticipated by the eucharistic bread), an image of plenty which will mark the completion of God's purposes. A reading oriented exclusively to God's future action, though, cannot exhaust the petition's meaning.

The other three options share some common ground, namely, God's provision of the (material) **bread** or food required for survival today. This emphasis receives some support, at least conceptually but not linguistically, from God's activity in Prov 30:8, "give me neither poverty nor riches; feed me with the food that I need" (see also Ps 146:7). It is akin to the daily supplying and collection of manna in the wilderness during the exodus (Exod 16). The petition recognizes God as sovereign over the earth, its creator who provides what is necessary today for existence. It asks this God to be faithful to these tasks in the daily lives of the community of disciples.

Implicit in this request is a recognition that **bread** and other necessities without which life would cease (Prov 30:8) come by way of the human community on earth. But God's will is not always done here (6:10). The petition recognizes that basic resources are not justly distributed, that many lack adequate access to what they need to sustain life (cf. Sir 31:23), and that some procure excessive bread by unjust means which deprive others. By asking God to give us our bread, the petition also asks God to ensure that others cooperate in, not hinder, this daily supply of what is necessary. It is a petition against the wealthy and greedy who hoard property and who through loans, interest, debt, high prices, limited supply, taxes, or tariffs enjoy the bread of injustice while ensuring that others do not have what is necessary for existence (12:1-4; 14:13-21). The petition is in line with the scenarios of 5:3, 5, 6, in which God's salvific reign reverses the injustice perpetrated by the elite and creates a different community—local and global—in which bread is shared, the homeless poor housed, the naked clothed, and the divided reconciled (so Isa 58:6-7).[25]

• 6:12

The prayer moves from a concern for a new human community which provides for material needs to a community of forgiveness.

Forgive us our debts. The language of **debts** is drawn from law and commerce (see Deut 24:10; 1 Macc 15:8; Matt 18:21-35) and is applied to relationships with God and others. Both **forgive** and **debts** appear in the sabbatical-year regulations (Deut 15) which require the cancellation of debt every seven years. This practice ensured that no one was permanently indebted, and it provided justice for the poor and needy (Deut 15:11). It recognized that humans are deeply enmeshed in sinful acts, relationships, and structures, always in need of renewal. The use of this language in prayer recalls the prophetic theme that worship and doing justice (remitting debt; ensuring that the poor have access to resources; new social structures) are interconnected (Isa 1:10-17; 58:5-9).

The language of **debts** depicts sin here, as in Matt 18:21-35, as an injustice, not meeting one's obligations (cf. 1:21, "missing the mark"). The exceeding righteousness required of disciples (5:20) concerns being faithful to one's commitments in various relationships (see 1:19; 3:15).[26] In context, these **debts** or unmet obligations constitute not living in relation with God or people in a faithful or righteous way. The request for **forgiveness** recognizes that the one praying has violated human dignity and not met divine and human demands. It requests God's faithful and inclusive love to set aside the debts and renew relationships and community. While God's final victory over all that opposes God's purposes might be in view, Jesus' mission of saving from sin is being enacted now (so 9:1-8). For God's forgiveness, see Pss 25:18; 32:1. There is a corollary:

as we also have forgiven our debtors. Asking God for such mercy means releasing others from their failed obligations also. So Sir 28:4; Matt 6:14-15.

• 6:13

The recognition of human frailty continues: **And do not bring us to temptation/the time of trial**.[27] Is this a petition not to enter into, or to persevere during, the time of temptation? And what is the form of human temptation in view?

1. Despite the assertion "God tempts no one" (so Jas 1:13), the tradition records numerous temptations by God, or at least God allowing people to be tempted to be unfaithful to the divine will or purpose (Gen 22 [Abraham]; Job; Tob 12:14-15; Sir 2:1-18; Wis 3:5-6; 11:9-10; Matt 4:1-11). Frequently some educative purpose is claimed for these experiences. At root they recognize how fragile are human attempts to be faithful. Does this petition pray against such temptation? While possible, it seems unlikely since the temptation not to be faithful is a constant struggle for disciples (cf. 7:13-14), faced by opposition on earth where God's will is not done (6:10). As long as the evil status quo remains, disciples face pressure to conform to cultural norms and not live the alternative lifestyle shaped by God's will.

2. Some have argued that the petition asks God to deliver disciples from **the time of trial**. This is the time of distress ("the eschatological woes") that precedes God's final victory. But the rest of the prayer asks God to accomplish those purposes and establish God's empire. It would be strange now to have a petition resisting that goal. In chapter 24 disciples are to persevere through such trials, not escape them (24:13).

3. A third approach rightly suggests that the petition concerns disciples tempting or testing God by doubting God's faithfulness or commitment to do God's will.[28] Israel tested God at Massah by doubting God's presence with the people and God's promise to deliver them and supply water (Exod 17:1-7; Deut 6-8; the noun **temptation/testing** appears in Exod 17:7; Deut 6:16; 7:19). This temptation is not far away for Matthew's audience. It derives from God's apparent inactivity, from the continuing, imperial status quo. If God really intends to establish God's will, justice, and reign, why has God not done so? Are human evil and imperial power too strong for God? The petition prays against despair, against being overwhelmed and paralyzed by this evil, against concluding that God is absent or has been rendered powerless.

How could God not **bring** disciples to this **temptation**? The prayer offers its answer in the final petition. **Rescue us from evil/the evil one**. As long as God has not completed God's purposes by hallowing God's name and establishing God's reign and will on earth, God tempts disciples to doubt. As long as God allows evil to continue, God allows a situation in which disciples can be unfaithful in doubting God's promises and power. **Do not bring us to temptation** is answered finally when God acts in **rescuing** disciples **from evil**. **Evil** results in part from the **evil one**, the devil (4:1-11, esp. 4:8, Rome), but also from the human heart (15:19-20) and human systems, whether the imperial regime of Rome's Herod supported by the religious elite (ch. 2) or the socioeconomic misery inflicted by the greed of the elite as envisaged by 5:3-6. It results from God's still unfinished salvific work.

The final escape is for God to complete God's purposes. The verb **rescue/save/liberate** or **deliver** designates God's action in various national and personal settings: in the liberation from slavery in Egypt (Exod 6:6; 14:30), from exile in Babylon (Isa 44:6; 48:17, 20), from the Seleucid threat (1 Macc 12:15), and from Rome (*Pss. Sol.* 17:45). In addition to these imperial situations, the righteous actions of a faithful king save the needy and poor from "oppression and violence" (Ps 72:12-14) and rescues them from personal enemies such as the wicked who pursue and hurt the petitioner (Ps 71:2, 4, 11). God saves from sickness (Ps 22:4, 8, 20; Matt 4:23-24). See also *T. Reu.* 4:9-11 for God's rescue of Joseph from Beliar, the prince of the demons, especially from promiscuity and accusations, and from his brothers (*T. Sim.* 2:8; *T. Gad* 2:5), and for God's rescue from various personal enemies, difficult circumstances, and vices (*Jos. Asen.* 12:7, 11, 12; 13:12; 27:10; 28:4; *Pss. Sol.* 4:23; 12:1; 13:4).

This petition for **rescue** is very broad and concrete. It is God's overcoming of all **evil** that resists God's life-giving and just reign, whether imperial (Rome) or personal. That resistance is under way already in the embodiment of God's empire in the community of disciples (**us**). But with a deep awareness of the disciples' fragility in difficult circumstances, the petition yearns impatiently for God's final accomplishment of God's salvific purposes. A marginal and minority community cannot sustain this difficult alternative existence for long periods of time.

The prayer thus constructs a worldview and shapes the community which prays it to live accordingly.[29] (1) The prayer builds a world of heaven, the abode of "our Father" and the place where God's will is done, and earth, the location of the pray-ers and a place of rebellion. Sin, evil/the evil one, and temptation threaten God's order on earth. Against these, the prayer seeks the full and final manifestation of God's empire and salvific will on earth. (2) The prayer reinforces the existence and identity of a community of children on earth. This community knows God as Father, yearns for the completion of God's purposes, does God's will in the midst of the threats of sin, evil, and temptation, and depends on God's grace and goodness to sustain its existence. (3) To pray this prayer is to seek nothing less than the total transformation of life on earth. It is to reject the status quo and pray for its complete realignment in terms of God's will. In a world dominated by Roman imperial rule, praying this prayer for God's empire and will is a profoundly subversive act. It seeks Rome's demise as part of God's future cosmic transformation, and those who pray it commit themselves to embody God's purposes even now in a communal life contrary to dominant cultural practices.

• 6:14-15

Elaborating the petition about forgiveness (6:12), these verses underline the connection between God's forgiveness and forgiveness of other humans. The same verb (**if you forgive others/people**) connects them to 6:12, though the concept of sin has changed from obligations or debts to **trespasses**, a term that stresses more the breaking of requirements.[30]

Both relational forgiveness and the request for God's forgiveness are necessary if **your heavenly Father will also forgive you**. The future tense is logical rather than eschatological. Jesus enacts his commission to save from sin by forgiving people now (9:1-8). This **heavenly Father** has been described in 6:4, 6 as "seeing in secret" and as all knowing in 6:8, so there is no escape. The **others/people** are not primarily disciples (though they are not excluded; see 5:23-24!). This term is used for outsiders to whom disciples go in mission (4:19; 5:16). Forgiveness is extended to them in imitation of God's love (5:43-45). The importance of forgiving is underlined by its negative restatement in 6:15: **if you do not forgive others, neither will your heavenly Father forgive your trespasses**. On **heavenly Father**, see 5:16, 45, 48; 6:1. See Sir 28:4; Plutarch urges mutual forgiveness ("On Brotherly Love," *Moralia* 489C).

6:16-18—A THIRD ACT OF JUSTICE: FASTING

• **6:16**

After almsgiving (6:2-4) and prayer (6:5-15), fasting offers a third warning against seeking societal rather than divine approval. Fasting, as with almsgiving in 6:2 and prayer in 6:5, 7, is assumed, **And whenever you fast**. It is a traditional Jewish religious practice,[31] associated with benefits such as atoning for sin (*Pss. Sol.* 3:6-8; cf. Sir 34:31), healing diseases, and casting out demons (*Apoc. El.* 1:21). Jesus fasts (4:2). There is criticism of fasting when it is separated from doing justice (Isa 58:3-14; Jer 14:12; Sir 34:31). Note two Gentile comments. Suetonius has Augustus say to Tiberius, "Not even a Jew . . . fasts so scrupulously on his sabbaths as I have today" (*Augustus* 76.2). And Martial derisively includes among unpleasant smells, "the breath of fasting Sabbatarian women" (*Epig* 4.4). Plutarch recognizes that fasting has health, but not religious, benefits ("Advice About Keeping Well," *Moralia* 128A, 132E, 134F, 135A; also Seneca, *Ep* 18).

As with almsgiving and prayer, Jesus distinguishes the practice of the community of disciples first by a negative portrayal **do not look dismal/sullen like the hypocrites**. Again the picture is hyperbolic. On **hypocrites** as those who seem genuine in obeying God, but whose inner motivation (known only to God) is for their own honor, see 6:2, 5. A negative reference to the synagogue is missing here, probably because the link was made in 6:2, 5, and the reference to the Jewish practice of fasting assumes it. The **dismal/sullen** look, associated with sadness and loss (Gen 40:7; Neh 2:1; Sir 25:23), is expanded with a puzzling reference, **they cover/disfigure their faces**. The verb **disfigure** (ἀφανίζω, *aphanizō*) can mean "to render invisible or unrecognizable" (BAGD, 125), so it could indicate covering the face with a cloth (cf. Jer 14:4) or ashes (1 Macc 3:47), or being unkempt (the contrast with washing the face in v. 17). Whatever the exact behavior, that which covers the face ironically reveals their motivation: **so as to show others/people that they are fasting**. Again as in 6:1, 2, 5, the approval of **people**, not God, is sought. An act of worship has become theater. That is **their reward**. See on 6:2, 5.

• 6:17
The alternative practice of the community of disciples is outlined. **But when you fast, put oil on your head and wash your face**. Fasting does not display itself; normal daily hygiene renders it inconspicuous (2 Sam [LXX 2 Kgdms] 14:2; Jdt 16:7). Plutarch advises a bride to use oil on her head and wash her face ("Advice to Bride and Groom," *Moralia* 142A).

• 6:18
Its rationale is the same as that of almsgiving and praying: **so that your fasting may be seen not by people but by your Father who is in secret;** see on 6:4, 6. In contrast to public attention, **your Father who sees in secret will reward you**. See 5:12; 6:1, 2, for **reward** as that which follows faithfulness, the intensification of communion with God known now in faithful service.

6:19-34—JUSTICE AND MATERIALISM

Since 5:21 Jesus has been illustrating the "exceeding justice/righteousness" which comprises the alternative and distinct lifestyle of the marginal and minority community of disciples: on murder and anger (5:21-26), adultery (5:27-30), divorce (5:31-32), oaths (5:33-37), nonviolent resistance (5:38-42), indiscriminate love (5:43-48), almsgiving (6:1-4), prayer (6:5-15), fasting (6:16-18). Along with 5:3-16, God's empire shapes this way of life. The audience is also to discern from these examples ways of living that are appropriate to other circumstances. The examples continue in 6:19-34 with a focus on materialism and daily necessities:

6:19-21	Warning against being distracted by material things
6:22-23	A single focus on God's empire
6:24	Material things and God compete for the human heart
6:25-34	Focus on God's empire and righteousness by trusting God to supply the necessities of life.[32]

A section on materialism is appropriate. (1) The sermon has been concerned with numerous aspects of daily life but has not yet explicitly addressed this topic. (2) Integral to 5:3-6:18 has been criticism of the current economic structures of the Roman empire, which oppress and subjugate the poor (5:3, 4) and deprive them of access to the earth and resources (5:5) through injustice (5:6). (3) How are disciples to respond? They are to give alms to those whose lives are reduced to desperate want by these structures (5:42; 6:1-4) and to pray and live for God's complete transformation (6:9-13), including an adequate supply of "daily bread" (6:11). Yet disciples also engage in fasting (6:16-18). Is deprivation the alternative to the greed, injustice, and unequal accumulation and distribution evidenced everywhere?

This section recognizes the necessity and goodness of material provision, but warns against a quest for material goods, which defines the identity and lifestyle of those seeking goods. The community of disciples is defined by a different goal: their encounter with God's reign manifested by Jesus directs them to the yet-future completion of God's empire and righteousness (6:33). They are to live in the light of, focused on, this end.

Wealth and poverty are important topics in the gospel (in addition to those discussed already, note ch. 10; 13:22, 44-46; 16:24-28; 19:16-30 as a preliminary list). For economic distress and misery as a staple of the experience of the audience in a city such as Antioch, see the Introduction, section 5.

6:19-21—WARNING: THE HEART'S COMMITMENT

• 6:19-21

These verses introduce a recurring theme through the section: the commitment of the heart. Misplaced commitment accumulates and overvalues material goods: **Do not store up for yourselves treasures on earth**. The initial negative command **do not store up** (literally, **treasure**) continues the "over-against" definition evident in the sermon. The negative command assumes that **treasuring or storing up** is a common practice. There is abundant evidence that wealth was widely regarded as a key indicator of social status and respectability (e.g., Juvenal, *Sat* 14, e.g. 14.119-51, 284-331).[33] The elder Seneca has Porcius Latro say that wealth (or its lack) reflects a person's virtue (*Controversiae* 2.1.17). Plutarch, though, describes anxious searching for and greedy accumulation of wealth ("On the Love of Wealth," *Moralia* 523C-528B). He attacks the greedy wealthy who borrow in order to acquire more ("That We Ought Not to Borrow," *Moralia* 827D-832A).

The verb **treasure or store up** denotes both the act of acquiring and the attitude of valuing material goods. Such valuing can mean, as 5:3-6:18 has indicated, greed, injustice, excessive accumulation, and disregard for others. The reflexive **for yourself** denotes the selfish focus of the action. Since wealth was regarded as a limited commodity,[34] excessive accumulation meant lack and distress for many who in the urban-rural setting of Antioch were deprived of what was needed to survive (5:3; 6:11). **Treasures** are material goods vulnerable to **moth and rust**. In 2:9 the term refers to gold, frankincense, and myrrh, and in 13:44 to something valuable that can be sold. See also Gen 43:23; Judg 18:7; Prov 3:14. **Earth**, in contrast to heaven, is the place where God's will is not done (see on 6:11). To **treasure** material goods on earth typifies the neglect of God's will. The community of disciples is not to participate in such injustice.

Treasuring is also futile (so Prov 23:4-5). **Earth** is the place of decay: **where moth and rust consume** (this verb ἀφανίζω, *aphanizō,* in 6:16 means either "cover" or "disfigure"). Moth (Job 13:28) threatens cloth (clothing), and rust[35] threatens metal. In addition to natural decay, social disarray threatens because the deprived take desperate measures—**thieves break in and steal**.

• 6:20

Instead (**but**) of this futile fixation, the community of disciples is to **store up for yourselves treasures in heaven**. The same vocabulary of valuing and accumulating is now applied to **treasures in heaven** (for the concept, see Tob 4:8-9; Sir 29:8-13; *Pss. Sol.* 9:5; *4 Ezra* 7:77). These **treasures** are recorded in the heavenly books (*2 Bar* 24:1). They are heavenly rewards (see Matt 6:1, 4, 6; cf. *4 Ezra* 8:33), whereby God justly honors and rewards actions that do God's will. These actions include those commended in chapters 5-6. Particularly in relation to wealth, they include actions that are not self-serving in greedy accumulation by injustice or in securing one's honor through reciprocity and patronage. They are indiscriminate acts of mercy done in secret to sustain the life of all (see 5:42, 45; 6:2-4).

• 6:21

The right attitude to and use of material goods center on the **heart's** commitment. **For where your treasure is, there your heart will be also**. The heart is the center of human commitment and decisions; see 5:8, 28. The unjust accumulation of goods reflects a heart committed to them. A **heart** committed to heavenly treasure means commitment to God's empire and will (cf. 6:33) enacted in daily decisions to use material goods not for one's own gain and honor through reciprocity, but mercifully, for the benefit, not distress, of others (5:42; 6:2-4). Cf. Deut 28:12; *T. Ash.* 1:8-9.

6:22-23—A SINGLE FOCUS ON GOD'S EMPIRE

• 6:22-23

This very difficult passage, part of a series of sayings about material possessions (6:19-24), elaborates the claim of 6:19-21 about the heart. The language is both literal and metaphorical.

The eye is the lamp of the body. While contemporary thought understands the eye as letting light into the body, the ancients understood the eye to be like the sun, letting light within the body out (so 6:23) to guide a person's way (2 Sam 12:11; Dan 10:6; Sir 23:19; *Jos. Asen.* 14:9).[36] Two contrasts (**healthy** and **evil**; **light** and **darkness**) develop this statement. **So if your eye is healthy, your whole body will be full of light.** The term **healthy** (ἁπλοῦς, *haplous*) includes not only physiological meanings ("sound," "healthy") but also ethical terms such as "single, simple, sincere, generous" (BAGD, 86). This person "does not desire gold . . . does not defraud neighbor . . . long for fancy foods . . . want fine clothes," is not distracted by women, has no envy, malice, or avarice "but awaits only the will of God" (*T. Iss.* 4:1, 2, 6; also 3:1-8; 5:1, 8; 6:1; 7:7; *T. Benj.* 6:6-7).[37] The word **healthy** suggests wholehearted focus and integrity. A **healthy eye** with a single focus on God's will signifies a **body full of light**.

The converse is asserted, **If your eye is unhealthy/bad**. The adjective **unhealthy** is everywhere else in Matthew translated as **bad** or **evil** (so 5:11, 37, 39, 45; 6:13). The common expression "evil eye" indicates envy, jealousy, hostility, hexing, and cursing.[38] Such evil seeing, which is not single-minded but divided, envious, jealous, and destructive reflects the state of one's body and the "light" within it: **your whole body will be full of darkness**. The so-called **light in you** has become so corrupted that it is now **darkness, how great is the darkness**.

What is the **light within you** in contrast to the **darkness? Light** in 4:16 is God's salvific presence and life (Ps 27:1), manifested in the **darkness** of sinful structures of oppression and exploitation (see 4:15-16). This **light** defines the worldwide mission (Isa 42:6; 49:6) in which God's people walk or live (Ps 56:13; Isa 2:5). The community of disciples continues this mission as the light of the world (5:14-16). The **light in you** is nothing other than God's salvific presence and empire, which have come "in/on you" (so 12:28). While this light should illumine every part of a disciple's existence, these verses (6:22-23) especially connect the presence of God's reign with how disciples view and use material goods. To "not treasure treasures," to "treasure heavenly treasures" (so 6:19-21) requires a single focus. It is to seek the presence and yet-future completion of God's purposes and empire (6:33). Such a goal reflects the commitment of one's heart (6:21). If disciples "treasure treasures," they have an evil or envious or greedy eye, revealing dark darkness within.

Such a teaching on single focus applies to a wealthy, as well as a poor, audience. For a wealthy audience, single focus on God's empire means the end of greedy and exploitative accumulation. It requires the divesting of wealth in merciful almsgiving (see 19:21). For a poor audience, single focus on God's empire means a lifestyle of trust in God and one another, free of obsessive anxiety about material provisions.

6:24—SERVE GOD, NOT MATERIALISM

• **6:24**

No one can serve two masters. The image is religious, imperial, and social. To **serve** or be enslaved denotes relationship with God/gods (Exod 23:33; Deut 13:4; Judg 2:7) in Jewish and Greco-Roman religions. The image evokes the God's ownership and power and the worshiper's dependence (see Matt 20:26-27).[39]

The image, along with the language of **slave**, defines subject people whether to Egypt (so Exod 14:5, 12) or to Rome, both Jews ("subjects . . . of the absolute emperor" [Philo, *Gaium* 115]; Josephus, *JW* 5.364, 422) and Iberians and Britons (*JW* 2.374-75, 378). It also evokes a basic social institution of the Roman empire, that of slavery.[40]

Where is the good news in using such an oppressive image to identify disciples as **slaves**? As O. Patterson and T. Wiedemann show, slaves occupied a marginal or liminal location, outsiders to (free, male) society yet necessary participants. But the character and status of a slave's owner determined the daily experience of slavery. While some slaves suffered terribly, others with educational, medical, business, and political skills who served an honored, powerful, and wealthy master could acquire considerable benefits of power and status-by-association. The slave Helicon, for example, in the service of the emperor Gaius Caligula, exercised considerable power in thwarting Philo's delegation (*Gaium* 26.166-78).[41] Plutarch refers disapprovingly to slaves as farm managers, masters of ships and traders ("Education of Children," *Moralia* 7B). Such examples in no way justify a humiliating and dehumanizing structure, but they do indicate that not all slavery was created equal. Like the image of children (see 5:9), being slaves is, on the one hand, an image of social shame and humiliation. The image reflects the social location of the marginal and minority community of disciples which lives on the edge of society. Yet, on the other hand, in the gospel's worldview this existence is honorable. In part it imitates and shares the existence of Jesus a slave (20:28). But also to be God's slave is to be committed to God's empire; it ensures access to God's saving power and protection and anticipates participation in the completion of God's purposes. To choose to serve God, the most revered of all, honored a person precisely because God is the master (cf. Philo, *De Cherub* 107).

No one can serve two masters. The verse declares both common sense and a legal principle concerning slaves. It warns that material goods can enslave disciples and usurp loyalty that rightfully belongs to God. The situation of being caught between competing and incompatible demands is elaborated with a double clause: **for a slave will either hate the one and love the other or be devoted to the one and despise the other**. The **hate/love** contrast is less about emotions that about comparative valuing, so that **hate** means "love less than" (Gen 29:30, 31, 33; Deut 21:15-17 [where the NRSV translates the verb "hate" as "dislike"]). The verbs **be devoted to** and **despise** can have more moderate meanings of "pay attention to" (BAGD, 73) and "disregard" (BAGD, 420), less than the absolute commitment, loyalty, and obedience required.

You cannot serve God and wealth forbids disciples from trying to live with divided (not sound/healthy, 6:22) loyalties. To **serve God** is incompatible with serving **wealth** or mammon (a Greek form of an Aramaic word meaning property or wealth or possessions). Others warned about dangerous wealth: Amos 5:10-12 (the oppressive rich); *Ps.-Phoc.* 42-47; *1 En* 38:4-5; 46:1-8; 48:1-10 (judgment on rulers [kings] and wealthy landowners); the common property of Qumran (1QS 1:11-13). Plutarch condemns the insatiable greed of the rich ("On Love of Wealth," *Moralia* 523E-F, 524C-D, 525C-D, 528B); see also Horace, *Sat* 1.1; 2.3.82-280. The cynics Epictetus (*Diss* 3.22.45-49) and Pseudo-Diogenes recognize that wealth is not necessary or desirable for the good life.[42] Yet they are minority voices. Juvenal claims that *Pecunia* (wealth), even without its own altar, is the most honored god among Romans (*Sat* 1.112-14; 3.162-63).[43]

By personifying the **serving (of) mammon**, the verse recognizes that the things which people possess become the possessors and masters of people. Not so for the community of disciples. God's empire removes any such claim or power from material things. By encountering the reign of God, by having this light provide the priority and focus of daily living (6:22-23), by serving God (6:24), the community learns not to treasure (or despise) mammon (6:19-21) but to use it mercifully and justly, with the completion of God's purposes as their priority.

6:25-34—TRUST GOD: NO ANXIETY
FOR MATERIAL GOODS

An audience's social location shapes its interaction with this section. For the haves, it offers great challenge; for the have-nots, it offers encouragement.

• 6:25

As God's authoritative spokesperson, Jesus (**I tell you;** see 5:18) elaborates a benefit of serving God (**therefore**), namely, that God will faithfully carry out God's duty to supply what slaves need.[44] The section urges trust in God to do this, over against a misplaced and excessive focus on materialism: **Do not worry about your life/self, what you will eat or what you will drink, or about your body what you will wear**. Like 6:19 the argument begins with a negative command (**do not worry**). It forbids what many, in an age of anxiety, clearly do, provoked by political and socioeconomic injustices as well as by philosophical and religious uncertainties.[45] Again Jesus defines the community of disciples over against a cultural norm (cf. 5:3-16, 21-48; 6:1-18; 6:19-24). The verb **worry** occurs five more times (6:27, 28, 31, 34 [twice]) to unify the passage.[46] **Worry** has to do with priorities, with "that which monopolizes the heart's concerns," with excessive concern to secure life in this world. The heart is not to be primarily concerned with **what you will eat or . . . drink or . . . wear**. Along with housing, Sir 29:21 identifies food, drink, and clothing as "necessities of life." Subsequent passages show these commodities often to be in short supply for the majority poor in imperial economics (see 14:13-21; 15:32-39; 25:31-46). **Not worrying** does not mean that nourishment and clothing do not matter. What is forbidden is a materialism that monopolizes human actions and commitments and defines identity and lifestyle. **Is not life more than food, and the body more than clothing?** This concluding rhetorical question, introduced by οὐχί (*ouchi*), elicits the audience's agreement that **life** (**life** and **body** are synonyms) for disciples consists of **more than** providing nourishment and clothing (as important as that is, cf. 6:11); it is focused on God's empire (6:33). Nourishment and clothing are the means, not the sum and goal, of human existence.

The community is to exhibit an alternative practice. It is to trust God's rule and provision demonstrated in creation (Gen 1; Ps 24:1; Matt 5:45), the provision of sabbatical years for the land (Lev 25:18-24), the blessings of the covenant (Deut 28:4-14) and the daily rising of the sun and falling of rain (Matt 5:45). Since 5:3, both the adequacy and abuse of God's provision and sovereignty have been asserted in various circumstances of distress and anxiety. See

Ep. Arist. 140-41, for a similar cluster of themes concerning God's omnipotence in creation, focus on God, not being distracted by food and clothing, and God's sovereignty. Materialistic living ("live to shop") indicates a treasuring of treasures (6:19-21), a heart making wrong decisions about priorities and commitments (6:21), an evil eye (6:22-23), serving mammon (6:24).

• 6:26-30
This section turns to the created world for examples of the argument of v. 25 that excessive attention to material needs is unnecessary because God provides for the needs of creatures—food (6:26) and clothing (6:28-30) (so Job 12:7-10 [cattle]; Prov 6:6 [ant and bees]; Epictetus, *Diss* 1.16). A contrast with Solomon occurs in 6:29 as one who did not trust God but resorted to oppressive means to secure excessive wealth. Recall 5:45.

• 6:26
The audience is directed first to observe (**look at**) the **birds of the heaven**, where God's will is done, and from which extends God's empire (see 4:17; 5:16, 34; 6:11). Discernment is crucial for this alternative lifestyle. The **birds**, created by God (Gen 1:20-22), **neither sow nor reap nor gather into barns** (traditional outdoor male roles). Instead **your heavenly Father feeds them** from creation (so Gen 1:30; Job 12:10; Ps 104:10-17; *Pss. Sol.* 5:9-10). The use of **your** along with the familiar image of **heavenly Father** (see 5:16, 45, 48; 6:1, 9) connects the birds' experience with the community of disciples. God's provision is certain.

Are you not of more value than they? Another rhetorical question elicits the audience's assent. The emphatic personal pronoun **you**, and the *a minore ad maius* argument (moving from the lesser to the greater) connects birds and disciples. What God does for the birds, God surely does for disciples. Therefore, if the birds trust God's provision and are not anxious, disciples should also trust and not be anxious. The image does not preclude work and activity (God and birds work), or God's provision through other people (6:2-4). The issue is of trust and worry.

• 6:27
And can any of you by worrying add a single hour[47] to your span of life? Worrying is not only distrustful; it is futile. This argument draws from human experience. Again agreement is sought with a rhetorical question and personal address (**you**). The attempt to control the future, which belongs to God, is absurd and arrogant because it usurps God's sovereignty. It is precisely this sovereignty that disciples are to trust, not usurp.

• 6:28-30
The example now moves to clothing, first mentioned in v. 25: **Why do you worry about clothing?** The audience's attention is again directed to creation, but with a more intense verb, **examine/learn closely from the lilies of the field**, and with greater focus: **how they grow**. The comparison with the

lilies/grass is not to underline human fragility (as in Isa 40:6-8) but God's care for the flowers, which **neither toil nor spin** (traditional female roles).

Another comparison is introduced: **yet I tell you even Solomon in all his glory was not clothed as one of these**. Is this a positive reference to **Solomon,** as most claim, that God's provision for the flowers is greater than Solomon's splendid clothing? More likely, the reference to Solomon is negative.[48] Solomon is the model distrustful and anxious person. Whereas the flowers show how to trust God, Solomon shows how not to do it.

This view can be supported by the following: (1) The introductory phrase **yet I tell you** has appeared thirteen times (5:18, 20, 22, 26, 28, 32, 34, 39, 44; 6:2, 5, 16, 25), each time introducing a contrast. (2) **Solomon** was introduced negatively in 1:6-7. (3) As a king he is associated with numerous negative references to kings (so 1:6-11; ch. 2). (4) The phrase **in all his glory** indicates something that rightly belongs to God (4:8; 5:16; 6:2) but can be usurped. The pronoun **his** indicates Solomon's concern with his own glory, not God's— behavior typical of kings' misdirected ambition (so Plutarch, "On Love of Wealth," *Moralia* 525D). (5) Solomon's reign in 1 Kgs (cf. LXX 3 Kgdms) shows that he violates God's will for kings set out in Deut 17:15-17b and 1 Sam 8. He acquires many wives, horses, and great wealth, by military conscription, forced labor, requisitioned property, heavy taxation, and slavery. He gains great wealth not by trusting God but by demonstrating such anxiety about material possessions that he employs the typical unjust and exploitative strategies of imperial powers which God had forbidden. By contrast, the flowers trust God, and God clothes them in a way superior to that of the distrustful anxious Solomon.

If God so clothes the grass of the field, which is alive today and tomorrow is thrown into the oven, will he not much more clothe you of little faith? Again an *a minore ad maius* argument (from the lesser to the greater) secures the connection (so 6:26). If God treats disposable grass with such care and splendor, disciples can trust God to provide for them just as God has done since creation (Gen 3:21). The essence of "worry" is clearly identified by the description of disciples as **you of little faith**. This term, used three more times (8:26; 14:31; 16:8) of disciples when they doubt Jesus' power, indicates not the absence of any faith, but little faith which must grow stronger and not be swamped or paralyzed by apparently overwhelming circumstances. It is to grow by discerning God's immensely powerful, faithful, and gracious sovereignty in creation, which Jesus promises is available to trusting disciples.

• 6:31-32
Jesus returns to the central contrast—worry and God's gracious provision. The repeated command **Do not worry** and dramatic questions **What will we eat? . . . drink? . . . wear?** recall the worry of 6:25. Such materialism, worried **striving** for material goods as the goal of life, belongs to the **Gentiles,** not disciples. Again the distinct practice and identity of disciples are defined over against a negative portrayal of **Gentiles** (5:47; 6:7). The disciples have a different practice because **your heavenly Father knows that you need all these**

things. This theological claim about God's all-knowing nature determines the practice of prayer (6:8). Now it extends to material goods as a basic feature of the disciples' lifestyle and identity. God supplies not excess or luxury, such as the Gentiles seek, but what **you need**.

• 6:33

Instead of the Gentiles' striving for material goods as the object of life (6:32), disciples **strive for** (same verb) a different goal and priority: **strive first for the empire/reign**[49] **and its justice/righteousness**. How? God's empire or reign is already among disciples in the ministry of Jesus (4:17; 12:28) though God's purposes are not completed. To **strive for** the empire is to pray for it (6:10), to live now the distinctive identity and lifestyle which it creates and which Jesus teaches, and to anticipate the goal of the completion of God's purposes (7:13-14).

Striving is not passive but an active doing. This lifestyle, marked by **justice/righteousness** (see 5:6, 10, 20; 6:1), means actions created by God's saving presence and faithful to God's purposes. These actions seek to return structures and practices to their God-given role in right relation in God's empire (cf. 5:3-12). The establishment of God's **empire** where all things are in just relationship (**justice/righteousness**) means that **all these things** (adequate material needs, 6:25, 31) **will be given** (the passive indicates that God gives what is needed for life) **to you as well**.

• 6:34

So do not worry about tomorrow repeats the negative command of 6:25, 30. The reference to **tomorrow** sums up the attempts to secure the future with adequate material provisions and to lengthen one's life (6:27). For concern about the future, see Prov 27:1 and the pervasive petitions for knowledge about the future in the Greek Magical Papyri. Plutarch urges meeting "the future without fear or suspicion, with their hopes cheerful and bright" not because of trust in God, but because calm that originates in controlled emotions allows one to accept whatever Fortune brings ("On Tranquillity of Mind," *Moralia* 477F).

One thing remains certain about tomorrow: **tomorrow will bring worries of its own**.[50] The issue of **worry** about the uncertainties of life is not settled once for all, but confronts disciples each day. While the present and future are out of human control, God's faithful and gracious provision remains. In the midst of tomorrow's worries, the assurances of the heavenly Father's gracious and adequate provision, which stem from God's sovereignty over creation, stand. To worry today about tomorrow is, in the light of God's sovereignty, unnecessary and unfaithful. Likewise for today and its **evil/trouble**. While **today's trouble/evil is enough for today**, God's gracious provision is more than adequate. Note **worry** and **trouble/evil** as the pervasive contexts in which disciples live (cf. 7:13-14). Therefore disciples are, without distraction, to seek God's empire and its righteousness, present and future, trusting God to meet their material needs.

CHAPTER 7

Jesus Teaches

The Sermon on the Mount Concludes

The sermon continues to provide a vision or examples of life shaped by God's empire (4:17).[1] Following instruction on material goods and economic relationships (6:19-34), 7:1-6 examines the role of correction in the community of disciples. Matthew 7:7-11 concerns seeking God in life and prayer; 7:12 is often read as a summary of the whole section from 5:17. Several units (7:13-14, 15-20, 21-23, 24-27) close out the sermon by emphasizing accountability in the judgment. All the material shapes the audience so that it can continue to discern a way of life appropriate to God's empire and in contrast to Rome's empire.

7:1-6—A COMMUNITY OF COMPASSIONATE
CORRECTION, NOT CONDEMNATION

• 7:1

A negative command marks a new subsection (also 6:19, 25, and within 6:25-34 at vv. 31 and 34). **Do not judge** translates the verb κρίνω (*krinō*). The verb has a broad range of meanings: "separate, distinguish . . . judge, think, consider . . . decide, propose . . . bring to trial, dispute, quarrel . . . condemn, punish . . . pass an unfavorable judgment on, criticize, find fault with . . ." (BAGD, 451-52). One can, with some interpreters, understand it as a prohibition on every act of judgment. But this view is not sustainable. (1) The command itself, directed against judging, is a judgment that would violate itself. (2) Most of the rest of the passage, notably v. 2a, and vv. 3-6, requires critical or discerning thinking by disciples. (3) In 18:15-20 the community must deal with a member who is discerned to need correction. (4) Through the sermon and the gospel, the disciples and the audience are being trained to discern practices appropriate to God's reign. Not everything is acceptable. (5) Jesus "judges" people: synagogue practices represent hypocrisy (6:2, 5); Gentiles don't know how to pray (6:7) and are inappropriately focused on material goods (6:32). To understand this verb in a broad sense would set up patent contradictions.

A more restricted translation is necessary. A clue comes from 19:28, where the verb appears in a scene of final judgment.[2] This suggests that the judgment prohibited by the four uses of the verb **judge** in vv. 1-2 is eschatological judgment. Disciples must not usurp God's role and decide someone's future destiny. Such "writing off" of a person is prohibited, not only because it lacks mercy or compassion (5:7, 22) but because only the all-seeing and all-knowing God can exercise that role (6:4, 6, 8, 18, 32; cf. 13:36-43, 47-50) in the future close of the age. Hence a translation **Do not condemn (to hell)**, or **Do not play God**, would be appropriate. To usurp God's role betokens such arrogance that future condemnation awaits the disciple who dares to do so. To refrain from usurping God's role means **you may not be condemned to hell**. The future passive indicates God's judgment. Compare 5:22.

• 7:2

The underlying principle of justice is now stated: **For with the judgment/condemnation you make you will be judged/condemned, and the measure you give will be the measure you get.** The future passives look to God's final judgment. To deprive others of mercy means to deprive oneself of it (so Sir 16:14b; 28:4; *T. Zeb.* 5:3). The eschatological scenario warns disciples not to make eschatological decisions about other community members.

Verses 1-2 identify the community of disciples as a community of the imperfect, of those who journey on the way to life (7:13-14). Growth in perfection (5:48), in greater righteousness (5:20), continues until that final destination. It is a community in which every member trusts himself or herself to God's mercy.

• 7:3-4

These two verses function as a transition. They look back to 7:1-2 to show why humans must not usurp God's role (humans have imperfect vision). They parody unacceptable correction of others in order to present a legitimate practice of correction (not judging), which is elaborated in v. 5 with a caution in v. 6.

Imperfect vision, the concern of 5:28-29, 38; 6:22-23,[3] is demonstrated in the caricature: **Why do you see the speck in your neighbor's/brother or sister's eye, but do not notice the log in your own?** The graphic contrast of size in **speck** and **log** emphasizes the inability to see one's own faults and the heightened but distorted ability to see the lesser faults of others.[4] The pretension of seeing the other's **speck** is ridiculed by the lack of self-knowledge in the second clause. The kinship language **brothers and sisters** indicates that relationships among the children of the heavenly Father (disciples) are in view (4:18-22; 5:9, 22). Verse 4 continues the ridicule. Attempting to correct the other by offering to remove their **speck** while still retaining one's own **log** shows how extensively vision is impaired.

• 7:5

Community members cannot condemn others to hell. Nor can they correct one another in the manner parodied in 7:3-4. Jesus, though, provides an alternative practice. He directly and negatively addresses the one who in v. 4 offers inappropriate correction, **You hypocrite**. For this harsh judgment, see 6:2, 5, 16. Correction of the other begins with and follows self-correction. The **first** requirement is to **throw out/take the log out of your own eye** ("know thyself"; "examine yourself" [Sir 18:20]). Then **you will see clearly**, an intensified form of the verb διαβλέπω (*diablepō,* 7:3). Now **removing the speck from** the other's **eye** is possible. Correction follows self-examination that is shaped by the presence and future of God's empire. Aware of one's own limitations and formed by God's reign, merciful and life-giving correction of another is possible. See Lev 19:17-18, where reproof, rather than revenge or bearing a grudge, expresses love for one's neighbor. The community of disciples takes seriously each other's journey to participate in the fullness of God's empire. A minority and marginal community will not survive otherwise.

• 7:6

While correction is to be given to a brother or sister, however, its reception and effectiveness as an act of love in the service of God's empire cannot be guaranteed. This strange verse[5] cautions that correction should not be pressed with those who will not receive it. Some are less receptive.

The term **the holy** comes from passages such as Exod 29:33 and Lev 2:3, which refer to sacrificial offerings set apart for divine service (see 4:5; 6:9). The correction offered to other community members serves God's empire and furthers God's purposes. But **Do not give what is holy to the dogs**. The term **dogs** (as pets, see Tob 6:1) is widely used to express hostility and contempt for opponents.[6] The **dogs** will not receive correction. This is the first of two negative animal images. It expresses the perspective of the obedient in identifying those who will not yield to the character-forming work of God's reign and of the community of disciples.

So **do not throw your pearls before swine**. This essentially repeats the point. Like "the holy," **pearls** are valued (13:45-46; also *T. Jud.* 13:5), whereas **swine** are despised (Lev 11:7; Prov 11:22; *1 En* 89:42-43, 49; Horace, *Ep* 1.2.26; 2.2.75 [negative references to pigs and dogs]). In this context, there is no point offering valuable correction when it will be despised and rejected, **trampled under foot**. The one providing it will be in danger: they will **turn and maul you**. But even in such circumstances, the rejected one is not permitted to consign them to hell (cf. 7:1; 13:36-43, 47-50).

7:7-11—SEEKING GOD IN LIFE AND PRAYER

After elaborating the greater justice/righteousness required of disciples in a distinctive and alternative identity and lifestyle (5:21-6:18), after exhorting trust in God to provide adequate material supplies (6:19-34), and after instructions about compassionate correction (7:1-6), this section reminds disciples of their focus on God and reassures them of God's gracious response in providing them with the necessary **good things** (7:11; 6:8, 32). While prayer is in view

(7:11), H. D. Betz correctly argues that the language of asking, seeking, and knocking is not exclusively the language of prayer, though it is that, but is language that describes a lifestyle of focusing on and doing God's purposes.[7] The section links prayer and human action.

• 7:7

Three parallel pairs assume a situation of want and lack. They combine the activity of searching with the certainty of success. **Ask, and it will be given you; search, and you will find; knock, and the door will be opened for you**. The language of the pairings abounds in biblical traditions.[8] It denotes seeking God, wisdom, knowledge, justice, the divine will or presence, and so on, either in a specific act of prayer or in a more general, everyday searching.[9] The particular prayer pairing of "cry/call" and "answer" (Isa 30:19; 58:9; 65:24; Jer 33:3) is not used. Sometimes this seeking is contrasted with misguided seeking (Ps 4:2; Prov 29:10; Isa 31:1; Jer 10:21). The verb **ask** has appeared twice, referring to prayer (6:8) and to seeking human support (5:42); **search** appeared in 6:33 instructing the audience to focus and live on the basis of God's empire and justice.

The three imperatives (second person plural present) require disciples to **ask . . . search . . . knock**. The present tense indicates not only tenacity in prayer but also an ongoing, faithful disposition and way of life focused on God. The first and third responses (**it will be given**; **will be opened**) employ the future passive,[10] suggesting God's response to the disciples' activity (**you will find**). Thus this faithful way of life focused on God, as well as the specific activity of prayer, is sustained by the disciples' continued focus and by God's response (see 7:11).

• 7:8

The imperatives of v. 7 become indicatives. The actions bring certain responses. **For everyone who asks, receives, and everyone who searches finds, and for everyone who knocks the door will be opened.** The "you" of the imperatives becomes a generalizing **everyone** that refers to the community of disciples. These changes (**for** links the two verses, as does almost the same vocabulary) verify the instruction of v. 7 from experience. The present tense for **receives** and **finds** indicates God's ongoing response. The two verses offer encouragement and assurance that the difficult quest for, and focus on, God's will, even in circumstances of hostility and/or competing claims, will not meet with disappointment.

• 7:9-10

A domestic example, presented in two rhetorical questions to solicit the audience's assent, reinforces this assurance. It also lays the basis for the theological claim that clinches the argument in v. 11. **What man among you, if his son asks for bread, will give him a stone? Or if he asks for fish, who will give him a serpent?** The example evokes household experience, common to the males in the audience (**what man** and **his** son). A father faithfully fulfills household duties to provide for the child without harming him (**a serpent**). It employs the vocabulary of **asking** and **giving** which appeared in 7:7a.

• 7:11

The argument proceeds from human to divine behavior, from an earthly father to the heavenly Father, from the lesser to the greater (*a minore ad maius*), from those who are **evil** to one who is good. **If you, then, who are evil know how to give good gifts to your children**. The **evil** of earth's inhabitants who refuse to do God's will has been everywhere present throughout the sermon (see, e.g., 5:11, 37, 39, 45; 6:13, 23), and disciples resist it (5:39-42) by praying for deliverance from it (6:13) and seeking God's empire constantly (6:33; 7:7-11). For disciples as **children**, see 5:9, 16, 45; 6:9; 18:1-6; 19:13-15.

This kind action of a human father provides the basis for understanding the greater (**how much more**) action of **your Father in heaven** (see 4:17; 5:16, 34, 45; 6:9-10) who **gives good things to those who ask him**. The verbs **ask** and **give** complete the assurance of the imperative and indicative in 7:7-8. The assurance of **good gifts** continues the claim of 6:8, 32 that God knows the needs of the community of disciples. The **good gifts** are not specified, but in the context of chapters 5-6, they include everything disciples need to live the challenging identity and lifestyle created by the presence and future completion of God's reign.

7:12—SUMMARY (5:17-7:12)

• 7:12

In everything do to others as you would have them do to you. The so-called golden rule is not Jesus' creation.[11] It appears in positive ("do to others . . .") and negative ("do not do . . .") forms in Hellenistic literature (Herodotus, *Hist* 3.142; Isocrates, *Demonicus* 14; *Nicocles* 61; Diogenes Laertius, *Lives* 5.21 [Aristotle]) as well as in Jewish (Lev 19:18, "you shall love your neighbor as yourself") and in Hellenistic Jewish texts (Tob 4:15; *Ep. Arist.* 207; Sir 31:15). It also appears in subsequent rabbinic writings and other religious traditions. Some claim that it is a universal ethic which expresses the wish of all people to be treated with decency and justice. While that may be so, it does not adequately express its meaning in this context near the end of the sermon and in relation to Jesus' vision of an alternative way of life. The reference to **the law and the prophets** recalls 5:17. Verse 12 encases the middle section of 5:17-7:11, which has offered examples of the "better justice/righteousness" of 5:20 as it points to the type of lifestyle created by God's empire. How does this context impact its interpretation?

A literal translation highlights the significant construction of the beginning of the verse: **everything, therefore, whatever it may be that you wish that people do to you**. The **therefore** connects the verse to Jesus' teaching that has preceded it. The **everything that you wish people to do to you** is not a blank check that the audience can fill in for any selfish or destructive living. The content of **everything** is circumscribed by the context of Jesus' teaching in the sermon about a way of life that embodies God's gracious, transforming, indiscriminately loving, generous, and good empire (5:43-48).

How does this way of life come about? **So thus you do to them**. **Do** refers in 3:8 and 6:1 to a way of life. The pronoun **them** refers to **people**, a term that names nondisciples in 4:19; 5:13, 16; 6:1, 2, 5, 18. So the audience is to live its distinct identity and lifestyle as a community of disciples, shaped by God's empire and articulated by the sermon, in order to influence others to encounter God's empire and to live accordingly. The verse states an ethical principle which sums up the whole sermon and provides direction for discerning how to live in all sorts of situations.

The final clause, **for this is the law and the prophets**, recalls Jesus' claim in 5:17 to "fulfill the law and prophets" (see 5:17). In his teaching and actions Jesus lives out what the scriptures proclaim as the will of God. He provides the definitive interpretation of the scriptures, as 5:21-48, for instance, has demonstrated. **This** refers to his teaching of a way of life in God's empire marked by indiscriminate love for all (cf. 5:43-48; 22:34-40) which is faithful to the scriptures. Disciples live this life, but they have been warned in the sermon (5:10-12, 38-48) that the imperial and synagogal powers will not always welcome their alternative structures and practices. Disciples live a lifestyle that is out of step with and resistant to Rome's imperial ways (see Introduction, section 9). In these difficult circumstances, they must remain focused on God's empire, strengthened not only by the words of Jesus and disciplines of prayer and fasting (6:1-18), but also by one another.

7:13-27—ESCHATOLOGICAL SCENES

This section concludes the sermon. It consists of three subsections; 7:13-14 on two gates and two roads/ways; 7:15-23 on discerning false prophets; 7:24-27 on hearing and doing God's will. The section maintains a focus on the completion of God's purposes as the goal of the life of discipleship. This eschatological horizon, which, with its emphasis on judgment, asserts God's, not Rome's, ultimate sovereignty, has been present throughout the sermon. What is the relationship between this eschatological goal and the way of life sketched in chapters 5-7?

This relationship can be understood in at least three ways.[12] (1) A *deontological* approach emphasizes knowing God's will. The sermon is the authoritative declaration of God's eternal will. They know what God requires of them. Disciples are to live now according to the standard that will be applied to them at the judgment. If they obey they will be vindicated. If they disobey and break God's rules, they condemn themselves.[13]

(2) A *consequentialist* or *teleological* approach understands the sermon as a form of moral argument which seeks to persuade or motivate disciples to live this way of life. The problem is not their lack of knowledge (as in no. 1) but their lack of will. The eschatological scenarios function to persuade disciples to

live this way. They spell out the consequences of reward or punishment, thereby motivating or persuading the audience.[14]

(3) A *perfectionist* approach focuses on learning to discern God's ways and purposes. The problem is not a lack of knowledge or will but a lack of discernment. It understands the sermon as offering a vision of life in God's empire. It sketches a symbolic world in which disciples are to live, and by which they are to see, understand, derive direction, and make sense of their lives and world. Hearing the sermon resocializes disciples into this symbolic world focused on God's reign. Important in this process of resocialization is that disciples grow in discernment. Their character is shaped in learning to discern behavior and practices appropriate to God's empire The eschatological scenes stipulate the horizon of God's purposes and provide models for the audience to imitate of discerning true and false ways of living.[15]

The first approach scares disciples into obedience; the second woos them, while the third trains them to discern an appropriate way of life. In the discussion that follows, I will emphasize the third approach, as I have been doing throughout, though I recognize that the three understandings are not totally exclusive, and elements of the other two will be present.

7:13-14—TWO ROADS/WAYS AND TWO GATES

• 7:13

Enter through the narrow gate. The initial imperative **Enter** (also 6:19, 25; 7:1, 7, 15) is used in 5:20 in relation to the justice necessary for "entering the empire of the heavens." The instruction concerns entering God's empire (see also 7:21: 18:3; 19:23-24; 23:13). But since disciples have already encountered the reign in Jesus' ministry (4:17-22; 5:3, 10), participation in the yet-future completion of God's purposes is in view. The **narrow gate** is a common image of entry to the afterlife.[16] The adjective **narrow** suggests difficulty, and provision for small numbers.

The **narrow gate** is contrasted with another **gate** which **is wide and the road/way is easy**. The metaphor of the two **roads/ways** was common and diversely understood. In Jewish writings, it was a metaphor for how one lives, one's loyalties and practices (Deut 11:26; 30:15-20; Josh 24:15; Ps 1:6; Jer 21:8-10; Wis 5:7; Sir 15:14-17; *T. Ash.* 1:3-5:4; *T. Abr.* 11-12 perhaps dependent on Matt 7:13-14). This easy **road/way leads away to destruction**, a common term in Christian writings for condemnation in the judgment (John 17:12; Rom 9:22; Phil 1:28; 3:19; Rev 17:8, 11). And it is popular—**there are many who take it/who enter in through it**. Disciples must discern that the majority way will not mean participation in the completion of God's purposes. The community knows a minority, alternative identity, lifestyle, and goal.

Gates and **roads** were familiar physical structures. They were instruments of Roman control and propaganda. Above Antioch's Eastern gate, built by Tiberius, was the she-wolf nursing Romulus and Remus, Rome's legendary founders, a monument to Rome's sovereignty.[17] Titus displayed spoils from the defeated Jerusalem temple on the gate leading to Daphne (Introduction, section 9). Vespasian and Titus began their triumph in Rome at the Triumphal Gate (*Porta Triumphalis;* Josephus, *JW* 7.130-31, πύλην, *pylēn,* the same Greek word). The construction of **roads** and bridges was a Roman trademark. Aristides celebrates it as a means of spreading civilization and order (*Roman Oration* 101), while the threatened Calgacus, prince of Britanni, bemoans the fact that a Roman victory will mean the certain loss of "life and limb" in the enforced construction of roads (Tacitus, *Agricola* 31.1). Roads carried Roman troops and ensured Roman control (Josephus, *JW* 3.118, 141-42). They enabled economic exploitation in carrying goods to cities such as Rome, especially tax levies and tribute, and in taxing the movement of other goods.[18] Gates and roads, then, attest military might, violent and enforced submission, and economic exploitation. God's empire shapes a way of life that differs greatly from this imperial way.

• 7:14

After sketching the **way** and destination to be rejected, focus returns to the **narrow gate,** which the audience was exhorted to **enter** at the beginning of v. 13 (*4 Ezra* 7:3-18). **For the gate is narrow and the road/way is hard/oppressed/afflicted/distressed** (BAGD, 362). This last word (a perfect passive participle) appears only here in Matthew. Elsewhere the verb θλίβω (*thlibō*) indicates personal danger from various sources (Mark 3:9; 2 Cor 1:6; 4:8; 7:8; 1 Thess 3:4; 2 Thess 1:6-7) and persecution (Heb 11:37). The related noun θλῖψις (*thlipsis,* "oppression, affliction, tribulation" [BAGD, 362]) denotes persecution or hardship because of the word and mission (13:21; 24:9), and the woes or hardship that the end brings (24:21, 29). The term describes the alternative existence which the sermon has illustrated, a mission way of life that participates in God's empire, challenges unjust imperial practices and social structures, and enacts God's empire in and through the community of disciples. The hardship or persecution results from the tension between societal participation and a distinct lifestyle, as disciples discern and challenge the evil of life under Roman rule. It also results from the journey nature of discipleship, in which disciples continue to learn this new way of living (cf. 6:14-15; 7:6; 18:15-20). Such an understanding of discipleship differs greatly from the approach to life represented by Plutarch and Seneca, for instance.[19]

Disciples are assured that this **hard/oppressed road/way leads to life**. The term **life** is a synonym for "entering the empire of the heavens" (5:20), for "eternal life" (19:16-17, 29; 25:46), and an antonym for "hell of fire" (18:8, 9) and "eternal punishment" (25:46). It denotes the goal of God's activity and of the journey of disciples. God's purposes and empire are life-giving. Their completion means a return to the initial creation (1:1; 14:32).

But the assurance brings a warning: **there are few who find it** (cf. *4 Ezra* 7:47-48, 51, 60-61 [few saved]). The verb **find** recalls 7:7-8 and the exhortation and assurance that continual focus on (asking, seeking and knocking) and discerning of God's empire in daily living are needed (6:33). The **few** denote the marginal and minority community of disciples out of step with the majority, living against the grain, often in tension or conflict with, or oppressed by, the majority (Introduction, section 7). It is on a hard journey and there is no guarantee that all will make it. It too awaits the division of judgment (13:36-43, 47-50). This claim of minority status has a long tradition, either for groups within Israel or in relation to the nations: see Gen 6 (Noah); 1 Kgs 19:10 (Elijah); Jer 11:18-20; 15:10-21 (Jeremiah); Sir 36:1-22; *Ep. Arist.* 136-39; *Pss. Sol.* 17; 1QS 1:5; 5:1-2, 10-11; 9:5, 8-9, 20-21; *4 Ezra* 7:45-61.

Verses 13-14 set out the shape of discipleship. It is a journey that begins with the call of Jesus (4:18-22). Its goal is the completion of God's purposes and the establishment of God's reign. In between, disciples as an alternative "antistructure" community, in tension with their society yet participants in it, discern a way of life that enacts God's empire. This marginal or liminal vision of discipleship, of life in and toward God's reign, continues to be elaborated through the gospel (Introduction, section 10).[20]

7:15-23—DISCERNING FALSE PROPHETS

• 7:15

Another imperative introduces a new section, **Beware** (so 6:1; 7:13) **of false prophets**. **False prophets** are one of the dangers or hardships on the road. They have not been discussed previously. **Prophets** were mentioned positively in 7:12, and prophets who correctly anticipated the ministry of Jesus are honored (1:22: 2:5, 15, 17, 23; 3:3; 4:14), as Jesus claims to enact the divine will which they revealed (5:17; 7:12). "True" prophets will appear in 10:41 (in the context of mission) and 23:34. In the LXX the falseness of **false prophets** (Zech 13:2-5; Jer 6:13; 26[LXX 33]:7, 8, 11, 19; 27[LXX 34]:9; 28[LXX 35]:1; 29 [LXX 36]:1, 8) consists of wrong messages, greed, false dealing, disagreement with Jeremiah, and results from demonic activity (Zech 13:2).[21] The term, then, is a harsh negative label for opponents whose commitments and practices do not conform to Matthean discipleship, but which could be understood, if J. Reiling is correct, to manifest the devil's power. In 7:21 they know the Christian confession of Jesus as Lord and they work miracles, but any more specific identification seems impossible.[22] The lack of specifics suggests either that the audience's knowledge of these prophets is assumed or that this generic and vague description anticipates some future danger from false prophets who will divert disciples from the hard way (7:14).

The community is warned because the false prophets are hard to identify. They feign genuineness while disguising their real destructive identity (cf. 23:25-26). They **come to you in sheep's clothing but inwardly are ravenous wolves**. The verb **come** may suggest outsiders who enter the community rather than the actions of insiders. Their adoption of **sheep's clothing** indicates an acceptable identity among disciples. The image of **sheep** is common for God's people (Num 27:17; Ps 100:3; *1 En* 89-90; for shepherds as leaders, see Ezek 34; Matt 2:6). **Wolves** provide an image of wicked people who bring danger and destruction (Gen 49:27; LXX Prov 28:15 [NRSV "bear"]; Isa 11:6; 65:25;

Jer 5:6; Hab 1:8; Sir 13:17 [a sinner]; *T. Benj.* 11:1; *1 En* 89:10-27, 55; *4 Ezra* 5:18; Epictetus, *Diss* 1.3.7 ["faithless, treacherous, and hurtful"]; Matt 10:16). Ezek 22:27 compares the people's leaders with destructive wolves, and 22:28 names prophets who cover up dishonest gain with false visions and words from God.

• 7:16-20

The challenge for disciples is to identify the wolves. These verses propose a somewhat flawed method whereby disciples can discern these disguised false prophets.

• 7:16

You will know them by their fruits. The imagery has changed from animals to plants and trees on the assumption that humans can learn from the created order (cf. 6:28-33; 5:45). The principle that external practices and behaviors manifest internal commitments is not original to Jesus (Sir 27:6 [speech]; Epictetus, *Diss* 2.1.21-24). On **fruit** as actions that indicate a way of life, see 3:8, 10; and Ps 1:1-3; Hos 9:16 [its absence]; Isa 27:6; Jer 17:7-8 [those who trust in God]; 17:10; Ezek 17:8-9, 23; Sir 23:25; *Ep. Arist.* 232. In 12:33-37, the fruit consists of words and speech. The **fruits,** or way of life, that evidence their falseness are contrary to the life shaped by the reign which the sermon envisions. Two examples follow. Presented as rhetorical questions and introduced by μήτι (*mēti*) to signal the expected answer no, they elicit the audience's assent: **Are grapes gathered from thorns, or figs from thistles?** The image is common, illustrating the point that good actions cannot come from bad people, that like produces like (Jer 13:23-24; Job 14:4; Jas 3:12; Seneca, *Ep* 87.25).[23]

• 7:17-18

The principle is now applied (**in the same way**) to the tree. **Every good tree bears good fruit**. The tree is recognized as good by its fruit. Conversely **the bad tree bears evil fruit**. The false prophets participate in and contribute to the pervasive **evil** context in which disciples live. Verse 18 moves the argument forward by stressing the impossibility (**cannot**) of a tree acting contrary to its nature. **A good tree cannot bear bad fruit, nor can a bad tree bear good fruit**. The type of fruit attests the type of tree. The problem with this criterion is that the false prophets disguise themselves as (true) sheep (to revert to the image of 7:15). But they cannot fool God.

• 7:19

The example is drawn more closely to the false prophets by describing the fate of the tree that bears bad fruit. **Every tree that does not bear good fruit is cut down and thrown into the fire**. John the Baptist has previously employed this image of judgment in 3:10. The singular **every tree** depicts the fate of each individual. The judgment is described twice, first as **cut down**, an image prophets use to describe the fall of powerful nations (Isa 10:33-34 ["the lofty" Assyrians]; Ezek 31:11-12 [Assyria]; Dan 4:9-27 [the Babylonian ruler Nebuchadnezzar]). Then it is **thrown into the fire**. This second image is also a prophetic image of judgment (Isa 10:15-19 [Israel]; Amos 7:4 [Israel]; Ezek 38:22 [Gog]) as well as an apocalyptic one (Zeph 1:18; *1 En* 90:24-27; 48:9; 54:1-2 destruction of "kings and potentates"). See 3:11. God, not disciples, carries out the judgment as the passive verbs indicate (**is cut down and thrown**; so 7:1-6).

• **7:20**

This verse repeats 7:16a, **You will know them by their fruits**. After the examples and application of 7:16-19, the repetition underlines the principle of discerning false prophets by their practices and lifestyle. It is important to note, especially in the light of the church's frequent use and oppressive misuse of this text,[24] that the emphasis falls on discerning false prophets, not on condemning them (so 7:1-6). The gospel will subsequently provide a rehabilitation process for repentant members (18:15-17).

The task of discerning is difficult, not only because the false prophets disguise themselves but because the gospel is very suspicious of human behavior and claims. It repeatedly addresses the issue of hypocrisy. It is very aware of evil eyes and poor vision. Given these factors, a criterion of discerning falseness from external fruits is limited, compromised both by the false prophets' acting ability, and by the unreliable vision of disciples. God will judge the false prophets.

• **7:21-23**

It is no surprise that the section concludes by developing the judgment reference of 7:19, with the emphasis on the risen Christ's role. That is where the final and true discernment and condemnation of false prophets take place (consistent with 7:1-6). It is not the role of disciples in the present.

• **7:21**

This verse announces a principle that the risen Jesus will employ in the judgment to determine whether people can or cannot enter God's empire. It begins by indicating the limits of one criterion of judgment: **Not everyone who says to me "Lord, Lord," will enter the kingdom of heaven**. Saying **"Lord, Lord,"** an address to Jesus used only by disciples, will not guarantee that the false prophet (or anyone else) **enters** (see on 7:13). But the formulation **not everyone** leaves open the possibility that some who say this will enter. What counts is that their saying **"Lord, Lord,"** is part of a more fundamental context: **but only the one who does the will of my Father in heaven**. That is, the words without matching commitment expressed in appropriate actions, such as those outlined by the authoritative teaching of Jesus in the sermon, are of no avail. But the words accompanied by these appropriate practices will mean vindication in the judgment. The point is not that the false prophets do nothing. They will list numerous accomplishments in v. 22, actions that Jesus also does. The issue concerns what the actions signify or enact.

The actions must do **the will of my Father in heaven**. While Jesus has frequently referred to God as "your Father" (see 5:16, 45, 48; 6:1, 4, 6, 8, 9, 14, 15, 18, 26, 32; 7:11; 10:32-33; 11:27; 12:50; 16:17; 23:9), this is the first time he has employed **my Father**. God has referred to Jesus as son (2:15; 3:17), designating Jesus as God's chosen agent or representative, just as the king (Ps 2:7), or Israel (Hos 11:1), or a wise person (Wis 2:13, 15, 18) was understood to be an agent of God's will. So the term reciprocates the relationship and function. It is important here because Jesus functions in this scene as the agent of God's judgment. The closeness indicated by **my Father** underlines Jesus' role as the revealer and interpreter of the divine will in the sermon, and now as the one who judges according to the revealed divine will. Disciples must discern Jesus in both these roles. Jesus will appear again as heavenly judge (Son of Man) in 25:31-45.

• 7:22-23

The principle outlined in 7:21 is now enacted in a description of the judgment. Judgment scenes appear in Egyptian, Greek, and Jewish texts (Wis 4:20- 5:23; Dan 12:1-3; *T. Mos.* 10; *1 En* 62-63). They are revelations which lift the curtain to glimpse the goal of God's purposes. They assure that the wicked will be destroyed and the righteous vindicated. Disciples see how the judgment is conducted so that they can live accordingly now. **On that day** evokes the prophetic tradition of "the day of the Lord," a day of judgment (Isa 10:20; Joel 2:1; Hos 1:5; 2:21; Amos 9:11; Zech 14:4, 6, 8, 9, 13, 20; *1 En* 45:3). The clause **many will say to me** recalls the image of the well-populated, easy road and wide gate which **many** travel in 7:13 (in contrast to the few on the hard road). The **many** address Jesus with claims of relationship (**Lord, Lord**) and accomplishments: **did we not prophesy in your name, and cast out demons in your name, and do many deeds of power in your name?** The false prophets have performed miraculous actions which seem honorable and desirable. Others such as "the law and the prophets" (11:13) and Isaiah (15:7) **prophesy**. Jesus **casts out demons** (9:33, 34; 12:24-27) as disciples are to do (10:8), and he performs **deeds of power** (11:20-23; 13:54, 58). They claim three times to have done these deeds **in your name,** which suggests using his name as a formula of power (cf. Acts 19:13-17) or invoking his authority. Compare Jer 14:14 and 27:15 where God exposes false prophets who tell lies in God's name.

• 7:23

But Jesus judges their claim to be false. **And then I will declare to them, "I never knew you."** Why this renunciation and judgment? It cannot be because of disapproval of miraculous actions, since Jesus, like numerous religious teachers in the ancient world, performs them (4:23-25; chs. 8-9) and instructs his disciples to do so (10:7-8). Rather it must be that Jesus, in a way reminiscent of God's special sight and knowledge (6:4, 6, 8), discerns that these external actions are not part of a lifestyle committed to doing **the will of my Father**. These miraculous deeds are not matched by other merciful and transformative actions of the type envisioned throughout the sermon. They lack an integrity between inner commitment and external actions (6:1-18). Miracles alone are not sufficient to enter the reign.

Judgment consists of disowning and dismissal from Jesus' presence, from the presence of God. **Depart from me, you evildoers**. See 13:41-42. Jesus quotes Ps 6:8-9 with minor changes. Some have seen the term **evildoers** (literally, "workers of lawlessness" [ἀνομία, *anomia*]) as disclosing the identity of the false prophets as those who teach that the law is not to be obeyed, in contradiction to Jesus' statement in 5:17-19. But its use here, and in 13:41; 23:28; 24:12, as well as in Ps 6 (also Pss 5:5; 53:4), suggests a comprehensive reference to all that is contrary to the divine will, including speaking falsehood and doing actions that destroy others.

7:24-27—THE TWO BUILDERS

A third and concluding judgment scene ensures that the audience discerns both the goal of discipleship and the appropriate way of life necessary to reach that goal. Though the term is not used, a parable[25] of two brief scenes contrasts two responses to Jesus' teaching and two eschatological destinies. The parable warns and exhorts (see ch. 13).

• 7:24

The parable is closely linked (**then**) to the preceding three chapters. It begins with a description of the discerning and faithful disciple: **Everyone then who hears these words of mine and acts on them**. The **everyone** is defined by the inseparable pairing of **hearing** and **acting on**. Those who hear and act are the disciples who assemble as the audience in 5:1-2. **Everyone** is repeated from 7:17, 19, to link **hearing** and **doing** with the tree image, in which external practices reveal internal commitments, and from 7:21, to recall that those who do not do the will of God do not enter the reign. The parable's focus continues the focus of 7:13-27.

Disciples must hear and do **these words of mine**, a reference to Jesus' teaching in the sermon. The initial possessive μου (*mou*, **mine**) underlines Jesus as its source. The one who exercises judgment (7:21-23) provides the instruction that enables disciples to be vindicated, not condemned, in the judgment. To **hear** the teaching is not merely physical audition but submission to the teacher (4:18-22) exhibited in a way of life formed by the teaching (to hear is to understand in 13:23). To **act on** them is to do the will of God (so 7:21; also used in 7:17, 18, 19, 21, 23; previously in 5:19, 32, 36, 46, 47; 6:1, 2, 3; 7:12). That is, the parable is introduced by, and the sermon ends with, a reminder that Jesus has articulated God's will (i) in definitively interpreting the tradition (5:21-48), (ii) in countering false practices, whether of the hypocrite (6:1-18), the Gentile (6:7, 32), the anxious person (6:25), the hypocritical judge (7:1-6), or the false prophet (7:15-20), and (iii) in announcing what God blesses, desires, and does (5:3-12, 45, 48; 6:1, 4, 6, 8, 14-15, 18, 26, 30, 32-33; 7:19, 21-23). The purpose of this articulation is a way of life for which there is accountability in the judgment.

The faithful and discerning disciple is compared to a **wise man/person**, a regular character in wisdom literature. The wise person does not trust his or her own understanding but turns from evil and fears the Lord (Prov 3:7), gaining understanding (Prov 14:6; 15:2, 21; 18:15; 20:5), correction (17:10; 19:25), education (Sir 21:21), and learning to speak wise words (Sir 21:17, 25). In the parable of the ten bridesmaids (concerning the unknowability of the time of Jesus' return), the five **wise** bridesmaids (the same Greek word) are ready and looking for the bridegroom's return (25:2, 4, 8, 9), and they enjoy the feast of God's empire.

This **wise man built his house upon a rock**. Construction is an image of human commitments and thoughts (Sir 22:16-18). The **house** in wisdom literature depicts human life as part of the larger world which is ordered either according or in opposition to the divine will. Lady Wisdom builds a house (Prov 9:1-6; 14:1; 24:3) wherein are evidenced understanding (Prov 9:6; 14:8; 24:3-4), righteous living (14:2), the fear of the Lord (9:10), and life and insight (9:6). Her house is to be sought (Sir 14:20-27). The house of the righteous endures (Ps 127; Prov 12:7; 15:6). The **rock** provides a solid foundation. Here the wisdom tradition receives christological modification to represent the teaching of Jesus which disciples hear, and on which they build their lives. Since a community of disciples is in view (4:18-22), the house should also be thought of as a collective, or ecclesiological, reference. This dimension will be made explicit in 16:18-19.

• 7:25

The rain fell, the floods came and the winds blew and beat on that house. This **rain** is not the merciful, life-giving rain that God graciously and indiscriminately sends to all (5:45). Storm imagery depicts the difficult lives that the righteous live, assailed by the wicked in various ways (Ps 69:1-4; Prov 28:3 ["A ruler who oppresses the poor is a beating rain that leaves no food"]). It also depicts God's judgment (Isa 28:2, 17-18; 29:6; Ezek 13:11-13; 38:20-22; Wis 16:16, 22-24; Sir 40:13) including the approaching end (*2 Bar* 53; *4 Ezra* 13:1-3; Matt 24:39 refers to Noah's flood). See further on 8:23-27. The image then depicts discipleship as under attack as the end approaches (the hard road of 7:13-14). Disciples must remain faithful against and in the midst of overwhelming challenges and threats to their very existence, sure that vindication will result.

But it also depicts the judgment, which disciples with houses built on the right foundation will survive. Thus **it did not fall because it had been founded on rock**. The repetition of **rock** from 7:24 underlines its importance. The verb **founded** commonly denotes foundations, whether of the universe (Pss 8:3; 24:2; Prov 3:19), Zion (Ps 48:8), or the temple walls (Sir 50:2). It also appears in writings concerned with education to denote the foundations of a person's life (Quintilian, *Instit* 1, pref. 4-5; 7, pref. 1; 8.5.27; 8.6.63; 9.4.27; 10.3.3; 12.6.2; 12.8.1; Epictetus, *Diss* 2.15.8).[26] Here Jesus' teaching provides the foundation for the life that endures through judgment. The present lives of disciples are to be consistent with the standard utilized in the future judgment.

• **7:26**

The contrast is now established with **everyone who hears these words of mine and does not do them**. Those who do not do the teaching are compared to the **foolish man**, who lacks understanding (Sir 21:14; 22:11), is senseless and misguided (Sir 16:23), abusive (Sir 18:18), full of empty gossip and chatter (Sir 19:12; 21:16, 26; 27:13), godless (Sir 22:12), without resolve (Sir 22:18). The fool does not seek Wisdom's house but Lady Folly and her house, a wicked woman, who builds a house of death (Prov 9:13-18) and evil (Prov 2:18; 5:3-10; 7:5-27). Such a character lacks any of the distinctive traits of disciples (see on 5:13). In the parable of the ten bridesmaids (the unknowability of the time of Jesus' return), the five **foolish** ones (the same Greek word) are not ready or looking for the bridegroom's return (25:2, 3, 8) and so are excluded from the reign. Not surprisingly, the **foolish man built his house on sand**, not the solid foundation of Jesus' teaching.

• **7:27**

As in 7:25 there is a storm (see on 7:25). Both the wise and foolish live simultaneously. But unlike the wise man's house, built on the solid foundation of rock, this house **fell—and great was its fall**. Such is the fate of the house of the wicked and godless who forget God (so Job 8:13-16; also Prov 14:11; 15:25; Sir 21:4; 27:3). The storm has revealed the lack of an adequate foundation. Their journey to destruction is completed (7:13) with separation from Jesus and God's presence (7:23). For disciples there is both a warning of the terrible consequences of hearing and not doing, and encouragement that if they hear and do Jesus' teaching, they will be vindicated through the judgment. The pictorial and contrasting presentation is aimed at ensuring that they discern both the goal of discipleship and the means of attaining it.

7:28-29—THE CROWD'S RESPONSE

• **7:28-29**

The sermon concludes with a formula that will also close Jesus' four other major speeches: **Now when Jesus had finished saying these things** (see 11:1; 13:53; 19:1; 26:1). This closure and transition formula somewhat resembles that used of Moses in Deut 32:45 (also 31:1). It continues the links between Moses and Jesus as teachers of God's will (see 5:1-2; also 8:1). The response of the overhearing **crowds**, not the disciples to whom it was addressed (see 4:25; 5:1-2), is highlighted.[27] The focus on the **crowds** highlights the existence of these two distinct groups, **crowds** and disciples. While **crowds** are not disciples, they remain here open to Jesus' ministry as in 4:23-25.

Their response is that they **were astonished at his teaching** (for **teaching**, see 4:23); **his** keeps Jesus center stage, as does the nature of their response.

Their astonishment, though, does not lead the crowd to engage Jesus with further inquiry into his teaching (as it will do for the astonished synagogue in 13:54 and the astonished disciples in 19:25, 27), nor does it motivate obedience (see 7:24-27). This is not surprising, since Jesus has warned that the many (cf. 4:25, "great crowds") occupy the wide and easy road, not the hard or oppressed road (7:13-14).

They do, though, praise Jesus' style: **as one having authority, and not as their scribes**. On the political and religious authority, as well as conserving the role of the **scribes,** see 2:4. **Authority** will be a feature of Jesus' ministry (9:6, 8; 28:18) that is debated and disputed by his opponents, the religious leaders (21:23-24, 27), and is delegated to his disciples (10:1). The opening chapters make clear to the audience the origin and goal of this authority. It comes from God, who has commissioned Jesus to save from sin and manifest God's saving empire (see 1:21-23; 3:15-17; 9:8; 11:27; 28:18). God gives Jesus a share in God's authority. Here Jesus has expressed his authority ("But I say to you" [5:22, 28, 32, 34, 39, 44]; "my words" [7:24-27]) as the revealer of God's will. He does not exercise his authority in the oppressive manner of the imperial Gentiles (20:25-28). The gospel redefines the nature of power and the goals to which it is directed.

The **crowds** discern that there is something different about Jesus, even if they cannot name it (so 9:8). He is superior to the religious elite, **their scribes** (see 2:4), who lack authority (just as his required righteousness is superior [5:17-20]; see also 6:1-18). The harsh polemic against Jewish religious leaders continues, perhaps reflecting the community's struggle with a synagogue group after 70 C.E. (see Introduction, Section 8). If **authority** comes from God, then the scribes are declared to be illegitimate, lacking God's authorization for their teaching (see on 2:4; 5:20; 15:12-14). The scribes derive their authority from their knowledge and training and from their association with the politically and religiously powerful chief priests (2:4; 16:21; 20:18; 21:15; 26:57; 27:41), Pharisees (5:20; 12:38; 15:1), and elders (16:21; 26:57; 27:41). They exhibit their authority with power over people's lives. But Jesus' authority is not based on birth (the priests), training and knowledge (the scribes), or wealth and birth (the elders); it derives from his commission by God and is expressed in his words and actions (chs. 8-9).[28] Jesus will continue to be in conflict with the alliance of religious leaders throughout the gospel until the blistering and harsh denunciations of 22:29 and chapter 23. Their participation in Jesus' crucifixion (26:57; 27:41) will confirm that the **scribes** are opponents of God's purposes. The use of **their** further distances the **crowds** from the disciples and Jesus, though their openness to Jesus' ministry, at least at this stage, also distances them from the **scribes** and the rest of the political and religious elite who have no interest in Jesus' ministry (2:4). The crowds occupy this middle position between disciples and opponents. In 27:15-26 Jerusalem crowds will call for Jesus' death.

CHAPTER 8

God's Empire Displayed
in Jesus' Actions

After three chapters of teaching, chapters 8 and 9 depict Jesus performing miraculous and nonmiraculous actions.[1] The chapters include ten miracle accounts (8:1-4, 5-13, 14-15, 23-27, 28-34; 9:1-8, 18-19/23-26, 20-22, 27-31, 32-34), with two summary passages in 8:16 and 9:35-36.[2] Six of the miracles are healings (leprosy, paralysis [twice], fever, hemorrhage, and blindness), with two exorcisms, a rescue-epiphany miracle, and a raising from the dead. In addition, Jesus engages in dialogue about discipleship: faith (8:9-12, within a miracle story), the cost of following (8:18-22), and mission (9:37-38). He also forgives, calls a disciple, eats with the marginalized, and talks with John's disciples (9:1-17).[3]

The chapters present five perspectives on Jesus' actions. (1) Jesus demonstrates God's empire (8:11-12; 9:35) in accord with his commission (1:21-23; 4:17). His actions elaborate the summary presentation of 4:17-25 in which Jesus begins his ministry of manifesting God's saving presence (1:21-23) by proclaiming God's empire, teaching the gospel of the reign, calling disciples, and healing.[4] Chapters 5-7 elaborate his teaching (also ch. 10), while chapters 8-9 elaborate his healings and other acts.[5] Jesus' actions and words carry out God's commission to manifest God's saving presence and reign (1:21, 23; 4:17). The scripture citation in 8:17 confirms that he does the divine will.

(2) Three statements about Jesus' purposes and motivation explicate the divine will. In 9:13, citing Hos 6:6, Jesus identifies mercy as central. In 9:16-17 he recognizes the interaction of the old and the new. And 9:36 identifies compassion for harassed people as motivating his transformative work. His power is an instrument not of oppressive death but of mercy and life.

(3) The display of God's empire collides with assertions of Rome's sovereignty. God's empire brings the wholeness which Rome's rule cannot provide (8:5-13), and it will effect Rome's demise (8:11-12, 28-34).

(4) His actions are questioned by the elite. The town leaders ask him to leave (8:34). Opposition grows through chapter 9. The religious elite reject any claim that his ministry enacts God's authority (9:3). They wonder why he associates with marginalized people (9:11). They attribute his actions to the devil, not to God (9:34). Jesus laments that the people are leaderless (9:36).

(5) In contrast, those on the margins recognize God at work. They cry out in faith and are healed/saved. Others become disciples (9:9). Disciples struggle to discern God's presence (8:25-27), demons recognize Jesus to be God's agent (8:29), and the crowd recognizes God's authority in him (9:8).

Miracle Stories

Miracles comprise a significant percentage of the actions. Miracle stories often unfold in a predictable, fourfold pattern with standard features. In chapters 8-9, these include:[6]

Introduction

Approach of the Miracle Worker	8:1, 5, 14, 28; 9:1, 18, 23, 27
Apearance of Crowd	8:1, 10; 9:23
Appearance of Distressed Person/s	8:2, 14, 23, 28; 9:2, 20, 27, 32
Presence of Representatives	8:5; 9:2, 18
Kneeling	8:2; 9:18
Respectful Address	8:2, 6, 25, 29(?); 9:27
Expressions of Trust	8:2; 9:18, 21
Request for Help	8:2, 25; 9:18, 27

Elaboration

Description of Distress	8:6, 14, 24-25, 28; 9:18, 20
Discussion	8:8-12, 26, 29-31; 9:4-6, 28
Conflict or Opposition	8:29; 9:3, 24

The Miracle

Miracle by Touch	8:3; 9:25, 29
Miracle by Word	8:3, 13, 26, 32; 9:6, 22, 29
Miracle at Distance	8:13
Report of Miracle to Confirm	8:3, 13, 32; 9:7, 22, 30, 32
Demonstration of Miracle	8:4, 15, 26; 9:25, 30, 32

Conclusion

Wonder/Acclamation	8:27; 9:8, 32
Alternative Explanation	9:34
Dismissal	8:4, 13; 9:6
Command to Secrecy	8:4; 9:30
Spread of News	8:33-34; 9:26, 31

This structure emphasizes Jesus' central role, the distress and often marginalized status of the sick, the means of the miracle and its transforming effect, and responses of wonder or opposition.

What function do these stories of Jesus working miracles perform? (1) As H. W. Pleket notes, the Roman world increasingly emphasized the power (δύναμις, *dynamis*) of gods in religious experience.[7] This focus was appropriate to an age hungry for revelation, transformation, and personal allegiance (or community).[8] The stories show the power of God's empire.

(2) The stories also demonstrate the compassionate nature of God's empire. In an age in which many understood sickness to derive from sin, from the devil and demons, from angry gods and hostile people, Jesus shows God to rule over all such forces (see 4:23-24; 8:15, 16, 28-34). God's reign or empire, a term that initially suggests destructive and authoritarian rule, is powerful and compassionate, transformative and life-giving. It disrupts conventional structures (8:21-22), contests Rome's oppressive claims (8:23-27), and anticipates Rome's demise (8:11-12, 28-34).

(3) Jesus' actions anticipate the establishment of God's new and just creation marked by plenty and wholeness (1:1; 14:32). He enacts the expectation that God's anointed one, the Christ, would establish God's reign over disease in the new creation (*2 Bar* 73:1-2). His acts anticipate the time when God's empire will be established in full (8:11-12). That age is dawning in Jesus' ministry (4:17; 9:35).

(4) In the meantime, God's empire is social, political, economic, and ecclesial in its impact. G. Theissen argues that Jesus' healings and exorcisms particularly attract the lower socioeconomic strata and the marginal.[9] Using social-science models, he notes that exorcisms, for example, reveal a "profound alienation in social relations." Hierarchical imperial society benefits the small elite at the expense of the vast and impoverished majority. But Jesus' actions manifest God's blessing among the poor (5:3-12). Chapters 8-9 are peopled with the nonelites, those on the margins of "either the socio-economic or the cultic system, lepers, women, tax-collectors and sinners."[10] Jesus' actions target debilitating physical disease to transform its destructive economic (no work), social (isolation), political (oppression) and religious (marginalized or cursed) dimensions (see 4:23-24).[11]

The chapters continue the gospel's identity and lifestyle-shaping work. The community is to address the casualties of imperial society, everywhere evident in the squalor and misery of Antioch.[12] These two chapters prepare for the extension of Jesus' ministry in chapter 10 whereby disciples are to imitate Jesus in performing healing actions (10:7-8).

8:1-4—JESUS HEALS THE LEPER

• 8:1

Jesus came down from the mountain and great crowds followed him. References to both **the mountain** (cf. 5:1) and **the crowds** (7:28-29) link Jesus' actions with his teaching in chapters 5-7.[13] Words *and* actions manifest God's empire. The phrase **When Jesus had come down from the mountain** resembles Exod 34:29, Moses' descent from Sinai. Echoes of Moses, which established Jesus as a revealer and liberator in chapters 1-7, continue. The **crowds** (see 4:25; 5:1; and 7:28-29) continue to **follow** him. Here the verb denotes physical movement, not a discipleship response to Jesus' call (see 4:18-22).

•8:2

And behold signals something important (so 1:20, 23; 2:1, 9, 13, 19; 3:16, 17; 4:11), here the entry of a new character, **a leper came to him**. His[14] skin disease is not the contemporary Hansen's disease, whose symptoms differ from Lev 13-14.[15] The term **leper** embraces a spectrum of skin diseases and of varying contagions. As an attack on the skin, the boundary of a person, "leprosy" threatens or attacks the boundary and "integrity, wholeness and completeness of the community and its members."[16] One response was social isolation. The leper in Lev 13:45-46 was to warn others to avoid contact by shouting out "unclean." Social and cultic isolation were enjoined (Lev 13:44-46; Num 5:2). Lepers were to live outside a city (2 Kgs 7:3-4) or in a separate house (2 Chr 26:21; see also Josephus, *Ant* 3.261, 264; *Con Ap* 1.281) until leper, clothing, furnishings, and house were cleansed (Lev 14). W. D. Davies and D. C. Allison note evidence for leper colonies.[17] Whether this biblical material had any impact on, or attests practices akin to, first-century practices in a city like Antioch is unclear. In 2 Kgs 5, the powerful Naaman, commander of the king's army, is certainly not isolated socially. Nor is the man's relation to the crowd clear in this scene. In Matt 26:6 Simon, who hosts Jesus and the disciples, is described as a leper, but the scene does not clarify whether it is a current or a past disease. S. J. Roth notes, though, that there is no command to care for lepers.[18]

Compounding the man's possible physical suffering and social isolation, as well as the uncertainties of this scene, was a view that saw leprosy as God's punishment for sin (Deut 24:8-9; Num 12:10; 2 Kgs 5:25-27; 15:4-5; 2 Chr 26:16-21). But the scene does not indicate if the man's illness is a divine punishment. God, though, is able to heal it (Num 12:10; 2 Kgs 5:1-14 [Naaman; Elisha is God's agent]). On sickness and healing, see 4:23-24.

The **leper came to him and knelt before him**. He has no name, age, or social rank. The verb **came** (προσέρχομαι, *proserchomai*), often used in the LXX to approach God in worship, frequently signifies respectful recognition of Jesus' authority (see 4:3, 11; 5:1),[19] as does **knelt** (see 2:2, 8, 11 [the magi]; 4:9-10).[20] Both terms describe approach to a ruler or emperor.[21] Philo expresses disdain for the custom of *proskynēsis* in Rome (*Gaium* 116-17). The **leper** approaches not an emperor or religious elite but King Jesus, who manifests God's presence as Emmanuel (1:21; 2:2).

He addresses Jesus as **Lord**, a title only disciples and those who believe in Jesus and depend on his authority as God's agent or Christ call him. It is also a title used for the emperor.[22] The **leper** appeals to Jesus' transforming power and compassionate will: **if you choose, you can make me clean**.[23] To be made **clean** is to be healed physically, and, depending on one's circumstances, to experience social, economic, and religious rehabilitation.

• 8:3

He stretched out his hand and touched him saying, "I do choose; Be made clean!" Jesus' yes to the leper's prayer is immediate by touch and word (also 9:29). While the **hand** can be an image of oppression (Exod 3:8; Ps 31:15), it also expresses God's work in saving and liberating people from oppressive nations and enemies (Exod 3:19-20 [from Egypt]; Ps 82:4 [from the wicked]; Isa 41:20 [from exile in Babylon]). As God's agent, Jesus' **hand** and **touch** save the man from his disease. God's power prevails (cf. Isa 43:13).

Jesus also speaks: **"I do choose. Be made clean."** He manifests God's compassion and will in a life-giving (Gen 1) and healing word (Ps 107:19-20) which accomplishes what God intends (Isa 55:11). The report, **And immediately his leprosy was cleansed**, confirms Jesus' impact. Disciples are given the same task in 10:8.

• **8:4**

No responses are described. **And Jesus said to him, "See that you say nothing to anyone** (also 9:30);[24] **but go, show yourself to the priest, and offer the gift that Moses commanded as a testimony to them."** The religious elite must confirm the man's healing in accordance with Lev 14:4, 10 to allow his reintegration into society. As Jesus' teachings comply with the traditions (5:17-48), so does this action. The man's **testimony** (or **witness**) **to them** declares Jesus' identity (so 11:5). This healing enacts the expectation that God's anointed one, the Christ (see 1:1), would establish God's reign over disease in the new creation (*2 Bar* 73:1-2). If the priest does not accept the **testimony**, the testimony is *against* him. Given their record (2:4; 3:7-10), this outcome is likely.

8:5-13—JESUS HEALS THE CENTURION'S SERVANT

This bold, subversive, and witty scene brings together two empires (Rome's and God's), two ethnicities (Gentile and Jew), and two people with different social roles (centurion and Jesus), yet two people who for different reasons occupy the margins (foreigner, prophet). The centurion is an agent and enforcer of the imperial status quo, whether as an agent of Rome or of Herod Antipas. He is stationed in Capernaum with troops to represent imperial control, enforce public order, and collect taxes from fishing. Jesus demonstrates God's empire in healing the centurion's servant and asserts God's supremacy in accomplishing what Rome's empire cannot do despite the propaganda claims of Aristides and Josephus that Rome has healed a sick world (4:23-24).

Yet Jesus' act is limited. While he heals a person enslaved by imperial power, he does not free him from slavery, but returns him, able-bodied, to active service. The healing can be understood to support the empire, especially if, as some have argued, paralysis is a psychosomatic protest against imperial power (see 4:23-24), or if his paralysis results from being beaten (see 8:6). Jesus' reference to God's future empire (8:11-12), however, contextualizes the act. The healing anticipates the very different world and time of God's empire established over all (*2 Bar* 73:1-2).

Ambiguity surrounds the Gentile centurion. He represents an occupying power, is responsible for public order, and protects the interests of the elite. Yet vis-à-vis Israel's elite, he occupies the margins as a foreigner and as a model of faith. His plea for help and dependence (discipleship features) surpasses the response of many Jews. While affirming Jesus' authority and the need for faith, the story also affirms the place of Gentiles with Jews in God's purposes (cf. the women in 1:1-17; 2:1-13; 3:7-10; 5:13-16).

• 8:5

In Roman-controlled Galilee (see 4:14-16, 23), Jesus **enters Capernaum**, his hometown (4:13). **A centurion came to him**. The term **centurion** denotes officers in the armies of Moses, David, and Judas Maccabeus (Num 31:14, 48, 52; 1 Chr 13:1; 1 Macc 3:55). Samuel warns that they are vital to the oppressive policies of kings (1 Sam [LXX 1 Kgdms] 8:12). In the Roman army a centurion was responsible for up to one hundred foot soldiers (Josephus, *JW* 2.63; 3.124; *Ant* 14.69; 17.282).[25]

The **centurion** initiates the meeting (cf. 15:22). Like the leper in 8:2, he approaches Jesus respectfully (**came**, 8:2). Surprisingly, he subordinates himself to one who, as a Jew, is under his authority. He **appeals** to Jesus. The verb expresses a request for consolation or help (so 2:18 and 5:4).[26]

• 8:6

He addresses Jesus with a term commonly used for the emperor but used by disciples of Jesus, **Lord** (see 8:2). The noun further allies him with the leper (8:2). The centurion describes the suffering which his military-political muscle cannot fix: **my servant** (or **child/son;** so BAGD, 604-5)[27] **is lying at home paralyzed, in terrible distress**. No reason for the centurion's concern, whether human decency or inconvenience, is offered. His act on behalf of **my servant** emphasizes the slave's marginalization: he cannot speak for himself or seek his own healing, he is owned by his master, with few legal rights, no economic opportunities, and is useful only in furthering his owner's imperial interests (see 6:24). While compassion for a slave was not unknown (cf. Cicero's concern for Tiro [*Fam,* book 16]), it was not normative.[28]

No cause of the slave's paralysis is given. Does it symbolize resistance to Rome (4:23-24)? Is it the work of a demon, as in *T. Sol.* 18:11? Does it result from a beating or torture? The adverb **terribly** and verb **distressed/tormented** describe intense suffering (so 8:29; 14:24; see 4:24 for the cognate **pains**). The verb describes the torture of resistant Jews by the imperial tyrant Antiochus Epiphanes.[29] Beating slaves and children signified their marginal status in relation to adult male society.[30] If so, Jesus' healing counters the short-term damage inflicted by imperial power, in anticipation of the wholeness of God's future reign (*2 Bar* 73:1-2). Jesus heals the **paralyzed** in 4:24 (and 9:2, 6); for **house** as a place of encountering Jesus, see 2:11.

• 8:7

Hearing the report, Jesus answers with a resistant, rhetorical question which expresses doubt about helping a Gentile: **Will I come and cure him?**[31] His reluctance expresses his commission to work only in Israel (so 10:5-6; 15:24). S. McKnight points out ambivalent Jewish attitudes to Gentiles.[32] The verb **cure/heal** is the most common of Matthew's healing vocabulary (see 4:23).

• 8:8

The centurion faces a great obstacle. Jesus will not help, yet the centurion's servant needs help. So he, a representative of the imperial power which imagines it rules the world, further subordinates himself to Jesus' authority. He recognizes it in his address to Jesus as **Lord** (see 8:2, 6) and in his appeal, which names the limits of his own power and points to Jesus' much greater power. **I am not worthy to have you come under my roof**. His strategy of submission is clear, but the reason for his unworthiness is not: Does he think that a Jew visiting a Gentile's house is culturally inappropriate? Is he embarrassed that he, an agent of imperial power, is asking for this figure's help? Is he aware that the visit would make Jesus an inferior client?[33] Is it shaped by Jesus' statement that his mission is restricted at this stage to Israel (10:5)? Either way, the centurion knows that while his power can do nothing in the situation, Jesus' power can cross any political and ethnic boundary. Jesus need **only speak the word, and my servant will be healed**. See 8:3 for healing by the word.

• 8:9

The centurion justifies his absolute confidence in Jesus' word by citing how he exercises the authority entrusted to him: **"For I also am a man under authority with soldiers under me**. His orders get things done; **and I say to one 'Go,' and he goes, and to another 'Come,' and he comes, and to my slave, 'Do this,' and the slave does it."** The explanation (**I also**) recognizes an analogy with Jesus' **authority** as one commissioned by God to manifest God's empire over sin and disease (1:21, 23; 4:17; 7:29). As the centurion's orders get things done, so do Jesus'. Jesus need only speak the healing word. The centurion's recogition of Jesus' authority separates him from the rest of the resistant elite.[34]

• 8:10

Jesus appreciates the analogy (**he was amazed**), a rare glimpse into Jesus' emotions in this ancient biography (9:36; 14:14; 20:34; 26:37). More often disciples and crowds are amazed (8:27; 9:33; 15:31; 21:20; 22:22; 27:14). Jesus comments to **those who followed him**, the crowd who physically accompany (see 8:1) and disciples committed to him (4:18-22, **I tell you** [plural]). Jesus' response is solemn (**truly;** see 5:18, 26; 6:2, 5, 16), emphatic in contrasting the centurion's faith and Israel's lack of faith (**in no one**), and comprehensive (**in Israel**, God's covenant people): **in no one in Israel have I found such faith.** It does not mean that no one from Israel will exhibit faith or that Israel is excluded from God's purposes. Other Jews believe (4:18-22 [disciples]; 9:2). Matt 8:11-12 indicates that God's future purposes include Jews and Gentiles.

Jesus identifies the centurion's statement as an expression of **faith**. Recognition of Jesus' authority, understanding of his identity, and reliance on his power are characteristic of disciples. Faith or believing[35] is the means of encountering God's saving power in miracles (8:13; 9:2, 22, 28, 29; 15:28; 17:20; 21:21; 27:42). The terms further denote understanding of, commitment to, and trust in Jesus (God's agent) or in God (18:6; 21:22, 25, 32), expressed in a lifestyle marked by merciful and just actions (23:23).[36] It is not instant but grows and develops ("little faith," 6:30; 8:26; 14:31; 16:8). **Faith**, not ethnicity (cf. 3:9-10), status (membership in the religious or political elite), birth, wealth, or gender, constitutes the identity and lifestyle of the community of disciples.

• 8:11-12

Jesus identifies a further implication. **I tell you many will come from east and west and will eat with Abraham and Isaac and Jacob in the kingdom of heaven**. Who are the **many**? Most commentators see Jesus generalizing the centurion's faith to refer to Gentile nations making a pilgrimage to the eschatological banquet to worship Israel's God in Jerusalem as God's reign is established over all (for this imperialistic scenario, see Isa 2:2-4; 25:1-9; Mic 4:1-8 [including the lame]; Zech 2:11-12; 8:20-23; Tob 13:10-12; 14:6-7; Matt 2:1-12 reverses the motif).[37]

W. D. Davies and D. C. Allison, though, restrict the reference to diaspora Jews.[38] They note the following: (i) The phrase **from east and west** refers to the ingathering of Jews from the nations (Ps 107:3; Isa 43:5; Zech 8:7; Bar 4:37; 5:5; *Pss. Sol.* 11:2) especially Egypt (west) and Babylon (east). (ii) Only in texts relating to the return of diaspora Jews is the feast mentioned (Ps 107; Isa 25-27; 49; Ezek 37-39). They conclude that Jesus contrasts not Jews and Gentiles, but privileged Jews in the land who do not receive Jesus; (**in Israel** is a geographical, not an ethnic, reference) and those in the diaspora outside, who do.

Davies and Allison have made the case for the inclusion of diaspora Jews, but they have not disproved a reference to Gentiles. The prophetic texts do not rigidly separate Gentiles and diaspora Jews; "all peoples" are involved in God's purposes (Isa 2; 25; Mic 4; Zech 8). Nor can the context of Matt 8:8-10 be ignored. Jesus encounters a Gentile in Israel. The faith of the centurion anticipates the participation of Gentiles and diaspora Jews.

The centurion's action solicits Jesus' blessing for a slave, a marginal person. Cultural nobodies are included in God's purposes. These too comprise the **many**.[39] The use of the meal image (**eat**) for the establishment of God's empire is similarly significant. God's empire repairs the Roman world and creates a world in which all have access to adequate resources. Just as Jesus' healings anticipate the health and wholeness of that reign, his acts of feeding the hungry anticipate its plenty (see 12:1-8; 14:13-21; 15:32-39; 25:31-46).

Jesus warns Israel that the time of enacting God's purposes **in the empire of the heavens** (already present in part in Jesus' ministry [so 4:17] but not yet completed) is imminent. They need to repent and trust themselves to God's empire and saving presence (4:17), as the centurion has done. Otherwise **the heirs/children of the empire will be thrown into outer darkness**. The heirs, who are under threat, do not include all Jews since **Abraham and Isaac and Jacob** are present at the banquet. Some Jews have already responded to Jesus with faith (disciples [4:18-22]; the leper [8:1-4]), and more will do so as Jesus' ministry continues through disciples (ch. 10; 28:18-20). There is still time to repent (19:28; 21:43; 23:39; 28:18-20).

Otherwise their lot will be **darkness**, an image of rejection and punishment, the absence of God's light or saving presence enjoyed in the festive dining hall (see 4:15-16; Wis 17:21; Tob 14:10-11; *4 Ezra* 7:93; *1 En* 63:6-8; *Pss. Sol.* 14:9; 15:10; cf. Matt 4:15-16). **Weeping and gnashing of teeth** reflect condemnation (cf. Matt 13:42, 50; 22:13; 24:51; 25:30), anger (Ps 112:10), and perhaps regret for not responding with faith and worship (see the condemned oppressive kings and landowners in *1 En* 63).

• **8:13**

After commending the Gentile centurion's faith, Jesus addresses the **centurion** (last named in 8:5), again (cf. 8:10) emphasizes his faith, and heals the slave at a distance. **Go** (see 8:4, 32; 9:6); **let it be done for you according to your faith**. For another distance miracle involving a Gentile, see 15:21-28(?); for faith and healing, see 9:2-7 (a paralytic); 9:29; 15:28. Jesus acts across ethnic (on behalf of a Gentile) and status (a slave) boundaries. The healing anticipates the establishment of God's reign over all, including disease and Rome. The report (**the servant was healed in that hour**) confirms the effective combination of Jesus' authoritative word and the centurion's faith.

8:14-17—JESUS HEALS PETER'S MOTHER-IN-LAW AND MANY OTHERS

• **8:14-15**

The location of this third miracle story is Peter's house (**When Jesus entered Peter's house**).[40] The name **Jesus** recalls his mission to save from sins (1:21) enacted in part in his miracles (see 4:23-24 on sin and demons as causes of sin). In 4:18-20, **Peter** left his fishing business to follow Jesus. While it seems that he left everything and everyone (cf. 19:29), this scene suggests a more complex picture. Peter has a house, possessions, and a household. His wife is not named here but is in 1 Cor 9:5; Andrew is his brother (4:18-20). Following Jesus does not mean escape from society or abandonment of it; it is lived out in everyday life (see chs. 19-20). Detachment from, yet participation in, society comprises the ambivalent existence of discipleship.[41] Important things happen in houses (see 2:11; 5:15; 7:24-27; 8:6; 9:10, 23-28; 10:12-14). Followers of Jesus in Antioch met in houses (Introduction, section 7). These stories legitimate this meeting place and raise expectations of similar encounters with Jesus.[42]

Jesus **sees** (as in calling the first disciples, 4:18, 21) **Peter's mother-in-law**

in bed (literally, **burning up**) **with a fever**. She is not named, but is introduced in relation to her son-in-law. Her **fever** suggests more than a physical illness. The cognate noun "fever" (cf. 8:15) denotes in Deut 28:22 a sickness with which God curses people (so also Philo, *On Rewards and Punishments* 143; Josephus, *JW* 1.656; *Ant* 17.168 [Herod]). In *T. Sol.* 7:5-7; 18:20, 23, demons cause **fever**. Josephus attributes his fever after falling from his horse in battle to a demon (δαίμονος, *daimonos,* in *Vita* 402-4). See 4:24. Neither sin nor demon is indicated here. But to heal a fever expresses God's blessing and power and anticipates the wholeness which God's empire will establish (*2 Bar* 73:1-2). Is it significant that Jesus overcomes the illness to which, in one tradition, the emperor Claudius succumbs (Seneca, *Apoc* 6)?[43] That this action involves a Jewish woman after a scene involving a Gentile man suggests that male and female, Jew and Gentile participate in God's purposes.

She does not speak. Having noticed her need, Jesus initiates her healing. **He touched her hand** (see 8:3) **and the fever left her**. Her healing may also be a victory over sin, since the verb **left** is used for forgiveness in 6:12, 14-15 (also 9:2 5, 6; 12:31-32; 18:21-35). It may also suggest an exorcism, since in 4:11 the verb is used of the devil after Jesus resists him (cf. 12:28). Her response, **she got up,** attests the power of God's reign. The verb is associated with resurrection and new life (9:25; 16:21; 28:6).

She **began to serve him**. The verb **serve** denotes a life of doing the will of God whether by angels (see 4:11), Jesus (20:28, which followers are to imitate), or the women (27:55). It contrasts a life of Gentile domination (cf. 20:25). Made whole by Jesus' action, she responds with faithful service. The pronoun **him** maintains the focus on Jesus.

• 8:16

A summary statement shows Jesus performing many such healings (4:23-24 and 9:35). Some bring themselves (8:1) and others assist the dependent sick (see 4:24; 9:2, 32; 12:22; 14:35; see also 19:13; 25:31-46). **They brought to him many who were possessed with demons and he cast out the spirits with a word.** Some understood demons to cause sickness (see 4:23-24; in *T. Sol.* demons are agents of the devil who are opposed to God's reign). Jesus' exorcisms express the victory of God's reign over Satan (4:1-11; 12:24-28) and anticipate its final establishment. For Jesus' action by the **word,** see 8:3, 8, 13. Demon possession often accompanies situations of political, social, and economic stress (see 4:23; and introduction to ch. 8). To label someone as possessed can be a means by which the elite control a threat (so 9:34; 12:24), while the behavior can be a way of resisting oppressive power (see on 4:24). In the gospel, exorcism represents not support for but the demise of the status quo through a release from imperial power. Jesus overcomes Satan's power, which controls the nations (4:8), and anticipates the full establishment of God's empire (cf. 12:28).

The final phrase, **And he healed all who were sick**, borrows vocabulary from 4:24 (anticipating also 9:35); **all** underlines Jesus' authority and effectiveness; for **healed**, see 4:23.

• 8:17

**This was to fulfill what had been spoken through the prophet Isaiah,
"He took our infirmities and bore our diseases."** The verse provides
perspective on Jesus' healings. Like the events of his birth (see 1:22-23; 2:15,
17-18, 23), his ministry in general (4:14-16), and his teaching (5:17-20, 21-48),
they are actions in accord with God's will previously revealed in scripture (**This
was to fulfill what had been spoken;** see 1:22-23; 2:15). The citation legit-
imizes Jesus' authority to perform healings among the marginals (a leper, a
slave, a woman) as God's will. It restates God's perspective so that the audience
can understand his actions in relation to God's purposes, which involve the present and future display of God's empire (4:17). By the same perspective, it can
judge the error of the religious elite's opposition and alternative analyses (9:3
[blasphemy]; 9:34 [agent of the devil]). It prepares for the instruction in 10:7-
8 for disciples to do the same actions (for cognates of **infirmities**, see 10:8 and
25:36, 39, 43, 44).

The citation is, as in 1:23 and 4:14-16, **through the prophet Isaiah**. It translates the Hebrew text of Isa 53:4, part of the fourth servant song (Isa 42:1-4; 49:1-
6; 50:4-11; 52:13-53:12).[44] The prophet (Deutero- or Second Isaiah) addresses
the people exiled in the sixth century B.C.E. by the imperial power Babylon, and
promises their return to the land. Exile was commonly understood as punishment
for sin (Isa 53:6; Matt 1:11-12). The return is God's faithful and merciful act of
salvation. In Isa 53, the prophet celebrates God's strange and alternative ways,
which do not imitate imperial militaristic might. He pictures not a powerful military figure but a battered and disfigured servant, perhaps Israel or a group within
it. The servant's terrible suffering (Isa 53:3) is incorporated within God's purposes: "The Lord has laid on him the inquity of us all" (Isa 53:6, 10). It benefits
the rest: "he was wounded for our transgressions, crushed for our iniquities."

The citation, applied to Jesus, claims that God works in the midst of imperial power and terrible sickness through Jesus. He is God's servant or agent, one
who suffers on behalf of and for the benefit of God's people. He **took our infir-
mities/weaknesses and bore our diseases**. The **our** refers to the community
which shares this confession, which discerns the presence of God in Jesus'
actions, and which recognizes him as God's agent or servant. For the term **diseases**, see the summaries of 4:23-24 and 9:35.

Whereas Isaiah's servant suffers within himself, Jesus heals the sickness of
others. What draws the two imperial situations, Babylon and Rome, together is
the affirmation that God works through a figure who suffers to benefit others.
Jesus crosses social, religious, and ethnic boundaries into the suffering of the
isolated and rejected (8:1-4, the leper), the oppressed and paralyzed (8:5-13, the
slave), the sick and demon-possessed (8:14-15, 16, 28-34) to bring healing. On
the margins, not in the center; by life-giving touch and word, not military
defeat; by actions that benefit rather than subjugate or oppress, the merciful
(9:13), compassionate (9:36), and liberating power of God's empire is encountered as Jesus carries out his God-given mission. For physical wholeness as part
of the completion of God's purposes and victory over sin and death, see 11:4-
6; Isa 35:5-6; *2 Bar* 73:1-2.

8:18-22—COSTLY DISCIPLESHIP

After three healing stories (8:1-15), a summary (8:16), and the scripture cita-tion (8:17) come two brief, parallel but contrasting scenes about following Jesus.[45] The first is negative (8:18-20), the second positive (8:21-22). The two scenes emphasize two themes: (1) Jesus' authority as God's commissioned agent (1:17 [Christ], 21-23; 2:15; 3:17);[46] and (2) the hardship and uncompro-mising cost of discipleship as a marginal and countercultural existence, the hard and narrow way (7:14). Both emphases shape the audience's identity and lifestyle as followers of Jesus.

• 8:18
The opening clause recalls the crowds of 8:16 (**Now when Jesus saw great crowds around him**). **Jesus** initiates a departure (**he gave orders to go over to the other side**). To whom does Jesus give orders? To the crowds to follow as disciples, or to the disciples to arrange the boat? The latter is more convincing since **command** (κελεύω, *keleuō*) does not call people to become disciples (14:9, 19, 28; 18:25; 27:58, 64).[47] And only one boat sails in 8:23. **The other side** includes the Decapolis and Gaulanitis, administrative regions under a pre-fect attached to the province of Syria, which included Gentile (Syrian) and Jew-ish inhabitants (Josephus, *JW* 3:56-58).

• 8:19
The first scene (8:19-20) shows how not to become a disciple. **A**[48] **scribe then approached**. Three previous references to **scribes** as members of the reli-gious elite are negative (see 2:4; 5:20; 7:29). With two exceptions (13:52; 23:34), seventeen negative references follow (including their role in Jesus' death, 16:21; 20:18; 26:57; 27:41; see Introduction, section 8).

The verb **approached** recognizes Jesus' authority (see on 8:2, 5), but the scribe addresses Jesus inadequately as **teacher** (not Lord; so 8:2, 5). Oppo-nents, not disciples, use this term (12:38; 17:24; 19:16; 22:16; though see 10:24-25; 23:8; 26:18).[49] While Jesus and Greek religious and philosophical teachers commonly choose followers,[50] the scribe chooses Jesus as his teacher: **I will follow you wherever you go**. The scribe has usurped Jesus' authority (see 4:18-22; 9:9; 10:1-4). On **follow**, see 4:18-22.

• 8:20
In rejecting the scribe, Jesus expands on the scribe's reference to **wherever you go**. Jesus informs him, **"Foxes have holes and birds of the air** (literally, **heavens) have nests, but the Son of Man has nowhere to lay his head."** Jesus contrasts his itinerant existence with the homes of **foxes** and **birds** (cf. 6:25-34). There may be a contrast between Jesus' itinerant existence and the settled political elite. Suetonius calls the greedy Vespasian a fox (*Vespasian* 16.3). Herod is called a **fox** in Luke 13:32, and **the birds of the air** are Gen-tiles in 13:32. If so, Jesus compares his alternative, marginal, itinerant existence

of life-giving service (20:26-28) with the security of the settled elite (so Herod and the magi in ch. 2).

How is **nowhere to lay his head** to be understood? It probably does not mean literal homelessness, since Jesus owns or has access to a house in Capernaum (9:10, 28; 13:1, 36; 17:25). But it does emphasize the basic itinerant quality of his ministry. J. D. Kingsbury sees this quality as an image of repudiation,[51] akin to Jesus withdrawing to minister elsewhere (2:13-14; 12:14-15; 14:12-13; 15:12-14, 21; 16:1-5). So also in 8:34. But his itinerancy illustrates a quality of discipleship, a preference for mobility, not stasis and institution,[52] for an unsettled, dispossessed existence often in tension with the dominant society. He lives as a "voluntary marginal" in solidarity with the marginalized and broken.[53] The ambivalence of discipleship means separation from, yet participation in and mission to, society. Without Jesus' sustaining call, such a lifestyle is impossible for this scribe.

The scribe's address to Jesus (**teacher**) contrasts Jesus' self-reference as **Son of Man**. This latter term, first used in the gospel here, can refer to a human being who serves God (so Ezekiel, over eighty times; cf. 2:1, 3, 6, etc.) or to a heavenly figure (Dan 7:13) who asserts God's reign in the final judgment (*1 En* 37-71; *4 Ezra* 13). In Matthew it is used of Jesus' earthly ministry, his passion, and his future return in power. It primarily denotes Jesus' interaction with the world, especially his frequent rejection, and his judgment on the world.[54] Here the term is appropriate since the scribe does not understand Jesus. In contrast even with the foxes (Neh 4:3; Cant 2:15; Lam 5:18; *1 En* 89:42) and birds (Deut 28:26; Jer 7:33 [who take care of unburied bodies]), the heavenly judge presently has no home.

• 8:21

A contrasting positive scene follows. **And another (man), of the disciples, said to him, Lord, first let me go and bury my father**. This is a **disciple** (cf. 5:1), not a scribe, and he calls Jesus **Lord**, not teacher. He has the familial responsibility to bury his **father**. The use of **first** establishes this act as, at least, his temporal priority. Burial of one's parents was an important act of piety that derived from the command to honor one's parents.[55] Not burying was a curse and a means of shame (Deut 28:26; 2 Macc 5:10; 9:15; *Pss. Sol.* 4:19-20; Josephus, *JW* 2.465; 4.317, 383-5). Suetonius has Vespasian ensure that Lepidus and Gaetulicus, conspirators against Gaius Caligula, are further shamed in being "cast out unburied" (*Vespasian* 2.3). Lucian's Cynic rebels against the high value placed on burial ("The smell will bury me") and is content for his dead body to be eaten by dogs and birds as a "service to some living creatures" (*Demonax* 65-66).

• 8:22

Jesus' response is stunningly iconoclastic. But Jesus said, "**Follow me, and let the dead bury their own dead.**" The demand to **follow** repeats the discipleship call of 4:18-22 to recognize Jesus' authority as God's agent and to live accordingly. Its repetition highlights a commitment that must be constantly renewed. It has highest priority, even over familial duties and obligations of piety (cf. 10:37). Sometimes piety expresses that commitment (so 6:1-18; 15:1-20) and sometimes, as here, it gets in the way. Jesus demands more than Elijah, who allowed Elisha to say farewell to his parents (1 Kgs 19:19-21), but the same as God, who did not allow Ezekiel to mourn his wife (Ezek 24:15-24).

Jesus' command to ignore the dead father violates the dominant cultural familial practice. He joins a minority philosophical and religious tradition which subjugated familial ties to religious commitment[56] and which saw household divisions as a feature of the approaching end of this age and dawn of the new age (Mic 7:5-7; *1 En* 99:5; 100:1-2; *Jub.* 23:16-17; *2 Bar* 70:6; Matt 10:34-39). Tacitus expresses the elite's fears that foreign religions like that of the Jews undermine patriarchal households by teaching converts to "set at nought parents, children and siblings" (*Hist* 5.5). While Jesus redefines households in 12:46-50 on the basis not of birth but of obedience to God's will, not all household responsibilities, including caring for one's parents, are voided (cf. 8:6, 13, 14-15; 15:1-9). Such duties can express loyalty to Jesus and obedience to God's will (15:1-6). Why is this burial denied to this follower? Perhaps Jesus speaks metaphorically, or perhaps he speaks illustratively, as in 19:21 when he instructs the rich man, but not every follower, to sell his possessions.

Jesus' alternative is to **let the dead bury their own dead**. Who is to bury the **dead**? If it is the literal **dead**, his instruction is a sharp dismissal, "leave the matter alone." If it is a metaphor for the "spiritual" dead, the task is left to those who refuse to follow Jesus. Either way, discipleship is hard, countercultural, single-minded, marginalized, a difficult and liminal lifestyle of absolute and continuing commitment to Jesus amidst participation in society.[57]

8:23-27—STORMY DISCIPLESHIP AND JESUS' AUTHORITY

Discipleship means traveling the hard and narrow road (see 7:14). Or to change the metaphor, it means being tossed around in a boat with Jesus when all hell seems to have broken loose.[58]

• 8:23

After the contrasting exchanges of 8:19-22, Jesus is on the move again (8:18). Christological and discipleship qualities are immediately apparent: Jesus leads (**When he got into the boat**) and **the disciples followed him**. On **follow,** see 4:18-22 (contrast 8:19 [the scribe]); on **disciples,** see 5:1; 8:21. The **boat** portrays the community of disciples threatened by an evil world yet reassured by Jesus' presence (Tertullian, *De Baptismo* 12).

• 8:24

And behold indicates something special (so 8:2): **A windstorm arose on the sea, so great that the boat was being swamped by** (literally, **being hidden under**) **the waves.** This scene (compare Jonah 1:4)[59] assumes the ancient

Near Eastern view of the sea as a threatening, chaotic force which God controls (Gen 1:6-10; Gen 6-10 [the flood and Noah's ark]; cf. Job 38:8-11). The evil powers of chaos rebel against God's created order. God's sovereign power subdues them (Ps 89:8-11; 107:23-30; 1QH 3:13-18).

Stormy waters represent political unrest (Plutarch, "Precepts of Statecraft," 19) and tyranny which God overcomes. God parts the water to liberate the people from the tyrant Pharaoh (Exod 14; 15:10). Deutero-Isaiah sees the release from Babylonian oppression as a new exodus (Isa 43:1-2) in which God again overcomes the sea (cf. Isa 51:9-10; so also Ps 46:3, for God's control of the restless nations). The stormy waters depict being threatened or overwhelmed by evil or chaotic situations from which God rescues or saves (Pss 69:1-3, 30-36; 124; also Jonah 1 [cf. Matt 12:41]; *T. Naph.* 6).[60] A **windstorm** (σεισμός, *seismos*) can represent the hardship of discipleship before Jesus' return (24:7; also 27:54; 28:2). To follow Jesus is a stormy confrontation with cosmic, political, social, economic, and religious powers. Recall the testing of the houses by storms and floods in 7:24-27. Attempts to identify the **storm** as empire-wide persecution of Christians by the emperor Domitian in the 80s-90s are shipwrecked on a lack of evidence.[61] In view are the general socioeconomic hardships of imperial reign, as well as personal hardships such as local persecution (5:10-12). While the storm raged, Jesus **was asleep** (cf. Jonah 1:5-6). **Sleep** is not powerlessness or neglect here as in 25:5 and 26:36-46; here it shows trust in God's power and safekeeping (Pss 3:3-5; 4:8).[62]

• 8:25

In these threatening circumstances, the disciples, rightly, seek Jesus' help. **And they went and woke him up, saying, "Lord save us! We are perishing!"** For **they went** as respectful approach, see 5:1; 8:2, 5, 19; for **Lord** as a term used by disciples to recognize Jesus' authority as God's agent, see 8:2, 6, 8, 21. These terms, used in 8:19, 21 connect the two scenes. The disciples' cry/prayer **save us** coheres with Jesus' mission (1:21). See the watery Ps 69:1, and Jonah 1:6, 14 for **save** and **We are** (not) **perishing.**

• 8:26

Jesus' saving action is not immediate (cf. 8:5-13). In dialogue, he challenges and affirms them, **"Why are you afraid, you of little faith?"** His question emphasizes their struggle for faith, suggesting that fear, faith's opposite, dominates their response. They do not share his confidence in God, nor do they emulate the Gentile centurion's faith (8:6-10). They are anxious, not trusting (6:25-34). But Jesus also affirms them, in recognizing that they have faith enough to seek his help (**save us**). It is a **little faith** (6:30; also 14:31; 16:8) which must grow (cf. 15:28, "great faith").

Then comes the miracle. **Then he got up and rebuked the winds and the sea; and there was a dead calm**. The verb **rebuked** (cf. the exorcism of 17:18) suggests that demons cause the storm (see *T. Sol.* 16:1-3). But Jesus' word (like God's) puts the sea in its place (cf. Gen 1:6-9). Jesus manifests God's reign not only over sin, disease, and demons but also over creation (Gen 1; Exod 14;

15:10; Pss 69:1-3, 30-36; 107:28-31; 124) and demonic distress, which threatens to destroy disciples. Like the house on the rock (7:24-25), they survive this storm.[63]

Martial claims that the emperor Titus rules the sea ("On the Spectacles," 28). Valerius Flaccus asserts that the deified Vespasian, *sancte pater* ("holy father") controls the fleets of "Greece, Sidon and Nile" (*Argonautica* 1.10-21). Philostratus has Apollonius call Domitian "master of sea and land" (*Apollonius* 7.3), while Juvenal calls him "master of lands and seas and nations" (*Sat* 4.83-84). An inscription from Pergamum addresses "son of a god, the god Augustus, of every land and sea the overseer."[64] The story contests these imperial claims by asserting God's sovereignty.

• 8:27

The disciples **were amazed** (cf. Jesus in 8:10), as the crowds are after an exorcism (9:33) and further healings (15:31). But unlike the crowds, and the elite (see 9:33; 15:31; 22:22; 27:14), the amazed disciples question the act's implications (so 21:20). They ask, **What sort of man is this, that even the winds and sea obey him?** The audience knows that Jesus is Christ or Messiah, anointed to manifest God's saving presence and reign (1:17, 21-23; 4:17). As God's agent or son (2:15; 3:17), he carries out this commission in announcing (4:17; chs. 5-7) and enacting (chs. 8-9) God's empire. The audience is to follow this Lord in the midst of the adversities of stormy discipleship. But the disciples are still discovering Jesus' identity, and therefore their own identity and lifestyle.

8:28-34—JESUS CASTS OUT DEMONS

The displays of Jesus' authority continue with the first exorcism scene (see 4:24; 8:16; also 8:26).[65] With demoniacs, tombs, and pigs charging into the sea, the scene is like a political satire or cartoon, which mocks the empire's pretensions with visions of demise. Casting out the demons resists and rejects the devil and the devil's leading empire, Rome (4:8-9), and anticipates the future triumph of God's empire over all.

• 8:28

When he came to the other side (cf. 8:18, 23), **to the country of the Gadarenes.**[66] Roman presence was evident in trade, buildings, settled veterans, and troops.[67] Josephus notes Syrian and Jewish inhabitants (*JW* 3.56-58). As in other Decapolis areas, there was violence between Jews and Gentiles in Gedara in the late 60s, with property burned and people killed in attacks and reprisals (Josephus, *JW* 2.458-60, 478).

Of all the people Jesus could meet, attention focuses on two marginal people: **two demoniacs coming out of the tombs met him**. The catalogue of marginal folks builds. The **two demoniacs** belong to the expendables, the bottom level of society (see Introduction, section 5). For possible links between demon possession and social conflict and oppression, see 4:23-24, and introduction to ch. 8.

They live in **the tombs**, outside urban areas but near major routes, so that the living could honor and care for the dead by supplying food and participating in sacramental meals to assist them in the afterlife.[68] The two men live physically on the margins, away from households, which defined gender and social roles, and economic and political involvement.

They were so fierce that no one could pass that way.[69] The word **fierce** (χαλεποί, *chalepoi*) can mean "violent" or "dangerous" (BAGD, 874) and describes animals (Dio Chrysostom, *Disc* 5.5) and rulers (*Ep. Arist.* 289; Cleopatra in Josephus, *Ant* 15.98). They approach Jesus in a confrontational manner; **met** has a hostile sense of **oppose** (BAGD, 837). They intend to maintain their isolation. Compare *T. Sol.* 17:2-3.

• 8:29

Unlike the respectful approaches of 8:2, 5, this meeting is loud (**they shouted**) and hostile (cf. *T. Sol.* 5, 7). The demoniacs fire off two quick questions. The first (**What have you to do with us, son of God?**) uses an idiom ("What business do we have with each other?") which highlights their differences with Jesus and their lesser authority as the questioners.[70] They address Jesus, not the emperor,[71] as **son of God** and acknowledge him as God's agent (1:21-23; see on 2:15; 3:17; 4:3, 6). The second question (**Have you come to torment us before the time?**) reveals awareness of Jesus' role as the eschatological judge (so 3:11-12). Some Jewish apocalyptic traditions understood demons to be active until the judgment and establishment of God's new creation and empire (*1 En* 16:1-2; *Jub.* 5:10-11; *T. Levi* 18:12). The **time** of judgment is dawning in Jesus' ministry (12:24-28), though not yet in full. For the verb **torment**, see 8:6 ("distressed").

• 8:30

Jesus does not answer their question. Attention moves to **a large herd of swine feeding at some distance from them**. The **swine's** proximity indicates a Gentile context. For many Jews, pigs were unclean and not to be eaten (Lev 11:7-8; Deut 14:8). Gentiles such as the Seleucid tyrant Antiochus Epiphanes mocked these views (1 Macc 1:41-50; 2 Macc 6:18; 7:1, 7, 42; Tacitus, *Hist* 5.4; Juvenal, *Sat* 6.159-60; 14.96-99; Epictetus, *Diss* 1.22.4; Philo, *Gaium* 361-62). Josephus has Antiochus sacrifice swine in the Jerusalem temple (*Ant* 12.253; 13.243). Vespasian or Titus is said to throw a pig's head onto the altar of burnt offerings as the siege of Jerusalem ends (*Aboth R. Nathan* 4.5).

Gentiles used pigs in various ways. (1) Roman soldiers raised them for food and commerce (Tacitus, *Ann* 13.54-55),[72] as did towns in their organized agricultural production (Columella, *On Agriculture* 7.9-11; Varro, *On Agriculture* 2.4.7 [on breeding pigs]). (2) Pigs were used in religious rituals which sought divine blessing on agricultural production,[73] and in burial rites to feed the dead, sanctify a grave, or propitiate dead ancestors (Cicero, *De Leg* 2.55-57). (3) The pig was a symbol of the Tenth *Fretensis* Legion stationed in Syria, which fought against Jerusalem in the 66-70 war.[74] In later talmudic literature, the pig symbolizes Rome.[75] The subsequent destruction of the pigs is not only an economic loss, but suggests a coded depiction of Rome's demise.

• 8:31

The demoniacs try a plea bargain. They concede Jesus' power over them (**If you cast us out**) and request a new home, **send us into the herd of swine** (12:43-45; for exorcisms, see Josephus, *Ant* 8:45-49; *JW* 7.185; Philostratus, *Apollonius* 4.20).

• 8:32

Jesus' first word in this scene powerfully demonstrates his authority: **Go** (so also 8:4, 13). The response is instant: **And they came out and entered the swine, and behold** (so 8:2, 24, 29) **the whole herd rushed down the steep bank into the sea and perished in the water.** God's empire destroys the pigs, symbols of Roman commercial, religious, and military power (see on 8:30), possessed by demons, agents of the devil's reign (4:8).[76] The water may be a place to control, not destroy the demons, until the judgment (so 8:26; *T. Sol.* 5:11; 11:6; for demons and desert/waterless places, see 4:1; 12:43). The representatives of Roman power end up in the same place as Pharaoh's armies (Exod 14:23-15:5). The story celebrates Jesus' liberating reign, which subverts claims made by religious and imperial powers and points to God's sovereignty over Rome.

• 8:33

The **swineherds ran off, and on going into the town, they told the whole story about what had happened to the demoniacs**. No mention is made of the former demoniacs. Focus falls on the disruptive impact of Jesus' actions. Jesus' act which benefited the demoniacs has destroyed a source of livelihood, wiped out animals used for various religious practices, and violated a mascot which represents political/imperial claims. The **swineherds** are witnesses. Herodotus (*Hist* 2.47) notes that in Egypt the rustic **swineherds** are so despised by the elite, they must intermarry!

• 8:34

The conflict is introduced by **And behold** (see 8:2, 24, 29, 32).[77] The *whole town* is impacted. **Then the whole town came out to meet Jesus**. This is not a friendly welcoming of a celebrity or of a Roman official at his *adventus* (see 21:1-11);[78] the verb **meet** has, as in 8:28, a hostile sense. In **opposing** Jesus, the townspeople, from whom the demoniacs had been physically isolated, now behave as the demoniacs did. In 2:3 when "all Jerusalem" is upset with Jesus, the threatened leaders lead the "all," so probably here (also 27:25).

The conflict has multiple levels: *economic,* since the pigs are a source of food and income from sale and taxes; *political,* since Jesus has challenged their control and destroyed a symbol of Roman imperial control; *social,* since Jesus has taken the side of the expendables, at the expense of the elite; *ethnic,* since Jesus is a Jew asserting his authority among Gentiles; *religious,* since Jesus has destroyed an animal with important roles in religious rites. **When they saw him** (the singular focuses on Jesus, not the two demoniacs), **they begged him to leave their neighborhood** (so 8:20). They respond to the disruptive presence of Immanuel (1:23) not with respectful address (8:2, 5), cries for help (8:2, 25), or faith (8:5-10, 26), but with resistance, as do the Jerusalem elite (so ch. 2). For different uses of **beg** (παρακαλέω, *parakaleō*), see 8:5, 31.

The alternative existence of discipleship means conflict, because it threatens the (in)vested interests of the urban elite by following Jesus' commitment to benefit the marginal.

CHAPTER 9

Jesus' Actions and God's Empire

9:1-8—JESUS HEALS AND FORGIVES
A PARALYZED MAN*

• 9:1

Jesus returns to Galilee (8:28-34). The words **getting into the boat, he crossed the sea** recall the epiphanies of the **boat** episode in 8:23-27. **He came to his own town.** Previous events there include both the encounter with the Gentile centurion (see 8:5), and his move to Capernaum in 4:13, interpreted in 4:14-16 as the coming of light—God's presence and reign—into the darkness of the distress and death of imperial rule. This retrospection provides the interpretative framework for 9:2-8. Jesus carries out his commission to manifest God's saving presence. A marginal person benefits, while the religious elite challenge him.

• 9:2

The customary **and behold** (NRSV: "and just then"), anticipating something special,[1] opens the scene. **They were bringing a paralyzed man to him lying on a bed**. The antecedent of **they** is unspecified, though it probably refers to relatives or neighbors. The imperfect tense **were bringing** suggests a protracted action; for its two previous uses to indicate the socioeconomic dependence of sick people, see 4:24; 8:16. Twice Jesus has healed a **paralyzed person**; see on 4:24; 8:6, 13. The lame[2] are excluded from the priesthood (Lev 21:18) but promised future healing (Isa 35:6).

Jesus interprets (**sees**) their action in bringing the man as expressive of **their faith**. **Their** may include the paralyzed man, though in 8:5-13 there is no mention of the slave's faith. For **faith** as dependence on Jesus' power, see 8:10, 13, 26; faith also means lived commitment to Jesus (18:6; 21:25; 23:23; 27:42). Jesus assures **the paralyzed man, "take heart, son"** (9:22; 14:27). Moses uses the same verb to reassure the people of God's saving power before their liberation from the Egyptians through the sea (Exod 14:13; 20:20 [Sinai]); and Uzziah similarly exhorts the people before God uses Judith to deliver them

---

*Introductory comments for chapter 8 apply to chapter 9 as well.

215

from the imperial tyrant Holofernes (Jdt 7:30). The term **son** expresses endearment (2:18; 3:9; 7:11).

Jesus takes the initiative (cf. 8:14-15) to announce **Your** (sing.) **sins are forgiven**. The declaration is strange when the man's sins have not been mentioned. Jesus assumes the common link between sickness and sin (cf. John 9:2; Matt 4:23-25). To forgive is to remove sin and to heal. The healing anticipates the establishment of God's reign (*2 Bar* 73:1-2), which includes the removal of sin (Isa 35:1-8). The passive present verb indicates God's action experienced in Jesus' words (cf. Exod 34:7 [exodus]; Isa 43:25 [exile]). Jesus performs his God-given mission to save from sin (1:21; 20:28; 26:28). The scene makes explicit the significance of Jesus healing the leper (8:1-4), the centurion's slave (8:5-13), Peter's mother-in-law (8:14-15), the crowds (8:16), and the demoniacs (8:28-34; also 8:17) and the healings of 9:18-38, that God's saving power is encountered in Jesus' actions (1:21-23).

• 9:3-6a

For the first time the religious leaders and Jesus openly clash. **And behold** (see 9:2; NRSV "then"), **some of the scribes said among themselves, "this man is blaspheming."** For **scribes**, see 2:4; 5:20; 7:29; 8:19. As members of the religious elite, and authorities on and interpreters of the traditions, they do not perceive God to be at work in Jesus. To **blaspheme** is to dishonor God (Lev 24:10-16; Isa 52:5; Tob 1:18; 1 Macc 2:6; 2 Macc 8:4; cf. Matt 12:31; 26:65). Presumably the **scribes** think Jesus dishonors God by announcing forgiveness, something that they claim he has no authority to do.[3] In their theological worldview, God does not designate humans like Jesus to announce forgiveness. But the audience knows that God has commissioned Jesus to this role (1:21). Jesus challenges their verdict, their authority to make such a determination, and their theological framework. Their concern about where God's forgiveness is encountered may reflect the post-70 debates about how atonement is experienced now that the temple has been destroyed (see Introduction, section 8).

• 9:4

Again Jesus **sees** beyond actions. While he discerned faith in 9:2b, here he discerns **their (evil) thoughts** (cf. 12:25; 22:18). Religious figures such as the oracle of Clarian Apollo (Tacitus, *Ann* 2.54) and God (Matt 6:3-4, 7-8; 1 Sam 16:7; Jer 11:20; 2 Chr 6:30) know human thoughts. His discernment demonstrates God's presence with him, but they cannot see it. He challenges them openly: **"Why do you think evil in your hearts?"** What the scribes see as a faithful defense of their traditions, Jesus names as **evil**. **Evil** resists God's purposes for Jesus. It derives from the evil one (6:13), who tried to tempt Jesus from God's purposes (4:1-11), who works among disciples (5:37), from whom they pray for deliverance (6:13). Jesus identifies the scribes as the devil's agents (cf. 16:1; 19:3).[4] On **hearts** and human willing and thinking, see 5:8, 28; 6:21.

• 9:5-6

His questions continue: **For which is easier to say, "Your sins are for-given," or to say "Rise and walk"?** Neither is easy, but the latter is visible. But Jesus is not offering an alternative. Since sin and sickness are linked (see 4:23-24), so are healing and forgiveness. Healing demonstrates forgiveness. Jesus challenges their view that only God can forgive by demonstrating to them, as to the priests in 8:4, that God has authorized him to be an agent of God's forgiveness: **But so that you** (plural; the religious leaders) **may know that the Son of Man has authority on earth to forgive sins, he said to the paralytic, "stand up, take your bed and go to your home."** See Isa 35:6 for healing physical deformities as a sign of God's reign. To **know** is to experience; on **son of man** and Jesus' interaction with the world, see 8:20; on **authority** see 7:29. The location **on earth** may contrast the Son of Man's future role in heaven as eschatological judge (*1 En* 46-48; cf. Dan 7:13-14). If so, it emphasizes that **on earth**, the arena of humans where God's will is to be done (6:10, 19), forgiveness is found now after the fall of the temple in 70 C.E. in Jesus (1:21; 12:6; 26:28).

• 9:7

The man's response is immediate and mirrors Jesus' command in 9:6b: **And he rose and went to his home**. His healing shows Jesus' authority to forgive. The emperor Vespasian's healing of a lame man with Serapis's help expresses divine favor and augments his status (Suetonius, *Vespasian* 7.2-3).

• 9:8

Response, the typical concluding element in miracle stories, comes not from the scribes or disciples, but from **the crowds,** distinguished from disciples in 5:1; 8:18, 23 (see 4:25; 5:1; 7:28-29; 8:1, 18)[5] and mentioned here for the first time in this scene: **When the crowds saw it, they were afraid/filled with awe**. See 1:20; 2:22 for **afraid** as trepidation in divine presence (cf. 17:6; 28:5, 10). While they lack the "little faith" of disciples (8:26), they can, unlike the scribes, discern God doing something in Jesus: **They glorified God, who had given such authority to human beings** (cf. 5:16). The plural (**to human beings**) indicates that Jesus is not unique. His role extends to the community of disciples, which also exercises forgiveness (5:21-26; 6:12, 14-15; 18:15-35) and healing (10:1, 8) as a sign of God's empire, forgiveness, and salvation.

9:9—JESUS CALLS MATTHEW

• 9:9

Jesus' call of Matthew resembles the call stories of 4:18-20, 21-22. (i) In motion, (ii) Jesus sees a named person engaged in everyday life, (iii) and calls him to follow, to discipleship. (iv) He responds at once. Both scenes involve activities embedded in the imperial world, fishing (see 4:18) and tax collection. Jesus' call disrupts these commitments. Following him means encountering

God's empire. The story legitimates discipleship as an alternative way of life which originates in Jesus' ministry.

The name **Jesus** (**As Jesus passed on from there**) recalls his commission to save from sins (1:21) and provides the interpretive framework. Jesus takes the initiative (**he saw a man called Matthew . . . and he said to him**) as in 4:18, 21 (cf. 8:14-15). **Matthew** appears in eighth position on the list of disciples in 10:3, and not again in the gospel. Perhaps this story legitimates the gospel's author as Jesus' companion, and/or as one whose name is theologically significant ("gift of God"), and/or as one who is a model disciple in following Jesus' call, and/or as one whose name symbolizes a "learning disciple" (Matthew sounds like "disciple" and "learn" [9:13] in Greek; see Introduction, section 4).[6]

˙ Matthew is **sitting at the tax booth**, a public building[7] near or in Capernaum on a main road. **Matthew** (cf. 10:3) collects not taxes on land and individuals (collected by the Roman or local administration) but tolls on transported goods. Individuals contracted to collect a certain amount; any surplus was theirs. Taxes served the empire's ruling elite (Tacitus, *Ann* 3.52-54; Josephus, *JW* 2.372). They secured an infrastructure in conquered areas to consolidate and extend Rome's power (roads, bridges, settlements, armies; see Aristides, *Roman Oration* 101; Tacitus, *Ann* 1.56, 61), and ensured the elite's comfortable lifestyle through imported treasures, food, clothing, building materials, games, entertainment, and so on (Aristides, *Roman Oration* 11; Tacitus, *Ann* 2.33; 12.43).[8] Tacitus reports alarm that Nero's plan to abolish indirect taxes meant, if implemented, "the (certain) dissolution of the empire" (*Ann* 13.50). At the local level, the system encouraged greed and exploited poor peasants and other producers (fishermen) who transported goods to urban markets. Tax collectors belonged to the retainer class (see Introduction, section 5), but though they had some political-economic power, they had little social status. The gospels and other writers attest how deeply despised they were by associating them with shameful characters such as beggars, thieves, extortioners, brothel owners, adulterers, and corrupt governors (Matt 5:46; 11:19; Luke 3:12-13; 5:29-30; 7:34; 15:1-2; 18:11; Cicero, *De Off* 1.150;[9] Josephus, *JW* 2.287; Dio Chrysostom, *Disc* 14.14; Philostratus, *Apollonius* 8.7.11).[10]

The socially despised **Matthew** belongs, then, with the cast of marginal characters in chapters 8-9. Jesus calls him to **follow me** (see 4:18-22), a call that welcomes him into God's life-giving empire. His instant response, **he rose and followed him**, signifies this encounter and start of a new way of life. It means abandoning his invested interests (cf. 6:19-24), disrupting his life based on greed and exploitation, and forsaking the imperial structure which his occupation sustains. To not collect taxes is to undermine the empire's way of life and control.[11]

The father of Vespasian and grandfather of Titus and Domitian (emperors when this gospel was written) collected taxes. Suetonius (*Vespasian* 1) assures his readers that they need not be ashamed of this origin. He says the grandfather had a fine military career (though there is some doubt). Inscriptions in cities of Asia honored him ("To an honest tax-gatherer"). The story of Matthew's call offers a very different perspective. Despised tax collectors (even emperors!) can walk away from the oppressive imperial tax system to find in God's saving presence manifested in Jesus a new life and an empire that is life-giving and merciful. It is a profoundly subversive, and witty, story.

9:10-13—A DINNER PARTY

This scene shows Jesus' call of Matthew to be a typical act, expressive of God's mercy among the marginal and constitutive of a new community. But opposition to Jesus' actions and conflict with the religious leaders grow (cf. 9:3-6).

• 9:10

Jesus hosts a dinner: **As he reclined at dinner**[12] **in the house** at Capernaum (4:13; 8:14 [perhaps Peter's house?]). Significant acts happen in houses: worship (2:11), merciful healing, and intimate, social relationships (8:6, 14; 9:6-7). Houses symbolize faithful and unfaithful responses to God's will revealed in Jesus (7:24-27).

M. Douglas argues that meals express patterns of social relations. "The message is about different degrees of hierarchy, inclusion and exclusion, boundaries and transactions across the boundaries."[13] In the ancient world, meal customs reflected and reinforced hierarchical order, social relations, and status through invitations, different qualities and quantities of food, types of tableware and eating utensils, and seating order (Pliny, *Letters* 2.6). Some groups, especially religious, philosophical, and funerary groups (Isis; Serapis; Cynics) resisted these conventions by including slaves and women of varying social rank in meals.[14] Jesus' actions belong with this countercultural trend. He upholds a different, inclusive, and more egalitarian social order. See 6:11; 8:11 for the meal as a symbol of eschatological inclusion.

And behold signals the unusual (9:2, 3): **many tax collectors and sinners were coming and sitting with him and his disciples**. Eating with despised people is common for Jesus (9:11-12). On **tax collectors**, see 9:9; 5:46.

Who are the **sinners**? One view identifies them as those who disobey God's will, such as Gentiles outside the covenant (1 Macc 2:48; Tob 13:6; *Pss. Sol.* 1:1; 2:1-2; Matt 5:46-47) and any whose "manner of life was basically antithetical to the will of God."[15] J. D. G. Dunn argues that **sinner** divides not only Jew from Gentile but also "faithful" Jew from "unfaithful" Jew.[16] **Sinner** is a polemical term. It identifies, distinguishes, and disapproves of those not living in accord with a group's claims. It expresses a group's disapproving perspective, denial of covenant status, and conviction that, in the user's perspective, judgment awaits them. The term indicates conflict between groups (so 9:11 [the Pharisees]).

But the criticism that follows in 9:11 is reframed here as an affirmation! Jesus welcomes and eats with people excluded and disapproved of by others, those whom others have judged fit only for God's judgment. As agent of God's saving presence (1:21-23), he indicates that no one is beyond God's mercy

(9:13), except perhaps those who deny it to others. Jesus' actions protest human decisions about future destiny (so 7:1-5). The present is the opportunity to encounter God's saving presence and empire.

K. Corley points out on the basis of developing Greco-Roman meal practices and the link between tax collectors and prostitutes in 21:31-32 that **sinner** probably includes women of varying social status. Those who upheld traditional gender and social divisions disapproved of the increasing presence of women at public meals. Such women were regularly labeled "prostitutes" or "slaves," regardless of their social status or role at the meal; Plutarch charges the Epicureans with using prostitutes (*Moralia* 1086E, 1129B).[17] Jesus welcomes to meals despised people marginalized by other groups, whether by occupation, gender, religious (non)observance, socioeconomic status, actions, and so on. Jesus forms an open, alternative, inclusive community/society not constituted by conventional status markers (ethnicity, wealth, etc.) and gender hierarchies but centered on himself as agent of God's empire.

• 9:11

The Pharisees (see Introduction, sections 1 and 5; 2:4; 3:7; 5:20), members of the elite alliance of religious leaders opposed to Jesus,[18] and members of the governing class committed to maintaining the unjust, hierarchical, societal status quo, criticize Jesus' practice and the inclusive social order he enacts. They continue the conflict of 9:3 (the scribes) over the significance of Jesus' actions. Their criticism is expressed indirectly (also 9:3) **to his disciples, "Why does your teacher eat with tax collectors and sinners?"** The designation **your teacher** (see 8:19) distances the **Pharisees** from Jesus and the disciples (disciples address him as Lord; see 8:2, 6), but links the **Pharisees** and scribes together (8:19). The reason for their opposition is, typically, not stated (cf. 9:3). It is reasonable, though, to infer from the gospel that they understand God's will to be for a social order that is more differentiated and devout or "righteous."[19] They support the current imperial hierarchy (cf. 5:20). They oppose Jesus' more inclusive, less hierarchical, nonconventional order.

• 9:12-13

The disciples do not respond because Jesus interprets his actions (see 9:31). **Hearing,** Jesus makes three counterassertions which articulate his authority (cf. 9:6, 8) to manifest God's empire. The first is parable-like (note parables against the leaders in 21:23, 28-22:14; 21:45; 22:15): **Those who are well have no need of a physician, but those who are sick**. This proverb-sounding statement (Plutarch, "Sayings of Spartans," *Moralia* 230F; Diogenes Laertius, *Lives* 2.70) restates the link between sin and disease that is assumed in 4:24 and 8:16 and made explicit in 9:2-8, by imaging sin as a disease (cf. Isa 1:5-6). The **sick** are **Matthew** and the **tax collectors and sinners** with whom Jesus eats.

Those who are well suggests power and strength, but its two previous uses have been negative. In 5:13 salt that has lost its saltiness "is strong/good for nothing" and is tossed out; in 8:28 the demoniacs are so fierce that "no one is strong/able to pass through." These uses depict not doing or being what should be done, and further condemn the Pharisees. Like the scribes in 9:3, they are resistant to God's purposes manifested in Jesus. The **physician** is Jesus, enacting God's will to heal and forgive (Ps 103:2-3; Hos 5:13; Isa 53:4-5, 10; Matt 8:17; 9:6-7). In this proverb, Jesus restates his commission. Eating with tax collectors and sinners, as with healing and teaching, expresses his salvific mission (1:21-23; 4:17). In opposing Jesus, the religious leaders resist God's purposes and empire.

• 9:13

A second statement clarifies his motive and repeats the claim that his actions enact God's will. Jesus answers their question (and subsequently: 12:3-8, 11-12; 15:3-9; 19:3-9; 21:42; 22:29-33, 41-46) by reminding them of what they already know: **Go and learn what this means**. The command to **learn** is ironic, since through the gospel the religious leaders learn nothing from Jesus.

Jesus quotes Hos 6:6: **I desire mercy, not sacrifice**.[20] The scribes in 2:4-6 and scribes and Pharisees in 5:20-48 do not know how to interpret the scriptures in relation to Jesus. Nor do they accept Jesus' interpretation of the scriptures, which the gospel presents as authoritative (cf. 22:29). They cannot be disciples (**learn** is a cognate form of the noun "disciple").

The northern eighth-century prophet Hosea announces judgment on Israel but holds out the possibility of repentance. The text expresses God's yearning for Israel's covenant faithfulness (*ḥesed*) in lives of trust, justice, and merciful obedience. The text is chosen partly for its emphasis on **mercy** (steadfast love as part of covenant loyalty) as well as for its relegation of sacrifice. It reinforces Jesus' forgiveness of sin in 9:1-8. After the fall of the temple in 70, various ways of making atonement became operative.

Jesus' actions provide the immediate referent for **mercy**. The context in Hosea suggests that **mercy** is part of a fundamental commitment of covenant loyalty. Jesus cites the text, then, to sustain his claim that his eating with sinners is consistent with God's will.

The text has polemical (**Go and learn**) and formational claims. Jesus indicates that the religious leaders, who are opposed to his actions, lack mercy. Their vision of differentiated, not inclusive, communities and their refusal to recognize that Jesus' act of eating with the marginals manifests God's saving reign indicate that they do not understand that God's will centers on God's mercy and steadfast love (Exod 34:5-6; Matt 15:13; 21:18-22:46). They must learn a faithfulness which enacts God's all-embracing and indiscriminate love (5:45) and destroys all gender, status, class, religious, political, and socioeconomic barriers. **Mercy** is not pity or condescension, but doing God's justice, which challenges the exclusionary practices and structures of the imperial status quo and seeks to establish a life-giving community of shared resources and sustaining relationships (see 5:7, 20; 6:3-4). For the gospel's audience, the saying legitimates its distinctive practice.

Jesus' third statement relates his actions to his life's mission **I have come not to call the righteous but sinners**. This is the third of seven **I have come** statements (5:17a, 17b; 9:13b; 10:34a, 34b, 35; 20:28) which elaborate Jesus'

God-given commission from 1:21-23.[21] Three key words, **I, call,** and **sinners,** make this connection. The **I** refers to Jesus, named in 9:2, 4, 9, 10 (cf. 1:21). **Call** is used in 1:21b and 23 to name and commission Jesus to manifest God's presence which saves from sins. To **call sinners** is to make available God's saving presence (1:21-23). To save from sin is, for now, to forgive it (9:2, 5, 6) and in the future to end it completely. **Sinners** (see 9:10, 11), the object of God's mercy, is a cognate of sins (1:21; 9:2, 5, 6). Eating with the marginalized, along with healing (9:2-8) and teaching (chs. 5-7), carries out Jesus' mission. Contrast the inclusive and merciful nature of Jesus' mission to all and any with Apollonius's teaching that the "holy deserve blessings and the wicked the contrary," and that the gods bless "the healthy, whole and unscarred by vice," while they pour out wrath on the sinful and corrupt. Apollonius teaches that Asclepius, the god of healing, does not welcome the wicked, even if they offer wealth (Philostratus, *Apollonius* 1.11).

On **sinners**, see 9:10. The identity of the **righteous** and the reason for no mission to them are not clear. But the contrast with the receptive sinners indicates that they may be the religious leaders who resist Jesus' mission. The term would, then, be ironic.

9:14-17—WITH ALL THIS FEASTING, WHAT ABOUT FASTING?

• 9:14

A new group replaces the religious leaders: **The disciples of John came to him**. John (see 3:1-12, 13-14) was last mentioned in 4:12 when he was arrested (see 4:12-16). John's **disciples** have not been mentioned previously. Their approach (**came to him**) recognizes Jesus' authority (see on 4:3, 11; also 5:1; 8:2, 5, 19, 25).

Jesus' meals raise questions about fasting: **Why do we and the Pharisees fast often, but your disciples do not fast?** Implicit is the issue of Jesus' authority to create a distinct way of life (Jesus addresses this issue in 9:16-17). The inclusion of **often** perhaps suggests a contrast not of "fasting and no fasting" but "much fasting and little fasting." Jesus' practice (4:2) and teaching in 6:16-18 on fasting point to this conclusion.

• 9:15

Jesus responds with three parable-like analogies from everyday life. They pull together unlikely elements: weddings, mourning, and fasting. The first, a rhetorical question expecting the answer "no" (signaled by the initial μή, *mē*), uses the wedding image: **Wedding guests cannot mourn while the bridegroom is with them, can they? The days will come when the bridegroom is taken away from them and then they will fast.** The term **bridegroom** is a rare image for God (Isa 62:5);[22] it also describes the people God clothes with "the garments of salvation" and "robe of righteousness" (Isa 61:10). If the former referent is taken, it denotes Jesus, through whom God's presence is manifested (1:23). If the latter referent is used, it denotes those who have in chapters 8-9 been clothed with God's salvation manifested in Jesus (cf. 1:21). Either way, to **mourn** is not the appropriate response. In the context of the disciples' question, **mourning** refers to fasting.

Fasting is inappropriate for two reasons. (1) It accompanies solemn and distressing circumstances of repentance and confession (1 Kgs 21:27-29; Neh 1:4; Dan 9:30). That is not the mood of chapters 8-9. Joyous celebration to honor God's action is more appropriate (Isa 12:6; 25:9; 29:19). (2) Fasting is inappropriate because that which it seeks—forgiveness and atonement for sin (Dan 9:3; *Pss. Sol.* 3:6-8; *Apoc. El.* 1:21), healing, and exorcism (*Apoc. El.* 1:21)— is now available in Jesus' ministry. He has evidenced forgiveness, healing, and exorcism in the events of chapters 8-9.

Is fasting ever appropriate? The rhetorical question and the statement anticipate a time **when the bridegroom is taken away**. This is the time for **fasting**. Jesus will be **taken away** in his crucifixion. The time between his resurrection and *parousia* or return in triumph (24:3), the "now" of the gospel's audience, is a difficult time of bold discipleship (cf. 5:3-12, 13-16, 21-48; 6:1-18, 19-34; 7:1-6, 7-11, 12, 13-23, 24-27). The phrase **the days will come** signals a time of judgment and distress (Isa 39:6; Jer 7:32; Amos 4:2) in which God's purposes are established through the line of David (Amos 9:13-15; Jer 23:5; Matt 1:1, 17). In this "in-between" time, fasting is necessary. As a spiritual discipline, it sustains disciples (6:16-18) in an appropriate way of life. God's chosen fast is to loose the bonds of injustice, to break every yoke, to let the oppressed go free, and to feed the hungry, house the homeless, clothe the naked (Isa 58:6-14; Matt 5:3-12; 25:31-46).

• 9:16

Jesus has answered the question about fasting, but two more images from everyday life address the larger issue of Jesus' authority to manifest God's empire and the distinctive way of life it creates. The first image posits the unlikely situation of using **unshrunk cloth** to patch **an old cloak**. Everybody knows **no one** does this, **for the patch pulls away from the cloak, and a new tear is made.** Likewise with Jesus' display of God's merciful reign. It creates a different way of life. This does not mean that Jewish traditions knew nothing of God's merciful presence, forgiveness, reign, or salvation. These traditions provide the source of Matthew's vision. Nor does it mean that the community of disciples is outside Judaism. Rather, there is continuity and discontinuity in a reformist perspective. Matthew's vision, comprising elements from the tradition, is a different configuration centered on Jesus, whom God has chosen (1:18-25; 2:15; 3:17). It threatens the theological understandings and practices of the religious elite (9:3, 11), as well as their role in determining communal norms.

• 9:17

The third image restates the point. It evokes the unlikely scene of putting **new wine into old wineskins**. With fermentation **the skins burst and the wine**

is spilled, and the skins are destroyed. Instead, **new wine is put into fresh wineskins, and so both are preserved**. Likewise with Jesus' ministry. **Wine** depicts both God's judgment (Ps 75:8; Isa 24:7, 9, 11) and merciful salvation, whether in a return to the land (Jer 31:12), a sign of God's everlasting covenant and steadfast love (Isa 55:1-3), or part of the feast that celebrates the salvation and return of the people to Zion, and the removal of death and tears (Isa 25:6-10a). Salvation, including Jesus' manifestation, does not leave people, structures, and relationships unchanged. It creates new relationships, shared resources, and just structures (**wineskins**). This does not mean a new or separated religion. The gospel maintains continuity with God's previous acts of salvation (1:1-17; 1:22-23; 2:5, 15, 18). It does, though, mean new structures or community centered on Jesus (4:18-22; chs. 5-7; 12:46-50; 16:18-19; 18:18-20; chs. 19-20) with distinctive and merciful practices.

9:18-26—JESUS HEALS A RULER'S DAUGHTER AND A WOMAN

The chapter returns to miracles to demonstrate God's reign and anticipate its future full establishment marked by plenty and wholeness (*2 Bar* 73:1-2). Jesus heals five people (9:18-34). Matthew 9:18-26 uses intercalation. It inserts the healing of the woman with a hemorrhage (9:20-22) into the story of the raising of the daughter (9:18-19, 23-26). This technique highlights similarities (two females, hands/touch [9:18, 20, 25], faith [9:22], powerlessness, Jesus' power) and differences in age, healing and death, indirect and direct advocacy, and public and private suffering.

• 9:18
The Greek genitive absolute construction (**While he was saying these things**) links Jesus' words (9:14-17) and actions of eating (9:10-13) with this healing as means of accomplishing his God-given mission (1:21-23; 4:17). **Behold/suddenly** signals a new element (see 9:2), **a ruler/leader**[23] **came in and knelt before him**. The ruler's approach is respectful (**knelt**), like the magi and the leper (see 2:2, 11; 8:2; also 4:9-10). It is not specified over whom he is **a ruler,** though the term indicates a member of the social elite.

My daughter has just died. As with the Gentile centurion in 8:5-13, the leader is powerless to do what really matters, give life in a situation of death. Like the centurion (8:6-9), he does a godly thing in being kind to the dead (Sir 7:33) and intervenes on behalf of a powerless person (on the marginal status of children, see 2:8). He confidently seeks Jesus' help: **come and lay your hands on her and she will live**. For **hands** as instruments of God's work, see 8:3; for acting on behalf of a child, see Philostratus, *Apollonius* 3.38; for God as the only one who can help the dead, see Ps 88:4-6, 9-18; Isa 26:19.[24] To **live** has a double significance—physical life and participation in God's eschatological purposes, the goal of the difficult but rewarding way of discipleship (7:14).

These actions contrast this **ruler/leader** with "the leaders/rulers of the Gentiles who lord it over others . . ." (20:25) and with "Beelzebul ruler of the demons" (9:34; 12:25), who opposes God with a reign of death. A.-J. Levine notes a contrast with the ruler Herod, who kills children (including daughters; 2:16-18), and Herod Antipas, who, powerless to retract his oath, and in a context of quite different music (9:23), brings death because of a daughter (14:1-12). Instead of such destructive power, this **leader/ruler** recognizes his limits, seeks Jesus, brings life, and benefits another person. He offers an alternative pattern of leadership appropriate to the community of disciples.[25]

• 9:19

Jesus **rose and followed him with his disciples.** While **follow** usually denotes discipleship (see 4:18-22), here Jesus **follows**. It may be literal accompanying,[26] but it also presents Jesus as a model disciple following a leader who rightly uses his authority (cf. 10:24-25). In chapters 8-9 Jesus models the mission he will entrust to disciples (10:7-8).[27]

• 9:20

The action is interrupted as a new story begins: **And behold** 9:18; see 9:2), **a woman who had been hemorrhaging for twelve years**. A woman is healed in 8:14-15, and women are surely included in the summary passages (4:23-25; 8:16; 9:35). Nothing identifies this woman's status; does she contrast with the elevated status of the ruler and his daughter?[28] Nor is her **hemorrhage** specified. The verb (αἱμορροέω, *haimorroeō*) appears in Lev 15:33 to denote defiling bodily discharges (semen and menstruation). But its meaning is not limited to menstruation or vaginal discharge; it includes any bleeding (Liddell and Scott, 39; Hippocrates, *Coac* 292, 300). Nor does the story mention the impurity or social ostracism so prevalent in discussions of it.[29] The emphasis falls on her suffering: sick **for twelve years.** Jesus' power must overcome this common obstacle in healing stories (cf. Philostratus, *Apollonius* 3.38 ["two years"]; 6.43 ["thirty days"]). No mention is made of other medical help. Is she too poor, or was it ineffective? Does she have a household?

The **woman came up** (for respectful approach, see 4:3, 11; 5:1; 8:2, 5, 18, 25; 9:14, 20) **from behind and touched the fringe of his garment**. This **fringe** (see 14:36; 23:5) reminded wearers of their covenant requirements, their identity as set apart for God's service, and God's saving the people from Egypt (Num 15:38-41; Deut 22:12). Jesus serves God in making available God's saving power (1:21) in healing the woman.

• 9:21

The rare access to a character's internal world indicates the intentional nature and goal of her act. She knows her need and Jesus' power to help: **for she said to herself, "If I only touch his cloak, I shall be made well/saved."** For **touch** rather than a word (8:8-10; 9:6) to transfer power for healing, see 8:3, 15. Her goal to be **made well/saved** (σώζω, *sōzō*) is consistent with God's will to save manifested in Jesus (1:21; also 8:25).

• 9:22

Her touch gets Jesus' attention: **Jesus turned and seeing her** (see 9:2) **he said, "take heart, daughter** (see on 9:2) **your faith has saved you."** With Godlike knowledge (so 6:3-4, 8, which gives the scene a prayerlike quality), Jesus knows who has touched him, why, and with what effect. He interprets her touch as **faith** or active dependence on his transforming power (see 8:10; 9:2; contrast the disciples' little faith in 8:26). Jesus manifests God's power to **save** her from her sickness. The perfect tense indicates continuing consequences of wholeness and a different way of life. **And instantly** (literally, **from that hour**) **the woman was made well/saved**. The third use of **saved/made well** in two verses underlines its importance. Her healing anticipates the wholeness which will mark the future fullness of God's empire (*2 Bar* 73:1-2).

• 9:23

The first story resumes: **When Jesus came to the ruler's house** (9:18-19) **and saw the flute players and the crowd making a commotion**. Again a **house** is the location (8:6, 14-15; 9:10). For **flute players** and mourning, see Josephus, *JW* 3.437. Whereas **the crowd** in 9:8 recognized God as the source of the authority demonstrated in Jesus' healing and forgiveness, here (unlike the ruler) they give no thought to transformation. Their mourning underlines that the daughter is dead, and death is final.

• 9:24

The situation deteriorates. Jesus instructs them, **"Go away for the girl is not dead but sleeping."**[30] They do not look for his life-giving work (faith). **And they laughed at him**. Their response allies them with the resistant scribes (9:3), Pharisees (9:11), and disciples of John (9:14).

• 9:25

Jesus, again not deterred by negative responses, exercises his authority: **But when the crowd had been put outside, he went in and took her by the hand** (cf. 8:3, 15) **and the girl was raised** (a passive verb indicating God's action). The verb **raised** recalls the healing/forgiving miracle of 9:5-7 (three times) and prepares for the mission instruction to disciples in 10:8, for Jesus' assertion of his messianic identity in 11:5, and for Jesus' resurrection (16:21; 17:23; 20:19; 27:52, 63, 64; 28:6, 7). Like the girl, Jesus, also the child of a ruler, will die and be raised.[31] The talk of newness in 9:16-17 is balanced with an action continuous with the actions of Elijah (1 Kgs 17:17-24; Sir 48:5) and Elisha (2 Kgs 4:32-37). For other raisings, see Pliny, *NH* 7.124; 26:14-15; Apuleius, *Metamorphoses* 2.21-30; Philostratus, *Apollonius* 4.45.

• 9:26

No specific responses (the girl, her parents, the crowd) are indicated. **The report of this went out into all that land**, presumably the area around Capernaum, and perhaps Galilee (4:15-16). Jesus' act manifests the light of God's saving reign (1:21-23) in the region of death and darkness (4:15-16).

9:27-31—JESUS HEALS TWO BLIND MEN

• 9:27

Jesus is again on the move, **And as Jesus passed on from there**. His name, **Jesus,** indicates that his itinerancy serves his God-given mission to save from sins (1:21). **Two blind men followed him**. The cast of marginalized characters continues. Blindness was thought to be hereditary or to be caused by poisons, bright lights, disease, or war.[32] As with other sicknesses and physical deformities, some saw it as punishment for sin and covenant disloyalty (Deut 28:29; Isa 59:1-15, esp. 10; *Ep. Arist.* 316). Note both divine punishment and imperial violence in putting out Zedekiah's eyes in 2 Kgs 25:7. Seneca thinks blindness is a deserved curse for evil people, but everything is to be accepted as God's will (*De Prov* 5.1). The blind suffer religious exclusion in not serving as priests (Lev 21:16-20) and social harassment as victims of cruelty (Lev 19:14; Deut 27:18; 2 Kgdms [NRSV 2 Sam] 5:6-10). They are economically vulnerable in relying on family support or sustaining themselves with shameful begging (Sir 40:28-30; Mark 10:46; John 9:8). Epictetus refers to people turning away from dirty beggars (*Diss* 3.22.89). The poor and the blind are linked in Job 29:12-17. Care for the blind is a righteous action (Job 29:12-17). They are promised God's future healing (Isa 29:18-20; 35:4-6; 42:6-7; *2 Bar* 73:1-2), the wholeness under way in Jesus' ministry (cf. Matt 11:5).[33] Blindness can be a metaphor for resistance to God's will (13:13-17 [the crowds]; 15:14; 23:16, 17, etc. [religious leaders]).

The blind men's **following** of Jesus may signify a discipleship action (see 4:19). Blindness and healing could have literal (physical) and metaphorical (spiritual) significance (Isa 42:18-19),[34] but there is some doubt about their discipleship since **following** is usually in response to Jesus' call (4:19, 21; 8:22; 9:9), which is absent here.[35] Their final act (9:31) reinforces the doubt.

A second trait of discipleship appears, their prayer to Jesus, **crying out, have mercy on us**. Their request for **mercy** does not specify what they want, but, as with the woman's request in 9:21-22 to be saved, **mercy** is consistent with Jesus' mission (9:13). **Mercy** means not Jesus' condescension or pity, not only a healing, but a transforming act which opens up a new way of life (see 5:7; 6:3-4).

A third trait of discipleship is the respectful title of address **son of David**.[36] David is associated with miraculous actions. His music exorcised the evil spirit from Saul (1 Sam 16:14-23; Ps.-Philo 60; Josephus, *Ant* 6.166-68). The term **son of David** commonly denotes David's son Solomon,[37] who in subsequent traditions is a healer and an exorcist (see Wis 7:15-22a, esp. 20; Josephus, *Ant* 8.2, 5; esp. *Testament of Solomon;* for the title, see *T. Sol.* 1:00; 1:7; 5:10). In *Testament of Solomon* (perhaps influenced by the gospels), Solomon confronts demons who kill children (*T. Sol.* 9:5-6; 13:3; cf. Matt 9:18-19, 23-26), produce festering sores (*T. Sol.* 9:6; cf. Matt 9:20-22), blind (*T. Sol.* 13:4; 18:7; Matt 9:27-31), overturn boats (*T. Sol.* 16:1-3; cf. Matt 8:23-27), and paralyze (*T. Sol.* 18:11; cf. Matt 9:2-8). The gospel criticized Solomon's oppressive rule in 6:29, but here evokes life-giving qualities.

Jesus is **son of David** (1:1), the one anointed by God (Christ; cf. *Pss. Sol.* 17:23, 32) in David's line, to whom God promises a reign forever (2 Sam 7:12-13). Jesus represents God's reign marked by justice which defends the poor, delivers the needy, and crushes the oppressor (Ps 72:1-4, 12-14). In this scene, two of the poor and needy, not the resistant elite (9:3, 11), recognize Jesus as God's agent. Jesus enacts God's empire in delivering the needy. By contrast, David attacked the blind and the lame (2 Sam 5:6-10) and could not raise a dead child (9:23-26; 2 Sam 12:13-23). Jesus is a **son of David** faithful to God's purposes.

• 9:28

Further features of discipleship follow. Jesus, again on the move (9:27a), **enters the house** (his own in 9:1, 10? Peter's in 8:14? another?), a place where God's presence is encountered (see 9:10). The blind men **approach him** respectfully (see 4:3; 9:14, 20). Jesus questions them about their faith (also 8:7-13a, 25-26; 9:2-6a): **Do you believe that I am able to do this?** As in 9:2 and 22, Jesus interprets their approach as **faith**, their active dependence on his transforming power without which their life situations cannot change (see 8:10). They affirm their faith and address Jesus as disciples do, **Yes Lord** (see 8:2).

• 9:29

Their healing is effected by Jesus' **touch** of **their eyes** (see 8:3, 15; 9:18, 20-21, 25) and words (**and said**; see 8:3, 8, 16, 26, 32; 9:6, 22). His words emphasize their **faith** (so 8:13). While faith is found among the marginalized, it is lacking from the religious elite (8:10; 9:3, 11), who remain blind to God's purposes and reign manifested in Jesus.

• 9:30

Their eyes were opened. God's promised restoration of sight is a reality (Isa 29:18-20; 35:4-6; 42:6-7). Numerous deities restored sight, including Aesculapius, Isis, and Serapis, who heals through Vespasian (Suetonius, *Vespasian* 7.2-3; Tacitus, *Hist* 4.81; see also Tob 3:16-17; Philostratus, *Apollonius* 3.39).[38] Anything the gods and emperor can do, Jesus can do, and much more in anticipation of the full establishment of God's reign. As in 8:4, **he sternly ordered them, "See that no one knows of this."** In 8:4 Jesus acts in accord with 5:17-20 to ensure testimony to the religious elite. Here the command has ecclesial and christological functions. (1) Followers need formation before they proclaim and act. Disciples, called in 4:18-22, have had instruction (chs. 5-7) and on-the-job training (chs. 8-9), while they witness Jesus carrying out his mission (8:23;

9:10, 19). Faith, understanding, and adequate words (8:26-27; 9:11; 16:16-21) take time to grow. Only then is their commission elaborated (4:19; ch. 10) and only after Jesus' death and resurrection do they go in mission (28:16-20).[39] (2) In not promoting his actions, Jesus shows his humility in accomplishing God's purposes (11:29; 12:16-21; 21:5) in contrast to gods who demand recognition.[40]

• 9:31

But despite having prayed for Jesus' help and having expressed insight into who he is (9:27), despite having confessed faith in him (9:28) and having named him Lord (9:28), and despite having encountered God's saving power through regaining their sight (9:30), they do not obey. **But they went away and spread the news about him throughout the district**. Compare 9:26.

9:32-34—JESUS EXORCISES A MUTE DEMONIAC

• 9:32

As they (Jesus and the disciples? the two men?) **were going away, behold** (see 9:2) **they** (unspecified) **brought** (see 9:2) **to him a deaf-mute demoniac**, another marginal person. The term **deaf-mute** (κωφός, *kōphos*),[41] indicates not hearing and not speaking (Wis 10:21; Hab 2:18; Philo, *Spec Leg* 4.197-98) and is often paired with "blind" (Exod 4:11; Isa 43:8; Matt 9:27). Like the blind, the deaf-mute are to receive care (Lev 19:14) and are promised God's future action to receive hearing and speech (Isa 29:18-20; 35:5-6). See 4:24 for muteness as an effect of imperial control. Not hearing can be a metaphor for not hearing God (Isa 42:18-19; 43:8; 44:11). This man's condition results from **demons** (see 4:24).

• 9:33

Jesus does God's work in giving speech (Exod 4:11; 35:5-6). **When the demon had been cast out** (cf. 8:31-32), **the deaf-mute spoke**, to confirm that the demons have been cast out. Jesus saves him from Satan's reign (4:1-11; 12:25-28). **The crowds**, positive in 9:8 but negative in 9:23-24, continue their roller-coaster ride. They **marveled** (cf. disciples in 8:27), a response of some insight (cf. Jesus in 8:10): **Never has anything like this been seen in Israel**. They perceive something special happening in Jesus without articulating it or following him.

• 9:34

Their response contrasts with the negative response of the religious elite, **the Pharisees** (see 3:7; 5:20; 9:11, 14). Their evaluation is that, **"By the ruler of demons he casts out demons."** Their labeling of Jesus as ruled by demons is a typical strategy whereby the elite demonize opponents and seek to control them.[42] This ruler is Satan, or Beelzebul (*T. Sol.* 3:1-6), the opponent of God's purposes (4:1-11; 10:25; 12:22-32). The Pharisees again fail to discern God's purposes in Jesus (1:21-23; 4:17). Jesus will respond to their misinterpretation in 12:22-32.

9:35-38—JESUS' MANY MIRACLES AND COMPASSION

These verses provide retrospection and anticipation as a transition to chapter 10. They summarize chapters 8-9 and 4:23-25 to underline Jesus carrying out his God-given commission (1:21-23) among the marginal. They anticipate chapter 10 by establishing a great need to expand Jesus' ministry through other laborers.

• 9:35
This verse repeats the summary of Jesus' threefold ministry (**teaching, preaching, healing**) from 4:23 (see 4:23 for comments).[43]

• 9:36
Seeing the crowds (9:2, 9, 22; 5:1), **he had compassion for them because they were harassed and helpless**. To **have compassion** (14:14; 15:32; 18:27; 20:34; 4 Macc 14:13) derives from "entrails," "bowels," or "guts," the location of merciful, loving action (BAGD, 762-63). Jesus expresses God's mercy in his acts (see 5:7; 9:13).

He sees crowds suffering from violence. **Harassed** can mean flaying or skinning (BAGD, 758), violence and plunder.[44] **Helpless** can mean a throwing down and a laying down, often in violent contexts, including abandonment (Gen 21:15; 37:20, 24), imperial violence (Exod 1:22 [Pharaoh]), war and death (Josh 8:29; 10:27; Judg 4:22; 9:53; 1 Macc 5:43; 7:44; 11:4, 51), and divine destructive judgment on unfaithfulness (Isa 22:18; 33:12; 34:3; Jer 7:15; 14:16; Wis 5:22; note the exodus context in Exod 7:9, 10, 12; 15:1, 4, 21). Jesus sees people who are oppressed, downtrodden, beat-up, and crushed. The historical and literary contexts indicate Rome and the religious elite as those who inflict social, economic, political, and religious abuse with misrule (9:18, 34).

So too do the intertextual links of the description, **like sheep without a shepherd** (Num 27:17; 2 Chr 18:16; Jdt 11:19). **Sheep** are God's people, and **shepherds** their often unfaithful leaders (Ps 100:3; Isa 53:6; Jer 23:1-4; Ezek 34:5-6; *1 En* 90:6; *2 Bar* 77:13). Jesus' comment attacks the misguided leadership of the elite (see 2:6, where Jesus is "a ruler who will shepherd my people"). The image echoes Ezek 34, in which God attacks false shepherds for caring for themselves but harming the sheep/people by depriving them of food and clothing, by not strengthening the weak, not healing the sick, not binding up the injured, not seeking the lost (34:2-4). "With force and harshness you have ruled them" (34:4, 17-19). Their misrule has meant that there is no shepherd (34:8). God is against the false shepherds and will destroy the "fat and strong" (34:10, 16). The sheep have been devoured and starved by the rulers (34:10, 29), and enslaved, plundered, and insulted by the nations (34:29).

Through Jesus, God will care for them, free them from the nations (Rome), and provide food, justice, security, healing, strength, and a Davidic shepherd (34:8-31).[45] Such is the ministry of Jesus, Immanuel (1:23). For the link of disease with socioeconomic and political oppression, see 4:24.

• 9:37

Then he said to his disciples, "The harvest is plentiful." This is a frequent image of God's judgment (see Matt 3:12; 13:39-42; Isa 18:4-5; 27:12-13; Joel 3:13; *4 Ezra* 4:26-37; *2 Bar* 70:1-2). **But the laborers are few**. Jesus' ministry, the manifesting of God's saving power which vindicates or condemns, is limited in its extent. A **few laborers/workers** (disciples; 10:10) will extend it. For the **few** as the minority and marginal community of disciples out of step with and in tension with its societal context, see 7:14.

• 9:38

Jesus' response to the great opportunity (**therefore**) is not despair but prayer. **Pray that the Lord** (God, 1:22; 2:15) **of the harvest will send out workers into his harvest**. Both the community's existence and missional nature result from God's commission enacted by Jesus (so 4:17-22; see ch. 10). Now Jesus will send his own disciples into this mission field.

CHAPTER 10

Jesus' Second Teaching Discourse

Mission

In 4:17-25 Jesus begins his God-given commission to manifest God's saving presence (1:21-23) in a world of sin dominated by the religious and Roman elite. He proclaims God's empire, calls disciples, preaches, teaches, and heals. Chapters 5-10 elaborate this mission, first as Jesus teaches the community of disciples (chs. 5-7) and then in chapters 8-9 through Jesus' miraculous and non-miraculous actions. Chapter 10 expands his call to disciples to join his liberating mission ("fish for people," 4:19).

The final scene of chapter 9 focuses this emphasis. The chapter's closing verses underline Jesus' compassion for the downtrodden crowds (9:36), their great need, and the lack of workers (9:37). Disciples are to pray for more workers (9:38). In chapter 10, God answers their prayers by sending them in mission.

The chapter divides into four main sections.[1]

10:1-4	Call and Commission of an Alternative Community
10:5-15	Four Aspects of the Mission
10:16-23	The Hardship of Mission: Inevitable Persecution
10:24-42	The Courage, Impact, and Reward of Faithful Mission

This mission signifies the community of disciples' relation to its society. (1) There is no flight from society, nor is there an acceptance of imperial society as "the way things are." (2) Mission is not a sporadic or optional activity for disciples. It is the reason for the community's existence. (3) It is a communal way of life that requires courage, hope, and the conviction that God's purposes are a matter of life and death. The chapter continues to shape the identity and lifestyle of the community of disciples. (4) Mission confronts Rome's world of injustice, power, greed, false commitments, and death, with God's mercy and justice. It challenges (in)vested interests despite conflict, division, suffering, and rejection. It offers an alternative to Rome's mission that employs military violence and cultural imperialism in order to "rule the nations with your power" (Virgil, *Aeneid* 6.851-53; see comments on 28:16-20). (5) Mission means

232

participation in God's purpose to transform human existence by saving it from sin (9:35-38). The disciples' mission imitates and parallels Jesus' mission (1:21-23; 4:17). Response to the mission involves eschatological consequences of vindication or condemnation. (6) To follow Jesus by proclaiming and doing God's empire is marked by "itinerancy, poverty, defenselessness, and love."[2]

10:1-4—CALL AND COMMISSION
OF AN ALTERNATIVE COMMUNITY

• 10:1

Jesus enacts God's response to the prayer of 9:38 for workers to carry out God's saving purposes. Then Jesus **called his twelve disciples** (4:18-22; 5:1; 9:10, 37). Just as God **calls/commissions** Jesus to save from sins (1:21-23), so Jesus **calls/commissions** (compound form of the same verb) disciples to continue his mission. The community of disciples is constituted not by birth (the priesthood) but by God's action in Jesus. Is it based on restrictive gender (male) and ethnicity (Jewish)? Though neither women nor Gentiles are included in this list, the final chapter will show women as the first to proclaim Jesus' resurrection and will show the expansion of this mission to include Gentiles. The number **twelve** recalls Israel's twelve tribes, who form a tribal confederacy marked by tribal self-governance, egalitarian structure, and resistance to oppressive Canaanite city-states.[3] The selection of **twelve disciples** points to the formation of a similar community. Jesus' community is to be an alternative community of different social patterns, shared resources, and resistance to oppressive structures (cf. chs. 5-7).

The link to and expansion of Jesus' mission is also evident in that **he gave them authority**. Jesus exhibited his God-given **authority** in preaching and healing/forgiving (7:29; 9:6, 8). Their tasks are his tasks: **over unclean spirits, to cast them out** (4:24; 8:16, 26, 28-34; 9:32-34), **and to cure every disease and every sickness** (4:23-24; 8:1-4, 5-13, 14-16; 9:1-8, 18-26, 27-31, 35). They are to transform the squalor and misery of cities like Antioch by manifesting God's liberating reign in these acts. (See each reference for discussion.) Disciples follow in a long line of key figures who are commissioned for key roles in God's purposes: Moses (Exod 3), David (1 Sam 16), prophets such as Isaiah (Isa 6) and Jeremiah (Jer 1).

• 10:2-4

The twelve (10:1) are called **apostles**. Deriving from the verb "to send" (10:5), the noun **apostles** highlights Jesus' authority, their commissioning, their identity, and their mission task ("sent out," 9:38). They are named, the first four—**first Simon also known as Peter, and his brother Andrew; James son of Zebedee, and his brother John**—in order of being called (4:18-22). **Simon** has a double name in anticipation of 16:16-19 (**Peter**); **first** also anticipates his subsequent prominence as spokesperson. On **brother** as an ecclesial term, see

4:20. Of the remaining names (**Philip, Bartholomew, Thomas, James son of Alphaeus, Thaddaeus, Simon the Cananaean**) only two are qualified: **Matthew the tax collector** recalls 9:9, 10-13, and **Judas Iscariot, the one who betrayed him,** anticipates the passion (chs. 26-27).

10:5-15—FOUR ASPECTS OF ITS MISSION

• 10:5a

A restatement of Jesus' authority, the communal structure (**These twelve Jesus**), and the extension of his mission to them (**sent out**) introduces teaching on four aspects of the mission task (**with the following instructions**): its arena (10:5b-6), tasks (10:7-8a), material support (10:8b-10), and impact (10:11-15). For Cynics "sent as messengers by Zeus to people," see Epictetus, *Diss* 3.22.19-26.[4]

• 10:5b-6

First, the mission's arena. Two negative commands (**do not go**; **do not enter**) establish that their mission is not **among the Gentiles** and **Samaritans**. A positive command (**go rather**), emphatic by its final position and contrasting content, sends them **to the lost sheep of the house of Israel**. As a parallel to **Gentiles** and **Samaritans**, the **lost sheep** are not a group within **Israel** but all Israel, misruled and abused by false shepherds, but for whom God promises life-giving rule (see 9:36; cf. Ezek 34:4, 16 [**lost sheep**]; 34:30-31 [**Israel**]). Why no **Gentiles** and **Samaritans**? This focus generally imitates Jesus' mission (2:6; 4:12-9:38). But he has been engaged by a few Gentiles (8:5-13, 28-34; 15:21-28) and calls disciples "salt of the earth" and "light of the world" (5:13, 16). These images anticipate worldwide mission. The focus on Israel, then, is temporary in that Israel has salvation-history priority in God's purposes. After the resurrection, the disciples' mission will extend to Gentiles (10:18; 28:16-20). On **Gentiles**, see 5:47; 8:28.

• 10:7-8a

Second, the mission's tasks. Disciples are to **proclaim**, as Jesus does (see 4:17, 23; 9:35). Their message is the same as Jesus' (4:17) and John's (3:2): **The empire of the heavens is at hand**. See 3:2; 4:17. This claim on human allegiance challenges all other reigns, including Roman imperial power and the religious elite's control. It announces that God's empire is encountered in Jesus. Chapters 4:17-9:36 have shown that God's reign is life-giving, not death-bringing, committed to justice for, not the exploitation and domination of, the poor and needy (Ps 72; Matt 5-7; 8-9). Four further tasks, expressed as imperatives, imitate Jesus' actions (see 10:1), demonstrate God's life-giving reign, and anticipate the wholeness which God's empire establishes in full (Isa 35:5-6; *2 Bar* 73:1-2). **Heal the sick** (see 4:23-24; 8:13, 14-16; 9:2-8, 20-22, 27-31, 35), **raise the dead** (9:24-26), **cleanse lepers** (see 8:1-4), **cast out demons** (see 4:23-24; 8:16, 28-34; 9:32-34). L. Keck notes that their tasks are the same as Jesus', but there is no reference to the Spirit's empowering (however, see 10:20).[5]

• 10:8b-10

Third, the mission's material support. The disciples are to conduct their mission without charge to its beneficiaries to ensure access for the poor (5:3): **You received without payment; give without payment**. In not profiting from the work, they imitate Jesus' practice toward them (cf. 4:18-22; 9:9; 10:1), and God's gracious act in commissioning Jesus (1:21-23).

Moreover, they are to travel as inconspicuously as possible. They are not to draw attention to themselves with conventional traveling apparel and so minimize anticipated opposition (see 10:16-17). **Do not take** as payment **gold, or silver, or copper in your belts, no bag for your journey, or two tunics** (a luxury), **or sandals or a staff**. A **staff** offered protection (Epictetus, *Diss* 3.22.50; Diogenes, *Epistle* 7).[6] But they are forbidden "normal" supplies for a journey (Exod 12:11; Josh 9:4-5); wandering philosophers carried **bags** (Epictetus, *Diss* 1.24.11; Diogenes, *Epistles,* 7; 13; 46).[7] According to Josephus, Essenes carried nothing except a staff for protection against brigands (*JW* 2.125). Minimizing signs of a journey increases safety.

The opening imperative (**Do not take**) does not only mean "take along with" you, but also (do not) **"receive/acquire** gold (in order to put it) into your money belts" (BAGD, 455). Disciples must not profit from the mission, but must embrace the margins of poverty and powerlessness. There they experience God's power and resources, **for laborers are worthy of their food** (or resources). They must trust God (6:24-34).

• 10:11-13a

Fourth, the mission's impact, positive (vv. 11-13a) and negative (vv. 13b-15). Their mission requires decision; there will be division. **Whatever town or village you enter** (like Jesus in 9:1, 35), **find out who is worthy in it**. In context, the **worthy** are those who, like disciples (10:10), respond with faith to their preaching and actions. **Stay there until you leave**. As the respondents have received without payment, so they will provide for disciples. **Houses** are important for the disciples' mission, as for Jesus' (see 8:14; 9:10, 23, 28). Disciples discern a worthy house by **greeting** it/them . . . **and let your peace come on it**. As **peacemakers**, disciples are advocates not of Rome's destructive peace but of God's merciful empire, which brings wholeness and well-being to the broken and the oppressed (see 5:9; Ps 72). To **greet** is to proclaim God's empire. Those who are worthy receive, benefit from, and commit to God's **peace** or reign.

• 10:13b-14

The negative response (**But if it is not worthy**) denotes those who do not believe and follow, who do not embrace God's **peace** made available in the disciples' proclamation and acts. To **not welcome you** means **they do not listen to your words** about God's empire (cf. 10:7). What are disciples to do? They are not to force changes or devise other ways to dominate or subdue. **Leave that house or town**. They are, though, to perform an act which symbolizes the consequences of this response: **shake off the dust from your feet**. To **shake** a garment invokes judgment (Neh 5:13). It also represents having discharged one's responsibility and the end of interaction (Acts 18:6; 13:51). The act recognizes that disciples have been faithful to their charge.[8]

• 10:15

This section on the mission task (10:5-15) ends with a solemn warning that those who reject the disciples' mission condemn themselves in the judgment. With a legitimation formula (**Truly I tell you**), used to claim authority by one whose status is superior to those addressed (see 5:18, 21-48),[9] Jesus declares, **"it will be more tolerable for the land of Sodom and Gomorrah on the day of judgment than for that town." Sodom and Gomorrah** were proverbially wicked cities (Gen 18:20; Deut 29:23; Jer 49:18) destroyed by God (Gen 13:10; 19:24-25) for their great sin (Gen 18:20). Their sin is variously identified as covenant unfaithfulness, especially idolatry (Deut 29:15-29); social injustice (Isa 1:9-10, 17; Amos 4:1, 11); immorality (Jer 23:14; *T. Levi* 14:6; *T. Benj.* 9:1); and not recognizing the Lord's angels (*T. Ash.* 7:1). But on the anticipated **day of judgment** (vindication and punishment; see 7:22; chs. 24-25; also *Pss. Sol.* 15:12; *Jub.* 4:19), God will deal even more harshly with **towns** who reject the disciples. The comparison (**more tolerable . . . than**) indicates that the disciples' mission has given greater opportunity to encounter God's saving presence than was given to **Sodom and Gomorrah**. The punishment will be worse. Jesus' words reveal God's actions on the yet future **day of judgment**.

10:16-23—THE HARDSHIP OF MISSION: INEVITABLE PERSECUTION

• 10:16

Jesus' actions and teaching demonstrate that to confront the elite's system of self-interest and domination means conflict and suffering (see 2:1-23; 5:3-12; 9:3, 11; 16:21; chs. 26-27). So also for disciples. **Behold/see I am sending you out like sheep into the midst of wolves.** The initial **behold/see** signals a further dimension to Jesus' authoritative **sending out** of disciples (so 10:1, 2, 5). As **sheep,** members of God's people (see 9:36; 10:6) conduct their mission in the midst of dangerous **wolves.** These **wolves** are the sociopolitical and religious elite who oppress and harass the people. See 9:36; in Ezek 34:5, 10 the oppressed and leaderless sheep are food for wild beasts and their own leaders. (Sir 13:17-19; *1 En* 56:5: "kings as hungry hyenas among their own flocks"). On **wolves**, see 7:15; also Philostratus, *Apollonius* 8.22; Philo, *Rewards and Punishments* 86. Note the proverb "holding a wolf by the ears," used to denote dangerous political opponents (Suetonius, *Tiberius* 25). Epictetus calls "faithless, treacherous and hurtful" people **wolves** (*Diss* 1.3.7). But since their mission is also to all the people, **wolves** also include any hostile reactions to disciples. P. Freire notes the frequency with which the humiliated oppressed turn on each other.[10]

What are disciples to do? Obey Jesus' teaching to **be wise as serpents and innocent as doves** in their mission actions. The **serpent's** discerning craftiness in achieving its ends is proverbial (Gen 3:1). To be **wise** is to hear and do Jesus' words (Matt 7:24). To be **innocent as a dove** or to be "pure, untainted" (Louw and Nida, 1:746; *Ep. Arist.* 145), knowing only the good and not the evil (Rom 16:19), suggests a single-hearted commitment to the task. This will not protect disciples from danger, but it will ensure their focus and integrity (cf. 5:48; 6:1-18, 19-24).

• 10:17-18

Suffering is inevitable, **beware of people**. Two sources are named, the first Jewish, as befits the limitation of 10:5, the other Gentile to anticipate the expanding mission. (1) **For they** (unspecified in ethnicity, societal role, or status, but see 10:21) **will hand you over**, as happened to John (4:12) and will happen to Jesus (10:4; 16:21-22; 17:22), **to councils** (presumably a local court or council)[11] **and they will flog you in their synagogues** (cf. 23:34). This punishment derives from Deut 25:1-3. The offense is not specified.[12] The punishment is not life-taking, but it inflicts violent suffering, as will happen to Jesus, though not in a synagogue (20:19; 27:26). On conflict with synagogues, see 4:23; 6:2; 9:35; see Introduction, section 8.

(2) **You will be dragged before governors** (as Jesus will be taken before the Roman governor Pilate in 27:1, 11, 15, 27) **and kings because of me as a testimony to them and the Gentiles**. Again the offense is not specified, though it centers on Jesus (**because of me**; cf. 5:11) and will derive from proclaiming and demonstrating God's empire, which challenges the status quo (10:7). Even **before governors and kings** there is mission. Disciples present **a testimony to them** and through them to other **Gentiles**. See 8:4 for the healed leper's **testimony** to the priests. Persecution is both a consequence of, and an opportunity for, mission.

• 10:19-20

Jesus promises help for this act of "speaking truth to power." **When they hand you over** (10:17), **do not worry**: disciples are to trust God (6:25, 31, 34), not resort to revenge (cf. 5:44-45) or succumb to intimidation. **... how you are to speak or what you will say; for what you are to say will be given to you at that time.** The passive **will be given** points to God's intervention. Recall Moses (Exod 4.12) and Jeremiah (Jer 1:6-10). **For it is not for you to speak but the Spirit of your Father speaking through you**. Just as the Spirit empowered key figures and Jesus (see 3:16; 12:18, 28; cf. Isa 61:1-2), so it empowers disciples. The Spirit originates with **your Father**. The term **father** recalls the new family to which disciples belong as children of God (see Matt 5:9, 16, 45, 48; 6:9; 11:25; 16:17; 23:9; etc.).

• 10:21-22

Evoking the new family is important because the locus of much of this strife is very close to home. The statements of 10:17 now have more specificity (**Brother will hand over** [10:17] **brother . . . and a father a child**) and intensified consequences (**to death**). **And children will rise against parents and have them put to death**. The verb **rise against** is used in relation to murder (Deut 22:26b) and opposition to the righteous (Ps 3:1). See also Mic 7:6 and 10:34-36 below. For ambivalent interaction with households, and redefinition of the patriarchal household because of the claims of Jesus, see 4:18-22; 8:14-15, 21-22; 12:46-50; 15:1-20; chs. 19-20.

The intensity continues (**and you will be hated**), but the focus immediately broadens (**by everyone**). There is no safe haven or escape. Again no specific reason is given for the hatred, though it derives from faithfully carrying out this mission which confronts and transforms the status quo (**because of my name**; 5:11; 10:18). **Name** represents Jesus' presence, which manifests God's empire and saving presence expressed in the mission. While disciples are faithful in continuing and imitating Jesus' mission, they suffer. Yet this too is an opportunity, though for a reason further to that offered in 10:18. Jesus offers a reassuring promise: **The one who endures to the end will be saved**. The **end** is likely the return of Jesus and completion of God's purposes at the day of judgment (10:15, 23; chs. 24-25). The promise is repeated in this context in 24:13. But in the context of 10:21, **the end** may also be the death of a disciple before the return. Either way, **to be saved** is to participate in the completion of God's saving purposes already being manifested in Jesus' mission (1:21) and by the disciples.

• 10:23

When (not if) **they persecute you**, restates the harsh rejection detailed in 10:17-18, 21-22. The same verb (διῶκω, *diōkō*) in 5:10-12 names persecution as a situation in which God's presence is encountered (a blessing; cf. 10:22b). It refers there to "reviling you" and "speaking false evil against you," and promises God's reward (see 5:10-12). In 23:34 persecution comes from the religious leaders. In 5:44 disciples are to love and pray for persecutors. Here they are to **flee to the next (town)**. Being "wise as serpents" (10:16) means discerning which strategy is appropriate. **Fleeing** is both escape and opportunity (also 10:18, 22) to further the mission.

This section (10:16-23) ends, as did 10:5-15, with an eschatological assertion (see 10:15). Again introduced by the legitimation formula (**For truly I tell you**) emphasizing his authority, Jesus declares, **you certainly will not** (οὐ μή, *ou mē;* strong, emphatic negative) **finish the towns of Israel**. The verb **finish** (NRSV "go through") is a cognate form of **the end** in 10:22 and suggests eschatological dimensions. Does it mean they will not finish their mission in every town before Jesus returns (10:5) or that they will not run out of towns to which to flee (10:23a)? Given that persecution is an opportunity for mission (10:18) and mission means persecution, both seem to be in view.

They will not finish their task of mission to Israel **until the Son of Man**

comes. In the context of the eschatological promise in 10:22b, this coming is not Jesus' preaching ministry (for **Son of Man** as Jesus' self-reference in his earthly ministry, see 8:20). It refers, rather, to Jesus' return to judge and establish the fullness of God's empire (13:40-43; 19:28; 24:27-31; the verb **comes** appears with **Son of Man** in 16:27, 28; 24:30, 44; 25:31; 26:64; cf. 10:15; Dan 7:13-14; *1 En* 46:3-8).[13] This event ends the disciples' suffering and makes possible their reward, participation in the fullness of God's empire, for which they have worked. The focus here is on a continuing mission to Israel, but hints of a Gentile mission (10:18) anticipate mission to "all the nations" (28:19), both Jewish and Gentile, until Jesus' coming.

10:24-11:1—THE COURAGE, IMPACT, AND REWARD OF FAITHFUL MISSION

• 10:24-25

The section begins by reprising the connection between Jesus and disciples: inevitable persecution is the dominant response to their missions. Generally the world does not welcome its challenge and alternative. **A disciple is not above his teacher, nor a slave above his master.** For the christological and discipleship language, see 5:1 (**disciple**); 8:19 (**teacher**); 6:24; 20:26-27 (**master and slave**). But disciples are to be **like** their teacher and master in imitating his mission, as 10:1-23 has emphasized. Jesus gives an example of this likeness: **If they have called the master of the house Beelzebul, how much more those of his household**. The **they** are the religious leaders who accuse Jesus of casting out demons by "the prince of demons" (9:34; also 12:24). **Called** is a compound of the verb used to "call" Jesus to his mission in 1:21, and disciples in 10:1. The religious leaders miscall/misname Jesus because they do not accept his identity. **Beelzebul** is "ruler of demons" (*T. Sol.* 3:6) or Satan/the devil. **Master of the house** (in parables, 13:27, 52; 20:1, 11; 21:33; 24:43) identifies Jesus as the head of a new and different household or family (see 10:20; 12:46-50). Disciples are the **household**; for relationships within this alternative household, which contest patriarchal, hierarchical structures, see chs. 19-20. **How much more** cannot indicate greater persecution, since Jesus pays the ultimate price in being put to death by crucifixion. It is a statement of certainty; persecution is inevitable.

• 10:26-31

After this restatement of harsh treatment and inevitable persecution and rejection, Jesus offers comfort and exhortation by placing persecution in the context of God's purposes. The passage utilizes three "fear not" commands (10:26, 28, 31) to emphasize the revelation (10:26-27) of God's sovereign control over the future (10:28) and present (10:29-31). Jesus promises that faithful disciples will be rewarded in the judgment (10:32-33).

• 10:26a

The opening command **Therefore do not fear them** rules out fear as a response to inevitable persecution. The **them** must refer to those who hand disciples over to Jewish (10:17) and Gentile (10:18) authorities, including family members (10:21) and religious leaders (10:25). **Fear** is commended in 10:28b, so there is appropriate and inappropriate fear. The fear being dismissed is, in the context of 10:1-25, that which paralyzes disciples and prevents them from proclaiming (10:7) and enacting (10:8) God's saving power and reign manifested in Jesus. The emphasis on "acknowledging me" in 10:32-33 confirms this.

• 10:26b-27

Instead of paralyzing fear, disciples have the task of proclaiming what God reveals through Jesus. Four statements emphasize this task. The first two statements are parallel, with future passive verbs **will be revealed** and **will be made known** to indicate God's action. God reveals what is **covered up**; God makes known what is **secret**. This language is often found in apocalyptic literature to express the disclosing of God's reign at the judgment (1 Cor 4:5; *2 Bar* 83:1-8, esp. v. 3). So it is here, but with variations in time and means as the next two clauses indicate. The revelation of God's empire is already under way in Jesus' ministry (4:17). His life and teaching (**what I tell you**) begin to reveal God's reign and purposes, which have been **covered up** and **secret** (1:21-23; 4:17; 10:7-8). Disciples are to proclaim it (**tell in the light**). The thought is repeated for emphasis. **What you hear in the ear, proclaim it** (cf. 10:7) **from the housetops** (a prominent space). Disciples participate now in a process of disclosing God's purposes and empire, which God has already initiated and will complete at the judgment. Fear of hostile responses must not derail the revelation of God's reign.

• 10:28

With a second **do not fear** command, Jesus teaches what he has demonstrated (9:23-26; 10:8; 11:5), namely, that death is subject to God's empire. Fear of death, fear for their personal safety and survival, must not force disciples into apostasy, because beyond death they are accountable to God.

And do not fear those who kill the body. Martyrdom is a possibility for disciples (10:21). 4 Maccabees 13:14, possibly written in Antioch and concerned with martyrdom (see 4:24), offers a similar exhortation. Why not **fear**? Because the power of **those who kill** is limited to one aspect of human existence. They think that in killing the body, they destroy a person. But they are mistaken; they neglect and **cannot kill the soul** (cf. *T. Job* 20:3). Like 2:20 and 6:25 (10:39 below), **soul** (ψυχή, *psychē*) means the whole self and life in relation to God. But here it also contrasts with **body** to refer to the disembodied soul which survives bodily death but, subject to God's power, is reunited with the body in resurrection (Wis 16:13-15; 2 Macc 6:30; 7:9, 14, 23, 29). Only God has power that extends over the whole person and beyond death to determine human destiny. Since God has this ultimate power, disciples will please God by not commiting apostasy but trusting themselves to God. Hence the present-tense exhortation to continue to **fear the one** (God) **who can destroy both soul and body in hell**. On **hell** as the place of punishment for the wicked, see 5:22. While "killing the body" is terrible (cf. 2 Macc 7; 4 Macc), physical death by persecutors is not as bad as total destruction. This destruction is to be feared; decisions have consequences. To **fear** God means a life of faithful mission.[14] On the function of scenes of eschatological judgment for faithful discipleship, see 7:13. Compare Epictetus's resignation to the inevitability of death (*Diss* 3.5.5-11; 4.1.103-110; 4.10.8-17).

• 10:29-33

The prospect of judgment asserts God's sovereign power over everything, including future destiny. The following verses, 10:29-31, offer another and more gentle image of God. The judge is also the loving father whose sovereign care is known in the present. The argument moves from the lesser (the sparrow's demise) to the greater (God's care for disciples).

• 10:29

The opening rhetorical question abruptly changes focus to **sparrows**, evokes common knowledge about them as cheap food,[15] and solicits agreement (the initial οὐχί, *ouchi*: **Are not two sparrows sold for a penny?** The next assertion is somewhat surprising: **Yet not one of them will fall to the ground without the knowledge and consent of** (BAGD, 65) **your Father**. The sparrows illustrate experience of God (Ps 102:7; 124:7; Jer 8:7; also Matt 6:26)—here God's knowledge of, not prevention of, their fall. The personal pronoun (**your**) and common image for the loving God of disciples (**Father;** see 5:16, 45-48), prepares for a parallel with disciples.

• 10:30

The parallel is delayed with a new image to emphasize God's intimate knowledge of disciples: **And even the hairs of your head are all counted** (the passive indicates by God). The image employs a tradition which contrasts God's knowledge with human ignorance (Job 38:37-38; Sir 1:2; *1 En* 93:14; *4 Ezra* 4:7-12).[16]

The point is not that sparrows do not fall/die, not that God will rescue disciples from persecution, which 10:1-25 has established as inevitable, but that what happens to disciples is within the compassionate knowing and purposes of God. The experience of persecution has a future solution (vindication for faithfulness, 10:28) and a present strategy, to trust God's all-wise and compassionate purposes, even when incomprehensible to disciples.[17]

• 10:31

The third **fear not** clause elaborates (**therefore**) the image of the sparrows for disciples: **you are of more value than many sparrows**. If God's compassionate knowing embraces the fall of sparrows, how much more the faithful lives and deaths of disciples?

• 10:32-33

Eschatological consequences (**therefore**) follow fearless faithfulness and fearful unfaithfulness. Jesus addresses **everyone who acknowledges me**. To

acknowledge me indicates what is not to be feared (10:26a, 28, 31): do not fear to be loyal to Jesus in proclamation, mission acts, and martyrdom (10:7-8, 28). Hostile responses must not prevent the mission. This loyal relationship with Jesus (**me**), even in persecution, brings reciprocal benefits. Acknowledgment *of* Jesus means acknowledgment *by* Jesus: **I also will acknowledge before my Father in heaven**. This is the day of judgment (10:15) after the Son of Man comes (10:23), when faithful disciples who have endured to the end will be saved (10:22). His role in the judgment is to advocate **before my Father in heaven**, with whom he has intimate relationship (7:21; 11:27; 12:50; 23:9). God who carries out this vindication is the loving **Father** (10:29) who loves indiscriminately (5:45-48), to whom disciples have prayed (see 6:9), whose empire they display on earth (see 10:20). While fear of condemnation motivates discipleship (10:28b), so too does the hope of life consistent with God's will and empire in its fullness.

The negative follows. **Denial** of Jesus, the failure to acknowledge him by living in loyal and trusting relationship to Jesus expressed in a missional existence, means denial before God. This is condemnation on the day of judgment (10:15, 28b).

• 10:34-39

The disciples' mission derives from and imitates Jesus' mission. That mission claims continual exclusive loyalty to Jesus. Its disruptive impact on households means persecution.

• 10:34

The focus moves from the disciples' mission to Jesus' mission with three **I have (not) come** sayings (see 5:17; 9:13).[18] The opening **do not think** counters a mistaken view (5:17): **I have come to bring peace on earth**. This denial is surprising after Jesus' blessing on peacemakers (5:9) and instruction to extend peace (10:13). Various traditions understood God to inaugurate a future age of peace or wholeness (Isa 8:23-9:7; 11:6; 66:25; Zech 9:9-10; *T. Levi* 18:2-4; *1 En* 5:7-10; *2 Bar* 73:1). But the story has also indicated Jesus' threat to the political and religious elite, and its violent responses (ch. 2; 9:3, 11; 10:17-18). For **earth** as the realm of doing God's will, see 2:6, 20-21; 4:15; 5:13, 18, 35; 6:10, 19; 9:6; 10:29. A second negative statement emphasizes the disclaimer (**I have not come to bring peace**). The fullness of God's purposes, the reign of peace, has not yet dawned in Jesus' ministry. Rather Jesus has come to bring **a sword**, creating a striking juxtaposition of **peace** and **sword**, and evoking struggle, conflict, war, violence, and death as elements of the establishment of God's empire. Naming these dimensions indicates that God's empire imitates regrettable elements of contemporary imperial practice (see Introduction, section 1).

• 10:35-36

The nature of this **sword** appears in a third **I have come** saying. The image denotes division and God's judgment of those, especially the elite, who reject

God's life-giving purposes (Wis 5:2; Sir 39:30; *1 En* 62:12; 63:11-12 [kings, governors, high officials, landlords]; 90:19; 91:11-12 [blasphemers, oppressors]; *Pss. Sol.* 15:7-9 [sinners]). Those who reject God's reign experience judgment through Jesus' words and actions. This judgment cuts through households: **to set a man against his father, and a daughter against her mother, and a daughter-in-law against her mother-in-law; and one's foes will be members of one's own household.** Micah 7:6 describes a time of turmoil before deliverance (cf. *1 En* 56:7; 100:1-2; *2 Bar* 70:2-6. R. Tannehill suggests that these divided family relationships are focal instances; what is true in these examples applies to many relationships. Nor is the division accidental or temporary; it is the very purpose of Jesus' mission, as some find salvation, others judgment.[19]

• **10:37-39**

After declaring his purpose, Jesus exhorts unsurpassed loyalty to himself from disciples. This means, first, redefining conventional household relationships. **Whoever loves father or mother above me is not worthy of me; and whoever loves son or daughter above me is not worthy of me.** The patriarchal household, claimed since Aristotle (*Pol* 1.2.1-2) to be central to any city or state and a microcosm of empire,[20] is undermined. Primary loyalty extends to Jesus, not the household. This does not mean the end of household obligations, required by the Decalogue (Exod 20:12; Deut 5:16; cf. Matt 8:14-15; 15:1-9). But it does mean that loyalty to Jesus is primary (see 8:21-22; 12:46-50; chs. 19-20). The verb to **love** (φιλεῖν, *philein*) is rarely used in Matthew and only to express disapproval (6:5; 23:6; 26:48). Here to **love** is to place any relationship and obligation above Jesus. To do so is to be **not worthy of me**. The **worthy** hear the good news, believe, and obey (10:11-14); the not worthy do not, and face judgment (10:15). A minority tradition of writers and groups exhorted the subordination of family ties because of commitment to God (Philo, *Spec Leg* 1.316-17; Josephus on the Essenes, *JW* 2.120-21) or to a philosophical school (Cynics: Epictetus, *Diss* 3.22.45-48, 69-72; Stoics: Musonius Rufus 16; Neopythagoreans: Philostratus, *Apollonius* 1.13).[21]

• **10:38**

Loyalty to Jesus means, second, not just household division and rejection but societal conflict: **and whoever does not take up the cross and follow me is not worthy of me**. To **take up the cross** evokes a political image of shame, humiliation, pain, social rejection, marginalization, condemnation, and death.[22]

Crucifixion, as employed by Rome, was a cruel means of execution (Tacitus, *Ann* 15.44.4; Seneca, *De Ira* 1.2.2; Josephus, *JW* 7.203 ["most pitiable of deaths"]). It was not used for Roman citizens (Cicero, *Pro Rabirio* 9-17, except for treason), but for sociopolitical marginals such as "rebellious" foreigners (Josephus, *JW* 2.306, 308; 5.449-53; Philo, *In Flaccum* 72, 84), violent criminals and robbers (Martial, *On the Spectacles* 9), and slaves (Cicero, *In Verr* 2.5.162; Juvenal, *Sat* 6.219-224; Tacitus, *Ann* 13.32.1). The cross was a means of dividing citizen from noncitizen, the socially acceptable from the rejected. It was the ultimate form of societal exclusion. Crucifixion in public places was intended to deter noncompliant behavior (Josephus, *JW* 5.550); carrying the cross-beam (*patibulum*) to the place of execution could be part of the precrucifixion torture and humiliation (Plutarch, "On the Delay of Divine Vengeance," *Moralia* 554B). Some Jewish traditions associated crucifixion with the curse on those hung on a tree (Deut 23:21; Gal 3:13; 11QTemple 64:6-13). The scandalous call of Jesus the crucified to **take up the cross and follow me** (see 4:18-22) is, then, a call to martyrdom. It is to resist even to death, as Jesus does (9:15; 10:4, 21, 28, 29; also 16:21; 17:22; 20:17-19; chs. 26-27). Such is the risk of Jesus' work of proclaiming and demonstrating God's empire (10:7-8).[23]

On another level, Jesus' words are a call to choose a way of life of marginalization, to identify with the nobodies like slaves, and with those some understood to be cursed by God. It is to identify with those who resist the empire's control, who contest its version of reality, and who are vulnerable to its reprisals. It is to identify with a sign of the empire's violent and humiliating attempt to dispose of those who threatened or challenged its interests. To so identify is not to endorse the symbol but to reframe its violence. As the end of the gospel indicates, it is to identify with a sign that ironically indicates the empire's limits. The empire will do its worst in crucifying Jesus. But God raises Jesus from death, thwarting the empire's efforts. And Jesus will return to establish God's empire over all including Rome (24:27-31). To not respond positively to such a call is to not be a disciple (**not worthy of me**; see 10:37).

• 10:39

Loyalty to Jesus, third, has eschatological consequences. The initial **finding-losing** paradox is difficult but is clarified by the context and the contrast in 10:39b. To **find one's life** (existence; 2:20; 6:25; 10:28) is to decide against the way of the cross and its confrontation with the status quo. It is to decide for what is safe, for self-interest. It is to be intimidated into compliance by the elite's threat to crucify those who resist. It is to preserve one's life from the persecutors. But this choice for safety is to **lose** life in the judgment (already under way) because a disciple has not been constant in acknowledging Jesus (10:32-33).

Conversely in the context of 10:16-38, to **lose one's life for my sake** (10:18, 22) is to die because of life lived in relation to God, at the hands of persecutors in the task of mission to which Jesus sends disciples. It is to identify with those who resist and contest the empire, with the marginal (10:38). On **for my sake** see 10:18, 22. But death is not the end (10:28). To **find** life in the subversive way of the cross is to **find** it in an act that refuses to give the elite the power of intimidation and conformity which it craves. To **find** (future tense) life is to enter into the fullness of God's purposes in the new age (10:15, 22b, 32-33).

• 10:40-42

After presenting the disciples' mission in relation to Jesus' call (10:1-4), their tasks (10:5-15), hardship and persecution (10:16-31), eschatological destiny (10:28, 32-33, 39), Jesus' mission (10:34-36), and loyalty to Jesus (10:37-

39), the chapter concludes by announcing that a favorable response to the disciples expresses a positive response to Jesus (10:40-42).

• 10:40

Whoever welcomes/receives you welcomes/receives me. The verse connects new disciples, missioning disciples, Jesus, and God, to reveal Jesus' presence in the disciples' mission. To **welcome/ receive** the missioning disciples is to accept their message, to listen to (= trust) their words, which proclaim God's reign (10:7, 14), to encounter Jesus, and to become his disciple. Responsiveness to disciples is equated with receiving (= committing to) Jesus, present through the mission of the sent ones (10:2).

There is a further link: **Whoever welcomes/receives me receives/welcomes the one who sent me**. Jesus' teaching reveals that God is present with him and through the disciples' mission. God's presence with Jesus is again affirmed (1:21-23; 3:17; 5:17; 9:13; 10:34-35). A central element of the disciples' mission is to make possible an encounter with God's saving presence and empire. New disciples are created. Unstated is the opposite conclusion. To reject disciples is to reject Jesus and God.

• 10:41-42

A threefold statement elaborates the reward of these new disciples. The context, parallel construction, and similar language (**Whoever welcomes . . . shall welcome**) indicate that the terms **prophet**, **righteous/just person,** and **little ones**, refer not to the long and honorable traditions of Hebrew Bible figures, but to missioning disciples. The qualifying of **little ones** in 10:42 with **in the name of a disciple** supports this claim. Nor do the three separate terms identify separate groups among the disciples.[24] Rather the terms highlight different aspects of the mission addressed by the previous verses. Like their Hebrew Bible predecessors, **prophets** proclaim and do miraculous actions (cf. 7:15), so the term evokes the tasks (10:7-8). Occupying a liminal societal location, **prophets** conflict with the center and challenge its commitments and priorities with a vision of life in relation to God (see ch. 3). **Righteous/just people** are those who are faithful to God's requirements (see 1:19), so the term suggests faithfulness and perseverance in the difficult task of doing justice. **Little ones** suggests vulnerability and danger for a minority group (Introduction, section 7). It recalls the context of persecution and exhortation to persevere which is evident throughout the chapter. To **receive/welcome** (see 10:40) involves not only believing the message but sharing hospitality (10:11-14), symbolized by **giving even a cup of cold water to one of these little ones**. Some suggest that this act indicates a double level of disciples, some in mission and some who support. But the verse does not support this division. It attests initial responsive action, not a permanent role. All disciples are called to the mission task, though without precluding different roles.

To receive a prophet/righteous person is to **receive a prophet's reward**. The reward is double. In the present it is a reward **of or from prophets**, which is to hear their words, the proclamation which makes possible the blessed encounter with God's empire (cf. 5:3-12). In the future (**will receive**) the reward is the eschatological **reward** that follows faithful participation in the task of mission (see 5:12; cf. 10:15, 28, 32-33, 39). It is the experience of life in the fullness of God's empire. Faithful, continual doing of Jesus' teaching leads to such a reward. **Truly I say to you** (as a conclusion to the two earlier sections, see 10:15, 23) **none of these will lose their reward**.

• 11:1

Now when Jesus had finished instructing his twelve disciples. Jesus' first major teaching discourse, the Sermon on the Mount, ends with a similar clause (7:28; so also 13:53; 19:1; 26:1), which provides both closure and transition to the ongoing ministry. **Twelve disciples** forms an inclusion with 10:1-4. The narrative does not indicate that the disciples go in mission. Rather, attention returns to Jesus, who **went on from there to teach and proclaim his message in their cities** (see 4:23; 9:35). The link of these actions with healing in 4:23 and 9:35, as well as with various actions in chapters 11-16, suggests the whole range of demonstrations of God's saving presence and empire. The **cities** of Galilee continue to be the focus (cf. 4:12-16); **their** suggests some distancing and hostility (see 4:23; 7:29; 9:35; 10:17).

PART III

The Third Narrative Block

*Responses to Jesus' Ministry
(11:2-16:20)*

CHAPTER 11

Responding to Jesus

The second narrative block has shown Jesus faithfully carrying out his God-given commission in words and actions (4:17-11:1). The third narrative block (11:2-16:20) focuses on people's responses to Jesus. The opening scene (11:2-6) poses the central question about Jesus' identity: "Are you the one who is to come?" (11:3). The closing scene restates the focus, "Who do people say that I am?" (16:13). The key scene (11:2-6) also provides the means of determining that Jesus is the one commissioned by God to manifest God's empire. Jesus' ministry testifies to his identity (11:4-5). Those who discern from his actions and words his identity as God's commissioned agent or Christ are blessed (11:6). The rest of the narrative block will elaborate these concerns of Jesus' identity and responses to him.

The logic of the gospel's narrative emerges. While 1:1-4:16 emphasizes God's initiative in commissioning Jesus, and 4:17-11:1 shows how Jesus faithfully carries out this commission in his words (chs. 5-7, 10) and actions (chs. 8-9), 11:2-16:20 indicates the necessity of discerning Jesus' identity from his actions and words, and of responding with commitment or rejection.[1]

These concerns shape the organization of chapter 11. After 11:2-6, two sections (11:7-19, 20-24) focus on discerning Jesus' identity and depict negative responses. The fourth section (11:25-30) celebrates a positive response from the marginalized "infants" and invites others to respond positively.[2]

1. 11:2-19   The Identity of and Negative Response to Jesus and John
    11:2-6   John's question about Jesus' identity
    11:7-15   Jesus' statement about John's identity
    11:16-19   The negative response to and rejection of both

2. 11:20-24 The Negative Response to Jesus
    11:20   Statement of rejection of Jesus
    11:21-24   Curses on Chorazin, Bethsaida, Capernaum

3. 11:25-30 The Revelation of Jesus' Identity to the "Infants"
    11:25-26   The positive response of the "infants"
    11:27   Jesus the Revealer
    11:28-30   Jesus invites the weary and burdened to respond.

11:2-19—THE IDENTITY OF AND NEGATIVE RESPONSE TO JESUS AND JOHN

11:2-6—JOHN'S QUESTION ABOUT JESUS' IDENTITY

• 11:2-3

John, out of view since his arrest (4:12; cf. 14:1-12) and his disciples' inquiry about fasting (9:14; see 3:1-12, 13-17), **hears in prison about the works of the Christ** (1:1). Presumably John hears from his disciples, who included tax collectors and prostitutes (21:32). Some traditions expected the messiah to work miracles (4Q521; *2 Bar* 29:6-7; 73:1-2; *4 Ezra* 7:123). The term **works** reviews Jesus' public ministry, words, and deeds, in 4:17-11:1 ("hear and see" is used in 11:4, and preaching in 11:5). From this report, and through **his disciples**, John seeks to discern Jesus' identity: **Are you the one who is to come or are we to wait for another?** This is the key issue. **You**, the first word and in pronoun form, is emphatic. In 3:11 John spoke of **the coming one** in his testimony about Jesus' ministry. Is John's question strange after this testimony and John' baptism of Jesus (3:14)? Somewhat. But there was no uniform, widespread messianic expectation (see 1:1). Jesus' ministry has demonstrated **power** (3:11) in authoritative teaching (chs. 5-7, 10) and miracles (chs. 8-9) and has offered salvation and promised judgment (10:32-33; 3:11-12). But no cosmic judgment has taken place. John seeks confirmation. His question underlines the means of recognizing Jesus' identity.

• 11:4-5

Jesus instructs John's disciples, **Go and tell John what you hear and see**. He describes his merciful ministry with the marginalized (see 4:23-24; chs. 8-9): **the blind receive their sight** (so 9:27-31), **the lame walk** (so 9:1-8), **the lepers are cleansed** (so 8:1-4), **the deaf hear** (see 9:32-34), **the dead are raised** (so 9:18-19, 23-26), **and the poor have good news preached to them**. See 4:23; 9:35 for **good news** as God's liberating action, not imperial oppression; also 5:3 for the **poor** as lacking resources, hope, opportunity, and subject to oppressive forces.[3] The list recalls Jesus' acts in chapters 8-9, the passives (**cleansed, raised, preached**) point to God's action in Jesus, and the language is shaped by Isaiah's visions of God's liberating work and reign, Isa 26:19 (**the dead**), 29:18-19 (**the deaf, blind, poor**), 35:5-6 (**the blind, deaf, lame**), 42:7 (**the blind**), 61:1 (**poor, blind**). Jesus' healing ministry enacts the healing anticipated in the fullness of God's empire (*2 Bar* 73:1-2). He performs God's will, embraces the marginalized, challenges the elite's power and self-interest, and creates new social roles for some. He is God's anointed.

• 11:6

Jesus emphasizes recognition of and response to his actions: **Blessed is anyone who takes no offense at me**. Jesus employs a beatitude. It states what God deems to be honorable. It declares God's favor on a present situation, promises future reversal or reward, and exhorts hearers to live accordingly (see 5:3). The blessing focuses on Jesus (**me**). It recognizes that his works attest his identity and express his commission as Christ, the one anointed by God to manifest God's empire over all that opposes God's life-giving purposes: sin, the devil and demons, the sociopolitical and religious elite, death (1:21-23; 4:17). The blessing affirms a positive response (cf. 10:32-33). To encounter Jesus is to encounter God's reign (see 10:40).

But a beatitude implies a curse. The negative **takes no offense** suggests that offense is possible. The verb's meaning of "causing one to sin" (see 5:29-30; 13:21; 18:7) names offense at Jesus as a sinful response.

11:7-15—JESUS' STATEMENT ABOUT JOHN'S IDENTITY

• 11:7-9

As they (John's disciples) **went away** (same verb as Jesus' command to go in 11:4 to demonstrate Jesus' authority), **Jesus began to speak to the crowds** (absent since 9:36) **about John.** Now the roles are reversed. John the questioner (11:2) is the focus of Jesus' six rapid-fire questions, as Jesus the questioned urges the crowd to understand John's identity and mission. To comprehend who John is means to understand Jesus' identity and mission.

The first question, **What did you go out into the wilderness to look at?**, recalls John's call to repentance and witness to Jesus, and his marginal location and status. See 3:1-6. The second question offers a possible answer: **A reed blown about by the wind?** Reeds were a common sight in the Jordan valley, but the term has rich symbolism. In 3 Macc 2:22 it images God's punishment of the Ptolemaic tyrant Philopator. Moreover, the reed was Herod Antipas's symbol on coins commemorating the founding of Tiberias (cf. Jesus as "king" in 27:29). John challenged and conflicted with the religious (3:7-10) and political elite including Herod Antipas, son of Herod (so 14:1-11; ch. 2). Did they go out to see Herod "blown about," attacked by John's critique of urban power, wealth, and alliance with Rome, and/or punished by God?[4] Or perhaps it evokes (with **wilderness**) the Sea of Reeds (Exod 13:18) blown back by the east wind (Exod 14:21) as God frees the people from Egyptian slavery. Did they go into the wilderness to see a new exodus, a new act of liberation, as others did (Josephus, *Ant* 20.97-98 [Theudas]; *JW* 2.261-63 [an Egyptian]; *JW* 7.437-38 [Jonathan])?[5] The third question repeats the first and pursues the issue of John's identity, **What then did you go out to see?**

Jesus' fourth question is ironic: **Someone dressed in soft robes?** The expectation of luxurious clothing, signs of elite status, wealth, and tyranny,[6] highlights John's prophetic stance toward the elite. His clothing is not conventional and resembles Elijah's (see 3:1-6), who confronted King Ahaz and Jezebel. Jesus' comment mocks any thought of John's alliance with the elite: **those who wear soft robes** [live] **in royal palaces**, places of power and luxury, not the wilderness, which John frequents.

After again asking, **Why did you go out?** Jesus' sixth question names John's identity, **a prophet?** This term embraces, not negates, the previous possibilities. The term covers a wide spectrum of figures (see 3:1-6):[7] biblical prophets who critique political-economic and religious personnel, structures, and practices; eschatological prophets who declare God's coming intervention, perhaps through messianic deliverers; miracle workers (see 7:15; Josephus, *Ant* 18.85-87; 20.97-98; 20.167-72); those who predict the future (Josephus predicts that Vespasian will be emperor [*JW* 3.400-402]); people who reveal a god's will (Delphi oracles; Joshua ben Ananiah declares doom against Jerusalem [Josephus, *JW* 6.300-309]). The gospel's audience knows from 3:1-12 that **yes**, John is a prophet who confronts the status quo and announces repentance to prepare for God's imminent intervention, which will manifest God's reign over all that opposes it. Jesus' questions confirm all this. He then moves beyond it. **But he is more than a prophet**. How so?

• 11:10

John's **more than** role is clarified by scripture, which indicates his role in preparing for Jesus' ministry (see 3:1-12), **about whom it is written, "See, I am sending my messenger ahead of you . . ."** This quote comes from Exod 23:20; the first half of the line is also close to Mal 3:1 ("I am sending out my messenger"). In Exod 23:20 God promises the people (**you**) a guide after their liberation from Egypt (probably a heavenly figure or angel; perhaps Moses). The verse, though, has new meanings in Matthew's new context. A verse about the people (**you**) becomes a verse about Jesus (**you**). What stays the same is God's way of working. Just as the messenger prepares the people to enter the land, so God sends John (**my messenger**) to prepare them to enter God's empire revealed by Jesus (**you**). In Mal 4:5, the prophet warns of God's coming judgment and a messenger, Elijah, is sent to prepare the people. The verse (as with Exod 23:20) is now understood to speak of John (**my messenger**) and his task to prepare for Jesus' coming (3:1-12). The second part (**who will prepare your way before you**) is not taken from either Exodus or Malachi, though both verses refer to **the way** as living God's will. John's task is to **prepare the way** for Jesus, an echo of Isa 40:3 (cited in 3:3), which recalls God's liberation of the people from Babylonian exile. John prepares the way for God's saving work to continue in Jesus in a world ruled by Rome.

• 11:11

Jesus affirms John's special role in preparing people for Jesus' mission: **truly I tell you** (see 5:18; 10:15, 23, 42), **among those born of women no one has arisen greater than John the Baptist; yet the least in the empire of heaven is greater than he**. Given the emphasis on John's importance, the last clause is striking. Is Jesus putting John's present greatness in the context of the coming future reign, which will redefine greatness? Or is he indicating that John is excluded and is inferior to those in the reign? Does Jesus speak of himself with humility as **the least** and with honor for John? The first possibility is not likely, since the reign is already present in part. The second is undercut by 11:12, which places John in the reign. The last option is consistent both with

John's subordinate role (3:1-12) and with Jesus' authority, which redefines greatness as service, not domination (11:25-27; 18:4; 20:25-28).

• 11:12

Yet despite, or because of, their importance in God's purposes, both know violent opposition.[8] **From the days of John the Baptist until now the reign/empire of heaven is violently attacked**[9] **and the violent take it by force**. The displays of **God's reign** in word or action provoke resistance. Herod and religious leaders (3:2, 7-10; 14:1-12) oppose John; Herod (ch. 2), the devil (4:8-11), demons (8:29), elite townspeople (8:34), religious leaders (9:1-13) allied with Rome (chs. 26-27), and crowds (9:24) oppose Jesus; households, Jewish councils, and Gentile kings and governors assault disciples (5:10-12; 10:17-18, 21-22, 34-36). The powerful protect their interest/s and resist God's claim and final victory. In the tradition of Ezek 34 the leaders do not enact God's will (see 9:36). They ensure their own well-being but do not "strengthen the weak, heal the sick or bring back the lost . . . but rule with force and harshness" (Ezek 34:3-4). They neglect the jubilee requirements of returning land, freeing slaves, and canceling debts (Lev 25:43, 46). Various traditions expected a time of eschatological birthpangs or woes, an intensifying conflict of good and evil, to precede the establishment of God's reign.[10] Things get worse before they get better.

• 11:13

John's link with God's empire and his (and Jesus') violent rejection is explained (**for**) as the enactment of what **all the prophets and the law prophesied until John came**. The unusual order (prophets preceding law; contrast 5:17) emphasizes the prophetic function of the whole tradition. It prepares for and now confirms John's special role and the rejection of John and Jesus.[11]

• 11:14-15

The affirmation **and if you are willing to accept it, he is Elijah who is to come** returns to the citation of Mal 3:1 and 4:5 in 11:10, which warned of judgment and announced a messenger, Elijah, to prepare the people. John carries out what Malachi predicted (11:13). He performs Elijah's prophetic role (see Sir 48:1-10). This identification matters (**let anyone with ears listen**) because to understand John's role as the messenger who prepares for God's coming enables one to understand Jesus' identity, that in him God's presence and reign are manifested (1:23). To understand John's identity helps people to respond appropriately to Jesus. To **have ears** is a metaphor that points beyond literal hearing to discerning significance (contrast Isa 6:9; Ezek 3:7, 27; 12:2).

11:16-19—THE NEGATIVE RESPONSE TO AND REJECTION OF JOHN AND JESUS

• 11:16-17

The opening clause is ominous (**To what will I compare**). This formula of comparison is prevalent in God's lawsuits against the people (Isa 40:18, 25).

The term **this generation**[12] denotes not so much time but character. It is essentially pejorative, first appearing in 1:17 to sum up the largely unfaithful history of the people with God. In 12:39 and 16:4 **this generation** is "evil and adulterous," a prophetic image of unfaithfulness (Jer 3:8; Ezek 23:37). In 17:17 it is "faithless and perverse." These adjectives evoke the "faithless," "evil," "sinful" wilderness generation who, despite God's miraculous and faithful interventions, did not trust God and were under God's judgment (Deut 1:35; 32:5, 20; *Jub.* 23:14). But it does not embrace everybody. In the flood generation, there were a faithful few like Noah (Gen 6:9; 7:1; *Jub.* 5:5; Sir 44:17), Enoch (*3 En* 7), and Caleb (Num 14:24), out of step with the rest. Like the people of the flood and the wilderness, **this generation** has witnessed God's liberating intervention but largely rejects God's saving presence and reign revealed in Jesus.

Their verdict on Jesus is misguided, self-deceiving, and self-incriminating. So **this generation** is **like children sitting in the marketplaces and calling to one another, "We played the flute for you and you did not dance; we wailed and you did not mourn."** The verb **sitting** can denote a judgment or court scene (so 27:19); likewise **in the marketplaces** (ἀγοραῖς, *agorais*) can designate not only a city's center, the center of public life, but particularly the courts and, in the plural as here, "court days."[13] The scene involves a law court and judgment. Seneca notes that children typically "play among themselves at being magistrates and in make-believe have their bordered toga, lictors' rods and tribunal . . ." (*De Const* 12.2).

This generation and its leaders condemn John and Jesus. But their wrong judgment reveals that they are marginal to the real center of God's purposes. While they claim the center in pronouncing judgment, they marginalize themselves by excluding themselves from God's purposes. They are **like children** who do not join in the game (2:8; 18:1-6). And in misjudging Jesus and John, they put themselves under God's judgment (cf. 11:16, **To what will I compare**).

• 11:18

John's ascetic lifestyle (**John came neither eating nor drinking** (see 3:1-6; 9:14; 11:8), an expression of God's call to repentance, is misinterpreted, **and they say, "He has a demon."** The **they** is not specified. Given the opposition expressed in 3:7-10 and 4:12, it could be the religious and political elite, but the reference in 11:17 to **this generation** suggests perhaps wider rejection. The elite label people as possessed to marginalize and dismiss them, and to deflect their challenge to the status quo. See 4:24; 9:34; 12:22-23.

• 11:19

Jesus' different lifestyle also provokes opposition: **the Son of Man came eating and drinking. Son of Man** denotes Jesus' interaction with and rejection by the world (see 8:20). Compared with John's ascetic behavior, his eating and drinking seems normal. But it too is misinterpreted: **they say, "Look, a glutton and a drunkard,"** a phrase indicating "a stubborn and rebellious son" who does not obey his parents and should be put to death (Deut 21:18-21). The irony is rich. From God's point of view, Jesus is an obedient son or child with whom God is well pleased (see 2:15; 3:17; 17:5). **They** (unspecified) declare a verdict that is totally at odds with God's. The second misinterpretation **a friend of tax collectors and sinners** evokes the meal scene (see 9:10-13), in which his demonstration of God's mercy to all regardless of economic, social, political, gender, or religious status aggravated the religious leaders. This alternative community challenges normative hierarchical divisions.

Yet, despite pervasive rejection from the elite and others, **wisdom is vindicated by her deeds**. Jesus is identified as **wisdom**, God's emissary sent to reveal God's ways but rejected (Prov 8-9; Sir 24; *1 En* 42:2). Numerous groups debated where wisdom, God's will and presence, was to be found: in Israel and the Jerusalem temple (Sir 24:8-12), in the law (Sir 24:23), in heaven (*1 En* 42:1-3), everywhere, and in human souls (Wis 7:24-26). This gospel's claim is that wisdom is found in Jesus (also 11:25-30; 1:21-23; 4:17; 13:54). Jesus' deeds, the actions and words of the Messiah (so 11:2), faithfully manifest his commission (1:21-23; 4:17), despite the wrong evaluations offered in 11:19. To reject him is to reject God (10:33). His deeds disclose his identity to those few (9:37) who can discern it (11:2-6).[14]

11:20-24—WOES ON TOWNS[15]

• 11:20
Then he began to reproach (5:11; 11:20; 27:44; here it means "curse," as 11:21-24 indicates) **the cities where most of his deeds of power** (cf. 11:2, 5, 19) **had been done because they did not repent**. Jesus' opening proclamation called for **repentance** (4:17). Repentance determines whether God is experienced as judge or savior (so 2 Chr 7:13-22; Jer 4:1-10; 7:5-34; 17:24-27). Jesus has taught that conflict and rejection would follow (5:10-12; also 10:17-18, 25), and it has been evident (9:3, 11, 34). **Cities**, the location of Jesus' and the disciples' ministry (9:35; 10:5, 11), suggest widespread rejection (evident in 10:14, 15, 23). Small cities are centers of power and of the elite's control over surrounding areas. Like Jerusalem they resist Jesus' ministry (ch. 2).

• 11:21-22
Jesus announces a double **Woe to you Chorazin! Woe to you Bethsaida!** Both towns were at the north of the Sea of Galilee. Neither was mentioned as a location for any of the "deeds of power" in chapters 8-9. For the first time Jesus declares, not threatens, judgment. The **woe**, a counterpart of blessings (see 5:3-12), announces God's grave disapproval and judgment on a disobedient and unresponsive people. See *1 En* 94:6-11 for a woe declaring God's destruction of oppressors, sinners, and the exploitative wealthy (also Deut 27:15-28; Isa 5:8-23; Amos 5:18; 6:1; *1 En* 97:7-10; 98:9-16; 99:1-2, 11-16; 100:7-9; *2 Bar* 10:7). Woes are announced on Moab (Num 21:29) and Jerusalem (Jer 13:27).

Chorazin and Bethsaida are cursed because they had opportunity to repent but didn't take it. **For if the deeds of power done in you had been done in**

Tyre and Sidon, they would have repented long ago in sackcloth and ashes.
Tyre and Sidon are two Gentile cities of ill repute on the Mediterranean coast,
denounced in Isa 23 and Ezek 27-28 for unjust and excessive wealth (Jer 47:4;
Zech 9:1-4). **Sackcloth and ashes** are worn in mourning and penitence.[16] If
even these wicked cities would have repented, how determined is **Chorazin
and Bethsaida**'s rejection. Why do they not recognize Jesus' identity from his
works (1:21-23; 4:17)? They do not see themselves as Jesus sees them, in need
of repentance, as the lost sheep of Israel (10:5). Perhaps they share the elite's
misplaced sense of well-being based on ethnicity (3:7-10).[17] Accordingly **But
I tell you** (see 10:15), **on the day of judgment** (see 10:15) **it will be more tolerable for Tyre and Sidon than for you.**

• 11:23a
The condemnation is repeated, directed now to **Capernaum**. This is tragic,
not only because it is Jesus' hometown (see 4:13; 8:5; 9:1) but his dwelling
there fulfills the divine will (4:14-16). **Will you be exalted to the heaven**? (an
image that emphasizes its fall). **No, you will be brought down to Hades**, the
place of the dead and here of condemnation and punishment.[18] *If* 9:1 refers to
Capernaum, a few respond positively even in this rejecting town: a paralyzed
man and his friends, Matthew and other tax collectors, the ruler, the woman
(9:1-26; cf. 7:13-14).

• 11:23b-24
Just as "Chorazin and Bethsaida" were compared with "Tyre and Sidon,"
Capernaum is contrasted with the notorious **Sodom**. **For if the deeds of power
done in you had been done in Sodom it would have remained until this day**.
Sodom would have repented and not been punished (see 11:20). **But I tell you
that on the day of judgment it will be more tolerable for the land of Sodom
than for you.** The rejection of Jesus is far worse. Capernaum's fate is worse
than that of the proverbial **Sodom**. On **Sodom**, see 10:15.

11:25-30—THE REVELATION OF JESUS' IDENTITY
TO THE "INFANTS"

Many have failed to perceive Jesus' identity (11:2-24). In this third section,
Jesus acknowledges God's revelation not to the powerful elite but to the receptive, marginal "infants" (11:25-26), celebrates his role as revealer and liberator
(11:27), and invites the weary and burdened to find salvation by acknowledging God's sovereignty, which will be established over all (11:28-30).[19]

• 11:25
The initial **At that time Jesus declared** relates Jesus' thanksgiving to this
rejection and to God's purposes. **"I thank you**[20] **Father, Lord of heaven and
earth."** Jesus combines several familiar titles that underline God's sovereign
rule. On God as a loving, life-giving **Father** with whom Jesus has close rela-

tionship, see 5:16, 45, 48; 6:9; 7:21 ("my father"); 16:17; 23:9. On God as **Lord** whose will is done on earth and in Jesus, see 1:20, 22, 24; 2:13, 15, 19; etc. The phrase **heaven and earth** (Jdt 9:12) acknowledges all of creation (Gen 1:1) to be subject to God's reign (cf. 5:45; 28:18; so Philo, *Gaium* 115, God is "Father and Maker of the world"). **Heaven** is God's dwelling place (5:16, 34; 6:9 ["our Father in heaven"]), disclosed by revelation (3:16), the place where God's will is done (6:10), the origin of God's empire manifested in Jesus (see 3:2; 4:17). **Earth** (cf. 2:6; 4:15) is the arena where God's saving will is to be done (6:10; 9:6, 34).

Similar claims are made for imperial power. Statius calls the emperor Domitian "Lord of the earth" (*Silv* 3.4.20), "Great Father of the World" (4.1.17), and "ruler of the nations" (4.2.14-15). Philostratus (*Apollonius* 7.3) identifies him as "master of sea and land." Invoking God's sovereignty contests these claims and relativizes Rome's rule (23:9).

Jesus gives thanks **because you have hidden these things from the wise and intelligent**. In context, **these things** refers to the significance of Jesus' deeds (11:2, 19) as expressing his God-given commission to manifest God's empire and saving presence (1:1, 17, 21-23; 4:17; so 11:2). God has **hidden** Jesus' identity and role, which means **the wise and intelligent** do not encounter God's purposes. Why has God done this? Is the gospel anti-intellectual? Is God mean-spirited and unfair in not giving all a fair chance?

The phrase **the wise and intelligent** evokes a tradition critical of those, often leaders and the elite, who refuse to recognize God's ways and purposes (Isa 29:9-24, esp. 14; Dan 2:1-13; *2 Bar* 46:5; 1QS 11:6). They are not humble before God and do not fear God (Prov 3:5-7; Sir 1:16, 27; 2:15-17). They are unreceptive to God's revelation, protective of their own interests and control. While **you have hidden** emphasizes God's role (1QS 4:6; 1QH 5:25-26), human responsibility is implied. Who are not open to God's disclosure in Matthew? The political (ch. 2; 10:18) and religious elite (3:7-10; 9:34; 10:17; 11:19) have not recognized Jesus as God's agent. But nor have some crowds (9:24), cities (11:20-24), and households (10:21, 35-36).

The converse of this hiding, and the second reason for giving thanks, is **you have revealed them/these things to infants**. Various traditions affirm God's revelations of Torah, wisdom, historical and eschatological purposes.[21] Thanks are given for God's revealing activity (Dan 2:22-23; *1 En* 39:9-11; 69:27). God's new age awaits further revelation (Jer 31:34; Hab 2:14). Revelation comes to the young who are faithful (Dan 1:4), those who seek (Sir 4:11; Wis 6:12-18), the simple (Ps 19:7), the dumb and the infants (Wis 10:21). Here **infants** are the small community of disciples who have responded to Jesus' call (4:18-22; 9:9; 10:1-4, 13 [the worthy]; Introduction, section 7), and the marginal in chapters 8-9 who have welcomed (cf. 10:14) God's saving presence and empire. **Infants** is a metaphor for the lowly and teachable (Pss 116:6; 119:130), the beginner and pilgrim (Philo, *Mig* 29-31; *Probus* 160), the righteous (Ps 19:7). Frequently it denotes the vulnerable child, physically endangered by war, capable of being deceived, of wrong action and foolishness.[22] On children, see 2:8; 18:1-6. The metaphor recognizes both receptiveness to God's revelation and the marginal and vulnerable social locations in which the desperate live. The wise and intelligent, the elite cocooned in power, comfort, and the arrogance of their own pretensions, do not discern God's purposes.

• 11:26

The claim of v. 25 that God reveals to the marginal Jesus' identity as God's agent through his actions and words while hiding it from the elite and others, is confirmed: **yes, Father, for such was your gracious will**. The noun **gracious will** is a cognate of the verb in 3:17, "with whom I am well pleased." God's revelation of God's reign is a good, if unappreciated, gift. This affirmation confirms that the minority (7:13-14; 9:37), against-the-grain, community of disciples of Jesus exists as God's will.

• 11:27

Jesus explicates his role as God's revealer. **All things have been handed over to me by my Father**. The **all things** refers, in context, to God's commissioning of Jesus as God's agent to reveal God's saving purposes and reign (1:1, 17, 21-23; 4:17) and Jesus' role as eschatological judge (10:23, 32-33). There is no mention of how or when knowledge is **handed over** to Jesus **by my Father** (see 7:21; 11:25), but the claim is polemical. Judaism after 70 struggled to make sense of Rome's destruction of Jerusalem and its temple, of intensified Roman occupation, and to discern God's will, presence, and means of atonement in a new situation (Introduction, section 8). Various writings and revealer figures were prominent: Abraham, Moses, the Torah, rabbis, Pharisees, scribes (wisdom), *2 Baruch, 4 Ezra, 1 Enoch,* etc.[23] Roman imperial theology asserted that the Flavian emperors manifested the will of Jupiter (see Introduction, section 9). In a context of diverse and competing claims, the verse asserts definitive revelation of God's purposes in Jesus (cf. 1:18-25).

This knowledge derives not from the usual apocalyptic means—angels, mediators, visions, heavenly journeys, secret writings—but from a unique and reciprocal relationship: **No one knows the son except the Father, and no one knows the Father except the son**.[24] Jesus' relationship with God reflects that between God and wisdom: they know each other (Job 28:12, 23-28; Prov 8:30; Wis 7:24-25; 8:3-4; 9:4, 9; Sir 1:6-9; 24:9); wisdom reveals God and calls people to share life with God (Prov 8:1-21; 9:1-6; Wis 8:3-4; 9:17-18; 10:10; Sir 1:19; 24:19-23). Jesus is wisdom (11:19). To **know** is intimate experience or encounter (Gen 4:1). The mutual, intimate relationship of **Father and Son** (rare in this unqualified form) provides the basis for Jesus' revelation. Jesus knows God's saving purposes and life-giving empire and reveals them in his actions and words. The father knows Jesus as the faithful son or agent commissioned by God to this task. On **son**, see 2:15.

Legitimated by this relationship, Jesus performs God's work of revelation, **and anyone to whom the son chooses to reveal him**. The verb **reveal** is the same as in 11:25. Jesus is God's agent. To "receive" Jesus is to receive God (10:40). The **any** is partly defined by **infants** in 11:25, but further clarified by Jesus' invitation in 11:28-30.

• 11:28

Jesus invites people to **come to me** to encounter God's saving presence. The imperative **come** recalls the first disciples (4:19), parallels the term "follow" (see 4:20, 22), and is a synonym of the verb "call" (see 4:21), which denotes Jesus' commission. The call requires allegiance to Jesus (**me**; cf. 11:6) as the one who reveals God's saving empire. It echoes wisdom's call (see 11:27; Prov 8:1-7; 9:4-5; Sir 24:19; 51:23-27) and extends to **all** (cf. "anyone" in 11:27) **who labor/are wearied and are heavy laden**. Given the echoes of 4:18-22, Jesus does not call those who are already disciples, but others (**all**) to become disciples, especially the harassed and helpless crowds (9:36). The term **heavy laden** is rare. In Sir 40:1 it refers to the "heavy yoke" of daily life. The term **wearied/labor** refers in the LXX to beatings, weariness, physical tiredness from work or heat or battle. It often identifies the afflicted, trouble, "oppressive labor and sorrow," the human lot from which only God can save.[25] The **wearied/beaten**, then, are not those "oppressed" by the law, as some argue, but those who are burdened by life under Roman imperial control and its unjust political and socioeconomic structures. They are afflicted by disease and demons (see on 4:23-24), by hard labor, by payment of taxes, tolls, and debts to the political, economic, and religious elite, and by the control of social superiors (5:3-12). Jesus saves from the punishment of Roman rule (21:41; 22:7; 1:21) in establishing God's empire, now in part and at his return in full (4:17; 24:27-31).

Jesus' promise is **I will give you rest**. Both Moses (Exod 33:14) and wisdom (Sir 6:28; 51:27) promise **rest**. It consists not of existential peace of mind but of God's presence with a people who live according to God's revealed will and free of tyranny from imperial powers (Deut 5:14; 12:9; 25:19; Isa 14:3-4; 65:10; Ezek 34:15, 27). **Rest** cannot happen under imperial domination (Deut 28:65; Lam 5:5) but means the removal of that power. Rome's rule is fated. God's **rest** is the creation vision of Gen 2:2-3, in which God, after creating, rests with all creation in just relation with God and itself. Only with God's transforming intervention can such a world be created. Eschatological visions anticipate a return to the begining, which ends all oppressive and death-bringing activity and reestablishes God's empire and rest (*2 Bar* 73-74 [farmers and reapers] will not be weary; *4 Ezra* 2:24; 7:36-38, 123; 8:52; *1 En* 5:7-10; 51:5; *T. Dan* 5:8-13). God's work of giving **rest** is under way through Jesus (11:27), God's agent, and will be completed at his return (chs. 24-25; 1:1; 14:32). Healings and exorcisms anticipate the wholeness of God's reign (chs. 8-9; *2 Bar* 73:1-2). Jesus' teaching instructs disciples to live lives that embody God's reign (so chs. 5-7, 10) until that day of new creation.

• 11:29

Jesus repeats the invitation with a parallel imperative, **Take my yoke upon you**. The **yoke** was a measurement or scales (Lev 19:35; Amos 8:5 [false scales]; cf. Job 6:2) and a means to control yoked animals (Num 19:2). Vespasian's power is such that an ox breaks its yoke plowing, bursts into the dining room, and falls at his feet (Suetonius, *Vespasian* 5.4).

The dominant and widespread use of **yoke**, though, refers to oppressive rulers and nations including Egypt, Assyria, Babylon, and Rome.[26] God breaks this oppressive rule in freeing the people: Lev 26:13; Isa 9:4; 10:27; 14:5; Jer 37[NRSV 30]:8; Ezek 34:27; *1 En* 103-4). Instead of the oppressive **yoke** of nations, God's people take the different **yoke** of serving God (Jer 2:20; *Pss. Sol.* 7:9), expressed variously as the **yoke** of obeying Torah (Jer 5:5; *2 Bar* 41:3), of salvation (Lam 3:27), of wisdom (Sir 51:26; cf. 6:30), the messiah (*Pss. Sol.* 17:30, by Gentiles), and written revelation (*2 En* 48:6-9). Again the gospel resorts to an imperial image to denote the accomplishment of God's purposes.

Jesus' invitation **take my yoke,** then, does not, as is frequently claimed, invite people to escape from the burdensome law with its 613 "legalistic" commands, which the Pharisees demand to be obeyed. They are not in view here (cf. 23:4). Torah is God's gift (Exod 19-24). Jesus does not reject it but demands a greater justice, which resists the status quo with an alternative way of life (see 5:20) and reveals God's will with its correct interpretation (see 5:17-48). As wisdom, he reveals God's purposes (11:19, 27).[27]

His call **take my yoke** is double-sided. It is to experience in *his* words and actions God's liberating presence and life-giving empire that free from everything and everyone, including political and religious elites who deprive people of the just life which God intends. Particularly that means freedom from Rome's reign, which will be accomplished at Jesus' imminent return (24:27-31). Second, to **take** Jesus' **yoke** is to live under God's reign in the meantime, in the struggle against such power and in anticipation of the full establishment of God's empire.

God's reign creates a distinctive, alternative way of life marked by justice, not oppression, and liberation, not subjugation. This life is not natural in the imperial world dominated by the elite. Jesus teaches it, **Learn from me** (Sir 51:23-26). The verb **learn** is a cognate of the noun "disciple." To take Jesus' yoke means learning from the actions and words of Jesus the liberator, revealer (11:27), and teacher (10:24) a life of alternative practices, structures, priorities, relationships, and perspectives (see chs. 5-7). It is to further his liberating work through proclamation and actions (10:7-8).

The explanatory **for I am gentle and humble in heart** says something about God's empire and about Jesus the teacher. The word **gentle** is translated as **meek** in 5:5, the powerless and humiliated righteous who do not take revenge on (or imitate) the wicked by resorting to violence, but who live faithfully and expectantly in trusting God to save them and transform the unjust structures. **Humble** is essentially a synonym, the righteous lowly who lack resources but who witness God overthrowing the rich and powerful (Pss 10:17-18; 34:18; Isa 11:4; 49:13; Sir 10:13-17, esp. 11; 12:5; 13:21-22; 29:8). Jesus is one of these (cf. 21:5), the opposite of the wicked and elite who oppress, the one who manifests God's life-giving empire in such situations.[28] On **heart** as the center of a person's commitment and identity, see 5:8.

Through learning a way of life that participates in God's saving purposes and empire, **you will find rest for yourselves**. This quotes Jer 6:16, which affirms that **rest** is found in God's "ancient . . . (but rejected) good ways," which contrast with the current "greed for unjust gain" and shameful actions. **Rest** acknowledges God's sovereign reign and anticipates participation in the completion of God's purposes. See 11:28. On **find**, see 7:8, 14.

• 11:30

Jesus offers a final explanation **for** finding rest: **my yoke is kind/good, and my burden is small**. The common translation "easy" is linguistically not accurate and makes little sense of the life to which Jesus calls disciples (cf. 10:17-25). Appropriately, Jesus describes his "yoke," the establishment of God's empire, as "kind" or "good." This adjective appears nearly thirty times in the Septuagint, most commonly to describe God as "good" or "kind" (Pss 25:8 [LXX 24:8]; 34:8 [LXX 33:9]; 119:68 [LXX 118:68]; Nah 1:7; *Pss. Sol.* 2:36; 10:7). It appears with numerous other descriptive words and phrases that confirm and elaborate this sense. God is kind/good, but also strong, just, and merciful (2 Macc 1:24), ready to forgive and merciful (Ps 86:5 [LXX 85:5]), compassionate (Ps 145:9 [LXX 144:9]), true, patient, and ruling all things in mercy (Wis Sol 15:1), and, most frequently, exhibits steadfast love/mercy that continues forever (see Pss 100:5 [LXX 99:5]; 106:1 [LXX 105:1]; 136:1 [LXX 135:1]; Jer 33:11 [LXX 40:11]; Dan 3:89 [Prayer of Azariah]). See also three of its seven New Testament uses—Luke 6:35; Rom 2:4; 1 Pet 2:3. So Jesus' "yoke," God's empire, is **kind** and **good,** in displaying God's mercy, justice, and compassion and in liberating those who wearily toil and are burdened by Rome's exploitative and cruel yoke. The eschatological establishment of God's empire is life-giving and just (cf. 7:13-14) and restores access to land (5:5) in a new creation (19:28; 5:18; 24:35). But it is not yet established in full. This "not yet" dimension comprises the **burden** of Jesus' yoke in the present in the midst of Roman imperialism. But that burden is **small** (Exod 18:26; the adjective is rare in the Septuagint and New Testament) in anticipation of Jesus' return (24:27-31) and is sustained by Jesus' presence and teaching in the meantime.

CHAPTER 12

Discerning Jesus' Identity

The emphasis in chapter 11 on discerning Jesus' identity from his actions and words continues. Negative responses dominate, though some people are receptive. See the introduction to chapter 11.

Changing topics divide chapter 12 into five units. Jesus conflicts twice with the religious leaders over the sabbath (12:1-14); his ministry is interpreted as that of the servant in Isa 42 (12:15-21). In a lengthy and nasty scene, Jesus conflicts with the religious leaders over the source of his ministry (12:22-37). He announces doom on this generation (12:38-45) and defines the alternative community of disciples (12:46-50). As in chapter 11, scenes of conflict and rejection (12:1-14, 22-45) alternate with scenes that affirm Jesus' identity (12:15-21, 46-50).

12:1-14 JESUS, THE SABBATH, AND ACCESS TO FOOD

Various elements prominent in 11:25-30 continue in 12:1-14:[1]

- The elite's failure to recognize Jesus' identity
- Jesus' authority as revealer of God's will
- Jesus' alliance with those who are weary and heavy burdened
- The link of rest and sabbath (see Deut 5:14; Matt 11:28)
- Jesus' display of liberating mercy for those in need

In this scene Jesus joins Jewish debates about sabbath praxis. This may well have been a point of conflict between the Matthean community(ies) and a synagogue in Antioch (Introduction, section 8). The scene is a "focal instance." It involves a specific conflict that has much wider implications.[2] Jesus confronts a view of the sabbath, represented by the Pharisees, which honors the sabbath by strictly observing God's prohibition against work on this day. The story shows that the impact of this observance is to prevent access to food resources. Jesus advocates a different praxis to honor the sabbath—to show mercy and do good. In the dispute over the disciples' hunger, Jesus makes God's command to alleviate human need a priority. This criterion evaluates and critiques not only sabbath practice but any system or structure that restricts access to basic resources such as food. Jesus' alternative praxis of showing mercy and doing good propels the community of disciples into missional work in Antioch (cf. ch. 10).

• 12:1

The opening **At that time** connects 12:1-8 to the rejection and invitation of chapter 11. This scene exemplifies Jesus' liberating yoke and struggle against destructive power (11:29-30). Jesus is on the move again (**Jesus went**). His name indicates that his mission "to save from sins" (see 1:21) is enacted here. The setting, both temporal (**on the sabbath**) and physical (**through the grain-fields**), suggests that control of and access to food provide the central example in the debate over the sabbath.

The temporal setting **on the sabbath** evokes three dimensions:

1. The sabbath celebrated deliverance from Egypt (Deut 5:12-15). In this scene Jesus continues God's liberating work by rescuing the sabbath from controls detrimental to human well-being. Significant for this scene is that **sabbath** is first mentioned in scripture in connection with the food God supplies in the wilderness, "as much as each of you needs" and double for the sabbath. Any excess spoils, a rebuke to greed and an emphasis on God's adequate daily supply (Exod 16:16-30; *Jub.* 50:10).[3] The sabbath recognizes both God's liberating work and God's provision of sufficient food. The day evokes God's justice.

2. The sabbath recalls God's covenant with Israel (Exod 31:16; Jer 17:19-27; Ezek 20:12; Neh 9:13-14). Sabbath observance expressed Jewish distinctiveness, privilege, and separation from the Gentiles (*Jub.* 2:17-22; 1 Macc 1:43, 46; 2:29-41; Josephus, *Ant* 14:241-46, 258, 263-64; Philo, *Abr* 28-30; *De Dec* 96-101).

3. The sabbath recalls creation, especially God's rest on the seventh day (Gen 2:2-31), and anticipates the completion of God's just purposes (see 11:28). The requirement of no work on the sabbath imitated God's rest and provided an opportunity to recognize and celebrate God's reign over the created world (Exod 20:8-11; Deut 5:12-15; Isa 1:13; 58:13-14 [a joy]; see *m. Shab.* 7:2 for thirty-nine forbidden activities). That reign was further recognized in a sabbath year every seven years. This year extended the sabbath day's humanitarian concern with vast social and economic consequences: rest for the land and food for the poor (Exod 23:10-11; Lev 25:1-7; *Jub.* 50:1-5; cf. Tacitus, *Hist* 5.4), freeing of slaves (Exod 21:2-6), and forgiveness of debt (Deut 15:1-18). And a jubilee year every fifty years meant, if it was observed, the return of property and land to their original holders, freedom for slaves, and forgiveness of debt (Lev 25). Celebrating God's creation involved a distinctive social structure and responsibility. Its egalitarian impulse challenged more hierarchical systems.[4] In recognition of God's ownership of the land (Lev 25:23), the redistribution of wealth was to prevent the emergence of both an elite with massive wealth and power and a permanent poor class with inadequate means of support.[5] In this scene Jesus resists controls on the sabbath which harm the poor by limiting access to food resources.

These three dimensions of sabbath indicate that this scene concerns not merely a quick snack but fundamental justice issues of access to food resources and alleviating human need. And while the dispute is about interpreting the divine will for the sabbath, the critique extends to any system—political, economic, or religious—that denies fair access to and distribution of resources.

Gentiles generally had little understanding of the sabbath's religious significance. They understood it as a distinctive Jewish practice (Martial, *Epig* 4.4; Suetonius, *Augustus* 76.2), generally mocked its observance as a waste of time and as an expression of Jewish preference for inactivity, misunderstood its origin (Tacitus, *Hist* 5.4; Josephus, *Con Ap* 2.20-27), could not understand not fighting on it (Plutarch, "Superstition," *Moralia* 169C), and associated it with fasting (see 6:16).[6]

The emphasis on food continues in the setting **through the grainfields**. The place appears in Gen 1:29 as part of what the creator God gives to human beings "for food." The term recalls that God's sovereignty, honored by the sabbath, extends over the food-producing earth. God's purposes conflict with those who claim the land and its production for themselves through ownership, indebtedness, taxes, and tolls (frequently paid in produce), without concern for their impact on others (see Introduction, sections 5-9).[7]

A third food detail follows: **his disciples** (see 5:1) **were hungry**. All around them is God's food supply. Yet their attempts to alleviate hunger (**they began to pluck heads of grain and eat it**) raise profound issues. While the hungry were entitled to food as a gift ("not for profit," Lev 25:35-37) or from gleaning after harvest (Lev 19:9-10; 23:22; Deut 23:25), work on the sabbath was not permitted (Exod 20:8-11; 31:14; 34:21; Deut 5:12-15; *Jub.* 2:26; 2:29; 50:9, 12; Philo, *Moses* 2:21-22 [no plucking fruit]).

Grain was a basic food resource. Hunger and food shortages were not unusual for natural (weather, disease, crop failure) and human (hoarding, profiteering, war) reasons. The impact of food shortages followed lines of wealth and social strata, falling hardest on those with limited access to resources, especially urban laborers, crafts workers, and traders. Philostratus (*Apollonius* 1.15) describes civil conflict and famine in the town of Aspendus in Pamphylia, where the rich and powerful withheld corn in the hope of profiting from its export. In a time of high prices and food shortage, one of Trimalchio's guests comments that the "jaws of the upper classes" do well while "the little people come off badly," and he blames the government for the situation (Petronius, *Satyricon* 44). Cities like Antioch regularly experienced food crises (e.g., famine in 46-47 C.E.). Most cities lacked institutions and laws to protect people from starvation.[8]

• 12:2

The religious leaders (**the Pharisees**; see 3:7; 5:20; 9:11) resume the confrontational stance evident in their last appearances in 9:11, 34. They maintain the intensity of 9:34 in asserting rather than questioning (as 9:11): **"Look, your disciples are doing what is not lawful on the sabbath."** The disciples violate something that the elite upholds. The **Pharisees** assess the disciples' actions not in relation to the "legalistic casuistry" with which many interpreters are concerned[9] but in relation to a high and serious view of God's covenant prohibitions against work on the sabbath. As far as they are concerned, Jesus' disciples have acted contrary to God's will. Twice in two verses the disciples are defined in relation to Jesus (**his, your**). Their actions reflect on him. If Jesus allows them to behave in this way, he cannot be God's commissioned agent (the key issue of 11:2-16:20).

• 12:3-4

Jesus does not dispute what the disciples have done but contests the Pharisees' evaluation of it. The Pharisees' quietistic approach to the sabbath, despite its noble intentions, functions to restrict access to food resources, and so should be violated. He argues that sabbath praxis should be shaped by the merciful divine mandate to meet basic needs. Jesus supports feeding the hungry (cf. 25:35-44).

Jesus' two questions (12:3, 5) appeal to the Pharisees' knowledge of scripture (**Have you not read**) and suggest that if they did know the scriptures they would not be expressing the view of v. 2. They should have discerned God's merciful will in the scriptures.

The first scripture passage concerns David (1 Sam 20:1), on the run for his life from King Saul (1 Sam 19:11; 20:31). He breaks the law by commandeering the bread of the presence from the altar in the sanctuary at Nob. The bread was eaten only by priests (1 Sam 21:1-6; Lev 24:5-9). Jesus' formulation (**what David did when he and his companions were hungry**) draws a general analogy between David and his companions and Jesus and the disciples.[10] Both are hungry. Both break the priestly regulations in a situation of human need (see the revised sabbath practice in 1 Macc 2:39-41). Both eat (12:1, 4). David is not punished by God. God seems to approve and strengthens David to continue his task. Likewise Jesus supports, rather than reproves, the disciples. Both David and the disciples set aside one divine requirement (no work; no harvesting) in order to enact another, namely, that people in need have a right to basic resources which sustain life (Lev 23:22; 25:35, 37). Jesus interprets sabbath demands in the light of, and subordinates them to, this divine demand. Jesus' argument counters the Pharisees' attempt to claim a strict observance regardless of its impact on people's lives. By extension, he critiques any religious or political-economic structure that deprives people of resources needed for daily life.

• 12:5

Having asserted his authority in making this determination, Jesus asks another question, which also appeals to their knowledge of scripture and of God's merciful will. Like 12:3-4 this scripture passage concerns actions **in the temple/house of God** (12:3). Referring to setting out the bread of the presence (Lev 24:8) or offering the sabbath sacrifice (Num 28:9-10), which required priests to work, Jesus asks, **"Or have you not read in the law that on the sabbath the priests in the temple break the sabbath yet are guiltless?"** How are the priests **guiltless**? Some sabbath work must be permissible. In this case, requirements of temple service surpass sabbath requirements. Sabbath observance must be assessed in relation to greater divine demands and human needs.

• 12:6

Therefore, **I tell you** (an authoritative declaration; see 5:18; 10:15), **something greater than the temple is here**. Jesus refers to himself as God's agent. He carries out functions associated with the temple, saving from sin (1:21), manifesting God's presence (1:23) and reign (4:17), proclaiming God's will (passim). He is **greater**. In what way? He, unlike the temple, was not destroyed by Rome. He, unlike the temple, is raised not razed.

Jesus employs an *a minore ad maius* approach in arguing from the lesser to the greater (*qal wahomer;* also 6:26, 30). If priests serving God in the temple can set aside divine commands, how much more can Jesus, who is **greater than the temple**? The disciples' action in taking food is legitimate. The divine command to meet human need allows them to work for food even on the sabbath. The disciples' action, upheld by Jesus, protests against and undermines the restrictive control of the religious leaders. This is the basis for an alternative praxis.

• 12:7

Jesus again attacks their understanding of scripture and so of God's will, **If you had known what this means**. He again quotes Hos 6:6 (see its previous polemical use against the religious leaders in 9:13): **I desire mercy not sacrifice**. In context the verse supports the actions of David, the priests, and the disciples (endorsed by Jesus) as doing God's will and shows that the religious leaders are wrong to **condemn the guiltless**.[11] Doing practical mercy, acquiring basic resources for life, meeting human need is the divine will for the sabbath. Mercy is not pity but doing God's justice, which challenges the restrictive practices and structures of the status quo and seeks to establish a life-giving community of shared resources and sustaining relationships. If piety hinders the doing of God's merciful justice and loving kindness, the piety is set aside (see 9:15). While the dispute is about interpreting the divine will for the sabbath, it implies critique of any system, political or religious, that denies access to and fair distribution of resources. Feeding the hungry is one expression of God's will to "break every yoke," which the prophet Isaiah identifies (Isa 58:6-7; cf. Matt 11:29). Doing **mercy** was not a highly valued virtue in many philosophical traditions (see 5:16).

• 12:8

The christological basis for Jesus' teaching, his authority to make such determinations of God's will, is stated: **The Son of Man is lord of the sabbath**. The term **Son of Man** denotes Jesus' interaction with, frequent rejection by, and judgment of the world. See 8:20. His instruction, which does not rescind the sabbath (cf. 5:17-20), legitimates a merciful, life-giving praxis as the divine will. This praxis is faithful to God's creation purposes and to the eschatological vision to restore God's just creation. It continues God's liberative work in setting people free from oppressive structures, upholds the sabbath recognition of "the earth and its fullness" as belonging to God, not people, and continues the sabbath association with fair access to and adequate distribution of food necessary to sustain existence (see introduction to 12:1; 6:11). Living this way means alleviating the "chronic urban misery" in a city like Antioch.[12] It also provides a praxis that may distinguish the community of disciples from the more quietistic synagogue sabbath practice.

• 12:9-14

A further sabbath dispute, provoked by a healing, restates and demonstrates Jesus' praxis, and intensifies the conflict.

• 12:9

He left that place (the grainfields) and entered their synagogue. The pronoun **their** indicates distance; while Jesus has taught in synagogues (4:23; 9:35), he also condemns some practices and warns of conflict (6:2, 5; 10:17).

• 12:10

And behold signals a new character and situation, **a man was there with a withered** (literally, "dried up") **hand**. The **dried up hand** points to a long-term though not life-threatening disfigurement. The man functions as a visual aid for a more general question which others initiate: **And they** (presumably from 12:14 and 12:2-8 the Pharisees) **asked him, "Is it lawful to heal on the sabbath?"** On **heal**, see 4:23-24. The issue of appropriate sabbath praxis continues from 12:1-8. Their question utilizes vocabulary from 12:2 (**is it lawful**; **on the sabbath**). Their question (not assertion, 12:2) indicates that they have heard Jesus claim authority to interpret the tradition. They question him **so that they might accuse him**, or better, **bring charges in court** (BAGD, 423; 27:12). Death is the formal penalty for breaking the sabbath (Exod 31:14; 35:2; Num 15:32-36; *Jub.* 2:25-27; 50:8, 13; CD 10:22-23; 11:1), though as the next verse indicates it does not seem to have been enforced. The religious leaders' purpose takes their conflict with Jesus to a new level.

• 12:11

Jesus' response evokes an everyday scene and appeals to their survival instincts in protecting a valuable asset (cf. 18:12-14): **Suppose one of you has only one sheep and it falls into a pit on a sabbath; will you not lay hold of it and lift it out?** The question, introduced by οὐχί, *ouchi* expects a "yes" answer. Deuteronomy 22:4 requires this action for any animal but does not discuss the sabbath, while CD 11:13-14 forbids it on the sabbath.

• 12:12

Jesus assumes the leaders' assent and moves again from the lesser to the greater (see 12:6): **How much more valuable is a human being than a sheep!** Kindness to human beings in need is the required behavior (12:7; so also CD 11:16-17; 4Q251 2.6-7). Jesus generalizes the conclusion, **So it is lawful** (12:2,

10) **to do good on the sabbath**. **To do good** is to show mercy, to benefit another, to love (5:44; 7:12), to feed the hungry and heal the sick. This is God's will for the sabbath as interpreted by Jesus (see 12:8). His declaration endangers the status quo because it places the needs of the marginal and desperate ahead of the religious leaders' control. His emphasis embraces more than the immediate question of healing. This view of the sabbath challenges any system which protects the elite's self-interest and accumulation of wealth and power and which withholds needed resources.

• 12:13

The healing follows Jesus' instruction. He acts consistently with his own teaching, unlike the hypocritical religious leaders who know what is right (12:11-12) but do not do it. Jesus heals not by touch but by his word, which is powerful to declare and effect God's will: **he said to the man, "Stretch out your hand."**[13] The man obeys (**he stretched it out**) and the healing is demonstrated: **it was restored as sound as the other**. The verb **restored** will appear in 17:11 with an eschatological reference (cf. Mal 3:23). Jesus' healings effect wholeness, which is part of and anticipates the restoration of creation to God's just purposes (see 4:23-24; *2 Bar* 73:1-2; Matt 1:1; 14:32). See 11:28.

• 12:14

The Pharisees went out and conspired against him, how to destroy him. They reject Jesus' claim that God has commissioned him to manifest God's saving presence and empire (11:2-6). His words challenge their control and societal vision, so they fight back. The verb **destroy** describes Herod's actions against Jesus in 2:13 and so allies them in active opposition. Jesus warned in 10:17-18, 28 that this was inevitable. His merciful justice will cost him his life.

12:15-21—THE MINISTRY OF JESUS
THE SUFFERING SERVANT

• 12:15-16

This summary of Jesus' ministry (see 4:23-25; 9:35-36) shows his extensive acts of mercy. Sabbath actions are a way of life that enact God's just and merciful reign over all things. This is Jesus' yoke and rest (11:28-30). But this lifestyle that challenges the powerful provokes opposition. **Jesus knew/became aware of** the emerging plot against him. He **departed/withdrew**, not intimidated into inactivity but to carry out his ministry elsewhere (see 4:12-14; 14:13 [for **withdrew**]; also 10:23).

As in 4:25; 8:1, **the crowds** are the recipients of Jesus' life-giving mercy and teaching (9:36; 11:7), often with some insight (9:8, 33) but not the commitment of discipleship.[14] **He healed all of them** (see 4:23-35) **and he ordered them not to make him known**. See on 8:4; 9:30. As with 9:30, the crowds need much more insight than the healings to make an adequate proclamation.

• 12:17

. . . so that what was spoken through Isaiah the prophet might be fulfilled. See the same phrase in 1:22; 3:3; 4:14. Again a scripture citation follows withdrawal (so 2:14-15; 4:12-16).[15] Does the citation refer only to 12:15-16 (Jesus' miracles; the silence of the healed; Jesus' withdrawal)? Or does it have a wider referent, aspects of chapters 11-13 such as Jesus' God-given authority (12:8, 28, 40), God's spirit at work in him (12:24-32, 43-45), rejection (11:16-19; 12:38-42), judgment on unbelievers (11:20-24; 12:31-37, 41-42; 13:39-43), his preaching to the nations (12:41-42, 46-50)? J. Neyrey correctly argues that it has a wider referent. All of this accomplishes God's will proclaimed by Isaiah.

Also important is the origin of the citation from Isa 42:1-4.[16] In Isa 40-55 the prophet proclaims to the defeated exiles in sixth-century Babylon that their exile is ending and they will return home. God's servant Israel (or a group or individual within Israel) is chosen by God as a light to the nations. In contrast to the imperialist powers of Babylon and Persia, this task does not subjugate and oppress but brings life and justice. It is not carried out with destructive force and crushing military might, not carried out by a ruler or a king, but by a people with gentle care. The citation is a definitive "no" to usual (Roman) imperialist means and ends, and a "yes" to God's life-giving means and ends. Matthew employs the text in a Roman imperial context and sees God at work in this way, now through Jesus. See 8:17 for another Isaianic servant text applied to Jesus' healing ministry.

• 12:18

The citation begins by emphasizing Jesus' identity in relation to God's perspective and actions. **Here is my servant whom I have chosen, my beloved with whom my soul is well pleased.** Three expressions underline Jesus' identity as God's favored one and agent. First, Jesus is **my servant** (or **child**). His function is to do God's will. This term has not been used for Jesus previously. See 2:16 (children); 8:6, 8, 13 (servant), and 6:24 (disciples). It places Jesus in a long line of God's servants (Jacob [Gen 32:10], Moses [Josh 1:7, 13; Num 9:24; 2 Chr 1:3], David [1 Chr 17:17-19; 2 Chr 6:15-17], Solomon [2 Chr 6:19; Job 42:8]), who in subordinate but honorable relation to God do God's will (see 6:24; 20:20-28). The second expression underlines God's initiative. As God's **chosen** (also David and Solomon [1 Chr 28:4, 10], Israel [Ezek 20:5], Zerubbabel [Hag 2:23]), Jesus is called not because others are rejected but to carry out the mission God gives him (1:21, 23; 4:17). The third statement stresses God's pleasure in Jesus. He is **my beloved with whom my soul is/I am well pleased**. The clause evokes the baptism (see 3:17), designates the relationship between God and Jesus as one of love, and suggests love as the motivation for God's choosing Jesus (cf. Ps 60:5).

God empowers Jesus for his mission, **I will place my spirit upon him**. Jesus is conceived by the Spirit (1:18, 20); the Spirit descends on him at his baptism (see 3:16), and it leads him (4:1). In accord with Isa 61:1, the Spirit empowers his ministry to proclaim good news to the oppressed (see 4:23-25) and to bring liberty and release to the broken (chs. 8-9; 12:9-14, 15). The task of proclaiming is particularly emphasized: he will announce justice to the **nations**, both Israel and Gentiles. To announce justice is to proclaim God's purposes and empire (1:21-23; 4:17, 23). For some, especially the marginal (cf. 12:21), salvation and a transformed lifestyle follow, while judgment and rejection result for others, especially the elite. The religious leaders fail to discern, and so resist, God's purposes enacted in him (12:14).

• 12:19

He will not wrangle/quarrel or cry aloud. The common views that this behavior reflects his withdrawal from conflict (12:16), silence in the face of oppression (12:14), the command to the healed to be silent (12:16), and general defenselessness are inadequate. Jesus has frequently engaged, not avoided, conflict (9:1-8, 10-13; 12:1-14, 25), will continue to do so in chapters 12-17, is not silenced by or defenseless before opposition (9:10-13; 12:1-15, 22-45), and withdraws to further his ministry (12:15). Perhaps it indicates that while conflict happens, he is not diverted from doing his mission. Or perhaps[17] it indicates Jesus' refusal to engage in a certain type of dispute, namely, publicly defending his identity and credentials. Neyrey points to his refusal to produce a sign in 12:38-39. His ministry of word and deed attests his identity, as 11:2-6 claims at the outset of this third section. There are more than enough signs.

Nor can the clause **nor will anyone hear his voice in the streets** mean that he does not proclaim and teach (4:23-25; chs. 5-7; 9:35; ch. 10; etc.), or that he passively does not engage in conflict, or does not defend himself. Matthew 12:1-14, 22-45 undermine the last two views. The clause describes response, rather than Jesus' activity. He does proclaim but many do not **hear his voice**. Since chapter 9, rejection has been growing from religious leaders (9:1-8, 10-13, 34; 10:17; 11:19, 25; 12:14), Gentile political leaders (10:18; 11:25), households (10:14, 21-22, 34-36), crowds (9:24-25; 13:14-15), this generation (11:16-19), and cities (11:20-24).

• 12:20

The style of his mission, among those who receive it, is mercy: **He will not break a bruised reed or quench a smoldering wick**. Both images of a **bruised reed** and **smoldering wick** suggest the battered and broken, the "harassed and helpless" (see 9:36), the "weary and heavy burdened" (see 11:28), the marginal and oppressed for whom life in a Roman imperial context is difficult because of hard work, poor nutrition, inadequate resources, disease, taxes, debts, and a lack of options. Toward them Jesus is compassionate with healings, exorcisms, and the formation of an alternative community with resistant (5:39-41), inclusive, and life-giving practices (5:42; 12:1-8). See chapters 8-9; 11:2-6; 12:15 for the marginals' receptivity to God's empire.

Jesus' ministry anticipates God's eschatological goal (cf. 10:32-33), **until he brings justice** forever[18] or **to victory**. Each healing or exorcism is a victory of God's reign over that which opposes it (4:1-11; 12:24-28), and anticipates the establishment of God's empire in full, in which wholeness, plenty, and justice will prevail (cf. *2 Bar* 73:1-2). The "rest" which Jesus now manifests means the future restoration of God's original created order (see 11:28).

• 12:21

Response to Jesus determines participation in God's future; **And in his name the nations will hope**. Jesus is named as God's authorized agent (1:21; 1:1, 17 [Christ]), Son of Man (12:8), God's servant (12:16) and son/child (2:15; 3:17). His mission to Jew and Gentile enacts God's purposes to bless all the nations of the earth (Gen 12:1-3; Matt 1:1 [son of Abraham]). On Gentile inclusion, see 1:3-6; 2:1; 3:7-10; 4:15-16; 5:13-16; 8:5-13; etc. On continuing mission to Israel (22:1-14; 28:19) and Israel's inclusion, see 23:39. The religious leaders, who do not discern his identity from his actions (11:2-6), have other names for him (9:34; 12:24, 38).

12:22-37—CONFLICT: THE SOURCE OF JESUS' MINISTRY

As with 12:9-14, a miracle provokes debate about Jesus' ministry and identity. An exorcism (12:22) leads to three differing evaluations of Jesus' identity from the crowds (12:23), the religious leaders (12:24), and Jesus (12:25-37). The scene exemplifies his claim of 11:2-6 that his actions provide the means by which people can discern his identity. But many, especially the religious leaders, do not see or hear (12:19b).[19]

• 12:22-24

The miracle and responses largely reprise 9:32-34. The dependence of the man is immediately stated (**was brought**; see 4:24; 8:16), as is his physical brokenness (**a blind and dumb demoniac**). His social and economic marginality is assumed. On muteness and imperial control, 4:24; on sin and sickness, 9:2-8; on blindness, see 9:27; on **dumb/deaf-mute**, 9:32; on demoniacs and casting out demons, 4:23-24; 8:16, 28, 33; 9:32. Jesus **heals him** (how?). Evidence of his efficacy follows in that he **who had been mute could speak and see**. This act frees the man from the devil's control, restores wholeness, makes available a new way of life, and anticipates the fullness of God's empire.

The first response comes not from the man but from **the crowds**. They **were amazed** (only here; cf. its synonym "marveled" in 9:33). The response indicates curiosity about Jesus' identity but not insight, **This is not the son of David, is it?** The gospel's audience knows that Jesus is the **son of David** (see 1:1, 25; 9:27 on David and Solomon as miracle workers), commissioned as God's agent (Christ; see 11:2-3 for miracles and the Messiah) to manifest God's reign, which defends the poor and crushed (see 9:27; 1:1; 3:17; 4:17; cf. Ps 72). But the crowds' question, introduced by μήτι (*mēti*) "an interrogative particle in questions that expect a negative answer" (BAGD, 520), suggests that the crowds know none of this. The crowds raise the possibility only to dismiss it. However, μήτι (*mēti*) can also introduce questions "where the questioner is in doubt" (BAGD, 520). If it is a genuine inquiry, the context of the miracle suggests that their inquiry may be focussed on the tradition of Solomon the miracle worker (see 9:27).

Either way, the religious leaders respond to the crowds' question with a very negative view. On **Pharisees**, see 3:7; 12:2, 14. Their verdict (see 9:34) is that **this one casts out demons only by Beelzebul, the ruler of demons**. On **Beelzebul**, see 4:1-11. Instead of discerning God's empire in his actions (11:2-6), and in stark contrast to God's declaration that Jesus is God's servant (12:18), they attribute his works to the devil. They resort to name calling, which discredits Jesus before the crowds as a deviant or agent of the devil.[20] Marginalizing him attempts to limit his influence and bolster their control of the crowds (so 9:34).

• **12:25**

Again Jesus **knows their thoughts** (12:15; 9:4) and confronts them (see 12:19). He makes two arguments against the leaders' analysis (12:25-26, 27), explains the significance of his actions (12:28), and offers a third argument (12:29). His observation that **every kingdom, city, or house divided against itself is laid waste** (so Josephus's analysis, in part, of the fall of the Jerusalem)[21] begins his counterattack to undermine the credibility of the Pharisees.

• **12:26**

Jesus applies the analogy to their charge that he is Satan's agent (cf. 12:24). **If Satan casts out Satan, he is divided against himself; how then will his kingdom stand?** Verse 25 has established that it cannot. To claim that he is Satan's agent is nonsense because it means that Satan is engineering his own downfall. The statement assumes that Satan has an evil kingdom with demons who do his bidding against God (cf. 4:8-10, 23-24; *Jub.* 10:1-14; *T. Ash.* 1:8-9; 1QS 3:16-26; *T. Sol.*). This kingdom opposes God's empire which Jesus manifests (4:17). Jesus thus rejects their charge.

• **12:27**

Jesus offers a further argument which extends the leaders' claim to their own exorcists. **If I cast out demons by Beelzebul** (as the religious leaders charge in 12:24), **by whom do your own exorcists cast them out?** By their own logic, they would have to recognize Satan as the source of their own exorcists' power, something they of course will not do. For other exorcisms, see Tob 6:6-18; 8:1-3; Josephus, *Ant* 8.45-49; *JW* 7.185; Philostratus, *Apollonius* 4.20; *T. Sol.* Jesus is willing to grant that God is at work in their exorcisms, though the crowds have testified to the superiority of Jesus' actions (9:8). Jesus' exorcisms display his identity (11:2-6) as the Christ commissioned to manifest God's reign (12:28; 1:1). These exorcists and their deeds **will be your judges**. They condemn the leaders at the judgment for not recognizing God at work in Jesus' exorcisms also.

• 12:28

Now Jesus asserts the significance of his own exorcisms in relation to his mission of manifesting not the devil's but God's empire (4:17). He begins by recognizing God as the source and means of his power: **But if it is by the Spirit of God that I cast out demons**. The **Spirit of God** recalls God's equipping of Jesus with power for his messianic tasks at the baptism (see 3:16). The citation in 12:18 links the Spirit with God's election of Jesus and his mission of proclaiming good news to the oppressed (4:23-25) and liberty and release to the broken (cf. Isa 61:1).

Empowered by the Spirit, Jesus' exorcisms manifest that **the empire of God has come to you** (see 3:2; 4:17). The exorcisms enact his mission (1:21-23; 4:17). He saves people from Satan's reign (including its political and social consequences; see 4:8, 24) by asserting God's reign over the demons. God's reign is known now in Jesus' ministry.[22] For the first time (also 19:24; 21:31, 43), and addressing the religious leaders, the gospel designates the kingdom or empire as **of God** rather than the usual "of the heavens."[23] This change intensifies the contrast with Satan. God's reign contrasts with Satan's kingdom/reign (12:26). The alternative is stark without neutral or middle ground. God's kingdom manifested in Jesus assails and overpowers Satan's kingdom in anticipation of its future establishment in full. The expected eschatological defeat of Satan is already under way (*1 En* 55:4; *T. Mos.* 10:1; *T. Zeb.* 9:8; cf. Matt 24-25).

• 12:29

Jesus offers a third argument (**Or**) against their claim that he casts out demons as Satan's agent by depicting his exorcisms as breaking into Satan's house whereby he overpowers Satan's rule and frees captives from its domination. **How can one** (Jesus) **enter a strong man's house** (Satan's kingdom, 12:26) **and plunder his property** (those under Satan's control) **without first tying up/binding the strong man?** (perhaps Jesus' successful overcoming of Satan's temptations in 4:1-11). For **binding** the devil or evil spirits and healing diseases, see *Jub.* 10:7, 11, 12-13; Tob 8:3; *1 En* 10:4, 11-13; 13:2; Rev 20:1-3. For **the strong man** as the Babylonian tyrant from whom God rescues the people in exile, see Isa 49:24-25; recall Matt 4:8 for Satan's control of the kingdoms or empires. **Then indeed the house can be plundered**, by Jesus' exorcisms, which liberate people from Satan's rule. Again the gospel uses violent language to picture the triumph of God's empire (see Introduction, section 1).

• 12:30

The three arguments lead to three warnings (12:30, 31-32, 33-37). **Whoever is not with me is against me**. Jesus, God's agent, is the key player as the threefold use of the pronoun **me** indicates. The phrase **with me** refers to a life of discipleship (4:19; cf. 26:71). Commitment to him means life in God's empire now and in the future (10:32-33), and resistance to Satan's rule or domination. Resistance to Jesus is resistance to God's purposes in alliance with the devil (see 4:1-11).

The eschatological context and goal of Jesus' work are emphasized in the second part, **Whoever does not gather with me scatters**. The verb **gather** is drawn from either shepherding (Isa 13:14; cf. 10:6) or harvesting (Matt 3:12; 13:29-30). It denotes God's liberating presence with God's people (Isa 40:11), and merciful, future in-gathering of the dispersed people of God (Ezek 34:13; Tob 13:5; *Pss. Sol.* 11:1-9; 17:26; Matt 24:31). **Gathering** means participation in God's eschatological purposes. The verb **scatter** denotes resistance to God's purposes, especially by unfaithful leaders (Jer 23:2). The warning invites the opponents to commit themselves to Jesus and to participate in, not resist, God's purposes.

• 12:31-32

The second warning follows all of 12:22-30 (**Because of this**), especially Jesus' claim in 12:28 that the Spirit, not Beelzebul, empowers his exorcism. It is introduced by the authoritative **I say to you** (5:18, 21-48; 10:15, 23, 42; 11:11) and structured as two contrasting statements. The first part affirms Jesus' salvific mission (1:21; 9:1-8): **every sin and blasphemy will be forgiven among people**. The passive **forgiven** denotes God's activity through him. In turn God's forgiveness requires changed practices, behaviors, and structures (6:14-15). It states the all-encompassing extent (**every**) of God's purposes. **Blasphemies** are sins that especially dishonor God (see 9:3; 26:65).

The second part names one exception: **but blasphemy against the Spirit will not be forgiven**. If blasphemy, that which dishonors God, is forgivable, why not blasphemy against the Spirit? The Spirit is the power at work in Jesus which accomplishes his liberating work of saving from sin and establishing God's empire (12:18, 25, 28). This power brings the beginning of the end, the completion of God's purposes under way in Jesus. To blaspheme against the Spirit is to refuse to recognize God's eschatological, liberating work under way in Jesus. It consists not of doubt, a misspoken word, or unknown or unwitting sin, but of a sustained refusal to recognize that Jesus' works, powered by the Spirit, enact God's eschatological goal (cf. 11:2-6). The religious leaders do precisely this in 12:24.

A similar contrast follows in 12:32. One sin is forgivable: **Whoever speaks a word against the Son of Man** (see 8:20) **will be forgiven.** But a sin against the Spirit is not: **but whoever speaks against the Holy Spirit will not be forgiven, either in this age or in the age to come**. The personal construction (**whoever speaks**) intensifies the threat. For many interpreters the verse intensifies mystery also. The difficult issue is the nature of the contrast. Wherein lies the difference? Is rejection of Jesus the man forgivable but not rejection of the Spirit? Is backsliding after experiencing the Spirit's work not forgivable? Some commentators understandably declare themselves "stumped."[24]

The two statements in v. 32 are parallel, word for word the same except for a couple of obvious changes: **but** and **Son of Man/ Holy Spirit** and **not**. There is one other change: perhaps the use of the singular **a word** in the first clause and its omission from the second clause provides a clue to their difference. **A word against the Son of Man** suggests an isolated instance of opposition or failure. This is forgivable (Peter in 26:75; yet 28:7, 16). But the removal of **a**

word in the second clause suggests not an isolated instance but a sustained, continued opposition of always **speaking against the Spirit**. It suggests a constant refusal to see God's Spirit empowering Jesus. This is not forgivable because it is a sustained rejection of God's work. That is, this second part of the second statement essentially repeats the claim of v. 31b. The reference to **either in this age or in the age to come** emphatically removes all opportunity.

• 12:33-37

A further warning and exhortation follow as Jesus exposes the evil that underlies the leaders' words (12:24) and warns of judgment. The image of the tree and its fruit is used of false prophets in 7:16-20. Words reveal a person's commitments.

• 12:33

The initial expression is awkward. Probably the best option for translation is "suppose" or "take as an example" (BAGD 682, I.e.β): **take as an example the good tree, its fruit is good; take for example the bad tree, its fruit is bad**. The principle is clear, **for the tree is known by its fruit**. See 7:16-17. The verse assumes a similarity between the created order and human behavior, typical of wisdom literature, and utilizes a traditional image. The type of fruit reflects the type of tree. Words and external behaviors reflect internal character and commitments. Both John (see 3:8, 10) and Jesus (see 7:16-20) have employed it previously.

• 12:34

Jesus applies the image to the religious leaders with a personal (**You**) and graphic denunciation of their evil, dangerous, and poisonous character. He insults them with a reference to their evil origin, **brood/offspring of vipers**. See 3:7; 15:13-14. Their attributing Jesus' works to the devil reveals their inner evil character: **How can you speak good things, when you are evil? For out of the abundance of the heart the mouth speaks**.

To call the religious leaders **evil** demonizes them (see Introduction, section 1; 4:11). The devil is identified as the **evil one** in 6:13. Speaking falsely has already been linked to the devil, the **evil one**, in 5:37. And in 9:4 Jesus accuses the religious leaders of thinking **evil** in deeming him a blasphemer. These links suggest more than the usual claim that all humans are evil or sinful (so 7:11). They regrettably link the religious leaders with the devil. Like the devil they do and speak **evil**, that which is contrary to God's will. Jesus has turned their claim about him in 12:24 back on them! It is impossible (**how can you...?**) for them **to speak good things** concerning God's purposes and Jesus' identity. For **the heart** as the core commitments of a person, the center of human willing, thinking, and deciding, see 5:8; 6:21.

• 12:35

The link of inner character and external actions is emphasized with a contrast: **The good person brings good things out of a good treasure, and the**

evil person brings evil things out of an evil treasure. **Treasure** and **heart** are linked in 6:21; **treasure** denotes fundamental commitments (see 6:19-21) which are evidenced in speech and actions. The religious leaders' evil words reflect their commitment to evil and the evil one.

• 12:36-37

An authoritative reminder of judgment (**I tell you**, see 12:31) ends the section. While this threatens the religious leaders, it also spells out a principle that applies to all: **On the day of judgment** (see 10:15), **you will have to give an account for every careless word you utter**. What is the **careless** word? Do these include jokes, social pleasantries, spontaneous expressions of annoyance? Probably not. Jesus has taught against angry words (5:22-26), oaths (5:33-37), empty prayers (6:7), unforgiving words (6:14-15), anxious words (6:31; 10:19), words of judgment (7:1), hypocritical words (7:4-5), words of false confession (7:21-22), presumptuous words (8:19), fearful words (8:26), and, more immediately, words that resist Jesus' mission and God's purposes (9:11, 34; 10:33; 12:2, 24, 31-32). Careless words, then, express disobedience to Jesus' teaching and rejection of God's purposes.[25] Underlying this reckoning is the awareness that God is all-seeing and hearing (see 6:4, 6). On speech and judgment, see 5:21-26. Words are decisive in the judgment: **for by your words you will be justified and by your words you will be condemned.** They reveal a person's fundamental commitments (12:34b-35). The religious leaders' verdict about Jesus in 12:24 is, then, a verdict about themselves if they persist in it. To be **justified** is to be recognized to be in faithful relationship with God and so vindicated as Jesus is (11:19), not **condemned** in the judgment. See the cognate "justice/righteousness" in 3:15.

12:38-45: JESUS ANNOUNCES DOOM
ON THIS GENERATION

• 12:38

Then some of the scribes and Pharisees said to him, we wish to see a sign from you. The new exchange has an ominous beginning. Jesus' exorcism in 12:22 provoked their misguided words in 12:24. Jesus has already pointed to his actions as revealing his identity as God's agent (11:2-6). What makes their demand so misguided is that they already have access to adequate sources of insight if they truly want it. On the negative presentation of **scribes** and **Pharisees**, part of the alliance of religious leaders, see 2:4; 3:7, and the conflicts of 12:2; 24.

The placement of this question after 12:25-37 shows the elite's determination to learn nothing from Jesus' words. They address Jesus as **teacher**. While disciples address Jesus as Lord, opponents use **teacher** (9:11; 17:24; 19:16; 22:16, 24, 36). See 8:19 for another scribe who asks an inappropriate question. They declare **we wish to see a sign from you**. Signs often verified claims of divine address or presence. Signs validate Moses' call to liberate the enslaved people (Exod 3-4), Saul's anointing as king (1 Sam 10:1-9), Elijah's conflict with the powerful Ahab and Jezebel (1 Kgs 18:17-40), Isaiah's message of deliverance from the imperialistic powers Israel and Syria (Isa 7:11-14), and God's purposes (Jer 44:29). Other figures promised signs of God's liberation (Josephus, *Ant* 18.85; 20.97-99, 169-71; see Matt 24:5, 11). Jesus has performed numerous miracles (chs. 8-9, 12:22), in accord with the scriptures (8:17; 11:3-5; 12:18-21) and predicts various cosmic signs as indicators of the near establishment of God's reign in full (24:24, 27-31). He has declared that his identity is knowable from these signs (11:2-6).

• 12:39-40

Jesus' response insults and denounces them. **An evil and adulterous generation** (see 11:16) **asks for a sign but no sign will be given to it except the sign of the prophet Jonah.** The passive **will be given** indicates God's refusal. The adjective **evil** again links them with the devil (contrast 12:24!; 12:34-35); **adulterous** labels them as illegitimate, depriving them of honor (cf. 12:34). The sign of Jonah[26] is explained: **For just as Jonah was three days and three nights in the belly of the sea monster** (compare LXX Jonah 2:1; NRSV 1:17b), **so for three days and three nights the Son of Man will be in the heart of the earth.** The emphasis falls not on miracles but on Jesus' death (12:14), with the title **Son of Man** emphasizing his rejection by the religious leaders (see 8:20). The sign will legitimate his doing of the divine will (so 16:21). The sign is his apparent powerlessness, his suffering. There is no explicit reference to his resurrection (or Jonah's deliverance), which has not yet been mentioned (so 16:21). The time period of **three days and nights**, though, anticipates it and the next verse assumes it. While the religious and political elite bring about Jesus' death, God will thwart their intentions.

• 12:41

The people of Ninevah will rise up at the judgment with this generation and condemn it. The scene is the resurrection (**will rise up**) at the final judgment, which involves everyone (5:21-22; 10:15; 11:22, 24; 12:18, 20, 36). For the people of Nineveh this is vindication **because they repented at the proclamation of Jonah** (Jonah 3). On **repented** as a changed way of life which experiences God not as judge but as savior; see 3:2; 4:17; 11:20-21. But for **this generation**, which Jesus has already condemned for not receiving his proclamation (see 11:16; 12:39), the news is worse. **Something greater than Jonah is here** (see 12:6). Though Jonah and Jesus are both commissioned by God, Jesus is **greater** because God has designated him to manifest God's saving presence and empire (1:21-23; 10:32-33; 11:27). Rejection of him is proportionally greater.

• 12:42

Jesus offers another example of a Gentile receptive to God's purposes. **The queen of the South** (the queen of Sheba; see 1 Kgs 10:1-13; 2 Chr 9:1-12) **will rise up at the judgment with this generation and condemn it.** Why?

Because she came from the ends of the earth (a great effort, and "with hard questions," 1 Kgs 10:1) **to listen to the wisdom of Solomon**. This **wisdom**, like Jonah's preaching, displays God's will (Prov 8-9; Sir 24; Wis 9-10; 1 Kgs 10:9). The religious leaders have questioned a king (2:2) but have not repented or recognized him as God's agent, a greater failure because **see, something greater than Solomon is here.** Jesus does not only teach wisdom, he embodies it (11:19, 27). For a negative reference to Solomon, see 6:29.

• 12:43-45

The key to interpreting these enigmatic verses is the context of 12:38-42. Jesus illustrates the plight of the religious leaders. Their rejection of Jesus means that they are even more in the service of evil now than before his ministry. The use of the wandering demon continues the regrettable linking of them with the devil. **And when the unclean spirit has gone out of a person, it wanders through waterless regions** (see 4:1) **looking for a resting place but finds none. Then it says, "I will return to my house from which I came."** See Philostratus, *Apollonius* 4.20. **When it comes, it finds it empty, swept, and put in order. Then it goes and brings along seven other spirits more evil than itself, and they enter and live there;** the level of evil has intensified. This is the devil's reign in control of the wicked (see 12:26; 4:8). The obvious conclusion is, **And the last state of the person is worse than the first.** The connection is made to Jesus' audience, **So it will be also with this generation**, which has not taken advantage of the opportunity to transfer from Satan's reign to God's empire. In rejecting God's purposes, the hold or reign of the devil over them is even greater.

12:46-50—THE ALTERNATIVE COMMUNITY OF DISCIPLES

The critique (12:25-45) of the religious leaders' failure to discern Jesus' identity, which has broadened to include others like them, might suggest that his ministry has been a failure. These verses show, though, a community or household committed to Jesus.

• 12:46-47

While much of 12:25-45 has been focused on the religious leaders, the crowds were present (12:23): **While he was still speaking to the crowds, his mother** (1:18-2:23) **and his brothers and sisters** (see 13:55-56) **were standing outside, wanting to speak to him**. No location for 12:22-45 was indicated. Now Jesus is inside not the synagogue (cf. 12:15) but a house (so 13:1; 9:10). Jesus' birth family (**outside, wanting to speak to him**) appears very respectful. The phrase **mother and brothers and sisters** appears five times.

• 12:48-50

Jesus' response is a question about the identity of his family: **"Who is my mother, and who are my brothers and sisters?"** Stretching out his hand to

his disciples he said, "Here are my mother and my brothers and sisters! For whoever does the will of my Father in heaven is my brother and sister and mother." The disciples are a separate entity from the crowds and contrast with the unrepentant religious leaders and "generation" of 12:22-45. Again (see 4:20-22), Jesus challenges the conventional patriarchal household based on kinship and centered on the husband/father/master. He redefines the household as centered on him (**my**) and committed to God's will (albeit God the **Father**; 5:16; 23:9). The new household is not based on birth, ethnicity, or gender; it is open to anyone who commits to Jesus and obeys his teaching of God's will. For the ambivalent relationship with birth families, see 8:14-15; 15:1-20; for household divisions and animosity to disciples, see 10:21-22, 34-37; for the structure of the new household, chapters 19-20. Subordination of household commitments to God or to different philosophical commitments was countercultural and not unique to followers of Jesus. It is also evident in Philo, Josephus, Qumran, and the Stoics and Cynics.[27] The use of **brother and sister,** which specifically includes women, indicates that the term **disciple** (12:49) must be understood expansively, not exclusively.

Ironically, while human patriarchy has no place in this household, the household derives from **my Father in Heaven** whose love is indiscriminate (see 5:16, 45, 48; 6:9; 7:21; 10:32-33; 11:27; 16:17; 23:9). Throughout, Jesus has revealed (11:27) the **will** of the Father, which is to be embodied in the daily living of the community of disciples (7:24-27). For **do** as living God's will, see 3:8-10; 5:19; 6:1-3; 7:12-26; 12:2, 3,12, 33. Disciples pray to **do** God's will (see 6:10). Jesus' teaching is "praxis-oriented."[28] Calling Jesus good names without **doing the will of my Father in heaven** means no encounter with God's empire (7:21). It is clear from chapter 10 that this missional community will confront and conflict with the status quo in living its alternative existence.

CHAPTER 13

Jesus' Third Teaching Discourse

Parables

Jesus' preaching and actions provide the means by which people can discern his identity as God's agent and encounter God's saving presence and empire (see 11:2-6; 1:21-23). But as chapters 11-12 have shown, many, both the elite and others, fail to discern his identity and oppose his ministry. God's reign brings division.

Chapter 13, Jesus' third major teaching unit (chs. 5-7, 10) addresses this division from both sides.[1] It explains to the gospel audience that this lack of receptivity derives not from Jesus' or God's failure but from human sinfulness and Satan's activity. On the other hand, the chapter affirms the audience's welcoming experience of "the empire of the heavens."

This divisive impact of God's empire is central to chapter 13. The word "reign/empire" appears twelve times, eight in the phrase "empire of the heavens" (13:11, 24, 31, 33, 44, 45, 47, 52), three times by itself (13:19, 38, 41), and once in a synonymous phrase (13:43). The audience already knows a considerable amount about God's empire from chapters 1-12 (see 3:2; 4:17):[2]

- It is manifested in Jesus' words and deeds.
- It is God's gracious gift, initiative, and action.
- It resists, rather than endorses, Rome's empire.
- It is divisive; some welcome it, while others, especially the elite, resist God's claim.
- It is disruptive and disturbing, reversing previous commitments, imperial structures, practices and priorities, while creating a new way of life which counters dominant societal values.
- It conflicts and competes with the devil's reign.
- It is present in part, but for many life remains unchanged.
- Its present manifestation will be completed when God's reign is established over all including Rome's empire.

The parables in chapter 13 confirm these understandings. As narratives embedded within the larger narrative, they graphically re-present familiar material. The repetition is necessary since God's empire of justice is distinctive. The parables challenge the audience afresh to continue to live on this basis and toward the completion of God's purposes. That goal of God's cosmic purposes is shown to be vast and triumphant in contrast to the seemingly insignificant and ineffectual way in which God's empire is currently experienced in Jesus' ministry.

The chapter consists of seven parables. The genre of parable is difficult to define.[3] The word "parable" appears for the first time in the gospel in 13:3 (and eleven more times in the chapter). Yet there have already been several parables (7:24-27; 9:15; 12:43-45)! The term comes from the Greek word "to throw alongside" and so denotes a comparison in which one thing (God's empire) is set beside something else.[4] Most, but not all, of these short narratives are introduced by a formula of comparison: "The empire of the heavens is like" (13:24, 31, 33, 44, 45, 47).[5] The "something else" in chapter 13 consists of a series of narratives involving diverse situations and actions which lead to some resolution. Most of the situations come from everyday, familiar peasant life, with a twist or surprise that forces the audience to reconsider some aspect of the status quo in the light of God's empire.[6] B. B. Scott has helpfully defined a parable as that which "employs a short narrative fiction to reference a transcendent symbol."[7] That "transcendent symbol" in this chapter consists of God's empire.

The focus on God's empire and its eventual triumph over all things implies the demise of Rome. Rome's imperial claims to sovereignty over the world and to be the agent of the gods in manifesting divine presence and blessing are relativized by God's empire. God controls its destiny and will assert sovereignty over the world. Again, ironically, the gospel co-opts an imperial worldview in asserting the triumph of God's empire (Introduction, sections 1, 9).

Chapter 13 is organized around alternating audiences.

    13:1-9   Crowds (with Disciples)
        13:1-3a   Introduction
        13:3b-9   Parable of the Seeds and Soils
    13:10-23   Disciples Alone
        13:10-17   Purpose of Speaking in Parables
        13:18-23   Interpretation of Parable of the Sower/Soils
    13:24-35   Crowds (with Disciples)
        13:24-30   Parable of the Weeds
        13:31-32   Parable of the Mustard Seed
        13:33   Parable of the Leaven
        13:34-35   Purpose of Speaking in Parables
    13:36-53   Disciples
        13:36-43   Interpretation of Parable of the Weeds
        13:44   Parable of the Treasure
        13:45-46   Parable of the Pearl
        13:47-50   Parable of the Fish Net
        13:51-53   Conclusion: Discipled for the Reign
    13:54-58   Rejection by the Hometown Synagogue Crowd.[8]

The crowds, for whose allegiance Jesus and the religious elite struggle in 12:22-45, underline both the opportunity presented by Jesus' ministry and its rejection. The disciples, by contrast, are those who have encountered God's empire, at least in part, and are on a journey of discipleship.

13:1-9—JESUS ADDRESSES CROWDS (WITH DISCIPLES): SEEDS AND SOILS

• 13:1-3a

The opening phrase **on that day** closely connects the chapter with 12:15-50. The naming of **Jesus** recalls his mission (1:21). He **leaves the house** where he had underlined the identity of the disciples as an alternative household based not on conventional markers of birth, kinship, wealth, or gender but on doing God's will (12:46-50). His new location (**sat beside the sea**) recalls Capernaum located in Galilee, the land under Gentile rule in which the light of God's empire shines in Jesus (see 4:15-16). While **sat** can indicate teaching, it also indicates the authoritative exercise of a king's reign (5:1-2, 34).

Focus shifts to the **many crowds** (see 4:25)[9] who **gathered before him so that he got into a boat and sat down**, while **the whole crowd stood on the beach**. Jesus carries out his task of revelation (11:27), **And he told them many things in parables saying**. Solomon spoke in parables (1 Kgs 4:32; Sir 47:15-17], as did David (LXX 2 Kdgms 23:3), and God/Ezekiel (Ezek 17:2, against false ones, 12:22-23; 18:2). One greater than Solomon now does so (12:42).

• 13:3b-9

The opening line **A sower went out to sow** evokes a common scene of a male peasant trying to eke out a living in generally inhospitable conditions. Three lots of seed fall into poor ground and produce nothing: the **path** (13:4), **rocky ground where they did not have much soil** (13:5), and **among thorns and the thorns grew up and choked them** (13:7). The **birds** (13:4) and the **sun** (13:6) are also adversaries. Unmentioned are other obstacles: rent, tithes, taxes and tolls, seed for the next year, a household to support. Crop failure meant borrowed money; indebtedness meant defaulting on the loan, loss of land, and virtual slavery as a laborer. The sabbath and jubilee traditions (so 12:1-14) were intended to prevent this cycle of poverty. God's empire creates a community of redistributed resources and mutual aid (5:42; 6:1-4). Eschatological expectations celebrated the ultimate demise of great landowners (*1 En* 46:4-8; 62-63; cf. Matt 5:5).

But in such desperation, there is some hope. **Other seeds fell on good soil and brought forth grain, some a hundredfold, some sixty, some thirty.** Compared to the path, rocks, and thorns, this yield is abundant. Some scholars suggest that it is not extraordinary. Pliny (*NH* 18.21.95) identifies four-hundredfold yield as unusual and one hundred as very good, and Varro (*On Agric* 1.44) notes ten- and fifteenfold yields in some places and up to one hundredfold in Syria. But R. McIver suggests that these accounts have the feel of "tall tales told by travelers" about exotic locations.[10] Data on traditional cropping systems suggest typical yields of seven- to elevenfold. Columella (*On Agric* 3.3.4) suggests fourfold. If McIver's data are correct, the **hundredfold, some sixty, some thirty** yields are magnificently unusual, the excess of the anticipated Garden of Eden when God's empire is established in full (cf. 11:28; 12:1-14; cf. *1 En* 10:18-20; *Sib. Or.* 3:619-23, 741-61; *2 Bar* 74:1). Such yields anticipate the final establishment of God's just reign, which will provide abundant resources for all and will destroy the cycle of poverty.

No further explanation or referent for the parable's experience is given at this point. But Jesus appeals to the audience to discern further significance in his words (see 11:15 for **Let anyone with ears listen**).

13:10-23—JESUS ADDRESSES THE DISCIPLES

13:10-17—SPEAKING IN PARABLES

• 13:10

Then the disciples (a new audience; see 5:1) **came** (denoting respectful address which recognizes Jesus' authority; see 4:3; 8:2) **and said to him, "Why do you speak to them in parables?"** The disciples distinguish themselves from the crowds (**them**) by asking about Jesus' purpose in using this form of ministry.

• 13:11

Jesus' explanation reinforces and defines the distinction between disciples and the crowds, **To you** (emphatic) **it has been given to know the secrets/mysteries of the empire of the heavens.** The concept of disclosed **mysteries/secrets** is common in Greco-Roman religion, where members of groups (Eleusis, Isis) are initiated into the secrets and destinies of the gods, the cosmos, and life.[11] In Jewish wisdom (Wis 6:17-22) and especially apocalyptic sources, the concept denotes the revelation of God's ways and purposes, particularly the end of sin and sinful rulers (*1 En* 38:3-5) and the establishment of God's reign over all things in returning creation to its original just order (Dan 2:27-28; *1 En* 103:1-4; 1QS 9:17; *4 Ezra* 14:5-6; *2 Bar* 81:1-4; Matt 1:1; 14:32). These **mysteries** cannot be known apart from God's revealing action. They are disclosed to the minority, the few (cf. 7:14; 11:25-27; Introduction, section 7) and the wise who are receptive to God's purposes (cf. *2 Bar* 18:1-2; 48:3b; *4 Ezra* 12:34-39). They are hidden from the majority. The secrets revealed to a few reinforce the group's distinctive existence and identity.

Both division (so 12:46-50) and God's revealing action are evident here. To the few disciples, God (the passive construction, **has been given**) has made **known** God's empire in Jesus the revealer (11:25-27). Disciples encounter its presence in his ministry while understanding that it shapes their identity and lifestyle now (ecclesiology, ethics), and that God's purposes are not yet complete (eschatology). But God gives the revelation to a few, not so that they will keep it to themselves, but so that they will imitate God's action and disclose it to others (cf. 4:15-16; 5:14-16; cf. Israel's role in Isa 49:6; Matt 10:5-8; 24:14; 28:19-20).

The act of disclosing God's purposes, however, does not guarantee receptivity. **To them it has not been given.** This cannot mean that God has hidden the revelation from the crowds. Jesus' ministry has been public; the disciples are sent in worldwide mission (28:16-20). Rather, revelation that is not received has not revealed God's purposes. Parables simultaneously reveal to some and conceal from others. For the former, God's empire disrupts the status quo (cf. 5:3-12; 12:1-4), threatens power structures, initiates different practices and relationships, and redistributes resources. The elite, and others, do not welcome it and do not repent (11:20-24; 12:33-37).

• 13:12

To receive Jesus (**To those who have**) means in part living in God's empire until God establishes it in its fullness (13:30, 40-43, 47-50; 19:28; 24:27-31). The chapter provides further understanding (**more will be given and they will have an abundance**). Conversely, **but from those who have nothing**, those who have not welcomed Jesus' proclamation of God's reign, **even what they have will be taken away.** Jesus utilizes an economic principle of the wealthy's increasing wealth[12] to explain the response to the revelation of God's mysteries, but reverses and reapplies the principle. Now it is the vulnerable infants (see 11:25), the marginal, not the resistant elite and crowds, who gain more because they welcome Jesus.

• 13:13

Jesus explains his use of parables. **The reason I speak to them in parables is that "seeing they do not perceive and hearing they do not listen nor do they understand."** The placement of this explanation is crucial. The parables in chapter 13 follow nine chapters of ministry, which has often met with rejection, hostility, and unbelief. Jesus' parables assume that response. The crowds do not understand parables because they do not understand Jesus.

Two phrases which echo Isa 6:9 and Jer 5:21-23 (**seeing they do not see, hearing they do not hear**) sum up the crowds' general response as well as recall specific miracles of restoring sight (9:27-31; 12:22) and hearing (9:32-34), which the crowds witness. Both events appear in the summary of 11:5, which Jesus offers as evidence of his identity and the means by which people can know him. The terms (**see**, **hear**) are literal and metaphorical. They denote these events as well as the understanding (or not) of their significance. To **see and hear** is to discern God's empire in Jesus' ministry (11:4). To not **hear** is to not believe or follow (7:26; 10:14). This is the dominant response (12:19) though some believe (7:24; 12:42). The third phrase **nor do they understand** repeats the claims.[13] Though still learning, disciples **understand** or discern that

God's empire is manifested in Jesus. They welcome or receive God's revelation, but the rest do not.

• 13:14-15

This situation dominated by rejection enacts Isaiah's prophecy, **With them Isaiah's prophecy is certainly fulfilled**. This unusual formula introduces a citation close to the LXX text of Isa 6:9-10.[14] The text warns Isaiah that most people will not respond to his message of judgment, though there is some hope in a "holy seed" (Isa 6:13). Isaiah 7-9 (see Matt 1:22-23; 4:15-16) predictably depicts one of the powerful elite, King Ahaz, as unresponsive to Isaiah's call to trust God. An analogous situation exists with Jesus. The unusually intense form **certainly fulfilled** and its first-word placement emphasize the word. What happened in Isaiah's ministry is happening (present tense) in Jesus' ministry. The rejection of Jesus by many and the positive response of a few disciples (13:23; Introduction, section 7) occur within God's will.

The first two lines of the citation essentially restate the literal/metaphorical dynamic of v. 13: **You will indeed listen but never understand, and you will look but never perceive.** The people have shut themselves off to God's intervention. Why? **For** (which signals the explanation) **this people's heart has grown dull** or unresponsive to God (cf. Deut 32:15). The responsibility lies with the people in their **heart**, the center of a person's willing, thinking, knowing, deciding, and doing (see 5:8; 6:21). Not centered on God, **their ears are hard of hearing, and they have shut their eyes**. The further effect is **so that they might not look with their eyes and listen with their ears and understand with their heart and turn**. Their response prevents any repentance (cf. 11:20-24). The last phrase, **And I will heal them**, is ambiguous. It may mean that their rejecting response prevents any encounter with God's saving empire. Or preferably, it may indicate that while it prevents any repentance now, God **will heal them** subsequently (cf. 23:39); their rejection of God is not permanent.

• 13:16-17

By contrast, **Blessed are your eyes, for they see, and your ears for they hear**. The disciples' accepting response (13:11) is affirmed as God's will (see 5:3-12; 11:6). While they contrast with the elite and the crowds, they stand in continuity with others: **Truly I tell you** (an authoritative statement; see 10:15) **many prophets and righteous people longed to see what you see but did not see it, and to hear what you hear but did not hear it.** Many longed for what is happening in Jesus, the manifestation of God's empire as the beginning of the end when it will be established over all things including Rome's empire. Whereas in 10:41 **prophet** and **righteous** denoted disciples in mission, here, especially following 13:14, a much longer time span of the Hebrew prophets and all who were faithful to God's purposes (righteous; see 1:19) are in view. But, as in 10:41, both terms evoke hostile contexts of resistance to God's purposes and people marginalized by a center resistant to God's reign and justice (see 3:1). The disciples, blessed by God, are to be faithful to their commission to manifest God's empire (10:7-8).

13:18-23—INTERPRETATION OF THE PARABLE
OF THE SEEDS AND SOILS

• 13:18

Jesus explains the parable of 13:3b-9; **Hear then the parable of the sower**. An initial emphatic **you** indicates that he is speaking to the disciples who are capable of understanding (13:16), but have much to learn. Disciples are made. The verb **hear** emphasizes the same quality. While introduced as **the parable of the sower**, the explanation focuses on the fate of the seeds and the soil/ground.

• 13:19

The explanation of **what was sown on the path** (13:4) provides the first reason why many with "dulled hearts" (13:15) do not believe. The clause **When anyone hears the word of the empire** denotes Jesus' (4:17) and the disciples' (10:7) proclamation that God's life-giving reign is present. See 4:23; 9:35, "gospel/good news of the empire." They **do not understand it**. They do not discern God's reign manifested in Jesus (see 13:13). Such a person is subject to the devil's action in the **heart**. **The evil one** (see 6:13; 12:34) **comes and snatches away what is sown in the heart** (see 13:15). In 13:4 the birds eat the seed. Birds are agents of the devil in *Jub.* 11:10-12 (eating seeds); *Apoc. Abr.* 13. Seed (and harvest) are often metaphors for various aspects of God's relationship with Israel: Jer 31:27-28 (a new covenant); Ezek 36:9 (restoration); Hos 2:21-23; *4 Ezra* 8:6; 9:31 (Torah); *2 Bar* 70:2 (final tribulation); Matt 9:37-38 (judgment). They are also common Hellenistic images for learning, for inculturation (Seneca, *Ep* 38.2; Quintilian, *Instit* 5.11.24). The parable concerns socialization into an alternative culture constituted by God's empire and in conflict with the dominant values and structures of the surrounding cultures.[15]

• 13:20-21

A second reason explains the inadequate response of "dulled hearts." **As for what was sown on rocky ground** (cf. 13:5), **this is the one who hears the word** (about God's empire, 13:19) **and immediately receives it** (cf. 10:14) **with joy** (because they discern God's presence; see 2:10; 13:44). **Yet such a person has no root** (13:6) **but endures only for a while, and when trouble or persecution arises on account of the word, that person immediately falls away/is made to stumble.** Difficulties **arise on account of the word**. The person does not understand that God's empire confronts, threatens, and conflicts with cultural values and structures, and that "the empire" strikes back. The noun **trouble** recurs in 24:9, 21, 29 to denote the hatred, martyrdom, and general suffering that occur as part of the eschatological woes before Jesus' return (see 11:12). **Persecution** can be physical or verbal abuse (see 5:10-12), flogging in synagogues (10:17), and appearances before kings and governors (10:18) after household divisions and hatred (10:21-22). The person is unable to survive such pressure (cf. 7:24-27; 10:22) and **is made to stumble**, presumably in betraying their discipleship. They prefer the status quo—the majority position, not the minority counterculture. Stumbling means experiencing not God's blessing but curse (11:6).

• **13:22**

"Dulled hearts" do not accept Jesus because of Satan (13:19) and opposition (13:21). A third reason follows. **As for what was sown among thorns** (13:22), **this is the one who hears the word** (about God's empire, 13:19), **but the cares of the world and the lure of wealth choke the word and it yields nothing.** The **cares of the world** (see 6:25-34) comprise a misplaced focus on the necessities of life, a commitment to materialism, an anxiety to secure life by making these things the sum and goal of, not the means of, human life. In a world of injustice and poverty, the community of disciples is called to trust God's gracious provision (6:25-34; 10:8-10) and to distribute its resources (5:42; 6:2-4) to ensure adequate provisions. But some find this alternative way of life too difficult and abandon it. The **lure** (the word indicates deception in Jdt 9:10, 13 and seduction in Jdt 16:8) **of wealth**, that which is seductively deceptive, betokens a similar misplaced commitment (see 6:24). Wealth, not God, reigns over the heart. Their vote is for the status quo of injustice, greed, accumulation, material comfort, anxiety (see 6:29), and status defined by possessions and wealth. The personifying of **cares** and **lure**, and the use of the verb **choke** suggest their aggressive and fatal attack on the word. The word **yields nothing**.

• **13:23**

By contrast to these three scenarios of negative reception is the fourth: **But as for what was sown on good soil** (13:8), **this is the one who hears the word and understands it**. The empire takes root in disciples. They fight off the devil, can endure through persecution, and renounce the cares and lure of materialism. Unlike the rocky-ground person in 13:20-21, they endure and **indeed bear fruit** in lives that testify to the presence of God's empire and anticipate the completion of God's purposes (see 13:8). The same image condemns the religious leaders in 12:33-37 (also 3:8) and contrasts the two groups. Instead of yielding nothing (13:22), those who receive the word **yield in one case a hundredfold, in another sixty, and in another thirty** (13:8). It should be noted that three of the four scenarios, three-quarters of the seed (?), come to naught. This ratio suggests that the mission of Jesus and of the disciples is often unrewarding. Their surrounding society is generally resistant to the gift and demands of God's empire, and to the alternative community it creates.

13:24-35—JESUS ADDRESSES CROWDS
(WITH DISCIPLES): THE WEEDS

• 13:24

He put before them another parable. The **them** could be the disciples, the audience of 13:10-23. But crowds are clearly present in 13:34. Jesus talks to the crowds in parables (13:2, 10, 13) and offers disciples explanations (13:18-23, 36-43). Crowds, then, are the audience for this series of three short parables, weeds (13:24b-30), mustard seed (13:31-32), and yeast (13:33).

The parable is introduced by a clause not present for the previous one in 13:3a. The clause (**The empire of the heavens may be compared to**) both restricts and invites. It directs the audience to think about the story in relation to God's empire (see 3:2; 4:17), but leaves it to the audience to discern connections.

The parable begins by creating a scene similar to 13:3b, **someone who sowed good seed in his field**, though both **good** and **in his field** suggest a somewhat different emphasis. On **seed**, see 13:19.

• 13:25-26

This different emphasis appears quickly. An enemy sows **weeds among the wheat**. Weeds and wheat grow together.

• 13:27-30

Another difference emerges with 13:3-9. This sower is not a peasant with poor land but a wealthy **householder** with slaves and good land. The **slaves** ask **the master** about the presence of the weeds. The master declares **an enemy has done this**, but forbids the slaves to remove the weeds now lest they uproot the wheat. They are to wait **until the harvest** when the reapers will collect the weeds first and burn them, and then **gather the wheat into the barn**.

How are we to interpret the parable? One way is to see the whole scene as depicting God's empire: its presence, its coexistence with evil, the opposition it provokes, its culmination. This approach begins to draw equivalencies between aspects of the parable and realities outside the parable. It anticipates the allegorizing of the parable, which the gospel itself will do in some detail in 13:36-43. Until we reach that section, the audience can make several guesses about God's empire as it is presented in 13:24-30, guesses informed by the previous chapters:

1. The sowing activity has to do with the proclamation and demonstration of God's empire by Jesus (chs. 8-9, 11-12). He is identified as a householder or "master of the house" in 10:25, addressed as Master/Lord (8:2, 6, 8, 21, 25; 9:28; 12:8), and identifies disciples as slaves (10:24-25; cf. 6:24). Perhaps the identification of the sower also includes disciples, since they are given Jesus' tasks in mission throughout Israel (10:5-8). Seed is identified as "the word of the empire" in 13:19.

2. The scene of growing wheat suggests that God's empire is creative and

life-giving in providing food to sustain life, in anticipation of the abundance that will mark its full establishment (12:1-14; *2 Bar* 74:1-2).

3. Opposition arises which resists and hinders the reign but does not destroy it (13:20-22). The opponent is not clear. Unlike in 13:15, 20-22, it does not seem to be the heart but is external. It might be the devil or its agents (13:19), other opponents such as the political elite (ch. 2; 14:1-12) or religious elite or their agents evident in chs. 11-12, or one's own household that is opposed to disciples (10:36).

4. Harvest images judgment (see 9:37; 13:19). What is happening now is put in eschatological perspective. While the wheat grows impeded by the weeds now, the parable points to the ultimate accomplishment of God's purposes and the destruction of the evil that resists God's life-giving empire. There is an end to evil including Rome's empire as Satan's agent (4:8). This is one of the mysteries of the empire revealed to disciples (13:11).

• 13:31-32

Without offering any interpretation, Jesus **put before them another parable** (13:24). This parable also names its referent explicitly (**The empire of the heavens is like**, 13:24) and invites the audience to think about God's empire in relation to the short narrative. The link both restricts the audience's focus yet stimulates its reflection. This parable offers a further reason for the failure to respond to Jesus. In addition to dull hearts (13:15, 18-23) and the devil's action (13:19, 24-30), response is limited because of the strange and hidden manner in which God's empire is present.

The narrative concerns **a mustard seed which someone took and sowed in his field**. The emphasis on sowing continues from the previous two parables, but the shift from wheat to **a mustard seed** focuses attention not on the activity but on this seed. What is so special or unusual about the mustard seed? **It is the smallest of all seeds, but when it has grown it is the greatest of shrubs and becomes a tree.** The mustard-seed image highlights invisibility; for a while one does not know if anything is happening. It also depicts contrast (tiny seed; greatest shrub, huge tree) and continuity (the tiny seed produces the greatest of shrubs and a huge tree). There is a further element of growth as the seed becomes the shrub/tree, though the use of an aorist passive verb (**when it has grown**), not a present tense, deflects attention from the process of growth to the agent (the passive indicates it is God's life-giving work) and to the result or end product.

The empire of the heavens is like this. The link of mustard seed and God's empire reveals the following: (1) A contrast: what is happening in Jesus' ministry is at times invisible and tiny compared to the overwhelming future of God's reign. It is invisible to Rome and to the religious elite. (2) A continuity: Jesus' ministry is the beginning of, will lead to, a great culmination of God's purposes. (3) An element of inevitability, of certainty, that God will complete God's work. (4) Growth: God extends the empire to those who receive Jesus' words and who seek to live its alternative existence.

What is surprising is the use of "small" to describe Jesus' present ministry.

The narrative has not portrayed it in this way. Jesus cures "every disease and every sickness" in Galilee; "all the sick" come to him including from Syria; "great crowds" constantly follow him from everywhere (4:23-25; also 9:35); "many" with demons are exorcised and "all" the sick are healed (8:16); he has political, international, and cosmic significance (ch. 2); he has so upset the elite (kings and religious leaders) that they want to kill him (2:13, 16; 12:14). It is this widespread activity, popular interest, and intense impact (both acceptance and rejection) that is described as "small." Jesus' ministry is placed in perspective by the image of the glorious completion of God's reign. But while it is very small, it is not inconsequential, because his manifestations of the reign lead to this culmination.

The completion of God's purposes is the final thwarting of the imperial ways of empires. To this **greatest of shrubs and . . . tree, the birds of the heaven come and make nests in its branches**. The images of the tree concern power and rule. In Judg 9:7-15, Jotham's story of the trees anointing a king over themselves is told against his brother Abimelech, who is staging a coup. Ezekiel uses tree images to oppose military alliances with Egypt against Babylon and to proclaim God's reign ("I make high the low tree" [Ezek 17:22-24]). The imperial powers Assyria and Egypt (Ezek 31:1-18) and Babylon (Dan 4:10-26) are magnificent trees which are cut down by God (also Israel [Ps 80:8-13]). The **tree**, then, is an image of God's reign, notably God's sovereignty over the nations. The **birds of the heaven** symbolize the people of the nations who have lived under oppression (Ezek 17:23; 31:6; Dan 4:12), who will know a very different sort of empire. The tiny mustard seed begins and produces a tree, God's empire free of tyranny, which supports life rather than destroys it with injustice. Rome's power will not last forever. See also the eternal tree that will feed the righteous after the judgment in *1 En* 24-25 (cf. Rev 22:2).

• 13:33

The introduction (**He told them another parable** and **the empire of the heavens is like**) closely resembles 13:24 and 31 and links the parables. Again the audience is directed to think about God's empire in relation to the short narrative. The narrative is similar to 13:31-32 in that it involves something small that has profound impact.

The narrative moves from the outside male world of sowing (13:3-9, 24-30, 31-32) to the domestic female world of baking.[16] The woman is not identified as a slave, suggesting perhaps a change from the relative wealth of 13:24-30 to the peasant world of 13:3-9. God's empire is like **yeast/leaven which a woman took and mixed in with three measures of flour until all of it was leavened**. The initial link with **yeast/leaven**[17] (a piece of fermented dough) is striking since it was often regarded as contaminating (Plutarch, "Roman Questions," *Moralia* 289F) and corrupting (pure sacrifice [Exod 23:18; Lev 2:11; 6:16-17]). God's liberation of the people from slavery in Egypt is associated with *unleavened* bread (Exod 12:14-20), which is used because of urgency (Exod 12:34, 39). There wasn't time to wait for leaven to do its work. Leaven, then, depicts a time-consuming process, the passing of time.

The link with **a woman** is not strange for the audience. While the larger cultural context generally regarded women as secondary in male-dominated society and households (see Sirach), the gospel has recognized some women as receptive to God's empire (1:3-6, 16, 18; 8:14; 9:18-26).

She **hid/mixed** her leaven **in three measures of flour until all of it was leavened**. The amount of flour is enough to feed a hundred people at one meal.[18] It makes a great feast, an image of God's empire in 8:11; 22:1-14. In addition, the **three measures** comprise an "ephah," which evokes accounts of three people preparing food: Sarah in Gen 18:6, Gideon from the smallest tribe in Judg 6:19, and Hannah in 1 Sam 1:24. All have integral roles in God's purposes. All are in contexts where God asserts God's reign—over Sodom and Gomorrah (Gen 18), over the Midianite oppressors (Judg 6), and over the opponents of God's justice (1 Sam 2:1-10). Her action is connected with encountering God's reign and presence, but whereas in these three instances God's reign is very evident, in this story it is **hidden**, or invisible at least for a while.

But the hiding/mixing in of the **yeast/leaven** eventually has an impact—**all of it was leavened**. Like the previous parable, both contrast and continuity exist between the small amount of leaven and the huge quantity of flour. The small beginning effects a massive impact. The **yeast/leaven** has worked quietly, invisibly, hidden away, over time. Rome and the religious elite do not see it at all. Disciples could wonder if it was there at all, or achieving anything. But inevitably **all of it was leavened**. The passive indicates God's action. The **yeast/leaven** has done corrupting work in transforming the flour.

By comparison, God's reign works over time. In a similar way, it attacks the status quo. In doing transformative work, it shows that conventional life under imperial rule is unacceptable. God's ways are not human ways. God's empire is not the same as oppressive political, socioeconomic, and religious control. So Jesus heals the sick, casts out demons, eats with tax collectors and sinners, urges mercy, promotes access to shared resources, and constitutes alternative households. This is corrupting work in relation to the empire's status quo because it replaces an unjust hierarchical system which furthers the interests of the elite at the expense of the rest. But if a person is well adjusted in a sick society, corrupting is the only path to wholeness. In such a context, to be corrupted is to be transformed, saved, in encountering God's empire, in anticipation of its eventual completion in establishing God's life-giving reign over all things.

• 13:34-35

After these three parables, an editorial comment explains Jesus' use of parables (cf. 13:10-17), **Jesus told the crowds all these things in parables**. The point is repeated in negative form to underline its importance, **without a parable he told them nothing**. While the gospel's audience, along with disciples, continues to learn, the crowds do not understand (13:14-15).

A scripture citation shows that Jesus' use of parables reflects God's will previously declared in scripture, as do his conception (1:23), birth and early childhood (ch. 2), ministry (4:15-16), healing (8:17), and preaching and rejection (12:15-21). He uses parables **so that what was spoken through the prophet**

might be fulfilled. See 1:22. The citation comes from Ps 78:2, attributed to Asaph a member of a guild of musicians and singers in the Jerusalem temple charged with prophesying (1 Chr 25:1-2; 2 Chr 5:12; 29:30).[19] The first half is from the LXX, the rest translates the Hebrew (MT) text, **I will open my mouth to speak in parables; I will proclaim what has been hidden from the foundation of the world**. Psalm 78 reviews Israel's history with God from the exodus, occupation, time of the judges, through to the election of Zion and David. It emphasizes the rebellious nature of the people and God's punishing and forgiving acts. The psalm recites this material so that subsequent generations will appreciate God's acts and not repeat the mistake of being "a stubborn and rebellious generation" (78:8). The psalm's declared intent to "not hide" these things (78:4) is often suggested to be at odds with Jesus' use of parables. But while the parables are not understood by many, they are told publicly, and some (the disciples) do understand at least some of the time. The Psalmist likewise makes known God's acts, knowing that previous generations were not moved and without any guarantee that history will not be repeated. The psalm is, then, analogous to Jesus' ministry in that the gospel highlights God's miraculous interventions (Matt 8-9; 11:2-6), which fail to elicit repentance, faith, and obedience from many (Ps 78:32, 56; Matt 11:20-24; 12:14, 22-45; 13:10-17), though some (disciples) discern God to be at work. Yet the psalm indicates that rejection is not the final word. While God "utterly rejected Israel" (78:59), God started again with Saul and David (78:65-72). Jesus reveals God's purposes. Some understand, but it remains hidden from many. See 11:25; 13:11. There is yet salvation for the rejecting majority (1:21; 23:37-39).

13:36-53—JESUS ADDRESSES DISCIPLES

13:36-43—INTERPRETATION OF THE PARABLE OF THE WEEDS

• 13:36

The audience changes as Jesus **left the crowds** (4:25) **and went into the house** (cf. 13:1). The **house**, previously a place of worship (2:8), a model of lived discipleship (7:24-27), of healing (8:6, 14), of eating with marginals and of conflict with the religious elite (9:10-13), of raising the dead (9:23), of received and rejected mission (10:12-14), becomes a place of teaching as **the disciples** (see 5:1) **approached him** (reverential address, see 4:3) **saying, "Explain to us the parable of the weeds in the field."** The prominence of **the house** may reflect its significance for the gospel's first-century audience as a meeting place for worship, teaching, and encountering (the risen) Jesus. In referring to the parable of 13:24-30, the disciples highlight not the sowing, the seed, the field (13:3-9, 18-24), or the abundant harvest (13:31-32), but the weeds, which 13:38 identifies as the devil's offspring, who are condemned (13:39-42). That is, Jesus and the disciples experience opposition to God's purposes because of Satan's activity (13:19). But the introduction already antici-pates judgment for Satan's followers. The devil's days are numbered.

• 13:37-39

Jesus' response asserts referents for eight (but not all) aspects of the parable. The explanation is a revelation of the present state of the world and the coming triumph of God's empire.

1. **He who sows the seed** (13:24) **is the Son of Man**. See 8:20 and 25:31 for **Son of Man**, denoting Jesus' ministry (which is often rejected) and future judging of the world. Presumably he is the householder (so 10:25) and Lord (13:27), though no explicit identification is made here. For **Son of Man** with an everlasting rule, and as eschatological judge, see Dan 7:13-14; *1 En* 46, 48.

2. **The field** (13:24) **is the world** (13:38), the realm of everyday political, social, economic, and religious life, created by God (Gen 2:1) yet dominated by the devil (see 4:8) and in need of liberating (see 5:14). It is the sphere of Jesus' ministry in proclaiming and enacting God's empire in words and actions. It is a realm of rejection more than acceptance (three quarters of the seed comes to naught, 13:3-9, 18-24).

3. **The good seed** (13:24, 27) are **the children of the empire** (13:38). In contrast to the next clause, these children (cf. 18:1-6; 19:13-15) are disciples who have encountered God's empire. The same phrase appears in 8:12 to denote Israel, which, as yet, does not commit to Jesus.

4. **The weeds** (13:25-27, 29-30) **are the children of the evil one** (13:38), the devil. Verse 41 will elaborate their identity. As **children of the devil**, they oppose God's purposes. They are, then, the religious leaders (already so identi-fied in 12:33-37) and the political elite (see 4:8), who enact the devil's reign.

5. **The enemy who sowed them** (13:25, 28) **is the devil** (13:39), who opposes God (see 4:1-11; 6:13; 13:19) and has a reign and subjects (4:8; 12:26). The opposition to and rejection of Jesus (and disciples) is not only a matter of dull hearts (13:15) but is symptomatic of a cosmic struggle (4:1-11; 6:9-13; 13:19).

6. **The harvest** (13:30) **is the end of the age** (13:39). **Harvest** is a common image of judgment (see 9:37; 13:19). The phrase **end of the age** is the time (known only to God) of God's judgment, the removal of all evil, and establish-ment of God's empire and purposes over all including Rome (*4 Ezra* 7:113; *2 Bar* 13:3; 21:8).

7. **The reapers** (13:30) **are the angels** (13:39), agents of God's judgment (*1 En* 53:3-5; 63:1; they punish the oppressive kings and governors) and of God's will among humans (1:20; 2:13, 19).

With these seven definitions the explanation reveals key characters and their roles in Matthew's cosmic worldview. The devil struggles against God; the two empires and their adherents clash. Now is a time of adversity for Jesus and the disciples, but in the future judgment, the devil's reign will be overcome, and God's reign established.[20] An eighth identification emphasizes and elaborates the final stage in God's purposes.

• 13:40-42

8. **Just as the weeds are collected and burned up with fire** (13:30), **so will it be at the end of the age** (see 13:39). **The Son of Man will send his angels** (see 13:39), **and they will collect** (13:28-30) **out of his reign/empire all causes of sin and all evildoers**. Is the **reign/empire** the world (13:38), in which the devil is active and has kingdoms (4:8; 12:26)? Or is it the church, a mixed body (*corpus mixtum*) of good and evil which God judges? Both suggestions lose sight of the future "end of the age" scenario that is being depicted. The **reign/empire** is the victory of God's purposes, which Jesus as Son of Man and judge extends over all that opposes them. That process is being described in this verse. Again the gospel borrows imperial and violent images to depict the final triumph of God's purposes.[21]

The evil that is overcome includes **all causes of sin**, a cognate of the verb "cause to stumble/sin." These **causes** include anything that diverts or destroys disciples (5:29-30; 18:6-9) and that rejects Jesus rather than recognizes his identity as God's commissioned agent (11:6). It includes persecution and the tribulation or woes that precede the end (13:21; 24:10). As weeds sown by the enemy (cf. 13:19), all of this is seen as the devil's work through demons and people, though the emphasis on human actions in 13:15 precludes a defense of "the devil made me do it." The devil's actions and human responsibility exist together.[22] The **evildoers** are literally "the doers of lawlessness," those who act contrary to the divine will (see 7:23). In some eschatological scenarios such as *1 En* 62-63, judgment focuses on "the kings, governors, high officials, and landowners" who ignored God and practiced oppression.

Their destiny is that **they will throw them into the furnace of fire**. The phrase cites Dan 3:6, 15, 17, 20, 23, 26. Babylon's ruler Nebuchadnezzar misuses his power and demands worship. Daniel and his three companions remain faithful to God. Thrown into the furnace of fire, they are rescued by God and the tyrant's purposes are thwarted. But in the judgment the roles are reversed. There is no deliverance for those who have resisted God's purposes, especially the mighty and powerful. This image is also to be linked to Gehenna in 5:22 and the furnace of hell in *4 Ezra* 7:36. See also 7:19 for **fire** as a prophetic and apocalyptic image of judgment. **Weeping and gnashing of teeth** (see 8:12) denotes anger and perhaps regret (cf. *1 En* 62). The cosmic conflict is over.

• 13:43

After the emphasis on judgment, a brief note of vindication follows. **Then the righteous**, disciples of Jesus and others prior to them (cf. 8:11) who have lived in faithful relationship to God and God's purposes (see 1:19; 3:15; 10:41), are vindicated (cf. 10:32-33). They **will shine like the sun**. This traditional language for the new world (Dan 12:3; *1 En* 39:7) uses images of light and life to evoke the completion of God's purposes as God's **empire** is established over all resistance (**the reign/empire of their father**; see 5:16, 45, 48; 6:9; 16:17; 23:9; etc.). At the beginning of Jesus' ministry, the image of light depicted God's saving presence and reign which shines in the darkness and death of Galilee under Roman imperial rule (4:15-16). Its use here links the beginning of Jesus' ministry with its goal, the establishment of God's empire, which is life-giving, not death-bringing, which liberates and does not oppress. The closing exhortation, **Let anyone with ears** (see 11:15), returns to the distinction between the crowds and disciples (13:10-17). It exhorts disciples to discern the significance of Jesus' words and to live in the light of this glorious future, with perseverance, faithfully even in the midst of the weeds, knowing that the time of the devil's evil is measured.

13:44-50—THREE FURTHER PARABLES

• 13:44

With little transition, another sequence of three parables begins (cf. 13:24-33). They continue Jesus' address to the disciples. After the vision of the completion of God's cosmic purposes, the first two underscore the smallness and hiddenness, yet great value and worth of God's empire active in the present.

The parable begins with a familiar introduction (see 13:24, 31, 33): **The reign/empire of the heavens is like treasure hidden in a field which someone found and hid; then in his joy he goes and sells all that he has and buys that field.** The wealth or status of the **someone** is not specified. Several speculate that he is a day laborer, who discovers the treasure while plowing another's field. His poverty demands selling everything to buy it.[23] This is possible but not certain. Nor is the **treasure** identified. The term denotes the magi's valuable gifts in 2:11 of gold, myrrh, and frankincense, but in 6:19-21 it signifies anything a person values. Hiding valuable things in the ground is common. Philostratus (*Apollonius* 6:39) describes a man who "sacrifices to mother Earth in the hope of finding a treasure" and subsequently finds a buried jar with money in it. Josephus (*JW* 7.114-15) records wealth from Jerusalem found in the ground by the Romans (cf. *2 Bar* 6:7-9). Again the parable involves a **field** (13:24, 27, 31, 36, 38) and the sequence refers to something **hidden** (13:33, 35; cf. 11:25), which recalls the empire's apparently inconsequential presence, invisible to many, especially the elite and Rome, but known to a few (7:14; Introduction, section 7).

Finding the **treasure** disrupts normal daily life and promises a different way of life. The **treasure** is so valuable that it is worth doing new, joyful, risky, and costly things to possess it. **Joy,** typically associated with encountering God's presence, marks the magi's discovery and worship of Jesus (see 2:10), and the reception of Jesus' proclamation of God's reign (13:20). He **sells all that he has and buys that field**. This is a risky act which threatens his life, but it is worth losing even his life (see 10:37-39). The empire requires setting aside all other priorities (4:18-22; 8:19-22; 9:9) in wholehearted commitment. Possessions must not hinder one from encountering God's empire (6:19-34; 13:22).

• 13:45-46

Again, the empire of the heavens is like a merchant in search of fine pearls. It is difficult to conclude much about the merchant. Wealth does not have to be assumed. As for the status of merchants, most LXX references are negative. Sirach 26:29 notes that a merchant cannot keep from wrongdoing—presumably greed and unjust transactions. Isaiah 23:8 and Ezek 37 (using the word eleven times) condemn Tyre's commerical empire; see also 1 Kgs 10:15, 28; 1 Macc 3:41; 2 Macc 8:34. Cicero despises small merchants (*De Off* 1.150-51). If the term's connotations are negative, then the merchant's subsequent actions may represent repentance. He would be typical of the marginals who encounter God's empire (cf. 10:9-13). The merchant's act of **searching** is ambiguous. In the gospel, people search in ways that resist God's purposes (2:13, 20; 6:32) or, as here, in ways that actively embrace them (6:33; 7:7, 8). God's empire does not automatically overtake people. People must look for it (which in the context of chs. 11-12, the elite and crowds have not done). His searching leads **to finding one pearl of great value**. As with finding treasure (13:44), this discovery disrupts normal daily life and promises a different way of life. The **pearl** is so valuable that it is worth doing new, risky, and costly things to possess it (**he went and sold all that he had and bought it**). The merchant makes it everything.

• 13:47-48

A third parable follows. **Again the empire of the heavens is like a net that was thrown into the sea**. On fishing as a Roman-regulated activity, and as a symbol of God's resistance to imperial power and of mission, see 4:18-22. The **net** symbolizes the Chaldeans' imperial aggression (Hab 1:15-17), God's sovereign control in destroying Egypt (Isa 19:8) and in using Babylon to destroy oppressive Tyre (Ezek 26:5, 14). These initial details indicate a scene concerned not with the presence of the reign (as in 13:44-46) but with the future completion of God's (imperial!) purposes (so 13:24-30), which will establish God's empire over all those, including the imperial power Rome, who resist God's rule.

The universal scope (birth, gender, status, wealth, ethnicity, training, etc.) is underlined by two details in the narrative, **and caught fish of every kind** and **when it was full**—then comes the judgment, **they drew it ashore, sat down** (cf. 19:28; 25:31), **put the good into baskets and threw out the bad/rotten**. These latter are probably not the inedible or the unclean fish that lack scales and fins (Lev 11:9-12). The pairing of **good** and **bad/rotten** (BAGD, 742) is well established from 7:16-19 and 12:33 as contrasting ways of life. Like the weeds and wheat (13:29-30), good and evil practices, actions, and structures, which result from commitments to or against God, coexist until the judgment. Then come the separation and the condemnation. Again evil, whether of empires or individuals, does not have the final word. For **threw out** and judgment, see 8:12.

• 13:49-50

This reading is confirmed by 13:49-50, which emphasizes the final judgment. **So it will be at the end of the age** (see 13:39). **The angels will come out and separate** (see 13:39) **the evil from the righteous**. This well-established pairing, a synonym of "the good and the bad" in 13:48, emphasizes those who have or have not been faithful to God's requirements (see 13:43). The term **evil** recalls 13:38 and identifies those who resist God's purposes as the devil's agents (13:19; 6:13). In 4:8 the empires and rulers were in view; in 12:34-35 the religious leaders, but 12:39 broadened the referent to a generation that does not receive God's messenger. Their fate is that of the weeds, the causes of sin and evildoers, of 13:42. The repetition underlines their certain but terrible fate.

13:51-53—CONCLUSION

• **13:51**

Having told seven parables, Jesus asks the disciples, **"Have you understood all this?"** **All this** refers to God's present and future reign revealed in the parables (13:35). Certainly disciples have some understanding, while the outsiders, the elite and the crowds, lack it (see 13:13, 19, 23). And the disciples' answer, **"Yes,"** befits Jesus' role as teacher (10:25) and revealer (11:25-27) of God's purposes, and confirms their identity as recipients of Jesus' revelation about God's purposes and empire (13:11). But the subsequent narrative will indicate that they do not understand as much as they profess to understand. Their response is wittily ironic.

• **13:52**

Jesus' response identifies the disciples as **every scribe who has been discipled for the empire of the heavens**. Until now, scribes as interpreters of the laws and members of the religious elite allied against Jesus have had bad press (see 2:4; 5:17; 7:29; 8:19; 9:3; 12:38). Here the term is contrastive and positive. It is linked with the verb **discipled** to denote those who have encountered God's empire (4:18-22) and who understand its present way of life, mission, and future completion (chs. 5-7; 10; 13:1-50; cf. Sir 39:1-3). The verb **discipled** involves both commitment to Jesus (27:57 [Joseph]) and receiving instruction about the reign which he manifests, expressed in an appropriate way of life (28:19; cf. Plutarch, "Antiphon," *Moralia* 832B; "Isocrates," *Moralia* 837C). On **empire**, see 3:2; 4:17; and all of chapter 13 above.

Jesus then compares them **to the master of a household who brings out of his storehouse what is new and what is old**. The image of **master of a household**, used previously for Jesus in 10:25 and 13:19, suggests that Jesus is also **a scribe discipled for the empire** and offers a clue for interpreting the enigmatic **what is new and what is old**. From the outset of the gospel, Jesus is set in continuity with God's previous dealings with Israel. God has not abandoned Israel. Jesus' disciples, the church, have not superseded Israel. His teaching and ministry utilize Jewish traditions, perspectives and practices. Yet they are reinterpreted in the light of the claim that God has anointed him for a definitive role, to begin the end by manifesting God's empire and saving purposes (cf. 5:17). There is continuity and discontinuity.

This chapter provides several examples of continuity and discontinuity. (1) Numerous apocalyptic writers (*1 Enoch; 4 Ezra; 2 Baruch*) reveal the end. Jesus' revelation shares features with them (as noted above), yet makes distinctive claims that already God's empire is evident in his ministry (13:19, 31, 33, 37); he has a definitive role in its completion (13:41-43), and lived commitment to him determines one's destiny (13:19-23, 38-43, 47-50). (2) Twice in the chapter Jesus explicitly cites scriptural material (13:14-15, 35). In both instances there is something analogous between the texts' original use and the Matthean use. But Jesus reinterprets both texts to speak to new circumstances. (3) Jesus' teaching is continually influenced by scriptural symbols and images (sowing, leaven, tree, net, etc.). But repeatedly these images take on new dimensions in relation to Jesus' commission and revelation concerning God's empire. Disciples are to imitate Jesus the master scribe in recognizing this continuity of God's purposes, in understanding his teaching about God's empire, and in living a way of life appropriate to its presence and future. They are to pass on this understanding to others. But in their ongoing teaching and life as a community of disciples, they too must reinterpret the scriptural tradition and the teaching of Jesus for new and different situations (5:17; 16:19; 18:18). In so doing, they live and maintain the tension and praxis of **bringing out what is new and what is old**, in contrast to the religious leaders who can only produce evil from their treasure/storehouses (12:35).

• 13:53

Jesus' third teaching section (chs. 5-7; 10) ends with a transitional clause similar to that used to close the previous teaching sections in 7:28a and 11:1, **When Jesus had finished these parables**. As in the other two instances he travels, **he left that place** (the house; see 13:36) in anticipation of the next scene.

13:54-58—JESUS' REJECTION BY HIS HOMETOWN SYNAGOGUE

The scene exemplifies the emphasis of the gospel's third narrative section (11:2-16:20), that many cannot discern Jesus' identity as God's commissioned agent from his works (cf. 11:2-6). The synagogue consists of those who "see but do not perceive, hear but do not listen or understand" (13:13). They take offense at him (13:57) invoking curse, not blessing, on themselves (11:6).

• 13:54

He came to his hometown. Is this Nazareth (2:23) or Capernaum (4:13)? The link with Jesus' family in 13:55-56 suggests Nazareth. He engages in his normal activity of **teaching them in their synagogue**. See 4:23; 9:35; also 6:2, 5; 10:17; 12:9 for conflict with and distance from the synagogue. This location suggests that things will not go well.

In response, **they were astonished** just as the crowds are after the first discourse (7:28). Perceiving something unusual, they are surprised because they know Jesus and his family well, and they know he is acting above his family status. They inquire further, **Where did this man get this wisdom and these deeds of power?** The question about Jesus' origin is astute, and it could lead to their successfully answering the section's central question about Jesus' identity (11:2-16:20) and discerning God's empire to be at work in him (so 11:2-6). Or they could side with the religious leaders, who attributed Jesus' authority to the devil (9:34; 12:24). The terms **wisdom** and **deeds of power** refer to his preaching (**he taught them**) and miracles (see 11:20, 21, 23), which manifest God's presence and reign (see 11:19, 25-30). On the gospel's claim that **wisdom** is found in Jesus, see 11:19, 25-30 (1:21-23; 4:17).

• 13:55-56

But they cannot answer their own question successfully. Instead of discerning God's presence, they focus on Jesus' biological family. Instead of being open to a revelation, they retreat into the known and familiar. Instead of discerning his identity as one who is faithful to his identity as son or agent of his Father God (see 1:21-23; 2:15; 3:17; 4:17), they try to define him according to his earthly father's occupation. There seems to be a tone of rebuke for not being true to that origin in their question, **Is not this the carpenter's son?**[24] As with Joseph in 1:18-25, and the disciples in 12:46-50, Jesus rebuffs cultural norms and expectations. The occupation (**carpenter**) signifies the family's lowly status and Jesus' lowly origins, befitting the emphasis throughout on the lowly and marginal, not the elite. This is the first reference to Joseph, though not named, since 1:18-2:23. **Is not his mother called Mary? And are not his brothers James and Joseph and Simon and Judas? And are not all his sisters with us?** By focusing on Jesus' birth family, they employ conventional cultural categories to define him. But Jesus has already indicated that his faithful enactment of his God-given commission constitutes his identity. This commitment transcends any birth family (see 12:46-50). The repeated question, **Where then did this man get all this?** emphasizes the key issue of origin and their inability to answer it successfully. They fail the test of this third narrative section (11:2-6).

• 13:57

And they took offense at him. In 11:2-6 Jesus has blessed those who discern God's presence in his words and actions, and do not take offense. In taking offense, the people of his hometown reveal their failure to discern and to believe (13:58). The term **take offense** evokes 13:41. It identifies the synagogue as weeds, the agents of the devil, and its destiny of condemnation in the judgment. Nazareth joins the condemned towns of Chorazin, Bethsaida, and Capernaum in not repenting (11:20-24). Galilee, though distant from the rejecting elite in Jerusalem, is not a welcoming sanctuary. Verse 12 of chapter 4 suggested as much in linking Jesus' move to Galilee with John's arrest.

Jesus interprets their rejection not just in a long history of rejections of God's agents (see *Lives of the Prophets;* Matt 23:34-39) but of rejections by their places of origin: **Prophets are not without honor except in their own country and in their own house**. See Epictetus, *Diss* 3:16; Dio Chrysostom, *Disc* 47.6; Jer 1:1; 11:21-23. The use of **prophet** recalls John's arrest and anticipates 14:1-12.

• 13:58

The consequence is that **He did not do many deeds of power there, because of their unbelief**. The town's "no-faith" contrasts with the disciples' little faith (6:30; 8:26; cf. 14:31; 16:8). Its rejection does not stop him working miracles. Rather he refuses to do so because of its opposition. Compare with the telling of parables in response to unbelief in 13:13-15.

CHAPTER 14

God's Empire at Work

Opposition, Abundance, Compassion

Chapter 14 includes four units.

The chapter continues to work the agenda of this third narrative section (11:2-16:20), namely, the challenge to discern in Jesus' actions and words his identity as God's agent commissioned to manifest God's saving presence and life-giving empire. Despite the widespread rejection and opposition, God does not forsake the people and order Jesus to stop his mission. Rather, Jesus continues to demonstrate God's empire, which critiques imperial structures and reverses human misery and want (hunger, sickness) with plenty and wholeness. His miraculous and compassionate actions point to a different way of life, instruct disciples, and provide others with opportunities to discern his identity. But as with chapters 11-13, the elite respond with hostility to what God is doing (Herod [14:1-12]). Some respond positively (disciples [14:33]), while the crowds benefit from Jesus supplying food and healing but they do not commit themselves to or oppose Jesus (14:13-21, 34-36).

14:1-12—THE EMPIRE STRIKES BACK—AGAIN

John the prophet (see 3:1), who proclaims God's reign (3:2), confronts Herod Antipas, tetrarch of Galilee and Peraea from 4 B.C.E. to 39 C.E. and agent of Rome's imperial reign.[1] Josephus attests Herod executing John because of fears that John's popularity might incite an insurrection (*Ant* 18.117-19).[2] Matthew's account, while assuming some historical basis, reinforces three pastoral-theological dynamics for its audience: the politically powerful resist God's empire; unbelief is expressed in hostility and violence; God's empire requires faithfulness even to death.

301

Throughout the gospel, rulers and kings like Herod (14:9) have consistently ended up on the wrong side of God's purposes: the disobedient kings in the genealogy (1:6-11); the murderous Herod (father of Antipas) in chapter 2; Herod's threatening son Archelaus (2:22); the continual conflict between God's reign and the imperial context of injustice and oppression; the greedy and oppressive Solomon in 6:29; the persecuting actions of governors and kings against disciples in 10:18; John's denouncing of Herod in 11:7-8; the eschatological visions of the demise of those who resist God's purposes including the trees of the nations (13:32); the crucifixion of Jesus (20:19; 26-27). The political elite reject God's threatening reign (see also 17:24-27; 22:15-22).

Unbelief, leading to hostility and violence, has been evident in the responses to the disciples' mission (10:17-18) and the religious elite's plans to kill Jesus (12:14). John's death is more of the same. While Herod is a particular figure, he is typical of all tyrannical rulers. His actions evoke a long biblical line of the powerful who actively resist God's purposes,[3] just as John belongs with the faithful who are martyred (2 and 4 Macc; Matt 10:28, 38). The audience is warned that faithful discipleship encounters hostility and violence from the politically powerful. John's fate anticipates Jesus'.

• 14:1-2

The introductory phrase **At that time** (used in 11:25 and 12:1) links this episode to the conflicts over Jesus' identity evident in chapters 11-13 (most recently 13:54-56). After verdicts about Jesus from Jesus himself (11:25-27; 12:8, 40-42), the religious leaders (12:24), and the synagogue (13:54-56), **Herod** Antipas **the tetrarch/ruler** of Galilee (4:12-16) offers his. **Tetrarch**[4] denotes a "petty dependent prince" (BAGD, 814), and so underlines his role as Rome's representative. Rome's agent clashes with God's agents. Herod **heard the reports about Jesus**. In 4:24 these reports spread everywhere and many came to be healed. Proclamation can lead to faith (13:23) and provides the basis for discerning Jesus' identity (11:4-5). But **Herod** gets it wrong, announcing **to his servants** (officials with considerable delegated power [so 1 Macc 1:6, 8]), **"This is John the Baptist; he has been raised from the dead, and for this reason these powers are at work in him."** The phrase **this is** echoes God's declaration in 3:17 (again in 17:5), "this is my beloved son." The echo underlines how wrong Herod is in not recognizing Jesus as God's agent. His comment provides the first indication that the imprisoned John has died (4:12; 11:2). His term **powers** appears in two previous contexts in which people have witnessed the "deeds of the Messiah" (11:2) but have not repented and believed (13:54; 11:20, 21, 23). The reference to John having **been raised from the dead** (also 16:14) is ambiguous. Does he mean literally John has revived, or does he mean that Jesus continues John's work? Either way John and Jesus are linked as agents of God's purposes (so 3:2; 4:17; 11:2).

• 14:3-4

John's death is elaborated: **For Herod had arrested** (also used of Jesus in 26:4, 48, 50, 55, 57) **John, bound him** (also Jesus in 27:2) **and put him in**

prison (4:12; the same fate happens to the prophet Micaiah in 2 Chr 18:26 for a prophecy unfavorable to Israel's king). An explanation follows: **because of Herodias, his brother Philip's wife, because John had been telling him** (an imperfect tense indicating repeated statements), **"It is not lawful for you to have her."** Herod is planning to marry her (note the relationships in "Philip's wife" and "daughter of Herodias"), or has already done so. Either way it is contrary to God's will in Lev 18:16; 20:21. Josephus also expresses disapproval by complaining that Herodias "flouts the way of our fathers" (*Ant* 18.136). **Philip** may be the tetrarch, Herod's son by Cleopatra, or another son of Herod by Mariamme.[5] Ruling elites used intermarriage to build alliances, expand territory, and increase power. John, the prophet from the margins, resists a consolidation of the center's power. See 11:7-8. Herod refuses to listen to his proclamation of God's will.

• 14:5

Though Herod wanted to kill him (also used of Jesus in 16:21; 17:33; 26:4), **he feared the crowd because they regarded him as a prophet**. The crowd is correct, though Jesus calls John more than a prophet (11:9). John does not fear those who can kill the body (10:28). The same fate awaits disciples (24:9) and Jesus.

• 14:6

The initial cryptic clause **But when Herod's birthday came** recalls the birth, origin, and commission of another king (1:18; 2:1, 2, 4) and contrasts their two reigns (2:2). Whereas Herod brings oppression and death, Jesus' reign consists of life and justice. A party is under way. For meals, hierarchical social relations, and occasions of inclusion and exclusion, see 9:10-13, and 8:11-12 as an image of God's coming eschatological triumph. But this meal is a gathering of the political and social elite, predominantly male, though high-status women are present (14:6, 8).

The daughter of Herodias danced in the midst and she pleased Herod. In 13:25, 49, **in the midst** is associated with evil and judgment. K. Corley notes that women who attended public meals, traditionally male events, were commonly understood to provide sex whether they did so or not.[6] G. Theissen also argues that this act imputes "shabby morals" to the Herodian women.[7] The presentation assumes at least a stereotype of immoral rulers, if not actual knowledge in Antioch about the Herodian women from Galilee, the neighboring territory. Berenice, the sister of Agrippa II (died ca. 90) and known as Queen Berenice (Josephus, *Vita* 119; Tacitus, *Hist* 2.81), had been the subject of rumors since the 40s. She was accused of being a prostitute and of incest with her brother Agrippa II (Josephus, *Ant* 19.357; 20.145). Juvenal refers to a diamond ring which Agrippa gives to Berenice, his "incestuous sister" (*Sat* 6.156-60). In the 70s she is rumored to have an affair with the yet-to-be emperor Titus (ten years her junior) with whom she lived in Rome (Tacitus, *Hist* 2.2; Suetonius, *Titus* 7.1-2; Juvenal, *Sat* 6.156-60).[8] Illustrating the same claim,

Theissen notes that "the appearance of a king's daughter before drinking men signifies a sexual relationship."[9] The scene emphasizes the ill repute and immorality of the political elite and mocks the Flavian emperor Titus by association. The gospel may well have been written while Titus was emperor (79-81), or shortly after his death (see Introduction, section 4).

• 14:7

Herod is so pleased by the dancing **that he promised on oath to grant her whatever she might ask**. Theissen notes that Gaius Caligula permitted Agrippa I such a request. Agrippa asked Caligula to desist from desecrating the Jerusalem temple (Josephus, *Ant* 18.289-97). King Ahaseurus offers Esther a similar request (Esth 5:3-8; 7:2). She uses it to have Haman the hater of Jews killed, and to protect her people from genocide.[10] But in contrast to these noble ends, Herodias's request is more interested in removing a critic and securing power. Herod's **oath** is clearly unwise, and contravenes Jesus' teaching in 5:33-37.

• 14:8

The negative presentation of the women continues. **Prompted by her mother, she said, "Give me the head of John the Baptist here on a platter."** Their request matches Herod's desire to kill John (14:5), but provides him with the occasion to act. Ironically, the death order for one who "came neither eating or drinking" (11:18) comes in the context of a feast. Livy (*Epit* 39.43.2-4) narrates a similar meal scene involving a consul who misuses his power in the same way at the suggestion of a woman.

• 14:9-10

Herod Antipas is appropriately called **the king**. The title links him with his father Herod the murderer (2:1, 3, 9), establishes him as an opponent of God's purposes (10:18), and contrasts his death-bringing reign with King Jesus (2:2) and his life-giving reign. **The king was grieved** (why?), **yet out of regard for his oaths and for the guests, he commanded it to be given; he sent and had John beheaded in the prison.** Herod values social conventions of honor and household ties ahead of doing God's will (12:46-50; 13:53-58; 15:19; 19:18) and John's life. He is another of the "violent ones" who does violence to God's empire (11:12). His order demonstrates how corrupt and resistant the elite can be. Jesus teaches against oaths (5:33-37; 23:16-22).

• 14:11

The head was brought on a platter and given to the girl, who brought it to her mother. The one who "came neither eating or drinking" (11:18) is served up at a feast on a platter. His head ends up with Herodias, who prompted the request (14:8). But the blame is evenly spread since her request enacted Herod's will (14:5). Their exercise of power is destructive, whereas Jesus proclaims justice, is merciful and compassionate (9:36; 12:20).

• 14:12

His disciples came and took the body and buried it. For John's disciples, which include some women, see 11:2. For burial as an act of respect, see 8:21. Josephus (*JW* 5.570) uses the same term, **body,** for other victims of imperial violence, the thousands from the "poorer class" who starved to death during Titus's siege of Jerusalem in 69-70 C.E. One of Jesus' disciples will bury his body (27:57-61). **Then they went and told Jesus**, an action that further links John and Jesus. John has confronted imperial power and lost, it seems. Yet he has been faithful (10:21-22, 28, 38) and will have his reward (10:32). This is the way of it in a hostile world until God completes God's purposes. The links to Jesus intimate that God has not finished yet, and brings new life from death.

14:13-21—JESUS FEEDS MORE THAN FIVE THOUSAND

Jesus enacts God's will that hungry people be fed (Ps 22:26; Job 22:5-11; Isa 58:6-7; Ezek 18:5-9; 34:2-3, 8; Sir 34:25-27; *T. Jos.* 1:5-7; Matt 5:6; 6:11; 12:1-8). Through Jesus' deed, God acts faithfully to sustain creation in anticipation of the new creation in which God's reign is established in full and there is abundant food for all (Ezek 34:25-31; *1 En* 10:18-20; *Sib. Or.* 3:619-23, 741-61; *2 Bar* 29:4-8; 74:1-2; for the eschatological feast, see Isa 25:6-9; Matt 8:11-12; 9:10-13; 12:1-8; 22:1-10). Jesus' act attacks the injustice of the sinful imperial system which ensures that the urban elite are well fed at the expense of the poor (Aristides, *Roman Oration* 11; Tacitus, *Ann* 2.33; 3.53-54).[11] Jesus enacts an alternative system marked by compassion, sufficiency and shared resources. His action imitates God's actions in saving the people from the tyrant Pharaoh and feeding them in the desert (Exod 16). See comments on 12:1-8.

• 14:13

Now when Jesus heard this (the report from John's disciples about John's death, 14:12), **he withdrew from there in a boat to a deserted place/wilderness by himself**. Jesus is clearly in danger. If Herod thinks Jesus is John raised from the dead, then Herod is likely to kill Jesus (14:2).

For the fifth time in the gospel, **withdrawal** follows aggression from imperial power, just as Moses withdraws from Pharaoh (Exod 2:15), and Judas Maccabeus from Apollonius, commander of Antiochus Epiphanes (2 Macc 5:27). See 2:12-15, 22-23; 4:12-18; 12:15-21; also 15:21-28; 27:5-10).[12] To **withdraw** is to refuse to play in the tyrant's world and by the tyrant's rules. It is to make a space for a different reign, God's empire, marked by life-giving structures and compassionate practices such as healing and feeding. Such a space is not found in the urban centers with their sharply differentiated society, carefully controlled power, and protected self-interest (cf. 13:53-58). It is found on the margins, in an insignificant place, a **deserted place or wilderness**, a place of no use to the elite but of central importance to God's purposes and very threatening to the center (cf. 2:3-6; 3:1). The beneficiaries are not the powerful but the poor and marginalized.

On **deserted place/wilderness** as a place of liberation and safety, see 3:1. Again Jesus and John are linked. The setting recalls God feeding the people after their escape from political oppression in Egypt (cf. 14:1-12) and links Moses and Jesus (see 5:1; Exod 16; and the sabbath controversy in Matt 12:1-8).

His **withdrawal** means further ministry. Though God's empire is opposed, Jesus does not stop being faithful to his commission (1:21-23; 4:17). Moreover, in contrast to the elite, his withdrawal shows some to be receptive to his ministry. **But when the crowds heard it, they followed him on foot from the towns**. See 4:25; 8:1; 12:15 (also after withdrawing from danger from the religious elite). Although mobile, **the crowds** do not share the disciples' call and commitment. They are open, not hostile (though 9:23-25), to Jesus' ministry, unlike the elite. Perhaps also they keep Jesus safe, as they have done for John (14:5).

• 14:14

When he went ashore, he saw a great crowd; and he had compassion for them. For **compassion** as the motivation for Jesus' ministry, see 9:36. The link to 9:36 recalls its description of the people as "sheep without a shepherd" and its evoking of Ezek 34. The shepherds/leaders in Ezek 34 are condemned partly because they feed themselves but deprive others of food (Ezek 34:2, 8; so also the elite in Aspendus; see Philostratus, *Apollonius* 1.8; cf. Matt 12:1-8), and they do not heal the sick (34:4, 16). Ezekiel 34 declares that God will do these tasks, along with the Davidic prince (34:10, 14, 23-24, 29). Jesus as a son of David (9:27; 12:23) does God's will in expressing compassion and in doing both tasks of healing and supplying food (12:1-14). **And he healed their sick**, see 4:23-25; 8:16; 9:35; 12:15. On **healed**, see 4:23-24. The term **sick** means **powerless** (BAGD, 109). Jesus continues his work with the marginal, those without options, victims of the imperial world. His healings anticipate the wholeness that marks the establishment of God's empire (*2 Bar* 73:1-2; 74:1-2). See 4:23-24; chapters 8-9. Unlike Nazareth, there is at least some faith evident (cf. 13:58).

• 14:15

When it was evening (the time of previous miracles, see 8:16), **the disciples approached him** (with respect; see 8:2), **saying, "This is a deserted place/wilderness** (see 14:13), **and the hour is now late; send the crowds away so that they may go into the villages and buy food for themselves."** The disciples assume (or hope) that the village markets will be able to cope with crowds of five thousand plus. Contrary to Jesus' teaching, they look first to the imperial economy to supply the need, rather than to God (6:25-34). Note the frequent claim that the emperor, and through him various gods, is responsible for blessing the empire with adequate food. Statius (*Silv* 5.1.79-107) praises Domitian for doing so, while the coins of Titus and Domitian claim that the gods Annona and Ceres manifest their approval for these emperors in adequate grain supplies.[13] To the contrary, the scene asserts that the earth and its produce belong to and are supplied not by the empire and its elite but by God the creator (Lev 25:23; Ps 24:1; also Matt 6:25-34; 12:1-8; 15:31-39).

• 14:16

Jesus said to them, "They need not go away; you (emphasized with a pronoun) **give them something to eat."** Instead of trusting the village markets, Jesus puts the challenge back onto the disciples to practice what they have supposedly learned (13:51; 6:24-34). The scene echoes 2 Kgs 4:42-43 in which at Elisha's instruction, one hundred people are miraculously fed from twenty loaves and grain, with some surplus.

• 14:17

But the disciples don't have a plan. **They replied, "We have nothing here but five loaves and two fish."** For other protests in food-multiplying miracles, see 1 Kgs 17:11-13 (Elijah and the widow of Zarephath); 2 Kgs 4:43 (Elisha); Num 11 (where the wilderness people crave meat and fish [11:4-5, 22]). Recall the household scene of Matt 7:9-10 involving bread and fish as staples. The source of the food is not identified, nor is it clear how the disciples came to have possession of it.

• 14:18-19

Jesus takes control as the host of a meal. The contrast with Herod's banquet is stark (14:6-11). Whereas Herod and the elite trade in manipulation, immorality, and death, Jesus' meal includes the crowds, promotes their well-being with healing the sick and supplying adequate food, and anticipates God's different future, God's new creation and empire, in which there is abundance for all (*2 Bar* 73-74). Whereas the disciples look to the village markets, Jesus trusts God's power to supply what they need (6:25-34). **And he said, "Bring them here to me." Then he ordered the crowds to sit down on the grass. Taking the five loaves and two fish, he looked up to heaven** (the dwelling place of God; see 5:34), **and blessed and broke the loaves, and gave them to the disciples, and the disciples gave them to the crowds.** The language of **taking, loaves, blessed, broke, gave to disciples, ate, all** recurs in the Last Supper scene of 26:26-27. Jesus, aided by God's power and the disciples, does God's will of feeding the hungry (cf. 25:35, 37, 42, 44). He acts according to his prayer of 6:11. He does a Godlike thing. Just as God fed the people in the exodus wilderness (Exod 16), Jesus feeds this wilderness people by multiplying the available resources and distributing them so that all have enough.

• 14:20

And all ate and were satisfied. See Pss 107:9; 132:15. In the beatitude of 5:6, hungering and thirsting are caused by injustice and the lack of resources and are directed toward justice/righteousness, namely, God's intervention and reign, which will reverse the situation. God promises satisfaction. This scene glimpses and anticipates the establishment of that empire and new creation in which there is plenty for all (*1 En* 10:18-20; *Sib. Or.* 3:619-23, 741-61; *2 Bar* 29:4-8) and wholeness (*2 Bar* 74:1-2). See 6:11; 12:1-8; 15:31-39. Jesus demonstrates his lordship over food resources, just as he has shown his author- ity, and thereby God's empire, over the sabbath, disease, sin, demons, people's lives, nature, and the sea (chs. 8-9; 12). His actions criticize the elite who con- trol and misuse the food supply. In Ezek 34 the leaders fail to provide food for the sheep/people but keep it for themselves (34:2-3). God's intervention saves the sheep from "forceful and harsh rule" (34:4), darkness (34:12; see Matt 4:15- 16), and hunger, in supplying them with abundant food and pasture (Ezek 34:13-14, 26-29). Jesus shepherds God's people (see 2:6; 9:36).

And they took up what was left over of the broken pieces, twelve bas- kets full. There is surplus in the miracles of Elijah (1 Kgs 17:16) and Elisha (2 Kgs 4:6-7, 44). God is more than able to meet these needs. In 14:19-20 the disciples act as servants, a basic identity and praxis in the community of disci- ples (6:24; 10:24-25; 20:27).

• 14:21
And those who ate were five thousand men, besides women and chil- dren. The greatness of the miracle is underlined not by the responses of the crowd but by its size and inclusivity. Women, children, and men benefit from his action.

14:22-33—JESUS WALKS ON THE WATER

God's saving power is revealed to the disciples through Jesus as he controls the sea and rescues them and the doubting Peter. Jesus performs a series of Godlike acts, which manifest God's reign and show that the God who saved the people from oppression in Egypt by parting the sea (Exod 14) and feeding the people (Exod 16), and from Babylon (cf. the water in Isa 43:2, 16; 44:27; 49:10; 51:10) is at work through Jesus in this context of (Roman) imperial con- trol.[14] The scene also instructs disciples about reliance on Jesus' power in tough times. These momentous events again occur in an unimportant, insignificant place, away from the notice of or the supervision of important urban centers. It is in places marginal to the center that God's reign and power are especially manifested.

• 14:22
The expression of Jesus' authority, first over the disciples (**immediately he made the disciples get into the boat and go on ahead to the other side**) and then over the crowds (**he dismissed the crowds**, repeated for emphasis in 14:23), is appropriate following 14:13-21 and as preparation for this scene. The disciples are dismissed first to suggest a long period of time before they meet again in 14:25-26. Links between this scene and the miraculous healings and feeding of the previous scene are created by references to the **boat** (14:13), **disciples** (14:15, 19), and **crowds** (14:14, 15, 19, 21). Though the order is

reversed, there is perhaps a further echo of the exodus: the parting of the waters in Exod 14, the feeding in Exod 16? The **boat** has been prominent in several scenes around the Sea of Galilee: the call of the first disciples (4:21-22); calming the storm (8:23-24); the return from the exorcism in Gadara (9:1); telling parables (13:2; cf. 15:39). The disciples' previous experience in the storm (8:23-27) left them wondering "What kind of man is this?" This scene gives the audience the chance to see how much understanding they have acquired, especially after the confident declaration of 13:51-52 (cf. 13:11-17).

• 14:23

And after he had dismissed the crowds, he went up the mountain by himself to pray. The clause **he went up the mountain** repeats 5:1 and evokes Moses' ascent of Sinai, where he prays (Exod 32:30-34; 34:8-9). It also alludes to worship on Mt Zion (Isa 2:2-3; see Matt 5:1). For mountains as places of divine presence and rule, revelation, prayer, worship, and eschatological significance, see 5:1. This is the first scene involving a **mountain** since Jesus' descent in 8:1 at the end of the Sermon on the Mount. Jesus obeys his own teaching on secret prayer (6:5-6). Presumably from 6:7-15, he prays for the hallowing of God's name, the coming of God's empire, the doing of God's will, the provision of food and forgiveness, and for trust that God will accomplish God's purposes. The subsequent miracle derives from his relationship with God (cf. 11:25-27), hallows God's name, and expresses God's empire and will (see on 6:7-15). **When evening came** (so 14:15; 8:16) **he was there alone**. The repeated reference to Jesus being **by himself** and **alone** emphasizes his separation from the disciples, in preparation for the epiphany.

• 14:24

The focus returns to the disciples whom Jesus sent across the lake (14:22). **But by this time the boat, battered by the waves,** (so 8:24) **was far from the land, for the wind** (8:26-27) **was against them**. The disciples are a long way from shore and from Jesus (**far from the land**), impeded by the wind. For the stormy sea as the powers of evil and chaos in rebellion against God's rule, see 8:24. This is a dangerous world, apparently out of control, threatening to crush disciples. The verb **battered** evokes political tyranny; its use is pervasive in 2 and 4 Maccabees in relation to torture from Antiochus Epiphanes (see 8:6; also 8:29 in the conflict with demons). A cognate word, "pains" (see 4:24), suggests not only sickness but physical distress or torment from imperial presence. Storms of political tyranny, physical distress, and demonic activity (for demons and the sea, see 8:24) oppose disciples. But storms also anticipate theophanies or revelations of God (Exod 19:16; Ezek 1:4). Distress at sea anticipates God's rescue (Exod 14:13-31; Ps 107:23-32; Jonah 1:1-16; Matt 8:23-27).

• 14:25

They left in the evening (14:15; 14:22 "immediately"). Nearly the whole night has passed before Jesus joins them. **And very early in the morning** (literally, "in the fourth watch of the night") **Jesus came walking toward them**

on the sea. The timing of **early in the morning** evokes the deliverance from
Pharaoh, since the rescue from the sea occurs "at the morning watch" (Exod
14:24). **Walking on the sea** is something God does, expressive of God's sovereignty over the sea and creation. See Job 9:8 (same verb "walking" as here);
Ps 77:16-20, the exodus (same word "sea" as here). That this is an activity of
God, not of humans, is underlined by God's challenge to Job ("Have you
walked in the recesses of the deep?" Job 38:16). In **walking on the sea** Jesus
does what God does. He manifests God's presence and demonstrates God's
reign over the sea and all the opposing forces it represents. He removes what
impedes the disciples, enabling them to cross the sea.

The scene has a polemical edge. Numerous writers claim that emperors like
Domitian are "ruler of lands and seas and nations" (Juvenal, *Sat* 4.83-84). See
Matt 8:26, 11:25, 28:18.

• 14:26

And when the disciples saw him walking on the sea (the repetition emphasizes Jesus' action), **they were terrified**, as the sea is in Ps 77:16 when God
approaches (Isa 51:15; Herod in Matt 2:3, when Jesus, Immanuel, God with us,
threatens his world), **saying, "It is a ghost!"** The term is unusual, only here in
the New Testament and twice in the LXX (see Wis 17:15, discussing the Egyptians' fear in the exodus). The link between demons and the sea (see 8:24) perhaps accounts for their verdict and fear, **And they cried out in fear**. To **cry out**
can indicate resistance (8:29) or hope (9:27). **Fear** accompanies epiphanies in
1:20; 9:8; cf. Exod 3:6 (Moses).

• 14:27

**But immediately he spoke to them and said, "Take heart; I am; do not
be afraid."** Jesus' appearance does not mean an instant miracle. Initially he
assures the disciples. His first words are familiar (**Take heart**) and invoke
God's power and presence, see 9:2. Jesus identifies himself by talking as God
talks. He quotes God's statement of revelation, **I am**. See Exod 3:14 (to Moses
before the exodus); Isa 41:4; 43:10; 47:8, 10, to Israel in exile anticipating the
deliverance of the second exodus and return home. It reveals God's saving presence (so Jesus' commission of 1:21; also 11:25-27) in circumstances of distress.
Fear not often follows appearances or words of angels or God to assure
humans that God's purposes are good (Gen 15:1; Isa 43:1-2, 5; with water in
43:2, and "I am" in 43:3, 11, 15, 25).

• 14:28

Peter takes a central role. **Peter answered him, "Lord, if/since it is you,
command me to come to you on the water."** This is the fourth reference to
Peter. He is the first disciple to be called (4:18), Jesus heals his mother-in-law
(8:14), and he is the first to be named in the list of the twelve (10:2). These three
references give him some prominence (Andrew, James, John, and Matthew are
mentioned twice [4:18-22; 9:9; 10:2-4]; the other seven only once) and antici-

pates his subequent prominent roles. His initiative here is the first of several scenes between chapter 14 and chapter 19 which show his prominence among the disciples (16:22-23; 18:21), as their spokesperson (15:15; 16:16; 19:27), as specifically addressed by Jesus (16:18; 17:24-25), as Jesus' special companion (17:1, 4), as a typical disciple evidencing how (and how not) to be a disciple. The passion narrative will continue and expand these roles (26:33, 35, 37, 40, 58, 69, 73, 75).[15]

Peter's address is submissive yet daring. Though perhaps tinged with some doubt (**if/since it is you**) he calls Jesus **Lord**, recognizing that Jesus manifests and participates in God's rule over all creation. He asks permission (**command me**) to imitate Jesus in walking **on the water** (cf. 10:24-25). The request recognizes and trusts Jesus' authority over the sea.

• 14:29

"Come." So Peter got out of the boat (obediently and faithfully) **and walked** (same verb as for Jesus in 14:25-26) **on the waters and came toward Jesus**. Jesus' response shows him to have the authority to enable others to overcome the chaotic evil. Peter imitates Jesus, as disciples should (10:24-25).

• 14:30

But after a good start, Peter falters. **But when he noticed the strong wind** (so 14:24), **he became frightened** (cf. 10:28; 14:27), **and beginning to sink** (like a stone), **he cried out, "Lord save me."** Peter's cry quotes Ps 69:1, which also employs language of stormy seas and threatening waters, and the same verb **cried out** (69:3; see also 69:14-16). The disciples use these same words in 8:25. Paradoxically, Peter exhibits faith and a lack of faith.

• 14:31

Jesus extended/reached out his hand and caught him. Jesus' **hands** have been instruments of healing (8:3, 15; 9:18, 25) and of identifying disciples (12:49). Now they save a disciple. God's extended hand (same phrase) delivers people from oppressive slavery (Exod 3:20; 7:5) and from water and other difficulties (Ps 144:7). Moses stretches out his hand in liberating the people (Exod 4:4; 8:5, 6; 9:22 etc.). The phrase "stretch out one's hand" can also signify acts of danger from which humans need saving by God's outstretched hand (Gen 3:22; 22:10-11). So in **extending his hand** to save Peter, Jesus again does what God does (cf. walking on the water [14:25-26]; talking as God [14:27]). He continues to manifest God's empire in showing God's sovereignty over the world God created. **Extending his hand** enables Jesus to accomplish a further action of God. God saves distressed people from water. See Exod 14:13-31; Isa 43:15-16; 51:10 (rescue from Babylonian exile as a new exodus); Ps 107:23-32; Jonah 1-2 (cf. Matt 12:41); *T. Naph.* 6; Wis 14:2-7; 1QH 3:6, 12-18; 6:22-25). As Immanuel, so does Jesus.

Jesus speaks to Peter, first with a rebuke (**You of little faith**) and then a question (**why did you doubt?**). The rebuke **You of little faith** (see 6:30; 8:26) recognizes that Peter exercises some faith in obediently starting to walk on the water and in crying out as he began to sink. But he did not have enough faith in Jesus' word to persevere (cf. 10:22) in trusting Jesus' authority to overcome the stormy waves and winds. He trusted the waves and wind more to sink him than he trusted Jesus' word to empower him to walk on the water. His little faith meant that he was distracted and overwhelmed (cf. 17:14-20). Peter will not have learned this lesson by the time of Jesus' death (ch. 26), when he again focuses on the opposing forces rather than on Jesus' power. For **faith** as reliance on Jesus' word despite opposition, see 8:10, 13; 9:2, 22, 28-29. Faith divides disciples from the religious leaders and the crowds.

• 14:32

When they (Jesus and Peter) **got into the boat, the wind ceased**. The calming of storms is also God's work. See 14:31; also Job 26:11-12; Pss 89:9-10, (connected to destroying enemies); 107: 23-32; Sir 43:23; for God **ceasing** the rain after the flood, see Gen 8:1, 11; for Jonah and the **ceasing** of the storm, see Jonah 1:11-12. Jesus does not give a direct order (as in 8:26b) but his presence is responsible for the calm. For the fifth time in the scene (walking on water, talking as God, extending hand, saving from water, calming the storm), Jesus does a Godlike act, manifesting God's reign over the sea. The sea is subdued and set in its place as God intended it (Gen 1:6-13). This is another in a series of references to restoring creation under God's reign: the notion of rest in Matt 11:28, sabbath (12:1-8), the abundant yield (13:8, 23), plentiful food (14:20), the subdued sea. See 1:1.

• 14:33

And those in the boat worshiped him, saying, "Truly you are a son of God." The disciples' response is typical of responses to other epiphanies and rescues from the sea (Exod 14:31; Ps 107:31-32; Jonah 1:16) but vastly different from the end of the last storm scene (Matt 8:27). There they were left wondering who Jesus was. Now, after six chapters of accompanying and listening to Jesus, they understand much more. They discern from his actions (so 11:2-6) that Jesus is **God's son or child**. Their verdict, so different from the unrepentant towns (11:20-24), religious leaders (12:24), the synagogue crowd (13:54-56), and the murderous Roman puppet Herod (14:2), agrees with God's perspective on Jesus (see 2:15; 3:17; cf. 4:3, 6; 8:29) and with Jesus' self-disclosure (see 11:27). To name him **God's son** is to recognize him as the agent God has commissioned to reveal God's saving presence and empire, and who enjoys a special relationship with God (see 1:21-23; 4:17; 11:25-27). They have discerned in his five actions of walking on the water, of speaking God's words, of stretching out his hand, of rescuing Peter, and of calming the storm actions that God performs. In **worshiping** him, they align themselves with the marginal and subversive magi (see 2:2, 11), the leper (8:2), and the leader (9:18), directing their loyalty not to emperors and kings (see 4:9), not to the devil (so 4:9-10), but to God's anointed, who manifests God's saving presence and reign.

14:34-36—JESUS' COMPASSIONATE HEALING

• 14:34

This verse completes the sea scene and provides a transition to the next. **When they had crossed over** (so 9:1), **they came to land at Gennesaret**, perhaps the town rather than the plain[16] because the next verse refers to "place" and "region."

• 14:35-36

And after the people of that place recognized him, they sent throughout that whole region and brought to him all that were sick. The verb **recognized** appears twice in 11:27 indicating the relationship of father and son, and Jesus' revelation of the father. Is the audience to understand that these people, like the disciples in 14:33, discerned God's presence and reign in Jesus (so 11:2-6), or did they recognize Jesus only as a miracle worker who feeds and heals people (14:13-21)?

Perhaps the latter is more sustainable. The description of Jesus' activity follows, rather than precedes, their recognition. Jesus' actions involve healing but no proclamation or faith (8:10, 13; 9:2, 22, 28-29). The scene in fact resembles the other summary healing scenes (4:23-25; 8:16; 9:35; 12:15; 14:14), with which it shares key vocabulary (**brought, sick** [4:24; 8:16]; **all** [4:24; 8:16; 14:35]). The crowds are open to and benefit from Jesus' display of God's reign without committing themselves to him or discerning his role in God's purposes. The scene then exemplifies his compassion to the nonelite (14:14; cf. 9:36) more than it does their faith or discipleship. **And they begged him** (used variously in 8:5, 31, 34) **that they might touch even the fringe of his cloak** (cf. 9:21; 23:5); **and all who touched it were healed**. This compound of the verb "save" reminds the audience that Jesus' mission of saving from sin (1:21) is enacted in his healings (see 4:23-24), which anticipate the wholeness that will mark the establishment of God's reign in full (*2 Bar* 73:1-2).

CHAPTER 15

Jesus' Authority as God's Agent

Four scenes continue the focus of the third narrative block (11:2-16:20) on discerning Jesus' identity (see 11:2-6):

> 15:1-20   Jesus Denounces the Religious Leaders
> 15:21-28   Jesus and the Canaanite Woman
> 15:29-31   Summary of Healing (cf. 11:2-6)
> 15:32-39   Jesus Feeds the Four Thousand

In each scene Jesus demonstrates his authority as God's agent commissioned to manifest God's saving presence and empire (1:21, 23; 4:17). Some discern this identity while others do not.

15:1-20—JESUS DENOUNCES THE RELIGIOUS LEADERS

These verses divide into three subscenes with three audiences:

> 15:1-9   Jesus and the scribes and Pharisees in conflict
> 15:10-11   Jesus explains to the crowd
> 15:12-20   Jesus teaches the disciples

The section begins with the religious leaders' question (15:2), Why do the disciples not wash their hands before eating? Jesus refers to this issue again in v. 20. In between are references to the use of *korban* ("gift") to evade parental support (see 15:4-6) and to purity and defilement (κοινόω, *koinoō* [15:11, 18, 20]).

How does the material connect? Central is the issue of who reveals and lives God's will, the Pharisees and scribes as members of the ruling elite and allies with the imperial status quo, or Jesus and the disciples. Jesus, commissioned by God, attacks their "tradition" as being contrary to, rather than faithful to, God's word which he presents (15:3, 6, 9). He attacks them also as "blind" and false. They are not legitimated by God (15:13-14). Their status, or lack thereof, is confirmed in that they do not discern Jesus' identity as God's agent but are scandalized by his attack (15:12). In contrast, the disciples model the desired response in seeking to understand Jesus' teaching (15:12-20). This polemic may well reflect the struggle of Matthew's community(ies) with the leadership of a synagogue in Antioch over the value of the Pharisees' tradition. Jesus thinks that it has little value because it is at odds with God's will. He resists the way in which they use their power over people's lives. As with the sabbath in 12:1-8, Jesus does not abolish hand washing and purity concerns, but reinterprets them in relation to the heart's lived commitment to God's will, which he reveals.[1]

• **15:1**

The introductory verb and initially unspecified subject (**Then they approached Jesus**) create ambiguity. The verb describes the approach to Jesus of both opponents (the devil [4:3] and a scribe [8:19]) and of those allied with Jesus (angels [4:11], disciples [5:1; 8:25; 13:10, 36; 14:15], a leper [8:2], a centurion [8:5], John's disciples [9:14; 14:12], a woman [9:20], two blind men [9:28], servants [13:27]). The phrase **from Jerusalem** is also ambiguous. While the political and religious elite in Jerusalem are hostile and resistant to Jesus (2:1-12; cf. 16:21 [Jesus' death]), others from Jerusalem respond positively to both his and John's preaching (3:5; 4:25). Jerusalem remains God's city (5:35, Zion), a "holy city" set apart to serve God (4:5; 27:53), the object of mission (10:23).

But naming the **Pharisees and scribes** (5:20; 12:38; 16:21) as the verb's subject removes the ambiguity. References to both have been negative: on **Pharisees**, see 3:7; 5:20; 9:11, 14, 34; 12:2, 14, 24, 38; on **scribes**, see 2:4; 5:20; 7:29; 8:19; 9:3; 12:38; contrast 13:52. See Introduction, sections 1 and 5, for their involvement in the ruling elite and alliance with Rome. They are religious leaders opposed to God's purposes manifested in Jesus. In this third narrative block (11:2-16:20), they plan to kill Jesus (12:14; cf. 16:21), discern Satan, not God, to be at work in him (12:24), and demand further signs (12:38; 16:1-4). They are "bad shepherds" who oppress and exploit the people and are faithless to their responsibilities (see 9:36; 12:2).

• **15:2**

They question Jesus: **Why do your disciples transgress the tradition of the elders?** As in 12:1-8 they do not attack Jesus directly but take issue with the disciples' practice, which they claim is at odds with **the tradition of the elders**. This **tradition** (mentioned only in 15:2, 3, 6) consists, according to Josephus (*Ant* 13.297), of "certain regulations handed down by former generations and not recorded in the law of Moses."[2] This extrabiblical material guides the Pharisees' practice. The defining phrase **of the elders** appeals to various unnamed past leaders who authorize the instructions and practices. While authoritative for the Pharisees, other groups such as the Sadducees (Josephus, *Ant* 13.297-98) and the Qumran community (1QH 4:14-15) did not find it authoritative. Jesus' critique is not unique.

They sustain their accusation with a specific example of the disciples' violation: **For they do not wash their hands when they eat.** Washing of hands (and feet) was required of priests to remove defilement before entering the tent of meeting (Exod 30:19-21). Leviticus 15:11 requires hand washing by one with a bodily discharge so as not to contaminate others. Hand washing absolves from guilt (Deut 21:6) and precedes prayer (*Ep. Arist.* 305-6; *Sib. Or.* 3.591-95). But there does not seem to be a biblical instruction requiring hand washing before meals. The Pharisees' valuing of this practice derives from their tradition. It may reflect their understanding that Israel was a nation of priests and that all of life should be lived in service to God (Exod 19:6), and that temple purity rules should be extended into everyday life such as meals.[3]

• 15:3

Jesus, though, sees not an extension of God's will but its avoidance (cf. 12:1-8). He responds to their accusatory question with a countercharge: **And why do you transgress the commandment of God because of your tradition?** His question juxtaposes **God's commandment** and **your tradition** (for the distinction, see *T. Levi* 14:4; *T. Ash.* 7:5). He accuses them of **transgressing** or "turning aside from" or "breaking" God's commandment (BAGD, 611). But he does not explain how requiring hand washing is a transgression. Perhaps it is because they misrepresent it as God's commandment when it derives only from **your tradition.** Rather he offers an example of their breaking God's commandment (15:3) by withholding support from parents.[4]

• 15:4-5

Jesus provides an example (**for**) of his condemnation of their elevation of the tradition. The example, not about hand washing, highlights a clash between God's commandment and a practice of evasionary vows concerning property. Presumably the argument moves by analogy. Jesus quotes two scripture passages. The first cites Moses' words from Exod 20:12 and Deut 5:16: **For God commanded, "Honor your father and your mother."** Jesus does not abolish the law and the prophets (see 5:17), but affirms the commandment. A second, comparable citation from Exod 21:17 and Lev 20:9 emphasizes the point, **Let the one who speaks ill of father or mother surely die.** On ambivalent household relations, see 4:18-22; 8:14, 21-22; 12:46-50.

In contrast to what **God says**, the religious leaders have a different teaching and practice: **But you say, whoever tells father or mother, "Whatever support you might have had from me is an offering/gift (korban) to God," that person certainly[5] need not honor his father (or mother).** Jesus refers to a practice called *korban*, in which people made offerings or gifts to God, priests, the temple, and so on, including offering themselves and then fulfilling the vow by redeeming themselves with a payment (cf. Lev 2:1; 27:1-8; Num 7:11-12; Josephus, *Ant* 4.72-73).[6] Vows or oaths of such gifts had to be kept (Num 30:2-5). The Pharisees teach that people could deny benefits to others from their "possessions by declaring them to be (like) a *Korban*."[7] Here their teaching supports a son who avoids his duty to provide economic support for needy parents by declaring that support to be *korban*.

Jesus opposes the practice on several grounds: (1) it involves a vow, against which Jesus has already spoken (see 5:33-37); (2) it enables people to bypass God's explicitly stated will of honoring one's parents by providing economic support. The wording **need not honor his father** imitates and negates the commandment from Exod 20:12 and Deut 5:16; and (3) the religious leaders and institutions encourage the abuse of the elderly/needy in depriving them of the means of life. This religious/economic act sustains injustice and parallels acts of the social and political elite who oppress the poor by depriving them of necessities. Jesus again sides with those marginalized by such practices in protesting the center's exploitation of them. He shapes a different and just praxis.

We have noted ambivalent attitudes to households in the gospel. James and John leave their father and family fishing business to follow (see 4:21-22). Jesus redefines families, not in terms of birth but in terms of doing the will of God as interpreted by Jesus (see 12:46-50). Yet along with such disruption, following him means here adequate support for parents.

• 15:6

Jesus concludes: **So for the sake of your tradition, you make void the word of God**. God's word or will requires parents to be honored (including with economic support), but the practice of *korban* advocated by the Pharisees' tradition voids God's requirements. For the second time, Jesus juxtaposes their tradition with God's word (15:3).

• 15:7-9

Jesus appeals to scripture to confirm his verdict. He addresses the religious leaders directly: **You hypocrites** (see 6:2, 5, 16; 7:5). They play the public role of religious commitment but it is a false image. They avoid doing God's will in their social practices (5:20).

The scripture comes from Isaiah: **Isaiah rightly prophesied about you**. Isaiah is named for the sixth time (see 3:3; 4:14; 8:17; 12:17; 13:14). The previous citations have come from imperial contexts in Isa 6-9 (Assyria—Matt 1:23; 4:14; 13:14) and Isa 40-55 (Babylon—Matt 3:3; 8:17; 12:17). This one from Isa 29:13 (closer to the LXX than to the MT) concerns the judgment Assyria will enact on Judah (chs. 28-32) before Assyria itself is judged (Isa 33). Rome enacts this punishment on the leaders in the fall of Jerusalem in 70 C.E.

Though the prophecy is addressed to eighth-century Judah, Jesus understands it to refer to the Pharisees (**rightly prophesied about you**) since they share with Judah the characteristic of hypocrisy. While the citation begins with **this people**, the referent in this context is not all Israel but **the Pharisees and scribes**. Jesus has different things to say to the crowds (15:10-11) and disciples (15:12-20).

The verse's two contrasting clauses highlight hypocrisy. The leaders **honor me with their lips but their heart is far from me**. For the **heart** as the center of a person's willing, thinking, knowing, deciding, and doing, see 5:8, 28; 6:21; 11:29. There are three previous negative references to evil hearts. In 9:4 Jesus confronts the unbelieving scribes about thinking "evil in your hearts" after he has performed his God-given task of saving from sin by announcing forgiveness (cf. 1:21). In 12:34, after the Pharisees declare that Jesus casts out demons by Beelzeboul (12:24), Jesus notes that they speak from evil hearts. And in 13:19 he observes Satan's work in snatching away "the word of the kingdom" from the dull-hearted, those who do not understand.

The condemnation is restated, first in relation to false worship (**in vain do they worship me**) and then in relation to their false teaching (**teaching human**

precepts as doctrine). For the third time Jesus does not recognize their tradition as God's word (15:3, 6). The use of **human** (ἀνθρώπων, *anthrōpōn*) is especially derogatory. The term denotes not merely human beings (5:19; 7:9; 13:24; etc.) but nonfollowers (4:19) or society in general (5:13, 16; 6:1) among whom disciples live and conduct their mission (10:32-3), and from whom they often experience rejection (10:17). Their precepts or traditions originate from humans, not God, and from those who often reject God's purposes.

• 15:10-11

The exchange between Jesus and the Pharisees and scribes has ended with Jesus quoting scripture. The religious leaders vanish, though their reaction is reported in v. 12. Jesus does not dismiss them. The authority he has just demonstrated in his teaching is now exhibited in **summoning/calling** (cf. 10:1 [disciples]) **the crowd to him**. The **crowd,** though the recipients of Jesus' ministry (4:25; 9:36), often lacks both the understanding and faith of disciples (cf. 12:23; 13:10-17; 8:18, 23, 26; 12:46; 14:31), as well as the hostility and resistance of the religious leaders.[8]

Jesus' appeal (**Listen and understand**) is strange, given that this is precisely what the crowd generally cannot do (see 13:13-14 [also quoting Isaiah]; 13:23). Yet at times the crowd has discerned Jesus' authority (7:28; 9:8, 33). Jesus maintains a compassionate mission to it (9:35-38; 14:13-21), and some separate themselves from the crowd to act as disciples (see 8:2; 17:14). Jesus has not given up on the crowd.

Jesus' words are enigmatic, even if the crowd has witnessed the conflict of 15:1-9 (why does he need to summon them?): **it is not what goes into the mouth that defiles a person but it is what comes out of the mouth that defiles**. The saying introduces the key verb **defiles**. Jesus emphasizes moral rather than cultic defilement. As noted, purity issues underlie the hand washing question in 15:2.

• 15:12

Jesus does not explain the saying until vv. 15-20. In the meantime there are two developments. First, there are new characters: **then the disciples approached and said to him**. For the verb **approach**, see 15:1 (cf. 4:3). As in 13:10, 36, the disciples seek clarification of Jesus' teaching (15:15). In both those instances they engage him apart from the crowds. It seems then that 15:12-20 is instruction not for the crowds but for disciples.

Second (15:12-14), they report **that the Pharisees** (no scribes, 15:1) **were scandalized/caused to sin when they heard this saying**. Presumably the **saying** refers to Jesus' condemnation in 15:3-9, but the narrative context suggests that 15:11 should be included also (though addressed to the crowds). The verb **scandalized/caused to sin** (see 5:29-30) appeared in 11:6 in the key scene of this third narrative block as a negative response to Jesus. To be **scandalized** is to not recognize from his words and work that he is God's agent. The religious leaders do not discern Jesus' identity or accept his saying. They are cursed (11:6). Those who sin in this way face eschatological condemnation (13:41).

• 15:13-14

Jesus declares judgment on them: **Every plant which my heavenly Father has not planted will be rooted up**. Previous plant metaphors have exhorted the Pharisees to change their way of life or face judgment (3:7-10; 12:33-37). The image of **planting** commonly denotes God's election of the people and its right-eous way of life.[9] But Jesus does not recognize them, their traditions, and their practices, as **my heavenly Father's** work (see 5:16, 45, 48; 6:9; 7:21 [my Father]; 10:32). An issue of different practice has resulted in a pronouncement of divine rejection (see 3:7; 12:34, for an insult about their origin). **My** underlines the intimate relationship between Jesus and God (cf. 11:25-30), the basis for Jesus' pronouncement of God's verdict. On **heaven** as God's abode and the origin of God's empire, see 3:2, 16; 4:17; 5:34. These ones who are not faithful to God's word (15:3, 6, 9) will be **rooted up** (passive, by God) at the judgment (cf. 13:29-30; Jer 1:10; 12:17; 18:7). That is, Jesus' words announce now God's verdict at the judgment. In the meantime disciples are to **Let them alone** in accord with 13:24-30, 36-43, 47-50.

Jesus then changes the metaphor. Using standard polemic,[10] he designates the leaders as **blind guides** who do not know the way (cf. Isa 56:10-11; 59:10) and therefore mislead others. **And if a blind man leads a blind man, both will fall into a pit**—an image of disaster (Ps 7:15; Prov 26:27; *T. Reu.* 2:9; cf. Matt 12:11) and judgment (Isa 24:18; Jer 48:44) for the unrepentant wicked.

• 15:15-16

Having declared the Pharisees to be not commissioned by God, pronounced judgment on them (15:13), and declared their teaching misleading and destruc-tive (15:14), Jesus returns to the enigmatic v. 11. **Peter** asks him to **explain the parable/riddle** (see introduction to ch. 13) **to us**. Compare 13:36, which sug-gests that the **us** consists only of disciples. **Peter** is the spokesperson (see 14:28), appropriately here following the dismissal of the Pharisees' teaching and in preparation for his role in 16:18 in relation to Jesus' teaching. Jesus' response (**Are you still without understanding?**) rebukes them because they should know (13:11, 51). The emphasis on **understanding** Jesus' teaching of God's will separates disciples from the crowds (15:11; 13:10-17) and scandalized Pharisees (15:12).

• 15:17-18

Jesus elaborates the first part of v. 11 (**it is not what goes into the mouth that defiles a person**) in v. 17, and the second part (**but it is what comes out of the mouth that defiles**) in vv. 18-19.

Do you not see that whatever goes into the mouth enters the stomach, and goes out into the sewer? The reference is to food and drink. The claim that food does not defile (15:11) runs contrary to an extensive Jewish tradition which affirmed that some food did defile (Lev 11; Deut 14). Faithful observance expressed Jewish identity especially in the diaspora (Dan 1:8-17; Tob 1:10-13; cf. Tacitus, *Hist* 5.4-5; Philo, *Gaium* 361-62), in circumstances of imperial threat

(1 Macc 1:44-50, 62-63; 2 Macc 6:18-31; 7:1-2; Jdt 12:2, 19), and in danger from other Jewish groups (1QS 5:13-14; 6:13-23).

Does this statement mean, as some argue, that Matthew's Jesus has revoked the purity laws?[11] That reading is possible, but unlikely in the light of both 5:17-20 and the absence of a direct attack on Jesus for doing so. Jesus does not say that what goes into the mouth should be ignored, but that **it goes out.** Its impact is temporary and, as the next verse indicates, of lesser importance. He moves attention to the heart and a person's way of life. Did Matthew's community observe food purity? It seems likely that they did. Gentile believers probably engaged in minimal observance sufficient to ensure table fellowship with Jews (cf. Acts 15:21, 29 and Lev 17-18). The next three verses remind them that observance does not constitute their distinctive identity and way of life.

• **15:18-19**

But what comes out of the mouth proceeds from the heart, and this is what defiles. On **heart** as the center of a person's willing, thinking, knowing, deciding, and doing, see 5:8, 28; 6:21; 11:29; 12:34. Jesus' emphasis reflects God's concern with human commitment (**intentions**) expressed in societal praxis (15:8). **For from the heart come evil intentions, murder, adultery, fornication, theft, false witness, slander.** The **evil intentions** are expressed in six actions on a typical list of vices (cf. Wis 14:22-26; 4 Macc 1:26-27; *T. Reu.* 3:1-7; *T. Levi* 17:11). The list is based on the Decalogue: **murder** (Exod 20:13; cf. Matt 5:21-26), **adultery** (Exod 20:14; cf. Matt 5:27-32); **theft** (Exod 20:15); **false witness** (Exod 20:16; see Matt 19:18; 26:59-60; for evil speech, see 12:33-37). **Fornication**, distinct from adultery, probably means premarital intercourse; compare 5:31-32. There is a polemical edge to the list. The religious leaders are guilty of most of these sins: evil intentions (9:4), murder (12:14; chs. 26-27), adultery (12:38; 16:4), false witnesses (26:60-61), slander (9:34; 11:18-19; 12:24). The commitment of the heart expressed in the actions of daily life matters much more than food purity.

• **15:20**

These (v. 19) **are what defile a person, but to eat with unwashed hands does not defile.** Jesus returns to the accusation that the disciples transgress the tradition (15:2). This reference at the end of the unit draws together the three examples of hand washing (15:2, 20), the *korban* of neglecting parents (15:3-9), and food purity (15:10-11, 15-19). Why does Jesus think this Pharisaic tradition (not the Mosaic law) does not matter? First, hand washing and *korban* are not God's commandment. Second, they focus on things of lesser value, which distract attention from destructive evil, misguided intentions or commitments, and just social practices (cf. 23:23).

15:21-28—JESUS AND THE CANAANITE WOMAN

While the gospel's final word on mission to Gentiles does not come until 28:16-20, this scene continues the emerging theme that ethnicity does not constitute God's people and that believing Gentiles are included in God's purposes. Jesus does not here send disciples or insiders out in mission, but brings an outsider into an ethnically mixed community. The scene recognizes Israel's temporal priority in God's purposes as God's chosen people, but this understanding does not mean that Gentiles are excluded. Jesus a Jew is the agent of God's blessing for this Gentile woman.

The scene locates Jesus in a world of ethnic, cultural, economic, political, and religious barriers. Jesus is not exempt from these prejudices, but God's reign, responsible for wholeness and plenty (14:13-21, 34-36; 15:29-39), breaks them down. The scene continues to present the responsiveness of those on the margins. This Gentile woman is geographically on the margins of Israel (Jesus' focus, 15:24) and is, as a Gentile, marginal in Israel's worldview. As a Canaanite, a member of a cursed people, destined to be subjugated as slaves (Gen 9:25), she belongs to a people dispossessed by Israel's occupation and possession of the land. This Israelite victory was viewed as God's gift, was understood as an expression of Israel's elect status, and was celebrated in Israel's traditions.[12] Yet, though submissive, she challenges this excluding ideology. Her demand for inclusion constitutes her faith, the means by which she encounters the blessing of Israel's God. Jesus commends it as great (15:28), in contrast to Peter's and the disciples' little faith (14:31) and its absence from crowds and religious leaders. Numerous echoes of previous miracle stories (esp. chs. 8-9) recall significant themes.[13]

• 15:21

Jesus left that place and withdrew. This is a transition verse. On the verb **withdrew**, see 14:13. Jesus puts distance (literally) between himself and the Pharisees after condemning their tradition (15:1-20). They remain in their center of power while he moves and withdraws to Gentile territory (cf. 2:14; 4:12-15; 12:18-21) for further ministry. He goes not to a city (centers of rejection [ch. 2; 11:20-24]) but to a rural area, **into**[14] **the district controlled by Tyre and Sidon**. See 11:21-22, where these proverbially wicked Gentile cities, attacked by the prophets, are contrasted positively with nonresponsive Galilean cities, Chorazin and Bethsaida.

• 15:22

And behold (indicating something significant; see 2:1) **a Canaanite woman from that region came out**. Just as Jesus "came out" or left one place (15:21), the woman also "came out." They meet in an unspecified "nowhere" place in the boundary region of Galilee and Tyre-Sidon, the interface of Jewish and Gentile territory. It is a place of tension and prejudice: Josephus declares "the Tyrians are our bitterest enemies" (*Con Ap* 1.70), and there were clashes between Tyrians and Jews in the 60s (*JW* 2.478). Along with ethnic conflict, there are competing religious understandings (Israel is God's chosen people), economic needs (the urban centers Tyre and Sidon require food from rural areas), and political goals. Tyrian political aspirations for further territory and resentment of Roman rule ran high. Josephus notes that many followers of John of Gischala, who revolted against Rome, came from "the region of Tyre" (*JW* 2.588; cf. *Vita* 372).[15] The woman comes not from the cities of Tyre or Sidon but from **that region**, suggesting perhaps her poverty as a rural peasant.

The phrase **behold a woman** recalls Jewish women who benefit from Jesus' actions of healing (9:20-22) and feeding (15:22). She will demand the same blessed treatment. As with many characters, she is unnamed. Nor is she introduced in relation to a male (husband, brother, father). Is she a widow, an orphan, never married, or alienated from her family for some reason? As a **Canaanite** (cf. Rahab in 1:3-5, who also crossed ethnic lines to find a place in God's purposes), she is a Gentile (cf. 8:5-13, 28-34; 12:18-21; cf. Josephus, *Con Ap* 1.70). Her identity evokes the land that God gives the people (Exod 3:8; 6:1-4; 15:15; Num 13:2), a gift at the expense of the Canaanites.

Yet like other Gentiles (2:1-11 [the magi]; 8:5 [the centurion]), she defiantly crosses this ethnic boundary to seek help from a Jewish itinerant teacher and miracle worker. There is no indication of how she heard about Jesus. But, unlike the religious leaders, she has not been scandalized by Jesus (11:6; 15:12). She is the first woman to speak in the gospel; as is common in miracle stories, she **was crying out**, a verb that can denote prayer (8:29; 9:27; 14:26 [with fear], 30). The imperfect tense suggests her persistence. Further, she uses a liturgical phrase to pray: **Have mercy on me** (9:27; 9:13 [consistent with God's will]; 12:7; Pss 6:2; 27:7; 30:10). She calls Jesus **Lord** (as only disciples do; see 8:2, 6, 24) in recognition of his authority over demons (cf. 4:1-11; 17:15), and **son of David,** as do the two blind men (see 9:27-28; 20:30). The latter title recognizes Jesus' links with Israelite and Davidic rule, ideally on behalf of the broken (cf. Ps 72), as well as his miracle-working power (see 9:27).

Yet this submissive posture is only part of her identity. Her petition challenges Jesus' very identity and mission. It confronts Israel's imperialist ideology. She demands that Jesus make available to her what is available to Israel. More accurately, her petition is not for herself (cf. the centurion in 8:5-6) but for Jesus to release her **daughter** (cf. the ruler in 9:18-26) from the forces now possessing her; **my daughter is tormented by a demon**. On demon possession, see 4:24; 8:16, 28, 33; 9:32; 12:22; 17:14-20, for demons as an expression of Satan's resistance to God's will, and of imperial control. She asks that through Jesus' exorcism, God's reign be manifest (12:28). The exorcism is delayed until 15:28, directing attention to her exchanges with Jesus. It is not clear whether the daughter is with her or absent (at home?).

• **15:23**

Jesus responds not with instant help (cf. 8:2-4, 6-7, 14-15, 16, 28-34, etc.) but with silence: **But he did not answer her at all**. The benefits of God's empire do not seem to be available to a Gentile woman. No motive is given, though the ethnic, cultural, religious, economic, and political factors noted above, as well as her gender, suggest numerous reasons for Jesus to ignore her.

The disciples came and urged him. Their request is not clear. Do they ask him to **send her away** (the woman) or to **release/free her** (the daughter)? In Matthew, the verb frequently refers to divorce (1:19; 5:31-32; 19:3, 7, 8, 9); it also means "send away/dismiss" (14:15 [requested by disciples], 22, 23; 15:32, 39) and "release" (18:27; 27:15, 17, 21, 26). The latter option makes better sense of Jesus' next comment, but it would also suggest a significant contrast with their request to dismiss the crowd in 14:15. It would indicate that the disciples have now learned that Jesus can provide assistance. But 15:33 does not support that claim. Probably, then, it should be taken as a statement of rejection: **send her away, for she keeps shouting after us** (because Jesus is ignoring her [v. 23a]). Ironically the disciples have learned well from their master the lesson of exclusive election. They continue (cf. 14:15) not to expect his power to be at work, while she, the marginal person, looks for it.

• 15:24

Jesus explains why he ignores the woman. He does not respond to her because his mission upholds Israel's temporal priority. **I was only sent to the lost sheep of the house of Israel** (Jer 50:6; LXX 27:6). See 9:36; 10:6 for Israel without just leadership (cf. Ezek 34) and for Jesus as a shepherd/ruler (2:6). Jesus' nonresponse underlines Israel's temporal priority in God's purposes, consistent with the geographical limits he places on the disciples (10:5). Yet her request has challenged his ideology of chosenness, which restricts his mission and his disciples' mission to Israel. In the tradition of Abraham, she demands her share in God's blessing for all the world (15:29-39; 1:1-2). Her request protests an excluding focus on Israel and reclaims her place as a Canaanite and a Gentile in God's purposes.[16]

Yet Jesus has not been completely resistant to the notion of benefiting Gentiles per se (so 8:5-13; 10:18; 12:17-21; also 28:16-20). Rather, in the light of this Gentile presence, it seems that his objection concerns whether he will conduct his mission outside Israel now, at this time. Jesus' declaration affirms God's election of Israel, God's faithfulness to God's covenant purposes, Israel's priority in those purposes, Jesus' identity as commissioned by God, and Jesus' persistence in mission to Israel despite the hostility of the religious leaders and the noncommitted interest of the crowds. Israel is not rejected or replaced. But is the Gentile, Canaanite woman included in God's blessing or excluded permanently as a victim of Israel's election?

• 15:25

Undeterred by his nonrecognition of her as a person, the woman initiates a second approach, determined to share in the blessing which Israel's God offers. **But she came and knelt before him**. For kneeling as a recognition of authority, see 2:2, 8, 11; 4:8-9; 8:2; 9:18; 14:33. Again she calls him **Lord** and employs a common liturgical phrase, **help me** (Pss 41:3 [illness]; 44:26 [imperial power and exile]; 94:17 [the wicked]; 109:26 [enemies]). Yet along with this submissiveness, she asks again. She defiantly continues to challenge an ideology of chosenness.

• 15:26

Jesus responds directly to her this time, and again he avoids her request. He repeats his focus on Israel: **It is not fair to take the children's food** (the covenant term "children of Israel" [Exod 4:22; Deut 14:1; cf. Matt 5:9, 45]) **and throw it to the dogs** (opponents, here Gentiles; see 7:6). To refer to her as a dog or bitch, even a "little bitch" or puppy, since a diminutive form is used, is offensive and insulting (Josephus, *Con Ap* 2.85). Jesus seems to be "caught with his compassion down."[17]

Why does he use a food metaphor when she has not asked for **food**? G. Theissen suggests that Jesus' comment may reflect the bitterness of an exploited rural area that has supplied urban Tyre with food.[18] **Bread or food** has also been an issue in two previous stories (12:7-8; 15:1-20) that have involved conflict between traditions and God's will. Here the struggle concerns whether Jesus will be bound by cultural and historical conventions in resisting this woman from around Tyre and Sidon (see 15:21-22), or understand that faithfulness to his commission to manifest God's saving reign does not violate Israel's priority if he extends the reign to Gentiles. **Food**, then, is a metaphor for God's empire or salvation (1:21, 23; 4:17). Are the woman and her daughter among "his people" whom Jesus saves? While concerned for the children to have food (cf. 14:15-21), Jesus resists giving this Gentile child the food of wholeness.

• 15:27

The woman is not deterred by Jesus' response. Instead she wittily and bravely recasts Jesus' response. Whereas disciples do not understand Jesus' parable (15:16), she understands this one so well that she recasts it to accomplish her goal. His comment maintains the status quo of ethnic, cultural, religious, gender, and political division. But her response moves beyond these barriers to possibilities that are faithful to God's promises to bless all the nations of the earth (Gen 12:1-13). Without questioning the priority of the children (Israel), and while recognizing the authority of **the masters**, she reframes the significance of dogs (Gentiles). It is not a matter of food or no food (Jesus' alternative), but food for both. **Yes Lord** (for the third time) **yet even the dogs eat the crumbs that fall from their master's table**. She demands a place at the table, not under it. For the tradition of Gentile inclusion in God's purposes, see Isa 2:2-4; 45:20-23; Zech 8:20-23; contra Ezra 9-10 [9:1, separation from the Canaanites]; Neh 13:15-31 [Tyrians violate the sabbath, 13:16].

• 15:28

Her witty response opens up new possibilities for Jesus and her daughter. Jesus now responds positively to her continued recognition of his ability to help her and her persistent requests. **Then Jesus answered her, "O Woman, great is your faith! Let it be done for you as you wish." And her daughter was healed instantly**. The initial **O Woman** indicates considerable emotion (BDF §146.2,1b) as well as great (and newfound) respect. Her persistence in the face of Jesus' obstructions, her challenge to the ethnic, gender, religious, political, and economic barriers, her reliance on his power, and her recognition of his authority over demons comprise her **faith** (see 8:10; 9:2, 22, 29). In contrast to its lack among the religious leaders, and "little faith" of disciples (6:30; 8:26; 14:31; 16:8), she is like the Gentile centurion (8:10) in showing **great . . . faith**, the only time this adjective is used to describe faith in the gospel. Like the centurion, this despised woman calls Jesus Lord (cf. 8:6), engages him in dialogue (cf. 8:8-10), surprises him with her faith (8:10) and elicits a (long distance?) miracle from him (8:13). Both are included in the people saved not by ethnicity but by faith in Jesus (cf. 1:21).

The miracle is effected by Jesus' words (which suggests a distance miracle). **Let it be done** echoes the Lord's Prayer (6:10b). This Gentile's desire for her daughter to be freed is consistent with God's will (cf. mercy in 15:22). God's empire is evident (12:28). See also 8:13 (Gentile centurion) and 9:29 (the blind men). **And her daughter was healed instantly**. So too the centurion's servant (8:13) and the healing of the woman with a hemorrhage (9:22). In performing the miracle, Jesus overcomes ethnic, cultural, political, gender, and religious barriers.

15:29-31—SUMMARY OF JESUS' HEALING

Jesus' mission to the "lost sheep of Israel" (15:24) continues with another healing summary. See 4:24-25; 8:16; 9:35-36; 12:15; 14:14. The summary passages interact with the accounts of individual healings (see chs. 8-9; also 15:21-28) to show the extent of Jesus' ministry. He accomplishes his commission (1:21, 23; 4:17-25) and anticipates the wholeness which marks the full establishment of God's reign (*2 Bar* 73:1-2). In this third narrative block (11:2-16:20), displays of power are one means by which people can recognize Jesus' identity (see 11:2-6).

• **15:29**
And after Jesus had left that place (the Galilee-Tyre/Sidon border), **he passed along the Sea of Galilee**, where he had called the first disciples (see 4:18-22). **He went up the mountain where he sat down**. See 5:1 (the Sermon on the Mount) and 14:23 (a place of prayer after feeding the five thousand). On sitting as the exercise of power and life-giving rule, see 5:1; 19:28.

• **15:30**
Here the mountain is a place of gathering (**And great crowds came to him**), healing (**bringing with them the lame, the crippled/injured, the blind, the mute and many others. They put them at his feet and he cured them**), and feeding in 15:32-39. T. L. Donaldson rightly argues that this scene invokes Zion traditions.[19] Zion is the place to which God's people (scattered Jews and Gentiles) gather at the beginning of the new age (Isa 2:2-4; 35:8-10; Mic 4:1-4; Jer 31:10-12). Healing takes place (Isa 35:1-10, esp. 5-6; Jer 31:7-12; Mic 4:6-7), and feasting (Isa 25:6-10; Jer 31:12-14). His healings and feedings anticipate this

age. Instead of the temple, Jesus Immanuel is the center of this scene. The new age of the establishment of God's empire is under way. For the eschatological feast, see 8:12; on healing, see 4:23-24.

The **great crowds bring** him a cast of religious and socioeconomic marginals, victims of the imperial structures, common figures well known to an audience in any city like Antioch (see 4:24-25). In this scene, anticipating the eschatological gathering at Zion, the marginal, not the elite, are center stage. On **the lame**, see 9:1-8; 11:5; on **the blind**, see 9:27-28; 11:5; 12:22; on **the mute**, see 9:32-33; 11:5; 12:22. The **crippled/injured** (BAGD, 457) appear for the first time (elsewhere only in 18:8; absent from the LXX). The first three terms appear in 11:5; Jesus' actions reveal his identity. The same three terms appear in Isa 35:5-6, in a vision of God's healing work on Zion. That work is being accomplished in Jesus' ministry as he demonstrates God's reign over all that is contrary to God's purposes (cf. 11:2-6). The crowds **put them** at Jesus' **feet.** The same verb meaning "thrown down" or "helpless" appears in 9:36 to evoke Jesus' compassion for the shepherdless people whose false leaders do not heal the sick (cf. 14:14; Ezek 34:4, 16). The mention of Jesus' **feet** perhaps indicates recognition of his authority (cf. 5:35; 28:9). The **healing** of the people (see 4:23-24) means not only physical health, but also new economic and social possibilities.

• **15:31**

The crowd witnesses the healings (**the mute speaking, the maimed whole, the lame walking, the blind seeing**; repeated for emphasis, cf. 11:5; Isa 35:6). In response they **wonder** (cf. 9:33, a response of some insight), and **praise** (9:8) **the God of Israel** (a liturgical designation for God evoking the covenant relationship; Pss 41:13; 59:5; 68:35). But they do not seem to understand Jesus' special identity (11:2-6).

15:32-39—JESUS FEEDS MORE THAN FOUR THOUSAND

In 14:13-21 Jesus fed more than five thousand people. Why is there a virtual repetition of this feeding scene in 15:32-39?[20] J. C. Anderson notes that repetition enhances communication by highlighting material, emphasizing its importance, increasing understanding, and causing review.[21] Hence this scene recalls 14:13-21 to emphasize its themes of doing God's will in feeding the hungry, of God's faithfulness to and sovereignty over creation, of the inadequacies of the imperial system that ensure the elite's food supply at the expense of the poor, and of anticipating the abundance of God's future new creation and empire. The scene again evokes the exodus and God's provision for the people (see 14:13 introduction) and exhibits the new creation in which in God's empire there is abundant food for all (*2 Bar* 73-74). It identifies even now an alternative reign marked by compassion and shared abundant resources.

The recalling of 14:13-21 also highlights differences. Apart from the smaller numbers, there is a significant difference in location. This feeding occurs on a mountain. The Zion links noted in 15:29 anticipate the completion of God's purposes accomplished through Jesus, Immanuel.

• 15:32

Unlike 14:15, Jesus, not the disciples, initiates the action. **Then Jesus called the disciples**. See 10:1 for the verb **called** at the beginning of the mission discourse. Feeding the hungry is a mission task for disciples. He **said, "I have compassion on the crowd because they have been with me now for three days, and have nothing to eat; and I do not want to send them away hungry, for they might faint on the way."** The phrase **for three days** establishes that they have consumed any food they might have brought, which enhances the miracle. For **compassion** as the motivation for Jesus' ministry and the equivalent of mercy, see 9:36; 14:14. The link to 9:36 recalls the people as "sheep without a shepherd" and the condemnation of the shepherds/leaders in Ezek 34 partly because they feed themselves but no one else (Ezek 34:2, 8) and they do not heal the sick (34:4, 16). Ezekiel 34 declares God's will to save the sheep from "forceful and harsh rule" (34:4), darkness (34:12; see Matt 4:15-16), and hunger by supplying them with abundant food (Ezek 34:13-14, 26-29) and with the Davidic prince (34:10, 14, 23-24, 29). Jesus as a son of David (9:27; 12:23; 15:22) does God's compassionate will in doing both tasks of healing and supplying food. As in 14:15, the imperial market economy does not adequately supply the rural **wilderness**.

• 15:33

As in 14:15-17, and in contrast to the Canaanite woman (15:21-28) and crowds (15:29-31), **the disciples** do not expect Jesus to solve the problem. Despite having witnessed the previous feeding miracle, despite knowing the traditions of God's provision in **the desert/wilderness** (see 14:13), despite accounts of God supplying food in miraculous ways (see 14:17 for Elijah and Elisha), they cannot see past the difficulties: **Where are we to get enough bread in the desert to feed so great a crowd?** Although they have learned something from being with Jesus (compare 8:27 and 14:33), they are still without much understanding (15:16) despite Jesus' instruction about the secrets of God's empire (13:11, 51).

• 15:34

As in 14:18-19 Jesus takes control as the host of a meal. But instead of using meal etiquette to maintain social hierarchy and to exclude undesirables (see 9:10-13), he displays God's gracious, inclusive, and life-giving order. **"How many loaves have you?" They said, "Seven, and a few small fish."** Compare 14:17. The disciples make no connection with the previous scene. Again the source of the food is not identified.

• 15:35-36

And commanding the crowds to sit down on the ground, he took the seven loaves and the fish, and after giving thanks he broke them and gave them to

the disciples, and the disciples gave them to the crowds. Compare 14:19. Jesus again enacts an alternative to the imperial market economy by sharing and multiplying resources. Jesus, aided by the disciples, does God's will of feeding the hungry (cf. 25:35, 37, 42, 44). He acts according to his prayer of 6:11. Just as God fed the people in the exodus wilderness (Exod 16), Jesus feeds this wilderness people. He supplies adequate food and anticipates a different future (so the Zion traditions and Ezek 34; see Matt 15:30, 32 above).

• 15:37

And all of them ate and were filled. See 14:20; Pss 107:9; 132:15. The scene anticipates the establishment of God's satisfying reign, imaged as a banquet (see 8:12), in which there is plenty for all. See also 6:11. Jesus shepherds God's people (see 2:6; 9:36) in contrast to the elite, who evade God's will (15:1-20).

And they took up the broken pieces left over, seven baskets full. The surplus attests God's abundant provision. As in 14:19-20 the disciples act as servants in feeding the crowds, a basic identity and praxis in the community of disciples (6:24; 10:24-25; 20:27). Recall R. Stark's view (see Introduction, sections 5-8) that the meeting of people's daily needs in harsh urban contexts like Antioch was a primary act for Christian communities like Matthew's, and a factor in the movement's growth.

• 15:38

Those who had eaten were four thousand men, besides women and children. Compare 14:21. God's blessings include women, children, and men. No response from the crowd is given. While they partake of God's blessing through Jesus, they do not seem to recognize his special identity (cf. 11:2-6; 15:21).

• 15:39

After sending away the crowds (cf. 14:22; also 14:15, 23; 15:32), **he got into the boat** (14:22; also 8:23-24; 9:1; 13:2; 14:13, 24, 29, 32, 33) **and went to the region of Magadan** (whose location is unknown).

CHAPTER 16A

Jesus' Identity

Verses 1-20 of chapter 16 complete the third narrative block (see 11:2-6). The religious elite continue to fail to discern Jesus' identity (16:1-4), in contrast to the disciples, who "understand" his teaching (16:5-12). A summary scene restates the central focus on Jesus' identity and its implications (16:13-20).

16:1-4—TESTING JESUS: REQUESTING A SIGN (CF. 12:38-42)

• **16:1**

The mix of recognition and resistance scenes, common through chapters 11-15, continues. After the Canaanite woman's faith (15:21-28) and Jesus' compassion for the crowds (15:29-39), **the Pharisees and Sadducees,** the religious elite, **came**. On **came** as respectful approach even from opponents, see 4:3, 11; 5:1. They approach Jesus presumably in the region of Magadan (15:39).

On these religious leaders as members of society's governing elite and allies of Rome, see Introduction, sections 1 and 5; 2:4; 3:7; 5:20, and the conflict scenes in 12:2, 14, 24, 38; 15:1. The **Pharisees** have been more prominent (9:11, 14, 34; 12:2, 14, 24, 38; 15:1, 12); the **Sadducees** have been absent since 3:7. In *Ant* 13.297 Josephus links the Sadducees with political power and the wealthy, and with high status people in *Ant* 18.17. At least one high priest was a Sadducee (*Ant* 20.199). Josephus shows the leading Pharisees as common allies of the chief priests, invested in maintaining their place in the social order sanctioned by Rome (*JW* 2.197, 410-14). Central to this scene is that the Pharisees and Sadducees represent and defend the current social order against Jesus' critique and alternative social practices and vision legitimated by God.[1]

The opposition of the Pharisees and Sadducees to Jesus is underlined by their motive for approaching Jesus. Their hostile purpose is **to test/tempt Jesus**. The verb previously denoted the devil's attempt to divert Jesus from God's will (4:1, 3). Its use allies the religious elite with the devil as opponents of God's purposes (cf. 15:12-14). This regrettable demonization (4:1-11; 9:4; 12:33-37) continues to present them as illegitimate leaders (9:36; 15:13-14; 21:40-41; 22:29).

They ask him to show them a sign from heaven. Spectacular **signs** such as those of Moses verify divine agency, address, or presence (see 12:38).[2] How is their request a test? Like the devil's temptations (4:1-11), the issue at stake concerns not Jesus' indisputable ability to do signs, but his allegiance. Does he perform their will or God's? If he performs a sign at their behest to prove his identity, he instantly betrays his identity as God's faithful agent and son. The sign would not be from heaven.

Two further aspects confirm that they wish to trap Jesus rather than benefit from a sign. (1) The request for a sign repeats 12:38. They have ignored Jesus' response, which pointed to his death as a sign (12:40). They do not want to learn. (2) The exorcism (15:28), healings (15:29-31), and feeding (15:32-39), demonstrations of God's liberating and merciful reign that transforms present injustice, have given them more opportunities to recognize Jesus' identity as commissioned by God to manifest God's saving empire and presence (see 11:2-6; 12:28). Like the wilderness generation that witnesses the exodus **signs**, they do not believe Jesus' existing signs (cf. Deut 29:2-4).[3]

• 16:2-4

Jesus refuses their request. He will not take instructions from them. His task is to do God's will. Jesus' refusal may also echo his rejection of Satan's second temptation (4:6-7) in refusing to test God (cf. Deut 6:16; Isa 7:12). The echo reinforces the elite's alliance with the devil.

Jesus' response falls into three sections. (1) He affirms their ability to interpret the weather. **He answered them, "When it is evening, you say, 'It will be fair weather, for the sky is red.' And in the morning, 'It will be stormy today for the sky is red and threatening.' You know how to interpret the appearance of the sky**. (2) He contrasts this ability with their failure to **interpret the signs of the times**. These religious leaders cannot discern what God is doing. In these **times**, judgment (see 8:29; 13:30) and revelation (see 11:25; 12:1) are under way in Jesus' ministry. But they cannot discern God's empire in Jesus' actions (11:2-6). (3) He again condemns them. **An evil and adulterous generation** (unfaithful and rejecting; see 11:16; 12:39) **asks for a sign** (12:38-40), **but no sign will be given to it** (the passive indicates "by God"; Jesus speaks on God's behalf) **except the sign of Jonah**. This reference recalls 12:40-41. The irony is that this sign is his death, of which the Pharisees are very aware since they are planning it (12:14)! They do not repent, unlike Nineveh. They are offended by Jesus (15:12). Jesus **left them and went away**.

16:5-12—THE DISCIPLES UNDERSTAND

• 16:5

Contrasting characters (**The disciples**) enter the scene, but several points of continuity with the previous chapters maintain the condemnation of the religious elite (cf. ch. 12).

Jesus reaches Magadan (15:39) ahead of the disciples, who do not witness the

scene of 16:1-4. **When the disciples reached the other side, they had forgotten to bring any bread.** The reference to **bread** recalls not only Jesus' two feedings (14:17-19; 15:33-38), and the Canaanite woman's response (15:26) but also
controversies with the Pharisees over hand washing and the tradition of the elders
(15:2), and over the sabbath (12:4). These scenes emphasize Jesus' authority to
reveal God's will about the sabbath, about feeding hungry people, about the
Pharisaic tradition, and about the inclusion of Gentiles and marginals in God's
purposes. His authority will be contrasted with the religious leaders.

• 16:6

**Jesus said to them, "Watch out, and beware of the yeast of the Pharisees
and Sadducees"** (see 16:1). What exactly the disciples are warned about is not
yet clear. But the image of **yeast/leaven** indicates something that effects corruption or contamination (see 13:33). For **beware** as a warning of danger, see 6:1;
7:15; 10:17.

• 16:7

The disciples understand Jesus' statement literally, perhaps not to eat bread
given them by Pharisees and Sadducees. **And they said to one another, "It is
because we have brought no bread."**

• 16:8-10

And becoming aware of it, Jesus said to them. On Jesus' special knowledge,
see 9:4; 12:15, 25; 26:10, which echoes God's seeing and knowing (see 6:1-4, 8).
The disciples' lack of understanding and anxiety about not having bread (despite
6:25-34; 14:13-21; 15:32-38) bring the rebuke, **you of little faith** (see 6:30; 8:26;
14:31), **why are talking about having no bread? Do you not perceive** (cf.
15:17) **and do you not remember the five loaves for the five thousand, and
how many baskets you gathered?** (14:13-21) **Or the seven loaves for the four
thousand, and how many baskets you gathered?** (15:32-38). Jesus reminds
them of his ability to supply food, which they should trust rather than be anxious
(cf. 6:24-34).

• 16:11

How could you fail to perceive (repeated from 16:8) **that I was not speaking about bread?** This question clarifies that he is not talking about literal leaven
or bread, but is speaking on a metaphorical level. So he repeats the warning from
v. 6, **beware of the yeast of the Pharisees and Sadducees** in preparation for its
metaphoric meaning. See 13:10, 36; 15:15, for the same technique of explaining
a parabolic saying.

• 16:12

Then they understood (as disciples, in contrast to crowds and the religious
elite, should: see 13:13, 14, 15, 19, 23, 51; 15:10; 17:13) **that he had not told
them to beware of the yeast of bread, but of the teaching of the Pharisees and
Sadducees**. The warning is repeated for the third time (16:2, 11, 12) to underline

its importance. The warning concerns **the teaching of the Pharisees and Sadducees**. This warning is no surprise, given Jesus' regular conflicts with the religious elite since chapter 9 over forgiveness (9:1-8), meals with sinners (9:10-13), exorcism (9:32-34; 12:22-37), the sabbath (12:1-14), signs (12:38-42; 16:1-4), their traditions and practices of hand washing, *korban*, and food purity (15:1-20), and Jesus' condemnation of them for neglecting the people (9:35-38; 15:6-9, 12-14). Their teaching corrupts (**yeast**, 16:6, 11, 12) and it is unreliable (see further 23:2-3). The warning may reflect the ongoing conflict between the gospel's audience and an Antiochene synagogue over authorized teaching and practice. The followers of Jesus claim that he, not the religious leaders, reveals God's will.

16:13-20—SUMMARY OF THE THIRD NARRATIVE BLOCK

This summary scene restates the central issue of this third narrative block (11:2-16:20), namely, Have people been able to discern from Jesus' ministry that he is God's Christ, the one anointed to manifest God's salvation and empire (cf. 11:2-6)?

• 16:13

The scene is set **in the district of/controlled by Caesarea Philippi** (cf. 4:15; 15:21), some twenty miles north of the Sea of Galilee south of Mt. Hermon. G. W. Nickelsburg notes it as a place of revelation and commission (*T. Levi* 2:5; *1 En* 12-16, esp. 13:7-8), important elements of this scene.[4] The site had been a shrine for the god Pan, god of flocks and shepherds (Josephus, *Ant* 15.363-64). But in this place, a very different shepherd is recognized. The one who shepherds/governs my people Israel (see 2:6), who has compassion for the crowds as sheep without a shepherd (9:36; Ezek 34), who is sent to the lost sheep of Israel (15:24) and who sends his disciples on a similar mission (10:6), the son of the shepherd David who manifests God's reign among the marginal (9:27; 12:23; 15:22), is again recognized as God's commissioned agent.

The location also underlines the issue of sovereignty. Its name **Caesarea Philippi** reflects its involvement with imperial power. King Herod built a marble temple there in honor of Augustus (Josephus, *JW* 1.404-5; *Ant* 15:360-64). Philip enlarged the city and named it Caesarea (*JW* 2.168; *Ant* 18.28). Agrippa enlarged it further and renamed it Neronias in honor of the emperor Nero (54-68 C.E.; *JW* 3.514; *Ant* 20.211). After Jerusalem fell (70 C.E.), Titus visited the city, and "many" Jewish captives were thrown to wild beasts or forced to fight each other (*JW* 7.23-24).[5] Its names, buildings (typically using local wealth [taxes and levies], labor, and materials), activities, and history attest Rome's claims and power. But in this place, God's purposes for Jesus and his followers are affirmed, purposes which contest Rome's claims that Jupiter determines human affairs, that history is under Rome's control, and that the emperor is the channel for the gods' blessing and presence (Introduction, section 9). Jesus, not Rome, is the agent of God's purposes, which will ultimately be triumphant.

Jesus **asked his disciples, "Who do people say that the Son of Man is?"** See

11:2-6 for this central question of the third narrative block. On **people** as the (unresponsive) society among whom disciples are to live in mission, see 4:19; 5:13, 16; 6:1. **Son of Man** may reflect its usage in Ezekiel (Ezek 2:1) meaning "I" (cf. 16:15). Typically the term denotes Jesus' interaction with the world/**people** (see 8:20). It occurs in key scenes of this narrative block: criticism of Jesus (11:19), sabbath controversy (12:8), forgiveness (12:32), the sign of Jonah and death (12:40), Jesus' mission (13:37), the eschatological judge (13:41; cf. *1 En* 48; 62; cf. Matt 16:27). All of these actions express Jesus' God-given authority and mission in contexts of conflict or challenge.

• 16:14

The disciples report various evaluations of Jesus: **some say John the Baptist** (cf. Herod in 14:2), **but others Elijah** (as was John, 11:14; 17:12-13; see 4:18-22 and 14:16-17 for similarities between Jesus' actions and Elijah's), **and others Jeremiah** (see 2:17; 27:9; a prophet of judgment[6]) **or one of the prophets**. All four responses locate Jesus in the prophetic tradition, as do the crowds and religious leaders (21:11, 46; 26:68). The gospel also links him with the prophetic tradition in the fulfillment citations (1:22-23; 2:5-6, 15, 17-18; etc.) and associates prophets with rejection and suffering (5:12; 13:57; 23:29-39). But God's perspective is that Jesus is more than a prophet (3:17) because of the intimate relationship they share. On the opposition of **prophets** to Roman power, see the introduction to chapter 3.

• 16:15-16

With the pronoun **you** positioned first-word, the question becomes more personal and emphatic, **"But who do *you* say that I am?"**

Simon Peter responds, as in 15:15, as the disciples' spokesperson and representative. **"You are the Christ"** or commissioned agent (see 1:1). This is the first time a disciple has used the term **Christ**, though the audience has known it since 1:1, 16, 17, 18 (cf. 2:4; 11:2) and disciples have made a comparable confession in 14:33. The disciples have answered the key question of 11:2-6 correctly, unlike the wider society (16:14) or crowds, and the political and religious elite.

Peter also confesses that Jesus is **the son of the living God**. This phrase agrees with God's perspective on Jesus (see 2:15; 3:17), with Jesus' own statements (11:25-27), and repeats the disciples' confession from 14:33. It underlines both Jesus' function as God's agent and his intimate relationship with God.[7] The phrase was commonly used to honor and elevate emperors, especially Augustus. It was part of a cluster of terms that recognized the emperors' identity as agents of the gods' will and power expressed through Rome's rule.[8] To designate Jesus as **son of God** is to contest and challenge those claims of sovereignty and agency.

As the **living God**, or God of life (Deut 5:26; Josh 3:10; 1 Sam 17:26, 36; 2 Kgs 19:4, 16; Pss 42:2; 84:2; Hos 1:10; Dan 6:20), God is creative, active, faithful, and just. As God's **son/child** or agent, Jesus expresses this life in his words and healings, feedings, exorcisms, and so on (cf. 11:2-6), and in creating a community that participates in God's empire. To recognize Jesus as God's agent confirms that he, not the emperor, manifests God's purposes.

• 16:17

Jesus greets Peter's response with a blessing or beatitude (cf. 5:3-12; 11:6; 13:16, also related to revelation). **Blessed are you, Simon Bar-Jona**. Does **Bar-Jona** link Peter with the prophetic tradition (12:39; 16:4) as the spokesperson of God's revealed word? Or is it a form of John (cf. John 1:42)? Jesus declares, **Flesh and blood has not revealed this to you**. The phrase **flesh and blood** denotes the human situation before God, not as one of mortality but as the inability to know God and God's ways. It underlines the limitations of "human intellectual, religious and mystical capacities" before God.[9] Instead, Peter's confession has come from **my Father in heaven** (5:45; 7:21; 10:32-33; 11:27; 12:50). It is consistent with God's verdict on Jesus (3:17; 17:5). God makes things known to disciples (13:10-17; 15:15-20; 16:5-12). The verb **revealed** denotes the disclosing of God's eschatological purposes (see 10:26b-27; 11:25, 27). Here the revelation concerns Jesus' role in those purposes. Jesus' function as revealer is rooted in his intimate relationship with God (son and Father, 11:25-27).

• 16:18

Discerning Jesus' commission in God's purposes means a commission for those who make this confession. Jesus gives Simon a second name, **And I tell you** (introducing an authoritative statement, 5:18) **You are Peter**. Peter was introduced as Simon "being called Peter" in 4:18 (also 10:2), but without any explanation of "Peter." In five subsequent instances, the narrator uses the name "Peter" (8:14; 10:2; 14:28-29; 15:15; 16:16). This scene explains the change of name.

Renaming often signifies a new role or change in status. Sarai becomes Sarah in anticipation of her giving birth (Gen 17:15-16), Abram is renamed Abraham as "the ancestor of a multitude of nations" (Gen 17:4-5; cf. Matt 1:1; 3:9), Jacob is renamed Israel (Gen 32:28), and Jesus is called Immanuel (1:21, 23). Names attest God's purposes (Isa 7-8; Hos 1:4-9; Matt 1:21).

Jesus elaborates Peter's role, **on this rock** (a wordplay in Greek with "Peter/rocky") **I will build my church**. What is **the rock**? U. Luz identifies four standard lines of interpretation: it is (1) Peter, the representative of every Christian; (2) Peter's faith or confession in 16:16; (3) Christ; (4) Peter the model bishop.[10] In context, Peter's confession (no. 2) seems to be the most justifiable answer, though the first option should be included. Peter is blessed for confessing Jesus' identity. But he is not uniquely blessed since the confession is one that the disciples have already made (14:33). Note Isa 51:1-2, where a **rock** is the foundation of a community (cf. 3:9).

Jesus **will build** on this confession of his identity and role in God's purposes. To **build** is a common metaphor for establishing a people (Jer 12:16; 18:9), notably in restoring God's people after the Babylonian exile (Jer 31:4; 33:7) or in restoring the Davidic line (Amos 9:11). In 2 Sam 7, David's descendant, the king as God's son (7:14), will build a temple (7:13). Jesus, son of David (15:22) whose reign means life and favor for the vulnerable and marginal (Ps 72), has been about the task of building a community since 4:17-22 through calling disciples (4:18-22; 10:1-4), teaching (5-7, 10, 13), and actions (chs. 8-9; Introduction, sections 2-3).

On this rock I will build my church (ἐκκλησία, *ekklēsia*). This community is built by Jesus, is based on the confession of Jesus' identity and role, and is committed to him (**my**). The term **church** (also in 18:18) means "called out." The common view of its origin and meaning is that the term derives from the LXX, where it denotes the assembled or called congregation of God's people (Deut 9:10; 31:30; 2 Chr 1:3; 1 Macc 2:56; cf. 1QM 4:10; Josephus, *Ant* 4.144; 6.86). Using this term suggests continuity for Jesus' followers in God's purposes, while the nonuse of "synagogue" distinguishes Jesus' group from those hostile and rejecting groups ("their synagogues" in 4:23; 9:35; 10:17; 12:9; 13:54; 23:34).

J. Y. Campbell has challenged this view, arguing that the term can designate nothing more than a variety of meetings and assemblies (Sir 31:11; Jdt 6:16, 21; Ezra 10:1, 8, 12, 14; Neh 13:1).[11] Frequently overlooked is the observation that the term *ekklēsia* is used in the political sphere.[12] It denotes the "duly summoned" (Liddell and Scott, 509) civic and political assembly of citizens in Greek cities which along with a council (the *boulē*) expressed the will of the assembled people (*dēmos*).[13] For Antioch, see Josephus, *JW* 7.47; for Alexandria, *JW* 7.412; for Ephesus, Acts 19:32, 39, 41; for Prusa in Bithynia, Dio Chrysostom, *Disc* 48:1). The assembly is not primarily cultic but political, social, cultural. It gathers to reinforce and administer the status quo under Roman control. As R. A. Horsley notes in discussing Paul's use of this term,[14] by claiming the same name, the community centered on Jesus exists in "pointed juxtaposition and 'competition' with the official city assembly . . . (as) an alternative society to the Roman imperial order . . . rooted in the history of Israel, in opposition to *Pax Romana*. . . . In God's guidance of human affairs, history, which had been running through Israel and not through Rome," continues in this countersociety with its alternative commitment and practices.

Such a community is bound to know conflict and threat. Jesus places that threat in a cosmic context (cf. 4:1-11) and promises: **and the gates of Hades will not prevail against it**. What does Jesus promise?[15] The phrase **the gates of Hades** is metonymy in which a part (**gates**) refers to the whole realm of **Hades** (Wis Sol 16:13; Isa 38:10; **gates** represent the city of Jerusalem in Ps 24 [LXX 23]:7, 9; Isa 3:26). **Hades**, associated with the dead, contains the demons and evil spirits of death and destruction (*1 En* 18:16; 21:6; 22:1-14; *Jub.* 5:10; 22:22; Rev 9:1-2; 20:1-3). Hades attacks Jesus' community (as the rock is attacked in Matt 7:24-27; cf. 14:24). The **gates of Hades** open to let the attacking demons out. Compare 1QH 3:17-18, 26-34; Rev 9:1-11. This attack is part of the eschatological woes which disciples experience as they conduct their mission before Jesus' return (10:16-25, 34-39; chs. 24-25). In 13:24-30, 38-39 the opposition comes from the devil. It can take all sorts of forms: domestic (10:21-22), religious and social (10:17; 16:21), cultural (13:21-22), and political, since the devil claims control of the nations (4:8; cf. 10:17-18). But Jesus promises that this diabolical opposition **will not prevail against** the community centered on Jesus (13:36-43).

• **16:19**

Jesus gives Peter a key role in this community, **I will give you the keys of the empire of heaven, and whatever you bind on earth will have been bound**[16] **in heaven, and whatever you loose on earth will have been loosed in heaven**. Often **keys** indicate access (Judg 3:25; 1 Chr 9:27) and authority or power: over the house of David (Eliakim in Isa 22:20-22), the temple (1 Chr 9:27), knowledge (Luke 11:52), death (Rev 1:18), and "stewardship of God's affairs on earth"[17] (2 *Bar* 10:18; 1 Chr 9:27).

What is Peter given authority over? And how does it relate to **the empire of the heavens**? God's reign originates in heaven (3:2; 4:17), the abode of God (5:34). It is manifested in Jesus' ministry in part now as Jesus extends God's reign over sin, disease, demons, and people's lives (4:17-25; 12:28).[18] Peter's role seems to be to continue the task (10:7-8). To use the "key" and "gates" metaphor, just as the gates of Hades open to let out the demons, Peter's key keeps heaven's gates open as God's reign is manifested among people and in struggles against demonic powers. How does Peter perform such a role? Revelation is, after all, God's prerogative (cf. 3:16-17; 16:4). But the revelation has already been entrusted to the disciples partly through the scriptures, partly through association with Jesus, and partly in the mission commission (10:7-8). Peter's role is that of the disciples, to enact God's reign in preaching, healing, exorcism, and the like.

This role clarifies the enigmatic metaphor **to bind and loose**. Scholars debate whether these terms refer to excluding/including people in the community (see 18:18), or, more commonly, to interpreting and teaching what God's will or law (the scriptures) forbids or permits as an expression of God's reign (see 5:19).[19] Both meanings have some support from rabbinic Judaism.[20] And both tasks are related in that they have to do with discerning an appropriate way of life shaped by God's empire.

Further, D. Balch has shown that the verb **loose** occurs in "Greek political discussions of a state's or a people's constitution and laws" (Josephus, *Ant* 4.310; Dionysius of Halicarnassus, *Rom Ant* 1.8.2; 2.27.3; 4.43.2; 4.72.1; 5.1.1). It appears in contexts which make a paradoxical assertion that the founder's laws (Romulus, Moses) are not to be abolished (cf. 5:17), yet they can be changed in order to adapt or abolish them for new circumstances. Jesus' charge gives Peter and the community of disciples (18:18) "a legitimate way to loose/annul even a great commandment . . . particularly Mosaic laws and even his own imperatives."[21]

Peter's role, and that of the community (anticipating 18:18) is concerned with understanding and doing what God's reign requires as declared by the scriptures and interpreted not by the religious leaders (15:1-20; 16:1-12; 23:2-7) but by Jesus, and by Peter and the disciples. They must understand God's empire (13:10-17, 52) and know Jesus' teaching about purity and food regulations (15:15), the illegitimacy of Pharisaic teaching (15:12-14; 16:1-12), the temple tax (17:24-27), forgiveness (18:21), and eschatological destiny (19:27) in order to interpret it for changing situations.

Is Peter's role as the foundation rock and teacher/interpreter unique? Is this authority given to Peter alone as bearer of the revelation, to guarantee and authorize the tradition, as some have argued?[22] Or is Peter the representative disciple or Christian, the "type" of all disciples?[23] Or does Peter's primacy lie only in his salvation-historical role of being the first to be called (4:18-20; 10:2) and otherwise he is a disciple like the others?[24]

The last view is the most sustainable. (1) Peter's confession in 16:16 is not unique. He repeats what the disciples confessed in 14:33. He is spokesperson for a group. (2) The blessing, then, in 16:17, while addressed to Peter the spokesperson, concerns all who make this confession. God has not revealed Jesus' identity and role in God's purposes to Peter alone. In 17:1-8 three disciples witness the transfiguration, and the group is entrusted with its proclamation (17:9). (3) Likewise in 16:18, Peter alone is not the sole foundation of the community Jesus is building. He is (so J. D. Kingsbury) the first to join (4:18-20) and so has salvation-historical priority. But all disciples are entrusted with the task of proclaiming and manifesting God's empire (10:7-8). His teaching/interpreting/transmitting role is shared with other disciples.

• **16:20**

Jesus sternly ordered the disciples not to tell anyone he was the Messiah. Why does Jesus enjoin secrecy when it has been the challenge since 11:2 to identify Jesus as God's agent? As the unfolding narrative will show, the disciples do not yet fully understand what Jesus is commissioned to do. There is more teaching for them in the fourth narrative block, which starts in 16:21. For previous instructions to silence, see 8:4a; 9:30; 12:16; 17:9.

PART IV

The Fourth Narrative Block

*Jesus Will Be Crucified
and Raised (16:21-20:34)*

CHAPTER 16B

The Way of the Cross
for Jesus and Disciples

16:21-28

In the key scene (16:21-28) of the fourth narrative block (16:21-20:34), Jesus teaches his disciples that God's purposes for him as God's agent ("the Christ, the son," 16:16, 20) involve his death at the hands of the religious and political elite, and his resurrection. He also begins to teach them that this event has profound consequences for discipleship, for "my church" (16:18). Chapters 17-20 will elaborate aspects of this life shaped by the cross.

• 16:21
The first of three predictions of Jesus' death intensifies the division between Jesus and the religious elite (17:22-23; 20:17-19). In predicting his death Jesus does what other great figures do (Socrates in Plato, *Apology* 39c; Moses in Philo, *Moses* 2.291; Sulla in Plutarch, *Sulla* 37). **From that time Jesus** (cf. 1:21; 4:17) **began to show his disciples** (see 5:1) **that he must go to Jerusalem**. The **must** is not blind fate. (1) He **must suffer** in Jerusalem because the center is always threatened by the margins and the empire strikes back at those who expose its injustice and promote an alternative empire. His suffering is the inevitable consequence of this collision course with the political, socioeconomic, and religious elite. He will suffer as many in Israel's history who have challenged the powerful have suffered. Pharaoh pursues Moses (Exod 14). Ahab and Jezebel threaten Elijah's life (1 Kgs 19:1-3). The strong oppress the weak (Ps 35:10, as do the "many," the enemies, and the wicked in Ps 3:1-2, 7). The "kings, the governors, the high officials and the landlords" oppress the "holy ones" (*1 En* 62). The rich oppress the poor (*1 En* 94:8). The sinners "who hate us" and "the officials" oppress the righteous (*1 En* 103:5-15). Princes and kings threaten (Ps 119:23, 46).

(2) It is also inevitable because through Jesus' suffering and death, God will expose the limits of the elite's power to punish and control. God will raise him to show that while the political and religious elite trade in death, God's sovereignty asserts life over death. They do not have the last word. Injustice and death-

bringing power do not prevail (16:18). Jesus is vindicated in anticipation of his return (24:27-31) to establish God's empire.

On **Jerusalem** as the center of the resistant religious and political elite, see 2:1; 15:1. Under their control, the city does not live out its special place in God's purposes (5:35 [Zion traditions]; cf. "holy city," set apart to serve God, in 4:5; 27:53). By contrast, some from Jerusalem are responsive to God's work (3:5; 4:25). In Jerusalem, Jesus will **suffer many things from the elders and chief priests and scribes and be killed.** Jesus foretells the plot of chapters 26-27. He will suffer through unfaithful disciples, an unjust trial, painful torture, an alliance of the religious and political elite, and the elite's misleading of the people (see 27:25). This suffering culminates his conflict with the religious elite that has been to the fore since chapter 9.[1]

The **elders** have not been mentioned previously as part of the ruling Jerusalem group (see 15:2 for a different sense). They were lay members of the Jerusalem Sanhedrin, members of leading families, probably supporters of the Sadducees (Josephus, *Ant* 18.17) but distinct by birth and wealth from other priestly families and scribes.[2] On **scribes** as Torah interpreters **and chief priests** as temple leaders and members of the Sanhedrin, see 2:4.[3] **Scribes** have opposed Jesus throughout (7:29; 8:19; 9:3; 12:38; 15:1; contrast 13:52). On the Sanhedrin, see 2:4; 26:3, 57.[4] Jesus names his killers as the religious establishment, members of the ruling elite and allies with Rome whose commitment is to protect the current hierarchical social structure (see Introduction, sections 1 and 5). **To be killed** is the fate of rejected prophets in 23:34. Jesus has taught that disciples should not fear those who kill the body, but those who kill the soul (10:28). Another part of the religious leadership has already begun to plot his death (12:14). This is part of the inevitable opposition from Hades (16:18).

Yet the worst that these representatives of the central religious elite can do by way of resisting and removing this marginal figure from Galilee is not final. **On the third day** (cf. 12:40) he will **be raised**. The passive construction indicates God's vindication of Jesus and thwarting of their destructive purposes, just as God circumvented the hostile Herod (ch. 2). Resurrection of the faithful from the dead emerges in a context of persecution and martyrdom as a means of participating in God's victory over imperial tyrants and death. See Dan 12:1-3; 2 Macc 7; 12:43-45; *2 Bar* 49-51. Jesus' resurrection will mean a resurrection of the faithful (27:51-54; ch. 28).

• 16:22

But the disciples do not understand the teaching of 16:21 (nor the earlier references to Jesus' death in 12:40 or 9:15 [?]). The spokesperson **Peter took him aside and began to rebuke him** (an echo of "began to show them" in 16:21) **saying, "God forbid it, Lord! This must never happen to you."** When Peter confessed Jesus as the Messiah/Christ, the son of God in 16:16, he got the words right in recognizing Jesus' role and relationship as God's agent, but he did not understand the specifics. Peter does not envisage apparent defeat and suffering. Just what he did expect (perhaps the triumphant Davidic king of *Pss. Sol.* 17:32 and *4 Ezra* 12:32?) is not stated. The contrast with 16:16 is stark. Whereas Jesus

rebukes the wind and sea, exercising authority over them (8:26) and over the crowds (12:16), Peter now turns the tables in **rebuking** Jesus and attempting to control him.

• 16:23

But he turned and said to Peter, "Get behind me, Satan!" Jesus' response shows that not only did Peter misunderstand, but he joined the opponents of God's purposes. (1) The command **Get/Depart** repeats Jesus' word to Satan in 4:10. But **behind/after me** calls him again to discipleship. This phrase is very close to that used in 4:19 when Jesus first calls Peter to follow "behind/after me." Jesus calls him to start over in a relationship and role in which the disciple is never above Jesus the teacher (cf. 10:24). (2) Peter performs **Satan's** role (cf. 4:1-11; 16:1-4) of distracting Jesus from doing God's will. (3) **You are a stumbling block/cause of sin to me.** Such "causes of sin" reflect Satan's disruptive work and are judged (see 13:39-41). On the cognate verb "cause to stumble" as that which is contrary to God's purposes, see 5:29-30; 11:6; 13:21, 57; 15:12. (4) In countering Jesus, Peter opposes God, **for you do not think the things of God**. Peter has opposed God's way of the cross. **But you think the things of human beings**, of human society which does not do God's will. Disciples are sent in mission to **human beings** (4:19; 5:16), but humans threaten disciples and God's will with distraction and false values (6:1, 5), with hostile opposition (10:17), and they often do not understand (16:13). Peter joins the religious elite in preferring "human precepts" to God's will (15:9).

• 16:24-28

Having instructed the disciples about God's purposes for him, Jesus states the implications for them, both its challenge (16:24b-26) and its eschatological reward (16:27-28). Christology and ecclesiology intersect. So do eschatology and ecclesiology/ethics, since disciples live toward the completion of God's purposes (see 7:13). The fourth narrative block will expand these concerns.

• 16:24

Then Jesus told his disciples, "If any want to become my followers, let them deny themselves." To be **followers** (literally, "to come after/behind me," as in 16:23; a present tense suggesting a continuing existence) is to renounce the practice of telling God and God's agent how God's purposes are best accomplished. It is to refuse to place oneself ahead of, or in the place of, the revealer.

To **deny** is to choose not to follow Jesus, not to be faithful to God's ways (10:33; 26:34-35, 75). It is to be intimidated by political and religious authorities and their power of death into renouncing commitment to Jesus and seeking safety and self-interest by siding with the elite. To **deny** oneself involves, then, turning from that which hinders faithful and lived commitment, and turning to trust oneself to God's purposes and unusual ways of Jesus' suffering and death at the hands of the elite.

To **deny oneself** and to **follow** is to **take up the cross**. This is the second time Jesus has invited disciples to do so (10:38). Here, the reference to the cross specifies how Jesus will be killed (16:21). His death and the way of discipleship are linked.

The **cross** utilizes a political image of shame, humiliation, pain, social rejection, marginalization, condemnation, and death. Crucifixion, as employed by Rome, was a cruel means of execution (Tacitus, *Ann* 15.44.4; Seneca, *De Ira* 1.2.2; Josephus, *JW* 7.203 ["most pitiable of deaths"]). It was not used for Roman citizens (Cicero, *Pro Rabirio* 9-17, except for treason), but for socio-political marginals such as "rebellious" foreigners (Josephus, *JW* 2.306, 308; 5.449-53; Philo, *In Flaccum* 72, 84), violent criminals and robbers (Martial, *On the Spectacles* 9), and slaves (Cicero, *In Verr* 2.5.162; Juvenal, *Sat* 6.219-224; Tacitus, *Ann* 13.32.1). Crucifixion in public places was intended to deter non-compliant behavior (Josephus, *JW* 5.550). Carrying the cross-beam (*patibulum*) to the place of execution could be part of the precrucifixion torture and humiliation (Plutarch, "On the Delay of Divine Vengeance," *Moralia* 554B). For some Jews, crucifixion could be associated with the curse on those hung on a tree (Deut 23:21; Gal 3:13; 11QTemple 64:6-13).

Jesus' scandalous call, then, to **take up the cross and follow** (cf. 4:18-22) is a call to martyrdom, to die as Jesus does (9:15; 10:4, 21, 28, 29; 16:21). Such is the risk of continuing Jesus' countercultural work of proclaiming and demonstrating God's empire (10:7-8).[5] On another level, it is a call to a life of marginalization, to identify with the nobodies like slaves, foreigners, criminals, and those understood to be cursed by God. It is also to identify with those who resist the empire's control, who contest its version of reality, and who are vulnerable to its reprisals. It is to identify with a sign of the empire's violent and humiliating attempt to dispose of all who threaten or challenge its interests. To so identify is not to endorse the symbol but to counter and reframe its violence. As the end of the gospel shows, it is to identify with a sign that ironically indicates the empire's limits. The empire does its worst in crucifying Jesus. But God raises Jesus from death to thwart the empire's efforts and to reveal the limits of its power.

• 16:25

W. Beardslee observes that sayings about gaining one's life by losing it are found in exhortations to soldiers before war (Xenophon, *Anab* 3.1.43; *Sayings of the Wise Menander* 65), and in discussions about loyalty in friendship or love (Pindar, *Nemean* 10).[6] Jesus reframes the first context to exhort resistance to, rather than the perpetration of, imperial power. And he utilizes the second to reinforce the loyalty of disciples to himself.

To **save one's life** (whole self, or existence, 2:20; 6:25; 10:28, 39) is to decide against the way of the cross and its confrontation with the status quo. It is to decide for what is safe, for self-interest. It is to be intimidated into compliance by the elite's threat to crucify those who resist it. But this choice for safety is, in Jesus' view, to **lose** life. Life based on intimidation is not God's way of trusting relationship. It is not God's saving way demonstrated in Jesus (1:21). God cannot honor such a choice in the judgment (10:32, 39).

Conversely, to **lose one's life for my sake** (cf. 5:11; 10:18, 39), to be loyal to

Jesus in the subversive way of the cross, at the hands of the elite, is to **find it** in an act which refuses to give the elite the power of intimidation and conformity that it craves. God will honor such a choice in the eschaton with a life that knows God's justice and empire in full.

• **16:26**

This life of faithfulness to God's purposes, of conflict with and challenge to the status quo, of future participation in God's accomplished purposes, is affirmed with two rhetorical questions. The first uses economic images, **For what will it profit them if they gain the whole world but forfeit their life?** See *2 Bar* 51:15. For **profit** as a harmful economic figure, see Matt 15:5. The **whole world** (see 4:8) is the realm of everyday political, social, economic, and religious life which, though created by God (cf. Ps 24:1; Matt 13:35), is claimed by the devil (4:8) and in need of saving (5:14; 13:38). The use of another term of economic profit (**gain**, cf. *Ep. Arist.* 270) reinforces the view that political-economic pursuits are in view (gaining "the sum total of earthly riches"; BAGD, 429). The verb **forfeit** denotes economic and social loss (1 Cor 3:15; Phil 3:8). To invest oneself in maintaining or increasing power, wealth, and status, even to the point of owning the world, is loss because it is not the means of participating in God's purposes now or in the eschaton. For warnings about wealth and power, see 6:19-21, 24, 25-34; 10:8-10; 13:22, 44-46; 19:16-30.

The second question, **Or what will they give in return for their life?**, reinforces the point. A life lost in these pursuits cannot be recovered.

• **16:27-28**

The eschatological goal of present faithfulness is underlined. This material does not instruct disciples to endure present injustice passively until they get to heaven. Rather, disciples resist injustice and oppression now (5:38-42; 17:24-27) with alternative practices, even to death (16:24). Their alternative way of life manifests God's empire in part now and anticipates the future full establishment of it (see 7:13).

For the Son of Man is to come with his angels in the glory of his Father. Jesus' return completes his life, death, and resurrection (16:21). What the political and religious elite intend as his defeat (16:21) turns out to be *their* defeat, his vindication, and the final establishment of God's empire marked by peace and wholeness (*2 Bar* 73:1-2). On **Son of Man** as the eschatological judge, see 10:23; 13:41. In Dan 7:13-14 this figure (perhaps a collective form of Israel) has an everlasting "dominion and glory and kingship" over "all peoples, nations, and languages," given to him by God at the judgment of the four kingdoms. He represents God's empire victorious over oppressive systems. In *1 En* 46:3-8 he judges "kings and mighty ones," whose "deeds are oppression," whose "power (depends) upon their wealth." This is the one disciples follow. They know that though Rome's control seems supreme, God's justice will prevail. The gospel continues to imitate imperial models in representing God's empire.

On **angels** as agents of God's will (cf. 1:20; 2:13) in the judgment, see 13:39,

41, 49; 25:31. **Glory** denotes God's power and presence (cf. 4:8; 5:16; 6:29) particularly evident in the Son of Man's role in the judgment and establishment of God's purposes (24:30; 25:31). On God as Jesus' **father**, see 11:25-27; 16:17.

At his coming, **he will repay everyone for what has been done**. This biblical theme attests God's faithfulness and watchfulness (Ps 62:12; Prov 24:12; Sir 35:22). The repayment will mean reward for disciples, an intensification of their relationship with God (see 5:12; 6:1), and punishment for the wicked (cf. 13:39-42).

• 16:28

Jesus ends the scene with an enigmatic saying. **Truly I say to you** (5:18, 22), **there are some standing here who will not taste death before they see the Son of Man coming in his kingdom**. Does Jesus refer to his resurrection (16:21), or his transfiguration (17:1-8), or the fall of Jerusalem (ch. 24), or his return/*parousia*? In favor of the last possibility is the context of 16:27. If Jesus' statement is taken literally, he is mistaken. If it is taken nonliterally, it warns the audience to be ready for Jesus' imminent return. The urgency of **not tasting death** (which suggests a brief interim period) is reflected in another **Son of Man coming** statement in 10:23. The repetition underlines the sure establishment of God's empire, and Jesus' role in it.

CHAPTER 17

The Way of the Cross

Five short scenes elaborate Jesus' announcement in 16:21-28 of imminent suffering and resurrection.

17:1-8   Jesus Is Transfigured
17:9-13   Elijah Is John the Baptist
17:14-20   A Difficult Exorcism of an Epileptic Boy
17:22-23   A Second Passion Prediction
17:24-27   The Tax in the Fish's Mouth

17:1-8—JESUS IS TRANSFIGURED

This rich and polyvalent scene divinely legitimates and elaborates Jesus' statement in 16:21-28 about his terrible death and glorious resurrection and return.[1]

1. Central to the scene is God's declaration that Jesus is God's son (17:5; repeating 3:17). (i) God's words confirm the disciples' confession of Jesus' identity in 14:33 and 16:16. This confession constitutes the community which Jesus is building (16:18). (ii) God's word also confirms what being "son of God" entails. The audience knows from Jesus' teaching in 16:21, 26-28 that as God's son Jesus will suffer and be vindicated. God's word in 17:5 repeats God's declaration made at Jesus' baptism in 3:17 to confirm Jesus' teaching that sonship involves his crucifixion. The new words, "listen to him," urge the audience to attend carefully to Jesus' teaching in 16:21-28 that he must die and be raised (16:21), that discipleship involves conflict with the status quo and suffering (16:24-26), and that Jesus will return in glory after his resurrection (16:27-28). Though Peter discounted it (16:22-23), God confirms what Jesus has taught.

God's approval for Jesus' teaching is presented in a typical revelation scene. God regularly discloses God's self and will on a mountain.[2] Clouds denote God's (hidden) presence and accompany revelations (see on 17:5). The heavenly voice speaks (Exod 24:16; 1 Kgs 19; Dan 8:16; *1 En* 13:8; *T. Levi* 18:6; *T. Job* 42:1-3; Matt 3:17).

Significantly the announcement is not made to the political and religious elite. It is not made in Jerusalem or in Rome. It is made in a remote place, away from the centers, privately (17:1) to a small group of disciples. The audience knows that marginal locations are central to God's purposes (cf. 2:4-6).

2. God's statement about Jesus' identity confirms his path of suffering. In declaring Jesus is "my Son the beloved," God echoes Isa 42:1, a statement about God's servant (see 3:17). This servant does not use imperial violence and force (contrary to Babylonian power), but suffers in accomplishing God's will of "justice on the earth" (Isa 42:1-4). The echo of Isa 42:1-4 (see also Matt 8:17; 12:18-21) confirms Jesus' suffering as an integral part of God's purposes in overcoming all sinful imperial practices.

3. But the appeal to "listen to him" embraces Jesus' instruction not only about his suffering but also about his future glory through resurrection and his return to establish God's empire in full (16:21, 27-28). His transfigured appearance, face shining like the sun and dazzling white clothes, are common elements in scenes of eschatological vindication (see on 17:2).

T. L. Donaldson notes this eschatological dimension in God's declaration that Jesus is "my Son" (17:5).[3] This is "a typical enthronement formula" evident in a royal Psalm like Ps 2:7 (also 2 Sam 7:14). The transfiguration occurs on a mountain (Matt 17:1; cf. 15:29) which Donaldson identifies (typologically) as Zion, the place of God's throne (Pss 2:4; 48:2; 146:10) and of the anointed king (Ps 2:6). The future fullness of God's reign will be established on Zion (Isa 24:23; 52:7; Ezek 20:40; Zech 14:8-11; *1 En* 18:6-16), as will God's anointed (messiah) and judge (Ezek 17:22-24; *4 Ezra* 13:12-58; *2 Bar* 40:1-4). The scene confirms Jesus as God's son who manifests God's reign in the present (Matt 4:17; cf. Ps 72) and anticipates his installation as the eschatological king on Zion after his resurrection and at his return. See further images of Jesus' enthronement in 28:18-20 and 25:31-46.

4. Prominent through the scene are echoes of Moses receiving the Decalogue from God on Mount Sinai in Exod 24 and 34.[4]

Feature	Jesus in Matthew	Moses in Exodus
Six days later	17:1	24:16
Mountain	17:1	24:12, 15-18; 34:3
Special select group	17:1	24:1
Shining face and skin	17:2	34:29-35
Bright cloud	17:5	24:15-18; 34:5
Voice from cloud	17:5	24:16
Fear of the bystanders	17:6	34:29-30

In addition to these links with Exod 24 and 34, four connections with the larger exodus story exist. (i) Peter's proposed booths or tents (17:4, σκηνή, *skēnē*) recall the "tent of meeting" (Exod 33:7, 8, 9, 10) where Moses met with God and around which was the cloud of God's presence (Exod 33:9-10). The term also denotes the tabernacle in which the ark of the covenant is placed (Exod 40:2, 17, 18, 19, 21, 22; Num 1:50-51). God commissions Joshua as Moses' successor there (Deut 31:14-15) and it enters the land of Canaan (Josh 18:1; 19:51). The term also refers to the thanksgiving festival of tabernacles/booths (*sukkot,* Deut

16:13), a festival which celebrates God's creative faithfulness, and which in Zech 14:16-19 anticipates God's reign.

(ii) The "overshadowing" cloud (ἐπισκιάζω, *episkiazō*, 17:5) appears in Exod 40:35 to overshadow the tent of meeting. In Wis 19:7 (σκιάζω, *skiazō*) it accompanies the exodus through the sea.

(iii) The words "listen to him" appear in Moses' words about "a prophet like me" to whom the people will listen (Deut 18:15). As 16:14 attests, "prophet" is one category for Jesus, though not fully adequate (16:16).

(iv) Both Moses and Elijah (17:4) are associated with Sinai (Exod 24; 1 Kgs 19) in the context of challenging dangerous rulers. In Exodus 34 Moses, having led the people from slavery under Pharaoh, reascends Sinai because the people have rejected God by creating the golden calf (Exod 32) and Moses has smashed the stone tablets (32:19). Elijah, having challenged King Ahab at Carmel, retreats to Horeb/Sinai under a death threat from Ahab and Jezebel (1 Kgs 19:1-2), there to be recommissioned by God. Jesus too has experienced rejection and misunderstanding and is also under a death threat from the elite (12:14; 16:1-12, 13-20, 21-28).

These connections with Moses underline four aspects of Jesus' mission. He is a liberator who frees people from oppressive rule (Rome). He reveals God's will. His ministry is contested, opposed, and rejected, though vindicated by God. Yet he has a greater role than Moses in his death, resurrection, and return.

• 17:1

The temporal marker is vague; **six days later** than when? It recalls Exod 24:16, God's presence on Sinai. The adjective "sixth" appears in 27:45 (also 20:5) to mark the time of darkness prior to Jesus' death, perhaps linking the two scenes, since his resurrection and return presuppose crucifixion (cf. 16:21). **Jesus took Peter and James and his brother John**, three of the first four disciples called (4:18-22; 10:2). (Why is Andrew excluded?) Compare Exod 24:1. And **he led them up a high mountain by themselves**. On **mountains** as places of temptation, see 4:8; of teaching, 5:1; of prayer, 14:23; of gathering, healing, and feeding, 15:29-38. On links with Mounts Carmel, Zion, and Sinai, see above.

• 17:2

And he was transfigured before them. The verb means "transform, change in form" in a visible way (BAGD, 511). Philo uses it of Moses (*Moses* 1.57; cf. *Gaium* 95). J. Behm notes Hellenistic mystical and magical traditions of deification, like that of the Isis initiation in Apuleius, *Metamorphoses* (11.29-30), but he locates this account in Jewish apocalyptic expectations in which the faithful receive a new form in the resurrection (*2 Bar* 51:3).[5] Certainly the description of Jesus' transfigured form derives from those traditions' presentations of the experience of divine power and presence. For **his face shone like the sun,** see Dan 12:3; *1 En* 14:20; 38:4; *T. Levi* 18:4; *4 Ezra* 7:97; 10:25; *2 Bar* 51:3, 10; cf. Philo, *Moses* 2.70 (also Sir 50:1-7 for the high priest Simon son of Onias emerging from the "Most Holy Place"). In Matt 13:43 the righteous, vindicated in the judgment, "shine like the sun." Jesus' vindication in resurrection (cf. 17:9) and his return (16:27-28) anticipate that of the righteous. Heavenly beings and the resurrected righteous have bright clothing (**and his clothes became dazzling white**); see Dan 7:9; *1 En* 14:20; 62:16. This is the destiny of Jesus and his community (16:18). But the way is that of the cross (16:21). **White** garments can also indicate martyrdom (Rev 3:5, 18; 4:4; 6:11; 7:9, 13).

In addition to this anticipation of future eschatological vindication, it should be noted that *light* marks Jesus' present ministry of manifesting God's saving reign in the darkness and death of an imperially controlled world (4:15-16). There are three implications. Already God's future reign is being manifested. The future glorious completion of God's purposes is in continuity with Jesus' present mission. And Jesus' community of disciples as "the light of the world" is given the task of continuing his mission (5:14; 10:7-8). Christology and ecclesiology are intertwined.

• 17:3

Suddenly there appeared to them Moses and Elijah talking with him. The same verb is used in Exod 34:35 for Moses speaking with God. Why **Moses and Elijah**? The question will be partially answered by 17:9-13. Both are foundational figures in shaping God's people.[6] Perhaps they represent the law and the prophets, which Jesus interprets and accomplishes (5:17; 7:12). We have noted above that both encounter God on Sinai/Horeb in situations of rejection. Traditions attest that both did not die (Josephus, *Ant* 4.326, despite Deut 34:7; *Ant* 9.28; 2 Kgs 2:9-12). Do they provide Jesus with further revelation? Jesus is located in the tradition of God's previous dealings with God's people.

• 17:4

Then Peter (still the spokesperson; see 14:28; 15:15; 16:16) **said to Jesus,** "**Lord** (the term of address used by disciples, 8:2), **it is good for us to be here; if you wish** (Peter submits to Jesus this time; contrast 16:22-26), **I will make here three tents, one for you, one for Moses and one for Elijah.**" On **tents** as evoking the exodus story and God's presence, see above (4,i). Does Peter intend to enshrine or prolong what is an important but not final moment? Jesus has a cross awaiting him.

• 17:5

God talks Peter down. **While he was still speaking, suddenly a bright cloud overshadowed them**. On a **cloud** as a sign of God's (hidden) presence, see Exod 16:10; 19:9; Ezek 1:4; Dan 7:13; *4 Ezra* 13:13; 2 Macc 2:7-8; Wis 19:7; Sir 50:6. On **overshadow** evoking Moses, see 4,ii above. God speaks, **and a voice from the cloud said**, (see 1 above; 3:17) "**This is my Son/Child, the beloved; with him I am well pleased.**" On the importance and function of God's declaration, see introductory comments. See on 3:17 (and 2 above) for echoes of Isa 42:1 (suffering servant who redeems the people but not by violence), Ps 2:7 (the Davidic king anointed to manifest God's power in a just reign which sustains the oppressed and vulnerable; Ps 72), Gen 22:2 (Abraham offers his beloved son Isaac), and Exod 4:22-23 (Israel as God's son or covenant people). See also Matt

2:15 for God's son/child not as a divine being but as God's agent, whether the people (Exod 4:22; Hos 11:1), the king (Ps 2:7), the wise person (Wis 2), or heavenly beings (Job 38:7). On Jesus as God's **son** in an intimate relationship of love which forms the basis for Jesus' revelation and faithfulness, see 2:15; 3:17; 4:3, 6; 7:23; 11:25-27; 16:16. At the crucifixion Jesus is confessed as son of God (27:43, 54).

On **listen to him** as God's legitimation of Jesus' teaching, see introductory comments. God mandates that the disciples **listen** to what Jesus has already taught and will yet teach. There are different kinds of **listening** in the gospel: some prior listening needs revising by Jesus' teaching (5:21, 27, 33, 38, 43), some listening involves hearing Jesus' word and doing it. Listening that does not lead to action has severe eschatological consequences (7:24, 26; cf. 10:14; 13:19-23). In contrast to the crowds, disciples hear and understand Jesus' teaching (13:10-17, 23; cf. 15:10). But hearing and understanding are not automatic. The devil can disrupt the process so that faithful discipleship does not follow (13:19). Persecution (13:20-21), daily concerns, and wealth (13:22) can do the same thing. To **listen**, then, is to understand and live by taking up one's cross (16:24-26). To **listen** is a central quality of discipleship.

• 17:6-7

When the disciples heard this, they fell to the ground and were overcome with fear. In **hearing** (the same verb as "listen"), the disciples discern God's presence and address. Their response is typical of people who encounter divine presence. On **falling**, see the magi in 2:11; by contrast the devil's demand in 4:9; see also Gen 17:3 (Abram); Lev 9:24 (the people); Num 16:22 (Moses and Aaron); Josh 5:14 (Joshua); Ezek 1:28 (Ezekiel); Dan 8:17; 10:9 (Daniel). On **fear** in divine presence, see Matt 1:20; 9:8; 14:27; Gen 15:1 (Abram); 26:24 (Isaac); 28:13 (Jacob); Judg 6:23 (Gideon); Dan 8:17. The same phrase translated **overcome with fear** denotes the onlookers' response at Jesus' death (27:54), further connecting the two scenes. See 17:1, 5; 16:21. Both crucifixion and vindication are legitimated.

Jesus reassures them: **But Jesus came and touched them, saying, "Get up and do not be afraid."** On **came**, see 4:3. Twice Jesus approaches disciples (here and 28:18). His **touch** has effected healing (8:3, 15; 9:29; 20:34; also 9:20-21; 14:36). On **touch** and divine appearances, see Isa 6:7; Jer 1:9; Dan 10:10, 16.

• 17:8

And when they looked up, they saw no one except Jesus himself alone. Moses and Elijah have departed.

17:9-13—ELIJAH AND JOHN THE BAPTIST

Elijah's appearance in 17:3 raises a question. How does Jesus' eschatological role announced in 16:21-28 and prefigured in 17:1-8 relate to traditions about Elijah as the forerunner of God's judgment? The scene elaborates an emphasis of 16:21-28 and revisits the role of John the Baptist.

• 17:9

The scene begins with a transition: **As they were coming down from the mountain**. The clause echoes Jesus' descent in 8:1a (significant things happen coming down the mountain) and Moses' descent from Sinai (Exod 34:29). **Jesus ordered them, "Tell no one about the vision until after the Son of Man has been raised from the dead."** The transfiguration in part prefigures Jesus' resurrection (28:16-20). On the command for silence and the need for the disciples to understand the crucifixion and resurrection before making an accurate proclamation, see 16:20.

Jesus identifies the transfiguration as a **vision**. The word denotes revelation from God by verbal or visible means (a theophany) (Gen 15:1 [Abram]; 46:2 [Isaac]; Exod 3:3 [Moses]; Dan 1:17; 7:1; 8:1 [Daniel]; the word is used about twenty-four times). It underlines the revelatory significance of 17:1-8. On **Son of Man**, see 8:20; 16:21. On Jesus being **raised from the dead**, see 16:21. The disciples (**them**) Peter, James, and John are witnesses who ensure continuity between Jesus and the community's proclamation. How does this corporate commission relate to that given to Peter in 16:16-19? Just as Peter's confession was not unique his roles of interpreting and proclaiming are not unique but are shared with community members.

• 17:10-11

And the disciples asked him, "Then why do the scribes say that first Elijah must come?" He replied, "Elijah is indeed coming and will restore all things." On the negative presentation of **scribes**, see 2:4; 15:1; 16:21. Jesus does not disagree with their focus, but the scribes have (typically) missed a crucial piece. As in 2:5-6 they know the scriptures but do not connect them to Jesus.

Prompted by their encounter with Elijah (17:3), the disciples refer to a diverse tradition expecting Elijah's return to prepare for the completion of God's purposes. In Mal 4:5, Elijah is to reconcile households before the judgment. In Sir 48:10 he will "restore the tribes of Jacob," a verse that uses a form of the same verb (**restore**) to refer to the ingathering of the disapora. In *Sib. Or.* 2:187-90, he displays three unspecified signs. The disciples wonder how this expectation fits with Jesus' eschatological role (16:27-28), which has been confirmed in the transfiguration (17:5). Jesus' answer confirms Elijah's key role as preparer or restorer.

• 17:12-13

But there is a twist. Elijah's coming is not future but past, not an eschatological display but a prophetic ministry that challenged the religious (3:7-12) and political (14:2-12) elite in preparation for Jesus' work in manifesting God's empire. **But I tell you** (authoritative speech, 5:18) **that Elijah has already come, and they did not recognize him, but they did to him whatever they pleased. So also the Son of Man is about to suffer at their hands." Then the disciples understood that he was speaking to them about John the Baptist**. As in 16:12, *how* the disciples understand is not made clear. The emphasis falls on the fact *that* they do understand (so 17:5, "listen"). Jesus does not say explicitly here that John is Elijah. He did so in 11:14, but the disciples seem to have missed it. The text shows their growing understanding which will secure their post-Easter proclamation (17:9).

Jesus' claim that Elijah has already come reinforces the view of the present as the time in which God's final purposes are under way. Jesus' summary of John's experience (**not recognized**) emphasizes the rejection narrated previously in 4:12; 11:7-19; 14:1-12. As in 11:18-19, Jesus allies himself with John in terms of the elite's nonunderstanding and rejection in killing him. It is the way of the world, and of prophetic ministry, which disciples also encounter (10:17-18). Jesus' death is inevitable (16:21).

17:14-20—A DIFFICULT EXORCISM OF AN EPILEPTIC BOY

The exorcism (the last in the gospel) is not difficult for Jesus, but it does prove too much for the disciples. Their faith must grow if they are to overcome Satan's reign and remain faithful on the difficult way of the cross (16:22-26).

• 17:14-15

The scene of 17:9-13 happens as they descend from the mountain. As in 8:1-4, that descent brings Jesus and the three disciples back **to the crowd** and its needs (cf. 9:36). The crowd is the constant context for Jesus' ministry, lacking both the hostility of the elite and the little faith of the disciples (e.g., 12:15, 23, 46; 13:34; 14:13, 14, 15, 19; 15:10, 30, 32). See 4:25.[7]

A man came to him. On **came** for reverential approach and recognition of authority, see 4:3, 11; 5:1; 8:2, 5, 19, 25; 9:14, 20, 28; 13:10, 27, 36; 14:12, 15; 15:1, 12, 23, 30; 16:1. This is the first use of **knelt**, a submissive posture. On **Lord** as the form of address used by disciples, see 8:2, 6. He begs for **mercy** (also 9:27; 15:22; 20:30) for his **son**. For other parents seeking Jesus' help on behalf of their children, see 9:18; 15:22 (a demon). On the marginal place of children, see 2:8; 18:1-6; 19:13-15. The man believes that Jesus can transform the situation with healing.

The unnamed man describes his **son's** situation, **for he is an epileptic and suffers terribly; he often falls into the fire and often into the water.** The man's social and economic circumstances, both present and future, are serious. A demon-possessed son probably means social ostracism for the family as others keep their distance. A son who cannot work cannot contribute to the family support or continue the family line of work, whether a small business or land. And since a child is its parents' old-age insurance policy, their outlook is bleak. The man is desperate.[8]

On the term **epileptic**, see 4:24. The term is better translated "moonstruck" and reflects understandings of the evil power of the moon, or of the moon goddess "Selene." The term also has imperial implications in denoting the moon-blessed success of Rome, with its destructive effect on people's lives. The alliance with demons is indicated in 17:18. The moon/demon/goddess threatens the boy's life in destructive acts.

So far the scene appears to be a predictable exorcism or healing scene. Its opening verses have established that the man, in seeking help from Jesus, has recognized his authority and shown faith in him, and that the echo of 4:24 recalls Jesus' previous success in overcoming this situation.

• 17:16

The man introduces a new factor; **And I brought him** (the sick are dependent on others for help; see 4:24; 8:16; 9:2, 32; 12:22; 14:35; cf. 15:30; healing means a new communal role) **to your disciples, but they could not cure him**. On **cure**, see 4:23. The disciples have been given authority to heal and cast out demons in 10:8 (same verb), but cannot. Chapters 14-17 have seen the disciples "fail" numerous times: 14:15-17, 26, 30-31; 15:15-16, 23, 33; 16:5-11, 22-23; 17:4.

• 17:17

Jesus' response is a strong condemnation, **You faithless and perverse generation, how much longer must I be with you? How much longer must I put up with you?** Who is Jesus condemning? It is not the father, who has shown exemplary faith in 17:14-15. In 11:16, 12:39, and 16:4, Jesus uses similar language to condemn the religious elite, but they are not present here. Perhaps he rebukes the crowd, but their role is minimal. The most likely recipients of the rebuke are the disciples. They are not "evil and adulterous" (12:39; 16:4) but (perhaps like the crowd?) **faithless and perverse** (only here in Matthew, and once of Israel in Deut 32:5 as a "perverse generation" which has not responded to God). The charge of being **faithless** will be elaborated in 17:20. Jesus' hometown displays this characteristic (13:58). The disciples have, in this instance, not evidenced what should distinguish them from the crowd.

The phrase **how much longer** commonly appears in psalms of lament to protest God's supposed inactivity and failure to show mercy or do something to change a threatening situation (Pss 13:1-2; 79:5; 89:46). Jesus laments God's lack of revealing activity (cf. 16:17) and the disciples' lack of understanding even though they have made some progress (13:10-17, 51; 16:12; 17:13). Compare 2 Kgs 4:18-37, where Elisha's servant cannot raise a dead child but Elisha can.

• 17:18

"Bring him to me." Jesus rebuked the demon and it came out of him and the boy was cured instantly. The man's faithful recognition of Jesus' authority is honored as Jesus heals his son. For previous exorcisms, see 4:24; 8:16, 28-34; 9:32-34; 12:22-24; 15:22-28. In the exorcisms Jesus overcomes Satan's reign (12:28) and manifests God's life-giving empire, which restores people to health (cf. *2 Bar* 73:1-2) and to new social roles. For the link of demon possession and imperial control, see 4:23-25.

• 17:19

But the central focus is not on the man's faith or Jesus' authority. It is on the lack of faith of the would-be exorcists. **Then the disciples came to Jesus privately and said, "Why could we not cast it out?"** Jesus and the disciples have **private** interaction and instruction on several occasions (17:1; 20:17; 24:3). The verb **cast out** appears in 10:8 when Jesus gives them authority to do so. Why have they been unable to live out their commission?

• 17:20[9]

Jesus' explanation concerns their faith. **He said to them, "Because of your little faith** (see 6:30; 8:26; 14:31; 16:8). **For truly I tell you if you have faith the size of a mustard seed, you will say to this mountain, 'Move from here to there,' and it will move; and nothing will be impossible for you."** There are two problems here. (1) In 17:17 Jesus called them "faithless" but now they have "little faith" (17:20a). (2) What accounts for their failure in 17:20a (their little faith) is commended to them in 17:20b. They are told that they need a little faith **(the size of a mustard seed)** to work great miracles. Then they will be like God and move mountains (Isa 40:4; 49:11). In 13:31 Jesus describes the mustard seed as the smallest of seeds. Its size seems to depict the disciples' "little faith" (6:30; 8:26; 14:31; 16:8), which is inadequate for this task (17:20a).

Part of the resolution seems to lie in understanding 17:17 as describing a lapse in the disciples' basic disposition of "little faith," or as hyperbolically expressing Jesus' frustration.

Beyond this, "little faith" seems to be an ambivalent state. Little faith is inadequate (17:16, 20a) when such faith knows God can transform a situation but does not rely on or trust God's power, graciousness, or sovereign will to do so. The disciples have witnessed Jesus' miracles but do not trust God to do miracles through them. They were rendered faithless by the demon's power and forgetful of God's reign over Satan. They were duped into thinking that God's power could not change this demonic situation. Just as the boy is thrown about and falls over (17:15), the disciples are diverted from their task of manifesting God's empire. In part, they do not understand God as a loving and merciful father who powerfully blesses all (5:45). But also, they misunderstand their own identity. They are a community which Jesus has authorized to continue his mission (10:8). Jesus has given them this authority to manifest God's good reign, in reliance on God's power and mercy. Their faith is "little" in that while it has grown, they still do not seek God's aid with any surety.

On the other hand, "little faith" is adequate when in desperation it cries out to God to act to accomplish God's life-giving purposes in a specific situation. While adequate for a particular situation, it must then develop into a way of life.

In this discussion of faith, Jesus does not say anything about trying to manipulate God to do any and everything which humans demand. This is not faith, as his responses in 4:5-7 show. Faith seeks to enact God's life-giving, merciful, and inclusive purposes.

17:22-23—JESUS' SECOND PASSION PREDICTION

• 17:22

Jesus repeats his teaching from 16:21 and 17:12 that he will be killed and raised. The repetition underlines its importance.[10]

The setting is vague geographically (**As they were gathering in Galilee**) since Jesus has been in Galilee since 4:12. But it is significant thematically because it recalls the context of imperial control in which his ministry occurs (see 4:15-16). Throughout, his proclamation and demonstration of God's empire have challenged the status quo and its political and religious leadership. It is inevitable that this alliance strikes back. **Jesus said to them,** (presumably the disciples, the audience for 16:21 and 17:12), **"The Son of Man is going to be arrested/ betrayed into human hands**. On **Son of Man** denoting Jesus' public ministry and rejection, see 8:20.

The verb **arrested/betrayed** is polyvalent and difficult to translate. (1) It means **arrest**. In 4:12 it denotes John's arrest (linking Jesus and John; also 5:25; 10:17, 19; 18:34). (2) It can also mean **betray**. In 10:4, linked with Judas' name, it anticipates Jesus' betrayal (also 10:21; note the different sense in 11:27). 3) It expresses a sense of **being in the control of** (especially with the phrase "into the hands of"). In Dan 7:25, "the holy ones . . . will be given into his power for a time." This common LXX phrase is translated variously as "delivered into the hands of" (Lev 26:25) or "handed over to" (Deut 1:28). Here, **the human hands** that will control Jesus are unspecified, though in 16:21 the religious elite are identified as the agents of Jesus' death (so also 20:18). The Romans also participate (20:19; ch. 27).

(4) But the irony of the phrase should not be lost. While these **human hands** of the religious and political elite "control" Jesus in putting him to death, their attempts will be thwarted and God's purposes will prevail. The verb **hand over/ control** often denotes God's action (Num 21:34; Deut 2:24; etc.) indicating that these events happen in the divine purposes ("must" in 16:21) and with Jesus' consent. This fourth sense is reinforced by the final clauses; though **they will kill him, on the third day he will be raised** (the passive form suggests "by God"; see 16:21). On **kill**, see 16:21, 24; also 17:2 for martyrdom. (5) The verb can denote God's **punishment**. See Jer 21:10; Ezek 11:9-11; the suffering servant (cf. Matt 8:17; 12:18-21; 17:5) in Isa 53:6, "the Lord has laid on him the iniquity of us all" (also 53:12). Why is Jesus being punished (20:28)? The audience must discern which meaning/s are appropriate in each usage.

The disciples **were greatly distressed**. Absent is any response comparable to Peter's in 16:22-23. This response suggests that they have understood that Jesus' death is imminent, and perhaps indicates they have understood that his death shapes their way of life (16:24-26). But have they heard that he will be raised, or is their faith as yet too little to understand (17:9, 17-20)?

17:24-27—THE TAX IN THE FISH'S MOUTH

Most readings of this enigmatic scene are apolitical and tax-free.[11] Most commentators argue that the scene provides the Matthean community with a theological object lesson that has nothing to do with paying taxes. Rather they suggest that it instructs the community variously about God as a loving father, about sonship (Jesus' and the disciples'), about Peter, about the rejection of Israel, about freedom from the temple cult, about giving as a voluntary action rather than as theocratic taxation, and, especially, about exercising Christian freedom responsibly, either in relation to the state or, more commonly, so as not to offend or cause a community member to stumble (so 18:1-14).

However, this scene uses the setting of Jesus' day to instruct the gospel's audience in its post-70 setting about paying a post-70 tax. This tax for the temple of Jupiter Capitolinus was levied by Rome on Jews, including Matthew's (largely) Christian-Jewish community. While this tax is to be paid, payment is not a matter of pragmatic survival for a marginal community, nor an acknowledgment of or submission to Roman sovereignty, as paying imperial taxes usually denotes. Rather, paradoxical as it may seem, payment is a defiant testimony to God's sovereignty. Payment expresses the community's allegiance to and anticipation of God's empire, which will overcome Roman rule.

Why is the story positioned here? It further elaborates Jesus' announcement of his imminent suffering and death repeated in the previous scene (17:22-23; cf. 16:21-22). The disciples are "greatly distressed" (17:22). It seems as though "the hands of people" (the religious and political elite) are in control. This scene reassures them and the audience that it is not so, that even in the face of Roman power God is sovereign. It also prepares for chapter 18. To live as a marginal community in these circumstances requires not only a resisting and subversive praxis which anticipates God's future victory and represents it in present actions (paying the tax), but also a strong communal life marked by vigilant support (18:1-14), discipline (18:15-20), and forgiveness (18:21-35) for community members.

• 17:24

The scene is set in **Capernaum**, where Jesus lives (4:13), as does Peter (8:5, 14). It has not been receptive to Jesus' ministry (11:23). But it does provide a ready supply of fish. **The collectors of the half-shekel tax came to Peter.** The **half-shekel tax** (δίδραχμα, *didrachma*; so Josephus, *JW* 7.218, and Dio Cassius 65.7.2) was levied annually after 70 by Rome on Jews.[12] Before 70, Jews paid this tax to support the Jerusalem temple (Josephus, *Ant* 18.312; *JW* 7.218; Philo, *Spec Leg* 1.78). With the fall of Jerusalem and the temple in 70 C.E., Rome established an imperial treasury (the *fiscus Ioudaicus*) to oversee a new use for the tax. The emperor Vespasian co-opted it to rebuild and sustain the temple of Jupiter Capitolinus in Rome. That which had formerly proclaimed the Jewish God now provided a rebuilt temple for the triumphant Jupiter, patron god of the Flavians and the empire (see Introduction, section 9). The tax had punitive and propaganda value. Its payment reminded Jews of Roman political, military, economic, and religious sovereignty and superiority sanctioned by Jupiter. The tax defined Jews, including Matthew's audience, as "a defeated race punished for [their] nationality."[13]

Should Matthew's community, committed to Jesus, pay such a tax? The **collectors of the tax** set up a scene in which Jesus instructs the gospel's audience.

They ask Peter, **Does your teacher not pay the tax?** Though they address **Peter**, the plural pronoun **your** indicates a communal concern (9:11; 23:8). **Peter** represents the community of disciples (see 16:16-19). The collectors refer to Jesus as **teacher**. The verb **pay,** with a different meaning ("finish"), concludes Jesus' teaching discourses (7:28; 11:1; 13:53; 19:1; 26:1) and underlines his teaching authority. Peter's positive answer (**He said, "Yes"**) confirms that Jesus pays it (17:25a). Disciples are to imitate his practice (10:24-25).

If the scene were only about actions it could end here. But the subsequent material suggests that more is at issue. The scene is concerned with that which shapes or interprets their practice.

• 17:25

When Peter returns home,[14] **Jesus spoke of it first saying. . . .** Jesus was not present in 17:24. He has exhibited similar special knowledge previously (9:3-4; 12:14-15, 25) and will do so again in the next discussion about taxes (22:18). His mysterious knowledge enhances his authority.

Jesus' question to Peter, called here Simon,[15] expands the focus. **"From whom do kings of the earth take toll or tribute?"** The noun **toll** refers to various "taxes, customs duties and tribute money,"[16] while **tribute** is a poll tax paid on the basis of a census.[17] The two terms embrace a broad spectrum of taxation. Rome regarded taxes as the price for maintaining peace (the Roman general Cerialis in Tacitus, *Hist* 4.74), as the means of supporting the Roman way of life (Tacitus, *Ann* 13.50), and as an expression of sovereignty since the refusal to pay was regarded as rebellion against Rome.[18] See 9:9.

Jesus invokes the traditions of **the kings of the earth**. The phrase has negative associations. It designates kings opposed to God's purposes and sovereignty, but over whom God has control. See Pss 2:2; 76:12-13; 89:27-28; 102:16; 138:4; 148:11. Moses (Deut 17:14-17) and Samuel (1 Sam 8:9-18) warned of the oppressive and exploitative ways of kings who tax and requisition labor and property in order to expand their destructive power and maintain military might. Herod has demonstrated such power (see Matt 2), as have Archelaus (2:22), Solomon (6:29), and Herod Antipas (14:1-12). The phrase is generic, referring variously to Egyptian, Assyrian, Babylonian, Persian, Seleucid, and Roman rulers. But **the kings of the earth** do not hold ultimate sway or determine human destiny. The kings' ways are not God's ways but they are subject to God's power. See Josh 12:1; Ezra 9:7; Lam 4:12; Ezek 27:33; *1 En* 48:8; *4 Ezra* 15:20; Rev 1:5; 6:15. The tradition of **the kings of the earth** affirms that God's empire, manifested in Jesus, will be victorious.

Jesus asks Peter who pays the **tolls and tribute** which **the kings of the earth** employ to control and subjugate subjects. Do they levy them **from their children or from foreigners/others?**

Suggestions that **children** should be read as the king's nation are not convincing. Kings did tax their own people. The **children** are the ruler's immediate physical offspring, the future, the apparently inevitable successors to and ominous continuation of the ways of the kings of the earth. They alone are exempt from taxation.

• **17:26**

The answer to Jesus' question, then, is obvious to anyone familiar with the taxing ways of kings. Taxes are paid **"from others."** Jesus states the corollary, **"Then the children are free."** This is the everyday imperial situation, well known to those who live with the taxing presence of empires. The elite privileges its own at the expense of the rest. Peter answers correctly, and Jesus confirms Peter's answer. There is no implicit comparison or analogy with God, no claim that kings act toward their children *as* God acts toward God's children. The "kings of the earth" (see 17:25) act in a manner contrary to God's purposes.[19]

• **17:27**

The only option for Jesus and Peter (and all disciples) is to pay the tax. **And**[20] **so that we do not give offense to them**, they pay, as Peter in v. 25 and Jesus in v. 26 have already indicated. To **scandalize/offend** the powerful elite would bring trouble. Paying makes pragmatic sense in order to survive.

But doesn't paying signify submission to Rome's sovereignty? Does it not acknowledge Jupiter's superiority over Israel's God, since Jupiter's will is done in destroying the Jerusalem temple and in establishing the Flavian dynasty? Where is God's sovereignty which thwarts the wicked? The "kings of the earth" tradition celebrates God's control over the nations and the kings. God laughs at their puny rebellion and holds them in derision (Ps 2:4). But the nations seem to have won! Where is the derisive laugh in this scene? Where is God's empire which Jesus is to manifest?

Jesus instructs Peter to **go to the sea and cast a hook; take the first fish that comes up; and when you open its mouth, you will find a coin** (στατήρ, *statēr*[21]); **take that and give it to them for you and me.** This miraculous procurement does not emphasize Jesus' voluntary payment, as some argue. The scene has shown that Jesus has no option but to pay. Rather it highlights God's provision.

The gospel's audience knows three previous stories about fish in the gospel; see 7:10; 14:13-21; 15:32-39. In each, God overcomes impossible circumstances to demonstrate compassion and sovereign power by supplying fish. Peter's procuring of the coin from the fish's mouth to pay the tax at Jesus' bidding emphasizes the same qualities. Fish are subject to God's sovereignty. God ensures that it is caught. God supplies both fish and coin.

This affirmation of God's powerful sovereignty is profoundly significant in a world that believed the emperor's *numen* or *genius* (personal power) influenced not only people but also birds, animals, and fish to recognize him as master and worship him. Martial (*Epig* 4.30.4-5) notes fish wishing to lick Domitian's hand, and Juvenal, in parody, describes a large fish given to Domitian, "the ruler of lands and seas and nations," because it "wished to be caught" (*capi voluit*).[22] The fisherman's motive for giving Domitian the fish attests Domitian's (oppressive) sovereignty. Numerous informers crowd the shoreline. So fine a fish was bound to be seized since "every rare and beautiful thing in the wide ocean . . . belongs to the imperial treasury" (*Sat* 4.51-55). For Rome's control of the sea and fish, see 4:18-22. But in Matthew's story, the fish is subject to God's sovereignty, not Rome's. For God's sovereignty over the sea, see 8:23-27; 14:22-33.

The tax is also in God's sovereignty. God ensures not only that a fish is caught but that the tax coin is in its mouth (17:27). The tax too falls within the sphere of God's sovereignty. Rome imposes the tax to assert its supremacy and to subjugate, humiliate, and punish. But this story shows that the tax is subject to God's power and sovereignty. Paying the tax, then, is no longer for disciples of Jesus an action defined by Rome, no longer an action that acknowledges the all-controlling power of the (Roman) kings of the earth and the oppressive sovereignty of the empire. Paying what God provides attests God's sovereignty. Paying the tax becomes, for those with eyes to see, a subversive not a subjugating act, a defiant act which symbolizes Rome's limited power subordinate to God. Rome imagines that it rules, but for the community which knows this story, there is the reassurance—and in paying the tax a visible sign—that the destiny of the nations is in God's hands and that God's empire will be established. See 9:9; 22:15-22.

For similar subversive actions which provide an alternative to the usual options of "fight or flight," violence or complicity, see 5:38-42. Here the act benefits the community of disciples. The story strengthens its identity and reminds the gospel's audience in Antioch that Roman power, which crucified Jesus and which must be taken seriously as a daily reality, is not the final or determinative reality. God's sovereignty will triumph.

The scene's posture is summarized in the oft-noted, anonymous proverb, "As the ruler/general/king passes by, the peasant bows—and farts."

CHAPTER 18

Jesus' Fourth Teaching Discourse

A Community of Sustaining Relationships and Practices

To live the way of the cross which Jesus outlines in 16:21-17:27 is difficult. It is a marginal lifestyle, lived as participants in the dominant society with its centers of empire and synagogue, yet in tension with it as a countercultural, alternative community. Its commitments and practices embody God's empire and challenge those of the dominant society.

To support this way of life, Jesus instructs the disciples in chapter 18, the fourth of his five major discourses (chs. 5-7; 10; 13; 24-25), about being a community of sustaining relationships and practices. Key repeated vocabulary and distinct themes mark out six sections. This alternative community lives as marginal children (18:1-5). Members do not cause each other to stumble (18:6-9). They take care of each other (18:10-14). They exercise communal reproof and restoration (18:15-20). They forgive repeatedly (18:21-22), never forgetting that God's forgiveness of them requires them to extend forgiveness to each other (18:23-25). With these practices they sustain one another in the demanding way of the cross.

The chapter includes four references to God's empire or reign (18:1, 3, 4, 23). The community is brought into existence by God's empire manifested in the call and ministry of Jesus (4:17-25). That reign shapes practices and relationships which differ greatly from Rome's empire. Instead of the empire's arrogant privileging of the center and mistreatment of the rest, instead of its hierarchical structure whereby a few control the many, this community practices humility, includes the marginalized, and exercises care for one another. Instead of exterminating or excluding dissenters, it seeks inclusion and relationship (18:15-20), forgiveness and reconciliation (18:21-35).[1]

18:1-14—SUSTAINING RELATIONSHIPS

18:1-5—LIKE A CHILD

• 18:1

The disciples initiate the discourse (so 13:10; 15:12, 15, 33; 17:10, 19): **At that time the disciples came** (see 4:3; 5:1) **to Jesus and asked, "Who is the greatest in the empire of heaven?"** On **empire**, see 3:2; 4:17; chapter 13 passim. Why do they ask this question? (1) Perhaps it is spurred by the role that Jesus gives to Peter and by his uneven behavior in 16:16-19, 22-23; 17:4, 24. (2) Perhaps Jesus' evoking of the "kings of the earth" tradition (17:25) in which their pretensions to greatness are relativized in relation to God's purposes provokes it. What then is greatness and who has it? (3) Perhaps it derives from Jesus' words about the way of the cross in 16:24. The cross is a way of shame and exclusion in the imperial world. What does greatness look like on that way? (4) Perhaps it derives from their cultural context, in which greatness comprises status accumulated from wealth, education, birth, patronage, office, and power exercised over others for one's own benefit and status (cf. 20:25). Is Jesus' new community (16:18) the same or different? Jesus has anticipated the issue in indicating that doing and teaching his instruction mean being great in God's reign (so 5:19).

• 18:2

Jesus' response is to define greatness not in terms of the empire's quest for territory, control, wealth, prominence, and so on, but in terms of the margins. **He called a child whom he put among them**, as he has **called** disciples (10:1; 15:32) and a crowd (15:10). The selection of a **child** as the visual aid is crucial. For **child** as excluded from the adult male center, as insignificant, as vulnerable, as dangerous and unpredictable, see 2:8 and 19:13-15.[2] Note their vulnerability in a violent and dangerous world subject to imperial violence (2:8, 9, 11, 13, 14, 20, 21), hunger (14:21; 15:38), sickness including paralysis (8:6; 9:2), death (9:18), and demon possession (15:26; 17:18; see 4:23-24). The phrase **among them** appears in 14:6 when Herodias's daughter dances at Herod's party. Jesus' community contrasts to that of the political elite.

• 18:3-4

While Jesus values marginalized children (18:2), the child becomes a metaphor of discipleship. **And he said, "Truly I tell you** (see 5:18) **unless you change/turn and become like children, you will never enter the empire of heaven. Whoever becomes humble like this child is the greatest in the empire of heaven."** To become **like a child** is defined as being **humble**. This is not a personal characteristic (certainly not the post-Enlightenment emphasis on the innocence and purity of children) but a social location of powerlessness (see 18:2).

Disciples form a community of children, marginal and without status as far as their societal structures are concerned yet central to God's purposes (cf. Bethlehem in 2:6).

Jesus describes himself with a cognate form of **humble** in 11:29, a synonym for "meek" (see 5:5; 11:29; Ps 37). These terms denote the humiliated righteous, who experience the destructive impact of the oppressive wealthy and powerful elite, who challenge it by looking to God to transform unjust situations and social relationships, and to restore adequate resources. That disciples live this (missional) lifestyle is not a new teaching but repeats what Jesus has already said (5:3-12; 11:28-30). But disciples must **change/turn**; they must learn this new identity and lifestyle, a process of being socialized out of dominant cultural patterns and into new practices and relationships appropriate to God's empire.

To **enter God's empire** is not a call to become disciples (4:18-22; 10:2-4) but anticipates participating in God's purposes beyond the judgment (5:20; 7:21; 19:23-24). To be vindicated in the judgment, to participate fully in God's purposes, requires this way of life.[3] On the **empire of heaven**, see 3:2; 4:17; chapter 13. Its threefold use in vv. 1-5 emphasizes that God's reign creates and shapes this community.

• 18:5

Whoever welcomes one such child in my name welcomes me. Is Jesus speaking of welcoming a literal child or using **child** as a metaphor for a disciple? Without dismissing the importance of the former, several factors emphasize the latter sense. (1) The link of disciples and children has been made in vv. 3-4. (2) The further links with the meek and humble depict the mission lifestyle of disciples which requires response from others. (3) The language of **welcome/ receive** was prominent (same verb) in 10:14, 40-41 to denote trusting response to disciples in mission. (4) There the same link of receiving a disciple (listening to and believing their words about God's empire, 10:14) and receiving Jesus is made (10:40). (5) The phrase **in my name** emphasizes this link and its missional significance. Jesus' **name** represents his mission of saving from sin (1:21). But disciples will be hated because of Jesus' **name** (10:22), because they embody his mission in their lifestyle. Their lifestyle challenges the current social structure and its legitimating worldview. But some will welcome them.

18:6-9—DO NOT CAUSE ONE ANOTHER TO STUMBLE

Such a way of life is demanding. It is possible only as the community of disciples sustains one another. There are dire warnings for those who divert or impede this existence.

• 18:6

The opening clause, **If anyone of you puts a stumbling block before one of these little ones who believe in me**, introduces the key concern. Causing other disciples to stumble or sin and fall away is a serious offense. To **scandalize**, or

to put a stumbling block before, or **to cause to sin** recurs in 18:8, 9, and its cognate noun appears three times in 18:7. The verb has appeared already in 5:29-30 referring to body parts which cause sin, in 11:6 (also 13:57; 15:12) to denote a negative response to Jesus, and in 13:21 to describe a disciple who begins to believe the word but ceases to be a disciple because of trouble or persecution (also 24:10; 26:31, 33). In 13:41-42 the noun denotes eschatological judgment on sinners and in 16:23 Peter is a stumbling block for Jesus.

The term for disciples **one of these little ones who believe in me** expresses the vulnerability of disciples in their difficult, against-the-grain, existence centered on Jesus. The term applies to all disciples, not a special group, because all disciples are vulnerable and all **believe** in Jesus. As **little ones,** they are weak and few (7:13-14; Introduction, section 7); they seem powerless before the political, social, economic, and religious elite. Yet they are Jesus' agents (10:42), commissioned by him (10:1-15), enabled by the Spirit (10:20), and assured of participation in the completion of God's purposes if they remain faithful in the midst of opposition (10:32-33). Here their allegiance to Jesus is defined as **believing in me**. This is a synonym for following Jesus (4:18-22). Jesus has looked for faith or trust or dependence on him throughout his mission and has usually found it not among the elite but among the marginal (see 8:10, 13; 9:2, 22, 28-29; 15:28; 17:20). Disciples exhibit it (little faith, 6:30; 8:26; 14:31; 16:8) but the crowds and elite do not.

To divert or destroy the faith of a disciple or follower will mean dreadful punishment: **it would be better for you if a millstone were fastened around your neck and you were drowned in the depth of the sea.** A millstone brings death (Judg 9:53; Rev 18:21 [destruction of Babylon/Rome]); among other punishments, Augustus used stones around necks to drown some because of "acts of arrogance and greed" (Suetonius, *Augustus* 67). On **sea,** see 8:23-27; 14:22-33. Again Jesus bullies disciples into obedience with a threat that imitates imperial practices.

• 18:7

Jesus follows this threat with two woes. This form of speech expresses God's disapproval and judgment (see 11:21). First, a general **woe** expresses disapproval **on the world,** the realm of everyday political, economic, social, and religious life over whose empires the devil claims control (see 4:8). The world is tempting (16:26), a source of inevitable (**it is necessary**) stumbling blocks with its different priorities and structures (cf. 13:22). Their inevitability derives from the devil's work, which intensifies toward the completion of God's purposes (cf. 13:41; 24:10). Some individuals also become agents of that opposition (Peter in 16:22-23). So the general **woe** is followed by a much more specific one; **woe to the one by whom the stumbling block comes!**

• 18:8-9

Two hyperbolic and graphic verses urge disciples to rid themselves of whatever causes them to sin, whether **hand, foot,** or **eye**. Presumably this will ensure their participation in God's future (**to enter life;** cf. 7:14; 19:16-17; 25:46), rather than being condemned (**thrown into the eternal fire/hell of fire**; see 5:22) as well as prevent others from being caused to sin or stumble. Sin must not reign in this community. The two verses (in reverse order and with some minor emendations) essentially repeat 5:29-30, where they warned against destructive male lust and adultery.

18:10-14—A COMMUNITY OF CARE

Having been warned against harming or destroying other disciples, the community is exhorted to active care and respect.

• 18:10
The exhortation to caring relationships is first stated negatively: **See that you do not despise one of these little ones**. As is clear from 18:6, the exhortation concerns relationship with all disciples, not a special group. The opening imperative **see** introduces severe warnings (8:4; 9:30; 16:6; 24:6). The phrase **one of these little ones** links the sections (18:6, 10, 14) and highlights the disciples' vulnerability and marginality. In 6:24, the verb **despise** parallels "hate" and contrasts with "be devoted to" and "love." To **despise** is to disregard other disciples, to not be committed or loving to them. With such attitudes and practices, the marginal and hard-pressed community will self-destruct.

The exhortation is supported (**for**) with Jesus' disclosure (**I tell you**) of both the value of every disciple to God, and of God's all-seeing presence; **in heaven their angels continually see the face of my Father in heaven**. Various traditions attest angels who watch over people and nations.[4] Angels enjoy God's presence (Tob 12:12-15; *1 En* 20; 1QH 6:13; Luke 1:19). Through these angels, the community is within God's care and purview. While that is reassuring, there is an implicit command: if this is how it is in heaven, so it must be among disciples on earth (6:10). There is also an implicit threat. The all-seeing **Father** (5:16, 45; 6:1-18; 11:25-27; 12:50; 23:9) knows if disciples make others stumble or despise them (18:6-9, 10a) and will punish as promised in 18:6-9.

• 18:12[5]
A double question introduces a story that exemplifies God's care for every disciple. The first question, **What do you think?**, will introduce another parable in 21:28; it requires an audience to consider a matter or offer an opinion (17:25; 22:17, 42; 26:66). The second question asks for agreement that a shepherd would pursue a straying sheep: **If a shepherd has a hundred sheep, and one of them has gone astray, does he not leave the ninety-nine on the mountains and go in search of the one that went astray?** The common shepherd-sheep image evokes the tradition of God's people as sheep and their leaders/king/God/Jesus as shepherd (cf. Ps 100). See Matt 2:6; 9:36; 10:6, 16; 12:11-12; 14:14; 15:24. The image has affirmed the identity of disciples as part of God's people. But it has also critiqued the religious leaders, especially in Ezek 34, for their failure to fulfill their calling in misleading and harassing the sheep. In this verse, echoes of

Ezek 34:16 reinforce that critique.[6] In contrast to the unfaithful religious leaders, God will *seek* the *lost* and return the *strayed* sheep. Ezek 34:16 and this verse use the same Greek words.

In addition, the **sheep** image attests (1) the capacity of sheep to **go astray** (used twice). In the context of 18:1-10, the sheep who goes astray is a disciple who has not remained faithful, because of other disciples, or because of "persecution or distress, the cares of the world or lure of wealth" (cf. 13:21-22). (2) Yet **one** straying sheep in a flock of one hundred is valued. The surprising[7] action of the shepherd in putting the rest at risk while retrieving that one sheep (Jesus' action in his ministry to Israel, cf. 9:36) attests its value.

• **18:13**

And if he finds it, he rejoices over it more than over the ninety-nine that never went astray. As with parables of the treasure and merchant (13:44-45), here the act of finding the straying disciple is celebrated with great rejoicing. The emphasis on the joy of restoring the one downplays the faithfulness of the ninety-nine and their exposure to danger in the shepherd's absence. That joy is greater perhaps because finding the one sheep is not certain (**if**). Do the numbers (**one hundred**) suggest anything about the size of the Matthean community?

• **18:14**

The shepherd exemplifies God's will: **So it is not the will of your Father in heaven that one of these little ones should be lost/perish.** Straying disciples can **be lost/perish**, a verb that can denote eschatological condemnation (5:29-30; 16:25) as well as a situation of lostness from which God saves (8:25; 10:6; 15:24). How is God's saving will accomplished? God's **will** is to be done by disciples (6:10; 7:21; 12:50). The statement of God's will conveys a command to the community of disciples to imitate the shepherd (God/Jesus) in being vigilant and active in seeking any disciple that wanders. For **will** and **Father in heaven**, see 7:21; 12:50; 21:31; 26:42. For God as a **father** who loves and blesses inclusively and indiscriminately, see 5:45; 18:10.

18:15-20—COMMUNAL REPROOF AND RESTORATION

So far Jesus' teaching has identified five features of the community of disciples. (1) The image of being like a child indicates a social location of insignificance, marked by powerlessness and marginality. (2) There it lives an alternative, against-the-grain life of the cross, the paradoxical way of greatness. (3) Given this difficult existence, disciples must not cause each other to fall or sin. (4) They must care for one another, actively vigilant in guarding one another as God guards them. (5) In this they embody God's love.

Yet despite such exhortations, conflict is inevitable among humans, especially among a hard-pressed, minority, and marginal community. How a community handles such conflict is crucial to its survival. Verses 15-20 outline a procedure of communal reproof and conflict resolution.

Numerous communities and groups in the first century developed procedures for reproving members and resolving conflict. R. C. Douglas notes that Hellenistic-Roman cities administered their affairs often through councils/assemblies (or *ekklēsiai;* see 16:18), which exercised disciplinary power including exclusion (Sir 23:24; Acts 19:38-39; Josephus, *Ant* 19.332).[8] Some Jewish groups drew on a tradition of reproof from Lev 19:15-18 (see Sir 19:13-20:3; *T. Gad* 4:1-3; 6:1-6). For Qumran, see 1QS 5:24-6:1; CD 9:2-8.[9] Voluntary associations (see Introduction, section 10) provided for reproof and exclusion from the group.[10] D. Duling discusses procedures from the *Iobachoi* (ca. 150 C.E.) for dealing with quarreling, uncivil behavior, demeaning, insults, taking someone's place (of honor?), and fistfights.[11] There is no private reproof (contrast Matt 18:15), but there is a public process involving two witnesses (evidence), a pecuniary punishment, and exclusion until the fine is paid. S. C. Barton and G. H. R. Horsley discuss an inscription from Philadelphia (*SIG*[3] 985) for a group founded by Dionysius at Zeus's urging. Loss of membership and expulsion follow a failure to comply with social and sexual codes.[12]

Matthew's instruction has clear affinities with these groups. But it "is not as explicitly developed as . . . the voluntary associations . . . and especially the Dead Sea Scrolls."[13] Lacking, for instance, are clear decision-making procedures in the assembly, roles for stipulated officers or leaders, specified penalties and fines, and a formal means of readmittance. The instructions resist punitive provisions and emphasize "unbounded reproof." They recognize conflict and offense, but seek above all to restore the offender to reconciled relationships in the community.

• 18:15

Jesus' exhortations in 18:1-14 recognize that the community is not perfect. What happens **if your brother or sister sins against you**. On **brother or sister** as a term for members of the family or household of disciples, see 12:46-50. What constitutes sinning is not specified with examples. But from the following procedure it involves observable, public behavior (witnesses) which impacts another (**against you**).

The first step is initiated by the wronged (**Go and point out the fault**) in a private meeting (**when the two of you are alone**). This step recognizes that sinning against another is serious, breaks relationship, and needs restorative action. The offended is to act as the shepherd does in 18:10-14 and seek out the one who has erred. See Lev 19:17. Could **pointing out the fault** involve others as witnesses to the offense? The purpose seems to be to establish agreement on the nature of the act and to effect reconciliation through forgiveness (6:14-15; 18:12-14, 21-35). **If the member listens to you, you have regained that one.** To **listen** is more than literal hearing; it is understanding what is at stake in the exchange (cf. 13:10-17; 17:5). This would involve acknowledgment of fault, repentance, and forgiveness, in order to achieve the goal of reconciliation.

• 18:16

But this outcome is not guaranteed: **But if you are not listened to**. Step 2 involves a further visit and witnesses. **Take one or two others along with you so that every word may be confirmed by the evidence of two or three witnesses**. The legal principle of two or three witnesses is clear in Deut 19:15 and evident in the voluntary associations' processes. The witnesses represent the community's authority and desire for reconciliation.

• 18:17

This visit may effect reconciliation. But that is not certain either: **But if the member refuses to listen to them, tell it to the church**. For the verb **refuses to listen** (only in this verse in the gospel) see Esth 3:8; Tob 3:4. For the **church** as Jesus' community, an alternative to city assemblies under the empire's control, see 16:18. What initially involved two members, then two or three witnesses, now involves the whole assembly.

This is a further opportunity to effect reconciliation, but that outcome is not certain. **If the offender refuses to listen even to the church, let such a one be to you as a Gentile and a tax collector.** What do this attitude and practice (**let such a one be to you as**) involve? Is a formal act of excommunication in view? Or is it a more informal recognition that the relationship has been broken, that the offender has put him- or herself outside the community by refusing to do God's will taught by Jesus? The latter seems more in keeping with the conciliatory emphasis and the lack of highly developed procedures. But either way, to be as **a Gentile and a tax collector** is not to be shunned or excluded permanently. The terms designate distinct and different groups in contrast to disciples, who are to surpass them in displays of inclusive love (5:43-48). Jesus associates with tax collectors (9:9, 10-13; 11:19). He benefits Gentiles (8:5-13; 12:18, 21; 15:21-28). **Gentiles and tax collectors** are objects of mission, people to be won over to the community of disciples. The three efforts to reconcile the person outlined in 18:15-17 do not finish the process. Though unspecified, restorative efforts continue.

• 18:18-19

The community's response to the situation is ratified by God. **Truly I tell you** (authoritative speech; 5:18; 10:15), **whatever you bind on earth will be bound in heaven, and whatever you loose on earth will be loosed in heaven.** See 16:19, where Peter represents the whole community's task of interpreting God's will in the scriptures and in Jesus' teaching. Their communal task is to discern a way of life expressive of God's empire. In the context of 18:15-17, **binding** and **loosing** refer to the same task of establishing appropriate conduct. The community must discern the presence or absence of repentance and forgiveness and determine whether the offender is within or outside the community.

But the emphasis continues on reconciliation. **Again** (repeating v. 18's point for emphasis) **truly I tell you if two of you on earth agree about anything you**

ask, it will be done for you by my Father in heaven. What is ratified is not the offender's *permanent* exclusion. Like God (18:10-14), the community pursues the difficult task of restoration. For this it must pray as it does its reconciling work (18:17). The verb **ask** denotes prayer in 6:8. To **agree** in praying for the offender's restoration expresses the willingness of community members (including the aggrieved?) to forgive the offender and to effect reconciliation.

• 18:20

This missioning, reconciling, and praying community of disciples committed to Jesus (**in my name**) is the place of Jesus' presence, represented by and encountered in these acts. **For where two or three are gathered in my name, I am there among them.** Jesus manifests God's saving presence and empire (1:21-23; 4:17; 9:1-8; 10:40; 12:28; 28:20). There may well be a polemical edge to the claim. Post-70 Judaism debated several issues, including where and how God's forgiving presence and will were encountered now that the temple was destroyed.[14] Matthew's answer is Jesus. See Introduction, section 8. Does the verb **gather**, a cognate of the noun "synagogue," heighten this distinction? Further, against claims that the emperor and empire manifest the gods' presence in a hierarchical and controlled society which executes its offenders (see 16:21, 24; 17:22; 20:17-19), God's presence is found in a merciful, inclusive community committed to reconciliation and forgiveness (see Introduction, section 9).

18:21-22—A COMMUNITY OF REPEATED FORGIVENESS

• 18:21-22

To prevent exclusion from the community, or to effect reconciliation within it, requires constant and repeated forgiveness. **Peter** is again the spokesperson (see 4:18-20; 10:2; 14:18-29; 15:15; 16:16-18, 22-23; 17:4, 24; 19:27). **Then Peter came and said to him, "Lord** (as disciples' address for Jesus, see 8:6), **if my brother or sister sins against me, how often should I forgive? As many as seven times?"** The question is not about the offending person's responsibilities. They were made clear in 18:15, namely, "to listen," which involves recognizing sin and asking for forgiveness. Rather, Peter's question focuses on the offended person's role. The generous offering of forgiveness does not negate the seriousness of sin or the community's responsibility to reprove the offender, even to the point of recognizing that he or she has become an outsider (for whom prayer and mission are required).

Why the number **seven**? Perhaps it simply denotes numerous offenses and generous forgiveness. Or it may echo Lev 16 (Lev 19 was evoked by 18:15), which requires sprinkling of blood on the mercy seat seven times (Lev 16:14, 19). Jesus' response effectively knows no limits: **Not seven times, but I tell you, seventy-seven times** (or **seventy times seven**).

18:23-35—GOD'S FORGIVENESS MANDATES COMMUNAL
FORGIVENESS: HOW NOT TO DO IT

The parable of the unforgiving servant asserts a basic point: God requires disciples to forgive one another. The forgiven but unforgiving slave[15] portrays the disastrous consequences which befall the disciple who "does not listen" (18:16, 17 [twice]), who does not effect forgiveness with others. The parable makes the point by drawing an analogy between forgiving a debt/loan and sin (linked in the Lord's Prayer, 6:12, 14-15).[16]

But various details and implications pose difficulties, particularly two literary inconsistencies. (1) While the parable's general link with its context is clear (imitating and embodying God's forgiveness is a norm in the community of disciples; not forgiving others brings terrible consequences; see 18:15-17), a connection with 18:21-22 is problematic. The connective "for this reason" in 18:23 links the parable with 18:21-22. But while these verses exhort repeated forgiveness, the parable does not. Not only does the king not forgive repeatedly; he takes back the forgiveness already offered when the servant fails to forgive just once.

(2) The king and his reign are usually understood as images of God and God's empire (18:35). But the gospel has established that God's empire manifested in Jesus is generally not like the death-bringing and oppressive reign of Rome and typical kings (17:25; 20:25). Yet the parable evokes precisely this scenario! The king is a tyrant who, like Rome (see 18:24), collects excessive tribute, and in the end inflicts vicious torture on a servant. Of course he has an apparently generous moment when he forgives the huge debt, but it is short-lived. Biblical traditions know the experience of God as an oppressive presence.[17] But the gospel has sought to establish a quite different image of God.

What should an audience do with these inconsistencies? One solution is to blame the author's lack of skill. Another is to change details in the parable to try to improve it. Both approaches have obvious shortcomings. It seems preferable not to allegorize this parable's details, to recognize the story's main point in vv. 34-35, and to discern what in the parable has pastoral-theological significance and what belongs to the parable's narrative world.

That which causes the problem, the parable's relation to the rest of the gospel, its intratextuality, also enables the audience to discern what should not be pressed. While "king" is a common image for God, the audience also knows that "king" has been used negatively in the gospel for unfaithful and oppressive rule (1:6b-11; ch. 2; 6:29; 14:1-12; 17:25; 20:25). It knows by chapter 18 that God has predominantly been presented as a merciful, forgiving God (5:45). Though capable of great destruction at the judgment, God is not an exploitative tyrant. The audience also knows after 18:1-20 that one mistake is not sufficient for God to subject a disciple to continuous torture. Yet it also knows from chapters 7 and 13 that failure to live God's will has eschatological consequences.

The audience must use these links carefully in its meaning-making and reading/hearing process. The initial presentation of the king, after the reference to God's empire, is unsettling. It evokes the familiar image of God as king, but the imperial scenario of exploitative and oppressive reign which the parable evokes (see below) indicates that this figure cannot be God. The audience can discern that God's empire is not like this, is not oppressive, does not deal in self-serving "mercy" (see on 18:27), does not forgive just once only to revoke it. Most of the parable establishes a contrast with God's reign. It is about God's forgiveness only by implication and by contrast. The focus is on forgiveness between people, on how disciples who have encountered God's reign treat one another.

The surprise comes at the end as the parable suddenly imitates the imperial practice it rejects. While God is not like this king, in one aspect, and one aspect only, God *is* like the king. Like the king, God gets justifiably angry when the divine will is constantly ignored and severely punishes the one who does not forgive ("so my heavenly father will do to you"). The king is and is not God. See 22:7 for another king in a parable who displays what the gospel regards as justifiable anger.

• 18:23a

The scenario in the parable as a whole, like those in 13:18, 24, 31, 33, 44, 45, 47, says something about God's empire: **The empire of heaven is like a king**. In 18:1 the disciples asked about greatness in the **empire**, only to be told that it consists of a societally marginal and vulnerable way of life ("like a child"). The empire's connection here with the societally most powerful and central figure of **a king** suggests that the parable will proceed in terms of contrast. In the gospel kings have had mixed press. They are frequently presented negatively (1:6-11; ch. 2 [Herod]; 6:29 [Solomon]; 10:18; 14:1-12 [Herod Antipas]; and especially 17:25), though both God (5:35) and Jesus (2:2) have been identified positively as kings. For God as **king**, see 1 Sam 8:7; Ps 72:1; 93:1; 97:1; 99:1. The aorist verb **is like** indicates that the parable is concerned with what the empire is effecting in the present (as in 13:24).[18]

• 18:23b-24

This king **wished to settle his accounts with his slaves. When he began the reckoning, one who owed him ten thousand talents, was brought to him**. The setting is political, a world which Matthew's audience has probably never experienced firsthand, but has "heard about" and has definitely felt the impact of its policies. This is the world of "every king," a king's court with its elite class of aristocrats and retainers, clients or servants of the patron ruler who carry out his military, administrative, financial, and religious policies (see Introduction, section 5).[19] Here attention is directed to the financial sphere, to the likely collection of taxes or tribute which finance the king's power. Recall 17:25. This king is doing what "the kings of the earth do." Particularly, attention focuses on one of the retainers whose task was to practice the "proprietary theory of the state." This theory saw a territory's resources as legitimate plunder for the ruler. The official or retainer's task was to transfer wealth "from the producers to the political elite."[20] For **slave** as designating a king's official or retainer, see 1 Sam 29:3; 2 Kgs 5:6; cf. Matt 14:2. The term denotes his loyalty to the king and his role of doing the king's bidding, rather than poor socioeconomic circumstances. The matching term **lord** will recur frequently to emphasize the dynamics of power, loyalty, and ownership (18:25, 27, 31, 32, 34). The king is not God.

The king is overseeing his financial matters (**settle his accounts; the reckoning**). A **slave** is **brought** to give account. He has particular responsibilities in raising revenue, probably by tribute.[21] The sum of **ten thousand talents** is the amount Rome, notably Pompey, extracts from newly conquered Judea in the 60s B.C.E. (Josephus, *Ant* 14.78). It is a large amount compared with some other tributes: Antiochus demands a thousand talents (1 Macc 15:31); Herod Antipas takes two hundred talents from Galilee and Peraea; Archelaus takes six hundred from Idumaea, Judea, and Samaria (Josephus, *Ant* 17.317-20). Josephus also notes Joseph, who promises Ptolemy that he will double the eight-thousand-talent tribute from Syria, Phoenicia, Judea, and Samaria (*Ant* 12.175-76). So the figure evokes Rome's action and reflects proverbial notions of the wealth of kings and of oppressive taxation. In addition, it enhances the status of the **slave**. To be charged with such a responsibility shows him to be at the highest levels of skilled financial administration, a man of great political skill and influence.

• **18:25**

But this time his skill and vast influence have failed him. **As he could not pay, his lord ordered him to be sold with his wife and children and all his possessions, and payment to be made.** The failure to raise the amount flouts the king's authority. The king is not amused. The verse underlines the king's power. It calls him **his lord** (over the slave; cf. 20:25). He exercises power (the verb **ordered**), and he sells the official, his household, and considerable possessions into slavery. The king has shown that he has power of life and death, has reasserted his authority, punished the man, and made an example of him for others. Compare the comparable situation of Bion's father, a tax-farmer, who is sold into slavery after failing to raise his contracted amount (Diogenes Laertius, *Lives* 4.46-58). Also Neh 5:3-5; Isa 50:1; Amos 2:6; 8:6.

• **18:26**

But the slave is not done. In this world of power, **the slave fell to his knees before him** (for the political act of *proskynēsis* or prostration before a ruler, see 4:9), **saying, "Have patience with me and I will pay you everything."** The slave submits himself to the king's authority and promises to accomplish the king's will.

• **18:27**

The king's honor is satisfied. He can now afford to change his mind. Moreover, if this official has not been able to raise this amount of tribute, it is probably not procurable. **And out of pity for him** (see 9:36), **the lord of that slave released him and forgave him his debt.** Compare King Demetrius's freeing Jews from tribute, salt tax, and crown levies in 1 Macc 10:29. Does the king's act model God's forgiveness? The reference to **pity** evokes Jesus (9:36; 14:14; 15:32; 20:34). But it contrasts the two kings, rather than parallels them (2:2; cf. "the kings of the earth" in 17:25). The audience knows that Jesus' mercy is constantly expressed in actions which transform and benefit a desperate person. But the king's "pity" is not of this kind. His decision is calculated for his own benefit. It does not improve the slave's life. In fact, the slave is now even more indebted to him and more easily controlled. His valuable skills and network are not lost to the king so he can accomplish the king's will. And the king has shown magnanimity to at least some of his subjects in not pursuing the amount. But he'll be able to raise other amounts by other means. The king's act is calculated and self-serving, the momentary (v. 34) act of a tyrant.

• 18:28

In the second part of the parable, the roles are reversed. Now the slave is in the place of the king. **But that same slave, as he went out, came upon one of his fellow slaves who owed him a hundred denarii.** The similar language closely links this situation with what has just happened. It involves **that same slave**, immediately after the king restores him (**as he went out**). The **fellow slave** is one of the slave's clients, a lower-level official in the court. A **hundred denarii** was a significant sum but not vast. Day laborers in 20:2 receive a denarius for a day's work. Compared with ten thousand talents, it is small. It is repayable.

This world is marked by demand and physical violence. **Seizing him by the throat, he said, "Pay what you owe."** Why this immediate demand? W. R. Herzog helpfully locates this demand and his subsequent brutal action in the dynamics of court political intrigue. This is the slave's damage control, a means of reasserting his power after his shaming experience before the king which exposed his vulnerability.[22] In monetary terms the wealthy slave could forgo repayment for a period of time, set up a "time payment," even cancel/forgive the debt. But the exchange is about power more than it is about money. As a patron to lower-level clients, he asserts his power in demanding repayment of the loan. The act sends a message to the rest. He holds the power of their life and death.

• 18:29

The lower-ranked official knows what to do just as his patron knew what to do before the king (18:26). He too **fell down and pleaded with him, "Have patience with me and I will pay you everything."** The term **fellow slave**, rather than client, underlines their similar situations, as does the use of the same words.

• 18:30

But there is no mercy. He refused; **then he went and threw him into prison until he would pay the debt.** His action is brutal. The slave's pleading is not sufficient to reestablish his power. A more ruthless act is needed. To forgive would be to choose not to assert power over him. It would be a tiny but significant step toward a more just order. To not forgive is of course quite inconsistent with the "mercy" the king has shown to him. But in a sense it is quite similar. Both engage in bullying behavior. Both assert their power over another to control him and make an example for others to notice (20:25). The king's so-called act of "mercy" was an act of control. The lower-ranked official is imprisoned until **he would pay the debt.** He will need another patron to do so.

• 18:31

When his fellow slaves saw what had happened, they were greatly distressed. The slave's action puts them in a very vulnerable position, subject to his assertions of power. Their only defense is to seek the protection of a more powerful patron. **They went and reported to their lord all that had taken place.**

• 18:32-34

The king is not pleased and reminds the slave of his own experience (18:26-27). **Then his lord summoned him and said to him, "You wicked slave! I forgave you all that debt because you pleaded with me. Should you not have had mercy on your fellow slave as I had mercy on you?" And in anger his lord handed him over to be tortured until he would pay his entire debt.** Why is the king so upset that he withdraws his earlier forgiveness and now tortures the slave? Is he angry that, having received "pure generosity," the slave has ignored mercy's demand to show it to others?[23] Is he angry that the slave has missed the opportunity to continue to break the cycle of exploitation which the king has initiated?[24] Probably not. We have observed that the king's so-called act of mercy in 18:27 is more a calculated act of power and domination. The king's anger seems as hypocritical as the slave's action. The slave has simply acted as the king usually acts in coercing money out of people through taxes and tribute.

The king's reaction has to be understood in the same context of imperial power. The slave's ruthless act has shamed the king by exposing him to be somewhat soft. While the king's forgiveness of the debt served him well, it could also be interpreted as weakness. In contrast, the slave's act is quite unambiguous. The slave has shown himself to be better at, more ruthless at, the imperial game than the king. Doing so of course dishonors the king.[25] The slave has now twice exposed the king to ridicule. His act is a challenge to the king's honor. The king's response is clear. He revokes his "pity" and tortures the slave, the perennial punishment of tyrants. Removing the slave prevents another such situation and shows that the king is not weak but powerful and ruthless.

• 18:35

Up to this point the empire of the heavens has not been like this king's reign. The king has not represented God's empire and God does not support oppressive reign. But now comes a surprise. **So my heavenly father will also do to everyone of you if you do not forgive your brother or sister from the heart.** The king's *final* act does represent something God will do! Drawing on this cultural image, the ending shows that God will act as a tyrant king if God's will to extend forgiveness is not done. As much as the parable rejects the king's bullying ways, it resorts to them to bully readers/hearers into compliance with God's will. Failure to enact God's will, failure to forgive and to sustain the community of disciples, means eschatological consequences from God's wrath. Warnings dominate the first part of chapter 18; see 18:3, 5, 6-7, 8-9, as well as previously in the gospel; see 7:15-27; 13:29-30, 36-43, 47-50; ch. 24.

The gospel's strategy can be understood as a deontological approach which makes God's will known and warns disciples of the consequences of disobeying.

Or it can be understood as a teleological or consequentialist form of moral argument which uses eschatological scenes to persuade or motivate (bully?) disciples to do God's will. Or it can be seen as a perfectionist approach which requires disciples to discern what is or is not appropriate to God's empire and to live accordingly (see introduction to 7:13-27).

This warning is introduced with **my heavenly Father** (at times but not always in relation to eschatological scenes; see 7:21; 10:32-33; 11:27; 12:50; 16:17; 18:10, 19; 20:23; 23:9; 26:29, 39, 42, 53). While **father** denotes God's indiscriminate love (5:45-48), that love must produce a way of life for which disciples are held accountable. The link between receiving God's forgiveness and extending it to others has been made in 6:12, 14-15. God's forgiveness or mercy is a transforming power which mandates a forgiving way of life. This verse underlines the great seriousness of this connection. Forgiveness is a normative practice within the community of disciples (**forgive your brother or sister**). On **heart** as the core of a person, the center of a person's willing, thinking, knowing, deciding, and doing self, see 5:8; 6:21. What happens in **the heart** is vitally connected to how one lives (5:28; 9:4; 11:29; 12:34; 13:15, 19; 15:8, 18, 19; 22:37; 24:48).

God's empire is like any other reign in that there is accountability and punitive consequences for disobeying the ruler. To ignore Jesus' teaching on forgiveness means eschatological consequences.

CHAPTER 19

The Alternative Households
of God's Empire

Part 1

Chapters 19-20 form a distinct subunit to conclude this fourth narrative block (16:21-20:34). In Matt 19:1, Jesus' community discourse delivered to disciples in chapter 18 ends. He leaves Galilee, where he has been in ministry since 4:17 (cf. 4:12-16), and enters Judea to travel to Jerusalem, which he will enter in 21:1. Chapters 19-20 narrate this journey.

In addition to the journey, what holds the 6 scenes of chapters 19-20 together?

19:3-12	Marriage and Divorce
19:13-15	Children
19:16-30	Wealth
20:1-16	Parable of the Householder
20:17-28	Being Slaves
20:29-34	Healing Two Blind Men

The coherence of these two chapters resides in pervasive cultural understandings of households.[1] Discussions of household management continued after Aristotle (*Pol* 1.2.1-2) in an Aristotelean tradition (the *Oeconomica*; *Magna Moralia*; Philodemus; Arius Didymus, *Epitome*; Hierocles, *On Duties*), in Stoicism (Seneca; Epictetus; Dio Chrysostom), among Neopythagoreans (Okkelos; Callicratidas; Perictyone; Phintys), and in Hellenistic Judaism (Pseudo-Phocylides, Josephus, Philo). These traditions regarded the ideal household as the basic unit of a state or kingdom or city, and a microcosm of imperial society (Dionysius of Halicarnasus, *Rom Ant* 2.24.2; Philo, *Jos* 38-39; 54). They understood the household to consist of four dimensions, namely, three relationships (husband–wife; father–children; master–slave) and the male's task of earning wealth. A power dynamic controlled the relationships in which the husband/father/master *ruled over* the wife/children/slaves. The household was hierarchical and patriarchal in that the male held power over women and children.[2] It was marked by strict gender differentiation. The woman was to attend to household tasks while the man represented the household in society (Dio Chrysostom, *Disc* 3.62, 70). Under the pressures of daily existence, many households, especially at the lower societal levels, may well have functioned in ways that differed significantly from this pattern. Yet these writings indicate that this structure continued to be advocated aggressively.

The sections of chapters 19-20 reflect this household pattern: the husband–wife relationship (including divorce, 19:3-12), children (19:13-15), procuring wealth (19:16-30), being slaves (20:17-28). In addition, 20:1-16 is a parable about a householder administering his estate and hiring workers.

But while the chapters utilize this household structure, they do not endorse this cultural norm. Rather, siding with some other minority cultural views, the two chapters subvert this hierarchical and patriarchal structure by instructing disciples in a more egalitarian pattern (cf. 20:12). Husbands are not to rule over wives but to participate in a "one-flesh" relationship (19:3-12); all disciples are children, there are no parents (19:13-15); following Jesus, not procuring wealth and status, defines discipleship (19:16-30); all disciples are slaves like Jesus, there are no masters (20:17-28). The parable of the householder in 20:1-16 exemplifies God's distinctive and different ways of ordering life. The concluding story of Jesus healing the blind men who beg for mercy offers disciples hope that they too will be enabled by Jesus' power to live this alternative and against-the-grain existence (20:29-34). That is, as Jesus journeys to Jerusalem to die, the chapters provide disciples with instruction on an alternative household that befits the empire or reign of God.

In countering societal norms, this household embodies the way of the cross. The two chapters continue to elaborate the alternative, socially shameful, resistant way of the cross named by Jesus in 16:24 in the central scene of this narrative block (16:21-28). Disciples live a marginal existence, as societal participants yet as outsiders, over against dominant social values. Their households resist hierarchical and patriarchal patterns and embody God's empire in more egalitarian structures. Other attempts to minimize or eradicate fundamental gender distinctions brought sharp resistance from the elite, who considered such actions to be socially and politically subversive.[3] In their dangerous and subversive existence, disciples are bound to meet with resistance.

19:1-2—TRANSITION

• **19:1-2**

These two verses close the teaching discourse of chapter 18 and begin Jesus' journey from Galilee (cf. 4:12-16, 17) to Jerusalem to die (16:21; 17:22-23). The clause **When Jesus had finished saying these things** has ended the previous discourses in 7:28; 11:1; 13:53 (note 26:1, "*all* these things") and draws his teachings together. A new location (Judea), audience (crowds), and activity (healing) mark this new subsection. Jesus' ministry in "Galilee under the Gentiles" (see 4:12-16) has ended: **He left Galilee and went to the region of Judea beyond the Jordan**, probably the region of Peraea, not Samaria (cf. 10:5).

Large crowds followed him, and he cured them all. For previous **healing** summaries and healing as a display of God's merciful and life-giving reign and anticipation of its fullness, see 4:23-25; 8:16; 9:35-36; 12:15-21; 14:14, 35-36; 15:30-31. For the **crowds** as the context of Jesus' ministry who do not share either the elite's hostility or the disciples' faith, see 4:25. These summary scenes remind the audience of the extent of Jesus' ministry. **Followed** does not here have discipleship implications, lacking Jesus' call and their commitment. See 4:19; 8:1.

19:3-12—MARRIAGE, DIVORCE, AND REMARRIAGE

This scene involves three exchanges, the first two involving Jesus and the Pharisees (19:3b-6, 7-9), the third Jesus and the disciples (19:10-12).[4]

• 19:3
Some Pharisees came to him. The Pharisees initiate the exchange with a question about the grounds for divorce. On **came** as underlining Jesus' authority even when used by opponents, see 4:3. **Pharisees** as part of the religious elite have resisted Jesus' ministry throughout; so 3:7; 9:11, 14, 34; 12:2, 14, 24, 38; 15:1, 12. In their last appearances, Jesus declared that they are not God's agents (15:12-14) and warned against their teaching (16:1, 6, 11, 12). The expectation of conflict is confirmed by the verb **test/tempt**. The verb denoted the devil's attempt to turn Jesus from God's purposes (4:1, 3) and the Pharisees' similar effort in 16:1. The Pharisees are the devil's agents (see 4:1-11). Here the **test** involves Jesus resisting their diabolical, patriarchal view of marriage and faithfully announcing God's alternative will. They are challenged to accept Jesus' teaching.

The **Pharisees** ask a question that assumes divorce is normative. They focus on the grounds for it, if any. **Is it lawful for a man to divorce his wife for any/every cause?** The opening **Is it lawful** recalls the conflict over the sabbath, their desire to accuse Jesus (12:10), and their plans to kill him (12:14). Their question is male-centered, concerned with what a man can do. While women had the right to divorce (*P. Eleph.* 1 [Demetria]; Josephus, *Ant* 18.136; 20.142-47; Philo, *Spec Leg* 3.82), it is not in view.[5] In asking about divorce **for every/any cause**, the Pharisees posit a husband's "natural right" to exercise unrestricted male power over his inferior, submissive, obedient, children-producing, home-focused wife in a patriarchal household (Aristotle, *Pol* 1.5.1-8; *Oeconomica* 3.2; *Magna Moralia* 1.33.17-18; Josephus, *Con Ap* 2.201).[6] As is appropriate to their position as members of the social elite, the Pharisees' question upholds the current hierarchical social order. Questions of marriage, divorce, and remarriage are life-and-death matters, as John the Baptist found out (14:1-12).

Their question reflects dominant Jewish and Greco-Roman attitudes to women and divorce. The schools of Hillel and Shammai disputed the interpretation of Deut 24:1 and legitimate reasons for divorce. Hillel's school allowed divorce for any reason (also Sir 25:8-26; 7:26), while Shammai held a more restrictive view (*m. Git.* 9:10; Philo, *Spec Leg* 3.79-82). The dominant cultural perspective of the Greco-Roman world regarded male power over women as unrestricted and divorce as legitimate for most reasons, including stealing money (Cicero, *Att* 11.24), adultery and being drunk (*Aulus Gellius* 10.23.5), loss of looks (Juvenal, *Sat* 6.142-47), arguments with one's mother-in-law and unpleasant temperament (Suetonius, *Augustus* 62), sickness (Plutarch, *Sulla* 35.2), and unpleasing behavior (Josephus, *Vita* 426). Several, though, complain about frequent divorces which undermine social stability. Juvenal notes a woman who has initiated eight divorces in five years (*Sat* 6.224-30). Seneca complains about women who reckon their years not by consuls but by divorced husbands (*De Ben* 3.16.2-3).[7]

• 19:4

Jesus' response to their question about divorce is to talk about the view of marriage which their question assumes. Instead of talking about a man's domination of a woman expressed in divorce, he recalls God's will for marriage from Gen 1:27. **He answered, "Have you not read that he who made them from the beginning made them male and female**." The opening question **Have you not read** rebukes them (as in 12:3, 5) as people who ought to know God's will but don't (also 15:1-9; see the same construction and rebuke in 21:16, 42; 22:31). In revealing God's empire, Jesus seeks to restore God's original reign over creation (**from the beginning**, Gen 1:1; cf. Matt 1:1; 13:35; 14:32; 19:5, 8).

• 19:5-6

To this statement about God's creation of male and female, Jesus adds Gen 2:24 about their unity in marriage, a consequence of God's creation. **For this reason a man shall leave his father and mother and be joined to his wife, and the two shall become one flesh?** The marriage does not extend the father's household. Rather, the son leaves that household and is joined to his wife in a new and different relationship. Their unity is emphasized by the last two clauses of 19:5 (**joined . . . one flesh**) and by the repetition of **one flesh** in 19:6a. This **one-flesh** relationship is marked by "unity, solidarity, mutuality, equality,"[8] a strange, against-the-grain identity in a culture that stressed gender differentiation, male superiority and domination, and female subordination as norms in the patriarchal household. The one-flesh marriage forms a relationship of "solidarity, trust and wellbeing."[9]

God intends this relationship to be permanent: **Therefore what God has joined together let no one separate**. Jesus' response contrasts this relationship of mutuality and permanence with the Pharisees' concern to uphold male power and patriarchal structures in divorce. Jesus' strict view parallels Mal 2:16 and Philo (above). His insistence on mutual, not hierarchical and exploitative, relationship between husband and wife runs counter to prevailing hierarchical and patriarchal attitudes and practices, but finds affinity with some changing attitudes and practices.[10]

• 19:7

The second exchange brings an immediate objection from the Pharisees that Jesus is at odds with Moses in Deut 24:1 who supports their practice of divorce. **They said to him, "Why then did Moses command us to give a certificate of dismissal and divorce her?"** Moses' provision of a certificate of divorce recognized a marriage had been terminated.

• 19:8

Jesus' response is not to trade scriptures but to interpret Moses' words. As in 15:1-9 (also 12:1-14; 16:5-12; 17:9-13) the religious elite do not know how to interpret scripture (22:29). **He said to them, "It was because you were so hard-hearted that Moses allowed you to divorce your wives but from the beginning it was not so."** Jesus argues that Moses' words in Deut 24:1 were not a command as the Pharisees claim in 19:7, but a concession (**Moses allowed**) for **hard-hearted** males living a patriarchal marriage. The **heart** is the center of a person's willing, thinking, deciding, knowing, and doing, the core of a person's commitments (see 5:8, 28) directed to God (6:21; 18:35) or to the devil in opposition to God's will (13:15, 19). The religious leaders have been identified as having hearts far from God (15:8). The term **hard-hearted** denotes Israel's stubbornness in not walking in God's ways of justice, and not loving or serving God (Deut 10:12-22, esp. 16). God's response is wrath (Jer 4:4; Sir 16:10). But Jesus is not only talking about past generations. The direct address (**you were so; allowed you**) and possessive pronoun (**your wives**) identifies these Pharisees as **hard-hearted** in resisting God's will for permanent and mutual marriage relations. Jesus reiterates God's will **from the beginning** (repeated from 19:4). He enacts God's empire envisaged from creation. For a new creation dawning in Jesus' ministry, see 1:1.

• 19:9

Only now, after recalling God's will since creation for mutual and permanent marriage relations, does Jesus speak of divorce. **And I say to you** (see 5:18; also 5:22, 28, 32, 34, 39, 44), **whoever divorces his wife except for unchastity/adultery, and marries another commits adultery.** While this is a very difficult verse, one thing is clear. Against the Pharisees' contemplation of unrestricted male power over a woman, which includes divorce for any/every reason, Jesus severely curtails that power by allowing one reason for divorce. While guided by God's will "from the beginning," like Moses he recognizes a concession. See 5:32.

The clause **except for unchastity/adultery** has provoked much debate. (1) It does not mean "including adultery," forbidding divorce *even in* situations of adultery, or "setting aside adultery" in the sense of a parenthesis whereby adultery is not discussed by the verse. (2) Some have suggested a reference to incest as defined by Lev 18, but the absence of the noun πορνείας (*porneias*) from Lev 18 rules this out.[11] While the word can have wide meaning, the context here of marriage confirms a meaning of **adultery**. (3) The exceptive sense is the most convincing. Divorce is not permitted except in situations of adultery.

Or to restate it, divorce is permitted in circumstances of infidelity. So Joseph in 1:19.[12] The concern with adultery reflects the seventh commandment (Exod 20:14; Deut 5:18; Matt 19:18).

Also difficult is the reference to remarriage. Does the phrase **except for unchastity/adultery** refer to the act of divorcing only, leaving one free to remarry if the divorce was because of adultery; or does it refer to both divorce and remarriage, whereby divorce in circumstances of adultery is permissible but remarriage is never allowed? The first option has been a traditional Protestant reading since Erasmus. The second option, a dominant patristic reading, has been revived more recently.[13] While recognizing the complexity of the debate, and pastoral implications for contemporary readers of Matthew, five factors suggest that the second option is a correct reading.[14]

1. If the exceptive clause was placed after "and marries another," it would treat divorce and remarriage as one unit, permissible in circumstances of adultery. But placed after the first verb, it refers only to the first:

Divorce, except in circumstances of unchastity, is adultery;

Remarriage is (always) adultery.

2. Matthew 5:32 has already prohibited remarriage for a divorced woman. It is adultery for a man to marry such a woman. This verse now expands that prohibition to a man. Jesus places man and woman on the same footing by removing male privilege.

3. A comparison with four other verses in the gospel where Matthew uses this same construction of a protasis (or clause beginning with "if") with two verbs (5:19 [twice]; 7:24; 10:14) shows that the apodosis (or main clause) refers to both situations. Committing adultery applies to both divorce and remarriage.

4. To read 19:9 as permitting remarriage after divorce misses Jesus' emphasis on the permanence of marriage which God has effected and no one else can break (19:4-6, 8). It is the understanding of marriage as a permanent bond that shapes this verse's understanding of divorce. That is why when the Pharisees talk divorce initially in 19:3, Jesus talks marriage. Jesus allows divorce after adultery because the bond has been fractured by that infidelity. Divorce recognizes and formalizes that fracture. But God's work in creating the "one flesh" relationship is such that adultery and divorce cannot erase it. Remarriage is not possible.

5. The disciples' response in 19:10 makes better sense if 19:9 not only restricts divorce but also forbids remarriage.

Are contemporary readers bound by this verse, or can we read against the text? While the passage's view of marriage, and subsequently of divorce and remarriage, upholds a wonderful understanding of mutual and permanent marriage relationships created by God, and does so in resistance to destructive patriarchal relationships, it offers little sympathetic recognition that humans live in a world very different "from the beginning." Jesus' teaching risks trapping women and men in relationships that are far from "one flesh," or consigning them to a future that forbids significant intimate relationships. It provides little concession to the "not yet" nature of the present, that humans live in a world in which God's reign is not yet established.

Moreover, the verse does not seem sufficiently faithful to the vision of God's empire expressed throughout the gospel. Intent on resisting patriarchy and offering the different vision of God's empire, it omits key aspects of that reign, namely, mercy, love, forgiveness, and the giving of new life. These dimensions of God's empire surely create a third option in which God's empire might be manifested in new relationships, where the past is mercifully forgiven, and a loving and life-giving future is possible.

• 19:10

The third exchange involves the disciples.[15] The Pharisees have been exposed and shamed as not knowing or being receptive to God's will. The disciples, though, seek clarification as they have previously (13:10, 36; 15:15). **His disciples said to him, "If such is the case of a man with his wife, it is better not to marry."** Anticipating 19:13, 25, they misunderstand Jesus' teaching. His emphasis on mutual and permanent relationships, restriction on divorce, and ban on remarriage makes little sense to their view of unlimited male power over a wife, even in divorce. Their (extreme) conclusion that it was better not to marry echoes some other groups: Josephus, *JW* 2.120 (Essenes); Epictetus, *Diss* 3.22.45-49, 67-82; Philostratus, *Apollonius* 1.13.

• 19:11

Jesus' response underlines that his teaching is definitely a minority and countercultural view. **But he said to them, "Not everyone can accept this teaching/word."** The verb **accept** has the sense of receive or welcome or make space for something (BAGD, 889-90; cf. 15:17). Does Jesus refer to the disciples' statement in v. 10 about celibate living, or to his own teaching in 19:9 or vv. 3-9? Given the use of **word** in 7:28 and 19:1 to refer to Jesus' teaching, it probably does so here also. Matthew 19:9 is the more immediate referent, but not to be detached from 19:3-8.

While the disciples focus on the difficulty or impossibility of his teaching, Jesus focuses on its gift, **but only those to whom it is given.** These to whom it is **given** can accept it. To **give** has frequently indicated God's actions to disciples (7:7, 11; 10:19; 20:23) including knowledge of "the secrets of the empire of heaven" in 13:11. Here, what is **given** is both an understanding of God's will as well as the strength to do it. God's will concerns male disciples giving up the power to exercise unlimited power over their wives, including divorcing them for any reason, and includes their commitment to mutual and permanent marriages. But in the light of 19:12, it also concerns the harsh claim of 19:9 that believers who divorce forgo remarriage.

• 19:12

Jesus identifies these divorced disciples (and disciples who choose not to marry) as a third category, **eunuchs. For there are eunuchs who have been so from birth and there are eunuchs who have been made eunuchs by others**. The first two clauses identify two categories of eunuchs, those who are born so and those who are subsequently made so, presumably by castration (common for slaves) or by accident, Jesus adds a third category, **and there are eunuchs who have made themselves eunuchs for the sake of the empire of the heavens.** These are not literal eunuchs like the first two. They are eunuchs because of their commitment to **God's empire**.

The image of divorced and single disciples as **eunuchs** is very rich and significant.[16] Eunuchs were permanent outsiders, dishonored marginal figures, often despised and socially alienated, with a distinct identity, yet participants in society and often with powerful or elite positions.

1. There was no place for eunuchs in patriarchal households with their carefully defined and separated roles for male and female, husband and wife, parent and child. The eunuch participated in none of these relationships. Eunuchs violated this order, threatened it (cf. Sir 20:4) and the future of the household and survival of the race because they could not produce children (Josephus, *Ant* 4.290; Philo, *Spec Leg* 3.37-42; cf. *Ps.-Phoc.* 175-76). Without children or family, sexually ambivalent, scorned (cf. Sir 30:20) and abused, eunuchs did not belong.

2. Yet as slaves, or as freedmen (Pliny, *NH* 12.5), eunuchs often had specialized societal roles. Josephus's son's tutor is a eunuch (*Vita* 429). Eunuchs frequently occupied powerful positions in the political or social arenas as loyal officials mediating between a ruler and the ruled. Herodotus notes that Xerxes respected the eunuch Hermotimus "more highly than any of his other eunuchs" (8.104-6), though Hermotimus describes himself as "no man but a thing of naught" (10.6). Pliny (*NH* 7.39) refers to the high price paid for Sejanus's eunuch Paezon, a "payment for lust and not for beauty." He also notes a wealthy eunuch who as a freed man joins the emperor Claudius's household (*NH* 12.5). See also Esth 2:14-15; Jdt 12:11; Josephus, *Ant* 16.229-40, and *JW* 1.488-91 for Herod's three chamberlains; Acts 8:27-28. As with many slaves, sexual duty was part of their lot. Suetonius attests the emperor Titus's passion for eunuchs and catamites (*Titus* 7.1). Though asexual, they were lovers, both homosexual and heterosexual.[17]

3. Eunuchs (**made eunuchs by others**) suffered personal violence and abuse often at an early age. Herodotus (8.104-6) tells of the Persian king Xerxes' eunuch Hermotimus who, embittered by his castration, enacts revenge on the man who castrated him by forcing Panionius to castrate his four sons, and then forcing them to castrate their father. The emperor Domitian, though passionate toward the eunuch Earimus, passes a law against castration (Suetonius, *Domitian* 7.1; Dio Cassius 67.2-3). Pseudo-Phocylides (187) bans castration.

4. Eunuchs had ambivalent roles in religion. Excluded from worship (Deut 23:1; a castrated animal in Lev 22:24) and from priestly service (Lev 21:20), they were included in God's favor at the eschaton (Isa 56:3-5; Wis 3:14). Eunuchs served as priests in cults of Cybele, Attis, and Artemis (Juvenal, *Sat* 8.175-76).[18]

In identifying divorced and unmarried disciples as **eunuchs**, Jesus utilizes a most appropriate symbol of the identity and lifestyle of disciples. (1) Both live a marginal existence on the edges of, yet are participants in, society. (2) Both experience estrangement from families and households (10:34-39). (3) Both face physical abuse and social hostility (5:11-12; 10:17-18). (4) Both know bodily mutilation (whether literal or metaphorical; 5:27-30; 18:8-9). (5) Both have powerful roles whether in the political-social arena (eunuchs) or in God's reign (disciples, 10:7-8; 19:28). (6) Both are slaves (6:24; 10:24-25; 20:26-28). (7) Both are considered religious outsiders by the elite.

In 19:12 another similarity emerges. O. Patterson argues that the essential characteristic of eunuchs is their paradoxical nature. They are androgynous, neither male or female. The eunuch's body

> both acknowledged and resolved symbolically most of the conflicts surrounding male-female relationships. The eunuch appeared to be both male and female, both weak and strong, both dirty and pure, both a sex object (as homosexual and heterosexual lover) and asexual, and both mother and wife.[19]

The mutual, permanent "one-flesh," husband–wife relationship of 19:3-6 also acknowledges and resolves the conflicts of male–female relationships with which patriarchal society was so concerned. But instead of doing so with the conventional hierarchy and subordination, with male superiority and female subordination, male control and female submission, it posits an alternative relationship of unity, permanence, and mutuality ("one flesh"). Divorced disciples forbidden to remarry and disciples who choose not to marry are given a similar identity. They are not excluded from a household concerned only with marriage. Rather, they share a similar one-flesh identity as **eunuchs because of the empire**. Their identity as eunuchs unites male and female and opposes the hierarchy and patriarchy that pervade the dominant culture.

The section ends with Jesus' call, **Let anyone accept this who can**. The present tense requires an ongoing openness to God's presence and will to guide disciples in this one-flesh identity.

19:13-15—DISCIPLES ARE CHILDREN

One image of marginal identity leads to another, that of children. The second element in conventional, hierarchical, patriarchal household structures concerned the rule of father over children.[20] Children must be trained for their future civic (male) and domestic (female) roles. Children depend on, submit to, and obey their parents. Children have no rights and are marginal to the adult, male-centered world. They are often viewed with suspicion, as threats to social order, ignorant, lacking reason, unpredictable, vulnerable (so Matt 2). One way to insult an adult is to call him a boy. Children, like slaves, are beaten as a means of establishing domination.

That is not to say that children were not loved or valued. Numerous writers attest close bonds between parents and children (Pliny, *Ep* 9.12) and parental grief at the death of children (Plutarch, "Consolation to His Wife," *Moralia* 608B-612B; Quintilian, *Instit* 6. pref 6-16). Nor is it to deny that there were changing or diverse understandings of children.[21] But fundamentally, children have a subordinate role in households. They are not valued for their present destabilizing and threatening presence, but are trained for their future roles in sustaining a differentiated and adult (male) society. They are marginal to that adult world, yet future participants in it.

• 19:13

Then little children were being brought to him. The dependence of the children is underlined by the passive verb **brought**. The verb has been used commonly for bringing sick people to Jesus for healing (4:24; 8:16; 9:2, 33; 12:22; 14:35; 17:16). It also describes bringing gifts to God or Jesus (2:11; 5:23, 24; 8:4). It denotes, then, reverent approach as people seek God's or Jesus' blessing and life-giving power. Contrast the very different, hostile opening involving the religious elite in the previous scene (19:3).

The term **children** says nothing about their age, since the term is used of children in the womb (Gen 25:22) and children of marriageable age (Tob 7:10-11; Sarah has been married seven times!). Rather, it underlines their cultural (lack of) status, namely, their vulnerability, marginality, powerlessness, and source of threat to the adult world. The same term figured prominently in chapter 2 (2:8, 9, 11, 13, 14, 20, 21), where Herod is threatened by the child Jesus and wreaks destructive havoc on the expendable and vulnerable children of Bethlehem. Yet even there the child Jesus receives divine protection and mercy. Recall also 18:1-6, where "child" appears four times associated with humility or the lack of status and power in the adult male world.

The identity of those bringing the children is not disclosed, but their good motives are underlined. They bring the children to Jesus **in order that he might lay his hands on them and pray**. While **hands** can cause disciples to stumble (5:30; 18:8), can be a matter of controversy with the religious elite (15:2, 20), and will destroy Jesus (17:22), Jesus' **hands** have previously effected healing (8:3, 15; 9:18, 25 [a child]), expressed his relationship with disciples (12:49), and saved the doubting-believing Peter (see 14:31). They make God's saving presence and power available in these situations. On Jesus **praying**, see 5:44; 6:5-9; 14:23.

The action, though, is resisted by the disciples. **The disciples spoke sternly to those who brought them.** The disciples again (cf. 19:10) exhibit the values of the patriarchal household and try to exclude the insignificant children. They have not yet learned a different structure from Jesus' actions of healing children (see 19:14) and of using a child as a model for discipleship (18:3). Old patterns take time and effort to shake. The verb **spoke sternly** is the verb "rebuke." When Jesus rebukes, God's will is accomplished (the storm [8:26]; the newly healed [12:16]; the demon [17:18]). But when disciples or people rebuke as here, God's will is resisted (Peter [16:22]; the crowd [20:31]).

• 19:14

Jesus exhibits a contrasting practice in his words and actions. **But Jesus said, "Let the little children come to me."** He emphasizes his welcome by repetition and a negative, **do not stop them**. His reason? **For it is to such as these that the empire of heaven belongs**. While Jesus' welcome is surprising to disciples, it is not for the audience. The mercy he received from God as a child (ch. 2) he extends to other children (cf. 18:35). He has healed children (9:18-26; 15:21-28), fed them (14:13-21; 15:29-39), held them up as a model for disciples (18:3), and will in 21:15 receive their praise. On **empire of the heavens**, see 3:2; 4:17; ch. 13.

Jesus' welcome affirms two things. Children belong within God's empire. In the alternative households of disciples, children have a legitimate, not marginal, place. Second, in addition to affirming the inclusion of literal children, the term **children** becomes a metaphor with the phrase **such as these**. The children represent disciples to whom the empire belongs (also 18:1-6).

1. As in 18:1-6 the children represent the powerless, the marginal, the insignificant, the threatening, the outsiders, the weak, the little ones. As the beatitudes of 5:3-12 indicate, or the healing and call stories of chapters 8-9 demonstrate, the culturally marginal encounter God's empire through Jesus' words and actions, while the powerful center does not. It is precisely on the margins that God's presence and empire are known. So it is with disciples.

2. As children, disciples live a continuing existence on the margins, an alternative way of life which challenges the hierarchical and patriarchal order.

3. Just as children are in transition preparing for a future role, so disciples also live toward the future, toward the fullness of God's reign in which they will participate (cf. 19:27-30).

4. All disciples are called children. Parents have no place in the alternative households. Their absence indicates a basic rejection of a hierarchical and patriarchal structure in which power is exercised over others and the creation of a different social order among disciples, in which all are equal (20:12). Disciples recognize God alone as father (23:9; cf. 5:45). The distinctive identity and way of life created by God's empire are a more egalitarian existence.

• 19:15

Exhibiting the consistency expected of a good character in a Greco-Roman biography, Jesus does what he says. **And he laid his hands on them and went on his way**.

Jesus' double-level affirmation of both (literal) children and disciples resists the power structure and values of the patriarchal household. It belongs with a minority countercultural stream which saw in the first century some emerging different attitudes and practices.[22] M. Manson attests emerging understandings of children as children and of the value of play. Quintilian evidences these qualities (*Instit* 1.1.32-34; 1.3.10-12; 2.1.20). He shows a growing respect for children (1.1.24), recognizes their powerlessness and the need for adult consideration (1.3.17), and advocates less beating in education 1.3.13-17). Musonius Rufus (16) recognizes situations in which a child should not obey his father. Jesus' vision belongs with these changing views.

19:16-30—DISCIPLESHIP, WEALTH, AND PRIVILEGE

A third aspect of conventional household structures, the acquiring of wealth, is the focus.[23] Josephus (*Con Ap* 2.207-8) discusses wealth and property after marriage (2.199-203), children and parents (2.204-7), as do Philo (*Hypothetica* 7.3-4), and Pseudo-Phocylides (153-227). Aristotle identified this element as the "art of getting wealth" (*Pol* 1.3.1). What is "necessary and useful" for life is available, and each household (notably the male) is to procure it (*Pol* 1.3.3-29). Subsequent discussions rehearse and elaborate these emphases. While Aristotle stressed the fair distribution of limited resources, wealth is a key marker of social status and a means of requiting favors and gaining power and influence (Cicero, *De Off* 2.15.43-49). Juvenal complains that property and income are more important than "extraction, birth, merit, personal liberty and education for determining one's social status."[24] R. MacMullen's "Lexicon of Snobbery" attests the derision in which the wealthy held the poor and the honor in which they held themselves.[25] Seneca the Elder claims that wealth reflects a person's virtue (*Controversiae* 2.1.17). See Introduction, sections 5, 6, and 9; 6:16-18, 19-34.

The passage divides into three subsections: 19:16-22, Jesus' dialogue with the rich man who exhibits the harmful effect of acquiring wealth; 19:23-26, Jesus' general statement on the rich, wealth, and salvation; 19:27-30, a contrast between present wealth/poverty and future reward. Themes of wealth (19:21, 22, 23, 24, 27, 29) and eternal life (19:16, 17, 29) draw the section together.

• 19:16

Then (literally, "And behold"; signaling something new, 1:21; 8:2) **someone came to him**. The grammatical form indicates that **someone** is a man. He is unnamed. Not until 19:22b-24 is he identified as "a rich man" (twice) and his "many possessions" are noted. He is one of the societal elite, of privileged status with economic, social, and political power. The verb **came** indicates respectful address to an authoritative figure, but its use in 19:3 signals the likelihood of conflict. By the end of this subscene it will be clear that Jesus' authority conflicts with the man's commitment to wealth.

He addresses Jesus as **Teacher**, the title used by nondisciples and opponents (8:19; 9:11; 12:38; 17:24; 22:16, 24, 36). This is a further indication that things will not go well. His question reveals a religious concern with his personal destiny. He seeks divine vindication: **What good thing must I do to have eternal life? Eternal life** (a synonym for "enter life" [19:17], "be perfect" [19:21], "enter the empire of heaven" [19:23, 24], "be saved" [19:25], "inherit eternal life" [19:29]) refers to living or participating in the final accomplishment of God's purposes, in the reestablishment of, or a return to, God's life-giving empire "in the beginning"; see 7:14; 18:8-9; 14:32; 25:46. Compare Dan 12:2; 2 Macc 7:9; *Pss. Sol.* 9:5; 14:8-10; 4 Macc 15:3; *4 Ezra* 7:48, 129.

His question concerns the **good** he must do (cf. Cicero, *De Off,* book 1, "Moral Goodness"; Epictetus, *Diss* 1.7.1-4; 2.8), the human actions necessary to enjoy life (Lev 18:5). In 19:26 Jesus will indicate that there are limits to those actions. Is the rich man thinking he can acquire eternal life just as he acquires possessions?

• 19:17

Jesus indicates that the man's compliment is inappropriate (applicable only to God) and turns his attention to God's revealed will. **And he said to him, "Why do you ask me about what is good? There is only one who is good** (Pss 27:13; 73:1). God has made **the good** known as in Mic 6:8, "What is good . . . to do justice, love kindness and walk humbly with your God." **If you wish to enter life** (19:16), **keep the commandments**. There life is to be found (Lev 18:5; Deut 30:15-20).

• 19:18-19

The man seeks clarification. **He said to him, "Which ones?"** Jesus points him to the Decalogue, especially its requirements of just societal relationships (Exod 20:12-15; Deut 5:16-20), a key issue in the procurement and use of wealth. **And Jesus said, "You shall not murder** (cf. 5:21-26); **You shall not commit adultery** (cf. 5:27-30; 19:3-12); **You shall not steal; You shall not bear false witness; Honor your father and your mother"** (15:1-9). Jesus adds the summary from Lev 19:18, **also you shall love your neighbor as yourself** (5:43; 7:12; 22:37-39). True to his claim in 5:17-20, Jesus does not abolish these commandments.

• 19:20

The young man said to him, "I have kept all these." His claim contradicts Jesus' statement that "only one is good." He tries to make himself "good" like God. The (in)accuracy of his claim is exposed by his considerable wealth. In a world that understood, or at least in which the poor understood, that there were limited but adequate resources for all, one person's excess meant another's shortfall.[26] This man's abundance means greed, violence and oppression. He has impoverished, not loved, his neighbor (22:39). He has stolen what belongs to another. Prophetic critiques also suggest that abundant wealth results from merciless oppression and deprivation of the poor (Isa 5:8-10; 10:1-3; Ezek 22:6-31; 27; Amos 2:6-7; 5:10-12; 8:4-8; see Matt 6:19-34). Horace protests against those who greedily seek wealth (*Sat* 1.1; 2.3.82-280). Philostratus (*Apollonius* 1.15) narrates an incident in Aspendus in Pamphylia during Tiberius's reign (14-37 C.E.). Apollonius arrives to find starvation and riots because "the rich men had shut up all the grain and were holding it for export from the country." Its export meant higher profits. The burning of the land registers and debt records in Jerusalem at the outset of the 66 C.E. revolt (Josephus, *JW* 2.427) and in Antioch ca. 70 C.E. (*JW* 7.55, 60-61) was a similar protest against exploitative means by which the rich increased their wealth. Jesus has demanded throughout a unity of commitment and appropriate actions (6:24; 7:19, 24-27; 12:33-37). The man's wealth indicates that he does not have this.

Yet he asks a further question: **What do I still lack?** His question indicates that he correctly knows that he does not have eternal life through the commandments.

• 19:21

Jesus clarifies the man's lack. **If you wish to be perfect**. To be **perfect** is a synonym for "have eternal life" (19:16) and "enter life" (19:17). It is to imitate God in indiscriminate loving which benefits the other (5:43-48). He must do four things:

1. **Go**: This command commonly expresses Jesus' authority over the devil (4:10; 8:32; 16:23), disease (8:4, 13; 9:6), sin (9:6), estrangement (5:24; 18:15), and imperial power (5:41). Jesus' command here will have the same effect. If the man obeys, it will overcome Satan's power in choking the word (13:19-22, 38). It will effect his healing from the disease of acquiring wealth and forgiveness for the sin of obsession with mammon. It will accomplish a small act of social reconciliation in an unjust, greedy, and hierarchical system ruled over by Rome.

2. **Sell your possessions** (liquidate your assets): This command is not given to all who become disciples. Peter, Andrew, James, and John "leave" family and business but do not sell it (4:18-22). Matthew leaves his tax office (9:9). Joseph of Arimathea has wealth (27:57). Jesus does not regard all wealth as evil per se. As 6:19-34 has established, its use and place are more important issues. The presence here of the command to **sell** suggests that possessions are an issue for this man. Jesus has warned of the enslaving power of wealth (6:24-35; 13:22). Included among his possessions will be his house. It is "a central symbol of status and honor" which attests one's lineage, wealth, family reputation, achievements, and social standing. It is the location for the morning *salutatio* in which friends and clients greet a powerful patron. One's house is the place to display family military, commercial, or political accomplishments.[27]

3. **Give to the poor**: This is a further act of repentance. The term denotes the literal, physical **poor**, those without resources, exploited and oppressed by the elite—the stranger, the orphan, the widow, the needy, the sick, the physically disabled, the powerless. See 5:3. Giving to the poor in part follows 5:42a (give to beggars), but goes beyond 5:42b in that this is a gift, not a loan, and beyond 6:1-4 (giving alms) in that it involves everything. It is an act of restitution. It is a means of transforming unjust hierarchical social structures, practices, and attitudes by divesting one of the wealthy elite and by redistributing his resources more equitably among the poor. Jesus seeks to enact the jubilee traditions which brought about God's empire in just practices, which redistributed wealth and prevented the establishment of an elite with massive wealth and power at the expense of the poor (see Lev 25; Matt 12:1).

Jesus confronts elitist practices that equated wealth with virtue, turned away from "dirty beggars" (Epictetus, *Diss* 3.22.89), despised the poor as "dirt . . . scum . . . rabble" (Juvenal, *Sat* 8.44-48), denied them legal access, often engaged in self-promoting acts of civic charity, expected reciprocity (see 5:42; 6:1-4), sought to maintain hierarchical distinctions, and thought that while some carefully measured charity was a duty, there was little point in helping some poor (Seneca, *De Vita Beata* 24.1).[28] Jesus' approach is different. In giving to the poor, in effecting social justice, **you will have treasure in heaven**. See 6:19-20, for this view that God honors the doing of God's will in the judgment. Jesus resists a dominant value that regarded wealth as an automatic sign of divine favor (contra Deut 8:11-20; 28:1-14, esp. 11).

4. **Come, follow me**: For this call to discipleship and to encounter God's saving reign, see 4:17-19; 9:9. In calling him, Jesus challenges his loyalty to mammon (6:24). He is to live in relation to Jesus (to **follow**), God's agent commissioned to manifest God's saving reign. Jesus controls eschatological destiny. Life is entered through his call to discipleship (4:18-22; 7:24-27; 18:1-9). The man is also to live in new social relationships. The call means joining a new community (4:18-22), not of the center but of the margins (19:1-15), a community of children, eunuchs, and one-fleshers, not constituted by birth, conventional gender roles, inherited or acquired wealth, hierarchy, or "ruling over" others, but by doing God's will, with just economic practices (5:42; 6:1-4) and patterns of social interaction (12:46-50; 18:1-35).

19:22 Jesus has offered the man what he lacks, the opportunity to repent of his service to the normative cultural valuing of wealth and to know service of God. But he declines the offer. **When the young man heard this he went away grieving; for he had great possessions.** While he wishes for eternal life (19:17, 21), he does not act to encounter it. Wealth rules his heart (6:24). His social status matters too much. He will not sell his possessions or give to the poor. He has heard the word but wealth has choked it (13:22). He has forfeited life (16:26). He is a rich man (19:23-24), defined by his wealth and not by following Jesus.

• 19:23

Jesus interprets what has happened for his disciples by generalizing it. While commitment to wealth can prevent entry to God's empire, God's power is able to overcome it.

And Jesus said to his disciples, "Truly I tell you (see 5:18, 22), **it will be hard for a rich man to enter the empire of heaven."** While wealth might reflect divine favor (Deut 28:1-14), it was not an automatic link (so Job). According to an extensive Jewish tradition of hostility to wealth,[29] the pursuit of wealth corrupts (greed) and causes social injustice and destructive behavior (Sir 31:4-7; 34:20-22; *Ps.-Phoc.* 42-47). The wealthy exploit the poor (Sir 13:4, 19-22). Judgment awaits those who acquire wealth by oppression (*1 En* 62-63; 97:8-10; 100:6), and God will compensate and reward the poor with riches (*T. Jud.* 25:4). Qumran practiced voluntary renunciation (CD 1:11-13; 1QS 6:19, 22). Some Greco-Roman writers (often Stoics and members of the wealthier elite!) protest the greedy quest for wealth and advocate more moderate practices (Plutarch, "On the Love of Wealth," *Moralia* 523C-528; Musonius

Rufus, 13B, 20; Seneca, *De Vita Beata* 22.1-5). Cynics such as Pseudo-Diogenes advocated a literal abandoning of wealth because it marked social status, caused dissension and envy, and enslaved.[30] On **entering the empire** as eschatological vindication, see 5:20; 7:21; 18:3.

• 19:24

Jesus repeats the point with a graphic and witty metaphor. **Again I tell you** (5:18, 22), **it is easier for a camel to go through the eye of a needle than for someone who is rich to enter the reign of God.**[31] What was hard (19:23) has now become impossible (cf. 19:26). A big animal will not go through a little hole! The rich cannot enter. Repentance and redistribution (19:21) are needed. Then they will not be rich. This metaphor, critical of the economic elite (= the greedy and oppressive), cannot be tamed.

• 19:25

The disciples respond: **When the disciples** (see 5:1-2) **heard this, they were greatly astounded and said, "Then who can be saved?"** They again miss the point (19:10, 13). They seem to equate wealth with divine favor (Deut 28:1-14), a view Jesus has rejected in calling the rich man to sell his possessions. They seem to think that if the divinely favored and socially prestigious wealthy cannot be saved, no one can. On **saved**, see 1:21; 8:25; 10:22.

• 19:26

But Jesus looked at them and said, "For mortals it is impossible, but for God all things are possible." Jesus has offered this wealthy man salvation. This involves (1) his personal liberation from an identity and life enslaved to wealth. If he does what Jesus commands in 19:21 he ceases to be a rich man. And (2) it involves a social transformation whereby the rich stop their exploitation of the poor and redistribute resources more equitably. Jesus has offered him a new allegiance and identity, a new community and set of social interactions and economic practices. Such a transformation happens, not by doing good things (19:16) but by trusting and doing Jesus' instructions to sell, give, and follow (19:21). In this way God makes salvation possible, an empire in which the rich do not dominate the poor. But the man is possessed by his possessions.

• 19:27

The third subsection contrasts the rich man's refusal to sell his wealth with the disciples' response of leaving family and possessions.[32] Peter speaks on behalf of the disciples (see 15:15; 16:16, 22; 17:4; 18:21). **Then Peter said in reply, "Look we have left everything and followed you. What then will we have?"** Peter's comment recalls the crucial call scenes of 4:18-22 and their leaving the fishing contracts and family, and of 9:9 for Matthew leaving his tax-collecting business. But leaving does not mean permanent separation, as the references to Peter's mother-in-law in 8:14, to the mother of James and John in 20:20-21, and to "the house" in 9:10, 28; 13:1, 36; 17:25 (Peter's? Jesus'?) indicate. They do not sell everything, but they have not been prevented from following Jesus by their possessions. They have sacrificed wealth and family ties for so great a thing (cf. 13:44-45). These actions attest their profound commitment. This reordering of priorities and cultural norms is a central feature of Matthean discipleship and of the new, restructured households which befit God's empire.

Picking up on Jesus' promise to the rich man of "treasure in heaven" (19:21), Peter asks about the disciples' eschatological reward, **What then will we have?** The plural pronoun and form of his question (**we**), Jesus' response **to them**, and Jesus' use of plural forms indicate that Peter asks as a representative of the disciples.

• 19:28

Jesus does not dispute their "leaving everything" but clarifies their eschatological destiny. **Jesus said to them, "Truly I tell you** (5:18, 22) **at the renewal of all things, when the Son of Man is seated on the throne of his glory."** Jesus depicts something of the eschatological scene in which God's empire is established over all. The return of the **Son of Man** (see 8:20) to complete God's purposes, to exercise judgment, and establish God's reign has frequently been indicated (10:23; 13:39-43; 16:27-28; 24:27-31, 36-44; 25:31-46; 26:64; cf. Dan 7:9-27; *1 En* 46-48, 62-63). **Seated** indicates the exercise of power (5:1; Suetonius, *Nero* 13). In the judgment scene of *1 En* 62:5 in which the Son of Man judges the oppressive "kings, governors, high officials and landlords," he is **seated on the throne of his glory** (also *1 En* 69:29, the end of the judgment and evil). Jesus' judgment and rule mean **the renewal of all things**. This term refers to the new age and world (BAGD, 606),[33] a new heaven and earth, both temporal and spatial (so 5:18; 24:35; cf. *1 En* 45:4-5; 91:16; *2 Bar* 44:12; 57:2), a new creation (1:1; 14:32; 19:4, 8), God's salvation and empire, which ends the oppressive imperial world under the control of the devil (4:8), of Rome and its gods.

Jesus has recalled his role; now he articulates the disciples' role: **you who have followed me will also sit on twelve thrones, judging the twelve thrones of Israel.** Jesus' vindication means vindication for disciples. Is their role of **judging** to be understood as exercising judgment, or as ruling? While various traditions envisage Israel judging the Gentiles (Wis 3:8; *T. Abr.* A 13:6) or the elect/righteous judging the nations (1QpHab 5:4; 1QS 5:6-7; 1QM 6:6; 11:13-14), several observations count against the first option here. (1) Judgment of others is not something disciples are permitted to do (cf. 7:1-2; the same verb κρίνω [*krinō*]). (2) In the eschatological scenes, the Son of Man and his angels enact judgment (13:39-43; 25:32), not disciples.

In support of the second option of **ruling** as their role are scenarios such as Dan 7 (involving the Son of Man) in which the saints reign in "an everlasting kingdom" (7:27), and traditions in which the twelve patriarchs rule gathered Israel (1QM 2:1-3). What sort of ruling is in view? In Matt 20:20-21, the mother of James and John asks for prominent seats in a reign which differs greatly from that of the Gentiles (20:25). Jesus rejects her request. Their rule is not ruling over or dominating others. Nor does it seem to be an exclusive role

for the twelve. Jesus promises this role to **you who have followed me**, all disciples, not just the twelve. The scene, then, envisages disciples participating in
the fullness of God's empire, along with faithful Israel and believing Gentiles
who enter the reign (8:11-12; 23:39). See further 20:25-28.

• 19:29

Jesus elaborates the abundant eschatological reward for all faithful followers. **And everyone who has left houses** (see 19:21) **or brothers or sisters or
father or mother or children or fields on account of my name will receive
a hundredfold, and will inherit eternal life.** The list (seven items—representing all loss?) includes possessions and the means of procuring wealth
(**houses, fields, inheritance**), as well as family relationships. The future tenses
(**will receive, will inherit**) and reference to **eternal life** indicate future, abundant (the hyperbolic **a hundredfold**) eschatological reward in the new creation
with its plentiful provision (see 14:13; *2 Bar* 74:1-2). But something of God's
empire, including restructured socioeconomic relationships, is known now in
the community/households of disciples (chs. 5-7; 12:46-50; 19-20).

• 19:30

In this context Jesus' final comment anticipates the reversal of the coming
judgment. **And/But many who are first will be last, and the last will be first**.
But to whom does it apply? (1) Does it function as a summary of 19:16-30 to
contrast the rich man as one of the societal elite (the **first**) who has rejected salvation and will be condemned at the judgment (**last**), with the obedient disciples who have left all (the **last** in societal rankings) and followed Jesus but who
will be vindicated at the judgment (**the first**)? (2) Or does it relate to 19:29 and
offer a contrast and warning? While the disciples are **first** in the reverse values
and practices of God's empire, they are warned that without continued faithful
following, they may yet be **last**, excluded at the judgment (cf. 7:21-23).

The conjunction **and/but** (δέ) can have both connective (no. 1) and contrastive (no. 2) functions. Both possibilities are consonant with the Matthean
worldview. It seems preferable to respect the polyvalent nature of the saying
rather than choose one of these meanings.

CHAPTER 20

The Alternative Households of God's Empire

Part 2

Chapter 19 has outlined the first three aspects of the alternative, against-the-grain households which embody God's empire (see the introduction to chapter 19). Chapter 20 will complete the fourth element of household structures, that of slaves, in 20:17-28. The preceding (20:1-16) and following (20:29-34) sections attend to the larger issues of understanding and living the alternative identity and more egalitarian lifestyle created by God's empire.

20:1-16—THE PARABLE OF THE HOUSEHOLDER

The opening, comparative formula signals a change of form in 20:1.[1] How does this parable connect to chapter 19? (1) The parable pictures God's empire, the central theme of Jesus' words and actions since 4:17. Life shaped by God's reign has been to the fore in this fourth narrative block (16:28; 18:1, 3, 4, 23; 19:12, 14, 23, 24) and continues to be in this chapter (20:1, 21).

(2) The parable concerns a householder. Chapter 19 has outlined households of one-fleshers, eunuchs, and children, shaped by God's empire. This householder will, in some regards, act in a surprising against-the-grain way that befits the alternative households being outlined in chapter 19. His main action displays the more egalitarian, less hierarchical emphasis evident in chapter 19 (20:12), which he affirms as both "right" (20:4) and "good" (20:15).[2] The parable continues the vision of households shaped by God's saving presence or empire. These households are part of the way of the cross to which Jesus calls disciples (16:21-28).

(3) Chapter 19 ended with a reversal motif involving the first and the last. The same pairing appears in 20:8, 16, while "first" is used in 20:10 and "last" in 20:12, 14. Moreover "first" appears in 20:27 to link the parable to the subsequent scene about being slaves. In depicting life shaped by the empire, this parable, like 18:23-35, emphasizes relationships among disciples.

This emphasis on the parable's contribution to the emerging alternative household structure being outlined in chapters 19-20 differs from other readings. Misled by mistranslations of v. 15, many see "generosity" as the key. But while generosity is evident in the payment to some workers (20:9), the householder is not consistently generous (20:10-11). J. Breech and J. Drury find a salvation-history perspective. They argue that the parable depicts all Christians receiving the same reward regardless of when they became Christians. Jesus' emphasis on greater or lesser rewards undercuts this claim (5:19). J. Lambrecht claims that it warns Christians against resenting God's mercy displayed in the judgment. But in addition to ignoring the present-tense focus of the comparative formula of 20:1, this approach neglects, as do the others, the household connections outlined above.[3]

• 20:1

The opening **For** indicates a connection with chapter 19. The parable will provide an example. On **the empire of the heavens**, see 3:2 4:17, 23; 12:28; chapter 13 (introduction). On the present-tense comparison formula **is like** emphasizing present dimensions of God's empire, see 13:31, 33, 44, 45, 47 and the introduction to chapter 13 (also for the parable form). The parable is not about the final judgment.

The parable divides into two scenes. Matthew 20:1-7 deals with hiring laborers, and 20:8-16 with paying them. The first scene further divides into four subunits in which the householder hires laborers at different times: early morning (20:1-2); the third (20:3-5a), sixth (20:6b), and eleventh (20:6-7) hours. The marking of time prepares for the key issue of payment in the second half.

The **empire of the heavens** is compared to a situation involving **a householder**. Jesus has been called a householder in 10:25. Epictetus (*Diss* 3.22.4) and Philo (*Somn* 1.149) use this image for God. The householder figures in other parables (Matt 13:27, 52; 21:33; 24:43), but we should not assume that the householder is God/Jesus (cf. the king in 18:23-35). Intertextual clues such as his large accumulation of land (cf. 19:21) and subsequent inconsistent behavior in not addressing the inequality of his own wealth suggest that that identification would be inappropriate.

The householder's first act is to go **out early in the morning to hire laborers for his vineyard**.[4] The references to the **householder**, **his vineyard**, **hiring laborers**, and **his manager** (20:8) depict an everyday scene of the male head of a patriarchal household doing what discussions of household management say he should do, acquiring wealth for its support (see introduction to 19:16-30). Vineyards[5] involved significant initial investment until they became productive. They were high yield and more profitable than basic survival crops involving grains. This man is probably very wealthy, like the rich man of 19:16-30. He is probably a member of the urban elite, managing (one of?) his estate. Did he inherit his land? Has he added to it by loans to peasant farmers at high interest rates, allowing him to force foreclosure when they could not repay?

The householder's act of going **out early in the morning to hire day laborers for his vineyard** is somewhat unusual. This is usually the manager's task

(20:8). Why does the owner do it? W. R. Herzog argues that the parable "codifies systems of oppression in order to unveil them and make them visible to those victimized by them."[6] Jesus shows both the manager and the householder making the daily decisions from which the workers suffer. His involvement prepares for the later confrontation.

Day laborers were a common sight in the *agora,* or marketplace (20:3) as they waited to be hired for work. They were a readily available pool of cheap labor for wealthier landowners and urban dwellers. Commonly uprooted from peasant farms taken over by wealthy landowners after foreclosing on debt, or forced from family plots because they could not support the household, they looked for agricultural or urban work, usually day by day and at minimal rates. During planting and harvest, work was readily available, "for vintage and haying" (Varro, *On Agric* 1.17.2), but in between times it often was not. For these "expendables," or involuntary marginals (see Introduction, section 5), life was unpredictable, marked by unemployment, malnutrition, starvation, disease, minimal wages, removal from households, and begging.[7] Their situation was more precarious than slaves since an employer had no long-term investment in them.[8]

• 20:2

The householder hires the laborers: **After agreeing with his laborers for a denarius a day, he sent them into his vineyard**. The pay rate of **a denarius a day** is not generous. In fact it is about normal for cheap labor (as much as we can tell;[9] see Pliny, *NH* 33.3). It pays perhaps enough for a subsistence existence, if the day laborer could not find regular daily work. What they are to do in the **vineyard** is not stated. It is, though, likely to be either planting or harvest.

• 20:3-4

The householder hires more laborers. His need for more laborers reinforces the sense of his great wealth. **When he went out about nine o'clock, he saw others standing idle in the marketplace**. That there were unhired laborers available at this time suggests oversupply and unemployment (Josephus notes eighteen thousand out of work at the completion of the temple [*Ant* 20.219-20]). He likewise sends them **into the vineyard** promising, **I will pay you what is right**. This is a key phrase. It involves the concept of meeting expectations and obligations (cf. 1:19). But in contrast to v. 1, the householder does not negotiate a specified price. The laborers, and the audience, can calculate what they think would be **right** in this situation relative to the denarius of v. 1 and compare with the householder's action in vv. 10-15.

• 20:5-7

Three more times the householder hires more laborers. **When he went again about noon and about three o'clock, he did the same. And about five o'clock he went out and found others standing around; and he said to them, "Why are you standing here idle all day?" They said to him,**

"Because no one has hired us." He said to them, "You also go into the vineyard." The term **idle** does not indicate laziness. They are available for work but there is none. Nothing is said about the level of payment for these subsequent hirings. The question of what is **right** remains open.

• 20:8

The second part of the parable begins. The issue is now payment. **When evening came, the owner of the vineyard said to his manager, "Call the laborers and give them their pay."** The owner's involvement is again unusual (see 20:1). It emphasizes the confrontation between householder and laborers. Paying the laborers at the end of the day is the right thing to do (Deut 24:14-15; Tob 4:14). The owner orders the payment to begin **with the last and then go to the first**. Those hired first see the whole payment process.

• 20:9

The payment process of those hired at nine and noon is collapsed into the payment of the last hired to create two groups. **When those hired about five o'clock came each of them received a denarius.** The householder pays them for a day's work (v. 1), though they have done less than a day's work. Until now he has appeared competent and predictable in his management. But this is a surprising and unusual act which will need explaining. This is what he considers to be right (20:4).

• 20:10

Then those hired first are paid. **Now when the first came, they thought they would receive more**. These laborers overlook their agreement (20:1) and calculate higher payments for more work. They are disappointed. **But each of them also received a denarius**. If the householder had paid them more, the issue would be generosity. How is this act **right**?

• 20:11-12

The parable's focus falls on how the two groups of laborers regard each other. The last paid are not pleased. Their energy and work have been slighted and dishonored. **And when they received it, they grumbled against the landowner saying, "These last worked only one hour, and you have made them equal to us who have borne the burden of the day and the scorching heat."** Their **grumbling** evokes that of the Israelites against God after liberation from slavery (same verb; Exod 17:3; Num 11:1; 14:27, 29). They are angry because the householder has not acted according to what they consider to be normal practices. He has surprised them by doing something quite different.[10] Instead of maintaining differentiation among the laborers based on performance, instead of reinforcing the superiority of some at the expense of the rest (cf. ch. 19; 20:20-28), he has evened out the distinctions and treated them in solidarity as **equals**.[11] Instead of using wages to reinforce distinctions, he uses them to express equality and solidarity. That this householder, with great wealth, should enact this egalitarian gesture is surprising, especially when he is blind to greater equalizing actions that he might perform (cf. 19:21)!

• 20:13-16

In response to their complaint against this "equal" treatment, the householder makes a double response consisting each time of statement, question, and command/question to help them and the audience comprehend this different reality (20:13-14a, 14b-15). **And he replied to one of them, "Friend** (cf. 22:12; 26:50, used of people in the wrong) **I am doing you no wrong/have not defrauded or cheated you**." His equalizing action bites at competitive drives whereby the oppressed acquiesce in the elite's divide-and-conquer strategy and use violence to oppress one another.[12] The owner has not wronged them, at least in this payment. **Did you not agree with me for a denarius?** He has paid them the agreed daily wage. **Take what belongs to you and go**.

Another explanation follows. **I choose to give to this last the same as I give to you. Am I not allowed to do what I choose with what belongs to me? Is your eye evil because I am good?** The householder asserts his privilege as owner to dispose of his wealth as he chooses without complaint, question, or comment. It is an elitist privilege and strategy. It overlooks other criteria that might guide his disposal of his wealth, such as maximum benefit for others (19:21).

But here a much smaller, though significant, action is in view. He asserts that in paying them all the same and treating them as equals, not only has he done "what is right" but he has done something **good**, something that, given the echo of 19:17, reflects God's ways (though he is certainly not God!). His final question (not command as in 19:14a), **Is your eye evil?**, challenges the workers and the audience to recognize "equal" treatment as a good, Godlike thing. The **evil eye** has nothing to do with generosity (so NRSV, RSV translations) but consists of jealousy or envy,[13] evil that is opposed to God's purposes. The question leaves open the workers' and audience's response, while it solicits their/our agreement. The parable challenges audiences of disciples to embrace this alternative egalitarian lifestyle and to view social structures and interactions from that perspective which is fundamental to God's empire. That reign challenges hierarchical and patriarchal structures (**the last will be first and the first will be last;** cf. ch. 19) with its transformative power to shape an alternative way of life.

The supreme irony and surprise of the parable are that the householder has the most to lose and to gain (16:24-26; 19:16-30) from clearly "seeing" and consistently enacting the principle of egalitarian treatment which he has demonstrated and articulated in this one transaction in the parable! The parable presents him as a cartoon figure with exaggerated and ironic characteristics.

20:17-28—IT SHALL NOT BE SO AMONG YOU

The shaping of the alternative households of God's empire continues. The fourth element of normative hierarchical households consists of masters ruling over slaves (Aristotle, *Pol* 1.2.1; 2.2-23; 5.3-12). Sirach 7:19-28 discusses wife (7:19, 26), slaves and cattle (7:20-23), children (7:23-25), and parents (7:27-

28). Pseudo-Phocylides discusses wealth and labor (153-74), marriage (175-206), parents and children (207-17), kinsfolk (218-22), and slaves (223-27). Also Josephus, *Con Ap* 2.199-216.

This section presents Jesus as a slave and calls disciples to live a marginal existence as slaves. As in chapter 19, the cultural pattern is subverted. The household or community of disciples is a community of slaves, of the marginal and of equals, which has no masters except God (6:24; cf. 23:10-11). Instead of relationships of "ruling over," which dominate and oppress, it is marked by service.

Numerous commentators treat the passion prediction of 20:17-19 as separate from 20:20-28. But several factors point to 20:17-28 as one section. (1) Jesus' death pervades the section. It is predicted in 20:17-19, discussed in 20:22-23 ("the cup"), and restated in 20:28. Introduced by *hōsper* (ὥσπερ, "just as") in 20:28, his death is a model for the disciples' way of life. (2) Jesus' resurrection draws the section together. It is asserted in 20:19 and is the basis for the mother's question concerning her sons' place in God's empire (20:20-23). His answer consists of further instruction concerning a lifestyle appropriate for God's reign (20:24-28). (3) The theme of "ruling over" is pervasive. The Gentiles put Jesus to death (20:19). Their "ruling over" destroys (20:25). Jesus contrasts it with the way of service which is to be evident in the present (20:26-28) and future (20:20-23) expressions of God's empire. (4) The disciples' way of life provides a further thread. They accompany Jesus to the cross (20:17), and their future roles and present lives are the focus of 20:20-28.

• 20:17-18a

Jesus again announces his imminent death (17:12, 22-23), first declared in the central scene (16:21) of this fourth narrative block (16:21-20:34). The repetition elaborates its importance[14] and prepares for the passion narrative (chs. 26-27).

The opening line recalls Jesus' departure from Galilee and move into Judea (19:1): **While Jesus was going up to Jerusalem**. The narrative underlines in two ways the disciples' close involvement in what is happening. First, Jesus **took the twelve disciples aside by themselves** (cf. 14:13, 23; 17:1, 19). Second, he includes them in a plural pronoun, **See we are going up to Jerusalem**. Compare 16:21; 17:12, 22-23, where the focus is on Jesus. **Jerusalem** has been the place of political opposition (ch. 2; 16:21), of the devil's temptation (4:5), and of organized resistance from the religious elite (15:1), along with some interest and responsiveness from the nonelite (4:25). The disciples walk the way of the cross with Jesus (16:24). His fate and their fate are linked as 20:20-28 will elaborate. Christology and ecclesiology are intertwined.

• 20:18b-19

The announcement adds more detail about Jesus' suffering and about its agents. **The Son of Man will be handed over/arrested/betrayed/delivered** (see 17:22) **to the chief priests and scribes and they will condemn him to death** (see 26:47-56, 57-68). The **chief priests and scribes**, the religious elite, were named as agents of his death in 16:21. See 2:4; 12:14; 16:21. They **condemn to death** the **Son of Man** (see 8:20; 17:22), who has the ultimate power in the judgment and over the new heaven and earth (19:28).

The Sanhedrin cannot put someone to death, but must gain Roman support.[15] So they **will deliver him/hand him over** (same verb as 20:18b) **to the Gentiles** (see 27:1-14). This is new information. Matt 16:21 referred to the religious elite and 17:22 to "the hands of people." Again the religious and political elite are shown as allies against Jesus. Rome and the religious elite have good reason to execute him. His proclamation of God's empire in "Galilee under the Gentiles" (see 4:15; 12:18) has challenged Rome's authority and legitimacy (taxation, 17:24-27). He has criticized exclusive Gentile communities (5:47), prayer practices and theology (6:7), and material priorities (6:32). Shortly he will criticize their oppressive exercise of power (20:25). The empire strikes back.

They will **mock** him (27:29, 31, 41; cf. 2:16 [the magi mock Herod]). The term describes violence against the righteous (1 Macc 9:26; 2 Macc 7:10; cf. Joseph in Gen 39:14, 17), the people's rejection of God's messengers and prophets, which results in punishment by destroying Jerusalem in 587 B.C.E. (2 Chr 36:16; cf. Rome's victory in 70 C.E.). Imperial Babylon mocks kings (Hab 1:10) and Jerusalem (Ezek 22:5). God mocks enslaving Egypt (Exod 10:2; 1 Sam 6:6). It also denotes the terrible violence in the rape and murder of the Levite's concubine (Judg 19:25). Jesus' death will be a violent mocking of a righteous man (cf. 27:19), a rejection of God's commissioned agent by imperial Rome. But through it God will mock Rome with its defeat at Jesus' return (24:27-31).

They will **flog** him as synagogues do to disciples (10:17) and to prophets, sages, and scribes (23:34; cf. 27:26). Cf. 2 Macc 6:30 the old man and martyr Eleazar. Slaves (cf. 20:26-28) were frequently beaten not so much out of fear of insubordination as because they were regarded as marginal beings, outside the boundary of the community of citizens in which social intercourse is marked by rational discourse and moral decisions.[16] On **crucified**, see 10:38; 16:24; 23:34; 27:33-50. But his death is not the Roman Gentiles' victory. **On the third day he will be raised**, by God. See 16:21; 17:23; 28. The last will be first (19:30). Jesus' prediction is accurate as the references to the passion narrative indicate. It functions to underline his credibility and as a plot summary foreshadows the end of the story.

• 20:20

Such an announcement could be expected to elicit expressions of concern or support for Jesus from the disciples. But they are silent, perhaps an ironic improvement on Peter's protest of 16:22. The refusal to accept his way of faithfulness, which leads to suffering and humiliation, is expressed by a new character. Her approach and question are closely linked to 20:17-19 by **then**. Instead of compassion, there is ambition and a desire for power among the disciples; **the mother of the sons of Zebedee came to him with her sons and kneeling before him she asked him for something**.[17] She (unnamed, but introduced by her place in a patriarchal household as mother and wife) has not been mentioned previously, though Zebedee figured in the call story as James and John left the family fishing contract to follow Jesus. The two brothers have some prominence in being called in the first group of disciples (4:21-22; 10:2) and in witnessing the transfiguration (17:1-8). While the spotlight falls on the mother and her ambitious request, the two sons do not resist. Her question seems to be theirs (cf. 20:22-24).

Though present to hear Jesus' prediction in vv. 17-19, they are concerned not with him but with their positions in the future empire. The reference to resurrection (20:19), as well as his instruction about reward in the future reign (19:27-30), prepare for this focus. Her approach is deferential in recognizing Jesus' authority. The respectful verb **came** (see 4:3; 5:1; 8:2) is reinforced by the act of **kneeling**, an action of disciples (2:2, 11; 8:2; 9:18; 14:33) and of another woman who seeks Jesus' help for a child (15:25). Her **asking for something from him** is an act of prayer (6:6; 7:7, 8, 9, 10, 11; 18:19). These three verbs, along with her association with her two sons, the context of private instruction (20:17), and her subsequent appearance at the cross with other women (27:55-60) suggest that she is a disciple. Perhaps she has left husband and house to follow (cf. 19:29). But disciples are capable of inappropriate requests and actions (19:10, 13). The three verbs also express hostile approach (19:3), false worship/kneeling (2:8; 4:9), and murderous requests (14:7-12, with a woman as subject).

• **20:21**

Jesus invites her to make her request: **And he said to her, "What do you want?"** The same verb denotes inappropriate requests in 19:17, 21. The deference and respect evident in 20:20 recede as she commands Jesus: **"Declare** (an imperative) **that these two sons of mine will sit, one at your right hand and one at your left, in your empire."** Compare the requests of other parents for healing, not for power, for their children (9:18-19, 23-26; 15:21-28; 17:14-18). Her question, though, shows some understanding. She knows that Jesus will be victorious, will establish God's empire, and that disciples will share in that reign (19:28). But they want their thrones now! She and her sons have failed to understand the nature of God's empire and their role in it. They are to be with the marginal and humiliated (18:1-14). They are children (19:13-15). Their "rule" (19:28) does not consist of domination, prestige, and importance for themselves (**left** and **right** are places of proximity and honor). It does not imitate imperial structures and hierarchical societal patterns (anticipating 20:25). Rather it is a different way, that of humiliation and service.

• **20:22**

Jesus' response is in the plural as he rebukes the mother and sons. **But Jesus answered, "You do not know what you are asking. Are you able to drink the cup that I am about to drink?"** The metaphor of **drinking the cup** refers to the suffering which imperial powers (often as agents of God's wrath) bring on people (Ezek 23:31-34; Jer 49:12). Jerusalem experienced this suffering in its fall to Babylon in 587 (Isa 51:17-23; Jer 25, esp. 15, 17, 28-29; Ezek 23:31-33). In turn Babylon experiences it (Isa 51:23; Jer 25:12-14), as does Jerusalem at Rome's hands (*Pss. Sol.* 8:14-15). **Cup**, though, can also denote God's salvation (Pss 16:5; 116:13). Through Jesus' suffering at the hands of the elite, God's salvation will be accomplished. He will return to establish God's empire. Disciples participate in that victory (1:21; 19:27) through faithfulness in the present distress (10:16-39; 24). The mother and disciples affirm that they can remain faithful (**We are able**).

• 20:23

Jesus does not contest their declaration, but he emphasizes that the way of the cross, of suffering, humiliation, shame, marginality, and death, is before them: **He said to them, "You will indeed drink my cup."** Not only have they underestimated the way of the cross; they have also overlooked that it is *God's* empire. Only God can determine what they have requested, **but to sit at my right hand and at my left, this is not mine to grant, but it is for those for whom it has been prepared by my Father**. Jesus recognizes his own limited knowledge (cf. 24:3, 36). He is commissioned to manifest God's saving presence (1:21, 23), empire (4:17; 12:28), and will (11:25-27), but God's authority is supreme. On **my Father**, see 5:16, 45, 48; 7:21; 10:32-33; 11:25-27; 16:17; 18:35; 23:9.

• 20:24

The dialogue among the mother and two sons broadens. **When the ten heard it, they were angry with the two brothers.** It is not clear whether they are angry at their ambition and lobbying, at their failure to understand chapters 18-19, or because they forced Jesus to explode a myth about their future power and glory. What is clear is that the disciples are not "at home" in their new identity and way of life in households of equals.

• 20:25

Jesus instructs all the disciples about the way of life which God's empire requires. God's empire shapes a community of slaves.

But Jesus called them to him. His **calling** recalls their summons to be disciples (10:1), to live the identity and social role of children (18:2). He **said, "You know** (invoking their everyday knowledge) **that the rulers of the Gentiles lord it over them, and their great ones are tyrants over them."** K. W. Clark has complained that the translations **lord it over** and **tyrants over** are unjustifiably perjorative, that the verbs are neutral in designating the exercise of rule. What Clark overlooks is that rule is never neutral in an imperial situation![18] Their rule embodies a hierarchical system in which the powerful (military, political, economic, social) exploit the majority poor for the former's benefit. Clark's appeal to linguistic data fails because he does not look "from below" to examine the effects of imperial rule, whether military, political, economic, social, cultural, legal, or religious.[19]

Moreover, the verbs **lord it over** and **are tyrants over** provide some clue as to why this rule is condemned. Both verbs are cognates of words used for God/Jesus, the first of "Lord" (κύριος, *kyrios*), the second of "authority" (ἐξ-ουσία, *exousia*). "Lord" usually denotes God's salvific will and authority over the heaven and earth, and human existence (1:20, 22, 24; 2:13, 15, 19; 3:3; 4:7, 10; 5:33; 11:25; 22:37). It denotes Jesus' life-giving authority over judgment (7:21-22), disease and demons (8:2, 6, 8; 9:28; 15:22, 25; 17:15), death (8:21), the sabbath (12:8), creation (8:25; 14:28, 30), disciples (10:24-25). "Authority" involves the revelation of God's will (7:29), healing and forgiveness (9:6, 8; 10:1), God's authority over all things (28:18).

The vocabulary suggests that the tyrannical rule of the **Gentiles and their great ones** is condemned because it claims to exercise the authority and rule that rightly belong to God/Jesus. Authority over heaven and earth belongs to its Lord (11:25; 28:18). The offense is twofold. In part, imperial rule commits an act of hubris in overstepping all limits and in claiming the authority and rule of God. Second, it does not accomplish God's purposes. It subverts God/Jesus' life-giving purposes and empire in bringing poverty, misery, political control, and, above all, death to God's agent (20:19).

The community of disciples has been contrasted with **Gentiles** previously, with exclusive Gentile communities (5:47), with prayer practices and theology (6:7), and with priorities set on material goods (6:32). Gentiles inflict suffering on disciples (10:18; 24:9), even as disciples are sent in mission to them (24:14; 28:19), and some Gentiles become disciples (2:1-12; 8:5-13; 15:21-28). Now their praxis of power is contrasted. Instead of exercising destructive power over others as the **great ones** do, and as they will do to Jesus (20:19), disciples are great in the reign by humility (18:1-4). The term **ruler** has both positive and negative links. In 9:18, 23 it denotes a local leader who is powerless to give life, but looks to Jesus to do so. In 12:24 it denotes Beelzeboul, the ruler of demons (an accusation against Jesus). The use of the same term in 12:24 and 20:25 again links the devil and the imperial structure (so 4:8).

• 20:26-27

Jesus strongly states the contrast between this normative imperial and societal structure and the alternative political and social praxis of the community of disciples. **It shall not be so among you**. Jesus' words are an outright rejection of such a system. He offers an alternative praxis of power and community. **But whoever would be great among you must be your servant.** In 18:1-4 to be great in God's empire means being as a child, one who is socially marginal, powerless, vulnerable, insignificant, dangerous as far as the center is concerned. Likewise here. Jesus again locates the identity and lifestyle of disciples on the margins. The point is repeated in equating **great** and **first**, **servant** and **slave**. **Whoever would be first among you must be your slave**. See 6:24; 10:24-25.

The linking of rule and servanthood is present in a Hellenistic tradition of the ideal king as the servant of his people (Plato, *Republic* I.347D; VII.540B; Dio Chrysostom, *Disc* 1.12-34; Musonius Rufus 61-65). Cynics utilized the tradition to describe the philosopher-ruler, whether literally a king (Seneca, *Ep*

90.5; Musonius Rufus 65-67) or as one who shares in Zeus's reign over all humankind by ruling, serving, and giving one's life (Epictetus, *Diss* 3.22.54-61, 77-85; 4.30-32).[20] Clearly this tradition is an ideal one. Jesus attacks the reality of imperial rule as experienced by the nonelite.

In using images of **slave/servant**, Jesus evokes a widespread, accepted, and complex system of domination in the first-century world. The discussions of household management since Aristotle (cf. *Pol* 1.2.1) attest the rule of master over slave/s as the third household relationship (husband–wife; father–child; see 19:16).[21] Seneca, despite some more noble sentiments (*Ep* 47), affirms this system of domination; "the more upright and capable of good action" rules over the inferior and obedient (*De Ben* 3.19.1-38.3). Slaves are subservient, dependent on their master, owned, lacking any self-determination, at the mercy of their owner, expected to obey, powerless, with few legal rights, beaten, alienated from any legitimated social existence, without honor, despised by the elite. See 8:9; 13:27-28; 18:23-24, 26-27.

Commenting on this outsider status, T. Wiedemann says, "In a world where the [male adult] citizen was at the center of human activity, slavery represented the other pole of minimum participation in humanity, and the slave came to symbolize the boundary of social existence."[22] The slave was a marginal person, physically alive but socially dead, an outsider existing on the edge of society and the household, yet a participant in human society only by service to a master.[23]

There was little questioning of the existence or normalcy of slavery. Certainly slave experiences were very diverse, depending on the type of work and nature of the master. Some have observed some amelioration in conditions through the first century and attributed it variously to a scarcity of slaves, to increased numbers of slaves raised in households, greater social interaction with slaves in voluntary associations, more prestigious and powerful positions held by educated and skilled slaves, and Stoic influence.[24] But for all that, Seneca (*De Ben* 3.21; *Ep* 47:14), like Cicero in the previous century (*De Off* 1.13.41; 3.23.89-92), still has to insist on a master's duty to provide adequately for a slave. And no matter how improved its conditions, slavery remained a system of domination and ownership of one human being by another.

Why, then, does Jesus invoke this image to identify disciples as **slaves** of God (6:24)? Why does the gospel again borrow this image from the imperial world it resists? (1) The image applies to all disciples. There are no masters (cf. 23:10), no ruling over other disciples. Instead of hierarchy there is equality of function as disciples seek to live God's will faithfully and for the benefit of each other. Enslavement to God, not domination of others, marks their identity and the social structure of this community which embodies God's empire. (2) The image embraces dimensions of the disciples' social interaction. Disciples, like slaves, know suffering and scorn (5:10-12; ch. 10). They practice obedience to their master's will (7:24-27; 12:46-50).

(3) Discipleship shares a similar temporal structure.[25] Slaves live in the time between their enslavement and their yet-future and hoped-for manumission or release from slavery. Disciples live in the time between their call and the future

completion of God's purposes and their eschatological vindication. (4) D. Martin has shown that for some slaves, slavery was an honorable existence.[26] Honor could be derived from serving a prestigious and benevolent master (for instance, slaves in the imperial household). Philo complains about the slave Helicon who influences Gaius Caligula against the Jewish delegation from Alexandria (*Gaium* 26.166-78, 203-6; see Matt 6:24). Some slaves accrued honor from indispensable skills (especially in business and commerce, medicine, and education) whereby their master's welfare was integral to their own. To be a slave of the one who is "Lord of heaven and earth" (11:25) provides great honor by association. To serve this master faithfully is a disciple's/slave's highest calling (24:45-51; 25:14-30), regardless of scorn or opposition. Faithful service guarantees final vindication.

• 20:28

The model (**even as**) of faithful service for the benefit of others is Jesus. **The Son of Man came not to be served but to serve**. On **Son of Man**, see 8:20; 17:22; 19:28; 20:18 (the focus here is on his death). On **came** as part of several statements that identify Jesus' mission, see 5:17; 9:10-13; 10:34-36; 11:19.[27] On Jesus as God's **servant** doing God's will, see 8:17; 12:18-21; 16:21.

His means of service is expressed in the second half, **to give his life/himself/his existence a ransom for many**. On **life** as oneself, see 2:20; 6:25; 10:28, 39. Jesus **gives his life** as a willing and chosen act in death (16:21). His death is not the victory of the religious and political elite. He does what he teaches disciples to do (16:24-26). Though he has referred to his death in 16:21; 17:12, 22; 20:17-19, here he interprets its significance.

Jesus' death is a **ransom**. This term derives from a word group meaning redemption,[28] freedom, or liberation. God redeems or liberates Israel from slavery in Egypt (Exod 6:6; Deut 7:8) and from exile under Babylon (Isa 43:1). **Ransom** often refers to the price paid for freedom or deliverance such as to free or manumit slaves[29] and prisoners of war (*Ep. Arist.* 22; Josephus, *Ant* 12.27-28; 14.107; *JW* 1.274-75, 384; *Vita* 419). In the LXX, it is a payment which is "a substitute for a person's life."[30] Levites are a substitute to release the first-born, which God claims in remembrance of the exodus (Num 3:12, 46, 48, 49, 51; Lev 18:15). In the provisions for the jubilee year, a ransom redeems or buys back land (Lev 25:24, 26) or a kinsperson who has sold him- or herself into slavery (25:51-52). Sometimes there is no ransom or price. A murderer is not to be ransomed (Lev 35:31, 32). In Isa 45:13 God promises to use Cyrus to free Israel from exile in Babylon, but there is no ransom. This redemption is a free act of God's power. See 1:21.

Jesus' death is a **ransom for many**. It affects more than his own life. It results from an act of violence by the religious and political elite intended to dispatch and silence a disruptive prophet. But in God's purposes it accomplishes more than they can control or envisage. It is **for many**; **for** means "in the place of" and "for the benefit of" others. Note Josephus, *Ant* 14.107; the priest Eleazar pays a Roman a gold bar *instead of, in the place of*, his plundering the temple treasures (λύτρον ἀντὶ πάντων). Jesus' ransom, his life, is "a substitute for another's life," a payment which liberates and frees others who live in the sinful world of imperial control (1:21). There is no indication that a price is paid to either God or the devil, as later theologians debate. The metaphor's emphasis falls on the liberation that it effects.

This notion of a death benefiting others is not original. It is evident in the faithful and suffering servant in Babylonian exile of Isa 53:5, 10-12 (cf. Matt 8:17; 12:17-21) and in the martyrs tortured by the imperial tyrant Antiochus Epiphanes in 4 Macc 1:11; 6:25-30; 17:17-22. Josephus offers his own life— "take my blood as the price of your own salvation"—if it will mean that the people do not wage war against Rome (*JW* 5.419). It is also evident in Sophocles' *Antigone*, in several women characters in Euripides' plays—Iphigenia in *Iphigenia at Aulis*, Alcestis in *Alcestis*, Macaria in *Heraclidae*[31]—and Seneca (*Ep* 24.4, Socrates' death frees people from the fear of death and imprisonment), Epictetus (*Diss* 4.1.159-69 [Socrates]), Silius Italicus (*Punica* 6.531-51 [Regulus]), Tacitus (*Ann* 16.35 [Thrasea]).[32]

How do **the many** experience Jesus' liberating ransom on their behalf/in their place? The gospel does not say, but by attending to 20:17-28 and by anticipating the end of the story we can make an informed guess.[33] (1) Jesus' death results from a "moral confrontation" with Gentile power that lords it over others (20:18-19, 25). His death reveals the nature and impact of imperial and religious power. That power is, first, intolerant, brutal, and destructive in stopping Jesus. His death demonstrates their abusive use of power in protecting their own interests. Second, that power has overstepped all limits in daring to resist God's purposes by crucifying God's agent. It is sinful.

(2) But God will raise him (20:19). Jesus' resurrection exposes not only the death-bringing and hubristic nature of their power, but also its pretense and relativity. His resurrection demonstrates that God's empire is not confined by imperial and religious power, violence, sin, and death. Their power is limited; it is not ultimate. It cannot enforce its will regardless of its propagandistic claims. Such power is subject to God's life-giving reign (cf. 19:28). What seems to be their victory is their defeat.

(3) This perception, this knowledge, has ecclesial and social consequences. It provides disciples with a perspective on, a way of seeing, the status quo. It exposes the nature of the present as a world in which sinful, brutish, and death-bringing power operates (20:25). But Jesus' resurrection shows that that is not the only way in which power can be used, that God's life-giving power overcomes abusive imperial power. That perception informs and forms the community of Jesus' followers. It lives not wanting to imitate such power (20:26). It lives knowing there is an alternative use of power that is life-giving and that seeks the good of the other (servanthood, 20:26-27). And it lives knowing that the alternative is possible because imperial power has been shown not to have the final word. The perception functions to enable members of this community to sustain one another in living its alternative existence shaped not by these authorities but by Jesus' revelation of God's will. It can be a community of "resistance and solidarity."[34]

(4) Moreover the notion of resurrection is eschatological. It belongs to the

cluster of final events including Jesus' return, in which God's empire is established in victory over all including Rome (so 1:21; 16:21; 19:28; 22:7; 24:27-31). To speak of Jesus' resurrection is to anticipate the general resurrection (27:52-53) and establishment of God's empire in full. Disciples as slaves live now toward this goal. His death and resurrection, as a ransom for many, offer hope, the conviction that they will participate in God's final salvation and new creation.

20:29-34—JESUS HEALS TWO BLIND MEN

How does this story connect with the rest of chapters 19-20? These chapters have outlined the alternative household structure required of disciples. The emphasis on more egalitarian relationships and the use of marginal identities as images of disciples (eunuch, children, the poor, slaves) set these households over against the culturally dominant, hierarchical and patriarchal household structures.

Jesus has called disciples to a difficult, against-the grain, marginal lifestyle and identity. This story of two blind men who in desperate circumstances persistently call out to Jesus for healing offers encouragement. It underlines that God's compassionate mercy and power are available for all disciples who, in the midst of difficult circumstances, recognize their inadequacy and call for God's help. Jesus, who is present with them, makes God's mercy and power available.[35]

The scene has a further function in relation to Jesus' ministry since 4:17 (see introduction to ch. 8). Apart from a short (but significant) reference to healing in 21:14, this is the last healing story in the gospel. Hence the scene functions as a summary healing which recalls important features of Jesus' previous miracles (see references below, esp. 9:27-31). It involves a marginal person, a prayerlike request for mercy, respectful and trusting address to Jesus, difficulty or opposition to be overcome, Jesus' compassionate response, an effective healing and transition from a desperate marginal situation to a new life and community. This larger context recalls that healings are (1) demonstrations of God's empire in anticipation of the full establishment of God's reign (see 4:23-25; chs. 8-9; *2 Bar* 73:1-2); (2) demonstrations of Jesus' identity as God's commissioned agent and the means whereby people can recognize his identity (11:2-6); and (3) demonstrations of the special place that the marginal have in God's purposes as recipients of God's life-giving mercy. This display of God's reign over disease and sickness also prepares for chapter 21 and Jesus' entry into Jerusalem (see further 21:1-17).

• 20:29

Jesus is on the move again. **As they were leaving Jericho, a large crowd followed him**). Movement, not stasis, often provides the context for welcoming and experiencing, rather than resisting, God's presence. Compare static Jerusalem and the itinerant magi in chapter 2.[36] Jesus is on his way to Jerusalem through Judea (19:1-2). **Jericho** was a center of a fertile agricultural area (Josephus, *JW* 4.459-75) and a "winter resort for Jerusalem's aristocracy." Herod built a large palace complex (including Roman-style baths) with extensive royal estates, and also built a hippodrome, theater, and amphitheater there.[37] Vespasian took the city unopposed in 68 (Josephus, *JW* 4.449-51). The **crowd**, not the elite, show interest in Jesus. On **crowd** as the recipients of Jesus' ministry yet exhibiting neither the faith of the disciples nor the hostility of the elite, see 4:25. Also 4:25 for this nondiscipleship use of **following**.

• 20:30

And behold draws attention to two particular characters. **Two blind men were seated beside the road**. Their social marginality is emphasized not only by their blindness (see 9:27-28; 12:22), but by their location outside a major social entity, Jericho, and by their being **seated beside the road**. They are not part of the city, nor of the crowd, nor of the human traffic and intercourse on **the road**. Presumably they are **beside the road** to beg, a shameful activity (Sir 40:28-30) which suggests that their households are too poor to support them. Epictetus notes people turning away from "dirty beggars" (*Diss* 3.22.89).

Significant things happen along **roads** (2:12; 4:15; 7:13-14; 10:10; 13:4, 19; 15:32). Roads were crucial to maintain imperial control: movement of soldiers, transport of tribute, spread of Roman influence, trade (see 7:13-14). Jesus, though, uses them for other purposes. In 20:17 on the **road** Jesus instructs his disciples about what the religious and political elite will do to him in Jerusalem. **Road** or way is also a metaphor for God's purposes (3:3; 7:13-14; 11:10). Outside Jericho, a center for the wealthy and powerful elite, Jesus focuses on the poor and needy.

In addition to this marginal location and affliction of blindness, the number **two** underlines their significance. In 20:20-21, 24, two disciples and their mother sought a privileged position in God's empire only to learn that the way of God's reign is found among marginal slaves. Two sets of two brothers become disciples in 4:18-22; two demoniacs encounter Jesus (8:28); two blind men seek sight (9:27); two fish (with five loaves) feed a crowd (14:17, 19); two hands or feet can keep a disciple out of the reign (18:8-9); two disciples can keep a disciple in the reign (18:15-16); two disciples know Jesus' presence (18:20); two become one (19:5-6).

When they heard (from the noise of the crowd?) **that Jesus was passing by** (9:9 [the call of Matthew]; 9:27 [the two blind men]), **they shouted, "Lord, have mercy on us, son of David!"** In **shouting out**, they imitate displays of desperation and faith from two other blind men (9:27), from disciples (14:26, 30), and the Canaanite mother (15:22-23). The desperate cry of two marginal and maimed beggars contrasts the question with which the wealthy man engages Jesus (19:16-22). They address Jesus with the dependent and reverent discipleship language of **Lord** (8:2, 6, 8, 21, 25; 9:28; 10:24-25; 14:28, 30; 15:22, 25, 27; 16:22; 17:4, 15). This is the language of slaves (10:24-25; 20:25-28). They join other marginal "nobodies" in calling for **mercy** (9:27 [two blind men]; 15:22 [Canaanite mother]; 17:15 [father of demon-possessed boy]).

On **mercy** as God's life-giving power which restores not only their sight but which also challenges exclusionary social, economic and religious practices, and opens up a new community to them, see 9:27. They ask for what is consistent with God's will manifested by Jesus (9:13; 12:7). On **son of David**, see 9:27; 1:1. As a king in David's line (1:1), Jesus enacts God's merciful reign among the needy (Ps 72). This title also links him with traditions which ascribed miracle-working power to Solomon, son of David. The blind men address Jesus with two titles of respect in contrast to the mother of James and John, who uses none (20:21).

In addressing Jesus (correctly) as **Lord** and **son of David**, the men express spiritual insight, a feature of disciples (13:13-17). Jesus' opponents, especially the religious elite, are blind, a conventional polemical term in the Greco-Roman world (see 15:14; 23:16, 17, 19, 24, 26). Jesus' merciful power demonstrates that blindness need not be permanent (9:27-31; 12:22; 15:30-31).

• 20:31

Jesus has warned disciples of persecution "on my account" (5:11; 10:16-39). **The crowd sternly rebuked them to be quiet.** A feature of these two chapters has been the use of opposition to clarify God's will. Like the Pharisees in 19:3-9, the disciples in 19:10, 13, the rich young man in 19:16-22, and the religious and political elite in 20:17-28, the crowd resists God's will (cf. 11:5). In 21:9-11 the crowd will exhibit a very different response. But faced by the crowds' opposition, the two blind men like faithful disciples **shouted even more loudly, "Have mercy on us, son of David!"** The repetition (20:30) underlines their respectful and faith-full address and their need for mercy.

• 20:32

Their faithful persistence is rewarded. In the midst of opposition and blindness, Jesus responds. **Jesus stood still and called them saying, "What do you wish/want me to do for you?"** Jesus' words are an implicit and public rebuke to the crowd (he will not be deterred from doing God's will), a signal to the blind men (he is ready to serve them, 20:28) and an invitation to them to name their need (can they express their faith?). This is the eighth uses of the verb **wish/want** in chapters 19-20 (θέλω, *thelō*). There are appropriate and inappropriate wishes: 19:17, 21 (to enter life and to be perfect); 20:14-15 (egalitarian treatment); 20:21 (the mother's request); 20:26-27 (to be great/first is the way of slavery). While the disciples and their mother wish for status and power, while the rich man wishes to hold onto his wealth even if it costs him life, the blind men wish to know God's saving reign.

• 20:33

Their response is clear and immediate. **They said to him, "Lord, let our eyes be opened."** Again they address Jesus with respect and dependence (**Lord**, 20:30). Their reference to **eyes** recalls not only the previous healings of blind people (9:29-30; so also **open**, 9:30) but also the challenge of the householder to the laborers in 20:15 to determine whether his eye is evil or good.

These blind men have determined that Jesus' purposes are good. On the importance of eyes and seeing for disciples, see 5:29; 6:22-23; 7:3-5; 13:15-16; 18:9).

• 20:34

Jesus responds. He is **moved with compassion**, a synonym for mercy (20:30), and the motivation for Jesus' ministry/service (20:28) to the crowds. See 9:36; 14:14; 15:32. **Jesus touched their eyes. Immediately they regained their sight**. Their healing is demonstrated by open eyes. What is impossible for humans is possible with God (19:25-26). On **touch** in Jesus' previous healings, see 8:3 (a leper); 8:15 (Peter's mother-in-law); 9:20-21 (the woman with a hemorrhage); 9:29 (the blind men); 14:36 (the sick in the region of Gennesaret). These men are associated with the marginals and desperate who seek Jesus' transforming power.

Their experience of that power is also confirmed in their response. **They followed him**, on the way of the cross (16:21-24). That the scene has been as much a call story as a miracle story has been evident in their address to Jesus as Lord, their overcoming of the crowds' resistance, and their dependence or faith in him. Now they do what disciples do. Mercy experienced is not only a gift but a mandate to show it to others in a way of life (5:7; 9:13; 12:7; 18:33-35). On **follow**, see 4:18-22.

PART V

The Fifth Narrative Block

Jesus in Jerusalem:
Conflict and Death
(21:1-27:66)

CHAPTER 21

Jesus in Conflict

The fifth narrative block (chs. 21-27) begins as Jesus enters Jerusalem.[1] His entry (21:1-27) provides the key incident or scene which advances the plot in two ways. First, it brings Jesus into Jerusalem, the center of religious power and the place where he has predicted he will be crucified (16:21; 20:17-19). Second, it answers a question that the fourth narrative block (16:21-20:34) raised: How will Jesus' death come about? The scene shows that Jesus' death results in part from a deadly conflict with the political and religious elite. Jesus' entry parodies Rome's military and political power and represents God's empire.[2] His attack on the temple and the issue of his authority provide the religious elite with motivation and opportunity (26:61) to kill him. These conflicts are developed through the parables of chapters 21-22, the curses of chapter 23, the eschatological discourse in chapters 24-25 (the end of Roman rule), and the passion narrative (chs. 26-27).[3]

Chapter 21 divides into six sections. The initial contrast with Rome gives way to conflict with the religious elite:

21:1-11   Making an Ass out of Rome: Entering Jerusalem
21:12-17   In the Temple
21:18-22   The Fig Tree
21:23-27   Jesus' Authority
21:28-32   The Parable of the Two Sons
21:33-46   The Householder, the Vineyard, and the Tenants

21:1-11—MAKING AN ASS OUT OF ROME: ENTERING JERUSALEM[4]

This scene employs a cluster of features common to traditions of Jewish and Greco-Roman entrance processions.[5] These entrances include triumphs, military victories, or the arrival (*adventus;* παρουσία; *parousia;* cf. 3 Macc 3:17) of a king/governor at a city.[6]

Features of Entrance Processions	*Jesus*
• appearance of the ruler/general with troops (and prisoners in a triumph)	Matt 21:1, 7
• a procession into the city	Matt 21:8, 10
• welcoming and celebrating crowds	Matt 21:8-9
• hymnic acclamation	Matt 21:9
• speeches from the local elite, who must gain the newcomer's favor if they are to have any (derived) power[7]	_____
• cultic act (often sacrifice) in a temple by which the ruler takes possession of the city	Matt 21:12-17

Entrances, like triumphs, expressed the imperial mind-set. "The triumph . . . revealed a deep tendency in human nature to conceive of human greatness in terms of power, acquired by the military or political victory over actual or potential enemies and to demand public recognition of such greatness."[8]

But Jesus conceives of human greatness in terms of service (20:25-28). His entry to Jerusalem, the center of power, is a prophetic sign action (see 3:1), "choreographed street theater."[9] He adopts some trappings from Greco-Roman entrance processions and triumphs, but reframes them in a different context (God's empire) and for a different goal (to serve not dominate, 20:25). His action evokes Zech 9-14, in which God enters Jerusalem in victory over all (see 21:5).[10] Jesus' entry imitates imperial behavior in order to parody it and to contrast two very different empires. He "protest(s) against the spirit which animated [Roman triumphs] to show a better way of fulfilling the meaning of human destiny."[11] Invoking God's victorious reign relativizes Rome's claims even as it replaces one imperial reign with another.

Jesus' entry differs from imperial entrances in three key aspects. (1) Two-thirds of the narrative concerns the animal (21:2-7). The ass has ambivalent significance. It is a royal animal. It carries the representatives of God's reign, the new king Solomon (1 Kgs 1:33-48) and the eschatological king in Zech 9:9 (21:5).[12] It also carries those who make claims to kingship (Absalom [2 Sam 18:9]; Mephibosheth [2 Sam 19:27]). But it is also an everyday beast of burden (Job 1:3, 14; Tob 10:11; Judg 2:17), so necessary that it is protected from coveting (Exod 20:17; Deut 5:21) and required to have sabbath rest (Deut 5:14). Moreover, it was a symbol of derision and scorn. Some Gentiles mocked Jews for worshiping an ass's head in the temple (Josephus, *Con Ap* 2.80-88, 112-120; Plutarch, "Table Talk," *Moralia* 670F; Tacitus, *Hist* 5.3-4). And it recalls the story of God's liberation of the people. Moses rides a donkey as he returns to Egypt to lead the people from slavery (Exod 4:19).

This common and scorned animal, not a war horse (cf. *Pss. Sol.* 17:33) or chariot of triumph (or of Israel's enemies in Zech 9:10), bears Jesus. Imperial entrance processions (soldiers, prisoners, officials, symbols like the *fasces;* see 3:10) were intended to demonstrate authority, to intimidate, and to ensure submission. Instead of celebrating captivity and domination with a parade of military might and violence, Jesus chooses what is royal but common, derided but liberating (cf. 11:28-30).

(2) He is a different sort of king (2:2). Jesus' entry occurs in the context of his proclamation and enactment of God's empire since 4:17. This reign is not like the oppressive and tyrannical reign of Rome, which has claimed divine agency and overstepped the mark (20:25-28; Introduction). It is not based on military violence and does not employ social and economic exploitation or legal privilege. It is merciful, inclusive, life-giving, and marked by servanthood and peace. This son of David enacts God's reign, which protects the needy, supplies the weak (Ps 72), and heals the sick (Solomon; Matt 9:27). He comes not to fight for the city, but to serve it (20:28).

(3) Absent are three elements. He is not welcomed by the powerful local elite. They offer no speeches, no escort. They are absent initially and resistant subsequently. Nor does the city welcome him (21:10). It does not know who he is. The center of power continues to resist (ch. 2), while the rural traveling crowds who enter Jerusalem with Jesus are prominent. Nor does he offer sacrifice in the temple. Rather he disrupts and judges it.

• 21:1-2

Since 19:1 Jesus has been traveling to Jerusalem: **When they had come near Jerusalem and had reached Bethphage at the Mount of Olives**. Jerusalem is hostile and under the control of the religious and political elite (ch. 2; 15:1); yet it retains its calling to serve God as a "holy city" (see 4:5; 5:35; 27:53). The **Mount of Olives** is a place of eschatological judgment and salvation in Zech 14:4, as Matt 21:5 emphasizes.[13] On "the day of the Lord" (Matt 7:22; 10:15), God enters the city to overcome Israel's enemies and establish God's reign and era of peace. See 24:3. For those with eyes to see, the establishment of God's empire over all is under way in Jesus, in anticipation of God's coming triumph. Again the gospel imitates the imperial worldview that it resists.

Jesus arranges the donkey. **Jesus sent two disciples saying to them, "Go into the village ahead of you, and immediately you will find a donkey tied, and a colt with her; untie them and bring them to me."** On the number **two**, see 20:30. On the **donkey**, as a royal and common animal, and symbol of scorn, prejudice, and liberation, see introductory comments above. Kings and their delegated representatives had the power of impressment, or *angaria,* over property or labor (see 5:41; 27:32). But his detailed instructions sound either like special knowledge (compare 9:3-4; 12:14-15, 25; 17:25) or a prior arrangement. With his commitment to return the animal (21:3) the scene is more a borrowing that exhibits Jesus' kingly authority and control than an impressment.[14]

• 21:3

Anticipating a possible difficulty, Jesus gives further instructions. **If anyone says anything to you, just say this, "The Lord needs them." And he will send them immediately.** Jesus seems to have made prior arrangements. For previous uses of **Lord** as a self-designation, see 10:24-25; 12:8. Again Jesus exerts his lordship over nature (cf. 8:23-27; 14:25-33) and exercises Adam's authority over the animals in Gen 1:26-31. For this theme of new creation in Jesus' ministry, see 1:1; 12:1-14; 14:32.

• 21:4-5

This act of procuring a donkey, on which Jesus will ride into the city, is consistent with and interpreted by scripture. **This took place to fulfill what had been spoken through the prophet, saying.** . . . For previous fulfillment citations, see 1:22-23; 2:15, 17-18, 23; 4:14-16; 8:17; 12:17-21; 13:35. **Tell the daughter of Zion, "Look your king is coming to you, humble and mounted on a donkey, and on a colt, the foal of a donkey."** Most of the citation comes from Zech 9:9 (cf. Matt 27:9-10). It mostly uses the LXX, though influence of the MT version of Zech 9:9 is evident in the concluding phrase. The opening words, **Tell the daughter of Zion**, come from Isa 62:11. They replace Zechariah's "rejoice greatly daughter of Zion," perhaps because of Jerusalem's nonwelcoming response in chapters 21-27. Isaiah 62 celebrates God's imminent salvation for Jerusalem after Babylonian exile. Zechariah 9:9 is part of Zech 9-14, which celebrates God's defeat of Israel's enemies and the establishment of God's reign. The verse anticipates that victory under way in Jesus' ministry.

The first phrase, **Tell the daughter of Zion,** invites a response of welcome. But while the traveling crowds welcome him, the city does not know who he is (21:10). Ultimately they will ally with the religious elite against Jesus (27:20-25). Jesus has been identified as **king** in 2:2. But his reign is not tyranny over others (20:25; 17:25; 18:23; cf. 4:17), and his entry is not the imposition of imperial will. Rather he is **humble/meek**. See 5:5 (citing Ps 37); 11:29.[15] Jesus is among the humble righteous, who, in contrast to the oppressive and powerful wicked, trust God to manifest God's reign over the wicked by restoring just structures and access to resources. That empire is manifested in Jesus. See 20:25-28 for the link of kingship and servanthood.

• 21:6-7

The disciples went and did as Jesus had directed them. The disciples are obedient and Jesus' word is trustworthy (7:24-27; 12:46-50). **They brought the donkey and the colt, and put their cloaks on them, and he sat on them.**[16] On **sitting** as the act of a king, see 5:2; also 1 Kgs 1:33-48—Solomon sits (the same verb in the LXX) on his donkey.

• 21:8

So far the action has involved Jesus and the disciples. Now **the crowd**, a key element of entrance processions and source of honor for the welcomed figure, is involved. But in a twist to the conventions of the entrance tradition, this is not the Jerusalem populace. Their response is not stated until 21:10. This is a journeying crowd of pilgrims and rural peasants. **A very large crowd** (see 4:25) **spread their cloaks on the road.** This act recognizes his authority. Other crowds **spread** garments in proclaiming Jehu king (2 Kgs 9:12-13; Josephus,

Ant 9.111). Roman soldiers perform this act in fond farewell to their commander Cato (Plutarch, *Cato the Younger* 12.1).

Others cut branches from the trees and spread them on the road. Branches are part of the celebration when Simon liberates Jerusalem from "the yoke of the Gentiles" (cf. 1 Macc 13:41, 51; Matt 11:29), and when Judas Maccabeus rededicates the temple after ending the tyranny of Antiochus Epiphanes (2 Macc 10:7-9). The branches, then, portend God's reign over Jerusalem and its Roman occupiers. The double reference to **the road/way** recalls 20:30, in which this king, son of David, heals the blind and offers new life to the marginal. See also 7:13-14.

• 21:9

The crowds surround Jesus and establish him as the scene's focus. **The crowds that went ahead of him and that followed were shouting, "Hosanna to the son of David! Blessed is the one who comes in the name of the Lord! Hosanna in the highest heaven!"** They shout from Ps 118:25-26. This psalm, recited during festivals such as the imminent Passover, gives God thanks for victory over "all the nations" (118:10). The theme of God's victory reinforces Zech 9-14, quoted in 21:5. Here it is directed to Jesus as **son of David** (1:1). In *Pss. Sol.* 17 the son of David is victorious over the Romans. In the gospel, the title is particularly associated with Jesus' healing mercy shown to marginal people (9:27; 15:22; 20:30-31) as a sign of God's empire (4:17-25; cf. Ps 72). **Hosanna** literally means "save now" (Ps 118:25), but in parallel to **blessed** here it means "praise."

• 21:10-11

Whereas the rural pilgrim-peasant crowd gives praise, the urban center of the city, which was threatened by news of Jesus' birth (see 2:3) and which allied itself with Herod's brutish power, is predictably disturbed by Jesus' entry. **When he entered Jerusalem, the whole city** (cf. 2:3, "all Jerusalem") **was in turmoil, asking, "Who is this?"** In the entrance traditions, the city crowds welcome the ruler/general. Jerusalem does not recognize God's anointed king but is **in turmoil**, "shaken or agitated" (BAGD, 746) by him. Jesus will continue to have this impact. The same verb is used for the earthquake that accompanies Jesus' death and splits the temple curtain (27:51; the cognate noun in 27:54), and for the angel who overwhelms the guards and announces that Jesus is risen (28:4; the cognate noun in 28:2). Earthquakes are part of the eschatological woes (24:7), the intensified turmoil that precedes the end (10:16-23, 34-39; ch. 24). For those with eyes to see, Jesus' entry to Jerusalem is part of these earth-shattering events.

The journeying crowd answers Jerusalem's question: **The crowds were saying, "This is the prophet Jesus from Nazareth in Galilee."** Their answer is not wrong. Jesus has just performed a prophetic sign action which contrasts God's empire and Jesus the meek king with imperial militarism and tyranny. He will perform further sign actions in 21:12-17, 18-22. And Jesus called himself a **prophet** in 13:57. But it is an ominous confession. Jerusalem is a city with a reputation for killing prophets (23:37). Nor is the confession adequate in God's perspective. God calls Jesus "my son" (3:17; 17:5), a confession that disciples make (14:33; 16:16).

21:12-17—IN THE TEMPLE

True to entrance procession traditions, Jesus heads to the temple, the center of cultic life and of the Jewish political, economic, and social leadership under Rome. But unlike those traditions where the conqueror/ruler sacrifices or prays for the favor of the city's gods, Jesus goes to a place of opposition. He has predicted that the elders, chief priests and scribes, the Sanhedrin (see 2:4; 16:21; 21:23) will put him to death (20:18). Going to the temple means confrontation with this leadership. He disrupts the temple, first by attacking the sacrificial economy (21:12-13), and, second, by healing those who have been previously banned from the temple (21:14-17).

On this side of Rome's destruction of Jerusalem and the temple in 70 C.E., Jesus' actions denote not reform or cleansing but God's judgment and curse, actions which anticipate and interpret Rome's destruction of Jerusalem and its temple in 70 C.E. (24:2; 26:61).[17] He is greater than the temple (12:6). He manifests God's forgiving presence (1:21, 23; 9:1-8; 18:18-20; 28:28-30).[18] He is the means whereby sin is forgiven (26:28). God does not want sacrifice (9:13; 12:7). The gospel shifts attention from the temple as the central sacred place to Jesus and his community.

Through both first and second temple eras, various prophetic and apocalyptic traditions expressed profound misgivings about the temple and its corrupt and immoral personnel and/or unacceptable rituals (Isa 1:10-23; Mal 3:8-10). Some sought its reform (2 Kgs 22-23; 1 Macc 4:36-59; 2 Macc 10:1-9; *1 En* 25:5; 1QM 2:1-6; 7:4-10; *Pss. Sol.* 17:30[?]); others predicted its doom (Jer 26:1-9; Josephus, *JW* 6.300-309) or anticipated its rebuilding (Ezek 40-43; Tob 14.5; *Jub.* 1:17; *T. Benj.* 9:2; *1 En* 89-90; 91:13).[19]

• 21:12
Then Jesus entered the temple and drove out all who were selling and buying in the temple. In 2 Chr 29:5, the verb **drove out** denotes Hezekiah's reform of the temple. But the same verb also frequently denotes exorcism (twelve of twenty-eight times; Matt 7:22; 8:16, 31; 9:33, 34; 10:1, 8; 12:24, 26, 27, 28; 17:19). Jesus' act is in part an exorcism. (1) A connection between the devil and the temple is suggested by the location of the second temptation on the temple pinnacle (4:5-6). (2) The religious leaders, a narrative alliance of priests, Pharisees, scribes, and Sadducees who appear in various combinations in opposition to Jesus, have previously been demonized by the terms "evil" (6:13; 9:4; 12:34) and "tempt" (4:1, 3; 16:1; 19:3; 22:18), which are used of the devil. (3) The chief priests, Jesus' opponents since 2:4, are allied with Herod. The devil has claimed power over all the empires of the world (4:8), which places Herod and his alliance with the chief priests under the devil's control.

(4) The Pharisees, opponents since 3:7, with a vision to extend priestly identity (Exod 34:6) and temple purity service to all of life,[20] are declared in 15:13-14 not to be God's planting. In the gospel's dualistic cosmic framework, that allies them with the devil. The verb **drove out** suggests that the religious elite and its central place are under the devil's control, contrary to God's purposes.

Further, the verb **drove out** denotes judgment (8:12; 22:13; 25:30). Jesus' act is one of judgment on the unfaithful temple leadership. The same verb ("I will drive them out of my house") appears in Hos 9:15 as God's judgment on the unjust elite.

Those **thrown out** are **all who were selling and buying**. These could be worshipers who were buying sacrifices, but Jesus' argument is with the temple leaders who control its "user pays" commerce. More likely the verbs refer to those who were buying for and selling to the temple treasury (2 Macc 3:6) materials necessary for its operation (oil, salt, wine, sacrifices, etc.).

Jesus attacks others involved in the economic control of the temple. **He overturned the tables of the money changers and the seats of those who sold doves**. **Money changers** provided shekels and half-shekels for temple dues (Exod 30:13). **Doves** were sacrifices for the poor, those not able to afford animals like a sheep (Lev 5:7; 12:8; 14:1-2), for women and for cleansing lepers (Lev 12:6; 14:22). Jesus' attack disrupts the whole temple sacrificial operation. He does not propose an alternative, acceptable action. This is not reform; it is judgment. What the buyers and sellers have done wrong is clarified by the next verse.

• 21:13

Jesus interprets his action from scripture. **He said to them, "It is written, 'My house shall be called a house of prayer'; but you are making it a den of robbers."** This citation combines two contrasting verses, Isa 56:7 and Jer 7:11. The Isaiah citation is part of a vision of God gathering sabbath and covenant-observant foreigners and eunuchs (cf. Matt 19:12) into God's people to pray and sacrifice in the temple. But the religious leaders (**you are making it**) do not live out this inclusive vision. They do what Jeremiah condemns in a harsh denunciation of the people. They trust that the temple will provide them sanctuary and cover (Jer 7:4) but they do not do God's will. They engage in social injustices against the poor, immoral acts, and false worship (cf. Mal 3:5-12). Their greed exploits the poor even in this place of worship. They live out a commitment to mammon (Matt 6:24), are not open to Jesus' teaching, and neglect God's will (3:7-9; 12:22-37; 15:1-9; 21:28-32). The temple is far from what God desires. Judgment awaits them. Jeremiah 7 provides an explanation for Jerusalem's fall to Rome in 70 C.E. It is God's punishment on the religious elite, carried out by Rome, God's agent (see 21:12-13, 18-19, 41-43; 22:7; 27:25).

The term **robbers** can mean "robber, bandit . . . insurrectionist" (BAGD, 473; 27:38, 44). In addition to charging the temple personnel with being criminals who rob the poor through dues and sacrifices, the subsequent reference to the crowds coming from the chief priests with swords and clubs (26:47) suggests some violence in extorting money (cf. 26:47 and Josephus, *Ant* 20.181, 206-7).

• 21:14

Jesus follows this act of disruption and judgment with a second. **The blind and the lame came to him in the temple and he cured them.** Since 4:23-25 Jesus has healed the sick to demonstrate and anticipate God's merciful and powerful empire. For previous healings of the **blind and the lame**, see 9:27-28; 11:5; 12:22; 15:30-31; 20:30. Given the assumed link of sin and disease (see 4:23-25; 9:1-8), Jesus' healing signifies God's forgiveness, mercy (9:13; 12:7) and presence available in him, the new temple. This is the final act of healing in the gospel (cf. 20:29-34).

The presence of **the blind and the lame** recalls 2 Sam 5:8. They are excluded from David's city (also Lev 21:16-24). Josephus notes that people with gonorrhea and leprosy are excluded from the city (*JW* 5.227). If God is understood to be especially encountered in the temple, the exclusion of the maimed from the city and temple appears to be an attempt to exclude them from God's presence. Jesus, son of David, who manifests God's inclusive and merciful empire (9:27-31; 12:23-24; 15:21-28; 20:29-34), welcomes them into God's presence (1:23; 18:20; 28:20) and includes them in God's transforming benefits (in accord with Mic 4:6-7; Ezek 34:15-16).

• 21:15

Jesus has directly challenged the authority and control of the powerful and prestigious religious leaders over the temple space and they are not pleased. **But when the chief priests and the scribes** (cf. 2:3-4; 16:21; 20:18; 21:23) **saw the amazing things he was doing** (the events of 21:12-14) **and heard the children crying out in the temple, "Hosanna to the son of David," they became angry.** Their opposition to healing and to the praise from children renders these members of the powerful and ruling elite ridiculous (see Introduction, sections 1 and 5). The **crying out of the children** continues the theme of the marginal, who, like the blind and the lame (21:14), experience God's presence in Jesus (1:23; 18:20) but who face the anger of the elite. For the marginality of children, see chapter 2; 18:1-6; 19:13-15. For **Hosanna to the son of David**, see 21:9. For **son of David**, especially healing like Solomon, 9:27.

• 21:16

The contrasting responses of the praising marginal children and the angry priests and scribes are developed as the religious elite confront Jesus, **"Do you hear what these are saying?"** Their antipathy to the title **son of David** (also in 12:23-24) expresses a refusal to recognize Jesus as commissioned by God to manifest God's merciful reign as a king (2:2) in David's line (2 Sam 7; Ps 72). The children's confession is dangerous and threatening.

Jesus said to them, "Yes." Contrary to their conviction that the title is misapplied and Jesus should resist it, he accepts it as appropriate. The religious leaders are caught opposing God. Again Jesus defends children (11:25; 19:13-

15; cf. **nursing babies** in danger, Moses [Exod 2:7, 9]; Lam 4:3, 4; *1 En* 99:5). **"Have you never read?"** The question is a rebuke. If they had read, they would not be opposing him. But they cannot interpret the scriptures (22:29; see 2:4-6). See 12:3, 5, 7; 19:4; 21:42, where Jesus uses the same question with the Pharisees.

He quotes Ps 8:2. **"Out of the mouths of infants and nursing babies, you have prepared praise for yourself."** Psalm 8 celebrates God's majestic creation and regard for human beings. Here, the citation affirms the inclusion of the marginal children, indicates both God's approval for their praise, and identifies God as the *source* of their declaration that Jesus is son of David. God (**you**) has **prepared** their **praise**. Children had important roles in religious celebrations because these marginal beings were understood to be effective in making contact with the gods and speaking oracles (Plutarch, "Isis and Osiris," *Moralia* 356E; Dio Chrysostom, *Disc* 32.13).[21] The children's praise, words inspired by God, are revelations which express God's legitimation of Jesus. See 11:25 for **infants**, not the wise and powerful, as recipients of revelation about Jesus; also Wis 10:25. The vulnerable **nursing babies** can be an image for God's people protected by God (Num 11:12; Deut 32:13). Here they receive God's revelation, unlike the **chief priests and scribes**.

• 21:17

He left them. Does this signify God's presence leaving the temple, a further disqualification of the temple? **He went out of the city to Bethany and spent the night there**.

21:18-22—THE FIG TREE

In 21:18-20 Jesus performs another sign action or enacted parable. His cursing of the fig tree symbolizes the cursing of or judgment on the temple and the religious leaders (not Israel as a whole), enacted by Rome in Jerusalem's defeat in 70 C.E. By contrast, 21:21-22 present the community of disciples as an alternative community of prayer, faith, and life-giving power.

• 21:18

This sign action (see 3:1) is linked to those of 21:1-17 by time (**In the morning**; cf. "night" in 21:17) and by place, **when he returned to the city** (21:1, 10, 12, 17), **he was hungry** (4:2).

• 21:19

And seeing a fig tree by the side of the road, he went to it and found nothing at all on it except leaves. Then he said to it, "May no fruit ever come from you again!" **Leaves** should evidence **fruit** (Pliny, *NH* 16.49.113). In the context of 21:1-17, the referent for Jesus' action must be the temple leadership (chief priests and scribes [21:15, 45]; elders [21:23]; cf. Pharisees, Herodians, and Sadducees [22:15, 16, 23, 34]), who do not recognize Jesus as commissioned by God to manifest God's saving presence and empire (1:21, 23; 4:17). They do not welcome him (21:10); their operation of the temple is defective (21:12-13); they resent his healing in the temple (21:14-15). Because they do not recognize that he is from David's line, they do not think he should receive praise (21:15-16). The absence of **fruit** describes the lives of the religious leaders which are not pleasing to God (3:7; 12:33-37; cf. 7:16-20). In cursing the fig tree, Jesus, greater than the temple (12:6), announces God's curse on them. Rome, God's agent, enacts the judgment in the defeat of them and their temple in 70 C.E. (see 21:12-13, 41-43; 22:7).

Jesus' curse or word of judgment is immediately and visibly effective. **And the fig tree withered at once**. A **fig tree** with fruit signifies God's blessing (Num 20:5; Deut 8:7-8; 1 Macc 14:12). A **withered fig tree** symbolizes judgment (Isa 34:4; Jer 8:13; 29:17; Hos 2:12; 9:10, 16). In the Greco-Roman world, fig trees were also portents or omens of forthcoming events (Pliny, *NH* 15.18.77-78; 17.38.241-45).[22] The withering of a grove of trees foreshadowed Nero's death in 68 C.E. and the end of the Julio-Claudian dynasty (Suetonius, *Galba* 1). Tacitus writes that in 58 C.E. the fig tree in the forum (*ficus Ruminalis*), under which the wolf was said to have suckled Rome's founders, Romulus and Remus, withered as a "portent" of Nero's terrible reign (*Ann* 13.58; Pliny, *NH* 15.18.77-78). The withered fig tree is an omen that represents the judgment Jesus has announced on the temple, on the religious leaders, and on their Roman allies.

• 21:20

The disciples' question allows Jesus to contrast the condemned temple leadership with the alternative community of disciples. **When the disciples saw it, they were amazed,** (cf. 8:27; 9:33; 15:31; 22:22) **saying, "How did the fig tree wither at once?"**

• 21:21-22

Jesus' house/community is marked by prayer (21:13), faith, and life-giving power. **Jesus answered them, "Truly I tell you** (5:18, 22)**, if you have faith and do not doubt, not only will you do what has been done to the fig tree, but even if you say to this mountain, 'Be lifted up and thrown into the sea,' it will be done." Faith** is an attribute of discipleship and a means of encountering God's power and favor (see 6:30; 8:10, 13, 26; 9:2, 22, 28-29; 14:31; 15:28; 16:8; 17:20 18:6; 21:25, 32; 23:23). Jesus' cursing of the **fig tree** makes Jesus a model of this powerful faith, and discipleship an imitation of him. What **mountain** does Jesus refer to? In the context of 21:12-17, it is the temple mount. To **throw it into the sea** recalls the judgment on the demons/pigs as representatives of Roman military power in 8:28-34. The temple system with its exploitation of the poor and advancement of the elite's interests goes the same way. **Faith**, then, is the means of encountering God's empire, and of anticipating, imagining, living for, and praying for a new world under God's just and merciful reign. With the fall of the temple in 70 C.E., something of this new world is possible for the Matthean audience.

Whatever you ask for in prayer with faith, you will receive. The presence of **faith** suggests that the request will be in accord with God's will. On the important place of **prayer** for the marginal and alternative life of discipleship, see 5:44; 6:5-15; 7:7-11; 14:23; 18:18-20; 19:13; 26:39-44.

21:23-27—JESUS' AUTHORITY

• 21:23

Jesus' confrontation with the religious leaders resumes from 21:15-17. The scene confirms why Jesus has announced judgment on them. They refuse to recognize his authority as one sent by God. **When he entered the temple, the chief priests and elders of the people came to him as he was teaching.** In 21:15 "the chief priests and scribes" were allied against Jesus. The alliance keeps changing (see 2:4; 15:1; 21:15). **The elders** are members of wealthy powerful lay families allied with the priestly elite and Pharisaic scribes in the Sanhedrin. This is the ruling body in Jerusalem, which had religious, economic, and legal jurisdiction under Roman sanction.[23] The **elders** were named in 16:21 with the chief priests and scribes as those who would kill Jesus. This alliance includes the Pharisees (12:14; 15:1; 21:45).

The **temple**, a place of prayer in 21:13 and of revelation and God-inspired praise in 21:15-16, is now a place of **teaching**. What Jesus had done previously in "Galilee under the Gentiles" (4:16, 23; 5:2; 7:29; 9:35; 11:1; 13:54) he now does in Jerusalem. But the religious elite interrupt, do not listen. Their own authority, centered on the temple, is clear. They are the social, economic, political, and religious elite allied with and legitimated by Rome. Their authority consists of social status and power over others (cf. 20:20-28) and is based on birth (chief priests), training (scribes), wealth (elders), and political alliances.[24]

But they want to know what Jesus' legitimation is, an issue raised by his actions in 21:1-22. **By what authority are you doing these things, and who gave you this authority?** Jesus' authority to teach (7:29), to heal and forgive (9:6, 8) has been shown to be superior (also 28:18), but they have refused to recognize its origin (God) and nature (life-giving service). **These things** include the entry, the destruction in the temple and disruption of its sacrificial system, healing, and receiving praise of 21:1-22. His actions have challenged the political and religious elite. Their question is a trap. If he claims his own authority, he admits to having no institutional or cultural legitimation, and appears to have acted against God's purposes and certainly against theirs. If he claims God's authority, he blasphemes (9:3) and violates their jurisdiction.

• 21:24-25

In this challenge of honor, Jesus does not respond directly but outwits them. The central issue is not his identity but whether they will recognize it. The questioners become the questioned. **Jesus said to them, "I will also ask you one question: if you tell me the answer, then I will also tell you by what authority I do these things. Did the baptism of John come from heaven, or was it**

of human origin?" The question about John's **baptism** evokes John's whole ministry and his challenge to the religious and political elite (3:1-12; 14:1-12). **From heaven**, the abode of God (5:34), denotes God-given authority; **human origin** means its absence. Asking about John is astute. The gospel links John and Jesus closely: John prepares for Jesus (3:1-12) and baptizes him (3:13-17); they preach the same message about God's empire (3:2; 4:17); Jesus confirms John as the one who prepares for his coming (11:7-19; 17:9-13); both are identified as prophets (11:9; 21:11). To decide about John is to decide about Jesus.

The religious leaders debate among themselves. The gospel's audience sees them try to answer the question not by discerning God's verdict but by a calculated attempt to protect their own honor and position. **And they argued with one another, "If we say 'From heaven,' he will say, 'Why did you not then believe him?'"** To **believe** John would mean accepting his preaching, repenting, and being baptized (3:1-12). It would mean accepting John's testimony about Jesus as one sent from God, demonstrated in John's baptism of Jesus in which God declares Jesus to be "my beloved son" (see 3:17). But they are not about to do that.

• 21:26

They consider the other option. **"But if we say, 'Of human origin,' we are afraid of the crowd; for all regard John as a prophet."** Jesus has testified to John's being (at least) a prophet. To agree with the crowd would be to agree with Jesus, and with God. It would mean having to accept the prophet's testimony about Jesus. But the elite will concede no ground to the **crowd** whom they fear.

• 21:27

So they answered Jesus, "We do not know." They choose a path of noncommitment, which, ironically, betrays their commitment. To not answer displays not genuine ignorance (their debate in 21:25 shows they know the options) but deliberate resistance. In refusing to say that John's ministry comes from God, they reject the claim that John and Jesus have God-given authority. To refuse this recognition is to reveal their own illegitimacy. Like the Pharisees and their tradition (15:1-9), they are not God's planting (15:13-14). They are **of human origin**. Jesus has now exposed and discredited the whole religious leadership. Judgment on them and their temple is inevitable. **And he said to them, "Neither will I tell you by what authority I am doing these things."**

21:28-32—THE PARABLE OF THE TWO SONS

Three parables directed to the religious leaders (not to all Israel[25]) follow (21:28-32, 33-45; 22:1-14). The parables clarify the leaders' failings and place in God's purposes, and warn disciples not to repeat their mistakes. The first parable focuses on their not doing the father's will. Jesus tells the parable in 21:28-30, and its content is interpreted with allegory in 21:31-32.[26] The religious elite inflict economic and social harm through their greedy and unjust leadership.

• 21:28-29

Jesus' question to the religious leaders introduces the parable: **What do you think?** The question invites their engagement (17:25; 18:12; 22:42). The parable concerns a vineyard (20:1-16). **A father had two sons; he went to the first and said, "Son, go and work in the vineyard today."** The use of **son** invokes household relationships in which children honor parents by obeying. The **vineyard** and the instruction to **work** recall standard household economic responsibilities (chs. 19-20). The **son** is expected to obey. But surprisingly, the son **answered, "I will not."** But after the passing of time, **later he changed his mind and went**.

• 21:30

A contrasting situation occurs with the second son. **The father went to the second and said the same; and he answered "I go, sir."** His positive response is expected. But then, **he did not go**. The use of **sir** recalls 7:21 (Lord).

• 21:31

Jesus poses the central issue: **Which of the two did the will of his father?** The religious leaders answer correctly. **"The first."** The first son, though initially refusing, does what his father wants. The second son, though saying he will do it, does not. The focus on the **father** and discussion of **doing his will** suggests an allegory about doing God's will (cf. Exod 20-23; Deut 5; Matt 6:9-10; 7:21; 12:50).[27] The leaders' answer corresponds to Jesus' teaching about doing God's will (7:24-27; 12:46-50) and to his condemnation of hypocrisy (6:2, 5, 16; 7:5; 15:7; cf. 22:18; 23:13, 15, 23, 25, 27, 29; Jer 6:10-21; Isa 1:10-20).

With the answer they condemn themselves for not doing God's will. **Jesus said to them, "Truly I tell you** (see 5:18, 22), **the tax collectors and the prostitutes are going into the empire of God ahead of you."** While the religious elite do not enter God's empire, the socially marginal and despised **tax collectors and the prostitutes** do.[28] On **tax collectors and prostitutes** (as part of the sinners), see 9:9-13. Do **tax collectors and prostitutes** give up their occupations and economic benefits for the sake of God's empire (cf. 13:44-45; 19:16-22)? The present tense **going into the empire** suggests a present participation in God's active reign.[29]

• 21:32

The elite's nonresponsiveness is emphasized. **For John came to you in the way of justice/righteousness and you did not believe him.** The descriptions of people being baptized by John did not highlight tax collectors and prostitutes (3:5-6). Scenes do, though, describe Jesus' merciful and transforming association with the marginalized tax collectors (9:10-11; 10:3 [cf. 9:9]; 11:19) and sinners (9:10-13; 11:19). That is, tax collectors and prostitutes have believed

John in that they have repented and are already experiencing God's saving presence manifested in Jesus, for whom John prepared the way and to whom John bore witness.

The **way of justice/righteousness** is a scriptural metaphor for living according to God's just and transforming purposes (Prov 8:20 [wisdom]; 12:28; 16:31; cf. Matt 5:6, 10, 20; 6:1, 33; 7:13-14; 10:5, 10; 20:17). It recalls John's role in proclaiming "the way of the Lord" (3:3) by repentance and baptism as the means of preparing for God's coming in Jesus. **Justice/righteousness** indicates the enactment of God's previously declared purposes, faithful human action in accord with and shaped by God's purposes and just activity (cf. Jer 22:13-17; Matt 3:15).[30] John comes in accord with God's salvific purposes to preach and do God's will and to prepare for the coming of Jesus, but the religious leaders have not recognized or believed him (3:7-10). On **believe/faith** as trusting and living God's empire, see 21:21. Their not believing John means not believing Jesus.

But their plight is even worse. Since their initial rejecting response, there has been time to change their mind (the first son) or to live out their commitment (the second son). **But the tax collectors and prostitutes believed him; and even after you saw it, you did not change your minds and believe him.** The marginal bear witness to God's empire, but the elite have not availed themselves of this time or testimony (**even after you saw it**). The **tax collectors and prostitutes** are like the first son, saying no to God's will initially but then repenting with the coming of John/Jesus. The elite resemble the second son, saying yes initially but not doing God's will and not taking advantage of the protracted opportunity to **change their mind** (21:29). There is division within Israel—the excluded powerful elite (the hard-hearted of 19:8) and those from the margins who believe.

21:33-46—THE PARABLE OF THE HOUSEHOLDER, VINEYARD, AND TENANTS

This second parable, also concerning a vineyard, repeats the condemnation of the religious leaders by depicting the fateful consequences of their persistent rejection of God's purposes, especially in Jesus the son.[31] They are rejected as caretakers of the vineyard. It identifies another group to take over the role of the displaced leaders as God's agents to ensure the fruitfulness of the vineyard Israel. The parable announces judgment on the unfaithful leaders and interprets the defeat of Jerusalem by Rome in 70 C.E. as punishment of them. God commissions a new group but does not condemn all Israel. The vineyard Israel is not destroyed but is given new tenants to care for it. To change metaphors, the unfaithful greedy shepherds are removed (9:36; Ezek 34) and new shepherds are installed to care for the sheep.

The parable employs familiar symbols from the tradition in its allegorical reading of salvation history. The vineyard is Israel initially (cf. Isa 5:7), then Jerusalem (21:39), then God's empire (21:43). Unlike 20:1-16, the householder is God. The tenants (21:33, 40-41) are the condemned religious elite. The produce (21:34) is a way of life pleasing to God. The rejected slaves (21:34-36) are prophets. The rejected son (21:37-39) is Jesus. The other tenants (21:43) are the church entrusted with producing fruit from the vineyard.

This parable of salvation history utilizes a struggle over land and resources, raising questions about ownership and just use. The parable evokes a dominant economic practice of the Greco-Roman world where high rents, civic and religious taxes, acquiring seed and feed for the next crop and for livestock, and the need to trade or barter for other goods not produced on a farm, made subsistence existence difficult for many. The religious elite as tenants experience not only the desperation many experienced, but the desperation they helped to cause. The presentation of God as the householder depicts God as the tyrannical landlord who presides over such a system. Again the gospel imitates the very system it seeks to oppose (cf. 18:35; 20:1-16). The tradition, though, presents a very different view. If God is the owner of all land (Lev 25:23), land is a trust from God, to be used for God's life-giving purposes for all, not to benefit only the elite.

• **21:33**

The initial **Listen to another parable** indicates a further statement to the religious elite about their failing to accomplish God's purposes (21:23, 45). For the gospel audience the parable serves to clarify its place in those purposes.

The scene is the establishment of a vineyard. **There was a landowner/ householder who planted a vineyard, put a fence around it, dug a winepress in it, and built a watchtower.** The **householder** is God (13:27), who owns all the land (Lev 25:23). In 21:40 he is identified as the vineyard's master or Lord, the term used for God (1:20, 22, 24; 2:13, 15, 19; 3:3; 4:7, 10; 5:33; 7:21-22; 9:38; 11:25; 21:9, 42). His establishing the **vineyard** by **planting**, **hedging around**, **digging** and **building** uses verbal parallels to recall Isa 5:1-7 and Jer 2:21 in which God **plants** or calls Israel into being. See 15:14. The actions denote considerable economic investment and expectations of high returns. In utilizing Isaiah, Jesus renews his prophetic attack on the elite.[32]

Then he leased it to tenants and went to another country. The owner's absence is a crucial element. It provides not only an element of realism in reflecting a common economic practice of the elite (absentee landlords) but also prepares for the tenants' having to give account to the owner at the harvest.

• **21:34-36**

When the harvest time had come, he sent his slaves to the tenants to collect his produce. On **harvest** as a time of judgment or accountability, see 9:37; 13:19, 39-43. **But the tenants seized his slaves and beat one, killed another, and stoned another. Again he sent other slaves, more than the first; and they treated them the same way.** The elite have become tenants, but they resist the role. They violently refuse to pay and reject the owner's repeated and intensified efforts to collect the rent (**more than the first**). The tenants dishonor the master's authority as sender of the **slaves** and as owner of the vineyard. On beating slaves, see 8:6. In refusing to supply the owner with fruit, they steal from him. They exhibit the greed and extortion evident in the temple management (21:12-13). On slavery, see 20:17-28.

In the allegory of salvation history, the **slaves** represent the prophets sent to Israel. Prophets are frequently identified as God's **slaves**/servants (Jer 7:25; Amos 3:7). Though sent by God they experience conflict with and rejection by the people's leaders (cf. 1 Kgs 18:4; Jer 7:25-26; 25:4; 26:5, 20-23; 29:19; 35:15; 2 Chr 36:15-16; Neh 9:26; Dan 9:6 ["we have not listened to your servants the prophets"]; *Jub.* 1:12-13). Particular prophets are identifiable from the descriptions of their fate.[33] The gospel has previously identified persecution as a fundamental aspect of the prophetic experience (Matt 5:12); see also the lament for Jerusalem's killing and stoning the prophets in 23:37. By dishonoring the owner, stealing his produce, and killing the messengers, the tenants break God's covenant commandments to honor God, not to kill, and not to steal (Exod 20:1-17; Deut 5:6-21).

• 21:37-39

Finally he sent his son to them, saying, "They will respect my son." But when the tenants saw the son, they said among themselves, "This is the heir; come, let us kill him and get his inheritance." So they seized him, threw him out of the vineyard, and killed him. Though some have debated it,[34] the murdered **son** is Jesus, crucified in Jerusalem (see 2:15; 3:17; 4:3, 6; 11:27; 14:33; 16:16; 17:5). The passion predictions (16:21; 17:12, 22; 20:17-19; also 12:14) have indicated that Jesus must die at the hands of the violent religious leaders. His death occurs in a long line of violent salvation history. The leaders agree **among themselves** to **kill** him, just as the religious leaders debated "among themselves" (21:25) how to avoid recognizing John and Jesus' authority. The tenants **kill the son, the heir,** to possess his **inheritance** (the vineyard) and be their own masters. They violate the first commandment (Deut 5:6). Greed, robbery, and injustice are their style, as in the temple (cf. 21:12-13; cf. Isa 5:8).[35]

• 21:40

Jesus invites the leaders to complete the plot. **Now when the owner of the vineyard comes, what will he do to those tenants?**

• 21:41

This question traps them into self-condemnation, as do his questions in 21:16, 24-25. **They said to him, "He will put those wretches/evil ones to a miserable death."** They identify the tenants as **wretches** or, literally, "the evilly evil ones." They condemn the very behavior in which they as elite engage, and unwittingly agree with Jesus' previous verdict on them as "evil" (9:4; 12:34-35, 39; 16:4) like the devil (6:13). They predict their own destruction at the hands of Rome in 70 C.E. This gospel, along with numerous other post-70 Jewish texts, interprets the defeat of 70 as divine punishment (see Introduction, sections 1, 9, 10; 1:21; 21:12-13, 18-19; 22:7; 23:37-39). Those who resist God's authority will be totally subjected to it in death. He **"will lease the vineyard to other tenants who will give him fruits in their seasons."** The last phrase ironically recalls Psalm 1's description of the righteous in contrast to the wicked (Ps 1:3).

• **21:42**

Jesus does not dispute their response but builds on it by citing Ps 118:22-23. He introduces it with the same question he has used previously to expose their ignorance of God's purposes declared in the scriptures and being manifested in Jesus (12:3, 5; 19:4; 21:16). **Jesus said to them, "Have you never read in the scriptures: 'The stone that the builders rejected has become the cornerstone; this was the Lord's doing and it is amazing in our eyes'?"** Psalm 118, cited in 21:9, gives thanks for Israel's victory over "all the nations." Here it celebrates God's vindication of Jesus after his rejection by the elite. The leaders do not recognize **the Lord's doing** or rejoice that **it is amazing in our eyes,** just as they did not recognize the significance of the response of the tax collectors and prostitutes (21:32). As in 20:15, their evil eyes prevent them recognizing God's purposes in Jesus. The image of a building (**cornerstone** and **builders**) continues from 16:18, Jesus' community of prayer (21:13a, 21-22) in contrast to the condemned temple.

• **21:43**

Because they have not recognized God's work in Jesus, **Therefore I tell you the empire of God will be taken away from you and given to a people that produces the fruits of the empire.**

For transferring the **empire** to another, see 1 Sam 15:28 (from Saul to David); Dan 7:27. On the **empire,** see 3:2; 4:17; chapter 13; on **the empire of God** (as here), see 12:28.

From whom is it taken and to whom is it given? With the focus on the religious leaders, and Jesus' address to them in 21:23-27, 28, 31, 33, 40, 42, 43, and especially 45, it is taken from the elite. His statement confirms the verdict that they offer in 21:41 and utilizes the contrast of 21:28-32. Jesus does not exclude all Israel.[36] The vineyard remains intact, owned by its owner. It is the tenants who are punished by losing their position as its caretakers. This punishment is understood to happen in Jerusalem's defeat by Rome in 70 C.E. (see Introduction, section 10; 1:21; 22:7; 27:25). New tenants are appointed. The new tenants are **a people that produces the fruits of the reign.** On **fruit** as an image of faithful obedience to God's will and reign, see 21:19. In context it means doing what the religious leaders did not do: acknowledging the owner's claim and authority, not stealing what is his, not rejecting and killing his slaves, living according to his purposes.

Who is this **people**? Gentiles or the mixed Jewish-Gentile church?[37] Certainly Gentiles do not replace Jews, but the emphasis in 21:41, 43 on "bearing fruit" underlines its ethical, not ethnic, nature. Nor does the parable's allegory replace the vineyard/Israel (there is no new Israel). The owner wants fruit from it. What changes is the group of **people** or "small subgroup"[38] charged with the responsibility to ensure it produces fruit. These are disciples constituted by encounter with God's empire present in Jesus' words and actions (4:17-23; 5:3, 10; 11:2-6, 12; 12:28; 13:11, 19, 24, 31, 38). They have been sent in mission to Israel to proclaim and demonstrate the presence of God's empire (10:7-8; cf. 15:24).[39] This people, the *ekklēsia* (16:18; 18:18) which includes Jews and Gentiles, exists as agents of God's empire in seeking fruit from the vineyard for God.

The future tense **will be taken away** (the passive indicates by God) is puzzling. When does the transfer take place? After the death of the son (21:39)? After Jerusalem's fall to Rome? The judgment? What is certain is that the group taking over the tenancy of the vineyard must live faithfully and fruitfully, aware of what has happened to the previous tenants and knowing that it must give account in the judgment (7:15-27; 10:32-42; 18:21-35).[40]

• 21:45

The chapter closes with an emphasis on the religious elite's response.[41] **When the chief priests and the Pharisees heard his parables, they realized he was speaking about them.** The alliance of religious leaders involves chief priests (21:15, 23, 45), scribes (21:15), elders (21:23 [Sanhedrin]), and Pharisees (21:45). See Introduction, sections 1 and 5; 2:4; 3:7; 5:20; 9:36. Josephus consistently locates this alliance of chief priests, the "most notable Pharisees" and the Sadducees among the ruling group ("the notables" or "powerful ones"; οἱ δυνατοί, *hoi dynatoi*) as defenders of the societal status quo and as allies of Rome (*Ant* 13.297; 18.17, Sadducees; *JW* 2.197, 320, 411, 414, chief priests and Pharisees; *Vita* 20-23). The plural **parables** links both parables (21:28-32; 21:33-46) as a double condemnation of the leaders.

Ironically, while the leaders perceive that *Jesus* spoke about them, they do not recognize that they had spoken about themselves (21:31a, 41), and that Jesus has confirmed their self-condemnation. Nor do they accept Jesus' depiction of them as disobedient sons or greedy, murderous thieves who resist his authority and refuse to give the rightful fruit to the owner. They do not repent or use this opportunity to reconsider their stance toward Jesus (21:28-32). They maintain their unbelief despite Jesus' direct disclosure of his identity as God's son (21:37) commissioned by God to reveal God's reign. This key perspective, enunciated by the scriptures (2:15), by God (3:17; 17:5), by Jesus (11:27), and by disciples (14:33; 16:16), is not general knowledge but is insight gained from divine revelation (cf. 16:17).[42] The parable could function as their moment of revelation. But just as they do not recognize John's baptism as being "from heaven" (21:23-27), they do not recognize Jesus as God's agent. They confirm Jesus' analysis of them and his claim about the divisive impact of parables in 13:10-17. The leaders are among those who "see but do not see, hear but do not hear, nor do they understand" (13:13).

• 21:46

Instead they try to silence the story teller. **They wanted to arrest him but they feared the crowds, because they regarded him as a prophet.** They seek to do what the tenants in the parable had done to the son (21:37-39; cf. 12:14; 16:21). Again they exhibit their evil and condemn themselves to the very fate they articulated for those tenants (21:41). They do not arrest him because of the **crowds'** understanding of Jesus as a prophet (cf. 21:11). The leaders continue the same stance as they evidenced with John (cf. 21:26) of seeking to maintain their own authority with the crowds while not recognizing God's. While identifying Jesus as a prophet is inadequate (cf. son of God), it is more positive than the leaders' opposition to Jesus. The crowds' inadequate but somewhat positive confession provides a starting point for the fruitful work of the "other tenants," for "the group of people" to whom the oversight of the vineyard has been given.[43]

CHAPTER 22

Conflict over Jesus' Authority

In the central scene (21:1-27) of the fifth narrative block (chs. 21-27), Jesus and religious leaders conflict over Jesus' authority. Chapter 22 elaborates the conflict. In the third of three parables (21:28-22:14), Jesus continues to announce God's punishment of the religious elite and their rejecting city (22:1-14). Then in three conflict stories, Jesus demonstrates his authority as he verbally bests the Pharisees and Herodians (22:15-22); the Sadducees (22:23-33); and the Pharisees (22:34-45). By the chapter's end the rift with the religious elite is so great and his superiority so established that "they dare not ask him any more questions" (22:46). It is now a struggle to the death.

22:1-14—THE PARABLE OF THE WEDDING FEAST

In two previous parables, the two sons in 21:28-32 and the vineyard tenants in 21:33-46, Jesus has addressed the religious leaders (not all Israel). They have rejected God's purposes and Jesus as God's son. Judgment awaits them. This third parable, also addressed "to them" (22:1; cf. 21:15, 23, 45) and also an allegory, rehearses the elite's rejection and outlines their judgment.[1] The repetition underlines the gravity of the elite's response, accounts for the fall of Jerusalem in 70 as an act of God's judgment carried out (unwittingly) by Rome, confirms the ongoing place of both Israel and disciples within salvation history, and impresses on the audience as the new tenants charged with mission to Israel the need for fruitfulness and faithfulness in carrying out their mission, especially among the poor.

Many have noted that along with the basic verisimilitude that the parable creates, there are a significant number of unrealistic aspects:[2] the double invitation (22:3-4), the universal rejection of the king's invitations (22:3-5), the shameful treatment and killing of his servants (22:6), the king sending troops to burn the city (22:7), the chronology of proceeding with the wedding immediately after the burning (22:8), the setting for the wedding in the burned city, the invitation to the unlikely guests (22:9-10), the inspection of the wedding guests' clothing (22:11), the exclusion of a poor guest for not having a wedding garment (22:11-14). B. B. Scott comments: "the destruction of the verisimilitude forces attention away from the story's story (from what happens) to its discourse (to what it means)."[3]

The parable is an allegory that continues the symbolism of 21:33-46 and assumes the audience's scriptural knowledge. The king (God) has a son, Jesus. The king sends slaves (prophets; cf. 22:3 and 21:34) several times (22:4 and 21:36) to invite people (the religious leaders) to the wedding feast (the eschatological age). But they kill the slaves (cf. 22:6 and 21:35, 38-39; also 23:34, 37; 26:4 anticipating the passion). Judgment is enacted as Rome destroys their city (Jerusalem in 70). God acts as an imperial tyrant. Disciples are to invite others, notably the nonelite, who will also face judgment.

• 22:1

The opening verse, **Answering, once more Jesus spoke to them in parables**, connects this parable to the two in 21:28-46 (**once more**), responds to the leaders' hostility in 21:45-46 (**answering**), identifies the speaker as **Jesus** (cf. 1:21), identifies the hearers as the religious leaders addressed by the previous two parables (21:15, 23, 45), and names the form of the discourse (**parable**; see ch. 13). The link with 21:28-46 recalls important themes: God's repeated invitations; frequent rejections; the exclusion of those who do not wish to participate; the inclusion of others.

• 22:2

The parable lays **the empire of heaven** beside (**may be compared to**) the action of the story. The interaction between the two discloses and envisions God's reign. See 3:2; 4:17; 12:28; chapter 13. Since the parables about God's empire in chapter 13, fourteen references to the **empire** have emphasized the responsibilities of the community of disciples created by the empire's presence (16:19; 18:1, 3, 4, 23; 19:12, 14, 23, 24; 20:1; 21:31, 43) and have indicated accountability in the future judgment (16:28; 18:23-35; 20:21-28). The aorist passive form **may be compared to** (cf. 13:24; 18:23) rather than the future passive ("will be like"; 7:25, 27; 25:1) focuses attention initially on the present experience of the reign.[4]

The central character is **the king**, a common image for God in the scriptures. God the king reigns over the world (Pss 24; 93:1-2) and over the affairs of nations (Ps 47:3). God challenges the nations' gods (Isa 41:21). Particularly, God reigns over Israel as God's people (1 Sam 8:4-9; Pss 97:1-5; 99:1-5; Isa 44:6), brings deliverance from exile (Isa 52:7), and entrusts a just reign to a human king (Ps 72). The day is coming when all nations will acknowledge God as king (Isa 24:23). The audience has also encountered the image previously in Matt 5:35 (Jerusalem as God's city) and with an ambivalent use in a previous parable in 18:34-35, where the king is not and is God! Jesus is a king (2:2; 21:5) whose reign contrasts negatively with the violent and unjust rule of Herod (2:1, 3, 9; 10:18) and Herod the tetrarch (14:9). But here God's violent and punitive act is very reminiscent of imperial tyrants.

The king gives **a wedding banquet for his son**. The son, Jesus, was prominent in the previous parable (see 21:37-39). And **son** is God's designation for Jesus (2:15; 3:17; 11:27; 16:16: 17:5; 20:18). The parable's king, then, represents Israel's God. The reference to **a wedding banquet** evokes several traditions. (1) Marriage is used in several prophets as a metaphor for God's covenant relationship with God's people (Hos 1-3; Jer 2:2-3; 3:1-10; Ezek 16:8-63). In Matt 9:15 Jesus the bridegroom is present with disciples.

(2) Feasting and eating indicate participation in God's purposes. In the exodus, God provides food for the grumbling people in the wilderness (Exod 16; Ps 78:23-25). The passover festival and meal ensure the continuing celebration of God's relationship with the people (cf. Exod 12). The return from exile and the making of "an eternal covenant" are celebrated in the invitation to feast on "rich food" (Isa 55:1-3). Lady Wisdom, a manifestation of God's presence and way, symbolizes the offering of life and instruction in God's way (Prov 8:32-36) by inviting people to a feast (Prov 9:1-2; cf. Matt 11:19). A meal also symbolizes the yet-future completion of God's purposes, when God's empire is established in full. Isaiah envisions God's future triumphant return to Zion, where God will make "for all peoples a feast of rich food" (Isa 25:6-10; cf. Matt 15:32-39; *2 Bar* 29:3-8). Jews and Gentiles will eat this meal (Matt 8:11; 25:10). In the parable those who refuse to attend the wedding celebration are excluded, while those who come participate in God's purposes (cf. 9:10).

(3) The wedding feast also invokes associations built up through the gospel around eating.[5] Food is a gracious gift from God, a symbol of God's justice and provision of adequate resources for all (6:11, 25-31; 14:15-21; 15:32-39), of God's goodness (7:9-11; 15:26-27) and transforming presence (13:33). Jesus' meals with the marginals such as "tax collectors and sinners" show the all-inclusive extent of God's goodness and mercy, which Jesus Immanuel manifests (9:10-13; 11:18-19). Unlikely people will participate in God's mercy in this feast too (22:8-10).

Meals also signify division and conflict. Providing food to disciples in mission indicates one's "worthy" acceptance of their proclamation in contrast to those who do not (10:10-15). The religious leaders have objected to the people Jesus eats with (9:10-13; 11:18-19), to the time and place of eating (12:1-8, the sabbath), and to the disciples' nonobservance of the ritual requirements of eating (15:1-20). In turn Jesus has used food to warn disciples about the teaching of the religious leaders (16:1-12). The setting of a feast alerts the audience to division.

• 22:3

As does the householder in 21:33, the king **sent his slaves to call those who had been invited to the wedding banquet, but they did not wish to come.** The parable assumes a typical political context. The invited guests are the elite among the king's subjects. They are clients, political dependents who owe allegiance to the king. But they snub the king's authority. Refusing the king's invitation is tantamount to rebellion.

The **slaves**, a common image of the prophets sent by God (see 21:35-36), are rejected by the religious leaders (21:45-46; 22:1).[6] The image of **slaves** who obediently carry out their task emphasizes the authority of the king.[7] So does the verb **send** (cf. 21:34, 36, 37). God is designated as "the one who sent" Jesus (10:40; cf. also 15:24) and John (11:10, using Mal 3:1). Jesus also has authority to send; see 10:5, 16; 13:41. The verb **call** not only underlines the king's authority but recalls God's calling of Jesus to carry out God's saving purposes (1:21, 23; 2:15; see also 4:21; 5:9; 9:13; 21:13 to denote a summons to the divine will and purpose). In being sent, the slaves extend God's **call**.

Though honored by an invitation, the invited do not reciprocate his honor or value his authority. They publicly shame him. Like the second son, they say yes but don't go (21:30). Like the tenants, they do not keep their agreement (21:34-39). They **do not wish to come**.

• 22:4

The king (in an unlikely but generous gesture) sends more slaves. **Again he sent other slaves saying, "Tell those who have been invited: Look I have prepared my dinner, my oxen and my fat calves have been slaughtered, and everything is ready; come to the wedding banquet."** The descriptions of sumptuous food attest his generous goodness (cf. 20:15). But the invited reject his goodness as well as his authority.

• 22:5-6

Again the recipients dishonor the king's authority. This time some use great violence (cf. 21:35-39) and heighten their wrong. **But they made light of/disregarded/neglected it and went away, one to his farm, another to his business, while the rest seized his slaves, mistreated them, and killed them.** They go about their daily tasks (farm, business) undisturbed by the king's invitation.[8] They show no interest in benefiting from his goodness. But in a surprising escalation of the conflict, some **mistreat** (on beating slaves see 8:6) and kill the **slaves**. See 21:46 for **seized/arrest**, and 26:4, 48, 50, 57. Violence awaits prophets (5:10-12; 23:29-31, 37), Jesus (16:21; 17:22-23; 20:17-19; chs. 26-27) and disciples (10:16-25; 23:34).

• 22:7

Their violent response, which amounts to insurrection, brings their own destruction. **The king was enraged** (cf. 18:34 for another king with justifiable anger). **He sent** (cf. 22:3, 4) **his troops, destroyed those murderers, and burned their city.** Knowledge of imperial habits, historical events, and religious traditions indicates that this event interprets Rome's destruction of Jerusalem in 70 C.E. as God's punishment for the elite's rejection of God's son or agent, Jesus (see 1:21; 21:12-13, 18-19, 41; 27:25; Introduction, sections 4, 9).

1. Destruction of cities and towns, killing, looting, and burning are common means of subjugating and punishing a defiant people. See Antiochus Epiphanes (1 Macc 1:19, 29-32); Judas (1 Macc 5:5, 27-28, 35, 50-51, 65); Pompey (*Pss. Sol.* 2:1-6; 8:1-5, 19-21); Cestius the governor of Syria in 66 C.E. (Josephus, *JW*

2.504-5, 508, 530). In envisaging God acting in the same way, the gospel is again co-opted by the very imperial world it seeks to resist.

2. Rome's destruction of Jerusalem in 70 C.E. was seen by others as God's punishment of the city (*4 Ezra* 3:24-36; 4:22-25; 5:21-30; *2 Bar* 1:1-5; 4:1; 6:9; 32:2-3; Josephus, *JW* 4.386-88; 5.559; 6.96-103, 409-11; 7.323-36, 358-60). The temple was burned (*2 Bar* 7:1; 80:3; Josephus, *JW* 2.395-97; 6.249-408). Given that this parable, as with the two previous ones, is directed to the religious leaders (21:45; 22:1), it is their rejection of God's messengers and God's son that accounts for the punishment.[9] Rome functions as God's agent of this punishment, as did Assyria (Isa 10:1-7), Babylon (Jer 25:1-11), Persia (Isa 44:28; 45:1-13), Antiochus Epiphanes (2 Macc 6:12-17; cf. *Pss. Sol.* 2:1-14 on Rome). God will subsequently punish Rome at Jesus' return, just as God judged Assyria (Isa 10:12-34), Babylon (Jer 25:12-14; 27:7), and Antiochus Epiphanes (2 Macc 7:32-36; on God's future punishment of Rome, see *Pss. Sol.* 2:16-25, 30; 17:21-34; *2 Bar* 1:4-5; 5:1-4; 8:1-5; 13:11-12; Matt 1:21; 24-25).

3. Traditions speak of God bringing judgment on God's people for unfaithfulness to the covenant. The Deuteronomist accounts for the sixth-century Babylonian exile in these terms (Deut 28-30; 1 Kgs 9:1-9; cf. Jer 25). See also the description in Isa 5 (cf. Matt 21:33 the vineyard) of judgment on Jerusalem. Isa 5:24-25 uses fire to image God's judgment. The **burning** of the city coheres with the image of fire for judgment in the prophets (Amos 1:4, 10; Ezek 38:22; 39:6; Mal 4:1), in the preaching of John the Baptist (Matt 3:10, 12) and in Jesus' parables in chapter 13 (13:30, 40, 42, 50).

• 22:8-9

But this act of punishment does not mean the king is finished with the city.[10] **Then he said to his slaves, "The wedding is ready, but those invited were not worthy"** of the honor shown them because they rejected the invitation. The religious leaders' unworthiness consists of their failure to live lives of obedient actions which reflect repentance (3:8, "worthy of repentance"), their failure to "receive" or "listen to" Jesus' proclamation of God's empire (10:13-14), and their failure to "take [their] cross and follow" Jesus (10:37-38; 21:32, 37-39).

Go therefore into the street crossings, and invite everyone you find to the wedding banquet. When the elite do not come, they are replaced by those of the lower social orders, not of a different ethnicity. On **invite** as calling people to participate in God's saving purposes, see 22:3. This sending of more slaves to **everyone** indicates the church's mission as tenants of the vineyard (see 20:25-28; 21:43; ch. 10; 24:14). Their mission is God's command. The **street crossings** were commonly a location for the shameful activity of begging (Sir 40:28-30). Responsiveness is found not in the corridors, great houses, temples, and town centers of the powerful elite but on the margins among the poor.

• 22:10

This time the inviting is effective. **Those slaves went out into the streets and gathered all whom they found, both good and bad; so the wedding hall**

was filled with guests. Gathering **all whom they found** may include Gentiles,[11] male and female, of any socioeconomic level, especially the poor.[12] Ethical types are particularly emphasized (**both good and bad**). In the parables of chapter 13, the mission and community of disciples incorporate the wheat and weeds (13:24-30), the "doers of lawlessness" and the righteous (13:40-43), the good and the bad, the evil and the righteous (13:48-49; cf. "the just and the unjust" in 5:45). Now is not the time to separate the good from the bad; this task belongs not to the community of disciples but to God at the judgment.

• 22:11-13

When the king came in to see the guests, he noticed a man there who was not wearing a wedding robe, and he said to him, "Friend how did you get in here without a wedding robe?" The absence of the wedding garment is a serious offense (whatever the practicalities of the recent invitation). He is not wearing what is appropriate to this festive occasion. On **friend**, see 20:13; 26:50. **And he was speechless** (cf. 22:34 [the Sadducees]). **Then the king said to the attendants, "Bind him hand and foot, and throw him into the outer darkness where there will be weeping and gnashing of teeth."**

The absence of the wedding garment suggests a failure to discern and honor the authority and goodness of the king.[13] He is one of the "bad" who has failed to behave or live in a manner appropriate to the status of being invited by the king. The language is that of judgment scenes: **bind** (13:30), **outer darkness** (cf. 8:12; 25:30), and **weep and gnash their teeth** (8:12; 13:42, 50; also 24:51; 25:30). In 13:41-42, 49-50 angels separate false disciples. These scenes result from the failure to accept or believe Jesus and live his proclamation (cf. 8:10-12; 13:3-9, 18-23, 36-38). This guest, though inside the wedding feast, is guilty of the same sorts of offenses as the elite leaders who did not honor the invitation, and suffers the same fate.[14]

• 22:14

Jesus provides a closing commentary. **For many were called, but few are chosen**. The opportunity to participate in God's saving purposes is offered to many (on **called**, see 22:3-4, 9) but **few** (7:13-14) availed themselves of the hard and narrow road (Introduction, section 7). To be called *and* chosen means honoring God (22:37-39) and doing God's will (7:24-27; 12:46-50) until the judgment.[15]

The parable shows judgment not only on the religious elite for rejecting God's purposes in Jesus but also on disciples. The final scene (22:11-14), unparalleled in the previous two parables of 21:28-46, functions to warn and encourage the audience. The audience, like the man, has heard and responded to the call by coming to the wedding. But his lack of honor for the king leads to his exclusion. The audience of disciples of Jesus is warned that responding to the call is the beginning of a life committed to God's purposes and requires ongoing faithfulness and fruitfulness (21:43). There is no room for gloating or smugness. Judgment also awaits the community of disciples.

22:15-22—CONFLICT WITH THE PHARISEES
AND HERODIANS OVER PAYING TRIBUTE TO ROME

Unlike 21:45-46, the religious elite do not respond directly to the parable of the wedding feast. They leave and plan to match Jesus' attack on them with an attempt to trap him.

• 22:15-16

Two verses prepare for the trap. **Then the Pharisees went and plotted/took counsel to entrap him in what he said. So they sent their disciples to him along with the Herodians.** (1) The initial focus falls on **the Pharisees,** who in 21:45-46 want to arrest Jesus. They are named first; they scheme (**plotted**) and initiate the action (**they went**). As defenders of the unjust social order, they seek to maintain their privileged place in the status quo against Jesus' attack. (2) Their action of **plotting/taking counsel** recalls 12:14, where they plot to kill him, and anticipates both 27:1, where the chief priests and elders (part of the alliance of religious elite) do the same, and 28:12, where they plot to bribe the guards to lie about disciples stealing Jesus' body. The action is one of opposition, violence, and deception. (3) Their motives are to **entrap** Jesus **in what he said,** but how they will do so is not clarified until 22:17. (4) They **sent their disciples** as their agents, the first reference to these disciples. Why not go themselves? They avoid direct encounter; the indirect approach heightens the subterfuge and the gap with Jesus. (5) They ally with **the Herodians**, also not mentioned previously. Their name suggests that they are identified with Herod as supporters of Rome.

(6) **"Teacher, we know that you are sincere, and teach the way of God in accordance with truth, and show deference to no one; for you do not regard people with partiality."** They address Jesus as **teacher** as they have done previously (9:11; 12:38), a title used not by disciples but by opponents or nonfollowers (8:19; 17:24; 19:16). If they truly respected him as a **teacher** they would not be trying to trap or oppose him.

(7) Their opening comments praise Jesus in terms unmatched anywhere in the gospel. If genuine, these remarks would render them disciples, but disciples do not attempt to trap Jesus. Rather the comments show them to be hypocrites (22:18), and are ironic, spoken more truthfully than they know. Although the elite do not recognize it, Jesus is **sincere/true** in being faithful to God's purposes (cf. 17:5). He does **teach the way of God**, which, like "the way of righteousness" in 21:32, refers to a way of life which God requires and which is focused on God. Like God (Lev 19:15; Rom 2:11; Matt 5:45) Jesus shows no **deference** or **partiality**. He takes no heed of the opinions or status of any others except God. He has engaged the powerful and the lowly equally with beneficial power (8:1-13), though the powerful are generally resistant. By commending his lack of deference, the elite dare Jesus to speak his mind openly on the controversial topic that they name in v. 17.

• 22:17

They ask his opinion. **Tell us, then, what you think.** The opening imperative **tell us** inappropriately compels an answer! In 21:28 Jesus asked them what they thought (same verb), and twice in response to his question (21:31, 40-41) they condemn themselves. Now they employ the same strategy (see also 22:42). **Is it lawful to pay taxes to the emperor or not?** A question about what **is lawful** is bound to bring controversy (as in 12:2, 4, 10; 14:4; 19:3; 20:15). Their question about taxes suggests that it is a matter of some debate. Their astute question is a trap in that if Jesus speaks against paying tribute, he attacks Rome's sovereignty (see below); if he encourages payment, he appears to be a collaborator and loses credibility as a prophet (21:11). The trap is clear, but futile. Jesus has already indicated that he will die at the hands of the Romans (20:19).

Their question concerns direct **taxes** or tribute, which were often paid in kind (cf. 17:25; 18:24), and were levied on landed property including crops and livestock and on personal property.[16] Since Roman occupation in 63 B.C.E., Judea paid tribute (Josephus, *JW* 1.154; *Ant* 14.74). Tribute was a means of subjugation, of establishing authority (1 Macc 1:29). It was a source of Rome's wealth and a means of sustaining its people (Josephus, *JW* 2.383, 386) and militarily imposed peace (Tacitus, *Hist* 4.74). Through the first century, in Judea and Syria (Tacitus, *Ann* 2.42, 17 C.E.; Syria in 36 C.E., *Ann* 6.41) and in other parts of the empire, resentment against taxes at times boiled over into tax revolts.[17] Judas the Galilean had in 6-9 C.E. exhorted the nonpayment of tribute to Rome since not Rome but "God was their Lord" (Josephus, *JW* 2.117-18), a viewpoint apparently revived by his son Menahem in the 66-70 war (*JW* 2.433-40). Josephus has Agrippa tell the people in revolt against Florus (66 C.E.) that not paying the tribute is "an act of war" against Rome (*JW* 2.403-4).

• 22:18

Jesus discerns their intent (cf. 9:3-4; 12:14-15, 25; 17:25; like God, 1 Sam 16:7). **Jesus, knowing their evil, said, "Why do you tempt me, hypocrites?"** Jesus has called them **evil** previously in 9:4; 12:34-35, 39; 16:4 (cf. 6:13), and they have been presented as **tempting/testing** him in 16:1; 19:3; 22:35 (cf. 4:1, 3). In calling them **hypocrites** (see 6:2 for this polemical term), he underlines that their apparently genuine public words and question express something that differs from their internal (evil) state (22:16).

• 22:19

Without waiting for a response he orders, **"Show me the coin used for the tax." And they brought him a denarius**. That he does not have a coin and that **they bring him the denarius** does not prove that Jesus refused to carry a coin which bore the emperor's image and titles, nor does it indicate their attitude to the tax. It is unclear whether they have a coin or have to go and procure one to bring to him. Jesus requests a **denarius** because "the Roman tribute was to be paid in Roman money."[18]

• **22:20-21a**

The coin is a visual aid. More than that, imperial coins were portable bill-boards, instruments of propaganda which reminded users of the emperor's political power and Rome's status as the favored of the gods (Introduction, section 9).[19] **Then he said to them, "Whose head is this, and whose title?" They answered, "The emperor's."** Denarii from Jesus' time, probably minted in Lugdunum in Gaul and bearing the **head** of the emperor Tiberius and **title** identifying him as Caesar, son of the deified Augustus and Pontifex Maximus (high priest), have been found. After defeating Jerusalem in 70, Vespasian issued denarii that depicted a dejected and bound female with the words IVDAEA CAPTA, and his own bust.[20]

• **22:21b**

Then he said to them, "Give therefore to the emperor the things that are the emperor's, and to God the things that are God's." Jesus' answer avoids an either/or response by combining the two options! What is the relationship of the two clauses and the meaning of the whole? Does the second clause annul the first: pay nothing because everything, including the land (Lev 25:23), belongs to God? Or does it endorse the first: the emperor does God's will and is to be honored as such? Or does it contextualize and relativize the first: pay the emperor while recognizing God's greater demand of loyalty? That is, does Jesus urge outright revolt, accommodation, or nonviolent subversion of Rome?

This last option is more convincing. The proclamation of God's empire in the world of *Pax Romana*, a reign that will eventually mean the end of Rome's rule (chs. 24-25), prohibits unquestioning loyalty to the empire. The instruction of 17:24-27 to pay (subversively) the Jewish tax to Rome eliminates revolt but commends the third. Certainly Jesus upholds paying the tribute (**give to the emperor**), as he does the tax in 17:24-27. But his teaching of 17:24-27 indicates that a tax can be paid without payment being a vote of support for Rome. The second clause here functions in a way similar to God's supplying of the didrachma (see 17:27). The clause recognizes payment within the context of God's far greater gifts and authority. It relativizes tribute payment, and establishes loyalty to God and God's purposes as the ultimate loyalty. Jesus has demonstrated this loyalty in the journey to Jerusalem, in his healing (21:15) and teaching (21:23-22:46) in the temple. Disciples, who live in God's world and Rome's world, are challenged to live faithfully to God "in both" worlds until Jesus returns to establish God's empire over all (19:28; 24:27-31).

• **22:22**

There is no verbal response from the disciples of the Pharisees and Herodians. They are effectively silenced (cf. 22:15, 34, 46). **When they heard this, they were amazed; and they left him and went away**. The response of being **amazed** (Jesus [8:10]; disciples [8:27; 21:20]; crowds [9:33; 15:31]; Pilate [27:14]) underlines that something truly important has happened.

22:23-33—CONFLICT WITH THE SADDUCEES OVER RESURRECTION

A second controversy scene follows. Just as the previous scene set loyalty to God's purposes above loyalty to Rome, this scene contrasts another staple of the present social structure, patriarchy, with God's future, where that structure no longer exists. At the heart of the dispute are differing understandings of God's will and power, and the nonpatriarchal structure of God's future empire, at least in regard to human interactions. See 5:45.

• **22:23-24**

The same day some Sadducees came to him, saying there is no resurrection. In their two previous appearances (3:7; 16:1, 6, 11, 12), **Sadducees** have been presented as opponents of John and of God's purposes (3:7), and as allies with the Pharisees against Jesus, who warns his disciples about their teaching (16:1, 6, 11, 12). Many have noted that their alliance with the Pharisees is unlikely: Sadducees lost their leadership position in the 66-70 war; doctrinal differences including resurrection and differing approaches to tradition separate the two groups; and in terms of social appeal, Josephus associates the Sadducees with the wealthy and notes a lack of popular support for them but considerable support for the Pharisees (see *JW* 2.162-66; *Ant* 13.297-98; 18.11). In the gospel, they are part of the Jerusalem elite centered on the temple opposed to Jesus.

Their claim that **there is no resurrection** sets them at odds with Jesus, who has previously proclaimed his own resurrection (see 16:21; 17:23; 20:19). They resist an eschatological view of God's purposes, which includes resurrection as part of a cluster of events that comprise the establishment of God's intentions for creation ("at the beginning," 19:4) in the fullness of God's just empire.

They asked him a question saying, "Teacher, Moses said, 'If a man dies childless, his brother shall marry the widow, and raise up children for his brother.'" Their topic is levirate marriage, an economic, religious, and patriarchal practice which ensured the continuation of a man's line, property, inheritance, and name, and which affirmed the woman's (widow's) childbearing place in her husband's family.[21] Levirate marriage served a patriarchal structure of households[22] already critiqued in chapters 19-20.

• **22:25-27**

They illustrate Moses' teaching by sketching the dilemma of a widow and seven brothers. **Now there were seven brothers among us: the first married, and died childless, leaving the widow to his brother. The second did the same, so also the third, down to the seventh. Last of all, the woman herself died.**[23]

• **22:28**

They ask Jesus to interpret Moses' teaching in relation to this example and the resurrection in which they do not believe. Unlike 22:15, 35 ("trap", "test"), no motive is given for their question, but its content betrays their motivation. The question mocks the notion of resurrection, challenges Jesus the teacher to find a solution to an absurd and apparently impossible situation, and seems intent thereby on undermining his credibility. **In the resurrection, then, whose wife of the seven will she be? For all of them had married her.** Their question concerns which brother will "own" the woman. While *they* do not believe in resurrection (22:23), their question requires Jesus either to dismiss the resurrection (contradicting his own previous statement of God's will) or to concede that she will have multiple husbands. The "proper" interpretation of scripture has been a major part of Jesus' ministry (5:17-48; the fulfillment citations whereby his life and actions enact God's will; see 1:22-23), and a significant point of division between Jesus and the religious leaders (12:1-14; 15:1-20; 19:3-12; 21:12-17; 22:41-45; 23:2-4).

• 22:29

Jesus' answer comes in three parts, a rebuke (22:29), a counter to their understanding of marriage and resurrection life (22:30), and a scriptural rebuttal of their rejection of resurrection (22:31-32). He rejects their limited understanding of God and challenges them to envisage God's transforming power.

Jesus' rebuke begins with a direct repudiation, **You are wrong/err** (cf. 18:12-13). Jesus' subsequent comments indicate that this declaration refers to their dismissal of resurrection, to their attempt to link levirate marriage to resurrection, and to their assumption that patriarchal marriage is a permanent state.

He then asserts their ignorance: **because you know neither the scriptures nor the power of God**. Their ignorance of **the scriptures** may refer to the link of resurrection and marriage which their question assumes, or to their denial of resurrection, or both. The charge that they do not know **the power of God** suggests that they cannot envisage God overcoming death and accomplishing resurrection, and cannot imagine God transforming the present world into one without the sinful structure of patriarchal power. To **know** is an experiential term (Gen 4:1).

• 22:30

Jesus counters their understanding of marriage and resurrection life. **For in the resurrection they neither marry nor are given in marriage**. The assumption of the Sadducees' question is that the present marriage structures, from which they as wealthy males benefit, continue indefinitely. Jesus' teaching indicates that God's future envisages different structures. **But (they) are like angels in heaven.** That humans will become like angels is attested in other apocalyptic texts (1QS 4:6-8, 11-13; 1QM 12:1-7; *1 En* 104:4; *2 Bar* 51:3, 10; *2 En* 22:10). Angels are immortal (cf. *1 En* 15:3-7). Fallen angels have intercourse with humans and abandon eternal life and immortality (*1 En* 62:13-16). But being vindicated in the resurrection means an immortal existence in which reproduction and marriage are not necessary. The category of patriarchal levirate marriage is irrelevant to resurrection life and the establishment of God's empire over all. God's reign transforms the norms of the present hierarchical, patriarchal, socioeconomic, and religious system and envisions a different future of communal equality (20:12).

• **22:31**

Jesus moves to the underlying difference between himself and the Sadducees and employs a scriptural rebuttal of their rejection of resurrection. **And as for the resurrection of the dead, have you not read what was said to you by God?** The questioning of their reading of scripture (12:3, 5; 19:4; 21:16, 42) occurs in situations of conflict which present Jesus as the definitive revealer and interpreter of God's will, and the religious elite as both ignorant and resistant. The phrase **to you by God** personalizes God's address to them and their rejection.

• **22:32**

Jesus quotes Exod 3:6 (omitting "of your father") in which God addresses Moses. The Sadducees valued the Pentateuch (the first five books), so Jesus quotes their own authoritative material against them. **"I am the God of Abraham, the God of Isaac, the God of Jacob." He is God not of the dead but of the living.** The use of the present tense (**I am**) when Abraham, Isaac, and Jacob were physically dead at the time of God's speaking indicates existence apart from physical death and a relationship with God not interrupted by death. They are among **the living** not **the dead**. The Sadducees' rejection of resurrection is a rejection of the God of Moses whose teaching they profess to accept (22:24)!

Jesus' citation is vague about the nature of the patriarchs' existence (resurrection of the body? immortality?) and the means of attaining it. A tradition that Abraham, Isaac, and Jacob did not die physically (4 Macc 7:19; 13:17; 16:25) but "live to God" also attests ongoing existence but without specifying its form. The context here of the exchange with the Sadducees suggests a resurrected state. One would expect that resurrection would accompany judgment (12:41-42; 22:30), yet the opening of the tombs in 27:52-53 suggests that this resurrection may begin with Jesus' resurrection, or is at least related to it. Jesus affirms that human existence is not bound by death, that God's power is not limited by patriarchal structures, but without going on to define the nature of that existence in this saying.

The phrase **the God of Abraham, Isaac, and Jacob** evokes God's covenant promises of land and descendants and God's faithfulness to that promise and people (Exod 33:1; Lev 26:42; Deut 1:8; 6:10; 1 Chr 16:16-18; etc.). God's life or power, not a patriarchal system based on male succession, guarantees the resurrection future. But ironically, this affirmation of a different future is guaranteed by citing God's faithfulness to three patriarchs without reference to Sarah, Rebekah, or Leah (see on 1:2)! Again the gospel is partially co-opted by the very structure which it resists.

• **22:33**

While the exchange has been between Jesus and the Sadducees, the crowds respond (not the Sadducees; see 22:22, 34, "silenced"). **And when the crowds**

heard it, they were astounded at/struck by his teaching. The same verb has described the crowds' responses to Jesus' teaching in 7:28 and 13:54 (also 19:25 for disciples). Their response highlights Jesus' dominance in the verbal sparring, and again distances the crowds from the religious elite (cf. 21:11, 15-16). His authority has been demonstrated here, and will be, finally, in his resurrection (28:18).

22:34-46—CONFLICT WITH THE PHARISEES

A third conflict scene with the religious elite follows. On the Pharisees and Sadducees as members of the ruling elite, see 2:4; 3:7; and 21:45.

• 22:34

The opening clause links this scene with the previous one. **When the Pharisees heard that he had silenced the Sadducees, they gathered together**. The Sadducees' lack of response in 22:33 is now explained. They were not merely silent, but Jesus' teaching caused their silence. Focus moves to their allies against Jesus, the **Pharisees**, whom he thwarted in their previous attempt to trap him (through their disciples) in 21:15. While they oppose the Sadducees on resurrection and may well be pleased that Jesus had won a victory over them, they seem more intent here in allying with the Sadducees against Jesus. The verb **gathered together** (also 22:41) underlines the opposition. The verb is used in Ps 2:2 for "the kings of the earth/the rulers (see Matt 17:25) who gather against/take counsel against the Lord and his anointed." The Pharisees oppose Jesus as God's agent.

• 22:35-36

A representative of the Pharisees tests Jesus. **One of them, a lawyer, asked him a question to test him. Teacher** (see 22:16, 24), **what kind of commandment is great in the law/Torah?"** On **test** as indicating opposition, see 22:18. The **lawyer** or teacher of the law is a scribe who belongs to the Pharisees (see 2:4; 5:20; 12:38; 15:1). How is his question to rank the commandments a **test**? Does the lawyer (mistakenly) think Jesus will speak against the law? Or does he hope Jesus will somehow trip himself up in answering and undermine his own authority? Or does he hope Jesus will elevate some laws and dismiss the rest? Various biblical writers had summarized the tradition; see Mic 6:8; Isa 33:15-16; 56:1; Amos 5:1. The test does not seem as astute as the questions of 22:17, 27. It is a last-ditch effort.

• 22:37-38

He said to him. "'You shall love the Lord your God with all your heart, and with all your soul, and with all your mind.' This is the greatest and first commandment." Jesus has spoken about "the law and the prophets" in 5:17-7:12, the heart of the Sermon on the Mount. Jesus' answer here quotes Moses from Deut 6:5.[24] Moses' exhortation in Deut 6 requires love for God to be lived in daily, social obedience. The terms **heart, soul,** and **mind** are parallel terms denoting the whole of human existence (Deut 10:12-13; 30:10; Matt 6:21-25). On **heart** as the center of a person's willing, thinking, knowing, deciding, and doing, see 5:8, 28; 6:21; 9:4; 11:29; 12:34, 40; 13:15, 19; 15:8, 18, 19; 18:35; 24:48. On **soul** as one's life or daily existence given either to God's service or to something else, see 2:20; 6:25; 10:28, 39; 11:29; 12:18; 16:25-26; 20:28; 26:38. **Mind** is used only here in Matthew. The terms denote the whole self in daily living oriented to God. **Love** for God, then, is a disposition and way of life, a direction and a life of actions according to God's will revealed by Jesus' words (7:24-27; 12:46-50) and actions (cf. 9:36).

• 22:39

Love for God cannot be separated from love for people. **And a second is like it: "You shall love your neighbor as yourself."** The coupling of the two (**is like it**) is not unique or original to Jesus. See *T. Iss.* 5:2; 7:6; *T. Dan* 5:3; Philo, *De Dec* 108-10 (where these two demands summarize the Decalogue); *Spec Leg* 2.63. Jesus has already asserted a very close link between treatment of people and of God in 10:40, where to welcome a disciple is to welcome Jesus and God. It will be asserted again in 25:31-46. **Love** demonstrated in practical acts of establishing God's justice through feeding the poor, housing the homeless, clothing the naked, and so on, is love for Jesus and God.

Jesus quotes Lev 19:18. The command presents not just an exhortation to occasional loving acts but a societal vision. Lev 19 requires just human relations, including respect for parents (Lev 19:3), provision of food for the poor and alien (19:9-10), no stealing, lying, false dealing or swearing falsely by God's name (19:11-12), no defrauding or reviling of the deaf and blind (19:13-14), no biased judgments or slander (19:15-16), no hatred or vengeance (19:17-18). The religious leaders have failed to create this sort of society (Matt 9:36; 15:13-14; 21:43). They allow parents to be deprived of support (15:3-6). Their sabbath laws deny people access to food (12:1-8; cf. 14:13-21; 15:32-39). They revile the blind and the lame by banning them from the temple (21:14).

Jesus has upheld this vision and its summary command to love one's neighbor. He has countered the religious elite's practices, healed the sick (4:23-24), has upheld the commands to honor parents, not steal and not bear false witness (19:18-19), and has forbidden oaths (5:33-37) and revenge (5:38-42). He has previously interpreted this command to mean a life of indiscriminate loving. Loving one's **neighbor** includes praying for one's enemies (see Matt 5:43-46) and, in 19:19-21, freeing one's heart from wealth (cf. 6:24) by selling possessions and giving the proceeds to the poor. Love for God and neighbor are intertwined. See also 7:12. To **love the neighbor** by seeking his or her welfare also involves loving **yourself.** One's own welfare is intertwined with that of the other.

• 22:40

On these two commandments depend all the law and the prophets. See 5:17 for **the law and the prophets** as the revelation of God's will which Jesus enacts and interprets. Jesus has answered the scribe in a way that asserts what is at the heart of God's will revealed in Torah. The reference to **all** and the use of the verb **depends** suggest an interconnection among God's revelation which Jesus has identified. While the lawyer asked him to distinguish some commands, Jesus has underlined the unity or coherence, as well as the center, of God's will. In so doing he has identified what is to shape the lifestyle of the community of disciples. Love is to inform and be expressed by its mission and daily life. There is no retreat from its world. There is no passivity induced by vast human needs or by false assurances from eschatological destiny. Love is lived faithfulness and active compassion. It manifests the presence and power of God. By citing Deut 6:5 and Lev 19:18, Jesus claims the authority of this God-given tradition. It is "by this authority" (21:23) that he teaches and lives as he does.

• 22:41-45

Jesus, a clear winner so far in this game of verbal challenges, goes on the offensive in asking the Pharisees two questions which challenge them to recognize his identity and role. This scene engages the central issue that divides Jesus and the religious elite, his identity. Jesus' question forces them into a dilemma. They recognize that he is God's authorized agent (something they have refused to do), or they denounce him again as lacking God's authority (cf. 12:23-24) and alienate the crowds (21:46).[25]

• 22:41

Now while the Pharisees were gathered together, Jesus asked them this question. Jesus' question is his rejoinder to their challenge about the commandments. The verb **gathered together** repeats v. 34 from the beginning of this scene, holds the two parts together, and continues the echo of Ps 2:2. The relationship continues to be adversarial. They oppose God's anointed.

• 22:42

Though the question is introduced as one, Jesus asks two questions, which are held together by a common issue, his identity. **What do you think of the Messiah? Whose son is he?** The question is about Jesus, who was identified as the **Messiah** in 1:1 (cf. 1:16, 17, 18; 2:4). His identity is discernible from his actions (11:2-6) and is recognized by disciples (16:16, 20). The religious elite are given another opportunity to recognize his God-given commission. Jesus introduces the question with **What do you think?**, the same question with which he began this sequence of three parables and three conflict stories in 21:28 (21:28-22:46). The elite put the same question to Jesus in 22:17 (paying tribute to Rome). Its use here closes the unit and, given the absolutely crucial nature of his question, ends any chance of dialogue between Jesus and the elite.

The gospel's audience knows the answer to his question. Jesus has been identified as **son/child** of David (see 1:1; 9:27; 12:23; 15:22; 20:30, 31) by the marginal poor and the sick whom Jesus heals.[26] The crowds and children address Jesus with this title (21:9, 15) as he enters Jerusalem. The chief priests and scribes, though, contest its use for Jesus (21:15-16), just as the Pharisees had earlier declared him not to be David's son but an agent of Beelzebul (12:23-24). But while Jesus' connection to David enacts God's promises to David of descendants and a reign forever (2 Sam 7; Ps 2:7; *Pss. Sol.* 17:21), God has identified him as "my son" (2:15; 3:17; 17:5). To be a disciple involves, among other things, agreeing with God's designation and confessing Jesus to be God's **son**, the one commissioned by God (14:33; 16:16). Those who are not disciples do not make this confession. To be God's son denotes a relationship and function (see 2:15; 11:25-27). As God's son or agent, he does the task that God entrusts to him, to manifest God's saving presence or empire among people (1:21, 23; 4:17).

The term **son** recalls the parables of 21:28-22:14. In the allegory of 21:37-38, the owner's son/Jesus is killed by tenants/the religious elite. In 22:1-10 they refuse to honor the king's son (see 22:2), not attending his wedding feast, for which they and their city are destroyed (by Rome as God's agents). His question again gives them the opportunity to condemn themselves if they do not welcome or honor God's son.

The Pharisees give the expected answer. **They said to him, "The son of David."** They give expression to a leading (though not the only) messianic expectation (see 1:1), but they give no indication that Jesus is David's son despite the testimony of the healed sick and crowds. It is not that they don't know (12:22-24; 21:15-16). It is that they refuse recognition.

• 22:43-45

Their answer is not wrong, but they do not connect it with Jesus (cf. 2:4-6). Nor is it the whole story. Jesus tries to point them beyond this Davidic connection to himself by citing Ps 110:1. **He said to them, "How is it then that David by the Spirit calls him Lord, saying 'The Lord said to my Lord, "Sit at my right hand until I put your enemies under your feet"'? If David thus calls him Lord, how can he be his son?"** The form of **under your feet**, an image of subjection and dominion, may derive from Ps 8:7, the psalm that Jesus quotes in 21:16 against the religious elite and in defense of the children's praise for him as son of David.

1. Psalm 110 was in its preexilic context a royal psalm, celebrating the coronation of a king (a son of God, Ps 2:7) whom God (**the Lord**) places on the throne (110:1). To **sit at the right hand** is the favored position of blessing and power over others (Gen 48:14-19; Exod 15:6, 12; cf. Matt 25:33-34), which only God can give (cf. 20:21, 23). On **seated** as signifying a king's rule, see 5:1. God promises the king that he will manifest God's power to destroy enemies and be a priest forever.

2. Matthew's Jesus shares the tradition's claim (as presumably do the Pharisees) that **David** wrote the psalm under the inspiration of **the Spirit** (cf. 2 Sam 23:2; Josephus, *Ant* 6.166). That is, what David writes is reliable and accurate.

3. But whom does David speak about in referring to **my Lord**? If David were speaking about the coronation of a king, why would he refer to one of his descendants or sons as **Lord**? This may be how sons address their fathers (so

21:29) but not vice versa. Who is this one commissioned by God to share in God's reign, and called both **son** and **my Lord** by David? On **call** (the verb appears seven times in the chapter: 22:3 [twice], 4, 8, 9, 43, 45; a cognate in 22:14) as recognizing someone's place and participation in God's purposes (see 1:21, 23; 2:15; 4:21; 5:9; 9:13; 21:13).

• **22:46**

The Pharisees have no solution to this riddle. **And no one was able to answer him a word.** See 22:12, 22, 34. Their silence attests his superior teaching. But having shamed them into silence, Jesus offers no explanation.

By contrast, the gospel's audience of disciples is supposed to know. The audience has learned since 1:21-23 and 2:5-6 that the scriptures are to be interpreted in relation to Jesus. The religious leaders, though, do not do so (see 2:5-6). Matthew understands David, inspired by the Spirit, to speak of the Messiah, Jesus. The psalm is understood to depict God (**the Lord**) commissioning the Messiah-king (**my Lord**, Jesus) to manifest God's empire over the nations in the judgment (Ps 110:6), a role given to Jesus (Matt 13:37-43; 16:27-28; 19:28; 25:31-46; 28:18-20). Note especially Matt 26:64, which depicts Jesus seated at the right hand and returning in power for the judgment. The Messiah is of David's line (David's son), but David recognizes one far greater than himself (Matt 12:42), a ruler of the nations, and **calls him (my) Lord**. Jesus has referred to himself as **Lord** (see 10:24-25; 12:8), as have others, particularly disciples (see 8:2, 6, 28; 14:28, 30; 16:22; etc.). **Lord** appears with **son of David** in 9:27-28; 15:22; and 21:9 in relation to Jesus. That is, while the term **son of David** says something important about Jesus' God-given task of showing healing mercy, it does not fully express his identity as God's son, commissioned by God to manifest God's saving presence or empire. As **Lord**, Jesus represents God's authority (28:18). This identity and role the religious elite refuse to confess. In so refusing, they oppose not only Jesus but God.

Their inability to answer this central question of Jesus' identity and role in God's purposes means there is nothing more to talk about. Jesus has decisively gotten the best of them in three challenges; **nor from that day did anyone dare to ask him any more questions**. By not engaging him in further conversation, they express their lack of openness to any insight about his identity and role.

CHAPTER 23

Jesus Attacks the Scribes
and Pharisees

The conflict with the religious elite over Jesus' authority (21:1-27) has intensified through three parables (21:28-22:14) and three conflict stories (22:15-45) to the point that Jesus has silenced his opponents (22:46). They refuse to recognize his God-given authority and identity as God's anointed agent or Christ, just as he has refused to accept their social vision (5:20; 9:10-13) and to recognize their legitimacy (15:12-14) and teaching (16:11-12).

Chapter 23 marks this impasse in three ways.[1] In 23:1-12, Jesus, addressing the disciples and crowds, differentiates the practices of the community of disciples from the illegitimate practices of the Pharisees. In 23:13-36 Jesus delivers a blistering series of seven woes or curses against the Pharisees that condemn them for their inappropriate, sinful practices and rejection of God's messenger. This attack implicitly justifies the disciples' different practices and way of life. And in 23:37-39 Jesus laments elite Jerusalem's rejection of him, but anticipates a future positive welcome. The chapter increases the hostility between Jesus and the religious elite and prepares for his crucifixion in chapters 26-27.[2]

For many Christian readers, this is a very embarrassing chapter. This vicious attack on the Jewish religious leaders is unacceptable. Equally unacceptable is the way in which Christian readers through the centuries have regarded this litany of hate as a factual record of Jewish unfaithfulness. Assisted by vv. 31 and 37, for example, they/we have generalized this specific attack on one group of religious leaders into a verdict on all Jews and Jewish religious leaders for all time. This way of reading must end. Neither the chapter nor the gospel asserts God's rejection of Israel or Israel's rejection of God. The chapter is directed against a particular set of religious leaders.

One way of ensuring that such readings do not continue is to take account of three factors which show the limits of the applicability of the material. First, it is important to note its place in the gospel's *plot* (see the first two paragraphs above). It is part of an increasing, life-and-death conflict between Jesus and the religious elite as characters in this story.

Second, we need to recall the *historical context* or circumstances surrounding the gospel. Many Jews struggled to make sense of the defeat of Jerusalem in 70 C.E. by Rome (cf. *4 Ezra* 3:30; *2 Bar* 11:2; Matt 21:12-13, 18-19, 41-43; 22:7). Post-70 debates to reformulate Jewish practices without a temple and a priesthood involved various groups and issues (see Introduction, section 8). Matthew's group participated in these debates but did not carry the day. The gospel interprets Jerusalem's fall as punishment for the elite's rejection of God's anointed one Jesus (22:7). Leaders who reject Jesus cannot, in the gospel's perspective, be regarded as legitimate (15:13-14). This chapter shows why these leaders are not legitimate and why the community of disciples of Jesus is legitimate (21:43). It does not show God's rejection by or of Israel. There is no such rejection in the gospel.

Third, we must recognize the *polemical and stereotypical nature of the language* in chapter 23. In a very helpful article, L. Johnson discusses "conventions of ancient polemic."[3] He shows that much of the language in chapter 23 is common to attacks made by various Gentile and Jewish philosophical, religious, and ethnic groups on other groups in the ancient world. It is a standard way of talking (a *topos*), not bothered by the facts, but which functions to show another group to be opponents. "If sophists are by definition blind, and Apion is blind (Josephus, *Con Ap* 2.132, 142) and Alexandrian pagans are blind (Philo, *Vita Cont* 2.10), and Zealots are blind (Josephus, *JW* 5.343, 572), and men of the pit are blind (Qumran, 1QS 4:9-14), should we be shocked to see scribes and Pharisees called 'blind guides' by Matthew . . . ?"[4] Nor should we be surprised to imagine that other groups are saying these same things about Matthew's community. Gentile philosophical groups say these things about other philosophical groups; Gentiles say them about Jews; Jews say them about Gentiles; and Jews say them about other Jews. Johnson calls it "the world of rhetorical hardball."

For example, a disciple of Epicurus calls his (Gentile) opponents "buffoons, charlatans, assassins, prostitutes, nincompoops" (Plutarch, *Moralia* 1086E). Plutarch replies by charging that Epicureans are noted for a "lack of friends, absence of activity, irreligion, sensuality and indifference" and for using prostitutes (*Moralia* 1100C; 1129B).[5] In his work *Contra Apion*, the Jew Josephus constantly trades numerous insults with the Gentile Apion by charging him with sedition, religious nonsense, envy, lies, ignorance, being a charlatan, and the like. The Jew Philo responds to attacks from Gentile Alexandrians by calling them "the promiscuous and unstable rabble," "more brutal and savage than fierce wild beasts," "adept at flattery and imposture and hypocrisy . . . with their loose and unbridled lips," and worthy allies of the emperor Gaius Caligula, who was "thinking that he was God" (*Gaium* 120, 131, 162).[6] Josephus says very negative things about the Sicarii, a group of fellow Jews whom he regards as largely responsible for the war against Rome in 66 C.E. They are "imposters and brigands . . . slaves, the dregs of society, and the bastard scum of the nation . . . ," guilty of cruelty, avarice, murder, atrocities, lying, oppression, evil (*JW* 2.264; 5.443-44; 7.255-58). W. D. Davies and D. C. Allison summarize fourteen charges that numerous Jewish groups make against other Jewish groups: good in appearance only, hypocrites, misleaders, blind, foolish or ignorant, teachers of wrong halakah, guilty of economic sins, guilty of sexual sins, unclean, persecutors and/or murderers of the righteous, like sinful generations of the past, snakelike, destined for eschatological judgment, the cause of God's forsaking the temple.[7]

This is standard polemical language, which Gentile and Jewish groups used to slander other groups. "The polemic signifies simply that these were opponents and such things should be said about them. The attempt either to convict first-century Jews of hypocrisy or vindicate them from it is irrelevant as well as futile."[8] The name calling is not intended to reform the other group. It is for internal consumption, affirming a group's own identity as distinct from other groups. Chapter 23 affirms the community of disciples in its commitment to Jesus and in practices that differ from those attacked in this chapter.

Identifying this way of talking as standard slander and polemic does not trivialize it or excuse it. It is intense rhetoric, and millennia later it is still hateful and destructive. Christians must understand what type of rhetoric it is. Identifying the conventional polemical language does help to show that we are not reading the results of a careful, "scientific" survey. We are, in fact, reading stereotypical polemical language that says much more about the experience of its users (a small, powerless, marginalized group attacking a larger, more successful group) than the historical and moral/religious reality of the described. Perhaps its only lasting value may be in self-examination to warn disciples against condemnation for similar actions.[9]

23:1-12—THESE TWO GROUPS ARE NOT LIKE THE OTHER

• 23:1

The verse establishes the chapter's audience, **Then Jesus said to the crowds and to his disciples**. On **crowds** as the recipients of Jesus' ministry, who show neither the faith of disciples nor the hostility of religious leaders, see 4:25. On **disciples**, see 5:1. The audience does not include the religious elite.

• 23:2-3

Jesus describes the elite's powerful social and religious position in regulating everyday life (see further below):[10] **The scribes and the Pharisees sit on Moses' seat**, but warns against imitating their practices: **therefore do whatever they say to you and follow/keep it; but do not do as they do, for they do not practice what they preach**. Both **scribes and Pharisees** participated in the alliance of the religious elite who as part of the ruling elite opposed Jesus in chapters 21-22. The combinations are fluid: 21:15, scribes and chief priests; 21:23, 45, Pharisees and chief priests; 22:15-16, Pharisees and Herodians; 22:34, Pharisees. On **scribes**, see 2:4; on **scribes and Pharisees**, see 5:20; 15:1 from Jerusalem; on **Pharisees**, see 3:7 and Josephus, *JW* 2.410-14, for their alliance with the chief priests and "powerful" or "notable" citizens in support of Rome. The two groups will be the particular focus of the curses in 23:13, 15, 23, 25, 27, 29.

Scholars usually interpret their **sitting on Moses' seat** and the reference to **doing whatever they say** as indicating their teaching role in *interpreting* scripture (with the **seat** perhaps being a piece of synagogue furniture). On this common reading, their teaching/interpretation is to be listened to, while their failure to practice what they preach is condemned in v. 3.

But this contrast is not convincing. It is not clear that **sitting on Moses' seat**, whether understood literally or metaphorically, refers to teaching and interpreting. The gospel's audience knows by this stage that the religious elite's teaching is not legitimate. Jesus has repeatedly declared their teaching to be wrong. See 9:10-13, associating with "sinners"; 12:1-14, sabbath; 15:1-20, hand washing and offerings; 19:3-12, divorce. He has warned disciples against it (16:1-12). He has declared that the leaders do not originate with God (15:13-14). They are failures in overseeing God's vineyard (21:33-45), and full of evil (9:4; 12:39, 45; 16:4; 22:18). They are a source of temptation (16:1; 19:3; 22:18); their teaching lacks authority (7:29). After all of this, Jesus does not now suddenly commend their teaching.

The verb **to sit** has other meanings, such as exercising rule or authority (see 5:1; 19:28; 20:21, 23; 25:31). M. A. Powell suggests that Jesus is not talking here about their teaching. Rather, Jesus acknowledges (without endorsing) their "powerful social and religious position that they occupy in a world where most people are illiterate and copies of the Torah are not plentiful."[11] Since the beginning of the gospel their power to shape society and human actions has been emphasized. They are based in Jerusalem, as part of the political and religious elite (2:4; 15:1). Jesus recognizes their powerful political, religious, and social position, before he goes on to attack it. The chapter collects examples of how they misuse their authority. What, then, is it that **they say** if it is not their teaching? Part of their power lies in citing the scriptures, and using it to legitimate their agenda. That is how they are introduced (2:4-6), and it has been prominent in the previous chapters (19:7; 22:24 [Moses], 42; 27:6). While they cite the scriptures, Jesus frequently condemns them for not knowing how to interpret them (12:3, 5; 19:4, 8-9; 21:16; 22:29, 44-45). He is the right interpreter of scripture.

The disciples and crowds, then, are to **do or keep** what the religious leaders **say** only in the sense of obeying what they *read from scripture*, but not in terms of their interpretation. Disciples and the crowds are not to **do as they do, for they do not practice what they preach.** The leaders read accurately from scripture, but they cannot interpret or enact it (22:29). They are hypocrites (6:2, 5, 16; 15:7; 22:18) who do not do in public the will of God as revealed in scripture. The accusation of hypocrisy is a standard feature in Greco-Roman and Jewish polemic against opponents (Plutarch, "Reply to Colotes," *Moralia* 1117D; *Pss. Sol.* 4:6-7; 1QS 4:14; Philo, *Gaium* 162; Josephus, *Con Ap* 2.71, 142-44).

• 23:4

Jesus provides an example of their wrong practice. **They tie up heavy burdens hard to bear, and lay them on the shoulders of others; but they themselves are unwilling to lift a finger to move them.** (1) The **heavy burdens**

hard to bear are their teachings concerning meal regulations (9:10-13), restrictive sabbath limitations (12:1-14), and required hand washing (15:2), which Jesus has attacked because they hinder doing mercy and good (9:13; 12:7, 12). His subsequent comment in 23:23 suggests that they miss the big picture of doing God's will of "justice and mercy and faith." (2) The elite do not help people carry these burdens. They seem indifferent to the harmful effect of their teaching on people. They lack mercy in wielding their considerable social and religious power. (3) In contrast, Jesus' teaching is light (11:28-30) and his presence constant (18:20; 28:20).

• 23:5-7

A second example of their wrong practice follows. They have wrong motivation (23:5a): **They do all their deeds to be seen by others**. Jesus has warned disciples against this desire for public glory (see 6:1-18). Compare Josephus's critique of the Pharisees for taking pride in their observance (*Ant* 17.41). They lack Jesus' motivation of a life of service (20:26-28). The quest for public approval (cf. *Pss. Sol.* 4:2) is also a common polemical theme that writers like Dio, Epictetus, and Lucian use against opponents.[12]

Jesus offers five examples of their misguided efforts to impress others. (1) **For they make their phylacteries long and their fringes long**. The **phylacteries** were boxes containing scriptures which they wore on the arm or forehead (so Exod 13:9, 16; Deut 6:4-9; 11:18-21). While they might express genuine faithfulness, here long boxes are interpreted as drawing attention to the wearer's piety.[13] The **fringes** are tassels worn on the corners of the outer garment (Num 15:38-39; Deut 22:12). Jesus wears them in 9:20; 14:36, so the critique is not against the practice itself, but against the alleged misuse to which it is put. Their misuse reflects their misinterpretations of scripture (15:1-9; 19:3-12; 22:29, 41-45).

(2) **They love to have the best place at the banquets**. Public meals attest someone's social status by type and quantity of food and drink they are served, type of tableware, and seating order (see 9:10-13). The **best place** was the "place of honor at a dinner beside the master of the house or the host" (BAGD, 725). The emphasis on **love** for public honor is damning. Jesus had summarized the law in terms of love (different verb) not for one's own honor but for God and neighbor (22:37-39).

(3) The same behavior is evident in the synagogue: **they love to have the best seats in the synagogue.**

(4) It is evident in the marketplace: **they love to be greeted with respect in the marketplace.** Greeting recognizes one's importance. Contrast the dishonorable images used for disciples in chapters 19-20: eunuch, children, the poor, slave.

(5) **And to have people call them rabbi**. The meaning and use of **rabbi** is not clear in the late first century. It seems to have been a general term of honor which could also mean a teacher or authoritative leader, meanings that became prominent in the developing rabbinic tradition.[14]

• 23:8-12

By contrast, the community of disciples is not to seek public glory.

• 23:8

The contrast is emphasized by the emphatic pronoun in the opening **But you**. Three imperatives and explanations follow. **You are not to be called rabbi**. In keeping with the alternative, more egalitarian, nonhierarchical ethos of the community/household of disciples (20:12, 25-28; chs. 19-20), there is to be no elevated public rank. **For you have one teacher** who is Jesus (9:11; 10:24-25; 17:24; 26:18; 23:10), **and you are all brothers and sisters**. The family image is again invoked for the community, a family defined not by birth order, ancestry, or gender, but by Jesus' call (4:18-22), doing God's will (12:46-50), and here recognizing Jesus' authority to shape the life of the community. The **all** is emphatic and inclusive.

• 23:9

A second imperative continues the contrast. **Call no one your father on earth**. The term **father** denotes religious, imperial, and social authority (see 5:16, 45; Introduction, section 1). In addition to the head of the patriarchal household (see 19:13-15), it referred to Zeus (see 5:16), to religious teachers (Prov 4:1; Sir 3:1; 4 Macc 7:1, 5, 9, 11), to the emperor (the senate calls Augustus the *Pater Patriae*, father of the fatherland; Statius calls Domitian "father of Rome" and "of the world" [*Silv* 4.8.20; 3.4.48]), and to patrons of *collegia* or voluntary associations.[15] Included among the latter was the Mithras mystery cult, a culturally conformist group "which replicated . . . the systems and values of the secular" and was particularly supported by soldiers and imperial personnel. The title "Father" was given to those who had achieved the highest of the cult's seven grades and who bore the greatest authority among its members.[16]

But the gospel bans such authority from this community (20:25-28). Its theology shapes a very different, alternative social reality. **For you have one Father, the one in heaven.** On God as the **Father** of the community, see 5:16, 45, 48; 6:9; 11:25-27. This **one Father** means all disciples are equal as brothers and sisters (12:46-50). Again we have the ironic situation in which the gospel resists a dominant cultural structure and seeks to establish an alternative, yet uses the language of the dominant culture to do so and creates a cosmic patriarchy. While people do not have authority over others, God the Father has all authority, even though God's intent is life-giving and loving to all (5:45-48).

• 23:10

A third imperative and explanation follow to reinforce the community's egalitarian social structure. **Nor are you to be called instructors/tutors, for you have one instructor/tutor, the Messiah.** The term **instructor/tutor** is a title of honor, which denotes a personalized learning relationship.[17] Disciples are also banned from using this title. This is the only time in the gospel Jesus refers to himself as **Messiah**. See 1:1. The third command against formal authority structures may indicate an attempt to resist a trend among the gospel's audience in this direction.

• **23:11-12**

Two generalized exhortations to continued status reversal conclude the section. **The greatest among you will be your servant**. The exhortation repeats previous material on humility and the servant identity of the community (18:1-6; 19:13-15; 20:20-28). The experience of the social margins, not the centers of power, shape this community. So too does its eschatological destiny. **All who exalt themselves will be humbled, and all who humble themselves will be exalted** (cf. 11:23; 18:4). The future passives indicate God's action in the judgment. See 7:13 for discussion of the functions of eschatological scenarios.

23:13-36—SEVEN WOES AGAINST THE PHARISEES

Jesus the prophet (cf. 21:11) delivers seven woes against the religious elite. The woes demonstrate the eschatological humbling of the socially and religiously powerful elite (23:2) who are not God's planting (15:13-14). If beatitudes indicate what is desirable and honorable for the community of disciples (see 5:3-12), then these woes indicate what is dishonorable, illegitimate, and unacceptable. The woes continue the task of distinguishing the two groups, delegitimating the scribes and Pharisees and legitimating the community of disciples. For woes in the prophetic tradition as public denunciations of unresponsive people, see 11:20-24.[18] Four observations can be made about their content:

1. While the religious leaders are condemned in chapters 21-22 for not recognizing Jesus' authority, the emphasis in the first six woes falls on their inappropriate practices which hinder God's purposes. The seventh woe highlights their response to Jesus. The two emphases show their lack of legitimacy.

2. The condemned practices present the perspective and verdict of one group about another. We can be quite sure that no faithful Pharisee sought to lock people out of God's empire or consign their converts to hell or evade God's will. Quite the reverse in fact. But the verdict of the gospel's writer is that that was the effect of their action. This is, of course, an opinion, a point of view, impressionistic polemic. Inner motives and eschatological effects cannot be derived from verifiable data.

3. The content of the woes is not new. Jesus has accused the religious leaders of these failings previously (see comments on each woe). The concentrated repetition of the denunciations provides the impact.

4. The woes occur in pairs. The first two (23:13-15) emphasize the elite's destructive impact on others. The next two (23:16-24) show their ability to focus on minor things and miss the big picture of God's will. Woes 5 and 6 (23:25-28) emphasize the disparity between their outer religious acts and inner motives. The seventh woe (23:29-36) depicts a lengthy history of rejecting God's messengers, including Jesus.

• 23:13

The first woe condemns them for excluding others from God's empire.[19] **But woe to you scribes and Pharisees, hypocrites!** The **woe** (see 11:20-24) is directed against and addressed to the scribes and Pharisees (**you**). It is not clear if they are present and silent (22:46) or if they are spoken about to the crowds and disciples (23:1). Either way the material is for the benefit of the community of disciples; the **you** is accusatory. On **hypocrites** as playing a public role, see 6:2, and 15:7; 22:18 for previous denunciations as hypocrites.

For you lock people out of the empire of heaven. For you do not go in yourselves, and when others are going in, you stop them. The image of **locking people out** recalls 16:19, where the keys of God's empire are given to Peter. He has the authority and task to keep its gates open to allow people access to God's empire by its proclamation and demonstration. In contrast, the religious leaders shut themselves and others out. Cf. Baruch's instruction to the priests to return the keys of the temple to God because they are "false stewards" (*2 Bar* 10:18).

Their effect on others is emphasized by being mentioned twice. How they prevent themselves and others from **going in** is not stated (cf. 5:20). The context of 23:4-7 (and chs. 12-16) suggests that their teaching does it by laying heavy burdens on others, and their desire to impress others disqualifies them because they miss the big picture of "justice, mercy, and faith," which constitute a life of doing God's will. Moreover, they do not recognize Jesus as God's anointed (9:33-34; 12:23-24; 21:15, 28-22:46), and so they do not exhort others to follow him and encounter God's reign. On **going into/entering** God's empire, verbs which link the doing of Jesus' teaching with eschatological destiny, see 5:20; 7:13, 21; 18:3, 8, 9; 19:17, 23.[20]

• 23:15

The second woe also emphasizes their harmful impact on others. They make them miss God's purposes. It begins the same way: **Woe to you scribes and Pharisees, hypocrites! For you cross sea and land to make a single convert, and you make the new convert twice as much a child of hell as yourselves.** Conversion to Judaism and/or to a particular Jewish group including Pharisaism is well attested.[21] The term **convert** in the LXX denotes foreigners or resident aliens who live permanently with a clan (Exod 22:21; 23:9) and are included in the religious life of the people including the covenant (Deut 29:10-14). They observe the sabbath (Exod 20:10; 23:12; Deut 5:14) and festivals such as Weeks (Deut 16:10-11) and Booths (Deut 16:13). Subsequently in Hellenistic Jewish writings the term comes to denote Gentiles who convert to Judaism and submit to Torah (Jdt 14:10; Josephus, *Ant* 18.82; Philo, *Somn* 2.273; *Spec Leg* 1.51-52, 308-9). The requirements of conversion, though, were variously understood. Not all groups required communal commitment in the manner of Qumran. The Ammonite Achior converts and is circumcised (Jdt 14:10), while others such as King Izates of Adiabene initially resist circumcision but are subsequently persuaded (Josephus, *Ant* 20.34-48). Josephus reports "multitudes of Greeks" being attracted to religious ceremonies in Antioch "and these they had in some measure incorporated with themselves" (*JW* 7.45). Horace (*Sat* 1.4, 139-43) and Tacitus comment negatively on Jews "compelling" others to join them. They view this act as one which threatens societal order by undermining religion, patriotism and households. Jews teach Gentile converts to "despise the gods, to disown their country and to regard their parents, children and brothers as of little account" (*Hist* 5.5).[22]

Matthew does not object to mission and converting efforts since disciples are instructed to do the same (ch. 10; 28:18-20). The problem is the impact of the Pharisees' work and teaching. If they cannot interpret and discern God's purposes and not acknowledge Jesus as Messiah, then their converts do not receive, in the gospel's perspective, what they need to enter God's empire. Their destination is **hell/Gehenna** (see on 5:22).

• 23:16-17

The third (23:16-22) and fourth (23:23-24) woes change focus from harmful impact to misguided teaching and practice, which Jesus has previously attacked (12:1-14; 15:1-20; 16:1-12). The third woe attacks their use (or misuse) of oaths. Distinctions of binding and nonbinding oaths (23:16-17, 18-19) miss the point of doing God's will. They are a means of evading God's will and exposing their users as people intent on doing so. On oaths, see 5:33-37, where Jesus deems them unnecessary for disciples. Here the elite's use of them is assumed but not made normative for disciples. A different introduction is used: **Woe to you blind guides.** The term recalls 15:14 and emphasizes their misleading teaching, a common element of polemic against other groups (see introduction to ch. 23). On **blind**, see 20:29-34.

The elite's teaching is summarized and ridiculed. They **say, "Whoever swears by the sanctuary is bound by nothing, but whoever swears by the gold of the sanctuary is bound by the oath."** A carefully formulated explanation for the distinction may exist,[23] but the absence of any rationale leaves the assertion of a distinction unsupported and ridiculous. Why should **the gold of the sanctuary** (highlighted as the only difference between two very parallel **whoever** clauses) be binding but **the sanctuary** is not? The distinction seems arbitrary (what about the gold makes it so special?). It raises suspicions about the group's sincerity.

The condemnation is harsh (**You blind fools!**). On **blind** as standard polemic, see introduction to chapter 23. **For which is greater, the gold or the sanctuary that has made the gold sacred?** The question is of course rhetorical, since the opponents are not present to offer a defense. The question offers a counter perspective which suggests that temple and gold are of equal importance (23:21). The absence of a rationale or response renders the practice ridiculous and suggests that those who teach it are more interested in avoiding obligations than in fulfilling them.

• 23:18-19

This method of attack is repeated. Another fine distinction is named, left unsupported, and mocked. Again the teaching of the elite is initially quoted.

**And you say, "Whoever swears by the altar is bound by nothing, but who-
ever swears by the gift that is on the altar is bound by the oath."** No reason
for distinguishing **altar** and **gift** is offered, but it is condemned. **How blind you
are!** (23:17; 15:14). **For which is greater, the gift or the altar that makes the
gift sacred?** The unanswered question suggests that any attempt to distinguish
them is suspect and evasionary.

• **23:20-22**

Jesus has already indicated in 5:33-37 that oaths are not necessary. Speech
should have integrity. There is no place for avoiding commitments and God's
will by ingenuine oaths. So what follows in vv. 20-22 is not alternative or contradictory teaching on the right use of oaths. Jesus has forbidden oaths. Rather
these verses elaborate the arbitrary nature of the practice of binding and nonbinding oaths and explain what is wrong with the religious leaders' approach.

So whoever swears by the altar, swears by it and everything on it. This
is not an instruction to swear by the altar, but a rebuttal of the distinction
claimed in vv. 18-19. Gift and altar are interconnected. To swear by one is to
swear by the other. Likewise in v. 21, **whoever swears by the sanctuary,
swears by it and by the one who dwells in it.** This is a rebuttal of the distinction between the sanctuary and its gold in v. 17. Their oneness is asserted since
God, who is understood to reside there (Ps 135:21), makes the sanctuary special and the oath binding. Verse 22 reinforces the point; **whoever swears** by any
sacred object or place, whether temple or **by heaven, swears by the throne of
God, and by the one who is seated on it.** They are rendered sacred by God's
presence; there is no room for hair-splitting or evading commitment. Jesus'
comments show the untenability of their practice and interpretation of God's
will.

• **23:23-24**

The fourth woe emphasizes their missing the big picture of doing God's will.
Again they misinterpret and wrongly teach and practice God's will (so also
12:1-14; 15:1-20).

The introduction returns to the first two woes (23:13, 14): **Woe to you
scribes and Pharisees, hypocrites! For you tithe mint, dill, and cummin.**
Their practice of tithing herbs extends the commands to tithe (give a tenth of)
flocks, wine, grain and oil, to support Levites, temple, and the poor (Lev 27:30-
33; Num 18:21-32; Deut 14:22-29; 26:12-15; Mal 3:8-12). These texts do not
mention tithing herbs. Jesus recognizes the extension, but notes that it has come
at the neglect of what Jesus considers to be more serious matters: **and have
neglected the weightier matters of the law: justice and mercy and faith.**
Twice Jesus has summarized the tradition in terms of love for God and neighbor (7:12; 22:37-39). These qualities of **justice and mercy and faith** comprise
dimensions or expressions of love.

Justice (κρίσις, *krisis*) denotes the eschatological day of accountability for
doing or neglecting God's will (5:22; 10:15; 11:22, 24; 12:36, 41, 42). In 12:18,
20, Jesus' task is the proclamation of **justice**, which is to be understood in rela-

tion to his proclamation of God's empire or reign (4:17). In the LXX, the term frequently translates the Hebrew *mišpaṭ,* which refers to fair judicial processes for the great and little, wealthy and poor (Lev 19:15; Deut 1:17), rescue for the oppressed, and advocacy and protection for the widow, orphan, weak, and poor (Isa 1:17, 21-23; 3:13-15). God's will of **justice** requires unexploited social relations and access to adequate resources, precisely the character of God's empire displayed in Jesus' teaching (cf. 5:3-12). The chapter began by noting the religious leaders' exalted social position (23:2). They have not used it to effect **justice** and will be humbled (23:12; cf. 9:36 and Ezek 34).

Mercy, a divine requirement of covenant loyalty (*ḥesed*), indicates God's transforming favor, which, enacted by humans, extends through social and religious barriers to the desperate and needy. Mercy brings money, community, food, healing, forgiveness, a new life (see 9:13; 12:7; cf. 6:2-4; 9:27; 15:22; 17:15; 18:33; 20:30). The religious leaders exhibit its lack in 9:10-13; 12:1-8. **Faith** is openness to Jesus which seeks his power, trusting it to overcome obstacles and transform situations of need (8:10; 9:2, 22, 29; 15:28; 17:20; 21:21). The scribes and Pharisees have not shown **mercy** or **faith**; in fact they have contested and resisted Jesus' displays of merciful power among the poor and needy (9:3, 11, 34; 12:2, 14, 23-24). And by concentrating on "lighter matters" such as tithing herbs they have missed these **weightier matters** and not produced them from the vineyard (21:43). **It is these you ought to have practiced without neglecting the others**. Jesus does not indicate that they should not bother with tithing. This is upheld, but it is a lesser matter.

Again they are condemned as **blind guides**; so 23:16, 19 (cf. 15:14). Their teaching is misleading; they are unreliable guides who lead people not into the empire of God but into hell (23:13-15). **You strain out a gnat but swallow a camel!** While the language is witty, hyperbolic, and ridicules the elite, it is derived from several important pieces and closely fits v. 23. (1) In Lev 11:41 swarming creatures like gnats are not to be eaten. (2) The verb **strain out** concerns filtering wine to remove impurities (Plutarch, "Table Talk," *Moralia* 692D; Amos 6:6). (3) Camels are not to be eaten (Lev 11:4; Deut 14:7). So while the Pharisees and scribes seek to be obedient in the tiniest detail, they err by overlooking and thereby neglecting big matters (**swallow a camel**).

• 23:25-26

The fifth and sixth woes change focus from misdirected teaching and practice to a disparity between their inner and outer lives. Yet there is some continuity. Their focus on public appearance rather than integrity evidences their ability to neglect the more weighty matters (23:23). The opening is the same as that of three of the previous four woes (except the third in 23:16), **Woe to you, scribes and Pharisees, hypocrites!**

The washing of plates and cups is a metaphor for their lives. **For you clean the outside of the cup and plate, but inside they are full of plunder and self-indulgence.** There is a disparity between their public appearance (**clean**) and their inner life, which is marked by **plunder**. This strong term refers to violation of neighbors by robbery (Lev 6:2), to imperial oppression by violent attack, exile, and slaughter (Tob 3:4; Jdt 2:11; 1 Macc 13:34; 4 Macc 4:10; cf. Josephus, *JW* 1.34), and to the acts of "the elders and princes" and legislators who take away the rights and spoil of the poor, orphans, and widows for themselves (Isa 3:14 [taxes?]; 10:2). See also Heb 10:34; Josephus, *Ant* 5.25; *T. Jud.* 23:3. The term denotes social, political and religious exploitation and violence, the misuse of power to oppress others and benefit oneself (Matt 21:13). The leaders are charged with this abuse (9:36; cf. Ezek 34). They have ignored justice, mercy, and faith in their interpretation and living of God's will.

The second term, **self-indulgence/lack of self-control**, refers to various unrestrained actions, whether imperial and religious persecution (Josephus, *JW* 1.34 [Antiochus Epiphanes]), sexual activity (Josephus, *Ant* 8.191 [Solomon]; *Con Ap* 2.244; 1 Cor 7:5) or intemperate accusations (Josephus, *Con Ap* 1.319 [Lysimachus]). Both terms are standard accusations in polemics (*Pss. Sol.* 4:1-5; *T. Levi* 14.5-6; *T. Mos.* 7.5-10), as is the more basic issue of hypocrisy (23:13, 15, 23, 25, 27, 29).[24] The failure of the religious elite (23:2) to **clean** their inner lives contrasts them with the marginals who cry out to Jesus for cleansing (8:2-3; 10:8; and 11:5).

Their inability to discern what is more important (integrity rather than religious/social window dressing) identifies them as a **blind Pharisee** (singular). See 23:16, 17, 19. Their practice and their teaching are misguided and misleading. Instead of public pretense, Jesus orders them to **first cleanse the inside of the cup and of the plate, that the outside also may be clean**. The focus on the **inside** parallels Jesus' previous concern with the heart, the center of human willing, deciding, doing, commitment (see 15:11, 18-19; 5:8; 6:21; 12:34; 22:37).

• 23:27-28

The beginning of this sixth woe (**Woe to you, scribes and Pharisees, hypocrites!**) remains the same, as does the condemnation (the lack of integrity), though the memorable metaphor changes. **For you are like whitewashed tombs, which on the outside look beautiful, but inside they are full of the bones of the dead and all kinds of filth.** The contrast of outside appearance that covers over a repulsive inside continues. **So you also on the outside look righteous to others, but inside you are full of hypocrisy and lawlessness**. The public image of being **righteous** (faithful to God's will, so 1:19; 3:15; 5:6, 10, 20, 45) betrays a fundamental unfaithfulness. The term **lawlessness** has described people who do not enter God's empire and face condemnation (7:21; 13:41) and names a characteristic of the time immediately before the end (24:12). The irony of the term here is its use for a group that defines itself in relation to Moses (23:2) but which does not know or correctly interpret or live the scriptures (cf. 22:29).

• 23:29-30

The same beginning marks the seventh and final woe (23:29-36), **Woe to you, scribes and Pharisees, hypocrites!** Verses 29-30 provide three statements which name actions and words that supposedly honor the prophets and righteous. But v. 31 shows these acts to be false and self-incriminating.

(1) **For you build the tombs of the prophets and** (2) **you decorate the graves of the righteous**. Tombs for Isaiah, Ezekiel, Haggai, and Zechariah are mentioned (*Lives of Prophets* 1.9-13; 3.3-4; 14.2; 15.6). Josephus refers to fine tombs for Abraham's family (*JW* 4.532) and for David (*Ant* 7.392-94). Note also the Maccabean tomb monument, high with polished stone and pyramids (1 Macc 13:27-30). This honoring of the prophets sits uneasily with some previous references to prophets (including John and Jesus) in which the elite persecute or reject them (5:12; 10:41 in context of 10:34-39; 14:5; 21:11, 46).

(3) Not only do they honor them in death with building and decorating fine tombs, but they honor them in their words. **And you say, "If we had lived in the days of our ancestors we would not have taken part with them in shedding the blood of the prophets."** As in 23:16, 18, their words are quoted to expose their falsity. The Pharisees plan to kill Jesus (12:14) and arrest him (21:46). The religious elite are named as those who will kill him (16:21; 20:18-19). Their present words and planned actions falsify any claims about different behavior in the past. For the tradition of killing the prophets, see Neh 9:26; 1 Kgs 18:4, 13; 19:10, 14; 2 Kgs 21:16; 2 Chr 36:15-21; *Lives of the Prophets* 1.1; 2.1; 3.2; 6.2; etc.; *Ascen. Is.* 1:9; 5:1-16; Josephus, *Ant* 10.38-39; Matt 5:10-12; Heb 11:37.

• 23:31-32

Jesus states the conclusion. **Thus you testify against yourselves that you are descendants of those who murdered the prophets.** On **murdering the prophets**, see 5:10-12; 23:30. Their plans in 12:14 and 21:46 to kill Jesus show that they are not guilty merely by association or descent. Rather, they actively continue this murderous tradition. The gospel has previously used this polemical technique of associating present opponents with well-known notorious figures or places from the past (11:20-24 [Tyre, Sidon, Sodom]; 24:37-39 [Noah's generation]). In other examples of this polemical technique, Josephus (*JW* 5.411, 566) compares pre-70 Jerusalem under attack by Rome to the sixth-century exile generation and to Sodom; *T. Levi* 14.6 also uses Sodom. To put Jesus to death will be an action consistent with their ancestors: **Fill up, then, the measure of your ancestors**. This act will complete "the fullness of their sins" (2 Macc 6:14) and bring God's punishment.

• 23:33

That punishment is certain. **You snakes, you brood/offspring of vipers! How can you escape being sentenced to hell/Gehenna?** John had warned them about eschatological punishment (see 3:7). Jesus' ministry is again linked with John's (cf. 3:2; 4:17). On the insulting questioning of their (illegitimate) origins, see 3:7; 15:13-14. Calling opponents **snakes** is also standard polemical fare (3:7; see Philo, *Gaium* 166, 205; *Pss. Sol.* 4:9). On **hell/Gehenna**, as the place of fiery punishment for the wicked, see 5:22, and 23:15. Declaring opponents to be destined for hell or condemnation in the judgment is common in the gospel (cf. 7:21-23, 26-27; 10:33; 11:24; 12:32, 41; 13:39-42, 49-50; 18:35; 22:11-14; 23:15) and in other polemical writings (1QS 2:7-9; *1 En* 62-63; *Pss. Sol.* 14:6-9).

• 23:34-36

The tradition of rejecting the prophets continues with these leaders. These three verses function as a transition section, concluding the woes and preparing for the lament on Jerusalem in 23:37-39.

• 23:34

This verse restates the tradition of "murdering the prophets" named in v. 31, which the religious leaders deny in v. 30. But now the tradition is updated to include their rejection of Jesus and the community of disciples.

The opening line sums up the tradition: **Therefore I send you prophets, sages, and scribes**. It emphasizes divine commissioning as the origin of those sent. God **sends** numerous slaves/prophets (see 21:34, 36), John (11:10), and Jesus (10:40; 15:24; 21:37) who **sends** disciples (10:5, 16). Who are the **prophets, sages, and scribes**? One possibility is to understand them as a chronological summary of salvation history, but the terms do not seem that precise. Previously in the gospel, the term **prophet** includes both Hebrew Bible prophets (killed by the elite; cf. 21:35; 22:6) and disciples (5:10-12; 10:41). Both **sages and scribes** have been used negatively (11:25; see 2:4; 7:29; 15:1, 13-14 [not planted by God]) without recognition of being sent by God (though disciples as scribes have been positively named in 13:52). It is preferable to see the terms, then, as referring to all those sent by God.

The rest of the verse, with four future tenses, focuses on the fate of Jesus and disciples at the hands of these leaders; **some of whom you will kill and crucify, and some you will flog in your synagogues and pursue from town to town.** Jesus has previously told disciples they will be **killed** as they engage in mission activity (10:28; 24:9). He has announced his own **killing** by the religious leaders allied with Rome (16:21; 17:23; 21:38-39; 26:4). He has also announced that he will be **crucified** (20:19; 26:2; see also 27:22, 23, 26, 31, 35; 28:5). He has warned disciples to expect to be **flogged in your synagogues** (10:17) and announced it will happen to him also (20:19). For **your synagogues** as an expression of distance, see 4:23, and as places of hostility, see 10:17. For disciples pursued **from town to town** in mission, see 10:23, and as an expression of persecution, see 5:10-12, 44.

• 23:35-36

Punishment is inevitable as v. 32 has indicated. These actions will "fill up their sins" and punishment follows, **so that upon you may come all the righteous blood shed on earth, from the righteous Abel to the blood of Zechariah, son of Barachiah, whom you murdered between the sanctuary and the altar.** The notion of filling up the sins explains why **all the righteous blood shed on earth** will be avenged on this group, including murders committed long ago such as **Abel** (Gen 4:10) and **Zechariah**. The identity of this Zechariah is difficult. The post-exilic prophet **Zechariah, son of Barachiah** named in Zech 1:1 does not seem to have been murdered, and he prophesied when the temple had not yet been rebuilt. A **Zechariah** murdered in 2 Chr 24:20-22 is son of Jehoiada. In favor of this last identity (perhaps confused with the prophet) is the observation that Abel is the first murder in the Hebrew canon and Zechariah in 2 Chr 24 is the last (2 Chronicles closes the Hebrew Bible). God will avenge all of this violence. **Truly I tell you** (see 5:18, 22 for a certain, authoritative declaration) **all this will come upon this generation**. The reference to **generation** does not condemn all the people (cf. 11:16; 12:39, 41; 16:4; 17:17; 24:34), since the whole chapter has been directed against the religious leadership. It is a chronological reference to the religious elite addressed by Jesus, which anticipates and interprets the fall of Jerusalem to Rome.

23:37-39—LAMENT AND HOPEFUL ANTICIPATION

• 23:37-39

The chapter closes with a lament against the leaders' city, **Jerusalem** (cf. Baruch's lament in *2 Bar* 10:6-19).[25] Previously, it has been identified as their center of power (2:1-12; 15:1), power that it is willing to use against children in resisting God's will (2:16-18). It is the place where Jesus is to die (16:21; 20:17-18), which dispatches religious leaders to conflict with him (15:1), and whose elite do not welcome Jesus (21:1-11). But while its leadership is resistant, its crowds are somewhat receptive in receiving John's baptism (3:5) and Jesus' healing (4:24). It remains God's city (5:35), a holy city (4:5; 27:53) called to serve God. The destruction of the city in 70 cannot, then, be seen as rejection of Israel as a whole. Judgment falls on its leaders, who mislead the people (21:12-13, 18-19, 41-43; 22:7; 27:25). Compare *2 Bar* 1-2; 9:1-2, where God warns of destruction of the sinful city so that "those like you" (the righteous) can escape.

Jesus addresses the personified city directly, **Jerusalem, Jerusalem**, and for the fourth time (23:30, 31, 34) describes it from the perspective of rejecting God's messengers, **the city that kills the prophets and stones those who are sent to it!** On **killing the prophets**, see 23:30; on **stoning**, see 1 Sam 30:6 [threatened against David]; 2 Chr 24:22-24 [Zechariah]; *4 Bar* 9:21-32 [Jeremiah]; Josephus, *Ant* 4.22. On **sent**, a passive denoting God's act, see 23:34.

Jesus expresses a longing for a positive response. **How often have I desired to gather your children together as a hen gathers her brood under her wings, and you were not willing/desiring!** The image of a bird's wings expresses God's merciful care and guidance (Deut 32:11), a refuge (Ruth 2:12; Ps 36:7) and protection from the wicked (Pss 17:8; 57:1). Defeated Jerusalem is a mother in *2 Bar* 3:1-3; 10:16, whose children have been taken into exile. Jesus' desire to **gather Jerusalem's children together** contrasts with the religious, political, and social divisions that the elite maintain (23:2). A fundamentally different vision of human society created by God's empire divides

Jesus and the leaders. But while Jesus **desired** this, the city's leaders did not **desire** it. The verb is the same in both instances and the same as 22:3, where the elite do not **desire** to come to the king's wedding feast (cf. also 23:4, "but they are unwilling . . . to move them").

• **23:38**

Accordingly there is condemnation. **See your house is left to you, desolate**. Is the **house** the temple or the city? In 21:13 it refers to the temple, and Jesus follows this statement with another in 24:1-3 proclaiming its imminent destruction. But in 23:37 he laments the city's downfall, not specifically the temple's. A rigid distinction cannot be drawn. Jesus refers to Rome's destruction of both Jerusalem and its temple in 70. Rome is God's instrument of punishment, but will subsequently also be subjected to God's punishment (see 21:12-13, 18-19, 41-43; 22:7; Introduction, section 9). The leaving of the temple/city **desolate** as a punishment for sin is a commonplace interpretation of the 587 B.C.E. defeat of Jerusalem and Babylonian exile. God has departed from the sinful people (1 Kgs 9:6-9; Isa 64:10-12; Jer 12:7; 22:5; Ezek 8:6). The fall of Jerusalem in 70 C.E. is similarly interpreted: "The Deity has fled from the holy places and taken His stand on the side of those with whom you are now at war" (Josephus, *JW* 5.412; 6.300; cf. also *2 Bar* 8:2; Tacitus, *Hist* 5.13).

Leaving the house **desolate** cannot be understood as God's final and utter rejection and abandonment of Israel. (1) Chapters 21-23 have concentrated on the elite's rejection. In 21:43 the vineyard remains, and the tenants responsible for it are replaced. (2) Chapter 23 concerns the religious leaders, the scribes, and Pharisees, not the whole populace. (3) The term **desolate** can also mean **a desert or wilderness** (BAGD, 309 no. 2). It is difficult to hear this term without thinking of the exodus or return from exile. The **desert/wilderness** is both a time of punishment and new beginnings. See 3:1 on John's preaching. (4) Verse 39 points to future hope.

• **23:39**

The focus moves to Jesus' death (**not see me again**) and return (**until**), in anticipation of a quite different reception from the leaders. **"For I tell you, you will not see me again until you say, 'Blessed is the one who comes in the name of the Lord.'"** Commonly this citation from Ps 118:26a is seen as a reference to Jesus' return in final judgment, in keeping with the condemnation of the rest of the chapter. But there are several problems with the emphasis on condemnation. The verse should be read as a reference to Jerusalem's final salvation (cf. 13:34-35).

1. In 21:9 the Galilean crowd cites Ps 118:26a positively in welcoming Jesus to Jerusalem. To attribute an opposite meaning to the same verse two chapters later is difficult to sustain.

2. Psalm 118 celebrates deliverance and God's steadfast love. Its use here to denote judgment would be odd. God's steadfast love delivers the people from their enemies.

3. Their welcome for the one who comes in the name of the Lord happens "from the house of the Lord" (Ps 118:26b). Clearly in chapter 23, those presently responsible for God's house (temple or city) do not welcome this one. Hence the judgment of v. 38. The scene of blessing and welcoming of the one who comes in the name of the Lord in v. 39 must denote another time. What is that time?

4. The verb for **blessed** occurs in contexts in which people recognize God's presence and favor (14:19; 21:9; 26:26). Especially to be noted is 25:34, where it indicates God's eschatological favor.

5. By contrast, those not favored, those who are condemned in the eschaton, do not bless. They weep and gnash their teeth (13:42, 50; 24:51), language that is absent from here. This is a scene of eschatological salvation.

6. G. N. Stanton has highlighted a threefold pattern of "sin-exile-return" in Deuteronomic and Christian writings (Justin, *Dialogue* 108; *Testaments of the Twelve Patriarchs* [with Christian editing]). This pattern interprets the events of 70 as punishment for sin and expresses the hope of Israel's future conversion or return to God. He suggests that this pattern is present in 23:37-39. Here the sin and punishment have been outlined to the end of v. 38. Verse 39 points to Israel's leaders welcoming the Messiah at his return.[26] W. D. Davies and D. C. Allison agree but argue further, on the basis of reading **until** as conditional, that Jesus' return is contingent on the leaders blessing him. When they bless him, Jesus will return.[27] There is no final rejection of Israel or its leaders. God remains faithful to the covenant promises. The verse anticipates their salvation.

CHAPTER 24

Jesus' Fifth Teaching Discourse

The Final Establishment of God's Empire (Part 1)

After three chapters of bitter conflict between Jesus and the religious leaders (chs. 21-23), and before the elite's final act of crucifying him (chs. 26-27), Jesus addresses his disciples (chs. 24-25). Jesus takes up the role of eschatological prophet or seer to announce signs of his return, or *parousia*, and the establishment of God's empire (24:3).[1] This is Jesus' fifth, and final, major teaching discourse (chs. 5-7 [Sermon on the Mount]; ch. 10 [mission instruction]; ch. 13 [parables]; ch. 18 [community instruction]).

There has been much debate about the content of Jesus' teaching in these two chapters. (1) D. Garland, for example, sees 24:3-35 as Jesus' answer to the disciples' first question about the timing of the destruction/judgment of the temple (24:2-3). These verses concern the pre-70 situation leading up to the temple's destruction in 70 C.E., while the following verses (24:36-25:46) answer their second question about the end of the age. In a time of testing and decision, disciples are exhorted to be faithful.[2] But this approach is not convincing. While some parts of 24:3-35 may evoke events surrounding the fall of Jerusalem (see commentary below), they are not restricted to that time period. Verses 6-14, 20-22, 23-24, 27-31 provide examples of elements that refer to, but are not exhausted by, the events of 70 C.E.

(2) D. Hagner thinks the chapter is concerned with both the fall of Jerusalem and the parousia, but the two events are not to be separated. Both are imminent. The questions of v. 3 indicate that the temple's destruction means Jesus' return and the end of the age.[3] Three factors render this approach unconvincing. The gospel's likely origin in the 80s separates destruction and return. Other references to Jesus' return do not include the destruction of Jerusalem (see n. 1). And the gospel's reference to the fall of Jerusalem in 22:7 locates the event in an ongoing history (sending out more invitations), not in relation to the return of Jesus.

(3) Another approach (D. J. Harrington, J. Gnilka) sees the events of chapters 24-25 in the eschatological future.[4] The events of 70 are not in view. The

chapters depict the last days of the age still in the future. But it is difficult to imagine that, for example, references to false messiahs and prophets (24:4-5, 11, 23-24) and to wars (24:6-7 bears no relation to the events of 66-70, at least in part, or that references to persecution and mission (24:9-10, 14) do not relate to the present experience of Jesus' disciples.

(4) The inability to divide the material's referents between Jerusalem's fall and Jesus' return, as well as the futility of trying to exclude any reference to contemporary happenings, commends an approach which embraces all of these elements within an overarching category. Davies and Allison argue more convincingly that the chapters depict "the entire post-Easter period, interpreted in terms of the messianic woes . . . [The chapters concern] the past, the present, and the future. What has happened will continue to happen and only get worse" until the return of Jesus.[5] The present, which stretches from Jesus' ministry to his return, is a time of tribulation or woes which will end with Jesus' return. This time of tribulation impacts all disciples, Jew or Gentile.[6]

The disciples' double question in 24:3 is answered, then, in these terms. The destruction of the temple is part of these woes or tribulation which point toward Jesus' return, which could occur at any time. Disciples are to be faithful and watchful. Numerous Jewish apocalyptic texts expect natural catastrophes, wars, and increased evil prior to the final establishment of God's reign (*Jub.* 23:8-25, 26-31; *4 Ezra* 4:51-5:13; 8:63-9:4; *2 Bar* 24-28).

The function of the chapter is diverse. D. Sim argues that Matthew's apocalyptic material, content that discloses the final establishment of God's empire, has five functions (see 7:13).[7] (1) Chapters 24-25 continue the dualistic understanding of the world. They again identify Matthew's community as the righteous community, and all those opposed to it and Jesus as the unrighteous. This division serves to legitimate the identity and way of life of the marginalized community of disciples within God's cosmic purposes. (2) The chapters explain the current difficult circumstances of suffering which the community of disciples faces in relation to other Jewish communities and the Roman empire. Their conflicts and adversity are placed in a cosmic context, are shown not to be a surprise or a defeat, and are depicted as temporary before the certain triumph of God's purposes. (3) The chapters thereby offer hope and encouragement. The present is not permanent. It requires faithfulness and watchfulness in the knowledge that God's glorious future is certain. (4) They also provide consolation. In the light of this future, the present distress is worth enduring whatever the cost. God will overcome all that opposes the community and God's purposes. One of the concerns of this chapter is the faithful survival of the community of disciples through these hardships. (5) The chapters foster group solidarity by controlling appropriate behavior (note the numerous imperatives), urging faithfulness, and offering eschatological rewards or punishment.

Such claims continue the fifth narrative block's attempts to delegitimize the elite. Chapter 23's denunciation of the Jewish religious leadership continues in this assertion of the ultimate triumph of the Son of Man whom they have rejected. By contrast, the reassertion of his return recalls the hope of 23:39 that Israel with new leaders will repent and welcome him. Moreover, Rome's claims to rule the world at the will of the gods and its means of conquering and forcibly subordinating all to its will, claims and means that were mocked by Jesus' entrance to Jerusalem (see 21:1-11), are placed in the context of God's cosmic purposes and shown to be false (see Introduction, section 9). E. Käsemann has argued that the basic question of apocalyptic material is, "To whom does the sovereignty of the world belong?"[8] Chapters 24-25 are an unequivocal assertion of God's ownership, God's right to determine cosmic destiny. Judgment falls on those who do not acknowledge God's sovereignty. Rome's empire, or any empire, is not ultimate. Eternal Rome is not the future (cf. *4 Ezra* 11:37-46). It is mortal (24:28) and subject to God's empire.

This critique of Rome gains some force because of the material's proximity to the struggle of 66-70. Rome's victory and destruction of Jerusalem suggest invincible power. But chapters 24-25 contextualize this power in God's purposes, thereby revealing it to be limited and under judgment (see 22:7). Moreover, as U. Mauser has argued, the frequent references to false prophets and messiahs (24:5, 11, 23-26) show that the chapter rejects the way of violence adopted by those who took up arms as the means of trying to throw off Roman oppression (see commentary below).[9] While the goal of liberation was commendable, the means was not. Armed revolution is a false way just as passive compliance was rejected previously in the gospel (see 5:38-42; 17:24-27). Ultimately God will bring the promised salvation through Jesus' return and the establishment of God's empire (so 1:21). In the meantime, the Matthean community is to live its alternative, countercultural existence of active, subversive, nonviolent resistance in the sure hope of God's coming triumph.[10]

On the basis of its subject matter, the chapter divides into six sections:

24:1-2	Jesus Predicts the Temple's Downfall
24:3-26	The Signs of Jesus' Return: Messianic Woes and Tribulation
24:27-31	The *Parousia:* The Coming of the Son of Man and the End of All Human Empires, especially Rome's
24:32-35	The Parable of the Fig Tree
24:36-44	The Unknown Time: Be Vigilant
24:45-51	The Parable of the Faithful and Wise Slave

24:1-2—JESUS PREDICTS THE TEMPLE'S DOWNFALL

• 24:1-2

Jesus entered the temple in 21:23 (the setting for 21:23-23:39). The end of his conflict with, and speech against, the religious leaders is marked by his departure (**As Jesus came out of the temple and was going away**) and by God's departure from the "deserted house" (see 23:38; 1:23; *2 Bar* 8:2; Josephus, *JW* 5.412; 6.300; Tacitus, *Hist* 5:13).

His disciples came (respectful approach; see 4:3, 11; 5:1; 8:2) **to point out to him the buildings of the temple.** Their approach and attention to the proverbially splendid temple (cf. Josephus, *JW* 5.184-226; 6.260, 267; Philo, *Gaium* 198) provide the context for his prophecy. **Then he asked them, "You see all these, do you not? Truly I tell you** (authoritative speech; see 5:18, 22), **not one stone will be left here upon another; all will be thrown down."** Jesus joins other rejected prophets (21:11) in predicting the temple's downfall (Mic 3:12; Jer 7:8-15; 9:9-11; Jesus son of Ananias in Josephus, *JW* 6.300-309; Baruch in *2 Bar* 1:4; 3:5).[11] His declaration means the demise of the priestly elite's central location, their religious, political, and economic power over people's lives. Not surprisingly, a form of this prediction will figure significantly in the elite's condemnation of Jesus in 26:61 and 27:40. The empire always strikes back.

The positioning of a prophecy which the gospel's audience knows was fulfilled by the events of 70 C.E. (cf. Josephus, *JW* 6.249-287; 7.1-4; *2 Bar* 10:2-3) at the outset of the chapter underlines the reliability of the rest of Jesus' words about God's purposes.

24:3-26—THE POST-EASTER ESCHATOLOGICAL WOES

Attention moves to the time between Jesus' resurrection and return.

• 24:3

Jesus' instruction is given **when he was sitting on the Mount of Olives**. For **sitting** as a position both of teaching/revelation and of ruling, see 5:1. For teaching on a **mountain**, see 5:1 (14:23; 15:29; 28:16; Exod 19:10-24:18; Ezek 40-48; *2 Bar* 4:5; 13:1). The setting on the **Mount of Olives** accentuates important themes in the discourse. The place is associated with a display of God's power and presence (glory; see Ezek 11:22-24). It is also a place of eschatological judgment and salvation in Zech 14:4 (cf. Matt 21:1, 5) in which "on the day of the Lord" (cf. Matt 7:22; 10:15), God enters the city, overcomes Israel's enemies, and establishes God's reign and era of peace. Jesus' presence and teaching anticipate that day. God's empire is being established but not yet in full.

The disciples came to him privately (17:1, 19; 20:17) **saying, "Tell us, when will this be** (the temple's destruction, 24:2), **and what will be the sign of your coming and of the end of the age?"** Other apocalyptic texts identify signs of the end (Dan 12:6-7; *4 Ezra* 4:33-35, 51-52; 5:1-2, 9-10; 6:7; 8:63; *2 Bar* 21:19; chs. 25-28). The question indicates that the disciples have understood some of Jesus' previous teaching about his return (10:23; 13:36-43, 47-50; 16:27-28; 19:28; 20:20-28; 23:37-39) and seek further instruction. It provides Jesus with an opportunity to offer insight into present circumstances, hope for the future, and clarity about the expected way of life in the meantime.

They call Jesus' **coming/arrival** a *parousia* (παρουσία; Latin, *adventus*). The term denotes presence (Jdt 10:18; Josephus, *JW* 4.345), but more importantly it has military (2 Macc 8:12; 15:21), political, and religious significance. It denotes the arrival of a king (Polybius, *Hist* 18.48.4), or emperor, governor, military commander (Josephus, *Vita*, 90-91), or other important official in a city or town (3 Macc 3:17; the *adventus* coins of Nero and Hadrian; see 21:1-11).[12] The arrival was often preceded by a special payment in tax or goods to cover expenses. The welcoming ceremony indicated submission to the official's power. In religious traditions, it refers to the appearing of a god or of God (to Elisha, Josephus, *Ant* 9.55), including God's "coming" to establish God's reign at the end of the age (Dan 7:13).[13] With this term, the gospel establishes Jesus' future **coming** as an event that asserts God's supreme authority (cf. 28:18), an event of life and blessing for those who welcome him but of condemnation and death for those who do not. Again the gospel employs imperial images to present the final establishment of God's empire.

On **the end of the age** as a time of judgment and establishment of God's empire, a time known only to God, see 13:39, 49; 28:20.

• 24:4-5

Jesus' response begins with a general warning, **Beware that no one leads you astray.** The concern with **leading astray** (common in other lists of signs preceding the end; *T. Moses* 7:4; *T. Levi* 10:2; 16, cf. Matt 27:63-64 describing Jesus) will be repeated three more times (24:5, 11, 24) in relation to false messiahs and prophets. The repeated warning indicates that the time before the end is one in which disciples are vulnerable. They are to remain focused on Jesus and to be discerning about various claimants.

Many will come in my name, saying, "I am the Messiah!" and they will lead many astray. Mauser links this saying in part to the 66-70 war and Josephus's account of numerous figures who across the century misled people by offering "release from prevailing horrors" (*JW* 6.286-88). Mauser notes Simon (*JW* 2.57-59), Athrongaeus (2.60-65), Menachem (2.433-40), and Simon bar Giora (4.503-13), who, though not claiming the title "Messiah," establish themselves as (or are regarded as) kings, an anointed figure, and resort to violent military action against the elite, both Roman and Jew. Jesus rejects their claims and methods. **Many** indicates a repeated and continuing phenomenon, and so a significant period of time. The warning against false messiahs and prophets echoes warnings against other groups and the religious elite who can lead the community astray (7:15; 10:17; 16:6, 11, 12).

• 24:6-7a

Jesus names a second feature typical of the final days. **And you will hear of wars and rumors of wars.** See Dan 11:2-45; *Jub.* 23:13, 20; *4 Ezra* 5:9; 6:24; 13:31; *2 Bar* 27:3, 5, 11-12; 70:3-4.

Numerous commentators cite Tacitus's reference (*Hist.* 1.2) to the period under review as being "terrible with battles, torn by civil struggles, horrible even in peace . . . there were three civil wars, more foreign wars, and often both at the same time." **See that you are not alarmed; for this must take place, but the end** (of the age, 24:3) **is not yet**. Jesus warns against misinterpreting the significance of wars. They do not threaten God's purposes or sovereignty (**this must take place**) nor signify **the end**. The war of 66-70 is included within the eschatological distress, but does not signal Jesus' coming. The messianic claimants are false because they misread the signs of the times. **For nation will rise against nation, and empire against empire**.

• 24:7b

A third feature involves disasters, **famines and earthquakes in various places**. A **famine** could result from natural phenomena (bad weather, disease, pests, poor seed/yield) or could result, as P. Garnsey demonstrates, from war, piracy, greedy trade practices, the control of resources by the elite, inept administration, and so on (see 12:1; 14:13-21).[14] **Famine** occurs in lists of signs (*4 Ezra* 6:22; *2 Bar* 27:6) as do **earthquakes** (Zech 14:5; *4 Ezra* 6:13-16; *2 Bar* 27:7; 70:8). Antioch suffers **earthquakes** in 37, 42, and 115 C.E., and **famine** in 46-47 C.E.[15] The plurals (wars, earthquakes, famines) emphasize recurring phenomena over a period of time.

• 24:8

These events are not the end but point toward it. **All this is but the beginning of the birth pangs.** The image of **birth pangs** for the new age which is being born out of the present distress or messianic or eschatological woes also occurs in Isa 13:8; 26:17-18; 66:7-8 (God's salvation); 1QH 3:7-10; *1 En* 62:4; *4 Ezra* 4:42. The image denotes the inevitability of this life-giving process, as well as the suffering associated with it.

• 24:9-14

A fourth sign that indicates the end is near but has not yet happened involves hostility toward disciples. **Then they will hand you over to tribulation and they will put you to death**. Who will do this is not specified, but the theme of persecution evokes 5:10-12; 10:16-31, 34-39; 13:21; 16:24-26; 21:34-36; 22:6; 23:34, where households, and the religious and political elite are responsible for persecuting disciples. On the polyvalent **hand you over**, see 17:22. In being **handed over** and **killed**, disciples imitate Jesus (10:28; 16:21; 17:22-23; 20:18-19; 21:35-39; 22:6; 23:34; 26:2). **You will be hated by all nations because of my name.** So 5:43-44; 10:22. Hostility is the normal reaction from the status quo to the disciples' mission of proclaiming and enacting the disruptive and transformative empire of God (5:3-12; 10:7-8).

• 24:10-12

Persecution can cause apostasy and division among disciples. **Then many will be made to stumble**, that is, to abandon their following of Jesus, a grave and serious matter with eschatological consequences. See the previous warnings in 5:29-30; 11:6; 13:21, 57; 15:12; 18:6-9. The disciples do precisely this in 26:31-33, 56. Such failure, though, is not final (so ch. 28).

They will betray one another and hate one another. See 10:21, 34-36; *4 Ezra* 5:9. The vulnerability to external pressure of this minority, alternative community is very evident. The warnings of increasing tribulation alert and prepare the community to remain faithful through them. The links with chapter

18 (stumbling, 18:6-9) invoke relationships which value other community members (18:10-14) and which look for reconciliation, not alienation (18:15-35). Only with such relationships, and the presence of God in their midst (1:23; 18:20; 28:20), encountered especially in spiritual disciplines like prayer (18:19-20; 6:1-18), can the community resist these pressures and prevent internal collapse.

• 24:11

One of the causes of the stumbling is repeated from 24:5. **And many false prophets will arise and lead many astray.** See 7:15. In opposing God's purposes they are agents of the devil. As noted in 24:5, Mauser suggests some reference to the pseudo-prophets so active in the 66-70 struggle with Rome. Josephus records many deceptive prophets (*JW* 6.286-88): "deceivers and imposters under the pretense of divine inspiration foster revolutionary changes [and look for] tokens of deliverance" (*JW* 2.258-59). Rome often responded with military violence. Josephus notes six thousand killed after being deceived by a false prophet into looking for deliverance in the temple (*JW* 6.283-85). See Matt 24:5, the Egyptian false prophet (Josephus, *JW* 2.261-63) and Theudas (*Ant.* 20.97-99).

• 24:12

And because of the increase in lawlessness, the love of many will grow cold. The term **lawlessness** (see 7:23; 13:41; 23:28) summarizes the growing tribulation and wickedness evidenced by false prophets, wars, famines, earthquakes, persecution, alienation and apostasy named in 24:3-12. **Love** that **grows cold** embraces both **love** for God and love for others (22:37-39), including persecutors (5:43-44) and other disciples (24:9-10).

• 24:13

By contrast to those who stumble (24:10) and whose love grows cold (24:12), **the one who endures to the end will be saved**. Again chapter 10 is recalled (so 10:22). In context, **enduring** means remaining faithful through the tribulation (cf. 4 Macc 1:11; *4 Ezra* 6:25), and expressing faith in Jesus (18:6) through obedient action, by not stumbling or breaking from the community and not letting one's love grow cold. Ethnicity, elevated socioeconomic status, or religio-political power does not effect salvation. The **end** is the arrival of Jesus (24:3, 6, 27-31; cf. 16:27-28; 19:28-30; 23:39). To be **saved** is to participate in the completion of God's purposes, which overcome all resistance to God's life-giving purposes (1:21; 19:25) and establish God's empire over all, including Rome, at Jesus' coming (24:3).

• 24:14

Hostility and persecution do not mean retreat from the world. The present is a time of mission activity and decision throughout the world. **And this good news of the reign/empire will be proclaimed throughout the world, as a testimony to all the nations.** The disciples **proclaim** (10:7) God's action manifested in Jesus. Those who are given an opportunity to hear the **good news** in the time before the coming are **all the nations,** Jew and Gentile, **throughout the world,** all the "inhabited **world**" (BAGD, 561).

The **good news of the reign/empire** consists of Jesus' announcement of the end of Rome's rule and the establishment of God's life-giving reign. See 4:23; 9:35. This **good news** of God's sovereignty competes with Rome's assertion of sovereignty over all the world. The news that Vespasian has become emperor is hailed as **good news** "from every quarter of the world"; Josephus uses the same term for **good news** (*JW* 4.655-56). But with its call to allegiance to God and declaration of the demise of all who refuse to acknowledge it (cf. 4:8), the gospel about God's empire challenges Roman imperial claims to control and rule the world. Like any empire, God's empire tolerates no rivals. The disciples' mission work is necessary to hasten the *parousia.* It is the means whereby people can repent and welcome God's agent (23:39) or reject him (10:18, 22). Hence the proclamation is **a testimony** to and against its hearers (cf. 8:4; 10:18). Various traditions envisage the conversion of the nations to God before the end (Isa 2:2-4; 25:1-9; Mic 4:1-8; Zech 8:20-23; Tob 13:10-12; 14:6-7; cf. Matt 8:11-12).

• 24:15-20

So far, four signs have marked the time of tribulation which stretches from Jesus' crucifixion to his return: false prophets and messiahs, wars, famines and earthquakes, and hostility to disciples. Endurance and proclamation are required. Jesus now offers a fifth, and more specific and immediate, sign which signals a change in circumstances and strategy. It is the time to flee.

So when you see the desolating sacrilege standing in the holy place, as was spoken of by the prophet Daniel (let the reader understand). The **desolating sacrilege** referred to by **Daniel** (Dan 8:9-27; 9:27; 11:31; 12:11; 1 Macc 1:54-59; 6:7; 2 Macc 6:1-5) was an altar to Olympian Zeus which the Seleucid tyrant Antiochus IV Epiphanes set up in the Jerusalem temple in 168-167 B.C.E. But the verse's evoking of this past event referred to by Daniel does not exhaust its referent. Unlike the numerous references to the fulfillment of what was previously spoken by or through a/the prophet/s (1:22; 2:15, 17, 23; 4:14; 8:17; 12:17; 13:35; 21:4; 26:56; cf. 3:3), this verse is not yet fulfilled. It points to another or future **desolating sacrilege** yet to be established.

In 40 C.E. Gaius Caligula had tried to establish a statue of himself in the temple (Josephus, *JW* 2.184-203; *Ant* 18.256-309; Philo, *Gaium* 188-98, 207; Tacitus, *Hist* 5.9), and in 70 Titus's troops sacrificed in the temple to their standards, which bore the empire's eagle, and hailed Titus as ruler (Josephus, *JW* 6.316). It is the way of tyrants to desecrate the temple and to flaunt their imperial authority in the face of God (cf. 17:25, "the kings of the world"). It will happen again. The events of 70 are not the end, though they are part of the tribulation leading to the end. The exhortation **let the reader understand** directs the audience's attention to this yet-future and unspecified key event. It is a sign of hope (Rome's downfall is imminent) but also of the community's flight in a time of intensified hardship and suffering.

• 24:16-19

When the desolating sacrilege is seen, **those in Judea must flee to the mountains**. The call to **flee** means not defending the city. Such a sacrilege in the temple indicates its defeat. But all is not finished. The term **mountains** or **hill country** is the location which God's people use so effectively in over-throwing the Canaanite overlords while occupying the land (Josh 2:22-23; Judg 1:19) and in resisting Antiochus Epiphanes (1 Macc 2:28). Flight is the means whereby Jesus (2:13) and the magi (2:12) escape Herod's violent persecution. Disciples are also to flee persecution from Gentile and Jewish opponents (10:17-18, 23; inappropriately in 26:59).[16]

The flight is urgent, like the escape from Pharaoh in Egypt (Exod 12:11-12, 33-36): **the one on the housetop must not go down to take what is in the house; the one in the field must not turn back to get a coat**. Possessions are abandoned; they must not impede disciples (cf. 6:19-34; 10:9-11; 13:22). **Woe to those who are pregnant and to those who are nursing infants in those days!** The flight brings particular hardships for these women (cf. the impact of imperial destructiveness in 2:18). The introductory **woe** suggests possible destruction (cf. 11:21; 18:7; 23:13, 15, 16, 23, 25, 27, 29; 26:24).

• 24:20

Pray that your flight may not be in winter/in the rainy and stormy season or on a sabbath. The first, **stormy or rainy weather** (16:3; BAGD, 879), presents obvious difficulties for flight. The **sabbath** has been variously inter-preted. G. N. Stanton summarizes six views:[17] (1) Strict sabbath observance would prohibit the flight. (2) The audience no longer strictly observes the sab-bath, so flight on a sabbath would draw attention to them. (3) The anachronis-tic verse, referring to earlier traditions, is no longer relevant to Matthew's (Gentile) audience. (4) The sabbath is to be honored so as not to offend other Jews, even though Matthew's community does not strictly observe it. (5) Flight on a sabbath would increase the tribulation. (6) The reference is anachronistic to the time of Jesus' disciples and irrelevant to the time of Matthew's audience.

Explanations (3) and (6) do not explain the verse in the gospel's final form; number (5) lacks support. Number (2) does not take sufficient note of diverse attitudes to the sabbath (compare Josephus, *JW* 2.392-94, and 634; cf. 1 Macc 2:29-41) but could be persuasive (so also numbers 1 and 4) if Matthew's audi-ence includes within it or lives in a setting with other Jews who observe the sab-bath strictly and "do not leave their place" on a sabbath (Exod 16:29). The dispute of 12:1-14 may support such a view since Jesus rejects a strict or pas-sive sabbath observance and advocates its active use for doing good and show-ing mercy. Flight on a sabbath would in this situation divide and expose the community to danger.

• 24:21

For at that time, presumably the time of the desolating sacrilege and the flight for safety, **there will be great suffering/tribulation** (13:21; 24:9, 29),

such as has not been from the beginning of the world until now, no, and never will be. The verse summarizes the intensified suffering surrounding their flight.

• 24:22

With the intensified tribulation, **if those days had not been cut short, no one would be saved; but for the sake of the elect those days will be cut short**. The **elect** names those who respond with active faith and an appropriate way of life to the call to participate in God's salvation (see 22:14). Some texts pray for God mercifully to speed the time of salvation (cf. the frequent appeal in the Psalms for God to act: Pss 68:1-2; 83; 94:1-7; Sir 36:8; *2 Bar* 20:1-2; 54:1; 83:1-2; *4 Ezra* 4:33-43.

• 24:23-25

The warning about false messiahs and prophets is repeated for the third time for emphasis (see 24:5, 11, especially for a connection with the 66-70 war). **Then if anyone says to you, "Look! Here is the Messiah!" or "There he is!"—do not believe it. For false messiahs and false prophets will appear and produce great signs and omens, to lead astray, if possible, the elect. Take note, I have told you beforehand.** The time before the end requires the community of disciples to be unbelieving about such figures. Even the display of miraculous powers does not guarantee a genuine figure (cf. 7:15-23; in Deut 13:1-5 false prophets test the people's loyalty). They have been forewarned. They should be neither surprised to witness such phenomena nor deceived by them. Instead their response is faithful endurance in the midst of the tribulation and suffering (24:13, 21), trusting/believing only the actions and teaching of Jesus (8:13; 9:28; 18:6; 21:22, 25, 32). His coming will be unmistakable (24:27, 30-31).

• 24:26

The warning continues. **So if they say to you, "Look! He is in the wilderness," do not go out.** The **wilderness** recalls Moses' wilderness miracles (e.g., Exod 14 [the sea]; Exod 16 [quails and manna]; Exod 17 [water]), John's testimony to Jesus (3:1-12), and the tradition especially evident in Josephus of figures who led people into the wilderness looking for God's liberation, often to be slaughtered by Rome (*JW* 2.259; 261-63; *Ant* 20.167, 188). This is not God's way to accomplish salvation from Rome.

If they say, "Look! He is in the inner rooms," do not believe it. The warning is repeated. In 6:6 the **inner room** is a place for prayer; here it is a place to be avoided. Throughout, **believing**, notably believing in Jesus, is the means of participating in God's salvific purposes (8:13; 9:28; 18:6; 21:22, 25, 32; 24:23). Believing in him precludes believing any false prophet or messiah, or proclamation about them. The community of disciples must remain firm in its commitment to Jesus.

24:27-31—THE *PAROUSIA:* THE COMING OF THE SON OF MAN AND THE END OF ALL HUMAN EMPIRES, ESPECIALLY ROME'S

• 24:27

How can disciples be sure that reports of false messiahs and prophets are wrong? How can they be sure that the method of armed revolt is not God's way of establishing God's empire? How can they be sure that they will not miss Jesus' coming? His coming will be so spectacular that no one will miss it. **For as the lightning comes from the east and flashes as far as the west, so will be the coming of the Son of Man**. The **east** is the place of origin of the marginal and Gentile magi in 2:1; **east and west** span the area from which the "many" come to the eschatological banquet in 8:11.

Lightning is often associated with divine appearances or theophanies which disclose God's presence and assert God's will and sovereignty (Exod 19:16; Ezek 1:13; Dan 10:5; Wis 5:15-6:11, esp. 5:21). Significantly, **lightning** is also closely associated with Jupiter/Zeus. It is often represented on the coins of emperors, including Domitian (81-96 C.E.), the likely emperor when this gospel was written.[18] **Lightning** wielded by emperors as Jupiter's designated agents symbolized Jupiter's rule and world order, which was manifested through the emperor in war and in the defeat of those who threatened Rome's way of life. The lightning "epitomized the entire conception of divine power exerted against the forces of barbarous hubris and on behalf of civilized existence."[19]

Or so the empire imagined it. By associating lightning with Jesus' coming, the gospel offers a counterperspective. Here **lightning** portrays not Jupiter's sovereignty, but *God's* power and sovereignty established over all things through Jesus' **coming** (*parousia*; see 24:3, 37, 39). Ironically, that which symbolized Rome's power is turned against Rome to signify the end of Rome's, or any, empire and the establishment of God's empire. On Jesus as **Son of Man**, see 8:20; 10:23; 13:37-43; 16:27-28; 19:28; 25:31; also Dan 7:13-14, where the "one like a Son of Man" seems to be either collective Israel or an angelic figure Michael; *1 En* 37-71; Matt 24:30, 36, 37, 39, 44 below).

• 24:28

The judgment on Rome is depicted in a graphic and clever saying which invokes a battle scene and involves multiple meanings. **Where the corpse is, there the eagles/vultures will gather.**[20] The term **eagles/vultures** usually designates birds of prey who feed on corpses (Job 9:26; 39:27-30; Prov 30:17; 4 Macc 9:15; cf. Seneca, *Ep* 95.43; Martial *Epig* 6.62.4). But **eagles/vultures** also denote imperial powers such as Babylon, who are instruments of God's judgment on God's people (Deut 28:47-53, esp. 49; Jer 4:13; Lam 4:19; Ezek 17:1-21; Hab 1:8; Dan 7:4). Rome has played that role in 70 C.E. but defeat always follows for imperial agents (cf. 22:7).

Significantly, literary and numismatic evidence attests **the eagle** as the well-known symbol of Rome. Josephus describes the **eagle** displayed on the military standards, or *aquilae,* carried into battle by Roman soldiers as "the symbol of empire . . . an omen of victory" (*JW* 3.123; *Ant* 18.120-21). Ovid laments the Parthian victory over Crassus and his son Publius in 53 B.C.E. and the shameful capture of the Roman eagle standards. They were regained by Augustus in 20 B.C.E. (Ovid, *Fasti* 585-90). Herod, puppet king of the Romans, insensitively displays the eagle on the temple gate (Josephus, *Ant* 17.151-63). In 66, Jews "routed" the governor of Syria and "took one of his eagles" (Suetonius, *Vespasian* 4.5). Often coins bring the symbols of the eagle and of lightning together by depicting the eagle clutching lightning in its claw to symbolize Roman military power, which enacts Jupiter's will.[21]

The verse, then, utilizes symbols of Roman power and domination. But it does not assert Rome as the victorious eagle or vulture. Rather it depicts its demise. The coming of the Son of Man, God's agent, to establish God's empire or reign over all things (24:27-31) means not the victory but the defeat of Rome's, or any, empire. The battle scene is the defeat of the imperial power Rome at the coming of Jesus. The **eagles** do not soar over the **corpses**, but **gather** among or with the **corpses**. The **eagles** are Rome's fallen military standards which are cast about on the ground in defeat with the **corpses** of Rome's soldiers. Rome's military might, the basis for its empire, is humbled by and subordinated to God's sovereign power.[22] Again the gospel borrows images of imperial power to depict the defeat of that which it resists, and to present God's victorious empire.

The verb **will gather** sustains such a reading. It commonly refers both to the elite who oppose Jesus (including Pilate and the Roman military; 2:4; 12:30; 22:34, 41; 26:3, 57; 27:17, 27, 62) and to judgment (3:12; 22:10; 25:32). The scene depicts judgment on Rome. Note Ezek 39:17, in which birds, or *Sib. Or.* 3:644, in which vultures eat the dead destroyed in the final battles.

• 24:29

Jesus' coming is not only a political shakeup on earth but a cosmic transformation. **Immediately after the suffering/tribulation of those days the sun will be darkened, and the moon will not give its light; the stars will fall from heaven, and the powers of heaven will be shaken**. The loss of light from the sun, moon, and stars is a common feature in the judgment scenarios of the "day of the Lord" (Amos 5:20; Ezek 32:7-8; Joel 2:2; *1 En* 80:4-7; *4 Ezra* 5:4-5; cf. Matt 7:22; 10:15). The language and details of this scene particularly echo Isa 13:10; 34:4. Significantly, both scenes depict God destroying the nations (Isa 34:2) or the tyrants, imperial Babylon (Isa 13:1, 5, 9, 11; cf. Egypt in Ezek 32), along with the heavenly deities that guide their actions and success. The scenes present the establishment of God's sovereignty over all including the heavenly bodies. The establishment of God's empire is a return to the edenic, pre-sin world of Gen 1-2 (Matt 19:28).

Not surprisingly, Rome's emperors claimed the blessing of the sun and moon. Caligula and Nero added "New Sun" to their titles; Nero had a statue to the sun placed in front of his palace; Nero and Vespasian issued coins depicting themselves wearing the "radiate crown" (crowned with rays of the sun) associated with the sun god. Domitian issues coins depicting the goddess Aeternitas (Rome and the Flavian dynasty forever) with the sun and moon.[23] Malalas (*Chron* 260-61) reports that Vespasian had set up a statue in honor of Selene the moon goddess outside Antioch because Selene's light (moon light) helped secure Jerusalem's conquest in 70 C.E. The coming of Jesus is the end of such imperial claims. It is "lights out" time for all tyrants. Jesus' coming returns the whole created cosmos to God's sovereignty.

• 24:30

From vv. 4-26 Jesus has named events that are part of the tribulation before the end, but do not signify his coming. Now he directly, but mysteriously, answers the disciples' question of v. 3 about "the sign of your coming." **Then the sign of the Son of Man will appear in heaven**. Unlike the reports of false messiahs or false prophets who claim to be "in the wilderness" or "in inner rooms" (24:26), this sign is **in heaven**, abundantly evident to all. What is the **sign**? It may be the glorious coming itself (24:30b, **they will see**), the cross (a traditional identification, but the crucifixion has not been in view), or, in keeping with the battle imagery of vv. 27-31, and especially the influence of Isa 13, it may be God "raising a signal" to summon "warriors" (Isa 13:2-3; 11:12; 18:3) to overthrow God's opponents.

Then all the tribes of the earth will mourn. Mourning accompanies the day of God's coming to Jerusalem (Zech 12:10-14). It is not stated why **all the tribes** or nations mourn. Is it repentance or fear at imminent judgment?

They will see the Son of Man coming on the clouds of heaven with power and with great glory. The scene's language recalls Dan 7:13-14 in which God destroys the last of the human empires and gives the one "like a Son of Man" an "everlasting dominion . . . and kingship that will never be destroyed." For a heavenly Son of Man exercising judgment, especially over "the kings, the governors, the high officials and the landlords," see *1 En* 62-63. On **Son of Man,** see 8:20. **Clouds** denote God's presence: in the deliverance from slavery in Egypt (Exod 13:20-22), in the revelation from Sinai (19:9), in the tent of meeting and tabernacle (33:9; 40:34-38). Recall Matt 17:5 for God's revelation. This is a revelation of God's **power**, more powerful than the "powers of heaven" and any human empire (24:27-29). On **glory** as a display of God's power and presence in Jesus' coming, see 16:27; 19:28; 25:31.

• 24:31

While judgment has been to the fore in 24:27-30, now the attention turns to salvation and the vindication of the elect. **And he will send out his angels with a loud trumpet call**. The diverse dimensions of this event are indicated by the **trumpet,** which can signal military engagement and victory (Num 10:9; Josephus, *Ant* 12.410), the anointing of a king (1 Kgs 1:34), God's revelation (Exod 19:16, 19), the ingathering of God's people in deliverance from the nations (Isa 27:13; Zech 9:14, 26; *Pss. Sol.* 11:1-2; *Apoc. Abr.* 31:1), God's reign (Ps 47:2-8), and the day of the Lord, or judgment (Joel 2:1; Zeph 1:16).[24] The Son of Man acts with his own authority (cf. 28:18) in **sending out angels**. On the diverse roles of angels, see 1:20, 24; 2:13, 19; 4:6, 11; 18:10; 22:30. In 13:41, 16:27, and 25:31, angels accompany the Son of Man in his coming. In 13:39-43, 49-50, the **angels** separate the evil from the righteous in the judgment. Here the focus is on **gathering** (13:30; 23:37) **his elect** (22:14; 24:22, 24) **from the four winds, from one end of heaven to another**. See 8:11-12 for the language of gathering God's people, both Gentiles and diaspora Jews.

24:32-35—THE PARABLE OF THE FIG TREE

• **24:32-33**

A short parable (cf. ch. 13) underlines the point of recognizing the signs that lead up to Jesus' imminent coming. **From the fig tree learn its lesson: as soon as its branch becomes tender and puts forth its leaves, you know that summer is near**. In 21:18-22 the fig tree taught a lesson in relation to the temple. Here it teaches concerning the end. **So also when you see all these things, you know that he is near**. The phrase **all these things** refers in 24:8 to the false prophets, wars, famines, and earthquakes named in 24:3-7 and elaborated through to v. 26. These are the tribulations which disciples face in the present, prior to the end or coming described in vv. 27-31.

• **24:34-35**

These events are happening currently. **Truly I tell you** (see 5:18, an authoritative statement), **this generation will not pass away until all these things have taken place**, that is, the events described in vv. 4-26 preceding the *parousia*. This generation refers to Jesus' contemporaries, a sinful people who will be judged (so 11:16; 12:39-45; 16:4; 17:17; 23:36). **Heaven and earth will pass away**, previously affirmed in 5:18 and 19:28, **but my words will not pass away**. Jesus' authoritative words (cf. 7:24-27) have abiding significance, like God's (Isa 40:8; *4 Ezra* 8:22-24).

24:36-44—THE UNKNOWN TIME: BE VIGILANT

The closing verse of the section states its main point, the need for constant vigilant living, since the time of Jesus' coming is unknown (established in 24:36). Verses 37-43 offer four examples of people surprised by or ready for (vv. 37-39, 40, 41, 43) Jesus' coming, with v. 42 exhorting readiness. The repeated exhortations to be alert and the four examples express an awareness of the vulnerability of the marginal and minority community of disciples before the end. External and internal pressures and distractions can prevent faithful discipleship.

• **24:36**

Having delineated aspects of the present tribulation (24:4-26), described his future coming (24:27-31), and urged the recognition of the signs that precede it (27:32-35), Jesus concedes, nevertheless: **but about that day and hour** (in context, the time of Jesus' coming), **no one knows, neither the angels of heaven, nor the Son, but only the Father.** His confession of ignorance is sur-prising, given the intimate relationship of **Father** and **Son** in 11:25-27, his rev-elation of various heavenly mysteries (cf. 22:29-33), and the instruction of 24:1-35. It is, though, consistent with other declarations in apocalyptic texts that only God knows the time of the coming of the Messiah (*Pss. Sol.* 17:21) or of the end (*2 Bar* 21:8; 54:1; contrary to Daniel's updating efforts to identify the time; cf. Dan 7:25; 8:13; 9:27; 12:7, 11, 12). On God as **Father**, see 5:16, 45; 6:9; 7:21; 11:25-27; 23:9; 25:34.

• 24:37-39

The unknown timing of Jesus' coming is compared to the days of Noah. Verse 37 asserts a connection: **For as the days of Noah were, so will be the coming of the Son of Man**. Verses 38-39 show that the connection lies in the suddenness of the flood/coming, which surprises most people who are going about the activities of their daily lives unprepared. **For as in those days before the flood, they were eating and drinking, marrying and giving in marriage until the day Noah entered the ark, and they knew nothing until the flood came and swept them all away, so too will be the coming of the Son of Man**. The activities that are named (**eating, drinking, marrying and giving in mar-riage**) are normal, everyday activities which sustain ongoing human life. But **they knew nothing** of the flood until it **swept them all away**. Their ignorance and unpreparedness (not their sinfulness or unbelief) lead to their destruction. The community of disciples is warned. The issue is not missing the coming of Jesus. Verses 27-31 have shown that it will be evident to all. Rather, the point concerns not being distracted or diverted from God's purposes, but living faith-fully for this goal. They must be focused even if the rest of society is not. On **coming**, see 24:3, 27; on **Son of Man**, see 24:27, 30, 36, 44.

• 24:40

A second example concerns two men engaged in the same activity with vastly different consequences. **Then two will be in the field; one will be taken and one will be left**. Presumably one is ready or alert for the Son of Man's coming by not being distracted by reports of false prophets, wars, famines, or earthquakes, by remaining a faithful follower/disciple/believer through perse-cution and mission work, by fleeing, by seeing the sign in heaven. But which one is taken? Is the righteous taken or is the unrighteous taken and consigned to hell? It is not at all certain. In favor of the latter is 13:40-42, 49-50; but in favor of the former is (1) 24:31, in which the angels gather the elect; (2) the verb **take** in 2:13, 14, 20, 21, which indicates salvation from danger (note that Jesus is the subject of the verb **takes** and disciples its object in 20:17; 26:37); (3) in 24:37-39 those who go in the ark are saved while those who are left are not; (4) the verb **left** indicates judgment in 23:38 and 24:2.

• 24:41-42

A third example of everyday activity follows involving two women (the par-ticiple "grinding" and form of the number "one" are feminine). **Two women**

will be grinding meal together; one will be taken and one will be left. The same division takes place (24:40), prompting a repeated warning: **Keep awake therefore, for you do not know on what day your Lord is coming.** Disciples, like their master, do not know the time (24:36). To **keep awake** is an active, alert stance of getting on with the tasks at hand. It means being a community (the imperative and pronouns **you/your** are plural) of faithful followers (26:38, 40-41) who live God's will (24:45-51) until God's purposes are completed in Jesus' coming (cf. 25:13).

• 24:43

A fourth example underlines alertness/preparedness for an event whose timing is unknown. **But understand this: if the owner of the house had known in what part of the night the thief was coming, he would have stayed awake and would not have let his house be broken into.** The image of Jesus as a thief is striking. If disciples are not alert or prepared with a life of faithful and active discipleship, Jesus' unexpected coming will "steal" the joy of eschatological participation in God's purposes from them.

• 24:44

The conclusion is clear: **therefore you** (plural, addressing the community of disciples) **also must be ready,** unlike the man in the field, the woman grinding meal, and the owner of the house. **For the Son of Man is coming at an unexpected hour**. For the fourth time, "not knowing" is emphasized (24:36, 39, 42), as it will be in the next two parables (24:50; 25:13). Disciples must be watchful, alert, and living faithfully as the following parable illustrates.

24:45-51—THE PARABLE OF THE FAITHFUL AND WISE SLAVE

Another parable illustrates the need to be alert and watchful in the light of Jesus' coming at a time which is not known.[25] It contrasts in 24:45-47 and 48-51 two sets of behaviors and two responses at the master's coming. The image of a slave again locates disciples with the marginal and despised (see chs. 19-20).

• 24:45-46

The parable opens with a question (18:12; 21:28) which engages the audience's attention, requires a response, and challenges the audience to live appropriately. **Who then is the faithful and wise slave?** The noun **slave** has been used previously to identify disciples (10:24-25; 18:23-35; 20:27); the parable is an allegory for disciples in the time of waiting for Jesus' coming.

While the adjective **faithful** has not been used previously, its cognate noun "faith" (8:10; 9:2, 22, 29; 15:28; 17:20; 21:21; 23:23) and verb "believe/trust/ have faith" (8:13; 9:28; 18:6; 21:22, 25, 32; 24:23, 26) have named qualities which disciples exhibit in encountering and trusting God's saving power and living accordingly. The adjective **wise** has also denoted desirable qualities: hearing and doing Jesus' teaching (7:24), the need for appropriate behavior in mission in a dangerous world (10:16; preparation in 25:1-10). The opening question of v. 45 requires the audience to identify these qualities in operation.

The first slave's actions are described, **whom his master has put in charge of his household, to give the other slaves their allowance of food at the proper time? Blessed is that slave whom his master will find at work when he arrives**. The slave, with management skills, has faithfully carried out his master's instructions to ensure the welfare of his fellow slaves (20:26-27). He is ready for his master's coming by being faithful to these instructions. Ensuring that people have access to adequate **food** has been an important theme through the gospel (6:25-34; 10:10-15 [response to mission]; 12:1-8 [sabbath]; 14:13-21; 15:32-39; 16:5-12; 24:7; 25:31-46). On **master** as an image for Jesus in eschatological contexts, see 7:21-22; 24:42. To be alert/ready/prepared for his coming (24:3, 36-43) is to be obedient to the divine will, which means actions that strengthen the community of disciples.

• 24:47

The slave gains more responsibility: **Truly I tell you** (see 5:18), **he will put that one in charge of all his possessions**.

• 24:48-49

A second scenario contrasts the first. **But if that wicked slave says to himself, "My master is delayed," and he begins to beat his fellow slaves, and eats and drinks with drunkards. . . .** The master's coming is now presented differently. Whereas he was absent in 24:45-47 and the time of his coming is not known, now the unknown time is labeled a **delay**, suggesting that his expected coming has not come about. Readiness or alertness means not only faithful living until his sudden coming at any time (24:39, 43) but also continuing active faithfulness and obedience when his expected coming is delayed and the time period drawn out.

This slave does not stay alert for the master's coming with faithful, obedient living. He takes advantage of the delay to abuse others with his power (cf. 18:23-35; cf. 24:10-12) and pursue his own pleasure (on beating slaves, see 8:5-6). His behavior imitates that of masters in patriarchal households and of Gentiles who lord it over others (see 20:20-28). He does not belong in the alternative community of disciples marked by service.

• 24:50-51

Whereas the "faithful and wise slave" is rewarded, the "wicked slave" is surprised and punished. **The master of that slave** (so 24:46) **will come on a day when he does not expect him and at an hour that he does not know** (cf. 24:36). **He will cut him in pieces and put him with the hypocrites, where there will be weeping and gnashing of teeth**. Violence against slaves was commonplace, an expression of an attitude that saw slaves as marginal beings outside the boundaries of normal social intercourse.[26] In this violent image of judgment, the gospel again borrows from and imitates aspects of the very world it seeks to resist. On **hypocrites**, see chapter 23 (also 6:2, 5, 16; 7:5; 15:7; 22:18). The slave, an unfaithful disciple whose way of life does not honor Jesus, faces the same destiny as the religious leaders who resist him. Eschatological condemnation is described as **weeping and gnashing of teeth** in 8:12; 13:42, 50; 22:13; 25:30. The gospel seeks to bully its audience into faithful, alert living.

CHAPTER 25

Jesus' Fifth Teaching Discourse

The Final Establishment of God's Empire (Part 2)

The chapter division is artificial in that Jesus' eschatological discourse continues from chapter 24. See the introductory comments there. Jesus has described the time between his resurrection and his coming, including the fall of the temple (24:1-2) and general tribulation (24:3-26). His *parousia,* or coming, will be evident to everyone as God's empire is established over all things, including Roman power (24:27-31). In the present time of tribulation, disciples must be ready for and alert to Jesus' eschatological coming as Son of Man, since they do not know the time of this (delayed) event, which could occur at any moment (24:32-51).

In 25:1-13 and 25:14-30, two further parables continue the emphasis on readiness and preparation in 24:32, 36-51. The final scene of the eschatological discourse depicts the judgment that follows the Son of Man's coming (25:31-46).

25:1-13—GOD'S EMPIRE IS LIKE THE SITUATION OF THE TEN MAIDENS

Jesus has exhorted disciples to be ready for his return, but the time of his coming is unknown (24:36, 42, 44, 50) and delayed 24:48). The emphasis on being ready for his delayed coming (25:5) continues in this parable. Disciples are to live as faithful and obedient slaves (24:45-51) through the delay.

As with previous parables (18:23-35; 21:28-32; 22:1-14; 24:45-51), two contrasting groups of characters exemplify the instruction to "keep awake" (cf. the two groups of 24:37-41; 25:14-46). Again allegory is used: suddenly (24:39, 43-44, 50) Jesus comes (the delayed bridegroom; cf. 24:48; 25:19) at the beginning of the new age (the wedding) to be greeted by alert, prepared, and faithful disciples (the five wise maidens; 24:13, 42-44; 25:14-30) while unprepared, unfaithful disciples (the foolish maidens) experience eschatological exclusion (24:39-41). The parable variously scares and bullies disciples into obedience, persuades them to live for this desired future, or provides models of faithfulness which they imitate so as to participate in God's future (see 7:13).[1]

• 25:1a

The opening comparative clause indicates that **the reign/empire of the heavens** is compared to or laid beside the story of the ten maidens: **Then the reign/empire of the heavens will be like this,** that is, like the situation of the ten maidens. The gospel's educative work about God's transformative and alternative empire continues (see 3:2; 4:17, 23; 12:28; ch. 13; etc). The future passive form of the introduction **will be like** directs attention to the judgment at the coming of the Son of Man (24:3, 27-31; 13:39-43; 16:27-28; 19:28). This future passive form of the common parabolic, comparative formula (cf. 13:24, 31, 33, 44, 45, 47; 18:21; 22:2) has occurred only twice previously. At 7:24, 26, it introduces the future judgment of the wise and the foolish, the former to vindication and the latter to condemnation.

• 25:1b-4

The parable's opening section establishes the situation. **Ten maidens took their lamps and went to meet the bridegroom.** While God is identified as Israel's bridegroom (Isa 54:5; Jer 31:32; Hos 2:16), Jesus is the bridegroom here (9:15). The verb **meet** is used twice, both in relation to Jesus at 8:28 and 28:9. The parable of 22:1-14 utilized the setting of a wedding.

The bride is a noncharacter in the parable. Instead, the focus is on the way in which the maidens handle the bridegroom's delayed arrival. They are perhaps waiting for the bride and groom to come from the bride's house to the place of the wedding banquet, perhaps the groom's family's house (25:10). The ten women represent the community of disciples, Jew and Gentile, male and female, of any social status. So also the women of 24:41. Their providing of light (**lamps**) recalls the community's commission to be light for the world (see 5:14). Their faithfulness in this task of proclaiming and living God's saving presence and reign will be judged. Why **ten**? They may represent perfection (Philo, *Moses* 1.96; Ten Commandments) shattered by the inadequate responses.

• 25:2

The ten are divided into two groups. **Five of them were foolish and five of them were wise.** The naming of the **foolish** first highlights their inappropriate behavior and reinforces the warning. The terms **wise** and **foolish** identify those who obey and do not obey Jesus' teaching in 7:24-27. For this common division in wisdom literature, see 7:24-27. The **wise** are vindicated in the judgment; the **foolish** are condemned. Used elsewhere, the terminology of the **wise** denotes disciples in faithful mission to a rejecting world (10:16), and slaves who faithfully obey their master's instructions while he is delayed (24:45). The **foolish** include the religious leaders, who reject Jesus (23:17). The division and designations signal the outcome of the parable's plot and its main point. **Five** of the maidens will behave in a way that ensures their vindication in the judgment at the bridegroom's arrival. **Five** will be condemned. How will this come about? Wherein lies their foolishness or their wisdom?

• 25:3-4

When the foolish took their lamps, they took no oil with them; but the wise took flasks of oil with their lamps. Their foolishness or wisdom is revealed in their preparation, or lack thereof, for the delay of the bridegroom. Not knowing the time of his coming requires focus and readiness.

What preparation is necessary? What does the lamp oil represent, if anything? While some have attempted specific answers (good deeds[2], the Holy Spirit), in the absence of any particular indication, it seems that a generic reference to faithful and obedient discipleship as defined by the whole gospel is more convincing. (1) The context supports this. The maidens are to be like the slave (24:45-47) who actively, faithfully, and obediently carries out what he has been instructed to do. (2) The echoes of 7:24-27 (wise, foolish) point to this conclusion also. They are to "hear and do" Jesus' words (7:24-27). (3) God's word is described as "a lamp for my feet" in Ps 119:105.

• 25:5-8

Their lack of preparation is exposed by the bridegroom's delay. The time of his arrival is uncertain, and they have not prepared accordingly. **As the bridegroom was delayed, all of them became drowsy and slept.** Their sleeping is not condemned. Both groups do it. What matters is that when they are awakened, they are prepared for his arrival (in living a life of active and faithful discipleship). **But at midnight there was a shout, "Look! Here is the bridegroom! Come out to meet him." Then all those maidens got up and trimmed their lamps. The foolish said to the wise, "Give us some of your oil, for our lamps are going out."** By not taking extra oil (25:3-4), the **foolish** have not prepared for the delay. They, or more accurately the disciples they portray, have not believed Jesus' word that no one knows the time of his coming (24:36). They expected it to be soon rather than delayed. They did not remain focused, prepared, and alert to the end.

• 25:9

But the wise replied, "No! there will not be enough for you and us; you had better go to the dealers and buy some for yourselves." By contrast **the wise** have prepared. Whereas the foolish had too much time previously, now they do not have enough.

• 25:10

Their departure to get oil contrasts with the bridegroom's (Jesus') arrival. **And while they went to buy it, the bridegroom came, and those who were ready went with him into the wedding banquet; and the door was shut.** The **ready** are the wise who heeded Jesus' words of warning (24:44; 7:24-27). On God's empire as a wedding feast, see Isa 62:5; Matt 22:1-14; also 8:11-12. The wise/ready are with the bridegroom in the wedding banquet. The phrase **with him** recalls Jesus' commission in 1:23 (cf. 28:20) as Immanuel, to manifest "God with us." The establishment of God's empire means the experience of God's saving presence and the completion of Jesus' mission (see 4:17).

• 25:11-12

Attention moves to the fate of the foolish maidens. The scene is one of judgment. **Later the other maidens came also, saying, "Lord, lord open to us."** The repeated **Lord, lord**, the same term as is used frequently of Jesus (cf. 24:42), recalls the pseudo-discipleship of 7:21-22. **But he replied, "Truly I tell you** (cf. 5:18)**, I do not know you."** They have failed to be ready at his delayed coming. Compare 22:11-14 for exclusion from the wedding feast. Peter uses the phrase **I do not know (the man)** in 26:74.

• 25:13

Keep awake/Be ready, therefore, for you know neither the day nor the hour. So 24:36. The closing exhortation to the audience recalls the two key emphases: the time of the coming is unknown (sudden; delayed), but disciples must be ready for it by always living faithfully and obediently to Jesus' teaching.

25:14-30—BE READY FOR THE MASTER'S RETURN

A third parable (24:45-51; 25:1-13) presents another allegory encouraging and warning disciples to be ready for Jesus' return:

the master	Jesus
the slaves	disciples
the long time	the present
the master's coming	Jesus' (delayed) return
rewards	eschatological vindication
punishment	eschatological punishment

The scene develops 24:45-47 in that the master gives his slaves talents which they are to use for the master's benefit while he is gone. The use or nonuse of the talents provides the basis for the master's verdict. This element specifies what is involved in being ready or watchful for the master's return, an important but somewhat vague emphasis in the previous parables and exhortations. They are to be actively seeking their master's good, faithfully carrying out the tasks he has entrusted to them. His delay means that the present is a time of opportunity, to be lived in faithful anticipation of God's future.

But there is a problem with identifying Jesus as the master, much like the problem with identifying the king as God in 18:23-35.[3] In this parable the master behaves in tyrannical ways that imitate dominant cultural and imperial values (25:25-30) and contradict Jesus' previous teaching. He rewards the first two slaves for their accumulation of wealth and punishes the third slave for not doing so. The parable takes the perspective of the wealthy elite and legitimates a "rich-get-richer and poor-get-poorer" approach. It punishes the one who subverts the system.

But throughout Jesus has sided with the nonelite and challenged this oppressive economic status quo (5:3-12). In 19:16-22 he challenges a rich man to divest his wealth and give to the poor in a move toward a more just society. In a "limited good" perspective, his wealth exemplifies greed; his accumulation means deprivation for others (see 19:20).

On the basis of Jesus' teaching in 19:16-22, the master and the first two slaves could rightly be rebuked for their greedy and acquisitive actions. The third slave should be commended for not adding to the master's wealth by not depriving others! He should be praised for refusing to play this unjust economic game. He seems more faithful to Jesus' teaching in 6:24-34, which challenged disciples not to seek security and identity from mammon, but to seek first God's empire (cf. 6:1-4, almsgiving). And in his resistance to the imperial scheme he reflects both Jesus' actions and Jesus' fate as one who will also be expelled from this society.

It seems that again the gospel has coopted dominant cultural values in picturing the establishment of God's empire. God's empire imitates, rather than provides an alternative to, Rome's empire, in which the wealthy and powerful become even more so at the expense of the rest. Such co-option is not surprising, given that the gospel's author is a creature of his cultural context.

What perhaps has happened is that the emphatic exhortation to disciples to be faithful and active slaves of Jesus until his return so dominates the shape of the story that the larger issues are neglected. The gospel audience's experience of compliant slaves who materially and socially benefit their master is assumed in order to exemplify faithful discipleship, but no critique of that socioeconomic structure or of their particular activities (accumulating wealth at the expense of others) is given at this point. The exhortation to faithful discipleship overrides all other concerns. The audience must hear the exhortation as well as supply the critique of the parable's content from the larger gospel context. The specific socioeconomic commitments of the master and the activities of the first two slaves are not to be imitated.

The parable falls into four readily identifiable scenes. The master entrusts property/tasks to the slaves and goes away (25:14-15); the slaves attend to their responsibilities (25:16-18); the master returns and rewards two of the slaves (25:19-23), while he punishes the third (25:24-30).

• 25:14-15

Unlike 25:1, no opening comparative clause identifies what the parable's situation compares. The context of 25:1-13 suggests a focus on the coming of Jesus and the establishment of God's empire/reign. God's reign/empire is like the situation of the master who commits tasks/talents to his slaves, goes away, and then suddenly returns. **For it is as if a man, going on a journey, summoned his slaves and entrusted his property/wealth to them**. The parable presupposes the identification of disciples as **slaves** in 20:26-27, and therefore, the **man** is Jesus. There is nothing unusual about educated and skilled slaves functioning as business managers. The verb **summoned/called** earlier expresses God commissioning Jesus to manifest God's saving presence (1:21, 23, 25; 2:15). In turn, Jesus' calling of disciples (so 4:21; 5:9; 9:13; 10:1; 22:3-9) is a means of enacting that commission and commissioning them to "fish for people" (cf. 4:19; 10:7-8; 28:18-20).

The act of **entrusting property/wealth** recalls 24:45-47 and is elaborated in v. 15. Here the **property** is money, hence the translation, **wealth**. **To one he gave five talents, to another two, and to another one, to each according to his ability.** A **talent** (cf. 18:24) was a large amount, consisting of six thousand denarii (a denarius being wages for a day's work; so 20:1-16).[4] The size points to the great importance of what has been entrusted to Jesus' disciples. No instruction is given as to what they are do with the talents. But well-trained slaves know that the master's wealth is to be increased. A gift is a task.

Then he went away. Disciples live in a time when Jesus is not present, yet paradoxically he is present in the community of disciples gathered for worship (18:20) and for mission (25:31-46; 28:20). The mode of his presence is not stated. The telling of the gospel story renders him present by enabling the audience to hear his words and actions (24:35).

• 25:16-18

What do the slaves do with the talents? **The one who had received the five talents went off at once and worked with them, and made five more talents. In the same way the one who had the two talents made two more talents.** These two slaves put forth effort (note the verbs of which they are the subjects: **went . . . worked . . . made**) and double their master's wealth. Exactly how they do so is not indicated; the emphasis falls on the result. By contrast, **the one who had received the one talent went off and dug a hole in the ground and hid his master's money/silver.** For the practice of burying money or treasure as a means of protecting it, see 13:44. While this act protects the talent, it does not increase its value. Compared with the other slaves, this last slave appears lazy or irresponsible. He has not faithfully and actively put the talent to work.

• 25:19-23

After a long time the master of those slaves came and settled accounts with them. The length of time of the master's absence is emphasized. Consistent with 24:48 and 25:5, his coming, or *parousia* (24:3, 27, 37, 39), is delayed. The issue, then, is how slaves/disciples live during the delay. They are not to be found engaging in abusive (24:49), careless (25:8-10), or neglectful (25:24-30) practices, but in faithful attention to the master's business (24:19-23). Recall the **settling of accounts** in 18:23.

• 25:20-21

The judgment begins with the vindication of those who have been faithful. **Then the one who had received the five talents came forward, bringing five more talents, saying, "Master, you handed over to me five talents: see I**

have made five more talents." The slave emphasizes his efforts and their
results. **His master said to him, "Well done, good and trustworthy slave."**
The commendation recalls 24:45. The faithful or **trustworthy slave** is one who
carries out the expected task, who acts in a manner consistent with the slave–
master relationship and his identity as a slave. The slave is called **good**, which
designates action reflective of and consistent with his inner commitment (7:17-
18). His living imitates God who is good (19:17; 20:15; 7:11) and contrasts
those, such as the religious elite, who are evil and do not do God's will (12:34-
39). **You have been trustworthy in a few things, I will put you in charge of
many things** (cf. 24:47); **enter into the joy of your master.** The verb **enter
into** is commonly used in verses about entering into life or God's reign/empire
(5:20; 7:13, 21; 18:3, 8, 9; 19:17, 23) and so maintains the scene's eschatological nature. **Joy** accompanies the experience of God's presence or empire (2:10;
13:20, 44; 28:8).

• **25:22-23**
    The scene is repeated with the second slave. **And the one with two talents
also came forward, saying, "Master, you handed over to me two talents: see
I have made two more talents." His master said to him, "Well done, good
and trustworthy slave; you have been trustworthy in a few things, I will put
you in charge of many things; enter into the joy of your master."** This slave
has also been faithful in carrying out the tasks committed to him.

• **25:24-30**
    Commendation gives way to condemnation, the celebration of faithfulness
to the cursing of faithlessness, vindication to vanquishment.

• **25:24-25**
    The third slave appears. **Then the one who had received the one talent
also came forward, saying, "Master I knew that you were a harsh man,
reaping what you did not sow, and gathering where you did not scatter
seed; so I was afraid, and I went and hid your talent in the ground** (25:18).
Here you have what is yours." While he uses the term of address **Master**, he
does not do the master's will or faithfully perform his responsibilities (cf. 7:21-
23).

• **25:26-27**
    But his master replied, "You wicked (contrast the "good" of vv. 21, 23)
and idle/lazy/indolent (BAGD, 563) **slave."** For denunciations of laziness, see
Prov 6:6, 9; 20:4; 21:25; 26:15; Sir 22:1-2. The designation **wicked** links the
slave with those opposed to God's purposes: the elite who misuse their power
(5:39), the devil (6:13; 13:19); religious leaders and this generation (12:33-42;
16:4). The slave is condemned for making no effort to increase the master's
wealth. Vigilance or preparation for the master's coming consists not of passive
waiting but of active and consistent service. **You knew, did you, that I reap**

where I did not sow and gather where I did not scatter? Then you ought to have invested my money with the bankers, and on my return I would have received what was my own with interest. See introductory comments.

• 25:28-29

So take (who is being commanded?) **the talent from him, and give it to the one who has ten talents. For to all those who have** (been faithful to the responsibilities/tasks entrusted to them by the master), **more** (talents/responsibilities) **will be given, and they will have an abundance; but from those who have nothing** (to show from the talent/s they have because they have not used them faithfully), **even what they have will be taken away** (by God).

• 25:30

The slave is condemned. He has not pursued the master's business in his absence. **As for this worthless slave, throw him into the outer darkness, where there will be weeping and gnashing of teeth.** The motifs of **darkness** (8:12; 22:13) and **weeping and gnashing of teeth** (8:12; 13:42, 50; 22:13; 24:51) commonly describe eschatological condemnation, and contrast with the destiny of the first two slaves (25:21, 23). The slave's destiny is that of those who do not respond to Jesus with faith and obedient lives.

25:31-46—JESUS SON OF MAN AND THE JUDGMENT

The two-chapter eschatological discourse culminates with a judgment scene.[5] After the lengthy tribulation or eschatological woes (24:3-26), the awaited, delayed, and glorious arrival of the Son of Man (24:48; 25:5, 19) takes place (24:27-31, 37, 39, 44). Accompanied by angels (24:31, 36), he executes judgment, vindicating the righteous (24:45-47; 25:10, 19-23) and punishing the wicked and unprepared (24:40-41, 48-51; 25:11-12, 24-30).

Judgment scenes are common in apocalyptic writings. Standard features include the majestic judge, angels, the assembling of the people to be judged, the separation, the reward of the righteous and punishment of the wicked, the establishment of God's empire. See Joel 3:1-3; Dan 7:7-27; *1 En* 62-63 (both involve the Son of Man); 90:20-39; *4 Ezra* 7:31-44; *2 Bar* 72-74. The scenes are usually presented from the perspective of the underdog. Powerful empires are defeated; the rich, the landowners, the rulers, get their just rewards for their oppressive tyranny. The oppressed are freed to enjoy God's just and life-giving rule. The scenes reveal what the judgment will be like and the basis for the separation. They function to encourage the oppressed minority to persevere, to remain faithful to God's purposes in difficult circumstances. The scene reveals that the present injustice is not a permanent way of life. God's action will reverse it.

There has been much controversy in interpreting Matthew's scene. Some of the language is ambiguous. Nor does the gospel offer one coherent judgment scene throughout.[6] Details differ in various references. For example, what role do the angels play? Here in 25:31 they seem to do nothing (also 16:27), but in 13:41, 49 they separate the righteous and wicked, and in 24:31 they gather the elect. And who is judged? In 13:41 the angels separate "out of his reign/empire all causes of sin and all evildoers," suggesting a judgment of Christians (also 24:45-51; 25:14-30), whereas in 13:49 they divide "the evil from the righteous." Everyone is judged (16:27; 24:30).

Not surprisingly, then, scholars have interpreted Matthew's judgment scene here in numerous ways. Basically there have been two approaches. (1) Some have seen it as the judgment of all people on the basis of how they have treated the poor, the marginalized, and the needy. (2) Others have interpreted it as the judgment of all people on the basis of how they have responded to Christian disciples and the proclamation of the good news.

In my view, while the first view is very appealing, the second approach has much better exegetical support. I will outline five factors here which support it and sustain them in the comments on the appropriate verses below.

1. The judgment follows the worldwide mission work of the community of disciples. This mission "to all people" is one of its tasks in the time between Jesus' ministry and the end (24:14; cf. 28:18-20). Judgment follows the opportunity that all have to respond to the disciples' proclamation.

2. The phrase "all the nations" (ἔθνη, *ethnē*, 25:32; see further below) includes Jews and Gentiles. The term "nations" does not refer only to Gentiles. In 24:9, 14 it is a synonym for the "whole inhabited world."

3. The phrase "the least of these my brothers and sisters" (25:40, 45) uses language that refers in the gospel not to all marginalized people but to Jesus' disciples (cf. 10:40; 12:46-50).

4. The scene has, as numerous discussions have noted, a rich and important Christology. It is significant that Jesus, the powerful Son of Man, enacts the judgment which involves actions done to Jesus, the suffering servant. Moreover, the gospel has insisted that commitment to Jesus is crucial for participating in God's purposes (4:19 [follow me]; 13:3-9, 18-23, 24-30, 36-43 [receiving the word]; 18:6 [believe in me]). In 7:24-27 hearing and doing the teaching of Jesus are the basis for vindication in the judgment. To claim that the judgment is on the basis of how people treat the poor does not deal adequately with this christological focus.

5. The blessed are described twice in the scene as "righteous" (25:37, 46). This term and its noun, "righteousness," describe a way of life consistent with God's purposes which disciples are to live (1:19; 6:33). This way of life begins with following Jesus and continues as an ongoing demonstration of God's love and mercy for all people, especially for the poor and marginalized, those not valued by the dominant society obsessed with power and wealth.

The scene divides into four sections. In vv. 31-33 the Son of Man quickly effects the division of the judgment. Verses 34-40 provide justification for the vindication of the righteous in a conversation between them and the Son of Man/king. Verses 41-45 use a similar conversation to justify the condemnation of the wicked. Verse 46 concludes the scene with the two groups being led to their respective eschatological destinies.

• 25:31

While the previous verses (24:36-25:30) have emphasized the unknown time, and delayed coming, of Jesus the Son of Man (24:27, 30, 37, 39, 44), and the need to be ready for the judgment, now that coming takes place and the judgment it represents is described. **When the Son of Man comes in his glory, and all his angels with him.** . . . The description of his coming is minimal, compared with the more detailed description already given in 24:27-31. See also 16:27-28; 19:28-30; Dan 7:13-14. On **Son of Man**, see 8:20. **Then he will sit on the throne of his glory**. For **sitting** as a position of ruling, see 5:1; 19:28; 20:21, 23; in contrast 23:2. The Son of Man sits on the throne to judge in *1 En* 61:8; 62:2-3. The emperor Nero sits to rule (Suetonius, *Nero* 13).

• 25:32

All the nations will be gathered before him. The gathering of the nations before God (the passive also indicates by God) at the end is typical of eschatological scenes (Isa 66:18; Zech 14:2; Joel 3:2, 9-21; *3 Ezra* 7:37; 13:37-38; *2 Bar* 72:2). Jesus enacts the role and will of God. W. D. Davies and D. C. Allison note six suggested meanings for **all the nations**: all non-Jews; all non-Christians; all non-Jews who are not Christians; Christians; Christians alive when Jesus comes; all humanity.[7] Given the repeated exhortations to be ready for the return in 24:36-25:30, the exclusion of Christians is unconvincing. Does the judgment include Jews and Gentiles or only Gentiles? There is no indication that Jews are already excluded. Christian mission to the whole of the inhabited world continues until the end (24:14; 28:18-20). The meaning of the term **nations** (ἔθνη, *ethnē*) can vary;[8] its context determines whether it denotes Gentiles in contrast to Jews (so 10:5, 18), or Gentiles *and* Jews as in 24:9, 14, where it is a synonym for the "whole inhabited world." Mission to Jew and Gentile precedes the judgment. The judgment, then, includes all people— Christians, Jews, and Gentiles (so also 8:11-12; 12:41-42; 13:36-43). As A.-J. Levine argues, ethnicity is not an issue in the scene. The emphasis falls on social factors, especially the treatment of the politically, socially, and economically marginal.[9]

And he will separate people one from another as a shepherd separates the sheep from the goats. The image assumes a Syrian-Palestinian (not Greco-Roman) practice of a single, mixed herd/flock of sheep and goats (in which both are valued). The two animals are separated just as wheat and chaff (3:12), weeds and wheat (13:24-30), and types of fish (13:47-50) are **separated**; just as two men in a field, two women grinding wheat, slaves and maidens are **separated** (24:36-25:30) at the coming of the Son of Man.[10] On Jesus as a **shepherd** protecting sheep from oppressive rulers, see 2:6; 9:36; cf. Ezek 34. The term **sheep** designates disciples in 10:16; 18:12; 26:31. So the gospel's audience identifies with the sheep. There is encouragement and challenge for faithful living in order to participate in this vindication.

• 25:33

Very quickly the two animals are divided. **And he will put the sheep at his right hand and the goats at his left.** The **right** side was a place of honor and blessing (Gen 48:13-20; Ps 110:1; *T. Benj.* 10.6), the better way (Eccl 10:2, the fool's heart moves toward the left), whereas the **left** could be regarded as the negative, unlucky, or cursed side (cf. the Latin word *sinister*, "left"). But note that in 20:21 both left and right are honored.

• 25:34

Here, the right side is the preferred side. **Then the king will say to those at his right side**. . . . The Son of Man in 25:31-33 is now identified as **king**. The reference to **right side** establishes the two terms as referring to the same figure. The term **king** has had diverse previous uses. In 2:2 the new king Jesus threatens King Herod and the elite in Jerusalem and is threatened by them. In 21:5 he is the humble, not conquering, king of the triumph. By contrast, other kings persecute disciples (10:18; cf. 14:9, King Herod and John the Baptist) and resist God (17:25). This judgment scene depicts Jesus exercising God's rule over all and sharing God's authority (cf. 28:18). The title prepares for the ironic mocking of Jesus as **king** throughout the passion (27:11, 29, 37, 42). The one who judges all people is condemned by those who will be judged by him and led "away into eternal punishment." The elite imagines that it exercises power, but it has no idea that its power is subject to God's purposes and authority.

Those on the **right side** receive God's favor and participate fully in God's empire. The language used of them identifies them as faithful disciples and their vindication in the judgment as the culmination of lives spent answering Jesus' call to follow.

(1) As faithful disciples (cf. 24:45-25:30), they **are blessed by my Father**. They have received God's blessing (5:3-12). While God is Jesus' **Father** (7:21; 10:32; 12:50), they also know God as "y/our Father" through Jesus.[11] The promise of 10:32 is accomplished. Jesus confesses before his Father those who have confessed him before people. (2) Jesus, as the eschatological Son of Man and king, now invites them to **come**, to complete the process that began with his same invitation (see 11:28). (3) They **inherit the empire**. To **inherit** is in 19:29 to share in God's life, which belongs to the new age. It is to **inherit** the earth, the end of oppressive systems and exploitative societal relationships, and the fair access to the necessary resources for life (see 5:5). The verb, then, denotes participation in God's eschatological purposes.

(4) God's **empire**, first announced and demonstrated in the ministries of John and Jesus (see 3:2; 4:17; also 10:7-8), is the establishment of God's saving presence and reign over all things including Rome. Disciples, in contrast to the crowds, have begun to understand this mystery through Jesus' ministry

(13:11). God has been working for this end since creation (**prepared for you from the beginning of the world**), by saving people (cf. 1:21, 23) from all that resists God's purposes. The establishment of God's reign in the judgment completes God's purposes for the world (6:10; 7:21). The end is a return to the beginning (13:35; 19:4, 8, 28).

• **25:35-36**

And how do people participate in this reality? **For** (signaling an explanation) **I was hungry and you gave me food, I was thirsty and you gave me something to drink, I was a stranger and you welcomed me, I was naked and you gave me clothing, I was sick and you took care of me, I was in prison and you visited me.** In 10:40-42, meeting the needs of disciples in mission, notably giving them something to drink, is a way of receiving Jesus. The reference to "little ones" in 25:40 also recalls this scene. But this welcoming action is only the beginning of a way of life marked by similar acts.

The six actions are traditional (Job 22:6-7; Isa 58:6-7; Ezek 18: 5-9; Tob 4:16-17; Sir 7:32-36; *T. Jos.* 1:5-7). Jesus performs them to manifest God's reign/empire or saving presence in a world of sinful oppression (see below). He has taught disciples to perform them as they carry out their mission of manifesting God's reign/empire. In Isa 58:6-7, these actions counter injustice and break the yoke of oppression enacted by wicked empires (cf. 11:29). Their acts of mercy reflect their commitment to Jesus. It is the good fruit from the good tree (7:17-18; 12:33-35). It is the "greater righteousness" (5:20), the doing of God's will which results from encountering God's saving righteousness.

On feeding the **hungry**, see 12:1-8; 14:13-21; 15:32-39, where it is an act that counters the mismanagement and greed of the elite. Giving **drink** to the **thirsty** is a response of welcome to disciples as they conduct their mission (10:42). To welcome **strangers** is to do Jesus' teaching of indiscriminate love (5:43-48) especially for the marginalized, whether in casting out demons (9:32-34), healing the broken, including foreigners (8:1-4, 5-13; 15:21-28), or eating with sinners (9:9-13; 11:19). Giving **clothing** to the **naked** expresses the same indiscriminate and practical love. To **take care** of the **sick** is to continue Jesus' healing work in imitation of his compassion (4:23-24; 8:14-17; 9:36; cf. 9:13; 12:7), and in obedience to his command (10:7-8). To **visit** those in **prison** is to provide food, drink, and clothing. See 5:42; 6:1-4 for such actions which are to be contrary to dominant cultural practices in that they are nonreciprocal and are concerned for the needs of the other, not the honor and social credit of the giver.

These actions are typical of those required of the **sheep**/disciples. To live this way is to be ready for the judgment. The actions describe typical needs among the majority (nonelite) population of a city such as Antioch, the likely place of Matthew's audience.[12] Among the unsanitary and overcrowded living conditions, the uneven and inadequate food and water supply, limited sewage disposal, the epidemics and infections fed by urine, feces, trash, corpses, decay, and insects, and the general misery of poverty, lack, and debt, disciples are to use their limited resources to meet these basic human needs of the poor.

• 25:37-39

These are the acts of the **righteous**, those who welcome Jesus and continue to live the will of God as revealed to them in relation to Jesus (Joseph, 1:19). They hunger and thirst for God's justice even when persecuted (5:6, 10). They continue in faithful mission (10:41), and are vindicated in the judgment (13:43, 49) for following and imitating Jesus the righteous (27:19).

They are surprised that Jesus, the king and Son of Man, identifies himself with the social and economic poor. And they do not recall doing any of these things for him. **Then the righteous will answer him, "Lord, when was it that we saw you hungry and gave you food, or thirsty and gave you something to drink? And when was it that we saw you a stranger and welcomed you, or naked and gave you clothing?"**

• 25:40

And the king will answer them, "Truly I tell you (an introduction to an authoritative statement, 5:18), **just as you did it to one of the least of these my brothers and sisters, you did it to me."** The identification of Jesus with **one of the least of these my brothers and sisters** is central to the scene. The phrase **one of the least of these my brothers and sisters** has provoked much debate. Are these any who are in need, or disciples?[13] In favor of the latter: (1) **The least** is an intensive form of the term "little ones," which refers to vulnerable and marginal disciples. In 10:42 it names disciples in mission and positive responses to their mission. In 18:6 the little ones are those who humble themselves like marginal children and "believe in me." They are very precious to God (18:10, 14). (2) The term **my brothers and sisters**, apart from natural birth relations (cf. 4:18-22; 10:2), refers to disciples who do God's will as revealed by Jesus (5:47; 7:3-5; 12:46-50; 18:15-21; 23:8; 28:10). (3) The identification of Jesus with the marginalized community of disciples has already been made in 10:40. To welcome (a metaphor for believing the gospel preaching in 10:11-14) a disciple is to welcome Jesus and God, "the one who sent me." This is the very criterion used here (cf. Prov 19:17). Jesus is present with the disciples as they engage in mission (cf. 1:23; 18:20; 28:20), though *how* he is present is not clear. The righteous, then, have responded positively to the mission proclamation, and in becoming followers of Jesus they commit to a lifestyle that imitates and continues Jesus' life of service among the poor.

• 25:41-43

The third section consists of Jesus' address to the condemned on the left. **Then he will say to those at his left hand, "You that are accursed, depart from me into the eternal fire prepared for the devil and his angels."** On **fire** as the key marker of the place of condemnation, see 3:10; 5:22; 7:19; 13:40, 42, 50; 18:8, 9. The fire is for those who do not do the will of God, and who resist God's purposes. They are **angels** or agents of the devil whose empire of opposition to God is now overthrown (4:1-11; 12:28; 13:24-30, 36-43). The command to **depart** (cf. 7:23) contrasts with the invitation to the righteous to "come" in 25:34.

They have not responded positively to the disciples' mission (10:40-42) and have not lived a lifestyle of performing these actions as expressions of God's will and empire, so they are condemned. For **I was hungry and you gave me no food, I was thirsty and you gave me nothing to drink, I was a stranger and you did not welcome me, naked and you did not give me clothing, sick and in prison and you did not visit me.**

• **25:44**

Like the righteous in 25:37, they are also surprised by the claim that Jesus, Son of Man, was among the poor. **Then they will also answer, "Lord, when was it that we saw you hungry or thirsty or a stranger or naked or sick or in prison, and did not serve/take care of you?"** Their question reveals their failure to recognize Jesus anywhere. The final verb translated **did not take care of** literally means "to serve." It is the verb by which Jesus sums up the mission of the Son of Man in 20:28 ("not to be served but to serve"). It denotes actions by angels (4:11), and by women disciples (8:15, giving him food and drink, welcoming him; 27:55). Its cognate noun "servant" names the identity of disciples as a marginal, low-status community in 20:26; 23:11 (cf. 24:45-51; 25:14-30). The condemned have not lived as disciples. They have not recognized Jesus' authority over their lives, despite calling him **Lord** (cf. 7:21-23).

• **25:45**

The Son of Man's response resembles but contrasts his words to the righteous in 25:40. **Then he will answer them, "Truly I tell you, just as you did not do it to one of the least of these my brothers and sisters, you did not do it to me."** See 25:40. They did not recognize Jesus' presence in the mission proclamation of the disciples (10:42) and have not lived a life of active mercy in faithful obedience to Jesus' teaching.

• **25:46**

The explanations are finished and the judgments are enacted. **And these will go away into eternal punishment, but the righteous into eternal life.** Compare Dan 12:1-3. On the **eternal punishment** of fire, darkness, weeping and gnashing of teeth, see 25:30, 41. On **righteous**, see 25:37. **Eternal life** is literally "life of the age," life which participates in the full establishment of God's empire, life which enjoys God's presence without all that presently opposes God's purposes (death, sin, tyranny, oppression, hunger, disease, Rome). See 4:23-24; 7:14; 12:1-8; 14:13-21; 18:8-9; 19:16-17, 29. The establishment of God's empire ends Rome's imperial reign, which benefits the powerful elite at the expense of the rest. Disciples are presently among the dishonored poor, the marginalized, and the oppressed (those lacking adequate food, housing, clothing, etc.). They will be vindicated in the judgment.

CHAPTER 26

The Passion Narrative

Part 1

The sequence of chapters is startling. After a vision of King Jesus executing universal judgment at his return, chapter 26 narrates events leading to his crucifixion.[1] Those he will judge first judge him and determine their fate in his judgment.

In a further irony, Jesus is condemned as a righteous person. He follows in the tradition of Joseph in Pharaoh's court (Gen 39-40); Esther under Haman's genocidal policy; Shadrach, Meshach, and Abednego under the edict of King Nebuchadnezzar requiring worship (Dan 3); Daniel under King Darius's similar edict (Dan 6); Susanna and the lustful elders; the martyrs (seven brothers and their mother) who refuse to comply with Antiochus Epiphanes' demands (2 Macc 7); or the afflicted wise person of Wisdom 2-5. Jesus, the righteous person, refuses to compromise his commitment to God's just empire and is persecuted and martyred by the religious and political elite. He will be vindicated by God after his suffering.[2] The repeated evoking of Psalms of the Righteous Sufferer (Pss 22; 69) and of Isaiah's suffering servant throughout chapters 26-27 underlines this presentation.[3]

Jesus' crucifixion in Jerusalem primarily results from proclaiming and embodying God's reign or empire. The life-giving and just power of God's empire conflicts with and challenges the hierarchical, exploitative, and oppressive practices of Rome's empire and the allied religious elite. Jesus dies because of his commitment to God's different world order, present and future. The religious elite condemn him as a blasphemer. Rome crucifies him as a treasonous insurrectionist. His death reveals both the center's desperate, self-serving, and brutal use of power to protect their own interests against those on the margins, and the power of his commitment to a different way of life.

But their violence does not triumph, as the vision of Jesus' return and the establishment of God's empire in chapters 24-25 has shown. Jesus is complicit in his own death. He declares that it will happen (16:21; 17:12, 22-23; 20:17-19). He goes to Jerusalem, the elite's center of power. He is aware of the threatening impact of his proclamation and enactment of God's empire on his opponents, but maintains his faithfulness and resoluteness to God's justice and life-giving reign in the face of their opposition, his own struggles (26:36-46), and his abandonment by his disciples and (seemingly) by God (26:36-46, 56; 27:46). His resistance is costly and its suffering inevitable.

By contrast, Jesus' disciples, the alternative community formed by God's empire, wilts under the pressure and deserts him, while Judas betrays him. Disciples have yet to learn what it means to carry and live the way of the cross (16:24-26). One of the functions of telling this story is to inspire faithfulness.

Moreover, the narrative emphasizes that mysteriously through Jesus' conflict, faithful suffering, and death, God's purposes are being accomplished. Jesus has previously indicated that giving his life in death is an act that is consistent with his identity as God's slave. It impacts not only himself but is a "ransom in the place of and for the benefit of many" (see 20:28). It is a means of liberation from a sinful imperial world. It effects release or forgiveness from sin (26:28). But just how this is accomplished is not made clear in chapters 26-27. It seems that God does not answer his cries of abandonment but leaves him to die. The audience has to read on into chapter 28 to see what God will do.

These characters and emphases weave their way through the chapter's seven sections:

26:1-16   The Preparation: Four Perspectives
26:17-35   The Last Supper
26:36-46   Agony in Gethsemane
26:47-56   Jesus' Arrest
26:57-68   Jesus' Trial before Caiaphas and the Sanhedrin
26:69-75   Peter's Betrayal

26:1-16—THE PREPARATION: FOUR PERSPECTIVES

Four short scenes (26:1-2, 3-5, 6-13, 14-16) identify diverse perspectives on, and the various roles of, key players in Jesus' death: Jesus predicts his own death; the religious elite plan it; a woman disciple recognizes it while other disciples do not; and Judas assists by betraying Jesus.

• 26:1-2

The chapter opens with a transition clause, **When Jesus had finished saying all these things.** The clause concludes chapters 24-25, Jesus' discourse about the signs of his future coming to establish God's empire in full. It also recalls Jesus' four previous teaching discourses (chapters 5-7, 10, 13, 18), which have concluded in the same way (7:28; 11:1; 13:53; 19:1). The addition of **all** provides a note of finality to Jesus' teaching. He has revealed God's will and shaped the identity and way of life of the community of disciples. The clause also echoes words used of Moses' teaching in Deut 31:1; 32:45. Moses and Jesus teach God's will.

Jesus speaks **to his disciples**; see 5:1; 10:1-4. **"You know that after two days the Passover is coming and the Son of Man will be handed over to be crucified."** Again Jesus announces his imminent death. He remains faithful to his God-given commission in a context of tyranny and the inevitable retaliation of the center. His previous passion predictions (16:21; 17:12, 22-23; 20:17-19) have not mentioned that his death will take place at **Passover**. Perhaps **know** should be read as an imperative not an indicative. This festival, another link with Moses, celebrates the liberation of God's people from slavery in Egypt (Exod 12-13; Josephus, *JW* 4.402). God's victory over tyrannical rule past and future provides the context for Jesus' death. On **Son of Man,** see 8:20; the proximity to its numerous uses in chapters 24-25 supplies great irony (24:27, 30, 37, 39, 44; 25:31). The one who will judge the world and condemn the resistant and oppressive elite is to be subjected to their destructive, though limited, power. On the polyvalent **handed over/arrested/betrayed,** see 17:22; 20:18, 19. What happens to Jesus happens also to disciples (10:17, 19, 21; 24:9, 10). On **crucified** as a means of political execution and imperial control, see 10:38; 16:24; 20:19.

• 26:3-5

The focus quickly moves to the religious elite, who will unwittingly accomplish what Jesus has just predicted. The opening **then** closely links the two scenes. **Then the chief priests and the elders of the people gathered in the palace of the high priest, who was called Caiaphas.** Jesus has previously signaled the role of the religious elite, the **chief priests and elders**, and the Sanhedrin[4] in Jerusalem in his death (16:21; 20:18; cf. 26:47; 27:1, 3, 12, 20, 41). Despite knowing what they plan, he remains true to his mission. The chief priests and elders are members of the governing class, allies with Herod (2:4) and Pilate (27:62-66), beneficiaries and protectors of the status quo and its unjust hierarchical practices. Josephus notes their alliances with the "leading Pharisees" and the "powerful" or "notable" citizens in support of Rome (*JW* 2.410-14). They value their privileged role legitimated by birth, gender, wealth, social position, tradition, and political alliance, and so do not appreciate Jesus' critique of the unfaithfulness of the religious leadership (cf. 5:20; 9:36; 20:25-28; ch. 23). Tension between them and Jesus has increased since chapter 21. In 21:15, 23, angered by his actions and reception in the temple, they challenge his authority and refuse to recognize him as God's agent ("Christ," 1:1, 16, 17, 18, 21-23; 3:15). In 21:45 they, with the Pharisees, plan to arrest him after he condemns them for unfaithful leadership and for rejecting God's messengers (21:28-44). In opposing God's anointed they enact the role of the nations, "kings of the earth" and rulers in Ps 2:2 (see Matt 17:25). This is not surprising since the **chief priests** were introduced in 2:4 as King Herod's allies. By identifying the birthplace of the Christ from the scriptures, they assist Herod's attempt to kill Jesus. At the end of the gospel story they continue the same death-dealing work as allies of the political elite.

Significantly, the Pharisees, with whom Jesus has also increasingly conflicted since chapter 21 (21:45; 22:15, 34, 41; ch. 23) and who in 12:14 plan to kill him, are not mentioned. They will appear with the chief priests in 27:62 (cf. 21:45) and are clearly involved in Jesus' death. Numerous groups comprise an alliance of the religious elite in opposition to Jesus. The prominence of one group (such as the chief priests) evokes all the religious elite.

The conspirators meet in a location of power, **in the palace of the high priest, who was called Caiaphas**. This is the first reference to Caiaphas as the high priest (also 26:57). His collusion with Rome is prepared for by 2:4-6 and by 20:18-19, which identifies Jesus' killers as both the chief priests and Gentiles (= Rome).[5] The term **high priest** is the same as that used for the **chief priests**. The plural is not strictly correct since there was only one high priest in office. The plural signifies, rather, the leading, socially elite, priestly families from whom the chief priest was selected. This whole social and religious entity is opposed to Jesus. Jesus, founder of an egalitarian, marginal community of disciples (cf. 23:8-12), conflicts with this group at the top of hierarchical society (see Introduction, section 5).

• 26:4-5

And they conspired to arrest Jesus by stealth and kill him. The verses largely repeat the elite's intent stated in 21:45-46. The element of **stealth** seems misplaced when Jesus has declared their purposes four times previously (16:21; 17:22-23; 20:18; 26:2). But it highlights their vicious and underhanded means of proceeding. The term frequently describes the unjust acts of the wicked against the righteous in the Psalms. The oppressed righteous seek God's deliverance from them (Pss 35:20; 52:2).

Jesus has already predicted that they will **kill** him (16:21; 17:23). He has identified **killing** as one of their common traits (10:18; 21:35, 38, 39; 23:34; 24:9). The verb **arrest/seize** (common in the chapter, 26:48, 50, 55, 57) is used for Herod's arrest of John in 14:3 (also **kill** in 14:5). The religious elite do to Jesus what the political figure Herod does to John. The similarities in the presentation of John and Jesus continue, as does the alliance of religious and political forces. The verb also denotes violent actions against others in 18:28 and 22:6. Ironically, by contrast, it indicates Jesus' life-giving actions (9:25; 28:9).

But they are somewhat frustrated in their plan: **But they said, "Not during the festival, or there may be a riot among the people."** Their concern recalls the crowds' welcome of Jesus in 21:1-17. Riots would necessitate greater Roman involvement in everyday control and a loss of power and face by the religious elite. They will succeed in their plans by winning over the crowd (27:20-26). Contrast their vagueness about when they will arrest Jesus with his reference to a specific time slot of "after two days" (26:2). The festival of liberation is the occasion for their act of tyranny.

• 26:6-13

This scene again indicates Jesus' awareness of his death (26:12). But in contrast to the religious leaders (and disciples), a woman anoints Jesus, an act that depicts her as a prophet and priest, and recognizes him as a king who will die in an act of service to God.[6]

• 26:6

This scene of recognition occurs not in the hostile, scheming, and opulent location of the elite's palace (26:3-5) but in the home of a marginal leper. **Now while Jesus was at Bethany** (cf. 21:17) **in the house of Simon the leper**. On the physical suffering, social isolation, religious exclusion, and economic difficulties of lepers, see 8:2. Jesus heals them (8:1-4; 11:5) and instructs disciples to do the same (11:5). Is Simon healed, but still identified by his disease? Has Jesus healed him?

• 26:7

An unnamed woman anoints Jesus. **A woman came to him with an alabaster jar of very costly ointment, and she poured it on his head as he sat at the table**. Pliny notes that **alabaster** containers provide good storage for perfumes (*NH* 13.3). **Perfume** had various uses: to cover odor (Pliny, *NH* 13.1), sacred (Exod 30:25; 1 Chr 9:30), sexual (Cant 1:3, 4; 4:14; Judg 10:3), to display opulence (Amos 6:6; Isa 39:2), to anoint the dead (2 Chr 16:14). Her perfume is **very costly**. Either she is a wealthy woman or has saved what little she has for this costly act. Wealth is to be used to serve others and Jesus (so 2:11; 19:16-30; 27:57).

Her action, which she does not interpret, evidences deep caring and respect for Jesus. Jesus will link it in v. 12 to his death. Certainly the disciples are upset by it (v. 8). What does it signify? Was it a customary gesture appropriate to a feast? Two factors indicate another significance: (1) The verb **came** signifies respectful address including to a ruler (see 4:3, especially 8:2 for references). The verb along with her actions style Jesus as a king and the woman as a loyal slave. (2) The act **poured it on his head** is one of hospitality performed at meals (so Agrippa in Josephus, *Ant* 19.239). But it also suggests anointings of priests (Exod 29:7; Lev 21:10; cf. Ps 133:2; a priestly action in 2 Macc 1:31), and especially of kings (1 Sam 10:1 [David by the prophet Samuel]; cf. 1 Sam 16:6; 24:7 [the king is the "anointed one"]; 1 Kgs 19:16; 2 Kgs 9:3, 6). Anointing by pouring liquid on the head expresses a commission to perform a special role in God's service. Her anointing of Jesus shows him to be God's king (cf. 2:2; 27:11, 29, 37, 42), who represents God's empire, which is being established and anticipated in his ministry (4:17; 12:28; 24:27-31). In this role, he will be crucified as a rebel against Rome's rule.

• 26:8-9

The disciples are not impressed by her action. **But when the disciples saw it, they were angry and said, "Why this waste? For this ointment could have been sold for a large sum, and the money given to the poor."** The disciples' anger (so also 20:24 against the inappropriate request of two disciples) seems well placed after Jesus' exhortation to relieve the poor's suffering in 25:31-46.

• 26:10

Jesus, though, has a different perspective. **But Jesus, aware of this** (for his special knowledge of thoughts or comments, see 12:15; 16:8; 22:18), **said to** them, "Why do you trouble the woman? She has performed a good service for me." Jesus values her act as a **good work/service**. The same phrase describes the actions that disciples do to embody God's empire (5:16). The phrase **for me** emphasizes Jesus as its focus and beneficiary. Her commitment to him as a disciple motivates her action.

• 26:11

Jesus agrees with the disciples' concern for the poor. **For you always have the poor with you, but you will not always have me.** Jesus recognizes an ongoing situation of poverty (cf. Deut 15:11) without endorsing it or dismissing it. Such is life until imperial control ends (cf. 5:3-12). But within that reality, he has called disciples to relieve poverty through gifts and loans (5:42), almsgiving (6:1-4), redistribution of surplus wealth to the poor (19:16-22), and constant practical mercy (25:31-46). The point here is timing. She recognizes the moment while the disciples do not. Since he will not always be with the disciples as a physical presence (so 26:2), her devotional act is appropriate.

• 26:12-13

Jesus interprets her act. **By pouring this perfume on my body, she has prepared me for burial.** Her action is a prophetic sign-action (see 3:1), which points beyond itself in significance to Jesus' destiny of suffering and death at the hands of the elite. See 8:21-22 for the importance of burial.

Unlike the disciples (26:8-9), she has recognized that his identity as king means he will suffer and die at the hands of the empire. The contrast between the woman and the male disciples sets the stage for the rest of the passion, in which the male disciples struggle to be loyal (26:14-16, 20-25, 33-35, 40-43, 47-52, 56, 69-75), while women remain with him (27:19, 55-61; 28:1-10).

Jesus commends her action very highly. **Truly I tell you** (5:18), **wherever this good news is proclaimed in the whole world, what she has done will be told in remembrance of her.** What she has done is recognize the way of suffering and death as inevitable for those who resist the empire's ideology, methods, and structures. The **good news** (see 4:23; 9:35; 11:5; 24:14) concerns not the emperor's birthday or the empire's supposed benefits to all, but God's empire, which is present in Jesus' words and actions (4:17; 12:28) and which will be established over **the whole world** in full at his return (24:27-31). He is king of a life-giving empire, one that contrasts with and abolishes Rome's oppressive rule at his return, but only after that empire has tried to crush Jesus in putting him to death. The proclamation of Jesus' death and resurrection **in the whole world** means reciting her action because her act recognizes his kingship in and through his death.

• 26:14-16

In contrast to the woman's costly act of service, and at about the same time (**then**), a male disciple asks the religious elite for money to betray Jesus. **Then one of the twelve, who was called Judas Iscariot, went to the chief priests and said, "What will you give me if I betray him to you?"** Judas was introduced in 10:4 in the list of twelve disciples as the betrayer. Now this description is elaborated. He takes the initiative, approaches the **chief priests** (see 26:3-5), and seeks money to betray Jesus. On the polyvalent **hand over/arrest/betray**, see 17:22; 20:18, 19. In 26:2 Jesus has announced that this act of betrayal will happen, though without specifying how. Judas's motivation seems to be the acquiring of money, against which Jesus has warned disciples (6:19-34; 10:9-10; 13:22; 19:16-30). **They paid him thirty pieces of silver.** The value is not clear. In Exod 21:32 this amount is compensation for a slave gored by an ox. In Zech 11:8-14 it seems to be wages for a month's shepherding work. Either way, Jesus is not highly valued. But Judas has enough: **And from that moment he began to look for an opportune time to betray him**. The phrase **from that moment he began to** has, ironically, appeared in 4:17 and 16:21 with Jesus as the subject to refer to Jesus' first proclamation of God's reign and to announce his imminent death. Judas's **opportune time** to have Jesus put to death is Jesus' "opportune time" (26:18) to give his life in faithfulness to God's empire (cf. 20:28).

Judas's role is strange. The chief priests know who Jesus is. They do not need help to arrest him, only a compliant crowd. Judas cooperates with them to accomplish something they can do without his aid. His actions, though, continue a trend evident in 26:8-9 and culminating in 26:56 and 69-75 as the disciples progressively abandon Jesus.

26:17-35—THE LAST SUPPER

• 26:17-19

Preparations are made for Passover, the time of Jesus' being handed over to be crucified (26:2). **On the first day of Unleavened Bread the disciples came to Jesus, saying, "Where do you want us to make the preparations for you to eat the Passover?"** Their question contrasts with Judas's question in 26:15. While he seeks to betray Jesus, these disciples seek to obey him. Have they been rebuked by the woman's actions in 26:6-13?

Jesus instructs them: **He said, "Go into the city to a certain man, and say to him, 'The Teacher says, My time is near; I will keep the Passover at your house with my disciples.'"** Jesus' instructions suggest previous arrangements rather than an impressment (compare the donkey, 21:2-3). Jesus refers to himself as **teacher** (10:24-25; 23:8-10, a synonym for Christ?), frequently a title used by opponents (8:19; 9:11; 12:38; 19:16; 22:16, 24, 36). Jesus' **time** is that of his crucifixion (26:2) and resurrection. It is the same opportune time Judas is seeking (26:16), but with different significance. Jesus' celebration of Passover **with my disciples** is appropriate, given that they are his household or family (12:46-50). This community, focused on God's anointed, contrasts with the elite's intent to destroy him (26:3-5).

The disciples obey Jesus' instruction (7:24-27; 12:46-50). **So the disciples did as Jesus had directed them, and they prepared the Passover meal.**

Jesus' prophecy in 26:18 is accurate; he is authoritative and in control of what is happening.

• **26:20-25**

The Passover meal is under way. For Jesus' previous meals and their significance, see 9:10-13; 11:19; 14:13-21; 15:32-39. Jesus' focus here is on betrayal and the breaking of the community's solidarity. **When it was evening, he took his place with the twelve and while they were eating, he said, "Truly I tell you, one of you will betray me."** The polyvalent word **betray** is the same as in 26:2, 4, but there it has the sense of "arrest" or "hand over." Its use here to indicate that one of the disciples will **betray** him is news to the disciples, though not to the gospel audience, since the verb recalls Judas's question in 26:15 (and 10:4). As in 26:18, Jesus' words predict a future event. The word **twelve** recalls their history with Jesus: their call (10:1, 2, 5), his teaching (11:1), their future (19:28), the way of the cross (20:17), and Judas's betrayal (26:14, 47).

• **26:22-24**

And they became greatly distressed (also 17:23 after the second passion prediction) **and began to say to him one after another, "Surely not I, Lord?" He answered, "The one who dipped his hand into the bowl with me will betray me. The Son of Man** (cf. 26:2; 8:20; 17:12, 22; 20:18, 28) **goes as it is written of him, but woe to the one by whom the Son of Man is betrayed! It would have been better for that one not to have been born."** The disciples' question (**Surely not I?**) is introduced by *mēti* (μήτι), which expects a negative answer and expresses their confidence that they will remain loyal. They call him **Lord**, a term that expresses trust in his power over diseases, demons, nature, and people (8:2, 8, 25; 9:38; 12:8; 14:30; 15:22; 25:37). But subsequently they will not trust him (26:56).

The focus narrows to one person. Jesus seems to know who the betrayer is but does not name him. The general reference to the scriptures without a particular verse in view (**as it is written of him**) reinforces the sense that Jesus is in control, that he is not surprised by what will happen, not a victim of Judas's actions. The **woe** underlines the grave eschatological consequences of Judas's decision to reject God's commissioned agent (11:21; 18:7; 23:13, 15, 16, 23, 25, 27, 29). Recalling the repeated woes of chapter 23 further links Judas the betrayer with Jesus' opponents (26:14-16).

• **26:25**

Jesus clarifies the prophecy that "one of you" will betray him. **Judas, who betrayed him, said, "Surely not I, Rabbi?"** The qualifier **who betrayed him** (10:4; 27:3) shows Jesus' prediction to be correct. Judas prefaces his question with *mēti* (μήτι), which expects a negative answer and shows Judas to be deceitful. He is already looking for an opportunity to betray Jesus (26:16). The term **Rabbi** also betrays Judas. Whereas the rest of the disciples call Jesus **Lord** in

26:22, as they usually do, Judas uses a title which Jesus has forbidden to disciples in 23:7-8. Jesus receives Judas's response without challenge or correction, **You have said so**.

• 26:26-29

While his death is an act of betrayal, it has other dimensions. Jesus explains to the disciples the significance of his imminent death by interpreting the meal's food.[7]

• 26:26

First it is a violent act of self-giving. **While they were eating, Jesus took a loaf of bread and after blessing it he broke it, gave it to his disciples, and said, "Take, eat; this is my body."** The blessed and broken bread represents Jesus' **body** or self (5:29, 30; 6:22-23; 26:12). The act of **breaking** the bread suggests the violence of his death by crucifixion. Giving it to the disciples indicates a self-offering. He does not escape the consequences of being faithful to God's empire and its collision with the elite. **Eating** the bread, like eating the Passover, is a means of solidarity with Jesus in the way of the cross (16:24) and of participating in the benefits of his death, previously described as "a ransom for many" (see 20:28). Numerous commentators have seen in the imperatives **Take, eat** a reflection of the community's liturgical celebration of this meal whereby the community looks back on and participates in Jesus' death.

• 26:27-28

Jesus interprets the cup to signify a covenant of liberation and release. **Then he took a cup, and after giving thanks he gave it to them, saying, "Drink from it all of you."** The imperative **drink**, which parallels the instruction to eat in 26:26, also probably reflects the community's liturgical celebration. Drinking is the means of participation in Jesus' death. **For this is my blood of the covenant, which is poured out for many for the release/forgiveness/jubilee from sins**. The cup (see 20:22) is identified as Jesus' **blood**. Blood is traditionally associated with life (Lev 17:14), so it signifies Jesus' giving of his life.

Blood is especially significant in the exodus. It is the means whereby God's people are saved from Egyptian oppression (Exod 12:12-13); it ensures their **release** from captivity. Moreover, the phrase **blood of the covenant** recalls Moses' act in Exod 24:8. After God's revelation on Mt. Sinai and gift of the Decalogue, blood from sacrifices seals the covenant between God and the people as the people commit to obey God's will. Likewise, Jesus' death seals a covenant marked by God's release from sins and obedience to God's will manifested in Jesus' teaching. A new exodus, this time involving a world dominated by Roman not Egyptian power, is under way. God's liberating work continues.

This covenant is sealed through Jesus' sacrificial death. He is **poured out**, a verb that refers to blood from sacrifices (Lev 4:7, 18, 25, 30, 34) as well as to the violent death of the righteous, killed by those who resist God's purposes (Matt 23:35).

In addition to God's liberation through the exodus from Egypt, another event in salvation history, the release from Babylonian captivity, is evoked. Like the suffering of the servant of Isa 53, who bears the suffering and sins of others for their benefit (Isa 53:4, 10; cf. Matt 8:17; 12:17-21), Jesus' death as a righteous person at the hands of the imperial powers benefits **many**. His blood/life is **poured out for many** (see 20:28 for **for many**). His death effects their **release** (BAGD, 125) **from sins**. This carries out in part his God-given commission to save from sins (1:21; 9:1-8).

But what is this **release from sins**? The noun **release** (ἄφεσις, *aphesis*) is usually translated "forgiveness," but it denotes much more than a personal restoration to fellowship with God (though it includes this). In Lev 25 the noun appears at least fourteen times to designate *the year of jubilee* or forgiveness (see 5:5).[8] Leviticus 25 provides for a massive societal and economic restructuring every fifty years, in which people rest from labor, land and property are returned and more evenly (re)distributed, slaves are freed, and households are reunited. In Deut 15:1-3, 9, the noun refers to the remission of the debts of the poor every seven years. In Jer 34 (LXX 41):8, 15, it refers to release of slaves (but note v. 17). In Isa 58:6 it defines part of God's chosen fast, "to let the oppressed go free," which parallels "to unloose the bonds of injustice; to undo the thongs of the yoke . . . and to break every yoke," an image of ending political oppression (see 11:28-29). In Isa 61:1, God's anointed is "to proclaim liberty/release to the captives, good news to the oppressed, to bind up the brokenhearted" (see Matt 5:3-6). In Esth 2:18 and 1 Macc 13:34 it indicates relief from imperial taxes.

The elite's central sin—the rejection of Jesus, for which Jerusalem and the religious elite are punished by Rome in the catastrophe of 70 (see 1:21; 21:12-13, 18-19, 41; 22:7; 27:25)—means a world contrary to God's just purposes. Jesus' death, like the exodus from Egypt, the return from exile in Babylon, and the year of jubilee, effects release from, a transformation of, sinful imperial structures which oppress God's people, contrary to God's will. His death establishes God's justice or empire, including release from Rome's power. **Release from sins**, then, has personal and sociopolitical and cosmic, present and future dimensions.

How does Jesus' death accomplish this **release . . . for many**? As with the image of ransom in 20:28, the gospel does not explicitly say. Some guesses are appropriate. In part it happens through the resurrection, in which God overcomes the worst that the elite can do. Their sinful power and way of structuring the world are shown not to be the final word. The community of disciples seeks to live an alternative existence in accord with God's will. Moreover, Jesus' death and resurrection anticipate his return, in which the elite's sinful rule is destroyed and God's life-giving and just empire is established over all, including Rome (24:27-31; 26:29).

• 26:29

This return and final victory or release from sins are made explicit as Jesus predicts both his death and return (so chs. 24-25). **I tell you, I will never again drink of this fruit of the vine** (because of his imminent death) **until that day** (on the day of the Lord/the day of judgment; see 7:22; 10:15; 11:22, 24; 12:36; 24:36, 42) **when I drink it new with you in my Father's empire/reign**. The present meal of Jesus and the disciples anticipates their participation together (**with you**; 26:18, 20) in the future establishment of God's empire. The image of the eschatological banquet is evoked (see 8:11-12; 22:11-4) in the emphasis on drinking wine (Isa 25:6; Joel 2:24; 3:18). The phrase **my Father's reign/ empire** anticipates the completion of God's purposes, the establishment of God's justice in full and Rome's vanquishment (see 8:11-12; 13:43; 19:28; 24:27-31).[9]

• 26:30-35

The supper scene concludes with further predictions which anticipate major elements in the passion story. Jesus will die (27:45-50) and be raised (ch. 28). All the disciples will desert him (26:56) but be reunited in Galilee (28:16-20). And Peter will deny Jesus three times before the cock crows (26:69-75).

• 26:30-31

When they had sung the hymn, they went out to the Mount of Olives (21:1; 24:3). **Then Jesus said to them, "You will all become deserters/stumble because of me this night."** The roller-coaster presentation of the disciples continues. They misunderstand and resist the woman who anoints Jesus (26:6-13); one of them sets out to betray Jesus (26:14-16); they serve and obey him in preparing for the Passover (26:17-19). Now they will **all** desert him (**because of me**). Jesus has previously predicted their unfaithfulness (using the same verb; 13:21; 24:10). The disciples join numerous others who have been **scandalized/stumbled** by Jesus' call to the way of the cross (11:6; 13:57; 15:12). On other uses of the verb **desert/stumble/scandalize**, see 5:29-30; 17:27; 18:6, 8, 9.

Their flight contrasts his faithfulness to God's purposes in the face of deathly opposition. But the scriptures indicate that their desertion is not final. **For it is written, "I will strike the shepherd, and the sheep of the flock will be scattered."** Jesus cites Zech 13:7-9, though he does not exactly quote either the Hebrew or LXX texts. Zechariah speaks of God's punishment of Jerusalem, which will scatter and destroy two-thirds of the people but one-third will be restored in a reestablished covenant.

Here the scene is christologized. The image of Jesus as **shepherd** has appeared previously in 2:6 and 9:36, where Jesus' compassionate and transformative actions have been contrasted with the religious and political elite, who have failed to care justly for God's people. In 25:32 as the eschatological judge, Jesus is the shepherd who divides the sheep and the goats. On **sheep** as God's people, see 9:36; 10:6, 16. The influence of Ezek 34 on the image of the shepherd and sheep is likely. Ezekiel 34 condemns the false shepherds for oppressing and exploiting the people (34:1-4, 7-10), but looks for a Davidic shepherd (Jesus in Matt 1:1; 9:27; 15:22; 20:30-31; 21:9, 15; 22:41-45) who will save them "from the hands of those who enslaved them" (Ezek 34:23-24), gather the scattered sheep (Ezek 34:5-6, 12-16) and rule faithfully in a new age (Ezek 34:23-30).[10] To **strike the shepherd** is to kill him as both the context and the verb's usage in Exod 2:12 indicate. Jesus again predicts his death.

• **26:32**

But true to Zech 13 there will be restoration. The disciples' fall will not be permanent. **But after I am raised up I will go ahead of you to Galilee.** Jesus has spoken of being **raised** after his death in 16:21; 17:23; 20:19. His resurrection, not *parousia,* is in view as the references to meeting with his disciples in **Galilee** in 28:7, 10, 16-20 indicate. Again his words turn out to be trustworthy.

• **26:33**

While Jesus has spoken of all the disciples ("You will all . . ."; 26:31), attention focuses on Peter as he brashly tries to exempt himself from Jesus' word and the scriptures. **Peter said to him. "Though all become deserters because of you, I will never desert you."** The vocabulary copies Jesus' statement in 26:31 closely. The addition of **never** intensifies the denial, while **because of you** keeps commitment to Jesus center-stage.

• **26:34-35**

Jesus counters Peter's claim with another detailed prediction. **Jesus said to him, "Truly I tell you, this very night, before the cock crows, you will deny me three times."** But Peter again resists Jesus' words, just as he rejected Jesus' first announcement of his imminent death (16:21-23). He makes a second bold statement of his loyalty, which in effect asserts that Jesus and the scriptures are wrong in predicting he will stumble. **Peter said to him, "Even though I must die with you, I will not deny you."** The double use of **deny** ironically recalls 16:24 (also 10:33) where Jesus, having made his first passion prediction, calls disciples to deny themselves and take up the cross. Peter's words do not mean self-denial, but they jeopardize his status before God (10:33). Peter's words in the protasis, or conditional clause (**even though**), anticipate the situation of possible death in which he will soon find himself (26:69-75). But he will not live up to the claim of the main clause. On Peter's previous roles in the gospel, see 4:18; 10:2; 14:28-31; 15:15; 16:16-19, 21-23; 17:1-4. All the disciples follow him in denying the truth of Jesus' prediction: **And so said all the disciples**.

26:36-46—AGONY IN GETHSEMANE

Thus far Jesus has been resolute in his commitment to God's empire and to his destiny of death in the face of the opposition of the political and religious elite. This scene, though, depicts great inner distress and struggle as he faces his martyrdom.

• 26:36-38

Then Jesus went with them to a place called Gethsemane. Presumably this is on the Mount of Olives (26:30; cf. Zech 14 the site of God's eschatological victory). **And he said to his disciples, "Sit here while I go over there and pray." He took with him Peter and the two sons of Zebedee.** These three disciples form something of an inner group. They (with the absent Andrew— why?) were the first to be called in 4:18-22 (cf. 10:2); they experienced the transfiguration in 17:1-8; and James and John, with their mother, sought the top places in God's empire and confidently declared they could drink from or share Jesus' cup or suffering (20:20-24). Their confidence is about to be shown to be misplaced. They, like Peter (16:22), have trouble understanding the cross as a consequence of Jesus' faithfulness and as preparation for the establishment of God's empire. Despite predicting their desertion, Jesus vainly seeks their support and solidarity.

Jesus **began to be grieved and agitated**. Three of the four previous uses of the verb **grieved** express distress in situations of danger and threat (17:23; 18:31; 19:22; cf. 14:9; Ps 55:2; Tob 3:1, 10). The verb **agitated** is rare (only here in Matthew). **Then he said to them, "I am deeply grieved, even to death; remain here and stay awake with me."** The phrase **I am deeply grieved** (literally, "my soul is downcast") quotes a refrain from lament psalms (Pss 42:5, 11; 43:5) in which the Psalmist looks for God's deliverance from oppressive enemies and a do-nothing God (Pss 42:9-10; 43:1-2; cf. 55:1-6). Jesus is located among the righteous sufferers who cry out to God whose inactivity is, ironically, as much the cause of Jesus' suffering as the opponents. The intensity of Jesus' distress is underlined by **to death**. Jesus does not in this scene embrace his death calmly as did Socrates, or nobly, "willingly and generously" as did the Maccabean martyrs (2 Macc 6:28, 19-20).

• 26:39

And going a little farther, he fell on his face and prayed. Jesus has prayed alone previously (14:23). But in chapter 26 his isolation is increasingly emphasized, by physical separation from most of the disciples (26:36), here by distance from three of them, then by their continual sleeping (26:40-45), then through Judas's betrayal (26:46), and supremely by a silent God who does not answer his desperate and repeated prayers. To **fall on his face** is a common biblical position for prayer and encountering the divine (Gen 17:3, 17; Num 22:31; Dan 8:17), and a position of desperation and anguish (Num 14:5; 1 Sam 20:41; 2 Sam 9:6). His prayer is to not face death by crucifixion. **"My Father, if it is possible, let this cup pass from me."** Exemplifying his own teaching in 6:9, he addresses God as **Father** (cf. 5:16; 11:25; 23:9; 26:29) and prays to escape the terror and humiliation of crucifixion (see 16:24). The **cup** (in context and consistent with 20:22) refers to this imminent and overwhelming suffering of death by crucifixion. Though he has been resolute until now, Jesus now shrinks from the horror of being faithful to his charge. Asking God to change plans is not uncommon or faithless in the biblical tradition (Moses [Exod 32:10-14]; Hezekiah [2 Kgs 20:1-6]; Judas [1 Macc 3:58-60]).

God makes no response. Jesus resigns himself to doing the divine will. **Yet not what I want but what you want**. No indication of the depth of struggle to reach this point of resolution is offered (cf. 7:24-27; 12:46-50). But the resolution is not solid, and the struggle continues through two more sessions of prayer.

• 26:40-41

Then he came to the disciples and found them sleeping. They are unable to obey Jesus' charge to **remain here and stay awake with me** (26:38). **He said to Peter** (the group's representative), **"So could you not stay awake with me one hour?"** He renews their task: **Stay awake and pray that you may not come into the time of trial**. The reference to the **time of trial** echoes the sixth petition of the Lord's Prayer (6:13a). What is this **time of trial**? Jesus does not instruct them to pray against being tempted to unfaithfulness. Temptation seems inevitable since Jesus has already predicted it with scriptural support (26:31-35). Nor does he command prayer to escape the time of tribulation. That time is the present, the time in which disciples live between Jesus' ministry and return, as chapters 24-25 make clear. They have already entered it and will remain in it until Jesus returns.

Rather, as with 6:13a, Jesus' instruction concerns the temptation to doubt God's faithfulness or commitment to do God's will.[11] Israel tested God at Massah by doubting God's presence and God's promise to deliver them and supply water (Exod 17:1-7; Deut 6-8; the noun **temptation/testing/time of trial** appears in Exod 17:7; Deut 6:16; 7:19). The temptation to doubt God's plans, goodness, faithfulness, and ability is not far from Jesus or the disciples in the story, or from Matthew's audience. Unless disciples truly understand that Jesus' imminent death is a consequence of his commission and is not the end of God's purposes to establish God's empire, they will readily doubt God's commitment and ability to accomplish God's purposes in the face of human evil and imperial power. Jesus urges them to pray against despair, against concluding that God is absent, inactive, or has been rendered powerless by, or been defeated in, Jesus' death.

The spirit is willing but the flesh is weak. The terms **flesh** and **spirit** identify not parts of the human being in conflict with each other, but the whole person considered from two different perspectives.[12] In 16:17 **flesh** designates the human situation as weak and limited in its accomplishments. In contrast, humans can intend or hope for what they cannot accomplish (26:33, 35). While the disciples (and Jesus?) hope to stay loyal to God's purposes (**spirit**), they will struggle to do so (**flesh**).

• 26:42-44

Jesus' struggle continues in another round of prayer. **Again he went away for the second time and prayed, "My Father, if this cannot pass unless I drink it, your will be done."** Now he resigns himself to the consequences of being faithful to God's will. For the third time he invokes the Lord's prayer, citing the third petition (6:10b) word for word (**your will be done**). He returns to his disciples but they have not been attentive to his last exhortation. **Again he came and found them sleeping, for their eyes were heavy.** He prays a third time. **So leaving them again, he went away and prayed for the third time, saying the same words**.

• 26:45-46

But nothing changes. **Then he came to the disciples and said to them, "Are you still sleeping and taking your rest?** There is, though, fresh urgency. **See, the hour is at hand, and the Son of Man is betrayed into the hands of sinners.** Jesus' **hour** seems to be more than the immediate arrest. It is the whole series of events which comprise his death and resurrection (possibly his return; see 24:36, 44), the consequence of his faithfulness to God's commission. On the verb **is at hand** indicating both nearness and arrival, see 3:2; 4:17. On **Son of Man**, see 8:20. Its use in the eschatological discourse (24:27, 30, 37, 39, 44; 25:41) creates a strong irony. The one who as **Son of Man** judges the cosmos and establishes God's empire is condemned by the religious and political elite and betrayed by a false disciple (26:2, 24). On **betrayed/given over**, a key word with various nuances, see 17:22; 26:2, 15, 16, 21, 23, 24, 25. Here the **handing over** involves Judas's betrayal, the elite's opposition, God's purposes, and Jesus' consent. The phrase **into the hands of sinners** resembles "into the hands of human beings," which names the agents of Jesus' death in the second passion prediction of 17:22. **Sinners** is a polemical term indicating opponents (see 9:10-13; 11:19). Here they are the religious and political elite responsible for Jesus' death. **Get up, let us be going. See my betrayer** (Judas, 10:4; 26:14-16, 25) **is at hand** (the same verb as is used with my hour, 26:54). The betrayer and the hour are interwoven.

26:47-56—JESUS' ARREST

• 26:47

Judas's opportunity to arrest and betray Jesus has arrived. The initial **While he was still speaking** overlaps this scene with the last to show Jesus' identification of "the hour" (26:45) to be correct. **Behold** (to highlight what is happening), **Judas, one of the twelve, arrived; with him was a large crowd with swords and clubs, from the chief priests and elders of the people.** The phrase **one of the twelve** underlines the tragedy of the events. One whom Jesus called, commissioned, accompanied, and instructed (see 10:1, 2, 5; 11:1; 20:17; 26:20) betrays him, just as Jesus predicted (26:2, 14-16, 20-25).

The presence of **a large crowd with swords and clubs** highlights both the physical violence of the process and the crowds' nonunderstanding of Jesus, who has set aside violent resistance (5:39). Behind these events are **the chief priests and elders** (26:3-5, 14-16). Josephus records that ca. 59 C.E. the chief priests had used mobs to fight the mobs of the priests and leaders of the people. The weapons were verbal abuse and stones. High priests also used slaves and mobs to forcibly remove tithes for themselves from threshing floors. This act caused poor priests to starve. The elite typically resorts to violence to impose its will, assert control, and secure its resources (*Ant* 20.181, 206-7).

• 26:48-50

Now the betrayer (Judas's whole existence is defined by this one act) **had given them a sign, saying, "The one I will kiss is the man."** A **kiss** is a gesture of welcome and respect (cf. Acts 20:37; Rom 16:16), but Judas uses it to enact his evil. Neither Jesus nor the gospel audience is fooled by the gesture, since both know Judas to be the enemy (cf. Prov 27:6).[13] The verb **arrest/seize him** is the same verb that states the religious elite's intent in v. 4; Judas carries out their will. **At once he came up to Jesus and said, "Greetings, Rabbi!"** (cf. 26:25, 22) **and kissed him. Jesus said to him, "Friend** (the term is ironic, as in 20:13 and 22:12, where appropriate behavior is absent and a rebuke is given) **do what you are here to do." Then they came and laid hands on Jesus and arrested him.** Whereas here **hands** denote betrayal, hostility, and violence (as they have in 26:23, 45, 51), Jesus has used his hands to heal (8:3, 15; 9:18, 25), to define his community/family (12:49), to save (14:31), and to bless (19:13, 15).

• 26:51

Attention moves from Judas to another disciple. This one uses force to resist the arrest (26:51-54). **Suddenly/And behold** (to indicate surprising and sudden action), **one of those with Jesus put his hand on his sword, drew it, and struck the slave of the high priest cutting off his ear**. Being **with** Jesus (or Jesus being with disciples) has been a common expression in the chapter (26:18, 20, 23, 29, 36, 38, 40, 51, 69, 71). **One of those with Jesus** seems to be a disciple. He, though, has not heeded Jesus' teaching in 5:38-42. What is a disciple doing with a sword? Nor has he understood that Jesus' arrest and death are inevitable (16:21), and that Jesus consents to them (as recently as 26:42-46). The **high priest's slave** is a slave with considerable prestige derived from his powerful and honored master (see 20:27), yet as a slave he remains marginal to the center of power. On violence to slaves, see 8:5-6. Is it significant that his **ear** is cut off? Does it emphasize that the elite, in contrast to the community of disciples, have refused to listen to Jesus (13:9, 14-16, 43)?

• 26:52-53

Jesus rebukes the action with a specific instruction: **Then Jesus said to him, "Put your sword back into its place."** The verb **put back** occurs elsewhere in Matthew only in Jesus' teaching about nonviolent resistance (5:42; see 5:38-42). He rejects violent defense by asserting its inevitable consequences; **for all who take the sword will perish by the sword**. These consequences were demonstrated in Rome's crushing of Jewish military opposition in 70 C.E. (cf. 24:5, 11, 24). Rome, whose empire is built on military might (Josephus, *JW* 3.70-109), will in turn meet its end in Jesus' return to establish God's empire in its fullness (24:27-31).

Jesus rejects the military option. **Do you think** (introducing Jesus' questions in 17:25; 18:12; 21:28; 22:42) **that I cannot appeal to my Father, and he will at once send me more than twelve legions of angels?** Available to Jesus is enormous power, armies or **legions of angels** (Josh 5:14; Ps 148:2; Dan 12:1; 1QM 7:6; 13:10; *2 Bar* 7:1-8:1; 63:5-11; 2 Macc 3:[13-21], 22-34; 10:29-31; 11:6; 15:20-24; 4 Macc 4:8-11; Zeus also had heavenly warriors; BAGD, 468). Angels will accompany him at his return to establish God's empire (13:41; 16:27; 24:27-31; 25:31). **Legion** is a Latin loanword. A **legion** comprised about six thousand soldiers (BAGD, 467-68). There were three or four stationed in Antioch (see Introduction, section 5). Jesus could call on seventy-two thousand angels, more than enough to overwhelm the crowd with its swords and clubs, and more than enough to deal with the whole of the local Roman military! All it needs is an **appeal to my Father** (26:29, 39, 42).

But he does not do so. He has accepted in Gethsemane (26:36-46) that faithfulness to his God-given commission to manifest God's saving presence and empire means inevitable death at the hands of the religious and political elite, who will truck no opposition or alternative. He must die. He refuses holy war and angelic help (also 4:5-7). He refuses to use his power except to benefit (serve, 20:28) others in healing, exorcism, and miracles concerning food and safety. Instead, he takes the way of nonviolent resistance (5:38-42) and remains faithful to God's commission even to death. Moreover, his fidelity exposes the misdirected, intolerant, destructive nature of their power, as well as, in his resurrection and return, its limited and condemned nature. His action again compels disciples after 70 still under Roman control to find alternative and nonviolent ways to resist the empire's definition of reality and control until Jesus' return.

• 26:54

This way is rooted in scripture. **But how then would the scriptures be fulfilled, which say it must happen in this way?** He does not cite a specific scripture. Perhaps Zech 13:7 is in view from 26:31 since it speaks of "striking the shepherd." Or perhaps a series of texts and stories is implied: the rejected prophets of 23:34-37; the suffering righteous of the lament psalms like Pss 42-43 evoked in Matt 26:38; the suffering servant of Isa 52-53. Texts throughout the scriptures speak consistently of the fate of the righteous who refuse to yield to the center, who refuse to submit to unjust tyrants and oppressors, and who suffer for their fidelity to God's just ways (see 16:21).

• 26:55-56

Jesus now addresses the crowd (cf. 26:47). **At that hour** (cf. 26:45) **Jesus said to the crowds, "Have you come out with swords and clubs to arrest me as though I were a bandit?"** The word **bandit** can refer as in 21:13 to economic exploiters or thieves. Those who are truly thieves treat Jesus as one. Recall that in 26:47 Judas and the crowd come from the religious elite. But here (and in 27:38, 44) the term more likely refers to Robin Hood-like peasant bands with a recognized leader who were alienated by harsh economic conditions such as indebtedness and were involved in social unrest and violent civic uprisings against the elite (including an attack on Stephen, a slave of Caesar [Josephus, *JW* 2.228-29]). Terrorists raided property, forcibly gained booty, food, and land, and killed landlords, before themselves being killed in pursuit, or crucified. See Josephus, *JW* 2.238, 253, 264-65, 271-76, 540-55, 587; 4.84-127, 406-9; *Ant* 20.124, 160-72, 215, 255-56.[14] Does the use of this term prepare for the focus on Jesus being "King of the Jews" in chapter 27? Jesus rejects any such violent action (see the criticism of the insurrectionists in 24:5, 11, 23-26), though he is accurately identified with those on the margins who find the suffering and deprivation of the status quo, dominated by the oppressive and greedy elite, to be unacceptable. His strategy, though, has been quite different. It has involved active nonviolent resistance, the establishment of a community with alternative practices, and eschatological hope (5:3-12, 38-48).

Jesus is not violent, nor is he in hiding. He has been quite accessible to the religious elite; their stealth (26:4) is not necessary but casts them in dishonest light. **Day after day I sat in the temple teaching** (24:3; on sitting, see 5:1-2; 13:1-3), **and you did not arrest me.** Presumably it is evening (26:20; cf. 27:1); the action of the crowd at night enacts the religious elite's intent to arrest him "by stealth" (26:4). **But all this has taken place so that the scriptures of the prophets may be fulfilled.** This thought is repeated from v. 54 to underline its importance. **All this** embraces all the passion events, not just Judas's betrayal, or the arrest or the flight. While Jesus remains steadfast to the fate of a rejected prophet, **all the disciples deserted him and fled**, just as he predicted (26:31-35). They demonstrate not the way of the cross, of losing their life to find it (16:24, 25b), but by trying to save it, they risk losing it (16:25a).

26:57-68—JESUS' TRIAL BEFORE CAIAPHAS AND THE SANHEDRIN

The arrested Jesus is taken to the Sanhedrin, the Jerusalem council under Caiaphas (see 26:3), which comprises priests, scribes, and laity. They condemn Jesus for blasphemy. As with the subsequent trial before Pilate, the central issue has to do with power. They refuse to recognize Jesus as God's commissioned agent (1:1, 21-23) because that would mean yielding their power and position to him as the interpreter of God's will and as the agent of God's empire. They prefer to remove this threat.

• **26:57**

Those who had arrested Jesus took him to Caiaphas the high priest, in whose palace the scribes and elders had gathered. The action moves back to the center, to Caiaphas's house, in which the religious elite had gathered at the beginning of the chapter and conspired to arrest and kill Jesus (see 26:3-5 for similar vocabulary). With Judas's help (26:14-16, 47-56), the goal to arrest him has been accomplished. Now they must kill him. On **arrest**, see 26:4, 48, 50, 55. On **scribes** as part of the religious elite opposed to Jesus, trained in the law's interpretation, see 2:4; 9:3; 15:1; 16:21; 23:2, 13, 15, 23, 25, 27, 29, 34.

Elders are also part of the Sanhedrin, lay members from leading families; see 16:21, where Jesus has indicated their involvement in his death.

• 26:58

While all the disciples fled (26:56), Peter still follows. **But Peter was following him** (a verb of discipleship; see 4:20, 22) **at a distance, as far as the courtyard/palace of the high priest; and going inside, he sat with the guards to see how this would end.** All the focus centers on Caiaphas's place. Peter's presence prepares for his denial scene in 26:69-75. Just what Peter thinks he might achieve by being in the vicinity is not stated.

• 26:59

Now that the cast is assembled, the trial begins. The narration highlights its corrupt nature, consistent with the negative presentation of the religious elite throughout. **Now the chief priests and the whole council/Sanhedrin were looking for false testimony against Jesus so that they might put him to death.** As presented, the Sanhedrin does not seek truth or justice, but Jesus' **death**. They ignore the ninth commandment of the Decalogue not to bear false witness (Exod 20:16; Deut 5:20). This is the only testimony in which they are interested.

• 26:60-61

But they found none, though many false witnesses came forward. This is an enigmatic comment with the two clauses seeming to conflict with each other. Does it indicate that they heard no "credible" false testimony, or that no two false witnesses told the same story (two being needed to sustain a charge; Deut 19:15)? But **at last two came forward and said, "This fellow said, 'I am able to destroy the temple of God and build it in three days.'"** This testimony is useful because two agree. It is false testimony. The gospel has not presented Jesus as making this claim, either in 21:12-17 or 24:1-2 (v. 2 uses the same verb **destroy,** but Jesus is not the destroyer). But while Jesus has not said it, ironically they speak more truly than they know.[15]

The statement is quite consistent with Jesus' actions and words in 21:12-22 against the temple. It also reflects his claim in 12:6 to be greater than the temple and to have assumed the temple-related functions of manifesting God's presence (1:23; 18:20; 28:20) and forgiving sin (9:1-8; 26:28). Moreover, it is consistent with his sayings about his return as Son of Man (16:27; 19:28; 24:27-31), since some expected that in the new age when God's reign or empire was established, the temple would be rebuilt (*1 En* 90:28-9; 91:13-14; *Jub.* 1:17; Tob 14:4-6). Perhaps Jesus will accomplish this expectation (although in what form is not clear). And in 70, the Romans did destroy the temple, an action already presented as God's punishment on the city for rejecting Jesus (21:12-13, 18-19, 41; 22:6-7; 23:34-39; 27:25; cf. Josephus, *JW* 6.99-110).

The religious elite find the statement of the two witnesses condemning for two reasons. (1) They did not tolerate threats against the temple and city. A prophet who predicts the fall of its walls is killed (Josephus, *Ant* 18.169-70), and the peasant Jesus son of Ananias who predicts the temple's demise is whipped (Josephus, *JW* 6.300-309). Jesus' words threaten the center of the religious elite's power and status, its way of life, and its means of maintaining control over the people's lives through taxation, ritual, and teaching. (2) Jesus' claim exudes great power (**I am able**). It assumes a privileged position in God's purposes akin to his earlier statements about his future role (16:27; 19:28; 24:27-31; 25:31-46). Since the elite do not accept his claim to be God's commissioned agent (Christ), his claims sound not only dangerous but also blasphemous.

• 26:62-63

Caiaphas demands an explanation. **The high priest stood up and said, "Have you no answer? What is it that they testify against you?" But Jesus was silent.** Compare Jesus ben Ananias's silence in Josephus, *JW* 6.302, 305. Does Jesus' silence reflect contempt for the court, consent to the charge, or conformity to Isa 53:7, where the suffering righteous servant does not seek to talk his way out of his fate? Or is it nonviolent resistance which forces the elite to determine the truth of the accusation?

The truth of the saying lies in the identity of Jesus. Only God's anointed agent could build the temple (cf. 2 Sam 7:13-14 [God's son]), so the chief priest's next question concerns Jesus' identity. **Then the high priest said to him, "I put you under oath before the living God** (contrary to Jesus' teaching in 5:33-37), **tell us if you are the Messiah, the Son of God."** His question reformulates Peter's confession from 16:16. Expectations about Messiahs were diverse and not uniform in first-century Judaism (see 1:1). The word "Messiah" could have various meanings (recall Peter in 16:16-23). Something of the chief priest's thinking in asking the question may be indicated by 27:55, where Jesus asked the armed crowd sent by the chief priest if they think he is a bandit or brigand who stages armed attacks on the elite. The chief priest's question may be accusing Jesus not only of threatening the temple but also of being a false messiah, a sociopolitical-religious insurrectionist. Both accusations reflect a threat to their position and power.

The audience knows Jesus is the messiah, but not of this sort. He has been identified as the **Messiah** or God's anointed agent from the outset (see 1:1, 16, 17, 18; 2:4; 11:2; 16:16; 22:42; 23:10). He is commissioned to proclaim and demonstrate God's merciful reign or empire (11:2-6). But only disciples have recognized him. The religious elite have not, despite opportunities to hear his teaching and observe his actions (11:2-6; 22:42-45). God has identified Jesus as **God's son** (see 2:15; 3:17; 17:5), primarily a term of agency and intimate relation (11:25-27). The disciples have agreed with God's verdict (14:33; 16:16) but the elite have not.

• 26:64

Jesus responds with a public proclamation. **Jesus said to him, "You have said so."** As in 27:11 the answer is ambiguous. Jesus neither confirms nor denies it, but leaves it to them to prove.[16] He proceeds with a revelation of his future role, which means power over all including the religious elite. **But I tell you, from now on you will see the Son of Man seated at the right hand of Power and coming on the clouds of heaven.** This **Son of Man** saying (see 16:13-16 for the equation of Messiah and Son of Man; also *1 En* 46:3 and 48:10) belongs with others which concern his post-resurrection existence: his vindication and return, judgment and establishment of God's empire (13:39-43; 16:27-28; 19:28; 24:27-31; 25:31). The **seated Son of Man,** which assumes his crucifixion and vindication in resurrection, evokes the rule of the anointed king (Ps 110:1; Matt 5:1) and the power of the Son of Man in the judgment and in establishing God's empire (cf. Dan 7:13-14; *1 En* 62-63 [over rulers]; Matt 19:28; 25:31). **Power** is, in context, a most appropriate name for God in that the establishment of God's empire overpowers all other claimants. The **right side** recalls the dispute about places of honor in God's reign in 20:21-23, and Jesus' role in the judgment (25:31-33). God gives Jesus the place of honor and authority. His **coming** was the focus of chapters 24-25 (24:3). It will follow the present time of tribulation, but will be so majestic that none will miss it (24:27-31) as he executes judgment and establishes God's empire. As they do elsewhere in the biblical tradition (Exod 13:21-22; 16:10; 19:9, 16; 33:9; 40:34-38), **clouds** denote God's power and presence (Matt 17:5; 24:30). In Jesus' return, God's power and presence mean the establishment of God's empire or rule over all (cf. Dan 7:13-14).

• 26:65-66

A revelation requires a decision, either worship or rejection. **Then the high priest tore his clothes and said, "He has blasphemed! Why do we still need witnesses? You have now heard his blasphemy."** True to his conviction that Jesus is not God's anointed, the high priest is shocked by Jesus' claim. The **tearing of clothes** expresses dismay in various contexts (especially grief, Josh 7:6; Job 1:20; Jdt 14:19). Perhaps the most illuminating parallel is 2 Kgs 19:1. Hezekiah tears his garments after Rabshakeh the Assyrian has, in Hezekiah's view, arrogantly "mocked the living God" (2 Kgs 19:4) by claiming that Hezekiah's reliance on God to deliver the people from the Assyrians is misplaced (19:28-35). Caiaphas's **tearing** of his clothes, then, is consistent with his words, which deem Jesus' revelation to be blasphemy, a mocking or dishonoring of God (so 9:3; 12:31), a "violation of the power and majesty of God,"[17] because he claims such a privileged relationship to God and exalted role for himself in God's purposes.

Caiaphas demands from the Sanhedrin **your verdict? They answered, "He deserves death,"** the penalty for blasphemy (Lev 24:16). Note the wicked's announcement of death on the righteous in Jer 26:11; Dan 3:15; 6:12-13; Wis 2:20; 2 Macc 7:1-6. As chapter 27 shows, the Sanhedrin cannot enact this penalty itself but needs Rome's consent. Of course the supreme irony of the scene is that the Sanhedrin commits blasphemy (mocks and dishonors God) by resisting, rejecting, and condemning the one whose role is to enact God's purposes for the cosmos.

• 26:67-68

Having condemned Jesus for claiming such a lofty and exalted role, the Sanhedrin mocks and humiliates him. **Then they spat in his face and struck him; and some slapped him saying, "Prophesy to us, you Messiah! Who is it that struck you?"** The act of **spitting** can indicate guilt (Num 12:14; Deut 25:9). But also, in **spitting on**, **striking and slapping** Jesus, they insult him (cf. Job 30:9-10 for spitting; also Isa 50:6; Matt 27:30). They treat as an inferior the one who will share God's authority (28:18). Slaves and children are beaten as reflections of and reinforcement of their marginal status (see 5:39; 8:6). The religious elite continue the pattern of salvation history of beating and rejecting the prophets (21:35-36; 22:6; 23:34-38). Jesus models his own teaching of 5:38-42. The taunt to **prophesy**, to guess who strikes him, mocks his prophetic revelation of his future role in 26:64, a role which, ironically, will see Jesus judge and condemn them.

26:69-75—PETER'S BETRAYAL

• 26:69-70

Now Peter was sitting outside in the courtyard. Peter's presence at the high priest's palace was noted in 26:58 after Judas had betrayed Jesus (26:47-56) and all the disciples had fled (26:56). This scene develops his presence in v. 58 to depict the enactment of Jesus' prophecy about Peter's denial in 26:33-35. The scene immediately follows the soldiers' mocking of Jesus' prophetic ability, and comes three verses after the high priest and Sanhedrin have decided his prophecy about his future role cannot possibly be true. The demonstrable fulfillment of Jesus' prophecies about Judas (26:20-25, 47-57), the disciples (26:31-32, 56) and now Peter show his eschatological prophecy to be reliable.

A servant-girl came to him and said, "You also were with Jesus the Galilean." The accusation is made by one who in terms of gender in an androcentric society is Peter's inferior. Though a slave, she has some status as the slave of the high priest (cf. 20:25-28). The narrative again exhibits the power of the margins. Her description of Jesus as a **Galilean** identifies his outsider status, marginal to the Jerusalem center. On being **with** Jesus, see 25:51. She is right. Peter has followed Jesus since 4:18-20. **But he denied it before all of them, saying, "I do not know what you are talking about."** The verb **deny** recalls 26:35 and 10:33, which puts the action in eschatological perspective and Peter in eschatological danger (though 26:31 indicates restoration, as does ch. 28). See also 16:24-25. Peter speaks correctly and ironically; he does **not know** what being with Jesus on the way of the cross means.

• 26:71-72

A second denial follows. **When he went out to the porch, another servant-girl saw him and she said to the bystanders, "This man was with Jesus of Nazareth." Again he denied it with an oath, "I do not know the** man." The accuser (**another servant-girl**) and the charge remain essentially the same. **Nazareth** is more precise than Galilee; the place again denotes distance from, inferiority to, and suspicion by the center Jerusalem. But Peter's denial is more intense (**with an oath**; contrary to Jesus' teaching in 5:33-37) and more personal (**the man**).[18]

• 26:73-74

The third denial occurs. **After a little while, the bystanders came up and said to Peter, "Certainly you are also one of them, for your accent betrays you." Then he began to curse, and he swore an oath, "I do not know the man!"** The third denial is even stronger, involving an **oath**, and **cursing**. **At that moment the cock crowed,** probably signaling the approaching morning (27:1).

• 26:75

The final verse spells out the connection with 26:34. **Then Peter remembered what Jesus had said: "Before the cock crows, you will deny me three times." And he went out and wept bitterly.**

CHAPTER 27

The Passion Narrative

Part 2

As with the chapter division between chapters 24 and 25, any division between chapters 26 and 27 is artificial. The passion narrative (see introduction to chapter 26) continues through to Jesus' death and burial. There are six scenes:

27:1-2	Jesus Is Handed over to Pilate
27:3-10	Judas's Money
27:11-26	Jesus' "Trial" before Pilate
27:27-44	Jesus Is Crucified
27:45-56	Jesus Dies
27:57-66	Jesus' Burial

27:1-2: JESUS IS HANDED OVER TO PILATE

• **27:1-2**

This scene concludes Jesus' trial before the Sanhedrin (26:57-68), the narrative of which was interrupted by Peter's failure (26:69-75). The events since 26:20 have happened in the evening or overnight. Now it is the next day (cf. 27:45, 46, 57, 62). **When morning came, all the chief priests and the elders of the people conferred together against Jesus in order to bring about his death**. On the **chief priests'** roles, see 2:4; 16:21; 20:18; 21:15, 23, 45; 26:3, 14, 47, 51, 57-65. On the **elders,** see 16:21; 21:23; 26:3, 47, 57. They have deemed Jesus' revelation about his future role in God's purposes (26:64) to be blasphemy, which merits the death penalty (26:66). But the Sanhedrin (see 26:2) needs Roman permission to execute.[1] **They bound him, led him away, and handed him over** (see 17:22; 26:45) **to Pilate the governor**. The three verbs with Jesus as the object indicate his subordination to their power (cf. the suffering servant of Isa 53:7-8) even though he has previously predicted their actions (10:18; 20:19).

This is the first of numerous references to **Pilate the governor** (27:11, 13,

14, 15, 17, 21, 22, 24, 27, 58, 62, 65).[2] D. Weaver notes that, like King Herod in chapter 2 and Herod the tetrarch in 14:1-12, Pilate has the vestiges of enormous power.[3] To him belong oversight of the tasks of provincial government: military occupation, tax collection, and supervision of public order, which includes the power of life and death.[4] Before him Jesus seems powerless. But, Weaver argues, Pilate is unmasked through the scene as "a powerless puppet" who acts at the behest of the crowds and religious elite (27:15-26) and is powerless to do what he knows is right. As chapter 28 will show, he who represents Roman imperial power is powerless to accomplish the elite's goal of keeping Jesus dead. The narrative in no way exonerates Pilate or Rome. While the "trial" may be technically correct,[5] Roman "justice" is shown to be self-serving and expedient. The religious and political elite ally to kill Jesus.

27:3-10—JUDAS'S MONEY

The scene plays out Jesus' woe which announced tragic consequences on his betrayer, Judas (26:64). The section "follows the money" that Judas receives for betraying Jesus. He returns it to the religious elite, who buy ground for burial. The scene highlights Judas's demise, Jesus' innocence, the scheming of the religious leaders, and God's purposes.

• 27:3-5

The initial focus is on Judas's suicide. **When Judas, his betrayer** (10:4; 26:14-16, 21-25, 46, 48; but no longer "one of the twelve," as in 26:14, 47), **saw that Jesus was condemned, he repented and brought back the thirty pieces of silver to the chief priests and the elders** (26:14-16). Judas's conclusion that Jesus is **condemned** is interesting in that it agrees with Jesus' prediction in 20:17-19, yet it *precedes* Pilate's decision. It attests that Jesus' death is inevitable because of the elite's alliance. It is in the interests of both to kill Jesus.

The genuineness of Judas's repentance has been variously assessed. Is it genuine if he does not seek forgiveness from Jesus but goes to the enemy, the religious elite, and hangs himself? The gospel places his actions under the valued rubric of **repentance** (two different words: see 3:2; 4:17; 11:20-21; 12:41; 21:29, 32). He returns the money and does not profit from it. He confesses his sin and witnesses to Jesus' innocence. **He said, "I have sinned by betraying innocent blood"** (a serious offense, Deut 27:25; 2 Kgs 21:16; 24:1-4; Jer 7:5-7; 1 Macc 1:37; 2 Macc 1:7-8). And this shed **blood** will in God's purposes effect release or forgiveness from sins (see 26:28; cf. 23:34-35).

The callous indifference of the religious elite contrasts with Judas's seemingly genuine remorse. They accept the money he discards, an ironic and tacit admission of guilt. They hear testimony (not false; cf. 26:59-62) that declares Jesus' innocence, but they do not investigate further or conduct a new trial. **But they said, "What is that to us? See to it yourself."** Their money, which Judas returns, bears witness to their corruption and that of the temple. **Throwing down the pieces of silver in the temple, he departed; and he went and hanged himself.** In his suicide he enacts the penalty for taking another's life

(Lev 24:17). The clause **went and hanged himself** recalls David's adviser Ahithophel (meaning "traitor"), who hangs himself after rebelling with Absalom against David (2 Sam 17:23). Both Ahithophel and Judas are allied in betraying (Davidic) rulers commissioned by God.[6]

• 27:6-8

The return of the betrayal money causes the elite an ironic pang of conscience and provokes a charitable deed. **But the chief priests** (the elders of v. 3 are included in this designation; compare 26:3 and the Pharisees), **taking the pieces of silver, said, "It is not lawful to put them into the treasury, since they are the price for blood."** Their concern with what is **lawful** is selective. They have had no problem with false witnesses (26:59-62) nor with condemning one who is innocent (27:4). **After conferring together** (the same verb as in 27:1), **they used them to buy the potter's field as a place to bury foreigners. For this reason the field has been called the Field of Blood to this day**.

• 27:9-10

Typically, the elite's purchased betrayal of "innocent blood" is shown to be in accord with God's will. **Then was fulfilled what had been spoken through the prophet Jeremiah.** This is the final fulfillment citation. See 1:22-23; 2:15, 17-18, 23; 4:14-16; 8:17; 12:17-21; 13:35; 21:5. Though **Jeremiah** is named as the source, the words mostly come from the difficult Zech 11:13. Scholars have accounted for this mistake in various ways: a copying error, the author's faulty memory, or a deliberate invoking of Jeremiah, the prophet of doom, gloom, and rejection. More persuasive is the recognition that while the *words* mostly come from Zechariah, they (along with the preceding verses) reflect the content of Jer 18-19 and 32:6-15 (19:4 innocent blood; 32:9 bought with silver; potter's field; place for burial).[7] In Jer 19 Jeremiah buys a potter's field, which signifies God's judgment on the unfaithful leaders (19:1) and people. Zechariah 11, which in its context has nothing to do with Judas, also concerns punishment and the rejection of a shepherd by the sheep/people (cf. Matt 26:31). Instead of offering faithfulness to God, the people prefer to pay the shepherd who pays his month's wages to the temple treasury (thirty pieces of silver; cf. Matt 26:14-16; 27:3).

"And they took the thirty pieces of silver, the price of the one on whom a price had been set, on whom some of the people of Israel had set a price, and they gave them for the potter's field, as the Lord commanded me." The choice and placement of the citation create several links between it and Judas's situation: the rejected shepherd (26:31), the thirty pieces of silver (26:14-16), the price which some impose (the religious elite), giving it to the temple, hostile leaders, the buying of the field, the theme of judgment (in the fall of Jerusalem for rejecting Jesus; see 21:41; 22:6-7; 23:37-38; 24:2). All of this lies within God's plans.

27:11-26—JESUS' "TRIAL" BEFORE PILATE

The story line about Jesus resumes from 27:2 after the focus on Judas in 27:3-10. Condemned, Jesus is taken from the Sanhedrin to Pilate for execution.

The term "trial" flatters the proceedings, which lack careful questioning, investigation, oaths, witnesses, and a defense. Influenced by the religious elite and worried about the crowd, Pilate oversees a process and verdict worthy only of the name "injustice." He abuses his power to join the religious leaders in executing a king who threatens their very existence and future, even though Pilate is not convinced that Jesus poses a threat.

Far from exonerating Rome, christianizing[8] or minimizing Pilate's role,[9] these verses offer a terse and scathing indictment of Roman justice "from below." K. Wengst notes the educated Roman's view that Rome's mission, legitimated by Jupiter, was to spread its superior law as part of the gift of *Pax Romana:*[10] "justice enthroned above all injustice" as Seneca calls it (*De Clem* 1.1.7-8), "to crown peace with law" (Virgil, *Aeneid* 4.231; 6.851-52), or "to impose tributes, laws and Roman jurisdiction" (Tacitus, *Ann* 15.6.4). In reality, this meant often that the law served the interests of the elite. Tacitus, for instance, records that Mucianus, the governor of Syria and supporter of Vespasian in the civil war, administered provincial justice with "an eye not for justice or truth but only for the size of the defendants' fortunes," a practice he continued "later in time of peace" (*Hist* 2.84). Suetonius (*Titus* 7) notes that the emperor Titus could be bribed in cases. The interests of the elite govern proceedings, as this account of Jesus' "trial" indicates.

• 27:11

Now Jesus stood before the governor (for disciples, see 10:17-18), **and the governor asked him, "Are you the King of the Jews?"** Herod is called king of the Jews in a situation of Roman control (Josephus, *Ant* 15.373; 16.311; cf. the magi in Matt 2:1-3). The title here means "leader of the resistance,"[11] given its use by kingly pretenders Judas, Simon, and Athrongeus (Josephus, *Ant* 17.271-72, 273-76, 278-84, 285) and at the time of the 66-70 revolt, Simon bar Giora (Josephus, *JW* 4.507-13).[12] Any relationship between this charge and the "blasphemy" conviction of 26:64-66 is not obvious. What is clear is that **the chief priests and elders** provide continuity between the two scenes (26:57, 59, 62, 63, 66; 27:12). Though a division of religious and political spheres is not very apt, they have presumably translated their religious concerns about blasphemy into political rhetoric of interest to an imperial power, namely, that Jesus claims kingship (26:63-4; cf. 2 Sam 7:13-14; Ps 2:1-7; 110:1). He has not denied Davidic links (21:15-17; cf. 21:5). He has announced the presence yet future fullness of God's empire (see 4:17; 12:28; ch. 13), in which he has a key role (19:28; 24:27-31; 25:31-46; 26:63-64). For the status quo with ears to hear, the title **King of the Jews** represents treasonous and seditious claims. It implies nothing less than Rome's demise.

Pilate gives Jesus a chance to defend himself (cf. Acts 25:16), though in a situation of "he says/the elite says," his word is of no consequence here. He neither confirms nor denies the charge but leaves it to Pilate to decide: **Jesus said, "You say so."** Compare his similar response to Caiaphas in 26:64 (one of several parallels between the two "trials").

• 27:12-14

Another parallel with the Caiaphas "trial" follows in Jesus' silence (cf. 26:62-63; cf. 12:19; Isa 53:7). **But when he was accused by the chief priests and elders, he did not answer. Then Pilate said to him, "Do you not hear how many accusations they make against you?" But he gave him no answer, not even to a single charge, so that the governor was amazed.** On the **chief priests** and **elders,** see 27:1. At what is Pilate **amazed**? Assuming that the accusations relay something of 26:63-64 and elaborate the charge of 27:11 of being a king, Pilate might be impressed by the fact that Jesus remains silent (a tacit confession of guilt?) in the face of accusations about claims of participation in cosmic sovereignty. The verb denotes responses in which people are impressed by Jesus' miracles (8:27; 9:33; 15:31) and teaching (22:22) without discerning enough to become disciples. The verb suggests that Pilate does not understand Jesus. Jesus' behavior echoes the response of the suffering servant in Isa 52:14-15.

• 27:15

With the elite's accusations, Jesus' silence, and Pilate's amazement, the questioning is now finished! No witnesses; no clarification of the charges; no oaths; no verdict; not even a convinced judge. A new factor enters the process. **Now at the festival the governor was accustomed to release a prisoner for the crowd, anyone they wanted.** There is no historical evidence for this practice at Passover, though it appropriately expresses the significance of the festival of liberation. Governors could exercise discretion and release prisoners. Josephus reports that the governor of Judea in 62-64 C.E., Albinus, released many brigands (*Ant* 20.215; Seneca, *De Clem* 2.7.1-5).[13] Whatever the historical factors, in narrative terms this scene further exposes the injustice. Pilate carries out the whims of the crowd manipulated by the religious elite (27:20).

• 27:16-18

At that time they had a notorious prisoner called Jesus Barabbas. The term **prisoner** has broad meaning and does not specify his crime. In John 18:40 he is a bandit or violent terrorist, the same word as Matt 26:55. Perhaps the adjective **notorious** indicates that he has been arrested for terrorist-type activities. If so, Barabbas and Jesus contrast two forms of opposition to the elite's control—violent opposition and nonviolent resistance with the formation of alternative communities and practices (see 5:38-42) until Jesus returns. In asking the crowd to vote, Pilate, the representative of Roman rule, not very astutely offers a referendum on preferred means of opposition! Violence, the way chosen in the 66-70 war, and which Jesus rejects, wins (26:51-53). Pilate also offers them a choice between one who is, ironically, called "Jesus son of the Father" (Barabbas), and one who is, in the gospel's view, truly God's son or agent (2:15; 3:17; 11:25-27; 17:5).

So after they had gathered, Pilate said to them, "Whom do you want me to release for you, Jesus Barabbas or Jesus who is called the Messiah?"

Some suggest that Pilate hopes the crowd will call for the release of Jesus Messiah thereby giving Pilate the opportunity to release the one he thinks is innocent. But there is no textual indication of his preference. He is convinced of Jesus' guilt and he is aware of the religious elite's motives: they are envious of Jesus' power with the crowds (cf. 21:1-17) or envious of Jesus' religious claims and want to protect the temple and maintain their position by removing a rival. **For he realized that it was out of jealousy/zeal that they had handed him over** (a rare glimpse into a character's thinking). But this insight does not evidence his preference. If he was convinced of Jesus' innocence and/or wanted him free, the Roman governor could easily have accomplished it! But the scene exposes this representative of Roman justice. He is not motivated by truth and justice, but by the Roman way. He is testing the political waters, securing his own position, and playing his part as one of the elite.

• 27:19

In addition to his own doubts about Jesus (27:14) and his suspicions about the religious elite (27:15-18), a third factor could sway him. **While he was sitting on the judgment seat, his wife sent word to him**. This timing is important. The life-and-death decision process is still under way. His wife's testimony offers Pilate another chance. Pilate's location and posture are rich in irony. Pilate **sits** in **judgment** on one who "stands" before him (27:11). But Jesus has already announced in chapters 24-25 the end of Pilate's world and empire. Jesus will **sit** in judgment on him and the system he represents (25:31) as the returned Son of Man, and establish God's empire in full. On **sitting** as exercising rule and power, see 5:1, 19:28.

His wife sent word to him, "Have nothing to do with that innocent/righteous man, for today I have suffered many things because of a dream about him." Her appeal to **a dream** echoes the birth story, in which dreams reveal God's will, guard God's purposes, and guide appropriate behavior (see 1:19-20; 2:12, 13, 19, 22). The dream comes from God. Its testimony to Jesus' innocence underlines Pilate's guilt and effectiveness. Pilate does not receive the dream himself; perhaps he, like the religious elite, has already shown that he cannot recognize the truth even when it is before him. She **suffered many things because of the dream**, though the narrative does not specify them. In contrast to the male (Jewish) religious and political leaders, it is a (Gentile) woman who gains more insight into Jesus. Women generally in the passion narrative are more understanding and loyal than males, whether disciples or officials (26:6-13, 69-75; 27:55-61; 28:1). Pilate's **wife**, like Judas in 27:4, attests Jesus' **innocence/righteousness**, the same word that describes Joseph's faithfulness to God's will in difficult circumstances in 1:19 (another link with the opening chapters). Compare Nero's wife, Poppaea, who pleads with Nero on behalf of Jews (Josephus, *Ant* 20.195; *Vita* 16).

• 27:20

Pilate's response is not given immediately. In the meantime, the religious elite act swiftly to use their powerful social, religious, and political position to counter any claims of Jesus' innocence. **Now the chief priests and the elders**

persuaded the crowds to ask for Barabbas and to have Jesus killed. This **killing** is **the chief priests'** goal (26:4, 59, 66; 27:1; cf. 12:14) as Jesus has accurately predicted (16:21; 17:22-23; 20:17-19; 26:1-2). Galilean crowds have previously been the beneficiaries of Jesus' ministry (see 4:25; 7:28; 9:8, 36; 14:14-21; 15:29-39). But the religious elite control the Jerusalem crowds, first in aiding Jesus' arrest (26:47), and now in calling for his death. The **chief priests and the elders** are false shepherds, misleading the people in calling for the death of God's shepherd (cf. 2:6; 9:36; 26:31). This act is punished in the fall of Jerusalem (Introduction; 22:7).

• **27:21-22**

The religious elite prevail. **The governor again said to them, "Which of the two do you want me to release for you?" And they said, "Barabbas."** Though given a further opportunity to choose Jesus Messiah, the crowd is well schooled. **Pilate said to them, "Then what should I do with Jesus who is called the Messiah?" All of them said, "Let him be crucified."** Presumably the phrase **who is called the Messiah** indicates Pilate's verdict that Jesus is a messianic pretender. Notice that Pilate uses **Messiah** as a synonym for "King of the Jews." On crucifixion as a Roman form of political execution for non-citizens who threatened the empire, see 10:38; 16:24; 20:19, where Jesus predicts it. The verb will recur frequently over the next fifteen or so verses (27:23, 26, 31, 35, 38; plus the noun "cross" in 27:32, 40, 42).

• **27:23**

Pilate protests. **Then he asked, "Why, what evil has he done?"** He is suspicious about the religious elite's motives, and he has heard his wife's testimony. But Pilate is a coward who has no strength of conviction, especially before a crowd shouting (at the religious elite's initiative) for someone else. **But they shouted all the more, "Let him be crucified."**

• **27:24**

Pilate washes his hands of Jesus and implicates himself further. **So when Pilate saw that he could do nothing, but rather that a riot was beginning, he took some water and washed his hands before the crowd, saying, "I am innocent of this man's blood; see to it yourselves."** Pilate's futile attempt to wash away his responsibility and transfer it to the people (**see to it yourselves**) may reflect Deut 21:1-9, which provides a hand-washing ritual by which people declare they are not responsible for a death. See also Ps 26:1; *Ep. Arist.* 305-6. Greco-Roman texts attest various customs of using water to cleanse participation in evil acts: Homer, *Iliad* 6.266-68; Herodotus, *Hist* 1.35; Virgil, *Aeneid* 2.718-20. Pilate, who is in charge of events, pretends that he is not. But a quick hand washing and a few words cannot remove the legal responsibility with which Pilate is charged as governor and agent of Roman power. Nor can they absolve him of his guilt in the murder of an innocent man or transfer it to a faceless crowd. Roman justice is all washed up. It is not exonerated but exposed as expedient, allied with and co-opted by the religious elite who manipulate a crowd to accomplish its own ends.

• 27:25

Pilate's act provokes the crowd brazenly to claim its responsibility for Jesus' death. It does so in accord with Jesus' words (23:29-36) and using a biblical idiom (Lev 20:9; 2 Sam 1:16; Ezek 18:10-13; 33:1-4). The crowds in Galilee have been the beneficiaries of Jesus' ministry. The Jerusalem crowds also seem to be impressed: they hold Jesus to be a prophet (21:11, 46), and are astonished at his teaching (22:33; 23:1). But now, manipulated by the elite, they shout against Jesus (cf. Seneca's comments on the dangerous and fickle crowd, *Ep* 7).

Then the people as a whole answered, "His blood be on us and on our children!" Christian interpretations of 27:25 have propagated a virulent anti-Judaism by claiming that the saying attests Israel's rejection of God's anointed and God's permanent rejection of Israel. Such attempts are textually unsustainable and morally and religiously repugnant.[14]

1. In the narrative, the phrase **the people as a whole** cannot refer to all Jews for all time. It does not even refer to all Jews in first-century Jerusalem, Judea, Galilee, or the diaspora, or to a whole generation. The phrase is narrative-specific. It denotes a subgroup, the crowd in Jerusalem under the control of the religious elite who have arrested Jesus (26:47) and have shouted for his death (27:15, 22). This subgroup takes responsibility.

2. The term **people** (λαός, *laos*) has diverse meanings in the gospel. In 1:21 it seems to refer both to all Jews as God's people and to those (Jews and Gentiles) who will follow Jesus, whereas in 2:4 it denotes those in Jerusalem under the power of the religious elite (also 21:23; 26:3, 47, where crowd and people are synonyms; 27:1, 15). Context determines its significance. Here the **people** are those in Jerusalem controlled by the elite.

3. In claiming responsibility, the **people** do not alienate themselves from God forever. In 27:64 even the religious elite worry that they might hear and welcome the resurrection message.

4. In claiming responsibility for Jesus' death, they recognize punishment on themselves and the next generation. The phrase **and on our children** designates the next generation (Exod 17:3), who can be objects of God's favor or God's wrath (Exod 34:7). So Matt 7:11; 9:2; 10:21; 18:25; 19:29; 21:28; 22:24. Why might the Jerusalem crowd/people involve its children in the responsibility for Jesus' death, and in its punishment? How does this punishment come about? Many interpreters have seen here a further reference to Rome's defeat of Jerusalem in 70 C.E., a generation after Jesus' death. Matthew understands this event as punishment of the elite for rejecting Jesus and misleading the people (see 1:21; 21:12-13, 18-19, 41; 22:6-7; 23:37-38; 24:2; 27:10). This understanding of disasters as punishment for sin pervades the biblical tradition (so the fall of Jerusalem in 587 to Babylon [1 Kgs 9:1-9] and in the 160s to Antiochus Epiphanes; 2 Macc 7:32-38; 4 Macc 17:20-22). Josephus, along with *4 Ezra* and *2 Bar* (see 22:7) also see Jerusalem's fall in 70 as divine punishment, though for quite different reasons (*JW* 4.362, 366, 385-88; 5.367-68, 395-419, 559; 6.96-110; 7.34).

5. In connecting Jesus' death with the destruction of 70 C.E., and supplying a theological explanation for it (the rejection of Jesus by the Jerusalem elite and

supporters), the gospel makes a polemical claim (see introduction to ch. 23). One (predominantly) Jewish group accuses another Jewish group of bringing misfortune on the people and puts words of responsibility into their mouths! Of course, historical events are always much more complex. The single theological explanation ignores a host of other causes: social, economic, religious, military, international. But the narrative is not a work of twenty-first-century historiography. It is a narrative religious work, an in-house polemic, which sustains the identity and way of life of its own community.

6. R. Brown notes that the biblical tradition understands God's wrath to be short-lived, while God's mercy endures forever (Ps 30:6; 100:5). Note Lam 3:22-24, which affirms, in the midst of the distress of the 587 B.C.E. destruction of Jerusalem, that "the steadfast love of the Lord never ceases; God's mercies never come to an end; they are new every morning; great is your faithfulness." God's wrath is not permanent. The gospel does not propose for a moment the permanent rejection of all Jewish people.

7. Also to be noted is the use of the term **blood**. This term denotes Jesus' innocent death and the culpability of Judas, the chief priests, and their Jerusalem crowd for his death (23:35; 27:4, 6, 8, 24). Its one other use comes in 26:28 in which Jesus' **blood**/life is "poured out for the release from or forgiveness of sins." This connection suggests that their cry is, for the audience, not only a claim of responsibility but a recognition (echoing Exod 24:8) that God's forgiveness is available to all, including the chief priests' crowd, both now and in the future establishment of God's empire at Jesus' return (23:39).

• **27:26**

Pilate complies with the manipulated crowd's wishes, not with what might be just. **So he released Barabbas for them; and after flogging Jesus he handed him over to be crucified**. Jesus predicts flogging for himself (20:19) and for his disciples (10:17). As God's slave, he suffers the violent lot of numerous slaves (see 8:5). The **flogging** recalls the "stripes" of the suffering servant (Isa 53:5). It often preceded crucifixion and imposed near-fatal wounds (Josephus, *JW* 5.449; 6.304; 7.200-205). Pilate **hands** Jesus **over**, as Jesus has predicted (17:22; 20:18; 26:2). Pilate's responsibility is clear.

27:27-44—JESUS IS CRUCIFIED

The way to the cross is the way of derision. As with the trial before Caiaphas (26:57-68), the empire's enforcers humiliate and mock Jesus, now condemned by Pilate to die (27:27-31). They mock Jesus with conventional symbols of kingship.[15] But while the soldiers do not think him a king, or at least not one to be honored, the audience knows he is a king who will be genuinely worshiped (28:18) and whose kingship will, at his return, condemn the soldiers' empire and extend God's empire over all (25:31, 34).

• **27:27-29**

Then the soldiers of the governor took Jesus into the governor's headquarters (or official residence), **and they gathered the whole cohort**. The place exudes the power and authority of the empire which bears down on Jesus. The number of soldiers, about six hundred to a thousand in a **cohort**, presents an intimidating scene. **They stripped him and put a scarlet robe on him and after twisting some thorns into a crown, they put it on his head.** While a Gentile woman declares his innocence (27:19), these male soldiers celebrate his guilt with a fake coronation. The **scarlet robe** is probably a soldier's cloak (Romulus in *Rom Ant* 2.34.2) that substitutes for the royal purple cloak of kings worn by Herod (Josephus, *Ant* 14:173) and emperors like Tiberius and Domitian (Suetonius, *Tiberius* 25.2; Statius, *Silv* 4.1.21-22). Simon, son of Gioras, a leader in the 70 C.E. revolt, surrendered to the Romans in Jerusalem wearing a purple cloak (Josephus, *JW* 7.26-31). And those leading the animals in Vespasian and Titus's triumph are decked in purple and gold (Josephus, *JW* 7.137). Both **robe** and **crown** are traditional vestiges of royal power, status, domination, and wealth (Esth 8:15; 1 Macc 8:14; 10:20; 2 Macc 4:38), precisely what Jesus has abandoned in his life and death of service (20:28). **They put a reed in his right hand** as a mock scepter or symbol of power (cf. 11:9). The one who enacts cosmic judgment needs no scepter (25:31). **They knelt before him and mocked him** (as Jesus predicted in 20:19), **saying, "Hail, King of the Jews!"** The act of kneeling, or *proskynēsis,* belongs in the world of kings and emperor worship as a form of paying homage (see 4:9), as does the greeting **Hail**. Compare 28:9 for the worship of the risen Jesus. They pick up the title **King of the Jews** from 27:11. For them, it is a fitting title with which to mock Jesus, but they have no clue as to its significance in terms of 26:64. Ironically, despite themselves, they proclaim his identity.

• 27:30-31

They spat on him (as did the Sanhedrin [see 26:67] and the opponents of the suffering servant in Isa 50:6) **and took the reed and struck him on the head. After mocking him** (cf. 27:29), **they stripped him of his robe** (for a second time, 27:28) **and put his own clothes on him. Then they led him away to crucify him.** Throughout, Jesus does not retaliate, struggle, or waiver from his destiny. His silence and inactivity absorb their violence as he moves toward his inevitable death. The soldiers enact the style of Gentile rulers as Jesus has described it. They lord it over him as tyrants (20:25). If Matthew was trying to exonerate Rome by either distancing it from Jesus' death or showing its impeccable justice (as some suggest), then this description of officially sanctioned petty thuggery, overlaid with the heavy irony of the identity and future role of the mocked as the cosmic judge, is hardly the way to present a convincing picture.

• 27:32

The action now leaves the governor's residence and heads out toward the place of crucifixion. Rome parades its prisoner typically to intimidate and maintain social control. See Josephus *JW* 7.37-40 for Titus's parade and execution of prisoners after 70 through various cities, and *JW* 7.154, for the inclusion of numerous prisoners including the leader Simon bar Giora in Vespasian and Titus's triumph in Rome. Simon is paraded, whipped, and executed.

As they went out, they came upon a man from Cyrene named Simon;

they compelled this man to carry his cross. Cyrene was a North African city in present-day Libya, capital of the province of Cyrenaica.[16] No reason is given why Jesus does not carry his own crossbeam. Perhaps he is too weak from the whipping. Whatever the reason, there are two important discipleship details in the scene. (1) Jesus has previously used the same phrase and vocabulary to teach that every disciple must **carry his cross**. See 16:24. The phrase clearly has a literal meaning as well as symbolically denoting the difficult, humiliating, counterway of discipleship. Simon (perhaps a pilgrim in the city for Passover) demonstrates what disciples are to do. (2) The man's name, **Simon,** recalls the absence of the other Simon, Peter, who refused to believe Jesus would be put to death (16:21-23), who declared his loyalty to Jesus even to death (26:33-35), and who like the other disciples has fled (26:56) and has denied Jesus (26:69-75). In the absence of Simon Peter (and the other disciples), the African Simon from Cyrene carries Jesus' cross. He is **compelled** into this act. The verb **compelled** recalls 5:41 and the imperial practice of **angareia** or impressment of labor or goods in the empire's service (see 5:41).

• 27:33-34
They reach the place of crucifixion. **And when they came to a place called Golgotha (which means Place of a Skull), they offered him wine to drink, mixed with gall; but when he tasted it, he would not drink it.** Rome's preference was to crucify prisoners in public places thereby deriving maximum advantage of its power for deterrence (Quintilian, *Decl* 274, "the most crowded roads"). Josephus notes that Titus crucifies prisoners outside Jerusalem in view of the besieged city to "induce the Jews to surrender" (*JW* 5.449-51). The reference to **wine to drink** evokes Ps 69:21, a psalm of lament in which the persecuted righteous person cries out against his enemies for God's deliverance. This is the first of numerous echoes through this section involving similar scriptures, notably lament psalms (esp. Ps 22), Isa 52-53, and Wis 2:10-20.[17] Why he does not drink is not clear.

• 27:35-37
The actual moment of crucifixion, like Jesus' birth in 2:1, receives a scant mention in a subordinate clause: **And when they had crucified him**. As Jesus has predicted (20:19; 26:2), as the crowd has demanded (27:22), and as Pilate has ordered (27:26), Jesus is crucified. See 10:38; 16:24, for some details of this horrific means of execution, which was reserved largely for noncitizens and those with little status, like slaves and political or military threats.[18] Jesus' death penalty is the ultimate form of marginalization available to the elite.

If Deut 21:23 was understood to refer to crucifixion, Jesus appears to be cursed by God. Yet for the gospel audience, this is God's commissioned and chosen son or agent (2:15; 3:17; 17:5).

They divided his clothes among themselves by casting lots. This reference to Ps 22:18 is the first of several to Ps 22, a psalm of lament in which the persecuted righteous person cries out against his enemies for God's deliverance. The removal of **clothes**, and the crucifixion of a person naked, were normal practice. They form part of the shame and humiliation of this form of execution.

Then they sat down there and kept watch. Their sitting signifies in part imperial control and rule (also 27:19). It intimidates Peter in 26:58, 69. Yet it recalls Jesus' words that at his return *he* will be seated at the right hand of God (26:64), as God's empire is established over all. The verb thus reveals the limits of Rome's power even while it seems all-powerful in exercising the power of life and death. Their constant attention throughout his dying (**kept watch**) prepares for the confession of 27:54 and will continue in the efforts to guard his tomb (27:62-66). The soldiers of the empire ironically are able to do what Jesus' disciples could not do in Gethsemane (26:36-46).

Over his head they put the charge against him, which read, "This is Jesus, the King of the Jews." So 27:11, 29. This act continues to mock and humiliate him. This king's throne is his cross. This is what Rome does to those who threaten its empire and understanding of reality. But the situation is worse for them than their billboard announces. Jesus will share in the kingship of heaven and earth (28:18), which means Rome's demise.

• **27:38-44**

Part of the time between his crucifixion (27:35) and death (27:50) is marked by mocking from three groups.[19] If a "real" king receives worship and honor from his subjects, then this one deserves mocking from his opponents. The mocking betrays how much his opponents do not understand Jesus.

• **27:38**

The first group comprises two bandits, who are introduced in v. 38 and close out the subscene in 27:44. **Then two bandits were crucified with him, one on his right and one on his left.** If a "true" king has a court of elite worthies and notables, this one has a court of sinners and sociopolitical rejects (9:9-13; 11:19). True to Isa 53:12, he is "numbered with transgressors." For the term **bandits** as armed terrorists, see 26:55; 27:16. Jesus, who has taught against the way of violence (5:38-42), is crucified between two of its advocates (cf. 27:16, Barabbas, perhaps). Though he has advocated a different way, nonviolent subversive resistance, he is appropriately crucified with other opponents of the empire. James and John sought to be on Jesus' **left and right** in 20:21-22, and assured him that they could drink his cup of suffering. But they did not have this sort of scene in mind and fled (26:56).

• **27:39-40**

The second group of mockers are the passersby. **Those who passed by blasphemed/derided him, shaking their heads, and saying, "You who would destroy the temple and build it in three days, save yourself!"** Mocking from passersby was likely at a crucifixion. The one who has been condemned by the Sanhedrin for blasphemy in claiming to be God's anointed agent (see 26:65-66) is now **blasphemed** or derided (cf. 9:3; 15:19). The blasphemy lies in their not recognizing that God is at work in him, that he is God's agent commissioned to accomplish God's salvation (1:21-23). The **shaking of heads** is one of the derisive actions that wicked opponents make against the afflicted righteous person in Ps 22:7 (cf. Lam 2:15 [defeated Jerusalem]; Job 16:4; Sir 13:7 [the rich against the poor]). In a further link with the trial before the Sanhedrin (26:59-68), they repeat the charge about the **temple** from 26:61. Again it is ironic in that while Jesus has not said it, they speak truly. The gospel claims that the temple is destroyed by Rome in 70 because of Jesus in that the Jerusalem elite refuse to believe his claims (so 27:25 above; 22:6-7). In his return he will establish a temple and the worship of God in some form.

The trial echoes continue as they mock him as **son of God**. This term recalls Caiaphas's question about his identity in 26:63. **If you are the son of God, come down from the cross.** In addressing him as **son of God** they speak God's perspective (2:15; 3:17; 17:5; 21:37-39), though they do not recognize it and they do not understand what they are saying (so also Peter in 16:16-23). Their understanding of **son of God** precludes any notion of suffering and humiliation. Perhaps they understand it as kingship language and associate it with power and domination (2 Sam 7:13-14; Ps 2:7). For them, Jesus is an obvious pretender! Or perhaps they understand a son or child of God to be a righteous person (Wis Sol 2:12-20) who is not punished with suffering. Jesus is a fraud.

Throughout, the presentation of Jesus has been quite the reverse. It is informed by traditions such as the lament psalms (22, 69), the prophets and suffering servant (Isa 52-53), the faithful righteous (Daniel, Wis) and martyr stories (the Maccabean traditions). Faithfulness to God's just purposes inevitably brings conflict and rejection. Faithfulness as God's son/child has put him on the cross and keeps him there. As a faithful servant-king and son, he gives his life to benefit others (20:27-28). He knows he cannot **save** himself, but trusts that God's saving work will be done through him (cf. "be raised," 16:21; 17:23; 20:19; cf. the commission of 1:21). Out of fidelity, Jesus has already renounced asking God to send angels to save him (26:53).

The conditional construction (**if you are**) also invokes the devil's temptation of 4:3, 6. The mockers continue the devil's work of trying to divert Jesus from this faithful path of suffering. But Jesus is not sidetracked.

• **27:41-43**

The third group comprises the ever-present Sanhedrin, the chief priests (26:3, 14, 47, 51, 57, 58, 59, 62, 63, 65; 27:1, 3, 6, 12, 20, 62), scribes (26:57), and elders (26:3, 47, 57; 27:1, 3, 12, 20). They gathered with Caiaphas for the trial (26:57). Now they add insult to injury. **In the same way the chief priests also, along with the scribes and elders were mocking him saying, "He saved others; he cannot save himself."** They too have forgotten that God is the one who **saves** (Deut 33:29; Judg 2:16; etc.; Ps 3:7; 6:4; 69:1, 14, 35; etc.). Nor have they recognized that God's saving work is being done through Jesus (1:21) in his healings (9:21-22), in other works of power (8:25; 14:30), in his return (26:64-66), and even in his death (20:28; 26:28).

They too rehearse the claim about being **king of Israel** (27:11), a synonym for Christ (27:17), and recall Caiaphas's question about being the Messiah, the son of God (26:63). They, like the passersby (27:39-40), despite their theological learning and positions, and previous encounters with Jesus, cannot put accurate content to the term. They too think that crucifixion and suffering are incompatible with Jesus' claims, though their traditions attest the fate of those faithful to God's purposes. **Let him come down from the cross now, and we will believe in him.** They have previously demanded signs (12:38; 16:1). Their promise to **believe in him** seems empty after previous opportunities. It continues the pervasive atmosphere of untruthfulness. Jesus has offered them the sign of Jonah, which requires his death (12:38-40). But in calling for him now to escape death, they have not learned from his teaching or believed in him! They repeat their call to demonstrate their intransigence and mock him further. They use Ps 22:8. **He trusts in God; let God deliver him now if he wants to; for he said, "I am God's Son."** Again they evoke the trial (26:63). They do not understand in what sense Jesus is God's son.

• 27:44

The mocking of this king ends by returning to the bandits introduced in 27:38. **The bandits who were crucified with him also taunted him in the same way.** Their words parallel those of the passersby and of the religious elite.

27:45-56—JESUS DIES

The fifth scene of chapter 27 focuses on the last few hours and words of Jesus' life (27:45-50), and the startling cosmic (27:51-53) and confessional (27:54) acts that accompany it.

• 27:45

Darkness falls. **From noon on, darkness came over the whole land until three in the afternoon.** The markers of time (**noon, three in the afternoon**) emphasize the unusual **darkness** for this time of day. **Darkness** has diverse significance: the chaos before creation, oppression and imperial tyranny, exile, injustice, and judgment, especially that of the "day of the Lord," in which God judges the nations (for references, see 4:15-16; 24:29; cf. Amos 8:9; Zeph 1:15). Here two connections (without eliminating others) seem especially apt. (1) The darkness, and so Jesus' death, is part of the tribulation which precedes Jesus' coming to reign as Son of Man (24:27-31). It evokes, therefore, God's larger purpose as the context in which his death is to be understood. (2) Darkness and judgment are linked. His death reveals the hostility of Rome's ruling elite and its commitment to maintain its hold on power by removing anyone its allies, the religious elite, perceive to be a threat. Judgment will be the consequence of this rejection.

• 27:46

In the all-encompassing darkness Jesus cries out. **And about three o'clock Jesus cried out with a loud voice, "Eli, Eli, lema sabachthani?" that is, "My God, my God, why have you forsaken me?"** Like his opponents, Jesus also cites Ps 22, though with a different interpretation (27:43). See its use also in 27:35, 39-40, 42, 43, 44. Psalm 22:1 is the anguished cry of the righteous sufferer who, faced with the continuing opposition of enemies and opponents, feels abandoned by God. God seems unable and/or unwilling to deliver the sufferer (Ps 22:2) and does not reply to Jesus' cry. Jesus' abandonment has been progressive through chapters 26-27: Judas (26:14-16, 48-49), the disciples (26:56), Peter (26:69-75), the crowds (27:21-22), and now God. Jesus reaches the lowest point of agony and despondency. The cited verse from the *beginning* of Ps 22, though, indicates that this is not the final word. The Psalmist's sentiments change through the course of the Psalm; God's deliverance and goodness are encountered again, just as Jesus will subsequently encounter God's vindication.

• **27:47-49**

When some of the bystanders heard it, they said, "This man is calling for Elijah" mistaking **Eli** ("my God") for **Elijah**. The misinterpretation may be a deliberate mocking. Elijah did not die but was taken directly into heaven (2 Kgs 2:9-12). Perhaps they are joking that Jesus wants a similar escape (**to save him**). But Elijah doesn't come. **At once one of them ran and got a sponge, filled it with sour wine, put it on a stick, and gave it to him to drink.** Why the cry should provoke this response and the significance of the gesture are not clear. As in 27:34, the reference recalls another psalm of lament, Ps 69:21.

But the others said, "Wait, let us see whether Elijah will come to save him." Some expected Elijah's return in preparation for the final judgment (Mal 4:5; Sir 48:10; see Matt 11:14; 17:10-11). But Jesus has previously indicated that Elijah has already come as John the Baptist in preparation for Jesus' ministry (11:14; 17:12-13), and that Elijah/John have witnessed to Jesus as God's anointed (3:11-12, 13-17; 17:3). Ironically, these **others** call too late for Elijah (he has already been); they call for one who would witness against them (because he witnesses to Jesus, whom they reject); and they call for one who would not save Jesus (because he knows that the prophetic role involves conflict with, rejection by, and suffering from the elite [1 Kgs 18-19]).

• **27:50**

Jesus dies.[20] **Then Jesus cried again with a loud voice and gave up his spirit/breath.** The verb **cried out** recurs in Ps 22 (22:2, 5, 24) as the righteous one desperately seeks God's assistance, but God does not yet answer Jesus. Jesus' death at the hands of the political and religious elite is the final form of societal dismissal and marginalization. The elite have accomplished their goal. Jesus is another in a long line of prophets to be killed by the religious leaders (see 21:34-39; 23:34-38).

• **27:51-54**

Four miraculous signs immediately follow Jesus' death as God suddenly seems to spring into action to attest that Jesus has not been forsaken. Just as God's creation in the form of a star witnesses to his birth (2:1-12), so the sun and the earth attest his death and anticipate new life. Several traditions understood that God gives signs to mark an important figure's death (blood quenching a fire; 4 Macc 9:20; Josephus *Ant* 17.167 [eclipse of moon]). Numerous authors record unusual cosmic actions (e.g., the sun) at Romulus's "death" and deification (Cicero, *De Re Publica* 2.17; Dionysius of Halicarnassus, *Rom Ant* 2.56; Ovid, *Fasti* 2.493-95). Virgil (*Georgics* 1.463-97) notes terrestrial and celestial signs at Caesar's death; Dio Cassius notes comparable signs anticipating Augustus's death (56.29.1-4) and at Claudius's death (61.35.1).[21] But the signs accompanying Jesus' death do not attest only his death, but, like all of Jesus' ministry, they belong to the time of tribulation (24:3-26) and anticipate God's coming triumph, which his return in glory will establish (24:27-31).

1. **At that moment the curtain of the temple was torn in two, from top to bottom.** Which curtain is torn and what does it signify?[22] The word **curtain** (BAGD, 416) can refer to that which covered the holy of holies (Exod 26:31; Josephus, *Ant* 8.75), or to that which separated the entrance forecourt from the temple proper (Exod 26:37; Josephus, *Ant* 8.75; *JW* 5.212). Several factors suggest the outer, not inner, curtain (contra BAGD), and that the tearing designates the beginning of the judgment/destruction of the temple by Rome in 70 C.E. (i) In 27:54 the centurion *sees* these signs. If the torn curtain was the inner one, this would be impossible. (ii) Jesus has predicted the temple's destruction in 24:2. (iii) The temple is the center of power for the chief priests who have been the prime movers in Jesus' death (see 27:41). Judgment on them is quite appropriate (cf. 21:42; 22:6-7; 23:37-38; 24:2). The passive **was torn** indicates God as the one who does the action. (iv) Twice in the passion narrative, in 26:61 and 27:40, charges are made that Jesus said he would destroy the temple. That charge is false in that Jesus did not say it, but ironically true in that his rejection by the elite accounts for the destruction of Jerusalem and temple in 70 C.E. (see 27:25). (v) Moreover, I have noted in the discussions of 26:60-61 and 21:12-22 that several eschatological traditions expected the replacement of the temple in the new age. Two of the following signs, earthquakes and resurrection, anticipate the new age also.

2. **The earth shook, and the rocks were split.** Earthquakes are common indicators of the end of the present age and beginning of the new (*4 Ezra* 6:13-16; *2 Bar* 27:7; 70:8; Zech 14:4-5; Matt 24:7b) as well as of judgment (Isa 29:6; Ezek 38:19). That power is anticipated and demonstrated already in part in Jesus' ministry (8:24, 27; 28:2) as part of the tribulation before the end (24:7). Note that the created order attests Jesus' birth (2:2), just as here it signals his death, in 28:2 his resurrection, and in 24:27-31 his return.

3. In addition to judgment, some bodies are raised. **The tombs also were opened, and many bodies of the saints who had fallen asleep were raised. After his resurrection they came out of the tombs and entered the holy city and appeared to many.** The term **saints** identifies faithful people who have died (**fallen asleep**) and are now **raised** (Isa 26:19; Ezek 37:11-14; Dan 7:18, 22; 12:1-3; Zech 14:5) as a sign that anticipates the approaching end. This is not the general judgment and resurrection, but is localized in Jerusalem. Nor is it the first time people have been raised in association with Jesus' ministry (9:18-19, 23-26; 10:8; 11:5). The timing of their resurrection is strange. Verse 52 links it to Jesus' death, while v. 53 delays it until after his resurrection. Jerusalem was called **the holy city** in 4:5, set apart to serve God (see 4:5). In this context, when its elite have just killed God's anointed, the phrase is ironic, marking the calling from which the city has fallen. But there is no indication that that calling has been removed. In fact the risen saints **appeared to many** in the city. They attest its judgment for its wrong verdict on Jesus, but also God's power for new life.

4. Conversion occurs. **Now when the centurion and those with him, who were keeping watch over Jesus** (cf. 27:36) **saw the earthquake and what took place, they were terrified and said, "Truly this man was God's Son."** Soldiers have mocked Jesus with a coronation and physical abuse (27:27-31) and have enthroned him in crucifixion (27:34-37). They have done their imperial duty. Is this cry more mocking, or an acknowledgment of defeat after the fact, or a genuine confession which agrees with God's verdict that Jesus is God's agent (3:17; 17:5)? The latter view seems more justified. (i) The confession follows the amazing events of 27:51-53, which evidence God's power and presence. (ii) Traditions noted in 27:51 attest that unusual events mark the deaths of extraordinary people, and attest their specialness. (iii) The clause **they were terrified** appears in two other revelatory circumstances, the three disciples' response to the heavenly voice's revelation of Jesus' identity in the transfiguration in 17:5-6, and the risen Jesus' appearance to the women in 28:8-9. This suggests a revelatory experience here. (iv) Their confession employs the same words as disciples use in 14:33, and agrees with God's verdict in 3:17 and 17:5. (v) This confessing group of soldiers contrasts with the earlier mocking groups (27:31, 41).[23]

Some of the soldiers, including a higher-ranking centurion (see 8:5, 8), discern in these events something that their commander Pilate could not discern, **Truly this man was God's Son**. They hear the language of **God's Son** from the passersby (27:40) and from the chief priests, scribes, and elders, who refer to Jesus as both king, with which the soldiers are already familiar (cf. 27:29, 37), and God's son (27:41-43). Ironically, the mocking of Jesus by the passersby and the Sanhedrin functions as proclamation!

In the narrative their confession has four functions. (i) This is the same title (in anarthrous form, lacking a definite article) that disciples use to confess Jesus' identity in 14:33. The soldiers act as disciples in agreeing with God's evaluation of Jesus (2:15; 3:17; 17:5). (ii) The use of God's title for Jesus (**Son of God**) evaluates the events of chapter 27. The actions of the political and religious elite resist God's verdict, but in the midst of their death-working power, God's unchanged perspective is asserted. The title evokes the parables in 21:33-22:14, in which murderous actions against the son are avenged, as Jesus' death will be in 70 C.E. Hence the cry proclaims Rome's certain defeat. (iii) The title **Son of God** was also a common title for the emperor Augustus, and to a lesser extent subsequent emperors. It denoted the emperor's role as the agent of the gods, particularly of Jupiter, who had committed rule over the earth to the emperor (see Introduction, section 9).[24] Now the title is transferred by the emperor's agents in an act of submission to the one who, in the gospel's perspective is its rightful claimant. The confession **Son of God** (like "lord" and "one who saves") challenges and competes with claims made about the emperor. As God's Son, Jesus, not the emperor, is the agent of the one who is Lord of heaven and earth (11:25) commissioned to manifest God's saving presence and empire (see 1:21-23; 2:15; 3:16-17; 4:17). (iv) The soldiers' confession anticipates the general turning of Gentiles to God, which signifies the imminent completion of God's purposes (see 8:11-12). As Gentiles, they, like the centurion of 8:5-13, can be counted among the Gentiles who also comprise the people of God. Psalm 22 (from which the cry of v. 46 derives) ends with the confident declaration that "all the ends of the earth shall . . . turn to the Lord" (Ps 22:27-28). That of course does not mean Israel has been rejected or displaced but that Gentiles have been included.

• 27:55-56

Jesus' abandonment in death has seemed total. Even God was absent it seemed (see 27:46). But the final two verses of the scene disclose loyal women who have remained with the crucified Jesus, though inactive and at some distance.[25] **Many women were also there, looking on from the distance; they had followed Jesus from Galilee and had served/provided for him. Among them were Mary Magdalene, and Mary the mother of James and Joseph, and the mother of the sons of Zebedee.** The **many women** who are witnesses of this major event of crucifixion (**looking on**) are clearly disciples. They have **followed** Jesus, the verb which from the outset (see 4:20) signifies attachment and obedience to Jesus in response to his disruptive call. Moreover, they are said to imitate his central orientation (20:25-28). They **serve** him over a sustained period of time and distance in travel (**from Galilee**). Their service is not only a matter of providing food and/or hospitality, though that may well be an important dimension (cf. Peter's mother-in-law in 8:15). The verb denotes Jesus' giving his life in obedience to God and for the benefit of others (20:28; cf. 25:44). The term is all-embracing for Jesus' ministry. Likewise for the women. Whatever he does by way of this service they do also: proclamation, works of power, suffering, and so on (cf. 10:7-8, 24-25; 11:2-5).

Unlike the male disciples, they have not fled (26:56). The phrase **from the distance** links them with Peter, who also follows Jesus "from a distance" to the courtyard in 26:58. But whereas he denies Jesus and departs, the women remain faithful in walking the way of the cross (16:24-26).

The third woman identified in the group is **the mother of the sons of Zebedee.** She had asked Jesus in 20:20-21 for the seats of honor for her sons. It was a highly inappropriate request. She seems to have learned from his response and has remained faithful through his ordeal, unlike her two sons.

27:57-66—JESUS' BURIAL

The burial scene is transitional. It completes the crucifixion. But the burial, along with the guards, prepares for the resurrection of chapter 28.

• 27:57-58

Darkness covers the land at noon (27:45); Jesus cries out at three in the afternoon (27:46) and dies (27:50). It is now evening (**When it was evening**). **There came a rich man from Arimathea, named Joseph, who was also a disciple of Jesus.** Jesus' death brings to light another (male) disciple when the eleven have fled (26:56; 27:55-56). Jesus has previously encountered a rich man (19:16-22, 23-24) who declined Jesus' call to follow him, sell his possessions and redistribute the wealth to the poor. This man is both a **disciple** and **a rich man** (19:23-26), not required to dispose of his wealth but like all disciples required to use it in serving God (6:24; cf. the woman in 26:6-13). This Joseph will give to the poor (19:21) in burying Jesus. **He went to Pilate and asked for the body of Jesus; then Pilate ordered it to be given.** Just like John's disciples (14:12), Jesus' disciples provide his burial. There is some evidence for leaving the bodies of the crucified unburied as a further humiliation, often to be consumed by wild beasts and birds (Horace, *Ep* 1.16.48; Philo, *In Flaccum* 10.83-84; Petronius, *Satyricon* 111-12; Tacitus, *Ann* 6.29).[26] How different would Pilate's response have been if Joseph was not a wealthy man?

Joseph's act is a courageous one. Guilt by association, presumably one of the reasons the eleven fled, could bring about his own execution. His action as a wealthy person of some social standing in providing a decent burial for a marginalized, crucified criminal is certainly unusual. He resembles the Joseph of the Egyptian court who refuses to be swayed by imperial power (Gen 39). He also resembles the Joseph of the gospel's opening chapter. This Joseph also does a brave thing on Jesus' behalf in countering prevailing cultural attitudes in order to be faithful to God's purposes (see 1:19-20, 24-25).

• 27:59-60

So Joseph took the body and wrapped it in a clean linen cloth and laid it in his own new tomb, which he had hewn in the rock. Jesus' naked **body** (cf. 27:35) is covered and **laid** in a **tomb in the rock**. The description looks back to 27:51-53, where the rocks had been split open and some dead raised. Jesus' resurrection scene is prepared for in that **He then rolled a great stone to the door of the tomb and went away.**

• 27:61

Mary Magdalene and the other Mary (so 27:56) **were there, sitting opposite the tomb.** What are these women doing here? One obvious possibility is that they are grieving. **Sitting** can indicate mourning (Job 2:8, 13; Ps 137:1), though of course the posture is polyvalent (cf. 5:1; 26:64; 27:36). But against this view is the absence of any other features of mourning: weeping, wailing, beating of breast, flute playing, and noise (see 2:18; 9:23). Certainly these women provide continuity as witnesses for Jesus' death (27:55-56) and now his burial, as they will for his resurrection. Most likely, they are there awaiting Jesus' resurrection. They have followed him from Galilee (27:55). As disciples, they have had both the opportunity and the disposition to learn from his teaching, including his passion predictions, which foretold his death and resurrection (16:21; 17:23; 20:19). Whereas the male disciples have fled, these woman have not. They have seen the accuracy of his prediction of death; now they await resurrection.[27] See the discussion of 28:1 for confirmation.

• 27:62-66

Resurrection is not only on the minds of the women. The religious elite also know of his predictions and so with Pilate's help, arrange a guard for the tomb.

• **27:62-63**

It is now the sabbath of Passover: **The next day, that is after the day of Preparation**. Attention returns to the alliance of the religious elite and Rome. **The chief priests** are still being attentive to Jesus' fate; in 27:20 they persuaded the crowd to shout for his crucifixion and in 27:41 they checked up on the crucifixion. Now they worry about the effect of the Easter proclamation on the people. They are accompanied by **the Pharisees**, their only appearance in the passion narrative, but part of the religious alliance condemned by Jesus (21:45) and committed to his death (12:14; 21:45-46; 22:15; 23:29-36; cf. Josephus, *Vita* 21).

They **gathered before Pilate and said, "Sir/Lord, we remember what that imposter/deceiver said while he was alive, 'After three days I will rise again.'"** The verb **gathered** denotes opposition to Jesus (cf. 22:34; 26:3, 57); in 2:4 it describes their gathering with Herod against Jesus. In Ps 2:2 it describes the stance of the "kings of the nations" against God and his anointed (see Matt 17:25). Ironically, it also designates Jesus gathering all the nations in judgment in 25:32. They address Pilate, the representative of the imperial regime, as **Lord**, not Jesus. They accuse Jesus of being a **deceiver**, when they have misled the nation (9:36), the crowds (27:20-25), and the willing Pilate (27:12-14, 15-23). Jesus has designated another part of the religious elite (the Sadducees, 22:29) as deceived, and warned his disciples against deceivers in the time before the end (24:4, 5, 11, 24).

• **27:64**

They give Pilate orders. **Therefore command the tomb to be made secure until the third day; otherwise his disciples may go and steal him away and tell the people, "He has been raised from the dead," and the last deception** (the disciples' proclamation) **would be worse than the first** (Jesus' proclamation). It does not seem to occur to them that Jesus may be right (though they take his proclamation very seriously), or that there is nothing they or Roman military power can do about it. Their misreading of the situation is further attested by their concern for the disciples' actions. But the disciples have fled (26:56).

• **27:65-66**

Pilate approves and complies with their command. **Pilate said to them, "You have a guard of soldiers; go make it as secure as you can." So they went with the guard and made the tomb secure by sealing the stone.** Just as chapter 28 will expose the injustice of Rome's legal system and the powerlessness of its imperial power over life and death, it will also portray the limits of Rome's touted military machine. The effect of the guard is, ironically, the exact opposite of the elite's intent. It accentuates the miracle of resurrection by removing all other possibilities. Jesus is dead. His tomb is sealed with a stone and guarded by Roman soldiers. Yet despite the best that the imperial forces can do, he will be seen alive. The elite set the stage for the demonstration of God's power. That power will thwart the intentions and resources of the political and religious elite.

PART VI

The Sixth Narrative Block

God Raises Jesus (28:1-20)

CHAPTER 28

The Resurrection

Jesus has been crucified. Every normal expectation indicates that the story has ended with his defeat. He has been faithful and resolute through great suffering to death. It seems that his opponents, the allied religious and political elite, have triumphed. They have removed this threat who proclaimed and enacted God's empire and coming triumph, and who claimed his own pivotal role in God's purposes. They have exposed him to be a very fallible fraud.

But there is a sixth narrative block. Chapter 28 introduces a new phase, a new future where there seemed to be none. Jesus does not stay dead. In the key incident (28:1-10), an angel announces to the women that God has raised him, just as Jesus had previously predicted. The women (28:9-10) see him alive. Later, the disciples (28:16-20) will meet with him. Possessing all authority in heaven and earth, he commissions them to worldwide mission and to build a community of disciples. He promises to be with them. God's purposes have not been thwarted. But it is up to the disciples to be faithful to their charge, even though they know what happens to those who remain faithful to God's commission.

In the meantime, the religious and political forces maintain their opposition and deceit (28:11-15). Announcements of resurrection are not compatible with the empire's ideology and propaganda of power and control. The empire's soldiers and religious leaders agree to attribute the missing body to theft by the disciples. Jesus' resurrection neither silences them nor converts them. Disciples exist in this dangerous world of the elite's stubborn resistance, constant deceit, and deadly opposition until the completion of God's purposes signaled by the return of Jesus (19:28; 24:27-31; 25:31-45). Only then will this sixth narrative block be completed.

The chapter divides into three sections

28:1-10—JESUS IS RISEN

• 28:1

The scene is the dawn of the morning after the sabbath: **After the sabbath as the first day of the week was dawning, Mary Magdalene and the other Mary went to see the tomb.** These two women were among the "many women" who observed Jesus' crucifixion (27:55-56), and they attend his burial and tomb (27:61). Why do they come to the tomb? In Mark they bring copious spices to anoint the dead Jesus. They expect him to be dead and plan to keep him that way. But here there are no references to anointing and spices. Some attribute their coming to mourning and great sadness. But as with 27:61, there are no descriptions of mourning behavior. One result of their coming is that they will be witnesses to the risen Jesus as they were to his crucifixion and burial. But the verse attributes purpose to them, they **went to see the tomb**.

The use of a verb **to see** offers a clue. This verb appears only in 27:55 and 28:1 and connects the two scenes. But verbs of seeing have been especially important in the gospel. Having "eyes to see" or "seeing" are metaphors that denote understanding (9:2) or insight into Jesus' teaching, and experience of the reality to which it testifies (13:16-17; cf. 5:8). This quality divides disciples from the noncomprehending crowds who do not see (13:13-15). What is it that the women have understood that causes them **to see the tomb**? These women have followed (a discipleship verb) Jesus from Galilee (27:55). They have had numerous opportunities, direct and indirect, to hear his teaching that he must die and be raised (16:21; 17:22-23; 20:17-19). They have faithfully witnessed his accurate teaching about his crucifixion and burial. They come awaiting his resurrection.[1] It is no accident that three times in these opening ten verses of chapter 28, and once in the final scene, the verb "to see" denotes encountering the risen Jesus (28:6, 7, 10, 17). That is what the women wait to do.

It is significant that it is not the powerful or the elite, not the male disciples, who gather. It is the women, generally (though there are exceptions) regarded as somewhat marginal to the normative adult male world. Consistently the narrative has shown the marginal, not the elite, to be receptive to God's purposes.

• 28:2-3

Various signs attest God's presence and power at work.

1. **And behold/suddenly** (announcing something special), **there was a great earthquake**. Earthquake-like experiences (8:24, the same word) and **earthquakes** (24:7) occur in the time of tribulation in which disciples currently live before the end. An earthquake accompanies Jesus' death and splits open the tombs of the saints in Jerusalem who were raised (see 27:51, 54). This earthquake prepares for (but does not cause) the opening of Jesus' tomb.

2. **An angel of the Lord, descending from heaven came and rolled back the stone and sat on it.** The phrase **angel of the Lord** recalls the birth narrative. There angels accomplish God's purposes by announcing Mary's preg-

nancy to Joseph, guiding the escape from the tyrant Herod, and instigating the return from Egypt (1:20, 24; 2:13, 19). They also have significant eschatological roles as agents of God's will (13:39, 41, 49; 16:27; 24:31; 25:31). In this scene, the angel participates in God's triumph over the religious elite and political forces by revealing, and then interpreting, the empty tomb. The angel's origin from God (the devil also has angels or messengers, 25:41) is emphasized by both **of the Lord** and **descending from heaven**, God's abode (5:34). This repeated detail establishes the angel's legitimacy and authority, and prepares for his proclamation in v. 5. He **rolls back the stone** (27:60), presumably, since Jesus does not walk out but is already risen, to let others see that he is not in the tomb. The angel **sat on it**, a common posture through the passion (26:58, 69 [Peter and the guards]; 26:64 [the ascended Jesus]; 27:19 [Pilate]; 27:36 [the soldiers at the cross]; 27:61 [the two Marys at the tomb]).

The angel's **appearance was like lightning, and his clothing white as snow.** Not only does the angel come from God but his clothing is like God's (Dan 7:9, and like the transfigured Jesus in 17:2). **Lightning** is often associated with divine appearances, presence, and power (see 24:27, the coming of the Son of Man). It was also closely associated with Jupiter, a symbol of Jupiter's rule and world order which Roman emperors manifested in their reign. But here, the power over life and death belongs not to the empire's emperor, governor, or soldiers but to God. The lightning-like appearance asserts God's sovereignty even over death, something the empire cannot duplicate.

• 28:4

In 27:54 the centurion and those with him see the earthquake and other signs and confess Jesus as Son of God. But not these guards. They see the earthquake and the angel and tremble: **For fear of him the guards shook/earthquaked**. The verb is the cognate of the noun for "earthquake." They **became like dead men.** The elite have been so careful to secure the tomb (27:62-66), but neither the religious elite nor Roman political or military might can seal it against God's life-giving ways. In this place of resurrection, it is not Jesus but the empire's guards who are **like dead men**. God's power renders the empire and its mighty fighting machine lifeless, just as God drowns the Egyptian army in the sea (Exod 14:21-31); Gideon's three hundred troops confound the Midianites—"as thick as locusts"—with torches, jars, and trumpets (Judg 7:4-23); the boy David routs the Philistines by flooring the mighty Goliath (1 Sam 17:40-54); Elijah prevails over Ahab, Jezebel, and prophets of Baal (1 Kgs 18); God shuts the lions' mouths to protect Daniel against king Darius (Dan 6); Judith halts Holofernes, the invading general of the Assyrian king Nebuchadnezzar "king of all the earth" (Jdt 11:1) to save Israel (11-16); Judas Maccabeus turns back Antiochus Epiphanes (1 Macc). "God has brought down the powerful from their thrones . . ." (Luke 1:52). In anticipating God's victory over Rome, the gospel again resorts to imperial images to attest that God out-empires the empire.

• **28:5-6**

The angel addresses the women and announces Jesus' resurrection. The resurrection message comes from God (cf. the angel's origin in 28:2). **"Do not be afraid** (a common reassurance from angels; 1:20; Gen 15:1 [Abram]); **for I know that you are looking for Jesus who was crucified. He is not here for he has been raised as he said. Come see the place where he lay."** The angel proclaims that the tomb is empty (as the women are invited to affirm for themselves) not because the disciples have stolen the body (the act that the chief priests, Pharisees, and Pilate fear in 27:62-66) **but because he has been raised as he said**. The passive construction (**has been raised**) indicates God's work. The reference to Jesus' words (**as he said**) recalls his predictions of resurrection in 16:21; 17:22-23; 20:17-19. Jesus' words are reliable. The angel's announcement is a revelation, an interpretation of the empty tomb and missing body. It discloses God's work, which is not observed or witnessed (there is no description of the resurrection itself), but whose effects are open to several explanations. The imperial and religious elite will offer another interpretation in 28:11-15. The notion of resurrection arose in part in contexts of persecution and martyrdom and ensures participation in God's victory over imperial tyrants and death. See Dan 12:1-3; 2 Macc 7; *2 Bar* 49-51.[2] Jesus' resurrection means the resurrection of the faithful. Those buried and raised in Jerusalem (27:51-53) anticipate the yet-future general resurrection.

• **28:7-8**

The angel commands them, **Then go quickly and tell his disciples, "He has been raised from the dead and indeed is going ahead of you to Galilee; there you will see him. This is my message for you."** A woman was the first to anoint Jesus for burial (26:6-13). These women are the first hearers and recipients of the resurrection proclamation. The angel now sends them to be its first human proclaimers. Their congregation comprises the male **disciples**. They were last referred to as having fled (26:56) or, in Peter's case, having "gone out and wept bitterly" (26:75). No details are given about where they are or how the women are to locate them in order to make the proclamation.

The disciples are to go **to Galilee**, the place of so much of Jesus' ministry (see 4:12-16; 4:17-19:2) and of their call to discipleship (4:18-22; 10:1-4). There they will **see** or encounter the risen Jesus (so the women in v. 1). This meeting will not take place in the center of power, Jerusalem, but, typically, in what that center regards as a less significant and marginal area, yet an area that is central to God's purposes (cf. 2:5-6; 4:15-16). The angel's word is consistent with and recalls Jesus' teaching of 26:32.

The women trust the angel's proclamation and quickly obey without waiting to see Jesus. His previous promise of being raised has been confirmed by the angel and empty tomb. **So they left the tomb quickly** (cf. 28:7) **with fear and great joy** (compare the magi in 2:10, and the eschatological experience of the faithful slaves in 25:21, 23), **and ran to proclaim it to his disciples.** The verb **proclaim** is used of Jesus' mission in 12:18.

• 28:9-10

Not only are the women the first hearers, recipients, and proclaimers of the resurrection message; they are also the first to see the risen Jesus. An appearance story confirms the angel's interpretation of the empty tomb. **Suddenly/And behold** (see 28:2) **Jesus met them and said, "Greetings!"** The risen Jesus reveals himself to them while they are obeying the angel. Details of location, his approach, appearance, clothing, gestures, or any other circumstances are absent. The not common verb **met** adds little specific information (used of hostile demons in Matt 8:28, of wisdom in Wis 6:16; Sir 15:2; and of evil in Sir 12:17). Jesus, though, exemplifies his own teaching, not only in being raised as he said (16:21; 17:22-23; 20:17-19) but also, in enduring to the end, he is saved (10:22), in losing his life he finds it (16:24).

The women know instantly from seeing and hearing him that it is Jesus. **And they came to him** (a verb of respectful approach; see 8:2), **seized/took hold of his feet and worshiped him.** The verb **seized/took hold** indicates that he is not a ghost. Further, in 21:46; 26:4, 48, 50, 55, 57, this verb, translated as "arrest," denotes what the religious elite and Jesus' betrayer have done to him.[3] But these women **seize** him appropriately, not to betray, arrest, and kill him but to **worship him.** The verb **worship** designates the prostration required when greeting a ruler, initially in the east since Alexander. By the first century Rome's emperors had acquired a taste for the practice (see 4:9 for prostration before Gaius Caligula, Nero, and Domitian; also 18:26). Like other marginal characters—the magi in 2:2, 8, 11, the leper of 8:2, the ruler of 9:18, the disciples of 14:33, the Canaanite woman of 15:25— these women **worship** him as the ruler or king (see 25:34, 40; contrast 27:11, 29, 37, 42). His resurrection confirms that he is God's commissioned agent (Son and Christ) and that he manifests God's reign over death and the very worst that the religious and political elite can do to him. It also confirms his teaching about his yet future role in establishing God's empire (19:28; 24:27-31).

• 28:10

As the angel has done (cf. 28:7), Jesus also commissions the women with the same message. **"Do not be afraid** (cf. 28:5); **go and tell my brothers** (cf. 12:46-50)[4] **to go to Galilee** (cf. 26:32); **there they will see me"** (cf. 28:6, 7, 10).

28:11-15—THE ELITE'S ALTERNATIVE STORY

The empire strikes back—again. While the angel, the women, and Jesus proclaim that God has raised Jesus from the dead, the religious elite join with Rome's soldiers to create an alternative story. Their imperial propaganda, full of claims of Rome's commissioning by the gods, of Rome's power and control (see Introduction, section 9), cannot entertain the notion that it has been outpowered and outsovereigned. Likewise the religious elite cannot confess God's triumph and their own error, nor believe the sign of Jonah which Jesus provides (12:38-40; 16:1-4; 27:42). In rejecting any notion of resurrection (also 27:62-66), the elite reject God's purposes and proclamation in order to maintain its own privileged position and power in the imperial society as Rome's allies (see Introduction, sections 1 and 5; 2:4; 3:7; 16:21; 26:3, 27:1).

• 28:11

Even while the women obey, the religious and political/ military forces are planning their spin. **While they** (the women) **were going, some of the guard went into the city and told the chief priests everything that had happened.** The "dead men" guards have revived and report to the ubiquitous **chief priests** (26:3, 14, 47, 51, 57, 58, 59, 62, 63, 65; 27:1, 3, 6, 12, 20, 41, 62). Whereas the raised saints in 27:53 go **into the city** to witness to what God has done, the soldiers go **into the city** to witness against God's work. They tell the **chief priests everything that had happened**, though **everything** is significantly qualified by the fact that they were "as dead men" for much of the scene. Ironically the religious elite are condemned by their own words in 27:42. Jesus has come down from the cross but they have not believed.

• 28:12-14

After the priests had assembled with the elders (so 27:1, 12, 20, 41; for the somewhat fluid alliance of religious groups through the passion narrative, see 26:3-5), **they devised a plan to give a large sum of money to the soldiers.** Their leadership authority, based on birth, training, wealth, and social status, has again been challenged by God's action in Jesus. Having accused Jesus of being a deceiver (27:63), they continue their work of deceiving and misleading others. They naturally resort to deception and lies, just as they did in charging Jesus (26:59-61). One deception leads to another and greater deception (cf. 27:64). Their evil hearts are manifested in deeds of murder, false witness, and slander (15:19). They are shown again to be false shepherds (9:36), not God's planting (15:14), people who refuse to recognize Jesus' commissioning (21:23-27), who know neither the scriptures nor the power of God (22:29).

In various scenes in the passion narrative, the vocabulary of **assembled** (26:3, 57; 27:17, 27, 62) and **devised a plan** (27:1, 7; cf. 12:14; 22:15) has appeared. It binds these episodes together to underline the elite's consistent and sustained opposition to Jesus.

The gospel continues its warnings about the dangers of **money** (6:19-34; 10:8-9; 13:22; 19:16-30). Wealth distracts, chokes, rules, and deceives. Just as the religious elite paid Judas to betray Jesus (26:14-16; 27:3-10), now they try to buy off the resurrection. Their money buys the soldiers' willingness to declare, **"His soldiers came by night and stole him away while we were asleep."** The deception and cover-up are not convincing. Apart from the carelessness of sleeping guards (again Rome's military is mocked), how can the soldiers testify that the body was stolen when they were asleep and did not see the theft, let alone prevent it? The military takes the public fall for the religious elite. The gospel's audience is not deceived. Nor, it seems, will Pilate be deceived. So the religious elite commit to reassure him and cover up the false testimony. **If this comes to the governor's ears, we will satisfy him and keep you out of trouble.**

• **28:15**

So they took the money and did as they were taught/directed. And this story/word is still told among the Jews to this day. The use of **story/word** throws the two accounts of resurrection and theft into sharp contrast. The same term (λόγος, *logos*) denotes Jesus' teaching (7:24, 26, 28; 19:1, 22; 24:35; 26:1) and healing word (8:8), as well as the proclamation about him (10:14) and the word about (God's) reign/empire (13:19-23). Jesus has previously accused the religious elite of making void God's word while preferring their own tradition (15:6).

28:16-20—JESUS COMMISSIONS THE DISCIPLES

The gospel's final scene is a commissioning story as the risen Jesus commissions the disciples to form a worldwide community of disciples of Jesus.[5]

Introduction	28:16
Confrontation	28:17
Reaction	28:17
Commission	28:18-19
Protest	(not here)
Reassurance	28:20
Conclusion	28:20

The scene has significant christological elements. It is the risen Jesus who commissions the disciples. Jesus assumes the role that God plays in the prophetic commissionings. Jesus shares in God's cosmic authority and is able, like God, to be with the disciples forever, even though he is not physically present. It also has ecclesiological elements. The community of disciples, with its imperfections and doubts, is given (again, cf. ch. 10) the task of continuing Jesus' mission and is reassured of Jesus' presence with them. It has ethical dimensions in urging transmission of all Jesus' teaching, which shapes and informs the community of disciples in its alternative existence.

The small, minority, marginal community of disciples is commissioned to nothing less than worldwide mission in proclaiming obedience to Jesus and his teaching. But this mission is carried out in a dangerous and resistant world as the passion narrative and the immediately prior scene in 28:11-15 have made clear. There are rivals for human loyalty, who are, like this gospel's vision, intolerant of other claimants. There are competing understandings of what God and/or the gods want from humans. Post-70 Judaism struggles with diverse visions of its future without the Jerusalem temple, but many do not find the Matthean vision convincing.

This worldwide mission is bound to collide with the empire. Rome's worldwide mission is clear, frequently articulated (coins, monuments, festivals, poets, historians, etc.), and very successful. Its mission is to dominate the world, a mission entrusted to Rome by the gods and enacted through the emperor and military and political personnel (see Introduction, section 9). Livy (*AUC* 1.16) recalls Proculus Julius's announcement that Romulus "the father of the Roman city" descended from heaven to command, "Go and declare to the Romans the will of Heaven that my Rome shall be the capital of the world so let them cherish the art of war, and let them know and teach their children that no human strength can resist Roman arms."[6] In the underworld Anchises commissions Aeneas, "O Roman, rule the nations with your power" (Virgil, *Aeneid* 6.851-53). Seneca (*De Clem* 1.1.2) has Nero wonder: "Have I of all mortals found favor with heaven and been chosen to serve on earth as vicar of the gods? I am the arbiter of life and death for the nations" with the power to determine the survival, rise, or fall of kings, cities and nations. Statius celebrates Domitian's exercise of this mission: "a god he is, at Jupiter's command he rules for him the happy/blessed world . . . Hail ruler of men [*sic*] and parent of gods . . . the god who holds the reins of earth, he who nearer than Jupiter directs the doings of humankind" (*Silv* 4.3.128-29, 139-40; 5.1.37-39). Martial acknowledges Domitian as ruler of the world (*Epig* 5.3.3), and Josephus endorses Rome's worldwide dominance as God's will (*JW* 4.370; 5.60-61, 362-68, 376-78).

The community of Jesus' disciples resembles the empire in that its mission is worldwide and concerns allegiance. Its mission, though, is not a military one; it announces God's reign or empire. This announcement is in conflict with and poses some threat to Rome. It does not recognize Jupiter/Zeus as supreme or in control of the world and human destiny. It finds the divine purposes and blessing revealed not in the emperor but in Jesus, crucified and now risen. It calls people to recognize God's sovereignty as "Lord of Heaven and earth" (11:25). And it proclaims that God's purposes are supreme. The future is not that of eternal Rome, but of God's just and life-giving empire established over all (chs. 24-25). It is to this mission that the community of disciples is again sent by the one who claims "all authority in heaven and earth."

• 28:16

Now the eleven (recall Judas's demise from 27:3-10) **disciples went to Galilee, to the mountain to which Jesus had directed them.** The narrative refers only to the **eleven**, but the appearance of "many" faithful women in 27:55-56, their description in discipleship language ("having followed him," "served him"), and their prominent role in 28:1-10 suggests that they have been present throughout, even if often invisible in the narrative. Here then, while the (androcentric) focus is on the eleven, it seems reasonable to guess that other followers, women and men, also meet the risen Jesus. On **Galilee**, see 26:32; 28:7, 10. Galilee is a place not of escape but of engagement with imperial power, darkness, and death (see 4:12-16).

The location is a **mountain**. Significant things have happened on mountains:

Jesus has been tempted (4:8), has taught (5:1; 8:1; 24:3), prayed (14:23), healed the sick and fed the hungry (15:29), been transfigured (17:1, 9), and entered Jerusalem (Mount of Olives, 21:1; 26:30). Echoes of both Mt. Sinai and Mt. Zion traditions cluster around these references. Moses dies on a mountain with a glimpse of the promised land (Deut 34:1-5). Joshua is commissioned to continue his leadership. The scene here is one not of death but of commissioning in anticipation of God's empire being established over all the world. And instead of Jerusalem as the center of power, it is the (relatively) marginal location of Galilee (cf. Zion, Isa 2:2-3; 25:6-10). It should also be noted that the gods were said to live on Mt. Olympus, but it is not *their* authority that is celebrated, disseminated, and anticipated by this scene.

• 28:17

The focus is Jesus and the disciples' confrontation with and reaction to him. **When they saw him** (cf. 28:1, 7, 10), **they worshiped him** just as the women did in 28:9 and disciples had done in 14:33. See 28:9 for the verb **worship** and the recognition of Jesus' kingship. But unlike the women, **some doubted**, a verb with which Jesus addressed Peter in 14:31. There it suggests the presence of some faith even though it is insufficient, distracted, indecisive, and wavering ("little faith"; see 6:30; 8:26; 16:8; 17:20). Do some not think it is Jesus? Or are they doubtful that he has been raised? Or are they frightened? Or are some not sure what all this means?[7]

• 28:18

And Jesus came and said to them, "All authority in heaven and on earth has been given to me." Compare 11:27. The verse evokes Dan 7:13-14, where God gives "dominion and glory and reign/empire" to one "like a son of man." This transfer occurs after a struggle with imperial powers. The dominion (same word as "authority") is everlasting, as is the reign promised to kings in the line of David (2 Sam 7:13-14). Jesus, son of David (1:1; 9:27; 15:22; 20:30-31; 21:9, 15; 22:42-45), the king (2:2; 25:34), mocked by the empire's political-military representatives and by the religious elite (27:11, 27-31, 37, 42), participates in God's rule over all things, and will return to judge the earth (19:28; 24:27-31; 25:31-46).

Jesus has previously turned down Satan's offer of "all the kingdoms/empires of the world" in 4:8. To have accepted it there would have been to submit to Satan's will. But he would not have been God's agent or son in manifesting God's reign or empire (4:17). Here he receives "all authority" from God as God's beloved son or agent faithful to God's purposes (3:17; 17:5). Jesus has described God (and not the emperor or Jupiter!) as "Lord of heaven and earth," of all creation (11:25; cf. Gen 1:1; Lev 25:23; Ps 24:1). Jesus participates in God's reign over all things. That includes authority not only over Satan but also over the religious elite and Rome, who "handed him over" to be crucified.[8] For visions of this authority exercised fully in his return and judgment, see 13:41-43; 19:28; 24:27-31; 25:31-46. For its anticipatory expression in his ministry, see 7:29 in his teaching and 9:6-8 over sin and disease. The religious elite refuse to recognize it (21:23-27), while Jesus delegates it to his disciples to share in his mission (10:1).

• **28:19**

With this authority Jesus commissions the disciples as his agents. **Go therefore and make disciples of all nations**.[9] The verb **make disciples** draws on the noun "disciple," which has been so important in the gospel. A disciple is one who is called to follow Jesus, who has encountered God's reign/empire in his preaching and actions and responds positively in an ongoing, learned, and lived recognition of his authority as Lord (4:18-22; 5:1-2; 8:1-4). See 13:52 for the verb. The community of disciples is to secure the transfer of allegiance to Jesus in a life of ongoing recognition of God's sovereignty and empire (4:17, 18-22), and in anticipation of its establishment in full over all (chs. 24-25). This commission builds on and elaborates a series of previous mission commands in 4:19; 5:3-16; ch. 10; 13:18-23; 22:9-10; 24:9-14.

The arena and target audience are **all nations**. Some have argued that this mission is limited to Gentiles (see 25:32), but several factors indicate a mission to all people, Jew and Gentile. (1) There is no evidence that mission to Israel has ended. Jesus had earlier limited mission to Israel during his life (10:6), but has not declared its end. (2) Other incidents (2:1-12; 8:5-13; 15:21-29) suggest an expanding mission to Gentiles, not one that replaces Israel. (3) There is no indication in 21:33-45 and 22:1-14 of any replacement of Israel in God's purposes. God's salvific purposes include Jew and Gentile. (4) The term **nations** can mean Gentiles in contrast to Jews (10:5, 18) or Jews and Gentiles, the whole inhabited world as in 24:9, 14 (mission sayings) and 25:32. There is no contrast present here. (5) Verse 18 recognizes Jesus as having "all authority in heaven and earth." There is no exceptive clause. A mission to all the inhabited world, Jew and Gentile, is in view. (6) The phrase "heaven and earth" evokes the creation of Gen 1:1. God's purposes are universal and promise blessing to "all the families of the earth" (Gen 12:3). This blessing is made available through the community of disciples of Jesus, son of Abraham (1:1).

The command to **make disciples** is elaborated by two participles, **baptizing** and **teaching**, and a promise. In recognizing Jesus' participation in God's kingship, new disciples are to be initiated into a new community by baptism: **baptizing them in the name of the Father and of the Son and of the Holy Spirit**. Just as Jesus signified his allegiance to God's purposes by submitting to John's baptism (3:13-17), new disciples imitate him (10:24-25) and show their allegiance to him by submitting to baptism **in the name of the Father and of the Son and of the Holy Spirit**. The phrase **in the name of** represents commitment to, ownership, and protection (Ps 124:8). God the **Father** (see 5:16, 45; 6:9; 7:21; 10:32; 11:25-27; 12:50; 13:43; 16:17; 18:10, 14; 20:23; 23:9; 25:34; 26:29, 38, 42) and Jesus the **Son** (see 2:15; 3:17) have been linked in that Jesus the Son does the Father's salvific will (3:15) and reveals the Father (11:25-27). Disciples of Jesus do the Father's will (12:46-50). Their baptism is an indication of a life of obedience to God in following Jesus. The **Holy Spirit** presumably assists in living this life, just as the "Spirit of your Father" (10:20) assists in their speaking (and God's Spirit assists Jesus in his mission, 3:15; 12:18-21). For possible origins of baptism, see 3:5-6.

• 28:20

The initiation of new disciples is not the end of the task. Disciples are to form and inform the community of disciples by **teaching them to obey/guard everything that I have commanded you.** The activity of **teaching** has been Jesus' activity until now (4:23; 5:2; 7:29; 9:35; 11:1; 13:54; 21:23; 26:55). He is the sole teacher (23:8, 10).[10] Now it is entrusted to disciples. The same verb is used in 28:15; the soldiers "did as they were taught." Whereas the soldiers teach lies about Jesus (his body is stolen; he is not risen), the disciples teach what Jesus has taught concerning God's reign/empire and life shaped by it until the risen Jesus returns in power and glory. That life is marked by **obeying** (cf. 19:17; cf. 7:24-27; 12:46-50) or **guarding** (so 27:36, 54; 28:4) **everything that I have commanded you**. The clause encompasses the whole of the gospel story of Jesus, both what has been commended and what has, by contrast, been shown to be false. Jesus has revealed God's will in his teaching (hence the five big teaching blocks in chs. 5-7, 10, 13, 18, 24-25), in his conflicts with the religious leaders, in his actions. The community of disciples incarnates his teaching and actions in obedient lives.

And remember, I am with you always, to the end of the age. The community does not struggle on its own in this mission task with the inevitable difficulties created by an environment of deceit and hostility (28:11-15) and by faithless discipleship (chs. 26-27). Though Jesus is not physically present, his presence continues through the gospel's narrative of his words and actions, and, based on 10:20, through the assisting role of the Spirit. The demand of mission brings with it the gift of gracious presence and assistance. See 1:23; 18:20.[11] God promises divine presence to the people liberated in the exodus from Egypt (Deut 31:23) and from exile in Babylon (Isa 41:10; 43:5).

The alternative, countercultural life of discipleship is lived in the time between Jesus' life, death, and resurrection, and **the end of the age**, the culmination of God's purposes, when Jesus returns and God's reign is established over all things including Rome, and God's salvation is experienced in full (see 13:39, 40, 49; 19:28; 24:3; 25:31-46). Until then, the present is a difficult time of tribulation (chs. 24-25) and mission. But this final promise and temporal marker provide hope in that discipleship looks forward to the end of the present oppression and the new, transformed future of God's reign or empire.

What happens to Jesus? Clearly he does not intend to remain physically with the disciples. But unlike Luke, Matthew has no reference to Jesus' ascension (Luke 24:51; Acts 1:9-10). Yet Jesus leaves. Matt 28:18, along with 19:28, 25:31 and 26:64, suggests that he joins God in heaven. Again it is possible that the gospel reflects an imperial practice, that of apotheosis or deification. Rome's founder Romulus was understood to have been deified. He was caught up in a star with thunder and clouds and was no more on the earth (Livy, *AUC* 1.16.1-3; also Cicero, *De Re Publica* 2.17-18; Dionysius of Halicarnassus, *Rom*

Ant 2.56; Plutarch, *Romulus* 27; Ovid, *Fasti* 2.491-96; *Metamorphoses* 14.816-820). When an emperor died, the Senate could confer deified status on him, as it did for Vespasian and Titus but not for Domitian (Suetonius, *Deified Vespasian*; *Deified Titus*; *Domitian* 2.3). This act involved a ceremony through which the emperor was understood to join the gods, whence he continued to bless the world.[12] Seneca mocks claims of Claudius's deification in his work *Apocolocyntosis* or the "Pumpkinification" of Claudius.[13]

Perhaps Jesus is understood in somewhat similar terms to join God in heaven (5:34) and to share in God's ruling authority (28:18) until he returns to effect final salvation from Rome and all God's opponents, by establishing God's life-giving empire.

Appendix

The Plot of Matthew's Gospel

A particular understanding of the gospel's plot informs the divisions that I utilize in reading the gospel and that appear in the table of contents. This appendix provides a brief justification for that understanding, as well as some references to a much fuller discussion and bibliography.

Audiences of ancient biographies (see Introduction, section 2) expect an initial focus on the ancestry, birth, and upbringing of the main character. Scenes of great and virtuous actions and accounts of teachings should follow, with an account of the character's death to close the biography.[1] Matthew's gospel generally follows this pattern in its presentation of Jesus. The first two chapters narrate Jesus' ancestry, conception, and some early childhood experiences. Chapters 3-25 cover teaching and actions. Chapters 26-28 focus on his death and resurrection.

Within this chronological structure, a useful way of reading the narrative understands the gospel's plot to unfold in six major sections or narrative blocks, to use the language of Seymour Chatman.[2] Each narrative block has a key scene or inceptive incident, a "branching point" which significantly moves the action forward. The action of this key scene or incident is often elaborated by the other scenes in the narrative block.

Part 1: The First Narrative Block—1:1-4:16   51-116

In the context of God's lengthy history with Israel (1:1-17), God initiates this story in the conception and commissioning of Jesus to manifest God's salvation from Roman imperial control (1:18-25). This event forms the key scene of the section. God protects Jesus from the imperial backlash (ch. 2). Jesus commits himself to his God-given task in his baptism and resists the temptation of the devil, the controller of the world's empires (3:1-4:16). Jesus' mission is to manifest God's salvation or light in a dark world under imperial control (4:12-16).

Part 2: The Second Narrative Block—4:17-11:1   117-246

Jesus carries out this task of manifesting God's saving presence or empire in his public ministry of preaching (chs. 5-7, 10) and healing (chs. 8-9), as well as by bringing into existence and by shaping a community of followers (4:18-22; ch. 10). The key incident is 4:17-25. Jesus carries out God's commission in proclaiming God's empire or reign, in calling disciples, and in preaching and healing. The scenes in chapters 5-7 and 8-9 elaborate these actions.

Part 3: The Third Narrative Block—11:2-16:20   247-338

Jesus' actions and preaching of God's empire reveal his identity as God's commissioned agent. These actions and words require a response of acceptance or rejection from those who meet him. While some welcome him, others, especially the religious and political elite, do not. The key incident is 11:2-6, in which John the Baptist poses the central question of the identity of Jesus. The subsequent scenes show various characters trying to discern Jesus' identity.

Part 4: The Fourth Narrative Block—16:21-20:34   339-410

Jesus teaches his community of followers that God's purposes for him involve his death and resurrection at the hands of the rejecting elite. This event also shapes the distinctive and alternative existence of discipleship. The key incident is 16:21-28 in which for the first time Jesus names his imminent crucifixion and states its significance for discipleship. The subsequent scenes, especially his teaching on paying the tax (17:24-27), community relationships in chapter 18, and his outline of an alternative household in chapters 19-20, elaborate this significance as Jesus moves toward Jerusalem to his death.

Part 5: The Fifth Narrative Block—21:1-27:66   411-540

In Jerusalem, Jesus conflicts with the elite, condemns their temple, and is rejected by them. He dies at their hands. His death (26:28), like his return (24:27-31), is part of God's purposes to save people from the sins punished by Rome in the fall of Jerusalem in 70 C.E. The key incident is Jesus' arrival in Jerusalem and conflict with the religious leaders in the temple (21:1-27). This event leads to the final rift with the religious leaders (chs. 22-23) and precipitates his crucifixion (chs. 26-27). In chapters 24-25 Jesus teaches his disciples about the end of this age and his future role as judge of the world at his triumphant return that destroys Roman power. His crucifixion at their hands is not a defeat but furthers God's salvific purposes to establish God's empire or reign.

Part 6: The Sixth Narrative Block—28:1-20   541-554

God's saving purposes are not thwarted. God overcomes the religious elite's opposition by raising Jesus from death. The risen Jesus, who now shares in God's sovereignty over heaven and earth, commissions his disciples to worldwide mission and promises to be with them. The key incident is 28:1-10. Jesus' death is not the end of God's story. Jesus' resurrection anticipates his return to effect God's salvation and to establish God's empire over all things including Rome.

Notes

Preface

1. See, for example, the massive and superb, multivolumed commentaries by Davies and Allison, and Luz.

2. Harrington, *Gospel of Matthew.*

3. Wainwright, *Towards a Feminist Critical Reading.*

4. Stanton, *Gospel for a New People,* 146-68.

5. Note, for example, in 1999, (1) the comments of Minnesota's governor Jesse Ventura, "Organized religion is a sham and a crutch for weak-minded people who need strength in numbers" (quoted in *Newsweek,* October 11, 1999, p. 27); (2) the reported shooting of some Columbine High School students who professed to believe in God and who have been widely perceived, especially in more conservative religious circles, as martyrs; (3) the shooting of people gathered to worship in a Baptist church in Fort Worth, Texas.

Introduction

1. Wimbush, "Introduction: Interpreting Resistance, Resisting Interpretations."

2. Other religious figures and texts resist Rome's empire—for example, the German prophetess Veleda (Tacitus, *Hist* 5.13); magi and astrologers who predicted various disasters and were expelled in the 70s and 90s by the emperors Vespasian and Domitian (see Matt 2:1-11); numerous Jewish prophetic figures attested to by Josephus (see Matt 24:5); the *Sibylline Oracles;* Revelation; apocalyptic texts which envisage the triumph of God's reign over all tyranny including Rome's (*1 En* 37-71; *4 Ezra; 2 Baruch;* Qumran; Paul). On religious opposition to Rome, see MacMullen, *Enemies of the Roman Order,* 95-162; Momigliano, "Some Preliminary Remarks on the 'Religious Opposition,'" 103-29; also Bowersock, "Mechanics of Subversion," 291-320; Bauckham, "Economic Critique of Rome in Revelation 18"; Horsley (ed.), *Paul and Empire.*

3. As I complete this manuscript, I have just read W. E. Pilgrim's fine book *Uneasy Neighbors: Church and State in the New Testament.* His discussion throughout and his language of "uneasy neighbors" and, in relation to the Synoptics, of "critical distance" and "uneasy tension" (p. 38) to denote this relationship are very helpful and frequently consonant with the direction of this analysis. I do not, though, think Pilgrim pushes his Matthean analysis far enough. The dynamics of tension and critical distance are part of the gospel's resistance, a category Pilgrim reserves for Revelation and from which he exempts Matthew. But two factors that cause Pilgrim to differentiate Matthew and Revelation (satanic control and martyrdom) are part of the gospel's worldview. Attention to 4:8 requires recognition that this gospel does deem the present world order to be under the devil's control, while 10:28, 38-39 and 16:24-26 expect martyrdom for disciples.

4. The wording derives from Beker, *Paul the Apostle: The Coming Triumph of God.* It is with sadness that I note the death of this marvelous scholar and wonderful human being in July 1999.

5. Iser, *Act of Reading;* Carter, *Matthew: Storyteller,* 103-256.

6. Saldarini (*Pharisees,* 35-49) draws on the work of Lenski (*Power and Privilege,* 256-

66) and Kautsky (*Aristocratic Empires,* 81-83, 161-66) to locate the religious leaders among the elite. Josephus consistently identifies the chief priests and the "most notable Pharisees" as allies of Rome (*JW* 2.197, 320, 411, 414).

7. For elaboration, see Kingsbury, *Matthew as Story;* Powell, "Plot and Subplots"; Carter, *Matthew: Storyteller,* 119-241.

8. Freire, *Pedagogy of the Oppressed,* 27-51.

9. Ibid., 31.

10. Soares-Prabhu, "Jesus the Teacher," 256.

11. Kingsbury ("Rhetoric of Comprehension") notes 164 uses of verbs of "seeing" and "hearing" and 58 uses of verbs of cognition such as "know," "perceive," and "reveal."

12. Carter, "'To See the Tomb,'" 201-5.

13. Carter and Heil, *Matthew's Parables,* 8-17; Rabinowitz, "Whirl Without End," 85; idem, *Before Reading;* idem, "Truth in Fiction."

14. Burnett ("Exposing the Anti-Jewish Ideology") argues that this title is anti-Jewish in that it identifies God as the Father of followers of Jesus, but denies this to Jews, thereby denying access to election and salvation.

15. For examples, see 7:13-27; 12:29; 13:41-42, 47; 15:21-28; 16:27; 18:6, 23-35; 21:1-11; 22:7; 24:3, 14, 28, 50-51; 28:4, 20.

16. See Bowman and Swanson, "Samson and the Son of God or Dead Heroes and Dead Goats." Their naming of the problem is helpful. But their contention that in chapter 28 it becomes clear that the world needs saving from the sin of making divisions is appealing but unconvincing. The cross has already indicated a huge division, and the problematic violence of the separations in chapter 13 lies in the future.

17. For further reflection on the "reign of the heavens," see Carter, "Narrative/Literary Approaches," 3-27.

18. On the performative qualities of language, see Austin, *How to Do Things with Words.*

19. Kilpatrick, *Origins of The Gospel,* 59-100.

20. Stanton, "Origin and Purpose," 1906-21.

21. Bornkamm, Barth, and Held, *Tradition and Interpretation;* Kingsbury, *Matthew: Structure.*

22. Burridge, *What Are the Gospels?* For a more elaborate statement of this argument and extensive bibliography, see Carter, "Community Definition and Matthew's Gospel."

23. Burridge, *What Are the Gospels?* 109-90. Burridge identifies *Opening Features* (title, prologue), *Subject* (a focus on a central figure); *External Features* (prose narrative, length, chronological framework, different types of literary subunits, use of sources, characterization through the display of words and actions); and *Internal Features* (setting, topics which include ancestry, birth, education, deeds, virtues, death, consequences, a somewhat literary style, a serious and respectful atmosphere, characterization, a mixture of educated and popular tendencies, a variety of purposes).

24. Burridge, *What Are the Gospels?* 191-219.

25. Ibid., 80. Talbert ("Biography, Ancient," *ABD* 1:747-48) identifies several social functions: to portray the subject as an ideal figure so that readers will accept his authority; to defend the subject against misunderstanding; to discredit the subject; to indicate where the true tradition is in the present; to legitimate the subject's teaching or provide an interpretive clue to it.

26. Burridge, *What Are the Gospels?* 256.

27. Ibid., 214.

28. Ibid., 216; Stanton, *Gospels and Jesus,* 78.

29. Freyne, "Vilifying the Other and Defining the Self," e.g., 119, 129, 132.

30. Talbert. "Biography, Ancient," *ABD* 1:749.

31. See Sanders et al. (eds.), *Jewish and Christian Self-Definition;* Neusner and Frerichs (eds.), *"To See Ourselves as Others See Us";* Collins, *Between Athens and Jerusalem;* Barclay, *Jews in the Mediterranean Diaspora;* on Matthew, see Saldarini, *Matthew's Christian-Jewish Community.*

32. Freyne ("Vilifying the Other and Defining the Self," 143) lists eleven characteristics in chapter 23 for which scribes and Pharisees are denounced and about which disciples are also warned. For the language of belonging and separation in Paul, see Meeks, *First Urban Christians,* 84-110.

33. For this helpful emphasis on the center rather than the boundaries as a means of definition, see Saunders, "No One Dared Ask Him Anything More."

34. Nickelsburg, "Revealed Wisdom as a Criterion for Inclusion and Exclusion," 85-87; Harrington, *Gospel of Matthew,* 10-22; Carter, *Matthew: Storyteller,* 80-88; Deutsch, *Lady Wisdom.*

35. On worship, see Powell, *God With Us,* 28-61.

36. For the importance of groups as the basis and context for identity in the first century, Malina, *New Testament World,* 63-89.

37. Carter, "Recalling the Lord's Prayer," 522-30, citing the work of Driver, *Magic of Ritual,* part 3.

38. Rajak, "Jews and Christians as Groups in a Pagan World," 247-62; Carter, "Matthew 4:18-22 and Matthean Discipleship," 58-75.

39. For "evil" as the "root trait" of the characterization of the religious leaders, see Kingsbury, "Developing Conflict." But note that in 7:11 disciples (5:1-2) are described as evil.

40. For these terms as conventional terms for vilifying one's opponents, see Johnson, "New Testament's Anti-Jewish Slander"; Freyne, "Vilifying the Other and Defining the Self," 132-35; Malina and Neyrey, *Calling Jesus Names,* 152-57.

41. For apocalyptic rhetoric and the "language of annihilation," see Freyne, "Vilifying the Other and Defining the Self," 135, 142.

42. Stanton, *Gospel for a New People,* 146-68; Sim, *Apocalyptic Eschatology,* 23-69, 222-42; Hagner, "Matthew's Eschatology."

43. Ancient biographies share generic features with other works such as histories and encomia. Encomia are literary works that praise a people or a city, and in doing so they define that people or city. Encomia achieve this definition with a fixed pattern of three topics. See Burridge, *What Are the Gospels?* 55-81, esp. 61-69, and 66 for a diagram. Basic to my argument are Burridge's observations (pp. 61-69) on the interconnectedness of genre and on flexible boundaries and "the borrowing and sharing of generic features across boundaries," especially from "neighboring" genres such as history and encomia. For the relationship of biography and history, see Momigliano, *Development of Greek Biography,* 15 and passim.

44. For extended discussion and bibliography, see Carter, "Community Definition and Matthew's Gospel"; note Balch, "Two Apologetic Encomia: Dionysius on Rome and Josephus on the Jews."

45. Burridge, *What Are the Gospels?* 145-46, 178, 207.

46. Brown, *Birth of the Messiah,* 110-19; Allison, *New Moses,* 140-65; Davies and Allison, *Matthew,* 1:190-96. Hultgren ("Matthew's Infancy Narrative," 92-94, 98-99) stresses connections with Joseph and the emergence of a new community.

47. See Droge, "Call Stories in Greek Biography and the Gospels"; Carter, "Matthew 4:18-22 and Matthean Discipleship"; Zumstein (*La Condition du croyant,* 217), among others, emphasizes connections with the Elijah-Elisha episode in 1 Kgs 19:19-21.

48. Burridge, *What Are the Gospels?* 146, 179, 208.

49. Betz, *Sermon,* 166-97.

50. Balch, "Greek Political Topos," 68-84.

51. Betz, *Sermon,* 179. For discussion of the verb "fulfill," see Davies and Allison, *Matthew,* 1:484-87; Carter, *What Are They Saying About Matthew's Sermon on the Mount?* 84-88; Meier, *Law and History in Matthew's Gospel,* 73-81.

52. Balch, "Greek Political Topos," 72-76, passim.

53. Ibid., 68-69.

54. Ibid., 81; for discussion of options, see Davies and Allison, *Matthew,* 2:635-41.

55. Balch, "Greek Political Topos," 84, quoting James A. Sanders, "Adaptable for Life," 531-60; also Sanders, *From Sacred Story to Sacred Text,* 9-39.

56. Carter, *Households and Discipleship*, 19-24.

57. Ibid., 17-22, 56-192; Balch and Osiek, *Families in the New Testament World*, 130-35.

58. Carter, *Households and Discipleship*, 90-114.

59. Burridge, *What Are the Gospels?* 146, 179, 208.

60. For discussion of options, see Davies and Allison, *Matthew*, 1:325-27; Meier, *Law and History in Matthew's Gospel*, 76-80; Przybylski, *Righteousness in Matthew*, 77-123.

61. On mission to Jews and Gentiles, see Senior, "Between Two Worlds."

62. I explore some of this knowledge and experience in Carter, *Matthew: Storyteller.*

63. Carter, *Matthew: Storyteller*, 15-34.

64. Eusebius (d. ca. 340) in his *Ecclesiastical History* 3.39.14-15 cites the second-century bishop Papias, who claimed that he had learned from an elder that "Matthew collected the oracles (of Jesus) in the Hebrew language."

65. For possibilities and references, see Carter, *Matthew: Storyteller*, 24-25; Brown and Meier, *Antioch and Rome*, 18-27.

66. Allen, *S. Matthew*, 310; Plummer, *Exegetical Commentary*, xxxiii.

67. Viviano, "Where Was the Gospel?"

68. Overman, *Matthew's Gospel and Formative Judaism*, 159 n. 40.

69. Slingerland, "Transjordanian Origin."

70. Saldarini, *Matthew's Christian-Jewish Community*, 11, 26.

71. For discussion, see, e.g., Brown and Meier, *Antioch and Rome*, 15-27; Senior, *What Are They Saying About Matthew?* 7-20; Carter, *Matthew: Storyteller*, 15-34; Sim, *Gospel of Matthew*, 53-62.

72. In writing to the church in Smyrna, Ignatius summarizes their beliefs, including Jesus' baptism by John that "all righteousness might be fulfilled by him" (1.1). Only Matthew includes this formulation in the baptismal story (3:15). Other uses of Matthean material appear in letters to Polycarp (2.2 and Matt 10:16b), to the Philippians (3.1 and Matt 15:13-14), and to the Ephesians (19.1-3 and Matt 1-2). See Meier, "Matthew and Ignatius," 178-86.

73. Stanton (*Gospel for a New People*, 50-51) suggests that the author "would have composed such an elaborate gospel" not for "one relatively small group" but for several groups. He cites the small meeting space in houses as indicating a number of places (but see below). I will also point to the interaction of countryside and city as another factor suggesting a wider audience. The view offered in Bauckham (ed.), *Gospel for All Christians*, that the gospels were written for all Christians seems to confuse their subsequent effect with their initial focus.

74. For discussion, see Carter, *Matthew: Storyteller*, 35-76.

75. *4 Ezra* 3:24-36; 4:22-25; 5:21-30; *2 Baruch* 1:1-5; 4:1; 6:9; 13:1-10; 32:2-3; Josephus, *JW* 4.386-88. See Harrington, *Gospel of Matthew*, 10-16; de Lange, "Jewish Attitudes to the Roman Empire," 265-67; Esler, "God's Honour and Rome's Triumph"; Neusner, "Judaism in a Time of Crisis."

76. Carter, *Matthew: Storyteller*, 26-28.

77. The literature is extensive; see de Coulanges, *Ancient City;* Jones, *Cities of the Eastern Roman Provinces;* Sjoberg, *Preindustrial City;* Mumford, *City in History;* Hammond, *City in the Ancient World*, 148-329; Carney, *Shape of the Past*, 83-278; Finley, "Ancient City"; idem, *Economy and Society in Ancient Greece*, 3-23; Hopkins, "Economic Growth and Towns," 35-77; de Ste. Croix, *Class Struggle;* Meeks, *First Urban Christians;* Stambaugh, *Ancient Roman City;* Rohrbaugh, "Pre-industrial City in Luke-Acts," 125-50; Owens, *City in the Greek and Roman World;* Rich and Wallace-Hadrill (eds.), *City and Country*. For a survey and selective bibliography, see Rohrbaugh, "Preindustrial City," 107-25.

78. For Antioch, see Downey, *History of Antioch;* idem, *Ancient Antioch;* Lassus, "Antioch on the Orontes," 61-63; Finley (ed.), *Atlas of Classical Archaeology*, 222; Stark, "Urban Chaos and Crisis," in Stark, *Rise of Christianity*, 147-62; for an earlier and somewhat longer version, see Stark, "Antioch," 189-210.

79. For options and discussion, see Alcock, "Archaeology and Imperialism," 90-95; for

an example, see Goodman, *Ruling Classes of Judea*, 29-36; Brunt, "Romanization of the Ruling Classes," 161-73.

80. Charlesworth, *Trade Routes and Commerce*, 36-56.

81. Wengst, *PAX ROMANA*, 37-40. Aristides (*Roman Oration*, 31-30) confidently but naively proclaims that there is justice for all. See introduction to 27:11.

82. Chandler and Fox, *Three Thousand Years*, 81, 303.

83. Lassus, "Antioch on the Orontes," 62.

84. Stark, "Urban Chaos and Crisis," in Stark, *Rise of Christianity*, 149-50; idem, "Antioch," 149-50; MacMullen, *Roman Social Relations*, 62-63.

85. For example, Rohrbaugh, "Pre-Industrial City," 133-37.

86. The diagram is used by permission and derives from Arlandson, *Women, Class, and Society*, 22. This model was developed by G. Lenski and J. Lenski (*Human Societies*, 164-208, esp. 203; and Lenski, *Power and Privilege*, 284) and modified by Fiensy (*Social History of Palestine*, 155-76). See also Kautsky, *Aristocratic Empires*. Numerous New Testament scholars have employed it with various modifications; for a partial listing, see Duling, "Matthew and Marginality," 650 nn. 37-38, and 651 for Duling's modified version. Duling adds "speculative percentages." He ("Matthew and Marginality," 652-56) suggests further modifications to accommodate the model from the time of Jesus (ca. 20s C.E.) to that of the Matthean community (ca. 80-90). The Herodians have gone, the priestly power significantly diminished. He also expands the lower social strata, the involuntary marginals, with "a sample inventory implied in Matthew's gospel." Arlandson (*Women, Class, and Society*, 14-119) draws attention to women's participation throughout these social divisions. Note also Herzog, *Parables as Subversive Speech*, 53-73.

87. Figures for Antioch are not available. Broughton ("Roman Asia Minor," 814) notes councils in Asia Minor cities of between 30 and 650 in number. He offers nine examples, five of which number one hundred or under.

88. Wengst, *PAX ROMANA*, 25-26; Alcock, "Roman Imperialism," 5-34.

89. Wallace-Hadrill, "Elites and Trade," 241-72. He challenges the views of scholars such as MacMullen, who see landowners as the only members of the urban elite. Hopkins ("Introduction," ix-xxv) also sees a greater role for trade than Moses Finley's model of the ancient economy, which understood trade to be limited, local, and removed from the elite. Pleket ("Urban Elites and Business in the Greek Part of the Roman Empire," 131-44) argues for some involvement in trade by the elite through investment (ships) and subordinate dependents (e.g., slaves; Plutarch, "Education of Children," *Moralia* 7B, E).

90. Wallace-Hadrill, "Elite and Trade," 244-49.

91. For the religious leaders in the gospel (chief priests, Pharisees, Sadducees, scribes, elders) as members of the elite, see Saldarini (*Pharisees*, 35-49), who draws on the work of Lenski (*Power and Privilege*, 256-66) and Kautsky (*Aristocratic Empires*, 81-83, 161-66).

92. Josephus places three legions in Antioch in 40 C.E. (*JW* 2.186). Van Berchem ("Une inscription flavienne," 185-96) discusses an inscription which indicates four legions in the mid 70s. Tacitus asserts four legions in Syria but does not identify where they are stationed (*Ann* 4.5).

93. Wengst, *PAX ROMANA*, 1-54, esp. 11-26.

94. Horsley (*Archaeology, History, and Society*, 66-87) usefully contrasts the trade and tribute models, arguing that for Galilee (though he often generalizes the argument to all the empire [e.g., p. 80]) the former has been much overstated, and the latter needs much greater emphasis.

95. Rohrbaugh ("Pre-Industrial City," 134) posits little contact between elites and non-elites arguing that the bulk of the population were "physically and socially isolated from the elite." Wallace-Hadrill ("Elites and Trade," 249-64, e.g., 250), however, suggests that "socially and politically, contact with the commercial world of the towns was inevitable for the elite." Given some proximity in living location, the latter view seems more convincing. See Brunt, "Labour."

96. MacMullen, *Roman Social Relations,* 73.

97. Ibid., 62, 88-94, passim.

98. Rohrbaugh, "Pre-Industrial City," 128.

99. MacMullen, *Paganism in the Roman Empire,* 8; Whittaker, "Poor in the City of Rome."

100. MacMullen, *Roman Social Relations,* 116-19; Hands, *Charities and Social Aid.*

101. See, e.g., Malina and Neyrey, "Honor and Shame in Luke-Acts," 25-65; Moxnes, "Honor and Shame," 19-40. For helpful discussion of a number of the issues noted here, see Balch and Osiek, *Families in the New Testament World,* 36-87.

102. To name those identified from Juvenal's satires by Reekmans, "Juvenal's Views of Social Change," 124.

103. For consideration of gender constructs, and further references, see Balch and Osiek, *Families in the New Testament World,* 40-45, 54-64; Arlandson, *Women, Class, and Society,* 14-119; Boatwright, "Plancia Magna of Perge: Women's Roles and Status in Roman Asia Minor," 249-72.

104. See MacDonald, *Architecture of the Roman Empire,* 2.111-42.

105. Downey, *History of Antioch,* 621-22.

106. Ibid., 101-2.

107. Perring, "Spatial Organisation," 273.

108. MacMullen, *Roman Social Relations,* 70-71; Wallace-Hadrill, "Elites and Trade," 258; Rohrbaugh, "Pre-industrial City," 134-37.

109. Perring, "Spatial Organisation," 284.

110. Moxnes, "Patron-Client Relations," 241-68; Elliott, "Patronage and Clientage," 144-56; Saller, *Personal Patronage under the Empire;* Balch and Osiek, *Families in the New Testament World,* 48-54.

111. MacMullen, *Roman Social Relations,* 68-87.

112. Perring, "Spatial Organisation," 280-81. When Caesar built (rebuilt?) the theater it was well outside the city, though the city's subsequent expansion saw it included near the center. The amphitheater was on the southern edges of the city. See Downey, *History of Antioch,* 172, 180, 216; Finley, *Atlas of Classical Archaeology,* 222.

113. Finley, *Atlas of Classical Archaeology,* 222.

114. For discussion of the relationship between city and country, see the essays in Rich and Wallace-Hadrill (eds.), *City and Country;* Finley, "Ancient City"; de Ste. Croix, *Class Struggle;* Braund, "City and Country in Roman Satire," 23-47; Whittaker, "Consumer City Revisited"; idem, "Do Theories of the Ancient City Matter?"; Oakman, "Countryside in Luke-Acts," 151-79.

115. MacMullen, *Roman Social Relations,* 49. Much of his discussion, however, indicates pervasive conflict and exploitation (pp. 28-56).

116. Harper, *Village Administration,* 57-64.

117. Hopkins, "Economic Growth and Towns," passim; also Hopkins, "Taxes and Trade in the Roman Empire," 101-25.

118. Corbier, "City, Territory, and Taxation," 234.

119. MacMullen, *Roman Social Relations,* 1-56; Wallace-Hadrill, "Elites and Trade," 244-49.

120. Downey, *History of Antioch,* 101, 204-5, 628-29. Josephus's account (*JW* 7.54-62) emphasizes ethnic more than economic factors. See Dyson, "Native Revolts."

121. MacMullen, *Roman Social Relations,* 123-27.

122. Stark, "Urban Chaos and Crisis," in Stark, *Rise of Christianity;* idem, "Antioch." See also Whittaker, "Poor in the City of Rome."

123. Stillwell, "Houses of Antioch," 47-57.

124. Downey, "Water Supply of Antioch," 171-87.

125. In discussing stomach upsets from immoderate consumption of food, Plutarch ("Advice About Keeping Well," *Moralia,* 134D) evokes these turbulent ethnic mixes (and

reveals his own xenophobia) by asking his reader to "just imagine that anybody feeling much troubled at the crowd of Greeks living in his city, should fill up the city with Arab and Scythian immigrants!"

126. Stark, "Urban Chaos and Crisis," in Stark, *Rise of Christianity,* 160-61.

127, Duling, "Matthew and Marginality," 653-54.

128. Kingsbury, "Verb AKOLOUTHEIN ("To Follow")," 66-68; also Kilpatrick, *Origins of The Gospel,* 124-26; Smith, "Were the Early Christians Middle-Class?" 265-71.

129. The value of this observation needs questioning. Numerous scholars have argued that Mark originated in Rome, an observation that bears no relationship to the number of times the word "city" is used.

130. Kautsky, *Foundations of Christianity;* Deissmann, *Light from the Ancient East.* For discussion, see Malherbe, *Social Aspects,* 1-28; Keck, "On the Ethos of Early Christians"; Meeks, *First Urban Christians,* 51-73; Stark, "The Class Basis of Early Christianity," in Stark, *Rise of Christianity,* 29-47; Balch and Osiek, *Families in the New Testament World,* 91-102.

131. Judge, *Social Pattern of Christian Groups,* 52, 54, 60-61.

132. Scroggs, "Sociological Interpretation," 168-71; Meeks, *First Urban Christians,* 51-73.

133. Theissen, *Social Setting,* 69-119; Fee, *First Epistle to the Corinthians,* 78-88.

134. Theissen, *Social Setting,* 145-74; Fee, *First Epistle to the Corinthians,* 531-69; Meeks, *First Urban Christians,* 67-71.

135. Gillman, "Erastus," *ABD* 2:571; Meeks, *First Urban Christians,* 58-59.

136. Sordi, *Christians and the Roman Empire,* 27-28, 185-86.

137. Ibid., 185-88. On the role of women, see Schüssler Fiorenza, "Missionaries, Apostles, Co-Workers"; Gillman, *Women Who Knew Paul,* 43-81; Wire, *Corinthian Women Prophets.*

138. Malherbe, *Social Aspects,* 29-59; for evaluation of the author's "correct" Greek, see Moulton, *Grammar,* 29, 169.

139. Stark, "The Role of Women in Christian Growth," in Stark, *Rise of Christianity,* 95-128.

140. Stark, *Rise of Christianity,* 37-47.

141. Meeks, "The Social Level of Pauline Christians," in *First Urban Christians,* 51-73.

142. Murphy-O'Connor, *St. Paul's Corinth,* 153-61, esp. 161.

143. Stillwell, "Houses of Antioch," 47-57, esp. 49-50, 55.

144. This is certainly possible, given the size of the city. Its area was established with walls at its founding (ca. 300 B.C.E.) with an area of about a square mile. It grew to be about two miles long and one mile wide. So Lassus, "Antioch on the Orontes," 62.

145. Balch and Osiek, *Families in the New Testament World,* 201-3, also 5-35.

146. On the pervasive peristyle, see MacDonald, *Architecture of the Roman Empire,* 2:207-10.

147. Stillwell, "Houses of Antioch," e.g., 48, 49, 50, 51.

148. Stark, "Conversion and Christian Growth," in Stark, *Rise of Christianity,* 4-13, esp. 7. For discussion of Stark's approach to the early Christian movement, see the essays in *Religious Studies Review* 25 (1999) 127-39, and in the *Journal of Early Christian Studies* 6 (1998) 161-267, especially Hopkins, "Christian Number and Its Implication," 185-226. Hopkins agrees with Stark in emphasizing the tiny size of first-century Christian groups and the impossibility of any precision. Hopkins's estimates of about seven thousand Christians, or 0.01 percent of the population in the year 100 (p. 195), are comparable to Stark's.

149. Stark, "Urban Chaos and Crisis," in Stark, *Rise of Christianity,* 131, 149; Chandler and Fox, *Three Thousand Years,* 81, 303. Nevertheless, estimates of population are difficult, and much higher estimates of up to four hundred thousand have been offered.

150. For discussion, see Brown and Meier, *Rome and Antioch,* 11-86.

151. Grant, *Early Christianity and Society,* 7-8.

152. For contrary views, see Clark, "The Gentile Bias of Matthew"; Meier, *Vision of Matthew,* 17-25.

153. For example, Senior, "Between Two Worlds"; contra Sim, *Apocalyptic Eschatology.*

154. For discussion, see Kraeling, "Jewish Community"; Meeks and Wilken, *Jews and Christians in Antioch;* Barclay, *Jews in the Mediterranean Diaspora,* 242-58.

155. Barclay (*Jews in the Mediterranean Diaspora,* 244-45) notes Josephus's at times contradictory and vague material. See Trebilco, *Jewish Communities in Asia Minor,* 8-19, 167-72; for Jewish participation in daily life in the cities of Asia Minor, see pp. 173-83; see also Smallwood, *Jews under Roman Rule,* 138-43, 224-50, 284-92, 358-64, 369-71.

156. Barclay, *Jews in the Mediterranean Diaspora,* 254.

157. For discussion, see Downey, *History of Antioch,* 192-95, 198-201, 205-6.

158. Ibid., 109-11, 206; Kraeling, "Jewish Community," 143-44.

159. Horsley, *Archaeology, History and Society,* 131-53, esp. 145-53.

160. Barclay (*Jews in the Mediterranean Diaspora*) uses language of "Levels of Assimilation," "Cultural Convergence," and "Cultural Antagonism."

161. On redaction criticism, see Stanton, *Gospel for a New People,* 23-53.

162. This material is adapted from Carter, *Matthew: Storyteller,* 80-88. For further discussion, Stanton, *Gospel for a New People,* 85-206; Stegner, "Breaking Away"; Saldarini, "Boundaries and Polemics"; idem, *Matthew's Christian-Jewish Community.*

163. This is the only one of these six references that derives from Mark (Matt 4:23 = Mark 1:39). Matthew adds the other five, three to material drawn from Mark and two to material taken from Q. Compare Matt 9:35 with Mark 6:6a; Matt 12:9 with Mark 3:1; Matt 13:54 with Mark 6:2. For Q, compare Matt 10:17 with Luke 12:11; Matt 23:34 with Luke 11:49. Matthew omits Mark 1:23-28, the other pericope in which the phrase appears. The distinctiveness of Matthew's use can be seen in comparing it with Mark's "the synagogue" (Mark 1:21, 29; 3:1; 6:2; 12:39; 13:9).

164. The NRSV's phrase "leader *of the synagogue*" in 9:18 does not reflect the Greek text.

165. Compare Matt 12:14 with Mark 3:6. Matthew's omission of Mark's "Herodians" intensifies the focus on the Pharisees. Compare Matt 16:21 with Mark 8:31; Matt 20:18-19 with Mark 10:33-34; Matt 26:2-4 with Mark 14:1.

166. Matt 23:13, 15, 23, 25, 27, 29; cf. Matt 22:18 with Mark 12:15.

167. Compare Matt 9:11 with Mark 2:16; Matt 9:34, 12:24 with Mark 3:22; Matt 22:41 with Mark 12:35.

168. For Matthew's use of "teacher" by nondisciples, see 12:38, 19:16; 22:16, 24, 36.

169. The one positive image appears in 13:52 and seems to refer to disciples who have entered into the kingdom of heaven (cf. 4:17). Some scholars have seen this scribal image as being of great importance for Matthew's audience. See Duling, "Matthean Brotherhood," 172-80; Deutsch, *Lady Wisdom,* 111-41.

170. Stanton, *Gospel for a New People,* 146-68, esp. 154-57.

171. Causing much debate has been the possible role of the group of rabbis led by Rabbi Yohanan ben Zakkai (and later by Gamaliel II), who met at the town of Yavneh (or Jamnia) northwest of Jerusalem. Davies (*Setting of the Sermon on the Mount,* 259-72, 315) argues that Matthew's Sermon on the Mount was "the Christian answer to Jamnia," and that the *Birkath ha Minim,* a curse on heretics composed around 85 C.E. was responsible for the exclusion of Matthew's community from the synagogue. Most scholars have not been persuaded by such a direct link with Yavneh. The deliberations at Yavneh are considered more a process than an event; there is no evidence that Yavneh functioned as a central council issuing decrees to all synagogues to obey; the role of Christian groups as a primary target seems overstated; and the *Birkath* prays for God's destruction of the heretics, not for their exclusion from the synagogue. For discussion, see Kimelman, "*Birkat Ha-Minim* and the Lack of Evidence"; Katz, "Issues in the Separation," 63-75.

172. Stanton, "Origin and Purpose," 1906-8.

173. Scholars debate how great is the distance between the two groups. Some see Matthew's group as a subgroup within a synagogue (an internal or *intra-muros* conflict). See Kilpatrick, *Origins of The Gospel,* 122; Bornkamm, "End-Expectation," 39; Barth, "Matthew's Understanding," 58-164; Davies, *Setting of the Sermon on the Mount,* 290, 332;

Saldarini, *Matthew's Christian-Jewish Community,* 3, 11-26. Others (including Stanton) see a physical departure from the synagogue with a process of definition over-against the synagogue still under way. For discussion, see Stanton, *Gospel for a New People,* 118-24, 192-206; idem, "Origin and Purpose," 1911-16. Another view sees the dispute with Judaism as belonging to the past of a now predominantly Gentile community. See van Tilborg, *Jewish Leaders,* 171; Strecker, *Der Weg der Gerechtigkeit,* 34; Meier, *Vision of Matthew,* 17-23. For discussion, see Stanton, *Gospel for a New People,* 131-39; idem, "Origin and Purpose," 1916-21.

174. Harrington's discussion (*Gospel of Matthew,* 10-19) of rabbinic and apocalyptic strands of Judaism (*4 Ezra* and *2 Baruch*) in the post-70 era is helpful; see also Neusner, "Judaism in a Time of Crisis"; Stone, "Reactions to Destructions of the Second Temple"; Esler, "God's Honour and Rome's Triumph."

175. Neusner, *From Politics to Piety,* chapter 6; Cohen, *From the Maccabees to the Mishnah,* chapter 7.

176. The importance of claims about Jesus as the interpreter of God's will have often been recognized. See Bornkamm, "End-Expectation," 25. There has been less discussion of the other christological issues identified here. See Stanton, "Christology and the Parting of the Ways," in Stanton, *Gospel for a New People,* 169-91. He considers claims about Jesus as a magician and deceiver, and about the meaning of the title "Son of David."

177. See Carter, "'To Save His People.'"

178. Compare Matt 9:1-8 with Mark 2:1-12; Matt 12:31-37 with Mark 3:28-30.

179. For discussion of other claims to authoritative revelation in relation to John, see Carter, "Prologue and John's Gospel."

180. Saldarini (*Matthew's Christian-Jewish Community,* 107-16, passim) prefers the sociologically informed term "deviant," which he uses to designate the relationship between "Matthew's group and the larger Jewish community" (p. 107). While this term as defined and employed by Saldarini is useful, I will avoid it here because it places the focus almost exclusively on the relationship between Matthew's group and the synagogue. My focus incorporates that dimension but moves beyond it to the larger cultural context.

181. Wink, "Jesus and the Domination System," 268-84; idem, *Engaging the Powers;* Beck, *Anti-Roman Cryptograms,* 93-117. For the hierarchical nature of first-century, imperial society, organized for the benefit of the ruling Roman elite and its allies, see section 5 above. For a more extensive discussion of the shape and strategies of imperial society, see, among others, de Ste. Croix, *Class Struggle;* Carney, *Shape of the Past;* Luttwak, *Grand Strategy of the Roman Empire;* Williams, *Empire as a Way of Life;* Kautsky, *Aristocratic Empires;* Scott, *Weapons of the Weak;* Said, *Culture and Imperialism.*

182. Senior ("Between Two Worlds," 5) rightly notes that much attention is paid in contemporary Matthean studies to Matthew's relationship to Judaism and relatively little attention to the Gentile world. But in seeking to redress this situation, Senior does not specify which Gentiles the gospel might have in view. It is my contention that any discussion of "the Gentiles" must involve Roman imperial power.

183. I use the terms "imperial" or "imperialism" to denote a relationship of power, of ruler over subjects, the stronger over the weaker, for the former's benefit and at the latter's expense. Finley ("Fifth-Century Athenian Empire," 103-7) offers a "crude typology of the various ways in which one state may exercise its power over others for its own benefit" (p. 107): (1) restriction of freedom, (2) political interference, (3) compulsory service, (4) tribute, (5) confiscation of land, (6) economic exploitation or subordination. For Antioch, all except no. 5 seem applicable though in varying degrees. Said (*Culture and Imperialism,* 9) defines imperialism as "the practice, the theory, and the attitudes of a dominating metropolitan center ruling a distant territory."

184. Saldarini, *Pharisees,* 35-49.

185. Brunt ("Laus imperii," 173-74) lists four functions of provincial government: taxation, jurisdiction, supervision of local government, internal order and defense.

186. Downey, *History of Antioch,* 140-41.

187. For specific details see Downey, *History of Antioch,* 163-219.

188. Ibid., 181-82, 215.

189. Ibid., 183, 206.

190. Mitchell, "Imperial Building in the Eastern Roman Provinces," 356.

191. Downey, *History of Antioch,* 206.

192. Kreitzer, *Striking New Images,* 136-39.

193. Carter, "Paying the Tax to Rome."

194. Downey, *History of Antioch,* 163.

195. Brannigan, "Images—or Mirages—of Empire," 105; Nutton ("Beneficial Ideology," 209-21) notes that Greek provincial elite writers such as Aristides and Plutarch identify benefits of peace, freedom, common laws, a common fatherland, and material gifts to cities and officials.

196. For a Greek text, translation of and commentary on Aristides' *Roman Oration,* see Oliver, "Ruling Power."

197. Wengst, *PAX ROMANA,* 1-54, esp. 26-37.

198. Corbier, "City, Territory, and Taxation," 211-39; see also Garnsey, "Grain for Rome."

199. Wengst, *PAX ROMANA,* 21.

200. Ibid., 46-51; Scott, *Imperial Cult;* Brunt, "Laus imperii," 164-68; Fears, "Cult of Jupiter"; idem, "Theology of Victory at Rome"; idem, "Cult of Virtues."

201. Wengst, *PAX ROMANA,* 47.

202. Ibid., 48-49.

203. Fears, "Nero as Vicegerent," 486-96.

204. Rajak, "Friends, Romans, Subjects," 124, 133; Rajak, *Josephus,* 99-103.

205. For discussion of Pliny, and some modification of Fears's thesis, see Schowalter, *Emperor and the Gods.*

206. For examples and discussion, see Scott, *Imperial Cult;* idem, "Statius' Adulation of Domitian"; Fears, "Cult of Jupiter"; idem, "Theology of Victory at Rome"; idem, "Cult of Virtue"; idem, *Princeps a Diis Electus;* Carter, "Toward an Imperial-Critical Reading"; idem, "Contested Claims: Roman Imperial Ideology."

207. De Lange, "Jewish Attitudes to the Roman Empire," 255-81.

208. Josephus (*Vita,* 364-67) claims that King Agrippa approved of his presentation of the war.

209. See discussion on John the Baptist (3:1), and introduction to chapter 24.

210. Josephus shows "the chief priests and notables" to be allies of Rome in that they try to persuade the lower-rank priests "not to abandon the customary offering for their rulers" (*JW* 2.197). The "chief priests and powerful ones" subsequently agree that this refusal lays the foundation for the war with Rome. They send delgations to the Roman governor Florus and to Agrippa to express loyalty to Rome and to distance themselves from the priests' actions (*JW* 2.410-11).

211. De Lange, "Jewish Attitudes to the Roman Empire," 263; Bilde, "Causes of the Jewish War."

212. Neusner, *A Life of Rabban Yohanan ben Zakkai,* 104-28.

213. *4 Ezra* 3:24-36; 4:22-25; 5:21-30; 11:40-43, 45; *2 Bar* 1:1-5; 4:1; 6:9; 32:2-3; Josephus, *Ant* 20.162-64, 166, 218; *JW* 2.455; 4.323. See Bilde, "Causes of the Jewish War," 190-94; de Lange, "Jewish Attitudes to the Roman Empire"; Stone, "Reactions to Destructions of the Second Temple"; Esler, "God's Honour and Rome's Triumph."

214. On religious opposition to Rome, see Momigliano, "Some Preliminary Remarks on the 'Religious Opposition,'" 103-29; also Bowersock, "Mechanics of Subversion," 291-320.

215. Berger, *Sacred Canopy.*

216. Käsemann, "Primitive Christian Apocalyptic," 135.

217. Kee, "Imperial Cult," 112-28.

218. With modifications, I am drawing from Duling's fine paper "Matthew and Marginality."

219. Park, "Human Migration and the Marginal Man"; Stonequist, *Marginal Man.*

220. Stonequist, *Marginal Man,* 3.

221. Ibid., 8.

222. Lee, *Marginality,* 42-47.

223. Ibid., 47-53.

224. Germani, *Marginality.*

225. Ibid., 49-51.

226. Duling, "Matthew and Marginality," 645.

227. Turner, *Ritual Process;* Carter, *Households and Discipleship,* 49-55.

228. Turner, *Ritual Process,* 96, 131.

229. Ibid., 127, 132.

230. Ibid., 132. I argue in *Households and Discipleship* that Matthew presents discipleship as a normative and ideological *communitas.*

231. Duling, "Matthew and Marginality," 646-48, 659-63.

232. This "in-both" dimension, which holds together diverse tensions and recognizes both participation and resistance, significantly qualifies any dualistic notion of "center" and "margin."

233. Fischer, "Toward a Subcultural Theory of Urbanism," 1323.

234. Ibid., 1322-23.

235. Ibid., 1324.

236. Ibid., 1328.

237. For details, see Carter, *Households and Discipleship,* 44-45.

238. Price, *Rituals and Power.*

239. On *Tychē,* see Ferguson, *Religions of the Roman Empire,* 77-87, esp. 84; Downey, *History of Antioch,* 73-75, 220.

240. Trebilco, *Jewish Communities in Asia Minor,* 104-13; Brooten, *Women Leaders in the Ancient Synagogue.*

241. Downey, *History of Antioch,* 91-92; Norris ("Isis, Serapis and Demeter," 189-207) assesses the evidence of texts, a possible sanctuary, inscriptions, statues, coins, lamps, and mosaics.

242. *P Oxy* 1380.214-16, cited by Heyob, *Cult of Isis Among Women,* 52. Ambivalence, though, should be noted in the role of women in Isis cults. *P Oxy* 1380 affirms Isis as a model spouse and protector of marriage; see Heyob, *Cult of Isis Among Women,* 52, 53-80. In the early-second-century popular romance *Ephesiaca* by Xenophon of Ephesus, Isis defends the chastity of Anthia and reunites her with her chaste husband Habrocomes. In Apuleius's *Metamorphoses* (11.19), chastity is required of devotees.

243. Heyob, *Cult of Isis Among Women,* 81-110.

244. Witt, "Isis-Hellas," 62.

245. Balch, *Let Wives Be Submissive,* 65-67, 69-73.

246. For discussion, see Judge, *Social Pattern of Christian Groups,* 40-49; Wilken, "Collegia, Philosophical Schools and Theology," 268-91; Barton and Horsley, "Hellenistic Cult Group"; Duling, "Matthean Brotherhood"; Kloppenborg and Wilson (eds.), *Voluntary Associations;* Ascough, *What Are They Saying About the Formation of Pauline Churches?* 71-94.

247. Kloppenborg, "Collegia and *Thiasoi,*" 16-30.

248. Note Josephus, *Ant* 14.215-16, 235-36, 259-60; Philo, *Gaium* 312, 316.

249. Augustus "treated with great respect such foreign rites as were ancient, and well-established, but held the rest in contempt" (Suetonius, *Augustus* 93). Tiberius "abolished foreign cults at Rome, particularly the Egyptian and Jewish" (Suetonius, *Tiberius* 36). Claudius "disbanded the clubs which had been reintroduced by Gaius" (Dio Cassius 60.6.6). Nero dissolved "the illegal associations" in Pompeii (Tacitus, *Ann* 14.17). Trajan exercises tight control (Pliny, *Ep* 10.33-34, 92-93, 96-97). See Cotter, "Collegia and Roman Law," 74-89.

250. Most seem to be under a hundred, clustering in the twenty-to-fifty range. But see the discussion of a group of four hundred in McLean, "Agrippinilla Inscription," 239-70.

251. Ascough, "Translocal Relationships among Voluntary Associations," 223-41.

252. Some differences have been noted: the Christian worldview was much more excluding (commitment only to Jesus) and all-encompassing (present and future; heaven and earth) than, for example, a trade group; Christian groups were concerned with more than social interaction; membership of Christian groups spanned more of the social spectrum; associations were local while Christian groups were translocal (see Ascough's effective refutation).

1. The Origins of Jesus Messiah and His Followers

1. Johnson, *Purpose of the Biblical Genealogies,* 139-228; Brown, *Birth of the Messiah,* 66-84, esp. 66-69, 94-95, 587-96 and literature cited there; Waetjen, "Genealogy," 205-30; Bauer, "Literary and Theological Function," 129-59.

2. The structure of Matthew's genealogy, based on three sets of fourteen generations (1:17), presents several problems for the view that this genealogy is a historical record. (1) If one assumes forty years per generation (the biblical reckoning of a generation), the time spans extend over too few or too many years to be covered by fourteen generations (14 × 40 = 560 years). The period from Abraham to David traditionally covers about eight hundred years, from David (ca.1000) to the Babylonian exile in 587 B.C.E. about four hundred years, and exile to Joseph about six hundred years. (2) In 1:5, Salmon (1 Chr 2:11-13; Ruth 4:21-22) and Rahab are linked, even though Rahab (Josh 2) lives at the time of the conquest, a hundred or so years before Salmon. (3) In the second span (1:6b-11), Matthew omits fifty-nine years or three kings and a queen between Joram (d. 842) and Uzziah/Azariah (d. 783) in v. 8, and omits kings Jehoahaz and Eliakim/Jehoiakim from v. 11 to achieve fourteen generations (see 2 Kgs 23:31-24:6; 1 Chr 3:15-16). (4) In 1:13-15 eleven names cover about six hundred years from Zerubbabel, appointed governor of Judah by the Persians after the return in 539 B.C.E. of those exiled in Babylon, to the time of Joseph. (5) The third section (1:12-16) has thirteen names, not fourteen generations.

3. Quintilian, *Instit* 3.7, 10; e.g., Tacitus, *Agricola* 4; Josephus, *Vita* 1-6; Burridge, *What Are the Gospels?* 146, 178, 207; Mussies, "Parallels."

4. For other studies of retelling the biblical story, see Feldman, *Studies;* Eisenbaum, *Jewish Heroes of Christian History.*

5. Hultgren, "Matthew's Infancy Narrative."

6. Foley (*Immanent Art,* 1-60) discusses the metonymic function of oral-derived and performed literature, in which phraseology or names evoke much larger narratives or common traditions.

7. See Introduction, sections 5-10.

8. Brown, *Birth of the Messiah,* 68.

9. Chatman (*Story and Discourse,* 19-26) would call this discourse. The *story* includes the chain of events, characters, and settings—the "what" in the narrative. *Discourse* is the form of expression, the "how" which involves the specific medium and presentation of the content (structure, point of view). Carter, *Matthew: Storyteller,* 119-48.

10. See de Jonge, "Messiah"; Charlesworth (ed.), *Messiah.*

11. Käsemann, "Primitive Christian Apocalyptic," 135.

12. For discussion, see Brown, *Birth of the Messiah,* 71-74, 590-96.

13. Hanson, "Rahab the Harlot."

14. Bailey, "Eliam"; Herion, "Giloh."

15. Levine, *Social and Ethnic Dimensions,* 59-88, esp. 87.

16. Wainwright, *Towards a Feminist Critical Reading,* 61-69, 156-71. See also Anderson, "Matthew: Gender and Reading"; eadem, "Mary's Difference," 186-90; Levine, "Matthew," 253-54; Schaberg, "Feminist Interpretations," 40-46.

17. Levine, *Social and Ethnic Dimensions,* 59-88, esp. 82; eadem, "Matthew," 252-54.

18. Levine, *Social and Ethnic Dimensions,* 62.

19. There is even confusion in the different textual traditions over how many sons Hezron

has. The Hebrew text of 1 Chr 2:9 mentions three but the LXX version names four. Nor are the traditions agreed on whether the name should be Aram or Ram. The MT of 1 Chr 2:9 has Ram as the second son, while the LXX has Ram as the second son and Aram as a fourth son (and the father of Aminadab). The LXX version of Ruth 4:19 has Arran as Hezron's son.

20. For Solomon's actions, see Carter, "'Solomon.'"

21. On the form **Asaph**, see Davies and Allison, *Matthew,* 1:175.

22. Davies and Allison, *Matthew,* 1:176.

23. Brown, *Birth of the Messiah,* 74-84.

24. Only in the LXX of 1 Chr 3:19 is **Salathiel the father of Zerubbabel**; in the MT, Zerubbabel is the son of Pedaiah; but in support of the LXX, see Ezra 3:2, 8; Hag 1:1, 12.

25. Anderson, "Mary's Difference," 189.

26. This quotation identifying the relationship of kernels and satellites is from Chatman, *Story and Discourse,* 53-56; see Carter *Matthew: Storyteller,* 149-61.

27. Waetjen, "Genealogy," 217-18.

28. Anderson, *Matthew's Narrative Web.*

29. For these possibilities, see Schaberg, *Illegitimacy of Jesus,* 152.

30. Schaberg, "Feminist Interpretations," 52-57.

31. It is often suggested that Matthew emphasizes the virginal conception of Jesus to answer charges from outsiders that Jesus was illegitimately conceived.

32. Levine, "Matthew," 254.

33. Eilberg-Schwartz, *God's Phallus,* 223-37.

34. God's actions, which exercise complete control over Mary's womb without her knowledge and consent, raise disturbing questions. Note that she will need a male to "rescue" her from her "shame" and reincorporate her into patriarchal society. What sort of image of God does this scene present? How does the preceding and following material interact with this scene?

35. Philo (*De Cherub* 44-48) has God visit Sarah, Leah, Rebekah and Zipporah. They become pregnant and produce Isaac, Reuben, Jacob and Esau, and Gershom.

36. Rank, *Myth of the Birth;* for critique, see Horsley, *Liberation of Christmas,* 162-72.

37. Plato (Diogenes Laertius, *Lives of Eminent Philosophers,* "Plato," 2 [Apollo]), Alexander the Great (Plutarch, *Alexander* 2.1-3.4 [Zeus]); Romulus (Plutarch, *Romulus* 2.3-6); Augustus (Suetonius, *Deified Augustus* 94.4 [Apollo]). Note the skeptical comments on claims about Alexander's conception in Lucian, *Dialogue of the Dead* 13. Several writers also recognize human parents. In Matthew's text there is no direct intercourse between God and Mary; the Spirit is an intermediary.

38. Waetjen ("Genealogy," 226-27) argues that the main features of Joseph's presentation (chastity, love, long-suffering) parallel the image of Joseph in the *Testament of Joseph* in *Testaments of the Twelve Patriarchs,* rather than Genesis 37-50.

39. That is, the first understands a concessive relationship of the two clauses: even though he was righteous, he did not wish to expose her to public disgrace. The second understands a causal relationship: Because he was righteous, he did not wish to expose her to public disgrace.

40. For discussion, see Schneider, "δίκαιος," *EDNT* 1:324-25; Quell and Schrenk, "δίκαιος," *TDNT* 2:174-78, 182-91; Davies and Allison, *Matthew,* 1:325-27; Meier, *Law and History in Matthew's Gospel,* 76-80; Przybylski, *Righteousness in Matthew,* 77-123; Reumann, *Righteousness,* 124-35.

41. Cox, *Dreams in Late Antiquity,* 1-123.

42. Brown, *Birth of the Messiah,* 155-59.

43. Cyrus the Persian, Herodotus, *Hist* 1.107-8; Alexander the Great, Cicero, *De Div* 1.23.47; Suetonius, *Augustus* 94; *Tiberius* 14; *Vespasian* 5; *Titus* 2; Plutarch, *Romulus* 2.4; Josephus, *Ant* 2.215-16, on Moses. Talbert, "Prophecies of Future Greatness," 129-41, esp. 132-34. Note the portents of disaster for the hapless Vitellius in Suetonius, *Vitellius* 3.2.

44. Wells, *Greek Language of Healing,* 49 n. 350; 96.

45. For elaboration of Ps 130 and the name "Jesus/Joshua," see Carter, "'To Save His People.'"

46. Some want to restrict the term to acts that distance humans and God; so Davies and Allison, *Matthew,* 1:174, 210.

47. There are exceptions: the centurions in 8:5-13 and 27:54.

48. See MacMullen, *Enemies of the Roman Order,* 142-62, for the role of prophecy in resistance and attempts to control it; see also Potter, *Prophets and Emperors,* 171-82.

49. Carter, "Evoking Isaiah."

50. Eilberg-Schwartz, *God's Phallus,* 233.

2. The Empire Strikes Back

1. For a similar sociopolitical reading, see Horsley, *Liberation of Christmas,* 39-60.

2. Levine (*Social and Ethnic Dimensions,* 89-106) pursues this line.

3. For discussion of his political reign, Levine, "Herod the Great," *ABD* 3:161-69; Netzer, "Herod's Building Program," *ABD* 3:169-72; Horsley, *Liberation of Christmas,* 40-52; for his presentation in the gospel narrative, see Weaver, "Power and Powerlessness," 454-66.

4. Good, *Jesus the Meek King,* 39-60. In addition to this contrast, Good notes that Herod fails to live up to an ideal Hellenistic vision of kings who promote peace and justice (see *Letter of Aristeas* 291-92).

5. Braund, "Juvenal and the East," 45-52; Potter (*Prophets and Emperors,* 183-212) takes a somewhat different approach, emphasizing the authority of antiquity and the mystery of the east.

6. I am following, initially, Delling, "μάγος," *TDNT* 4:356-59, then Powell, "Magi as Kings"; idem, "Magi as Wise Men"; idem, "Neither Wise nor Powerful," 19-31; also Levine, *Social and Ethnic Dimensions,* 89-106; Horsley, *Liberation of Christmas,* 53-60.

7. Horsley, *Liberation of Christmas,* 53. Note the Moabite king Balak's summoning of the diviner Balaam, identified by Philo as a *magus* (*Moses* 1.276), to curse the Israelites, but instead Balaam blesses them and predicts their defeat of Moab (Num 22-24). See also the stories of the Armenian king Tiridates and his group, who as *magi* teach Nero magic (Pliny, *NH* 30.6.16-17), and of Gaumata, a *magus* who rebels against King Cambyses. See Henning, "Murder of the Magi." Eddy (*King is Dead,* 65-72) notes that magi frequently and ubiquitously proclaim liberation from evil kings.

8. See Cramer, "Expulsions"; Potter, *Prophets and Emperors,* 171-82; MacMullen, *Enemies of the Roman Order,* "Magicians," 95-127; "Astrologers, Diviners, and Prophets," 128-62.

9. Paraphrasing Powell, "Neither Wise nor Powerful," 25.

10. Jones, *Emperor Domitian,* 119-21; Cramer, "Expulsions," 9-50. Cramer notes expulsions in the reigns of Tiberius (Tacitus, *Ann* 2.32; Suetonius, *Tiberius* 36; Dio Cassius, 57.15.8-9), Claudius (Tacitus, *Ann* 12.52; Dio 61.33.3b), Vitellius (Tacitus, *Hist* 2.62; Dio 64.1.4; Suetonius, *Vitellius* 14.4), Vespasian (Dio 65.9.2; 65.13.2), and Domitian (Dio 67.13.2-3; Suetonius, *Domitian* 10; Philostratus, *Apollonius,* 7.3). See also Oster, "'Show Me a Denarius,'" esp. 108-11.

11. Levine, *Social and Ethnic Dimensions,* 89-105; for the development of Christian piety concerning the magi (= the three kings), see Luz, *Matthew,* 1:139-41; Powell, "Neither Wise nor Powerful," part 2.

12. Levine (*Social and Ethnic Dimensions,* 95-98) highlights the contrast of journey and stasis.

13. Scholars have attempted to identify the star as a supernova, Halley's comet, or a planetary conjunction of Jupiter and Saturn. See Brown, *Birth of the Messiah,* 170-73.

14. See Greeven, "προσκυνέω," *TDNT* 6:758-66; Taylor, "'Proskynesis' and the Hellenistic Ruler Cult," 53-62.

15. See n. 7 above.

16. Note his actions: inquires (v. 4); summoned, learned (v. 7); sent, go, search, bring (v. 8); sent and killed (v. 16).

17. Goodman, *Ruling Classes of Judea,* 113-16.

18. Kautsky, *Aristocratic Empires,* 326-27; Saldarini (*Pharisees,* 35-49) draws on the work of Lenski (*Power and Privilege,* 256-66) and Kautsky (*Aristocratic Empires,* 81-83, 161-66) to locate the religious leaders among the elite.

19. Van Tilborg, *Jewish Leaders;* Kingsbury, "Developing Conflict," 57-73; Anderson, *Matthew's Narrative Web,* 97-126; Carter, *Matthew: Storyteller,* 229-41.

20. Saldarini, *Pharisees,* 241-76; for the religious leaders in Matthew, see the preceding note.

21. Potter, *Prophets and Emperors,* esp. 171-82.

22. Heil, "Ezekiel 34 and the Narrative Strategy," 699-700.

23. For discussion, see Carter, *Households and Discipleship,* 90-114.

24. Crosby, *House of Disciples;* Carter, *Households and Discipleship.*

25. Luz, *Matthew 1-7,* 1:138.

26. Powell, "Neither Wise nor Powerful," 22.

27. Levine, "Matthew," 254.

28. See Allison, *New Moses,* 140-65. Allison's discussion includes not only biblical material but also various subsequent retellings of the Moses story.

29. This aspect of Good's argument ("The Verb ΑΝΑΧΩΡΕΩ," 1-12) is accurate. For discussion, see 14:13.

30. The Greek construction πάντας τοὺς παῖδας (*pantas tous paidas*) is masculine in form. It may denote only male children. But since masculine grammatical forms may be inclusive of male and female, a translation of children, rather than boys, is preferable.

31. The narrative does not address the question of why God is able to keep Jesus safe but does not prevent this horrendous act.

32. Horsley, *Archaeology, History, and Society,* 108-12.

33. Hertig, "The Multi-Ethnic Journeys of Jesus," 24.

3. John's Ministry

1. That is to say, I do not think 3:1 begins a major new section as some have argued. On John the Baptist, see Wink, *John the Baptist;* Meier, "John the Baptist," 383-405; Anderson, *Matthew's Narrative Web,* 83-90; Taylor, *Immerser;* Yamasaki, *John the Baptist.*

2. Amos 7:14-15; Wolff, *Joel and Amos,* 314: "probably among the well-off of his society."

3. A Samaritan invoked Moses, ascended holy Mt. Gerizim, and looked for liberation (Josephus, *Ant* 18.85-87). In the mid-40s, Theudas and his followers sought to reenact the crossing of the Jordan and reoccupy the land (Josephus, *Ant* 20.97-98). An Egyptian sought to overpower the Roman garrison in Jerusalem (*Ant* 20:169-71; *JW* 2.261-63). In the 60s the peasant Jesus ben Hananiah predicted woe for Jerusalem (*JW* 6.300-309). See Horsley and Hanson, *Bandits, Prophets, and Messiahs,* 135-89.

4. MacMullen, *Enemies of the Roman Order,* 128-62.

5. Matthew's John does not use the common LXX verb ἐπιστρέφω, but the less common μετανοέω.

6. See Kingsbury, *Matthew: Structure,* 28-31.

7. Josephus refers to this area as desert (*JW* 3.515, ἐρημίαν, *erēmian*), as do the Septuagint narratives of David's flight from Absalom (2 Kgs [2 Sam] 15:23 τὴν ἔρημον, *tēn erēmon,* 15:28; 17:16). It would seem possible that John's preaching and baptizing concentrated on the fords.

8. For translation issues, see Carter, "Challenging by Confirming," 401 n. 22. I will use

"empire" or "reign" throughout to highlight God's empire as resistance to and as an alternative to Rome's empire. The noun βασιλεία can indicate both "royal power" and "territory" (BAGD, 134-35). A survey of the usage in Josephus and the LXX confirms these dimensions. Sometimes the term refers to quite limited power and territory, but the term also refers to extensive empires—Babylonian, Median, Persian, and Alexander's in Dan 2:37-45, to Alexander's in 1 Macc 1:6, to Antiochus Epiphanes' and the Seleucids' in 1 Macc 1:16, 41, 51; Josephus, *JW* 1.40; 7.40, and to Rome's empire in Josephus, *JW* 5.409 (Vespasian). In Josephus, there are numerous references to Rome's apportioning power and territory to particular rulers in Judea, Galilee, and surrounding areas (e.g., *JW* 1.392, 396, 398, 457-58, 2.93-94, 215, 220, 247, 252, etc.).

9. For example, Daniel employs "kingdom" in three ways, a Jewish political kingdom (2:44), God's eternal reign (3:33 LXX; 4:4 NRSV), a future kingdom of angels and righteous humans (7:18, 27). See Collins, "Kingdom of God," 81-95, esp. 81-84.

10. Perrin, *Jesus and the Language of the Kingdom,* 29-34. For further discussion and bibliography, see Chilton, "REGNUM DEI DEUS EST," 261-70; Willis (ed), *Kingdom of God;* Carter, "Challenging by Confirming," 399-409.

11. Berkey, "ΕΓΓΙΖΕΙΝ, ΦΘΑΝΕΙΝ, and Realized Eschatology," 177-87.

12. Note that Matthew changes the last three words of the LXX (τοῦ θεοῦ ἡμῶν, "of our God") into a pronoun αὐτοῦ ("of him" or "his"). This change probably indicates that "Lord" should be read (at least in the first instance, given that Jesus is Emmanuel) as a reference to Jesus ("prepare the way of the Lord/Jesus") and not to God.

13. Michaelis, "ὁδός," *TDNT* 5:48-56.

14. Suggestions include the Mandean sect, levitical ritual washings, daily Qumran washings, other desert figures such as Bannus (Josephus, *Vita* 11-12), and proselyte washing. For discussion, see Beasley-Murray, *Baptism in the New Testament,* 1-44; Meier, *Marginal Jew,* 49-56.

15. Saldarini, *Pharisees,* parts 2 and 3.

16. See BAGD, s.v. ἐπί, III.1.b.ε; ἐπί with an accusative = "Esp. also if the feelings or their expressions are of a hostile nature toward, against . . . ." The lexicon lists Matt 3:7 under III.1.b.η expressing "goal, purpose, result."

17. Malina and Rohrbaugh, *Social-Science Commentary,* 38; Foerster, "ἔχιδνα," *TDNT* 2:815-16.

18. For a detailed discussion of wrath, see Kleinknecht, Grether, Fichtner, Sjöberg, Stählin, and Procksch, "ὀργή," *TDNT* 5:382-447. The **wrath to come** evokes from Greek and Roman thought notions of angry and punishing deities who, in response to perceived violations of the gods' will, punish humans with various misfortunes such as disease, inclement weather, adversity, civic strife, misfortunes.

19. BAGD, s.v. "μέλλω," 1, 2. Matthew uses the verb nine times (2:13; 3:7; 11:14; 12:32; 16:27; 17:12, 22; 20:22; 24:6). Setting aside 3:7, in six instances it refers to something about to happen without any eschatological referent (three times to Jesus' death). Only twice does it specify eschatological realities: in 12:32 it qualifies "age" in "the coming age" with a clear eschatological meaning, and in 16:27 the "coming" of the Son of Man with angels to judge.

20. For the covenantal nomism of first-century Judaism, see Sanders, *Paul and Palestinian Judaism*; for good summaries, see Dunn, *Romans 1-8,* lxiii-lxxii, 199-201.

21. Marshall, "Symbols and Showmanship," 130, 136. See Virgil, *Aeneid* 7.173; Horace, *Odes* 1.12.35; Livy 2.54.4; 3.36.3-5; Tacitus, *Ann* 3.2; Pliny, *NH* pref. 4; Martial, *Epig* 8.66.3; Dio 67.4.3.

22. For a listing of other possibilities, see Davies and Allison, *Matthew,* 1:312-14.

23. For discussion, see Davies and Allison, *Matthew* 1.316-18; Dunn, *Baptism in the Spirit,* 8-22.

24. The discussion of this clause is extensive. See the commentaries and Meier, *Law and History in Matthew's Gospel,* 73-81.

25. Cf. ποιεῖν (*poiein,* "do") 5:19; 7:12, 21, 24; 8:9; 12:50; 19:16; 21:6, 31; 23:3, 23; 26:19; τηρεῖν (*tērein,* "keep") 19:17; 23:3; 28:20; φυλασσεῖν (*phylassein,* "observe") 19:20.

26. Przybylski, *Righteousness in Matthew,* 1-79, 91-94, though I do not agree with the conclusion that 3:15 concerns God's demand; Reumann, *Righteousness,* 125-35; Powell, *God With Us,* 115-17; also Dunn, *Theology of Paul,* 340-46.

27. Here in 3:15, option 2 is unlikely. There is no biblical demand to submit to baptism, and the word **all** would make little sense. Option 1 overlooks Jesus and John.

28. Charette, "'Never Has Anything,'" 31-51.

29. The dove has invited much speculation. For sixteen options, see Davies and Allison, *Matthew,* 1:331-34.

30. See Parker, *Oracles of Zeus,* 34-45; Goodenough, *Jewish Symbols in the Greco-Roman Period,* 8:27-46, esp. 32.

4A. Diabolical Opposition and Imperial Darkness

˙1. Wink, *Unmasking the Powers.*

2. Beck, *Anti-Roman Cryptograms,* 97-102.

3. Von Rad and Foerster, "διάβολος," *TDNT* 2:72-79.

4. Edwards notes that this verb appears fifty-two times in Matthew (cf. five in Mark, ten in Luke, one in John) ("Use of ΠΡΟΣΕΡΧΕΣΘΑΙ," 65-74). He argues that ten times, as here in 4:3, the approach is "adversarial," yet the verb underlines Jesus' authority, which is vindicated by the subsequent scene (pp. 67-68).

5. Garnsey, *Famine and Food Supply.*

6. As numerous commentators acknowledge, Deut 8:1-10 contains several linguistic and thematic connections with 4:1-11: led (8:2), in the wilderness (8:2), test (8:2), hunger (8:3), forty years (8:4), a son/child (8:5), obedience (8:6), bread (8:9), stones (8:9), mountains (8:9).

7. For example, the sabbath is holy (Exod 16:23; 20:8-11), set apart for the special purposes for which God designates it; the nation is holy (Exod 19:6), set apart to serve God; temple offerings (Lev 2:3; 6:17), temple places (Lev 6:16), temple/priestly garments (Lev 16:4, 32), and temple personnel/priests (Lev 21:1, 6, 7, 8, etc.) are holy because they are set apart/consecrated to serve God.

8. Carter, "Toward an Imperial-Critical Reading," 296-324.

9. Käsemann, "Primitive Christian Apocalyptic," 135.

10. Gaius Caligula (Philo, *Gaium* 116-17, cf. 352-53; Suetonius, *Vitellius* 2.5; Dio Cassius 59.24.4); Nero (Tiridates, king of Armenia, worships/pays homage to Nero; Pliny, *NH* 30.6.16-17; Dio 62.23.3; 63.2.4; 63.5.2). Traditions (Suetonius, *Domitian* 13; Dio 67.5.7) also attest Domitian's wish to be addressed as *Dominus et Deus noster* (our Lord and God), though there is considerable doubt about whether this was Domitian's actual practice. For discussion, see Taylor, "'Proskynesis' and the Hellenistic Ruler Cult," 53-62; Good, *Jesus the Meek King,* 49-55.

11. The term may mean serving food, but it embraces a much wider range of meanings, including messengers and errands, contract killings, and numerous business tasks. See Collins, *Diakonia,* 3-95.

12. Note that Adam and Eve are guarded by angels (*Life of Adam and Eve* 33), but the devil tempts Eve in their absence; cf. Greek *Apoc. Ezra* 2:13-16.

13. For discussion and bibliography, see Levine, "Anti-Judaism," 9-36; and Carter, "Response to Amy-Jill Levine," 47-62.

14. Carter, "Evoking Isaiah."

15. Horsley, *Archaeology, History, and Society,* passim; Freyne, *Galilee from Alexander the Great,* 155-207, esp. 166-68, 180, 193-94.

16. Freyne, *Galilee from Alexander the Great,* 144.

17. Freyne, *Galilee, Jesus, and the Gospels,* 272, see 70-90 for Galilee in Matthew, and 135-218 for social, political, economic, and religious analysis of Galilee. Freyne, *Galilee from Alexander the Great.* Freyne's discussion of Galilee is challenged in various ways by

Horsley, *Galilee: History, Politics, People;* idem, *Archaeology, History, and Society;* Hertig, *Matthew's Narrative Use of Galilee,* 31-44, 82-109.

18. Horsley, *Archaeology, History, and Society,* 112-18.

19. Carter, "Evoking Isaiah."

20. Omitted from Isa 9:1 are the phrases "In the former time he brought into contempt" and "but in the latter time he will make glorious the way of the sea."

21. I cannot agree with Davies and Allison (*Matthew,* 1:380), who claim "a shift from literal destruction and political plight to moral and spiritual darkness." The political situation of Roman rule provides a parallel situation which negates any attempt to spiritualize the material. See Carter, "Evoking Isaiah."

22. In addition to the context, the genitive of relationship (Γαλιλαία τῶν ἐθνῶν, *Galilaia tōn ethnōn*) indicates possession. See BDF §162.5,7. For parallel constructions, see 15:21 and 16:13 (territory under the control of); 22:21 (τὰ Καίσαρος . . . τὰ τοῦ θεοῦ).

23. See Freyne, *Galilee from Alexander the Great,* passim, esp. 138-45.

24. Including the hiddenness and majesty of God (Deut 4:11; 5:22; 2 Sam 22:12; Ps 18:11).

25. Menander (Russell and Wilson, *Menander Rhetor,* 95-103 [2.378-82]) repeatedly uses images of light and sun shining in darkness to image both the emperor and the arrival of an imperial governor.

4B. The Beginning of Jesus' Public Ministry

1. See Carter, "Kernels and Narrative Blocks," 463-81, esp. 468-71, 474-77; Carter, *Matthew: Storyteller,* 160-64.

2. For bibliography and my preference for "reign" or "empire," not kingdom, see on 3:2; and Carter and Heil, *Matthew's Parables,* 36-63.

3. Berkey, "ΕΓΓΙΖΕΙΝ, ΦΘΑΝΕΙΝ, and Realized Eschatology," 177-87.

4. Chilton, "REGNUM DEI DEUS EST," 261-70; see Davies and Allison (*Matthew,* 1:604-5), who point to a tradition of the "coming of God" including Isa 35:4 (Isa 35:5-6 are partially cited in Matt 11:4-5); Isa 40:9-10; Zech 14:5; *1 En* 1:3-9; 25:3; etc. For Matthew, see Carter, "Challenging by Confirming," 399-409; a revised version appears in Carter and Heil, *Matthew's Parables,* 36-63; Carter, "Narrative/Literary Approaches," 3-27.

5. See Carter, "Matthew 4:18-22 and Matthean Discipleship," 58-75; Barton, *Discipleship and Family Ties,* 128-40.

6. Zumstein (*La Condition du croyant,* 217) notes a fourth element (Elisha wants to see his parents) not present in this scene.

7. Habel identifies a six-part form of Divine Confrontation, Introduction, Commission, Objection, Reassurance, Sign, from the calls of Gideon (Judg 6:11b-17), Moses (Exod 3:1-12), Jeremiah (Jer 1:4-10), Isaiah (Isa 6:1-13), Ezekiel (Ezek 1:1-3:11), and Deutero-Isaiah (Isa 40:1-11) ("Form and Significance," 297-323, esp. 317). Several aspects of this form are not evident in 4:18-22.

8. Droge, "Call Stories in Greek Biography and the Gospels," 245-57.

9. Carter, "Community Definition and Matthew's Gospel," 637-63.

10. Kingsbury, "Figure of Peter," 67-83.

11. See the declaration dating from 46 C.E. from "the fishermen of the shore of Berenicis Thesmophri" to the local agent of the emperor Tiberius that they will comply with their "public contract" not to catch "the likenesses of the divine oxyrhynchi and lepidoti" fish. Text in Braund, *Augustus to Nero,* 275-76.

12. Hanson, "Galilean Fishing Economy," 99-111.

13. Cited in Murphy-O'Connor, "Fishers of Fish," 23-27, 48-49.

14. Kingsbury, "Verb ("To Follow")," 56-73; Hengel, *Charismatic Leader,* 18-37, 50-73.

Hengel surveys various military and prophetic models, the calling to philosophy and Torah, John the Baptist's disciples, the differences from a rabbinic model, and argues that Jesus' call to follow displays his eschatological and messianic authority.

15. Anderson, *Matthew's Narrative Web.*

16. Carter, *Households and Discipleship,* 19-22, 55-218.

17. Ibid., 98-100.

18. Barton, *Discipleship and Family Ties,* 23-56.

19. Carter, "Matthew 4:18-22 and Matthean Discipleship," 69-75.

20. Powell, *God With Us,* 62-88, esp. 64-67; Soares-Prabhu, "Jesus the Teacher," 244-47.

21. Deissmann, *Light from the Ancient East,* 370-72; Friedrich, "εὐαγγέλιον," *TDNT* 2:721-26; for the Priene inscription, see Dittenberger, *Orientis Graeci Inscriptiones Selectae,* vol. 2, no. 458.

22. Wells, *Greek Language of Healing,* 229; see also Comber, "Verb THERAPEUŌ in Matthew's Gospel," 431-34.

23. Scarborough, *Roman Medicine,* 94-121.

24. Elliott, "Matthew 20:1-15," 52-56.

25. Betz, *Greek Magical Papyri.*

26. Garnsey, *Famine and Food Supply;* MacMullen, *Enemies of the Roman Order,* 180-85, 249-54. Thomas (*Devil, Disease and Deliverance,* 297), who does not discuss these wider understandings, notes that Matthew does not attribute sickness to God.

27. For Asklepios, see Wells, *Greek Language of Healing,* 1-101.

28. Downey, *History of Antioch,* 91-92, 208. Mosaics from Antioch depict Isis; see Levi, "Allegories of the Months," 258-59, 270-71.

29. For discussion, see Meier, *Marginal Jew,* 576-95. Meier discusses Apollonius of Tyana, Honi the Circle-Drawer and Hanina ben Dosa, Dead Sea literature figures, characters in Josephus, and Tacitus's and Suetonius's accounts of Domitian. See also Kee, *Miracle in the Early Christian World;* idem, *Medicine, Miracle, and Magic;* Theissen, *Miracle Stories.*

30. Downey, *History of Antioch,* 208.

31. Wise and Tabor, "Messiah at Qumran," 60-65.

32. Pilch, "Health Care System in Matthew," 102-6; idem, "Understanding Biblical Healing," 60-66.

33. See 4 Macc 5:6; 6:27, 30; 7:2, 10, 16; 8:9, 19; 9:5, 6, 16, 18; 10:11, 16; 11:1, 6; 14:5, 8, 11; 15:11, 18, 19, 20, 21, 22, 32; 16:1, 2, 17; 17:3, 7, 10, 23; 18:20, 21. It also appears in 9:9; 12:12; 13:15, promising the tyrant eternal torture. The term refers in 2 Macc 7:8 to the brothers' torture, and in 9:5 to God's punishment of Antiochus with bowel pain.

34. See Anderson, "4 Maccabees," *OTP* 2:534-37.

35. Wink, *Unmasking the Powers,* 43-50, esp. 47-48. Wink identifies the New Testament stories as examples of "elements introjected into the personality from the general pathology of the society (p. 52), what he calls "Outer Personal Possession," rather than the "Inner Personal Demonic." See Hollenbach, "Jesus, Demoniacs, and Public Authorities," 573; Theissen, *Miracle Stories,* 231-64. Also introduction to chapter 8 below.

36. Ross, "Epileptic or Moonstruck?" 126-28.

37. *3 Baruch* 9:1-7 suggests God's displeasure with the moon because the moon provided light for the serpent.

38. Betz, *Greek Magical Papyri,* 78-81, 86-88, 90-92.

39. Brown, "Techniques of Imperial Control," 366-68; Hollenbach, "Jesus, Demoniacs, and Public Authorities," 575-77.

40. Deborah Amos, "The Littlest Victims," *ABC News,* April 13, 1999, reporting on traumatized Kosovar children no longer able to speak, and citing medical research from Dr. Ron Dahl of the University of Pittsburgh Medical Center, and Dr. Murray Stein of the California Veterans Health Care System.

41. Carter, "Crowds in Matthew's Gospel," 54-67.

5. Jesus Teaches: The Sermon on the Mount Begins

1. See discussion and bibliography in MacArthur, *Understanding the Sermon on the Mount;* Kissinger, *Sermon on the Mount;* Bauman, *Sermon on the Mount;* Carter, *What Are They Saying About Matthew's Sermon on the Mount?;* idem, "Some Contemporary Scholarship on the Sermon on the Mount"; Patte, *Discipleship.* In terms of Patte's very helpful analysis, my reading is particularly akin to Readings C and D. See also Guelich, *Sermon;* Hendrickx, *Sermon on the Mount;* Betz, *Sermon.* On the history of interpretation, see Luz, *Matthew 1-7.*

2. Crosby, *House of Disciples,* 147-95.

3. It occurs another eight times in relation to the exodus and occupation of the land, sometimes indicating the people not going up Sinai (Exod 19:12, 13; Deut 5:5), and sometimes identifying other mountains from which to see or to fight for the promised land (Moses [Num 27:12; Deut 32:49]; the people [Deut 1:24, 41, 43]).

4. Wilkins, *Concept of Disciple.*

5. For discussion, see Betz, *Sermon,* 92-110; Guelich, *Sermon,* 63-66.

6. Hanson, "How Honorable! How Shameful!" 100-101. I amend Hanson's argument a little. He says that beatitudes present "the conditions and behaviors which the community regards as honorable." Perhaps, but this statement assumes a total overlap of the text and the actual Matthean community. I would prefer to say that the beatitudes present conditions and behaviors which God values or finds honorable, and which therefore the community of disciples is also to value and esteem. Some, of course, may not do so. See also Neyrey, *Honor and Shame,* 164-211.

7. For discussion, see Guelich, "Matthean Beatitudes"; Powell, "Matthew's Beatitudes." I generally follow Powell; see also Garland, *Reading Matthew,* 52-58.

8. Pobee, *Who are the Poor?* 14-31; Gallardo, "Matthew: Good News for the Persecuted Poor," 181-92.

9. Garland, *Reading Matthew,* 54.

10. Wengst, *PAX ROMANA,* 64-65; Gabriel, "Jesus' Economic Perspective," 201-6.

11. MacMullen, *Roman Social Relations,* passim.

12. Roth, *The Blind, the Lame, and the Poor,* 115-25, 132-41.

13. God intervenes on behalf of the poor, for example, with special laws (Exod 21-23), by answering in unspecified ways their cries (Ps 12:5), by entrusting their protection to righteous kings (Ps 72:1-14), in the rebukes of the prophets (Isa 3:14-15; 10:1-2; Amos 2:7; 4:1; 5:11), in the punitive destruction of the powerful and wealthy (Amos 5:11-27), in the merciful actions of the righteous (Prov 19:17; 28:27; Sir 4:1-4, 8).

14. See Martin and Phillips, "Consolatio ad Uxorem," 397-412.

15. Betz, *Sermon,* 121-23.

16. See, e.g., Good, *Jesus the Meek King,* passim, 72-74.

17. Ringe, *Jesus, Liberation and the Biblical Jubilee.*

18. Powell, "Matthew's Beatitudes," 468.

19. Betz notes its value in popular piety, but philosophical disapproval, especially from Stoics (*Sermon,* 133) . Seneca sums up a tradition of political understandings by arguing that while a ruler, the vice-regent of the gods, "restrains the mind from vengeance" (*De Clem* 2.3.1) or cruelty, he shows mercy by acting for the good of the state, which means maintaining the ruler's interests and power! In so ruling the ruler imitates the gods (1.7.1). Mercy is not pity (*misericordia*), which is sorrow or distress at the misfortunes of others (2.5.4), though the wise (Stoic) person can still act benevolently among such people. Statius in *The Thebaid* describes the Altar of Mercy in Athens (12.481-518) to which all unfortunates are welcome, "a common refuge for distressed beings" away from the "anger and threats of kings" and from Fortune (12.503-5). But while mercy provides a haven, there is no confronting or correcting these destructive forces. See Harris, "Idea of Mercy," 89-105.

20. For Hellenistic notions, see Betz, *Sermon,* 135.

21. Zampaglione, *Idea of Peace,* 135; Wengst, *PAX ROMANA,* 11-26.

22. Wengst, *PAX ROMANA,* 7-11, 11-54.

23. Scott, *Imperial Cult,* 25-26, 43, 51, 94-95.

24. Windisch, "Friedensbringer—Gottessöhne," 251-57.

25. Wengst, *PAX ROMANA,* 10; see also Introduction, sections 4-9.

26. Zampaglione, *Idea of Peace,* 157.

27. Reicke, "New Testament Conception of Reward," 196, 205.

28. Deatrick, "Salt, Soil, Savour," 41-48.

29. A synonym appears in Pss 14:1; 53:1, "A fool says in his heart, 'There is no God.'" Compare also Matt 7:24-27, where the foolish person does not do Jesus' teaching.

30. Campbell, "New Jerusalem," 335-63.

31. Mowery, "From Lord to Father," 652-53.

32. Schrenck and Quell, "πατήρ," *TDNT* 5:952-53.

33. Carter, "Jesus' 'I have come' Statements."

34. Betz, *Sermon,* 166-97, esp. 178.

35. Balch, "Greek Political Topos," 68-76.

36. See the commentaries for options; also Meier, *Law and History in Matthew's Gospel,* 65-89, esp. 73-76, 84-89; for a summary, see Carter, *What Are They Saying About Matthew's Sermon on the Mount?* 84-88.

37. Aune, *Prophecy in Early Christianity,* 164-65.

38. Käsemann ("Sentences of Holy Law in the New Testament," 66-81) identified the form of this statement as "a sentence of holy law" which outlines God's punishment at the judgment.

39. See Betz, *Sermon,* 192-97. esp. 194-96, for higher and lower justice derived from Aristotle's *Nicomachean Ethics.*

40. Sim, *Apocalyptic Eschatology,* 235-41.

41. Lapide, *Sermon on the Mount,* 45-46. Lapide calls them supertheses.

42. For example, Lambrecht (*Sermon on the Mount,* 101) sees the first two strengthening two commandments, while the rest abolish Old Testament regulations; Meier (*Law and History in Matthew's Gospel,* 125-61) sees the first two and the last as radicalizing the law, while sections 3, 4, and 5 revoke the law and replace it with Jesus' teaching.

43. Again the irony should be noted. In the judgment God seems to exercise revenge on those who have not obeyed (cf. 18:34-35).

44. Tannehill, "Focal Instance," 382-84.

45. The presence of this untranslated Aramaic word in this Greek text suggests its familiarity to the audience.

46. Milikowsky, "Which Gehenna?" 238-49.

47. On Plutarch, see Betz and Dillon, "De Cohibenda Ira (*Moralia* 452E-464D)," 170-97.

48. Improbable because post-70 there was no Jerusalem temple for such worship, and it is most unlikely that the gospel refers to its Antiochene audience's participation in some local "pagan" worship. Moreover, is it possible to leave one's gift at the altar and travel some distance to an unreconciled brother or sister? And what if the brother or sister refuses to reconcile?

49. Carter, *Households and Discipleship,* 72-87.

50. This could be translated "everyone who looks at a woman in order that she desires/becomes lustful." In this translation the woman has an active role.

51. Contrast Plutarch ("Advice to Bride and Groom," *Moralia,* 140B; 144B) and the Neopythagorean Perictyone ("On the Harmony of a Woman" in Guthrie and Fideler, *Pythagorean Sourcebook and Library,* 240), who counsels the wife's toleration of her husband's unfaithfulness while forbidding her to engage in such behavior.

52. See Carter, *Households and Discipleship,* 56-89, esp. 72-87.

53. Ibid., 78-80.

54. The school of Hillel was said to include a badly cooked dish (*m. Git.* 9:10). Josephus

(*Ant* 3.276-77; 4.253; *Vita* 426) and Philo (*Spec Leg* 3.30) advocate any cause. In 19:3, some Pharisees ask Jesus about this matter, "Is it lawful for a man to divorce his wife for every cause?"

55. The issue is well formulated by Luz, *Matthew 1-7,* 1:307-10.

56. As usual, Betz very helpfully outlines the larger philosophical and religious contexts for this focus (*Sermon,* 259-62). See also Fitzgerald, "Problem of Perjury," 156-77.

57. See Betz, *Sermon,* 267; Davies and Allison, *Matthew,* 1:535; Fitzgerald, "Problem of Perjury," 171-73.

58. I am following Wink, "Beyond Just War," 199. A revised form of this essay, which first appeared in *SBL 1988 Seminar Papers,* is "Neither Passivity nor Violence," 102-25. Tannehill ("Focal Instance," 377-83) draws attention to the form of this example. The specific and extreme examples create tension with ordinary human behavior to stimulate reflection and new insight about many other situations.

59. Betz, *Sermon,* 275-77.

60. Ibid., 278.

61. This word (ὁ πονηρός) could be translated "evil one" meaning "the devil," as in 5:37, but the examples in 5:39-42 indicate a human evildoer. As 4:1-11 has shown, the two are not unconnected.

62. See Rajak, "Friends, Romans, Subjects," 122-34.

63. Wink, "Beyond Just War," 199: LXX, 44 of 71 uses; Josephus, 15 of 17 uses; Philo, 4 of 10 uses. He also notes that its root is used in numerous compounds for violent uprising and war (nn. 6 and 8). My investigation of the LXX reaches comparable conclusions. In thirty-four instances military or violent action is clearly designated (exodus/entry to the land [Lev 26:37; Deut 25:18; Jdg 2:14]; David takes Jerusalem [2 Kgs 5:6]; Nebuchadnezzar, Holofernes, and the Assyrians [Jdt 2:25; 6:4; 11:18; 1 Macc 6:4; 14:29, 32]), but not so in thirty-five instances. Many of the latter category refer generically to trying to or not being able to resist God or wisdom.

64. Fitzgerald, *Cracks in an Earthen Vessel,* 103-7.

65. On the oppressed ones' difficulty of perceiving and resisting their oppression, see Freire, *Pedagogy of the Oppressed,* passim, esp. 25-51.

66. For a glossary of insulting terms which exemplifies the attitudes of the elite toward the disdained masses, see MacMullen, *Roman Social Relations,* "The Lexicon of Snobbery," 138-41.

67. See Wiedemann, *Adults and Children,* 27-30, citing Seneca, *De Const,* 12.3, among others.

68. As is often noted, one of the first places destroyed in the revolt of 66 C.E. was the place where debt records were kept in Jerusalem (Josephus, *JW* 2.427). Note a similar attack in Antioch ca. 70 C.E. (Josephus, *JW* 7.61).

69. Lewis, "Domitian's Order," 135-42. Lewis refers to similar orders from Germanicus in 19 C.E., from a prefect in 48 C.E., and from the prefect of Egypt in 68. Wink ("Beyond Just War," 203) cites the Theodosian Code which promises severe penalties for abusing this power.

70. Freire, *Pedagogy of the Oppressed,* 27-51, esp. 47.

71. Freire (*Pedagogy of the Oppressed,* 119-48) notes that after conquest, the strategies of divide and rule, manipulation and cultural invasion serve the goals of oppressors.

72. Betz, *Sermon,* 301-9.

73. See the collection of texts in Stern, *Greek and Latin Authors on Jews and Judaism,* 3 vols.

74. Downey, *History of Antioch,* 204-5; Josephus, *JW* 7.41-62.

75. Thompson, *Romans and Blacks.*

76. For a similar Stoic and Cynic emphasis, see Fitzgerald, *Cracks in an Earthen Vessel,* 103-7.

77. Stark, *Rise of Christianity,* 147-62.

78. Betz, *Greek Magical Papyri,* 46, 72; Rudolph, "Helios," *ABD* 3:123-25.

79. Donahue, "Tax Collectors and Sinners," 39-61; Badian, *Publicans and Sinners.*

80. McKnight (*Light Among the Nations,* 11-29) notes this tension, identifying "eight aspects of the integrating tendency" (universalism, friendliness, gentile participation in Judaism, citizenship, Hellenistic education, intermarriage, assimilation, apostasy) and "six different forms of Jewish resistance" (separation [social and verbal distance and distinctiveness], temple circumscription, warnings of idolatry, prohibition of intermarriage, revolting against reforms, vindictive judgment scenes).

6. Jesus Teaches: The Sermon on the Mount Continues

1. On the possible origin of this section, its genre, and the wider debates about appropriate cultic activity, see the commentaries, especially Betz, *Sermon,* 330-38.

2. On verbal self-promotion, compare Plutarch's instruction "On Inoffensive Self-Praise" (*Moralia* 539A-547F), in which he identifies the central problem: while many condemn self-commendation, they engage in it. Plutarch outlines some situations and techniques to render it beneficial to others (and to oneself).

3. Betz uses this comparison (*Sermon,* 353).

4. Hands, *Charities and Social Aid,* passim, esp. 26, 77.

5. Note 523F: "Indeed in what suffices no one is poor; and no one has ever borrowed money to buy barley meal, a cheese, a loaf, or olives." Plutarch takes a similar attitude to the poor who can't afford education ("Education of Children," *Moralia,* 11E).

6. MacMullen, *Roman Social Relations,* 109-20, and his "Lexicon of Snobbery," 138-41.

7. Stark, *Rise of Christianity,* 85-88, 147-62 (Antioch), 209-12.

8. Oakley, "Hypocrisy in Matthew," 118-35.

9. Deissmann (*Light from the Ancient East,* 110-12) notes that the phrase "received their reward" uses the image of giving a receipt. The transaction is finshed. There is nothing further.

10. For a similar notion in Greek religion for Zeus, see Betz, *Sermon,* 340; idem, *Greek Magical Papyri,* 15 (*PGM* II.89) "Hail, fire's dispenser, world's far-seeing king, O Helios, with noble steeds, the eye of Zeus which guards the earth, all-seeing one." The reference to **your father** recalls 5:16 and makes explicit which God is in view.

11. On 6:5-15, see Cullmann, *Prayer,* 16-69.

12. See Kiley et al. (eds.), *Prayer from Alexander to Constantine.*

13. See Lucius's prayer to the "blessed queen of heaven," whether Ceres, Venus, the sister of Phoebus, or Proserpine in Apuleius, *Metamorphoses* 11.2; or Catullus, *Poem 34: A Prayer to Diana* 21-22, which includes the line "Under whatever name you please, may you hallowed be"; or Cleanthes, *Hymn to Zeus,* which acknowledges that while Zeus is "praised above all gods, many are thy names."

14. Versnel ("Religious Mentality," 10-17) notes the request to Apollo about which gods should be sacrificed to for a good journey (Xenophon, *Anab* 3.1.5-6). The surviving enquiries from the sanctuary of Zeus at Dodona frequently request to know which god to address (Parker, *Oracles of Zeus,* 259-73). Other requests employ the Greek and Latin formulae "to all the other gods and goddesses"; see Betz, *Greek Magical Papyri,* e.g., 161-62.

15. Betz, *Greek Magical Papyri,* passim.

16. Pythagoras teaches people to pray simply for "all good things" and "not name them . . . as power, strength, beauty and the like" (Diodorus Siculus 10.9.8). Apollonius urges a short prayer, "O ye gods, grant unto me that which I deserve" (Philostratus, *Life of Apollonius* 1.11; also 4.40).

17. Versnel, "Religious Mentality," 26-42, on "Hearing Gods" and "Deaf Gods and Angry Men."

18. Again the polemical edge should be recognized. Seneca recognizes that brevity

comes from praying only that which can be named before people (*Ep* 10.4-5; *De Ben* 2.1.4); Martial, *Epig* 1.39.5.

19. Betz, *Greek Magical Papyri;* Versnell, "Religious Mentality," 4-10, 17-21; Parker, *Oracles of Zeus,* 113-14, 259-73. Parker divides the inquiries into categories of Public (from various peoples, cities, and states) and Private ("On general subjects," "On family questions," "On health" [including prosperity and safety in travel]). Compare the petitions to Asklepios (Wells, *Greek Language of Healing,* 13-101).

20. For surveys of and contributions to the rich discussion, see Betz, *Sermon,* 370-86; Davies and Allison, *Matthew,* 1:590-99; Carter, *What Are They Saying About Matthew's Sermon on the Mount?* 42-45, 93-95; Carter, "Recalling the Lord's Prayer," 514-30. For further reflection in relation to contemporary discipleship, see Crosby, *Thy Will Be Done;* Boff, *Lord's Prayer.*

21. See chapter 2, and Carter, *Households and Discipleship,* 95-114.

22. On the progressive understanding of the reign/God's empire through the gospel, see Carter, "Challenging by Confirming," 399-424; a revised version appears in Carter and Heil, *Matthew's Parables,* 36-63.

23. See Betz, *Sermon,* 394-96.

24. Hill, "'Our Daily Bread,'" 2-10.

25. See Gregory of Nyssa's fourth-century *On Prayer: Sermon 4,* which also interprets the petition in a material sense, with polemic against greed, excess, and injustice to one's neighbor effected in procuring the necessary bread. See *St Gregory of Nyssa: The Lord's Prayer,* trans. Graef, 57-70.

26. Kertelge, "δικαιοσύνη," *EDNT,* 1:326.

27. Betz (*Sermon,* 405-13) is very insightful.

28. Gerhardsson, *Testing of God's Son,* 28-31; Houk, "ΠΕΙΡΑΣΜΟΣ, The Lord's Prayer and the Massah Tradition," 216-25.

29. See Carter, "Recalling the Lord's Prayer."

30. Wolter, "παράπτωμα," *EDNT* 3:33.

31. Neh 1:4 and *T. Jos.* 4:8 (prayer); Dan 9:3 (confession and forgiveness); 1 Kgs 21:27-29 (repentance); Tob 12:8 (prayer, almsgiving, and righteousness).

32. The structure of 6:19-7:11 has perplexed many interpreters, and it would be fair to say that no proposal has carried the day. Bornkamm ("Der Aufbau der Bergpredigt") proposes that the section elaborates the Lord's Prayer, so that 6:19-24 develops the first three petitions on disciples' priorities, and 6:25-34 elaborates the fourth petition on "daily bread." For discussion, see Carter, *What Are They Saying About Matthew's Sermon on the Mount?* 42-45. Betz (*Sermon,* 423-28) suggests that 6:19-7:11 is governed by the golden rule of 7:12 and that 6:19-7:12 illustrates the difficult journey leading to life in 7:14. This suggestion is helpful as far as it goes, but it does not explain why the referent of 7:13-14 should be restricted to 6:19-7:12, and not 5:3-7:12.

33. See Reekmans, "Juvenal's Views of Social Change," 117-61; MacMullen, *Roman Social Relations,* 88-127; Carter, *Households and Discipleship,* 127-42.

34. Malina, "Wealth and Property," 354-67.

35. There is uncertainty whether βρῶσις (*brōsis*) means "rust" or the eating action of another insect. See BAGD, 148.

36. See Betz, *Sermon,* 442-49, on "Ancient Greek Theories of Vision."

37. Schramm, "ἁπλότης, ἁπλοῦς," *EDNT* 1:123-24; Bauernfeind, "ἁπλοῦς, ἁπλότης," *TDNT* 1:386-87.

38. Elliott, "Matthew 20:1-15," 52-65.

39. Pleket, "Religious History," 159-78.

40. See Patterson, *Slavery and Social Death;* Wiedemann, *Greek and Roman Slavery;* Carter, *Households and Discipleship,* 172-89.

41. Philo refers to Helicon as "riff-raff" and a "scorpion in the form of a slave." Helicon ingratiates himself with Gaius Caligula to poison Caligula against the Jewish delegation (*Leg. Gai.* 166-78, 203-206).

42. See Malherbe, *Cynic Epistles*, 91-108.

43. Carter, *Households and Discipleship*, 138-43; Schmidt, *Hostility to Wealth;* Hengel, *Property and Riches.*

44. That masters must provide adequately for slaves is a common theme in agricultural treatises: see Cato (d. 149 B.C.E.) *De Agricultura* 56-59, 107-15; Varro (d. 27 B.C.E.) *De Re Rustica* 1.17-18; and Columella, *De Re Rustica* (written 60-65 C.E.) 1.8. Seneca (*De Ben* 3.21; *Ep* 47.11-14) also urges the master's duty of adequate provision.

45. Dodds, *Pagan and Christian in an Age of Anxiety;* Betz, *Sermon,* 460-65. For the history of interpretation, see Luz, *Matthew 1-7,* 1:409-12.

46. Bultmann, "μεριμνάω," *TDNT* 4.589-93; Zeller, "μεριμνάω," *EDNT* 2:408-9.

47. The term πῆχυν (*pēchyn*) can also indicate a measure of size, a "cubit" based on a forearm, about eighteen inches (so RSV), but the context concerns sustaining, thereby prolonging life with food, not size.

48. See Carter, "'Solomon in all his Glory,'" 3-25.

49. Some manuscripts add **of God** after **kingdom**, but this reading is not to be preferred. It is missing from the great codices Sinaiticus and Vaticanus.

50. On the saying's proverbial nature, see Betz, *Sermon,* 484-85.

7. Jesus Teaches: The Sermon on the Mount Concludes

1. The sequence of sections in chapter 7 is puzzling. Bornkamm's stimulating analysis of 6:19-7:11 argues that it expands the Lord's Prayer ("Der Aufbau der Bergpredigt"). The first section, 6:19-24, develops the focus on priorities in the first three petitions of 6:9b-10; 6:25-34 elaborates the fourth petition on daily bread; 7:1-5 unpacks implications of the petition for forgiveness in a community free of judgment; 7:6 develops the sixth and seventh petitions asking for deliverance from evil in a life of faithfulness; 7:7-11 provides assurance that prayer is heard; and 7:12 concludes the larger unit from 5:17.

2. The verb appears six times, in 5:40 in a legal scenario, four times in 7:1-2 and 19:28. The meaning I suggest below is akin to the verb κατακρίνω; see BAGD, 412. In Rom 2:1 the two verbs are synonymous.

3. Contrast "good seeing" in 5:8; 6:26, 28.

4. On Greco-Roman material, see Betz, *Sermon,* 487, esp. nn. 492-94. For discussion of (excessive) knowledge of one's own faults and/or correction of others, see Cicero, *De Off* 1.146; Horace, *Sat* 1.3.25-28; Seneca, *De Ira* 1.15.1-16.7; 2.28.1-8; Plutarch, "On Tranquillity of Mind," *Moralia* 469B.

5. The meaning of this verse is uncertain, partly because its connection, if any, with its context and the meaning of "the holy," "pearls," and "swine" are not clear. Scholars invoke connections with other parts of the gospel to explain the meaning: (1) Bornkamm ("Der Aufbau der Bergpredigt," 419-32) reads it in relation to the final two petitions of the Lord's Prayer (6:13) as an exhortation to faithfulness in the face of temptation and evil. (2) Noting that "the pearl" refers to the reign in 13:45-46, and "dogs" to Gentiles in 15:21-28 (esp. 15:26), some have suggested that the saying forbids preaching the gospel to Gentiles. But the important roles for Gentiles so far in the gospel, as well as 28:19-20, suggest otherwise. (3) Others look outside the gospel for referents. Early interpreters understood "the holy" to refer to the Eucharist which was not to be given to unbelievers (*Did* 10:6), or "the pearls" to be doctrine that was not to be preached to outsiders (*Pseudo-Clementine Recognitions* 2.3). A contemporary version of these approaches (Betz, *Sermon,* 496) sees it as a possible reference to the Sermon on the Mount as a collection of Jesus' teaching, not to be seen by uninitiated outsiders. But just why such people should turn violent and vicious in response is not clear.

I will partly follow Davies and Allison (*Matthew,* 1:674), who initially suggest reading this verse in the context of, and as a part of, 7:1-5. However, my reading differs from their initial suggestion that it counters "too much laxity." Strangely, they do not follow through on this suggestion, proposing two pages later (p. 676) that the verse refers either to mission work or to not making "esoteric teachings and practices" available to outsiders. But their comments on the words and clauses in the verse do not relate particularly to any of these three readings!

6. See Matt 15:26; Deut 18:33 (Gentile prostitutes); *1 En* 89:41-50 (the nations); Isa 56:10 (Israel's blind leaders); 1 Sam 17:43 (Philistines). For opponents, see 1 Sam 24:14; Prov 26:11; Sir 13:15-20; Phil 3:2; Rev 22:15; Ignatius, *Eph.* 7.1; for Cynics, see Diogenes Laertius, *Lives* 6.60; Plutarch, "On Tranquillity of Mind," *Moralia* 468C.

7. Betz, *Sermon,* 501-2; see also Luz, *Matthew 1-7,* 1:424.

8. For "historical" texts, see Deut 4:29; 1 Chr 16:10-11; for prophetic texts, see Hos 5:15; Jer 29[LXX 36]:13-14; Isa 51:1; 55:6; for liturgical texts, see Pss 24:6; 26:8; 27:4; and for sapiential writings, see Job 8:5; Wis 1:1; 6:12; 8:2, 18; 13:6; Sir 2:16; 4:11; 6:27; Prov 2:3-4; 8:17; 14:6; 15:14; 18:15; 29:10.

9. Note that the language also appears, for instance, in Epictetus, *Diss* 1.28.20; 4.1.51, to exhort a seeking after philosophy.

10. The second **you will find** is a future active. Placed in between the other two responses, it suggests that God will enable the finding.

11. See Betz, *Sermon,* 508-19, for bibliography and discussion; also Luz, *Matthew 1-7,* 1:425-32, for history of interpretation.

12. In linking ethics and eschatology, I am summarizing and extending the helpful discussions of Ogletree, *Use of the Bible,* 15-34; and Patte, *Discipleship,* 269-350. For discussions of Matthew's eschatology, see Cope, "'To The Close of the Age'"; Sim, *Apocalyptic Eschatology;* Hagner, "Matthew's Eschatology."

13. Also Patte, *Discipleship,* 176-79.

14. Also ibid., 191-93.

15. Also ibid., 242-47, 248-51.

16. For Babylonian, Egyptian, Homeric, and Jewish uses, see Jeremias, "πύλη," *TDNT* 6:924.

17. Downey, *History of Antioch,* 181-82.

18. Wengst, *PAX ROMANA,* 26-28; MacDonald, *Architecture of the Roman Empire,* 2:5-73, on forms of roads, and 74-111, on gates.

19. Compare this recognition of the afflicted nature of existence and the goal of participation in God's purposes with Plutarch's claim that while there is much trouble for many ("On Tranquillity of Mind," e.g., 477E: "the greater part of life in lamentation and heaviness of heart and carking cares"), humans are to master their emotions and with self-control calmly face the future and whatever circumstances fortune brings (τύχη, *tychē*) "undaunted and confident" (475D-476A). Plutarch's approach reflects "the social world of the highly privileged upper classes of the Roman empire," who were "refined and wealthy enough to afford the idea of mental tranquillity," a world very different from that of the gospel's audience. So Betz, "De Tranquillitate Animi (*Moralia* 464E-477F)" in Betz (ed.), *Plutarch's Ethical Writings,* 198-208, esp. 205. Compare also Seneca's life goal of "peace of mind and lasting tranquility" (*Ep.* 92.3).

20. For Matthean discipleship as permanent liminality, see Carter, *Households and Discipleship,* 22-28, 49-55, passim.

21. Reiling, "Use of Ψευδοπροφητης," 147-56.

22. Scholars have usually argued that they are (1) Jewish opponents (such as Pharisees) or (2) Christian opponents (perhaps followers of Paul, those who do not think the law should be followed [cf. 5:18-19], or charismatic wonder-workers), or (3) nonexistent, because the verse offers a general and standard warning that false prophets will arise before the end. For discussion, see Betz, *Sermon,* 528, 34-35; Davies and Allison, *Matthew,* 1:701-2.

23. The image can also illustrate other claims: Plutarch, "On Tranquillity of Mind," *Moralia* 472F (an incomplete life); Epictetus, *Diss* 2.20.18-19 (the impossible).

24. See Luz, *Matthew 1-7,* 1:446-50.

25. See Carter and Heil, *Matthew's Parables,* 1-22, 23-35.

26. Betz, *Sermon,* 557-58.

27. Carter, "Crowds in Matthew's Gospel," 58-59.

28. Soares-Prabhu, "Jesus the Teacher," 247-53; on scribes, see Saldarini, *Pharisees,* 241-76; on their typical support for the status quo as interpreters of sacred texts and traditions, see Kautsky, *Aristocratic Empires,* 326-27.

8. God's Empire Displayed in Jesus' Actions

1. On chapters 8-9, see Held, "Matthew as Interpreter," 165-299; Kingsbury, "Observations on the 'Miracle Chapters,'" 559-73; Heil, "Significant Aspects of the Healing Miracles," 274-87; Vledder, *Conflict in the Miracle Stories.*

2. Davies and Allison (*Matthew,* 1:67-69; 2:3-4) entitle chapters 8-9 "a cycle of nine miracle stories" and divide them (2:xi) into three "triads of miracle stories" (8:1-22; 8:23-9:17; 9:18-34). But these claims are not convincing. The summary statement in 8:16 makes four miracle scenes in the first triad, the claimed third triad also has four stories (9:18-19/23-26, 20-22, 27-31, 32-34) with five people healed, and the separation from 9:35-38 in which many are healed is artificial. See their helpful review of other suggested structures (2:1-5).

3. Held ("Matthew as Interpreter," 246-53) has suggested thematic divisions for the two chapters: christology (8:2-17 [Moses performs ten miracles in Exod 7-12]), discipleship (8:18-9:17), and faith (9:18-31). But while this identifies important themes, the categories are not adequate (faith, for example, is commended in 8:10, 26; 9:2).

4. Carter, "Kernels and Narrative Blocks;" idem, *Matthew: Storyteller,* 159-75.

5. Note these key words in 4:17-22 that recur throughout chapters 8-9: Ἰησοῦς, Jesus (4:17; 7:28; 8:4, 10, 13, 14, 18, 20, 22, 34; 9:2, 4, 9, 10, 15, 19, 22, 23, 27, 28, 30, 35); κηρύσσειν, *kēryssein,* "preach" (4:17, 23; 9:35); βασιλεία, *basileia,* "reign" (4:17, 23; 8:11, 12; 9:35); περιπατέω, *peripateō,* "walk" (4:18; 9:5); θάλασσα, *thalassa,* "sea" (4:18 [twice]; 8:24, 26, 27, 32); ὁράω, *horaō,* "see" (4:18, 21; 8:4, 14, 18, 34; 9:2, 4, 8, 9, 11, 22, 23, 30, 36); δύο, *duo,* "two" (4:18, 21; 8:28; 9:27); ἀφίημι, *aphiēmi,* "leave, forgive" (4:20, 22; 8:15, 22; 9:2, 5, 6); ἀκολουθέω, *akoloutheō,* "follow" (4:20, 22, 25; 8:1, 10, 19, 22, 23; 9:9, 19, 27); καλέω, *kaleō,* "call" (4:21; 9:13).

Note these key words in 4:23-24 that recur throughout chapters 8-9: θεραπεύω, *therapeuō,* "heal" (4:23, 24; 8:7, 16; 9:35); πᾶσαν, *pasan,* "all, every" (4:23 [twice]; 9:35 [twice]); πάντας, *pantas,* "all, every" (4:24; 8:16); other forms of πᾶς, *pas,* "all, every" (8:32, 33, 34; 9:35); νόσος, *nosos,* "disease" (4:23, 24; 8:17; 9:35); μαλακία, *malakia,* "sickness" (4:23; 9:35); προσφέρω, *prospherō,* "bring" (4:24; 8:4, 16; 9:2, 32); κακῶς ἔχω, *kakōs echō,* "to be sick" (4:24; 8:16; 9:12); δαιμονίζω, *daimonizō,* "demon-possessed" (4:24; 8:16; 28, 33; 9:32); δαιμόνιον, *daimonion,* "demon" (9:33, 34); παραλυτικός, *paralytikos,* "paralytic" (4:24; 8:6; 9:2, 6); βάσανος, βασανίζω, *basanos, basanizō* "pain, distress" (4:24; 8:6).

6. So Theissen, *Miracle Stories,* 47-118, esp. 72-80.

7. Pleket, "Religious History," 178-83.

8. Johnson, *Writings of the New Testament,* 29.

9. Following Theissen, *Miracle Stories,* 231-64; Hollenbach, "Jesus, Demoniacs, and Public Authorities."

10. Levine, *Social and Ethnic Dimensions,* 107-10.

11. For "disease" as "the malfunctioning of biological and/or psychological processes," and "illness" as "the psychosocial experience and meaning or interpretation of the perceived malady," see Pilch, "Biblical Leprosy," 108-9.

12. Stark, "Antioch," 189-210.

13. On 8:1-4, in addition to the commentaries, see Kingsbury, "Retelling the Old, Old Story," 342-49; Held, "Matthew as Interpreter," 213-15.

14. The male pronouns in vv. 3b and 4 indicate a man. Nothing indicates his social level.

15. On leprosy, see Wright and Jones, "Leprosy," *ABD* 4:277-82; Pilch, "Biblical Leprosy," 108; Roth, *Blind, the Lame, and the Poor,* 108-9.

16. Pilch, "Biblical Leprosy," 111.

17. Davies and Allison, *Matthew,* 2:11-12.

18. Roth, *Blind, the Lame, and the Poor,* 108-9.

19. Edwards, "Use of ΠΡΟΣΕΡΧΕΣΘΑΙ," 65-74.

20. Greeven, "προσκυνέω," *TDNT* 6:758-66; Taylor, "'Proskynesis' and the Hellenistic Ruler Cult," 53-62; for kneeling in Greco-Roman religion, see Pleket, "Religious History," 156-57.

21. Edwards, "Use of ΠΡΟΣΕΡΧΕΣΘΑΙ," 66-67; Schneider, "προσέρχομαι," *TDNT* 2:683-84. See Matt 2:2, 8, 11; Josephus, *Ant* 7.348; 8.213, 390; 12.19 (a king); for **knelt,** Josephus, *Ant* 6.285 (David to King Saul); 7.187, 349, 354 (to David).

22. For examples of inscriptional use, see Bureth, *Titulatures impériales,* 37-40 (Vespasian), 40 (Titus), 41-45 (Domitian). Note Josephus, *JW* 7.407-19 on the struggle among Alexandrian Jews over calling the emperor "lord" (the synonym δεσπότης, *despotēs*); see Kingsbury, *Matthew: Structure,* 103-13. It should be noted that the term is used of God (1:20, 22) and as a very secular title of address (13:27). Pleket ("Religious History," 174-78) notes its common use in Greco-Roman religious observance as the corollary of the language of servant, denoting ownership and authority.

23. Wells (*Language of Healing,* 191-95) mistakenly identifies the verb as καταίρω, *kathairō.* It is καθαρίζω, *katharizō* (BAGD, 386-87, b.α).

24. Most commentators note vestiges of Mark's "messianic secret" (also 9:30; 12:16; 16:20; 17:9), which forbids people to proclaim because they cannot accurately understand Jesus until the cross (Tuckett [ed.], *Messianic Secret*). Matthean scholars must explain why Matthew omits some of Mark's commands to silence but incorporates others, while insisting that disciples have some understanding of Jesus' identity before the cross (cf. 14:33; 16:16). For another perspective, concerned mainly with Mark, see Pilch, "Secrecy in the Mediterranean World."

25. See Dobson, "Significance of the Centurion," 403-10; Davies, "Daily Life of the Roman Soldier," 299-338.

26. Levine, *Social and Ethnic Dimensions,* 110-11.

27. Determining the relationship is difficult. The term παῖς (*pais*) can mean child/ren (2:16; 17:18 [cf. υἱός, *huios,* in 17:15]; 21:15 [cf. v. 16]) and servant/s (12:18; 14:2). The reference to "slave" in v. 9 suggests servant. A filial relationship could be identified by υἱός (*huios*). Herod Antipas has servants (παισίν, *paisin,* 14:2). A ruler or official's servant could have considerable delegated power (cf. 1 Macc 1:6, 8).

28. Carter, *Households and Discipleship,* 172-92.

29. See 2 Macc 1:28; 7:13, 17; 9:6; 4 Macc 6:5, 10, 11; 8:2, 5, 27; 9:7, 15, 27, 30, 32; 11:16, 20; 12:4, 13; 13:27 15:22; 16:3, 15.

30. Patterson, *Slavery and Social Death,* 3-8, 46-51; Wiedemann, *Greek and Roman Slavery,* 9-11; idem, *Adults and Children,* 27-30; see the catalogue collected by D'Arms, "Slaves at Roman Convivia," 175-76, 179.

31. E.g., Levine, *Social and Ethnic Dimensions,* 111-13.

32. McKnight, *Light among the Gentiles,* 11-48. There is openness or integration (God creates all, Gentiles worship God, Gentile education, intermarriage, friendly coexistence in diaspora towns and cities), but also resistance (national and religious distinctiveness, bans on idolatry and intermarriage, resistance to enforced hellenization, proselytes, eschatological punishment of wicked Gentile sinners).

33. Malina and Rohrbaugh, *Social-Science Commentary,* 75-76.

34. Levine, *Social and Ethnic Dimensions,* 114.

35. The noun πίστις, *pistis* ("faith") occurs eight times; the verb πιστεύω, *pisteuō* ("I believe") occurs eleven times.

36. Barth, "Matthew's Understanding," 112-16; Ogawa ("Action-Motivating Faith") also highlights its noetic and volitional dimensions.

37. Hagner, *Matthew,* 1:205-6; Harrington, *Gospel of Matthew,* 114; Gundry, *Matthew,* 144-46.

38. Davies and Allison, *Matthew,* 2:26-29.

39. Levine, *Social and Ethnic Dimensions,* 126-30.

40. On Peter's house, see Corbo, "Capernaum," *ABD* 1:866-69; Strange and Shanks, "Has the House Where Jesus Stayed?" 26-37.

41. Carter, "Matthew 4:18-22 and Matthean Discipleship."

42. Carter, *Households and Discipleship;* Crosby, *House of Disciples;* Balch and Osiek, *Families in the New Testament World;* Davies and Allison, *Matthew,* 2:34.

43. Both Suetonius (*Claudius* 44.2) and Tacitus (*Ann* 12.67.1) attribute his death to poisoning.

44. Page, "Suffering Servant," 481-97.

45. In addition to the commentaries, see Kingsbury, "On Following Jesus," 45-59; Barton, *Discipleship and Family Ties,* 140-55; Hengel, *Charismatic Leader;* Vledder, *Conflict in the Miracle Stories,* 187-92.

46. Hengel, *Charismatic Leader,* 15 and passim.

47. So Kingsbury, "On Following Jesus," 46-47, contra Barton, *Discipleship and Family Ties,* 142-43; Vledder, *Conflict in the Miracle Stories,* 188-89.

48. For εἷς (*heis*) as an indefinite article, see 21:19; 26:69.

49. Because of a link of wisdom and teaching, some see a clash of opposing teachers, part of presenting Jesus as wisdom. See Deutsch, *Lady Wisdom,* 23-27, 43-45. For debate about wisdom and Matthew, see Pregeant, "Wisdom Passages in Matthew," 197-232; Johnson, "Reflections on a Wisdom Approach," 44-64.

50. On call stories in the Greek philosophical biographical tradition, see Droge, "Call Stories in Greek Biography and the Gospels," 257.

51. Kingsbury, "On Following Jesus," 50.

52. Levine, *Social and Ethnic Dimensions,* 7-8, passim.

53. So also Vledder, *Conflict in the Miracle Stories,*189.

54. Kingsbury, *Matthew: Structure,* 117; Luz, "Son of Man in Matthew," 3-21; Davies and Allison, *Matthew,* 2:43-52; Hagner, *Matthew,* 1:213-15; Carter, *Matthew: Storyteller,* 197-98; Deutsch, *Lady Wisdom,* 45.

55. Exod 20:12; Deut 5:16; Tob 1:17-18; 4:3-4; 6:14-15; 12:12-13; 14:11, 13; Sir 38:16-17; *4 Ezra* 2:23; Josephus, *JW* 5.545; Philostratus, *Apollonius,* 1.13.

56. Barton, *Discipleship and Family Ties.*

57. For the alternative households which reflect the reign's presence, see Carter, *Households and Discipleship.*

58. Bornkamm ("Stilling of the Storm," 52-57) interprets the scene as a discipleship story; Feiler highlights christological elements ("Stilling of the Storm," 399-406).

59. See Feiler, "Stilling of the Storm," 404-5.

60. Contemporary readers can think of numerous "watery" metaphors for human difficulties: swimming against the tide, drowning, being swamped, being pulled under, all adrift, and so on.

61. Jones, *Emperor Domitian,* 114-17.

62. Batto, "Sleeping God," 153-77.

63. Others are reputed to have overcome the sea: Aeneas (Virgil, *Aeneid* 4.553-83); Julius Caesar (Plutarch, *Caesar* 38). Apollonius is called "master of the tempest" (Philostratus, *Apollonius* 4.13).

64. Deissmann, *Light from the Ancient East,* 350.

65. Hollenbach, "Jesus, Demoniacs, and Public Authorities," 567-87; Johnson, "Mark 5:1-20," 50-74.

66. Three complications arise. (1) Matthew 8:32 clearly locates the event near the sea. (2) The manuscript traditions for Matthew (as well as Mark and Luke) identify three locations: Gadara, Gerasa, and Gergesa. Textually Gadara seems the strongest; see Metzger, *Textual Commentary,* 23-24. (3) These locations are problematic. Gerasa is about thirty miles southeast of the Sea of Galilee. There are two towns called Gadara, one the capital of Perea about fifty miles south of the Sea and closer to the Dead Sea (where the notes in the New Oxford Annotated NRSV locate the story), and the other in the Decapolis about six miles

from the Sea. Whether the audience is assumed to know any of this geography is difficult to assess. The narrative supplies the details necessary for the story.

67. Harding, *Antiquities of Jordan,* 79-85; Spijkerman, *Coins of the Decapolis and Provincia Arabia;* see the references to Gerasa and Gadara in Sperber, *City in Roman Palestine,* 195-96.

68. Jones, "Burial Customs," 813-14; Ferguson, *Religions of the Roman Empire,* 134-35.

69. See MacMullen, *Roman Social Relations,* 4, for the dangers associated with being away from the city.

70. Maynard, "ΤΙ ΕΜΟΙ ΚΑΙ ΣΟΙ," 582-86.

71. See the evidence collected in Kim, "Anarthrous υἱὸς θεοῦ," 221-41.

72. Wolmarans, "Who Asked Jesus," 87-92.

73. Firmage, "Zoology," *ABD* 6:1132; Stendebach, "Das Schweinopfer im alten Orient," 263-71; de Vaux, "Les sacrifices de porcs," 259-62. Cato indicates offering swine before harvest (*De Agricultura* 134), thinning a grove (139), tilling the ground (160), purifying the land and making atonement to Mars so that flocks and crops might flourish (161; for the same rite, see Suetonius, *Augustus* 2.97.1; *Tiberius* 21.1).

74. Michon, "Mélanges III. Note sur une inscription de Ba‘albek et sur des tuilles de la legion Xa Fretensis," 101-5 and pl. 1.

75. Wiesenberg, "Related Prohibitions," 221.

76. For demons as the interiority of institutions and structures, see 4:1-11; and Wink, *Engaging the Powers.*

77. Also Vledder, *Conflict in the Miracle Stories,* 197-98.

78. On the *adventus,* see Kreitzer, *Striking New Images,* 155-86, 212-19.

9. Jesus' Actions and God's Empire

1. See 1:20, 23; 2:1, 9, 13, 19; 3:16, 17; 4:11; 7:4; 8:2, 24, 29, 32, 34.

2. Roth, *Blind, the Lame, and the Poor,* 107-8.

3. Sand, *Das Evangelium nach Matthäus,* 192.

4. For the unfortunate demonizing of opponents, see 4:1-11, and Introduction, section 1.

5. Carter, "Crowds in Matthew's Gospel," 54-67.

6. See Carter, *Matthew: Storyteller,* 15-34, esp. 26-28; Kiley, "Why 'Matthew'?" 347-51; Duling, "Matthew," *ABD* 4:618-622.

7. Snell, "Tax Office," *ABD* 6:338.

8. For discussion and sources, see Wengst, *PAX ROMANA,* 26-35.

9. Cicero (*De Off* 150-51) links tax collectors with manual workers, mechanics, and those catering to sensual pleasures such as cooks, dancers, butchers, and fishermen. Agriculture is the best means of gaining wealth. Trade on a small scale is vulgar but on a large scale is not to be disparaged.

10. Duling, "Matthew," *ABD* 4:621; Donahue, "Tax Collector," *ABD* 6:337-38; Freyne, *Galilee from Alexander the Great,* 183-94.

11. Tacitus (*Ann* 13.50) narrates the story of Nero contemplating the abolition of indirect taxes, but his advisers persuade him not to do so because the empire would fall apart.

12. Smith, "Historical Jesus at Table," 468 n. 7; idem, "Greco-Roman Meal Customs," *ABD* 4:650-53; Smith and Taussig, *Many Tables,* 21-35.

13. Douglas, "Deciphering a Meal," 61, quoted by Smith, "Historical Jesus at Table," 469.

14. Smith, "Greco-Roman Meal Customs," *ABD* 4:652; Corley, *Private Women, Public Meals,* 24-79, esp. 31-34, 57; also eadem, "Jesus' Table Practice," 448-49.

15. Sanders, "Sin, Sinners (NT)," *ABD* 6:43; idem, *Jesus and Judaism,* 174-211.

16. Dunn, *Jesus, Paul, and the Law,* 61-88, esp. 71-77; idem, "Jesus and Factionalism," 156-75; Smith. "Historical Jesus at Table," 480-84; Corley, *Private Women, Public Meals,* 89-93.

17. Corley, *Private Women, Public Meals,* 24-79; eadem, "Jesus' Table Practice," 444-59. Note Juvenal's lament of loss of distinctions; see Reekmans, "Juvenal's Views of Social Change," 117-61.

18. Kingsbury, *Matthew as Story,* 17-23; idem, "Developing Conflict," 57-73; van Tilborg, *Jewish Leaders;* Saldarini, *Pharisees,* 35-49, drawing on Kautsky, *Power and Privilege,* and Kautsky, *Aristocratic Empires.*

19. While it is possible to know something of the beliefs and practices of first-century Pharisees (Neusner, *From Politics to Piety;* Saldarini, "Pharisees," *ABD* 5.289-303), my focus is on their presentation as characters in Matthew's story.

20. Hill, "On the Use and Meaning of Hosea 6:6," 107-13. For debate over the use of this text by Yohanan ben Zakkai in the post-70 reconstruction, see Neusner, *Development of a Legend,* 114, 130, who regards it as a late (ca. 130 C.E.) addition, while Davies (*Setting of the Sermon on the Mount,* 307) locates it in the 70s.

21. Carter, "Jesus' 'I have come' Statements," 54-57.

22. It designates most commonly the bridegroom in Song of Songs. Most of its other references refer to human bridegrooms, often in situations of catastrophe.

23. Note that, under the influence of Mark 5:22, the NRSV calls him "a leader of the synagogue," though acknowledging that the Greek text lacks "of the synagogue." The translation is both textually and theologically impossible. This gospel does not present a synagogue leader in such positive light.

24. Roth, *Blind, the Lame, and the Poor,* 110-12.

25. Levine, "Discharging Responsibility," 379-97, esp. 394-96.

26. Kingsbury, "Verb AKOLOUTHEIN ("To Follow")," 58.

27. Levine, "Discharging Responsibility," 393-94.

28. Arlandson, *Women, Class, and Society,* 1-119.

29. See the critique of Levine, "Discharging Responsibility," 384; also Cohen, "Menstruants and the Sacred," 273-99.

30. This is a difficult statement. It is unlikely to mean that Jesus knows she is unconscious not dead. The mourning is too advanced for such a deception (though this possibility appears in Philostratus, *Apollonius* 4.45). Moreover, the verb in 9:25 ("arose") points to death, as does the reference to "raising the dead" in 11:5. "Sleep" is a metaphor for death (Jdt 14:14-15; Matt 27:52) which seems to be doing double duty, referring to death but also evoking resurrection (so Dan 12:2; *1 En* 49-51; 1 Cor 15:6; Matt 27:52; so "arose" in 9:25). Her death is temporary, and, as from a sleep, she is about to be awakened/raised. The crowd understands a literal statement.

31. For other links, see Levine, "Discharging Responsibility," 396-97.

32. Schrage, "τυφλός," *TDNT* 8:270-94, esp. 270-71. Martial narrates the story of a man blinded while stealing the emperor's fish; blindness forces him to beg (*Epig* 4.30).

33. Roth, *Blind, the Lame, and the Poor,* 103-6.

34. Schrage, "τυφλός," *TDNT* 8:275-79, 281-82, 284-86, 291-93.

35. Kingsbury, "Title 'Son of David,'" 599.

36. Duling, "Therapeutic Son of David," 392-410; idem, "Solomon, Exorcism, and the Son of David," 235-52; Kingsbury, "Title 'Son of David,'" 591-602; Loader, "Son of David, Blindness and Duality in Matthew," 570-85.

37. 1 Chr 29:22; 2 Chr 1:1; 13:6; 30:26; 35:3; Prov 1:1; Eccl 1:1; note also Absalom in 2 Sam 13:1.

38. Schrage, "τυφλός," *TDNT* 8:274-75.

39. Contrast this audience-oriented focus on making sense of the material within the flow of the gospel's finished form with appeals to Matthew's clumsy redaction of Mark's messianic secret (see Davies and Allison, *Matthew,* 2:14-15), or to Jesus' intent not to exploit popular messianic expectations by proclaiming miracle-working power (Hagner, *Matthew,* 1:254).

40. Gundry, *Matthew,* 178; Garland, *Reading Matthew,* 106-7, quoting Versnel, "Religious Mentality," 60.

41. Roth, *Blind, the Lame, and the Poor,* 106-7.

42. Hollenbach, "Jesus, Demoniacs, and Public Authorities," 577.

43. In 9:35 **Jesus** replaces the pronoun "he" to recall his mission (1:21); **all the cities and villages** replaces "in all Galilee"; and "among the people" is omitted.

44. Allen, *S. Matthew,* 99.

45. Heil, "Ezekiel 34 and the Narrative Strategy," 698-708.

10. Jesus' Second Teaching Discourse: Mission

1. Essentially I follow (as I will frequently through this chapter) Weaver, *Matthew's Missionary Discourse,* 14-16, who notes formulaic closures ("Truly I tell you) in 10:15, 23, 42. Davies and Allison (*Matthew,* 2:160-62) identify seven sections (also Hagner, *Matthew,* 1:262-3) and offer a chiastic structure centered on the encouragement of 10:26-31. But 10:24-25 and 32-33 do not match. In the former, disciples imitate Jesus in persecution, while in the latter Jesus imitates disciples in confession. They also omit 10:1-4. Morosco ("Matthew's Formation," 539-56) suggests a structure based on a Hebrew Bible form of commissioning story, but the indirect speech of 10:1-4 is not a "confrontation," and there is no "objection."

2. Luz, *Matthew in History,* 54.

3. Gottwald, *Hebrew Bible,* 276-88.

4. Epictetus says they are to show people "that in the question of good and evil they have strayed and are seeking the true nature of the good and the evil where it is not" (*Diss* 3.22.19-26).

5. Keck, "Matthew and the Spirit," 145-55; Charette, "'Never Has Anything Like This.'"

6. Isaiah removes his sandals in announcing judgment against Egypt and Ethiopia enacted through Assyria (Isa 20:2-4). Does the absence of sandals also symbolize the judgment being enacted in the disciples' mission (so Matt 10:11-15)?

7. Downing, "Cynics and Christians."

8. Some later traditions have Jews shaking dust from sandals after leaving Gentile territory (*b. Sanh.*12a; *m. Ohol.* 2:3), an action redirected here.

9. Aune, *Prophecy in Early Christianity,* 164-65.

10. Freire, *Pedagogy of the Oppressed,* 27-51, esp. 47.

11. Lohse, "συνέδριον," *TDNT* 7:866.

12. Davies and Allison (*Matthew,* 2:183) speculate (1) that discipline may follow criticism of the religious leaders as causing disorder (cf. Josephus, *JW* 6.302); or (2) that claims that God has authorized Jesus to forgive sin may be seen as blasphemous (9:2-8).

13. Contra Hagner (*Matthew,* 1:279-80), who sees a reference to the fall of Jerusalem in 70 C.E.

14. Marshall, "Uncomfortable Words," 277-79.

15. Deissmann, *Light from the Ancient East,* 270-72.

16. Allison, "Hairs of Your Head," 334-36.

17. The issue is not theodicy (so Davies and Allison, *Matthew,* 2:210-11), because not all human suffering is in view. The suffering of disciples incurred while living faithfully to their missional task is in view.

18. Carter, "Jesus' 'I have come' Statements," 57-60.

19. Tannehill, *Sword of His Mouth,* 142-43.

20. Carter, *Households and Discipleship,* 19-22.

21. Barton, *Discipleship and Family Ties,* 23-56, 155-78; Carter, *Households and Discipleship,* 82-87.

22. Hengel, *Crucifixion.*

23. Griffiths, "Disciple's Cross," 358-64.

24. Contra Weaver, *Matthew's Missionary Discourse,* 120-21.

11. Responding to Jesus

1. Carter, *Matthew: Storyteller*, 149-75, esp. 164-67; idem, "Kernels and Narrative Blocks," 463-81, esp. 476-77.

2. Compare Davies and Allison, *Matthew*, 2:233-35; Hagner, *Matthew*, 1:298; Gnilka, *Matthäusevangelium*, 1:426-42; Verseput, *Rejection of the Humble Messianic King*, "Contents," 55-56, 152-54, 207-8, 280-81.

3. Compare 4Q521, which links a Messiah expected by its Qumran author(s) with healing the sick, raising the dead, and announcing good news to the poor. See Wise and Tabor, "Messiah at Qumran," 60-65.

4. Theissen, *Gospels in Context*, 25-42.

5. Schwartz, "Wilderness and Temple," 61-78.

6. For these associations in Cynic critiques of Greco-Roman culture, see the evidence summarized in Cameron, "'What Have You Come Out to See?'" 42-44.

7. Kramer, Rendtorff, and Meyer, "προφήτης," *TDNT* 6:781-828; Boring, "Prophecy (Early Christian)," *ABD* 5:495-502; Potter, "Prophecy and Personal Power in the Roman Empire," in *Prophets and Emperors*, 146-82; Aune, *Prophecy in Early Christianity*, 106-7, 121-52; Horsley, "Popular Prophetic Movements," 3-27; Horsley and Hanson, *Bandits, Prophets, and Messiahs;* Barnett, "Jewish Sign Prophets."

8. For this difficult verse, Davies and Allison (*Matthew*, 2:254-56) list seven possible readings; see also Hagner, *Matthew*, 1:306-7. For a range of views, see Moore, "ΒΙΑΖΩ, ΑΡΠΑΖΩ and Cognates in Josephus," 519-43; Cameron, *Violence and the Kingdom;* Catchpole, "On Doing Violence," 78-80; Barnett, "Who were the Biastai?" 65-70.

9. Not a middle voice denoting the empire's action but a passive denoting violence done to the reign. See Schrenk, "βιάζομαι," *TDNT* 1:609-14; the two clauses are essentially parallel.

10. *1 En* 46:4-8; 56:5-8; chs. 62-63; 91:5-6; 1QH 2; *4 Ezra* 5:1-13; 9:1-8; 16:18-50; Matt 24-25. See Allison, *End of the Ages*, 5-25, 120-24.

11. Meier, *Law and History in Matthew's Gospel*, 85-89.

12. Lövestam, "ἡ γενεὰ αὕτη Eschatology," 403-13.

13. I am essentially following Cotter, "Parable of the Children in the Market-Place," esp. 296-303. Cotter, though, sees the parable's central juxtaposition as "immaturity and dignity" (p. 298). By emphasizing the cultural associations of children (see 2:8), I am arguing that it consists of margins and center.

14. Suggs, *Wisdom, Christology, and Law.*

15. Comber, "Composition and Literary Characteristics," 497-504.

16. See Gen 37:34; 2 Kgs 19:1-2; Isa 37:1-2; 58:5; Job 42:6; Jonah 3:5-6; Esth 4:3; Jdt 4:8-12.

17. Patte, *Matthew*, 163.

18. Jeremias, "ᾅδης," *TDNT* 1:146-49.

19. For those who read the passage in relation to wisdom, see Deutsch, *Hidden Wisdom;* Betz, "Logion of the Easy Yoke," 10-24. Others contest this link; see Stanton, "Matthew 11:28-30: Comfortable Words?" Charette, "To Proclaim Liberty," 290-97. While wisdom connections cannot be denied (revealing God's will and presence), I think they offer starting, not ending, points. Charette points the way to eschatological expectations of God's sovereignty or reign which breaks the yoke of oppressive imperial rule. But Charette seems to think Matthew has spiritualized or metaphorized the tradition, makes no connection to Roman imperial power, and suggests little material significance for Jesus' ministry.

20. The verb means "confess" in 3:6. When addressed to God, it gives thanks for God's actions: BAGD, 277; cf. Sir 51:1; Ps 136:26; 1QH 7:26-27; 11:3-4, 15.

21. The giving of Torah (Exod 20; Sir 45:5), wisdom (Sir 24:3 [identified with Torah in 24:23]; *1 En* 37:1; *2 En* 28:1), the heavenly Son of Man (*1 En* 46-48), mysteries of creation (*1 En* 72-73; *4 Ezra* 4:7-11; *2 En* 24), of God's purposes in history (*1 En* 85-90, 93, 91:12-17) and judgment (*1 En* 46-51).

22. See 1 Sam 15:3; 22:19; 2 Kgs 8:12; Job 3:11; Ps 17:4; Isa 11:8; Jdt 4:10, 12; 7:22, 27; 16:4; Esth 8:11; Wis 12:24; 15:14; 18:5.

23. For brief overviews, see Harrington, *Gospel of Matthew,* 10-19; Carter, *Matthew: Storyteller,* 80-88; and the relevant sections of Carter, "Prologue and John's Gospel," 35-58.

24. For textual issues, see Deutsch, *Hidden Wisdom,* 34-35; Swanson, *New Testament Greek Manuscripts: Matthew,* 99-102.

25. Hauck, "κοπός, κοπιάω," *TDNT* 3:827-29.

26. Egypt (Lev 26:13); nations (Deut 28:48-49 [synonym κλοιός, *kloios*]); Rehoboam (2 Chr 10:4, 9, 10, 11, 14, and Josephus, *Ant* 8.213); the nations against God and Israel's king (Ps 2:3); Assyria (Isa 9:4; 10:27; 14:25, 29); Babylon (Isa 47:6 [43:14, κλοιός]; Jer 34[NRSV 27]:8; 35[NRSV 28]:11); the Medes (*Sib. Or.* 11:67; cf. Sir 28:17-20); the Egyptian Philopator (3 Macc 4:9); the Seleucid Demetrius (1 Macc 8:18, 31); "the yoke of the Gentiles" (1 Macc 13:41); slavery to Rome (*Sib. Or.* 8.125-30; cf. *Pss. Sol.* 17:30; Josephus, *JW* 5.365; 7.87); the wicked ("the sinners and the oppressors") who "hate us . . . scatter us and murder us" and the complicitous officials who cover it up in *1 En* 103:11-15. Strangely, references to this common metaphor are missing from most contemporary commentaries.

27. Suggs, *Wisdom, Christology, and Law;* Deutsch, *Hidden Wisdom.* Good (*Jesus the Meek King,* 61-64) rejects identifications with wisdom (Deutsch) and servant (Stanton) and argues that notions of kingship inform the verses. Good's suggestion is helpful, though a monolithic claim seems unlikely. Nor does she extend her analysis of the key notion of "yoke."

28. Good, *Jesus the Meek King.*

12. Discerning Jesus' Identity

1. On 12:1-14 in addition to the commentaries, see Verseput, *Rejection of the Humble Messianic King,* 153-294; Robbins, "Plucking Grain on the Sabbath," 107-41; Yang seems more interested in the historical Jesus (*Jesus and the Sabbath*).

2. Tannehill, "Focal Instance," 374-83.

3. On sabbath, see Dunn, *Romans 1-8,* lxiv-lxxii; idem, *Romans 9-16,* 804-6; Yang, *Jesus and the Sabbath,* 53-99; Kimbrough, "Concept of Sabbath," 483-502; Harrington, *Gospel of Matthew,* 174-77; Saldarini, *Matthew's Christian-Jewish Community,* 126-34.

4. Gottwald, *Tribes of Yahweh,* 615, 692-709.

5. Ringe, *Jesus, Liberation, and the Biblical Jubilee,* 16-32. She does not discuss 12:1-14.

6. Goldenberg, "Jewish Sabbath in the Roman World," 430-42.

7. Horsley, *Galilee: History, Politics, People,* 202-221; Garnsey, *Famine and Food Supply,* 43-48, 55-63.

8. Garnsey, *Famine and Food Supply,* 1-86; MacMullen, *Enemies of the Roman Order,* 180-85, 249-54.

9. Rightly critiqued by Schottroff and Stegemann, "Sabbath Was Made for Man," 118-29.

10. Numerous commentators (e.g., Cohn-Sherbok, "Analysis of Jesus' Arguments," 31-36) note clear differences. (1) David does not act on the sabbath; the disciples do. (2) David and companions eat the bread of the presence; the disciples work. (3) David has the primary role; no mention is made of Jesus eating. (4) David is fleeing for his life; the disciples are not.

11. The word ἀναίτιοι (*anaitioi*) describes the disciples here, the priests in 12:5 and David in Symmachus's translation of the Jewish scriptures in 1 Sam 19:5 (LXX 1 Kgdms 19:5).

12. Stark, "Antioch as the Social Situation," 189-210.

13. See 8:3-4; for healing by the word, see 8:5-13, 32; 9:6. For other healings of withered hands, see 1 Kgs 13:1-10; *T. Sim.* 2:11-14; and Exod 4:7 for Moses.

14. Carter, "Crowds in Matthew's Gospel."

15. Neyrey, "Thematic Use of Isaiah 42:1-4," 468-70.

16. The text, the longest of Matthew's citations, does not quote the LXX exactly, but appears to be a translation from the Hebrew text, somewhat influenced by the LXX.

17. Neyrey, "Thematic Use of Isaiah 42:1-4," 468-70.

18. Kraft, "εἰς νῖκος: Permanently/Successfully," 153-56.

19. Robbins, "Rhetorical Composition and the Beelzebul Controversy," 177-85.

20. On "deviance labeling," see Malina and Rohrbaugh, *Social-Science Commentary,* 97-98; Malina and Neyrey, *Calling Jesus Names,* 1-67; on Pharisees as part of the ruling elite, see Introduction, sections 1 and 5; 2:4; 3:7; 5:20; 9:11; Saldarini, *Pharisees,* 35-49.

21. Bilde, "Causes of the Jewish War," 186-94.

22. Berkey, "ΕΓΓΙΖΕΙΝ, ΦΘΑΝΕΙΝ, and Realized Eschatology."

23. There has been much discussion of this change. Most scholars see the two terms as synonymous, with the variants determined by either source or context issues. A few see conceptual differences. Pamment ("Kingdom of Heaven," 211-32) thinks "of the heavens" refers to the future and "of God" to the present. Mowery ("Matthean References to the Kingdom," 398-405) helpfully notes that "of God" is used with the religious leaders and "of the heavens" with disciples/crowds. Thomas ("Kingdom of God," 136-46) sees the changes as literary to highlight matters of concern to the community. All of these proposals come to grief, though, on 19:23-24, where the two terms are used without a temporal distinction, change of audience, or change of topic. Beck (*Anti-Roman Cryptograms,* 102) suggests that "kingdom of heaven" tones down the overtly political meaning of "kingdom of God" probably "partially in an attempt to try to protect Christians from additional political persecution by Roman authorities." The phrase would be, then, another "anti-Roman cryptogram." Beck, though, does not explain what persecution scenario he has in mind, nor why "kingdom of God" should be used four times. It seems to me that it is the word "kingdom/empire" rather than "God/heaven" that causes more political difficulty.

24. Davies and Allison, *Matthew,* 2:347-48.

25. Derrett ("Every 'Idle' Word," 261-65, esp. 265) calls them "unpropitious, not tending to the results which the religion requires . . . unedifying . . . unproductive for God."

26. Edwards, *Sign of Jonah.*

27. Carter, *Households and Discipleship;* Barton, *Discipleship and Family Ties,* 178-91.

28. Soares-Prabhu, "Jesus the Teacher," 246-47.

13. Jesus' Third Teaching Discourse: Parables

1. The bibliography is extensive. See Carter and Heil, *Matthew's Parables,* 1-22, 36-63, 64-95; Kingsbury, *Parables of Jesus;* Drury, *Parables in the Gospels;* Donahue, *Gospel in Parable,* 1-27, 63-125; Lambrecht, *Out of the Treasure.*

2. Carter, "The Parables in Matthew 13:1-52, as Embedded Narratives," in Carter and Heil, *Matthew's Parables,* 38-58.

3. Crossan, "Parable," *ABD* 5:146-52.

4. For discussion, see Carter and Heil, *Matthew's Parables,* 17-21.

5. Carson notes that the present tense in 13:31, 33, 44, 45, 47 highlights the present aspects of the reign, the aorist tense in 13:24 indicates what it has become like, while the future passive in 7:24, 26 emphasizes its future eschatological form ("ΟΜΟΙΟΣ Word-Group," 277-82).

6. Soares-Prabhu, "Jesus the Teacher," 253-56.

7. Scott, *Hear Then The Parable,* 8. Compare Dodd (*Parables of the Kingdom,* 5) ". . . the parable is a metaphor or simile drawn from nature or common life, arresting the hearer by its vividness or strangeness, and leaving the mind in sufficient doubt about its precise application to tease it into active thought."

8. Heil, "Narrative Progression in Matthew 13:1-52," in Carter and Heil, *Matthew's Parables,* 65-66, modified; Patte, *Matthew,* 185. For other attempts, see Davies and Allison, *Matthew,* 2:370-72.

9. Carter, "Crowds in Matthew's Gospel," 54-67.

10. McIver, "One Hundred-Fold Yield," 606-8.

11. Bornkamm, "μυστήριον," *TDNT* 4:802-19.

12. This increasing wealth is often at the expense of the poor, and is often condemned; so Prov 22:7, 16; Isa 5:8; Amos 5:11; Sir 13:2, 18-20; 34:24-27.

13. On συνιέναι (*sunienai,* "understand"), used four times in 13:13-19, see Barth, "Matthew's Understanding," 105-12.

14. Missing are several common features of citation introductions ("what was spoken by the Lord"; "through/by the prophet"). The use of **prophecy** as the subject is unique in Matthew, and the verb **certainly fulfilled** appears only here. Likewise only this one is a statement by Jesus rather than an editorial comment. A number of scholars (so Davies and Allison, *Matthew* 2:393-94; compare Hagner, *Matthew,* 1:373-75) think this citation is a later addition to the gospel.

15. Mack, "Teaching in Parables," 143-60.

16. Waller, "Parable of the Leaven," 99-109.

17. Windisch, "ζύμη, ζυμόω, ἄζυμος," *TDNT* 2:902-6.

18. Kingsbury, *Parables of Jesus,* 85.

19. Rogers, "Asaph," *ABD* 1:471.

20. On Matthew's eschatology, see Cope, "'To the Close of the Age'"; Sim, *Apocalyptic Eschatology;* Hagner, "Matthew's Eschatology," 163-81.

21. Bowman and Swanson, "Samson and the Son of God," 66.

22. Giesen, "σκανδαλίζω, σκάνδαλον," *EDNT* 3:248-50. The LXX use is quite diverse, in referring to military action (1 Macc 5:5; Jdt 5:1), idols (Ps 106:36; Hos 4:17), the nations who as God's instruments punish the disobedient people (Josh 23:13; Judg 2:3), conflicts with other people, especially the wicked (Pss 69:22; 140:5; 141:9). Loving the law, though, means no stumbling block (Ps 119:165).

23. Gundry, *Matthew,* 277-78; Garland, *Reading Matthew,* 151.

24. Though usually translated "carpenter" and with good support (2 Kgs 12:11-13; 1 Chr 14:1; Isa 40:20 [a builder from wood]), the term has a wider meaning of "maker" or "producer." It refers to a metal worker (1 Sam 13:19; 1 Kgs 7:14) and stone worker (2 Sam 5:11). Note the range in Isa 44:12-13. Perhaps "artisan" (1 Chr 4:14) would be accurate, signifying someone skilled in building. See Batey, "Is Not This the Carpenter?" 249-58.

14. God's Empire at Work: Opposition, Abundance, Compassion

1. For discussion, see Braund, "Herod Antipas," *ABD* 3:160; Theissen, *Gospels in Context,* 81-97; Corley, *Private Women, Public Meals,* 158-60; Weaver, "Power and Powerlessness," 454-66.

2. Josephus does not mention any attack on Herod by John. He presents John positively as a preacher who exhorts righteous behavior. Twice Josephus mentions that some Jews thought that God punishes Herod in a military defeat because of Herod's maltreatment of John.

3. For example, Pharaoh against Moses (Exod 5-15); Ahab and Jezebel against Elijah (1 Kgs 17-18); Nebuchadnezzar against Daniel; Nebuchadnezzar and Holofernes against Judith; Antiochus Epiphanes against Judas Maccabeus. See on 16:21; 17:25.

4. Herod was deposed and exiled by the emperor Gaius Caligula on the suspicion of sedition after he planned to ask for the title "king" (Josephus, *Ant* 18. 240-55, esp. 242-44).

5. See Braund, "Philip," *ABD* 5:310-11, #5; Herion, "Herod Philip," *ABD* 3:160-61.

6. Corley, *Private Women, Public Meals,* 24-79.

7. Theissen, *Gospels in Context,* 88, 91-96.

8. Crook, "Titus and Berenice."

9. Theissen, *Gospels in Context,* 92.

10. Ibid., 86.

11. Wengst, *PAX ROMANA,* 31-35; Garnsey, *Famine and Food Supply.*

12. Good ("Verb ΑΝΑΧΩΡΕΩ") notes the possible influence of imperial aggression (though of the seven references in 1 and 2 Macc which she lists, only one [2 Macc 5:27] actually uses this verb; two use related compounds; three use totally unrelated verbs translated by the English word "withdraw"; one has no textual basis) but strangely she sets aside the Matthean narrative contexts which evidence this reality to emphasize the influence of wisdom's withdrawal. But the argument lacks linguistic support. None of the texts she cites (Prov 1, 8; Sir 24; *1 En* 42; 84:3; 94:5; Bar 3:9-4:4; *2 Bar* 48:30), uses this verb (though wisdom does "withdraw" in 2 Esdr 5:9 but the text is in Latin). Further, she does not distinguish the subjects of the verbs—in 2:12, 13 the magi; in 2:14, 22 Joseph; and in 27:5 Judas. Are they wisdom personified as Jesus is (11:19)? Moreover, her claim of "seven instances of the three-fold pattern, hostility/withdrawal/prophetic fulfillment" (p. 1) is not accurate. It does not fit 2:12-13, 14:13, 15:21, 27:5, leaving four instances (2:14, 22; 4:12-16; 12:15-21). And finally, the claim on p. 10 that while wisdom influence is pervasive in the gospel, "one cannot say the same about extensive use of Maccabees or Exodus," is also not accurate.

13. Scott, *Imperial Cult,* 51-52, 91-96.

14. Heil, *Walking on the Sea,* 17-67, 84-117.

15. Kingsbury, "Figure of Peter," 67-83.

16. Edwards, "Gennesaret," *ABD* 2:963.

15. Jesus' Authority as God's Agent

1. Saldarini, *Matthew's Christian-Jewish Community,* 134-39, 154-56.

2. I am following the helpful article by Baumgarten, "Pharisaic *Paradosis,*" 63-77.

3. Neusner, *From Politics to Piety,* 73-84.

4. Through the scene Jesus teaches or reveals God's will as Moses did in the exodus. Note the similar sequence: both reveal after political tyranny (cf. Matt 14:1-12), feeding in the wilderness (Matt 14:13-21), and escape from water (Matt 14:22-33).

5. The Greek construction οὐ μή (*ou mē*) with a future is a strong negative (BDF, 365).

6. Josephus (*Con Ap* 1.167) claims that the practice is uniquely Jewish. The term *korban* is used in Matt 27:6 and *JW* 2.175 for the temple treasury where gifts were deposited. Josephus's reference records its violation by Pilate to finance an aqueduct.

7. Baumgarten, "Korban and the Pharisaic Paradosis," 16; Rengstorf, "κορβᾶν," *TDNT* 3:860-66.

8. Carter, "Crowds in Matthew's Gospel."

9. See Pss 1:3; 80:15; 92:13; 2 Sam 7:10; Isa 5:1-10; 60:21; Jer 32:41; Ezek 17:22-24; 19:10, 13; cf. Matt 7:16-20; especially for particular groups, 1QS 8:5; *1 En* 10:16; Wis 4:3-5 [the wicked]; *Pss. Sol.* 14:1-5 [the righteous].

10. Johnson, "New Testament's Anti-Jewish Slander," 435-40; Josephus, *Con Ap* 2.142 (Apion); *JW* 5.343, 572 (Zealots); Philo, *Vita Cont* 10 (Egyptian idolaters); Qumran, 1QS 4:9-14 (outsiders). See chapter 23.

11. For example, Meier, *Vision of Matthew,* 100-104.

12. On her dispossession, see Guardiola-Sáenz, "Borderless Women," 69-81.

13. For discussion in addition to the commentaries, see Dube, "Readings of *Semoya,*" 111-29; Wainwright, *Towards a Feminist Critical Reading,* 102-18, 217-47; Levine, *Social and Ethnic Dimensions,* 131-64; Ringe, "Gentile Woman's Story," 65-72; Dermience, "La péricope de la Cananéenne (Mt 15, 21-28)," 25-49.

14. Contra Levine (*Social and Ethnic Dimensions,* 136-38), who insists that Jesus travels

"toward Tyre and Sidon" but does not "enter the region of Tyre and Sidon." The preposition clearly indicates "into" the region; compare 2:12, 14, 22; 4:12. Does Jesus travel toward Galilee but not enter it (also 19:3, Judea)?

15. See Theissen, *Gospels in Context,* 61-80.

16. Guardiola-Sáenz, "Borderlesss Women," 69-72. Senior ("Between Two Worlds," 19) suggests Jesus' hesitations and words reflect the resistance of some in the Matthean community to the idea of a Gentile mission.

17. Ringe, "Gentile Woman's Story," 69.

18. Theissen, *Gospels in Context,* 79.

19. Donaldson, *Jesus on the Mountain,* 122-35.

20. My question, which concerns the narrative function of the material, differs from the usual investigations of possible sources and/or of numerous events in the life of the historical Jesus.

21. Anderson, *Matthew's Narrative Web,* 87.

16A: Jesus' Identity

1. Saldarini, *Pharisees,* 35-49, 277-308.

2. On "sign-prophets" (e.g., Theudas [Josephus, *Ant* 20.97-98]) who promised acts of liberation akin to those of Moses and Joshua, see Horsley, "'Like One of the Prophets of Old,'" 435-63.

3. On some of Jesus' claims, see 1:21, 23; 3:17; 5:17; 7:21-27; 8:11-12; 9:2, 5; 10:32-33; 11:2-6, 25-30; 12:8, 28, 40, 49-50; 13:35; 14:22-27; 15:1-20.

4. Nickelsburg, "Enoch, Levi and Peter," 575-600.

5. Kutsko, "Caesarea Philippi," *ABD* 1:803.

6. Witherup, "Jeremiah and the Gospel of Matthew," 10-11.

7. Carter, *Matthew: Storyteller,* 194-97.

8. Kim summarizes the data with its concentration on Augustus ("Anarthrous υἱὸς θεοῦ," esp. 225-38); Price, "Gods and Emperors," 79-95.

9. Schweizer et al., "σάρξ," *TDNT* 7:123-24.

10. Luz, *Matthew in History,* 57-74, esp. 57-63; Burgess, *History of the Exegesis of Matthew 16:17-19.*

11. Campbell, "Origin and Meaning," 130-42; for the standard view, see Küng, *Church,* 79-87; for discussion, see Marshall, "Biblical Use," 359-64.

12. Linton, "Ekklesia," *RAC* 4:906-7; Douglas, "Matthew 18:15-17 and the Hellenistic-Roman *Polis*"; Gomme, "Ecclesia," *Oxford Classical Dictionary,* 303-4.

13. Antioch had the institutions of the *boulē* and *dēmos* by the first century B.C.E. (Josephus, *JW* 7.107). For inscriptional evidence, Downey, *History of Antioch,* 114-15.

14. Horsley (ed.), *Paul and Empire,* 209.

15. Davies and Allison (*Matthew,* 2:630-32) helpfully summarize twelve views: (1) immortality for Peter; (2) immortality for his office; (3) Christ's preaching in hell; (4) Jesus' resurrection; (5) general resurrection; (6) the church's foundation; (7) gatekeepers; (8) death by martyrdom; (9) the church's preaching in Hades; (10) evil against Peter's teaching; (11) death; (12) the powers of the underworld (their choice). It is also essentially the view of Marcus, "Gates of Hades," 443-55, whom I generally follow here.

16. For this translation, see Marcus, "Gates of Hades," 448-49.

17. Garland, *Reading Matthew,* 172.

18. For this dynamic understanding, see also Marcus, "Entering into the Kingly Power of God," 663-75.

19. Collins, "Binding and Loosing," *ABD* 1:743-45.

20. Büchsel, "δέω (λύω)," *TDNT* 2:60-61.

21. Balch, "Greek Political Topos," 68, 78, 81, 84.

22. Hummel, *Die Auseinandersetzung,* 59-64. On the whole topic, see Brown et al., *Peter in the New Testament.*

23. Strecker, *Der Weg der Gerechtigkeit,* 198-206, esp. 205.

24. Kingsbury, "Figure of Peter."

16B. The Way of the Cross for Jesus and Disciples

1. See 9:3, 11, 32, 36; 10:17; 12:1-14, 24, 33-42; 15:1-20; 16:1-12; though recall 2:4-6.

2. Bornkamm, "πρέσβυς, πρεσβύτερος," *TDNT* 6:658-59.

3. For the chief priests as members of the ruling elite, see Lenski, *Power and Privilege,* 256-66.

4. Saldarini, "Sanhedrin," *ABD* 5:976; Lohse, "συνέδριον," *TDNT* 7:862-70.

5. Griffiths, "Disciple's Cross," 358-64.

6. Beardslee, "Saving One's Life," 60-64.

17. The Way of the Cross

1. For comprehensive discussion of various possibilities, see Davies and Allison, *Matthew* 2:684-709; Donaldson, *Jesus on the Mountain,* 136-56.

2. See Exod 24:12-18 [Sinai]; 1 Kgs 18:20 [Carmel]; 19:11-18 [Horeb/Sinai]; *T. Levi* 2:5-6; Matt 5:1.

3. Donaldson, *Jesus on the Mountain,* 146-48.

4. Allison, *New Moses,* 243-48.

5. Behm, "μεταμορφόω," *TDNT* 4:755-59.

6. Note traditions that Rome's famous sons, Aeneas and Romulus, did not die (Dionysius of Halicarnassus, *Rom Ant* 1.64.4; 2.56.2).

7. Carter, "Crowds in Matthew's Gospel."

8. Malina and Rohrbaugh, *Social-Science Commentary,* 115.

9. Because of weak manuscript attestation, the discovery of no good reason for the verse's omission if it were original, and the well-attested practice of scribal insertions of material from one gospel into another, many contemporary translations omit 17:21. It was probably added by later copyists influenced by Mark 9:29, "But this kind does not come out except by prayer and fasting." See Metzger, *Textual Commentary,* 43.

10. Anderson, *Matthew's Narrative Web.*

11. For a fine review, see Garland, "Temple Tax in Matthew," 190-209; also Chilton, "Coin of Three Realms," 269-82. For the following argument in greater detail and with extensive bibliography, see Carter, "Paying the Tax."

12. For discussion, see Smallwood, *Jews under Roman Rule,* 371-76; Goodman, "Nerva, the *Fiscus Judaicus* and Jewish Identity," 40-44.

13. Smallwood, *Jews under Roman Rule,* 374.

14. While there is ambiguity about who owns houses (9:1-10, 28; 13:1, 36 suggest Jesus does), the location of this house in Capernaum and the prominence of Peter suggest it is his house (8:5, 14; 17:24).

15. The change from "Peter" in 17:24 has perplexed interpreters. It may recall 16:17.

16. Louw and Nida, 1:578; BAGD, 812; Moulton and Milligan, *Vocabulary,* 630-31; Delling, "τέλος," *TDNT* 8:51, 52, 57; Cassidy, "Matthew 17:24-27," 572-73. Examples include Josephus, *Ant* 10.2 (tribute of submission to Sennacherib); *Ant* 12.169, 175 (tax-farming rights in submission to King Ptolemy); *Ant* 17.205 (taxes on "public purchases and sales"); Esth 10:1; 1 Macc 10:31; 11:35; Philo, *Mig* 139 (to God).

17. Louw and Nida, 1:578; BAGD, 430; Cassidy, "Matthew 17:24-27," 573.

18. See Josephus, *Ant* 12.158-59; *JW* 2.403-4; Tacitus, *Ann* 3.40-41; 4.72-73; 6.41. MacMullen, *Enemies of the Roman Order,* 212-14; Dyson, "Native Revolts," 254, 267, 269.

19. *Contra,* e.g., Davies and Allison, *Matthew,* 2:741, 745, 748; Hagner, *Matthew,* 2:511, 512. For further unconvincing attempts to allegorize this exchange about the children, see the discussion in Carter, "Paying the Tax."

20. The connective δέ (*de*) on its own (without μέν, *men*) should not be translated "however" to suggest a contrast, but as a connective "and" (BDF §§442-43).

21. Louw and Nida (1:63) identify it as a silver coin worth two didrachma.

22. Scott, *Imperial Cult,* 116-25. Juvenal, *Fourth Satire,* 63-128, esp. 65-71, 83-86. Martial (*On the Spectacles*) celebrates Titus's power or *numen* over wild beasts (12), an elephant (20), the sea (28), and hounds (33).

18. Jesus' Fourth Teaching Discourse: A Community of Sustaining Relationships and Practices

1. On chapter 18, see Thompson, *Matthew's Advice to a Divided Community.*

2. Carter, *Households and Discipleship,* 95-114.

3. Marcus, "Entering into the Kingly Power of God."

4. Over people: Pss 34:6; 35:5-6; 91:11; *1 En* 100:5; Tob 5:4; 6:1; passim; including Jesus in 2:13, 19; 4:6, 11; over nations: Dan 10:13; 12:1; Sir 17:17; *1 En* 20:1-7; 2 Macc 11:6.

5. The verse sometimes found as v. 11 ("For the Son of Man came to seek and to save the lost") is lacking from the earliest texts and was probably added from Luke 19:11. Metzger, *Textual Commentary,* 44-45.

6. Heil, "Ezekiel 34 and the Narrative Strategy," 704.

7. Huffman, "Atypical Features," 211.

8. Douglas, "Matthew 18:15-17 and the Hellenistic-Roman *Polis.*"

9. See Kugel, "On Hidden Hatred and Open Reproach," 43-61; Weinfeld, *Organizational Pattern;* Klinghardt, "Manual of Discipline," 251-70.

10. Weinfeld, *Organizational Pattern,* 38-43; Klinghardt, "Manual of Discipline"; Kloppenborg and Wilson (eds.), *Voluntary Associations.*

11. Duling, "Matthew 18:15-17: Conflict, Confrontation, and Conflict Resolution," 253-95, esp. 274-75.

12. Barton and Horsley, "Hellenistic Cult Group," 7-41.

13. Duling's fine discussion, "Matthew 18:15-17: Conflict, Confrontation, and Conflict Resolution," 281.

14. Neusner, "Judaism in a Time of Crisis," 313-27; Stone, "Reactions to Destructions of the Second Temple," 195-204. Sievers ("'Where Two or Three . . . ,'" 47-61) also recognizes this post-70, post-temple context. He cites a tradition of texts concerned with God's presence with judges (Exod 20:24; Ps 82:1b; Mal 3:6; *Mekilta Bahodesh* 11 on Exod 24). This would provide an alternative reading, a third assurance of Jesus' presence in the reproof process.

15. Beavis ("Ancient Slavery," 37-54) notes the reluctance of interpreters to recognize that the parable is about literal slaves.

16. In addition to the commentators and other contributions cited below, see Thompson, *Matthew's Advice to a Divided Community,* 203-37; Scott, *Hear Then The Parable,* 267-80; de Boer, "Ten Thousand Talents?" 214-32; Ringe, "Solidarity and Contextuality"; Heil, "The Unforgiving Forgiven Servant," in Carter and Heil, *Matthew's Parables,* 96-123.

17. Crenshaw, *Whirlpool of Torment.*

18. Carson, "ΟΜΟΙΟΣ Word-Group."

19. Both Derrett ("Law in the New Testament: The Parable of the Unmerciful Servant," 32-47) and Herzog (*Parables as Subversive Speech,* 135-46, 53-73) are helpful in drawing attention to the parable's political setting.

20. Lenski, *Power and Privilege,* 214, 246.

21. On tribute in Galilee, see Horsley, *Archaeology, History and Society,* 76-85.

22. Herzog, *Parables as Subversive Speech,* 143-44.

23. Davies and Allison, *Matthew,* 2:802.

24. Derrett, "Law in the New Testament: The Parable of the Unmerciful Servant," 42.

25. Malina and Rohrbaugh, *Social-Science Commentary,* 120.

19. The Alternative Households of God's Empire: Part 1

1. For the argument that follows, supporting Greco-Roman texts, and extensive bibliography, see Carter, *Households and Discipleship,* 15-28. For discussion of households, see Balch, *Let Wives Be Submissive;* idem, "Neopythagorean Moralists and the New Testament Household"; Balch and Osiek, *Families in the New Testament World,* passim, 130-36.

2. Lerner, *Creation of Patriarchy,* 239.

3. There are condemnations of religious groups (especially the cults of Dionysus and Isis) that collapse a strict hierarchical male domination of women and encourage more egalitarian male–female roles. Diodorus Siculus (*Hist* 1.27.1-2) condemns Isis groups and Egyptian practices of women ruling men; also Herodotus, 2.35. Octavian complains that Antony has let a woman control him (Dio Cassius 50.24-26). Josephus, in reporting on Herod's concern with Cleopatra's political aspirations, comments pejoratively on Antony being "basely enslaved as he was by his passion for her" (*JW* 7.302). Tacitus (*Ann* 14.1-2) attacks Agrippina's power over Nero. Epictetus insists on preserving differences among men, women, and children (*Diss* 3.1.44-45). He attacks men who adorn themselves elaborately and remove hair. Excellence resides in the man's reason and moral purpose (3.1.26, 40). Hair distinguishes a man from a woman; removing it along with male-female differences is contrary to nature (3.1.30) and unworthy citizenship (3.1.34-35). Pseudo-Phocylides (210-11) objects to men's long hair because it blurs the gender difference. Plutarch insists on rulers upholding the sacred social (i.e., patriarchal and hierarchical) order ("To an Uneducated Ruler," *Moralia* 780D-F). Balch, *Let Wives Be Submissive,* 65-80.

4. Carter, *Households and Discipleship,* 56-89.

5. Brooten, "Konnten Frauen im alten Judentum die Scheidung betreiben?" 65-80.

6. Carter, *Households and Discipleship,* 72-82.

7. For supporting data and some minority counterviews, see Carter, *Households and Discipleship,* 75-87.

8. Trible, *Rhetoric of Sexuality,* 98-102; Brueggemann, "Of the Same Flesh and Bone," 532-42.

9. Brueggemann, *Genesis,* 47.

10. Carter, *Households and Discipleship,* 72-87.

11. E.g., Fitzmyer, "Matthean Divorce Texts," 197-226.

12. Allison, "Divorce, Celibacy and Joseph," 3-10.

13. Among the vast contributions, see Wenham and Heth, *Jesus and Divorce.* For a summary and critique of the first option, see chapters 3-6; for the second option (their preference), see chapters 1-2. Also Wenham, "Matthew and Divorce," 95-107; idem, "Syntax of Matt 19.9," 17-23.

14. I am summarizing Carter, *Households and Discipleship,* 66-68.

15. For discussion of 19:10-12, see Quesnell, "'Made Themselves Eunuchs for the Kingdom of Heaven,'" 335-58; Moloney, "Matthew 19:3-12 and Celibacy," 42-60.

16. Schneider, "εὐνοῦχος," *TDNT* 2:765-68.

17. For discussion of eunuchs serving emperors in the fourth and fifth centuries, see Hopkins, *Conquerors and Slaves,* 172-96; also Patterson, *Slavery and Social Death,* 314-31.

18. Nock, "Eunuchs in Ancient Religion," 25-33.

19. Patterson, *Slavery and Social Death,* 326.

20. See Carter, *Households and Discipleship,* 90-114; Gardner and Wiedemann (eds.), *Roman Household,* 96-116; Wiedemann, *Adults and Children;* Rawson, "Children in the Roman Familia," 170-200; Manson, "Emergence of the Small Child in Rome," 149-59;

Marrou, *History of Education;* Rawson, "Family Life Among the Lower Classes at Rome," 71-83.

21. Carter, *Households and Discipleship,* 108-13.

22. See Oepke, "παῖς," *TDNT* 5:640; Wiedemann, *Adults and Children,* 176-208; Manson, "Emergence of the Small Child in Rome"; Carter, *Households and Discipleship,* 108-13.

23. Carter, *Households and Discipleship,* 115-45, and the material cited there; Balch and Osiek, *Families in the New Testament World,* 91-102; Malina, "Wealth and Property," 354-67.

24. Reekmans, "Juvenal's Views," 121.

25. MacMullen, *Roman Social Relations,* 138-41; see also his discussion of "Class" (pp. 88-120), but wealth is a pervasive issue in his discussions of rural and urban living (pp. 1-87).

26. For a "limited goods" economy, see Malina, "Wealth and Property"; Hengel, *Property and Riches,* 12-22.

27. Saller, "*Familia, Domus,*" 349; Carter, *Households and Discipleship,* 135-36.

28. Carter, *Households and Discipleship,* 136-38.

29. Schmidt, *Hostility to Wealth;* Carter, *Households and Discipleship,* 138-43.

30. Malherbe, *Cynic Epistles,* 91-108 (translation by B. Fiore).

31. Note that in 19:23 Jesus speaks of "the reign of the heavens" and here of "the reign of God." There is no difference despite numerous theories. See 12:28 and the literature cited there.

32. Barton, *Discipleship and Family Ties,* 204-15.

33. The word has Pythagorean and Stoic origins. See Büchsel, "παλιγγενεσία," *TDNT* 1:686-89. Its use ranges from cosmic rebirth (Stoics), to the post-flood world (Philo, *Moses* 2.65), to the rebirth of the soul after physical death (Philo, *De Cherub* 113-15), to Israel's reestablishment after the exile (Josephus, *Ant* 11.66), to Christian rebirth through baptism (Titus 3:5). On Philo, see Burnett, "Philo on Immortality," 447-70; idem, "Παλιγγενεσία in Matt 19:28," 60-72; Sim, *Apocalyptic Eschatology,* 110-14.

20. The Alternative Households of God's Empire: Part 2

1. For discussion and bibliography, see Carter and Heil, *Matthew's Parables,* 124-46; Carter, *Households and Discipleship,* 146-60.

2. Fortna, "'You Have Made Them Equal to Us,'" 66-72.

3. Breech, *Silence of Jesus,* 142; Drury, *Parables in the Gospels,* 92-95; Lambrecht, *Out of the Treasure,* 81-84.

4. Herzog (*Parables as Subversive Speech,* 79-97) is very helpful, though I do not agree with his conclusion. Nor do I understand why he consents to theologizing interpretations for Matthew but not for Jesus. The previous nineteen chapters attest Matthew's great interest in socioeconomic injustice, as we have seen.

5. Vineyards can represent Israel (Isa 5:1-7; Jer 12:10) if one chooses to read allegorically, not socially and economically. In 15:13-14 Jesus judges the religious elite not to be God's planting.

6. Herzog, *Parables as Subversive Speech,* 87.

7. Schottroff, "Human Solidarity and the Goodness of God," 129-47.

8. Scott (*Hear Then The Parable,* 295-96, also 205-8) misconstrues the relationship when he identifies the situation as that of patrons and clients. Basic aspects of this relationship are missing. The householder makes no commitment to the laborers on a long-term basis, and no obligation (protection, benefit, honor, etc.) beyond a basic exchange of work and money.

9. Heichelheim ("Syria," 179-80) calculates about half a denarius as that which an adult needed for survival, and suggests that one denarius a day was the average daily wage.

10. Huffman, "Atypical Features," 208-10.

11. Schottroff, "Human Solidarity and the Goodness of God," 138.

12. Freire, *Pedagogy of the Oppressed,* 27-51, esp. 47; 119-48.

13. Elliott, "Matthew 20:1-15," 52-65.

14. Anderson, *Matthew's Narrative Web.*

15. Sherwin-White, *Roman Society,* 35-43.

16. Wiedemann, *Slavery,* 3-4, 25; Patterson, *Slavery and Social Death,* 3-8, 46-51, 89-92; for examples of beatings, see Carter, *Households and Discipleship,* 182-83.

17. Wainwright, *Towards a Feminist Critical Reading,* 118-21, 253-57.

18. Clark, "Meaning of [κατα]κυριεύειν," 207-12; for critique, see Carter, "Toward an Imperial-Critical Reading," 321-23, retracting previous comments in *Households and Discipleship,* 170.

19. Wengst, *PAX ROMANA,* 1-54.

20. Seeley, "Rulership and Service," 234-50.

21. Carter, *Households and Discipleship,* 172-89.

22. Wiedemann, *Slavery,* 3.

23. Patterson, *Slavery and Social Death,* 38-71.

24. Carter, *Households and Discipleship,* 184-89.

25. For discussion of slavery as a liminal existence, see Patterson, *Slavery and Social Death,* 45-51, 293, 340; Carter, *Households and Discipleship,* 172-92, esp. 177-78, 189-92.

26. Martin, *Slavery as Salvation,* 11-30.

27. Carter, "Jesus' 'I have come' Statements."

28. Morris, *Apostolic Preaching,* 11-64.

29. Deissmann, *Light from the Ancient East,* 331-34.

30. Procksch, "λύτρον," *TDNT* 4:329-31, 340-49; Shogren, "Redemption (NT)," *ABD* 5:654-57; Morris, *Apostolic Preaching,* 18-38.

31. Williams, *Jesus' Death as Saving Event,* 59-202.

32. Seeley, *Noble Death,* 113-41.

33. These thoughts are also stimulated by the fine article of Teselle, "Cross as Ransom," 161-69.

34. Welch, *Communities of Resistance and Solidarity.*

35. Carter, *Households and Discipleship,* 193-203.

36. Levine, *Social and Ethnic Dimensions.*

37. Netzer, "Jericho," *ABD* 3:738-40.

21. Jesus in Conflict

1. Carter, *Matthew: Storyteller,* 159-75, esp. 169-71; idem, "Kernels and Narrative Blocks," 463-81.

2. Tatum, "Jesus' So-Called Triumphal Entry," 129-43.

3. In turn, this material prepares for the sixth narrative block (ch. 28) by raising a further question: Does Jesus' death mean his opponents' victory and the thwarting of God's purposes?

4. For discussion, Catchpole, "'Triumphal' Entry," 319-34; Duff, "March of the Divine Warrior," 58-64; Tatum, "Jesus' So-Called Triumphal Entry," 132-33; Kinman, "Jesus' 'Triumphal Entry.'"

5. For example, Solomon (1 Kgs 1:32-40); the eschatological king (Zech 9-14); Alexander (Josephus, *Ant* 11.325-39, 342-45); Apollonius (2 Macc 4:21-22); Judas Maccabeus (*Ant* 12.312, 348-49; 1 Macc 4:19-25; 5:45-54); Jonathan Maccabeus (1 Macc 10:86); Simon Maccabeus (1 Macc 13:43-48, 49-51); Antigonus (Josephus, *Ant* 13.304-6; *JW* 1.73-74); Marcus Agrippa (*Ant* 16.12-15); Pilate (*Ant* 18.55-56); Romulus (Dionysius of Halicarnassus, *Rom Ant* 2.34.1-4), Antony (Plutarch, *Antony* 24.1-4); Gaius (Suetonius, *Gaius* 13-14); Vitellius (Suetonius, *Vitellius* 10-11); Titus (*JW* 4.112-20); Vespasian (*JW* 7.68-74) with Titus (*JW* 7.116-57). Note also Philostratus, *Apollonius* 4.1. See Kinman, *Jesus' Entry to Jerusalem,* 25-65.

6. Marshall, "Governors on the Move, 231-46; Versnel, *Triumphus;* MacCormack, "Change and Continuity," 721-52; Kinman, "Pilate's Assize," 282-95.

7. Russell and Wilson, *Menander Rhetor,* pp. 94-103, sections 378-82. For Menander, the speech of welcome to an imperial governor must employ a tone of joy, praise the emperor, celebrate the governor's virtues and actions, and warmly welcome him to the city.

8. Visser 't Hooft, "Triumphalism," 491; Brunt ("Laus imperii," 163) calls the triumph "the institutional expression of Rome's military ideal."

9. Duff, "March of the Divine Warrior," 55, citing C. Meyers.

10. Esler ("God's Honour and Rome's Triumph," 257) argues that *2 Bar* 40:1-3 employs Zion traditions to parody the Roman triumph in presenting God's defeat of the empire.

11. Visser 't Hooft, "Triumphalism," 491-504.

12. For further examples from the ancient Near East, see Hanfmann, "Donkey and the King," 421-26.

13. The Mount of Olives has diverse significance. It is a place of mourning for David (2 Sam 15:30), of unfaithfulness for Solomon (1 Kgs 11:7), of faithfulness and reform for Josiah (2 Kgs 23:13), of a display of God's glory for Ezekiel (Ezek 11:22-24).

14. Derrett, "Law in the New Testament: The Palm Sunday Colt," 241-58.

15. Good, *Jesus the Meek King.*

16. How many animals does Jesus ride? Meier (*Vision of Matthew,* 21-23) has concluded that the presence of two animals suggests Matthew did not know or misunderstood the Hebrew text (and so must have been a Gentile), but this hardly follows, especially when the past phrase of the citation comes from the MT. The presence of two animals may point to a literal fulfillment of Zech 9:9, or it may reflect the custom of keeping mother and foal together, even though Jesus rides only one.

17. Compare *2 Bar* 1:1-5; 13:2-10; *4 Ezra* 2:7; 3:2, 25-36; 4:23; 5:28-30; 6:18-19; 10:48; *Apoc. Abr.* 22-27, 28-32.

18. Neusner, "Judaism in a Time of Crisis," 319-20.

19. See the discussions of the historical Jesus in Sanders, *Jesus and Judaism,* 61-90; Watty, "Jesus and the Temple," 235-39.

20. Neusner, "Judaism in a Time of Crisis," 320-25.

21. Chapter 2; 18:1-10; 19:13-15. For support, see Carter, *Households and Discipleship,* 111-12.

22. On the fig tree's rich significance, see Telford, "More Fruit from the Withered Tree," 264-304; Ellul, "Dérives Autour d'un Figuier," 69-76.

23. Lohse, "συνέδριον," *TDNT* 7:862-70; Soares-Prabhu, "Jesus the Teacher," 247-53.

24. See Saldarini, *Pharisees,* 35-49, drawing on the work of Lenski, *Power and Privilege,* and Kautsky, *Aristocratic Empires.*

25. With Saldarini, *Matthew's Christian-Jewish Community,* 58-64; *contra* Drury (*Parables in the Gospels,* 96), who claims they "explain the momentous transfer of divine approval from orthodox Jewry to the unrespectable but responsive gathering of repentant sinners who make up the Church," and Lambrecht (*Out of the Treasure,* 104), who notes that they depict the Jews' "persistent hardening" upon which "Jesus pronounces their condemnation." My reading sees the parables accounting for the fall of Jerusalem to Rome in 70 C.E. because of the leaders' rejection of Jesus, but holding out to the leaders (and of course the people) of the author's own day the opportunity to do the will of God as revealed by Jesus. The parable employs but does not sever the father–son image. There is still the time and opportunity for the second son to change his mind and go to work in the vineyard. This view is similar to Donahue, *Gospel in Parable,* 88-89.

26. Textually I follow the Third and Fourth Revised Editions of the *Greek New Testament* (United Bible Societies, 1983, 1993), which have the first son responding in the negative but then going to the vineyard. For discussion, see Metzger, *Textual Commentary,* 55-56; Scott, *Hear Then The Parable,* 80-81.

27. The vineyard is a common image for Israel as God's special, though frequently erring,

people (Isa 5:1-7; Jer 12:10-11; Ezek 19:10-14; Hos 10:1). The metaphor of father and son or children also images the relationship of God and Israel. See Deut 8:5; 14:1; 32:6; Pss 68:5; 103:13; Isa 1:1-9; 64:8; Hos 11:1; Sir 23:1; Wis 14:3; 3 Macc 6:3, 8; 7:6. See Schrenk and Quell, "πατήρ," *TDNT* 5:970-82, though Schrenk's comments on the lack of "the spirit of true faith" in early Judaism (pp. 981-82) betray a regrettable anti-Jewish bias and ecclesial triumphalism that mandate caution.

28. Levine, *Social and Ethnic Dimensions,* 204-6.

29. Marcus, "Entering into the Kingly Power."

30. For righteousness as divine activity and human behavior, see Meier, *Law and History in Matthew's Gospel,* 76-80; see also Przybylski, *Righteousness in Matthew,* 1-12, 91-96; Reumann, *Righteousness,* 124-35.

31. For discussion, see in addition to the commentaries, Carter and Heil, *Matthew's Parables,* 159-68; Scott, *Hear Then The Parable,* 237-53; Kingsbury, "Parable of the Wicked Husbandmen"; Snodgrass, *Parable of the Wicked Tenants,* 72-110; Carlston, *Parables of the Triple Tradition,* 40-45; Herzog, *Parables,* 98-113.

32. On the construction and operation of vineyards, see Columella, *On Agriculture,* bks 3-5; Cato, *De Agricultura,* 11-26, 33.

33. Drury (*Parables in the Gospels,* 96-97) suggests particular prophets: Jeremiah is beaten (Jer 20:2), Uriah is killed (Jer 26:20-23; LXX 33:20-23), Azariah/Zechariah is stoned (2 Chr 24:21). The choice of verbs suggests some particular prophets: the *attempt* to kill Uriah but not the actual killing employs the verb ἀποκτεῖναι (*apokteinai;* Jer 33:21 LXX) used in Matt 21:35 (also 14:6 [John], 10:28; 24:9 [disciples], 16:21; 17:23; 26:4 [Jesus]), and the verb ἐλιθοβόλησαν (*elithobolēsan,* "stoned") appears in both 2 Chr 24:21 and Matt 21:35.

34. For examples including John the Baptist or no referent, see Carter and Heil, *Matthew's Parables,* 162 n. 34.

35. Derrett situates their action in viticultural and economic laws and practices ("Parable of the Wicked Vinedressers," in Derrett, *Law in the New Testament,* 296-305).

36. With, e.g., Harrington, *Gospel of Matthew,* 304; Gundry, *Matthew,* 430; Culbertson, "Reclaiming the Matthean Vineyard Parables," 267; Snodgrass, *Parable of the Wicked Tenants,* 109; *contra* Hare, *Matthew,* 248-49; Drury, *Parables in the Gospels,* 97 ("Judaism was condemned and Christianity authorized"); Stanton, *Gospels and Jesus,* 67.

37. See the commentaries and Snodgrass, *Parable of the Wicked Tenants,* 90-95; and Hare and Harrington, "'Make Disciples,'" 359-69; Meier, "Nations or Gentiles?" 94-102.

38. Saldarini (*Matthew's Christian-Jewish Community,* 59-60, 78-81) suggests that the small group of believers is a "voluntary association" (see Introduction). Meier ("Nations or Gentiles?") surveys the uses of ἔθνος (*ethnos*) in Matthew in three categories: (1) seven cases that refer to "Gentiles" (4:15; 6:32; 10:5, 18; 12:18, 21; 20:19); (2) two doubtful cases (20:25-26; 24:9), the latter of which he subsequently moves into the third category; (3) not meaning "Gentiles" but "nation/s" or "people," which includes Jews and Gentiles (21:43 ["people"]; 24:7 ["nation (probably the Jewish nation) against (a Gentile) nation"]; 24:14 ["nations," including Jews]; 24:9 ["nations," including Jews]; 25:32 ["nations," including Jews]; 28:19 ["nations," including Jews]). Also to be noted is that the noun appears in the singular only in 21:43 and 24:9 (twice).

39. Levine, *Social and Ethnic Dimensions,* 185-204.

40. Donahue (*Gospel in Parable,* 90-92) argues that the emphasis on bearing fruit indicates the primary recasting of the parable as a warning for the Matthean community against presumption and to emphasize the need for fruitful discipleship.

41. Verse 44 (as designated in some versions) is probably an interpolation from Luke 20:18. So Metzger, *Textual Commentary,* 58.

42. Kingsbury, "Parable of the Wicked Husbandmen," 646-52.

43. Donahue, *Gospel in Parable,* 92; Carter, "Crowds in Matthew's Gospel," 64-67.

22. Conflict over Jesus' Authority

1. For discussion, see Scott, *Hear Then The Parable,* 161-74; Saunders; "'No One Dared'"; also Van Aarde, "A Historical-Critical Classification," 229-47; Lemcio, "Parables of the Great Supper and the Wedding Feast," 1-26; Wainwright, "God Wills to Invite All," 185-93.

2. Gundry, *Matthew,* 433; Scott, *Hear Then The Parable,* 162.

3. Scott, *Hear Then The Parable,* 162.

4. Carson, "ΟΜΟΙΟΣ Word-Group," 277-82.

5. Note the article on Luke-Acts by Neyrey, "Ceremonies in Luke-Acts," 361-87.

6. Some argue that the slaves, or at least the second group in v. 4, represent disciples or Christian missionaries (so Hendrickx, *Parables of Jesus,* 124; Hare, *Jewish Persecution,* 121-22). Certainly **slave** refers to such in the mission discourse of 10:24-25, to disciples in the parables of 13:27-28 and 18:23, 26, 27, 28, 32, and to disciples in 20:27. But given the clear reference to prophets in the salvation-history allegory of 21:34-36, it seems best to take these references to prophets also. However, given also the continuity between prophets and the Christian community in terms of similar experiences of rejection (5:10-12; 13:10-17), the mission experiences of the gospel's audience are not far away.

7. Compare the centurion, who as one under authority (ὑπὸ ἐξουσίαν) commands his servant (δοῦλος) to "do this" and "he does it" (8:9).

8. Attempts to connect these activities with the Deuteronomic provisions for excusing men from military service (see Derrett, "Parable of the Great Supper," in *Law in the New Testament,* 126-55; Ballard, "Reasons for Refusing," 341-50; Palmer, "Just Married, Cannot Come," 241-57; Scott, *Hear Then The Parable,* 170-71) fail because Matthew lacks the important marriage claim.

9. For a dissenting view on 22:7, see Rengstorf, "Die Stadt der Mörder," 106-29; Gundry, *Matthew,* 436-37.

10. I cannot agree with Drury (*Parables in the Gospels,* 98), who claims that the destruction of the city is "the doom of Judaism"; nor with Hendrickx (*Parables of Jesus,* 121), who sees the whole parable illustrating the judgment of Israel; nor with Lambrecht (*Out of the Treasure,* 119, 123, 133, 137), who also sees the sealing of Israel's fate and its replacement. See Matt 28:18-20. *4 Ezra* and *2 Baruch* also evidence God's continuing relationship with Israel after punishment of Jerusalem in 70 C.E..

11. If Luz is right that Gentile mission is a recent post-70 commitment of the Matthean community and is being sustained by the gospel story (*Matthew,* 1:76, 84-87), the understanding of the third sending after the burning of the city (22:8-10) may well reflect the history of Matthew's audience. However, on the basis of my reading of 21:33-45, and on the lack of ethnic emphasis in 22:8-10, I disagree with Luz (*Matthew,* 1:88) that the "mission in Israel has come to an end."

12. So Levine, *Social and Ethnic Dimensions,* 211-15.

13. Derrett ("Parable of the Great Supper," 142) emphasizes that inappropriate clothing is an insult; Dillon ("Towards a Tradition-History," 37-41) thinks that the image recalls baptismal instruction.

14. This reformulates the argument of Sim, "Man Without the Wedding Garment," 165-78.

15. Meyer, "Many (= All) Are Called," 94-96; Donahue, *Gospel in Parable,* 95-96.

16. Bruce, "Render to Caesar," 253-54; Giblin, "'Things of God,'" 510-27.

17. Carter, "Paying the Tax," n. 69; Dyson, "Native Revolts."

18. Bruce, "Render to Caesar," 258, citing an inscription from Palmyra dated 136/7 C.E.

19. Sutherland, "Intelligibility of Roman Imperial Coin Types," 46-55; Oster, "'Show Me a Denarius,'" 107-15; Kreitzer, *Striking New Images.*

20. Hart, "Coin of 'Render unto Caesar . . . ,'" 241-48; Kreitzer, *Striking New Images,* 136-37; Esler, "God's Honour and Rome's Triumph," 246-54.

21. Kalmin, "Levirate Law," *ABD* 4:296-97.

22. I am following Schüssler Fiorenza, *In Memory of Her,* 143-45.

23. In Tob 3:7-15 Sarah marries seven husbands (though they are not said to be brothers). Each dies before consummating the marriage.

24. McBride, "Yoke of the Kingdom," 273-306.

25. See Saunders, "'No One Dared,'" 426-450; Hay, *Glory at the Right Hand.*

26. Duling, "Therapeutic Son of David."

23. Jesus Attacks the Scribes and Pharisees

1. On chapter 23, see Garland, *Intention of Matthew 23;* Saldarini, *Matthew's Christian-Jewish Community,* 46-52.

2. It is interesting to note that Kingsbury ("Developing Conflict," 70-72) omits any discussion of the chapter's place in the gospel's plot.

3. Johnson, "New Testament's Anti-Jewish Slander;" 419-41; see also Vaage, "Woes of Q," 582-607.

4. Johnson, "New Testament's Anti-Jewish Slander;" 440, with references added.

5. For this and other examples, see Johnson, "New Testament's Anti-Jewish Slander;" 430-33; Davies and Allison, *Matthew,* 3:258-59.

6. Johnson, "New Testament's Anti-Jewish Slander;" 434-36.

7. Davies and Allison, *Matthew,* 3:259-60; Johnson, "New Testament's Anti-Jewish Slander;" 434-36.

8. Johnson, "New Testament's Anti-Jewish Slander;" 441.

9. Garland (*Reading Matthew,* 229) notes the advice of Demetrius of Phaleron (*On Style* 5.292) that when making a direct critique to a group, a preferable rhetorical strategy is to direct the criticism to another group so that one's audience will be more receptive. Garland notes that disciples are guilty of these same offenses: 23:6, desire for first place (cf. 20:20-28); 23:25-26, discrepancy of inner and outer life (cf. 7:15); passim, hypocrisy (cf. 6:1-16, 16-18); 23:2-7, abuse of authority (cf. 24:45-51); 23:13, haughtiness that causes others to stumble and shuts them out of God's empire (cf. 18:6; 19:13); 23:28, inner lawlessness (cf. 7:23); 23:23, lack of mercy (cf. 18:21-35; 24:12).

10. I follow Powell, "Do and Keep What Moses Says," 419-35. See his summary (pp. 424-31) of ten different ways of reading these opening verses; see also Saldarini, *Matthew's Christian-Jewish Community,* 47-48.

11. Powell, "Do and Keep What Moses Says," 431-32; also Saldarini, "Delegitimation of Leaders," 670.

12. For references, see Johnson, "New Testament's Anti-Jewish Slander;" 432-33 n. 47.

13. Tigay, "On the Term 'Phylacteries' (Mt 23:5)," 46-48; Davies and Allison, *Matthew,* 1:16-18.

14. Lapin, "Rabbi," *ABD* 5:601-2.

15. See Lassen, "Use of the Father Image," 127-36; see p. 129 n. 12 for inscriptional support of its use for patrons of *collegia.* Lassen lists *Corpus Inscriptionum Latinarum* III, 7505; VI, 8796; 10234; IX, 2687; 5450; XIV, 37; 2408.

16. Beck, "Mysteries of Mithras," 176-85, esp. 178-81; also Merkelbach, "Mithras, Mithraism," *ABD* 4.877-78.

17. Winter, "Messiah as the Tutor," 152-57.

18. Also Vaage, "Woes in Q," 582-607.

19. For a discussion of "woes," see Garland, *Intention,* 64-90, who also sees them as announcing judgment.

20. On 23:14 as a later interpolation, see Metzger, *Textual Commentary,* 60.

21. Segal, "Costs of Proselytism and Conversion," 336-67.

22. Kuhn, "προσήλυτος," *TDNT* 6:727-34; Stuehrenberg, "Proselyte," *ABD* 5:503-5. See also the negative comments by Juvenal, *Sat* 14.96-106, and Dio 57.18.5; 67.14.2.

23. Garland (*Intention,* 134-35), for instance, suggests that the temple gold and altar gift (23:18) legitimate valid oaths because they are associated with *korban* (cf. 15:4-6), while the temple and altar themselves, not linked to *korban,* are invalid for binding oaths.

24. Davies and Allison, *Matthew,* 3:259, guilty of economic sins; guilty of sexual sins; hypocrisy.

25. Levine, *Social and Ethnic Dimensions,* 215-22.

26. Stanton, *Gospel for a New People,* 232-55, esp. 249-51.

27. Davies and Allison, *Matthew,* 3:323-24.

24. Jesus' Fifth Teaching Discourse:
The Final Establishment of God's Empire (Part 1)

1. Cf 7:21-27; 8:11-12; 10:15, 23, 32-33; 11:20-24; 13:36-43, 47-50; 16:27-28; 18:8-9, 35; 19:28-30; 22:23-33; 23:37-39.

2. Garland, *Reading Matthew,* 234-36.

3. Hagner, *Matthew,* 2:683-85, 688-89.

4. Gnilka, *Matthäusevangelium,* 2:309-33; Harrington, *Gospel of Matthew,* 331-41; Lambrecht, "Parousia Discourse," 319, "the phases of the future."

5. Davies and Allison, *Matthew,* 3:331.

6. For the universal emphasis of chapters 24-25, see Levine, *Social and Ethnic Dimensions,* 222-29.

7. Sim, *Apocalyptic Eschatology,* Summary, 222-42.

8. Käsemann, "Primitive Christian Apocalyptic," 135.

9. Mauser, "Christian Community," 50-51. Mauser notes the following links between Matthew 24 and Josephus's (disapproving) description of the Jewish Revolutionaries: (1) *Pseudochrists:* Matt 24:5, 24. In Josephus, Simon (*JW* 2.57-59), Athrongaeus (2.60-65), Menachem (2.433-40), and Simon bar Giora (4.503-13) establish themselves, or are treated, as king. (2) *Pseudoprophets:* Matt 24:11, 24. Josephus notes six thousand killed after being deceived by a false prophet into looking for deliverance in the temple (*JW* 6.283-85). He goes on to record many deceptive prophets (6.286-88). Cf. the Egyptian false prophet (2.258-63) and Theudas (*Ant* 20.97). (3) *Deceivers:* Four times Matthew 24 warns against deceivers (24:4, 5, 11, 24). Compare Josephus, *Ant* 20.98; *JW* 2.259; 6.287. (4) *The New Exodus:* Matt 24:24, 26. Josephus notes several groups who look in the desert for God's wonders and signs of freedom (*JW* 2.259, 261-63; *Ant* 20.169-72, 188; cf. in the temple, *JW* 6.285. Also Horsley and Hanson, *Bandits, Prophets, and Messiahs.*

10. The phrase originates from Beker, *Paul the Apostle.*

11. Evans, "Predictions of the Destruction," 89-147.

12. For examples of inscriptions and coins, see Deissmann, *Light from the Ancient East,* 372-78; *BAGD,* 630; Oepke, "παρουσία," *TDNT* 5:858-61; Kreitzer, *Striking New Images,* 146-86, 212-19; for later Christian uses, see MacCormack, "Change and Continuity," 721-52.

13. *BAGD,* 630; Oepke, "παρουσία," *TDNT* 5.860-65.

14. Garnsey, *Famine and Food Supply,* 20-21 in summary.

15. Stark, "Antioch," 206-7.

16. Note that the religious leaders are to flee God's wrath by repenting (3:7), something that in 23:33 seems impossible.

17. Stanton, "'Pray that your Flight may not be in Winter," in *Gospel for a New People,* 192-206; Wong, "Matthean Understanding," 3-18.

18. Kreitzer, *Striking New Images,* 66-67: an aureus depicting an eagle (see 24:28) with a lightning bolt in its claw.

19. Fears, "Theology of Victory at Rome," *ANRW* 2.17.2, p. 817. He provides further examples of coins. Also idem, "Cult of Jupiter," 79.

20. For eight other readings of this verse, none of which sees it representing Rome's judgment, see Davies and Allison, *Matthew,* 3:355-56.

21. Kreitzer, *Striking New Images,* 30-68.

22. Though Beck (*Anti-Roman Cryptograms,* 93-117) does not seem to discuss this chapter or verse as an "anti-Roman cryptogram," this verse provides a fine example of the coded messages of hope and liberation to which Beck helpfully draws attention.

23. Rudolph, "Helios," *ABD* 3:123-25; Scott, *Imperial Cult,* 32-33, 95.

24. Bockmuehl, "'The Trumpet Shall Sound,'" 199-225.

25. For discussion and bibliography, see Heil, "Final Parables in the Eschatological Discourse in Matthew 24-25," in Carter and Heil, *Matthew's Parables,* 190-92.

26. Carter, *Households and Discipleship,* 181-83.

25. Jesus' Fifth Teaching Discourse: The Final Establishment of God's Empire (Part 2)

1. For discussion, see Heil, "Final Parables in the Eschatological Discourse in Matthew 24-25," in Carter and Heil, *Matthew's Parables,* 193-96; Donfried, "Allegory of the Ten Virgins," 415-28.

2. So Donfried, "Allegory of the Ten Virgins," 423.

3. Rohrbaugh, "A Peasant Reading," 32-39; Mattam, "Judgement on the Present Economic Order," 176-80; Herzog, *Parables,* 150-68.

4. Powell, "Weights and Measures," *ABD* 6:907-8.

5. The bibliography for 25:31-46 is enormous (in addition to the following, see the listings in the commentaries of Hagner, and Davies and Allison). See especially Lambrecht, "Parousia Discourse," 329-42; Donahue, "'Parable' of the Sheep and the Goats," 3-31; Stanton, "Once More: Matthew 25:31-46," in Stanton, *Gospel for a New People,* 207-31, 401-3; Heil, "Double Meaning of the Narrative of Universal Judgment," 3-14. On the history of interpretation, see Gray, *Least of My Brothers.*

6. Donahue, "'Parable' of the Sheep and the Goats," 11.

7. Davies and Allison, *Matthew,* 3:422. Their preference is "all humanity."

8. Hare and Harrington ("'Make Disciples of All the Gentiles,'" 359-69) favor a consistent translation "Gentiles," while Meier ("Nations or Gentiles," 94-102) rightly favors a mixed usage dependent on context.

9. Levine, *Social and Ethnic Dimensions,* 233-39, esp. 236.

10. Weber, "Image of the Sheep and Goats," 658-59, 661.

11. On Father, see 5:16, 45, 48; 6:1, 9; 7:21; 10:32; 11:25-27; 12:50; 13:43; 16:17; 23:9; 28:19.

12. Stark, "Antioch," 189-210; idem, "Urban Chaos and Crisis," in Stark, *Rise of Christianity,* 147-62.

13. Davies and Allison (*Matthew* 3:428-29) note three other views which have had little support: Jewish Christians, Christian missionaries or leaders only, those who are not Christian missionaries or leaders.

26. The Passion Narrative: Part 1

1. On the passion narrative, in addition to the commentaries, Carter, *Matthew: Storyteller,* 211-28; Carroll and Green, "'His Blood on Us and on Our Children,'" 39-59; Brown, *Death of the Messiah;* Heil, *Death and Resurrection of Jesus;* Powell, "Plot to Kill Jesus," 603-13; Boff, *Passion of Christ;* Matera, *Passion Narratives and Gospel Theologies,* 86-149; Senior, *Passion of Jesus;* Hendrickx, *Passion Narratives.* Hendrickx and Brown start their discussions at 26:47 and 26:30 respectively.

2. Nickelsburg ("Genre and Function," 154-84) identifies the following components of

the genre: introduction, provocation, conspiracy; decision, trust, obedience; accusation, trial, condemnation, protest, prayer, assistance, ordeal, reactions, rescue; vindication, exaltation, investiture, acclamation, reactions, punishment.

3. See Marcus, "Old Testament and the Death of Jesus," 205-33.

4. See Saldarini, "Sanhedrin," *ABD* 5:975-80, for discussion of this "central council of the highest leaders with broad powers."

5. Historically, his collusion with Rome is attested by his appointment by a Roman official Valerius Gratus, and by his length of occupancy in the office—from 18 to 36 C.E. Josephus also notes that the chief-priestly vestments were kept by Rome in the Antonia Fortress adjacent to the temple (Josephus, *Ant* 18.90-91). Caiaphas's absence from Josephus's descriptions of insurrections against Pilate also suggests his support for Rome. See Chilton, "Caiaphas," *ABD* 1:803-6.

6. Wainwright, *Towards a Feminist Critical Reading,* 124-37; 257-83; Levine, "Matthew," 261.

7. The bibliography on 26:26-29 is enormous. See especially Hagner, *Matthew,* 2:768-70; Davies and Allison, *Matthew,* 3:478-81.

8. Lev 25:10, 11, 12, 13, 28, 30, 31, 33, 40, 41, 50, 52, 54. The NRSV translates it variously as "liberty," "jubilee, "free"; see also Lev 27:17, 18, 21, 23, 24.

9. On **Father**, see 5:16, 45; 6:9; 7:21; 10:32; 11:25; 13:43; 16:17; 23:9; 25:34; 26:29, 38, 42; 28:19.

10. Heil, "Ezekiel 34 and the Narrative Strategy."

11. Gerhardsson, *Testing of God's Son,* 28-31; Houk, "ΠΕΙΡΑΣΜΟΣ, The Lord's Prayer and the Massah Tradition," 216-25.

12. Brown, *Death of the Messiah,* 1:198-200.

13. Ibid., 1:254.

14. Horsley and Hanson, *Bandits, Prophets, and Messiahs,* 48-87; Shaw, "Bandits in the Roman Empire," 3-52.

15. In reading it as an ironic statement, I essentially agree with Senior (*Passion of Jesus,* 93-94). Three other approaches can be noted. (1) One approach asks if it is testimony based on a misunderstanding. Jesus has talked of the temple's destruction (24:2; by whom is unspecified; the passive could imply God, which does not rule out the possibility of human agents), an act that here is attributed to him. He has also talked of being raised **in three days** (16:21; 17:23; 20:19), which may here be misunderstood as a statement about the temple. (2) A second approach argues that while the statement is reported as being about the temple, Jesus may have spoken it about himself as a temple destroyed in crucifixion and built by being raised. So Davies and Allison, *Matthew,* 3:526; Hagner, *Matthew,* 2:798-99. Against this is that there is no evidence for such a statement. The passion predictions are not metaphorical, nor does Jesus claim power to raise himself (the verb is passive in 16:21; 17:9, 23; 20:19). (3) Brown (*Death of the Messiah,* 1.434-60) takes it as a statement made by Jesus. Against this is the absence of any such statement in the gospel.

16. Brown, *Death of the Messiah,* 1:489-92.

17. Beyer, "βλασφημέω, βλασφημία," *TDNT* 1:622; Brown, *Death of the Messiah,* 1.520-27.

18. More personal in that he now refers to "the man" rather than "I don't know what you are talking about." But "the man" is a far cry from "Jesus."

27. The Passion Narrative: Part 2

1. Sherwin-White, *Roman Society,* 35-43.

2. Pilate was governor from 26 to 37 C.E. For historical sources, Philo, *Gaium* 299-305; Josephus, *JW* 2.169-77; *Ant* 18.35, 55-64, 85-99, 177; Tacitus, *Ann* 15.44. See McGing, "Pontius Pilate and the Sources," 416-38; Schwartz, "Pontius Pilate," *ABD* 5.395-401; Brown, *Death of the Messiah,* 1.676-705; Bond, *Pontius Pilate in History and Interpretation,*

1-23, 120-37. I disagree with Bond's claims that Matthew's narrative relegates Pilate to a minor role, depoliticizes the scene and downplays relations with Rome.

3. Weaver, "Power and Powerlessness," 462-66.

4. Sherwin-White, *Roman Society,* 1-23, esp. 12. Governors could be held to account for excessive cruelty and financial extortion.

5. Sherwin-White, *Roman Society,* 32.

6. For further parallels, see Davies and Allison, *Matthew,* 3:565-66.

7. Brown, *Death of the Messiah,* 1:647-52, 657-60; Davies and Allison, *Matthew,* 3.568-71.

8. Gundry, *Matthew,* 561-65.

9. Bond, *Pontius Pilate,* 124-37.

10. Wengst, *PAX ROMANA,* 37-40. See Brown, *Death of the Messiah,* 710-22, 725-29, for comments about the genre and legal features of the narrative.

11. Sherwin-White, *Roman Society,* 24.

12. Horsley and Hanson, *Bandits, Prophets, and Messiahs,* 110-27.

13. For discussion, Brown, *Death of the Messiah,* 814-20.

14. The bibliography is enormous. For some discussion, see Saldarini, *Matthew's Christian-Jewish Community,* 32-34; Brown, *Death of the Messiah,* 1:830-39; Sullivan, "New Insights into Matthew 27:24-25," 453-57; Luz, "Matthew's Anti-Judaism"; Adam, "Matthew's Readers, Ideology, and Power"; Cargal, "'His Blood Be Upon Us and Upon Our Children,'" 101-12; Kosmala, "'His Blood Be Upon Us and Upon Our Children,'" 94-126; Levine, "Anti-Judaism"; Carter, "Response to Amy-Jill Levine."

15. Brown (*Death of the Messiah,* 873-77) discusses four types of mockings of kings in Greco-Roman sources.

16. Gasque, "Cyrene," *ABD* 1:1230-31.

17. Marcus, "Role of Scripture."

18. Hengel, *Crucifixion;* O'Collins, "Crucifixion," *ABD* 1:1207-10.

19. Donaldson, "Mockers and the Son of God," 3-18.

20. Edwards et al., "On the Physical Death," 1455-63.

21. Brown, *Death of the Messiah,* 2:1113-14; Hill, "Matthew 27:51-53"; Senior, "Death of Jesus and the Resurrection of the Holy Ones"; Witherup, "Death of Jesus and the Raising of the Saints."

22. De Jonge, "Matthew 27:51 in Early Christian Exegesis."

23. Contra Sim, "'Confession' of the Soldiers."

24. Also Kim, "Anarthrous υἱὸς θεοῦ."

25. Wainwright, *Towards a Feminist Critical Reading,* 140-42, 293-99.

26. Brown, *Death of the Messiah,* 2:1207-11, for discussion.

27. Carter, "'To See the Tomb': A Note on Matthew's Women."

28. The Resurrection

1. Carter, "'To See the Tomb.'"

2. Drane, "Some Ideas of Resurrection"; Perkins, *Resurrection;* Nickelsburg, "Resurrection (Early Judaism and Christianity)," *ABD* 5:684-91.

3. See its other uses in 9:25 and 12:11 for healing and merciful acts. The other three uses denote violence or arrest (14:3; 18:28; 22:6).

4. The androcentric perspective of the narrative highlights the special role of the eleven male disciples (28:7, 10, 16-20). But the text's attention to the significant and faithful role of the women undermines any attempt to reserve a privileged role for the male disciples. See Wainwright, *Towards a Feminist Critical Reading,* 143-46, 300-314.

5. Hubbard, *Matthean Redaction of a Primitive Apostolic Commissioning.* Hubbard identifies the form, or significant elements thereof, in twenty-seven Hebrew Bible narratives. See also Matt 4:18-22. On this passage, see Kingsbury, "Composition and Christology," 573-

84; Donaldson, *Jesus on the Mountain,* 170-90; Perkins, "Matthew 28:16-20"; eadem, *Resurrection,* 124-47; Smith, "Matthew 28:16-20, Anti-Climax or Key to the Gospel?" Smith helpfully highlights christological, ecclesial, and especially ethical dimensions of reading this text.

6. Also quoted by Davies and Allison, *Matthew,* 3:680.

7. See the helpful review of options in Hagner, *Matthew,* 2:884-85.

8. The verb "give" in this verse is *didōmi* (δίδωμι), while the verb "hand over" which has been so prevalent through the passion predictions and narrative is a compound form of the same verb *paradidōmi* (παραδίδωμι).

9. For discussion of this command in relation to its use in eighteenth- and nineteenth-century colonializing missions, see Sugirtharajah, "Postcolonial Exploration," esp. 95-100.

10. Soares-Prabhu, "Jesus the Teacher."

11. Van Unnik, "'*Dominus Vobiscum*'"; Kupp, *Matthew's Emmanuel,* 201-19.

12. Kreitzer, *Striking New Images,* 69-98; Scott, *Imperial Cult,* 61-82.

13. For discussion, see Eden (ed.), *Seneca: Apocolocyntosis.*

Appendix: The Plot of Matthew's Gospel

1. Burridge, *What Are the Gospels?* 109-219.

2. Carter, "Kernels and Narrative Blocks," 463-81; idem, *Matthew: Storyteller,* 149-75; Chatman, *Story and Discourse,* 53-56. Chatman identifies the key scenes as *kernels* and the remaining scenes in a narrative block as *satellites.* For other options, see Bauer, *Structure;* Carter, "Kernels and Narrative Blocks," 463-66.

Bibliography

Adam, A. K. M. "Matthew's Readers, Ideology, and Power." In *Society of Biblical Literature 1994 Seminar Papers,* edited by E. H. Lovering Jr., 435-49. SBLSP 33. Atlanta: Scholars Press, 1994.

Alcock, S. "Archaeology and Imperialism: Roman Expansion and the Greek City." *Journal of Mediterranean Archaeology* 2 (1989) 87-135.

———. "Roman Imperialism in the Greek Landscape." *Journal of Roman Archaeology* 2 (1989) 5-34.

Alexander, L. (ed.). *Images of Empire.* JSOTSup 122. Sheffield: Sheffield Academic Press, 1991.

Allen, W. *A Critical and Exegetical Commentary on the Gospel According to S. Matthew.* ICC. Edinburgh: T & T Clark, 1907.

Allison, D. *The New Moses: A Matthean Typology.* Minneapolis: Augsburg Fortress, 1993.

———. "Divorce, Celibacy and Joseph (Matthew 1:18-25 and 19:1- 12)." *JSNT* 49 (1993) 3-10.

———. "The Hairs of Your Head Are All Numbered." *ExpT* 101 (1990) 334-36.

———. *The End of the Ages Has Come.* Philadelphia: Fortress, 1985.

Anderson, H. "4 Maccabees." In *The Old Testament Pseudepigrapha,* edited by J. H. Charlesworth, 2:531-64. 2 vols. Garden City, N.Y.: Doubleday, 1983, 1985.

Anderson, J. C. *Matthew's Narrative Web: Over, and Over, and Over, Again.* JSNTSup 91. Sheffield: JSOT Press, 1994.

———. "Mary's Difference: Gender and Patriarchy in the Birth Narratives." *Journal of Religion* 67 (1987) 183-202.

———. "Matthew: Gender and Reading." *Semeia* 28 (1983) 3-28.

Arlandson, J. M. *Women, Class, and Society in Early Christianity: Models from Luke-Acts.* Peabody, Mass.: Hendrickson, 1997.

Ascough, R. *What Are They Saying About the Formation of Pauline Churches?* New York: Paulist, 1998.

———. "Translocal Relationships among Voluntary Associations and Early Christianity." *JECS* 5 (1997) 223-41.

Aune, D. *Prophecy in Early Christianity and the Ancient Mediterranean World.* Grand Rapids: Eerdmans, 1983.

Austin, J. A. *How to Do Things with Words.* Cambridge, Mass.: Harvard University Press, 1962.

Badian, E. *Publicans and Sinners: Private Enterprise in the Service of the Roman Republic.* Ithaca, N.Y.: Cornell University Press, 1972.

Bailey, R. C. "Eliam." *ABD* 2:459-60.

Balch, D. "Neopythagorean Moralists and the New Testament Household." *ANRW* 26.1 (1992) 380-411.

———. "The Greek Political Topos περὶ νόμων and Matthew 5:17, 19, and 16:19." In *Social History of the Matthean Community: Cross-Disciplinary Approaches,* edited by D. Balch, 68-84. Minneapolis: Augsburg Fortress, 1991.

———. "Two Apologetic Encomia: Dionysius on Rome and Josephus on the Jews." *JSJ* 13 (1982) 102-22.

———. *Let Wives Be Submissive: The Domestic Code of 1 Peter.* SBLMS 26. Chico, Calif: Scholars Press, 1981.

———— (ed.). *Social History of the Matthean Community.* Minneapolis: Fortress, 1991.

Balch, D., and C. Osiek. *Families in the New Testament World: Households and House Churches.* Louisville, Ky.: Westminster/John Knox, 1997.

Ballard, P. H. "Reasons for Refusing the Great Supper." *JTS* 23 (1972) 341-50.

Barclay, J. M. G. *Jews in the Mediterranean Diaspora: From Alexander to Trajan (323 BCE–117 CE).* Edinburgh: T & T Clark, 1996.

Barnett, P. W. "The Jewish Sign Prophets A.D. 40-70." *NTS* 27 (1981) 679-97.

————. "Who were the *Biastai* (Mt 11:12-13)?" *Reformed Theological Review* 36 (1977) 65-70.

Barth, G. "Matthew's Understanding of the Law." In G. Bornkamm, G. Barth, and H. J. Held, *Tradition and Interpretation in Matthew,* 58-164. London: SCM, 1963.

Barton, S. C. *Discipleship and Family Ties in Mark and Matthew.* SNTSMS 80. Cambridge: Cambridge University Press, 1994.

Barton, S. C., and G. H. R. Horsley. "A Hellenistic Cult Group and the New Testament Churches." *JAC* 24 (1981) 7-41.

Batey, R. "Is Not This the Carpenter?" *NTS* 30 (1984) 249-58.

Batto, B. "The Sleeping God: An Ancient Near Eastern Motif of Divine Sovereignty." *Bib* 68 (1987) 153-77.

Bauckham, R. "The Economic Critique of Rome in Revelation 18." In R. Bauckham, *The Climax of Prophecy: Studies in the Book of Revelation,* 338-83. Edinburgh: T & T Clark, 1993.

———— (ed.). *The Gospel for All Christians: Rethinking the Gospel Audiences.* Grand Rapids: Eerdmans, 1998.

Bauer, D. R. "The Literary and Theological Function of the Genealogy in Matthew's Gospel." In *Treasures Old and New: Contributions to Matthean Studies,* edited by D. R. Bauer and M. A. Powell, 129-59. SBL Symposium Series 1. Atlanta: Scholars Press, 1996.

————. "The Kingship of Jesus in the Matthean Infancy Narrative." *CBQ* 57 (1995) 306-23.

————. *The Structure of Matthew's Gospel: A Study in Literary Design.* JSNTSup 31. Sheffield: Almond Press, 1988.

Bauer, D., and M. Powell (eds.). *Treasures Old and New: Contributions to Matthean Studies.* Atlanta: Scholars Press, 1996.

Bauer, W., W. F. Arndt, F. W. Gingrich, F. Danker. *A Greek-English Lexicon of the New Testament and Other Early Christian Literature.* Chicago: University of Chicago Press, 1957, 1979.

Bauernfeind, O. "ἁπλοῦς, ἁπλότης." *TDNT* 1:386-87.

Bauman, C. *The Sermon on the Mount: The Modern Quest for Its Meaning.* Macon, Ga.: Mercer University Press, 1985.

Baumgarten, A. I. "The Pharisaic *Paradosis.*" *HTR* 80 (1987) 63-77.

————. "Korban and the Pharisaic Paradosis." *Journal of the Ancient Near Eastern Society of Columbia University* 16 (1984) 5-17.

Beardslee, W. "Saving One's Life by Losing It." *JAAR* 47 (1979) 57-72.

Beasley-Murray, G. *Baptism in the New Testament.* Grand Rapids: Eerdmans, 1977.

Beavis, M. "Ancient Slavery as an Interpretive Context for the New Testament Servant Parables with Special Reference to the Unjust Steward (Luke 16:1-8)." *JBL* 111 (1992) 37-54.

Beck, N. A. *Anti-Roman Cryptograms in the New Testament.* New York: Peter Lang, 1997.

Beck, R. "The Mysteries of Mithras." In *Voluntary Associations in the Graeco-Roman World,* edited by J. Kloppenborg and S. G. Wilson, 176-85. London and New York: Routledge, 1996.

Behm, J. "μεταμορφόω." *TDNT* 4:755-59.

Beker, J. C. *Paul the Apostle: The Coming Triumph of God.* Philadelphia: Fortress, 1980.

Berger, P. *The Sacred Canopy.* Garden City, NY: Doubleday, 1966.

Berkey, R. "ΕΓΓΙΖΕΙΝ, ΦΘΑΝΕΙΝ, and Realized Eschatology." *JBL* 82 (1963) 177-87.

Betz, H. D. *The Sermon on the Mount: A Commentary on the Sermon on the Mount, including The Sermon on the Plain (Matthew 5:3-7:27 and Luke 6:20-49).* Minneapolis: Augsburg Fortress, 1995.

————. *The Greek Magical Papyri in Translation Including the Demotic Spells.* 2nd ed. Chicago: University of Chicago Press, 1992.

————. *Plutarch's Ethical Writings and Early Christian Literature.* Leiden: Brill, 1978.

————. "The Logion of the Easy Yoke and of the Rest (Mt 11:28-30)." *JBL* 86 (1967) 10-24.

Betz, H. D., and J. M. Dillon. "De Cohibenda Ira (*Moralia* 452E- 464D)." In *Plutarch's Ethical Writings and Early Christian Literature,* edited by H. D. Betz, 170-97. Leiden: Brill, 1978.

Beyer, H. "βλασφημέω, βλασφημία." *TDNT* 1:621-25.

Bilde, P. "The Causes of the Jewish War According to Josephus." *JSJ* 10 (1979) 179-202.

Blass, F., A. Debrunner, and R. W. Funk. *A Greek Grammar of the New Testament and Other Early Christian Literature.* Chicago: University of Chicago Press, 1961.

Boatwright, M. T. "Plancia Magna of Perge: Women's Role and Status in Roman Asia Minor." In *Women's History and Ancient History,* edited by S. B. Pomeroy, 249-72. Chapel Hill: University of North Carolina Press, 1991.

Bockmuehl, M. "'The Trumpet Shall Sound': *Shofar* Symbolism and Its Reception in Early Christianity." In *Templum Amicitiae: Essays on the Second Temple presented to Ernst Bammel,* edited by W. Horbury, 199-225. JSNTSup 48. Sheffield: JSOT Press, 1991.

Boff, L. *Passion of Christ, Passion of the World.* Maryknoll, N.Y.: Orbis Books, 1987.

————. *The Lord's Prayer: The Prayer of Integral Liberation.* Maryknoll, N.Y.: Orbis, 1977.

Bond, H. *Pontius Pilate in History and Interpretation.* SNTSMS 100. Cambridge: Cambridge University Press, 1998.

Bonnard, P. *L'Evangile selon Saint Matthieu.* 2nd ed. Neuchâtel: Delachaux & Niestlé, 1970.

Boring, M. "Prophecy (Early Christian)." *ABD* 5:495-502.

Bornkamm, G. "Der Aufbau der Bergpredigt." *NTS* 24 (1977-78) 419-32.

————. "The Stilling of the Storm in Matthew." In G. Bornkamm, G. Barth, and H. J. Held, *Tradition and Interpretation in Matthew,* 52-57. London: SCM, 1963.

————. "End-Expectation and Church in Matthew." In G. Bornkamm, G. Barth, and H. J. Held, *Tradition and Interpretation in Matthew,* 15-56. London: SCM, 1963.

————. "μυστήριον." *TDNT* 4:802-27.

————. "πρέσβυς, πρεσβύτερος." *TDNT* 6:651-83.

Bornkamm, G., G. Barth, and H. J. Held. *Tradition and Interpretation in Matthew.* London: SCM, 1963.

Bowersock, G. W. "The Mechanics of Subversion in the Roman Provinces." In *Opposition et Résistances à L'Empire d'Auguste à Trajan,* edited by A. Giovannini, 291-320. Entretiens sur L'Antiquité Classique 33. Geneva: Fondation Hardt, 1987.

Bowman, R., and R. W. Swanson. "Samson and the Son of God or Dead Heroes and Dead Goats: Ethical Readings of Narrative Violence in Judges and Matthew." *Semeia* 77 (1997) 59-73.

Brannigan, K. "Images—or Mirages—of Empire." In *Images of Empire,* edited by L. Alexander, 91-105. JSOTSup 122; Sheffield: JSOT Press, 1991.

Braund, D. C. "Herod Antipas." *ABD* 3:160.

————. "Philip." *ABD* 5:310-11.

————. *Augustus to Nero: A Sourcebook on Roman History, 31 BC-AD 68.* London and Sydney: Croom Helm, 1985.

Braund, S. H. "Juvenal and the East: Satire as an Historical Source." In *The Eastern Frontier of the Roman Empire,* edited by D. H. French and C. S. Lightfoot, 45-52. BARIS 553 [i]. Oxford: B.A.R., 1989.

————. "City and Country in Roman Satire." In *Satire and Society in Ancient Rome,* edited by S. H. Braund, 23-47. Exeter Studies in Religion 23. Exeter: University of Exeter Press, 1989.

Breech, J. *The Silence of Jesus: The Authentic Voice of the Historical Man.* Philadelphia: Fortress, 1983.

Brooten, B. *Women Leaders in the Ancient Synagogue: Inscriptional Evidence and Background Issues.* Brown Judaic Studies 36. Chico, Calif.: Scholars Press, 1982.

————. "Konnten Frauen im alten Judentum die Scheidung betreiben?" *EvT* 42 (1982) 65-80.

Broughton, T. R. "Roman Asia Minor." In *An Economic Survey of Ancient Rome,* edited by T. Frank, 4:499-916. 6 vols. New York: Octagon Books, 1975.

Brown, J. P. "Techniques of Imperial Control: The Background of the Gospel Event." In *The Bible and Liberation: Political and Social Hermeneutics,* edited by N. Gottwald, 357-77. Maryknoll, N.Y.: Orbis Books, 1983.

Brown, R. E. *The Death of the Messiah.* 2 vols. New York: Doubleday, 1994.

————. *The Birth of the Messiah.* Rev. and updated ed. New York: Doubleday, 1993.

Brown, R. E., and J. P. Meier. *Antioch and Rome: New Testament Cradles of Catholic Christianity.* New York: Paulist, 1983.

Brown, R., et al., *Peter in the New Testament.* New York: Paulist; Minneapolis: Augsburg, 1973.

Bruce, F. F. "Render to Caesar." In *Jesus and the Politics of His Day,* edited by E. Bammel and C. F. D. Moule, 249-63. Cambridge: Cambridge University Press, 1984.

Brueggemann, W. *Genesis.* Atlanta: John Knox, 1982.

————. "Of the Same Flesh and Bone, Gen 2:23a." *CBQ* 32 (1970) 532-42.

Brunt, P. A. "Labour." In J. Wacher, *The Roman World,* 2:701-16. 2 vols. London and New York: Routledge, 1987, 1990.

————. "Laus imperii." In *Imperialism in the Ancient World,* edited by P. D. A. Garnsey and C. R. Whittaker, 159-91. Cambridge: Cambridge University Press, 1978.

————. "The Romanization of the Ruling Classes in the Roman Empire." In *Assimilation et résistance à la culture greco-romaine dans le monde ancien,* edited by D. M. Pippidi, 161-73. Bucharest: Editura Academiei, 1976.

Büchsel, F. "δέω (λύω)." *TDNT* 2:60-61.

————. "παλιγγενεσία." *TDNT* 1:686-89.

Bultmann, R. "μεριμνάω." *TDNT* 4:589-93.

Bureth, P. *Les Titulatures impériales dans les papyrus, les ostraca et les inscriptions d'Égypte.* Bruxelles: Fondation Égyptologique Reine Élisabeth, 1964.

Burgess, J. A. *A History of the Exegesis of Matthew 16:17-19 from 1781 to 1965.* Ann Arbor, Mich.: Edwards Brothers, 1976.

Burnett, F. W. "Exposing the Anti-Jewish Ideology of Matthew's Implied Author: The Characterization of God as Father." *Semeia* 59 (1992) 155-91.

————. "Philo on Immortality: A Thematic Study of Philo's Concept of παλιγγενεσία." *CBQ* 46 (1984) 447-70.

————. "παλιγγενεσία in Matt 19:28: A Window on the Matthean Community?" *JSNT* 17 (1983) 60-72.

Burridge, R. A. *What Are the Gospels? A Comparison with Graeco-Roman Biography.* SNTSMS 70. Cambridge: Cambridge University Press, 1992.

Cameron, P. S. *Violence and the Kingdom: The Interpretation of Matthew 11:12.* ANTJ 5. Frankfurt: P. Lang, 1984.

Cameron, R. "'What Have You Come Out to See?' Characterizations of John and Jesus in the Gospels." *Semeia* 49 (1990) 35-69.

Campbell, J. Y. "The Origin and Meaning of the Christian Use of the Word *Ekklesia.*" *JTS* 49 (1948) 130-42.

Campbell, K. M. "The New Jerusalem in Matthew 5:14." *SJT* 31 (1978) 335-63.

Cargal, T. B. "'His Blood Be Upon Us and Upon Our Children': A Matthean Double Entendre?" *NTS* 37 (1991) 101-12.

Carlston, C. *The Parables of the Triple Tradition.* Philadelphia: Fortress, 1975.

Carney, T. F. *The Shape of the Past: Models and Antiquity.* Lawrence, Ks.: Coronado Press, 1975.

Carroll, J. T., and J. B. Green. "'His Blood on Us and on Our Children': The Death of Jesus in the Gospel according to Matthew." In *The Death of Jesus in Early Christianity,* edited by J. T. Carroll and J. B. Green, 39-59. Peabody, Mass.: Hendrickson, 1995.

Carson, D. A. "The ΟΜΟΙΟΣ Word-Group as Introduction to Some Matthean Parables." *NTS* 31 (1985) 277-82.

Carter, W. "'To Save His People from Their Sins' (Matt 1:21): Rome's Empire and Matthew's Salvation as Sovereignty." In *Society of Biblical Literature 2000 Seminar Papers.* SBLSP 39. Atlanta: Scholars Press, 2000.

———. "Evoking Isaiah and Matthean Soteriology: An Intertextual Anti-Imperial Reading of Isaiah 7-9 in Matthew 1:23 and 4:15-16." *JBL* 119 (2000) 503-20.

———. "Paying the Tax to Rome as Subversive Praxis: Matthew 17:24-27." *JSNT* 76 (1999) 3-31.

———. "Contested Claims: Roman Imperial Ideology and Matthew's Gospel." *BTB* 29 (1999) 56-67.

———. "Response to Amy-Jill Levine." In *Anti-Judaism and the Gospels,* edited by W. R. Farmer, 47-62. Harrisburg, Pa.: Trinity Press International, 1999.

———. "Jesus' 'I have come' Statements in Matthew's Gospel." *CBQ* 60 (1998) 44-62.

———. "Toward an Imperial-Critical Reading of Matthew's Gospel." In *Society of Biblical Literature 1998 Seminar Papers: Part One,* 296-324. SBLSP 37. Atlanta: Scholars Press, 1998.

———. "Matthew 4:18-22 and Matthean Discipleship: An Audience-Oriented Perspective." *CBQ* 59 (1997) 58-75.

———. "Community Definition and Matthew's Gospel." In *Society of Biblical Literature 1997 Seminar Papers,* 637-63. SBLSP 36. Atlanta: Scholars Press, 1997.

———. "'Solomon in all his Glory': Intertextuality and Matthew 6:29." *JSNT* 65 (1997) 3-25.

———. "Narrative/Literary Approaches to Matthean Theology: The 'Reign of the Heavens' as an Example (Mt 4:17-5:12)." *JSNT* 67 (1997) 3-27.

———. *Matthew: Storyteller, Interpreter, Evangelist.* Peabody, Mass.: Hendrickson, 1996.

———. "'To See the Tomb': A Note on Matthew's Women at the Tomb (Matt 28:1)." *ExpT* 107 (1996) 201-5.

———. "Some Contemporary Scholarship on the Sermon on the Mount." *Currents in Research: Biblical Studies* 4 (1996) 183-214.

———. "Challenging by Confirming, Renewing by Repeating: The Parables of 'the Reign of the Heavens' in Matthew 13 as Embedded Narratives." In *Society of Biblical Literature 1995 Seminar Papers,* 399-424. SBLSP 34. Atlanta: Scholars Press, 1995.

———. "Recalling the Lord's Prayer: The Authorial Audience and Matthew's Prayer as Familiar Liturgical Experience." *CBQ* 57 (1995) 514-30.

———. *What Are They Saying About Matthew's Sermon on the Mount?* New York: Paulist, 1994.

———. *Households and Discipleship: A Study of Matthew 19-20.* JSNTSup 103. Sheffield: JSOT Press, 1994.

———. "The Crowds in Matthew's Gospel." *CBQ* 55 (1993) 54-67.

———. "Kernels and Narrative Blocks: The Structure of Matthew's Gospel." *CBQ* 54 (1992) 463-83.

————. "The Prologue and John's Gospel: Function, Symbol and the Definitive Word." *JSNT* 39 (1990) 35-58.

Carter, W., and J. P. Heil. *Matthew's Parables: Audience-Oriented Perspectives.* CBQMS 30. Washington, D.C.: Catholic Biblical Association, 1998.

Cassidy, R. J. "Matthew 17:24-27—A Word on Civil Taxes." *CBQ* 41 (1979) 571-80.

Catchpole, D. R. "The 'Triumphal' Entry." In *Jesus and the Politics of His Day,* edited by E. Bammel and C. F. D. Moule, 319-34. Cambridge: Cambridge University Press, 1984.

————. "On Doing Violence to the Kingdom." *IBS* 3 (1981) 77-91.

Chandler, T., and G. Fox. *Three Thousand Years of Urban Growth.* New York: Academic Press, 1974.

Charette, B. "'Never Has Anything Like This Been Seen in Israel': The Spirit as Eschatological Sign in Matthew's Gospel." *Journal of Pentecostal Theology* 8 (1996) 31-51.

————. "'To Proclaim Liberty to the Captives': Matthew 11:28-30 in the Light of OT Prophetic Expectation." *NTS* 38 (1992) 290-97.

Charlesworth, J. H. (ed.). *The Messiah: Developments in Earliest Judaism and Christianity.* Minneapolis: Fortress, 1992.

Charlesworth, M. P. *Trade Routes and Commerce of the Roman Empire.* 2nd rev. ed. New York: Cooper Square, 1970.

Chatman, S. *Story and Discourse.* Ithaca, N.Y.: Cornell University Press, 1978.

Chilton, B. "Caiaphas." *ABD* 1:803-6.

————. "A Coin of Three Realms (Matthew 17.24-27)." In *The Bible in Three Dimensions,* edited by D. J. A. Clines, S. E. Fowl, and S. E. Porter, 269-82. JSOTSup 87. Sheffield: JSOT Press, 1990.

————. "REGNUM DEI DEUS EST." *SJT* 31 (1978) 261-70.

Clark, K. W. "The Gentile Bias." In K. W. Clark, *The Gentile Bias and Other Essays,* 1-8. Leiden: Brill, 1980.

————. "The Meaning of [κατα]κυριεύειν." In K. W. Clark, *The Gentile Bias and Other Essays,* 207-12. Leiden: Brill, 1980.

Cohen, S. J. D. "Menstruants and the Sacred in Judaism and Christianity. In *Women's History and Ancient History,* edited by S. B. Pomeroy, 273-99. Chapel Hill: University of North Carolina Press, 1991.

————. *From the Maccabees to the Mishnah.* Philadelphia: Westminster, 1987.

Cohn-Sherbok, D. M. "An Analysis of Jesus' Arguments concerning the Plucking of Grain on the Sabbath." *JSNT* 2 (1979) 31-41.

Collins, J. J. "The Kingdom of God in the Apocrypha and Pseudepigrapha." In *The Kingdom of God in 20th-Century Interpretation,* edited by W. Willis, 81-95. Peabody, Mass.: Hendrickson, 1987.

————. *Between Athens and Jerusalem: Jewish Identity in the Hellenistic Diaspora.* New York: Crossroad, 1986.

Collins, J. N. *DIAKONIA: Re-interpreting the Ancient Sources.* New York: Oxford University Press, 1990.

Collins, R. "Binding and Loosing." *ABD* 1:743-45.

Comber, J. A. "The Verb THERAPEUŌ in Matthew's Gospel." *JBL* 97 (1978) 431-34.

————. "The Composition and Literary Characteristics of Matthew 11:20-24." *CBQ* 39 (1977) 497-504.

Cope, O. L. "'To The Close of the Age': The Role of Apocalyptic Thought in the Gospel of Matthew." In *Apocalyptic in the New Testament,* edited by J. Marcus and M. Soards, 113-24. JSNTSup 24; Sheffield: JSOT Press, 1989.

Corbier, M. "City, Territory, and Taxation." In *City and Country in the Ancient World,* edited by J. Rich and A. Wallace-Hadrill, 211-39. New York: Routledge, 1991.

Corbo, V. "Capernaum," *ABD* 1:866-69.

Corley, K. "Jesus' Table Practice: Dining with 'Tax Collectors and Sinners,' including

Women." In *Society of Biblical Literature 1993 Seminar Papers,* edited by E. Lovering Jr., 444-59. Atlanta: Scholars Press, 1993.

―――. *Private Women, Public Meals: Social Conflict in the Synoptic Tradition.* Peabody, Mass.: Hendrickson, 1993.

Cotter, W. J. "The Collegia and Roman Law: State Restrictions on Voluntary Associations 64 BCE-200 CE." In *Voluntary Associations in the Graeco-Roman World,* edited by J. S. Kloppenborg and S. G. Wilson, 74-89. London and New York: Routledge, 1996.

―――. "The Parable of the Children in the Market-Place, Q (Lk) 7:31-38: An Examination of the Parable's Image and Significance." *NovT* 29 (1987) 289-304.

Cox, P. C. *Dreams in Late Antiquity: Studies in the Imagination of a Culture.* Princeton, N.J.: Princeton University Press, 1994.

Cramer, F. H. "Expulsions of Astrologers from Ancient Rome." *Classica et Mediaevalia* 12 (1951) 9-50.

Crenshaw, J. *A Whirlpool of Torment: Israelite Traditions of God as an Oppressive Presence.* OBT 12. Philadelphia: Fortress, 1984.

Crook, J. A. "Titus and Berenice." *American Journal of Philology* 72 (1951) 162-75.

Crosby, M. *House of Disciples: Church, Economics and Justice in Matthew.* Maryknoll, N.Y.: Orbis Books, 1988.

―――. *Thy Will Be Done: Praying the Our Father as Subversive Activity.* Maryknoll, N.Y.: Orbis Books, 1977.

Crossan, J. D. "Parable." *ABD* 5:146-52.

Culbertson, P. "Reclaiming the Matthean Vineyard Parables." *Encounter* 49 (1988) 257-83.

Cullmann, O. *Prayer in the New Testament.* Minneapolis: Fortress, 1995.

D'Arms, J. H. "Slaves at Roman Convivia." In *Dining in a Classical Context,* edited by W. Sater, 171-83. Ann Arbor: University of Michigan Press, 1991.

Davies, R. W. "The Daily Life of the Roman Soldier under the Principate." *ANRW* 2.1.299-338.

Davies, W. D. *The Setting of the Sermon on the Mount.* Cambridge: Cambridge University Press, 1964.

Davies, W. D., and D. C. Allison. *The Gospel According to Saint Matthew.* 3 vols. ICC. Edinburgh: T & T Clark, 1988-97.

Deatrick, E. P. "Salt, Soil, Savour." *BA* 25 (1962) 41-48.

de Boer, M. "Ten Thousand Talents? Matthew's Interpretation and Redaction of the Parable of the Unforgiving Servant (Matt 18:23-35)." *CBQ* 50 (1988) 214-32.

de Coulanges, N. D. F. *The Ancient City.* Translated by W. Small. Garden City, N.Y.: Doubleday, 1873, 1976.

Deissmann, A. *Light from the Ancient East.* New York: Hodder & Stoughton, 1910.

de Jonge, M. "Messiah." *ABD* 4:777-88.

―――. "Matthew 27:51 in Early Christian Exegesis." *HTR* 79 (1986) 67-79.

de Lange, N. R. M. "Jewish Attitudes to the Roman Empire." In *Imperialism in the Ancient World,* edited by P. D. A. Garnsey and C. R. Whittaker, 255-81. Cambridge: Cambridge University Press, 1978.

Delling, G. "μάγος." *TDNT* 4:356-59.

―――. "τέλος." *TDNT* 8:49-87.

Dermience, A. "La péricope de la Cananéenne (Mt 15, 21-28): Rédaction et théologie." *EThL* 58 (1982) 25-49.

Derrett, J. D. M. "Every 'Idle' Word That Men [*sic*] Speak [Mt 12:36]." *Estudios Bíblicos* 56 (1998) 261-65.

―――. "Law in the New Testament: The Palm Sunday Colt." *NovT* 13 (1971) 241-58.

―――. "Law in the New Testament: The Parable of the Unmerciful Servant." In *Law in the New Testament.* London: Darton, Longman & Todd, 1970.

de Ste. Croix, G. E. M. *The Class Struggle in the Ancient Greek World.* Ithaca, N.Y.: Cornell University Press, 1981.

Deutsch, C. M. *Lady Wisdom, Jesus, and the Sages: Metaphor and Social Context in Matthew's Gospel.* Valley Forge, Pa.: Trinity Press International, 1996.

―――. *Hidden Wisdom and the Easy Yoke: Wisdom, Torah and Discipleship in Matthew 11:25-30.* JSNTSup 18. Sheffield: JSOT Press, 1987.

de Vaux, R. "Les sacrifices de porcs en Palestine et dans l'Ancien Orient." In *Von Ugarit nach Qumran: Beiträge zur altestamenlichen und altorientalischen Forschung,* edited by J. Hempel and L. Rast, 250-65. BZAW 77. Berlin: Töpelmann, 1958.

Dillon, R. J. "Towards a Tradition-History of the Parables of the True Israel." *Bib* 47 (1966) 1-42.

Dittenberger, W. *Orientis Graeci Inscriptiones Selectae.* 2 vols. Leipzig: Hirzel, 1903-5.

Dobson, B. "The Significance of the Centurion and 'Primipilaris' in the Roman Army and Administration." *ANRW* 2.1.395-433.

Dodd, C. H. *The Parables of the Kingdom.* New York: Scribner's, 1961.

Dodds, E. R. *Pagan and Christian in an Age of Anxiety: Some Aspects of Religious Experience from Marcus Aurelius to Augustine.* New York: Norton, 1965.

Donahue, J. R. "Tax Collector." *ABD* 6:337-38.

―――. *The Gospel in Parable: Metaphor, Narrative, and Theology in the Synoptic Gospels.* Philadelphia: Fortress, 1988.

―――. "The 'Parable' of the Sheep and the Goats: A Challenge to Christian Ethics." *TS* 47 (1986) 3-31.

―――. "Tax Collectors and Sinners: An Attempt at Identification." *CBQ* 33 (1971) 39-61.

Donaldson, T. L. "The Mockers and the Son of God (Matthew 27:37- 44)." *JSNT* 41 (1991) 3-18.

―――. *Jesus on the Mountain: A Study of Matthean Theology.* JSNTSup 8. Sheffield: JSOT Press, 1985.

Donfried, K. P. "The Allegory of the Ten Virgins (Matt 25:1-13) as a Summary of Matthean Theology." *JBL* 93 (1974) 415-28.

Douglas, M. "Deciphering a Meal." In *Myth, Symbol, and Culture,* edited by C. Geertz, 61-81. New York: Norton, 1971.

Douglas, R. C. "Matthew 18:15-17 and the Hellenistic-Roman *Polis.*" Unpublished paper.

Downey, G. *Ancient Antioch.* Princeton, N.J.: Princeton University Press, 1963.

―――. *A History of Antioch in Syria From Seleucus to the Arab Conquest.* Princeton: Princeton University Press, 1961.

―――. "The Water Supply of Antioch on the Orontes in Antiquity." *Les Annales archéologiques de Syrie* 1 (1951) 171-87.

Downing, F. G. "Cynics and Christians." *NTS* 30 (1984) 584-92.

Drane, J. W. "Some Ideas of Resurrection in the New Testament Period." *TynBul* 24 (1973) 99-110.

Driver, T. *The Magic of Ritual: Our Need for Liberating Rites That Transform Our Lives and Our Communities.* San Francisco: HarperSanFrancisco, 1991.

Droge, A. J. "Call Stories in Greek Biography and the Gospels." In *Society of Biblical Literature 1983 Seminar Papers,* edited by K. H. Richards, 245-57. SBLSP 22. Chico, Calif.: Scholars Press, 1983.

Drury, J. *The Parables in the Gospels: History and Allegory.* New York: Crossroad, 1985.

Dube, M. W. "Readings of *Semoya*: Batswana Women's Interpretation of Matt 15:21-28." *Semeia* 73 (1996) 111-29.

Duff, P. B. "The March of the Divine Warrior and the Advent of the Greco-Roman King: Mark's Account of Jesus' Entry into Jerusalem." *JBL* 111 (1992) 55-71.

Duling, D. "Matthew 18:15-17: Conflict, Confrontation, and Conflict Resolution in a 'Fictive Kin' Association." *BTB* 29 (1999) 4-22.

————. "Matthew 18:15-17: Conflict, Confrontation, and Conflict Resolution in a 'Fictive Kin' Association." In *Society of Biblical Literature 1998 Seminar Papers,* 253-95. SBLSP 37. Atlanta: Scholars Press, 1998.

————. "Matthew." *ABD* 4:618-22.

————. "Matthew and Marginality." In *Society of Biblical Literature 1993 Seminar Papers,* edited by E. H. Lovering Jr., 642-71. SBLSP 32. Atlanta: Scholars Press, 1993.

————. "The Matthean Brotherhood and Marginal Scribal Leadership." In *Modelling Early Christianity,* edited by P. F. Esler, 159-82. London: Routledge, 1995.

————. "The Therapeutic Son of David: An Element in Matthew's Christological Apologetic." *NTS* 24 (1977-78) 392-410.

————. "Solomon, Exorcism, and the Son of David." *HTR* 68 (1975) 235-52.

Dunn, J. D. G. *The Theology of Paul the Apostle.* Grand Rapids: Eerdmans, 1998.

————. "Jesus and Factionalism in Early Judaism." In *Hillel and Jesus: Comparative Studies of Two Major Religious Figures,* edited by J. H. Charlesworth and L. L. Johns, 156-75. Minneapolis: Fortress, 1997.

————. *Jesus, Paul, and the Law: Studies in Mark and Galatians.* Louisville, Ky.: Westminster/John Knox Press, 1990.

————. *Romans 1-8; 9-16.* 2 vols. WBC 38A. Dallas: Word, 1988.

————. *Baptism in the Spirit.* London: SCM, 1970.

Dyson, S. "Native Revolts in the Roman Empire." *Historia* 20 (1971) 239-74.

Eddy, S. *The King is Dead: Studies in the Near Eastern Resistance to Hellenism, 334-31 B.C.* Lincoln: University of Nebraska Press, 1961.

Eden, P. T. (ed.). *Seneca: Apocolocyntosis.* Cambridge: Cambridge University Press, 1984.

Edwards, D. R. "Gennesaret." *ABD* 2:963.

Edwards, J. R. "The Use of ΠΡΟΣΕΡΧΕΣΘΑΙ in the Gospel of Matthew." *JBL* 106 (1987) 65-74.

Edwards, R. A. *The Sign of Jonah in the Theology of the Evangelists.* SBT 18. London: SCM, 1971.

Edwards, W. D., J. Gabel, and F. E. Hosmer. "On the Physical Death of Jesus Christ." *Journal of the American Medical Association* 255 (1986) 1455-63.

Eilberg-Schwartz, H. *God's Phallus.* Boston: Beacon Press, 1994.

Eisenbaum, P. M. *The Jewish Heroes of Christian History: Hebrews 11 in Literary Context.* SBLDS 156. Atlanta: Scholars Press, 1997.

Elliott, J. H. "Patronage and Clientage." In *The Social Sciences and New Testament Interpretation,* edited by R. Rohrbaugh, 144-56. Peabody, Mass.: Hendrickson, 1996.

————. "Matthew 20:1-15: A Parable of Invidious Comparison and Evil Eye Accusation." *BTB* 22 (1992) 52-65.

Ellul, D. "Dérives Autour d'un Figuier: Matthieu 21:18-22." *Foi et Vie* 91 (1992) 69-76.

Esler, P. "God's Honour and Rome's Triumph: Responses to the Fall of Jerusalem in 70 CE in Three Jewish Apocalypses." In *Modelling Early Christianity,* edited by P. Esler, 239-58. London and New York: Routledge, 1995.

Evans, C. A. "Predictions of the Destruction of the Herodian Temple in the Pseudepigrapha, Qumran Scrolls, and Related Texts." *JSP* 10 (1992) 89-147.

Fears, J. R. "The Cult of Jupiter and Roman Imperial Ideology." In *ANRW* 2.17.1, 3-141. Berlin and New York. Walter de Gruyter, 1981.

————. "The Cult of Virtues and Roman Imperial Ideology." In *ANRW* 2.17.2, 827-948. Berlin and New York. Walter de Gruyter, 1981.

————. "The Theology of Victory at Rome: Approaches and Problems." In *ANRW* 2.17.2, 736-825. Berlin and New York. Walter de Gruyter, 1981.

————. *Princeps A Diis Electus: The Divine Election of the Emperor as a Political Concept at Rome.* Papers and Monographs of the American Academy in Rome 26. Rome: American Academy in Rome, 1977.

————. "Nero as Vicegerent of the Gods in Seneca's De Clementia." *Hermes* 103 (1975) 486-96.

Fee, G. D. *The First Epistle to the Corinthians.* NICNT. Grand Rapids: Eerdmans, 1987.

Feiler, P. "The Stilling of the Storm in Matthew: A Response to Gunther Bornkamm." *JETS* 26 (1983) 399-406.

Feldman, L. *Studies in Josephus' Rewritten Bible.* Leiden: Brill, 1998.

Ferguson, J. *The Religions of the Roman Empire.* Ithaca, N.Y.: Cornell University Press, 1970.

Fiensy, D. A. *The Social History of Palestine in the Herodian Period: The Land is Mine.* SBEC. Lewiston: Edwin Mellen Press, 1990.

Finley, M. I. *Economy and Society in Ancient Greece.* New York: Viking Press, 1982.

————. "The Fifth-Century Athenian Empire: A Balance-Sheet." In *Imperialism in the Ancient World,* edited by P. D. A. Garnsey and C. R. Whittaker, 103-26. Cambridge: Cambridge University, 1978.

————. "The Ancient City: From Fustel de Coulanges to Max Weber and Beyond." *Comparative Studies in Society and History* 19 (1977) 305-27.

Finley, M. I. (ed.). *Atlas of Classical Archaeology.* New York: McGraw-Hill, 1977.

Firmage, E. "Zoology." *ABD* 6:1109-67.

Fischer, C. S. "Toward a Subcultural Theory of Urbanism." *American Journal of Sociology* 80 (1975) 1319-41.

Fitzgerald, J. T. *Cracks in an Earthern Vessel: An Examination of the Catalogues of Hardships in the Corinthian Correspondence.* SBLDS 99. Atlanta: Scholars Press, 1988.

————. "The Problem of Perjury in Greek Context: Prolegomena to an Exegesis of Matthew 5:33; 1 Timothy 1:10; and Didache 2.3." In *The Social World of the First Christians: Essays in Honor of Wayne A. Meeks,* edited by L. M. White and O. L. Yarbrough, 156-77. Minneapolis: Augsburg Fortress, 1995.

Fitzmyer, J. A. "The Matthean Divorce Texts and Some New Palestinian Evidence." *TS* 37 (1976) 197-226.

Foerster, W. "ἔχιδνα." *TDNT* 2:815-16.

Foley, J. M. *Immanent Art: From Structure to Meaning in Traditional Oral Epic.* Bloomington: Indiana University Press, 1991.

Fortna, R. "'You Have Made Them Equal to Us' (Mt 20:1-16)." *Journal of Theology for Southern Africa* 72 (1990) 66-72.

Frankemölle, H. *Matthäus: Kommentar 1.* Düsseldorf: Patmos Verlag, 1994.

Freire, P. *Pedagogy of the Oppressed.* 1970. New rev. 20th-anniversary ed. New York: Crossroad, 1993.

Freyne, S. *Galilee, Jesus, and the Gospels: Literary Approaches and Historical Investigations.* Philadelphia: Fortress, 1988.

————. "Vilifying the Other and Defining the Self: Matthew's and John's Anti-Jewish Polemic in Focus." In *"To See Ourselves as Others See Us": Christians, Jews, "Others" in Late Antiquity,* edited by J. Neusner and E. S. Frerichs, 117-43. Chico, Calif.: Scholars Press, 1985.

————. *Galilee from Alexander the Great to Hadrian 323 BCE to 134 CE.* Wilmington, Del.: Michael Glazier; Notre Dame, Ind.: University of Notre Dame Press, 1980.

Friedrich, G. "εὐαγγέλιον." *TDNT* 2:721-36.

Gabriel, K. J. "Jesus' Economic Perspective As Presented in Matthew." *Bible Bhashyam* 22 (1996) 200-209.

Gallardo, C. B. "Matthew: Good News for the Persecuted Poor." In *Subversive Scriptures: Revolutionary Readings of the Christian Bible in Latin America,* edited by L. Vaage, 173-92. Valley Forge, Pa.: Trinity Press International, 1997.

Gardner, J. F., and T. Wiedemann (eds.). *The Roman Household.* London: Routledge, 1991.

Garland, D. *Reading Matthew: A Literary and Theological Commentary on the First Gospel.* New York: Crossroad, 1995.

———. "The Temple Tax in Matthew." In *Society of Bibical Literature 1987 Seminar Papers,* edited by K. H. Richards, 190-209. SBLSP 26. Atlanta: Scholars Press, 1987.

———. *The Intention of Matthew 23.* Leiden: Brill, 1979.

Garnsey, P. *Famine and Food Supply in the Graeco-Roman World.* Cambridge: Cambridge University Press, 1988.

———. "Grain for Rome." In *Trade in the Ancient Economy,* edited by P. Garnsey, K. Hopkins, and C. R. Whitaker, 118-30. Berkeley: University of California Press, 1983.

Garnsey, P., K. Hopkins, and C. R. Whitaker (eds.). *Trade in the Ancient Economy.* Berkeley: University of California Press, 1983.

Gasque, W. W. "Cyrene." *ABD* 1:1230-31.

Gerhardsson, B. *The Testing of God's Son (Matt 4:1-11 & Par).* Lund: C. W. K. Gleerup, 1966.

Germani, G. *Marginality.* New Brunswick, N.J.: Transaction Books, 1980.

Giblin, C. H. "'The Things of God' in the Question Concerning Tribute to Caesar (Lk 20:25; Mk 12:17; Mt 22:21)." *CBQ* 33 (1971) 510-27.

Giesen, H. "σκανδαλίζω, σκάνδαλον." *EDNT* 3:248-50.

Gillman, F. *Women Who Knew Paul.* Collegeville, Minn.: Liturgical Press, 1992.

———. "Erastus." *ABD* 2:571.

Giovannini, A. (ed.). *Opposition et Résistances à L'Empire d'Auguste à Trajan.* Entretiens sur L'Antiquité Classique 33. Geneva: Fondation Hardt, 1987.

Gnilka, J. *Matthäusevangelium.* 2 vols. HTKNT. Freiburg: Herder, 1986, 1988.

Goldenberg, R. "The Jewish Sabbath in the Roman World up to the Time of Constantine the Great." *ANRW* 19.1 (1979) 414-47.

Gomme, A. W. "Ecclesia." *Oxford Classical Dictionary,* 303-4. Oxford: Clarendon Press, 1961.

Good, D. "The Verb ΑΝΑΧΩΡΕΩ in Matthew's Gospel." *NovT* 32 (1990) 1-12.

———. *Jesus the Meek King.* Harrisburg, Pa.: Trinity Press International, 1999.

Goodenough, E. R. *Jewish Symbols in the Greco-Roman Period.* Vol. 8. New York: Bollingen Foundation/Pantheon Books, 1958.

Goodman, M. "Nerva, the *Fiscus Judaicus* and Jewish Identity." *JRS* 79 (1989) 40-44.

———. *The Ruling Classes of Judea: The Origins of the Jewish Revolt Against Rome A.D. 66-70.* Cambridge: Cambridge University Press, 1987.

Gottwald, N. *The Hebrew Bible: A Socio-Literary Introduction.* Philadelphia: Fortress, 1985.

———. *The Tribes of Yahweh: A Sociology of the Religion of Liberated Israel, 1250-1050 B.C.E..* Maryknoll, N.Y.: Orbis Books, 1979.

Graef, H. C. (trans.). *St. Gregory of Nyssa: The Lord's Prayer; The Beatitudes.* Ancient Christian Writers 18; Westminster, Md.: Newman Press, 1954.

Grant, R. M. *Early Christianity and Society.* San Francisco: Harper & Row, 1977.

Gray, S. W. *The Least of My Brothers: Matthew 25:31-46: A History of Interpretation.* SBLDS 114. Atlanta: Scholars Press, 1989.

Greeven, H. "προσκυνέω." *TDNT* 6:758-66.

Griffiths, J. G. "The Disciple's Cross." *NTS* 16 (1970) 358-64.

Grundmann, W. *Das Evangelium nach Matthäus.* THKNT. Berlin: Evangelische Verlagsanstalt, 1968.

Guardiola-Sáenz, L. "Borderlesss Women and Borderless Texts: A Cultural Reading on Matthew 15:21-28." *Semeia* 78 (1997) 69-81.

Guelich, R. *The Sermon on the Mount: A Foundation for Understanding.* Dallas: Word, 1982.

———. "The Matthean Beatitudes: 'Entrance Requirements' or Eschatological Blessings?" *JBL* 95 (1976) 415-34.

Gundry, R. *Matthew*. 2nd ed. Grand Rapids: Eerdmans, 1994.

Guthrie, K., and D. R. Fideler. *The Pythagorean Sourcebook and Library*. Grand Rapids: Phanes, 1987.

Habel, N. "The Form and Significance of the Call Narratives." *ZAW* 77 (1965) 297-323.

Hagner, D. "Matthew's Eschatology." In *Society of Biblical Literature 1996 Seminar Papers*, 163-81. SBLSP 35. Atlanta: Scholars Press, 1996.

———. *Matthew 1-13, 14-28*. 2 vols. WBC 33A, 33B. Dallas: Word, 1993, 1995.

———. "Matthew's Eschatology." In *To Tell the Mystery: Essays on New Testament Eschatology in Honor of R. H. Gundry,* edited by T. E. Schmidt and M. Silva, 49-71. JSNTSup 100. Sheffield: Sheffield Academic Press, 1994.

Hammond, M. *The City in the Ancient World*. Cambridge, Mass.: Harvard University Press, 1972.

Hands, A. R. *Charities and Social Aid in Greece and Rome*. Ithaca, N.Y.: Cornell University Press, 1968.

Hanfmann, G. M. A. "The Donkey and the King." *HTR* 78 (1985) 421-26.

Hanson, A. T. "Rahab the Harlot in Early Christian Tradition." *JSNT* 1 (1978) 53-60.

Hanson, K. C. "The Galilean Fishing Economy and the Jesus Tradition." *BTB* 27 (1997) 99-111.

———. "How Honorable! How Shameful! A Cultural Analysis of Matthew's Makarisms and Reproaches." *Semeia* 68 (1994) 81-111.

Harding, G. L. *The Antiquities of Jordan*. New York: Frederick A. Praeger Publishers, 1959, 1969.

Hare, D. R. A. *Matthew*. Interpretation. Louisville, Ky.: Westminster John Knox, 1993.

———. *The Theme of Jewish Persecution of Christians in the Gospel According to St. Matthew*. SNTSMS 6. Cambridge: Cambridge University Press, 1967.

Hare, D., and D. Harrington. "'Make Disciples of All the Gentiles' (Matthew 28:19)." *CBQ* 37 (1975) 359-69.

Harper, G. McL. *Village Administration in the Roman Province of Syria*. Princeton, N.J.: Princeton University Press, 1928.

Harrington, D. J. *The Gospel of Matthew*. Sacra Pagina 1. Collegeville, Minn.: Liturgical Press, 1991.

Harris, B. F. "The Idea of Mercy and Its Graeco-Roman Context." In *God Who Is Rich In Mercy,* edited by P. T. O'Brien and D. G. Peterson, 89-105. Homebush: Lancer Books, 1986.

Hart, H. St. J. "The Coin of 'Render unto Caesar . . .' (A Note on Some Aspects of Mark 12:13-17; Matt 22:15-22; Luke 20:20-26)." In *Jesus and the Politics of His Day,* edited by E. Bammel and C. F. D. Moule, 241-48. Cambridge: Cambridge University Press, 1984.

Hauck, F. "κοπός, κοπιάω." *TDNT* 3:827-30.

Hay, D. M. *Glory at the Right Hand: Psalm 110 in Early Christianity*. Nashville: Abingdon, 1973.

Heichelheim, F. "Syria." In *An Economic Survey of Ancient Rome,* edited by T. Frank. 4:121-257. 6 vols. New York: Octagon Books, 1975.

Heil, J. P. "The Double Meaning of the Narrative of Universal Judgment in Matthew 25:31-46," *CBQ* 69 (1998) 3-14.

———. "Ezekiel 34 and the Narrative Strategy of the Shepherd and Sheep Metaphor in Matthew." *CBQ* 55 (1993) 698-708.

———. *The Death and Resurrection of Jesus: A Narrative-Critical Reading of Matthew 26-28*. Minneapolis: Fortress, 1991.

———. *Walking on the Sea: Meaning and Gospel Functions of Matt 14:22-33, Mark 6:45-52 and John 6:15b-21*. Rome: Biblical Institute Press, 1981.

———. "Significant Aspects of the Healing Miracles in Matthew." *CBQ* 41 (1979) 274-87.

Held, H. J. "Matthew as Interpreter of the Miracle Stories." In G. Bornkamm, G. Barth, and H. J. Held, *Tradition and Interpretation in Matthew,* 165-299. London: SCM, 1963.

Hendrickx, H. *The Parables of Jesus.* London: Geoffrey Chapman, 1986.

————. *The Sermon on the Mount.* London: Geoffrey Chapman, 1984.

————. *The Passion Narratives of the Synoptic Gospels.* London: Geoffrey Chapman, 1984.

Hengel, M. *The Charismatic Leader and His Followers.* New York: Crossroad, 1981.

————. *Crucifixion.* Philadelphia: Fortress, 1977.

————. *Property and Riches in the Early Church.* Philadelphia: Fortress, 1974.

Henning, P. "The Murder of the Magi." *JRAS* (1944) 133-44.

Herion, G. A. "Giloh." *ABD* 2:1027.

————. "Herod Philip." *ABD* 3:160-61.

Hertig, P. *Matthew's Narrative Use of Galilee in the Multicultural and Missiological Journeys of Jesus.* Lewiston: Edwin Mellen Press, 1998.

————. "The Multi-Ethnic Journeys of Jesus in Matthew: Margin- Center Dynamics." *Missiology: An International Review* 26 (1998) 23-35.

Herzog, W. R. *Parables as Subversive Speech: Jesus as Pedagogue of the Oppressed.* Louisville, Ky.: Westminster/John Knox, 1994.

Heyob, S. K. *The Cult of Isis Among Women in the Graeco-Roman World.* Études préliminaires aux Religions orientales dans l'empire Romain 51. Leiden: Brill, 1975.

Hill, D. "Matthew 27:51-53 in the Theology of the Evangelist." *IBS* 7 (1985) 76-87.

————. "'Our Daily Bread' (Matt 6:11) in the History of Exegesis." *IBS* 5 (1983) 2-10.

————. "On the Use and Meaning of Hosea 6:6 in Matthew's Gospel." *NTS* 24 (1977) 107-19.

————. *The Gospel of Matthew.* NCB. Grand Rapids: Eerdmans, 1972.

Hollenbach, P. "Jesus, Demoniacs, and Public Authorities." *JAAR* 49 (1981) 567-88.

Hopkins, K. "Christian Number and Its Implication." *JECS* 6 (1998) 185-226.

————. "Introduction." In *Trade in the Ancient Economy,* edited by P. Garnsey, K. Hopkins, and C. R. Whitaker, ix-xxv. Berkeley: University of California Press, 1983.

————. "Taxes and Trade in the Roman Empire (200 B.C.-A.D. 400)." *JRS* 70 (1980) 101-25.

————. "Economic Growth and Towns in Classical Antiquity." In *Towns in Societies: Essays in Economic History and Historical Sociology,* edited by P. Abrams and E. A. Wrigley, 35-77. Cambridge: Cambridge University Press, 1979.

————. *Conquerors and Slaves.* Cambridge: Cambridge University Press, 1978.

Horsley, R. A. *Archaeology, History, and Society in Galilee.* Valley Forge, Pa.: Trinity Press International, 1995.

————. *Galilee: History, Politics, People.* Valley Forge, Pa.: Trinity Press International, 1995.

————. *The Liberation of Christmas: The Infancy Narratives in Social Context.* New York: Crossroad, 1989.

————. "Popular Prophetic Movements at the Time of Jesus: Their Principal Features and Social Origins." *JSNT* 26 (1986) 3-27.

————. "'Like One of the Prophets of Old': Two Types of Popular Prophets at the Time of Jesus," *CBQ* 47 (1985) 435-63.

Horsley, R. A. (ed.). *Paul and Empire: Religion and Power in Roman Imperial Society.* Harrisburg, Pa.: Trinity Press International, 1997.

Horsley, R., and J. S. Hanson. *Bandits, Prophets, and Messiahs: Popular Movements at the Time of Jesus.* San Francisco: Harper & Row, 1988.

Houk, C. B. "ΠΕΙΡΑΣΜΟΣ, The Lord's Prayer and the Massah Tradition (Ex 17:1-7)." *SJT* 46 (1963) 216-225.

Hubbard, B. J. *The Matthean Redaction of a Primitive Apostolic Commissioning.* SBLDS 19. Missoula, Mont.: Scholars Press, 1974.

Huffman, N. "Atypical Features in the Parables of Jesus." *JBL* 97 (1978) 207-20.

Hultgren, A. "Matthew's Infancy Narrative and the Nativity of an Emerging Community." *HBT* 19 (1997) 91-108.

Hummel, R. *Die Auseinandersetzung zwischen Kirche und Judentum im Matthäusevangelium.* BEvT 33. Munich: Kaiser, 1963.

Iser, W. *The Act of Reading: A Theory of Aesthetic Response.* Baltimore: Johns Hopkins University Press, 1978.

Jeremias, J. "πύλη." *TDNT* 6:921-28.

———. "ᾅδης." *TDNT* 1:146-49.

Johnson, E. "Mark 5:1-20: The Other Side." *IBS* 20 (1998) 50-74.

Johnson, L. "The New Testament's Anti-Jewish Slander and the Conventions of Ancient Rhetoric." *JBL* 108 (1989) 419-41.

———. *The Writings of the New Testament.* Philadelphia: Fortress, 1986.

Johnson, M. D. "Reflections on a Wisdom Approach to Matthew's Christology." *CBQ* 36 (1974) 44-64.

———. *The Purpose of the Biblical Genealogies with Special Reference to the Settings of the Genealogies of Jesus.* SNTSMS 8. Cambridge: Cambridge University Press, 1969.

Jones, A. H. M. *The Cities of the Eastern Roman Provinces.* 1937. 2nd ed. London: Oxford University Press, 1937, 1971.

Jones, B. W. *The Emperor Domitian.* London: Routledge, 1992.

Jones, R. "Burial Customs of Rome and The Provinces." In *The Roman World,* edited by J. Wacher, 2:813-14. London and New York: Routledge & Keegan Paul, 1987.

Judge, E. A. *The Social Pattern of Christian Groups in the First Century.* London: Tyndale, 1960.

Kalmin, R. "Levirate Law." *ABD* 4:296-97.

Käsemann, E. "On the Subject of Primitive Christian Apocalyptic." In *New Testament Questions of Today,* 108-37. Philadephia: Fortress, 1969.

———. "Sentences of Holy Law in the New Testament." In *New Testament Questions of Today,* 66-81. Philadelphia: Fortress, 1969.

Katz, S. "Issues in the Separation of Judaism and Christianity after 70 C.E.: A Reconsideration." *JBL* 103 (1984) 43-76.

Kautsky, J. *The Politics of Aristocratic Empires.* Chapel Hill: University of North Carolina Press, 1982.

Kautsky, K. *The Foundations of Christianity.* New York: Russell & Russell, 1953. Ger. 1908.

Keck, L. "Matthew and the Spirit." In *The Social World of the First Christians: Essays in Honor of Wayne A. Meeks,* edited by L. M. White and O. L. Yarbrough, 145-55. Minneapolis: Augsburg Fortress, 1995.

———. "On the Ethos of Early Christians." *JAAR* 42 (1974) 435-52.

Kee, A. "The Imperial Cult: The Unmasking of an Ideology." *Scottish Journal of Religious Studies* 6 (1985) 112-28.

Kee, H. C. *Medicine, Miracle, and Magic in New Testament Times.* Cambridge: Cambridge University Press, 1986.

———. *Miracle in the Early Christian World.* New Haven, Conn.: Yale University Press, 1983.

Kertelge, K. "δικαιοσύνη." *EDNT* 1:325-30.

Kiley, M. "Why 'Matthew' in Matt 9, 9-13?" *Bib* 65 (1984) 347-51.

Kiley, M., et al. (eds.). *Prayer from Alexander to Constantine: A Critical Anthology.* London and New York: Routledge, 1997.

Kilpatrick, G. D. *The Origins of The Gospel According to St. Matthew.* Oxford: Clarendon Press, 1946.

Kim, T. H. "The Anarthrous υἱὸς θεοῦ in Mark 15, 39 and the Roman Imperial Cult." *Bib* 79 (1998) 221-41.

Kimbrough, S. T. "The Concept of Sabbath at Qumran." *RevQ* 5 (1966) 483-502.

Kimelman, R. "*Birkat Ha-Minim* and the Lack of Evidence for an Anti-Christian Jewish Prayer in Late Antiquity." In *Jewish and Christian Self-Definition,* edited by E. P. Sanders, A. Baumgarten, and A. Mendelson, 2:226-44. Philadelphia: Fortress, 1981.

Kingsbury, J. D. "The Rhetoric of Comprehension in the Gospel of Matthew." *NTS* 41 (1995) 358-77.

———. "On Following Jesus: The 'Eager' Scribe and the 'Reluctant' Disciple (Matthew 8:18-22)." *NTS* 34 (1988) 45-59.

———. "The Developing Conflict between Jesus and the Jewish Leaders in Matthew's Gospel: A Literary Critical Study." *CBQ* 49 (1987) 57-73.

———. *Matthew as Story.* 2nd ed. Philadelphia: Fortress, 1988.

———. "The Parable of the Wicked Husbandmen and the Secret of Jesus' Divine Sonship in Matthew: Some Literary-Critical Observations." *JBL* 105 (1986) 643-55.

———. "The Figure of Peter in Matthew's Gospel as a Theological Problem." *JBL* 98 (1979) 67-83.

———. "Observations on the 'Miracle Chapters' of Matthew 8-9." *CBQ* 40 (1978) 559-73.

———. "The Verb AKOLOUTHEIN ("To Follow") as an Index of Matthew's View of His Community." *JBL* 97 (1978) 56-73.

———. "Retelling the 'Old, Old Story': The Miracle of the Cleansing of the Leper as an Approach to the Theology of Matthew." *Currents in Theology and Mission* 4 (1977) 342-49.

———. "The Title 'Son of David' in Matthew's Gospel." *JBL* 95 (1976) 591-602.

———. *Matthew: Structure, Christology, Kingdom.* Philadelphia: Fortress, 1975.

———. "The Composition and Christology of Matt 28:16-20." *JBL* 93 (1974) 573-84.

———. *The Parables of Jesus in Matthew 13: A Study in Redaction-Criticism.* Richmond: John Knox Press, 1969.

Kinman, B. *Jesus' Entry to Jerusalem.* Leiden: Brill, 1995.

———. "Jesus' 'Triumphal Entry' in the Light of Pilate's." *NTS* 40 (1994) 442-48.

———. "Pilate's Assize and the Timing of Jesus' Trial." *TynBul* 42 (1991) 282-95.

Kissinger, W. *The Sermon on the Mount: A History of Interpretation and Bibliography.* ATLA Bibliography Series 3. Metuchen, N.J.: Scarecrow Press and the American Theological Library Association, 1975.

Kleinknecht, H., O. Grether, J. Fichtner, E. Sjöberg, G. Stählin, and O. Procksch. "ὀργή, ὀργίζομαι, ὀργίλος, παροργίζω, παροργισμός." *TDNT* 5:382-447.

Klinghardt, M. "The Manual of Discipline in the Light of Statutes of Hellenistic Associations." In *Methods of Investigation of the Dead Sea Scrolls and the Khirbet Qumran Site: Present Realities and Future Prospects,* edited by J. J. Collins, M. O. Wise, N. Golb, D. Pardee, 251-70. Annals of the New York Academy of Sciences 722. New York: New York Academy of Sciences, 1994.

Kloppenborg, J. S. "Collegia and *Thiasoi*: Issues in Function, Taxonomy, and Membership." In *Voluntary Associations in the Graeco-Roman World,* edited by J. S. Kloppenborg and S. G. Wilson, 16-30. London and New York: Routledge, 1996.

Kloppenborg, J. and S. Wilson (eds.). *Voluntary Associations in the Graeco-Roman World.* London/New York: Routledge, 1996.

Kosmala, H. "'His Blood Be Upon Us and Upon Our Children': The Background of Mat. 27:24-25." *ASTI* 7 (1968-69) 94-126.

Kraeling, C. H. "The Jewish Community at Antioch." *JBL* 51 (1932) 130-60.

Kraft, R. "εἰς νῖκος: Permanently/Successfully: 1 Cor 15:54; Matt 12:20." In *Septuagintal Lexicography,* edited by R. Kraft, 153-56. Missoula, Mont.: Scholars Press, 1975.

Kramer, H., R. Rendtorff, and R. Meyer, "προφήτης." *TDNT* 6:781-828.

Kreitzer, L. J. *Striking New Images: Roman Imperial Coinage and the New Testament World.* JSNTSup 134. Sheffield: Sheffield Academic Press, 1996.

Kugel, J. L. "On Hidden Hatred and Open Reproach: Early Exegesis of Leviticus 19:17." *HTR* 80 (1987) 43-61.

Kuhn, K. G. "προσήλυτος." *TDNT* 6:727-44.

Küng, H. *The Church*. London: Search Press, 1968.

Kupp, D. *Matthew's Emmanuel: Divine Presence and God's People in the First Gospel*. SNTSMS 90. Cambridge: Cambridge University Press, 1996.

Kutsko, J. "Caesarea Philippi." *ABD* 1:803.

Lagrange, M.-J. *Evangile selon Saint Matthieu*. 7th ed. Paris: Lecoffre, 1948.

Lambrecht, J. *Out of the Treasure: The Parables in the Gospel of Matthew*. Louvain Theological and Pastoral Monographs 10. Louvain: Peeters/Eerdmans, 1992.

———. *The Sermon on the Mount: Proclamation and Exhortation*. Good News Studies 14. Wilmington, Del.: Michael Glazier, 1985.

———. "The Parousia Discourse: Composition and Content in Mt 24-25." In *L'Évangile selon Matthieu: Rédaction et théologie*, edited by M. Didier, 309-42. BETL 29. Gembloux: Duculot, 1972.

Lapide, P. *The Sermon on the Mount*. Maryknoll, N.Y.: Orbis Books, 1986.

Lapin, H. "Rabbi." *ABD* 5:600-602.

Lassen, E. M. "The Use of the Father Image in Imperial Propaganda and 1 Cor 4:14-21. *TynBul* 42 (1991) 127-36.

Lassus, J. "Antioch on the Orontes." In *The Princeton Encyclopedia of Classical Sites,* edited by R. Stillwell, 61-63. Princeton, N.J.: Princeton University Press, 1976.

Lee, J. Y. *Marginality: The Key to Multicultural Theology*. Minneapolis: Fortress, 1995.

Lemcio, E. E. "The Parables of the Great Supper and the Wedding Feast: History, Redaction and Canon." *HBT* 8 (1986) 1-26.

Lenski, G. *Power and Privilege: A Theory of Social Stratification* New York: McGraw-Hill, 1966.

Lenski, G., and J. Lenski. *Human Societies: An Introduction to Macrosociology*. 5th ed. New York: McGraw-Hill, 1993.

Lerner, G. *The Creation of Patriarchy*. New York: Oxford University Press, 1986.

Levi, D. "The Allegories of the Months in Classical Art." *Art Bulletin* 23 (1941) 251-91.

Levine, A.-J. "Anti-Judaism and the Gospel of Matthew." In *Anti-Judaism and the Gospels,* edited by W. R. Farmer, 9-36. Harrisburg, Pa.: Trinity Press International, 1999.

———. "Discharging Responsibility: Matthean Jesus, Biblical Law, and Hemorrhaging Woman." In *Treasures New and Old: Contributions to Matthean Studies,* edited by D. R. Bauer and M. A. Powell, 379-97. SBL Symposium Series 1. Atlanta: Scholars Press, 1996.

———. "Matthew." In *The Women's Bible Commentary,* edited by C. A. Newsom and S. H. Ringe, 252-62. Louisville, Ky.: Westminster/John Knox, 1992.

———. *Social and Ethnic Dimensions of Matthean Social History*. SBEC 14. Lewiston: Edwin Mellen Press, 1988.

Levine, L. "Herod the Great." *ABD* 3:161-69.

Lewis, N. "Domitian's Order on Requisitioned Transport and Lodgings." *Revue internationale des droits de l'antiquité* 15 (1968) 135-42.

Linton, O. "Ekklesia." *RAC* 4:906-7.

Loader, W. R. G. "Son of David, Blindness and Duality in Matthew." *CBQ* 44 (1982) 570-85.

Lohse, E. "συνέδριον." *TDNT* 7:860-71.

Louw, J. P., and E. Nida. *Greek-English Lexicon of the New Testament Based on Semantic Domains*. 2 vols. New York: United Bible Societies, 1988, 1989.

Lövestam, E. "The ἡ γενεὰ αὕτη Eschatology in Mark 13.30 parr." In *L'Apocalypse johannique et l'Apocalyptique dans le Nouveau Testament,* edited by J. Lambrecht, 403-13. BETL 53. Gembloux: Duculot, 1980.

Luck, U. *Das Evangelium nach Matthäus.* Züricher Bibelkommentare. Zurich: Theologischer Verlag, 1993.

Luttwak, E. N. *The Grand Strategy of the Roman Empire.* Baltimore: Johns Hopkins University Press, 1976.

Luz, U. *Matthew in History: Interpretation, Influence, and Effects.* Minneapolis: Fortress, 1994.

———. "The Son of Man in Matthew: Heavenly Judge or Human Christ?" *JSNT* 48 (1992) 3-21.

———. "Matthew's Anti-Judaism: Its Origin and Contemporary Significance." *CurTM* 19 (1992) 405-14.

———. *Matthew 1-7: A Commentary.* Minneapolis: Fortress, 1989.

MacArthur, H. *Understanding the Sermon on the Mount.* London: Epworth, 1961.

MacCormack, S. "Change and Continuity in Late Antiquity: The Ceremony of *Adventus.*" *Historia* 21 (1972) 721-52.

MacDonald, W. L. *The Architecture of the Roman Empire.* Vol. 2, *An Urban Appraisal.* New Haven, Conn.: Yale University Press, 1986.

MacMullen, R. *Paganism in the Roman Empire* (New Haven, Conn., and London: Yale University Press, 1981.

———. *Roman Social Relations.* New Haven, Conn.: Yale University Press, 1974.

———. *Enemies of the Roman Order: Treason, Unrest and Alienation in the Empire.* Cambridge, Mass.: Harvard University Press, 1966.

Mack, B. L. "Teaching in Parables: Elaboration in Mark 4:1-34." In *Patterns of Persuasion in the Gospels,* edited by B. Mack and V. Robbins, 143-60. Sonoma, Calif.: Polebridge, 1989.

Malherbe, A. J. *Social Aspects of Early Christianity.* 2nd ed., enlarged. Philadelphia: Fortress, 1983.

———. *The Cynic Epistles.* Missoula, Mont.: Scholars Press, 1977.

Malina, B. J. *The New Testament World: Insights from Cultural Anthropology.* Rev. ed. Louisville, Ky.: Westminster John Knox, 1993.

———. "Wealth and Property in the New Testament and Its World." *Interpretation* 41 (1987) 354-67.

Malina, B. J., and J. Neyrey. "Honor and Shame in Luke-Acts." In *The Social World of Luke-Acts: Models for Interpretation,* edited by J. Neyrey, 25-65. Peabody, Mass.: Hendrickson, 1991.

———. *Calling Jesus Names: The Social Value of Labels in Matthew.* Sonoma, Calif.: Polebridge, 1988.

Malina, B. J., and R. Rohrbaugh. *Social-Science Commentary on the Synoptic Gospels.* Minneapolis: Fortress, 1992.

Manson, M. "The Emergence of the Small Child in Rome (Third Century BC-First Century AD)." *History of Education* 12 (1983) 149-59.

Marcus, J. "The Old Testament and the Death of Jesus: The Role of Scripture in the Gospel Passion Narrative." In *The Death of Jesus in Early Christianity,* edited by J. T. Carroll and J. B. Green, 205-33. Peabody, Mass.: Hendrickson, 1995.

———. "Entering into the Kingly Power of God." *JBL* 107 (1988) 663-75.

———. "The Gates of Hades and the Keys of the Kingdom (Matt 16:18-19)." *CBQ* 50 (1988) 443-55.

Marrou, H. *A History of Education in Antiquity.* Madison: University of Wisconsin Press, 1956, 1982.

Marshall, A. J. "Symbols and Showmanship in Roman Public Life: The Fasces." *Phoenix* 38 (1984) 120-41.

———. "Governors on the Move." *Phoenix* 20 (1966) 231-46.

Marshall, I. H. "The Biblical Use of the Word Ἐκκλησία." *ExpT* 84 (1973) 359-64.

———. "Uncomfortable Words: VI. 'Fear him who can destroy both soul and body in hell' (Mt 10:28 RSV)." *ExpT* 81 (1970) 277-79.

Martin, D. *Slavery as Salvation.* New Haven, Conn.: Yale University Press, 1990.

Martin, H., and J. E. Phillips. "Consolatio ad Uxorem (*Moralia* 608A- 612B)." In *Plutarch's Ethical Writings and Early Christian Literature,* edited by H. D. Betz, 394-441. Leiden: Brill, 1978.

Matera, F. J. *Passion Narratives and Gospel Theologies: Interpreting the Synoptics Through Their Passion Stories.* New York/Mahwah, N.J.: Paulist, 1986.

Mattam, J. "Judgement on the Present Economic Order: Matthew Twenty Five." *Bible Bhashyam* 23 (1997) 174-82.

Mauser, U. "Christian Community and Governmental Power in the Gospel of Matthew." *Ex Auditu* 2 (1986) 46-54.

Maynard, A. H. "TI EMOI KAI SOI." *NTS* 31 (1985) 582-86.

McBride, S. D. "The Yoke of the Kingdom: An Exposition of Deuteronomy 6:4-6." *Interpretation* 27 (1973) 273-306.

McGing, B. C. "Pontius Pilate and the Sources." *CBQ* 53 (1991) 416-38.

McIver, R. "One Hundred-Fold Yield—Miraculous or Mundane? Matthew 13:8, 23; Mark 4:8, 20; Luke 8:8." *NTS* 40 (1994) 606-8.

McKnight, S. *A Light among the Gentiles: Jewish Missionary Activity in the Second Temple Period.* Minneapolis: Fortress, 1991.

McLean, B. H. "The Agrippinilla Inscription: Religious Associations and Early Church Formation." In *Origins and Method: Towards a New Understanding of Judaism and Christianity: Essays in Honour of John C. Hurd,* edited by B. McLean, 239-70. JSNTSup 86. Sheffield: Sheffield Academic Press, 1993.

Meeks, W. A. *The First Urban Christians: The Social World of the Apostle Paul.* New Haven, Conn.: Yale University Press, 1983.

Meeks, W. A., and R. L. Wilken. *Jews and Christians in Antioch in the First Four Centuries of the Common Era.* SBL Sources for Biblical Study 13. Missoula, Mont.: Scholars Press, 1978.

Meier, J. P. *A Marginal Jew: Rethinking the Historical Jesus.* Vol. 2, *Mentor, Message, and Miracles.* New York: Doubleday, 1994.

———. "Matthew and Ignatius: A Response to William R. Schoedel." In *Social History of the Matthean Community: Cross-Disciplinary Approaches,* edited by D. Balch, 178-86. Minneapolis: Fortress, 1991.

———. "John the Baptist in Matthew's Gospel." *JBL* 99 (1980) 383-405.

———. *The Vision of Matthew: Christ, Church, and Morality in the First Gospel.* Mahwah, N.J.: Paulist, 1979.

———. "Nations or Gentiles in Matthew 28:19?" *CBQ* 39 (1977) 94-102.

———. *Law and History in Matthew's Gospel.* Analecta Biblica 71. Rome: Biblical Institute Press, 1976.

Merkelbach, R. "Mithras, Mithraism." *ABD* 4:877-78.

Metzger, B. *A Textual Commentary on the Greek New Testament.* London: UBS, 1971.

Meyer, B. F. "Many (= All) Are Called, but Few (= Not All) Are Chosen." *NTS* 36 (1990) 89-97.

Michaelis, W. "ὁδός." *TDNT* 5:42-96.

Michon, E. "Mélanges III. Note sur une inscription de Baʿalbek et sur des tuilles de la legion Xa Fretensis." *Revue biblique* 9 (1900) 95-105.

Milikowsky, C. "Which Gehenna? Retribution and Eschatology in the Synoptic Gospels and in Early Jewish Texts." *NTS* 34 (1988) 238-49.

Mitchell, S. "Imperial Building in the Eastern Roman Provinces." *Harvard Studies in Classical Philology* 91 (1987) 333-65.

Moloney, F. J. "Matthew 19:3-12 and Celibacy." *JSNT* 2 (1979) 42-60.

Momigliano, A. *The Development of Greek Biography.* Expanded ed. Cambridge, Mass.: Harvard University Press, 1993.

———. "Some Preliminary Remarks on the 'Religious Opposition' to the Roman Empire." In *Opposition et Résistances à L'Empire d'Auguste à Trajan,* edited by A. Giovannini, 103-29. Entretiens sur L'Antiquité Classique 33. Geneva: Fondation Hardt, 1987.

Moore, W. E. "ΒΙΑΖΩ, ΑΡΠΑΖΩ and Cognates in Josephus." *NTS* 21 (1974-75) 519-43.

Morosco, R. "Matthew's Formation of a Commissioning Type-Scene." *JBL* 103 (1984) 539-56.

Morris, L. *The Apostolic Preaching of the Cross.* 3rd ed. Grand Rapids: Eerdmans, 1965.

Moulton, J. H. *A Grammar of New Testament Greek.* Edinburgh: T & T Clark, 1919.

Moulton, J. H., and G. Milligan. *The Vocabulary of the Greek New Testament.* Grand Rapids: Eerdmans, 1959.

Mowery, R. L. "From Lord to Father in Matthew 1-7." *CBQ* 59 (1997) 642-56.

———. "The Matthean References to the Kingdom: Different Terms for Different Audiences." *EThL* 70 (1994) 398-405.

Moxnes, H. "Honor and Shame." In *The Social Sciences and New Testament Interpretation,* edited by R. Rohrbaugh, 19-40. Peabody, Mass.: Hendrickson, 1996.

———. "Patron-Client Relations and the New Community in Luke-Acts." In *The Social World of Luke-Acts: Models for Interpretation,* edited by J. Neyrey, 241-68. Peabody, Mass.: Hendrickson, 1991.

Mumford, L. *The City in History: Its Origins, Its Transformations, and Its Prospects.* New York: Harcourt Brace, 1961.

Murphy-O'Connor, J. "Fishers of Fish, Fishers of Men." *Bible Review* 15 (1999) 23-27, 48-49.

———. *St. Paul's Corinth.* Good News Studies 6. Wilmington, Del.: Michael Glazier, 1983.

Mussies, G. "Parallels to Matthew's Version of Jesus' Pedigree." *NovT* 28 (1986) 32-47.

Netzer, E. "Herod's Building Program." *ABD* 3:169-72.

———. "Roman Jericho." *ABD* 3:738-40.

Neusner, J. *From Politics to Piety: The Emergence of Pharisaic Judaism.* Englewood Cliffs, N.J.: Prentice-Hall, 1973.

———. "Judaism in a Time of Crisis: Four Responses to the Destruction of the Second Temple." *Judaism* 21 (1972) 313-27.

———. *The Development of a Legend: Studies Concerning Yohanan ben Zakkai.* Leiden: Brill, 1970.

———. *A Life of Rabban Yohanan ben Zakkai.* Leiden: Brill, 1962.

Neusner, J., and E. S. Frerichs (eds.). *"To See Ourselves as Others See Us": Christians, Jews, "Others" in Late Antiquity.* Chico, Calif.: Scholars Press, 1985.

Neyrey, J. *Honor and Shame in the Gospel of Matthew.* Louisville, Ky.: Westminster John Knox Press, 1998.

———. "Ceremonies in Luke-Acts: The Case of Meals and Table Fellowship." In *The Social World of Luke-Acts: Models for Interpretation,* edited by J. Neyrey, 361-87. Peabody, Mass.: Hendrickson, 1991.

———. "The Thematic Use of Isaiah 42:1-4 in Matthew 12." *Bib* 63 (1983) 457-73.

Nickelsburg, G. W. "Resurrection (Early Judaism and Christianity)." *ABD* 5:684-91.

———. "Revealed Wisdom as a Criterion for Inclusion and Exclusion: From Jewish Sectarianism to Early Christianity." In *"To See Ourselves as Others See Us": Christians, Jews, "Others" in Late Antiquity,* edited by J. Neusner and E. S. Frerichs, 73-91. Chico, Calif.: Scholars Press, 1985.

———. "Enoch, Levi and Peter: Recipients of Revelation in Upper Galilee." *JBL* 100 (1981) 575-600.

———. "The Genre and Function of the Markan Passion Narrative." *HTR* 73 (1980) 154-84.

Nock, A. D. "Eunuchs in Ancient Religion." *ARW* 23 (1925) 25-33.

Norris, F. W. "Isis, Serapis and Demeter in Antioch of Syria." *HTR* 75 (1982) 189-207.

Nutton, V. "The Beneficial Ideology." In *Imperialism in the Ancient World,* edited by P. D. A. Garnsey and C. R. Whittaker, 209-21. Cambridge: Cambridge University Press, 1978.

Oakley, J. W. "Hypocrisy in Matthew." *IBS* 7 (1985) 118-35.

Oakman, D. "The Countryside in Luke-Acts." In *The Social World of Luke-Acts: Models for Interpretation,* edited by J. Neyrey, 151-79. Peabody, Mass.: Hendrickson, 1991.

O'Collins, G. "Crucifixion." *ABD* 1:1207-10.

Oepke, A. "παῖς." *TDNT* 5:636-54.

———. "παρουσία." *TDNT* 5:858-71.

Ogawa, A. "Action-Motivating Faith: The Understanding of 'Faith' in the Gospel of Matthew." *Annual of the Japanese Biblical Institute* 19 (1993) 53-86.

Ogletree, T. *The Use of the Bible in Christian Ethics: A Constructive Essay.* Philadelphia: Fortress, 1983.

Oliver, J. H. "The Ruling Power: A Study of the Roman Empire in the Second Century after Christ through the Roman Oration of Aelius Aristides." *Transactions of the American Philosophical Society* n.s. 43 Part 4 (1953) 871-1003.

Oster, R. "'Show Me a Denarius': Symbolism of Roman Coinage and Christian Beliefs." *Restoration Quarterly* 28 (1985-86) 107-15.

Overman, J. A. *Matthew's Gospel and Formative Judaism: A Study of the Social World of the Matthean Community.* Minneapolis: Fortress, 1990.

Owens, J. E. *The City in the Greek and Roman World.* New York: Routledge, 1991.

Page, S. H. T. "The Suffering Servant Between the Testaments." *NTS* 31 (1985) 481-97.

Palmer, H. "Just Married, Cannot Come," *NovT* 18 (1976) 241-57.

Pamment, M. "The Kingdom of Heaven According to the First Gospel." *NTS* 27 (1981) 211-32.

Park, R. E. "Human Migration and the Marginal Man." *American Journal of Sociology* 33 (1928) 881-93.

Parker, H. W. *The Oracles of Zeus.* Oxford: Basil Blackwood, 1967.

Patte, D. *Discipleship According to the Sermon on the Mount: Four Legitimate Readings. Four Plausible Views of Discipleship and Their Relative Values.* Valley Forge, Pa.: Trinity Press International, 1996.

———. *The Gospel According to Matthew: A Structural Commentary on Matthew's Faith.* Philadelphia: Fortress, 1987.

Patterson, O. *Slavery and Social Death.* Cambridge, Mass.: Harvard University Press, 1982.

Perkins, P. "Matthew 28:16-20, Resurrection, Ecclesiology and Mission." In *Society of Biblical Literature 1993 Seminar Papers,* edited by E. H. Lovering Jr., 574-88. SBLSP 32. Atlanta: Scholars Press, 1993.

———. *Resurrection: New Testament Witness and Contemporary Reflection.* New York: Paulist, 1984.

Perrin, N. *Jesus and the Language of the Kingdom.* Philadelphia: Fortress, 1976.

Perring, D. "Spatial Organisation and Social Change in Roman Towns." In *City and Country in the Ancient World,* edited by J. Rich and A. Wallace-Hadrill, 273-93. New York: Routledge, 1991.

Pilch, J. J. "Secrecy in the Mediterranean World: An Anthropological Perspective." *BTB* 24 (1994) 151-57.

———. "Understanding Biblical Healing: Selecting an Appropriate Model." *BTB* 18 (1988) 60-66.

———. "The Health Care System in Matthew: A Social Science Analysis." *BTB* 16 (1986) 102-6.

———. "Biblical Leprosy and Body Symbolism." *BTB* 11 (1981) 108-13.

Pilgrim, W. E. *Uneasy Neighbors: Church and State in the New Testament.* Minneapolis: Fortress, 1999.

Pleket, H. W. "Urban Elites and Business in the Greek Part of the Roman Empire." In *Trade in the Ancient Economy,* edited by P. Garnsey, K. Hopkins, and C. R. Whitaker, 131-44. Berkeley: University of California Press, 1983.

———. "Religious History as the History of Mentality: The 'Believer' as Servant of the Deity in the Greek World." In *Faith, Hope and Worship: Aspects of Religious Mentality in the Ancient World,* edited by H. S. Versnel, 152-92. Leiden: Brill, 1981.

Plummer, A. *An Exegetical Commentary on the Gospel According to St. Matthew.* London: E. Stock, 1909.

Pobee, J. S. *Who are the Poor? The Beatitudes as a Call to Community.* Geneva: WCC Publications, 1987.

Potter, D. *Prophets and Emperors: Human and Divine Authority from Augustus to Theodosius.* Cambridge, Mass.: Harvard University Press, 1994.

Powell, M. A. "The Magi as Kings: An Adventure in Reader-Response Criticism." *CBQ* forthcoming.

———. "The Magi as Wise Men: Rethinking a Basic Presupposition." *NTS* 46 (2000) 1-20.

———. "Neither Wise nor Powerful: Reconsidering Matthew's Magi in Light of Reader Expectations." *Trinity Seminary Review* 20 (1998) 19-31.

———. "Matthew's Beatitudes: Reversals and Rewards of the Kingdom." *CBQ* 58 (1996) 460-79.

———. "Do and Keep What Moses Says (Matthew 23:2-7)." *JBL* 114 (1995) 419-35.

———. *God With Us: A Pastoral Theology of Matthew's Gospel.* Minneapolis: Fortress, 1995.

———. "The Plot and Subplots of Matthew's Gospel." *NTS* 38 (1992) 187-204.

———. "The Plot to Kill Jesus from Three Different Perspectives: Point of View in Matthew." In *Society of Biblical Literature 1990 Seminar Papers,* edited by D. J. Lull, 603-13. SBLSP 29. Atlanta: Scholars Press, 1990.

Powell, M. "Weights and Measures." *ABD* 6:907-908.

Pregeant, R. "Wisdom Passages in Matthew." In *Treasures Old and New: Contributions to Matthean Studies,* edited by D. Bauer and M. Powell, 197-232. Atlanta: Scholars Press, 1996.

Price, S. F. R. "Gods and Emperors: The Greek Language of the Roman Imperial Cult." *Journal of Hellenic Studies* 104 (1984) 79-95.

———. *Rituals and Power: The Roman Imperial Cult in Asia Minor.* Cambridge: Cambridge University Press, 1984.

Procksch, O. "λύω, . . . λύτρον." *TDNT* 4:328-56.

Przybylski, B. *Righteousness in Matthew and His World of Thought.* SNTSMS 41. Cambridge: Cambridge University Press, 1980.

Quell, G. and G. Schrenk. "δίκη, δίκαιος, δικαιοσύνη." *TDNT* 2:174-225.

Quesnell, Q. "'Made Themselves Eunuchs for the Kingdom of Heaven.'" *CBQ* 30 (1968) 335-58.

Rabinowitz, P. J. "Whirl Without End: Audience-Oriented Criticism." In *Contemporary Literary Theory,* edited by G. D. Atkins and L. Morrow, 81-100. Amherst: University of Massachusetts Press, 1989.

———. *Before Reading: Narrative Conventions and the Politics of Interpretation.* Ithaca, N.Y.: Cornell University Press, 1987.

———. "Truth in Fiction: A Reexamination of Audiences." *Critical Inquiry* 4 (1977) 121-42.

Rajak, T. J. "Friends, Romans, Subjects: Agrippa II's Speech in Josephus' *Jewish War.*" In *Images of Empire,* edited by L. Alexander, 122-34. JSOTSup 122. Sheffield: Sheffield Academic Press, 1991.

———. "Jews and Christians as Groups in a Pagan World." In *"To See Ourselves as Others*

See Us": Christians, Jews, "Others" in Late Antiquity, edited by J. Neusner and E. S. Frerichs, 247-62. Chico, Calif.: Scholars Press, 1985.

————. *Josephus: The Historian and His Society.* Philadelphia: Fortress, 1983.

Rank, O. *Myth of the Birth of the Hero.* New York: Vintage, 1959.

Rawson, B. "Children in the Roman Familia." In *The Family in Ancient Rome,* edited by B. Rawson, 170-200. Ithaca, N.Y.: Cornell University Press, 1986.

————. "Family Life Among the Lower Classes at Rome in the First Two Centuries of the Empire." *Classical Philology* 61 (1966) 71-83.

Reekmans, T. "Juvenal's Views of Social Change." *Ancient Society* 2 (1971) 117-61.

Reicke, B. "The New Testament Conception of Reward." In *Aux Sources de la Tradition Chrétienne,* 195-206. Neuchâtel & Paris: Delachaux & Niestlé, 1950.

Reiling, J. "The Use of Ψευδοπροφήτης in the Septuagint, Philo and Josephus." *NovT* 13 (1971) 147-56.

Rengstorf, K. H. *A Complete Concordance to Flavius Josephus.* 4 vols. Leiden: Brill, 1975.

————. "Die Stadt der Mörder (Mt 22:7)." In *Judentum, Urchristentum, Kirche,* edited by W. Eltester, 106-29. Festscrift J. Jeremias. BZNW 26. Berlin: Töpelmann, 1960.

————. "κορβᾶν." *TDNT* 3:860-66.

Reumann, J. *Righteousness in the New Testament.* Philadelphia: Fortress, 1982.

Rich, J., and A. Wallace-Hadrill (eds.). *City and Country in the Ancient World.* New York: Routledge, 1991.

Ringe, S. "Solidarity and Contextuality: Readings of Matthew 18:21- 35." In *Reading from This Place,* edited by F. Segovia and M. A. Tolbert, 2:199-212. 2 vols. Minneapolis: Fortress, 1995.

————. *Jesus, Liberation and the Biblical Jubilee: Images for Ethics and Christology.* OBT 19. Philadelphia: Fortress, 1985.

————. "A Gentile Woman's Story." In *Feminist Interpretation of the Bible,* edited by L. Russell, 65-72. Philadelphia: Westminster, 1985.

Robbins, V. "Plucking Grain on the Sabbath." In *Patterns of Persuasion in the Gospels,* edited by B. Mack and V. Robbins, 107-41. Sonoma, Calif.: Polebridge, 1989.

————. "Rhetorical Composition and the Beelzebul Controversy." In *Patterns of Persuasion in the Gospels,* edited by B. Mack and V. Robbins, 107-41. Sonoma, Calif.: Polebridge, 1989.

Rogers, J. S. "Asaph." *ABD* 1:471.

Rohrbaugh, R. "The Preindustrial City." In *The Social Sciences and New Testament Interpretation,* edited by R. Rohrbaugh, 107-25. Peabody, Mass.: Hendrickson, 1996.

————. "A Peasant Reading of the Parable of the Talents/Pounds: A Text of Terror?" *BTB* 23 (1993) 32-39.

————. "The Pre-industrial City in Luke-Acts: Urban Social Relations." In *The Social World of Luke-Acts: Models for Interpretation,* edited by J. Neyrey, 125-50. Peabody, Mass.: Hendrickson, 1991.

Ross, J. M. "Epileptic or Moonstruck?" *Bible Translator* 29 (1978) 126-28.

Roth, S. J. *The Blind, the Lame, and the Poor: Character Types in Luke-Acts.* JSNTSup 144. Sheffield: Sheffield Academic Press, 1994.

Rudolph, K. "Helios." *ABD* 3:123-25.

Russell, D. A., and N. G. Wilson. *Menander Rhetor.* Oxford: Oxford University Press, 1981.

Said, E. *Culture and Imperialism.* New York: Random House, 1993.

Saldarini, A. J. *Matthew's Christian-Jewish Community.* Chicago: University of Chicago Press, 1994.

————. "Boundaries and Polemics in the Gospel of Matthew." *Biblical Interpretation* 3 (1995) 239-65.

————. "Delegitimation of Leaders in Matthew 23." *CBQ* 54 (1992) 659-80.

————. "Pharisees." *ABD* 5:289-303.

————. "Sanhedrin." *ABD* 5:975-80.

————. *Pharisees, Scribes and Sadducees in Palestinian Society: A Sociological Approach.* Wilmington, Del.: Michael Glazier, 1988.

Saller, R. P. "*Familia, Domus* and the Roman Conception of the Family." *Phoenix* 38 (1984) 336-55.

————. *Personal Patronage under the Empire.* New York: Cambridge University Press, 1982.

Sand, A. *Das Evangelium nach Matthäus.* RNT. Regensburg: Pustet, 1986.

Sanders, E. P. "Sin, Sinners (NT)." *ABD* 6:40-47.

————. *Jesus and Judaism.* Philadelphia: Fortress, 1985.

————. *Paul and Palestinian Judaism.* Philadelphia: Fortress, 1977.

Sanders, E. P., A. I. Baumgarten, A. Mendelson, and B. F. Meyer (eds.). *Jewish and Christian Self-Definition.* 3 vols. Philadelphia: Fortress, 1980-82.

Sanders, J. A. *From Sacred Story to Sacred Text: Canon as Paradigm.* Philadelphia: Fortress, 1987.

————. "Adaptable for Life: The Nature and Function of Canon." In *Magnalia Dei: The Mighty Acts of God: Essays on the Bible and Archaeology in Memory of G. Ernest Wright,* edited by F. M. Cross et al., 531-60. New York: Doubleday, 1976.

Saunders, S. "'No One Dared Ask Him Anything More': Contextual Readings of the Controversy Stories in Matthew." Ph.D. dissertation, Princeton Theological Seminary, 1990.

Scarborough, J. *Roman Medicine.* Ithaca, N.Y.: Cornell University Press, 1969, 1976.

Schaberg, J. *The Illegitimacy of Jesus: A Feminist Theological Interpretation of the Infancy Narratives.* New York: Crossroad, 1990.

————. "Feminist Interpretations of the Infancy Narrative of Matthew." *Journal of Feminist Studies in Religion* 13 (1997) 35-62.

Schmidt, T. *Hostility to Wealth in the Synoptic Gospels.* JSNTSup 15. Sheffield: JSOT Press, 1987.

Schneider, G. "δίκαιος." *EDNT* 1:324-25.

Schneider, J. "προσέρχομαι." *TDNT* 2:683-84.

————. "εὐνοῦχος." *TDNT* 2:765-68.

Schottroff, L. "Human Solidarity and the Goodness of God: The Parable of the Workers in the Vineyard." In *God of the Lowly,* edited by W. Schottroff and W. Stegemann, 129-47. Maryknoll, N.Y.: Orbis Books, 1984.

Schottroff, L., and W. Stegemann. "The Sabbath Was Made for Man: The Interpretation of Mark 2:23-28." In *God of the Lowly,* edited by W. Schottroff and W. Stegemann, 118-29. Maryknoll, N.Y.: Orbis Books, 1984.

Schowalter, D. N. *The Emperor and the Gods: Images from the Time of Trajan.* HDR 28. Minneapolis: Fortress, 1993.

Schrage, W. "τυφλός." *TDNT* 8:270-94.

Schramm, T. "ἁπλότης, ἁπλοῦς." *EDNT* 1:123-24.

Schrenk, G. "βιάζομαι." *TDNT* 1:609-14.

Schrenk, G., and G. Quell. "πατήρ." *TDNT* 5:945-1022.

Schüssler Fiorenza, E. *In Memory of Her: A Feminist Theological Reconstruction of Christian Origins.* New York, Crossroad, 1989.

————. "Missionaries, Apostles, Co-Workers: Romans 16 and the Reconstruction of Women's Early Christian History." *Word and World* 6 (1986) 420-33.

Schwartz, D. R. "Pontius Pilate." *ABD* 5:395-401.

————. "Wilderness and Temple: On Religion and State in Judea in the Second Temple Period." In *Priesthood and Kingship,* 61-78. Jerusalem: Zalman Shezer Center for the History of Israel, 1987.

Schweizer, E. *The Good News According to Matthew.* Atlanta: John Knox, 1975.

Schweizer, E., F. Baumgärtel, and R. Meyer. "σάρξ." *TDNT* 7:98-151.

Scott, B. B. *Hear Then The Parable: A Commentary on the Parables of Jesus.* Minneapolis: Fortress, 1989.

Scott, J. C. *Weapons of the Weak: Everyday Forms of Peasant Resistance.* New Haven: Yale University Press, 1985.

Scott, K. *The Imperial Cult Under the Flavians.* Stuttgart and Berlin: W. Kohlhammer, 1936.

—————. "Statius' Adulation of Domitian." *American Journal of Philology* 54 (1933) 247-59.

Scroggs, R. "Sociological Interpretation of the NT." *NTS* 26 (1980) 164-79.

Seeley, D. "Rulership and Service in Mark 10:41-45." *NovT* 35 (1993) 234-50.

—————. *The Noble Death: Graeco-Roman Martyrology and Paul's Concept of Salvation.* JSNTSup 28. Sheffield: JSOT Press, 1990.

Segal, A. F. "The Costs of Proselytism and Conversion." In *Society of Biblical Literature 1988 Seminar Papers,* edited by D. J. Lull, 336-67. SBLSP 27. Atlanta: Scholars Press, 1988.

Senior, D. *Matthew.* Abingdon New Testament Commentaries. Nashville: Abingdon, 1998.

—————. "Between Two Worlds: Gentile and Jewish Christians in Matthew's Gospel." CBQ 61 (1999) 1-23.

—————. *What Are They Saying About Matthew?* Rev. ed. Mahwah, N.J.: Paulist, 1996.

—————. *The Passion of Jesus in the Gospel of Matthew.* Collegeville, Minn.: Liturgical Press, 1985.

—————. "The Death of Jesus and the Resurrection of the Holy Ones (Mt 27:51-53)." *CBQ* 38 (1976) 312-29.

Shaw, B. D. "Bandits in the Roman Empire." *Past and Present* 102 (1984) 3-52.

Sherwin-White, A. N. *Roman Society and Roman Law in the New Testament.* Oxford: Clarendon Press, 1963.

Shogren, G. "Redemption (NT)." *ABD* 5:654-57.

Sievers, J. "'Where Two or Three . . .': The Rabbinic Concept of Shekhinah and Matthew 18:20." In *The Jewish Roots of Christian Liturgy,* edited by E. J. Fisher, 47-61. Mahwah, N.J.: Paulist, 1990.

Sim, D. *Apocalyptic Eschatology in the Gospel of Matthew.* SNTSMS 88. Cambridge: Cambridge University Press, 1996.

—————. "The 'Confession' of the Soldiers in Matthew 27:54." *HeyJ* 34 (1995) 401-24.

—————. "The Man Without the Wedding Garment." *HeyJ* 31 (1990) 165-78.

Sjoberg, G. *The Preindustrial City.* New York: Macmillan, 1960.

Slingerland, H. D. "The Transjordanian Origin of St. Matthew's Gospel." *JSNT* 3 (1979) 18-28.

Smallwood, E. *The Jews under Roman Rule: From Pompey to Diocletian.* Studies in Judaism in Late Antiquity 20. Leiden: Brill, 1976.

Smith, D. "Greco-Roman Meal Customs." *ABD* 4:650-53.

—————. "The Historical Jesus at Table." In *SBL 1989 Seminar Papers,* edited by D. J. Lull, 466-86. SBLSP 28. Atlanta: Scholars Press, 1989.

Smith, D., and H. Taussig. *Many Tables.* London: SCM, 1990.

Smith, R. W. "Matthew 28:16-20, Anti-Climax or Key to the Gospel?" In *Society of Biblical Literature 1993 Seminar Papers,* edited by E. H. Lovering Jr., 589-603. SBLSP 32. Atlanta: Scholars Press, 1993.

—————. "Were the Early Christians Middle-Class? A Sociological Analysis of the New Testament." *CTM* 7 (1980) 260-76.

Snell, D. C. "Tax Office." *ABD* 6:338.

Snodgrass, K. *The Parable of the Wicked Tenants.* WUNT 27. Tübingen: J. C. Mohr [Paul Siebeck], 1983.

Soares-Prabhu, G. "Jesus the Teacher: The Liberative Pedagogy of Jesus of Nazareth." *Jeevadhara* 11 (1981) 243-56.

Sordi, M. *The Christians and the Roman Empire.* Norman: University of Oklahoma, 1986.

Sperber, D. *The City in Roman Palestine.* New York: Oxford University Press, 1998.

Spijkerman, A. *The Coins of the Decapolis and Provincia Arabia.* Jerusalem: Franciscan Printing Press, 1978.

Stambaugh, J. *The Ancient Roman City*. Baltimore: Johns Hopkins University Press, 1988.

Stanton, G. *Gospel for a New People: Studies in Matthew*. Edinburgh: T & T Clark, 1992.

———. "Matthew 11:28-30: Comfortable Words?" In *Gospel for a New People: Studies in Matthew,* 364-77. Edinburgh: T & T Clark, 1992.

———. *The Gospels and Jesus*. Oxford: Oxford University Press, 1989.

———. "The Origin and Purpose of Matthew's Gospel: Matthean Scholarship from 1945 to 1980." *ANRW* 2.25.3, 1889-1951. Berlin: Walter de Gruyter, 1985.

Stark, R. *The Rise of Christianity*. Princeton, N.J.: Princeton University Press, 1996.

———. "Antioch as the Social Situation for Matthew's Gospel." In *Social History of the Matthean Community,* edited by D. Balch, 189-210. Minneapolis: Fortress, 1991.

Stegner, W. R. "Breaking Away: The Conflict with Formative Judaism." *Biblical Research* 40 (1995) 7-36.

Stendebach, F. J. "Das Schweinopfer im alten Orient." *BZ* 18 (1974) 263-71.

Stern, M. *Greek and Latin Authors on Jews and Judaism*. 3 vols. Jerusalem: Israel Academy of Sciences and Humanities, 1974.

Stillwell, R. "Houses of Antioch." *Dumbarton Oaks Papers* 15 (1961) 47-57.

Stone, M. "Reactions to Destructions of the Second Temple: Theology, Perception and Conversion." *JSJ* 12 (1981) 195-204.

Stonequist, E. V. *The Marginal Man*. New York: Charles Scribner's Sons, 1937.

Strange, J. F., and H. Shanks. "Has the House Where Jesus Stayed in Capernaum Been Found?" *BAR* 8 (1982) 26-37.

Strecker, G. *Der Weg der Gerechtigkeit*. FRLANT 82. Göttingen: Vandenhoeck & Ruprecht, 1962.

Stuehrenberg, P. "Proselyte." *ABD* 5:503-5.

Suggs, M. J. *Wisdom, Christology, and Law in Matthew's Gospel*. Cambridge, Mass.: Harvard University Press, 1970.

Sugirtharajah, R. S. "A Postcolonial Exploration of Collusion and Construction in Biblical Interpretation." In *The Post-Colonial Bible,* edited by R. S. Sugirtharajah, 91-116. Sheffield: Sheffield Academic Press, 1998.

Sullivan, D. "New Insights into Matthew 27:24-25." *New Blackfriars* 73/863 (1993) 453-57.

Sutherland, C. H. V. "The Intelligibility of Roman Imperial Coin Types." *JRS* 49 (1959) 46-55.

Swanson, R. (ed.). *New Testament Greek Manuscripts: Matthew*. Sheffield: Sheffield Academic Press, 1995.

Talbert, C. H. "Biography, Ancient." *ABD* 1:745-49.

———. "Prophecies of Future Greatness: The Contribution of Greco- Roman Biographies to an Understanding of Luke 1:5-4:15." In *The Divine Helmsman,* edited by J. L. Crenshaw and S. Sandmel, 129-41. New York: Ktav, 1980.

Tannehill, R. *The Sword of His Mouth: Forceful and Imaginative Language in Synoptic Sayings*. SBL Semeia Supplements 1. Missoula, Mont.: Scholars Press, 1975.

———. "The 'Focal Instance' as a Form of New Testament Speech: A Study of Matthew 5:39b-42." *Journal of Religion* 50 (1970) 372-85.

Tatum, W. B. "Jesus' So-Called Triumphal Entry: On Making an Ass of the Romans." *Forum* 1 ns (1998) 129-43.

Taylor, J. E. *The Immerser: John the Baptist within Second Temple Judaism*. Grand Rapids: Eerdmans, 1997.

Taylor, L. R. "The 'Proskynesis' and the Hellenistic Ruler Cult." *JHS* 47 (1927) 53-62.

Telford, W. "More Fruit from the Withered Tree: Temple and Fig-Tree in Mark from a Graeco-Roman Perspective." In *Templum Amicitiae: Essays on the Second Temple presented to Ernst Bammel,* edited by W. Horbury, 264-304. JSNTSup 48. Sheffield: JSOT Press, 1991.

Teselle, E. "The Cross as Ransom." *JECS* 4 (1996) 147-70.

Theissen, G. *The Gospels in Context: Social and Political History in the Synoptic Tradition.* Minneapolis: Fortress, 1991.

————. *The Miracle Stories in Early Christian Tradition.* Philadelphia: Fortress, 1983.

————. *The Social Setting of Pauline Christianity.* Philadelphia: Fortress, 1982.

Thomas, J. C. *The Devil, Disease and Deliverance: Origins of Illness in the New Testament.* JPTSS 13. Sheffield: Sheffield Academic Press, 1998.

————. "The Kingdom of God in the Gospel According to Matthew." *NTS* 39 (1993) 136-46.

Thompson, L. *Romans and Blacks.* Norman: University of Oklahoma Press, 1989.

Thompson, W. G. *Matthew's Advice to a Divided Community: Matt 17:22-18:35.* Analecta Biblica 44. Rome: Biblical Institute Press, 1970.

Tigay, J. "On the Term 'Phylacteries' (Mt 23:5)." *HTR* 72 (1979) 46-48.

Trebilco, P. *Jewish Communities in Asia Minor.* SNTSMS 69. Cambridge: Cambridge University Press, 1991.

Trible, P. *The Rhetoric of Sexuality.* Philadelphia: Fortress, 1978.

Tuckett, C. M. (ed.). *The Messianic Secret.* Philadelphia: Fortress, 1983.

Turner, V. *The Ritual Process: Structure and Anti-Structure.* Ithaca, N.Y.: Cornell University Press, 1969, 1977.

Vaage, L. E. "The Woes of Q (and Matthew and Luke): Deciphering the Rhetoric of Criticism." In *Society of Biblical Literature 1998 Seminar Papers,* edited by D. J. Lull, 582-607. SBLSP 27. Atlanta: Scholars Press, 1988.

Van Aarde, A. G. "A Historical-Critical Classification of Jesus' Parables and the Metaphoric Narration of the Wedding Feast in Matthew 22:1-14." In A. G. Van Aarde, *God-With-Us: The Dominant Perspective in Matthew's Story,* 229-47. Hervormde Teologiese Studies Supplementum 5. Pretoria, 1994.

van Berchem, D. "Une inscription flavienne du Musée d'Antioche." *Museum Helveticum* 40 (1983) 185-96.

van Unnik, W. C. *"'Dominus Vobiscum.'"* In *New Testament Essays,* edited by A. J. B. Higgins, 270-305. Manchester: Manchester University Press, 1959.

van Tilborg, S. *The Jewish Leaders in Matthew.* Leiden: Brill, 1972.

Verseput, D. *The Rejection of the Humble Messianic King: A Study of the Composition of Matthew 11-12.* Frankfurt am Main: Peter Lang, 1986.

Versnel, H. S. "Religious Mentality in Ancient Prayer." In *Faith, Hope and Worship: Aspects of Religious Mentality in the Ancient World,* edited by H. S. Versnel, 1-64. Leiden: Brill, 1981.

————. *Triumphus: An Inquiry into the Origin, Development and Meaning of the Roman Triumph.* Leiden: Brill, 1970.

Visser 't Hooft, W. A. "Triumphalism in the Gospels." *SJT* 38 (1985) 491-504.

Viviano, B. "Where Was the Gospel According to St. Matthew Written?" *CBQ* 41 (1979) 533-46.

Vledder, E.-J. *Conflict in the Miracle Stories: A Socio-Exegetical Study of Matthew 8 and 9.* JSNTSup 152. Sheffield: Sheffield Academic Press, 1997.

von Rad, G., and W. Foerster. "διάβολος." *TDNT* 2:72-81.

Waetjen, H. "The Genealogy as the Key to the Gospel According to Matthew." *JBL* 95 (1976) 205-30.

Wainwright, E. *Towards a Feminist Critical Reading of the Gospel According to Matthew.* BZNW 60. Berlin and New York: Walter de Gruyter, 1991.

————. "God Wills to Invite All to the Banquet: Matthew 22:1-10." *International Review of Mission* 77 (1988) 185-93.

Wallace-Hadrill, A. "Elites and Trade in the Roman Town." In *City and Country in the Ancient World,* edited by J. Rich and A. Wallace-Hadrill, 241-72. New York: Routledge, 1991.

Waller, E. "The Parable of the Leaven: A Sectarian Teaching and the Inclusion of Women." *Union Seminary Quarterly Review* 35 (1979-80) 99-109.

Watty, W. "Jesus and the Temple—Cleansing or Cursing?" *ExpT* 93 (1982) 235-39.

Weaver, D. "Power and Powerlessness: Matthew's Use of Irony in the Portrayal of Political Leaders." In *Society of Biblical Literature 1992 Seminar Papers,* edited by E. H. Lovering Jr., 637-63. SBLSP 31. Atlanta: Scholars Press, 1992.

———. *Matthew's Missionary Discourse: A Literary Critical Analysis.* JSNTSup 38. Sheffield: JSOT Press, 1990.

Weber, K. "The Image of the Sheep and Goats in Matthew 25:31-46." *CBQ* 59 (1997) 657-78.

Weinfeld, M. *The Organizational Pattern and the Penal Code of the Qumran Sect.* NTOA 2. Göttingen: Vandenhoeck & Ruprecht, 1986.

Welch, S. *Communities of Resistance and Solidarity: A Feminist Theology of Resistance.* Maryknoll, N.Y.: Orbis Books, 1985.

Wells, L. *The Greek Language of Healing from Homer to New Testament Times.* BZNW 83. Berlin and New York: Walter de Gruyter, 1998.

Wengst, K. *PAX ROMANA and the Peace of Jesus Christ.* Philadelphia: Fortress, 1987.

Wenham, G. J. "The Syntax of Matt 19.9." *JSNT* 28 (1986) 17-23.

———. "Matthew and Divorce: An Old Crux Revisited." *JSNT* 22 (1984) 95-107.

Wenham, G. J., and H. Heth. *Jesus and Divorce.* Nashville: Thomas Nelson, 1984.

Whittaker, C. R. "The Poor in the City of Rome." In *Land, City and Trade in the Roman Empire.* Aldershot: Variorum, 1993. Section 7.

———. "The Consumer City Revisited: The *Vicus* and the City." In *Land, City and Trade in the Roman Empire.* Aldershot: Variorum, 1993. Section 8.

———. "Do Theories of the Ancient City Matter?" In *Land, City and Trade in the Roman Empire.* Aldershot: Variorum, 1993. Section 9.

Wiedemann, T. *Adults and Children in the Roman Empire.* New Haven, Conn.: Yale University, 1989.

———. *Slavery.* Oxford: Clarendon Press, 1987.

———. *Greek and Roman Slavery.* Baltimore: Johns Hopkins University Press, 1981.

Wiesenberg, E. "Related Prohibitions: Swine Breeding and the Study of Greek." *HUCA* 27 (1956) 213-33.

Wilken, R. L. "Collegia, Philosophical Schools and Theology." In *The Catacombs and the Colosseum: The Roman Empire as the Setting of Primitive Christianity,* edited by S. Benko and J. J. O'Rourke, 268-91. Valley Forge, Pa.: Judson, 1971.

Wilkins, M. J. *The Concept of Disciple in Matthew's Gospel As Reflected in the Use of the Term μαθητής.* Leiden: Brill, 1988.

Williams, S. K. *Jesus' Death as Saving Event: The Background and Origin of a Concept.* HDR 2. Missoula, Mont.: Scholars Press, 1975.

Williams, W. A. *Empire as a Way of Life.* New York: Oxford University Press, 1980.

Willis, W. (ed.). *The Kingdom of God in 20th-Century Interpretation.* Peabody, Mass.: Hendrickson, 1987.

Wimbush, V. L. "Introduction: Interpreting Resistance, Resisting Interpretations." *Semeia* 79 (1997) 1-10.

Windisch, H. "ζύμη, ζυμόω, ἄζυμος." *TDNT* 2:902-6.

———. "Friedensbringer—Gottessöhne." *ZNW* 24 (1925) 240-60.

Wink, W. *John the Baptist in the Gospel Tradition.* Cambridge: Cambridge University Press, 1968.

———. "Beyond Just War and Pacifism: Jesus' Nonviolent Way." *Review and Expositor* 89 (1992) 197-214.

———. "Jesus and the Domination System." In *Society of Biblical Literature 1991 Seminar Papers,* edited by E. H. Lovering Jr., 265-86. SBLSP 30. Atlanta: Scholars Press, 1991.

————. "Neither Passivity nor Violence: Jesus' Third Way (Matt. 5:38-42 par.)." In *The Love of Enemy and Nonretaliation in the New Testament,* edited by W. M. Swartley, 102-25. Louisville, Ky.: Westminster/John Knox, 1992.

————. *Engaging the Powers: Discernment and Resistance in a World of Domination.* Minneapolis: Fortress, 1992.

————. *Unmasking the Powers: The Invisible Forces That Determine Human Existence.* Philadelphia: Fortress, 1986.

Winter, B. "The Messiah as the Tutor: The Meaning of καθηγητής in Matthew 23:10." *TynBul* 42 (1991) 152-57.

Wire, A. *The Corinthian Women Prophets: A Reconstruction Through Paul's Rhetoric.* Minneapolis: Fortress, 1990.

Wise, M. O., and J. D. Tabor. "The Messiah at Qumran." *Biblical Archaeology Review* 18 (1992) 60-65.

Witherup, R. "Jeremiah and the Gospel of Matthew: An Audience-Oriented Perspective." Paper presented to the Narrative Exegesis of the New Testament Seminar, Catholic Biblical Association meeting, Seattle, Washington, August 1997.

————. "The Death of Jesus and the Raising of the Saints: Matthew 27:51-54 in Context." In *Society of Biblical Literature 1987 Seminar Papers,* edited by K. H. Richards, 574-85. SBLSP 26. Atlanta: Scholars Press, 1987.

Witt, R. "Isis-Hellas." *Proceedings of the Cambridge Philological Society* 12 (1966) 48-69.

Wolff, H. W. *Joel and Amos.* Hermeneia. Philadelphia: Fortress, 1977.

Wolmarans, J. L. "Who Asked Jesus to Leave the Territory of Gerasa (Mark 5:17)?" *Neotestamentica* 28 (1994) 87-92.

Wolter, M. "παράπτωμα." *EDNT* 3:33-34.

Wong, E. K.-C. "The Matthean Understanding of the Sabbath: A Response to G. N. Stanton." *JSNT* 44 (1991) 3-18.

Wright, D. P. and R. N. Jones. "Leprosy." *ABD* 4:277-82.

Yamasaki, G. *John the Baptist in Life and Death: Audience-Oriented Criticism of Matthew's Narrative.* JSNTSup 167. Sheffield: Sheffield Academic Press, 1998.

Yang, Y.-E. *Jesus and the Sabbath in Matthew's Gospel.* JSNTSup 139. Sheffield: Sheffield Academic Press, 1997.

Zampaglione, G. *The Idea of Peace in Antiquity.* Notre Dame, Ind., and London: University of Notre Dame Press, 1973.

Zeller, D. "μεριμνάω." *EDNT* 2:408-9.

Zumstein, J. *La Condition du croyant dans l'Evangile selon Matthieu.* OBO 16. Göttingen: Vandenhoeck & Ruprecht, 1977.